Business Today

Seventh Edition

INTEGRATED VIDEO EXERCISES

McGraw-Hill, Inc.

THE *Business Today*

INTEGRATED VIDEO EXERCISES

Introduction

T he ability to drive home a point—to excite the human mind and to stimulate action—is what makes videos so incredibly powerful. Now this power is yours when you experience the drama and immediacy of real-world business in your own classroom.

The *Business Today* Integrated Video Series consists of 22 high-quality videos, one linked to each chapter of *Business Today,* Seventh Edition. They allow you to meet, on location, a cross section of real people who work for some of the world's most fascinating companies—including small, medium, and large firms as well as nonprofit and international organizations. The videos are designed as in-class field trips to bring to life the concepts and issues covered in your textbook. But most important, these videos challenge you with a unique set of instructive exercises.

In this section you will find a brief synopsis of each video and unique exercises that are specifically related to the *Business Today* Integrated Video Series. The videos and exercises are keyed to the text with a logo in the margin. You will be asked to react to the videos by responding to questions, making decisions, and taking the initiative to solve real business problems. Offering you a wide variety of assignments, the exercises for each video contain ten labeled components: analysis, application, decision, communication, integration, ethics, debate, teamwork, update, update research, or role playing. These critically acclaimed videos and highly effective exercises are unmatched in helping you understand how business principles and concepts in the chapter are applied in the workplace.

CHAPTER 1 VIDEO EXERCISE

Upstairs/Downstairs: Inflation Begins to Divide a Nation

SYNOPSIS

This video discusses the Consumer Price Index (CPI), the most commonly used measure of inflation in the United States. The video makes two key points. First, because the CPI is an average, it can conceal important information, such as the steep increase in housing costs in recent years. Second, the United States increasingly has a two-tiered socioeconomic structure, with people in the top tier ("upstairs") increasingly able to afford housing and other items that have shot up in price and people in the bottom tier ("downstairs") increasingly unable to afford housing. Beyond these particular issues, the CPI and inflation in general are two key issues for business leaders, whether it's a case of customers not being able to afford a firm's products, or the firm itself not making enough profit because of increases in the cost of materials and supplies.

EXERCISES

ANALYSIS
1. Discuss the CPI in relation to the Dow Jones Industrial Average, the Index of Industrial Production, and the Wholesale Price Index.
2. Relate the CPI to the supply and demand curve.
3. Is it possible that the CPI presents a confusing picture to various segments of the population? If so, why use it?
4. How does inflation influence the multiplier effect?
5. What role does scarcity play in inflation?

APPLICATION
Choose an industry and speculate on how the two-tier economy might affect its future. An example would be the art market. When a lot of money was flowing in the art market, galleries and auction houses grew and prospered. (Make sure you understand current conditions in the industry you choose; the housing and art markets, for instance, have fallen on tougher times since this video was produced.)

DECISION
Assume you're a manufacturer of mid-priced products, and you hear the statistic that the middle class is shrinking. Someone suggests that you add either low-cost or top-quality products in order to attract the growing number of people in the lower and upper economic tiers. What factors do you need to consider before making such changes?

COMMUNICATION
Write a brief description of inflation that could be easily understood by children in grade school.

INTEGRATION
Look ahead to the description of the "consumer's bill of rights" in Chapter 4. Write a one-paragraph response to the statement that the consumer should also be guaranteed reasonable prices (you can agree or disagree with the statement).

ETHICS
In response to rampant inflation in housing costs, New York City

once imposed rent controls that limited the amounts by which landlords could raise rents. Do you think such controls are fair?

DEBATE
Suppose someone reviewed the status of rent controls and decided that the same kind of controls should be applied to purchased housing as well. The specific proposal calls for limiting the price increase each time a house is sold, which would put an end to the huge jumps such as you saw for the house in the video. Option A: In a formal debate format, argue either for or against this proposal. Option B: Take either side and state your case in a brief summary report.

TEAMWORK
In a team of three or four students, pick a well-known product and identify the primary ingredients, parts, supplies, or services that are needed to create that product (pick a simple product in order to limit the number of items you have to worry about). Divide

the list among team members and find out how the price of each has increased (or perhaps decreased) in recent years and speculate on how future price changes might affect the overall cost of creating the product.

Do the research necessary to write a one-paragraph summary of either (a) the CPI over the last five years or (b) the current financial status of the U.S. middle class.

ROLE PLAYING
One student should play the role of a government economist, armed with the latest CPI figure. Two or three other students play reporters who question the economist on how this level of inflation is affecting consumers and businesses.

CHAPTER 2 VIDEO EXERCISE

The Body Shop: Structuring a Business for Profit and Social Good

SYNOPSIS

Anita Roddick's cosmetics company, The Body Shop, may participate in one of the global economy's slowest-growing sectors—retailing—but The Body Shop is anything but slow growing. After opening her first shop in England in 1976, Roddick took only a few years to expand The Body Shop into an international retail chain. She avoided the financial strain and the risk of rapid expansion by selling franchises (permission to use the name, the operation's techniques, and the products) throughout Great Britain, the United States, and more than three dozen other countries. The company's phenomenal growth is not the only thing unusual about The Body Shop, however. As the video explains, Roddick preaches and pursues a distinct brand of capitalism, one that puts as much emphasis on people, health, and the global environment as it does on profits.

EXERCISES

ANALYSIS
1. Would you like to work in a company like The Body Shop? Why or why not?
2. Would you want to own stock in the company? Why or why not?
3. What is likely to happen when the employees' position on an issue differs from the company's? What about the backlash against the company when the public disagrees with its politics?
4. How should the company handle management succession when Roddick retires?
5. What barriers to entry might await any company that tries to compete with The Body Shop?

APPLICATION
Choose three other businesses and describe how they could take an active social role. For instance, a restaurant could use its facilities to prepare meals for the homeless.

DECISION
Assume that an extremely wealthy weapons manufacturer is making a move to purchase controlling interest in The Body Shop. The company's CEO is running newspaper ads in New York and London, encouraging shareholders to

take the offer, which is 50 percent above the stock's current price. You're a shareholder, and you know you could sell out and use the extra money to help the poor. Should you take the offer?

COMMUNICATION

Write a brief letter (one page or less) to other Body Shop shareholders, explaining your decision.

INTEGRATION

It would be possible for another company to make and sell products that are as safe and healthy as The Body Shop's products, even though this other company might not pursue The Body Shop's activist agenda. Referring to the discussion of competition in Chapter 1, would this other company be able to compete with The Body Shop for the same group of customers? Explain your answer in a paragraph.

ETHICS

Store managers hold key positions in The Body Shop organization because they are the keepers of the flame, so to speak, in terms of guiding sales clerks in the ways of the company. What if a certain store needs to replace its manager, and the most qualified candidate has little interest in social causes—would it be fair to the company and the other employees to promote this person to store manager? Would it be fair to the employee to be denied the promotion based solely on personal beliefs?

DEBATE

Is there some inherent conflict between The Body Shop's social agenda and the fact that Anita Roddick is the fifth-richest woman in England? Option A: In a formal debate format, argue either for or against the notion that it is acceptable for Roddick to make so much money, given what her company claims to be all about. Option B: Take either side and state your case in a brief summary report.

TEAMWORK

With a team of three or four students, identify a cause or group that could benefit from "capitalistic intervention" of the sort practiced by Anita Roddick. For instance, beleaguered family farmers in Vermont get a helping hand from Ben & Jerry's Ice Cream, which buys cream from them rather than from huge corporate farms.

UPDATE RESEARCH

Do the research necessary to write a one-paragraph update on either (a) the number of Body Shop outlets currently in operation and the company's prospects for the next five or ten years or (b) the activities of other companies that are managed in a fashion similar to The Body Shop.

ROLE PLAYING

One student plays the role of a sales clerk; two others play the role of customers who are unfamiliar with The Body Shop's products and philosophy. The customers want to know why the store doesn't carry their favorite brands of mass-market cosmetics.

CHAPTER 3 VIDEO EXERCISE

Ray Kurzweil: Financing the Future

SYNOPSIS

In many respects, Ray Kurzweil represents the classic inventor/entrepreneur. On the one hand, he has a vision of technology helping humankind; from a computer that can read text for blind persons to a sophisticated synthesizer that lets a solo musician replicate the sounds of many different instruments. On the other hand, he knows that it's impossible to succeed without investment capital and strong business skills. This video introduces Kurzweil and a number of his inventions, and it chronicles his efforts to secure financing for each new creation. It also explains how ideas for new products come to him, including a meeting with musician Stevie Wonder that led to Kurzweil's foray into electronic music.

EXERCISES

ANALYSIS

1. Using the checklist in the chapter, do you think you have what it takes to succeed as a small-business owner?

2. How do you suppose Kurzweil finds new opportunities?

3. With the products described in the video, would franchising ever make sense for Kurzweil?

4. With respect to the amount of time it takes one of his inventions to return any profits, does equity or debt financing make more sense?

5. Which would be riskier: one of Kurzweil's high-tech breakthroughs or a new neighborhood dry cleaner? Explain your answer.

APPLICATION

The voice-input technology shown in the video might have quite a few applications in the business world. List as many potential uses for it as you can and in each case explain how the technology would increase productivity or quality or decrease costs.

DECISION

Let's say you're the chief financial officer at Xerox, and Ray Kurzweil is approaching you again to invest in his latest project. What are some of the factors you should think about before making the decision to invest?

COMMUNICATION

Identify a new product that you've seen recently, either in person or in an advertisement. Assume you're about to sell it to a potential customer; write a 30-second oral description of the product and its benefits.

INTEGRATION

Referring to the discussion of the service sector in Chapter 2, how might Kurzweil's various ventures participate in the service sector?

ETHICS

Is it ethical for Kurzweil to approach investors for money for new projects, even though only one of his existing product ideas has made any money so far?

DEBATE

Some might say that a talent such as Kurzweil's should be applied to more important problems than Stevie Wonder's need for a new keyboard. Option A: In a formal debate format, argue either for or against this statement. Option B: Take either side and state your case in a brief summary report.

TEAMWORK

In a team of four students, two of the students should propose a new product idea, describing the target customers and the benefits the product brings to them. The other two students should look for holes in their logic and point out ways to improve the proposal.

UPDATE RESEARCH

Do the research necessary to write a one-paragraph update on the current status of Ray Kurzweil's various business enterprises.

ROLE PLAYING

One student should play the role of an entrepreneur pitching a new business to two other students, who are playing the role of potential investors. The new business idea doesn't have to be something high-tech like Kurzweil's; a new dry-cleaning business or similar "low-tech" concept would be fine as well.

CHAPTER 4 VIDEO EXERCISE

When in Rome, Should You Really Do as the Romans Do?

SYNOPSIS

As global business grows, so does the challenge of global business ethics. And as complex as ethics can be inside a single country, ethical questions become much more difficult as soon as you cross the border into another country. The key problem with global ethics is the difference in ethical standards from one country to the next. This video addresses the problem of conflicting standards and values, and it presents several intriguing—and very realistic—ethical dilemmas. A discussion panel made up of ethics experts, international business executives, and business students discuss these dilemmas and expose the complexity of global ethical questions. The scenarios these people discuss are more than just academic exercises; they occur regularly in the world of global business.

EXERCISES

ANALYSIS

1. Why are colleges and universities putting more emphasis on business ethics?
2. Is it possible to teach ethics to adults, or are a person's behavioral patterns basically in place by the time he or she reaches adulthood?
3. If a global business situation involves conflicts between two countries' value systems, whose should prevail?
4. Is it proper for one country to "preach" its value system and ethical standards to the rest of the world?
5. What is your school's responsibility in terms of the overall topic of business ethics?

APPLICATION

Make the pesticide decision described in the video, then explain how you would handle whichever decision you reach. In other words, if you decide to sell the pesticide, explain what steps you'll take.

DECISION

Let's say your company is in a desperate financial condition, and if sales don't improve soon, you'll have to lay off dozens of employees. The economy is in dire shape as well, and you know that few of the laid-off employees will find other jobs. You're faced with a global ethics question on a big sales opportunity that could turn the company around. In any situation like this, what are some of the general questions you should ask yourself before making the decision?

COMMUNICATION

Assume that you're the CEO of a company that has just established a code of ethics. Write a memo to all employees, describing the code (make up any details you need) and emphasizing the company's position in terms of following and enforcing the new code.

INTEGRATION

Turning back to Chapter 1, review the description of per-capita in-

comes around the world. Do you think that these variations in economic prosperity around the world have an impact on global ethical challenges?

ETHICS

Nations in the Third World are often criticized by people in the United States and other developed countries for such environmentally unsound practices as cutting down rain forests. However, these less-developed countries make a good point when they respond that the vast majority of the world's pollution is generated by a comparatively small collection of industrialized countries. As one of the world's premier polluters, does the United States have any right to criticize, say, Brazil's destruction of the Amazon rain forest?

DEBATE

Some U.S. executives say that the Foreign Corrupt Practices Act puts them at a serious disadvantage in certain cases. One could even argue that the FCPA creates another ethical problem in that the U.S. companies that can't compete successfully may have to lay off employees, pay lower dividends to investors, and so on. Option A: In a formal debate format, argue either for or against the FCPA. Option B: Take either side and state your case in a brief summary report.

TEAMWORK
In a team of three or four students, research the Michael Milken

case and write a one-page summary of the situation, including both the charges against him and his defense in response to those charges.

UPDATE RESEARCH
Do the research necessary to write a one-paragraph update on the status of U.S. business involvement in either South Africa or the People's Republic of China.

ROLE PLAYING
One student should play the role of the CEO of a company whose international sales manager has recently crossed an ethical line in securing a deal (make up whatever details you need; you might find it easiest to base this on one of the scenarios from the video). Several other students play company directors. Together, decide how you will respond.

CHAPTER 5 VIDEO EXERCISE

Lotus Bridges the Cultural Gap in Japan

SYNOPSIS

Japan is something of an enigma to many U.S. companies, from its complex language to its unique cultural traditions to its unfamiliar management and business practices. A failure to grasp and respond to these often profound differences has left more than one U.S. firm frustrated and wondering if there is any way to crack the Japanese market. One of the leading software companies in the United States, Lotus Development Corporation, has shown that success in Japan is possible, with careful planning and a large dose of cultural sensitivity. This video explains how Lotus first sought out a liaison to help build its Japanese arm, then carefully selected an experienced Japanese manager to guide the operation. It also discusses the experiences of Lotus's Japanese employees as they try to blend traditional Japanese practices with innovative American management.

EXERCISES

ANALYSIS
1. What steps did Lotus take to increase its chances of success in Japan?
2. Do you know of any products created in other countries that have been successfully adapted for the U.S. market?
3. Can you think of any draw-

backs to hiring a Japanese national to head Lotus Japan?
4. Why would Lotus want to start its own organization in Japan, rather than simply exporting Japanese-language products from the United States?
5. If Lotus were facing a decision that involved both U.S. and Jap-

anese managers, which country's style of decision making should be used?

APPLICATION
Lotus Japan has successfully added an element of U.S. creative freedom to the Japanese elements of diligence and attention to de-

tail. Could the reverse be accomplished in Lotus's U.S. operations? In other words, is it possible to add the Japanese work habits to the creative culture in the U.S. arm of the company? In a page or less, outline a plan for doing so.

DECISION

Assume that Lotus's U.S. employees have started a newsletter that is sometimes critical of company management. Open criticism like this is practically unheard of in Japan, but the newsletter also has good information on competitors and creative ideas for new products. As head of Lotus Japan, should you distribute the newsletter to your employees?

COMMUNICATION

Write a one-page memo to the employees of Lotus Japan, announcing and explaining your decision regarding the newsletter.

INTEGRATION

Chapter 3 outlined numerous ways in which companies find new business opportunities. From the list in Exhibit 3.4, which concept did Lotus use in moving into Japan?

ETHICS

Assume that the current head of Lotus Japan is retiring and one of the leading candidates to replace him is a woman. She is the most qualified candidate, but you know some Japanese customers, distributors, and employees may resist a female top executive, and their reluctance may hurt Lotus's sales in Japan. Should she get the job?

DEBATE

Some employees think that Lotus Japan should loosen the reins on its employees in order to foster even more creativity. Two suggestions are no more white shirts and ties and no more bowing when one enters a manager's office. Option A: In a formal debate format, deliberate the wisdom of the two suggestions, taking into account tradition and expectations. Option B: Take a position either for or against the two suggestions and state your case in a brief summary report.

TEAMWORK

In a team of three students, pick a country that looks like a good market for Lotus software. One student should find out whether Lotus sells there now, another should find out if competitors sell there now, and a third should identify major barriers to entering the market. Summarize your findings in a report no longer than two pages.

UPDATE RESEARCH

Do the research necessary to write a one-paragraph update on either (a) the current status of Lotus in Japan or (b) the emergence of any competition in the Japanese-language spreadsheet market.

ROLE PLAYING

One student plays Lotus CEO Jim Manzi; another plays a U.S. manager who speaks fluent Japanese and who wanted the top job at Lotus Japan. Manzi needs to explain why the job went to a Japanese native, even though the U.S. manager was qualified otherwise. The student playing the manager can decide to accept the decision gracefully or to protest it.

CHAPTER 6 VIDEO EXERCISE

Gary David Goldberg: From Caveman to Leading-Edge Manager

SYNOPSIS

The list of successful Hollywood executives who lived for a time in a cave is probably rather short, but at the top of that list one would surely find Gary David Goldberg. This video chronicles his days from a carefree cave dweller in Greece to his current role as the

head of Ubu Productions, creator and producer of some of the most successful television shows on the air. It provides a backstage look at the creation and shooting of *Family Ties*, a phenomenally successful show that now reaps riches in syndication. But the video is more than an insider's look at a TV program. It also explains Goldberg's management philosophies and practices, from sharing the enormous wealth his shows generate to insisting that his employees be given an on-site day-care center so that they can more easily balance the demands of work and family life.

EXERCISES

ANALYSIS

1. Which managerial skills did you see Goldberg using?
2. For the production of a TV show, which set of skills is most important? Explain your answer.
3. Would Goldberg be an effective CEO of a major corporation, such as IBM or Toyota?
4. How would you describe Goldberg's leadership style?
5. Explain how management by objectives (MBO) could be used to produce a TV show.

APPLICATION

How might a manager in a less-glamorous business such as a steel mill apply Goldberg's creative, share-the-wealth management style?

DECISION

Assume that in a last-minute script-tuning session with his writers, Goldberg finds himself in disagreement with the entire staff regarding a scene change. He thinks the group's idea is out of character with the show's established tone, but he doesn't want to cause long-term friction by overriding their decisions. If you were in his shoes, what would you do?

COMMUNICATION

Just as many employees need day care for their children, some need care facilities for elderly relatives. Assume Ubu wants to add an elder-care facility; write a one-page memo to Paramount's chief financial officer, explaining why the facility is needed.

INTEGRATION

Chapter 1 identified three general types of competition. Which of these apply to the products created by Ubu Productions? Who are Ubu's competitors?

ETHICS

Goldberg seems to exhibit little tolerance for employees who can't or won't perform up to his expectations. Is this really fair in all cases? After all, people have different levels of intelligence and experience.

DEBATE

Assume that other managers in the entertainment business are pressuring Goldberg to stop paying his people so much, saying that not all shows are as profitable as his, so not all production companies can afford the salary increases that usually occur at Ubu.

Option A: In a formal debate format, take either Goldberg's position or the position of one of the managers pressuring him to stop paying so much. Option B: Take either position and state your case in a brief summary report.

TEAMWORK

In a team of five or six students, outline an episode of a currently popular TV show. When you're finished, share with the class how your team handled the four managerial functions of planning, directing, organizing, and controlling.

UPDATE RESEARCH

Do the research necessary to write a one-paragraph update on either (a) how Goldberg and Ubu are doing these days or (b) how much money *Family Ties* currently makes in syndication.

ROLE PLAYING

One student plays Goldberg, a second plays an actor, and a third plays a writer. The actor refuses to do a scene created by the writer, saying that it is embarrassing. Goldberg needs to mediate the dispute and get the team working together again.

CHAPTER 7 VIDEO EXERCISE

Springfield Remanufacturing Company Teams Up for Success

SYNOPSIS

Innovative management is often associated with high-technology and celebrity entrepreneurs, but this video shows that enlightened management works just as well in the unglamorous business of overhauling truck engines. SRC tripled its sales in six years after it adopted a management system that patterns business efforts after Americans' love of a good game. SRC bases its game of business on three principles. First, everyone is on the same team; the company is owned by its managers and employees. Second, everyone learns how to keep score; even entry-level workers are taught how to read financial statements so they can see how well the company is doing. Third, everyone has a stake in the company's success; as the company prospers and the value of its stock climbs, so does the financial health of the managers and employees who own it.

EXERCISES

ANALYSIS
1. What type of organization is operating at SRC?
2. Explain the role of authority in a team-oriented organization.
3. Using the chapter's clues for identifying a corporate culture, how would you describe the culture at SRC?
4. What role could intrapreneurship play at SRC and how might it be encouraged?
5. Would SRC's structure tend to be more centralized or decentralized?

APPLICATION
One of the reasons why SRC's employee-involvement approach works is that employees see long-term benefit in learning how to read financial statements, work extra hours when needed, and so on. How might this concept be applied to a business such as a convenience store, in which employees rarely work for more than a few years? In a page or less, out-line how SRC's approach could be applied by the owner of a convenience store.

DECISION
Assume that SRC has decided to purchase a company and make it a division. However, this company has a traditional, centralized corporate culture that emphasizes top-down control, not teamwork and participation. Identify the problems that SRC might encounter as it tries to infuse the new division with the SRC culture.

COMMUNICATION
Write a three-minute introductory speech that you would present to the employees and managers of the new division, describing SRC's culture and the company's reasons for introducing it to the new division.

INTEGRATION
Which of the three leadership styles described in Chapter 6 seems to be the norm at SRC?

ETHICS
Teamwork in the SRC style can be a boon to productivity and employee satisfaction, but it is sometimes hard for individual accomplishments to stand out in such an environment. A good sports analogy is the fate of linemen on a football team; they slug it out game after game for the benefit of the team but rarely get any individual glory. In this sense, is a strong emphasis on teamwork really fair?

DEBATE
Some people might say that becoming well-versed in corporate finance is too great a burden for some employees, particularly those who aren't all that interested in the business and just want to do a good day's work and not worry about anything else. Option A: In a formal debate format, take either side of this issue. Option B: Take either position and state your case in a brief summary report.

TEAMWORK

With three or four other students, develop a short presentation that teaches financial novices how to read an income statement. Chapter 17 offers an introduction to income statements, and you may want to use other sources as well.

UPDATE RESEARCH

Do the research necessary to write a one-paragraph update on either (a) the book that Bo Burlingham was writing, including its title, whether it is still in print, and any reviews it received in the business press or (b) SRC's current status.

ROLE PLAYING

One student plays the production manager, who is announcing to two other students (playing the role of production-line employees) that the company has received a large order that would require canceling the Thanksgiving holiday if the company accepts it. One employee wants to take the order; the other doesn't.

CHAPTER 8 VIDEO EXERCISE

Septor Discovers the Human Side of Automation

SYNOPSIS

Factory automation has often been seen as—and sold as—an automatic cure-all for quality and productivity problems. After all, the theory goes, if people are making the mistakes and causing the problems, the mistakes and problems will disappear when people are replaced by automated machinery. But this video shows how Septor, a U.S. auto-parts manufacturer, learned that removing human input can cause enormous problems of its own. The video compares Septor's factory with a Japanese factory that uses identical equipment, only minus the automation. In the Japanese factory, highly trained technicians and engineers keep a close eye on the machinery and solve any problems that creep in. In Septor's highly computerized factory, however, even a simple problem freezes production because the few employees, who have been reduced to passive caretakers, aren't even paying attention.

EXERCISES

ANALYSIS

1. How can we reconcile the apparent need for automation with the desire to keep as many people as possible employed?
2. From what you've seen in the video, what conclusions might you make about the differences between U.S. and Japanese management practices?
3. Why do you suppose these differences exist?
4. Should U.S. manufacturers try to closely copy Japanese manufacturing methods?
5. Did this factory appear to be using "hard" or "soft" manufacturing?

APPLICATION

The situation at Septor demonstrates the need for trained employees to be involved in even the most advanced production facilities. This also applies to service businesses that rely on automation, such as the information systems used by an insurance company to process claims. Assume you work for this insurance company; draw up some brief guidelines for making sure that employees stay involved in the process.

DECISION

In both manual and automated production facilities, managers sometimes have to stop production because of quality problems. The key factor in the decision to stop production is the minimum acceptable quality level, which is the lowest that quality can drop and still be acceptable. List the points you would have to consider when defining a minimum acceptable quality level for a manufacturer such as Septor.

COMMUNICATION

Just as lower-level employees at the Springfield Remanufacturing Company in the Chapter 7 video exercise had to learn the basics of corporate finance, employees in manufacturing companies such as Septor often have to learn statistical quality control methods in order to improve quality and pro-

ductivity. Draft a three minute speech to the production employees, explaining why this is an important subject for them to learn.

INTEGRATION

Referring to what you learned about motivation in Chapter 6, list several ways that the employees in the Septor plant might be motivated to pay closer attention to the machinery.

ETHICS

The issue of replacing employees with computers (or machinery of any kind) has long troubled some observers of the business world. The problem stretches back to the earliest days of the Industrial Revolution and promises to remain a key issue as companies struggle to increase productivity. Is it fair to replace a good employee with a machine?

DEBATE

When faced with the problem shown at Septor, some managers would be tempted simply to punish the employees who erred. Option A: In a formal debate format, argue for or against doing so. Option B: Take either position and

state your case in a brief summary report.

TEAMWORK

In a team of four students, outline a plan for automating a job that one of you now holds or has held in the past. One student should serve as "devil's advocate" when the plan is finished, searching for flaws.

UPDATE RESEARCH

Do the research necessary to write a one-page summary on either (a) current trends in employee training among U.S. manufacturers or (b) the current balance of trade between the United States and Japan, in terms of manufactured goods.

ROLE PLAYING

One student plays the role of a salesperson from a company that sells factory automation equipment, such as robots. The other student plays a manufacturing manager who is skeptical of the true benefits of automated production. The salesperson tries to convince the manager that, if implemented correctly, automation has much to offer.

CHAPTER 9 VIDEO EXERCISE

Au Bon Pain Moves Productivity and Quality to the Front Burner

SYNOPSIS

This video showcases the dramatic turnaround experienced by Au Bon Pain, a French-styled fast-food chain, after it motivated store managers by giving them more control over their own destinies. With its old approach, Au Bon Pain did little to motivate store managers and crews, with predictable results. Customer service was often poor, sales were way below potential levels, and even simple chores such as restocking restrooms with paper towels seemed to slip through the cracks. But after the company motivated store managers by giving them a share of their store's profits, the situation improved dramatically. The store managers worked hard to increase sales and reduce costs, and they in turn did their best to motivate their crews by offering substantial pay increases.

EXERCISES

ANALYSIS
1. Explain how Au Bon Pain is motivating its managers.
2. Explain how these managers are in turn motivating their crews.
3. Working in a fast-food outlet can be exhausting, demoralizing work. How could an Au Bon Pain manager keep crew morale high?
4. What effect might changing workforce demographics have on Au Bon Pain?
5. Referring to Herzberg's theory of motivation, list possible hygiene factors and motivators in the Au Bon Pain environment.

APPLICATION
Motivation programs that rely heavily on financial rewards tend to be less effective during slow economic periods, for the simple reason that even the most concerted efforts may yield only minor increases in sales. As a result, the company has less money to pay employees in terms of raises or bonuses. Outline a way in which you could apply Au Bon Pain's system to a real estate brokerage, but make allowances for the slow times that inevitably strike such businesses.

DECISION
Assume that you're an Au Bon Pain store manager listening to several employees who say they can make more money elsewhere. You don't want to lose them, but you've used all your discretionary finances already, and to give them a raise, you'd have to cut your own salary. What should you think about before giving them an answer?

COMMUNICATION
Assume that you've gone ahead and made a decision regarding raises for these employees. Now plan what you'll say when you give them the news. Limit your remarks to no more than three minutes.

INTEGRATION
Referring to the description of quality assurance in Chapter 8, list several ideas that Au Bon Pain could implement to assure higher quality and reduce waste.

ETHICS
The partner/managers in Au Bon Pain's system clearly have primary responsibility for the success of individual store locations. On the other hand, these store managers can't be successful without their crews. Do you think it is unfair to pay the manager $100,000 or more a year, while the people doing most of the work get far less?

DEBATE
One might be tempted to criticize Au Bon Pain's motivation system for relying too much on money and not enough on nonfinancial factors such as personal satisfaction, at least from the evidence presented in the video program. Option A: In a formal debate format, argue for or against the no-

tion that the system relies too much on money. Option B: Take either position and state your case in a brief summary report.

TEAMWORK
In a team of five students, identify ways that Au Bon Pain can help satisfy its employees at all five levels of Maslow's hierarchy. You may choose to work on each level as a team, or assign one level to each student.

UPDATE RESEARCH
Do the research necessary to write a one-paragraph update on either (a) Au Bon Pain's current status or (b) moves by any other companies to adopt similar motivational schemes for managers or employees.

ROLE PLAYING
Two students play the role of Au Bon Pain employees who are earning roughly $6 an hour. Their manager, played by a third student, is earning $115,000 a year. Even if the manager works 70 hours a week, this is well over $30 an hour. The employees complain that the manager isn't worth five times as much as they are, and the manager has to respond.

CHAPTER 10 VIDEO EXERCISE

General Dynamics: Are Employees about to Buy a Lemon?

SYNOPSIS

The former employees of an idle General Dynamics shipyard face a big dilemma: they have a chance to buy the shipyard from General Dynamics and manage it themselves, but the operation was previously shut down because of big losses. The employees and their union, however, believe that they can turn the yard into a success. They are banking on the pride and motivation that will come with ownership; if it is their yard, they will manage it more successfully and thus turn the financial situation around. The ownership vehicle they are considering is called an employee stock ownership plan (ESOP) that gives a corporation a tax break when employees buy stock in the company. However, as the video points out, ESOPs have a mixed record. Hyatt Clark Industries failed after an ESOP was introduced because employees invested in the company but didn't get much voice in how it was managed.

EXERCISES

ANALYSIS
1. Why have ESOPs generally failed to meet their objectives?
2. Who's in a better position to write a job description—a manager who oversees that job or someone with experience in the job?
3. Should the General Dynamics plant use peer review, a system in which employees appraise each other's performance?
4. What are some potential drawbacks of peer review?
5. Do you think employees would prefer benefits such as health-care insurance or an equivalent increase in their wages?

APPLICATION

Explain how the concept of employee ownership might work when the company is considering benefits. For instance, what's to stop the employees from simply voting in more vacation time, better health insurance, and other expensive benefits?

DECISION

What if the employee-owned shipyard had to lay off some employees during a tough period? How should the company pick who gets laid off and who doesn't?

COMMUNICATION

In a three-minute speech, explain to a group of bankers how, as owners, the employees will manage the facility better and make a profit.

INTEGRATION

Referring to Chapter 6, describe how planning might work in a democratically owned and managed company.

ETHICS

Is the idea of "lemon socialism" ethical? Should union leaders try to talk their members into buying a plant that is losing money?

DEBATE

One might argue that employees shouldn't have democratic control because the company's strategy and direction will change whenever prevailing opinions change. Option A: In a formal debate format, argue either for or against the validity of this notion. Option B: Take either side and state your case in a brief summary report.

TEAMWORK

In a team of three or four employees, assume that you've just bought your company from its previous owners. Assume further that you now can't agree on a compensation plan for yourselves. Figure out a way to work through this problem as a team.

UPDATE RESEARCH

Do the research necessary to find out whether or not the employees in Quincy bought the shipyard, and if so, how they are doing with their new investment today.

ROLE PLAYING

One student should play the role of an employee who supports the buyout plan, trying to convince two others who are skeptical.

CHAPTER 11 VIDEO EXERCISE

Labor Day: Labor and Management Try New Roles as Collaborators

SYNOPSIS

This video presents an unusual collaboration between management and organization labor—on a picket line. In this particular case, managers of several unionized grocery stores and the grocery workers' union are teaming up against a number of nonunion stores in the area. The nonunion stores are a threat to the union stores because their prices are lower, a situation made possible by lower, nonunionized wages. The union is concerned that if the nonunion stores run the union stores out of business, union workers will lose jobs. On the other hand, the nonunion stores view the union-management collaboration as unfair and possibly illegal. In addition to this particular struggle, the video also highlights a new attitude found among many unions these day, an attitude of working with, rather than against, management.

EXERCISES

ANALYSIS

1. How are consumers likely to react to pleas such as the one made by the union-management coalition?
2. What effect has unionization had on this community overall?
3. Why don't the managers of the union stores simply kick the union out and replace them with cheaper, nonunion labor?
4. Why did the union decide to work with management?
5. Should the grocery workers' union apply this model nationwide (i.e., should every local join forces with store managers to drive out nonunion stores)?

APPLICATION

Try to find any two groups that could benefit from the sort of cooperation demonstrated by the union grocery stores and the grocery union. Describe their current relationship, what they could do to cooperate, and the benefits each would get from such cooperation.

DECISION

As a consumer, whose side would you take if one of the union members pictured in the video called and asked you to stop shopping at nonunion stores?

COMMUNICATION

Put yourself in the position of the head of the grocery union, and write a "telepicketing" message that union members could use to sway consumers. People don't want to spend much time listening to a phone pitch; make sure the core of your message can be communicated in a minute or less.

INTEGRATION

What if the union-management boycott campaign doesn't work, and the Piggly Wiggly stores in the video stay in business? Referring to the description of competition in Chapter 1, outline ways that the union stores can compete with the nonunion stores. Keep in mind that the union stores' prices will be higher because of the union wages.

ETHICS

Assume that the union-management campaign works, and Piggly Wiggly and the other nonunion stores go out of business. What if the managers of remaining (union) stores decide to stop cooperating with the union once their common enemy (the nonunion stores) is out of the picture? Would such a shift on management's part be ethical?

DEBATE

The video raised, but didn't resolve, a key ethical issue: Is it fair for union stores to join together with unions in an effort to drive nonunion stores out of business? After all, it is perfectly legal to own and manage a nonunion store. Option A: In a formal debate format, support or reject the fairness of picketing against the nonunion stores. Option B: Take either position and state your case in a brief summary.

TEAMWORK

The union movement tends to provoke strong emotional reactions from some people. In a team of four or five students, conduct an informal survey of friends, relatives, and other people that you can reach conveniently. The entire team should first develop a brief questionnaire that will uncover feelings towards unions, then split up the task of polling people.

UPDATE RESEARCH

Do the research necessary to write a one-paragraph update on either (a) the status of the class-action lawsuit discussed in the video or (b) trends in union membership in the service sector of the U.S. economy.

ROLE PLAYING

One student plays the role of the union members in the video who were telephoning local residents, asking them to avoid shopping at the nonunion stores. Another student plays a resident who is sympathetic to the union's cause, and a third plays a resident who happens to have just lost his or her job at a nonunion store that recently closed because of the boycott.

CHAPTER 12 VIDEO EXERCISE

McDonald's Covers the World with Fast Food and Good Times

SYNOPSIS

The field of marketing covers quite a range of topics, from understanding your customers and designing products that they will find appealing to promoting your products in a persuasive manner and delivering them in ways that are convenient and satisfying. McDonald's is a superb example of the challenges and rewards of contemporary marketing, and this videotape gives you a guided tour of marketing according to McDonald's. You'll see that the marketing exchange offered by McDonald's is more than just food and beverages; it also includes a pleasant social and family experience, convenience, consistency, and value. You'll also see how McDonald's addresses the issue of social responsibility and the complexities of international business.

EXERCISES

ANALYSIS
1. How does McDonald's apply the four Ps?
2. What factors shown in the video influence the buying behavior of McDonald's customers?
3. What types of utility does McDonald's provide its customers?
4. How has McDonald's responded to changing consumer demands in recent years?
5. Does McDonald's do any market segmentation for its products?

APPLICATION
Identify a business you've seen or patronized and figure out if franchising would make sense for this business (assuming it's not already franchised).

DECISION
If you were purchasing a new McDonald's franchise and had the choice between locating next to a high school or a minor league baseball field, which would you choose?

COMMUNICATION
Pick an item from McDonald's menu and create a print (magazine or newspaper) ad for it. Think about the image you want to project, the graphical elements you'll want to use, and the words that will get your point across. (Rough sketches are fine in place of finished artwork.)

INTEGRATION
Refer to Chapter 3 and identify the advantages and disadvantages of buying a McDonald's franchise relative to the idea of creating a new restaurant from the ground up.

ETHICS
One of the issues McDonald's has had to grapple with in recent years is the healthiness of its foods. Some would say that McDonald's can't possibly be a good member of the community if it is feeding people high-calorie and high-cholesterol foods. Others say that McDonald's has made efforts to offer healthy foods and besides, each consumer has the right to decide what he or she is going to eat. What's your opinion?

DEBATE
Many people favor one fast-food chain over another. Option A: In a formal debate format, support either McDonald's or a well-known competitor operating in your area. Option B: Take either side and state your case in a brief summary report. With either option, consider how points in the cases for and against McDonald's could be used to improve its marketing strategy.

TEAMWORK
In a team of three or four students, identify a business that one or more of you is familiar with, a business that has established a strong relationship with its cus-

tomers. This can be anything from a restaurant to the college bookstore. Decide what it is that makes the place special to its customers, and write a list of general guidelines that other businesses could follow.

UPDATE RESEARCH
Do the research necessary to write a one-paragraph summary on ei-

ther (a) McDonald's menu changes in recent years or (b) the effect of any recent government regulation on the marketing of fast food.

ROLE PLAYING
One student plays the role of a McDonald's franchise owner trying to explain to his or her employees why it is a good idea to help out with a local charity event. Several

other students can play employees who agree to do it on their own time, a few others demand to be paid while doing it, and one or two don't want to participate at all.

CHAPTER 13 VIDEO EXERCISE

So Why Do Textbooks Cost So Much?

SYNOPSIS

This program addresses a marketing topic that is near and dear to every one of you: the price of textbooks. You can view this video at two levels. First, as a potential marketing manager you can gain insights into the risks of developing a new product and the challenge of setting prices. Second, as a consumer of textbooks, you would undoubtedly like to know why college texts cost as much as they do. This program answers that question by showing you the steps in the development process for textbooks and pointing out the costs behind the prices. When you realize that college bookstores see a profit of only 5 cents on the dollar and look at the expenses publishers incur as they develop books, then compare book prices with increases in tuition and other expenses, you'll realize that textbooks are a better deal than is commonly thought.

EXERCISES

ANALYSIS
1. What sort of buyer behavior is associated with a college's or instructor's decision to adopt a new textbook?
2. If the fixed costs of producing a textbook are $350,000, the variable costs are $10 per book, and the price the publisher receives from the bookstore is

$25, what is the publisher's break-even point?
3. Would your business textbook have the same product life-cycle curve as a basic math text? A classic work of literature?
4. How does the notion of product testing apply to textbooks?
5. How does the idea of packaging apply to textbooks?

APPLICATION
Can you think of any ways to reduce the cost and/or risks of producing textbooks?

DECISION
If you were a successful textbook author and wanted to apply brand extension to create another product (your highly regarded name is

basically the "brand" in this case), would you pick a textbook in a related field (e.g., go from a business text to a business law text) or a book aimed at professional managers?

COMMUNICATION
Assume you write a column in the student newspaper and your new assignment is to explain why textbooks cost what they do. In two or three paragraphs, express the information presented in the video in your own words.

INTEGRATION
Considering the issues of international business described in Chapter 5, do you think textbooks could be exported?

ETHICS
Do you think it is fair for authors and publishers to make a profit from students?

DEBATE
Some upper-level and specialized classes are taught without regular textbooks. The instructor instead collects relevant articles from magazines, journals, and books, then makes copies available for students. Do you think such an approach would work for this introduction to business course?
Option A: In a formal debate format, support or reject the idea.
Option B: Take either side and state your case in a brief summary report.

TEAMWORK
With a team of three other students, survey prices in your college bookstore. Make a list of all the texts that all team members are using during the current term, then identify the range of prices. Speculate why there is a range of prices, based on relative demand and product costs (e.g., a book

with color photographs is more expensive to print than one with black and white photos or no photos at all).

UPDATE RESEARCH
Do the research necessary to write a one-page update on the financial health of either a single publishing company or one of these three industry segments: textbooks, trade books (books for the population in general), or magazines.

ROLE PLAYING
One student should play the role of a college bookstore manager, and several others should play themselves—students faced with expensive textbooks. The manager should explain why the books cost as much as they do.

CHAPTER 14 VIDEO EXERCISE

McKesson Innovates through 150 Years of Successful Wholesaling

SYNOPSIS

This video profiles the innovations and customer support services offered by McKesson, the nation's largest wholesaler of pharmaceuticals and health and beauty products. You see some of the company's advanced technology in action, such as the "picking" machine that can count individual items (such as bottles of aspirin) and load each drugstore's order correctly and efficiently. Like other major wholesalers in this and other industries, McKesson also offers its customers a variety of services, from store design through special marketing assistance. As a wholesaler, McKesson is very interested in helping its customers, the retail stores, sell more to consumers because the more those consumers buy from retailers, the more those retailers buy from McKesson.

EXERCISES

ANALYSIS

1. The automation employed by McKesson doesn't come cheap; does it increase or decrease the final price that consumers pay?

2. Could McKesson afford to invest in automation if its competitors didn't?

3. How does McKesson help its customers compete?

4. What are the risks of investing so much money in distribution technology?

5. Could McKesson utilize its technology by expanding into other areas of wholesaling, such as groceries?

APPLICATION

Name three other industries that could benefit from the sort of high-tech distribution (such as the machines that can collect a variety of small products for shipment to a customer) illustrated by McKesson in the video.

DECISION

Put yourself in the shoes of a pharmacist who has been offered the McKesson Pharmacy Information Center. These computer terminals provide shoppers with information about drug dosages, side effects, and interaction with other medication. You'd like to provide the service for your customers, but you're afraid the terminal might attract a lot of people who don't buy anything from you but only come into the drugstore to get free information. Assuming that the terminal doesn't cost you anything, should you accept McKesson's offer?

COMMUNICATION

Review the points of "The McKesson Advantage" outlined in the video and draft a one-page sales brochure that McKesson could use to promote itself to drugstores.

INTEGRATION

Referring to Exhibit 12.1, explain how McKesson delivers the four types of utility to its drugstore customers.

ETHICS

A recurring dilemma for many wholesalers is the problem of supplying small, remote retail locations that don't buy much and cost a great deal to serve. However, if these retailers can't get wholesalers to supply them, they can't provide the goods their customers want and need. Does McKesson have a social obligation to serve these retailers, even if it must do so for little or no profit?

DEBATE

The video stated that McKesson can satisfy up to 80 percent of the retailer's product needs. Some people might question the wisdom of a retailer relying to such a great extent on a single supplier, even one with the sterling reputation of McKesson. Option A: In a formal debate format, assume the role of a retailer and argue for or against the notion of relying on a single wholesaler for the vast majority of your product needs. Option B: Take either position and state your case in a brief summary report.

TEAMWORK

In a team of three or four students, pick several different types of retail stores and make a list of the services that a wholesaler such as McKesson (or similar companies that serve other industries) could offer. Be sure to consider everything from marketing research to store design, and if time allows, visit representative retail stores to get more ideas.

UPDATE RESEARCH

Do the research necessary to write a one-paragraph summary on either (a) the current status of McKesson and the drug wholesaling industry or (b) trends in electronic data interchange (EDI).

ROLE PLAYING

One student plays the role of a "customer satisfaction" trainer employed by McKesson to help drugstore employees treat customers better. Several other students play store employees who have been accustomed to retail environments in which the emphasis was on selling, selling, selling. The trainer explains the meaning and importance of customer satisfaction in retailing.

CHAPTER 15 VIDEO EXERCISE

Accuvue Commercial Gives Consumers a New Look at Contact Lenses

SYNOPSIS

This video gives you a backstage view of the development of a television commercial. In this case, the commercial is for Accuvue, an innovative disposable contact lens recently introduced by a subsidiary of Johnson & Johnson. Accuvue differs from traditional contact lenses in that there is no cleaning involved. Accuvue wearers simply sign up to receive new pairs at regular intervals and toss out each pair as they get dirty. The video shows how the company and its ad agency identify the single most important benefit to consumers (no cleaning) and how they develop a commercial to communicate that benefit. You'll see how the company combines visual, verbal, and musical elements to create a distinct message.

EXERCISES

ANALYSIS
1. What type of advertising does the Accuvue commercial represent?
2. What role does the advertising agency play in this process?
3. What role do the clients play?
4. Why did the company choose a simple visual presentation, with just the lens, a blue background, and a collection of cleaning solutions that represent the competition?
5. Why did they pick the particular music that was used?

APPLICATION
Identify another product that could benefit from the sort of advertising created for Accuvue and explain how that product benefits customers. You can search back in time for a good example if you like.

DECISION
Would you have put some people in the commercial? If so, who?

COMMUNICATION
Suppose Accuvue's marketers want to back up the TV campaign with radio ads. Write 15 seconds of advertising copy that could be read in a radio commercial.

INTEGRATION
Consider the product life cycle described in Chapter 13. Where was Accuvue at the time this commercial was being created? Where were regular contact lenses?

ETHICS
Suppose the commercial had mentioned competitors by name, as many commercials now do. Do you think it is fair to mention competitors, since they don't have a chance to defend themselves in your ad?

DEBATE
One might argue that the complex photography required to shoot the lens falling in slow motion didn't add much to the ad's effectiveness? Option A: In a formal debate

format, argue for or against this notion. Option B: Take either side and state your case in a brief summary report.

TEAMWORK
With a team of three other students, design a print ad that communicates the same message as the TV commercial you saw in the video. (Rough sketches are fine in place of finished artwork.)

UPDATE RESEARCH
Do the research necessary to write a one-paragraph update on the success or failure of Accuvue.

ROLE PLAYING
With the ad created by your team in the Teamwork part of this exercise, reconfigure the teams with different people and have one person "pitch" the ad idea to the members of the new team, who play the role of clients.

CHAPTER 16 VIDEO EXERCISE

Apple Pulls Small Businesses into the Information Age

SYNOPSIS

This video, produced by Apple Computer to promote the use of its computers in the small-business sector, provides a good introduction to the benefits that computers offer today's managers. Although the video's target audience is the small-business owner, the information-processing ideas shown in it can be applied to virtually every business, from a one-person retail shop to a multinational conglomerate. You'll see computers being put to work in marketing, finance and accounting, planning, and project management. As you watch the video, imagine how computer technology might be applied to a job that you now hold or once held, or perhaps to a small-business venture that you'd like to launch some day.

EXERCISES

ANALYSIS

1. Would a big business apply these techniques in the same way? Why or why not?
2. Why do you suppose Apple aimed this video at small businesses instead of all businesses?
3. Is it possible for computers to slow down, rather than speed up, business operations? Explain your answer.
4. What are the benefits that Apple is promoting in this video?
5. Will your generation have an easier time applying computers to business than your parents' generation had or is having? Explain your answer.

APPLICATION

Pretend you own a baseball memorabilia shop (such as cards and posters). Your customer database includes names, addresses, favorite players, favorite teams, and amount spent. Speculate on some of the ways you could use these data to increase sales.

DECISION

Would you buy a computer for your small business even if you had no computer experience? Explain your answer.

COMMUNICATION

List several ways that computers can help with business communication both inside and outside the company.

INTEGRATION

Referring to the discussion of segmentation in Chapter 12, how could you use computerized customer lists to segment your markets?

ETHICS

All of the capabilities shown in this Apple video are available on IBM PC-compatible computers as well. In fact, in some cases, the very same programs are available on both types of computers. In view of this, was it ethical for Apple to refer to the software you saw in the video as "Macintosh software" when in fact the software (or at least its equivalent capabilities) is available for other computers as well?

DEBATE

You've probably received direct mail that the sender has tried to personalize by inserting your name into the letter, putting your name in the caption of a cartoon, and so on. Option A: In a formal debate format, argue for or against the suggestion that computer-personalized mailings are effective, based on your own response to such letters. Option B: Take either position and state your case in a brief summary report.

TEAMWORK

In a team of four students, research the respective competitive strengths of the Macintosh and DOS systems, Microsoft Windows, and OS/2. From these four system options, recommend the one you think is best for small-business owners.

UPDATE RESEARCH
Do the research necessary to write a one-paragraph update on either (a) Apple's current share of the personal computer market or (b) recent trends in white-collar productivity.

ROLE PLAYING
Divide into small groups based on computer experience; each group should have one experienced computer user. This user then plays the role of a company trainer trying to overcome the rest of the group's fear of computers (if the rest of the group isn't afraid of computers, they can just pretend to be).

CHAPTER 17 VIDEO EXERCISE

Just How Accountable Are Those Accounting Numbers, Anyway?

SYNOPSIS

One of the most important issues in corporate finance is placing a value on a company. Managers inside the company need to know how much the company is worth for several reasons, including judging how well they're handling the company's assets. People outside the company, particularly investors, need to know how much the company is worth so they have some idea of exactly what it is that they're investing in. As this video shows, valuing a company isn't quite as simple as you might think; you can't just walk around with the calculator and add up the value of the company's buildings, machinery, office furniture, and so on—the machinery might be gasping its last breath, for instance, making it far less valuable. And you can't just add up the price of all the company's stock, either; the video points out that stock prices usually far outpace "book value," which represents the best estimate of the company's tangible value.

EXERCISES

ANALYSIS
1. What role should intangibles such as brand names and customer goodwill play when one is placing a value on a company?
2. Does computing book value fall under the umbrella of financial accounting or management accounting?
3. If a company paid off its debts with cash that it had sitting in the bank, would this change the shareholders' equity?
4. Why do companies usually try to keep their debt burdens as low as possible?
5. You saw in the video that Gillette had a large portion of its total assets tied up in inventory; shouldn't it try to reduce the size of this inventory?

APPLICATION
Compute your own net worth, using the same process shown in the video: add up all your assets, then subtract all your liabilities (debts). (For the sake of privacy, feel free to omit any items that

you might not want discussed in class; but don't worry about the magnitude of your net worth—nobody expects college students to be wealthy.)

DECISION
When you computed your net worth in the previous question, how did you arrive at figures for clothes, car, and other personal belongings?

COMMUNICATION
Find a recent article that describes a stock that has dropped in price dramatically. Pretend that you're the CEO of this company, and write a letter to shareholders explaining the sudden drop.

INTEGRATION
Referring to the discussion of insider trading in Chapter 4, list some situations in which company insiders could be in a position to benefit from insider trading.

ETHICS
In terms of disclosing your company's financial health to investors, how far is far enough? For instance, what if you know that a major customer is about to switch to one of your competitors; would you be obligated to tell your shareholders?

DEBATE
When people buy shares in a company, they are basically betting that management will follow a sensible plan for reaching the company's goals. Option A: In a formal debate format, argue for or against the suggestion that management should have to reveal its strategic plans to investors. Option B: Take either position and state your case in a brief summary.

TEAMWORK
In a team of three or four students, obtain a company's annual report and compare the chairman's letter to shareholders with both the financial data contained in the report (see "How To Read an Annual Report" in the chapter) and any recent news that you can find about the company. Does the chairman's letter reflect what you've seen elsewhere?

UPDATE RESEARCH
Do the research necessary to write a one-paragraph update on either (a) recent news that affected Gillette's stock price or (b) any recent changes in accounting rules that affect what companies must tell shareholders.

ROLE PLAYING
Two students play the role of an investment-adviser team, and two others play customers who just received a "great tip" from a friend about a certain stock. The advisers should explain to the customers what they need to do in order to evaluate the stock.

CHAPTER 18 VIDEO EXERCISE

How Much Longer Can Traditional Banks Survive?

SYNOPSIS

This video explores the current plight of traditional banks in this country. Banking boils down to two primary functions: attracting depositors who like the interest rates that you'll pay them and then attracting borrowers who like the interest rates they'll have to pay you. The difference between the rates a bank pays its depositors and earns from its borrowers, minus expenses, is the bank's profit. As this video points out, however, traditional banks are getting squeezed on both fronts. On the deposit side, mutual fund companies such as Fidelity Investments often provide better returns for investors. On the borrowing side, consumers are increasingly turning to car companies for car loans and to specialized mortgage bankers for home loans, taking away two of the bank's biggest traditional customers. And large businesses often bypass regular banks as well, using specialized investment banks instead.

EXERCISES

ANALYSIS

1. How can Ford afford to offer such attractive rates on its car loans?
2. Why would a consumer decide to build, say, a retirement fund through Fidelity, rather than through a regular bank account?
3. How does Fidelity keep its costs so low?
4. With better rates elsewhere, why do consumers bother with traditional banks at all?
5. How much sympathy do you have for troubled banks?

APPLICATION

What are your options for financing your college education (assuming you weren't able to pay as you go and didn't receive a full scholarship)? Did your financing involve banks?

DECISION

Let's say IBM was considering getting into the credit-card business, as Sears and AT&T have done. What issues should IBM consider first?

COMMUNICATION

Write a brief description of investment banking, differentiating it from consumer banking and commercial banking.

INTEGRATION

Referring to the discussion of the business environment in Chapter 1, what are the environmental forces causing so much trouble for banks?

ETHICS

Is it fair to tie banks' hands, as the banking executive explains the government is doing?

DEBATE

Should taxpayers foot the bill for bailing out failed banks and savings and loan institutions? Option A: In a formal debate format, argue for or against the suggestion that taxpayers should pay. Option B: Take either position and state your case in a brief summary report.

TEAMWORK

With a team of three or four students, find out why banks were excluded from certain financial services back in the Great Depression, then decide if you think the exclusions are still necessary or fair.

UPDATE RESEARCH

Do the research necessary to find out whether banks are still prohibited from selling mutual funds and other securities.

ROLE PLAYING

One student should play a taxpayer advocate who is testifying to Congress that taxpayers shouldn't have to foot the bill for bank bailouts. Several other students play members of Congress.

CHAPTER 19 VIDEO EXERCISE

The Boston Celtics Slam Dunk the Stock Market

SYNOPSIS

This video bridges the gap between professional sports and big-time finance by explaining how the owners of the Boston Celtics made a sizable fortune by selling shares in the team to stock-market investors. The program takes a look at the role that logic and emotion play in stock-market investing as well: Celtic fans bought up the stock soon after it was first offered to the public, but dispassionate investors waited until the fan frenzy was over. The "real" investors were able to buy the stock at a lower price because after the initial emotional rush to buy, the stock's prices gradually fell. The video also considers the rather substantial risks that an investment in a sports organization entails, particularly given the age and health of Boston's current lineup.

EXERCISES

ANALYSIS

1. Why don't all companies adopt a "pay as you go" approach and finance their expansion through current sales, rather than selling shares to the public?

2. Beyond the initial emotional rush, do you think Celtics fans will keep investing in the team?

3. Would you make an investment that didn't give you any say in how the company is run?

4. How could investors minimize the risks of investing in sports teams?

5. Do you think players' salaries should be tied to team performance?

APPLICATION

Could a musical group make the same move the Celtics did, selling shares to the public?

DECISION

Would you buy stock in your favorite sports team?

COMMUNICATION

Pretend that you own a team that is about to sell shares to the public (use a real team if you want). Write a letter to fans explaining why you think this is a good investment for them to make.

INTEGRATION

Do any of the production management ideas discussed in Chapter 8 apply to a professional sports team?

ETHICS

How far should a sports team (or any company for that matter) have to go in terms of explaining risks to potential investors. For instance, should the Celtics make it very clear that Larry Bird can't be expected to play for too many more years?

DEBATE

Given the roller-coaster fortunes of most sports teams, some people would think it crazy to invest in one. Option A: In a formal debate format, argue for or against the wisdom of investing in a team. Option B: Take either position and state your case in a brief summary.

TEAMWORK

Team up with two or three other students and together decide how you would invest $10,000 in the stock market. Be prepared to explain your choices to the class.

UPDATE RESEARCH

Do the research necessary to write a quick summary of either (a) the recent price of Celtics stock or (b) moves by other pro teams to sell stock to the public.

ROLE PLAYING

Using the stock picks your team made in the Teamwork exercise, play the role of a stockbroker trying to convince customers to make these same investments. One or more students play the role of potential buyers.

CHAPTER 20 VIDEO EXERCISE

The ABCs of Investing: Getting Smart Is the First Step Toward Getting Rich

SYNOPSIS

This video offers a different sort of program than the others you've seen in this class—this one provides basic advice for anybody who wants to invest money, which presumably applies to just about everyone taking this class. You can use the concepts to improve your current investing skills or to get you started in investing if you haven't already. The video starts with the most important investment decision you have to make: setting your financial goals. Whether it's saving for retirement, a house, or a new car, investing is more successful if you have a clear, realistic goal in mind. The program then outlines the major classes of investments—stocks, bonds, and mutual funds—and explains how each one works, then it concludes with a look at how you can become a better-informed investor. (The program was produced by CNBC, an all-business cable TV channel, which explains the advice on watching CNBC for investment news.)

EXERCISES

ANALYSIS
1. Why would you buy mutual funds instead of individual stocks and bonds?
2. Who should be the more aggressive investor: a single 25-year-old or a 50-year-old with two kids in college?
3. If you work or have worked for a publicly traded company, would you buy some of its stock as an investment? Why or why not?
4. If your college or university were a publicly traded company, would you buy some of its stock as an investment? Why or why not?
5. Are bonds always a safer investment than stocks?

APPLICATION
Would it be a good idea to borrow money in order to invest in the stock market?

DECISION
If you were investing both your own money and your parents' retirement fund (let's assume that you're in your twenties and your parents are a dozen years or so from retirement), would you use the same style of investing?

COMMUNICATION
Pretend you just made an investment for a friend (pick any investment you like). Now write your friend a letter and explain why you made this particular choice.

INTEGRATION
Review the topic of business plans in Chapter 3, then list the points you would consider before investing in a new company.

ETHICS
Should stockbrokers be held responsible for their recommendations to customers?

DEBATE
Some people would never trust their own judgment in the stock market, whereas others always make their own buy and sell decisions. Option A: In a formal debate format, argue for the idea of always (or usually) making your own investment choices or for the idea of letting a professional make these decisions for you. Option B: Take either position and state your case in a brief summary report.

TEAMWORK
Assume that you and a team of three or four other students are partners in a small company that just received $1 million in a legal settlement. Decide how you should invest it, making up whatever details about the company that you need.

UPDATE RESEARCH
Do the research necessary to list the latest values of the Dow Jones Industrial Average, the S&P 500, and the NASDAQ Composite.

ROLE PLAYING
Two students should play the role of a couple who want to start investing but who are currently overloaded with consumer debt.

A third student plays the role of an investment adviser who gives them a plan to get out of debt and into investing.

CHAPTER 21 VIDEO EXERCISE

No Wonder People Call It the "Bank of Crooks & Criminals"

SYNOPSIS

The scandal involving the Bank of Credit and Commerce International (BCCI) was one of the largest the world has seen in recent years. Depositors were devastated as the bank crumbled after several governments learned of its illegal activities and clamped down on it. This video describes how BCCI was able to get away with as much as it did, and in the process explains the general state of global banking regulation. Some of the more interesting issues in this case include the way drug smugglers use renegade banks to harbor and hide their huge sums of cash and the problems created by vastly different government regulations and enforcement capabilities in various countries around the world.

AWAN: I'm not concerned further than that because, you know, I'm not really responsible for the morals of, um, of your customers. I deal with you.

EXERCISES

ANALYSIS
1. Why should the U.S. government ever allow foreign banks to do business here?
2. Why do you suppose BCCI didn't crumble after Bank of America backed out of the partnership?
3. Can you speculate as to why Bank of America ever got involved with BCCI in the first place?
4. How can a bank's owners influence banking regulations in a given country?
5. Why don't all countries simply band together to create one common set of banking regulations?

APPLICATION
List several others situations in which loopholes in global government regulations could adversely affect consumers in a given country.

DECISION
Let's assume you're about to open a savings account with the $10,000 you got for your birthday. In terms of safety, how would you decide which bank to use?

COMMUNICATION
Let's say a government regulator forced you, one of BCCI's owners, to write a letter of apology to all depositors. Assume for the mo-

ment that BCCI has no money left to repay these depositors. What will you say?

INTEGRATION
How did the Cayman Islands' use of a comparative advantage contribute to the BCCI scandal?

ETHICS
Should the Cayman Islands and/or Luxembourg repay the depositors who lost money in BCCI?

DEBATE
Some people might say that we should feel sorry for the depositors who lost money in BCCI but that

public funds (i.e., taxes) shouldn't be used to compensate depositors since it was either bad judgment or simply bad luck that got them into trouble. Option A: In a formal debate format, argue for or against the notion that depositors should basically be on their own. Option B: Take either position and state your case in a brief summary.

TEAMWORK

With several other students acting as cooperative researchers, prepare a presentation to the class on the whole BCCI story, from how the bank was formed to current legal action against the people involved with it.

UPDATE RESEARCH

Do the research necessary to write a one-paragraph update on either (a) the current legal status of Clark Clifford and the other owners of First American or (b) what happened to depositors in England and other countries who lost money when BCCI's accounts were frozen.

ROLE PLAYING

One student should play the role of a U.S. government official trying to convince several other students, representing the government of the Cayman Islands, that the Caymans have a moral responsibility to tighten banking regulations.

CHAPTER 22 VIDEO EXERCISE

It's Hard to Find Much Health in Our Health-Care System

SYNOPSIS

The state of health care in general and health-care insurance in particular is of great concern to consumers and business owners alike. Even as the United States continues as one of the world's leading economic powers, our health-care system sports some embarrassing features, such as one of the highest infant-mortality rates among industrialized nations and millions of people who have no health-care insurance and consequently little or no way to pay for health care. This video examines a proposal made by President George Bush aimed at improving the system. The first part of the program identifies the major points of the Bush plan, and the second part involves a discussion featuring experts on both sides of the political aisle. Don't be too surprised by the complexity of the discussion—it only represents the complexity of this nation's health-care situation.

EXERCISES

ANALYSIS

1. Have you or your family ever shopped around for health care (whether for insurance, for a family doctor, or for a specific medical procedure)? If you haven't shopped around, how did you reach a decision?

2. What is Representative Richard Gephart's major complaint about the Bush proposal?

3. Do you think the health-care issue in general is well understood by the average consumer and taxpayer?

4. How important is this issue to business owners and managers?

5. Summarize the current prob-

lems with our health-care system.

APPLICATION
Can you identify any steps that companies could take to reduce the amount of money that they and their employees spend on health care?

DECISION
What are the things you would think about when deciding whether or not to change health-insurance coverage from one insurance company to another?

COMMUNICATION
Assume that you're the owner of a small business that provides health insurance for its employees. Write a letter to your employees, explaining the need to economize on health-care expenditures and list several ways to do so.

INTEGRATION
Refer to the discussion of costs in Chapter 13. Are a company's health-insurance premiums a fixed or variable cost?

ETHICS
One of the most vexing issues in health-care today is the amount of money spent on innovative machines and procedures designed to prolong the lives of people with serious illnesses and injuries. Some observers say that we should spend less money on these advanced technologies (which the well-insured or the wealthy can afford) and more money on basic health care for all citizens (such as better prenatal care for poor mothers). What do you think?

DEBATE
Some people might question why companies ever got strapped with the burden of health-care insurance in the first place. Option A: In a formal debate format, argue for or against the suggestion that companies are obligated to provide (or at least share the cost of providing) their employees with health insurance. Option B: Take either position and state your case in a brief summary.

TEAMWORK
With a team of three or four other students, research the health-care crisis in this country and its effect on business, then prepare a brief presentation to the class on your findings.

UPDATE RESEARCH
Do the research necessary to write a one-paragraph summary on either (a) whatever happened to the Bush proposal or (b) any similar legislation currently before Congress.

ROLE PLAYING
One student should play the role of a business owner explaining to his or her employees that the company can no longer afford to provide health insurance for them. Several other students play the employees about to lose their coverage.

Business Today

McGraw-Hill, Inc.

New York St. Louis San Francisco Auckland Bogotá Caracas
Lisbon London Madrid Mexico Milan Montreal New Delhi Paris
San Juan Singapore Sydney Tokyo Toronto

Business Today

Seventh Edition

David J. Rachman

Department of Marketing
Bernard M. Baruch College
of the City University of New York

Michael H. Mescon

Regents Professor of Human Relations
and Holder of the
Bernard B. and Eugenia A. Ramsey
Chair of Private Enterprise
Georgia State University

Courtland L. Bovée

Professor of Business Administration
C. Allen Paul Distinguished Chair
Grossmont College

John V. Thill

Chief Executive Officer
Communication Specialists of America

BUSINESS TODAY

2 3 4 5 6 7 8 9 0 VNH VNH 9 0 9 8 7 6 5 4 3 2

ISBN 0-07-006821-6

This book was set in Caslon and Eras by York Graphic Services, Inc.
The editors were Bonnie K. Binkert, James Nageotte, and Bob Greiner;
the designer was Armen Kojoyian;
cover illustration by Roy Weimann;
the production supervisor was Annette Mayeski.
The photo editor was Elyse Rieder;
the photo manager was Kathy Bendo.
Exhibits were rendered by Fine Line Illustrations, Inc.
Von Hoffmann Press, Inc., was printer and binder.

Library of Congress Cataloging-in-Publication Data

Rachman, David J.
    Business today / David J. Rachman . . . [et al.].—7th ed.
        p.   cm.
    Includes index.
    ISBN 0-07-006821-6
    1. Business.   2. Management—United States.   I. Title.
    HF5351.R26   1993
    658—dc20   92-17433

Contents in Brief

Contents

CHAPTER 3

CHAPTER 11

SPECIAL FEATURES

▶ The Challenge of
Organizing Today's
Work Force 302

▶ Should Workers Strike
When the Public Welfare
Is at Stake? 306

▶ Keeping Current Using
*The Wall Street
Journal* 323

PART FOUR

CHAPTER 12

CHAPTER 13

Preface

To date, more than two million students have learned about business from *Business Today,* and its popularity continues. Although widely imitated, *Business Today* remains unique, conveying the excitement and flavor of American business better than any other textbook.

No other textbook is as trusted as *Business Today,* which is relied on for its topic coverage, currency, ancillary package, service, and commitment to students. *Business Today* presents a balanced view of business—the strengths, weaknesses, successes, failures, problems, and challenges. With its vast array of features, it gives students a solid underpinning for more advanced courses, and it explains the opportunities, rewards, and challenges of a business career.

Business Today, Seventh Edition, continues its respected tradition of excellence. Students not only read about business, they experience it firsthand through a variety of highly involving activities in every chapter that no other textbook can match. Students appreciate its up-to-date real-life examples, its carefully integrated in-depth coverage, its lively conversational writing style, and its eye-opening contemporary graphics. With its powerful video exercises, integration of international examples and concepts throughout the book, coverage of current events, exploration of important ethical and societal issues, activities that foster critical thinking, and wealth of assignments to improve students' business communication skills, this edition implements the guidelines for undergraduate business programs of the American Association of Collegiate Schools of Business.

The Seventh Edition has been extensively revised and updated, with two important goals in mind: (1) to provide a clear and complete description of the concepts underlying business, and (2) to illustrate with real-life examples and cases the remarkable dynamism and liveliness of business organizations and of the people who operate them. Every chapter in this edition has been improved and enriched to give students an even better learning experience.

▶ INTEGRATED VIDEO EXERCISES TEACH IMPORTANT CONCEPTS

The ability to drive home a point—to excite the human mind and to stimulate action—is what makes videos so incredibly powerful. Now you can harness this power and bring the drama and immediacy of real-world business into your classroom. The high-quality videos that accompany this text allow students to meet, on location, a cross section of real people who work for some of the world's most fascinating companies, including small, medium, and large firms as well as nonprofit and international organizations. But most important, these videos enable you to challenge your students with the unique set of exercises placed at the front of this book.

Business Today videos and exercises do more than simply relate to end-of-chapter cases. Each video is integrated with chapter material and keyed to the text with a logo in the margin. The exercises are far more involving than simple discussion questions. Students are asked to react to the videos by responding to questions, making decisions, and taking the initiative to solve real business problems. Closely integrated with the content of the chapter, and offering instructors maximum flexibility in selecting various types of student assignments, the exercises for each video contain ten labeled components: analysis, application, decision, communication, integration, ethics, debate, teamwork, update research, and role playing. These critically acclaimed videos and valuable exercises surpass those offered with any other text and are unparalleled in helping students understand how business principles and concepts in the chapter are applied in the workplace. Examples include

- The Body Shop: Structuring a Business for Profit and Social Good
- Lotus Bridges the Cultural Gap in Japan
- General Dynamics: Are Employees about to Buy a Lemon?
- The Boston Celtics Slam Dunk the Stock Market

▶ INTERNATIONAL EXAMPLES OFFER A GLOBAL PERSPECTIVE

When students enter the business world, they will most likely be facing competition not only from home but also from abroad. As it becomes harder and harder to separate the domestic business climate from the growing global economy, students have a vital need to understand international business. Thus today's business texts must have a global perspective, and *Business Today* integrates hundreds of international examples throughout its 22 chapters. These examples describe U.S. companies doing business overseas, as well as overseas organizations doing business in the United States and other countries. Specifically, coverage of international business includes

· A complete chapter (see Chapter 5) on international business

· A series of "Exploring International Business" boxes throughout the book

· Cases such as "Cautious Hope for a United Korea," "Pepperoni Wrapped in Red Tape," and "Making History in Hungary—Almost"

· A map of one or more countries in each chapter of the book—all carefully tied to the text

· Numerous examples throughout the book that focus on international principles and practices

· Video exercises focusing on multinational companies such as Lotus in Asia and McDonald's in Europe

▶ ETHICAL AND SOCIETAL MATERIAL EXPLORES TODAY'S MOST IMPORTANT ISSUES

Whether small enterprises or multinational corporations, companies throughout the world are attempting to resolve ethical dilemmas. Today's students need to understand social responsibility as it relates to the environment, consumers, employees, and investors. This edition includes a well-rounded chapter (see Chapter 4) that discusses ethical decision making on both the individual and the corporate levels.

This text fires students' enthusiasm and respect for business, but it doesn't pretend that business is without problems or critics. By pointing out ethical dilemmas and by reminding students of the responsibilities that accompany the rights of free enterprise,

Business Today helps prepare the next generation of conscientious businesspeople. Here are just a few of the social/ethical issues discussed in the text:

· AIDS in the workplace

· Credit reports

· Employee drug testing

· English-only on the job

· Environmental pollution

· Executive compensation

· Glass ceiling

· Negligent hiring

· 900 telephone numbers

· Privacy and marketing databases

· Product liability

· Sexual harassment

· Whistle blowers

In addition, a series of "Focus on Ethics" boxes appear throughout the book so that students can see that nearly every aspect of business presents ethical questions.

Business Today has no examples promoting alcohol. The authors certainly support companies' rights to market their products, but considering that many students taking this course are not of legal drinking age and that alcoholism among college students is increasing, the authors believe that an emphasis on alcoholic products in a textbook is inappropriate. *Business Today* also avoids tobacco examples (other than those instances in which tobacco products are the subject of critical discussion). The business literature offers thousands of great examples that students can relate to, and this edition takes advantage of those.

▶ SPECIFIC FEATURES STIMULATE AND DEVELOP CRITICAL THINKING

National test results show a serious weakness in the ability of U.S. students to reason, analyze, interpret, synthesize, and solve problems. According to respected reports on the state of higher education by the National Commission on Excellence in Education, the National Institute of Education, and the Association of American Colleges, fostering students' ability to think critically should be one of the major effects of an undergraduate education.

Moreover, labor forecasters predict that between now and the end of this century, the majority of the work force in the United States will change jobs, change careers, or need retraining. Therefore, if students are to make a successful transition from the classroom to the workplace and maintain uninterrupted, rewarding employment, they must apply the critical thinking skills that will make them adaptable workers.

Critical thinking calls for skills such as observing, classifying, interpreting, criticizing, summarizing, analyzing, comparing, hypothesizing, collecting and organizing information, making decisions, and applying knowledge to new situations. Specific features in *Business Today* have been designed to stimulate critical thinking and to develop these vital skills more effectively than any other introductory business text. These features include the questions at the conclusion of the chapter-opening "Facing a Business Challenge" vignettes, the chapter concluding "Meeting a Business Challenge" case study/simulations, chapter-ending review questions, chapter-ending cases, "Building Your Communication Skills" exercises, "Keeping Current Using *The Wall Street Journal*" exercises, and experiential video exercises.

In addition, *Business Today* offers a self-study *Critical Thinking Guide,* and a *Communication Skills Guide,* both available in quantity to adopters, and The Investment Challenge (portfolio management) game. Two computer simulations are also available: Threshold: A Competitive Management Simulation, and SHOES: A Marketing Simulation.

▶ SMALL BUSINESS TAKES CENTER STAGE

Today's business students, more than any other recent group of students, have strong entrepreneurial interests. Although comparatively few will ever be self-employed, many will work for small enterprises. In either case, they have an obvious need to understand the risks and rewards, the problems and the perils, of small business. An entire chapter is devoted to this subject (see Chapter 3), and throughout this book smaller businesses are used as examples.

▶ RELIABLE AND EFFECTIVE PEDAGOGY SPARKS STUDENT LEARNING

Business Today includes an extraordinary number of pedagogical devices that simplify teaching, facilitate learning, maintain interest and enjoyment, and illustrate the practical application of chapter concepts. In short, these devices make the new edition the most effective teaching tool for introductory business ever published.

"Facing a Business Challenge" Introduces Each Chapter

As a glance at the table of contents will reveal, each chapter begins with "Facing a Business Challenge," a slice-of-life vignette that attracts the students' interest by vividly portraying a business challenge faced by a real executive. The vignette closes with thought-provoking questions that help draw students into the chapter and that provide a rationale for studying the chapter. References throughout the chapter to the opening vignette help students see the connection between the chapter's content and the real world of business. The special dimension of reality provided by these vignettes helps students develop a genuine interest in the world of business, which is the first step in learning about it.

"Meeting a Business Challenge" Concludes Each Chapter

Each chapter concludes with an end-of-chapter case study/simulation that (1) elaborates on the actions taken by the executive featured in the vignette, and (2) analyzes the results in light of the concepts presented in the chapter. Then the student takes over, playing a role in the executive's organization by making business decisions in four carefully chosen scenarios. These case study/simulations include

· Microsoft: Struggling to Survive Success

· Campbell Soup: Organizing a National Kitchen

· Johnson & Johnson: Keeping Employees in the Pink and the Company in the Black

· Nike: Running a Race That Never Ends

· Orville Redenbacker: Personality with a Pop

Boxes Center on Five Well-Integrated Themes

Boxes, referred to as Special Features, are strategically placed in every chapter to help make the world of business come alive. They are based on extensive research in business literature, and they further enhance the practical flavor of the book.

Behind the Scenes

These boxes exemplify timely issues of vital importance to contemporary business by introducing companies, organizations, products, and people whose names have surfaced recently in the business media. Examples include "World-Class Manufacturing at Next," "The Mysteries of Product Packaging," and "Risk Management in the Entertainment Industry Is Serious Business."

Techniques for Business Success

These "how-to" guidelines demonstrate ways business concepts can be applied in a practical way. They include "Seven Common Mistakes Small Businesses Make—and How to Avoid Them," "How to Read an Annual Report," "How to Plan and Negotiate a Business Loan," and "How to Make a Stock Purchase."

Focus on Ethics

These boxes present current ethical issues in business. They include "Does Capitalism Cause Pollution?" "How Do Your Ethics Measure Up?" "Should Employees Speak English on the Job?" and "Should Companies Be Allowed to Withhold Information about Potentially Harmful Products?"

Checklist for Business Today

These boxes present information in a checklist format to guide students in organizing their thinking and to help them make decisions. Examples are "Have You Got What It Takes to Be a Small-Business Owner?" "Would You Make a Good Manager?" and "Stock Analysis: Calculating Prospects for Growth."

Exploring International Business

This series of boxes demonstrates to students the impact of international business on virtually every topic in this text. Examples include "Gift Versus Bribe: When a Friendly Exchange Turns into Risky Business," "How to Avoid Business Blunders Abroad," and "Can Universal Appeal Overcome Cultural Differences?"

Cases Present Challenging Business Problems

At the end of each chapter, "A Case for Critical Thinking" provides further illustration and practical application of key concepts. This classic device assists students in evaluating situations, using good judgment, learning to make decisions, and developing critical thinking skills. The case questions reinforce major points made in the chapter. Case topics include

- Mail Boxes Etc.: Putting a Stamp on the Market
- The Pizza Olympics: A Question of Dough
- High-Tech Time Bomb: The Spread of Computer "Viruses"—and Their Prevention
- Hub-and-Spoke Is Wheel of Fortune for Federal Express

Maps Help Develop Geographic Literacy

Each chapter features a map of one or more countries that relate to the text. The "Business Around the World" captions give a "news flash" description of relevant business concepts, topics, or challenges being dealt with by companies or governments in the countries identified. These maps enhance students' knowledge of geography and focus attention on the global nature of business.

New Exercises Build Communication Skills

The ability to communicate well—whether listening, speaking, reading, or writing—is a skill students must possess to have a successful career. Because of their extensive research and writing in the area of communication, the authors are especially equipped to help your students develop these skills. You'll find unique Building Your Communication Skills exercises near the end of each chapter. Students are called on to practice a wide range of communication activities, including one-on-one and group discussions, class debates, personal interviews, panel sessions, oral and written reports, and letter writing assignments.

Also available to adopters is a *Communication Skills Guide,* a supplement offering practical advice and hands-on exercises to help students improve their written and oral skills.

"The Wall Street Journal" Exercises Keep Students Current

To emphasize the link between today's business news and *Business Today,* a "Keeping Current Using *The Wall Street Journal*" exercise is provided at the end of each chapter. The exercises ask students to choose an article and then provide a structure for analyzing it in the context of the material covered in the chapter. These exercises offer interesting and useful ways to utilize *The Wall Street Journal* in the classroom and give students practice in the critical skill of interpreting business news.

Understanding Wall Street, a valuable supplement that takes the reader on an in-depth tour of the stock, bond, mutual fund, and commodities markets, is also available.

Real-Life Examples Translate Theory into Practice

Educational experiments demonstrate that students learn more and are more interested in their studies when actual people, organizations, and events are presented. True-to-life examples also help prepare students for the world of work by showing them how theory translates into practice. One of the most important characteristics of *Business Today* is its realism. In addition to having a factual chapter-opening vignette and real cases, each chapter contains abundant examples from businesses of every size and from a wide range of industries.

Learning Objectives Establish Benchmarks for Measuring Success

Each chapter begins with a list of objectives that summarizes exactly what students should learn as a result of studying the chapter. These objectives, which are organized to reflect the sequence of topics within the chapter, guide the learning process and help motivate students to master the material.

At the end of each chapter, the "Summary of Learning Objectives" restates the learning objectives and summarizes chapter highlights, a feature designed to reinforce learning of basic concepts.

A Four-Way Approach Reinforces Business Terminology

Because business has its own special terminology, an important goal of this textbook is vocabulary development. First, each key term is printed in boldface within the text. Second, a definition appears in the margin adjacent to the term. Third, at the end of each chapter is a list of key terms, in alphabetical order, with convenient cross-references to the pages where they are defined. And fourth, all marginal definitions are also assembled in an alphabetical Glossary at the end of the book. With this four-way method of vocabulary reinforcement, students should be able to learn the basic terminology of the course with ease.

Readable Writing Style Motivates Students

The reading level of this book has been carefully monitored to ensure accessibility for students. The lucid writing style makes the material pleasing to read and easy to comprehend. Every line of text has been carefully edited to ensure that it reads clearly and that there is a smooth transition from one idea to the next.

Full-Color Design and Graphics Reflect the State of the Art

Business Today, Seventh Edition, looks the way it does for more than just artistic reasons. Students are used to reading popular magazines with lots of headings, paragraphs, and boxed material. And because of the pervasive influence of television and film, students expect to be visually stimulated while they learn. To accommodate today's media sophisticates, *Business Today* has been designed to be engrossing and attractive yet still businesslike and professional.

Because of a firm belief that effective design serves both to invite the reader's interest and to reinforce learning, striking new three-dimensional artwork and graphic examples have been created for this new edition. The art program—numerous exhibits and photographs—amounts to a course in itself. Combined with the instructive captions, the art serves as both a preview and a review of each chapter. Boxes, photos, and illustrations appear at the top or bottom of the page or in the margin to avoid interfering with students' attention and concentration.

▶ COMPREHENSIVE RESEARCH PROVIDES A SOLID FOUNDATION

A successful textbook must be revised to reflect changes in the course for which the book is designed. For the Seventh Edition of *Business Today,* over 500 professors of business contributed their viewpoints on trends in instructional methodology for the introductory business course. Their recommendations, as well as those of a distinguished panel of more than 30 academic and business experts, helped shape this new edition.

In addition, the authors conducted an exhaustive study of the literature of business, including hundreds of the very latest articles, reports, monographs, and books. As a glance at the extensive References and Credits section near the end of this book will show, *Business Today* is the most carefully researched and documented introductory business textbook on the market. This attention to detail is in keeping with the goal of accurately portraying the changing nature and emerging trends of business.

▶ CAREFUL PREPARATION OFFERS THE UNIQUE ADVANTAGE OF CURRENCY

For any textbook to meet the needs and expectations of both students and professors, it must reflect the rapid changes occurring every day in the business world. Extraordinary measures have been taken to ensure that *Business Today* is the most up-to-date textbook on the market, with more 1992 references than any other text. Topic coverage includes

· The dramatic changes in the global network of economic systems, including the birth of the Commonwealth of Independent States and the growth of capitalism in traditionally socialist Latin America

· The new method adopted by the United States government for tracking and comparing nations' economies, the gross domestic product (GDP)

· The faltering growth of services in the 1990s (except for health care)

· The impact on business of the Americans with Disabilities Act

· The latest type of affirmative action program, as exemplified by the Pilot Mentor Protege Program

· The free-market approach to controlling pollution

· The issues faced by women in the workplace, including the mommy track, fetal protection, and the glass ceiling

· The practices of foreign companies within the United States and their employment of U.S. workers

· The European Community's unification into a single trading bloc and its agreement with the European Free Trade Association

· The fragile relationship between the United States and Japan

· The Boeing 777 widebody transport plane, high-definition television (HDTV), and magnetic levitation

· The trends toward telecommuting and home-based offices

· The management of global human resources

· The use of knowledge-based pay to motivate employees

· The growth of database marketing and the importance of brand equity

· The emergence of Wal-Mart as the nation's number one retailer

· The trends toward green marketing, electronic couponing, in-store radio networks, and shopping-cart calculators

· The environmental impact of transportation

· The march of technology toward artificial intelligence, including expert systems, natural-language processing, parallel processing, workgroup computing, and palmtop computers

· The health-care industry's attempt to deal with the astronomical costs of the AIDS epidemic

· The ethics and feasibility of medical rationing

· The Los Angeles riots and implications for business

To further assist your students in keeping abreast of current business trends, and to dramatize the latest business developments, selected readings from *Business Week* are available through PRIMIS, an electronic database.

▶ BUSINESS CAREER GRIDS OFFER VITAL GUIDANCE

This edition retains the career grids for each of the functional areas of business (see Appendix I). Each grid reflects current trends in specific fields and includes salary information, job descriptions, and information on the outlook for future growth.

A supplement, *Planning Your Career in Business Today,* is also available. It contains self-assessment material and in-depth career information.

▶ MAJOR REFINEMENTS ENHANCE THE BOOK

This is a brief overview of some of the refinements made in *Business Today,* Seventh Edition. For a more detailed list of changes, see the beginning of each chapter in the Creative Lectures in the Instructor's Manual. Revisions in this edition include

· Updating the dramatic changes in the global network of economic systems and explaining the effects of the increasing internationalization of business

· Examining how the latest recession has affected the service sector and explaining the impact both of favorable government policies and of tough management on the goods-producing sector

· Discussing partners' unlimited liability to include risk-cutting measures such as master limited partnerships, risk insurance, and malpractice insurance

· Reviewing the impact of the 1991–1992 recession and the resulting prospects for new businesses, discussing new legislation and the effect of business cycles, and expanding coverage of entrepreneurship among women and minorities

· Analyzing the Clean Water Act of 1990, explaining the free-market approach to controlling pollution, detailing recent industry efforts to reduce environmental damage, and explaining government attempts to crack down on misleading food labels

· Presenting information on foreign corporations operating in the United States and weighing the impact of the European Community's unification into a single trading bloc

· Introducing the concept of world-class production and discussing the current mandate for environmental responsibility among manufacturers

· Exploring the challenges presented by the culturally diverse work environment of the 1990s and new trends in telecommuting and home-based offices

· Adding new legal and ethical factors in hiring, weighing current challenges such as managing global human resources, and analyzing applications of basic-skills training

· Discussing strategic marketing planning and new insights into market segmentation, database marketing, and VALS 2

· Introducing the 1990s concepts of "brand equity" and "reverse channels," and amplifying the discussion of organizational products with contemporary terminology

· Describing the five classes of computer systems as well as the four basic groups of hardware (from palmtop to supercomputer)

· Updating the effects of the banking mergers, consolidations, and acquisitions of the 1980s along with an analysis of recent bank failures and a discussion of the solvency of the FDIC

· Presenting the implications of proposed legislation on interstate banking, corporate ownership of banks, and authorization for banks to sell securities and insurance

· Explaining contemporary issues such as asset allocation in portfolio management, efficient market hypotheses, and current program trading practices

· Tempering the discussion of deregulation to reflect the current mood of disillusionment, updating the section on government as tax collector, analyzing the impact of a recent Supreme Court decision on product liability, and expanding the section on bankruptcy

▶ INTEGRATED SUPPLEMENTARY MATERIALS MAKE *BUSINESS TODAY* A COMPLETE LEARNING PACKAGE

The supplementary package has been thoroughly revised, and several new elements have been added. The instructor's materials are not only comprehensive, but also totally integrated with the text.

Study Guide
Stanley Garfunkel, CUNY, Queensborough Community College
Dennis Guseman, California State University, Bakersfield

Creative Lectures (four-volume Instructor's Manual)
Judith G. Bulin, Monroe Community College

Test Bank and *Computerized Test Bank*
Stephen Cyrus, Montclair State College
Philip Weatherford, Embry-Riddle Aeronautical University

Business Week (selected readings on the PRIMIS system)

Acetate Transparency Program

Lecture Outline Transparency Master Program

The Business Today *Integrated Video Series*

"Integrated Video Exercises," prepared by Robert Goldberg, Northeastern University, at the front of the text, accompanies the Integrated Video Series. Solutions to the Video Exercises appear in the *Creative Lectures.*

Planning Your Career in Business Today
Les R. Dlabay, Lake Forest College

Critical Thinking Guide
William J. Hisker, St. Vincent College

Guide to Communication Skills
Courtland Bovée and John Thill

Understanding Wall Street
Jeffrey B. Little and Lucien Rhodes

The Investment Challenge (Portfolio Management Game)

Software:　*Testmaker* (Computerized Test Bank)
　　　　　Threshold: A Competitive Management Simulation
　　　　　PC Case: Computerized Cases
　　　　　Computerized Instructor's Manual
　　　　　Report Card: Classroom Management Software
　　　　　SHOES: A Marketing Simulation

▶ ACKNOWLEDGMENTS

A key reason for the continued success of *Business Today* is our extensive market research effort. For this revision, we once again sought the advice of hundreds of instructors around the country. We have worked very hard to create a textbook ideally suited to the unique needs of the introductory business market. Our sincere thanks are extended to the following individuals who responded to our market questionnaires.

The editorial, production, and design qualities of *Business Today,* Seventh Edition, are the result of the combined efforts of many people at McGraw-Hill. We are indebted to our publisher, June Smith, and our editor, Bonnie Binkert, for their support and excellent management of this project.

We are grateful to senior editing supervisor Bob Greiner and associate editor Jim Nageotte for their careful, conscientious work and deep commitment to quality in producing the text and accompanying materials; their outstanding coordination of all the details kept the project on schedule. Thanks are also due to Suzanne Thibodeau and Joe Murphy, editing managers, for their expert guidance; Dan Loch, marketing manager, for his creative suggestions; Carole Schwager, for her superb copyediting skills; Lee Medoff, for his editorial assistance; and Roberta Flechner, for her word processing skills. Caroline Izzo, front matter editor, coordinated and edited introductory portions of the text and ancillaries. And Scott Hardy deserves recognition for his efforts in securing the video segments that make up the video series that accompanies this edition.

Robert Goldberg selected video segments and prepared the analysis exercises to accompany the integrated video series. Valerie Raymond edited the art that appears in the Acetate Transparency Program, as well as the Lecture Outline Transparency Masters. Lisa Mitchell revised Appendix I and managed the updating of *Planning Your Career in Business Today.* Mary Eshelman provided editorial guidance for both *Guide To Communication Skills* and the *Critical Thinking Guide.*

Armen Kojoyian gave the book its clean, attractive design. Annette Mayeski's management of the production process was exemplary. Leon Bolognese's continued dedication to this project is appreciated. Jorge Ramirez coordinated many of the manufacturing details. Finally, Elyse Rieder's photo research under the guidance of Kathy Bendo lent the book a pedagogically sound visual program and an unparalleled appeal.

Specialty Reviewers

Paul Bolster, Northeastern University (MA); **David E. Booth,** Kent State University; **Larry Clark,** Louisiana State University; **Robert Eskew,** Purdue University; **Michael J. Houston,** University of Minnesota; **Frank Hoy,** Georgia State University; **Campbell R. McConnell,** University of Nebraska; **James McElroy,** Iowa State University; **James McHugh,** St. Louis Community College; **Norma Nielson,** Oregon State University; **Charles Parker; Jack L. Smith,** University of South Florida; **Michael L. Smith,** Ohio State University; **Lee Stepina,** Florida State University; **John Steiner,** California State University—Los Angeles; **Brian Toyne,** University of South Carolina; **Bill Werther,** University of Miami

Market Reviewers

Harvey Bronstein, Oakland Community College; **Philip Weatherford,** Embry Riddle Aeronautical University

Simulations Reviewers

Dr. Bertee Adkins, Eastern Kentucky University; **Professor Harold Babson,** Columbus State Community College (OH); **Professor John J. Balek,** Morton College (Il.); **A. J. Brunini,** Champlain College (Vt.); **Professor Larry Goodnight,** Western Nevada Comm. College; **Professor Jeri Harper,** Western Illinois University; **Professor Warren Helmstedter,** Bakersfield College (Ca.); **Professor Jehan G. Kavoosi,** Clarion University of Pennsylvania; **Professor Thomas Lerra,** Quinsigamond Community College (Ma.); **Professor Wayne Moore,** Indiana University of Pennsylvania; **Professor Martin St. John,** Westmoreland County Comm. Coll. (Pa.); **Professor Bill Syvertsen,** Fresno City College; **Professor Rita Thomas Noel,** Western Carolina University; **Paul J. Wolff, II, Ph.D.,** Dundalk Community College (Md.)

Survey Respondents

Professor Xenia A. Adoniou, Endicott College (MA); **Professor John Alderson,** East Arkansas Community College; **Professor Jack Amyx,** Cameron University (OK); **Professor Charles Armstrong,** Kansas City Community College; **Professor Robert Ash,** Rancho Santiago College; **Professor Bertee Atkins,** Eastern Kentucky University; **Professor Hal Babson,** Columbus State Community College (OH); **Professor Judy Baccarella,** Otero Junior College (CO); **Professor John Balek,** Morton College (IL); **Professor Helen Barbor,** Waynesburg College (PA); **Professor Mary Jo Boehms,** Jackson State Community College (TN); **Professor Karen Bradshaw,** Missouri Southern State College; **Professor Harvey Bronstein,** Oakland County Comm. College (MI); **Professor Julie Ann Brown,** Antelope Valley College (CA); **Professor A. J. Brunini, Jr.,** Champlain College (VT); **Dr. Carl Buckel,** College of the Canyons (CA); **Professor John Bunnell,** Broome Community College (NY); **Dr. David Byford,** Lee College (TX); **Professor Joe Cantrell,** DeAnza College (CA); **Professor Robert Carrell,** Vincennes University (IN); **Professor James Catrambona,** Norwalk Community College (CT); **Professor Gary Christianson,** North Iowa Area Community College; **Professor Michael Cicero,** Highline Community College (WA); **Professor Bernard L. Coffey,** Jefferson Community College (NY); **Professor Gilbert S. Cohen,** Montgomery County Comm. Coll. (PA); **Professor Diane Coleman,** Hutchinson Community College (KS); **Professor G. F. Conlin,** Savannah State College; **Professor Robert Connole,** University of Montana; **Professor Gary Cutler,** Dyersburg State Comm. College (TN); **Professor Irmagaard Davis,** Kapiolani Community College (HI); **Professor Nick Dietz,** SUNY-Farmingdale; **Professor Michael Dougherty,** Milwaukee Area Technical College; **Dr. John J. Doyle,** Springfield College (MA); **Professor Sam Dunbar,** Delgado Community College (LA); **Professor Donald Edwards,** Indiana State University; **Professor Darrell Erickson,** Butler County Community College (KS); **Professor John K. Evans,** New Hampshire College; **Professor John Feightner,** Craven Community College (NC); **Professor Francis Foley,** Berry College (GA); **Dr. Carl Gates,** Sauk Valley Community College (IL); **Professor Harold Gelderloos,** Muskegon Community College (MI); · **Professor Marlin Gerber,** Kalamazoo Valley Community College (MI); **Professor Ken Gibson,** Texas A & I University; **Professor Gary Gibson,** Maple Woods Community College (MO); **Professor James R. Glover,** Essex Community College (MD); **Professor Larry Goodnight,** Western Nevada Community College; **Professor Gorno,** Cypress College (CA); **Professor Jerome Guffey,** College of the Redwoods; **Professor Jeri Harper,** Western Illinois University; **Professor Fred Hazlett,** Brookdale Community College (NJ); **Professor Douglas G. Heeter,** Ferris State University (MI); **Professor Warren Helmstedter,** Bakersfield College (CA); **Professor Don Hiebert,** Northern Oklahoma College; **Professor William S. Idalene,** Kearney State College (NE); **Professor Richard Immenhausen,** College.of the Desert (CA); **Professor Michael R. Johnson,** Delaware County Comm. College (PA); **Professor Wallace Johnston,** Virginia Commonwealth University; **Professor George Katz,** San Antonio College; **Professor Robert Kaulfuss,** Middlesex Community College (MA); **Professor Chong W. Kim,** Marshall University (WV); **Professor Jeffrey Klivans,** University of Maine; **Professor Dale Konichek,** Houston Community College; **Dr. Bill Lacewell,** Westark Community College (AR); **Dr. Kenneth Lacho,** University of New Orleans; **Professor Rita Lambrecht,** Northeastern Junior College (CO); **Professor Tom Lerra,** Quinsigamond Community College (MA); **Professor Jean Macdonald,** Norwich University (VT); **Professor Albert Mahrer, Ph.D.,** Front Range Community College (CO); **Dr. Mallory,** Mesa State College (CO); **Professor Michael Martinoff,** Long Beach City College; **Professor Robert Masters,** Fort Hays State University (KS); **Professor Charles Mattox,** St. Mary's University (TX); **Professor Lauren Maxwell,** University of Central Arkansas; **Professor Ina Midkiff,** Austin Community College (TX); **Professor Linda Mitchell,** Lyndon State College (VT); **Professor Wayne Moore,** Indiana University of Pennsylvania; **Professor Bill Motz,** Lansing Community College; **Professor Pracheta Mukherjee,** Slippery Rock University (PA); **Professor Robert Mullins,** Delgado Community College (LA); **Professor Eric H. Nielsen,** College of Charleston (SC); **Professor Rebecca Oatsvall,** Meredith College (NC); **Professor Billye Peterson,** Central State University (OK); **Professor Melinda Phillabaum,** Indiana University; **Professor Bill Platzer,** Incarnate Word College (TX); **Professor Ken R. Rachal,** Nicholls State University (LA); **Professor Ravi Ramamurti,** Northeastern University (MA); **Professor Margaret Raney,** Northern Essex Community College (MA); **Professor Rose Raynak,** Delta College (MI); **Professor Margaret Rechter,** University of Pittsburgh; **Professor Deborah Roebuck,** Kennesaw State College (GA); **Professor Jill Russell,** Camden County College; **Professor Martin St. John,** Westmoreland Cty Comm. College (PA); **Professor Eugene Schneider,** Austin Community College—Rio Grande Campus; **Professor Henry W. Schoen,** Prince Georges Community College (MD); **Professor Ron Schoneberg,** McCook Community College (NE); **Professor Raymond Shea,** Monroe Community College (NY); **Professor Frank J. Siebold,** Pennsylvania State University; **Professor Kathleen Simmons,** Gainesville College; **Professor Gwen Smith,** Louisiana State University; **Professor Carl Sonntag,** Pike's Peak Community College (CO); **Professor Lee Sutherland,** Suffolk University (MA); **Professor Bill Syvertsen,** Fresno Community College; **Professor Zachary Taylor, Jr.,** LaGrange College (GA); **Professor John Thomas,** UC Riverside; **Professor Rita Thomas Noel,** Western Carolina University; **Dr. Sandra Toy,** Orange Coast College (CA); **Dr. P. A. Weatherford,** Embry Riddle Aeronautical University (FL); **Professor Rick Webb,** Johnson County Community College (KS); **Professor Jim Wells,** Daytona Beach Comm.

College; **Professor Allan Weintraub,** Tulsa Junior College Metro; **Professor Ron Weston,** Contra Costa College (CA); **Professor Patti Wilber,** Northwestern Oklahoma State University; **Professor J. Richard Williams,** Laramie County Comm. College (WY); **Professor Paul Wolff,** Dundalk Community College (MD)

Our thanks to Terry Anderson, whose outstanding communication skills, breadth of knowledge, and organizational ability assured this project of clarity and completeness. We are also indebted to Jackie Estrada, for her expertise and dedication. And a very special acknowledgment to the late Jane D. Pogeler, whose assistance for the past three editions is deeply appreciated.

David J. Rachman
Michael H. Mescon
Courtland L. Bovée
John V. Thill

A Preview of Business Today

CHAPTER 5

International Business

LEARNING OBJECTIVES
After studying this chapter, you will be able to

1 Differentiate between an absolute advantage and a comparative advantage in international trade.

2 Distinguish between the balance of trade and the balance of payments.

3 List and describe three international trade pacts.

4 Identify five techniques that countries use to protect their domestic industries.

5 Cite five drawbacks to protectionism.

6 Discuss the impact of a weaker dollar on U.S. companies.

7 List five common forms of international business activity.

8 Cite five things you can do to facilitate international business relationships.

Facing a Business Challenge at Pizza Hut
PEPPERONI WRAPPED IN RED TAPE

After opening Pizza Huts for PepsiCo's restaurant division in Africa, Eastern Europe, Scandinavia, and the Middle East, Andrew Rafalat figured he could start a Pizza Hut from scratch on the moon if he had to. The moon maybe—but Moscow was something else. "Setting up a business here was like setting up an island in an ocean," Rafalat explained. "You hoped it would survive the storm." No one could know how severe a storm was coming—or when. Before Russia joined eleven other republics to form the Commonwealth of Independent States (CIS), before the death of the communist party, before the ill-fated coup that attempted to restore old-guard communism to the people, and even before Gorbachev formally asked the West for help in moving his country toward capitalism, companies like Pizza Hut saw the promise of new markets in the ailing economy of the Soviet Union.

Actually, Rafalat was luckier than most Westerners trying to penetrate the Soviet system. He had the backing of a giant multinational corporation that had been doing business in the USSR for years. Pepsi's involvement there began in 1959 when Donald Kendall displayed the company's soft drinks at a trade show in Moscow. Kendall, who later became chairman and CEO of PepsiCo, was intrigued by the potential of selling soda pop to 290 million thirsty comrades. He was determined to find a way to get Pepsi-Cola into their hands. It took him 13 years, but in 1972 he finally negotiated a trade agreement providing for the bottling and sale of Pepsi in the USSR, making Pepsi the first foreign consumer product to cross the iron curtain. Today, Pepsi is the leading soft drink in the CIS and in much of Eastern Europe.

Having done so well with its cola, PepsiCo was eager to introduce other staples of the U.S. diet through its restaurant and snack food divisions, which include Pizza Hut, Kentucky Fried Chicken, Taco Bell, and Frito-Lay. Anatoli

▲ **LEARNING OBJECTIVES**
Each chapter begins with a concise list of objectives that students are expected to achieve. The end-of-chapter summary is keyed to these objectives so that important concepts are reinforced.

▲ **FACING A BUSINESS CHALLENGE**
Each chapter opens with a slice-of-life vignette that attracts the students' interest by vividly portraying a business challenge faced by a real executive.

Meeting a Business Challenge at Pizza Hut

When PepsiCo decided to get into the pizza business in the Soviet Union, it established some long-term goals to guide the effort. The company set a basic objective of blanketing the country with Pizza Huts; running a couple of isolated restaurants in Moscow simply wouldn't be profitable enough to justify the effort. Given this ambitious plan, the first two restaurants represented a chance to establish a model that could be duplicated in other parts of the country.

Andrew Rafalat's job, then, was not only to get the two Moscow Pizza Huts up and running, but also to lay the foundation for building a significant presence in the rest of the country. His plan was to set things up, iron out the wrinkles, and train Soviet managers to open similar facilities in other cities. "If we don't develop a construction, supply, and management infrastructure here in Moscow, then we don't have a future in this market," Rafalat explained.

Rafalat started with the Moscow City government. Under Soviet law at the time, foreign companies could not hold a majority interest in a Soviet business, and ownership of private property by Soviet citizens was still restricted. So Pizza Hut had to operate through joint ventures with government entities—in this case, the City of Moscow, which owns 51 percent of the two restaurants.

Rafalat had to pick sites for the first two Pizza Huts. Government officials, who weren't quite sure what a profit *is* and who had doubts about the morality of making one, offered to donate two cellars on the outskirts of Moscow. Rafalat pointed out that succeeding in the restaurant business generally involves putting the outlets where the people are. He eventually wrangled two reasonably decent spots, one with the capacity to seat 325 people; the other, 120 people. After an initial rush of heavy business, the two restaurants were expected to serve between 3,000 and 5,000 cus-

Andrew Rafalat (standing) of Pepsi-Co's Pizza Hut

tomers per day. The typical U.S. Pizza Hut serves approximately 1,200 customers per day, whereas the European average is 2,000 per day.

Although Rafalat originally planned to rely on local supplies to equip, furnish, and stock the restaurants, he quickly discovered that this was not practical. Nothing was available. He had to import virtually everything from the West, from building materials to tomato concentrate to pizza ovens and restaurant furniture. Eventually, he hopes to develop local sources, particularly for pizza ingredients.

Initially, though, he had to arrange to ship 45 different 20-foot containers from a collection point in London to Moscow. He tried at first to use an all-Soviet transportation route, but the initial shipments were lost for several weeks. Rafalat switched to a London-based shipping company that routed the containers through the port of Helsinki, Finland, and then transferred them to East European and Finnish trucks for the trip south to the Pizza Hut warehouse in Moscow. The warehouse soon had more food than the average Moscow supermarket, including 20 tons of mozzarella and 20 tons of meat toppings.

Rafalat needed to hire and train roughly 300 people—managers, chefs, and other kitchen and restaurant

help. He needed to teach them to make pizza, of course, but more important, he had to teach them about customer service. He hired teenagers rather than more experienced workers because it's easier to teach young people to smile. (At a typical state-owned restaurant in Moscow, customers wait an hour and a half to get seated, wait again for menus, and again to place an order. Then they wait a little longer to be told the kitchen is out of what they want—and no one smiles much.)

Rafalat tackled the training problem by importing five Pizza Hut managers from the West. They spent almost two months giving the Moscow employees a crash course in how to operate a restaurant. They discovered that competition excited the employees; everything from folding pizza boxes to sprinkling on the cheese topping became a team sport, a game to win. Rafalat also sent some of the management-level Soviet employees to London for on-the-job training in existing Pizza Huts. By the time the restaurants opened, the esprit de corps among the staff was incredible; the employees were having *fun*, and so were the customers, who had never seen a cheerful restaurant employee before.

Too bad the government officials weren't as cooperative as the new work force. Rafalat's biggest problem was coping with the many layers of government bureaucracy. Although some members of the government were eager to encourage capitalism and foreign investment, many traditionalists still clung to the communist doctrine and were extremely suspicious of Westerners. Rafalat eventually discovered that many of his problems with the government could be solved with a slice or two of "complementary" pizza.

Finally, after three years of planning and preparation, Rafalat opened Moscow's first two Pizza Huts on September 11, 1990. When he saw hun-

through the red tape and develop a reliable network of local people." Handle the following assignments, using your common sense and the principles discussed in this chapter.

1. Andrew Rafalat shakes his head in dismay as he looks at the accounting numbers. "We can't go on importing everything we need," he says. "It's just too expensive, particularly since most of our revenues are in rubles. We can't use them to buy supplies from the West. We have to start living off the land, so to speak, developing local sources. All we really need is the ingredients for dough, cheese, tomato sauce, and vegetable and meat toppings. Surely *somebody* in the country is producing those things. See what you can do." How should you proceed?
   a. Call the manager of the McDonald's that opened in Moscow shortly before the Pizza Huts opened and ask how they're handling the problem of obtaining ingredients.
   b. Seek help from the officials in the City of Moscow who are your joint venture partners. Perhaps they can use their connections to obtain

cult. In fact, a few days after your grand opening, a sanitation inspector closes both Pizza Huts, claiming that you have failed to file the required papers, that your employees have not been properly tested for disease, and that you are using dirty vegetables in your pizza. Rafalat asks for your advice about how to cope with the mess. What should you tell him?
   a. Defy the officials and reopen the restaurants.
   b. Invite the official who ordered the restaurants closed to return for a closer look at the situation. While the inspector is there, subtly indicate that you believe friendly officials should be rewarded with Western currency.
   c. Attempt to comply with all of the requirements as quickly as possible.
   d. Use PepsiCo's influence with highly placed officials to get the restaurants reopened immediately.

3. You accept both rubles and hard currencies from the West as payment at your restaurants. However, since you opened, the value of the ruble has been dropping dramatically as a result of economic changes. As long as you buy ingredients from the West

with Western money and sell pizza in Moscow for rubles, your profits are at the mercy of fluctuations in the value of the ruble. As the ruble falls, so do your profits. Until you can buy more of your ingredients locally, what is the best way to handle the problem?
   a. Raise prices across the board.
   b. Raise prices on all transactions conducted in rubles.
   c. Accept only rubles.
   d. Accept only Western money.

4. Among the many problems that Andrew Rafalat faces, adjusting to Moscow living conditions looms large. He has asked you to help him obtain an apartment before his wife and two children arrive from London, where they have been living while Rafalat checks things out. You have worked with your contacts in the Moscow City government, and they have pulled many strings to get a three-bedroom apartment with a private bath for Mr. Rafalat and his family. However, when you inspect the place you discover that it has no light bulbs, no medicine chest or mirror in the bathroom, no stove, and no drainpipe under the kitchen sink. Large mosquitoes are emerging from the heating vents. What should you do?
   a. Complain to the city officials and ask them to fix all of the problems.
   b. Thank the city officials for their help in finding such a nice apartment for Mr. Rafalat and ask for their advice on correcting these few "minor" things.
   c. Tell Mr. Rafalat that you think he should encourage his wife and children to remain in London indefinitely.
   d. Ask the people at the American embassy to get the names of reliable service people and sources of household appliances and supplies.[35]

KEY TERMS

◀

MEETING A BUSINESS CHALLENGE

Each chapter concludes with a unique case study/simulation relating to the chapter-opening vignette. To reinforce the concepts presented in the chapter, students are asked to make business decisions about four situations faced by the executive described in the vignette.

KEY TERMS ▶

At the end of each chapter is a list of key terms, in alphabetical order, with convenient cross-references to the pages where they are defined.

EXPLORING ▶ INTERNATIONAL BUSINESS

The first of five types of boxes demonstrates the impact of international business on virtually every topic in the text.

EXPLORING INTERNATIONAL BUSINESS

Can Universal Appeal Overcome Cultural Differences?

You've got a great product that's been selling like hotcakes in the United States. Now you want to market it in other countries. How do you go about it? Do you go into each country and conduct extensive market research so that you can adapt—or even create—the product, the packaging, and the promotion specifically for that culture? Or do you keep everything essentially the same for all countries, changing only the language on the package and in the advertising? In other words, do you go local or do you go global?

According to Harvard marketing professor Theodore Levitt, global is the only way to go. He argues that, thanks to telecommunications and cheap, easy travel, consumers the world over are becoming more and more alike. People everywhere share certain needs and desires, which allows marketers to sell standardized products at low prices the same way around the world. He points to Coca-Cola as the perfect example of a global product. In Levitt's view, adopting a global marketing perspective not only saves time and money in production and advertising outlays but also helps a company clarify its focus and objectives, making operations easier to manage and coordinate.

When Levitt's controversial ideas were first published in the early 1980s, many companies thought he made a lot of sense and jumped on the global bandwagon. But many more were wary of the whole idea. They saw numerous barriers to worldwide product standardization, including problems in technology (disparate electrical systems), packaging (colors, for example, can have different meanings in different cultures), consumer habits (it's difficult to sell cereal to Brazilians, who tend not to eat breakfast), and even physical characteristics of consumers (Japanese, on average, have smaller frames than Western people, and some products are too big or heavy for them).

Of course, some products are certainly global. On the streets of any major city in the world, you'll be able to stop for a snack at McDonald's, Pizza Hut, or Kentucky Fried Chicken. You'll see people wearing Levi's jeans and Swatch watches, carrying Gucci bags. They'll be driving Hondas and Volkswagens, shooting pictures with Canon cameras containing Kodak film, and then heading home to watch "Dallas" on their Sony TVs.

The market for such products, according to consultant Kenichi Ohmae, is primarily in what he calls

the "Triad": the United States, Europe, and Japan. In his book *Triad Power: The Coming Shape of Global Competition*, Ohmae suggests that what many consider to be "global" products—those with a universal appeal—have their greatest demand within the Triad because of the increasing homogeneity of consumers in these three major world areas. He notes that high educational levels, exposure to television, and high levels of purchasing power lead to a similar lifestyle in these areas, setting them off from the rest of the world. Ohmae does believe, however, that some modifications should be made to adapt to each market. Manufacturers should strive to make the "insides" of a product the same for all countries but modify the exteriors to meet specific consumer desires. For example, pianos can have the same basic design and components, but people in the United States prefer a woodgrain exterior (as a fine piece of furniture), whereas people in Japan want black enamel (as an educational tool for children).

Along these same lines, other experts have suggested that *products* can be standardized globally but that *brands* need to reflect local conditions in terms of positioning and promotion. One marketing authority has summarized this approach as "thinking global, acting local." Thinking global refers to looking for something that people in many countries have in common and appealing to that common need with a universal product or service or one that is easily modified. Acting local means basing marketing strategies on knowledge of consumer behavior and desires in specific target areas. Ohmae gives the example of Mister Donut's entry into Japan. The U.S. fast-food chain found that the Japanese weren't fond of cinnamon, a key ingredient in doughnuts. So for this particular market the amount of cinnamon was drastically reduced. However, over a five-year period the ingredient was gradually increased, and today the doughnuts in Japan have as much cinnamon as they do in the United States.

It seems, then, that global marketing is a great idea if (1) your product is one that lends itself to standardization and has universal appeal, and (2) you take local cultural conditions into account when it comes to the specifics of branding and promotion.

Levitt himself has clarified his position by stating that he is not against some modifications on a local basis. Whether all products can be marketed like Coke remains to be seen.

349

---

646   Part Seven / The Env

$1.80 per $100 to $3 p[...]
his insurance agent ha[...]
lines between telephon[...]
ground cable installers[...]

Workers' compensat[...]
for a variety of reasons[...]
rise; employees are no[...]
courts have expanded t[...]
and lawsuits have oper[...]
cially lung ailments fro[...]
in which workers' com[...]

To find less expens[...]
insurance programs for[...]
paying high premiums[...]
number of employee cl[...]
that aim in mind, man[...]
closely.

UMBRELLA LIABILIT[...]

Making sure employees have—and use—protective clothing and other safety devices is one way companies can reduce risk.

umbrella policies Insurance that provides businesses with coverage beyond what is provided by a basic liability policy

extra protection above[...]
Because of the unknow[...]
companies have recently raised their rates for umbrella coverage by up to 1,000 percent or have refused to issue this form of policy. As a result, some insurance buyers such as Du Pont have set up their own insurance companies to obtain additional coverage.

anagement and Insurance

tors, lawyers, accountants[...]
usually carry some form of[...]
h protects professionals from[...]
ts, is another form of insur[...]
itively—expensive. For ac[...]
l liability has tripled in only[...]
nalpractice insurance, thou[...]
abilities.[25] Because of the high[...]
are going bare (carrying no[...]
, .[26]

has expertise or experience[...]
erson insurance can be pur[...]
inancial impact of the death[...]
ompany, not the executive's[...]

Besides insuring their property and assets, most businesses buy coverage for risks to employees. Disease and disability may cost employees huge sums of money unless they are insured. In addition, death carries the threat of financia[...]

BEHIND THE SCENES

Risk Management in the Entertainment Industry Is Serious Business

As insurance broker Shel Bachrach tells it, he was sleeping soundly when a client telephoned at 2 a.m. to ask a question about his insurance coverage. It wasn't anything so pedestrian as an automobile policy. Says Bachrach, "They asked if they had coverage in place for a helicopter to fly over and film their concert." As a principal in Albert G. Ruben Company of Beverly Hills, Bachrach sells insurance to rock stars.

Bachrach advised his client that if there was an accident, the people inside the helicopter, their relatives, or their estates could sue under nonowned-aircraft liability. If the stagehands were hurt or killed, the client would need workers' compensation. If one of the backup singers couldn't sing anymore, they would need permanent total disability insurance. If the concert stage and field were damaged, third-party property damages would come in. If they

couldn't get the field ready in time for the football game scheduled there for the next day, they would need extra-expense coverage and more third-party property damage coverage. If the group couldn't appear the next day, they'd need nonappearance insurance. So Bachrach calmly advised his client that he could be at risk for hundreds of millions of dollars if he went ahead with the helicopter filming. Nevertheless, his client wanted to go for it. So Bachrach called around, set up the insurance, and his client filmed the concert three days later.

Rock bands with superstar status pay as much as $1 million a year in premiums to cover big-time mishaps. Lesser-known groups can get by on $100,000 a year in premiums. In his 1988 concert tour, rock star David Lee Roth "surfed" over the audience on an airborne surfboard. Had he fallen and hit someone in the audience, he could have been sued for millions.

Promoters say that of the average ticket price, 8 percent goes to pay the insurance.

Hollywood film producers sometimes face even more unusual risks than rock stars. For *Indiana Jones and the Last Crusade*, Lucasfilm had 2,000 rats specially bred for the scene in which Jones and his sidekick wade through a dank underground chamber. Lucasfilm asked Fireman's Fund to insure the rodents and cover the cost of any delays in filming if the production company lost a large number of the animals. The insurer, however, demanded a "1,000-rat deductible," meaning that it wouldn't pay any claims resulting from the loss of the first 1,000 rats. So as any good risk manager would do, Lucasfilm lined up an extra 1,000 rats as a cushion.

Filming delays are extremely costly in the movie business—as much as $500 a minute, or $250,000 a day. With films today costing an average of $19 million, the insurer of a major picture might have as much as $75 million on the line. The price of

such coverage is usuall[...]
budget.

Some observers are[...]
taking too big a risk in[...]
industry. Lloyd's of L[...]
MGM's filming of *Brai*[...]
died during filming, M[...]
movie and collect from[...]
at Lloyd's thought it w[...]
the film, using a stand-[...]
remained. Lloyd's got i[...]
about $8 million in cla[...]
lays.

Back in the 1950s, i[...]
tertainment industry w[...]
dom covered much bey[...]
however, little can be b[...]
limited only by the[...]
involved.

▲ BEHIND THE SCENES

The second type of box features timely issues of vital importance by introducing companies, organizations, products, and people whose names have surfaced recently in the business media.

society's legal and reg... brand, or a patent, or if yo... ...ng of becoming in... definitely need legal help. Many other situations require the hel...

TECHNIQUES FOR BUSINESS SUCCESS

Seven Common Mistakes Small Businesses Make—And How to Avoid Them

You can learn from others—if not always the secrets of success, then at least the most common causes of failure. Examinations of failed companies and studies of those stalled in the early stages of growth reveal a pattern of oft-repeated blunders and oversights that consistently spoil the dream of entrepreneurial success.

Consider the following mistakes (along with the guidelines for avoiding them) a survival guide for entrepreneurs:

1. Mistaking a hobby for a business. Would-be entrepreneurs often go into business for the wrong reason—namely, the dangerous and mistaken belief that a lifelong hobby can automatically be converted into a business. A hobbyist, no matter how skilled or creative, often lacks the critical business experience essential to success. For example, the ability to whip up a glorious soufflé is not reason enough to open a restaurant.

Hobbies can serve as promising springboards for business ventures, providing you complement your creative or technical skills with a strong foundation in business tech-

niques. You can get this experience in two ways. (a) Go to work for someone else before going into business for yourself. Consider this first step an apprenticeship in the sort of venture you want to start. Soak up all you can about the problems, the opportunities, and the necessary technical skills. (b) Go directly into busi... ...with a partner strong in management experience. ... ...t and an... ...enced restaurant mana... ...of skills to get a ventu...

2. Trying to make the... ...cally, the small-busine... the widest possible ra... scription for success. ... creates a company tha... rather than strong in... the company's focus, ... and marshaling the ... advertising, personnel... factor in it. For exam... (senior citizens or te... nomic group, and stic... prices, high fashion, ...

▲ TECHNIQUES FOR BUSINESS SUCCESS

The third type of box features "how-to" guidelines and demonstrates business concepts being applied in a practical way.

CHECKLIST FOR BUSINESS TODAY

The fifth type of box presents information in a checklist format to guide students in organizing their thinking and to help them make ▼ decisions.

A computer's calculations are made in the **central pro...** ...which performs the three basic functions of arithmetic, logic, and control/communication.[20] Actually, computer arithmetic is nothing more than addition; subtraction

CHECKLIST FOR BUSINESS TODAY

Buying a Computer

Buying a computer has its perils, but you can sidestep difficulties by asking yourself these questions before you shop:

1. What am I going to do with a computer? You need to have a clear idea of your main goal. Otherwise, you may end up either paying for extras you don't really need or owning a computer model that doesn't do enough.

2. How much money am I willing to spend? The cost of a microcomputer system varies considerably. Sometimes the lowest price translates into the shoddiest service. If you think you might like advice or other help from the dealer after you buy the computer, be prepared to spend 5 to 10 percent more.

3. How am I going to educate myself about what the computer can do and what software is available? Product reviews in computer magazines are a good place to start. Most bookstores also sell guides to buying computers.

4. Where should I shop for a computer? Before you start visiting stores, ask friends or business associates where they bought their computers and whether they were satisfied with the advice and the service they received. How was your friend treated after buying the computer and going back to the store with questions or complaints? The answer will tell you a great deal about how reputable the firm is.

5. What options do I need? Computers come with a variety of features. Check to be sure that the ones you need come with the machine you're buying.

6. What kind of software—and how much—is available for the computer I prefer? Some models have more than 10,000 software programs available. For others, only a few dozen are available. In fact, many experts suggest that you start your purchase process by picking out the software you want and then look for the computers that will run that software.

7. What kind of training and support will I get after I buy the computer? Who will be available when you're stuck and need someone to talk you through a program? Are there free classes on using your computer?

8. What kind of warranty exists? In addition to the standard manufacturer's warranty, the dealer may be able to offer service contracts that provide on-site maintenance and repairs by factory-trained specialists. Ask for references so that you can find out how other customers were treated when something went wrong with their computers.

9. Is the computer I prefer one that can grow with me? Don't buy a computer just for your immediate needs. Find one you will be able to do more with as your abilities grow and your needs change.

important... because ... condition... day's co... skills.

mission statement Putting the organization's mission into words

Goals a...

An orga... ...t... the organization supposed to do?" A **mission statement** sets the organization's purpose into words and defines the organization's scope of operations, allowing

FOCUS ON ETHICS

When Decisions Are More Than Right or Wrong

When you have all the facts, your information is clear-cut, and your choice is right or wrong, ethical decisions are easy. But situations can be clouded by conflicting responsibilities, incomplete information, and multiple points of view. Large ethical problems arise when a brokerage firm pays huge bonuses to top managers just before declaring bankruptcy, a government contractor hides the truth from customers, and a lawyer trades inside information. Less newsworthy issues include a boss who lies at your expense, a co-worker who pads her expense account, or a supervisor who uses the company's phone for personal calls. The way you handle such everyday ethical decisions shapes the overall ethics of your company, and handling them ethically may help you avoid the sort of front-page scandals that have been in the news lately.

Assume you are leaving your employer to start your own company. Is it ethical to take one or two co-workers with you? Is it ethical to take your employer's accounts with you? If you need to borrow money to make a go of your new business, is it ethical to withhold information from your banker? Three businesspeople faced these questions and made their own decisions.

▶ Andy Friesch founded Heartland Adhesives & Coatings in Germantown, Wisconsin. But before starting his own company, he was still a top sales producer for a very large company in the industrial adhesives industry. He believed that two co-workers would be assets to his own firm, so he asked them to join him in his new enterprise.

Says Friesch, "When it comes to corporate America, individuals have to do what's in their own best interest.

Corporations look out for themselves first and employees second." As it turned out, Friesch's co-workers did not go with him. "They were willing to talk about going off with me, but when it came right down to it they didn't want to make the sacrifice."

▶ John G. McCurdy founded Sunny States Seafood in Oxford, Mississippi. But he was still working for another Mississippi seafood distributor when several of his employer's customers asked to go with him. He believed taking his employer's customers was unethical, so he refused.

Says McCurdy, "I'm only 24 years old, I've got another 40 years left in business, and if I do somebody like that, somebody's going to do me like that." McCurdy is succeeding, but his former employer "got into debt and had to sell out to a big catfish company."

▶ W. Mark Baty, Jr., founded Accredited Business Services, a metals recycling business in Cleveland, Ohio. When approached by a big customer, he needed to purchase a $60,000 specialized truck with hydraulic lift in order to land the account. He asked his bank for a loan, knowing that his finances were a little shaky—he owed his parents and in-laws, his credit cards were stretched thin, and he was juggling his receivables and payables to keep his head above water. He did not lie to his banker, but neither did he reveal the amount of money he owed to relatives and on credit cards. He got the loan.

Says Baty, "You don't lie to a bank—but I certainly don't believe in offering them more information than they ask for." Baty paid off his loan, and his banker never learned of his overextended finances.

1. Given the same circumstances, what would you have done? Did these businesspeople make the right choices?

2. In this sort of ethical dilemma, is there ever a choice that is absolutely correct?

FOCUS ON ▶ ETHICS

The fourth type of box presents current ethical issues, encouraging students to become conscientious businesspeople.

CHARTS AND TABLES ▶

Charts and tables have been carefully constructed to amplify major points and to give the book exceptional visual appeal.

OUTSTANDING PHOTOGRAPHS AND AWARD-WINNING ADVERTISEMENTS

All of the photographs focus on real people, companies, or organizations, and the captions integrate illustrations with the text to reinforce important ▼ concepts.

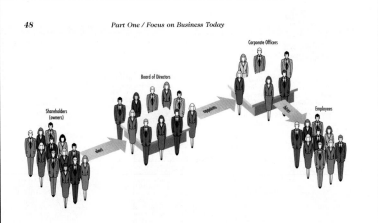

48   *Part One / Focus on Business Today*

EXHIBIT 2.6

The Corporate Framework
Theoretically, the corporate framework resembles a democracy in which shareholders vote to elect representatives (members of the board of directors) who will establish corporate policy and select competent managers to direct the employees. Actually, the real power in a corpora-

little or no voice in management. Shareholders who cannot attend the annual meeting in person vote by **proxy,** signing and returning a slip of paper that authorizes management to vote on their behalf.

BOARD OF DIRECTORS As a practical matter, the **board of directors,** which supposedly represents the shareholders, is responsible for guiding corporate affairs and selecting officers. The board has the power to vote on major management decisions, such as building a new factory, hiring a new president, or buying a new subsidiary. Depending on the size of the company, the board might have anywhere from 3 to 35 directors, although 15 to 25 is the typical range. In some corporations, several of the directors may be "insiders" who also serve as executives of the company. The outside directors are typically major stockholders, executives of other firms, or high-ranking officials connected with the compa-

---

Chapter 15 / Promotion   **431**

Product advertising, such as this ad for North Beach Leather, sells specific goods or services.

MARGIN GLOSSARY

Significant terms appear in boldface in the text, and each term is defined in the margin near where it is first mentioned. This gives immediate reinforcement of important terminology as well as a comprehensive reference for review and study. In addition, terms are included in a convenient glossary at ◀ the end of the book.

technique being used is **comparative advertising.** In some countries, comparative ads are tightly regulated and in some cases banned, but that is clearly not the case in the United States. Indeed, the Federal Trade Commission started the ball rolling by encouraging advertisers to use direct product comparisons with the intent of better informing customers. In fact, 40 percent of all advertising in this country is comparative.[14]

Comparative advertising is frequently used to challenge a dominant market leader, but it is useful in many situations because it focuses on the

comparative advertising An advertising technique in which two or more products are explicitly compared

432   *Part Four / Marketing*

Business Around the World

Belgium has some of the strictest advertising regulations in the world. For instance, comparative advertising is not allowed if it is denigrating, and no advertising of any type or style may be directed toward children.

product strengths that are important to customers. Burger King used it on McDonald's, Pepsi used it on Coke, and Ford finally got tired of getting slammed by Chevrolet truck advertising and decided to fight back with comparative ads. This is bare-knuckle marketing, and when done well, it is effective. However, comparative advertising sometimes ends up getting neutralized by look-alike campaigns from the competition. Analgesics (pain killers) is one category cited as an example of comparative advertising taken too far. There are so many claims and counterclaims in this "ad war" that consumers can't keep it all straight anymore.[15]

Comparative ads can cross legal and ethical boundaries in two ways. First, some ads tout a product's strengths, but they do so selectively, talking about only those areas in which the product beats the competition and ignoring the rest. In the analgesics category, for example, Johnson & Johnson distributed a "safety profile" to doctors, showing that its Tylenol brand exhibited fewer side effects than three of its competitors. However, the company didn't list some other possible side effects, including potential liver damage and greater risk of overdose, in which it lost out to the competition. Second, some comparative ads simply overstep the bounds of truth and embellish claims of superiority. For instance, Jartran, a truck-rental firm, claimed in its ads that it could "save consumers big money" compared to U-Haul. However, Jartran was promoting a temporary, introductory price, not its normal price. The court determined that the company deliberately tried to deceive customers.[16]

Another potential problem with comparative advertising is unfair portrayal of the quality or characteristics of competitors' products. To help bring an end to

MAPS

Each chapter features a map of one or more countries that relates to the text. These 22 maps enhance students' knowledge of geography and focus attention on the global nature of business.

A CASE FOR ▶ CRITICAL THINKING

End-of-chapter cases provide practical application of key concepts. This classic device assists students in evaluating situations, using good judgment, learning to make decisions, and developing critical thinking skills.

---

30   *Part One / Focus on Business Today*

A CASE FOR CRITICAL THINKING

Cautious Hope for a United Korea

For over 45 years, North and South Korea have remained enemies, split by a two-and-a-half-mile-long "demilitarized zone" over which 1.7 million opposing soldiers keep an anxious watch (among them 40,000 U.S. troops). This bleak situation developed at the end of World War II, when the defeated Japanese withdrew from Korea, leaving the Soviets to influence the north and the other Allies to influence the south. After the Korean civil war ended in 1953, the division became a powder-keg Cold War standoff, with the potential to erupt at any time into a major superpower conflict.

Today, that possibility is increasingly remote. Global politics are changing so rapidly that North Korea has become one of the last remaining hard-line communist dictatorships. Experts predict that its aging "Great Leader," Kim Il Sung, cannot maintain his policy of *juche* ("self-reli...

ing is five times higher than in the North, but it would be seriously threatened by the high cost of rapid reunification. Kee Woo-sik, a World Bank economist, suggests that the cost of reunification might be as high as $170 billion over a ten-year period. Paying only one-third of that without foreign aid would cost the South Koreans 18 percent of their national budget.

Another concern is the very real possibility of total economic collapse in the North, which could send billions of needy refugees to seek aid in the South. Stagnant conditions in self-isolated North Korea have nearly bankrupt the country. The dictatorship faces billions of dollars in unpaid foreign debt as its communist bloc trading partners vanish and its heavily controlled populace endures shrinking rice rations and intermittent electric power. North Korea's primary ally was the Soviet Union, now the Common...

already held a few diplomatic meetings to discuss the future. Although both sides are open to reunification, the North Koreans want to begin with a resolution of political and ideological differences, but the South Koreans believe the economic union must come first. They think the North Koreans will quickly recognize the advantage of a free-market system.

Meanwhile, many South Korean business leaders, such as Hyundai's powerful chairman Chung Ju-Yung, are pushing for a speedier union. They view North Korea as a potential source of cheap labor and raw materials to fuel the South's new position as an international economic competitor. Chung (who was born in the North) has already initiated trade with two former South Korean enemies: the former Soviet Union and the Chinese. These countries, in turn, have put pressure on Kim's regime to relax its internal and external strictur...

Other ...

BUILDING YOUR COMMUNICATION SKILLS

◀ Located near the end of each chapter, these exercises offer students practice in a wide range of communication activities. Exercises include one-on-one and group discussion, class debates, personal interviews, panel sessions, oral and written reports, and letter-writing assignments.

Chapter 13 / Product and Pricing Decisions   *385*

BUILDING YOUR COMMUNICATION SKILLS

Examine the life cycle of a product with which you are familiar. Locate an article in a magazine or book that describes the life cycle of that product. Note the factors affecting its introduction, its growth, and the strategies that have been used to maintain sales as it reached maturity. If this product has experienced a de-

cline, identify the causes, and describe the manufacturer's attempts to revive the product.

▶ As directed by your instructor, prepare a brief presentation describing the life cycle of the product.

▶ In a class discussion, identify the factors contributing to the various stages in your chosen product's life cycle, and compare them with those of products examined by other students. Identify common elements in the life cycles of all the products evaluated by class members.

KEEPING CURRENT USING *THE WALL STREET JOURNAL*

Scan recent issues of *The Wall Street Journal* for an article related to one of the following:

▶ New-product development
▶ The product life cycle
▶ Pricing strategies
▶ Packaging

1. Does this article report on a development in a particular company,

several companies, or an entire industry? Which companies or industries are specifically mentioned?

2. If you were a marketing manager in this industry, what concerns would you have as a result of reading the article? What questions do you think companies in this industry (or related ones) should be asking? What would you want to know?

3. In what ways do you think this industry, other industries, or the public might be affected by this trend or development in the next five years? Why?

KEEPING CURRENT USING ◀ THE WALL STREET JOURNAL

To emphasize the link between today's business news and *Business Today,* these exercises, provided at the end of each chapter, offer interesting and helpful ways of using *The Wall Street Journal* to give students practice in interpreting business news, a crucial business skill.

Integrated Video Exercises   *V-3*

CHAPTER 1 VIDEO EXERCISE

Upstairs/Downstairs: Inflation Begins to Divide a Nation

SYNOPSIS

This video discusses the Consumer Price Index (CPI), the most commonly used measure of inflation in the United States. The video makes two key points. First, because the CPI is an average, it can conceal important information, such as the steep increase in housing costs in recent years. Second, the United States increasingly has a two-tiered socioeconomic structure, with people in the top tier ("upstairs") increasingly able to afford housing and other items that have shot up in price and people in the bottom tier ("downstairs") increasingly unable to afford housing. Beyond these particular issues, the CPI and inflation in general are two key issues for business leaders, whether it's a case of customers not being able to afford a firm's products, or the firm itself not making enough profit because of increases in the cost of materials and supplies.

EXERCISES

ANALYSIS
1. Discuss the CPI in relation to the Dow Jones Industrial Aver-
... the Index of I...

DECISION
Assume you're a manufacturer of mid-...
... and you hear

once imposed rent controls that limited the amounts by which landlords could ...

INTEGRATED VIDEO ▶ EXERCISES

The 22 high-quality videos that accompany this text, one for each chapter, provide a powerful and engaging learning experience. A unique set of video exercises placed at the front of this book asks students to react to the videos by responding to questions, making decisions, and taking the initiative to solve real business problems.

PART ONE

Focus on Business Today

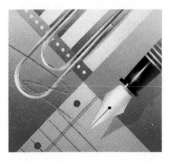

CHAPTER 1

LEARNING OBJECTIVES
After studying this chapter, you will be able to

1 Explain what an economic system is.

2 List the four factors of production.

3 Name the three major types of economic systems and differentiate their identifying characteristics.

4 Describe the relationship between profit and sales, and explain how profit motivates entrepreneurs.

5 Discuss three ways companies compete.

6 Explain how supply and demand interact to establish prices.

7 List the four major economic roles of the United States government.

8 Identify six trends that will influence the economy in the years ahead.

Foundations of American Business

*Facing a Business Challenge
at Johnson Publishing*
MAKING IT IN AMERICA

H ow do poor people become rich? One man who knows the answer is
John H. Johnson, publisher, chairman, and chief executive officer of
Johnson Publishing Company, the second largest black-owned company
in the United States. Johnson publishes *Ebony, Jet,* and *EM* (Ebony Man), and
he is one of the few African-Americans to have been listed on the Forbes roster
of America's 400 wealthiest people. In addition to publishing, his business interests include cosmetics, radio stations, television, and life insurance.

He's come a long way from his humble beginnings in Arkansas City, Arkansas.
In the process of building his fortune, he's created something significant—the
first mass circulation magazine for black audiences, a publication that has influenced millions of people. He's also taught corporate America that blacks represent a significant market, worthy of focused attention. But as Johnson himself
says, "I wasn't trying to make history. I was trying to make money. . . . The
reason I survived is that I refused to believe the signs that said I was defeated.
And I dared to do things I couldn't afford to do. . . . I used to lock myself up in
my office and say the word *success* out loud, over and over, like a Buddhist
monk chanting his mantra. I used to say to myself, 'John Johnson, you can make
it. John Johnson, you can make it. John Johnson, you can make it. John Johnson, *you can and must make it.*'"

There were many times when it was touch and go. Back in the early 1940s,
when Johnson got his start, prejudice was *the* predominant fact of life for
African-Americans. They couldn't try on hats in Baltimore department stores or
shoes or dresses in Atlanta. They couldn't live in downtown hotels in Chicago.
The only place to buy a meal in Washington, D.C., was at the train station. There
were no successful black magazines, no black advertising agencies, and no black
employees in white advertising agencies. Black models did not appear in ads for
"white" products. A black man could not walk into a bank and get a loan to start
a business.

In the early 1940s, when John Johnson was struggling to publish his first magazine, *Negro Digest,* he never dreamed it would develop into the conglomerate that today publishes *Ebony, EM,* and *Jet.*

Those were the rules of the game, and they weren't favorable. But Johnson was a motivated and inventive player, determined to win. He began his career in 1942 as an office boy for the Supreme Life Insurance Company, a black-owned firm in Chicago. There he caught the eye of Harry Pace, president of the company, who assigned Johnson the task of scanning newspapers and magazines so that he could brief Pace on what was happening in the black community. Pretty soon, Johnson knew more black news than anybody in Chicago. He was the center of attention at parties, where he entertained his friends with stories about blacks who were making it. The idea of publishing a magazine about blacks occurred to him. It would be sort of a *Reader's Digest,* a compilation and summarization of the best and most thought-provoking articles by and about blacks.

For two months, he went from office to office in black Chicago, looking for support. Finally, he went to New York to seek the advice of Roy Wilkins, then editor of *The Crisis,* the noncommercial house magazine of the NAACP. Wilkins said, "Save your money, young man. Save your energy. Save yourself a lot of disappointment."

When he had exhausted every avenue of support, Johnson fell back on his own resources. He asked himself, "What can I do by myself with what I have to get what I want?" He took a long hard look at his situation and asked himself some tough questions. How could a 24-year-old black man with no track record in publishing or journalism start a magazine? How could he raise the money for the first issue? How could he attract subscribers? How could he convince newsstands to carry his magazine?[1]

▶ THE IDEAL OF ECONOMIC FREEDOM

Like hundreds of thousands of people before him, John Johnson recognized that the United States is a land of opportunity—in an economic sense. We are free to work for someone else or for ourselves. We may choose our investments and our purchases. We have the chance to succeed—or fail—based on our own efforts.

The Nature of Economic Systems

economic system Means by which a society distributes its resources to satisfy its people's needs

What exactly is an **economic system?** Simply put, it's a basic set of rules used to allocate a society's resources to satisfy its citizens' needs. Although every nation has a unique way of distributing resources, economic systems all have certain features in common and may be measured in similar ways.

Factors of Production

factors of production Resources that a society uses to produce goods and services, including natural resources, labor, capital, and entrepreneurship

A society's resources are referred to by economists as the **factors of production.** One factor of production, natural resources, includes things that are useful in their natural state, such as land, forests, minerals, and water. The second, labor, consists of the human resources used to produce goods and services. The third factor of production is **capital,** which includes human-made inputs such as machines, tools, and buildings, as well as the money that buys other resources.

capital Funds that support a business and its tools (machines, vehicles, and buildings) to produce goods and services

entrepreneurs People who accept the risk of failure to organize the other three factors of production in order to produce goods and services more efficiently

A fourth factor of production is entrepreneurship. **Entrepreneurs** are people like John Johnson, the ones who develop new ways to use the other economic resources more efficiently. They acquire materials, employ workers, invest in capital goods, and engage in marketing activities. In some societies, entrepreneurs risk losing only their reputations or their positions if they fail. In the United States, entrepreneurs also risk losing their own personal resources. On the other hand, U.S. entrepreneurs reap the benefits if they succeed, which motivates them to take the risk of trying something new.

Although all economies rely on the same basic factors of production, not all are blessed with the same quantity and quality of resources. North America is more fortunate than most regions. We have a wealth of land and raw materials, an industrious and well-educated work force, a strong capital base, and an abundance of entrepreneurs. To a great extent, our prosperity derives from these plentiful resources.

Economic Goals and Measurements

Each society's economic system reflects the country's history, traditions, aspirations, and politics. What works for one culture might not work as well for another, and vice versa.

In measuring the success of different economic systems, the fairest approach would be to apply the standards that are valued by the people of that culture. Such goals as economic stability, job security, and equality of income and opportunity are given higher priority in some cultures than others.

One of the measures traditionally used for keeping economic score is **gross national product** (GNP)—the dollar value of all the final goods and services produced by an economy during a specified period (usually a year). GNP excludes profits from foreign-owned businesses within a nation's borders, and it includes receipts from overseas operations of U.S.-based companies.

The latest method used for tracking an economy is **gross domestic product** (GDP), which also measures the total output of goods and services. However, unlike GNP, the new GDP includes profits from foreign-owned businesses within a nation's borders, and it excludes receipts from overseas operations of U.S.-based companies. When GNP (or GDP) is compared over a number of years, a pattern appears. A rise in GNP (or GDP) is a sign of economic growth, indicating that the country has achieved at least one goal—a higher level of production, which can be distributed to the people.

GNP and GDP are also used to compare two or more economies. These measures can be adjusted for inflation and currency rates, but these figures may be misleading because of different population sizes. So economists often calculate per capita figures—a nation's total GNP (or GDP) divided by its population. For example, study the GNP figures in Exhibit 1.1. The per capita GNP of Canada is a little less than that of the United States, even though its total GNP is only a tenth of the total U.S. GNP. Bear in mind, however, that per capita GNP reveals nothing about the way in which the income is distributed among the people, nor does it indicate the quality of the goods and services produced.

Government policymakers and businesspeople use GNP and GDP to forecast trends and to analyze the economy's performance. Although the measure is well entrenched, many economists complain that it is sometimes misleading. The value of all the **underground economy,** for example, is not reflected in GNP or in GDP figures. Revenues from illegal drug sales, gambling, prostitution, and other crimes are not included because they are not reported (for obvious reasons). "Under the table" payments for jobs done off the payroll are also left out of these calculations. The proceeds from small-scale transactions between individuals are not usually reported either. Finally, the value of **bartering,** or trading, goods

gross national product Total value of all the final goods and services produced by an economy over a given period of time; includes receipts from overseas operations of U.S.-based companies, and excludes profits from foreign-owned businesses within a nation's borders

gross domestic product Dollar value of all the final goods and services produced by an economy during a specified period (usually a year); includes profits from foreign-owned businesses within a nation's borders, and excludes receipts from overseas operations of U.S.-based companies

underground economy Economic activity that is not reported

bartering Trading by exchanging goods or services directly rather than through a medium like money

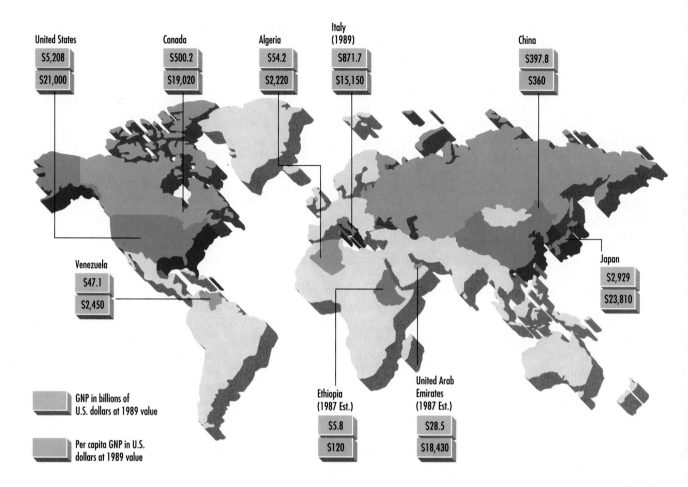

United States
$5,208
$21,000

Canada
$500.2
$19,020

Algeria
$54.2
$2,220

Italy
(1989)
$871.7
$15,150

China
$397.8
$360

Venezuela
$47.1
$2,450

Japan
$2,929
$23,810

GNP in billions of
U.S. dollars at 1989 value

Per capita GNP in U.S.
dollars at 1989 value

Ethiopia
(1987 Est.)
$5.8
$120

United Arab
Emirates
(1987 Est.)
$28.5
$18,430

EXHIBIT 1.1

**Total and Per Capita
GNP in Ten Nations**

The free-market system has
given people in the United
States one of the highest
standards of living in the
world, as measured by GNP.

and services cannot easily be measured because money is not used in the transaction. In some less-developed economies, "underground" sources of income like these make up a substantial portion of the GNP. Even in the United States, the underground economy is estimated to be worth as much as $842 billion a year, or 15 percent of GNP.[2]

Types of Economic Systems

Regardless of exactly how they operate, all economic systems must deal with the same basic questions: How should limited economic resources be used to satisfy society's needs? What goods and services should be produced? Who should produce them? How should these goods and services be divided among the population? These questions are addressed differently by the three main economic systems: capitalism, communism, and socialism (see Exhibit 1.2). The best way to distinguish among them is in terms of the freedom they give individuals to own the factors of production and to pursue their own economic interests.

Capitalism

The U.S. economic system is capitalism, which permits a high degree of individual freedom. Capitalism owes its philosophical origins to eighteenth-century

EXHIBIT 1.2 ▶ **Types of Economic Systems**

FACTORS	CAPITALISM	COMMUNISM	SOCIALISM
Careers and employment	Every individual has right to choose occupation and place of employment	Limited freedom in selecting occupations and places of employment; nearly everyone works for state	Individuals free to select occupations and employment of their choice within state-controlled economy
Business ownership	Private ownership of business and industry encouraged and sanctioned by government	All industries and virtually all farms owned by state	Major utilities, transportation, mining, and communications owned by government; mixture of private and public ownership
Competition	Competition encouraged by state; monopolies forbidden unless government regulated	No competition, because government owns and controls all businesses and industries	Competition encouraged in smaller businesses but restricted in key industries (usually owned by state)
Government planning	Business makes decisions independently of government but must conform to rules and regulations	Master plan for major economic and business decisions	Management of key industries must follow government plans
Consumer choice	Goods and services sold at prices based on supply and demand; a wide assortment available	Limited choice of goods; prices (higher) determined by state	Goods and services sold at prices based on supply and demand; a wide assortment available
Labor unions	Large-scale union participation with right to bargain collectively	Labor unions function as information channels for communist party; no power to negotiate wages, hours, or benefits	Large-scale union participation with right to bargain collectively
Taxation	Medium taxation; right to influence by vote	Heavy taxation in form of sales tax and large cost margins	Heavy taxation; right to influence by vote
Profits	All net profits kept by individual(s) incurring risk in business	All "profits" (margins) go to state	Businesses not owned by state may earn reasonable profits

philosophers such as Adam Smith, who advanced the theory of **pure capitalism.** In the ideal capitalist economy, all production and allocation decisions would be made by private holders of property or money. The market itself would serve as a self-correcting mechanism, an "invisible hand," to ensure the production of the goods that society wants in the quantities that society wants, without anyone ever issuing an order of any kind.[3] In reality, however, it is sometimes in everyone's best interest for the government to intervene. Because the government can use its power to affect prices and wages or to change the way resources are allocated, the economic system of the United States may be called **mixed capitalism.**

But even under mixed capitalism, private individuals are allowed to determine what is produced, by whom, and for whom. The pursuit of private gain is regarded as a worthwhile goal that ultimately benefits society as a whole. Other countries with variations of this economic system include Canada, Germany, and Japan.

Capitalist economies like these operate under a **free-market system.** Thus, they are often called **market economies.** In essence, this means that if you have

pure capitalism Capitalism in its ideal state, in which all resource allocations are controlled by the unfettered operation of the free market

mixed capitalism Economic system in which operation of the free market is influenced to some degree by government involvement

free-market system Economic system in which the way people spend their money determines which products will be produced and what those products will cost

market economies Economic systems in which goals are achieved by the action of the free market, with a minimum of government intervention

something to sell—whether it's a product such as a magazine for African-Americans or a service such as washing cars—you're free to charge any price you want and to sell to anyone willing to pay that price. Conversely, as a consumer you're free to buy whatever you want and can afford from whomever you choose.

In a free-market system, independent entrepreneurs and entrepreneurial leaders of existing businesses play an important role. They look for unfulfilled needs and bring together the resources required to meet those needs. Therefore, business is a major partner in U.S. society.

Communism

communism Economic system in which all productive resources are owned and operated by the government so that there is no private property

planned economies Economic systems in which resource-allocation decisions are made by the central government

The system that allows individuals the least degree of economic freedom is **communism.** Communist economies are characterized by state ownership of the factors of production and by planned resource allocation. The second feature is so important in these economies that they are frequently called planned economies. In a **planned economy,** social equality is a major goal, and private enterprise is generally regarded as wasteful and exploitative. Planned economies exist in such countries as North Korea and Cuba.

The degree to which communism is actually practiced varies from country to country. In its purest form, almost all factors of production are under state control. Private ownership is restricted largely to personal and household items. Resource allocation is handled through rigid centralized planning by a handful of government officials who decide what goods to produce, how to produce them, and to whom they should be distributed.

FOCUS ON ETHICS

Does Capitalism Cause Pollution?

Many people blame business for creating the lion's share of our pollution problems. According to conventional wisdom, greedy companies think nothing of exploiting the earth in their quest for profits. They'll dump toxic wastes in the rivers, strip the forests bare, dig huge open pits in the ground, and spew all sorts of vile stuff into the air. Incidents like the *Exxon Valdez* oil spill off Alaska confirm the public's perception that the free-enterprise system and the protection of the environment are inherently at odds.

Fed up with big business, people are pressing for stronger environmental rules and regulations and for tougher enforcement of laws already on the books. They argue that government intervention is required to stem the environmental abuses of capitalism. But if capitalism causes pollution and if government intervention is the answer, you'd expect communist and former communist countries like the Common-

wealth of Independent States, China, and the countries of Eastern Europe to be models of environmental purity, wouldn't you?

But these countries have some of the worst pollution in the world. Major cities in the former Soviet Union routinely dump untreated sewage and industrial wastes into the handiest body of water. The Volga River has so much oil floating on its surface that passengers on river boats are warned not to toss cigarettes overboard.

The picture is equally grim in Eastern Europe. The Polish railroad tracks are so polluted with acid rain that trains are not allowed to go over 24 miles an hour. Ninety-five percent of the water in Poland is unfit for human consumption; 65 percent can't even be used for industrial purposes because it's so toxic that it would destroy heavy metals used by industry. In what was formerly East Germany, 40 percent of the population suffers ill effects from air pollution: visitors have been known to vomit from simply

Planned economies have advantages and disadvantages. Because of their commitment to social welfare, there is less of a gap between rich and poor. Unemployment and inflation can more easily be controlled. On the other hand, without the opportunity to get ahead, entrepreneurs like John Johnson have little incentive to develop new products or more efficient ways of doing things. As a consequence, goods and services that people in the United States take for granted are often difficult to obtain. For example, in some ex-Soviet cities, the typical wait for an apartment is 15 years.[4]

Although pure communism still has its supporters, more and more communist countries are beginning to relax the central control of their economies and encourage individual initiative. The shift has been especially dramatic in Eastern Europe, where the issue is not whether to move toward capitalism, but rather how far to go and how to get there as painlessly as possible. What was once East Germany (now reunited with West Germany), Poland, Hungary, Romania, Czechoslovakia, and Bulgaria are all taking steps toward market-based economies. In what was the Soviet Union, the situation is complicated by political and economic issues, as the various ex-Soviet republics struggle to gain more regional control over their resources. In December 1991, the 74-year-old Soviet Union died, and Soviet communism with it. Eleven former republics formed the Commonwealth of Independent States (CIS), dedicated to far-reaching reforms intended to lead toward a market-based economy, private ownership of property, and decentralized planning. However, nobody expects the road to free enterprise to be a smooth one. Throughout the newly formed Commonwealth and Eastern Europe, the transition is marked by political upheavals, unemployment, inflation, and a temporary drop in living standards.[5]

breathing the air, and people often use their headlights in midday to see through the smog. In Czechoslovakia, the top 12 inches of much of the finest farmland is toxic, poisoned by overuse of fertilizers. Air pollution has destroyed 300,000 acres of forest; there's nothing left for 350 miles but stumps and skeletons of dying trees. The same problems haunt the cities and countryside in Bulgaria, Hungary, Romania, and Yugoslavia.

Information on pollution in China is difficult to obtain, but the facts that are available are not reassuring. Worldwatch Institute reports that air pollution has destroyed 90 percent of the pine trees in Sichuan province and 4,500 acres of forest in Chungking. Fish have all but disappeared from the Chinese diet, thanks to massive water projects that have destroyed the fish breeding grounds.

In fact, pollution exists wherever people live, regardless of their economic system or form of government. Capitalism, by itself, does not cause pollution. People do. We want luxury and convenience at an affordable price—disposable diapers, big cars, cool houses, hair spray, refrigerators that make ice cubes automatically, charcoal lighter fluid, soft drinks in plastic bottles. People in less-developed countries have more modest desires, but even though they lack the money for conspicuous consumption, they are just as likely to dump untreated sewage into their rivers or to decimate their forests for a profit. The real villain is not free enterpise but human greed. Corporations are simply responding to our demands. They are giving us what we want at a price we can afford.

If we want a clean environment, business will respond to that imperative—provided that we're willing to pay the price. If you'd rather drink from a paper cup than from one made of Styrofoam, McDonald's will oblige you. If you want a car that doesn't use much gas, you have plenty of options. If you prefer recycled paper, you can buy reams of it. Certainly there are many examples of corporate irresponsibility, but the times are changing, and business is changing too. The market has spoken, and companies are getting the message.

The empty shelves in Moscow are just one indication of the economic problems faced by former Soviets as they struggle to establish a market economy.

In China, even as hardline communists battle to prevent political reform, the country's businesspeople are taking small but steady steps toward a more market-based economy. Chinese managers are tremendously interested in Western-style management and economic reform.[6] However, such small steps aren't nearly enough for many businesspeople in Hong Kong. After 1997, Hong Kong will cease to be a British colony and will fall under the control of communist China. Thus entrepreneurs and professionals are fleeing Hong Kong, and their number one destination is capitalist Canada. A record 29,000 people immigrated from Hong Kong to Canada in 1990, and experts expect to see 200,000 more by 1997.[7]

Socialism

socialism Economic system characterized by public ownership and operation of key industries combined with private ownership and operation of less vital industries

The third major type of economic system, **socialism**, lies somewhere between capitalism and communism in the degree of economic freedom that it permits. Like communism, socialism involves a relatively high degree of government planning and some government ownership of land and capital resources. However, government involvement is limited to industries considered vital to the common welfare, such as transportation, utilities, medicine, steel, and communications. In these industries, the government owns or controls all the facilities and determines what will be produced and how the output will be distributed. Private ownership is permitted in industries that are not considered vital, and both businesses and individuals are allowed to benefit from their own efforts. But taxes are high in socialist states because the government absorbs the costs of medical care, education, subsidized housing, and other social services.

Like communism, socialism has been embracing elements of capitalism in the past decade. Private ownership of basic industries is on the rise. In Latin America, for example, Mexico and Chile are selling off state-owned enterprises such as their telephone companies and national airlines. Bolivia, Colombia, and Costa Rica began creating open-market economies in the mid-1980s and are enjoying a boom in manufacturing and exports. Argentina and Brazil are also jumping on the free-market bandwagon.[8]

▶ ECONOMIC FORCES AFFECTING BUSINESS

Countries around the world are becoming more capitalistic because they're impressed with the prosperity that seems to accompany the free-market system. By and large, people in capitalistic countries enjoy higher standards of living than people in communist or socialist societies. One appeal of capitalism is that it seems to work almost automatically.

The Profit Motive

The foundation of the U.S. economic system is **profit,** the difference between what it costs to produce and market something and what someone is willing to pay for it. If it costs you $1.00 to make a sandwich and you can sell the sandwich for $1.50, your gross profit is 50 cents.

profit Money left over after expenses and taxes have been deducted from revenue generated by selling goods or services

In the United States, the owner of a business is entitled to keep whatever profits the business produces (minus taxes, of course). Profit thus becomes the goal of most business enterprises. It takes effort, after all, to put a desirable product or service into useful form and then sell it to people. Furthermore, the entrepreneur may have to make a considerable investment in resources before a single product is ready to sell. And if the venture doesn't succeed, the entrepreneur stands to lose the investment.

Scarcity and Opportunity Cost

One fact of economic life is that resources are scarce. Only so much land, so many workers, and so much capital are available. Even the number of a business's potential customers is limited—and certainly their dollars are. Because of the scarcity of resources, individuals and enterprises are sometimes required to make hard economic choices. For example, if it's Friday night and you have $10 in your pocket, do you spend it on a good dinner? Do you use it to go shopping? Or do you save it for future use? You may choose any of these options, but as soon as you spend that $10, it's gone—you can't do anything else with it.

This simple concept is called **opportunity cost.** Say that you decided to spend the $10 on dinner. Not only would that decision cost you $10, but it would also cost you the opportunity of buying something else. Even if a friend invited you to dinner so that you could save your $10, the time you spend at dinner would not be available for other pursuits. In other words, whenever resources are limited, the decision to use some of those resources means that they will not be available for other, perhaps more worthwhile, uses. And the true cost of making an economic decision such as attending college, for example, is not only the cost of tuition but also the value of the next best alternative that can't be chosen.

opportunity cost Value of using a resource; measured in terms of the value of the best alternative for using that resource

Competition

Just as scarcity is an economic fact of life, so is competition. If you set out to sell a product or service in a free-market society, chances are that someone else will be trying to sell something similar. And because potential customers are free to buy where they please, you must compete with your rivals for those customers' business. You might choose to compete in one of three ways: price, quality, or innovation.

Competition and Price

Take the fast-food business, for example. A couple of years ago, Taco Bell, which competes with hamburger chains like McDonald's and Burger King, launched a full-scale price war by reducing the price of its tacos and burritos from 79 and 89 cents to 59 cents. When sales jumped by 27 percent, it slashed prices on 16 of its 23 menu items, and sales climbed another 19 percent. Meanwhile, sales in the fast-food business in general increased by only 3 percent. The catch, of course, is that Taco Bell now gets less money for almost every item it sells, and it still has to cover the same expenses—buying ingredients, paying employees, and so forth. How can the company charge less and still make a worthwhile profit? The answer is that the lower price attracts more customers. Even though Taco Bell makes less on each item, it's luring people away from its rivals and is consequently making more money than it used to. In fact, in 1990 Taco Bell's profits were up by 37 percent (to $150 million on a sales increase of 19 percent to $2.4 billion).

Stung by the competition, McDonald's followed suit by offering lower prices on certain items and special meal combinations. To one degree or another, Burger King, Wendy's, Hardee's, Carl's Junior, Del Taco, Pizza Hut, Domino's, and Kentucky Fried Chicken have all reduced their prices as well.[9] Now everybody in the fast-food business is feeling the profit squeeze.

So what are they all doing? They're trying to operate more efficiently, hustling to maintain their profit margins by tightening their grip on costs. And they're hoping that lower prices will continue to increase the number of visits made by customers who are heavy fast-food users (those who eat at fast-food restaurants more than 18 times per month, representing over 70 percent of sales in the industry). Head-on competition tends to keep prices down, which is good for the buying public. At the same time, it holds out the promise of great profits to the business that can sell more of its product or service than competitors do.

Competition, Quality, and Service

Instead of cutting prices, a business may decide to compete for customers by offering higher-quality goods or better service than its rivals do. El Torito and Taco Bell both appeal to customers who want Mexican food. El Torito charges more for its burritos than Taco Bell, but it provides larger portions, table service, ambience, and free tortilla chips with salsa. Although El Torito may attract fewer customers than Taco Bell, its customers spend more money on every meal.

A business that competes on the basis of quality or service may well end up with an equal or a greater total profit than a business that competes on price. This possibility provides a practical incentive for businesses to maintain high standards, and it increases the choices available to consumers.

Competition and Innovation

The free-market system not only encourages variations in quality and price but also encourages immense variety in the types of goods and services offered to the public. Changes in popular taste, technology, the economy, and the competitive environment are constantly creating new business opportunities. The possibility of profit, however remote, almost invariably attracts entrepreneurs willing to risk their time or money. The result is an astonishing diversity of businesses. Almost anything you might want to buy—any product or service, no matter how obscure—is probably sold somewhere.

Consumers gobbled up the bargains when Taco Bell launched a full-scale price war in the fast-food industry, proving once again that price reductions stimulate demand.

Supply and Demand

As we have seen, prices in a free-market system are influenced by the competitive strategies of rival businesses. Price levels are not determined solely by the decisions of business managers, however. Price levels usually respond to the forces of supply and demand. In economic terms, **supply** refers to the quantities of a good or service that producers will provide on a particular date at various prices; **demand** refers to the amount of a good or service that consumers will buy at that time at various prices. Basically, the theory of supply and demand is a matter of common sense. Consumers buy more when the price is low and less when the price is high. Producers offer more when the price is high and less when the price is low. In other words, the quantity supplied and the quantity demanded are continuously interacting, and the balance between them at any given moment is reflected by the current price on the open market.

In broad terms, the forces of supply and demand combine with the profit motive in a free-market system to regulate what is produced and in what amounts. For example, a movie studio might produce more comedies if ticket sales for similar films are brisk. On the other hand, it might decide to produce fewer comedies and more action adventure movies if attendance at comedies lags. The result of decisions like these—in theory, at least—is that consumers will get what they want and producers will earn a profit by keeping up with public demand.

supply Specific quantity of a product that the seller is able and willing to provide at various prices at a given time

demand Specific quantity of a product that consumers are willing and able to buy at various prices at a given time

How Prices Are Set

The forces of supply and demand determine the market price for products and services. Say that you're in the business of selling blue jeans. You have an inventory of 600 pairs on hand, which you hope to sell within a month. You have priced the jeans at $35. But since they aren't selling well, you have decided to mark them down to $18. Now the jeans start to move, so you decide to reorder, but at a lower price than before so that you can continue selling them at $18 and still make a good profit. You find, however, that the manufacturers are not interested in filling your order at the lower price. You have discovered that there is plenty of demand for inexpensive blue jeans, but no supply.

The question is: Is there a price that will make both the supplier and the customer happy? The answer is yes—the price at which the number of jeans demanded equals the number supplied.

This relationship is shown in Exhibit 1.3. A range of possible prices is listed vertically at the left of the graph, with the lowest at the bottom and the highest at the top. Quantity of blue jeans is represented along the horizontal axis. The points plotted on the line labeled *D* indicate that on a given day you would sell 10 pairs of jeans if they were priced at $35, 15 pairs if they were priced at $30, and so on. The line that describes this relationship between price and quantity demanded is a **demand curve.** (Demand curves are not necessarily curved; they may be straight lines.)

Now, think about the situation from your point of view. You will want to offer more pairs of jeans if you can price each pair at $35 rather than at $18; that is, for a higher price, you would be willing to take the risk of buying the jeans for $10, use precious floor space to display them, and mark them down if they don't sell well. In general, the quantity of a good or service that is supplied increases as the price rises, other things being equal. This relationship can also be depicted graphically. Again, look at Exhibit 1.3. The line labeled *S* shows that you would

VIDEO EXERCISE

demand curve Series of points on a graph showing the relationship between price and quantity demanded

EXHIBIT 1.3

The Relationship Between Supply and Demand

In a free-market system, prices aren't set by the government; nor do producers alone have the final say. Instead, prices reflect the interaction of supply **(S)** and demand **(D)**. The equilibrium price **(E)** is established when the amount of a product that producers are willing to sell at a given price equals the amount that consumers are willing to buy at that price.

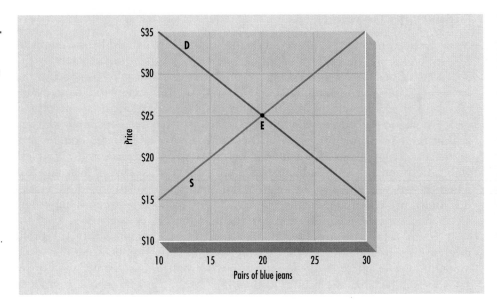

supply curve Series of points on a graph showing the relationship between price and quantity supplied

equilibrium price Point at which quantity supplied and quantity demanded are in balance

be willing to offer 30 pairs of jeans at $35, 25 pairs at $30, and so on. Your willingness to carry the item increases as the price you can charge and your profit potential per item increase. In other words, as price goes up, quantity supplied goes up. The line tracing the relationship between price and the quantity supplied is called a **supply curve.**

As much as you would like to sell 30 pairs of jeans at $35, customers are likely to want only 10 pairs at that price. If you offered 30 pairs, therefore, you would probably be stuck with some that you'd have to mark down. How do you avoid this problem? Look for the point at which the demand curve and the supply curve intersect, the point at which the intentions of buyers and sellers coincide. The point marked *E* in Exhibit 1.3 shows that when jeans are priced at $25, your customers are willing to buy 20 pairs of them and you are willing to sell 20 pairs. In other words, at the price of $25, supply and demand are in balance. The price at this point is known as the **equilibrium price.**

Note that this intersection represents both a specific price—$25 in our example—and a specific quantity of goods—20 pairs of jeans; it is also tied to a specific point in time. Note also that it is the mutual interaction between demand and supply that determines the equilibrium price. In a purely free-market economy, no outside interference disrupts that interaction.

As time passes, equilibrium points between supply and demand may shift. In the blue jeans business, clothing styles may change or other retailers may mark down their jeans and attract your customers. When this happens, you would need to reevaluate the profit potential of the jeans and adjust your buying and pricing policies accordingly.

How Prices Affect Whole Industries

Price affects the supply of a product throughout a whole economy by helping businesspeople decide which products to offer and which industries to invest in. For example, consider the commercial real estate business. During the 1980s, easy credit and good economic times encouraged developers to erect office buildings in major cities from Boston to San Diego. But just when many of these new buildings were nearing completion, the economy softened. Instead of expanding, businesses began to lay people off, and the need for additional facilities declined. Office vacancy rates soared: Hartford, 28 percent; Atlanta, 19 percent; Indianapolis, 22 percent; Minneapolis, 17 percent; Dallas, 26 percent; Phoenix, 28 percent. People with existing buildings for sale or rent were forced to cut prices, and their profits declined accordingly.[10]

This, in turn, discouraged additional construction and paved the way for the industry's eventual recovery. Ultimately, when the economy improves and all the existing office buildings are almost full, demand for facilities will bump up against supply. When that happens, builders will be able to raise prices, and a new cycle of construction will begin.

Theoretically, the law of supply and demand should operate just as well on a global scale as it does on a national scale. However, this is currently not the case. In many major industries like steel, automobiles, and textiles, large production facilities are more efficient than small ones, so producers are inclined to build big plants capable of producing large quantities—enough to supply their own domestic market and then some. To ensure that these plants operate efficiently, many governments pass protective trade measures to keep out competing goods from abroad. Some also provide financial support to help boost export sales. This interference with the market system prevents the self-correcting mechanism from operating. As a consequence, many major industries around the globe are burdened with excess capacity, a situation that depresses both profits and prices in these industries.[11]

How Prices Affect Labor Decisions

In addition to providing signals within industries and between buyers and sellers of goods and services, prices send signals between those who need workers and the workers themselves. Workers use the price of work to choose among available jobs, just as they use price to choose among blue jeans.

Perhaps you have had some personal experience with this phenomenon. In high school or during summer vacations, you may have discovered that the jobs for which you were qualified did not pay very well. Recognizing that your lack of training was holding you back, you decided to invest in a college education in order to qualify for a better job. Once you earn your degree, your improved earning power should more than compensate for the cost of college.

Workers have the option of selling their time where it is worth more. When enough of them leave one type of job to seek higher-paying jobs, employers can attract more workers only by increasing the wages they pay. Pay is generally lower in fields with an abundant pool of qualified workers. In other words, the labor market is subject to the same forces of supply and demand as the markets for goods, services, and investment capital.

Circular Flow

So far, this discussion has focused on the economic forces that affect individuals and businesses. However, some economic forces affect society as a whole. Perhaps the most important concept at this level is **circular flow,** which describes the movement of all resources within an economy. Just as the bloodstream carries oxygen to the body's cells and carbon dioxide from those cells back to

circular flow Continuous exchange of goods and services for money among the participants in an economic system

EXHIBIT 1.4

Circular Flow

Consumer households pay money for the goods and services that businesses provide. With this money, businesses pay for raw materials—and for the workers who produce goods and services. These workers come out of consumer households. (The circular pattern in this relationship can be seen in the pathways around the edge of the diagram.) Meanwhile, the government also buys goods and services as well as labor. (The government's role is represented by the straight-line pathways in the center.)

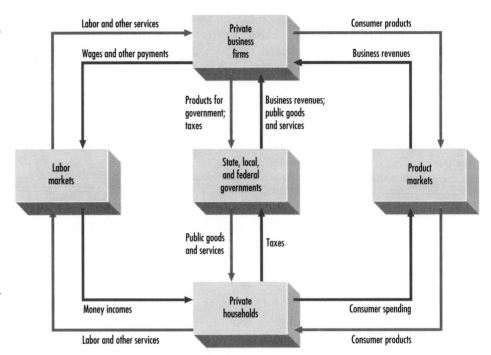

the lungs, the economy carries goods and services, which are exchanged for money, as seen in Exhibit 1.4.

1. Goods and services flow from businesses to households; households generate a return flow of money as compensation for these goods. Goods and services also flow from businesses to other businesses.

2. Governments provide goods and services (such as roads, courts, and education) to households and businesses, which send a return flow of money in the form of taxes.

3. At the same time, households provide services to businesses in the form of labor and receive a return flow of money in the form of wages and salaries.

The flow of money also involves the process of saving and investing. As a group, people in the United States have historically saved approximately 5 percent of their household income. This money is invested in bank accounts, stocks, bonds, and other forms of savings. Much of it eventually wends its way through the banking system and securities markets and ends up in businesses, where it can be used for capital improvements. Many economists are concerned because people in the United States tend to save a smaller percentage of their incomes than people in other industrial countries. This means that our companies have a relatively harder time financing expansion. To make matters worse, the household savings rate in the United States has declined in the last few years.[12]

As business becomes more international in scope, the flow of capital, labor, raw materials, and goods and services is taking on a global dimension. Companies in the United States employ foreign labor, build plants in other countries, sell their products abroad, and obtain capital from foreign investors. As a result, the flow of money is becoming increasingly dependent on decisions and events over which we have relatively little control. Our prosperity—or lack of it—

depends on what happens in places like Japan, Germany, Saudi Arabia, Australia, Poland, China, Mexico, and Canada.

The Multiplier Effect

The circular-flow diagram shows that all elements of our economy are linked. Because of the interrelationships, any change in one part of the economic system creates changes elsewhere. For example, if a university decides to construct a new dormitory, some construction workers will have more income. If some of these workers decide to spend the extra income on new boats, boatbuilders will have more income. The boatbuilders, in turn, might spend this income on beer, and the brewers might spend it on cars. Exhibit 1.5 shows how all economic decisions ripple through the system—the **multiplier effect.** Money never stays in one place, and every market decision has an impact on other markets.

The multiplier effect operates in the opposite direction as well. If a business needs fewer delivery trucks, truck assembly workers will have less income. The truck assembly workers may choose to cut back on air travel, and airline personnel with less income may choose to buy fewer bicycles. All economic events are linked this way.

multiplier effect Chain reaction whereby a change in one economic variable affects other variables, resulting in a ripple of changes throughout an economic system

EXHIBIT 1.5 ▶ **Multiplier Effect**

All economic decisions ripple through the economy. Spending 75 percent of each additional amount of revenue in each cycle would yield a series of spending cycles like this one.

HYPOTHETICAL SPENDING CYCLES	AMOUNT SPENT IN BILLIONS		CUMULATIVE AMOUNT SPENT IN BILLIONS
First cycle: Government buys $100 billion worth of missiles	$100	Missiles	$100
Second cycle: Missile workers have more income, spend it on $75 billion worth of new boats	$75	Boats	$175
Third cycle: Boatbuilders have more income, spend it on $56 billion in beer	$56	Beer	$231
Fourth cycle: Brewery workers buy $42 billion worth of new cars	$42	Cars	$273
Fifth cycle: Autoworkers spend $32 billion on air travel	$32	Air travel	$305
Sixth cycle: Airline personnel buy $24 billion worth of bicycles	$24	Bicycles	$329
Seventh cycle and beyond: Additional spending adds another $71 billion in sales	$71	Additional	$400

The United States spends roughly $300 billion per year to educate some 58 million students, operating on the theory that an educated population is essential to a free and productive society. Most students attend public schools, which are paid for with tax money.

public goods Goods or services that can be supplied more efficiently by government than by individuals or businesses

transfer payments Payments by government to individuals that are not made in return for goods and services

▶ THE ROLE OF GOVERNMENT

Although the market system generally works well, it is far from perfect. If left unchecked, the economic forces that make capitalism succeed may also create severe problems for some groups or individuals. The solution to these problems often requires government intervention. This intervention takes four basic forms: enforcing rules and regulations, providing public goods and transfer payments, fostering competition, and contributing to economic stability.

Enforcing Rules and Regulations

The federal government is creating new rules and regulations at the rate of 4,600 per year.[13] Meanwhile, state and local governments are adding their own provisions to the body of rules that limit what businesses and consumers can and cannot do. Mostly, the regulations just keep piling up, since relatively few of them are ever officially rescinded. Whether you're a department-store owner or a street vendor, you can't legally do business without a permit. If you run a restaurant, you need a certificate from the board of health. You can't practice medicine, sell stock, or drive a cab without a license. In some industries you can't sell your own services as a worker without joining a union. And you can't legally hold any job without having a Social Security number.

Nor is there unrestricted freedom of action in the marketplace. As a consumer, for instance, you can't buy some medications without a doctor's prescription, and you can't buy alcoholic beverages without a certificate proving that you're old enough. Some goods (such as endangered animal species) and services (such as contract murder) are not legally available at all.

Companies and individuals are also required to share their profits with the government. Whether those profits take the form of corporate earnings, stock dividends, personal wages, or winnings from a lottery, they are taxed, and the money is used for the common good.

Providing Public Goods and Transfer Payments

Although everybody hates to pay taxes, most of us are willing to admit they're a necessary evil. For example, if the government didn't take your tax money and buy national defense, would you be inclined to invest in a missile of your own? Similarly, it might not be practical to rely on individual demand to provide police and fire protection, to build roads, or to launch satellites. Instead, the government steps in and supplies the **public goods** that benefit everyone.

In addition, our society recognizes that some individuals are not capable of supplying enough labor to provide themselves a decent standard of living. We could each contribute voluntarily to care for these people, but instead we have chosen to let the government be our conduit. The government collects contributions in the form of taxes from those who are capable of supporting themselves and distributes the money to the less self-sufficient in the form of **transfer payments** such as Social Security, food stamps, welfare, and unemployment compensation. The individuals who receive these allocations are usually not required to provide any goods or services in return.

Fostering Competition

Because competition generally benefits our economy, we have passed laws to ensure that no single enterprise becomes too powerful. The theoretical ideal is

pure competition, in which no single firm or group of firms in an industry is large enough to influence prices and thereby distort the workings of the free-market system.

But in practice, pure competition works better in some industries than in others. Compare the dry-cleaning business, for example, with the auto industry. The nature of dry cleaning is such that small, independent firms operating on a local level are efficient. This is not the case in the auto industry, where economies of scale favor large manufacturers. An industry of this type, dominated by just a few producers, is called an **oligopoly.** Although oligopolies themselves are not illegal, the law prohibits oligopolists from artificially setting prices by agreeing among themselves. In addition, the government has the power to prevent combinations of firms that would reduce competition and lead to oligopolistic conditions in an industry.

Restrictions are also imposed to prevent the development of a monopoly in any particular industry or market. A **monopoly** is a company that has total control over products and prices and keeps other companies from competing. (Some monopolies, such as utilities, are legal but closely regulated.) By definition, therefore, monopolies undermine the principle of competition. True monopolies are prohibited by federal law and have been a subject of continuing government concern since the turn of the century.

A number of factors apart from government intervention help prevent the development of oligopolies and monopolies. In many instances, consumers can find substitute goods or services if the prices in one industry are higher than consumers wish to pay. For example, when the price of copper went up, the telecommunications industry turned to new technology such as fiber optics that didn't depend on copper wire and cable. Even if there are no domestic substitutes, consumers can often purchase foreign products, thereby discouraging oligopolists from raising prices.

In fact, many foreign governments prefer to have only one or two major companies in industries where economies of scale provide a distinct advantage. They argue that the larger firms will have a better chance of competing in the world market. U.S. producers up against this type of competition from abroad can make a very convincing case against strict enforcement of antitrust laws. Some even advocate the development of a national industrial policy that would cultivate specific industries and technologies that are vital to our international competitiveness. In these areas, the government would foster cooperation among U.S. companies so that they would be better able to compete on a global scale.

Contributing to Economic Stability

An economy never stays exactly the same size. Instead, it grows and contracts in response to the combined effects of such factors as technological breakthroughs, changes in investment patterns, shifts in consumer attitudes, world events, and basic economic forces. Since 1854, economists have charted 31 distinct cycles of growth and decline in our economy, including the recession that began in July 1990. On the average, the periods of expansion have lasted about three years, while the periods of contraction, or **recession,** have averaged 11 months, creating an upward trend overall.[14]

Although these up-and-down swings, known as the **business cycle,** are natural and to some degree predictable, they cause hardship. Once consumers start to buy less, factories must produce less; companies must, therefore, lay off workers, who in turn buy less; and so on. In an attempt to avoid these problems and

pure competition Situation in which so many buyers and sellers exist that no single buyer or seller can control the price of a product or the number of units sold

oligopoly Market dominated by a few producers

monopoly Market in which there are no direct competitors so that one company dominates

recession Period during which national income, employment, and production all fall

business cycle Fluctuations in the rate of growth that an economy experiences over a period of several years

to foster economic stability, the government adjusts the tax system, interest rates, and the total amount of money circulating in our economy. This complex of government action aimed at influencing the economy has two facets: fiscal policy and monetary policy. **Fiscal policy** involves changes in the government's revenues and expenditures to stimulate or dampen the economy; **monetary policy** entails adjustments to the nation's money supply. (Monetary policy is discussed more fully in Chapter 18.)

fiscal policy Use of government revenue collection and spending to influence the business cycle

monetary policy Government action to influence the economy by controlling the money supply

Employment and Unemployment

When the U.S. economy is strong, it has historically been able to employ about 95 percent of the people who are willing and able to work. Although unemployment approached 7 percent during the 1990–1991 recession, the U.S. economy is projected to add 18 million jobs between 1988 and 2000, increasing employment from 118 million to 136 million.[15]

During downturns in the business cycle unemployment may become a major social problem. The most extreme case in this century came during the Great Depression of the 1930s, when unemployment affected as much as 25 percent of the labor force. Today's welfare programs did not exist then, so most of the unemployed and their families went hungry. We have since been able to maintain higher levels of employment, largely through the manipulations of fiscal policy. For half a century now, whenever business activity has fallen off and large numbers of people have lost their jobs, we have encouraged government to borrow and spend money in order to keep businesses in operation and people employed.

Despite the past effectiveness of such fiscal policy, recent economic conditions make it more difficult to intervene in the business cycle. The government is already spending far more than it is taking in—roughly $250 billion to $300 billion more every year. Economists and politicians fear the consequences of piling up even more red ink. One of the problems is that government borrowing competes with business and personal borrowing. The nation has only so much money available for investment; if the government, businesses, and consumers are all trying to borrow the same funds, somebody loses out—and generally that somebody is not Uncle Sam. When government borrowing crowds out business and private borrowing, the economy suffers a decline in both capital and consumer spending. This, in turn, has a depressing effect on the GNP (or GDP). So instead of boosting the economy, an increase in government spending may actually make matters worse.[16]

Inflation and Disinflation

inflation Economic condition in which prices rise steadily throughout the economy

Fiscal policy is also related to **inflation,** which occurs when the prices of goods and services rise steadily throughout the economy. Although many factors (such as increases in the price of imported goods) contribute to inflation, government borrowing is a major factor. When the government borrows great sums of money to bolster the economy, the total amount of money circulating tends to increase. With more money chasing the same quantity of goods and services, inflation increases too.

Theoretically, the government is supposed to pay back its debt during inflationary times, thereby taking some of the excess money out of the economy and slowing inflation to a moderate level. This system worked relatively well throughout the 1950s and 1960s, but during the 1970s, inflation kept building. By the end of the decade, prices were increasing by almost 14 percent a year.

Inflation of this magnitude brings an unproductive mind-set. People become motivated to buy "before the price goes up," even if they have to borrow money to do it. With greater competition for available money, interest rates increase to a level that makes business borrowing riskier and business expansion slower. Businesses and individuals alike begin spending on short-term items instead of investing in things like new factories and children's education, which are more valuable to the nation's economy in the long run.

Because of the peculiar psychology that accompanies high inflation, slowing it has always been difficult. In addition, the causes of inflation are complex, and the remedies can be painful. Nevertheless, several factors conspired to bring about a period of **disinflation,** a moderation in the inflation rate, during the 1980s. A weakening of the oil **cartel** (a producers' group that keeps prices high by limiting production), deregulation of American industry, a decline in the power of labor unions, and restrictions on the amount of money put into general circulation yielded a modest annual inflation rate of 6 percent by the end of the decade.

Whether inflation will remain under control is debatable. The country is still vulnerable to outside shocks. When Iraq invaded Kuwait, oil prices suddenly shot up. Although they declined when U.S. and allied forces began attacking Iraq, the run-up was a reminder of our dependence on imported oil. Similarly, bad weather could jack up food prices, and political upheavals could limit the supply and boost the price of vital raw materials. Also, government efforts to stimulate the economy could rekindle inflation. When the economy slumps, the government is inclined to increase the money supply, which tends to drive prices up.

disinflation Economic condition in which the rate of inflation moderates

cartel Association of producers that attempts to control a market and keep prices high by limiting output and dividing market shares among the members

High and Low Dollars

Juggling the value of the dollar relative to foreign currencies is still another way in which the government tries to stabilize the economy. By manipulating the value of the dollar, Washington can stimulate or dampen imports and exports. Because international trade currently accounts for about one-fifth of the GNP, it has a profound impact on the country's economic health.

When the dollar is high, it buys a lot of Japanese yen, German marks, English pounds, or whatever, which makes foreign goods relatively cheap for people in the United States and U.S. goods relatively expensive for foreigners. In other words, a high dollar stimulates imports into the United States and hurts exports out of the United States. If the dollar is high, companies that rely on exports are hurt, and the country is likely to suffer a trade deficit with its trading partners. When the dollar is low, the opposite situation prevails.

One factor that determines the value of the dollar on international exchanges is the nation's monetary policy. When the government tightens the supply of money, interest rates in the United States go up and inflation falls. Foreign investors are attracted by this combination. Money flows into the United States from abroad, pushing up the value of the dollar relative to other currencies. This has two important consequences: (1) foreign companies are squeezed for investment capital, since money that would ordinarily be available to them is instead invested in the United States, and (2) U.S. exporters have a hard time selling their goods abroad, which means that production falls off and unemployment rises.

The value of the U.S. dollar determines international trade levels. A strong dollar increases imports and decreases exports; whereas a weak dollar decreases imports and increases exports. By manipulating U.S. monetary policy, the government can influence the balance of international trade.

Conversely, when the government loosens up on the money supply as it did when the 1990–1991 recession occurred, interest rates fall. This discourages foreign investment in the United States and pushes down the value of the dollar. Exports from the United States to other countries tend to rise, whereas imports tend to fall. Meanwhile, the decline in foreign investment means that the United States loses capital that would otherwise be available for business and government projects.

Striking the optimum balance between the value of the dollar and other currencies is a complex undertaking because it depends on decisions made by other countries as well as by our own. The fact is that as much as we would like to create the ideal financial climate, no force—not even government—can completely control the course of the economy.

▶ SHIFTS IN THE ECONOMIC CLIMATE

Such economic forces as the profit motive, scarcity and opportunity costs, competition, supply and demand, circular flow, and the multiplier effect are reasonably constant facts of economic life. Businesspeople can use these concepts when planning how to operate a business, even though they can't control the economic impact. At the same time, however, businesspeople must learn to cope with unexpected shifts in the economy, which have occurred throughout our nation's history and will undoubtedly continue into the future.

The History of Our Economy's Growth

Initially, the economic base in the United States was the small family farm. People grew enough food for their families and used any surplus to trade for necessary goods provided by independent craftsmen and merchants. Business operated on a small scale, and much of the population was self-employed. With fertile, flat terrain and adequate rainfall, farmers soon prospered, and their prosperity rubbed off on the townspeople who served them.

In the early nineteenth century, people began making greater use of the rivers, harbors, and rich mineral deposits. Excellent natural resources helped businesspeople accumulate the capital they needed to increase production, and the process of *capital accumulation* was aided by their cultural heritage. Saving played an important role in the European tradition, and in the United States, this tradition contributed to the habit of putting something aside today for the tools needed tomorrow.

By the mid-nineteenth century, the United States had begun the transition from an agrarian to an industrial economy. Entrepreneurs brought together the capital, technology, and labor required for heavy industrialization. The scale of business began to shift. Independent craftsmen were replaced by large-scale factories in which each person did one simple task over and over. The trend toward mass production and the division of labor was fueled by the arrival of millions of new workers who came to the United States from abroad.

As businesses increased in size, they increased in power. More and more industrial assets were concentrated in fewer and fewer hands, putting smaller competitors, workers, and consumers at a disadvantage. By popular mandate, the government passed laws and regulations to prevent the abuse of power by big business. At the same time, workers began to organize into unions to balance the power of their employers. The Great Depression of the 1930s further strengthened the hand of government and labor as people became disenchanted with the power of business to pull the country out of hard times.

World War II and the postwar reconstruction revived the economy and renewed the trend toward large-scale enterprises. The government, accustomed to playing a major role in the war effort, continued to exert a large measure of control over business and the economy. Stimulated by a boom in world demand and an expansive political climate, the country prospered throughout the 1960s.

Then, as Western Europe and Japan gradually grew stronger, the United States entered an era of diminishing growth. Ironically, the United States had

TECHNIQUES FOR BUSINESS SUCCESS

How to Predict the Future

Forewarned is fore-armed, as they say, which is why businesspeople try to predict the future of the economy. If you know what's coming, you can take advantage of shifting conditions to get one step ahead of the competition. Crystal balls and tea leaves have their adherents, but most companies turn first to the index of leading economic indicators published by the U.S. Department of Commerce. The index, which is a composite of 11 broad measures of economic activity, has successfully predicted every downswing and upturn in the business cycle since 1948.

The indicators are called "leading" because they change several months ahead of a change in the general economy. Typically, the index starts to fall 9.5 months before a recession officially begins, and it starts to rise 4.5 months before an expansion gets under way. One reason for the reliability of the index is that many of the indicators represent commitments to do business a few months downstream. Here are some of the key factors that make up the composite index:

▶ *Stock Market.* Stock prices are one of the most reliable economic signals we have, partly because they reflect what investors are doing and partly because they influence public perceptions. When the market starts to climb, a few people actually make money, and everybody else begins to feel a little more confident. As confidence in the future grows, people tend to spend money more freely, creating a snowball effect that perks up business. Conversely, when the market declines, pessimism increases and people start to buy less.

▶ *Consumer Confidence.* Like stock market activity, consumer confidence has an important psychological effect on economic activity. Consumer spending accounts for roughly two-thirds of the GNP, so when people are reluctant to spend money for fear of what lies ahead, the economy generally tumbles. At the same time, when people feel secure about the future, they're comfortable buying things.

▶ *Housing Starts.* One-fifth of the workers in this country are directly or indirectly involved in the construction industry, so when home building picks up or falls off, it's a fairly safe bet that the economy as a whole will be affected within a few months.

▶ *Business Orders.* Companies place orders for big-ticket items like new factories or machinery several months before they expect to take delivery. They place those orders because they're picking up clues that they'll need more production capacity to meet future demand—a good sign that a recovery lies ahead. When demand slips, companies cut back on capital expenditures.

▶ *Length of Workweek.* When companies start asking their employees to work overtime, chances are good that business is beginning to pick up. If new orders continue to come in, additional workers may be hired, which will raise the general level of employment and contribute to an economic recovery. Thus, the length of the workweek is often an early clue to swings in the business cycle.

Other factors that signal the onset of recessions or recoveries include fluctuations in the money supply, orders for durable goods, unemployment claims, export activity, percentage of companies receiving slower deliveries from suppliers, and the prices of raw materials that are especially sensitive to increases or decreases in demand. If you get in the habit of tracking these indicators in the newspapers or business magazines, you'll be among the first to know what lies ahead.

supplied its foreign competitors with the resources and know-how to stake a claim in the world marketplace. Inflation soared while the economy stagnated. The Vietnam War dulled U.S. optimism and made people question the wisdom of both big business and big government.

Throughout the 1980s, competition from abroad continued to increase. Business responded with an often ruthless effort to regain its competitive edge. Entire industries virtually disappeared. Some giant corporations gobbled one another up; others splintered into fragments. Whole levels of management were eliminated. During this period of upheaval, a subtle shift occurred. Small companies began reasserting their role in the economy, generating new jobs to employ some of the workers displaced by large corporations.

The Challenges Ahead

The U.S. economy has by no means reached the limits of its potential. It still has natural resources, labor, and capital that can be used more productively, and U.S. businesses seem to have an unlimited supply of the entrepreneurial vision that allows people like John Johnson to bring resources together to create needed goods and services as well as new jobs.

The 1990s will provide new problems and opportunities for companies and their employees. Global competition, changing technology, environmental concerns, and demographic shifts will prompt businesses to move in new directions and to experiment with various management approaches. How will the trends of tomorrow affect you and your career? A look at Exhibit 1.6 will provide some insight into the outlook for various occupational groups, and the following observations will give you some perspective on business today.

The Global Economy

The economic integration of the world will increase as multinational corporations continue to invest overseas and expand through international joint ventures. The lines between exports and imports will blur as companies become more international in scope. The United States will continue to face strong competition from Western Europe, Japan, and newly industrialized countries such as Taiwan, Korea, Singapore, and Hong Kong. At the same time, the move toward capitalism in Eastern Europe, in the new Commonwealth of Independent States, and in Latin America will provide U.S. businesses with new opportunities as well as new challenges. Third World countries will continue to supply raw materials and basic commodities. *The challenge:* Without resorting to the sorts of trade restrictions that would harm consumers or increase tensions among nations, the United States must find ways to keep businesses healthy and workers employed. To remain competitive, businesses must continue their efforts to control costs and boost quality.

Accelerating Technological Development

As older industries are consigned to lower-wage regions of the globe, the United States will rely more heavily on technology as its chief competitive weapon. New fields such as biotechnology, computers, robotics, lasers, fiber optics, and composite materials will serve as the mainsprings of economic growth. Developments will occur rapidly in these fields, putting a premium on our ability to

EXHIBIT 1.6 ▶ **Fastest-Growing and Fastest-Declining Occupations**

In the 1990s people looking for jobs in the service sector will generally have more opportunities than people looking for manufacturing jobs.

	EMPLOYMENT IN THOUSANDS		PERCENTAGE CHANGE
	1988	**2000**	**1988–2000**
FASTEST-GROWING OCCUPATIONS			
Medical assistants	149	253	70%
Home health aides	236	397	68
Radiologic technologists and technicians	132	218	66
Medical secretaries	207	327	58
Securities and financial services sales workers	200	309	55
Travel agents	142	219	54
Computer systems analysts	403	617	53
Computer programmers	519	769	48
Human services workers	118	171	45
Correction officers and jailers	186	262	41
Electrical and electronics engineers	439	615	40
Receptionists and information clerks	833	1,164	40
FASTEST-DECLINING OCCUPATIONS			
Electrical and electronic equipment assemblers, precision	161	91	−44%
Electrical and electronic assemblers	237	134	−44
Farmers	1,141	875	−23
Stenographers	159	122	−23
Telephone and cable TV line installers and repairers	127	100	−21
Sewing machine operators, garment	620	531	−14
Crushing and mixing machine operators	136	117	−14
Textile machine operators	227	197	−13
Machine feeders and offbearers	249	218	−13
Hand packers and packagers	635	560	−12
Packaging and filling machine operators	286	254	−11

respond quickly and reap a profit before a particular level of technology becomes obsolete. With the help of computers and sophisticated telecommunications equipment, workers will be freed to an increasing extent to work in scattered locations. *The challenge:* In the process of adopting new technology, business must create a process for retraining workers so that change does not occur at their expense. Business must also be careful to consider the implications of technology for overall quality of life, weighing the costs against the benefits so that enlightened choices can be made.

Environmental Concerns

Environmental issues top the list of America's social concerns. People are worried about acid rain, global warming, oil spills, chemicals in their food and water, pesticides, toxic wastes, endangered species, and polluted air. Rightly or wrongly, business gets blamed for causing many environmental troubles. People are pressuring companies to handle hazardous materials more carefully and to

Three-fourths of all Americans will be of prime working age in the 1990s. These midlife baby boomers will hit the peak of their earning power, creating demand for all sorts of goods and services that will make their lives more fun or more convenient. After a hard day at the office, they will turn to home, family, travel, and leisure.

provide products that take the environment into account. Meanwhile, the government is strengthening the rules and regulations that govern what companies must do to cut pollution. *The challenge:* Business must find ways to safeguard the environment in the most cost-effective way, balancing the risks of pollution against the potential loss of jobs and economic growth that may ensue if unnecessarily high environmental standards are established.

The Changing Labor Force

The labor force will change dramatically over the next several decades. As the "baby boomers" age, they will swell the ranks of middle and upper management, creating intense competition for jobs at the top. At the same time, employers will face a serious shortage of new workers as the "baby bust" generation enters the work force. To an increasing extent, new jobs will be filled by immigrants and ethnic minorities, many of whom will lack adequate training, which will force many companies to become educators as well as employers. Ethnic diversity will be accompanied by a more even balance between the sexes as women continue to increase their participation in the work force. *The challenge:* Business must find ways to make work satisfying for older people with limited opportunities for advancement and, at the same time, find ways to attract and train an adequate supply of new workers. Companies must also help two-job families cope with child-rearing and elder-care responsibilities.

Participative Management

Because of the changing attitudes of workers and because of increasing competition from abroad, managers can no longer rely on the old, paternalistic, bureaucratic style of getting things done. Instead, they must learn to coax and motivate and to lead by example, not edict. *The challenge:* Older executives must become more flexible, and younger executives must orient themselves toward people rather than toward organizational structures.

The Evolution of the Service Sector

The past decade was a period of explosive growth for companies that provide services: restaurants, hotels, retail stores, airlines, beauty parlors, health clubs, theme parks, financial planners. But in the 1990s, services are trimming—more than just the fat. Overexpansion, runaway costs, and increased competition are causing services to tighten their belts. *The challenge:* As the service sector slows in the 1990s, many service businesses will need to refocus. To sustain profits, service businesses will need to boost their productivity by operating more efficiently and by taking advantage of new technology.

SUMMARY OF LEARNING OBJECTIVES

1 Explain what an economic system is.
An economic system is a society's way of producing, distributing, and marketing the goods and services desired by its population.

2 List the four factors of production.
Natural resources, labor, capital, and entrepreneurship are the four factors of production.

3 Name the three major types of economic systems and differentiate their identifying characteristics.
Under capitalism, the factors of production are owned by individuals

who make all business decisions; citizens have a high degree of economic freedom but also face considerable economic risk. Under communism, the government owns all factors of production and makes all the business decisions; distinctions between rich and poor are minimized. Under socialism, the state owns and operates certain key industries but allows private ownership of many businesses; relatively high taxes permit the government to provide many social services.

4 Describe the relationship between profit and sales, and explain how profit motivates entrepreneurs.

Profit is the amount left over after expenses are deducted from revenues. The profits of the business add to its value and thereby increase the entrepreneur's return on investment.

5 Discuss three ways companies compete.

Companies compete on the basis of price, quality and service, and innovation.

6 Explain how supply and demand interact to establish prices.

When price goes up, the quantity demanded goes down, but the supplier's incentive to produce more goes up. When price goes down, the quantity demanded increases, but the quantity supplied declines. When the interests of buyers and sellers are in balance, an equilibrium price is established.

7 List the four major economic roles of the United States government.

The U.S. government enforces rules and regulations, provides public goods and transfer payments, fosters competition, and contributes to economic stability.

8 Identify six trends that will influence the economy in the years ahead.

In the coming years, the U.S. economy will become increasingly integrated with the world economy. Technology will continue to give U.S. companies an edge in certain businesses. Safeguarding the environment will become a major management priority. The labor force will change as the baby boomers are followed by the baby bust generation and as immigrants, minorities, and women increase their role in the work force. Companies will adopt a more participative style of management. The service sector will focus on meeting consumers' changing needs and boosting productivity.

Meeting a Business Challenge at Johnson Publishing

John Johnson had two factors of production already lined up when he decided to publish his first magazine, *Negro Digest*. He had labor (his own), and he had an entrepreneurial vision. What he lacked was capital—the financial resources to get under way. He found a partial solution at his fingertips. One of his least favorite duties at Supreme Life Insurance was operating the addressing machine for billing the company's 20,000 policyholders. While he was running the machine one day, an idea came to him. Why not write a letter to the people on the list, asking each one to buy a two-dollar prepaid subscription to *Negro Digest?* Johnson discussed the idea with his boss, who approved and even offered to donate the stationery for the project.

But there was still one hurdle: stamps. He would need $500 to mail 20,000 letters, and he didn't have anything close to $500. He did what any hopeful young man might do under the circumstances. He went to the bank. The loan officer turned him down; it was against bank policy to

John H. Johnson, publisher, chairman, and chief executive officer, Johnson Publishing

lend money to blacks, he said. Johnson was angry, but he kept his temper and asked, "Who in this town will loan money to people like me?" The bank employee gave Johnson the name of a man at a loan company,

who agreed to give Johnson the $500, provided he could offer some collateral. Johnson had no tangible property of his own, so he persuaded his mother to use her newly purchased furniture to back the loan.

With the money for stamps in hand, Johnson composed a sales letter to the 20,000 people on Supreme's mailing list. Fifteen percent sent in their $2.00 for a prepaid subscription, an amazing response rate for a direct-mail solicitation. That gave Johnson $6,000 to create the first issue of *Negro Digest*. Featuring articles by Carl Sandburg, Walter White, John P. Lewis, Rabbi Harry Essrig, Langston Hughes, and Bishop Bernard Sheil, it was an impressive accomplishment. But Johnson couldn't relax and enjoy it.

He had to pay the printer and cover the cost of mailing 3,000 copies to subscribers, and he was short of cash again. He needed to sell 2,000 copies at newsstands to meet his expenses. He contacted the Charles Levy Circulating Company, the biggest magazine distributor in Chicago, to get copies of *Negro Digest* into circulation. But Levy said, "Johnson, we don't handle colored books." Again, Johnson bit his tongue and kept his temper. "Is that because you're prejudiced or because colored books don't sell?" he asked. Levy denied being prejudiced. His decision was strictly business, he said. Johnson replied that *this* "colored" magazine would sell, and he left his card in case Levy changed his mind.

To give Levy a push in the right direction, Johnson asked 30 of his friends to drop by Levy's newsstands and ask for the exciting new publication *Negro Digest*. After about a week of this, Levy called to say he'd take a few magazines after all. Johnson talked him into stocking 1,000. To keep the ball rolling, he gave all 30 friends enough money to buy up all the newsstand copies. Levy was so impressed that he ordered another 1,000.

By this time, word was out among the newsstand dealers that the magazine was a hit. Whenever a black person walked by a newsstand, the vendor would call out, "Have you seen the new magazine, *Negro Digest?*" Demand fueled demand, and Johnson printed another 5,000 copies. Within six months, circulation reached 50,000 copies, and Johnson was on his way to building a publishing empire.

Looking back on those early days, Johnson recalls, "I never thought I would be rich. Never in my wildest dreams did I believe that *Negro Digest* would lead to the Johnson Publishing Company of today. If I'd dreamed then of the conglomerate of today, I probably would have been so intimidated, with my meager resources, that I wouldn't have had the courage to take the first step. . . . You can't get rich trying to get rich. What you need to do is dream small dreams, because very often when you try to see things in their largest form, you get discouraged, and you feel that it's impossible. But if you can somehow think and dream of success in small steps, every time you make a step, every time you accomplish a small goal, it gives you the confidence to go on from there."

Your Mission: You are an administrative assistant to Mr. Johnson, a position that's designed to serve as a management apprenticeship. Your duties are many and varied, ranging from scheduling Mr. Johnson's activities to drafting speeches and correspondence and conducting special studies. How would you handle the following situations?

1. Johnson has been asked to deliver the commencement address to the graduating class of Howard University, a predominantly black institution in Washington, D.C. The university has suggested that he speak on the topic of "Making It in America," and he has agreed. Your job is to develop the first draft. Which of the following main ideas do you think would be the most appropriate for Johnson and his audience?

a. Thanks to the free-market system, everybody in the United States has an equal chance to succeed in business.

b. Because of racial and economic inequality, it is almost impossible for a person from a minority group to succeed in business in the United States. If you want to make it, you will have to work harder and be smarter than your white counterparts.

c. If succeeding in business is your goal, you can make it in spite of the odds. The system may not be perfect, but opportunities exist if you're willing to take some risks and make some sacrifices.

d. Because the government has passed laws to protect minorities from discrimination in the workplace, African-Americans have a much better chance of making it today than they did in the 1940s when Johnson began his career.

2. One of Johnson's magazines, *EM* (EbonyMan), has been losing circulation during the recent economic downturn. The magazine, which focuses on fashion and lifestyles, competes with "white" publications such as *Gentlemen's Quarterly.* What should Johnson Publishing do to boost circulation?

a. Assume that the decline in circulation is a temporary phenomenon brought on by the recession; do nothing until the economy picks up. If circulation still lags, make changes at that time.

b. Cut the price of the magazine by 20 percent at the newsstands and offer discounts of 20, 35, and 50 percent for subscribers who sign up for one, two, and three years.

c. Compare the circulation of *EM* to the circulation of competing magazines to determine whether all are declining or whether a rival is gaining market share at *EM*'s expense. If sales of rival magazines are off by a similar amount, survey subscribers to determine why. If *EM* is losing share to rival magazines, analyze reasons such as price, promotion, and editorial content to identify opportunities for improving *EM*.

d. Cut back on the number of copies printed of *EM* each month until the supply-and-demand relationship gets back into balance.

3. A group of militant African-Americans has threatened to boycott Johnson Publishing's magazines because they tend to focus on upbeat topics. The magazines portray blacks who have succeeded and present a picture of them leading "the good life." The militants would like Johnson to change his editorial policy so that the magazines give more attention to the inequities of the free-market system. Johnson is preparing to meet with representatives of the group in hopes of convincing them to drop the boycott threat. He has asked you to suggest some points he might make.

a. Listen to the militants' point of view; objectively analyze their arguments. They may be right in thinking that the magazines should take a tougher, more adversarial position on some issues. Ask the militants to suggest some topics they would like to see covered—maybe they have some good ideas. Also ask them to critique past articles. Maybe they haven't *read* the magazines carefully enough to know what the editorial policy is. Show them some of the more thought-provoking articles that have appeared and challenge them to back up their contention that Johnson is poisoning the minds of black Americans with false hopes.

b. Johnson cannot afford to alienate his advertisers by running negative, adversarial articles. If he starts knocking the system, big companies may pull their ads. If that happens, the magazines will no longer be economically viable, and Johnson will be forced out of business.

c. Johnson's businesses are an extremely positive force for African-Americans. His publishing business alone employs over 2,000 people, many of whom are black. They use their paychecks to buy things from many black-owned companies, which in turn employ other blacks. His magazines have created opportunities for black advertising agencies, black models, black writers, black photographers, black printers, and black-owned magazine distributors. Because of his efforts to sell ad space in his publications, major corporations have become more aware that blacks as a group are an important market segment. It is unfair to accuse him of selling out to the white establishment when he has made such a positive contribution to the black community.

d. It's a free country. Johnson has every right to print what he wants, and the militants have every right

to think what they think and do what they will. If they want to boycott his magazines, that's their privilege, but they'd better not break any laws because if they do, he'll take action. His magazines don't appeal to African-American militants anyway, so he probably won't lose many readers.

4. Looking toward the future, Johnson is thinking of launching a new magazine to respond to changes in business and society. He has asked you to consider some of the changes occurring and to suggest ideas for a magazine that will respond to those shifts. Which of the following concepts best addresses the needs of future audiences?

a. A magazine that would focus not just on African-Americans but on all minorities who are trying to make it. The theme would be that diversity is good for society and that people from all groups need to understand one another and work toward the common good. Articles

would feature Asians, Hispanics, Native Americans, women, and immigrants from all over the world. The aim would be to create a sense of cohesion among the diverse subscribers.

b. A magazine that features black athletes. The magazine would be similar to *Sports Illustrated,* but it would emphasize the accomplishments of black sports figures.

c. A magazine for black homemakers, featuring articles on home decorating, gardening, child-rearing, cooking, and household crafts.

d. A magazine aimed at black businesspeople engaged in international activities. The focus would be on multinational business with an African-American twist. For example, articles might feature black-owned companies that do business abroad, black employees of multinational companies, black business and political leaders around the globe, and travel tips for African-American businesspeople.[17]

KEY TERMS

bartering (5)
business cycle (19)
capital (4)
cartel (21)
circular flow (15)
communism (8)
demand (13)
demand curve (13)
disinflation (21)
economic system (4)
entrepreneurs (4)
equilibrium price (14)

factors of production (4)
fiscal policy (20)
free-market system (7)
gross domestic product (5)
gross national product (5)
inflation (20)
market economies (7)
mixed capitalism (7)
monetary policy (20)
monopoly (19)
multiplier effect (17)
oligopoly (19)

opportunity cost (11)
planned economies (8)
profit (11)
public goods (18)
pure capitalism (7)
pure competition (19)
recession (19)
socialism (10)
supply (13)
supply curve (14)
transfer payments (18)
underground economy (5)

REVIEW QUESTIONS

1. How is capitalism different from communism and socialism in the way it achieves key economic goals?

2. The U.S. economic system is actually a form of modified capitalism. What are the benefits and drawbacks of this system (as opposed to pure capitalism) for the average citizen?

3. How do scarcity and opportunity cost affect the businessperson?

4. What role does competition play in a free-market economy?

5. Define the demand curve, the supply curve, and equilibrium price.

6. What role does the multiplier effect play in an economic system?

7. What happens when an economy shifts from a period of high inflation to a period of disinflation?

8. What major change in the American economy appeared during the mid-nineteenth century, and what were some of its effects?

A CASE FOR CRITICAL THINKING

Cautious Hope for a United Korea

For over 45 years, North and South Korea have remained enemies, split by a two-and-a-half-mile-long "demilitarized zone" over which 1.7 million opposing soldiers keep an anxious watch (among them 40,000 U.S. troops). This bleak situation developed at the end of World War II, when the defeated Japanese withdrew from Korea, leaving the Soviets to influence the north and the other Allies to influence the south. After the Korean civil war ended in 1953, the division became a powder-keg Cold War standoff, with the potential to erupt at any time into a major superpower conflict.

Today, that possibility is increasingly remote. Global politics are changing so rapidly that North Korea has become one of the last remaining hard-line communist dictatorships. Experts predict that its aging "Great Leader," Kim Il Sung, cannot maintain his policy of *juche* ("self-reliance") in the face of overwhelming economic and political realities. Reunification of the two Koreas—once a dream—is now considered inevitable.

This is exciting news to many South Koreans who fled their northern homes when Kim came into power. But others are urging a "go-slow" policy. Ten to twenty years would not be unreasonable, they say, pointing to the economic problems plaguing Germany as its capitalist West is forced to carry its communist East since the Berlin Wall collapsed and the two nations reunified. Although the political change is welcomed, the West Germans (61 million people) have had to absorb the needs of the East Germans (17 million). All have endured economic hardships, including rising taxes, bankruptcies, and unemployment.

South Koreans have been keeping close watch, frequently telephoning German diplomats to inquire about such problems as developing a joint currency system. Despite their new importance in international trade, the South Koreans don't believe their small nation (42 million population) is equipped to support needy North Korea (21 million). In the affluent and democratic South, the standard of liv-

ing is five times higher than in the North, but it would be seriously threatened by the high cost of rapid reunification. Kee Woo-sik, a World Bank economist, suggests that the cost of reunification might be as high as $170 billion over a ten-year period. Paying only one-third of that without foreign aid would cost the South Koreans 18 percent of their national budget.

Another concern is the very real possibility of total economic collapse in the North, which could send billions of needy refugees to seek aid in the South. Stagnant conditions in self-isolated North Korea have nearly bankrupt the country. The dictatorship faces billions of dollars in unpaid foreign debt as its communist bloc trading partners vanish and its heavily controlled populace endures shrinking rice rations and intermittent electric power. North Korea's primary ally was the Soviet Union; now the Commonwealth of Independent States demands hard currency for the oil imports North Korea needs to operate its heavy industry and military forces. Ironically, the "Great Leader" is turning to Japan as the last hope of infusing billions of dollars in war reparations.

Moreover, the South Koreans fear sudden political events that might force the issue before supporting infrastructure can be set in place. For instance, East and West Germany traded long before events forced their economic union. But until very recently, Kim's repressive regime has forbidden travel or even communication between the two Koreas. (Radio sets in the North are pretuned to keep out news from the South or from the rest of the world.) Their only trade has been conducted indirectly, mostly through Japan, where many Koreans now live.

Responding to economic pressure, the North Koreans have opened up their borders ever so slightly. The two countries fielded their first joint athletic teams for international competition recently, and both have applied to the United Nations for membership, setting the stage for future negotiations. Government officials have

already held a few diplomatic meetings to discuss the future. Although both sides are open to reunification, the North Koreans want to begin with a resolution of political and ideological differences, but the South Koreans believe the economic union must come first. They think the North Koreans will quickly recognize the advantage of a free-market system.

Meanwhile, many South Korean business leaders, such as Hyundai's powerful chairman Chung Ju-Yung, are pushing for a speedier union. They view North Korea as a potential source of cheap labor and raw materials to fuel the South's new position as an international economic competitor. Chung (who was born in the North) has already initiated trade with two former South Korean enemies: the former Soviet Union and the Chinese. These countries, in turn, have put pressure on Kim's regime to relax its internal and external strictures.

Other private business owners point out that reduced military spending could supply as much as $2 billion annually to support the cost of upgrading living standards in the North. The desire for reunification, according to Hyundai's Chung, "is not because we think there's a big market there or lots of raw material. It's because they are our brothers. We are the same people." And these people share a dream: seeing a unified Korea ultimately defeat old enemy Japan in the arena that now seems most significant—the global marketplace. For this reason, it may be the wheels of commerce that successfully replace the tread of tanks in the Korean peninsula.[18]

1. How could a free-market system help North Korea overcome its internal problems?

2. What steps would you recommend South Korea take to protect its own affluence while moving toward reunification with North Korea? Do you think trade negotiations with China are wise? Why or why not?

3. Should private business play a strong role in the reunification effort? Why or why not?

BUILDING YOUR COMMUNICATION SKILLS

Examine how the various economic forces affect a business operation by interviewing the owner or manager of a local business. If this is not possible, your library has journals and periodicals available from which you can select an article that profiles a business. Consider the following: profit motive, scarcity and opportunity, competition, and supply and demand. Present a brief discussion of your findings to several class members, or write a brief summary as directed by your instructor. Be prepared to discuss the method you used to locate information for this analysis.

KEEPING CURRENT USING *THE WALL STREET JOURNAL*

In the past decade, the following business developments have had a dramatic impact on sectors of the economy. Choose one of these factors. Then in recent issues of *The Wall Street Journal*, find three or more articles related to the topic you've chosen.

► The global economy

► Technological developments

► Environmental concerns

► The changing labor force

► Participative management

► Evolution of the service sector

1. What effects of this development are mentioned in the articles you've chosen?

2. What is the impact (or the expected impact) of this development on employment? What groups are most likely to be affected?

3. How do you think this development will affect the industry or job field that you hope to enter?

CHAPTER 2

LEARNING OBJECTIVES
After studying this chapter, you will be able to

1 Identify the two broad sectors of the U.S. economy and the eight subsectors.

2 List four factors that have contributed to the growth of the service sector.

3 Discuss the three basic forms of business ownership.

4 List five advantages and four disadvantages of forming a sole proprietorship.

5 Explain the difference between a general and a limited partnership.

6 List the three groups that govern a corporation, and describe the role of each.

7 Cite four advantages of corporations.

8 Describe the four waves of merger activity.

Forms of Business Enterprise

Facing a Business Challenge
at KPMG Peat Marwick

WHO'S IN CHARGE HERE?

How do you reach decisions when you have 6,100 partners in 117 countries, all of whom think they "own" the business? Answering that question is tricky indeed, as Jon C. Madonna discovered when he became chairman of KPMG Peat Marwick, the biggest of the Big Six accounting firms on a global basis. But to understand what he was up against, you must understand what went on before Madonna was elected chairman.

The previous chairman was Larry Horner, who made plenty of good moves. Perhaps his boldest stroke was the 1986 merger with the Dutch firm of Klynveld Main Goerdeler, which turned Peat into a global powerhouse capable of serving a multinational clientele. He also engineered another cross-border coup when he lured away the entire Canadian staff of Ernst & Whinney, a major competitor now part of Ernst & Young. In addition, Horner saw the opportunities for additional accounting work generated by the merger-and-acquisition boom of the 1980s, a new business area that augmented the firm's traditional tax and auditing practice.

As he steered the firm in some very profitable directions, Horner also fostered a liberal promotion policy. Between 1984 and 1991, Peat elevated 750 associates to the partnership level, bringing the total number of partners in the United States to 1,875. Much as this pleased the junior partners, it made the firm top-heavy compared to its domestic competitors. A typical accounting firm had 14 staff people for every partner, but at Peat the ratio was 7 staff people for each partner.

In good times, the imbalance between partners and associates was not a major problem. There was plenty of money for everybody. But good times don't last forever. As the 1980s drew to a close, the merger boom ended, and Peat's juicy merger business ended with it. Furthermore, after a decade of mergers, there were fewer big clients who needed tax and audit services, and Peat's U.S. rivals began to grab a bigger chunk of the remaining business. Then the recession hit in August 1990, and business fell off in general. After years of double-digit increases, Peat's earnings tapered off in 1989 and were flat in 1990.

As the economy softened, the partners began to feel the effects on their pay (part of which is keyed to profits), and the income squeeze added to a problem that had been simmering for some time: the gap between the compensation of senior and junior partners. Horner was making $1.2 million per year, and some of the junior partners were making one-tenth that amount, a difference they felt was excessive. Their annoyance increased when a study of the accounting profession revealed that Peat's partners were making less than their peers in other firms. In response to the criticism, Horner appointed a task force to study the compensation system. When the group recommended keeping the current structure, many newer partners were outraged, claiming the task force was stacked with senior people.

As the 1990 election of officers approached, Horner was faced with widespread opposition, and in August he announced that he would not seek reelection. Within 24 hours, several new contenders emerged. Jon C. Madonna, a young and charismatic figure, quickly pulled into the lead and was elected chairman of the U.S. operation. In December 1990, he became head of the international business as well.

But, having won the throne, Madonna faced two big problems: (1) the newer partners' desire for a more democratic distribution of power and pay, and (2) the firm's declining profits. How could he satisfy the people who elected him and at the same time exert the control required to increase profits?[1]

▶ HOW TO CATEGORIZE A COMPANY BY INDUSTRY SECTOR

When you look at a company, whether it's KPMG Peat Marwick, your local bank, Xerox, or Exxon, you generally try to draw some conclusions about it. Is it the kind of company you respect? Would you like to work there? Would you invest your money in it? Would you feel comfortable buying its products or services? To answer those questions, you need to figure out what makes the company tick.

service businesses Businesses that provide intangible products or perform useful labor on behalf of another

goods-producing businesses Businesses that produce tangible products

Most companies can be categorized by industry sector; that is, they can be described as providing primarily either services or goods. As Exhibit 2.1 illustrates, the **service businesses** include wholesale and retail trade, finance and insurance, transportation and utilities, and "other" services, such as the accounting advice dispensed by KPMG Peat Marwick. The **goods-producing businesses** include manufacturing, construction, mining, and agriculture. Broadly speaking, companies in these two major sectors of the economy differ in their growth rate, cycle of business, cost structure, company size, and geographic focus.

The relationship between services and the production of goods is not a battle for dominance. The two sectors are complementary parts of a whole, each dependent on the other. Producers need service businesses to buy and distribute products, and service businesses depend on the production of goods for survival. What would a clothing manufacturer do without department stores? And how could McDonald's dish up all those burgers without beef, buns, and grills?

In fact, the line between services and producers has blurred somewhat. Consider IBM, for example. Few IBM employees are involved in physically building a good. Most perform service tasks such as interacting with individual customers,

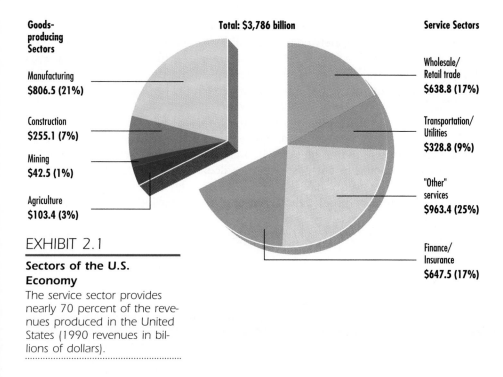

Total: $3,786 billion

Goods-producing Sectors

Manufacturing
$806.5 (21%)

Construction
$255.1 (7%)

Mining
$42.5 (1%)

Agriculture
$103.4 (3%)

Service Sectors

Wholesale/
Retail trade
$638.8 (17%)

Transportation/
Utilities
$328.8 (9%)

"Other"
services
$963.4 (25%)

Finance/
Insurance
$647.5 (17%)

EXHIBIT 2.1

Sectors of the U.S. Economy
The service sector provides nearly 70 percent of the revenues produced in the United States (1990 revenues in billions of dollars).

designing systems for them, or finding out what they need. Such activity ultimately results in selling a good, so you can't call it a service. But the activity itself does not actually produce a good, so you can't call it manufacturing either. The distinction between a good and a service is fuzzy here because what is produced cannot be separated from what is performed.[2]

Growth of the Service Sector

Between the end of World War II and the beginning of the 1990s, the relative balance between the two sectors shifted. In general, the service sector expanded more than the goods-producing sector. Today services account for roughly 72 percent of our nation's economic activity, and manufacturing is responsible for 23 percent of the GNP. Construction, agriculture, and mining account for the remainder.[3]

Services have always played an important part in the U.S. economy, accounting for half of all employment as long ago as 1940. But in the last decade or two, services became an increasingly vital force for a variety of reasons. For one thing, improvements in manufacturing made it possible for fewer people to turn out more goods, thus freeing a greater part of the work force to open restaurants, practice law, write songs, play baseball, and the like. Technological innovation is another important factor, giving birth to a host of new computer-based services that were scarce or even unknown a mere decade ago. The rise of services also reflected a growing trend among producers to let outside firms take over services that the producers used to perform themselves. Instead of having its own data-processing, advertising, or public relations department, for example, a company might hire outside professionals. In addition, foreign producers with access to inexpensive labor took over much of the world's manufacturing, furthering the shift to services in the U.S. economy.

Taken together, these factors led to a surge in employment in the service sector (see Exhibit 2.2). Between 1982 and 1990, service businesses were on a hiring binge, adding a whopping 19 million people to their payrolls. That boils down to virtually all of the new jobs created during the 1980s.[4] In contrast, manufacturing employment dropped from its postwar high of 21 million people to 19 million—about where it stood 20 years ago.[5]

But except for health care, services in the 1990s are faltering, much as goods-producing manufacturers faltered during the 1980s. As the U.S. economy slipped into a recession in August 1990, many service businesses began slashing their payrolls, hoping to cut costs as sales declined. The intense effort to cut costs and improve profits has led to job freezes, layoffs, consolidations, and takeovers. Economists predict that even once the recession is over, the service

BEHIND THE SCENES

The Public Sector

To get a complete picture of the U.S. economy, you need to look beyond the private sector (which consists of companies that aim to make a profit) and consider the public sector (which consists of federal, state, and local governments). Very few of the public sector's operations are profitable; in fact, very few of them break even, which is why the federal budget deficit is humongous and why many states are operating in the red.

Still, the public sector is a vital force in the economy. Roughly 15 percent of the working population is employed by federal, state, or local government agencies—and that doesn't include the people in the military services. In terms of revenue, the federal and state governments take in over $1.5 trillion each year, roughly $1 trillion at the federal level and $500 billion at the state level. The government is also rich in assets. Federal, state, and local governments own roughly 40 percent of all the land in the United States. They also own equipment and buildings worth over $3.9 billion, including the world's largest office building, the Pentagon, which houses 29,000 employees and receives 280,000 phone calls each day.

What does the public sector do with all its resources? It struggles to pay the interest on its debts. And it meets its payroll. It dispenses money through a bewildering array of social programs: about 40 million people collect Social Security, 11 million receive Aid to Families with Dependent Children, 22 million get Medicaid, and 19 million get food stamps. The government also builds and maintains roads, bridges, dams, and sewers. It collects garbage, delivers the mail, fights crime, defends the country, collects taxes, and generates an incredible amount of paperwork. Scattered throughout the massive bureaucracy are almost 4 billion records on individuals—roughly 20 files for every American. According to some estimates, 20 percent of the information in these files is wrong.

Coping with all these commitments is enough to give even a seasoned bureaucrat a headache. To ease the burden, many government agencies are turning to the private sector for help. Companies of all sizes are lining up to take over functions or property that have traditionally been in the government's domain. Firms in the private sector are now managing public libraries, municipal golf courses, and military airfields. In Seattle, Washington, a private company has relieved the city of its solid waste recycling chores. In Starr County, Texas, the jail is in private hands. Twenty-one percent of the public transit system in Denver, Colorado, is run by a profit-making business. A company in Maryland has signed on to handle the Veterans Administration's mail. And McDonald's is selling burgers on 400 military bases.

Can the private sector handle these activities more efficiently than the public sector? Will the trend toward privatization continue? Where should the line between government and business fall?

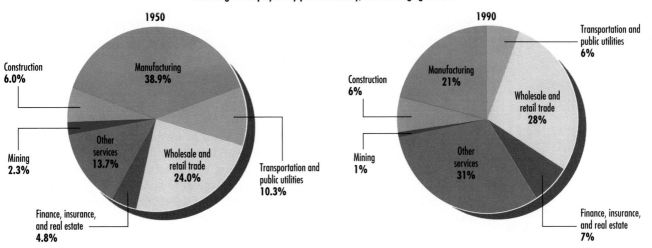

Percentage of employees by private industry, not including agriculture

1950

- Construction 6.0%
- Manufacturing 38.9%
- Mining 2.3%
- Other services 13.7%
- Wholesale and retail trade 24.0%
- Transportation and public utilities 10.3%
- Finance, insurance, and real estate 4.8%

1990

- Transportation and public utilities 6%
- Construction 6%
- Manufacturing 21%
- Wholesale and retail trade 28%
- Mining 1%
- Other services 31%
- Finance, insurance, and real estate 7%

sector machine will run at half speed through much of the 1990s.[6] Even under ideal economic conditions, the service sector may be due for a slowdown. The service sector has grown so quickly that demand must now catch up. After the boom of the 1980s, the country probably has more banks, retail stores, and restaurants than it needs.[7] However, the various groups within the service sector have different prospects.

Retailing and Wholesaling

The slowest-growing sector of the service industry—retailing and wholesaling—is also the largest in sales volume and total number of employees. In this category, you find many small, family-run businesses like the corner grocery, the gift shop, the neighborhood café, and the candy store. You also find the wholesale distributors and brokers who serve as intermediaries between producers and retailers.

For many years, these small businesses have been losing ground to larger competitors, like the department-store chains that dominate the shopping malls and the franchise outlets that line the highways from coast to coast. Now many of the big chains are in trouble, burdened with heavy debts, overbuilding, and aggressive competition. In February 1991, for example, Sears, Roebuck announced 21,000 job cuts.[8]

Finance and Insurance

The financial-services sector contains a relatively even mix of large and small businesses. On the one hand, giant insurance companies and banks have operations around the world; on the other hand, independent insurance agents, real estate brokers, and local banks operate within well-defined regions. Companies with fewer than 500 employees account for roughly half of the sector's employment and slightly less than half of its sales.[9]

On balance, the financial-services sector has expanded over the past decade, but some stormy days are dawning. The savings and loan industry is in dire straits, and many banks are not in the best of shape. Plagued with a bundle of

EXHIBIT 2.2

Shifts in Employment by Industry Sector
Since the end of World War II, the service sector has been responsible for creating virtually all job growth in the U.S. economy.

bad real estate loans, some 340 banks may fail between 1991 and 1993, according to government forecasts. And many of the surviving institutions may merge. At the same time, securities firms are retrenching. The Wall Street brokerage firms eliminated some 20 percent of their work force during the late 1980s, and more cuts are contemplated.[10]

Transportation and Utilities

Transportation and utilities have not grown much in terms of employment over the past decade. The federal government recently spent $700 million to develop magnetic levitation (a "maglev" train would float on invisible magnetic cushions). But some view maglev as a pipe dream. Deregulation has caused considerable turmoil in such industries as telecommunications and airlines. New airline carriers have sprung up, only to be devoured by larger companies, which have been merging and purging among themselves.

capital-intensive businesses Businesses that require large investments in capital assets

This segment of the service sector is dominated by large companies. Airlines, electric utilities, and telecommunications companies are **capital-intensive businesses.** It takes a great deal of money to buy airplanes, build power plants, or construct nationwide telephone networks. Small businesses simply lack the funds.

Other Services

The most rapidly growing service area is the group of "other" services, which includes such diverse businesses as beauty parlors, repair shops, private schools, health services, hotels, amusement parks, theaters, and business and professional services. Employment in these businesses has more than doubled since the 1950s.[11]

labor-intensive businesses Businesses in which labor costs are more important than capital costs

barriers to entry Factors that make it difficult to launch a business in a particular industry

By and large, this sector is composed of **labor-intensive businesses,** as opposed to capital-intensive ones. The most important factor of production is labor, supplied in many cases by the owner of the business. The partners at KPMG Peat Marwick, for example, are the firm's primary resource and its primary cost. In most labor-intensive businesses, the **barriers to entry** are relatively low; in other words, you don't need a lot of special knowledge, facilities, employees, or capital to open shop. All you need is a good idea, a little money, and a willingness to work. As a consequence, you see many small firms in this sector.

Production's Revival

In the early 1980s, the goods-producing sector was plagued by recession, unfavorable exchange rates between the dollar and foreign currencies, tough international competition, and relatively lackluster productivity. Producers regained much of their momentum in the late 1980s, however, because of supportive government policies and tough-minded management. The government's efforts to quicken the economy and bring down the value of the dollar did much to stimulate demand for products both here and abroad. At the same time, producers slashed costs by closing or modernizing inefficient plants, laying off underutilized workers, and pruning layers of bureaucracy.

productivity The measured relationship of the quantity and quality of units produced and the labor per unit of time; indicates the efficiency of production

Many of these changes were painful, but the goods-producing sector emerged in better shape. Fewer workers were able to produce more goods in the same amount of time, giving a much needed boost to **productivity,** measured as output per unit of time, usually per worker-hour. When productivity rises, the cost per unit of production falls, giving producers room to cut price or increase profits. Manufacturing productivity in the United States is currently growing by 3.6 percent per year, roughly three times as fast as in the 1970s and on a par with productivity growth in other industrialized countries.[12] This has been a big factor in helping U.S. companies compete more effectively in the global marketplace. Since 1985 exports of our manufactured goods have increased by more than 80 percent.[13]

Historically, the goods-producing sector has been more global in scope than the service sector, deriving 10 percent of its revenues from foreign customers versus 5 percent in the service sector. However, many of the leading firms in both sectors are counting on overseas sales to make up an increasing percentage of their business. For example, IBM, Boeing, and Merck already sell as much or more abroad as they do at home; Detroit's auto manufacturers expect 60 percent of the growth in the car market in the next 20 years to be in Asia; Compaq computer is looking for sales increases of 25 percent per year in Europe in the 1990s; McDonald's is now opening more outlets overseas than in the United States; Toys 'R' Us has launched stores throughout Europe and is now moving on to Asia; and KPMG Peat Marwick gets more than half of its revenues from overseas offices.[14]

It's interesting to note that the production of goods is inherently more volatile than the delivery of services. Production moves up and down depending on the state of the economy. When times get tough, consumers and businesses both defer their purchases of such products as cars, houses, major appliances, laboratory equipment, and machinery. Consumption of services, on the other hand, is less dependent on the business cycle. Despite recessions, people still go to the doctor, pay their insurance premiums, use their checking account, make telephone calls, go to the movies, and burn electricity. Some economists expect that as services account for an increasing share of the GNP, the economy will be less susceptible to recessions, since services will act as a cushion for the ups and downs of the goods-producing sector.

Manufacturing

Manufacturing is by far the largest category in the goods-producing sector, and it has improved most dramatically in recent years. By almost every measure—quality, sales, profits, international market share—U.S. factories are proving that they have what it takes to succeed. Large companies dominate the manufacturing sector.[15] Nevertheless, small businesses play an important role in the manufacturing sector, both as suppliers to large manufacturers and as pioneers of new technology. Many of the most exciting scientific developments of recent years have come from small high-tech companies involved in such fields as biotechnology, computers, robotics, lasers, and exotic materials.

Construction

Construction is one of the most cyclical businesses in the economy, responding to general economic conditions and to fluctuations in interest rates. When rates are high, the cost of borrowing money to build and buy property increases, so construction declines. The outlook for the industry in the 1990s is cloudy be-

Fixing shoes used to be a mom-and-pop service business, but not any more. In the past few years, several would-be shoe-repair tycoons have been reaching for a toehold in the national market. This Moneysworth & Best Quality Shoe Repair store in a Woodbridge, New Jersey, shopping mall is run by Donald Leafloor, operations manager. The Woodbridge store is part of an 87-store chain founded by Canadian entrepreneur Rick VanSant, who hopes to open 500 new stores in the United States within five to eight years. The shift from small, locally owned operations to national chains is sweeping through many segments of the service industry.

Advanced technology such as welding robots has helped the Chrysler plant in St. Louis boost its productivity. Thanks to labor-saving equipment, fewer workers are required to turn out more goods.

commodity business Business in which products are undifferentiated, so that price becomes the chief competitive weapon

cause the United States has an oversupply of commercial buildings. Unlike manufacturing, construction is made up largely of small, local businesses. Firms with under 100 employees account for two-thirds of the volume.[16]

Mining

Mining is another volatile business, subject to big swings in profitability depending on global economic conditions and on supply-and-demand relationships. One reason for this volatility is that mining is a **commodity business** with little distinction between one unit of production and another. Regardless of who produces it, oil is oil, gold is gold, copper is copper. Companies cannot do much to differentiate their products, so they are forced to compete on the basis of price. When the supply of commodity products exceeds demand, the producers all cut their prices, and profits fall throughout the industry. In recent years, the global supply of many minerals has increased because developing nations have expanded their mining capacity in order to build an export base. This has depressed profits for the mining sector as a whole.

Agriculture

Like mining, agriculture is a commodity business, so profitability hinges on supply-and-demand relationships. As more and more developing nations become self-sufficient in food production, American farmers have seen their profits shrink along with their export market. At the same time, farming has become more capital intensive as the price of equipment and land has increased.

The pressure of profits has forced many of the less successful farmers to sell out to larger concerns. Over the next several years, the number of commercial farms is expected to decline, and the average size of each farm is expected to increase.[17] Although farm employment represents only a small fraction of total employment in the United States, the health of the nation's farms ripples throughout the economy, affecting equipment makers, banks, and rural retailers.

▶ HOW TO CATEGORIZE COMPANIES BY FORM OF OWNERSHIP

Figuring out where a company fits in the industrial scheme of things gives you a general idea of its characteristics. Another way to get a feel for what makes a company tick is to look at its form of ownership. The three most common forms of business ownership are sole proprietorship, partnership, and corporation. As Exhibit 2.3 illustrates, corporations tend to be larger-scale operations, accounting for the lion's share of total receipts in all eight of the economy's industrial sectors. However, proprietorships are more numerous, particularly in the service sector.

Each form of ownership has a characteristic internal structure, legal status, size, and field to which it is best suited. Each has key advantages and disadvantages, and each offers employees a distinctive working environment with its own risks and rewards. Exhibit 2.4 on page 42 contrasts the characteristics of the three forms of business.

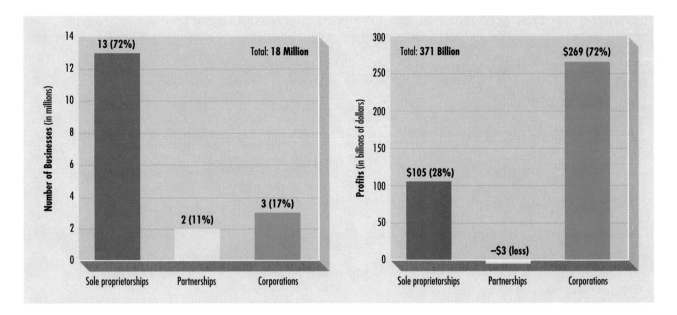

Sole Proprietorships

A **sole proprietorship** is a business owned by one person, although it may have many employees. It is the easiest and least expensive form of business to start. Many farms, retail establishments, and small service businesses are sole proprietorships, as are many home-based businesses.

Advantages of Sole Proprietorships

Sole proprietorship has a number of advantages. One is ease of establishment. All you have to do to launch a sole proprietorship is to obtain any necessary licenses, open your doors, and start selling your goods or services. Once you're under way, you have the satisfaction of working for yourself. You can make your own decisions—what hours to work, whom to hire, what prices to charge, whether to expand, and whether to shut down. Best of all, you can keep all the profits, assuming there are any.

You also have the advantage of privacy. As a sole proprietor, you do not have to reveal your performance or plans to anyone other than the Internal Revenue Service. Although you may need to provide financial information to a banker if you need a loan, you do not have to prepare any reports for outsiders as you would if you owned a corporation. Furthermore, as a sole proprietor you can set up a so-called Keogh account in which you may save some of your earnings for a pension. This money is not taxed until it is withdrawn from the account, usually at retirement when personal income and tax rates are likely to be lower.

Disadvantages of Sole Proprietorships

Although a sole proprietorship can theoretically be any size, most are relatively small businesses. Only 16 percent of them have receipts totaling more than $1 million.[18] The small scale of most sole proprietorships reflects their limited financial resources. A single person starting a company generally has less capital

EXHIBIT 2.3

Prevalence and Profits of the Three Forms of Business Ownership
Sole proprietorships are the most common type of business in the United States, accounting for 72 percent of all enterprises. However, corporations account for 72 percent of the profits earned by U.S. businesses.

sole proprietorship Business owned by a single individual

EXHIBIT 2.4 ▶ **Characteristics of the Forms of Business Ownership**

The "best" form of ownership depends on the objectives of the people involved in the business.

ASPECT	FORM OF OWNERSHIP		
	SOLE PROPRIETORSHIP	**PARTNERSHIP**	**CORPORATION**
Tax treatment	Profits and losses flow directly to the owner; are taxed at personal rates	Profits and losses flow directly to the partners; are taxed at personal rates; partners share income and losses equally unless the partnership agreement specifies otherwise	Profits and losses are taxed at corporate rates; profits are taxed again at personal rates when they are distributed to the investors as dividends
Owner's control	Owner has complete control	General partnerships: partners have control of the business; each partner is entitled to equal control unless partnership agreement specifies otherwise Limited partnerships: the general partner controls the business; limited partners don't participate in the management	Ownership and management of the business are separate; individual shareholders in public corporations are not involved in daily management decisions; in private or closely held corporations, owners are more likely to participate in managing the business
Owner's liability	Owner assumes unlimited personal liability for business	General partnerships: partners assume unlimited liability for business Limited partnerships: partners are liable only for the amount of their investment	Investors' liability is limited to amount of their investment
Liquidity of owner's investment	Owner must generally sell business to get his or her investment out of it	Partners must generally sell their share in the business to recoup their investment	Shareholders in public corporations may trade their shares on the open market; shareholders in private corporations must find a buyer for their shares to recoup their investment
Ease of formation	No expenses or formalities apart from obtaining necessary business licenses	No formalities or expenses apart from obtaining necessary licenses; however, advisable to have an attorney develop a written partnership agreement	Must follow procedures established by the state in which business will be incorporated; expense and complexity of incorporation vary from state to state; public corporations must also comply with requirements of their stock exchanges
Life span of the business	May be limited to the life span of the owner	Depends on the terms of partnership agreement	Unlimited

than a group of people and may also have more difficulty getting a loan. Furthermore, a sole proprietor may have to pay more for his or her money, because lending institutions are likely to charge higher interest rates to smaller companies than to large corporations.

In some cases, the sole proprietor's independence may be a drawback because it often means that the business depends on the talents and managerial skills of one person. If problems crop up, the sole proprietor may not recognize them or may be too proud to seek help, especially given the high cost of hiring management-level employees and professional consultants. In addition, many proprietors have a problem delegating responsibility.

The major disadvantage is the proprietor's **unlimited liability.** From a legal standpoint, the owner and the business are one and the same. Any legal damages or debts incurred by the business are the owner's responsibility. As a sole proprietor, you might have to sell personal assets, like your family's home, to satisfy a business debt. If someone sues you over a business matter, you might lose everything you own.

A final disadvantage is that proprietorships often have a limited life. Some sole proprietors pass their business on to their heirs as part of their estate. However, the owner's death may mean the demise of the business, particularly if the owner's skills are crucial to the operation.

Partnerships

If starting a business on your own seems a little intimidating, you might decide to share the risks and rewards by going into business with a partner. In that case, you would form a **partnership**—a legal association of two or more people as co-owners of a business for profit. You and your partners would share the profits and losses of the business and perhaps the management responsibilities as well. Your partnership might remain a small, two-person operation or it might grow into an international business with thousands of employees like KPMG Peat Marwick.

There are three basic types of partnership. In a **general partnership,** all partners are legally equal and are liable for the business's debts. In a **limited partnership,** however, one or more people act as general partners and run the business. The remaining partners are passive investors (i.e., they are not involved in managing the business). These partners are called limited partners because their liability is limited to the amount of their capital contribution. They cannot be sued for more money than they invested in the business. In a **master limited partnership** (MLP), firms act like corporations, selling partner units on a recognized stock exchange. MLPs have advantages similar to corporations (limited liability, unlimited life, and transferable ownership); moreover, if 90 percent of their gross income is passive (typically rental income or other income not requiring the physical efforts of the owners), they pay no corporate taxes (since profits are paid to stockholders who pay taxes at individual rates).

Advantages of Partnerships

Proprietorships and partnerships have some of the same advantages. Like proprietorships, partnerships are easy to form, although it's wise to get a lawyer's advice on the partnership agreement—the legal document that spells out the

Dale Roberts is the sole proprietor of The Horn Doctor in Charleston, West Virginia, where he repairs band instruments and sells music supplies. If the company grows, Roberts may want to incorporate to protect himself from liabilities associated with the business and to increase financing options.

unlimited liability Legal condition under which any damages or debts attributable to the business can also be attached to the owner, because the two have no separate legal existence

partnership Unincorporated business owned and operated by two or more persons under a voluntary legal association

general partnership Partnership in which all partners have the right to participate as co-owners and are individually liable for the business's debts

limited partnership Partnership composed of one or more general partners and one or more partners whose liability is usually limited to the amount of their capital investment

master limited partnership A business partnership that acts like a corporation, trading partnership units on listed stock exchanges; if 90 percent of income is passive, MLPs are taxed at individual rates

Jerry Scheer and Mark Cumins are partners in four T-Bones steakhouses, located in Augusta, Georgia, and Charleston, South Carolina. Both say their partnership is successful because they are so much alike. Proof of their teamwork is the way they rebuilt their first Georgia unit after it was wiped out by Hurricane Hugo.

corporation Legally chartered enterprise with most of the legal rights of a person, including the right to conduct a business, to own and sell property, to borrow money, and to sue or be sued

partners' rights and responsibilities. Partnerships also provide the same tax advantages as proprietorships, since profits are taxed at personal income tax rates rather than corporate rates.

In a couple of respects, partnerships are superior to sole proprietorships, largely because there's strength in numbers. When you have several people putting up their money and pooling their talents, you can start a more ambitious enterprise and increase your chances of success, assuming of course that you have picked good partners. As a partner, you may also have better luck than a sole proprietor in obtaining financing, since you and your partners are all legally responsible for paying off the debts of the group. Finally, by forming a partnership you increase the chances that the organization will endure since new partners can be drawn into the business to replace those who die or retire. For example, the founders of KPMG Peat Marwick died many years ago, but their firm, which was founded in 1897, continues. Provisions for handling the departure and addition of partners are usually covered in the partnership agreement.

Disadvantages of Partnerships

A fundamental drawback of a general partnership arrangement is the unlimited liability of the active partners. If one of your partners makes a serious business or professional mistake and is sued by a disgruntled client, you are financially accountable. You stand to lose everything you own. At the same time, you are responsible for any debts incurred by the partnership. Even though malpractice insurance or business risk insurance offers some financial protection, you pay a premium for your peace of mind. Faced with the risk of unlimited liability, many lawyers, doctors, and accountants are forming professional corporations rather than partnerships.

Another disadvantage of partnerships is the potential for interpersonal problems. Difficulties often arise because each partner wants to be responsible for managing the organization. Electing a managing partner to lead the organization may diminish the conflicts, but disagreements are still likely to arise. Moreover, you may have to face the question of what to do with unproductive partners. The inner circle at Peat Marwick had to face this very question in January 1991, when it became clear they had to dismiss some partners to become more competitive. And finally, in the ranks of the aspiring partners, competition is often fierce. The junior employees are vying for a limited number of partnership slots, and they view each other as rivals. This may give rise to political maneuvering or create a pressure-cooker environment in which everyone is working 80-hour weeks in hopes of looking good.

Corporations

The modern **corporation** evolved in the nineteenth century when large sums of capital were needed to build railroads, coal mines, and steel mills. Such endeavors required so much money that no single individual or group of partners could hope to raise it all. The solution was to sell shares in the business to numerous investors who would get a cut of the profits in exchange for their money. These investors got a chance to vote on certain issues that might affect the value of their investment, but they were not involved in managing day-to-day operations. To protect the investors from the risks associated with such large undertakings, their liability was limited to the amount of their investment.

It was a good solution, and the corporation quickly became a vital force in the nation's economy. As rules and regulations developed to define what corporations could and could not do, corporations acquired the legal attributes of people. Like you, a corporation can receive, own, and transfer property; make contracts; sue; and be sued.

The relationship between a corporation and its **shareholders,** or owners, is a source of enormous strength. Since ownership and management are separate, the owners may get rid of the managers (in theory, at least), if the owners vote to do so. Conversely, because shares of the company (known as **stock**) may be bequeathed or sold to someone else, the company's ownership may change drastically over time while the company and its management remain intact (as long as the company is economically sound). The corporation's unlimited life span, combined with its ability to raise capital, gives it the potential for significant growth.

A company need not be large to incorporate. Most corporations, like most businesses, are relatively small, and most small corporations are privately held. The big ones, however, are *really* big. The 500 largest corporations in the United States, as listed by *Fortune* magazine, have combined sales of over $2 trillion and employ 12.4 million people. General Motors alone has 760,000 employees; if all of them lived in one place, it would be one of the 12 largest cities in the United States.[19]

Types of Corporations

Corporations have evolved into various distinct types. The first distinction is whether a corporation is public, quasi-public, or private. **Public corporations** are formed by federal or state governments for a specific public purpose, such as running local school districts, making student loans, or developing major land areas (such as the Tennessee Valley Authority building an extensive dam system in the Tennessee River Valley). **Quasi-public corporations** are public utilities having a government-granted monopoly to provide such services as electricity, local phones, water, and natural gas. The companies on the Fortune 500 list are almost exclusively **private corporations**—that is, companies owned by private individuals or companies. These investors buy stock on the open market, which gives private corporations access to large amounts of capital. In return, the shareholders receive the chance to share in the profits if the corporation succeeds. Private corporations are the primary focus of this book.

Public and private corporations may be either not-for-profit or for-profit corporations. **Not-for-profit corporations** pursue goals other than economic ones, such as those targeted by charitable, educational, and fraternal organizations. The Public Broadcasting System (PBS), the American Heart Association, and Harvard University are all not-for-profit corporations. **For-profit corporations** are formed to earn money for their owners.

Corporations that are **publicly traded** (also called open corporations) actively sell stock on the open market. Both private and quasi-public corporations may be publicly traded, such as Ford Motors and Commonwealth Edison (which supplies power to the Chicago area). Corporations that are **not publicly traded** (also called closed corporations) withhold their stock from public sale, preferring to finance any expansion out of their own earnings or to borrow from some other source. This gives the owners complete control over their operations and protects the business from unwelcome takeover attempts. Such famous companies as Hallmark, United Parcel Service, and Hyatt Hotels have opted to remain

shareholders Owners of a corporation

stock Shares of ownership in a corporation

public corporations Government-owned corporations formed for a specific public purpose

quasi-public corporations Public utilities having a monopoly to provide basic services

private corporations Companies owned by private individuals or companies

not-for-profit corporations Incorporated institutions whose owners have limited liability and that exist to provide a social service rather than to make a profit

for-profit corporations Companies formed to earn money for their owners

publicly traded corporations Corporations that actively sell stock on the open market (open corporations)

not publicly traded corporations Corporations that withhold their stock from public sale (closed corporations)

professional corporations
Companies whose shareholders offer professional services (medical, legal, engineering) and set up beneficial pension and insurance plans

S corporations Corporations with no more than 35 shareholders that may be taxed as partnerships

limited liability companies Organizations that combine the benefits of S corporations and limited partnerships without the drawbacks of either

subsidiary corporations Corporations whose stock is owned entirely or almost entirely by another corporation

parent company Company that owns most, if not all, of another company's stock and that takes an active part in managing that other company

holding company Company that owns most, if not all, of another company's stock but that does not actively participate in the management of that other company

closed corporations. **Professional corporations** are not publicly traded, and their shareholders offer professional services (such as medical, legal, and engineering services). Popular because of their ability to set up beneficial pension and insurance plans, professional corporations are replacing partnerships in some parts of the country.

Another type of corporation, known as the **S corporation** (or subchapter S corporation), is a cross between a partnership and a corporation. Income and deductions from the business flow directly to the owners and are taxed at personal income tax rates, just as they are in a partnership. At the same time, the shareholders in an S corporation, like the shareholders in a regular corporation, have limited liability. S corporations can be extremely attractive under certain circumstances, but their freedom of operation is limited by a number of restrictions. For example, an S corporation can have no more than 35 shareholders; it cannot own more than 80 percent of the stock of another corporation; and it cannot derive more than 25 percent of its income from passive sources such as rent, interest, or royalties.

Companies can now combine the advantages of S corporations and limited partnerships, without having to abide by the restrictions of either. **Limited liability companies** (LLCs) allow firms to pay taxes like partnerships while protecting shareholders from personal liability beyond their investments. Moreover, LLCs are not restricted to 35 shareholders (although they must have at least 2 shareholders, whereas S corporations can have only 1). In addition, members' participation in management is not restricted (as it is in limited partnerships). Unlike a corporation, however, an LLC's existence is restricted to 30 years.[20]

Finally, not all corporations are independent entities. **Subsidiary corporations** are partially or wholly owned by another corporation known as a **parent company,** which supervises the operations of the subsidiary. A **holding company** is a special type of parent company that exercises little operating control over the subsidiary, merely "holding" its stock as an investment.

Corporations can also be classified according to where they do business. An *alien corporation* operates in the United States but is incorporated in another country. A *foreign corporation,* sometimes called an *out-of-state corporation,* is incorporated in one state (frequently the state of Delaware, where incorporation laws are lenient) but does business in several other states where it is registered. A *domestic corporation* does business only in the state where it is chartered. Exhibit 2.5 summarizes some of these distinctions among types of corporations.

Corporate Structure and Governance

Although a corporation's shareholders own the business, they are rarely involved in managing it, particularly if the corporation is publicly traded. Instead, they elect a board of directors to represent them. The directors, in turn, select and monitor the top officers, who actually run the company (see Exhibit 2.6).

SHAREHOLDERS   Theoretically, the shareholders are the ultimate governing body of the corporation, but in practice most individual shareholders in large corporations—where the shareholders may number in the millions—accept the recommendations of management. Indeed, the more shareholders there are, the less tangible influence each one has on the corporation. However, some shareholders have more influence than others. For one thing, some people own stock that carries no voting rights, and others own shares that are worth one vote

EXHIBIT 2.5 ▶ Major Types of Corporations

The most visible corporations are the large, public ones like General Motors, IBM, and Coca-Cola, but other types are also common.

TYPE	DEFINITION	EXAMPLE
Public corporation	Business formed by federal or state governments for a specific purpose	TVA
Quasi-public corporation	Profit utilities with a monopoly on providing basic public services	Commonwealth Edison
Private corporation	Businesses owned by private individuals or companies	General Motors
Not-for-profit corporation	Service or arts institution in which no stock-holder or trustee shares in the profits or losses and which is exempt from corporate income taxes	Harvard University
For-profit-corporation	Companies in business to make a profit	IBM
Professional corporation	Business whose partners offer professional services (medical, legal, engineering) and can set up beneficial pension and insurance packages	La Jolla Medical Group, Inc.
S corporation	Corporation with no more than 35 owners whose profits are taxed at personal income-tax rates rather than at corporate income-tax rates	Inland Asphalt
Limited liability company	Business that reeps the benefits of S corporations and limited partnerships without the drawbacks	Realatech
Parent company	Operating company that owns or controls sub-sidiaries through the ownership of voting stock	Sears, Roebuck
Holding company	Corporation organized for the purpose of owning stock in and managing one or more corporations; differs from a parent company in that it gener-ally does not conduct operations of its own	Intermark
Subsidiary corporation	Corporation that is entirely, or almost entirely, owned by another corporation, known as a parent company or holding company	Seven-Up

each. Furthermore, some people (or organizations) own more shares with voting rights than others do; a person with 1,000 voting shares, for example, has 1,000 votes and 10 times the impact of a person with only 100 shares.

In the last 20 years, **institutional investors** such as pension funds, insurance companies, and college endowment funds have accumulated an increasing share of the stock in the nation's corporations. They now own over half the stock in scores of Fortune 500 companies.[21] These large institutional investors want the value of their stock to increase, and they are beginning to play a more powerful role in governing the corporations in which they own shares. For example, public pension funds led by the New York City Employees' Retirement System convinced Exxon to appoint an environmentalist to its board following the company's disastrous 1989 oil spill off Alaska.[22]

At least once a year, all the owners of voting shares are invited to a meeting to choose directors, select an independent accountant to audit the company's financial statements, and attend to other business. Some states limit the type of issues on which shareholders may vote; thus the shareholders effectively have

institutional investors Organizations that own many shares of stock; typical examples are banks, mutual funds, pension funds, insurance companies, foundations

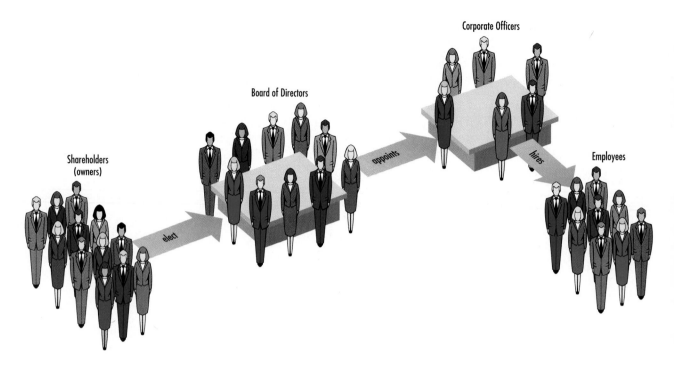

Shareholders
(owners)

Board of Directors

Corporate Officers

Employees

elect

appoints

hires

EXHIBIT 2.6

The Corporate Framework
Theoretically, the corporate framework resembles a democracy in which shareholders vote to elect representatives (members of the board of directors) who will establish corporate policy and select competent managers to direct the employees. Actually, the real power in a corporation often lies with the top executives who suggest a roster of board members for shareholder approval.

proxy Document authorizing another person to vote on behalf of a shareholder in a corporation

board of directors Group of people, elected by the shareholders, who have the ultimate authority in guiding the affairs of a corporation

chief executive officer Person appointed by a corporation's board of directors to carry out the board's policies and supervise the activities of the corporation

little or no voice in management. Shareholders who cannot attend the annual meeting in person vote by **proxy,** signing and returning a slip of paper that authorizes management to vote on their behalf.

BOARD OF DIRECTORS   As a practical matter, the **board of directors,** which supposedly represents the shareholders, is responsible for guiding corporate affairs and selecting officers. The board has the power to vote on major management decisions, such as building a new factory, hiring a new president, or buying a new subsidiary. Depending on the size of the company, the board might have anywhere from 3 to 35 directors, although 15 to 25 is the typical range. In some corporations, several of the directors may be "insiders" who also serve as executives of the company. The outside directors are typically major stockholders, executives of other firms, or high-ranking officials connected with the company's industry.

The board's actual involvement in running a corporation varies from one company to another. Some boards are strong and independent and serve as a check on the company's management; others act as a "rubber stamp," simply approving management's recommendations. Assertive boards are becoming more common these days, partly because board members recognize that they can be held financially responsible if they fail to perform their duties. This came as a rude shock to the directors of Trans Union Corporation, who accepted a takeover bid without soliciting competing offers for the company. The Delaware Supreme Court ruled that the directors had been too hasty in accepting the first bid and had therefore deprived the shareholders of money they might have received if other offers had been encouraged. The directors agreed to pay the shareholders $13.5 million of the $23.5 million settlement.[23]

OFFICERS   The real power in a corporation often lies with the **chief executive officer,** or CEO, who is responsible for establishing the policies of the company at the direction of the board. The chief executive officer may also be the chairman of the board, the president of the corporation, or both. In many instances, the CEO picks a slate of directors that includes friends and business associates and submits their names to the shareholders for approval. Since the directors in these companies owe their position on the board to the CEO, they tend to be loyal. However, in the past few years, boards at Alcoa, Pillsbury, United Airlines, and Mellon Bank have replaced their CEOs when the directors agreed that the shareholders' interests were being compromised by company management.[24]

Advantages of Corporations

No other form of business ownership can match the success of the corporation in bringing together money, resources, and talent; in accumulating assets; and in creating wealth. The corporation has certain significant advantages that make it the best vehicle for accomplishing these tasks. One of these advantages is the corporation's limited liability. Although a corporate entity can assume tremendous liabilities, it is the corporation that is liable rather than any of the private shareholders. Say you buy stock in a company that goes bankrupt. You may lose the money you invested in the stock, but you are not legally responsible for paying the company's debts. Of course, the board members and company management may be liable if they have acted irresponsibly or illegally, as illustrated by the Trans Union case already mentioned.

Public corporations also have the advantage of **liquidity,** which means that investors can easily convert their stock into cash by selling it on the open market. This makes buying stock in a public corporation attractive to many investors; getting your money out of a privately held corporation, a sole proprietorship, or a partnership can be extremely difficult.

liquidity An asset's ease of conversion to cash

A corporation's unlimited life span is another important advantage. It allows a firm to make long-range plans and to recruit, train, and motivate the best employees.

Disadvantages of Corporations

Corporations are not without some disadvantages. Publicly owned companies are required by the government to follow certain rules and to publish information about their finances and operations. These reporting requirements increase the pressure on corporate managers to achieve short-term growth and earnings targets in order to satisfy shareholders and attract potential investors. In addition, having to disclose financial information increases the company's vulnerability to competitors and to those who might want to take over the company. The paperwork and costs associated with incorporation can also be burdensome, particularly if you plan to sell stock to the public. The complexity varies from state to state, but regardless of where you live, it is wise to consult an attorney and an accountant before incorporating.

Although the tax rates for small corporations have declined in recent years, incorporated businesses still suffer from relatively *high taxes* when compared with unincorporated businesses. All corporations (with the exception of S corporations) pay a tax of 34 percent on annual profits between $75,000 and $100,000. In addition, shareholders must pay income taxes on their share of the company's profits received as dividends. This means that corporate profits are taxed twice, whereas the profits in a sole proprietorship or partnership are taxed only once, and at a lower rate.

Some large corporations claim that they are taxed too heavily and that society would benefit if companies could retain more of their earnings for reinvestment. Many critics of business counter that corporations have evaded their social responsibility by employing various tax-minimization techniques, such as doing business in Panama, the Bahamas, and Bermuda, which impose no income taxes. According to the critics, large corporations that take advantage of such options actually have a far lower tax rate than do small corporations or individuals.

Business Around the World

One of the ten biggest mergers of the 1990s was Philip Morris's acquisition of Jacobs Suchard, Swiss coffee and candy maker. The merger helps Philip Morris further reduce its dependence on tobacco products and continue to gain a foothold in Europe.

▶ MERGERS AND ACQUISITIONS

Regardless of what form a business takes—be it a sole proprietorship, a partnership, or a corporation—the chances are reasonably good that its form will evolve over time. Companies of all sizes and types achieve a variety of objectives by merging, dividing, and restructuring. A look at the Fortune 500 over the past decade illustrates the point. Almost 40 percent of the corporations listed at the start of the 1980s have merged with or have been acquired by other firms. Standard Brands, for example, was acquired by Nabisco, which was acquired by R. J. Reynolds, which was in turn acquired by KRK (Kohlberg Kravis Roberts). Of the 313 Fortune 500 corporations that survived the decade, 67 underwent radical restructuring, generally by purging themselves of tangential businesses.

TECHNIQUES FOR BUSINESS SUCCESS

Are You the Corporate Type?

Where's the best place to start your career—in a large corporation, a small company, or a business of your own? When *Business Week* posed that question to a group of students recently, only 14 percent of them answered "in a large corporation"; 41 percent thought starting their own business was the best bet; and 36 percent voted for working in a small company.

The poor showing of big corporations probably stems from the popular perception that they are uncaring, bureaucratic, boring, and impersonal. But that perception may be inaccurate. If you talk to the people who actually work in Fortune 500 companies, you find that the majority of them disagree. A *U.S. News & World Report* poll of middle managers in 20 major corporations revealed that 80 percent of them are deeply committed to their company because they feel the company has been good to them. Three out of four of these managers, all of whom are under 45, hope to spend their entire career with the same outfit.

Granted, working for IBM, AT&T, or GM may not be for everyone, but these companies and their companions on the Fortune 500 list employ some 20 million people. Although it's true that small companies are generating more new jobs than the corporate giants, there are still plenty of employment opportunities with the biggies. In 1989, an off year for hiring, the Fortune 500 were looking for 160,000 people to fill new jobs and thousands more to replace departing employees. So before you write off the Fortune 500 as being "not my type," think about what they have to offer:

1. Experienced people who can teach you a thing or two. Large corporations are likely to employ dozens of people who specialize in your field. You'll have a chance to learn about the diverse niches that might appeal to you. Your opportunities to find a mentor will be far greater than they might be in a small company that employs only a few people in any given specialty.

2. A broad range of activities and locations. If you think variety is the spice of life, a big corporation may be just the ticket. Most have formal rotation programs to help new

Mobil Oil sold off its nonenergy divisions; Colgate-Palmolive pruned its health-care businesses; and General Mills sold its toy, fashion, and retailing units.[25] At the same time, smaller companies from San Diego to Boston were mirroring the pattern of the Fortune 500, coming together, pulling apart, and reforming in new configurations.

Types of Mergers

The terms most often used to describe all of this activity are *mergers, acquisitions,* and *leveraged buyouts.* The difference between a merger and an acquisition is fairly technical, having to do with how the financial transaction is structured. Basically, in a **merger,** two or more companies combine to create a new company by pooling their interests. A recent deal of this type occurred when Time and Warner Communications combined to form Time Warner. In an **acquisition,** one company buys another company (or parts of another company) and emerges as the controlling corporation. The flip side of an acquisition is a **divestiture,** in which one company sells a portion of its business to another company. In the late 1980s, many acquisitions were **leveraged buyouts** (LBOs). In an LBO, one or more individuals purchase the company (or a division of the company) with borrowed funds, using the assets of the company they're buying to secure (or guarantee repayment of) the loan. The loans are then repaid out of the company's earnings, through the sale of assets, or with stock. Note, however, that LBOs do not always work.

merger Combination of two or more companies in which the old companies cease to exist and a new enterprise is created

acquisition Combination of two companies in which one company purchases the other and remains the dominant corporation

divestiture Sale of part of a company

leveraged buyout Situation in which an individual or a group of investors purchases a company with the debt secured by the company's assets

employees gain firsthand experience in various parts of the business. You'll have the chance to broaden your expertise and see which functions are your favorites. Since most Fortune 500 companies have operations in many locations, you may also have the chance to move from city to city, or even to another country if that's your goal.

3. *Major budget and program responsibility early on.* Because Fortune 500 companies operate on such a large scale, you may find yourself managing a significant program with a big budget before you know it. Outlays that would be enormous in a small company are routine in a larger operation. At the same time, mistakes are not such a big deal, since major corporations do not have all their eggs in one basket. If you gamble and lose, you will not sink the company. This gives you the freedom to learn to take sensible risks.

4. *Formal training.* Most large corporations offer extensive training to get their new recruits started on the right foot. In some organizations, you can learn as much on the job as you would in a graduate business program—and get paid for doing it.

5. *More resources to do the job.* Success often depends on the tools you have to work with. In a big corporation, you are likely to have advanced information systems, state-of-the-art equipment, a well-trained staff, and a large enough budget to get the job done. These resources will enable you to accomplish things you could not hope to achieve in a smaller organization.

6. *A chance to work on significant things.* Big companies do big things, and being part of that action can be exciting. Whether you're building a new hotel in Hong Kong or designing state-of-the-art telecommunications systems, you can participate in something on a grand scale. Furthermore, being associated with a large, well-known organization can open doors that might otherwise be closed to you. It's amazing how responsive people become when they know that you represent a powerful company.

7. *Opportunities for advancement.* Your chances of being promoted at a big company are greater than they are at a small company because there are more slots to move into. Since most large companies are committed to promoting from within, you will have the inside track. You will also have the benefit of a professional human resources department that will help you formulate and achieve your career goals.

8. *Excellent pay and benefits.* With few exceptions, big companies pay higher salaries and provide better benefits than small companies. Money may not be what motivates you, but it certainly helps pay the bills.

joint venture Enterprise supported by the investment of two or more parties for mutual benefit

consortium Group of companies working jointly to promote a common objective or engage in a project of benefit to all members

Mergers and acquisitions represent relatively radical ways in which companies are combined. On a more modest scale, businesses often join forces in alliances to accomplish specific purposes. In a **joint venture,** two or more companies combine forces to work on a project. The joint venture may be dissolved fairly quickly if the project is limited in scope, or it may endure for many years. Corning Glass Works and PPG Industries have worked together in a joint venture for over 50 years to create glass architectural materials.[26] A **consortium** is similar to a joint venture, but it involves the combined efforts of several companies. For example, the David Sarnhoff Research Center, General Electric's NBC, France's Thomson S. A., and the Netherlands' Philips Electronics formed an international consortium to design a system for high-definition television (HDTV). As one of five groups submitting proposals to the FCC for testing, their aim was to offer consumers razor-sharp television pictures.[27]

cooperatives Associations of people or small companies with similar interests, formed to obtain greater bargaining power and other economies of scale

Cooperatives also serve as a vehicle for joint activities. In a cooperative, a group of people or small companies with common goals work collectively to obtain greater bargaining power and to benefit from economies of scale. Like large companies, these co-ops can buy and sell things in quantity; but instead of distributing a share of the profits to stockholders, co-ops divide all profits among their members.

How Mergers Occur

hostile takeovers Situations in which an outside party buys enough stock in a corporation to take control against the wishes of the board of directors and corporate officers

About 95 percent of all mergers and acquisitions are friendly deals.[28] The ones that make the headlines, however, are usually the **hostile takeovers,** where one party fights to gain control of a company against the wishes of the existing management. If the "raider" succeeds in taking over the target company, the existing managers are generally dismissed. Needless to say, they fight tooth and nail to stave off their attacker.

tender offer Invitation made directly to shareholders by an outside party who wishes to buy a company's stock at a price above the current market price

A hostile takeover can be launched in two ways: the tender offer and the proxy fight. In a **tender offer,** the raider offers to buy a certain number of shares of stock in the corporation at a specific price. The price offered is generally more than the current stock price, so the shareholders are motivated to sell. The raider hopes to get enough shares to take control of the corporation and replace the existing board of directors and management. In a **proxy fight,** the raider launches a public relations battle for shareholder votes, hoping to enlist enough votes to oust the board and management. Proxy fights sound easy enough, but they are tough to win. The insiders have certain advantages: They know how to get in touch with shareholders, and they can use money from the corporate treasury in their campaign. In one study of 60 major proxy fights, researchers found that incumbent managers won 70 percent of the time.[29]

proxy fight Attempt to gain control of a takeover target by urging shareholders to vote for directors favored by the acquiring party

The Historical Perspective

trusts Monopolistic arrangements established when one company buys a controlling share of the stock of competing companies in the same industry

There is nothing new about deals of this sort. Companies have been combining in various configurations since the early days of U.S history. In fact, one of the biggest waves of merger activity occurred between 1881 and 1911, when capitalists created giant monopolistic **trusts,** buying enough stock of competing companies in basic industries like oil and steel to control the market. These trusts were **horizontal mergers,** or combinations of competing companies performing the same functions. The purpose of a horizontal merger is to achieve the benefits of economies of scale and to prevent cutthroat competition. The rise of a govern-

horizontal mergers Combinations of companies that are direct competitors in the same industry ment antitrust movement and the dissolution of Standard Oil in 1911 ended this wave, although in recent years the horizontal merger has reappeared.

A second great wave occurred in the boom decade of the 1920s. This era was marked by the emergence of **vertical mergers,** in which a company involved in one phase of a business absorbs or joins a company involved in another phase of that business. The aim of a vertical merger is often to guarantee access to supplies or to markets.

A third wave of mergers occurred in the late 1960s and early 1970s, when corporations acquired strings of unrelated businesses. These **conglomerate mergers** were designed to augment a company's growth and diversify its risks. Theoretically, when one business was down, another would be up, thus creating a balanced performance picture for the company as a whole. However, many of the superconglomerates of the late 1960s are currently being dismantled for a variety of reasons: to streamline operations, to build up capital for other endeavors, to get rid of unprofitable subsidiaries.

The most recent wave of mergers occurred in the 1980s, as Exhibit 2.7 illustrates. During the decade an incredible $3.7 trillion was spent on mergers, acquisitions, and leveraged buyouts.[30] Although many of these deals were made to improve the operations of the companies involved, the chance to make a quick profit was the motive in many cases. When the decade began, many companies were actually worth more than the combined value of all their stock. A clever takeover artist could borrow money, buy enough stock to control the company, sell off pieces of the company to repay the debt, and still come out with money left over.

When American Telephone & Telegraph launched its bid for NCR Corporation, it used a combination of a tender offer and a proxy fight. At NCR's annual meeting in Dayton, Ohio, the AT&T troops carried in enough proxy ballots to win four of the twelve NCR board seats up for reelection, including the one held by NCR's chairman. With a divided board, NCR was under pressure to negotiate AT&T's tender offer and accept a merger.

Mergers and Acquisitions Today

The rash of mergers and acquisitions that occurred in the 1980s kindled a heated debate. Opponents argued that the wave of mergers was creating an immense burden of high-risk corporate debt and diverting investment from productive assets. Instead of building new plants, said critics, companies were borrowing huge sums to finance an endless game of "musical" ownership. These companies would be in serious financial trouble if the economy slipped.

In many cases, the critics' warnings proved to be well-founded. A number of companies that took on heavy loads of debt to finance acquisitions subsequently went under. One of the most visible disasters was the fall of the Campeau retailing empire, which had been assembled by Toronto developer Robert Campeau in the 1980s. Campeau paid over $10 billion to acquire Allied Stores and Federated Department Stores, whose chains include Bloomingdale's, Stern's, and Jordan Marsh. Although the stores were popular with the public, they did not earn enough to cover the interest on Campeau's debt. In early 1990, he was forced to declare bankruptcy.

Critics also pointed out that mergers and acquisitions entail high costs for individuals and communities. Even in friendly deals, there are bound to be losers: executives whose careers come to a crashing halt, workers who are laid off through no fault of their own, communities that suddenly find themselves with empty factories because operations are consolidated elsewhere, consumers who face higher prices when competition diminishes. But in all the controversy about the takeovers of the 1980s, the hottest topic was the obscene amount of money the raiders were making on deals that were put together at other peoples' expense.

When some of the famous figures of the merger era, such as Ivan Boesky and

vertical mergers Combinations of companies that participate in different phases of the same industry

conglomerate mergers Combinations of companies that are in unrelated businesses, designed to augment a company's growth and diversify risk

EXHIBIT 2.7

Merger and Acquisition Activity in the 1980s

The decade of the deal climaxed in 1988 when the value of mergers and acquisitions reached $579 billion. As sources of financing began to dry up in 1989 and 1990, fewer deals were made and those that did occur were generally smaller.

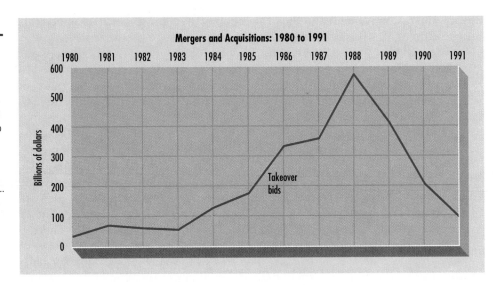

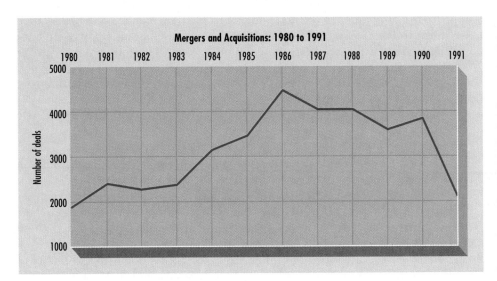

Michael Milken, were finally penalized for skirting securities laws, the public was generally delighted and corporate executives breathed a collective sigh of relief. The raiders' greed played a large part in bringing the merger mania of the 1980s to a halt, but other factors contributed as well. First, fewer undervalued companies were left as targets. Second, the sources of financing for highly leveraged deals dried up. And third, some 30 states passed antitakeover laws to protect corporations chartered within their borders.

Apart from the dealmakers, few people lamented the passing of the era. However, the mergers of the 1980s had their good points. Shareholders benefited from all the merger activity, which boosted stock prices and fueled big increases in the market value of takeover targets. In addition, the fear of becoming takeover targets forced many companies to become more efficient.

The mergers occurring in the 1990s are in sharp contrast to the bids by raiders in the 1980s. Today most of the deals are being done by large corporations for strategic purposes. Instead of using debt to take over and dismantle a company for a quick profit, corporate buyers are using cash and stock to selectively acquire businesses that will enhance their position in the marketplace. AT&T's bid for NCR is a good example: the acquisition strengthens AT&T's computer business. Frequently, the motivation behind a merger is to gain geographic strength. Of the top ten deals made in 1990, six involved foreign buyers or sellers. For example, Switzerland's Roche Holding, a health-care company, bought 60 percent of Genentech, a U.S. biotech firm, gaining both geographic scope and access to new technology.[31]

SUMMARY OF LEARNING OBJECTIVES

1 Identify the two broad sectors of the U.S. economy and the eight subsectors.

The economy consists of (1) the goods-producing sector, which includes manufacturing, construction, mining, and agriculture, and (2) the service sector, which includes wholesale and retail trade, banking and insurance, transportation and utilities, and other services.

2 List four factors that have contributed to the growth of the service sector.

In recent years, the service sector has expanded because (1) fewer workers are required in goods-producing businesses, (2) technology has created new service opportunities, (3) manufacturers are hiring outsiders to do service jobs formerly done by company employees, and (4) many manufacturing operations are done abroad where labor rates are lower.

3 Discuss the three basic forms of business ownership.

A sole proprietorship is a business owned by a single person. A partnership is an association of two or more people who share in the ownership of an enterprise. The dominant form of business is the corporation, a legally chartered entity having many of the same rights and duties as a person.

4 List five advantages and four disadvantages of forming a sole proprietorship.

Sole proprietorships have five advantages: (1) they are easy to establish, (2) they provide the owner with control and independence, (3) the owner reaps all the profits, (4) the company's plans and financial performance remain private, and (5) income is taxed at personal rates. The four main disadvantages of a sole proprietorship are (1) the company's financial resources are usually limited, (2) management talent may be thin, (3) the owner is liable for the debts and damages incurred by the business, and (4) the business may cease when the owner dies.

5 Explain the difference between a general and a limited partnership.

A general partnership is owned by general partners who are equally liable for the business's debts. A limited partnership is owned by at least one general partner, who runs the business, and limited partners who are passive investors and generally liable for no more than the amount of their investment.

6 List the three groups that govern a corporation, and describe the role of each.

Shareholders are the basis of the corporate structure. They elect the board of directors, who in turn elect the officers of the corporation. The corporate officers carry out the policies and decisions of the board. In practice, the shareholders and board members often follow the lead of the chief executive officer.

7 Cite four advantages of corporations.

Corporations have the power to raise large sums of capital. They offer the shareholders protection from liability, they provide liquidity for investors, and they have an unlimited life span.

8 Describe the four waves of merger activity.

The earliest mergers, occurring from 1881 to 1911, were horizontal mergers combining two companies that compete in the same industry. A second wave of mergers occurred in the 1920s. These were vertical mergers combining two companies that participate in different phases of the same industry. The 1960s and 1970s introduced a third wave of mergers known as conglomerate mergers, in which unrelated companies are combined. The most recent wave of mergers, which occurred in the 1980s, focused on the purchase of undervalued companies, which were then dismantled and sold off piece by piece.

Meeting a Business Challenge at KPMG Peat Marwick

One reason Jon Madonna was elected chairman of KPMG Peat Marwick was that he promised to make the firm more responsive to the younger partners. He quickly made a number of moves in that direction, advocating the creation of three new task forces to study compensation, retirement benefits, and the firm's governance structure. In addition, he engineered some important changes in the composition of the firm's board, reducing the power of the vice chairmen and giving more power to functional and area managing partners.

These changes partially satisfied the newer partners' appetite for a more favorable balance of power between themselves and the old guard. However, Peat was still far from being a democracy. Although each partner is part owner of the firm, some partners have more clout than others, by virtue of their tenure or talent. In addition to Madonna and the board, the executive ranks include the managing partners of the various offices, the heads of the practice groups such as tax and auditing, and members of assorted committees and task forces. When important decisions are made, they are often made behind closed doors without a vote of the entire partnership. However, those decisions are tempered by the knowledge that if enough partners object, the management team can be overthrown.

Madonna was well aware of that fact in January 1991 when he called a joint meeting of the firm's two most powerful groups, the management committee and the board of directors. The subject of the meeting was how to improve Peat's profits. Faced with an earnings slump, most businesses cut costs. But in a service business like accounting, where the main expense is salaries, cutting costs means cutting people. At KPMG Peat Marwick, which was already top heavy, the most logical people to eliminate would be partners, since a single partner costs the firm more than several associates. And because of the imbal-

KPMG Peat Marwick

ance between the pay of senior and junior partners, weeding out the senior partners would provide the most savings per termination.

However, very few accounting firms fire their partners. "Making partner" at a Big Six firm is like grabbing the brass ring on the merry-go-round. Partners can look forward to a long and profitable career with job security. Salaries average around $200,000, and those who become managing partners or vice chairmen earn closer to $1 million. On top of that, they earn interest on their shares in the partnership and reap the rewards of a generous pension and benefits program. Naturally, partners are expected to do their share of the work, to keep their clients happy, and to bring in new business. But if a partner has an off year or two, the others rally around and carry him or her for a while.

So far, the formula had worked well for KPMG Peat Marwick. But given the circumstances facing the firm early in 1991, Madonna felt that it was time to break with tradition. He proposed to the management committee and the board of directors that

the firm fire 265 U.S. partners. The group agreed, and the process began. The cost in severance pay was projected to be $52 million, but the remaining partners would see their average take-home pay increase by up to 19 percent within a few years. The long-term effects of Madonna's decision on both the firm's profits and morale remain to be seen.

Your Mission: You are a junior associate with Peat, and you have aspirations to advance to a management level, whether by making partner at Peat, by starting your own accounting practice, or by rising through the accounting/finance department of an industrial corporation. Assess the following situations and choose the best answer from the solutions presented.

1. The recent turmoil at Peat has made you stop and think about your career options. Looking back at your decision to join the firm 12 months ago, you wonder whether your decision was the right one. What should you do?
  a. Stay where you are.
  b. Look for a job in the service sector.
  c. Look for a job in the goods-producing sector.
  d. Look for a job in a nonprofit organization or government agency.

2. One thing that concerns you about staying with Peat is the impact that the partner cutbacks will have on your own prospects for advancement. Since one of the reasons for the layoffs is to improve the ratio of partners to associates, the firm may decide to hold back on electing new partners for a while. This will obviously limit your chances of moving up. What could the senior people at Peat do that would reassure and motivate you and the other associates?
  a. The managing partner in each office should explain the situation to each of the associates that the firm especially wants to keep. These

individuals should be reassured that they will eventually make partner so that they will not be discouraged and leave.

b. The firm should continue to invite its most valuable associates to become partners, but it should elect fewer of them each year. Without the lure of partnership, the best associates will leave regardless of what other carrots are dangled before them.

c. The firm should give the most valuable associates the same responsibilities and pay as the partners but not the same voting rights or the title of partner.

d. The firm should convert from a partnership form of ownership to a public corporation.

3. You have thought a good deal lately about forming your own accounting practice. You like the idea of being in business for yourself and of being able to work from your home. Which of the following forms of business ownership would be the best choice for your practice?
   a. A sole proprietorship.
   b. A partnership.
   c. A corporation.

4. You are currently assigned to work on an accounting project for a Fortune 500 company. You have become friendly with several of the people in your client's finance department, and one evening you all go out for dinner. As the night wears on, everyone loosens up and begins to talk frankly. You learn that your client is planning to make a hostile tender offer for a major corporation in a related industry. This information is told to you "in strictest confidence." What should you do?
   a. Report the information to the partner in charge of the assignment so that Peat can approach the corporation about using the firm's services to help with the tender offer.
   b. Advise your friends and relatives to buy stock in the target company, since the value of its shares is sure to increase when the tender offer is made.
   c. Do nothing.
   d. Send an anonymous letter to the chairman of the target company warning him that his company is about to face a hostile tender offer.[32]

KEY TERMS

acquisition (51)
barriers to entry (38)
board of directors (48)
capital-intensive businesses (38)
chief executive officer (48)
commodity business (40)
conglomerate mergers (53)
consortium (52)
cooperatives (52)
corporation (44)
divestiture (51)
for-profit corporations (45)
general partnership (43)
goods-producing businesses (34)
holding company (46)
horizontal mergers (52)

hostile takeovers (52)
institutional investors (47)
joint venture (52)
labor-intensive businesses (38)
leveraged buyout (51)
limited liability companies (46)
limited partnership (43)
liquidity (49)
master limited partnership (43)
merger (51)
not-for-profit corporations (45)
not publicly traded corporations (45)
parent company (46)
partnership (43)
private corporations (45)
productivity (38)

professional corporations (46)
proxy (48)
proxy fight (52)
public corporations (45)
publicly traded corporations (45)
quasi-public corporation (45)
S corporations (46)
service businesses (34)
shareholders (45)
sole proprietorship (41)
stock (45)
subsidiary corporations (46)
tender offer (52)
trusts (52)
unlimited liability (43)
vertical mergers (53)

REVIEW QUESTIONS

1. What factors have contributed to the revival of the manufacturing sector?

2. What is a sole proprietorship? Why is it the most common type of business in the United States?

3. What are the advantages and disadvantages of a sole proprietorship?

4. Define a partnership. In what fields are partnerships typical?

5. Discuss the advantages and disadvantages of partnerships.

6. Explain the difference between a private and a public corporation.

7. To what extent do shareholders control the activities of a corporation?

8. What are the two techniques used to conduct a hostile takeover?

A CASE FOR CRITICAL THINKING

Shareholder Activism

Whose interests are being served, shareholders' or management's? That's the question being asked by the California Public Employees' Retirement System (CalPERS), the largest pension fund in the United States. Each year, CalPERS analyzes the performance of the 1300 companies in which it invests, developing a "hit list" of those with consistently poor showings. If CalPERS determines that management's interests are being served to the detriment of shareholders, it goes to work to give shareholders a greater say in how the business is run.

With assets estimated at $58 billion and investments in over 1300 companies (about 1 percent ownership of each), CalPERS has considerable clout in the boardroom. The institutional investor has become a leader in shareholder activism, successfully influencing policy at such large corporations as Avon, General Motors, TRW, ITT, Inland Steel, Sears, Boise Cascade, Hercules, Whirlpool, Scott Paper, Lockheed, Occidental, and others.

When ITT's board of directors voted a 103 percent raise (to $11.4 million) for CEO Rand Araskog while company profits increased only 4 percent, CalPERS led a vehement protest by shareholders. Although unsuccessful, the pension fund did win an agreement requiring the board's future compensation committees to be composed of directors from outside the company. The compromise is typical

of the kind of success that is bringing CalPERS a lot of attention as an organization to be reckoned with.

"The belief is that improved corporate performance results when management is held accountable to shareholders," says CalPERS general counsel Richard Koppes. Frequently, the fund will submit a formal proposal for the formation of a shareholders' advisory committee. Hoping to avoid a messy public proxy fight but not wanting to relinquish too much management power, most companies have responded by agreeing to more frequent informal meetings with shareholders. At that point, CalPERS drops its formal proposals and sits down at the table with management.

To CalPERS CEO Dale Hanson, this kind of success is just fine. It wasn't too long ago that shareholders' interests were routinely ignored. When CalPERS first approached Avon, for instance, they couldn't even get a meeting with the chief executive. Now Avon has agreed to meet twice a year with its large investors.

Believing that outsiders will be more responsive to shareholders, CalPERS has also influenced companies such as General Motors to elect independent directors. "The board is our link to the company," Hanson says. "They're the individuals we have the right to nominate and vote for. That is really where you'll see a number of (institutional investors) focusing more and more attention."

When investor Harold C. Simmons

attempted a takeover of Lockheed Corporation, alleging poor management, CalPERS agreed and voted against Lockheed's board. The buyout was unsuccessful, but Lockheed's CEO Daniel Tellep started talking with CalPERS on a regular basis. "Ultimately, I came to realize that we should never have gotten into a position where CalPERS had to vote against us to get our attention, so I resolved to get to know them."

Although a few disagree with CalPERS's approach, most corporate executives respond positively once the door is opened. CalPERS and other shareholder activist groups have had considerable impact on corporate boardrooms in recent years, but they say they've just begun. The issue of the 1990s will be executive compensation—directors who approve lucrative pay packages for chief executives presiding over corporations whose stock values are falling. Nothing makes investors angrier or more committed to gaining influence in the boardroom.[33]

1. Who should control corporate governance, shareholders or management? Why?

2. What other techniques might a shareholders' organization use to gain an influence over management?

3. Name two examples of management strategies to repel a takeover that could adversely affect the interests of the companies' shareholders.

BUILDING YOUR COMMUNICATION SKILLS

Some critics believe that growth in the service sector has contributed to the decline of industry in the United States. Using information from the text, as well as from other resources, examine the increase in service-related businesses and the factors leading to their growth. Consider the

interrelationship between businesses in the goods-producing and service sectors. Be prepared to discuss both the advantages and disadvantages of a growing service sector for the overall economy.

▶ As a class, divide into groups of

two and discuss the pros and cons of this issue. Alternate taking a positive or negative position with your partner.

▶ Following discussion with your partner, develop a class chart listing the contrasting points of view.

KEEPING CURRENT USING *THE WALL STREET JOURNAL*

Find an article or series of articles in recent issues of *The Wall Street Journal* illustrating one of the following business developments:

► Merger

► Acquisition

► Divestiture

► Hostile takeover

► Leveraged buyout

► Consortium or joint venture

1. Explain in your own words what steps or events led to this development.

2. What results do you expect this development to have on (a) the company itself; (b) consumers; (c) the industry the company is part of? Write down and date your answers.

3. Follow your story in *The Wall Street Journal* over the next month (or longer, as your instructor requests). What problems, opportunities, or other results are reported? Were they anticipated at the time of the initial story, or did they seem to catch industry analysts by surprise? How well did you do at predicting the results in your answers to question 2?

CHAPTER 3

LEARNING OBJECTIVES
After studying this chapter, you will be able to

1 Differentiate between lifestyle businesses and high-growth ventures.

2 Discuss the demographic and economic factors that have affected small businesses in the 1980s and 1990s.

3 List four important functions of small business in the economy.

4 Identify three ways of getting into business for yourself.

5 Name ten topics that should be covered in a formal business plan.

6 Describe nine sources of financing available for new businesses.

7 Identify five managerial activities that are important to the success of a small business.

8 Explain the pros and cons of owning a franchise.

Small Businesses, New Ventures, and Franchises

HOW TO KEEP YOUR FEET ON THE GROUND WHILE TURNING AN INDUSTRY UPSIDE DOWN

The idea for Staples occurred to Tom Stemberg when he arrived for a job interview at a warehouse club, one of those vast discount barns that sell everything from tomato paste to computers. As Stemberg made his way through the store toward the executive offices, he noticed that the office supply section looked like it had been plundered by savages. The devastation told him that the merchandise was moving fast.

Lights flashed. Why not create a warehouse club for office supplies, a Toys 'R' Us for grownups that would offer low prices on everything from rubber bands to office furniture? It was an obvious idea, but nobody had thought of it. Perhaps the concept occurred to Stemberg because he had the right background to put two and two together. After earning a master's degree in business administration, he joined the management training program at the Jewel Companies and was placed with its supermarket division in Boston. He quickly rose through the marketing and merchandising functions, where he introduced the concept of "generic" products and earned a reputation for competing aggressively on price. He later joined another supermarket chain where he opened discount food warehouses.

With 12 years as a grocery executive behind him, Stemberg could see that big stores with low prices would transform the office-supply business, just as supermarkets had transformed the grocery business. He pictured customers wheeling shopping carts down wide, brightly lit aisles, loading up on items that, for economy's sake, were frequently bundled three or more to a package. Merchandise would be piled high on metal shelves, and the aisles would be numbered and identified with bright red signs to indicate product categories. Rows of checkout counters would welcome the departing shoppers, and boxes of candy and other impulse items would tempt the buyers waiting to pay.

Stemberg's market research confirmed his hunch that the office-products industry was both attractive and ripe for change. The potential market was huge ($100 billion in annual sales) and growing rapidly (11 percent per year). Better yet, a whole category of customers (small businesses) was getting a bad deal on price. While large corporations were buying their office supplies at quantity discounts from wholesalers and manufacturers, small businesses were paying full price at retail office-supply stores or ordering goods through catalogs at slightly reduced prices. This meant that a company like General Motors might spend $4 for a dozen yellow pads, and a small business might spend $11.50.

What Stemberg hoped to do was give those small businesses and individuals the same kind of price break that General Motors was getting. He knew how to do this: based on his experience building a chain of high-volume, low-priced food warehouses, he would buy directly from manufacturers, cut out the wholesalers, keep his costs down with a no-frills approach, and pass the savings along to the customers.

To make the concept work, however, he would need to open a number of stores in a short period of time. That would take both money and workers. He would also need to convince office-supply manufacturers to deal with him directly, a move that would upset their relationships with wholesalers. How could he raise the funds required for rapid expansion? How could he attract a group of managers capable of building a major business from scratch? And how could he gain the cooperation of office-products suppliers?[1]

▶ THE SCOPE OF SMALL BUSINESS

A quick look up and down a typical commercial street is enough to tell you that small businesses are an important element in the U.S. economy. However, determining just *how* important is surprisingly tricky, partly because there's no single reliable source of data on small businesses and partly because *small* is a relative term. A manufacturing firm with 500 employees might be considered small if it competes against much larger companies, but a retail establishment with 500 employees might be classified as big compared to its competitors. For official purposes, the Small Business Administration defines a **small business** as being a firm that is independently owned and operated, not dominant in its field, and relatively small in terms of annual sales and number of employees compared to other firms in its industry. From a practical standpoint, any company with fewer than 500 employees is generally considered small.

Small businesses are of two distinct types: Roughly 80 to 90 percent are modest operations with little growth potential. The self-employed consultant working part-time from a home office, the corner florist, and the neighborhood pizza parlor fall into this category of **lifestyle businesses** (sometimes called mom-and-pop operations).[2]

In contrast to lifestyle businesses, some small firms, such as Staples, are small simply because they are new. These **high-growth ventures** aim at outgrowing their small-business status as quickly as possible. Often run by a team rather than by one individual, they obtain a sizable supply of investment capital and then attempt to introduce new products or services to a large market.

The most rapidly growing of these ventures are listed by *Inc.* magazine every year. In 1990 the Inc. 500 had sales of $9.6 billion and created 56,858 new jobs. The average company on the list was growing at an annual rate of 103 percent, adding 23 new employees each year. Obviously, companies growing at that rate

small businesses Companies that are independently owned and operated, that are not dominant in their field, and that meet certain criteria for number of employees or annual sales revenue

lifestyle businesses Small businesses intended to provide the owner with a comfortable livelihood

high-growth ventures Small businesses intended to achieve rapid growth and high profits on investment

quickly cross the threshold from small to large. The firm that topped *Inc.*'s 1990 list was Cogentrix, a firm that develops and operates cogeneration power plants in Charlotte, North Carolina. In recent years, the list has been dominated by computer-related companies and firms involved in health care, environmental cleanup, and personnel services. Graduates of the *Inc.* list include such well-known companies as Domino's Pizza, Charles Schwab, and Microsoft.[3]

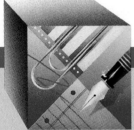

CHECKLIST FOR BUSINESS TODAY

Have You Got What It Takes to Be a Small-Business Owner?

This checklist will help you determine your potential for owning a small business.

A. Are you a self-starter?
  1. I do things on my own. Nobody has to tell me to get going.
  2. If someone gets me started, I keep going all right.
  3. Easy does it. I don't put myself out until I have to.

B. How do you feel about other people?
  1. I like people. I can get along with just about anybody.
  2. I have plenty of friends. I don't need anyone else.
  3. Most people irritate me.

C. Can you lead others?
  1. I can get most people to go along when I start something.
  2. I can give the orders if someone tells me what we should do.
  3. I let someone else get things moving. Then I go along if I feel like it.

D. Can you take responsibility?
  1. I like to take charge of things and see them through.
  2. I'll take over if I have to, but I'd rather let someone else be responsible.
  3. There's always some eager person who wants to look smart. I'm glad to let that person do the work.

E. How good an organizer are you?
  1. I like to have a plan before I start. I'm usually the one to get things lined up when the group wants to do something.
  2. I do all right unless things get too confused. Then I quit.
  3. When I get all set, something comes along and presents too many problems. So I just take things as they come.

F. How good a worker are you?
  1. I can keep going as long as I need to. I don't mind working hard for something I want.
  2. I'll work hard for a while. But when I've had enough, that's it.
  3. I can't see that hard work gets you anywhere.

G. Can you make decisions?
  1. I can make up my mind in a hurry if I have to. It usually turns out okay, too.
  2. I can if I have plenty of time. If I have to make up my mind fast, later I think that I should have decided the other way.
  3. I don't like to be the one who has to decide things.

H. Can people trust what you say?
  1. You bet they can. I don't say things I don't mean.
  2. I try to be on the level most of the time, but sometimes I just say what's easiest.
  3. Why bother if the other person doesn't know the difference?

I. Can you stick with it?
  1. If I make up my mind to do something, I don't let anything stop me.
  2. I usually finish what I start—if it goes well.
  3. If it doesn't go well right away, I quit. Why beat your brains out?

J. How good is your health?
  1. I never run down!
  2. I have energy for most things I want to do.
  3. I run out of energy sooner than most of my friends seem to.

Directions: If most of your checks were beside the first answer, you probably have what it takes to operate a business successfully. If not, you are likely to have difficulty and should consider getting a partner to compensate for your weaknesses. If most of your checks were beside the third answer, not even a good partner will enable you to overcome the deficiencies indicated.

Trends Affecting Small Businesses

America's small-business roots run deep. The country was originally founded by people involved in small businesses—the family farmer, the shopkeeper, the craftsman. Successive waves of immigrants carried on the tradition, launching restaurants and laundries, driving taxicabs, and opening newsstands and bakeries. These small businesses are the cornerstone of our economic system.

Yet despite our independent heritage, we have become a nation of employees. In 1800, some 80 percent of the working population was self-employed; today, the figure is 6 percent for women and 13 percent for men.[4] The trend away from self-employment began after the Civil War, when big business emerged as the primary economic force. Aided by improvements in transportation and communication, large producers were able to achieve **economies of scale,** which are the savings resulting from manufacturing, marketing, or buying large quantities of an item. These large producers could manufacture goods at lower costs than their smaller rivals, so they were able to charge lower prices. The small, independent businesses could not compete. As scores of them closed their doors, the dominant firms became increasingly powerful, making it virtually impossible for new rivals to enter many industries.[5]

In the last 15 or 20 years, however, the trend toward bigness has slowed. To some extent, this reflects the economy's shift toward services, where economies of scale are often elusive. But even in the manufacturing sector, small firms have been able to hold their own against larger rivals. In many industries, the advent of computer-aided manufacturing equipment has enabled small plants to operate just as efficiently as larger ones, eliminating the large-scale producer's advantage in economies of scale. Because of their simpler organization and management structure, these small plants can often provide customized service or deliver goods more quickly than their larger rivals.

At the same time, a number of other factors have encouraged more people to leave the corporate world and form businesses of their own. Demographic trends have had something to do with it. Baby boomers have reached their 30s and 40s, the prime age for starting businesses. Furthermore, many of these people are frustrated by their career progress. With so many baby boomers competing for the same positions in big companies, the odds of rising to the top are slim. Add the fact that many big companies have been laying off middle managers, and you get a large pool of frustrated, experienced people looking for a better option.

The movement of women into the work force has also been a factor. During the 1980s, over 2 million women started companies, bringing the number of firms owned by women in the United States to 4.6 million—nearly one-third of all small businesses. If present trends continue until the year 2000, women are likely to own as many businesses as men do.[6] For many of these women, self-employment provides an opportunity to combine a career with family life. Many of their businesses are operated from the home or are part-time ventures. However, to an increasing degree, women are launching companies in industries with significant growth potential.[7]

As a result of these forces, small businesses blossomed throughout the 1980s. During the decade, three times as many new businesses were incorporated as was the case during the 1960s.[8] Although much of the new business activity occurred in urban population centers, small businesses sprang up throughout the country, as Exhibit 3.1 indicates.

Whether the expansion of small businesses will continue throughout the

economies of scale Savings from manufacturing, marketing, or buying large quantities

Tom and Kate Chappell are husband and wife; they are also business partners. Their company, Tom's of Maine, has been manufacturing all-natural toothpaste since 1975 and also makes a line of natural health and beauty aids.

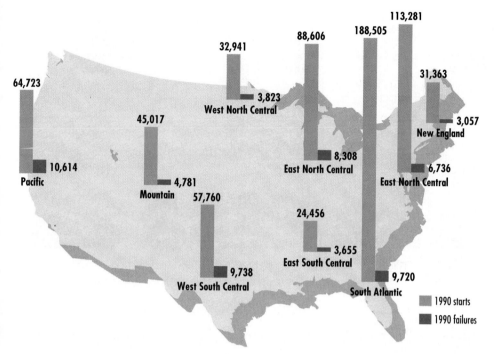

EXHIBIT 3.1

Regional Variations in Business Start-Ups
Throughout the 1980s, new businesses sprang up from coast to coast. As you might expect, the areas with the most rapid population growth were also the areas with the most new business activity.

1990s remains to be seen. As the United States slipped into a recession early in the decade, the number of business failures began to shoot up. The vast majority of the firms closing their doors were small ones.[9] New companies are particularly likely to feel the impact of economic downturns because many of them haven't accumulated enough capital to see them through hard times. As bankers grow more cautious about making loans, these firms find themselves strapped for cash.

Area Mountain Travel of Lincoln, New Hampshire, is a case in point. A few years ago Mary Garland created the company to provide a single toll-free reservation line for five ski resorts. In 1990 she had bookings of $350,000, a healthy increase over 1989 levels. Nevertheless, as the general economic climate deteriorated, her bank canceled her line of credit, leaving her company short of money to meet expenses. Most of the other bankers she approached wouldn't even return her phone calls. She has a viable business, but unless she can find financing, it may not be viable for long.[10] If finding money to *stay* in business is tough for a small company during a recession, finding money to *start* a business is even tougher.

The Men and Women Who Build Businesses

Roughly 200,000 people start new businesses every year.[11] Could you be one of them? Probably. You don't have to be a superhero of mythic proportions to launch a company. For the most part, those who take the plunge are ordinary people rather than glamorous adventurers. Roughly half of them start out with less than $20,000 and operate informally from their home, at least for a while.[12] As Exhibit 3.2 illustrates, good grades and an outstanding track record in business are not required. What does seem to be important is a willingness to work

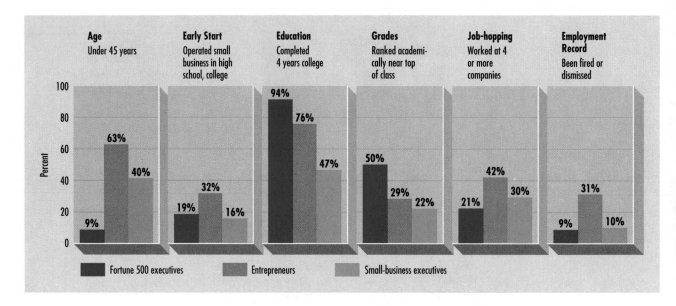

| Age | Early Start | Education | Grades | Job-hopping | Employment Record |
| Under 45 years | Operated small business in high school, college | Completed 4 years college | Ranked academically near top of class | Worked at 4 or more companies | Been fired or dismissed |

Fortune 500 executives   Entrepreneurs   Small-business executives

EXHIBIT 3.2

What Makes Entrepreneurs Different

The young and the restless are most likely to be entrepreneurs. The data in the chart are based on a telephone survey that the Gallup Organization did for **The Wall Street Journal**. Small-business executives own or manage a broad cross section of businesses with 20 or more employees but with sales of less than $50 million per year. Entrepreneurs are chief executives of companies listed by **Inc.** magazine as among the 500 fastest-growing smaller companies in the United States. The Fortune 500 executives are chief executive officers and other senior executives from **Fortune** magazine's list of the 500 largest U.S. corporations. The respondents were almost exclusively male. The entrepreneurs—55 percent of whom are under age 45—are a generation younger than the corporate executives.

start-up company New venture

long hours. Three out of four people who start their own company spend at least 50 hours a week on the job; a quarter of them put in 70 hours or more.[13]

Roughly two-thirds of the new business founders begin **start-up companies**; that is, they start from scratch rather than buying an existing operation or inheriting the family business. Only 11 percent take the franchising route. Before going into business for themselves, the vast majority of company founders are employed by small businesses rather than major corporations.[14] They are likely to draw on their experience in an industry or profession for their idea. Some 88 percent of them attribute their success to doing an ordinary thing especially well, as opposed to coming up with an extraordinary idea.[15]

Although the typical company founder is a white male, women and minorities also launch plenty of businesses. In recent years, women have been starting businesses at twice the rate of men and have been getting into a wide variety of industries such as mining, construction, manufacturing, transportation, communications, and utilities.[16]

Although minorities may have to overcome discrimination and language barriers in order to start a business, they are reasonably well represented among the ranks of company founders, launching roughly 6 percent of the 3,000 new ventures analyzed in a recent survey.[17] Asian-Americans and Hispanic-Americans are somewhat more likely than African-Americans to go into business for themselves.[18]

One black woman who serves as a role model for other women and minorities is Flori Roberts, founder of Flori Roberts, Inc., which manufactures and sells a line of cosmetics formulated specifically for African-American women. It took plenty of hard work for Roberts to convince department stores to carry her line. "Buyers would say, 'Our black customers use the cosmetics we already have,' or 'Blacks don't shop in department stores,'" she recalls. Roberts's persistence finally paid off when she convinced a department store in Newark, New Jersey, to stock her product. Black women flocked to the Flori Roberts counter to buy foundation, lipsticks, and eye shadows in colors that were right for them. Today the firm has sales of $25 million per year and its products are sold in 1,200 stores.[19]

The Economic Role of Small Businesses

People like Flori Roberts who build businesses perform a valuable service for the rest of us. Small businesses play a number of important roles in our economy.

Providing Jobs

Stop and think for a minute about the people you know who have jobs. Where do they work? For big companies? For the government? Or for small businesses? If you're typical, at least a third of your friends and relatives work for companies that employ fewer than 100 people.[20] And that number is likely to increase.

According to the Small Business Administration, slightly over half the new jobs created in the United States in the past decade have been in businesses with fewer than 100 employees.[21] As Exhibit 3.3 illustrates, most of that growth has occurred in the new high-growth ventures like Staples or like the firms on the Inc. 500 list. These rapid growers represent only 27 percent of all new businesses but create 60 percent of the new jobs.[22]

The jobs created by small businesses differ from those created by big companies in several key respects. For one thing, small businesses generally pay less in terms of both cash compensation and employee benefits. Roughly 25 percent of these jobs are part-time. They tend to be filled by employees who are either younger or older than the average big-company employee. Many of these employees have never worked before; many others have been out of work for a long time before finally finding a job with a small company. On average, employees in small businesses have less formal education than their counterparts in large companies. By hiring workers who don't quite fit the corporate mold, small businesses serve as an important safety net in our society.[23]

Introducing New Products and Services

Another important way small businesses contribute to economic growth is by fostering innovation. The National Science Foundation estimates that 98 percent of the nation's "radical" new-product developments spring from small firms, a staggering percentage given the fact that small companies spend less

Roxanne Givens, president of Legacy Management and Development Corporation of Edina, Minnesota, is one of the new breed of women entrepreneurs who are starting businesses in fields formerly dominated by men—fields such as mining, manufacturing, and construction. Givens's firm develops low-cost and senior-citizen housing.

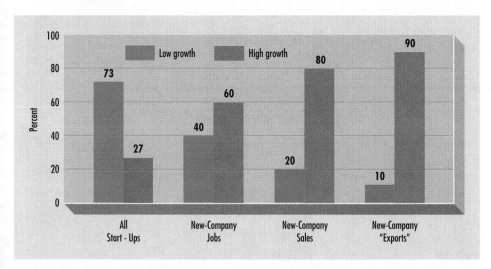

EXHIBIT 3.3

The Role of High-Growth Companies
Although they account for a relatively small share of all new businesses, the companies that grow rapidly are responsible for the lion's share of the newly created jobs, sales, and exports.

than 5 percent of the nation's research and development money.[24] Among the contributions that small businesses have made are the safety razor, the self-winding wrist watch, the helicopter, stainless steel, and the plain-paper copier.

Supplying the Needs of Large Corporations

Besides providing new products and jobs, small businesses fill an important role in the operation of large corporations, acting as distributors, servicing agents, and suppliers. In fact, some of the most successful companies in the country have based their business strategy on the use of small, outside suppliers. Consider Liz Claiborne, one of the leading firms in the fashion industry: The company has no factories, and all its garments are made on contract by outside suppliers, which gives Liz Claiborne the flexibility to change its designs quickly—an important competitive edge in the fickle world of fashion.[25]

Providing Specialized Goods and Services

Finally, many small businesses exist because they meet consumers' special needs. If you want to rent a Santa Claus suit, buy an odd piece of sheet music, or get your watch fixed, you naturally turn to a small business for help. Big companies tend to shy away from businesses of this type because the demand isn't sufficient to make mass production worthwhile.

Today, affluent consumers have custom tastes: They often seek out the individualized or different item. Some small businesses have thus become successful by meeting these far-fetched needs. If you're looking for a small, personal swimming pool, for example, you might check with SwimEx of Warren, Rhode Island. For a mere $22,000, they'll sell you a 6-by-12-foot personal pool that enables you

Specialization is one way that a small business can compete successfully against larger rivals. Just for Pets Superstore, in Peabody, Massachusetts, sells everything for pets and even has a pet bar with snacks for pets.

to swim in place against an adjustable current.[26] The market for personal pools may be limited, but businesses that offer such unique products can often find a niche.

▶ THE JOB OF BUILDING A BUSINESS

Suppose you decide to join the ranks of business owners. What are your chances of success? You may have heard some depressing statistics about the number of new ventures that fail. Some reports say your chances of success are only one in three; others claim that the odds are even worse, stating that 85 percent of all new ventures fail within 10 years.

Recent research suggests that your chances are somewhat better than that; however, a lot depends on the type of business you start and the general state of the economy. According to the Small Business Administration, roughly 40 percent of new businesses are still operating five years after they open their doors. The odds may be even better, judging by a study of 3,000 new ventures conducted by three authorities on small business, Arnold C. Cooper, William C. Dunkelberg, and Carolyn Y. Woo. Their conclusion is that roughly 80 percent of new businesses make it through their third year. It's worth noting, however, that those results were obtained during the late 1980s when the economy was strong. In general, the Cooper-Dunkelberg-Woo survey revealed that manufacturing firms have a better chance of surviving than retail businesses. Interestingly enough, one of the factors that seemed to make the most difference to a firm's survival was the founder's faith that the business would succeed.[27]

Finding an Opportunity

If you decide to take the risk, there are three ways to get into business for yourself: start from scratch, buy an existing operation, or obtain a franchise. Starting from scratch is the most common route, and probably the most difficult as well. Most of the people who succeed do so because they have enough experience to minimize the risks. They start with something they know how to do and capitalize on an existing network of professional or industry contacts. Tom Scholl, the CEO of an Inc. 500 ad agency, is a typical example. He spent 13 years working in the advertising industry before setting up his own agency and seeking out clients he thought his former employer (Young & Rubicam) was overlooking.[28]

If you lack work experience but still want to start a business, you might find a good idea by solving some problem that's been plaguing you. Chances are, a similar problem is plaguing someone else. Jean Griswold, the wife of a Presbyterian pastor, got the idea for her business when she was trying to line up volunteers to do errands and chores for elderly parishioners. When she couldn't find enough volunteers, she experimented with hiring students to do the work for a modest fee. The idea clicked, prompting her to found Special Care, a multistate firm with revenues of $10 million that provides full- and part-time help to elderly persons.[29] Exhibit 3.4 suggests some other avenues for developing entrepreneurial ideas.

Buying an existing business tends to reduce the risks—provided, of course, that you check the company out carefully. When you buy a business, you instantly acquire a known product or service and a system for producing it. You don't have to go through the painful period of building a reputation, establishing

EXHIBIT 3.4 ▶ **How to Get Good Ideas for New Businesses**

When looking for ideas for new companies, think in terms of what people want but can't get. According to the experts, "Inventing a fancy gizmo first and then finding out later that no one wants it is a waste of time."

CONCEPT	EXPLANATION	EXAMPLE
Upgrade	Take a basic product, and enhance it.	Designer blue jeans, gourmet cookies
Downgrade	Take a quality product, and reduce its cost and price.	No-frills motels, budget rental cars
Bundle	Combine products to provide double benefits.	Laundromats that sell food or beverages
Unbundle	Take a product that has multiple features, and offer only one of those features independently.	Term life insurance that has no savings value
Transport	Move a product that sells well in one area to another area.	"Ethnic" restaurants
Mass-market	Take a product that has been used for a specific purpose and find a larger audience for it.	Industrial cleaners repackaged for consumer markets
Narrowcast	Aim for a narrow portion of a large market.	Cable TV service for rural markets
Think big	Offer the broadest possible selection of a general category of goods.	Electronics "supermarkets"
Think small	Offer a complete selection of a specific type of product.	Bookstore that sells only mystery novels
Compete on price	Offer more value for the same price, the same value for a lower price, or lower quality at a far lower price.	"Warehouse" stores

a clientele, and hiring and training employees. And financing the venture is generally much easier; lenders are reassured by the history and assets of the going concern. With these major details already settled, you can concentrate on making improvements.

Obtaining a franchise is another alternative. The franchiser's name, product, and system are already established, and you can build on that base. However, owning a franchise is no guarantee that your business will succeed. According to one study, your chances are no better with a franchise operation than with a start-up.[30]

Deciding on a Form of Ownership

Once you have identified a promising opportunity, you need to decide on the form of business you will use. You can choose a sole proprietorship, a partnership, or a corporation, depending on your needs and the advantages and disad-

EXHIBIT 3.5 ▶ **Advantages and Disadvantages of the Three Forms of Business Ownership**

FORM OF OWNERSHIP	ADVANTAGES	DISADVANTAGES
Sole Proprietorship	Ease of formulation and dissolution	Limited potential for big profits
	Control and freedom	Restricted financial resources
	Secrecy of operations	Reliance on owner for all managerial skills
	Tax advantages	Unlimited liability
		Life of business limited to owner's interest or life span
Partnership	Ease of formulation	Unlimited liability of general partners
	Tax advantages	Ever-present danger of interpersonal conflict between partners
	Ownership opportunities for skilled persons	Potential for aggressive competition among employees for partnership status
	Legal standing in case of disputes	
	Increased capital and credit sources	Lack of clear-cut management responsibility
	Ability to continue despite changes in ownership	
Corporation	Limited liability for shareholders (owners)	Requirements for public disclosure
	Investment liquidity	Costs to establish and dissolve
	Unlimited life span	Tax rates

vantages of each (see Exhibit 3.5). For each type of organization, certain legal formalities must be met.

The sole proprietorship can be started by opening a checking account for the business, obtaining invoices and other forms, and accumulating the cash to pay a month's rent. But you may also have to obtain a business license and take care of other legal details, depending on the type of business.

To start a partnership, you need two additional things: a partnership agreement, which spells out the basic outlines of your arrangement with your partner or partners, and a buy/sell agreement, which defines what will happen if one of the partners dies.

For a corporation, you must choose the state in which you want to incorporate, file incorporation papers, form a board of directors, name officers, and also set up a stock-redemption plan, which serves the same functions as the buy/sell agreement in a partnership.

The best form of business for you depends on your circumstances: your financial situation, the type of business you're starting, the number of employees, the risks involved, and your tax position. For advice on this issue, it is generally worthwhile to consult a lawyer or an accountant who specializes in this area. Regardless of whether you form a sole proprietorship, a partnership, or a corporation, you need to obtain various licenses and permits. The requirements differ from state to state and from business to business. For information, contact the Internal Revenue Service or the chamber of commerce in your area.

Developing a Business Plan

One of the first steps you should take toward starting a new business is to develop a written business plan that explains what you're going to do. Preparing such a plan will help you decide how to turn your idea into reality, and if you need outside financing, the plan will also help you convince lenders and investors to back your business. Your business plan may be relatively informal if you're starting out on a small scale and using your own money, but at a minimum, it should describe the basic concept of the business and outline specific goals, objectives, and resource requirements.

Although the business plan has a simple, straightforward purpose, it requires a great deal of thought. Before you even open your doors, you have to make important decisions about personnel, marketing, facilities, suppliers, and distribution. A formal plan, suitable for use with banks or investors, should cover the following information:

1. *Summary.* In one or two pages, describe your product or service and its market potential. Also describe your company and its principles, highlighting those things that will distinguish your firm from the competitors. Summarize your financial projections and expected return on investment. And indicate how much money you need and for what purpose.

2. *Company and industry.* Give full background information on the origins and structure of your venture and the characteristics of its industry.

3. *Products or services.* Give a complete but concise description, focusing on the unique attributes of your products or services.

4. *Market.* Provide data that will persuade the investor that you understand your market and can achieve your sales goals.

5. *Marketing strategy.* Provide projections of sales and market share and outline a strategy for identifying and contacting customers, setting prices, servicing customers, advertising, and so forth.

6. *Design and development plans.* If your product requires design or development, describe the nature and extent of what needs to be done, including costs and possible problems.

7. *Operations plan.* Provide information on the facilities, equipment, and labor needed, including background on principals, directors, and key management personnel.

8. *Overall schedule.* Show development of the company in terms of completion dates for major aspects of the business plan.

9. *Critical risks and problems.* Identify all negative factors and discuss them honestly.

10. *Financial information.* Include a detailed budget of start-up and operating costs, as well as projections for income, expenses, and cash flow for the first three years of business.

VIDEO EXERCISE

Obtaining Financing

With your business plan in hand, you can begin the search for financing. The most common sources of funds for new businesses fall into two basic categories: debt and equity. **Debt** must be repaid; **equity** does not have to be repaid, but it entitles the investor to a piece of your company and a share of future profits. Most businesses are financed with a mix of debt and equity.

Once the business is launched, it will have a continuing need for money. You can't expect to obtain all the financing you need in one fell swoop. Although a few businesses do grow entirely through internally generated funds, most need repeated transfusions from outside lenders or investors.

debt Funds obtained by borrowing

equity Funds obtained by selling shares of ownership in the company

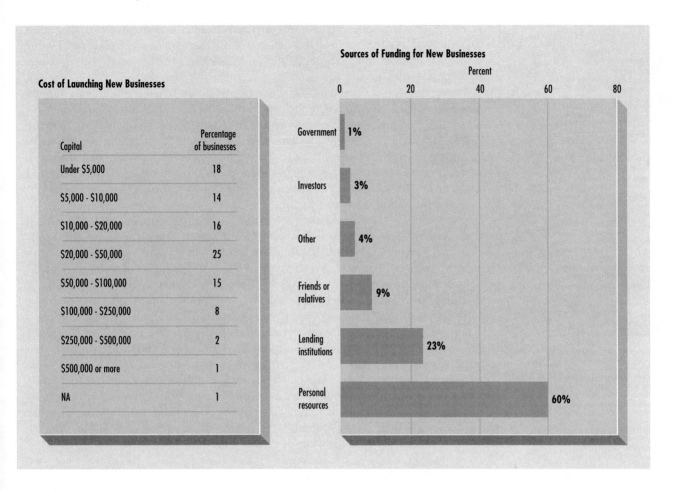

Cost of Launching New Businesses

Capital	Percentage of businesses
Under $5,000	18
$5,000 - $10,000	14
$10,000 - $20,000	16
$20,000 - $50,000	25
$50,000 - $100,000	15
$100,000 - $250,000	8
$250,000 - $500,000	2
$500,000 or more	1
NA	1

Sources of Funding for New Businesses

Percent

Source	Percent
Government	1%
Investors	3%
Other	4%
Friends or relatives	9%
Lending institutions	23%
Personal resources	60%

But say that you're just starting out. How much money will you need, and where should you turn first for capital? The answer depends on the size and type of business you want to launch. Retail and service businesses generally require less start-up cash than manufacturing companies or high-tech research-and-development ventures. On average, though, the majority of small businesses are launched with less than $20,000, as Exhibit 3.6 indicates.[31] Even entrepreneurs who found high-growth firms begin with a modest pool of capital. Three-fourths of the CEOs of the companies that have appeared on the Inc. 500 list since 1982 say they got into business with less than $50,000.[32] As Exhibit 3.6 also shows, finding the money was usually no problem. Sixty percent of the time, the founders reached into their own pockets.

Bank Loans and Other Sources of Debt

The second most common source of funds is bank loans, although banks are often reluctant to back new ventures. Most banks expect you to put up 25 to 50 percent of the money yourself, and they demand both collateral and personal guarantees to back the loan.[33] In addition, banks typically charge small businesses relatively high interest—two or three points above the prime rate available to large corporate clients. In periods when interest rates in general are high, this practice may impose a severe burden on small companies. It

EXHIBIT 3.6

How Much It Costs to Launch a Business and Where the Money Comes From

Most new businesses are started with relatively little money. The founders generally use their own savings to get under way.

Frederick Smith, founder of Federal Express, got his company off the ground with the help of an SBA-guaranteed loan.

pays to shop around for the most attractive rate. Banks have differing loan criteria and business objectives. Some cultivate small businesses and offer attractive interest rates or special services. It doesn't hurt to apply at two banks simultaneously.

If you apply to several banks and are turned down by all of them, you may be able to qualify for a loan backed by the Small Business Administration (SBA). To get an SBA-backed loan, you apply to a regular bank, which actually provides the money; the SBA guarantees to repay 85 to 90 percent of the loan if you fail to do so. The average SBA-backed loan is about $100,000; the upper limit is $750,000. In addition to operating its loan guarantee program, the SBA provides a limited number of direct loans to minorities, women, and veterans.[34]

From the businessperson's standpoint, SBA-backed loans are especially attractive because they generally have longer repayment terms than conventional bank loans—nine years as opposed to two or three. This translates into lower monthly payments. Unfortunately, demand for SBA loans vastly outstrips the agency's supply of capital. As a consequence, getting an SBA loan is difficult. In a typical year, only about 17,000 businesses are lucky enough to qualify.[35]

One of the best ways to borrow money for a small business is to obtain credit from suppliers. Say that you want to open a store. You might be able to convince a potential supplier to provide your initial inventory on credit. The supplier's risk is minimal in a deal like this; if you don't sell the product, the supplier can take it back. You might also be able to make some special arrangements with customers. Perhaps you can take a deposit for merchandise or arrange to be paid when the product is delivered. Later, you can ease your financial situation by negotiating liberal payment terms with your vendors or by using the money that others owe you to secure a loan.

Private Investors

Wealthy individuals are one of the most promising sources of equity financing, funding some 30,000 start-up companies every year.[36] However, finding a so-called angel may be difficult. Bankers, accountants, brokers, financial planners, and other entrepreneurs are often able to provide leads. One organized listing of private investors is the Venture Capital Network, a nonprofit corporation based in New Hampshire, which uses a computer to match investors and entrepreneurs.

Venture Capitalists

venture capitalists Investment specialists who provide money to finance new businesses or turn-arounds in exchange for a portion of the ownership, with the objective of making a considerable profit on the investment

In addition to looking for private investors, many high-growth ventures attempt to attract the interest of **venture capitalists,** investment specialists who raise pools of capital to fund ventures that are likely to succeed. The investment funds available to venture-capital firms come from corporations, wealthy individuals, pension funds, and other pools of capital, such as university endowments.

Venture capitalists, or VCs as they're called in entrepreneurial circles, do not simply lend money to a small business as a bank would. Instead, they provide capital in return for an ownership interest, which may amount to half of the stock or more. They often become involved in helping to run the business. In a typical scenario, the venture-capital firm buys part of the stock in the company at a low price—say, 50 cents a share—then, when the company goes public, the VC sells at a much higher price.

The problem with venture capital is that it's extremely hard to find. VCs fund fewer than 5,000 companies each year, and many of those companies are established firms ripe for expansion rather than raw start-ups. To catch the eye of a typical venture capitalist you need a business with pizzazz that has the potential to reach $50 million in sales within five years and provide an annualized rate of return of 40 to 60 percent over five to seven years.[37]

If your business doesn't fit the profile of a high-powered venture-capital firm, you might be able to raise money from one of the investment firms created by the Small Business Administration. Small Business Investment Companies (SBICs) and Minority Enterprise Small Business Investment Companies (MESBICs) are similar in operation to venture-capital firms, but they tend to make smaller investments and are willing to consider less glamorous businesses. They are federally licensed, shareholder-owned investment companies that have borrowed money at lower-than-market rates from the SBA to put into new ventures.

Corporate Sources

Yet another source of funding is big business. Companies like IBM, Motorola, and Eastman Kodak are making direct investments in small businesses.[38] In addition, many other large companies provide equity funding through investment pools run by venture capitalists.

In general, the large corporation's interests differ from the venture capitalist's. Apart from hoping for a profitable investment, most large companies want to gain access to promising technology, with the possible goal of acquiring the operation. Corporate investors often provide more than money. They sometimes share their marketing expertise or provide distribution capabilities that the new venture lacks.

State and Local Government Programs

In the past 10 years, state and local governments, hoping to boost their economies and create jobs, have launched hundreds of programs to help small businesses. All but four states now provide some sort of small-company financing; 28 have established venture-capital funds aimed at start-ups, and 30 provide research-and-development grants.[39]

In a related development, many state and local economic development offices and universities are forming "incubator" facilities to nurture fledgling businesses. In a typical incubator, new companies can lease space at bargain rates and share secretaries, receptionists, telephone equipment, financial and accounting advice, marketing support, and credit-checking services. Some incubators are open to businesses of all types, but many specialize. For example, the Spokane Business Incubation Center operates the Kitchen Center, where small food-processing companies can share a commercial kitchen. In 1990 385 incubators were in operation in 46 states, up from only 50 in 1984.[40] These facilities can make a big difference to the success of a start-up business. According to the National Business Incubation Association, 8 out of 10 businesses that are nurtured in incubators succeed.[41]

Public Stock Offerings

After a high-growth venture has been operating for a few years, it has the option of raising capital by **going public,** or selling stock in the company on the open

going public Act of raising capital by selling company shares to the public for the first time

market. Going public achieves two purposes: (1) It raises money for the company, and (2) it enables the founder and other early equity investors to make money by selling at a profit the stock they obtained at low prices.

The case of Bill Gates is an interesting example. Gates is the founder of Microsoft, a leading software systems company. In 1986, when Microsoft went public, Gates raised $58 million for the company. He also took a giant step down the road to personal wealth. Still in his 30s, Gates is the country's youngest billionaire thanks to his Microsoft stock.[42]

Although the potential rewards for going public are enormous, problems exist as well. Success depends on the public demand for stock in new companies, which varies considerably from year to year. Another problem with going public is the expense. Typically, when a company goes public, it might raise $10 million but spend $330,000 on various fees and printing costs and another $800,000 on underwriting commissions. Unless your company has annual sales of $15 million to $20 million and profits of $1 million or more, going public is not a viable option. Only about 5 percent of small businesses raise capital in this fashion.[43]

Managing the Business

Assuming that you obtain adequate financing to start or buy your own business, your next job is to run it. You may find yourself working 12-hour days week in and week out—with no boss to blame for your miseries! Not only is it common for small-business owners to put out the product—be it chopsticks, videotapes, homemade bread, or legal advice—but they also function as sales representative, secretary, personnel manager, financial planner, public relations expert, and janitor. Exhibit 3.7 shows where the time goes in a typical entrepreneur's week. With all the details to attend to, it's easy for the owner of a small business

EXHIBIT 3.7

How Entrepreneurs Spend Their Time

The men and women who found companies are jacks-of-all-trades, but their top priorities are selling and producing the product.

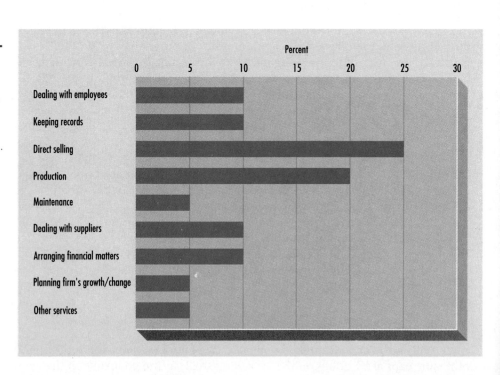

to lose sight of the big picture. Here are some of the broad managerial tasks that can make or break a small business.

Planning the Activities of the Business

You can find plenty of successful entrepreneurs who claim to have done very little formal planning, but even the most intuitive of them have *some* idea of what they're trying to accomplish and how they hope to do it. Before you rush in to supply a product, you need to be sure that a market exists. No amount of hard work can make a bad idea into a profitable one: The health-food store in a meat-and-potatoes neighborhood and the child-care center in a retirement community are probably doomed from the beginning.

You must also try to foresee some of the problems that might arise and figure out how to cope with them. What will you do if one of your suppliers suddenly goes out of business? Can you locate another supplier quickly? What if the neighborhood suddenly starts to change—even for the better? An influx of wealthier neighbors may cause such a steep increase in rent that your business must move. Also, tough competition may move into the neighborhood along with the fatter pocketbooks. Do you have an alternative location staked out? What if fashions suddenly change? Can you switch quickly from, say, hand-painted T-shirts to some other kind of shirt?

Marketing for the New Business

Marketing is especially important in a new business, because the company's ultimate success depends on building a customer base. Marketing encompasses a number of important activities such as product development, pricing, distribution, and promotion, which are discussed in detail in Chapters 12 through 15.

In terms of product development, small companies often have an edge over larger organizations because they can react more quickly. If a demand for broccoli pizzas arises tomorrow, a small restaurant can make them up almost as quickly as "Pop" can run out to the supermarket for the new ingredients and "Mom" can think of a way to incorporate them into the old family recipe. A chain, on the other hand, would probably not get wind of the new demand for months and would then need time to study the concept, formulate a new recipe, order ingredients in quantity, ship them to each outlet, and so on.

When it comes to prices, however, small companies may be at a disadvantage compared to larger firms. Because of their larger volume of business, big firms may have lower costs per unit and thus be able to charge lower prices. To set prices at the optimum level, you have to analyze with a critical eye your competition, your area, your costs, and your profit requirements. And once you've set those prices, you have to remain tuned in to changing conditions in the marketplace so that you don't get caught with too little demand for your supply or with too little reward for your risks.

Choosing the ideal outlet for your product is another problem. To build a distribution network, you must convince wholesalers or retailers to carry your product. You also need to analyze how to use your promotion budget to the fullest. For example, when Gretchen Scott started Nevica USA, she found an inexpensive way to get photographs of her firm's brightly colored skiwear into ski magazines. Her approach: Give free skiwear to photographers whose work

Marketing on a shoestring requires a little creative thinking. Gretchen Scott stretched the promotion budget for Nevica USA by giving photographers an incentive to use shots of Nevica-clad skiers in magazine articles.

appears frequently in ski magazines and pay them a fee whenever one of their pictures of a Nevica-clad skier appears in an article.[44]

Monitoring and Controlling Operations

In addition to marketing your product, you need to develop an effective record-keeping system that will handle customer files, billing, production and inventory data, employee information, and basic accounting functions. Many small businesses are solving the paperwork problem with personal computers. According to Neil Balter, that's what enabled him to turn his small carpentry business into the California Closet Company, a franchised chain of 135 closet-design shops with sales of $65 million per year.[45]

Coping with Red Tape

No business operates in a vacuum or under a glass dome—and like all other enterprises, new businesses are subject to the pressures and requirements of our society's legal and regulatory system. If you need a trademark, a company brand, or a patent, or if you are thinking of becoming incorporated, you will definitely need legal help. Many other situations require the help of a lawyer too.

TECHNIQUES FOR BUSINESS SUCCESS

Seven Common Mistakes Small Businesses Make—And How to Avoid Them

You can learn from others—if not always the secrets of success, then at least the most common causes of failure. Examinations of failed companies and studies of those stalled in the early stages of growth reveal a pattern of oft-repeated blunders and oversights that consistently spoil the dream of entrepreneurial success.

Consider the following mistakes (along with the guidelines for avoiding them) a survival guide for entrepreneurs:

1. Mistaking a hobby for a business. Would-be entrepreneurs often go into business for the wrong reason—namely, the dangerous and mistaken belief that a lifelong hobby can automatically be converted into a business. A hobbyist, no matter how skilled or creative, often lacks the critical business experience essential to success. For example, the ability to whip up a glorious soufflé is not reason enough to open a restaurant.

Hobbies can serve as promising springboards for business ventures, providing you complement your creative or technical skills with a strong foundation in business tech-

niques. You can get this experience in two ways. (a) Go to work for someone else before going into business for yourself. Consider this first step an apprenticeship in the sort of venture you want to start. Soak up all you can about the problems, the opportunities, and the necessary technical skills. (b) Go directly into business with a partner strong in management experience. A hobbyist chef and an experienced restaurant manager may have the right combination of skills to get a venture off the ground.

2. Trying to make the business appeal to everyone. Typically, the small-business owner believes that appealing to the widest possible range of consumers is a sure-fire prescription for success. Instead, this broad-brush approach creates a company that is likely to be weak in several areas rather than strong in one. A wiser approach is to narrow the company's focus, identifying a specific market segment and marshaling the necessary resources (merchandise, advertising, personnel, and so on) to become a significant factor in it. For example, appeal to a single age category (senior citizens or teen-agers) or focus on one socioeconomic group, and stick to a single selling point (discount prices, high fashion, or attentive customer service).

Likewise, you'll be coping with government regulations, many of which were written with larger businesses in mind but are applied to small businesses anyway. Disposing of hazardous wastes, for example, may be difficult for small companies, which typically lack their own waste-treatment facilities. Similarly, small businesses may have problems complying with the recently passed Americans with Disabilities Act, which is designed to ensure that disabled consumers receive the same level of services as other customers. Although small businesses have more time to comply with the law than large firms do, they may be required to make costly modifications to their facilities or prove that doing so would pose an economic hardship. One regulation, for example, requires that restaurants must either be accessible to the disabled or offer home delivery. Another requires that store aisles be wide enough to accommodate wheelchairs and that shelves be low enough so that a person in a wheelchair can reach the merchandise.

Adjusting to Growth

One of the most difficult management problems you may face in a new business is success. Trouble often occurs when the founder—fundamentally an "idea person"—assumes the role of manager. Many people who are good at launching companies lack the skills needed to manage them over the long run. The person

---

3. Starting out with too little cash. Very few companies move immediately into the black; most sustain losses for months, even years, before turning profitable. You should create a worst-case scenario, projecting on a monthly basis minimum revenue and maximum expenses for the first two years. Note the point at which income will cover expenses, and calculate the amount of money necessary to cover the shortfall until then. Add to this the amount of the initial investment required to launch the business and to cover ongoing expenses for inventory and equipment. This total is the minimum amount required to launch the business. In addition, you should try to arrange a line of credit at a bank so that you can draw cash to cover expenses as required. A reserve like this serves as a buffer between you and your creditors, allowing you to keep the business going even when income fails to cover expenses.

4. Failing to detect bad credit risks early. Implement an early warning detection plan to short-circuit emerging credit problems before they jeopardize the company's finances.

5. Setting the wrong price. The right price tag can make the difference between making a profit and losing money. Strike a delicate balance between the company's need for profits and the consumer's search for value.

6. Bleeding the business. Generous salaries, bonuses, and company cars are seen as the rewards of success. But they may also sow the seeds of catastrophe. Disaster can be averted by routinely saving some of the company's earnings. The best approach is to establish a set amount—perhaps a percentage of total earnings—and discipline yourself to leave that amount in the business.

7. Becoming isolated. Unlike their counterparts in large companies, small-business owners tend to run their ventures singlehandedly, making all key decisions without going through an elaborate approval process. Although there is strength in that approach (the company can respond faster to emerging opportunities), the owner is insulated from other points of view. The best way to overcome this problem is to bring in outside opinions by assembling an informal board of directors. Ask a banker, an accountant, and another local business owner to sit on the board, joining you once a month to discuss the company and to give their insights into its needs and requirements.

These seven mistakes are by no means the only ones you can make. But anticipating and tackling such common blunders may take you a long way toward building and maintaining a profitable company.

who excels during the start-up phase may not be able to delegate work well or may have problems figuring out how to expand the business.

And even if the person is flexible enough to adjust to changing conditions, there is a lot to learn as a company grows. Arranging additional financing, hiring new people, adding new products, computerizing the record keeping—all these activities are demanding.

▶ THE FRANCHISE ALTERNATIVE

franchise Business arrangement in which an individual obtains rights from a larger company to sell a well-known product or service

franchisee Person or group to whom a corporation grants an exclusive right to the use of its name in a certain territory, usually in exchange for an initial fee plus monthly royalty payments

franchiser Corporation that grants a franchise to an individual or group

One way to avoid some of the management headaches associated with starting a business is to invest in a **franchise,** an approach that enables you to use a larger company's trade name and sell its products or services in a specific territory. In exchange for this right, the **franchisee** (you, the small-business owner) pays an initial fee (and often monthly royalties as well) to the **franchiser** (the corporation).

Franchises are of three basic types. In a *product franchise,* the franchisee pays the franchising company for the right to sell trademarked goods, which are purchased from the franchiser and resold by the franchisee. Car dealers and gasoline stations fall into this category. In a *manufacturing franchise,* like a soft-drink bottling plant, the franchisee is licensed by the parent company to produce and distribute its products, using supplies purchased from the franchiser. In a *business-format franchise,* the franchisee buys the right to open a business using the franchiser's name and format for doing business. The fast-food chains typify this form of franchising.

If you are an average American, you already know something about franchises. In our economy, they are a factor of rising importance, as Exhibit 3.8 suggests. We buy our houses from franchised real estate brokers, get our hair cut in franchised beauty salons, and drive cars purchased from franchised dealers. The soda pop we drink is bottled by franchisers, and the food we eat is sold by franchises such as McDonald's, Wendy's, Pizza Hut, and Kentucky Fried Chicken. Franchises account for about one-third of all retail sales in the United States and employ over 7 million people. With sales growing at five times the

EXHIBIT 3.8

The Growth of Franchising
Both the number and revenues of franchises have increased dramatically over the past decade.

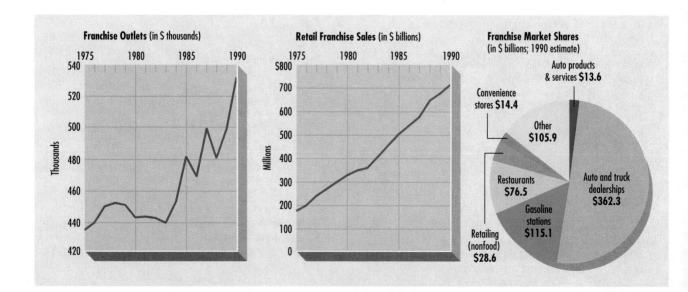

Franchise Outlets (in $ thousands)

Retail Franchise Sales (in $ billions)

Franchise Market Shares (in $ billions; 1990 estimate)

Auto products & services **$13.6**
Convenience stores **$14.4**
Other **$105.9**
Restaurants **$76.5**
Auto and truck dealerships **$362.3**
Gasoline stations **$115.1**
Retailing (nonfood) **$28.6**

rate of the GNP, franchises will be responsible for half of all retail sales within 10 years.[46]

Franchising is not a new phenomenon. It has been around since the nineteenth century, when such companies as Singer and International Harvester established dealerships throughout the world. Early in this century, Coca-Cola, General Motors, and Metropolitan Life Insurance Company (among others) used franchises to distribute or sell their products. But the real boom in franchising began in the late 1950s, with the proliferation of hotels and motels like Holiday Inn and of fast-food establishments like Baskin-Robbins and Dunkin' Donuts.

The 1980s saw a proliferation of service-oriented franchises that catered to the needs of busy baby boomers: day-care centers, cleaning services, auto maintenance centers, and video rental stores. The 1980s also saw a shift in the type of people buying franchises. It used to be that the typical franchisee expected to own and operate one store, but more and more franchisees are entering the business with broader ambitions. Their aim is to own a number of outlets and delegate day-to-day operations to employees.[47]

In the 1990s you can expect to see an increase in corporate franchising, with giant companies like PepsiCo operating a collection of franchise chains such as Kentucky Fried Chicken, Pizza Hut, and Taco Bell. You can also expect to see franchisers reaching overseas to sustain their customary growth rate, particularly if they have already saturated much of the domestic market. After all, how many more McDonald's does the United States need?

Advantages of Franchising

Why is franchising so popular? According to the president of the International Franchise Association, franchising has triple benefits: "The franchiser wins because he builds a strong foundation for his company. The franchisee wins because he can take advantage of the franchiser's proven business system. And the general public benefits from the consistency of the product or service."[48]

The biggest winners are generally the franchisers, who are able to expand their businesses through franchised outlets without depleting their own capital. For example, take the case of I Can't Believe It's Yogurt, Inc. The company was founded by Julie and Bill Brice, a brother-and-sister team who invested $10,000 of their own money in a frozen yogurt shop while they were still students at Southern Methodist University. With the help of friendly service, good promotion, and solid management methods, the Brices were able to show a profit within four months. They opened seven more company-owned stores within six years, but then they realized that further expansion would require debt. At that point, they turned to franchising to finance their business. The chain currently has over 300 outlets.[49] Franchisers not only expand their business using other people's money but also receive regular income from franchisees, who pass on a percentage of their gross revenues and help pay for advertising and promotional costs.

Investing in a franchise can also be good for the franchisee, because the *risk is reasonably low.* When you invest in a franchise, you know that you are getting a viable business, one that has "worked" many times before. You also have the advantage of *instant name recognition* and *mass advertising.* An independent hamburger stand can't afford a national TV advertising campaign, but McDonald's, Burger King, and Wendy's can.

In addition to giving you a proven formula, buying a franchise helps you solve

Every 15 minutes a new franchised store opens for business. The fastest-growing U.S. franchise—Subway Sandwiches & Salads—rolls out 23 new restaurants a week.

one of the biggest problems that small businesses face: lack of money. Franchisers generally use a number of methods to make sure the franchisee is on *firm financial footing*. First, before approving prospective franchisees, the franchiser weeds out those whose own finances are in unacceptable shape; a franchiser will not grant a franchise unless the applicant has enough money for start-up costs. (The franchiser, unlike many independent proprietors, has enough experience to estimate start-up costs realistically.) The investment required varies from a few thousand dollars to upward of a million, depending on the franchise. The initial investment covers such franchiser services as site location studies, market research, training, and technical assistance, as well as the costs associated with building or leasing the structure, decorating the building, purchasing supplies, and operating the business for 6 to 12 months.

Few franchisees are able to write a check for the amount of the total investment. Most obtain a loan to cover at least part of the cost. In some cases, the lender is actually the franchiser. Approximately one-quarter of *Entrepreneur Magazine*'s list of top 500 franchisers offer some sort of financial assistance to their franchisees.[50]

Besides financial aid and advice, the franchiser gives a new franchisee *training* in how to run a business. For example, I Can't Believe It's Yogurt operates a "Yogurt University" at company headquarters in Dallas, where new franchisees go through a 10-day indoctrination program. Their training includes role-playing exercises, in which some franchisees play the parts of salespeople while others act like temperamental customers. By offering this course, I Can't Believe It's Yogurt is able to teach standard procedures to each operator and thus maintain its distinctive image.[51] Many franchise organizations offer advice on advertising, taxes, and other business matters, as well as offering instructions in the day-to-day operation of the franchise.

Disadvantages of Franchising

Although franchising offers many advantages, it is not the ideal vehicle for everyone. For one thing, owning a franchise is *no guarantee of wealth*. It may be the safest way to get into business, but it is not necessarily the cheapest. According to some analysts, it costs 10 to 30 percent more to buy a franchise than to open a business independently.[52] And not all franchises are extremely profitable operations.

One of the most significant financial variables is the *monthly payment,* or *royalty,* that must be turned over to the franchiser. The fees vary widely, from nothing at all to 20 percent of sales. High royalties are not necessarily bad—if the franchisee gets ongoing assistance in return.

Another drawback of franchises is that many of them allow individual operators *very little independence*. Franchisers can prescribe virtually every aspect of the business, down to the details of employees' uniforms and the color of the walls. Franchisees may be required to buy the products they sell directly from the franchiser at whatever price the franchiser feels like charging. Franchisers may also make important decisions without consulting franchisees. In recent years, a growing number of disgruntled franchisees have filed lawsuits or formed associations in an attempt to even up the balance of power.

Although most franchise opportunities are legitimate, it pays to be wary. Franchises and "business opportunities" are *occasionally fraudulent*. Rose Gregg, a single mother from Cincinnati, Ohio, learned this painful lesson the hard way. After attending a weekend franchising and business opportunity show, she invested $5,500 with Atlanta-based American Legal Distributors, which claimed to be selling prepaid legal services franchises. According to Gregg, "They had the biggest booth at the show, surrounded by legitimate franchises I recognized. I spent a week in a training seminar. I talked to other people who said they'd been successful. They even sent a bouquet of flowers after I invested." But the flowers were all Gregg got. Like 375 other people who had invested in American Legal, she lost all of her money. The scam's organizer, Harold H. Pasley, collected more than $3 million before he was caught and sentenced to 15 years in prison.[53]

Evaluating the Franchise

The best way to protect yourself from a poor franchise investment is to study the opportunity very carefully before you commit yourself. Since 1978, the Federal Trade Commission has required franchisers to disclose information about their operations to prospective franchisees. By studying this information, you can determine the financial condition of the franchiser and ascertain whether it has been involved in lawsuits with franchisees. Before signing a franchise agreement, it's wise to consult an attorney. Exhibit 3.9 suggests some points to consider as you study the package of information on the franchise.

EXHIBIT 3.9 ▶ **Ten Questions to Ask Before Signing a Franchise Agreement**

A franchise agreement is a legally binding contract that defines the relationship between the franchisee and the franchiser. Because the agreement is drawn up by the franchiser, the terms and conditions generally favor the franchiser. You don't necessarily have to agree to everything on the first go-around. Maybe you can negotiate a better deal. Before signing the franchise agreement, be sure to consult an attorney.

1. Are your legal responsibilities as a franchisee clear? Are your family members similarly obligated?

2. Who is responsible for selecting the location of your business?

3. Is the name or trademark of your franchise legally protected? Can the franchiser change or modify the trademark without consulting you?

4. Has the franchiser made any oral promises that are not reflected in the written franchise agreement?

5. What are your renewal rights? What conditions must you meet to renew your agreement?

6. Do you have exclusive rights to a given territory, or could the franchiser sell to additional franchisees who would become your competitors?

7. Under what terms are you allowed or required to terminate the franchise agreement? What becomes of the lease and assets if the agreement is terminated? Are you barred from opening a similar business?

8. Under what terms and conditions are you permitted or required to sell some or all of your interests in the franchise?

9. Are you required to buy supplies from the franchiser or other specified suppliers? Under what circumstances can you choose your own suppliers?

10. Has your attorney studied the written franchise agreement? Does it conform to the requirements of the Federal Trade Commission?

Another good source of information about a franchise is other franchisees. You might want to spend a few months working for someone who already owns a franchise you're interested in. At a minimum, you should find out what other franchisees think of the opportunity. If they had it to do over again, would they still invest?

SUMMARY OF LEARNING OBJECTIVES

1 Differentiate between lifestyle businesses and high-growth ventures.

Most small businesses are lifestyle businesses, intended to provide the owner with a comfortable living. High-growth ventures, on the other hand, are businesses with ambitious sales, profit, and growth objectives.

2 Discuss the demographic and economic factors that have affected small businesses in the 1980s and 1990s.

The expansion of the small-business sector in the 1980s reflects a shift to services, a diminution in the advantages afforded by large-scale manufacturing, the maturation of the baby-boom generation, and an increase in the number of women in the work force. Although many of these trends will continue to favor small businesses in the 1990s, the recession that began in 1991 cast a cloud over their prospects.

3 List four important functions of small business in the economy.

Small businesses provide jobs, introduce new goods and services, sup-

ply the needs of large corporations, and provide specialized goods and services.

4 Identify three ways of getting into business for yourself.

You can start a new company from scratch, buy a going concern, or invest in a franchise.

5 Name ten topics that should be covered in a formal business plan.

A formal business plan should (1) summarize your business concept, (2) describe the company and its industry, (3) explain the product, (4) analyze the market, (5) describe your marketing strategy, (6) discuss design and development plans, (7) explain your operations plan, (8) provide an overall schedule, (9) identify risks and potential problems, and (10) provide detailed financial information.

6 Describe nine sources of financing for a new business.

New businesses may be financed through personal savings, commer-

cial-bank loans or loans from the Small Business Administration, credit from suppliers, private investors, venture capitalists, corporate sources, Small Business Investment Companies and Minority Enterprise Small Business Investment Companies, state and local programs, and public stock offerings.

7 Identify five managerial activities that are important to the success of a small business.

Success depends on planning the activities of the business, marketing, monitoring and controlling operations, coping with red tape, and adjusting to growth.

8 Explain the pros and cons of owning a franchise.

A franchisee has the advantages of wide name recognition and mass advertising, financial help, and training and support. However, owning a franchise involves considerable start-up expense, monthly payments to the franchiser, constraints on the franchisee's independence, and possibly questionable deals.

Meeting a Business Challenge at Staples

Tom Stemberg knew his idea for a chain of office-supply superstores was a good one, but he didn't realize *how* good until he started looking for money. One of his first calls was to Leo Kahn, an old adversary from Stemberg's supermarket days. One of the country's leading supermarket entrepreneurs, Kahn had recently sold

his food store chains for $80 million and, at age 68, was looking for new investments to liven up his retirement. Despite his previous rivalry with Stemberg in Boston's supermarket price wars, Kahn agreed to put up $500,000 in capital for the new venture and to serve as chairman of the board.

Stemberg and Kahn refined the idea for Staples and prepared a detailed business plan, which they circulated to venture capitalists. Although most would-be entrepreneurs have trouble raising money, Stemberg and Kahn received dozens of offers. "We could easily have raised $100 million," Stemberg recalls. What excited the venture capitalists was the "rightness" of the idea. As one investor said, "A lot of retail start-ups come by, but most of them are a twist on an old theme or a better presentation. Not Staples—it was an entirely new retailing category." Stemberg turned down most of the offers but accepted $4 million in start-up funds in exchange for 50 percent of the company, with commitments for $31 million later on.

With his money problems solved, he was ready to build a management team. Because he expected the business to grow rapidly, Stemberg wanted people who had worked for large-scale operations. He also wanted people with practical, hands-on experience in retailing, people who understood costs and customers. Not surprisingly, he turned to his contacts in the grocery business. Many of Staples's top people are, like Stemberg, graduates of the Jewel company's management training program. Although many of the people he recruited held high-paying executive positions, Stemberg persuaded them that joining Staples would enable them to get in on the ground floor of a company with enormous potential. In addition to offering competitive salaries, he promised his team stock in the company, which could be extremely valuable if Staples went public.

But before Stemberg could open his first store, he needed merchandise to stock the shelves. His plans called for a deep inventory of some 5,000 items, ranging from paper and pencils to coffee machines and computers— everything a small company might need to set up shop and run a business. However, vendors of office supplies were leery of doing business directly with Staples. Many major manufacturers didn't want to upset their relationships with their wholesalers, who would be cut out of the distribution chain by Staples. The wholesalers, in turn, were reluctant to sell to the company, because Staples demanded price discounts in exchange for volume orders. Furthermore, the wholesalers' customers— the retailers—would be hurt by Staples's low prices. In fact, several retailers threatened to stop doing business with wholesalers that supplied Staples. Meanwhile, the whole-

Tom Stemberg, founder of Staples, radically changed an entire industry when he launched the first deep-discount office-products superstore to sell paper and pens the way Toys 'R' Us sells bikes and balls.

salers were putting similar pressure on the manufacturers to prevent them from selling to Staples.

The manufacturers' reluctance to sell directly to Stemberg threatened the profitability of his entire concept, which depends on shortening the distribution chain to save on costs. To combat their fears, Stemberg and his vice president of merchandising, Paul Korian, invited a group of 100 major office-products manufacturers to a breakfast meeting. After hearing a presentation on the company's prospects and probable impact on the office-supply business, many of the manufacturers were convinced that Staples would revolutionize the industry and that cooperating with the firm would be the most profitable course. They agreed to supply the company; so with money, labor, and merchandise lined up, Stemberg was ready to open his first store in the Boston suburbs.

Your Mission: You are a new recruit in Staples's management training program. In addition to learning the business from the ground up, you handle special projects for Staples's top executives. They have asked for your help in analyzing the following issues:

1. Although Staples has satisfied its initial financing needs, it will need additional capital beyond the $35 million that it has lined up through venture capitalists. In fact, Stemberg is thinking in terms of raising another $35 million to $40 million. He has asked you to weigh some of the advantages and disadvantages of various funding alternatives and to recommend the one you prefer. Here are the options:
 a. Bank loans
 b. Additional venture-capital investments
 c. A public stock offering
 d. A combination of debt and equity

2. When Stemberg opened the first Staples store, he was disappointed that more customers didn't show up. But perhaps he shouldn't have been surprised. Most of Staples's target customers—owners and office managers of small businesses—are not used to shopping for office supplies in a warehouse. They customarily order over the phone from a wholesale catalog and have the supplies delivered to the back room. Why would they want to get in their cars, fight the traffic, find the store, and then push a shopping cart around a 15,000-square-foot warehouse with concrete floors and metal shelves, searching through 5,000 items to find computer paper, paper clips, and file folders? And why would they want to cart the stuff back to the office and unload it themselves? Why? To save 50 percent on office supplies. But first Stemberg must convince them to visit the store. Stemberg has asked for your advice on how to get the owners and office managers of small businesses to come in for an initial visit. Which of the following options do you recommend?
 a. Encourage Staples's managers and employees to join organizations where they might meet the target customers. Examples would be the chamber of commerce, Rotary Club, Kiwanis Club, and other networking groups. By attending meetings, the Staples team could make contacts with local businesspeople and introduce them to the company's advantages.
 b. Blanket the Boston area with radio, TV, and newspaper ads to introduce as many people as possi-

ble to Staples's first store.

c. Buy a list of the small businesses located within reasonable driving distance of the store and call them on the phone. Explain the Staples concept, ask how much the business spends on various supplies, and follow up with a free coupon for something the company uses often.

d. Identify 35 office managers of small businesses in Staples's area. Send each a check for $25, together with an invitation to come in and critique the store. Their comments will be useful, and they are likely to be impressed with the store and tell their friends about it.

3. Good ideas are quickly imitated. Before Stemberg could say "paper clip," he was confronted with competition from "me-too" office-supply warehouses. Although the rivals initially stayed in their own geographic territory, Stemberg could see that it was just a matter of time before Staples would face head-on competition. What strategy should he pursue in competing with the clones?

a. Expand as quickly as possible into as many geographic areas as possible in hopes of nailing down the best locations and developing an initial base of loyal customers before competitors can get up and running.

b. Working from Staples's original base in Boston, expand the chain throughout the heavily populated corridor from Washington, D.C., through New England. Concentrate on getting established in this area so that Staples will have a significant advantage when competitors try to move in. With the Northeast in hand, expand selectively into other metropolitan areas where small businesses are doing well.

c. Threaten to take legal action against competitors who copy Staples's format.

d. When competition surfaces, fight back by starting price wars and increasing Staples's advertising and marketing budgets.

4. Stemberg has asked you to investigate the advantages and disadvantages of franchising the Staples concept.

Which of the following points would you emphasize most strongly in your report to him?

a. Franchising would be a good way for Staples to expand rapidly throughout the country. Franchisees would supply much of the money and labor required to open stores in all of the major metropolitan areas, thereby enabling the company to get a jump on the competition and nail down the best locations.

b. Franchising would limit Stemberg's control over the quality and consistency of Staples stores and might jeopardize the company's long-term competitiveness.

c. Franchising would limit the value of the company to Stemberg and the other existing investors, since franchisees would own the stores and have a right to part of the profits.

d. Franchising would be beneficial overseas; the participation of foreign partners would help Staples overcome legal barriers to international expansion and would enhance the company's understanding of foreign markets.[54]

KEY TERMS

debt (72)	franchisee (80)	lifestyle businesses (62)
economies of scale (64)	franchiser (80)	small businesses (62)
equity (72)	going public (75)	start-up company (66)
franchise (80)	high-growth ventures (62)	venture capitalists (74)

REVIEW QUESTIONS

1. What qualities usually characterize the men and women who run successful small businesses, and why?

2. Why have small businesses been started in record numbers in recent years?

3. What class of business organization creates the most new jobs in the United States?

4. In what ways do small businesses complement big businesses in our economy?

5. Why do many new businesses fail, and how might such failures be avoided?

6. What are the principal sources of financing for new businesses?

7. What are the motives that encourage big businesses to support start-up companies?

8. How does a franchise operation work, and what are some of its advantages and disadvantages for the franchisee?

A CASE FOR CRITICAL THINKING

Putting a Stamp on the Market

Suppose you had a bright idea for a service business—a convenient place where people could rent a postal box, mail packages, buy office supplies and stamps, make copies, collect tele-

phone messages, duplicate keys, and send documents electronically by telex or fax. Say you did some market research and found that people liked the idea, and you thought you could

make a decent living by opening such a center. Being ambitious, you thought you might even open a bunch of centers. After all, if one is good, aren't two better? And why stop at two? Why not open centers in every town and neighborhood throughout the country? You had a few reservations, though. There was nothing patentable about your idea. Anybody with a little capital could duplicate your service. If you were successful, people might imitate you and grab the best locations before you could afford to expand. So what should you do?

Anthony DeSio, chief executive officer of Mail Boxes Etc. (MBE), solved the problem by franchising. To date he has sold franchises for over 1,386 MBE centers scattered across the country from Alaska to Florida. In fiscal year 1992, he expects to sell at least 300 more. DeSio estimates that the U.S. market can accommodate up to 20,000 centers of the MBE type, and he plans to lock up a dominant position before rivals such as Postal Annex can beat him to the punch. He also plans to expand internationally before the U.S. market becomes saturated.

During the expansion phase, MBE's primary source of revenues is the sale of both area and individual franchises. The company also receives royalties from franchisees and revenue from selling equipment and supplies to franchisees. As the MBE network matures and growth slows, DeSio anticipates that royalties and revenue from selling equipment and supplies will replace franchise fees as the main source of company income.

DeSio believes that building a nationwide network will eventually provide MBE with a major advantage over independent competitors. Economies of scale have already helped bring down the cost of operations. The centralized purchasing and shipping department obtains supplies and equipment in large quantities at reduced prices, and it passes the savings on to individual franchisees. The headquarters design and construction staff helps local owners plan their centers more efficiently and get good deals from national suppliers on cabinetry and fixtures. The MBE administration and franchise support departments provide customized computer software to help franchisees manage their accounting and inventory control.

DeSio believes that in the long run, MBE's success will depend on strong, positive relationships among the company's executive office, the area franchisees, and the individual franchise owners. He has created seven regional franchise advisory councils, composed of area and individual franchisees, to obtain feedback from the field. DeSio also supports the franchisees with training programs. He has opened two company-owned stores to experiment with new ideas and test new products and services. Ideas under investigation include selling airline tickets and money orders as well as distributing assorted merchandise that might appeal to MBE customers.[55]

1. Do you think DeSio was wise to rely on franchising to expand his business, or should he have attempted to retain ownership of all the stores? Explain your answer.

2. What are the pros and cons of starting your own mail-and-business-services center versus buying an MBE franchise?

3. If you were to invest in an MBE franchise in your area, what unique products or services would you offer in order to attract business?

BUILDING YOUR COMMUNICATION SKILLS

Using the section titled "Obtaining Financing" (p. 72) as a resource, investigate one of the sources of funding that is available to new business ventures. Either by letter or in a personal interview, contact a local financial institution or a state, local, or federal business advisor to find out what type of financing is available for new businesses. The reference section of your local library might also have information regarding local funding sources. Be sure to note the requirements necessary to obtain funding from each source. (For example, are sources limited to a specific type of business?) As directed by your instructor, prepare a brief report summarizing your findings and present it to the class.

KEEPING CURRENT USING *THE WALL STREET JOURNAL*

Scan issues of *The Wall Street Journal* for articles describing problems or successes with franchise operations. Clip or copy three or more articles that interest you.

1. What problem or opportunity does each article present? Is it an issue that faces many franchises, or is it specific to one chain or industry?

2. What could a potential franchise owner learn about the risks and rewards of franchises from reading these articles?

3. Have you ever considered purchasing a franchise? What impact did these articles have on your interest. Why?

CHAPTER 4

LEARNING OBJECTIVES
After studying this chapter, you will be able to

1 Identify four groups to which business has a responsibility.

2 List and explain four philosophical approaches to resolving ethical questions in business.

3 Name three kinds of pollution, and outline actions to control each.

4 Specify the four rights of consumers.

5 State the responsibilities of the Equal Employment Opportunity Commission.

6 Identify four issues that are of particular concern to women in the workplace.

7 Delineate two general ways in which investors may be cheated of their rightful profits.

8 List six actions that companies are taking to meet their ethical and social responsibilities.

Ethical and Social Responsibilities of Business

Facing a Business Challenge at Ben & Jerry's Homemade

CAN A COMPANY BE PROFITABLE AND SOCIALLY RESPONSIBLE AT THE SAME TIME?

B en & Jerry's Homemade makes more than premium ice cream; it makes an unusual effort to operate a business as a force for social change. The company has earned a nationwide reputation as an organization that stands apart in today's highly competitive, money-driven business environment. Making a profit seems to be less important to the founders than meeting the needs of employees and the surrounding community. And the company culture has always emphasized people, fun, and adventure.

Co-founders Ben Cohen and Jerry Greenfield intended to start an ice cream parlor, and once the business got going, sell it and move on. But there always seemed to be something that forced them to grow, such as a new competitor or the need to replace or fix equipment. Almost in spite of itself, the ice cream parlor became a growth company.

But growth brought increased profits and financial controls. The company was becoming less fun and more "businesslike." Cohen and Greenfield believed that if the company became like other corporations, they would have failed. So four years after starting the company, the two founders decided on a way to run it so that Ben & Jerry's Homemade would be a force for social change. The company would be held in trust for the community. Growth and profit would be a means to increased social responsibility, which would justify being more businesslike.

The co-founders' social responsibility goals are demonstrated in many ways. Of pretax profits, 7.5 percent goes to support social causes (the national average is 1.5 percent). The company is a leader in corporate recycling and environmental programs. Products are not only associated with peace, justice, and the environment, but they support these causes financially. For example, a percentage of sales from Peace Pops goes to promoting world peace. Rain Forest Crunch is made with nuts from the South American rain forest, which supports the native people directly and gives them a long-term financial incentive to nurture the forest rather than chop it down for lumber.

Today the company is a multimillion-dollar corporation, and double digit growth is once again challenging the culture and commitment to social change. There are now hundreds of people in the company, and not all of them share Cohen and Greenfield's idealism. The two founders worry that some managers have become too profit-oriented and that new projects are being evaluated for their ability to generate profit rather than social change. How can Cohen and Greenfield maintain their ideals as the company grows? What does it mean for a company to be socially responsible? Can a large corporation balance the desire to be socially responsible with the need to remain profitable?[1]

▶ FOUNDATIONS OF BUSINESS ETHICS

stakeholders Individuals or groups to whom business has a responsibility

As Ben Cohen and Jerry Greenfield realize, each company functions as part of an interactive system composed of various **stakeholders:** managers, owners, employees, consumers, and society at large. If a company's management consistently shortchanges any of these groups, the business will eventually cease to exist. Owners who are unhappy with the company's performance will withdraw their capital and invest it elsewhere. Workers whose needs are not met will quit and find other jobs. Consumers whose tastes and values are ignored will spend their money on other things. And if the concerns of society are disregarded, the voters will clamor for laws to limit offensive business activities.

Most business executives sincerely try to respond to the needs of these groups. Generally speaking, their efforts are successful. However, the interests of these groups sometimes conflict. When that happens, businesspeople are faced with a dilemma: how to reconcile competing interests. In trying to ensure profits, for example, a manager might be tempted to compromise product quality. Would the choice be justified? No, but it isn't always easy to know what's best.

The Evolution of Social Responsibility

Business ethics is more complicated than it used to be. Back in the "bad old days" before the turn of the century, the prevailing view among industrialists was that business had only one responsibility: to make a profit. Railroad tycoon William Vanderbilt summed up this attitude when he said, "The public be damned. I'm working for the shareholders."[2]

By and large those were not good times to be a low-level worker or an unwary consumer. People worked 60-hour weeks under harsh conditions for a dollar or two a day. The few bold people who tried to fight the system faced violence and unemployment. Consumers were not much better off. *Caveat emptor* was the rule of the day—"Let the buyer beware." If you bought a product, you paid the price and took the consequences. There were no consumer groups or government agencies to come to your defense if the product was defective or caused harm; if you tried to sue the company, chances were you would lose.

These conditions caught the attention of a few crusading journalists and novelists known as muckrakers. They used the power of the pen to stir up public

EXHIBIT 4.1 ▶ **Early Government Regulations Pertaining to Business**

Despite their reputation for being cold-blooded in business, many early tycoons were also philanthropists. For example, Andrew Carnegie, a pioneer in the steel industry, donated money to create public libraries in small towns throughout the United States. Nevertheless, government regulations were needed to ensure fair business practices.

GOVERNMENT REGULATION	DATE	EFFECT
Interstate Commerce Act	1887	Regulated business practices, specifically railroad operations and shipping rates.
Sherman Antitrust Act	1890	Fostered competition by preventing monopolies and noncompetitive mergers.
Pure Food and Drug Act	1906	Encouraged purity of food and drugs, specifically those transported across state lines.
Meat Inspection Act	1906	Encouraged purity of meat and meat products, specifically those transported across state lines.
Federal Trade Commission Act	1914	Controlled illegal trade practices through the creation of the Federal Trade Commission.
Clayton Act	1914	Eliminated price discrimination that gave large businesses an advantage over smaller firms.

indignation and agitate for reform. Largely through their efforts, a number of laws were passed to limit the power of monopolies and to establish safety standards for food and drugs (see Exhibit 4.1).

Despite these reforms, business continued to pursue profits above all else until the Great Depression. When the economic system collapsed in 1929, the public became disenchanted with business. With 25 percent of the work force unemployed, people lost their faith in unbridled capitalism, and pressure mounted for government to fix the system.

At the urging of President Franklin Roosevelt, Congress passed laws to protect workers, consumers, and investors. The Social Security system was set up, employees were given the right to join unions and bargain collectively, the minimum wage was established, and the length of the workweek was limited. Legislation was enacted to prevent unfair competition and false advertising, and the Securities and Exchange Commission was established to protect investors.

As the Depression drew to a close and World War II began, public confidence in business revived. Throughout the 1950s, the relationship among business, government, and society was relatively tranquil. But the climate shifted dramatically in the 1960s, as activism exploded on four fronts: environmental protection, national defense, consumerism, and civil rights. These movements have drastically altered the way business is conducted in the United States. Many of the changes have been instituted willingly by socially responsible companies, others have been mandated by government regulation, and still others have come about because of pressure from citizen groups.

But despite the efforts of various groups, public confidence in business remains low. Approximately two out of three people believe that business is not doing enough to provide job security for employees, help the community, keep the environment clean, price products fairly, and behave ethically.[3] Executives themselves also have doubts about the ethical standards of the business world. Eight out of ten upper-level managers think people are either occasionally or frequently unethical in their business dealings, and nearly one in four believes that ethical standards get in the way of career success.[4]

As stakeholders in their companies, today's employees have the right to bargain collectively. If negotiations break down, union members such as these telephone workers have the right to go on strike. When a company fails to meet the needs of its stakeholders, its prospects for success are dim.

The problem, some argue, is inherent in the nature of capitalism, which is based on the assumption that if people are free to pursue their own interests, they will all look out for themselves fairly effectively, and society as a whole will benefit. Thus the "invisible hand" of the market will juggle everyone's interests more effectively than laws or regulatory agencies. This assumption can be used to justify selfish behavior in business dealings and to support a "survival of the fittest" approach to ethical decisions.

Philosophical Bases for Social Responsibility

Although we tend to blame "business" for exerting a corrupting influence, in the final analysis, corporations are merely collections of individuals, each making choices with moral implications. If everyone behaves ethically, the organization as a whole will act in a responsible manner. The trick, then, is for each person to think through the consequences of his or her actions and make the "right" choice.

The trouble lies in determining what is "right" in any given situation. One approach is to measure each act against certain absolute standards. In our culture, these standards are generally derived from Judeo-Christian teachings: "Thou shalt not lie"; "Thou shalt not steal"; "Thou shalt not bear false witness against thy neighbor"; "Do unto others as you would have them do unto you." These principles provide the foundation for the laws and regulations of our society.

But rules have their limitations. Some situations defy clear-cut distinctions. In such situations, three other philosophical approaches are useful in identifying the "right" course of action: utilitarianism, individual rights, and justice.[5]

Utilitarianism

utilitarianism Philosophy used in making ethical decisions that aims to achieve the greatest good for the greatest number

According to the concept of **utilitarianism,** the "right" decision is the one that produces the greatest good for the greatest number of people. If you were a manager using this approach, you would try to figure out the impact of all the alternative actions on everyone concerned and then choose the alternative that created the most satisfaction for the most people. You would reject alternatives that catered to narrow interests or that failed to satisfy the needs of the majority. The value of this approach would depend on your skill in estimating the effect of your decisions. The challenge would lie in coming up with a decision that would benefit the most people.

Individual Rights

individual rights Philosophy used in making ethical decisions that aims to protect human dignity

Another approach is to be guided by a belief in the importance of **individual rights.** Because a belief in another person's rights implies that you have a duty to protect those rights, you would reject any decision that violated these rights. For example, you would not deceive people or trick them into acting against their own interests. You would respect their privacy and their right to express their opinion openly. You would not force people to act in a way that was contrary to their religious or moral beliefs. And you would not punish a person without a fair and impartial hearing. Although you might be guided by a desire to achieve the greatest good for the greatest number of people, you would reject any choice that violated the rights of even one person. In an era when individual workers expect and demand their rights, this philosophy is becoming a practical necessity. In dealing with issues related to AIDS or drug testing, for example, companies are trying to honor the individual's right to privacy without jeopardizing the group's rights to a safe working environment. In the last few years, in fact, the concept of individual human rights has been broadened to encompass the protection of plants, animals, land, water, air, and other natural elements of the environment.

FOCUS ON ETHICS

How Do Your Ethics Measure Up?

The solutions to many day-to-day questions in business are not simply right or wrong. Rather, they fall into a gray area. To demonstrate the perplexing array of moral dilemmas faced by businesspeople, here is a "nonscientific" test. Give it a try, and see how you score. In the space to the right of each statement, mark 0 if you strongly disagree, 1 if you disagree, 2 if you agree, and 3 if you strongly agree.

1. It's okay to withhold negative information about a product in order to make a big sale as long as the negative aspect isn't dangerous or life-threatening. _____

2. There are times when a manager must overlook contract and safety violations in order to get on with the job. _____

3. It is not always possible to keep accurate expense records. Therefore, it is sometimes necessary to give approximate figures. _____

4. There are times when it is necessary to withhold embarrassing information from the boss. _____

5. We should do what our managers suggest, even though we may have doubts about its being the right thing to do. _____

6. It is sometimes necessary to conduct personal business on company time. _____

7. Taking a friend to lunch and charging it to the company as a business expense is acceptable as long as the bill is reasonable and doing so doesn't become a regular habit. _____

8. I would quote a "hopeful" shipping date to get an order. _____

9. It is proper to use the company WATS line for personal calls as long as it's not being used for company business. _____

10. Management must be goal-oriented. Therefore, the end usually justifies the means. _____

11. If providing heavy entertainment and twisting company policy a bit would win a large contract, I would authorize it. _____

12. Exceptions to company policy and procedures are a way of life. _____

13. Inventory controls should be designed to report "underages" rather than "overages" in goods received. _____

14. Occasional use of the company's photocopying machine for personal or community activities is acceptable. _____

15. Taking home company property (pencils, paper, tape, and the like) for personal use is an accepted fringe benefit. _____

If your total score is:

0	Possible saint
1–5	Bishop material
6–10	High ethical values
11–15	Good ethical values
16–25	Average ethical values
26–35	Deficient ethical development
36–44	In trouble
45	Possible jailbird

Justice

justice Philosophy used in making ethical decisions that aims to ensure the equal distribution of burdens and benefits

In making your decisions, you might also apply criteria based on the principles of **justice**. These principles include a belief that people should be treated equally, that rules should be applied consistently, and that people who harm others should be held responsible and make restitution. A just decision, then, is one that is fair, impartial, and reasonable in light of the rules that apply to the situation.

These three approaches are not mutually exclusive alternatives. On the contrary, most people combine them to reach decisions that will satisfy as many people as possible without violating any person's rights or treating anyone unjustly. In applying these philosophical principles, companies must balance the needs of the various groups that have a stake in our economic system: the community and its environment, consumers, workers, and investors.

▶ BUSINESS AND THE ENVIRONMENT

The difficulty of this balancing act becomes apparent when you consider the case of Bofors Nobel, a manufacturer of paint pigments. The company disposed of the wastes from the manufacturing process on 68 wooded acres behind its plant in Muskegon, Michigan. When the government ordered the firm to clean up the site, the estimated cost came to $60 million. With annual sales of only $30 million, Bofors opted to close its doors.[6] Now the company is out of business, its customers are scrambling to line up new sources of pigment, the employees are out of work, and the toxic waste remains. In a situation like this, there are no winners.

The Pervasiveness of Pollution

pollution Threats to the physical environment caused by human activities in an industrial society

Toxic wastes are not the only form of **pollution** threatening our environment. Our air, our water, and our land are all paying dearly for our economic progress.

Air Pollution

As a resident of the United States, the chances are two out of three that you breathe air that fails to meet the standards of the Environmental Protection Agency (EPA).[7] How bad is this air? Bad enough to cause 50,000 premature deaths each year; bad enough to add an extra $10 billion to $25 billion annually to the nation's health-care bills.[8] Potentially bad enough to jeopardize the ecosystem and make the earth uninhabitable.

On a day-to-day basis, the most noticeable form of air pollution is probably smog, which is produced by the interaction of sunlight and hydrocarbons (gases released when fossil fuels are burned). On especially smoggy days, your eyes burn, your throat feels sore, and if you suffer from a respiratory disease, your activities are restricted.

Another sort of air pollutant is rain that has a high acid content, created when nitrous oxides and gaseous sulfur dioxide react with air. This "acid rain" has been blamed for damaging lakes and forests in southeastern Canada and the northeastern United States. Most of the harmful emissions come from coal-burning factories and electric utility plants.

Apart from contributing to acid rain, coal emissions have another disadvantage: They may contribute to a "greenhouse effect." The heated gases form a layer of unusually warm air around the earth, which traps the sun's heat and prevents the earth's surface from cooling. Some scientists believe that the greenhouse effect will eventually cause dramatic changes in the earth's climate, including a general increase in temperature, changes in rainfall, and a rise in the level of the oceans.

Another long-term threat of unknown proportions is the depletion of the earth's protective ozone layer caused by chlorofluorocarbons (CFCs), which are used as industrial cleansers, refrigerants, and ingredients in insulation and foam packaging. Scientists fear that if the ozone layer continues to deteriorate, the effects of the sun's rays will be magnified, increasing the incidence of a deadly form of skin cancer.

An air-pollution problem with more immediate health implications is posed by the airborne toxins that are emitted into the atmosphere during some manufacturing processes. Large corporations release some 2.7 billion pounds of these chemical wastes into the air each year, and small companies probably add a good deal more.[9] Although the effects of many of these substances are unknown, some are clearly carcinogens (cancer-causing agents).

Water Pollution

Our air is not the only part of our environment to suffer. Approximately 10 percent of our river and lake water is polluted.[10] In some areas, the harbors and coastal waters are in trouble as well. This pollution comes from a variety of sources: manufacturing facilities, mining and construction sites, farms, and city sewage systems. Although dramatic accidents like the *Exxon Valdez* oil spill in Alaskan waters capture our attention, the main threat is the careless day-to-day disposal of wastes from thousands of individual sources.

Land Pollution

Even if all wastewater were purified before being discharged, our groundwater would still be endangered by leakage from the millions of tons of hazardous substances that have been buried in the ground or dumped in inadequate storage sites. The cost for cleaning up U.S. toxic waste sites could eventually exceed $500 billion.[11] Many of these sites were created years ago by companies that carelessly—but legally—disposed of substances that are now known to cause cancer and other illnesses. Although some experts believe that 90 percent of these sites pose little health risk, the fact remains that nobody knows for sure just how dangerous they are. What is certain is that they are extremely difficult to clean up.

Government and Industry Response

Today an overwhelming majority of people in the United States consider themselves environmentalists. In fact, by a ratio of six to one, they want to reduce pollution even if it means paying higher prices.[12] Politicians and business executives are well aware of this fact, and they're responding accordingly.

Concern for the environment has gradually increased since the 1960s, when **ecology,** or the balance of nature, became a popular cause. In 1963 federal,

Business Around the World

In countries such as Egypt, the World Health Organization is investigating the spread of a debilitating disease through stagnant irrigation canals. Although the irrigation systems were built to increase agricultural production, the disease has cut worker output by as much as 35 percent.

ecology *Relationship among living things in the water, air, and soil, as well as the nutrients that support them*

state, and local governments began to enact laws and regulations aimed at reducing pollution. (A brief summary of major federal legislation appears in Exhibit 4.2.) But the bedrock legislation underlying federal efforts to control pollution is the National Environmental Policy Act of 1969, which established a structure for coordinating all federal environmental programs. This act was followed by a presidential order in December 1970, which established the Environ-

EXHIBIT 4.2 ▶ Major Federal Environmental Legislation

LEGISLATION	DATE	EFFECT
National Environmental Policy Act	1969	Established a structure for coordinating all federal environmental programs.
Order of Administrative Reorganization	1970	Established Council on Environmental Quality to advise president on environmental policy and to review environmental impact statements. Led to formation of Environmental Protection Agency and consolidation of federal activities under it.
AIR POLLUTION		
Clean Air Act	1963	Authorized assistance to state and local governments in formulating control programs. Authorized limited federal action in correcting specific pollution problems.
Clean Air Act amendments (Motor Vehicle Air Pollution Control Act)	1965	Authorized federal standards for auto-exhaust emissions. Set standards for 1968 models and thereafter.
Air Quality Act	1967	Authorized federal government to establish air-quality control regions and to set maximum permissible pollution levels. Required states and localities to carry out approved control programs or else give way to federal controls.
Clean Air Act amendments	1970	Authorized EPA to establish nationwide air-pollution standards and to limit the discharge of six principal pollutants into the lower atmosphere. Authorized citizens to take legal action to require EPA to implement its standards against undiscovered offenders.
Clean Air Act amendments	1977	Postponed auto-emission requirements. Required use of scrubbers in new coal-fired power plants. Directed EPA to establish system to prevent deterioration of air quality in clean areas.
Clean Air Act amendments	1990	Established schedule and standards for cutting smog, acid rain, hazardous factory fumes, and ozone-depleting chemicals.
SOLID-WASTE POLLUTION		
Solid Waste Disposal Act	1965	Authorized research and assistance to state and local control programs.
Resource Recovery Act	1970	Subsidized construction of pilot recycling plants; authorized development of nationwide control programs.
Resource Conservation and Recovery Act	1976	Directed the EPA to regulate hazardous-waste management, from generation through disposal.
Surface Mining and Reclamation Act	1976	Controlled strip mining and restoration of reclaimed land.
Resource Conservation and Recovery Act amendments	1984	Amended Solid Waste Disposal Act. Provided technical and financial assistance for recovery of energy and other resources from solid waste; regulated treatment, storage, transportation, and disposal of hazardous waste.

mental Protection Agency (EPA) to regulate air and water pollution by manufacturers and utilities, supervise auto-pollution control, license pesticides, control toxic substances, and safeguard the purity of drinking water.

The EPA's effectiveness has waxed and waned over the past 20 years, depending on who's in power in Washington, D.C. After slipping in influence during the Reagan years, the agency has regained some ground under the Bush administra-

LEGISLATION	DATE	EFFECT
WATER POLLUTION		
Refuse Act	1899	Prohibited dumping of debris into navigable waters without a permit. Extended by court decision to industrial discharges.
Federal Water Pollution Control Act	1956	Authorized grants to states for water-pollution control. Gave federal government limited authority to correct specific pollution problems.
Water Quality Act	1965	Provided for adoption of water-quality standards by states, subject to federal approval.
Water Quality Improvement Act	1970	Provided for federal cleanup of oil spills. Strengthened federal authority over water-pollution control.
Federal Water Pollution Control Act amendments	1972	Authorized EPA to set water-quality and effluent standards; provided for enforcement and research.
Safe Drinking Water Act	1974	Set standards for drinking-water quality.
Clean Water Act	1977	Ordered control of toxic pollutants by 1984 with best available technology that is economically feasible.
Water Quality Act	1987	Extended the current program of grants for sewage-treatment projects. Required states to develop and implement programs to control "nonpoint" sources of pollution (rainfall runoff from farm and urban areas, forestry, and mining sites).
OTHER POLLUTANTS		
Federal Insecticide, Fungicide and Rodenticide Act	1947	To protect farmers, prohibited fraudulent claims by salespersons. Required registration of poisonous products.
Federal Insecticide, Fungicide and Rodenticide Act amendments	1967, 1972	Provided new authority to license users of pesticides.
Pesticide Control Act	1972	Required all pesticides shipped in interstate commerce to be certified as effective for their stated purposes and harmless to crops, animal feed, animal life, and humans.
Noise Control Act	1972	Required EPA to set noise standards for major sources of noise and to advise Federal Aviation Administration on standards for airplane noise.
Pesticide Control Act amendments	1975	Set 1977 deadline (not met) for registration, classification, and licensing of many pesticides.
Toxic Substances Control Act	1976	Required testing of chemicals; authorized EPA to restrict the use of harmful substances.
Comprehensive Environmental Response, Compensation, and Liability Act	1980	Commonly called "Superfund Act"; created a trust fund (paid for in part by toxic-chemical manufacturers) to clean up hazardous-waste sites.
Superfund Amendments and Reauthorization Act	1986	Established schedules for clean-up and preferences for types of clean-up actions.

tion. Its current efforts are based on the premise that more will be accomplished by working with business to clean up and prevent pollution than by taking an adversarial stance. To an increasing degree, the EPA is moving away from a command/control posture toward a free-market approach, which emphasizes incentives for doing the right thing as well as punishment for doing the wrong thing. For example, in certain cities companies can buy and sell pollution rights. Each company is given an allowable "pollution quota" based on such factors as its size and industry. If a company voluntarily reduces pollution below its limit, it can sell its "credits" to another company. Although granting companies the right to pollute might seem counterproductive, it encourages them to clean up their operations as quickly and as thoroughly as possible. Ultimately, a national or even a global market could exist for trading pollution credits.[13]

The current approach to pollution control recognizes that the health threat posed by a given industrial pollutant must be weighed against the economic cost of limiting or eliminating its use. Many activities that cause pollution also produce socially desirable results. The waste dumps, factories, power plants, and pesticides that threaten the environment almost always meet a legitimate social need. Long-term solutions lie in giving business the motive and opportunity to find alternative ways to meet those needs.

One of the most promising new directions is emphasizing prevention as opposed to correction. Pioneering companies are reducing the flow of pollutants into the environment—and lowering their cleanup bills—by using alternative materials, changing production techniques, redesigning products, and recycling wastes. Since 1975, 3M has launched 2,500 projects aimed at reducing pollution. Far from costing the company money, these projects have actually saved $1 billion.[14]

Progress Toward Cleaner Air

The one good thing you can say about air quality in the United States is that it could be a lot worse. In the past 20 years, some modest progress has been made toward cleaner air, thanks to government standards and industry's efforts to comply. Companies are currently spending some $35 million per year to combat air pollution.[15] Cars account for 40 percent of our smog problem and are 96 percent cleaner than they were prior to 1970.[16] Factory emissions that contribute to smog and acid rain have declined. An agreement among 24 nations to limit the production of chlorofluorocarbons should help reduce the threat to the ozone layer. The fight against toxic chemical emissions is getting a boost from the passage of the Emergency Planning and Community Right-to-Know Act, which requires businesses to report the amount of toxic chemicals they release into the air, land, and water.

Preparing this information has been an eye-opener for many companies. When Richard Mahoney, chairman of Monsanto, saw how much toxic waste the company was generating, he was flabbergasted. He decreed that Monsanto would voluntarily cut toxic emissions by 90 percent. In the process of meeting that goal, Monsanto—like many other large companies—has discovered ways to save money and clean up the environment simultaneously by improving production processes and by recycling chemicals that used to pose a disposal problem. For example, one of the company's nylon fiber plants has cut its toxic air emissions by 90 percent since 1987 by capturing a toxic solvent in a mineral oil bath before it goes up the smokestack. Recycling the solvent saves the company several million dollars a year in raw material costs.[17]

In 1990 Congress passed a series of tough new amendments to the 1970 Clean Air Act. The sweeping measure calls for cuts in smog, acid rain, toxic emissions, and ozone-depleting chemicals. Businesses are required to phase in improvements through the year 2005. The legislation differs from previous laws in several important respects that should contribute to its effectiveness. For one thing, it applies to small companies as well as large ones. Believe it or not, local dry cleaners, bakeries, and other seemingly innocent businesses are a significant source of air pollution. Another important aspect of the new law is that instead of requiring companies to reduce pollution to virtually zero, it requires them to achieve whatever level of purity can be attained using the best technology available. This provision puts an end to a controversy over the meaning of "negligible health risk" that has tied up the implementation of previous laws.

Experts project that by the year 2005, the new law should knock out 75 to 90 percent of the pollutants being released into the air.[18] However, progress has a price. The cost to industry may run as high as $25 billion per year by early in the next century. Opponents of the measure contend that profits and jobs will be lost and that the economy as a whole will suffer. On the other hand, given the circular flow of money, one company's expenditures become another company's revenues, so the net economic effect may not be all that severe.[19]

The Battle for Cleaner Water

Since the passage of the Water Quality Act of 1965, the federal government has invested over $50 billion in the fight against water pollution, while state and local governments have contributed at least half again as much. Much of this money has been used to upgrade sewage systems, which handle wastes from homes and businesses alike. These improvements have gone a long way toward cleaning up harbors, lakes, and rivers that formerly served as cheap dumping grounds for raw sewage. One notable exception is the ocean off Cape May, New Jersey, which serves as the disposal site for sludge from both New York City and New Jersey.[20]

Industry has also made a major investment in treating wastewater. Factories that used to dump toxic chemicals into nearby waterways are discouraged from doing so by the National Pollutant Discharge Elimination System, which requires any company that pumps fluid into a river or lake to obtain a permit. However, even though this system has effectively stopped "point-source" pollution from industry, it does nothing to control nonpoint pollution—the runoff from farms and streets that accounts for 65 percent of the stream pollution in the United States.[21]

The War on Toxic Waste

For years, many industrial wastes were routinely dumped in landfills, whose protective barriers (if any) could not be counted on to prevent dangerous chemicals from leaking into the soil and eventually into the water supply. In 1980 Congress established the so-called Superfund to clean up the 1,189 most hazardous of these old dumps. The initial fund, financed by a special tax on chemical manufacturers, has received several additional transfusions of taxpayer money, bringing total government funding so far to $15.2 billion. When a site is targeted for cleanup, the EPA encourages the parties responsible for the pollution to pay the bill. If an agreement can't be reached up front, the cleanup is paid for out of the Superfund, and the EPA then tries to recover the costs by suing the compa-

Before you blame business for all of our environmental problems, consider that the average person in the United States discards 1,300 pounds of garbage a year. We are rapidly running out of places (like this dump in Phoenix, Arizona) to discard our trash. The answer to the solid-waste problem is not figuring out how to burn it or compact it; the answer is to reduce it.

nies most responsible for the environmental damage. These companies, in turn, may sue other parties that were involved in owning, operating, or sending wastes to the site. All too often, the effort to parcel out the burden of responsibility leads to lawsuits among hundreds of companies, tying up the cleanup effort for years. Companies generally end up paying about 60 percent of the cleanup costs, and the government pays the rest. Each site costs an average of $30 million to restore.[22]

Results to date have been discouraging. It's taken over 10 years to remove 60 sites from the Superfund list. There's a question, however, about whether the groundwater in some sites can ever be restored to drinking-water purity—the standard imposed by a 1986 amendment to the Superfund law. Some 19 locations that improved after initial treatment have subsequently reverted to a contaminated state. A more practical approach, some argue, would simply be to contain the damage, since only 11 percent of the sites pose a potential health threat to residents in a finite area.[23]

Although old sites will be a continuing problem far into the future, industry is making progress in reducing new hazardous-waste contamination. For one thing, more companies are now dumping wastes in their own controlled and environmentally sound sites, and fewer are leaving their wastes to independent disposal firms, which are notorious for illegal dumping. In addition, manufacturers are trying out several other methods of eliminating or neutralizing their hazardous by-products. Some use high-temperature incineration, some recycle wastes, some give their wastes to other companies that can use them (sometimes getting in return wastes *they* can use), some neutralize wastes biologically, and some have redesigned their manufacturing processes so that they don't produce the wastes in the first place.

▶ BUSINESS AND CONSUMERS

The activism of the 1960s that awakened business to its environmental responsibilities also made companies more sensitive to consumers. Crusaders such as Ralph Nader, author of *Unsafe at Any Speed,* shocked the public with exposés about poorly designed, unsafe, and unhealthful products. In response to the consumer movement, a number of businesses created their own consumer-affairs departments to handle customer complaints, and state and local agencies set up bureaus to provide consumer information and assistance. At the federal level, President John F. Kennedy announced a new "bill of rights" for consumers, which laid the foundation for a wave of consumer-oriented legislation (see Exhibit 4.3 on pages 102–103). These rights include the right to safety, the right to be informed, the right to choose, and the right to be heard.

The Right to Safety

The federal government imposes many safety standards, which are enforced primarily by the Consumer Product Safety Commission (CPSC), an agency created in 1972 to monitor the safety of some 15,000 products sold to consumers. Standards for some products, such as automobiles, drugs, foods, and medical devices, are established and monitored by special agencies. In addition, state and local agencies have regulations of their own.

Theoretically, companies that fail to comply with these rules are forced to take corrective action. However, many consumer advocates complain that a wide array of unsafe products slip through the cracks because the various regulatory agencies lack the resources to do an effective job. Roger Burrows is the lone CPSC inspector in San Diego, California, one of the 10 largest cities in the country. Burrows not only investigates all complaints received by the local CPSC office but also does spot checks to be sure the city's 27,000 retailers are selling safe products. His investigations of accidents involving all-terrain vehicles and lawn darts were instrumental in the nationwide banning of those two products.[24]

But even without government action, manufacturers are motivated to meet safety standards by the threat of product liability suits and declining sales. A poor safety record can do grave damage to a company's reputation. Consider the case of the Audi 5000 sedan, which reportedly is prone to sudden, violent acceleration when the transmission is put into drive. After a report on the problem was aired on "60 Minutes," Audi's sales plunged, declining by almost half in two years. Although Audi initially blamed the problem on inept drivers, it was ultimately forced to recall the car and modify the transmission. The firm has discontinued the Audi 5000 and is introducing new models, but according to industry experts, "It'll take five years to repair the damage" to Audi's reputation.[25]

The Right to Be Informed

One possible way to protect the safety of consumers is to explain any product risks on the label. If the danger is great enough, a warning label is required by law, as in the case of cigarettes. But warning labels can be a mixed blessing for consumers. To some extent, the presence of a warning protects the manufacturer from product-liability suits, but the label may do little to deter people from using the product. The warning labels on toys are a case in point. Every year, roughly 12,000 children are seriously injured by toys, many of which are clearly labeled "Not recommended for children under three years of age."[26]

Regardless of whether a product is harmful, however, consumers have a right to know what is in it and how to use it. At the same time, they have a right to know the costs of goods or services and the details of any purchase contracts. Over the years, the government has created a variety of rules and regulations that prevent companies from making false or misleading claims about the ingredients, features, or prices of their products and services.

During most of the last decade, the agencies responsible for labeling (the Food and Drug Administration, the Federal Trade Commission, and the Agriculture Department) were squarely aligned with the supporters of deregulation. But the laissez-faire policies of the recent past are fading. The Nutritional Education and Labeling Act of 1990 is now the basis for reregulating food labeling: The Surgeon General's office is leading an interagency task force to revamp the warning labels on alcohol, the FDA is cracking down on the food industry's use of false or misleading claims on labels, the FTC is investigating the unsupportable claims made by liquid-diet manufacturers, and the Agriculture Department is working on new labels for meat and poultry.

These agencies are concerned not only with safety but also with accurate information. For example, the FDA is seeking consistency in serving sizes (so that consumers can compare equal quantities), it's clarifying label language (so that consumers will know what terms such as *light* and *ultralight* really mean), and it's investigating the accuracy of health claims (so that consumers can identify which products are truly good for them). The FDA has made a few high-profile assaults on companies that were making misleading claims. For example, it seized shipments of Procter & Gamble's Citrus Hill Fresh *(continued on p. 104)*

This display of fruit and vegetables at Norman's in Miami looks healthful, doesn't it? But before you bite into any of the fruit, you might ask where it comes from. Of the 30 billion pounds of food imported into the United States each year—fresh, canned, packaged, or frozen—only 2 percent is tested by the FDA for bacteria and other impurities. Of the products tested, 40 percent fail to meet FDA standards.

EXHIBIT 4.3 ▶ **Major Federal Consumer Legislation**

LEGISLATION	DATE	EFFECT
FOOD AND DRUGS		
Food and Drugs Act	1906	Forbade adulteration and misbranding of food/drugs in interstate commerce.
Meat Inspection Act	1906	Authorized Department of Agriculture to inspect slaughtering, packing, and canning plants.
Federal Food, Drug, and Cosmetic Act	1938	Added cosmetics and therapeutic products to Food and Drug Administration's jurisdiction. Broadened definition of misbranding to include "false and misleading" labeling.
Delaney Amendment to the Food, Drug, and Cosmetic Act	1958	Prohibited use as food additive of any chemical found to induce cancer.
Kefauver-Harris Drug Amendments to Food and Drug Act	1962	Required manufacturer to test safety and effectiveness of drugs before marketing them and to include common or generic name of drug on label.
Wholesome Meat Act	1967	Strengthened standards for inspection of slaughterhouses of red-meat animals.
Orphan Drug Act	1983	Established incentives (such as tax credits, grants, and contract support) and granted exclusive marketing rights to promote the development of drugs for rare diseases and conditions.
Drug Price Competition/Patent Term Restoration Act	1984	Established abbreviated application procedure for generic versions of "pioneer" drugs; eliminated requirement for expensive retesting of generic equivalents of brand-name drugs developed after 1962.
Amendment to Orphan Drug Act	1985	Extended federal incentives to promote the development of drugs for rare diseases and conditions.
Nutrition Education and Labeling Act	1990	Required specific, uniform labels detailing nutritional information such as caloric levels, fat content, and cholesterol amounts in food items to be included on product labels; prohibited manufacturers from making certain nutritional claims about their products on the label when other equally important information (such as cholesterol level) has not been mentioned.
Pesticide Safety Improvement Act	1990	Required continuous updating of information on safety of pesticides, established user training, and set new registration standards.
Food, Agriculture, Conservation, and Trade Act	1990	Prevented the export of pesticides banned for use in the United States (to abolish U.S. pesticides showing up in food imported for U.S. consumption).
MISBRANDING AND FALSE OR HARMFUL ADVERTISING		
Wheeler–Lea Act	1938	Enlarged Federal Trade Commission's powers to cover deceptive practices in commerce and false advertising of foods, drugs, and cosmetics.
Wool Products Labeling Act	1939	Required fabric labeling (percentage of fabric components, manufacturer's name).
Fur Products Labeling Act	1951	Required that fur labels name animals of origin.
Textile Fiber Products Identification Act	1958	Prohibited misbranding and false advertising of fiber products not covered in the wool or fur labeling acts.

LEGISLATION	DATE	EFFECT
MISBRANDING AND FALSE OR HARMFUL ADVERTISING		
Federal Hazardous Substances Act	1960	Required warning labels to appear on items containing dangerous household chemicals.
Fair Packaging and Labeling Act	1966	Required honest, informative package labeling. In 1972, added requirement that labels show origin of product, quantity of contents, representation of servings, uses and/or applications.
Public Health Cigarette Smoking Act	1970	Banned cigarette advertising on radio and TV; strengthened required warning on packaging.
Country of Origin Labeling Act	1985	Required all items of clothing to carry a label indicating the country of origin.
PRODUCT SAFETY		
Flammable Fabrics Act	1953	Prohibited interstate shipment of apparel or fabric made of dangerously flammable materials.
Traffic and Motor Vehicle Safety Act	1966	Required manufacturers to notify purchasers of new cars of safety defects discovered after manufacture and delivery.
Child Protection and Toy Safety Act	1969	Provided greater protection from children's toys with dangerous mechanical or electrical hazards.
Poison Prevention Packaging Act	1970	Required manufacturers to use safety packaging on products that may be harmful to children.
Consumer Product Safety Act	1972	Created Consumer Product Safety Commission, an independent federal agency, and empowered it to set safety standards for certain products, such as power lawn mowers and children's toys; to require warning labels on unsafe products; and to order recalls of hazardous products.
CREDIT PROTECTION		
Truth-in-Lending Act (Consumer Protection Credit Act)	1968	Required creditors to inform individuals obtaining credit of the amount of the finance charge and the percentage rate of interest charged annually. Limited credit card holders' liability in unauthorized use.
Fair Credit Reporting Act	1970	Required agencies reporting consumer credit data to follow procedures assuring accuracy of their information. Required users of this information, upon withholding credit, to inform consumer of source of this information.
Magnuson-Moss Warranty Act	1975	Required all warranties to be written in ordinary language, to contain all terms and conditions of the warranty, and to be made available prior to purchase to facilitate comparison shopping.
Home Mortgage Disclosure Act	1975	Required banks and savings and loan associations to compile and make public information on mortgage loans that they make and the locations of those loans.
Fair Debt Collection Practices Act	1978	Prohibited deceptive and unfair debt-collection practices: calling at inconvenient or unusual times; harassing, oppressing, or abusing any person; making false statements when collecting debts.

orange juice, arguing that "fresh" is a misnomer for a product made from concentrate. It is also cracking down on the use of such claims as "low in cholesterol," "light," and "high in fiber."[27]

The Right to Choose

Business responds very well to the right to choose: The number of products available to consumers is truly amazing. But how far should this right extend? Are we entitled to choose products that are harmful—cigarettes and liquor, for example? Or sugar-coated cereal? Or rock music with suggestive lyrics? And to what extent are we entitled to learn about these products? Should beer and wine ads be eliminated from TV, as ads for other types of alcoholic beverages have been? Should advertising aimed at children be banned?

These are some of the issues that consumer groups are concerned about. No clear answers have been found. Generally speaking, however, business is sensitive to these issues. Recent public concern about drunk driving, for example, has led the liquor industry to encourage responsible drinking. Similarly, the movie industry has instituted a rating system to help the public gauge whether a film is appropriate for a particular audience. Like those in the liquor and movie industries, most U.S. businesspeople would rather help consumers make informed choices than be told what choices they can offer.

The Right to Be Heard

A final consumer right is the right to be heard. Here again, most businesses are extremely responsive. Over half of all companies with sales of over $10 million have toll-free consumer information numbers.[28] Most actively encourage feedback from customers, because this information helps the business correct past mistakes and make informed decisions about offering new products and services.

Consumers can often make their points more forcefully by working through advocacy groups such as the Consumer Federation of America, the National Consumers League, Mothers Against Drunk Driving, and the American Association of Retired Persons. These organizations, and hundreds of others that represent special interests, have the resources to lobby lawmakers and influence public opinion. They can also put pressure directly on businesses by staging demonstrations or boycotts.

▶ BUSINESS AND WORKERS

Over the past 20 years, dramatic changes have occurred in the attitudes and composition of the work force. These changes have forced businesses to modify their recruiting, training, and promotion practices.

The Push for Equality in Employment

discrimination In a social and economic sense, denial of opportunities to individuals on the basis of some characteristic that has no bearing on the ability of these persons to perform

minorities In a social and economic sense, categories of people that society at large singles out for discriminatory, selective, or unfavorable treatment

The United States has always espoused economic freedom and individual rights to pursue opportunity. Unfortunately, until the past few decades, many people in the United States were targets of economic **discrimination**, relegated to low-paying, menial jobs and prevented from taking advantage of many opportunities based solely on their ethnic background, race, gender, age, disability, religion, or other irrelevant characteristics.

The burden of discrimination has fallen on **minorities**, such outnumbered and easily distinguishable groups as African-Americans, Hispanics, Asian-

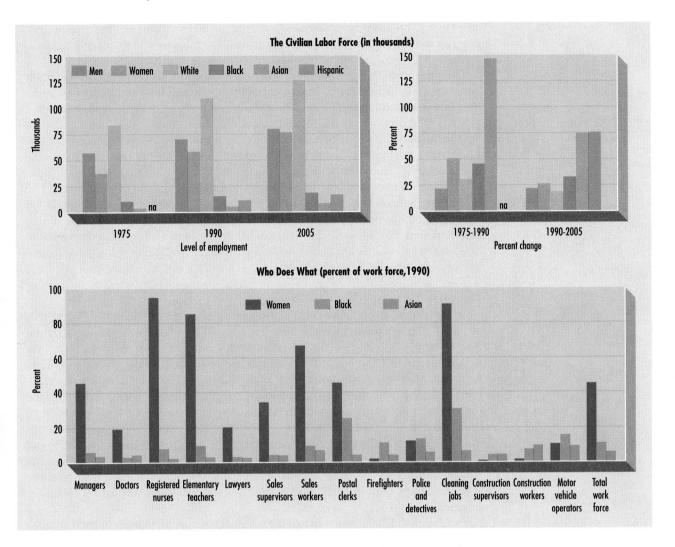

Americans, people with disabilities, and people who are elderly. In a social or economic sense, women are a minority as well. Even though they outnumber men in our society, women have also traditionally suffered economic discrimination.

Job discrimination, in particular, has been a "vicious cycle." Because they could not hope for better jobs, many minority-group members have had little incentive to seek an education. And because they have not been adequately educated, many have not been able to qualify for those jobs that might have been available to them. Exhibit 4.4 shows how discrimination has affected the job opportunities of key minorities.

Discrimination runs counter to the American ideal of equal opportunity for all. So when women, African-Americans, Hispanics, and other minorities have pressed for fair treatment, society has responded.

Government Action

Several branches of the federal government are instrumental in shaping the country's position on civil rights. Congress, the executive branch, and the courts

EXHIBIT 4.4

How Discrimination Has Affected Employment of Minorities

Discrimination has resulted in continuing low levels of employment for minorities and has narrowed their choice of career.

all play a vital role. In addition, state and local governments have their own programs and policies for helping minorities. As the composition of these groups changes, the government's policies on civil rights shift.

Over the past 25 years, there has been a constant tension in the government between those who want to create special programs to help minorities move up the economic ladder and those who prefer to minimize the government's intervention. The proponents of **affirmative action** believe that equal opportunity can best be achieved if disadvantaged groups are temporarily given special benefits. They argue that minorities deserve and require preferential treatment to make up for years of discrimination.

The opponents of government intervention believe that individuals should be judged on their own merits, regardless of race, sex, religion, or age. They argue that creating special opportunities for women and minorities creates a double standard that infringes on the rights of other workers and forces companies to hire, promote, and retain people who are not necessarily the best choice from a business standpoint. These affirmative-action opponents believe that the best way to help the disadvantaged is to promote economic growth, since "a rising tide carries all ships."

In the 1960s, strong advocates of affirmative action were in office. During this period, Congress passed the Civil Rights Act of 1964, which forbids discrimination in employment. The act established the Equal Employment Opportunity Commission (EEOC), a regulatory agency whose aim is to help bring minority-group members into the mainstream of the economy by countering job discrimination. Also during this period, President Lyndon Johnson issued a presidential order requiring all private companies that do business with the government to develop affirmative-action programs for hiring and promoting women and minorities. The EEOC was given responsibility for monitoring these programs and for investigating complaints of job-related discrimination. The EEOC has the power to file legal charges against companies that discriminate and to force them to compensate individuals or groups who have been victimized by unfair practices.

During the 1980s and early 1990s, the balance of power in government shifted to a more conservative group. Working through the Department of Justice, the Reagan administration, with its "less is more" philosophy, backed off the pursuit of civil rights violations. Perhaps the most important shift occurred with the gradual replacement of members of the Supreme Court. In a 10-year period, four relatively liberal justices were replaced by four conservatives. With the resignation of Thurgood Marshall and the confirmation of Clarence Thomas in 1991, the trend away from liberal support for civil rights is likely to continue.

The impact of this change in the composition of the Supreme Court became apparent in 1989 when six cases in three weeks sharply narrowed workers' ability to win race-, sex-, and age-discrimination suits (Exhibit 4.5). In the wake of these rulings, Congress tried in both 1990 and 1991 to pass a new civil rights bill that would reverse some of the effects of those decisions. In 1991 President Bush accepted the Civil Rights Act of 1991, which makes it easier for workers to sue for discrimination and gives women new legal tools against bias in the workplace.

Although points of disagreement remain about how far affirmative action should go, there is broad consensus on the basic concepts. Here is a brief summary of what employers can and cannot do:

affirmative action *Activities undertaken by businesses to recruit and promote minorities, based on an analysis of the work force and the available labor pool*

Voluntary affirmative action. Companies can adopt voluntary programs to hire and promote qualified women and minorities to correct an imbalance in their work force, even if there is no evidence of past discrimination.

Mandatory affirmative action. The federal courts can impose mandatory affirmative-action plans in cases where employers have clearly discriminated against women and minorities and have refused to take corrective action.

EXHIBIT 4.5 ▶ Supreme Court Rulings on Affirmative Action

YEAR	RULING
1978	**University of California Regents** v. **Bakke** Court strikes down (5–4) medical-school admissions plan that favored minorities, but upholds (5–4) race as one factor in admissions.
1979	**Steelworkers** v. **Weber** Court upholds (5–2) a voluntary affirmative-action plan for crafts training at Kaiser Aluminum & Chemical plants.
1980	**Fullilove** v. **Klutznick** Court upholds (6–3) Congress's decision to set aside a portion of public-works funds for minority businesses.
1984	**Memphis Firefighters** v. **Stotts** Court (6–3) limits judges' power to approve layoffs that disregard seniority and permit employees with less tenure to remain on the job.
1986	**Wygant** v. **Jackson Board of Education** Court rules (5–4) that the Constitution bars Jackson, Michigan, from laying off white teachers with more seniority than blacks who remain at work.
	Local 93 v. **City of Cleveland** Court approves (6–3) a plan of promotions for firefighters using a 1:1 ratio to increase the number of minorities in upper-level jobs.
	Local 28 v. **EEOC** Court rules (5–4) that a federal court properly set a goal of 29 percent minority membership in a Sheet Metal Workers local and made the union pay for training.
1987	**U.S.** v. **Paradise** The Court (5–4) upholds a 1:1 ratio for promoting black state troopers in Alabama, saying the Constitution doesn't prohibit this corrective action.
	Johnson v. **Transportation Agency** Court rules (6–3) that public employers, as well as private, may voluntarily implement affirmative action to correct sex discrimination.
1989	**Richmond** v. **Croson** Court votes (6–3) to strike down Richmond, Virginia, law requiring 30 percent of all city building contracts to go to minority companies.
	Wards Cove v. **Antonio** Court sets new standards (5–4) for suits challenging hiring or promotion practices that appear fair but that have a "disparate impact," resulting in proportionately more whites than minorities. Plaintiffs must specifically identify practices that have disparate impact and must prove that employer has no business need for the practice.
	Martin v. **Wilks** Court rules (5–4) that because some white firefighters in Birmingham, Alabama, had not been involved in two earlier suits charging discrimination, they had a right to sue over hiring and promotion policies.
	Patterson v. **McClean Credit Union** Court finds (5–4) that the right to sue for damages for racial job discrimination applies only to hiring, not to on-the-job harassment or other forms of bias after someone is hired.
	Lorance v. **AT&T Technologies** Court rules (6–3) that the statute of limitations for challenging a discriminatory seniority plan begins when the plan is adopted, not when the plan is applied to harm the plaintiff.
	Price Waterhouse v. **Hopkins** Court holds (6–3) that in discrimination cases in which the employer has made an employment decision for both legitimate and illegal reasons, the employers can avoid liability if they can justify decision on permissible, nondiscriminatory grounds.

Quotas. In specific cases, where companies have clearly discriminated against minorities, a federal court can impose rigid numerical hiring and promotion **quotas** for minorities. However, voluntary quota plans remain legally questionable.

Layoffs. Companies cannot lay off white males with job seniority in order to save the jobs of minorities with less seniority.

One other type of affirmative action was recently approved by Congress. For some time, the Department of Defense has been striving to award 5 percent of its contracts to minority-owned firms, but qualified firms were in short supply. In 1990 the Pilot Mentor Protege Program (a section of the Defense Authorization Act of 1991) became law. This new program aims to increase the number of qualified subcontractors by reimbursing prime contractors that adopt a minority-owned firm and offer technical and managerial assistance. By increasing the subcontractor's capability, the prime contractor is helping create its own supplier base, a plan applauded by all.[29]

Business's Response

Since passage of the 1964 Civil Rights Act, most businesses have taken an active role in complying with government requirements to set up affirmative-action programs to recruit members of minority groups and train them for jobs. With the passage of the 1991 civil rights compromise, companies have been given the incentive to train their managers and set up employment policies to ensure against bias in the workplace.

Although business has many reasons for its commitment to affirmative action, the most important is that the policy has worked. By and large, companies have had positive experiences with the people who have been hired and promoted under these programs. Furthermore, cultural diversity is rapidly becoming a fact of business life. By the end of the 1990s, 85 percent of the new hires will be women, African-Americans, Hispanics, or Asian-Americans. White males will become a minority of the work force, and employers who discriminate against women and minorities will be at a serious competitive disadvantage in attracting talented people.[30]

Women in the Workplace

In the past 20 years women have made significant strides in the workplace, thanks to a combination of affirmative action and changing attitudes among women. The feminist movement of the 1960s encouraged women to aspire to the same sort of career success that had previously been the province of men. As their assumptions about work shifted, women began to invest more time in career training and to opt for higher-paying professions. In the 1950s, only 20 percent of college undergraduates were women; today, women earn more B.A. degrees than men and their most frequent major is business. Roughly a third of all professional degrees are earned by women, versus 5 percent in 1960. In addition, 30 percent of all working women are professionals or managers, the same proportion as men.[31]

As women have moved into these higher-paying occupations, the gap between their earnings and men's earnings has narrowed from 60 percent in 1980 to 68 percent today.[32] But despite their progress, women continue to earn significantly less than men, even when they compete in the same occupations, as

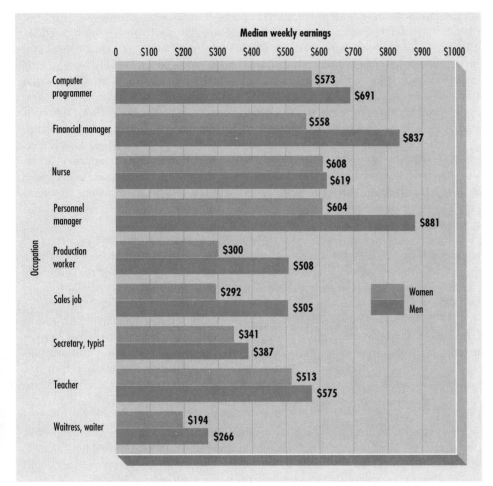

Median weekly earnings

Occupation	Women	Men
Computer programmer	$573	$691
Financial manager	$558	$837
Nurse	$608	$619
Personnel manager	$604	$881
Production worker	$300	$508
Sales job	$292	$505
Secretary, typist	$341	$387
Teacher	$513	$575
Waitress, waiter	$194	$266

EXHIBIT 4.6

Women's Earnings Versus Men's Earnings

Despite more than 20 years of fighting for equal opportunity, women still earn less than men in almost every field, even those dominated by women.

Exhibit 4.6 illustrates. Women are more likely than men to work part time or on an intermittent basis, which tends to put them behind their male peers on the career ladder. Also, many of the top positions in industry are held by men in their 50s and 60s who began their careers in the years before the women's movement.

Many women perceive a **glass ceiling,** or wall of subtle discrimination, barring them from moving up into the highest ranks. Only 3 of every 100 top jobs in the largest U.S. companies are held by women, about the same number as a decade ago.[33] Women are often passed up for promotion because people assume they will be less interested in the job and more tied to their family than their male associates are.

One way to counteract this prejudice, some argue, is to establish two separate career tracks for women: a fast track for those who consider work their top priority and a so-called mommy track for those who want to balance their career and family commitments more evenly. Although many women are troubled by the concept of the mommy track and feel it will be used to justify discrimination, 82 percent of a group of 1,000 professional women said in a recent poll that they would choose a career path with flexible full-time work hours and more family time but slower career advancement over one with inflexible hours and faster advancement.[34]

Meanwhile, blue-collar women are grappling with another type of career-

glass ceiling *The invisible barrier that keeps women out of the top positions in business*

versus-family issue—fetal protection. For a number of years, some major corporations have barred women of child-bearing age from jobs involving hazardous chemicals that might cause birth defects. Women have argued that these fetal protection policies effectively shut them out of 20 million relatively high-paying industrial jobs. The issue came to a head in 1991 when the Supreme Court ruled that fetal protection policies are an illegal form of sex discrimination. The court's ruling will give women, not companies, the final decision about whether they should take assignments that might be harmful to their unborn children.

Another sensitive issue concerning primarily women in the workplace is **sexual harassment.** As defined by the EEOC, sexual harassment takes two forms: the obvious request for sexual favors with an implicit reward or punishment related to work, and the more subtle creation of a sexist environment in which employees are made to feel uncomfortable by off-color jokes, lewd remarks, and posturing.

sexual harassment Unwelcome sexual advance, request for sexual favors, or other verbal or physical conduct of a sexual nature within the workplace that affects a person's job prospects or job performance

A recent survey reports that four out of ten women say they've experienced some form of sexual harassment on the job. However, only 5 percent of those four women ever reported the harassment. Moreover, five out of ten men say they've done or said something at work that could be considered sexual harassment by a female colleague.[35]

There's a good deal of subjectivity in deciding whether a particular action constitutes sexual harassment. The most recent court cases involving women use the "reasonable woman" standard. If a reasonable woman would find a situation objectionable, the court deems it sexual harassment. Another important factor is whether the employer has an effective internal grievance procedure that gives employees an opportunity to complain without suffering repercussions.

Honeywell, Corning, and Dupont are among the companies that have amplified their antiharassment programs with employee training, detailed handbooks, and workshops. AT&T says that 19 out of 20 complaints received are valid, and the company warns its employees that they can be fired for acts of sexual harassment. However, rather than offering separate training on the subject, AT&T offers voluntary classes on workplace diversity, believing the approach has more impact.[36]

People with Disabilities

In 1990 people with a wide range of physical and mental difficulties got a boost from the passage of the federal Americans with Disabilities Act (ADA), which guarantees equal opportunities for an estimated 50 million to 75 million people who have or have had a condition that might handicap them. As defined by the 1990 law, *disability* is a broad term that protects not only those with obvious physical handicaps but also those with less visible conditions such as cancer, heart disease, diabetes, epilepsy, AIDS, drug addiction, alcoholism, and emotional illness. For example, it is now illegal in most situations to require job applicants to pass a physical examination as a condition of employment. It is also illegal to terminate people who have a serious drinking or drug problem unless their chemical dependency prevents them from performing the essential functions of their jobs.

The law also says that all businesses serving the public must make their services and facilities accessible to people with disabilities. This means that restaurants, hotels, retail stores, beauty parlors, gas stations, libraries, airports, buses, taxis, banks, theaters, concert halls, sports stadiums, and so forth must make a reasonable effort to accommodate people who are disabled. A hotel, for example, must equip 5 percent of its rooms with flashing lights or other "visual alarms" for people with hearing impairments.[37]

Occupational Health and Safety

Every 18 seconds, someone in the United States is injured on the job; every 50 minutes, someone is killed in a work-related accident; every year, more than 70,000 people die from diseases directly related to their work.[38] Obviously, some jobs are more dangerous than others, as Exhibit 4.7 illustrates. Concern about workplace hazards mounted during the activist 1960s, resulting in passage of the Occupational Safety and Health Act of 1970, which set mandatory standards for safety and health and which established the Occupational Safety and Health Administration (OSHA) to enforce them.

OSHA is charged not only with preventing accidents but also with eliminating "silent killers": work-related diseases (such as black lung among coal miners) and injury from the toxic effects of chemicals, asbestos, and other harmful substances. OSHA employees investigate complaints and review company records to identify firms with higher-than-average accident rates. The usual penalty for safety violations is a fine. If the violation was intentional, OSHA turns the case over to the Justice Department for criminal prosecution. However, in the 1980s, OSHA referred only 30 cases, and the Justice Department prosecuted only four of them. No corporate executive has ever served in prison for federal safety violations that resulted in a worker's death, although six executives have been sentenced under state convictions.[39]

Even without tough government supervision, many companies are stepping up efforts to improve the health and safety of their employees, motivated both

EXHIBIT 4.7

Accidents on the Job
Although one might expect manufacturing jobs to be the most dangerous, service and government workers are among the most likely to be injured at work. Truck drivers run the greatest risk of a work-related injury, whereas chemical workers, surprisingly enough, are relatively safe.

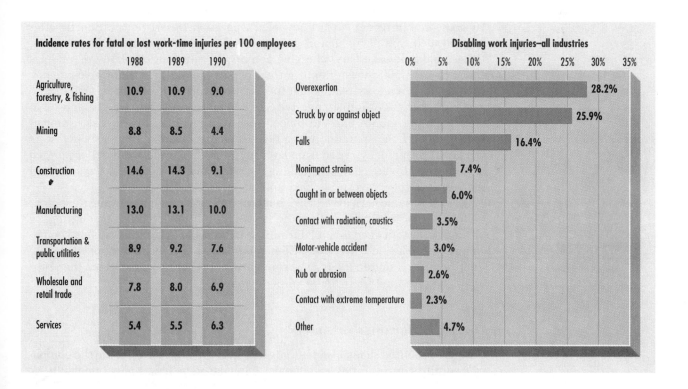

Incidence rates for fatal or lost work-time injuries per 100 employees

	1988	1989	1990
Agriculture, forestry, & fishing	10.9	10.9	9.0
Mining	8.8	8.5	4.4
Construction	14.6	14.3	9.1
Manufacturing	13.0	13.1	10.0
Transportation & public utilities	8.9	9.2	7.6
Wholesale and retail trade	7.8	8.0	6.9
Services	5.4	5.5	6.3

Disabling work injuries—all industries

Overexertion	28.2%
Struck by or against object	25.9%
Falls	16.4%
Nonimpact strains	7.4%
Caught in or between objects	6.0%
Contact with radiation, caustics	3.5%
Motor-vehicle accident	3.0%
Rub or abrasion	2.6%
Contact with extreme temperature	2.3%
Other	4.7%

by genuine concern and by the mounting costs of workers' compensation claims. Alcoa, the big aluminum company, has improved its safety record by 25 percent in three years and estimates that it saves $10,000 to $12,000 for every accident it prevents.[40]

If you think that nice office job is safe, think again. Almost half the reported cases of workplace illness involve ailments caused by repetitive motion such as typing at a keyboard. Although the problem first showed up in factories among assembly-line workers, it is increasingly common among clerical workers. Early warning signs include tingling fingers and loss of feeling.

▶ BUSINESS AND INVESTORS

In addition to its other responsibilities, a business must also keep in mind its responsibility to those who have invested in the company. Although a growing number of investors are concerned about the ethics of the companies in which they invest, most are chiefly interested in the company's financial performance. Thus, the company's major responsibility to investors is to make money on their behalf. Any action that cheats the investors out of their rightful profits is unethical. But a business can also fail in its responsibilities to shareholders by being too concerned about profits.

Cheating the Investor

Of all the ways investors can be cheated, most fall into one of two categories: misrepresenting the potential of the investment or diverting the earnings or assets so that the investor's rightful return is reduced.

Misrepresenting the Investment

Every year, tens of thousands of people are the victims of investment scams. Lured by promises of high returns, people sink more than a billion dollars per year in nonexistent oil wells, Lithuanian gold mines, and other fraudulent operations touted by complete strangers over the telephone.[41] One of the most popular come-ons in recent history involved Operation Desert Storm. Shortly after Iraq invaded Kuwait, regulators raided 32 telemarketing firms in Los Angeles, Dallas, and Salt Lake City, charging con artists with touting phony oil and gas deals. Some 3,500 investors put a total of $50 million into these investments, trusting the promotors' claims that the war would drive up oil prices. One retired postal worker, for example, invested $31,250 in gas wells that were supposed to yield $625 per month and did indeed receive a few monthly checks. Unfortunately, though, the operation was a **Ponzi scheme,** meaning that early investors were paid with money raised from later investors. The wells were either plugged or not owned by the company making the offer, and the scheme collapsed when the supply of new investors dried up.[42]

Ponzi scheme *Form of fraud in which money received from later investors is used to pay off the earlier investors*

A Ponzi scheme is clearly illegal, but other ways of misrepresenting the potential of an investment fall within the law. With a little "creative accounting," a business that is in deep financial trouble can be made to look reasonably good to all but the most astute investors. Companies have a certain amount of latitude in their reports to shareholders, and some firms are more conscientious than others in representing their financial performance.

Diverting Earnings or Assets

Business executives may also take advantage of the investor by using the company's earnings or resources for personal gain. Managers have many opportunities to indirectly take money that rightfully belongs to the shareholders. Perhaps the most common approach is to cheat on the expense account. Padding invoices and then splitting the overcharge with the supplier is another common ploy. Another possibility is selling company secrets to competitors or using inside information to play the stock market.

Insider trading—the use of knowledge gained from one's position in a company to benefit from fluctuations in stock prices—has been in the news frequently in recent years. Although insider trading is illegal, it is difficult to police. Say you're an accountant for a major corporation. You know the company is about to report a large, unexpected loss. When the news breaks, the price of the stock will undoubtedly fall. You could protect yourself by selling the stock you own before the word gets out. Who'd know the difference? And who'd care? Consider the people who might buy your shares; chances are *they* would care. And consider the other shareholders, the investors who actually own the company even though they have no day-to-day involvement with it. Would it be fair for you to profit while they did not?

insider trading Employee's or manager's use of information gained in the course of his or her job and not generally available to the public in order to benefit from fluctuations in the stock market

Overdoing the Quest for Profits

Most executives would agree that insider trading is damaging to shareholders. But what about trying to maximize profits? How can that possibly be bad? Few companies knowingly break laws in an attempt to gain competitive advantage. But many companies have employed questionable practices in their zeal to maximize profits. Managers are often caught in a gray area, where the legality and ethicality of a particular action are debatable. For example, should a company bribe a foreign official? You might say no, but be aware that bribery is considered customary in many cultures. The Foreign Corrupt Practices Act explicitly makes it illegal to bribe higher-level foreign officials, but "grease" payments to lower-level officials such as customs agents are permitted. As a manager, where would you draw the line between higher- and lower-level officials?

And what about spying on competitors? When does legitimate market research become unethical or illegal? Is it okay to buy a competitor's product and take it apart to see how it works? Is it all right to hire someone who previously worked for a competitor and ask probing questions about the company's plans and strategies?

A number of companies have recently been penalized for overdoing their quest for profits. Johnson & Johnson, one of the 10 most admired corporations in the country, has been ordered to pay $113 million to 3M for analyzing a sample of a soon-to-be-launched 3M material used in making casts for broken bones. J&J received the sample from a disgruntled 3M employee who offered to explain the technology for $20,000. Although J&J did not pay for any information, the company was able to use the sample in developing a similar product. What J&J should have done, according to an industrial security consultant, was report the situation to 3M and call the FBI.[43]

J&J is by no means alone. General Electric, another highly regarded company, was recently ordered to pay a $10 million fine for padding a defense contract.[44] And Chrysler faces a $7.6 million fine for selling 30 previously wrecked vehicles as new cars.[45]

None of the executives involved in these cases profited personally; their chief concern was to improve the financial performance of the company. Some might argue that these executives were guilty of nothing worse than loyalty to their company, or that their competitors were doing the same thing, or that the rules they broke were trivial. You be the judge. Were these companies right or wrong?

▶ THE EFFORT TO BECOME MORE ETHICAL

Most companies are concerned about issues like these, and many are trying to develop approaches for improving their ethics. At the same time, however, many individuals in both business and government are taking a hard look at the costs associated with programs designed to protect consumers, employees, and the environment.

How Companies Encourage Ethical Behavior

code of ethics *Written statement setting forth the principles that should guide an organization's decisions*

By and large, businesspeople are like the rest of us. They're waking up to their social and environmental responsibilities and trying to do the right thing. Three out of four large companies have adopted a written **code of ethics**, which defines the values and principles that should be used to guide decisions.[46] Many also run training programs to teach employees how to deal with ethical dilemmas. Some companies screen potential employees for honesty *before* they are hired. The simplest but least scientific way to do this is to ask questions during the interview process that reveal something about the applicant's values and moral principles. A more formal approach involves the use of written "honesty" tests designed to reveal a candidate's standards. For example, the test might ask, "If you

EXPLORING INTERNATIONAL BUSINESS

Gift Versus Bribe: When a Friendly Exchange Turns into Risky Business

Your company has sent you to an African country to conduct business. You think you've clinched the deal, but then your contact asks you for a "gift" of money to ensure that the deal goes through. Do you say, "Sorry, I don't give bribes," and stomp away in a huff? Or do you give him what he asks for and feel guilty for violating business ethics?

Deciding how to handle such situations requires knowing the customs of the country you're doing business in. Most non-Western countries, especially in Africa and Asia, have strong traditions built around exchanges of gifts. The savvy businessperson who can tap into these traditions will not only clinch today's deal but will also establish long-term business relationships—without compromising integrity.

American businesses that operate in non-Western countries need to be aware of three traditions underlying modern business dealings in those countries:

the inner circle, the future-favors system, and the gift exchange.

People in developing nations tend to see themselves as belonging to an inner circle that consists of relatives, friends, and close colleagues. All those in the inner circle are devoted to mutual protection and prosperity. Everyone else is an outsider, a stranger whose motives are to be questioned. Obviously, people prefer to conduct business with insiders—people they know and trust.

In a system of future favors, a gift or service obligates the recipient to return the favor at some future time—with interest. And once the favor is returned, the original giver becomes obligated to repay this greater favor. And so the system of obligations becomes a lifelong relationship, one that can provide access to the inner circle and that can serve as the basis of business dealings.

A third cultural tradition, intertwined with the

saw a co-worker stealing, would you turn the person in?" or "Do you agree or disagree that stealing from an employer is not the same as stealing from a friend?"[47]

Companies are also giving corporate responsibility an important place on the organizational chart. A number of leading corporations have appointed environmental or community affairs executives to oversee corporate-wide efforts to act in a socially responsible manner. For example, McDonald's created the post of vice president of environmental affairs in August 1990. Mike Roberts, the new VP, immediately set up a task force to work with the nonprofit Environmental Defense Fund. The resulting major waste-reduction program will cut the huge stream of waste from McDonald's 11,000 restaurants by 80 percent within a few years. The program goes far beyond the company's much publicized decision to switch from polystyrene packaging to coated paper boxes for sandwiches. At least 42 major changes in restaurant operations are involved—everything from composting food scraps to replacing plastic spoons with a biodegradable starch-based alternative. From now on, the entire company will view waste reduction as a top priority, along with quickness, cleanliness, and quality service. A cynic might say that the program is just a public relations gimmick, but there's more than hype involved. McDonald's plans to spend $100 million annually on waste-reduction efforts and expects its suppliers to incur additional costs as well.[48]

McDonald's is only one of many high-profile companies that are leaping on the "social responsibility" bandwagon. To bolster their image as corporate good guys, most of the leading consumer products companies are "going green"— inventing new products, repackaging old ones, and redoing their advertising

VIDEO EXERCISE

future-favors system, is the practice of gift giving. Giving or receiving a gift can be much more than a gesture of friendship—it can be the first in a long-term sequence of gift exchanges. As expert Jeffrey A. Fadiman noted, "The gifts are simply catalysts. Under ideal circumstances the process should be unending, with visits, gifts, gestures, and services flowing back and forth among participants throughout their lives."

By participating in the traditional exchange of gifts and favors and becoming part of an inner circle, American businesspeople can build trust, gain greater access to local markets and expertise, and minimize risk in a foreign environment.

The difficult part about participating in local gift-giving traditions is learning how to distinguish gifts from bribes. If your African contact asks you for money, is he engaging in extortion, or is he encouraging you to enter into the future-favors system? One clue is the size of the request—the smaller the amount, the less likely it is to be a bribe. Another clue is the person the money is to be paid to. If it is supposed to go to a third party—especially someone

in power—it is more likely to be a bribe.

Many large American corporations have developed clever and useful strategies for handling requests for payoffs. Instead of making private payments to individuals, they offer donations to build hospitals and schools, they provide engineering or other expert services for public works, or they donate jobs—all with the goal of creating goodwill in the host nation. Furthermore, they gain a reputation for providing social services instead of paying bribes, and the foreign officials who arrange the donation increase their prestige.

Having appropriate knowledge and using appropriate strategies, Western businesspeople can pursue successful dealings in non-Western countries without compromising their ethics. On the local level, gift giving serves an important traditional function that can be seen as a courtesy and not as a bribe. On broader levels, companies can circumvent questionable payoffs by providing important social services that benefit everyone and that establish long-term trusting relationships.

Unocal, the Southern California oil company, found a creative, relatively inexpensive way to save Los Angeles's air from 10.7 million pounds of smog-forming gases. For $6 million, the company bought and retired 8,376 pre-1971 cars, which belch out 60 times the pollutants of new cars. To achieve the same pollution savings at its local refinery, which is already equipped with sophisticated controls, Unocal would have had to spend $160 million.

campaigns to emphasize their virtue. Companies are also doing more cause-related marketing, in which they contribute a portion of the profit from sales of a product to a worthy cause. Ben & Jerry's uses this technique to promote its Rain Forest Crunch brittle. Forty percent of the profits go into a fund to protect the Amazon rain forest.

Many businesses are also trying to encourage ethical behavior among employees by setting an example of community involvement. Corporations donate over $5.6 billion to charity each year, and many executives also donate their time to community affairs.[49] At the same time, many corporations have begun to take a stand on moral issues, such as helping foster the growth of minority-owned businesses or fighting apartheid in South Africa.

Practical Limitations on Social Responsibility

Although most companies attempt to make ethical decisions, they are also concerned about the costs of their actions. Undertaking many socially responsible activities takes money. Just how much money is unclear, because no single source of information exists on business's expenditures for socially desirable activities.

Looking just at pollution control, a recent analysis by the Environmental Protection Agency estimates that the United States devotes 2 percent of its GNP to protect and clean up the environment; that figure is expected to increase to almost 3 percent, or $46 billion, by the year 2000. Is that too much? Can the country afford it? The answer depends on your priorities, but as a percentage of GNP, the amount is comparable to what other industrialized nations are spending. To put the figure in perspective, we spend roughly the same amount on illegal drugs each year, twice as much on clothing, and six times as much on defense.[50]

Regardless of exactly how much we spend, we need to be concerned about getting our money's worth. For example, say that you are the manager of a chemical-processing plant. For $2.2 million, you can remove 94 percent of the hazardous by-products from your wastewater. To remove 97 percent would cost you another $3.8 million. Is the additional reduction of 3 percent worth the price?

Because resources are limited, companies do not have the luxury of paying "whatever it takes" to save lives or to protect the environment. If they spend $1 million to save a few lives by cleaning their wastewater more thoroughly, they may not have another $1 million to spend on other safety measures that would save even more lives.

SUMMARY OF LEARNING OBJECTIVES

1 Identify four groups to which business has a responsibility.

Companies have a responsibility to society, to consumers, to employees, and to investors.

2 List and explain four philosophical approaches to resolving ethical questions in business.

In resolving ethical questions, companies may employ absolute standards based on religious teachings or apply the principles of utilitarianism (the greatest good for the greatest number of people), individual rights (respect for human dignity), and justice (fair distribution of the benefits and burdens of society).

3 Name three kinds of pollution, and outline actions to control each.

Air, water, and land pollution are all significant problems. The government has attacked these problems by passing the National Environmental Policy Act of 1969 and by establishing the Environmental Protection Agency to regulate the disposal of hazardous wastes and to clean up polluted areas.

In addition, many companies have taken steps to reduce the amount of pollution they produce and to dispose of hazardous wastes more safely.

4 Specify the four rights of consumers.

Consumers have the right to safety, the right to be informed, the right to choose, and the right to be heard.

5 State the responsibilities of the Equal Employment Opportunity Commission.

The EEOC is responsible for seeing that employers do not discriminate against members of minority groups. The EEOC investigates complaints of job-related discrimination and files legal charges against discriminating companies.

6 Identify four issues that are of particular concern to women in the workplace.

Women are concerned about the gap between male and female pay. They are also grappling with such is-

sues as the "mommy track," fetal protection, and sexual harassment.

7 Delineate two general ways in which investors may be cheated of their rightful profits.

Investors are cheated (1) when companies or individuals misrepresent the value of an investment and (2) when company representatives divert earnings or assets for their personal use, thus reducing the amount available to return to investors.

8 List six actions that companies are taking to meet their ethical and social responsibilities.

Companies are adopting codes of ethics, teaching employees the importance of maintaining high moral standards, screening job candidates for honesty, and appointing executives to oversee environmental and community affairs. In addition, companies are reviewing their operations and products in an effort to minimize waste and protect the environment. They are also setting a good example by giving time, money, and moral support to worthy causes.

Meeting a Business Challenge at Ben & Jerry's Homemade

Ben Cohen and Jerry Greenfield acknowledged the company was no longer what it had been. For one thing, there were now over 300 employees, not just two. Also, company stock had been sold publicly, making the company responsible not only to the community and employees but to stockholders as well. Even internal communication had changed. Monthly staff meetings, for all employees, had always been a part of the Ben & Jerry culture. But in the old days, employees split into small groups, talked over problems, and came back with solu-

tions. Now the meetings had become one-way communications, with managers talking at the employees.

Cohen and Greenfield wanted to make some changes to address these issues. First, they wanted management to be more responsive to employees, for they believed that communication had not kept pace with the other changes growth had brought to the company. Even though Ben & Jerry's ice cream promoted social causes, sales were based on the quality of the product. And they believed that the excellent product

would not continue to exist without better communication. Second, they wanted to do more for the employees. They wanted to put more power in the hands of lower management and to make life more enjoyable for everyone at the company.

But before making any changes, Cohen decided to consult the employees using the old format of the monthly staff meetings. He convened all the employees and asked what they considered to be the most pressing problems facing Ben & Jerry's. As in the old days, the employees talked over the problems and came back with some answers. The most pressing problem expressed was the need for the company to have a clearly stated direction. Employees were feeling caught between the managers, who wanted the company to grow and become more businesslike, and the co-founders, who wanted the company to be a force for social change. The old way of doing things was no longer working in the Ben & Jerry's of today.

The managers developed a strategy for Ben & Jerry's—the most comprehensive plan the company had ever had—but it was too businesslike for the co-founders, attuned to profits but not satisfactorily addressing the social agenda. Cohen and Greenfield wanted more creativity, so they pressed management to further explore the bounds of social responsibility. In the end, the co-founders got their social agenda, but the company also had to tend to business. The revised plan yielded an improved Ben & Jerry's. The company now had a clearly stated direction: Produce a product of the highest quality, demonstrate social responsibility, and remain economically viable. High product quality remained a company standard. The company's position regarding its social goals remained unchanged, true to Cohen and Greenfield. And the employees, still an important part of the organization, were given more room for input and discussion on business decisions.

Your Mission: As assistant to Ben Cohen and Jerry Greenfield, you are responsible for helping them keep the company on track with its new direction. Consider the following scenarios, and decide how you will act.

1. A group of the company's employees recently approached you with a concern about one of the social causes the company supports through the Ben & Jerry Foundation. They were opposed to the cause and did not want the company to support it. Of the following, what would be your best response to their concern?
   a. You do not believe all employees need to support all the social causes. It is the responsibility of the board to donate the money and

Ben Cohen and Jerry Greenfield believe in measuring their success in terms of more than money. Every year they donate 7.5 percent of Ben & Jerry's pretax profits to charity. They also believe in social responsibility on a smaller scale, providing a diaper-changing table in the men's room as well as in the lady's room.

then it is up to the Ben & Jerry Foundation to allocate the funds to social programs they choose. You convey this message to the employees.
   b. You decide to take the issue back to the employees. You convene an all-employee staff meeting and ask the employees to evaluate the social causes the company supports. The employees decide which issues to support.
   c. You realize from time to time this will happen. The employees have approached you in a very responsible manner and you feel obligated to act on their concerns. There are innumerable social causes to support. You decide to approach the board and ask them to withdraw support for this one.
   d. You personally believe in this cause and do not want to change anything. You use your influence to keep the funds flowing. You feel justified in using your influence this way because if it were not for your social beliefs, you'd be making a higher salary somewhere else.

2. A new ice cream promoting a healthy ozone layer has been proposed. Ingredients for the product are produced exclusively by environmentally sound practices, making the product more expensive to manufacture than competitor products. A pre-

liminary review indicates the product would pay for itself but would generate no profit. What should you do?
   a. The ice cream meets the company's social and product goals. You go ahead with the introduction since other products will make up for the lack of profit.
   b. You believe you are being disloyal to the stockholders if you do not maximize profits with every decision. You withdraw support for the product.
   c. You decide to compromise the product by changing some of the environmentally sound ingredients to reduce the cost. This may dilute the social message, but you need to keep the shareholders in mind.
   d. You believe the market will pay a higher price for a product associated with this issue. You raise the price, introduce the product, and hope for the best.

3. A congressional bill has been proposed to limit the fat content of manufactured foods. This directly affects your ice cream products. What do you do?
   a. You hire a professional lobbyist, who attempts to prevent the bill from becoming law. You believe people can decide for themselves what to eat and have the right to choose which foods they buy.
   b. You share the government's concern for consumer health. You develop a long-term strategy for reducing the fat content of all of Ben & Jerry's ice creams.
   c. You refute the findings relating fat content to adverse health. You initiate a campaign to educate the public on the benefits of dairy fat in the diet.
   d. You support the effort to reduce fat but you also believe in consumer choice. You propose an alternative bill to require accurate labeling of food containers.

4. As the environment becomes more important to both the government and the consumer, what is Ben & Jerry's responsibility in the manufacturing of a product?
   a. Ben & Jerry's must take full responsibility for reducing waste, no matter what the cost. To counteract

the pollution already in the environment, businesses must take the initiative in using safer resources and controlling every aspect of waste, regardless of the effect on profit.
b. Ben & Jerry's is only one company, and its impact on the environment is small when compared to all the other businesses. Since the

company must maintain profits in order to remain in business, and because it owes as much to its investors as it does to the environment, whatever attempt Ben & Jerry's makes to reduce and control waste will have to be enough.
c. In addition to meeting all government standards, Ben & Jerry's must decide which actions will yield the

most benefit for the least money.
d. Complying with government regulations is all that any company can do. With so many agencies dictating so many rules, it's difficult enough for Ben & Jerry's to keep up with requirements, regardless of other actions the company may want to take.[51]

KEY TERMS

affirmative action (106)
code of ethics (114)
discrimination (104)
ecology (95)
glass ceiling (109)

individual rights (92)
insider trading (113)
justice (94)
minorities (104)
pollution (94)

Ponzi scheme (112)
quotas (108)
sexual harassment (110)
stakeholders (90)
utilitarianism (92)

REVIEW QUESTIONS

1. How has business's sense of social responsibility evolved since the turn of the century?

2. How do individuals employ philosophical principles in making business decisions?

3. What are some of the things business has done to protect the environment from the dangers of pollution?

4. In what way do you think the consumer movement might actually benefit business?

5. In what ways is business legally accountable for helping to achieve equal opportunity for minorities?

6. What are the responsibilities of the Occupational Safety and Health Administration, and how does the agency carry out its mission?

7. What is "insider trading," and how does it harm an investor in a company?

8. In your opinion, is the United States spending too much, too little, or just about the right amount to prevent pollution and clean up the environment?

A CASE FOR CRITICAL THINKING

Benevolent Capitalism—An Endangered Philosophy?

Clessie Cummins believed in the solid principles of hard work, good products, and community involvement. When he founded Cummins Engine Company in 1919, he built his success on this foundation. Cummins engines are the pride and joy of truckers who drive Kenworth, Peterbilt, and Navistar rigs. The engines

log a full 600,000 miles before they need any major repair work, according to one fleet owner. That's 100,000 miles more than the competition. And they average 6.2 miles to the gallon, compared to 4.3 for other brands.

But to people in the heartland community of Columbus, Indiana (population 32,000), Cummins has

traditionally meant much more than a good product. For over 60 years, local high school graduates could look forward to a high-paying job on Cummins's factory floor, albeit with some stringent rules designed to maintain its reputation for quality. (The rejection rate at the end of the assembly line is a mere 1 percent, one-third the industry average.) And when was the last time you heard of a company lobbying the state government for higher corporate taxes so that it could contribute more to the community?

Cummins takes its social responsibilities seriously. The company has built a shelter for the homeless, financed drug counseling in local schools, and hired the best architects (at a cost of $9.9 million) to design 24 of Columbus's public buildings. Near its new factory in a slum area of Sao Paulo, Brazil, Cummins helped build a school, a clinic, and a gymnasium. The manufacturer sent engines and generators to hurricane victims in South Carolina in 1989, and it contributed more to charity than all but 95 of the Fortune 500 companies in 1988—both years when Cummins Engine Company made no profit.

But such steadfast benevolence may soon succumb to the relentless forces beating against the company. After decades of hefty profits, Cummins slammed into the economic hardships of the 1980s. In 1983 the company was forced to lay off employees for the first time, a painful step announced after executives met for prayer with 30 of the town's clergy. Subsequent plant modernization eliminated more jobs, putting a total of 4,000 Columbians out of work. As a result, the community is experiencing a dramatic increase in domestic and violent crime, and young people are moving away, disillusioned and frustrated.

Two hostile takeover attempts have further buffeted Cummins Engine, which made itself vulnerable by sacrificing short-term profits in order to slash prices and hold on to its market share against stiff foreign competition. Despite wagging fingers and shaking heads on Wall Street, Cummins managed to keep a 54 percent share of the U.S. market. And even though costs have been cut 22 percent, the company hasn't eliminated its research and development, as some would advise. It remains committed to long-term thinking and to Clessie Cummins's founding principles. In one annual report, chairman Henry B. Schacht described the company's goal as "being fair and honest and doing what is right even when it is not to our immediate benefit."

Thus far, Cummins's social investments in the surrounding community seem to be paying off. The wealthy Columbus banking family that originally financed Clessie Cummins's business put up $72 million to buy off a British conglomerate attempting a takeover. But other investors have made unwanted advances, and it remains to be seen whether socially committed Cummins will survive in an era of less caring, less committed corporations.[52]

1. How far should a company take its community involvement? Do you believe Cummins Engine Company was right to continue its philanthropy in years when it returned no profit to shareholders?

2. If you were Henry B. Schacht, what tactics and strategies would you institute to strengthen the company against outside forces?

3. Why would foreign investors be interested in a company like Cummins Engine, which seems rooted in an earlier era and which has stubbornly refused to move its operations to a location that would provide cheaper labor and lower taxes?

BUILDING YOUR COMMUNICATION SKILLS

As directed by your instructor, call or write a local business or franchise operation and request a copy of its code of ethics. As an alternative, visit the periodical section of your library and locate such a code in a business magazine or professional journal article dealing with business ethics. With a group of no more than three or four other students, evaluate the code. Consider its policies toward workers and consumers. Who is protected by this code? How does the company balance its obligations to workers and consumers with its goals of producing products and generating income?

KEEPING CURRENT USING *THE WALL STREET JOURNAL*

From recent issues, clip or copy a *Wall Street Journal* article related to one or more of the following ethical/social-responsibility challenges faced by businesses:

► Environmental issues, such as air and water pollution, acid rain, and hazardous-waste disposal

► Employee or consumer safety measures

► Consumer information/education

► Employment discrimination/ affirmative action

► Investment ethics

► Industrial spying and theft of trade secrets

► Fraud, bribery, and overcharging

► Company codes of ethics

1. What was the nature of the ethical challenge or social-responsibility issue presented in the article?

2. What lasting effects will be felt by (a) the company and (b) the agency or social group affected?

3. Was there any wrongdoing by a company or agency official? Was the action illegal, unethical, or questionable? What course of action would you recommend the company or agency take to correct or improve matters now?

CHAPTER 5

LEARNING OBJECTIVES
After studying this chapter, you will be able to

1 Differentiate between an absolute advantage and a comparative advantage in international trade.

2 Distinguish between the balance of trade and the balance of payments.

3 List and describe three international trade pacts.

4 Identify five techniques that countries use to protect their domestic industries.

5 Cite five drawbacks to protectionism.

6 Discuss the impact of a weaker dollar on U.S. companies.

7 List five common forms of international business activity.

8 Cite five things you can do to facilitate international business relationships.

International Business

PEPPERONI WRAPPED IN RED TAPE

A fter opening Pizza Huts for PepsiCo's restaurant division in Africa, Eastern Europe, Scandinavia, and the Middle East, Andrew Rafalat figured he could start a Pizza Hut from scratch on the moon if he had to. The moon, maybe—but Moscow was something else. "Setting up a business here was like setting up an island in an ocean," Rafalat explained. "You hoped it would survive the storm." No one could know how severe a storm was coming—or when. But before Russia joined eleven other republics to form the Commonwealth of Independent States (CIS), before the death of the communist party, before the ill-fated coup that attempted to restore old-guard communism to the people, and even before Gorbachev formally asked the West for help in moving his country toward capitalism, companies like Pizza Hut saw the promise of new markets in the ailing economy of the Soviet Union.

Actually, Rafalat was luckier than most Westerners trying to penetrate the Soviet system. He had the backing of a giant multinational corporation that had been doing business in the USSR for years. Pepsi's involvement there began in 1959 when Donald Kendall displayed the company's soft drinks at a trade show in Moscow. Kendall, who later became chairman and CEO of PepsiCo, was intrigued by the potential of selling soda pop to 290 million thirsty comrades. He was determined to find a way to get Pepsi-Cola into their hands. It took him 13 years, but in 1972 he finally negotiated a trade agreement providing for the bottling and sale of Pepsi in the USSR, making Pepsi the first foreign consumer product to cross the iron curtain. Today, Pepsi is the leading soft drink in the CIS and in much of Eastern Europe.

Having done so well with its cola, PepsiCo was eager to introduce other staples of the U.S. diet through its restaurant and snack food divisions, which include Pizza Hut, Kentucky Fried Chicken, Taco Bell, and Frito-Lay. Anatoly

Dobrynin, the former Soviet ambassador to the United States, was also eager to see a Pizza Hut open in Moscow, having developed a real taste for their pepperoni during his stint in Washington, D.C.

With Dobrynin's help, PepsiCo finally found the right opportunity to expand its Soviet operations through a complicated $3 billion deal that involved a lot more than pizza. In addition to opening the restaurants, Pepsi would build and equip 28 new bottling plants (in addition to the 26 already there). The Soviets would buy concentrate for the plants from PepsiCo, using vodka and its revenue from some oil tankers (rather than rubles) to pay for the concentrate. This peculiar form of payment was necessary because rubles could not be exchanged for dollars, which meant that money made in what was then the USSR was good only in the USSR—an obvious problem for a U.S. company.

With the umbrella deal in place, Rafalat arrived on the Moscow scene to tackle the task of opening two Pizza Huts. Despite his many years of experience in international business, he was not prepared for the complications he encountered. Even though the equipment for the restaurants was imported from the United States, setting things up was difficult because the Soviet transportation system was unpredictable. Supplies were lost for weeks on end. Lining up ingredients for the pizza was also difficult because the food distribution system was such a mess. And, of course, there was the problem of hiring and training 300 Muscovites to staff the restaurants. The biggest problem for Rafalat, though, was the red tape. A person needed a master's degree in bureaucratic intrigue to cope with the system. There was the Soviet government to consider then, not to mention the Russian Republic and the Moscow City government. "It seemed impossible," said Rafalat. "I had a problem even knowing whom to call."[1]

► THE DYNAMICS OF INTERNATIONAL BUSINESS

Like Pizza Hut, more and more enterprises are becoming global in scope, reaching out for opportunities to buy, sell, and manufacture products and services throughout the world. The shift to a worldwide focus poses obvious problems for managers like Andrew Rafalat, who must cope with unfamiliar ways of doing business. But on a broader level, it also poses problems for government policymakers.

What should national objectives be with respect to international business? When countries negotiate international trade agreements, should they try to promote the interests of domestic companies and protect them from foreign competitors? It was once assumed that the national interest and the interests of U.S. corporations were one and the same. "What's good for America is good for General Motors, and vice versa" was once a fairly accurate statement. Now the issue is much more difficult. General Motors derives 70 percent of its profits from non-U.S. operations; foreign-owned factories employ roughly 10 percent of U.S. manufacturing workers, and they provide the United States with some of its favorite products. For the past few years, the most popular car in the United States has been the Honda Accord, a "Japanese import" manufactured not in Tokyo but in Marysville, Ohio. If the U.S. government tries to protect GM from Honda, is it doing the country a favor? Should the U.S. government look out for its own corporations, workers, or consumers? Can a policy be devised to serve all three equally well?

Why Nations Trade

International trade occurs because no single country has the resources to produce everything well. The products a country decides to produce depend on what must be sacrificed to produce them; that is, whatever resources a country uses to produce one product are no longer available for producing some other product. Those things we have to give up in order to get more of what we want are called **opportunity costs,** and they determine what countries produce for trade.

For example, Saudi Arabia exports crude oil. The Saudis could have chosen to export wheat, but they lack the resources (the arable land, the water, the climate) to grow wheat efficiently. To devote their resources to producing wheat, the Saudis would have to foresake innumerable barrels of oil, an extreme opportunity cost. By choosing to produce crude oil, Saudi Arabia utilizes its resources in the most efficient manner.

The United States also produces both crude oil and wheat, but its opportunity cost is lower than Saudi Arabia's. Having smaller reserves of oil and more than ten times the arable land, the United States has to give up only a few barrels of oil (compared with Saudi Arabia's innumerable barrels of oil) to produce a bushel of wheat. Thus, in the production of wheat, the United States has a **comparative advantage;** that is, it has the ability to produce a given product at a lower opportunity cost than its trading partners.

Comparative advantage has nothing to do with the actual costs involved in production; it concerns the devotion of resources to produce one product rather than another. In fact, Saudi Arabia might be able to produce one bushel of wheat using fewer resources than the United States is using. An **absolute advantage** is a nation's ability to produce a particular product with fewer resources (per unit of output) than any other nation. This absolute advantage might exist because the Saudis have been growing wheat far longer than people in the United States or because the Saudis are simply more talented. But even if Saudi Arabia did have an absolute advantage in wheat production, that fact does not affect what the United States produces. If the United States has a comparative advantage in wheat production, then it must exploit that comparative advantage, regardless of any other country's absolute advantage.[2]

Because countries naturally specialize in what they do best, all countries are better off. Nations trade the goods they make most efficiently for goods that other countries produce more efficiently. In this way, specialization expands the total supply of goods and reduces their total cost. However, for political reasons, most countries try to remain reasonably self-sufficient in certain essential industries. For example, the United States does not want to become totally dependent on foreign oil because such dependence would make it vulnerable during a conflict such as the Persian Gulf War.

It's worth noting that a country's resources may change over time. No nation has demonstrated this fact more dramatically than Japan. Immediately after World War II, Japanese companies utilized their access to cheap labor; they specialized in producing things like plastic toys and inexpensive knickknacks. Over the years, however, Japanese wage rates have risen, and the country has cultivated other talents and resources: engineering expertise, production efficiency, investment capital. By developing these capabilities, Japan has shifted its comparative advantage. Today it specializes in machinery, precision instruments, consumer electronics, motor vehicles, and other sophisticated products of high quality.

Holland's comparative advantage centers on the flower industry, allowing the Dutch to export products resulting from their superior flower technology while importing those products not easily produced in Holland.

opportunity cost *The value of using a resource; measured in terms of the value of the best alternative for using that resource*

comparative advantage *Nation's ability to produce a given product at a lower opportunity cost than its trading partners*

absolute advantage *Nation's ability to produce a particular product with fewer resources (per unit of output) than any other nation.*

The Evolving Role of the United States in the World Economy

The comparative advantages of the United States are changing as well, partly because people in the United States are developing new skills and partly because other countries are cultivating their own capabilities and becoming more formidable competitors.

The Postwar Boom

To a great extent, perception of where the United States "belongs" in the world economy is a function of a unique combination of circumstances that gave it relatively more competitive advantages than other countries for roughly 20 years following World War II. While Europe and Japan faced the daunting task of rebuilding their economic base, the United States emerged from the war with its factories and transportation network in better shape than ever. The United States had geared up to meet the wartime emergency, and its corporations were eager to convert that capacity and technology to peacetime uses. The public was tired of wartime sacrifices and was hungry for consumer goods. Meanwhile the Europeans and the Japanese needed everything from food to machine tools, and much of their productive capacity was in shambles. With booming demand and few foreign competitors to contend with, U.S. corporations became the dominant players on the international business scene.

The Stimulus of Foreign Aid

Ironically enough, the postwar national policy eventually undercut U.S. competitive advantages. By providing aid to help its allies and former enemies rebuild, the United States gave foreign companies the boost required to get back in the game. At the same time, however, the United States helped its own businesses. Part of the $12 billion in aid that the U.S. poured into Europe through the Marshall Plan was spent on U.S. products, as was a portion of the $2.5 billion in grants and trade credits that the U.S. government provided to Japan between 1945 and 1955.[3]

Encouraged by the success of foreign aid in Western Europe and Japan, the United States turned its attention to the developing countries of Africa, Latin America, and Asia. In these areas, the goal was to help build industries where they had never existed before. Although the developing countries' economic problems turned out to be much more complex than originally thought, U.S. aid benefited not only the developing countries but U.S. companies as well. It was also a powerful stimulus for world trade.

The Rise of Multinational Corporations

Initially, most U.S. companies approached the growing foreign markets from bases in the United States. But as international business became an increasingly important source of profits, U.S. companies began to open foreign branches and sales offices, staffed by local workers. One step led to another, and soon U.S. companies were shifting production and assembly operations abroad to minimize transportation expenses, capitalize on lower labor costs, and take advantage of local raw materials. The ownership of some companies became increasingly international. Almost imperceptibly, these companies became **multinational corporations,** with operations in several countries. As the econo-

multinational corporations
Firms with operations in more than one country

mies of the other industrialized nations revived, their corporations began operating on an international scale as well.

In deciding where to put various functions, global managers began to make use of the comparative advantages of various countries, thereby optimizing the efficiency of the corporation as a whole. Marketing and sales activities might be located close to the customers, whereas research and design might be based near a pool of skilled engineers and scientists. Factories would be situated where labor rates were low and transportation was readily available. Based solely on economics, these decisions might or might not serve the national interests of the corporation's home country.

As managers at JVC (Japan Victor Company) know well, one key to future economic growth is the amount of money invested in new plants and equipment. On that score, the United States lags far behind Japan, spending only about half as much per person. The United States is also behind in spending for roads, bridges, and other public services that enhance a country's productivity.

Where the United States Stands Today

Not surprisingly, the U.S. lead in international business has gradually narrowed, losing dominance in such areas as steel manufacturing, textiles, machine tools, automobiles, and consumer electronics. In fact, some U.S. industries have virtually disappeared—most television sets and all VCRs and camcorders are now imported.

Does this mean that the United States is slipping? Some authorities think so, but others hold a more optimistic view. As Exhibit 5.1 illustrates, the picture is mixed. In terms of sheer magnitude, the United States still has the lead, a reflection to some extent of its large population base. The U.S. gross national product is twice the size of the combined GNPs of West Germany (not including reunited East Germany), Britain, and France and almost three times as large as Japan's. Its share of world manufacturing is on the upswing, and its factories are humming along efficiently. Although the rate of Japanese productivity growth has exceeded the U.S. rate for many years, the average U.S. worker is still the most productive in the world, churning out a third more than the typical Japanese worker. People in the United States enjoy a higher standard of living than their counterparts in Europe and Japan.[4] And despite all the hand wringing about the decline of U.S. competitiveness, many U.S.-made goods are considered the best in the world. They range from 3M Post-It Notes and Thermos bottles to Polaroid cameras, Remington shavers, Xerox copiers, Boeing airplanes, Levi's jeans, and the American Express card. Throughout the world, the United States is noted for its soft drinks, movies, disposable diapers, cowboy boots, cotton bath towels, and sirloin steaks, to name but a few generic products.

The Balance of Trade

One of the biggest sources of gloom about the U.S. position in the world economy is that for most of the past decade it has been buying more goods and services from abroad than it has been selling. In other words, the United States is **importing** more than it's **exporting**. The U.S. **balance of trade** is determined by the relationship between imports and exports. In years when the United States exports more than it imports, the balance of trade is favorable: People in other countries buy more from the United States than it buys from them, and money flows into the U.S. economy. In years when imports exceed exports, the balance of trade is unfavorable. Money flows out of the United States into the pockets of foreign suppliers.

As Exhibit 5.2 illustrates, the U.S. **trade deficit**—the amount by which im-

importing Purchasing goods or services from another country and bringing them into one's own country

exporting Selling and shipping goods or services to another country

balance of trade Relationship between the value of the products a nation exports and those it imports

trade deficit Negative trade balance

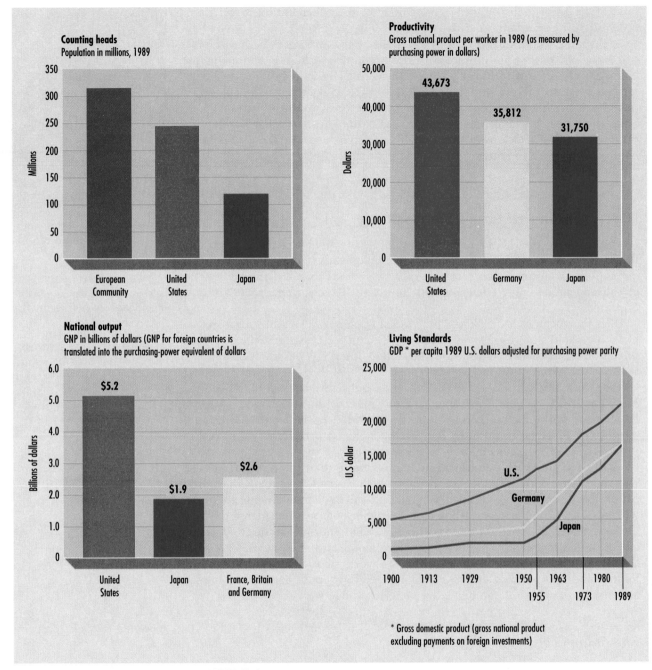

Counting heads
Population in millions, 1989

Productivity
Gross national product per worker in 1989 (as measured by purchasing power in dollars)

National output
GNP in billions of dollars (GNP for foreign countries is translated into the purchasing-power equivalent of dollars

Living Standards
GDP * per capita 1989 U.S. dollars adjusted for purchasing power parity

* Gross domestic product (gross national product excluding payments on foreign investments)

EXHIBIT 5.1

Where the United States Stands in the Economic Race
By many measures, the United States is still the world's dominant economic power, but Western Europe and Japan are closing the gap. The success of the market-based econo-mies is prompting a worldwide rush toward capitalism.

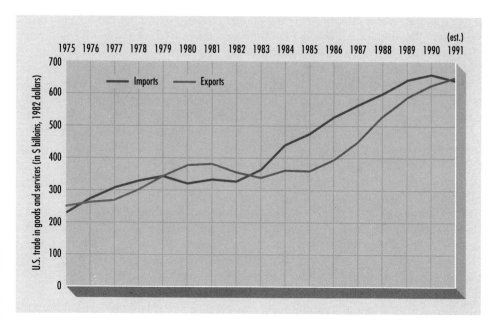

EXHIBIT 5.2

The U.S. Balance of Trade
In the past few years, the trade deficit has begun to narrow as the United States has boosted its exports and cut back on its consumption of imports.

ports exceed exports—peaked in 1987 when the value of the dollar was extremely high against other currencies, making foreign products relatively inexpensive in the United States and making U.S. products relatively expensive overseas. At that point the Reagan administration negotiated an international agreement to bring down the value of the dollar, and the deficit began to narrow. At the same time, U.S. manufacturers went on a relentless cost-cutting campaign to make their products more competitive in international markets. The gap between imports and exports narrowed still more during the 1990–1991 recession, when U.S. consumers cut back on the purchase of imported goods while foreigners continued to gobble up U.S. exports.

One thing to bear in mind about the trade deficit is that the gap between imports and exports does not necessarily mean that U.S. companies are losing their competitive edge. In many cases, they've simply moved some of their operations. The overseas subsidiaries of U.S. companies produce and sell abroad more than $700 billion a year in products that are not counted as "U.S. exports." If one-seventh of this production were shifted here and exported, the trade deficit would be wiped out.[5] Another offsetting factor is that many of the so-called imports into the United States are made by U.S.-owned companies operating abroad. AT&T, RCA, and Texas Instruments are among the largest exporters in Taiwan, and General Electric is the largest private employer in Singapore. These companies have set up factories to make components in countries where wage rates are low. When the parts are shipped back to the United States for assembly, they are called imports. This sourcing pattern accounts for a substantial portion of the U.S. trade imbalance with Mexico, Taiwan, South Korea, and Singapore.[6]

The Balance of Payments

The **balance of payments,** also known as the current account, is the broadest indicator of international trade, measuring the total flow of money into a coun-

balance of payments Sum of all payments one nation has made to other nations minus the payments it has received from other nations during a specific period of time

try minus the flow of money out of the country over a period of time (usually one year). The balance of payments encompasses not only the balance of trade but also payments of foreign aid by governments and direct investments in assets. For example, when a U.S. company buys all or part of a foreign company, that investment is counted in the balance of payments but not in the balance of trade. Similarly, when foreigners buy U.S. companies, stocks, bonds, or real estate, those transactions are part of the balance of payments.

For most of the 1980s, foreign investments in the United States exceeded U.S. investments overseas, yielding a deficit in the U.S. balance of payments (Exhibit 5.3). Whether this is good or bad is a subject of much debate. Some people worry that foreigners are buying up U.S. assets and compromising its economic independence. Others contend that the eagerness of foreigners to invest in the United States proves that its economy provides outstanding opportunities. One thing is certain: The money that poured into the United States from Japan and Europe in the 1980s helped fuel U.S. economic growth. During that period, the U.S. economy created twice as many jobs as Japan and Europe combined, even though those two economies have a population almost double that of the United States.[7]

Regardless of whether all that foreign money is good or bad, the United States is likely to attract far less of it in the 1990s than it did in the 1980s. In fact, in 1990, foreign purchases of U.S. stocks, bonds, real estate, and companies plunged $121 billion to $49 billion; and in the first quarter of 1991, the United

BEHIND THE SCENES

Business Makes a Run for the Border

United States businesses face increasing competition from companies in Taiwan, South Korea, Hong Kong, Singapore, and China—companies that have captured a share of the market with cheaper products, thanks to low domestic wage rates. How can American companies sell their products for less, maintain a desirable profit level, and still pay production costs? Once, the only solution for U.S. businesses hoping to withstand foreign competition was to go to Asia. The answer now is to make a run for the Mexican border.

The border towns in northern Mexico have become home to some 1,900 manufacturing plants, built by such companies as Ford, General Electric, General Motors, RCA, IBM, Honeywell, Memorex, and Digital Equipment Corporation, to name a few. These plants, called *maquiladoras,* manufacture waterbeds, computer keyboards, toys, refrigerators, shoes, and many other diverse items—practically anything that involves a high degree of labor.

Maquiladoras were authorized in 1965, but the real rush to build them didn't occur until 1982, when the devaluation of the peso reduced the cost of land, labor, and local materials from low to ridiculously low levels almost overnight. Wages have increased since then, but the average *maquiladora* worker still makes only $1 or $2 per hour, less than workers in most low-wage Asian countries and roughly one-seventh the U.S. rate. Because of Mexico's proximity to the United States, transportation costs are also reasonable—the trip across the Pacific from South Korea to Los Angeles costs nearly five times as much as the 200-mile road trip from Tijuana, which also takes less time. And finally, there are decided tax advantages: Under Mexican law, U.S.- and other foreign-owned companies can ship raw materials, components, and finished goods back and forth across the border without paying tariffs, as long as the end products are shipped out of the country. Duties are paid only on the "value added" by Mexican labor and any foreign-made parts that have been included.

These benefits have spurred interest in Mexico among other foreign businesses as well. Roughly 30 percent of the border plants are owned by the Japanese, who expect to build approximately 100 new plants each year, employing 1 million workers by 1996. The South Koreans are also shifting some of

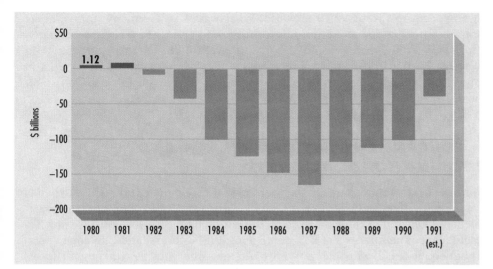

EXHIBIT 5.3

The U.S. Balance of Payments
Throughout the 1980s, more money flowed out of the United States than in, but the gap between outflows and inflows is narrowing.

States ran a surplus of $10 billion in the balance of payments—the first surplus in nine years.[8] The surplus occurred for a number of reasons, the most important being a decline in interest rates in the United States coupled with an increase in rates overseas. Foreigners could simply earn a better return on their money elsewhere. Then too, all sorts of interesting new investment opportuni-

their production to Mexico, and the Taiwanese are looking into the possibilities of doing the same.

Thanks in part to the stimulation of foreign investment in *maquiladoras*, the Mexican economy has blossomed in the past 10 years as the government has turned away from socialism and protectionism toward a full-fledged commitment to free enterprise and open markets. The output of goods and services is expanding by roughly 3 percent per year. The budget deficit has turned into a budget surplus. Inflation has dropped from a peak of 180 percent to 20 percent. Some 75 percent of all state-owned industries have been sold to private interests, and two-thirds of the economy is now open to foreign ownership. Tariffs and licensing requirements have been slashed.

Prosperity will get an additional shot in the arm if the North American free-trade pact among Mexico, the United States, and Canada is enacted. Among other things, the agreement would extend *maquiladora* privileges, which currently apply only to border areas, throughout Mexico. This would stimulate growth in the interior and take some of the pressure off the border towns, which have been overwhelmed by peasants from the countryside looking for work. Housing, roads, and sewage-treament facil-

ities have not kept pace with the influx of people.

Despite their successes, *maquiladoras* have plenty of critics on both sides of the border. Many Mexicans worry about the Americanization of their country, seeing the use of both English and the U.S. dollar spreading in the northern states. "I understand the people of New Mexico, Texas, and California better than I do the people in Oaxaca," says one businessman in Chihuahua City. "We have the same land, the same climate. We're doing the same things."

On the U.S. side of the border, union bosses are not happy about the number of U.S. jobs that may be going to Mexican workers, and environmentalists argue that companies are moving to Mexico to avoid tough enforcement of U.S. environmental laws. To deflect some of the criticism, the U.S. government has promised to provide some protection for import-sensitive industries in the United States if the free-trade pact passes, and it has promised to fund retraining programs for displaced U.S. workers. Meanwhile, the Mexican government is increasing its commitment to tougher enforcement of environmental regulations.

ties opened up throughout the world. What was West Germany, for example, started funneling its capital into Eastern Europe and what was East Germany. Meanwhile, the Japanese shifted some of their attention to opportunities in Western Europe and to the booming economies of the Pacific Rim. The Latin American countries are also soaking up capital as they begin to sell off state-owned businesses to private investors.[9]

▶ GOVERNMENT ACTIONS RELATING TO INTERNATIONAL BUSINESS

How the United States fares in its international economic relationships depends to a great extent on government actions with respect to trade, foreign investment, and currency values. Basically, the national objective is to devise policies that balance the interests of U.S. companies, U.S. workers, and U.S. consumers. Other countries, of course, are trying to do the same thing. As you might expect, the many players involved in world trade sometimes have conflicting goals.

Protectionist Measures

protectionism Government policies aimed at shielding a country's industries from foreign competition

People everywhere are inclined to keep their resources for themselves, to guard against "outside exploitation," and to nurture their own businesses. Motivated by **protectionism,** many countries erect legal fences aimed at shielding their industries from foreign competition. It has been estimated that nearly half of all world trade is restricted in one way or another as a result of protectionist measures.[10] The main types of protectionist measures are tariffs, quotas, subsidies, restrictive standards, and retaliatory measures.

Tariffs

tariffs Taxes levied on imports

Tariffs are federal taxes levied against goods imported into a country. In the past, tariffs were imposed primarily as a source of government revenue. Today, however, most tariffs are protective; that is, they make foreign goods more expensive, thereby giving domestic producers a cost advantage.

During the Great Depression, many countries tried to protect jobs at home by imposing higher and higher tariffs. But these tariffs stifled world trade and contributed to the downward spiral of the world economy. To avoid repeating the problem, the United States led a movement after World War II to reduce tariffs throughout the world. The effort resulted in an international agreement signed by 111 countries that has sharply reduced tariffs. This agreement, known as the General Agreement on Tariffs and Trade, is discussed in more detail later in the chapter.

Quotas

quotas Fixed limits on the quantity of imports a nation will allow for a specific product

As reliance on tariffs declined, many countries adopted other techniques to discourage imports. One of the most common is to impose **quotas,** which limit the number of specific items that may be imported. Often these quotas are negotiated; one trading partner "voluntarily" agrees to limit its exports to another country. Japan, for example, voluntarily restricts the number of autos it sells to the United States, which also has quotas to limit imports of steel, clothing, textiles, footwear, television sets, sugar, and peanuts.

In the most extreme form, a quota becomes an **embargo,** which prohibits trade in certain products or with specific countries altogether. After Iraq invaded Kuwait, for example, members of the United Nations voted to place an embargo on Iraqi oil. Although some embargoes are politically motivated, most are imposed to protect domestic industries or for health or safety reasons. To protect its dairy industry, for instance, Canada prohibits the importation of oleomargarine. The U.S. ban on toys with lead paint is motivated by health concerns.

embargo Total ban on trade with a particular nation or in a particular product

Subsidies

Rather than restrict imports, some countries prefer to subsidize domestic producers so that their prices will be substantially lower than import prices. The idea is often to help build up an infant industry until it is strong enough to compete on its own. The European Airbus, for example, is a subsidized joint venture in aircraft manufacturing supported by Germany, France, England, and Spain. By far the greatest amount of money goes to agricultural subsidies; major industrial countries spend $240 billion a year subsidizing their farmers. The European Community spent $80 billion subsidizing their farmers in 1990. U.S. consumers pay twice the world price for sugar, and Japanese consumers pay 7 to 8 times the world price for their own rice.[11] As such subsidies escalate, primarily benefiting the huge farm industries in the United States and Europe, the United States is trying to spearhead a movement to reduce agricultural price supports.

Restrictive Standards

One way to keep out imports is to establish standards that give domestic producers an edge. Many countries require special licenses for doing certain kinds of business, and then make it difficult for foreigners to obtain a license. In Brazil, import licenses are withheld for any domestically made product, effectively blocking 90 percent of imports.[12] Other countries require imports to pass special tests. The Japanese, for example, set standards for rice based on their claim that foreign rice is evil, unhealthy, and tastes bad. These standards make it impossible for foreign companies to enter the Japanese rice market.[13]

Retaliatory Measures

Although the United States has relatively few trade barriers compared to many countries, it tends to strike back against countries that engage in unfair practices. Under Section 301 of the Trade Act of 1988, the president is legally obligated to retaliate against foreign producers that use questionable tactics in approaching the U.S. market. The United States is particularly quick to act against foreign companies that try to build sales volume by selling goods at a lower price in the United States than in their home market. This practice, known as **dumping,** or predatory pricing, puts pressure on U.S. companies to cut their own prices in order to maintain sales.

dumping Charging less for certain goods abroad than at home

If a U.S. company presses for action and can support the dumping claim, the government typically responds by imposing an antidumping duty on the foreign import, which effectively raises its price to the U.S. level and protects U.S. producers. A recent case occurred when a Connecticut ball-bearing manufacturer complained that rivals in nine foreign countries were selling ball bearings for less in the United States than they were charging at home. When the government imposed a duty on ball-bearing imports from those nine countries, the Connecticut company was happy. However, customers such as General Electric and Black & Decker were annoyed because they were forced to pay substantially more for bearings.[14]

The Pros and Cons of Protectionism

Is protectionism a good idea or a bad idea? The Japanese have one of the most restrictive trade policies in the world, and their economy has thrived. On the other hand, many less developed countries that once imposed trade barriers to shield their emerging industries are now opening up their markets because trade restrictions were stifling their economies. At the same time, the former Soviet-bloc countries have abandoned the isolationist policies that insulated them from the rest of the world.

People in the United States have tended to waffle between an open market and protectionism. This apparent ambivalence reflects the political process by which U.S. trade policies are made. Both the executive and congressional branches of the government are involved, and they have historically viewed trade issues from different perspectives. Since World War II, U.S. presidents, looking at the overall economic picture, have advocated a reduction in trade barriers. Congress, on the other hand, has tended toward protectionism, responding to pressure from manufacturers and workers in their districts who are threatened by imports.

Although the issue is an emotional one, there are few good arguments for protectionism. In fact, study after study has shown that in the long run protec-

India has decided that protectionism may be partly to blame for its relatively poor economic record in the past 20 years. The country's per capita annual income is among the lowest in the world. In hopes of turning the economy around, the government has pledged to open India's doors to multinational businesses, scale back subsidies to domestic industries, encourage trade, and move toward capitalism. With a population of 850 million, the country is potentially one of the largest markets in the world.

tionism hurts everyone. Here are just a few of the arguments against protectionism:

1. Consumers are the ones who bear the brunt of protectionism. As already discussed, farm subsidies increase food prices. Existing U.S. trade barriers are estimated to cost U.S. consumers $80 billion a year in higher prices for imports.[15] In clothing alone, people in the United States pay $20 billion more than they would without restrictions.[16]

2. The cost of saving jobs in specific industries is enormous. Each job saved in the dairy industry, for example, costs consumers $220,000 annually. Other annual costs range from $30,000 (for jobs in the rubber-footware industry) to $750,000 (for jobs in the steel industry).[17]

3. The jobs that are saved in industries threatened by imports may be offset by jobs lost in other sectors of the economy. Workers who distribute or sell foreign goods are likely to suffer with protectionism. Companies that depend on low-cost foreign components may have to cut back on production and employment.

4. U.S. companies could be crippled by protectionist measures, since many businesses depend on imported components, materials, or equipment. Such U.S. multinationals as General Motors, IBM, and General Electric, which import nearly $80 billion in items from their foreign plants and affiliates, would be severely hampered by tariffs or quotas.[18]

5. A loophole exists for every "protectionist fix." For example, when the United States limited imports of cotton from China, the Chinese got around the barrier by switching to cotton blends.[19]

International Organizations

To prevent trade disputes from escalating into full-blown trade wars and to ensure that international business is conducted in a fair and orderly fashion, the countries of the world have created a number of international organizations to facilitate world trade. Philosophically, most of these groups support the basic principle of **free trade**. They agree that each nation ultimately benefits if it trades freely, because it is exchanging the goods and services it produces most efficiently for goods and services it produces less efficiently.

free trade International trade unencumbered by any restrictive measures

The General Agreement on Tariffs and Trade

The General Agreement on Tariffs and Trade (GATT) is a worldwide trade pact that was established in the aftermath of World War II. GATT is actually two things: a treaty and an organization of about 300 people in Geneva representing 111 nations who administer the treaty. Over the years, each GATT country has sent representatives to a series of meetings to iron out trade problems. The guiding principle has been one of nondiscrimination: Any trade advantage a GATT member gives to one country must be given to all GATT members, and no single GATT nation can be singled out for punishment.

GATT has been successful in reducing tariff barriers on manufactured goods, which have fallen from an average of 40 percent in pre-GATT days to 5 percent today. However, as tariffs fell, other nontariff barriers emerged to take their place. Eighty percent of all trade barriers these days are permitted under GATT. Furthermore, the agreement does not cover agricultural products or services.[20]

At the eighth and most recent round of GATT talks, which are now under way, representatives are attempting to deal with some of GATT's limitations.

Since the talks began in 1986, members have been arguing over agricultural subsidies, service exports, nontariff trade barriers, counterfeited goods, and technological piracy. Talks broke down in December 1990 but were resumed in the spring of 1991. A final agreement is not expected before the mid-1990s.[21]

Trading Blocs

trading blocs *Organizations of nations that remove barriers to trade among their members and that establish uniform barriers to trade with nonmember nations*

Although most GATT members continue to pay lip service to the concept of applying the same rules to all trading partners, they are actually moving in the direction of creating or strengthening regional **trading blocs.** Although specific rules vary from group to group, trading blocs generally eliminate special taxes and other trade barriers among members and establish uniform barriers against goods entering the region from nonmember countries.

One of the oldest and best known of these trading blocs is the European Community (EC), which includes most of Western Europe. Originally formed in 1957, the EC started as a loose alliance of trading partners. However, it is rapidly moving toward a much tighter economic and political unity. Its 12 members include Belgium, Britain, Denmark, France, Germany, Greece, Ireland, Italy, Luxembourg, the Netherlands, Portugal, and Spain. These nations are working to eliminate all trade barriers among themselves. This entails doing away with hundreds of local regulations, variations in product standards, and protectionist measures. When these restrictions are eliminated, the EC will function as a single market, much like the United States. Ultimately, the EC hopes to operate as a single monetary unit with one currency; some members are working toward a political union as well, although that will be more difficult to achieve.

With a combined GNP of approximately $5 trillion and a population of 325 million, the EC will be a commanding force in the world economy, on a par with the United States and significantly more powerful than Japan. The EC's clout is increased by its economic integration with seven neighboring Western European countries (Austria, Finland, Iceland, Liechtenstein, Norway, Sweden, and Switzerland) that belong to the European Free Trade Association (EFTA). The pact between the trading blocks attempts to put the EFTA in compliance with the EC's single-market plan. Although both blocks will remain separate, the pact is seen as the first step for many countries becoming full members in the EC.[22] When the trade barriers come tumbling down within the EC, the barriers to outsiders, like the United States and Japan, may become more restrictive. As an ounce of prevention, many U.S. and Japanese companies are rushing to establish or strengthen their presence in the EC. The idea is to become an "insider" before the EC institutes new and more restrictive barriers.

Meanwhile, another trading bloc is forming in the Western Hemisphere, and the United States is the dominant player. The United States and Canada have agreed that all tariffs and quotas between the two countries will be phased out by 1999. Negotiations are under way to extend the agreement to Mexico, creating a North American trading bloc with a population of 360 million and a combined GNP of $6 trillion. In Asia, where the regional economy is booming, Japan is strengthening its ties with Korea, Hong Kong, Taiwan, and Singapore.

Many economists are apprehensive about the growing importance of regional trading blocs, fearing that the world will split into three camps, centered around the United States, the EC, and Japan. They argue that this will undermine GATT and ultimately diminish world trade. Poor nations, particularly, might suffer if they do not fall conveniently into one of the "big three" economic regions.[23]

The International Monetary Fund and the World Bank

One of the major problems of international trade is that some less-developed countries are too poor to participate to any great extent in the world economy. They lack both the capital to develop their own industrial potential and the money to pay for much-needed imports. Two international organizations—the International Monetary Fund (IMF) and the World Bank—are especially helpful in channeling funds to these nations. The IMF, founded in 1945 and later brought into affiliation with the United Nations, lends money to countries that are having trouble with their balance of payments. The World Bank, officially known as the International Bank for Reconstruction and Development (and founded to finance reconstruction following World War II), provides low-interest loans for specific projects. Both the IMF and the World Bank are funded by contributions from the 135 member nations. The bulk of the funds come from the industrialized countries of Western Europe, the United States, and Japan.

In addition to the IMF and the World Bank, there are a number of regional development banks, including the European Bank for Reconstruction and Development, which funnels loans from Western Europe to Eastern Europe; the Asian Development Bank of Manila, funded primarily by Japan to make loans to emerging economies in Asia; and the Inter-American Development Bank, which provides money for loans to Latin America and which is dominated by the United States.

Apart from these quasi-governmental banks, the private banking system is also involved in international lending, although many banks are no longer as willing to make loans to less-developed countries because the countries are having problems repaying existing loans. The international debt of developing countries now totals $1.3 trillion, a sum that puts a severe strain on the economies of the indebted nations. Strapped with large loan repayments, they are unable to pay for imports and industrial development. To ease the burden, Treasury Secretary Nicholas Brady proposed that U.S. banks forgive a percentage of the loans.[24] The deal was good for Mexico, cutting debt payments by $4 billion a year between 1989 and 1994. The unintended effect on many other poor countries is the difficulty the United States is having in paying off its share of the Third World write-offs.[25]

Economic Summit Meetings

Apart from participating in formal organizations that facilitate world trade, some countries also hold occasional economic summit meetings with key trading partners. These policy-making sessions are generally attended by the finance ministers of the countries involved, and they usually deal with such issues as exchange rates and trade imbalances. Because they are attended by high-ranking government officials, these meetings are influential in shaping trade relationships.

In recent years, the United States has increasingly relied on such meetings to resolve perplexing trade problems among the Group of Five (the United States, Britain, France, Germany, and Japan), the Group of Seven (the Group of Five

Business Around the World

foreign sales corporations
Tax-sheltered subsidiaries of U.S. corporations that engage in exporting

plus Canada and Italy), or the Group of Ten (the Group of Seven plus Belgium, the Netherlands, Sweden, and Switzerland, which joined later). One of the most memorable summits in recent history occurred in July 1991, when the ailing Soviet Union met with the Group of Seven to enlist support for moving its economy away from communism and toward capitalism. At the meeting, the USSR was offered associate membership in the International Monetary Fund. Arrangements were also discussed for encouraging Western investment in the Soviet Union and for making the ruble convertible with other currencies.[26] Of course, before much formal progress could be made, the Soviet Union broke up into separate republics, eleven of which formed the new CIS.

U.S. Measures to Encourage Foreign Trade

In addition to promoting world trade through international groups, the United States has established domestic agencies and policies that help U.S. companies compete abroad. Over 15 federal agencies, including the Commerce Department, the Small Business Administration, and the Agriculture Department, are together spending more than $2 billion to help promote exports.[27] One of the most important agencies is the Export-Import Bank of the United States, which grants cheap financing to overseas buyers of U.S. goods. Such low-cost financing is particularly important when making sales to less-developed nations because these countries frequently have heavy debt burdens.

The United States has also passed several laws that encourage domestic companies to do business abroad. For instance, the Webb-Pomerene Export Trade Act of 1918 allows U.S. companies to cooperate in developing export markets without running afoul of the antitrust laws that limit joint activities in the United States. The Export Trading Companies Act of 1982 further eased antitrust rules for companies involved in international business. This act allows companies and banks to form export trading companies to market products abroad. In 1988 Congress enacted a sweeping trade bill that gives the president power to block any foreign purchase of U.S. companies that might endanger U.S. security. The act also requires the government to investigate the trade practices of countries that maintain numerous barriers to imports from the United States.

As an added incentive to exporting, the government grants tax benefits to companies engaged in international business. Companies are allowed to set up **foreign sales corporations** (FSCs), which are marketing subsidiaries that can exempt some of their income taxes on profits from exports.

The federal government offers insurance against some of the political and economic risks associated with doing business abroad. The government-sponsored Foreign Credit Insurance Association and the Overseas Private Investment Corporation offer coverage for losses due to expropriation (the takeover of a business by a foreign government), war, revolution, insurrection, credit defaults, and currency-exchange problems.

When it comes to encouraging foreign companies to do business in the United States, most of the action occurs on the state and local level. Most of the states and many of the major cities have agencies that try to convince foreign companies to open regional facilities that will employ U.S. workers.

Adjustments in Currency Values

Perhaps the most potent weapon the federal government has used to help U.S. companies compete internationally is lowering the value of the dollar relative to foreign currencies. This adjustment makes U.S. products cheaper abroad and increases the price of imports in the United States (Exhibit 5.4).

Because each country has its own currency, trade between countries involves an exchange of currencies. When a company in one country sells its products abroad, the price must be converted from one currency to another. For example, every time a Japanese trading company buys a ton of soybeans from the United States, it must obtain U.S. dollars to pay for them. It may do so by exchanging Japanese yen for dollars at one of the international banks that buy and sell **foreign exchange,** foreign currency that is traded for domestic currency of equal value. The number of yen, francs, or pounds that must be exchanged for every dollar, mark, or lira is known as the **exchange rate** between those two currencies.

International traders operate under a **floating exchange rate system,** a flexible system governed by the forces of supply and demand, which is reflected in foreign exchange markets around the world (in banks and elsewhere). Exchange rates change rapidly because supply and demand are always changing. The relationships among the rates are determined in part by what is happening in local economies. If Italy's economy is suffering from severe inflation and unemployment, the value of Italian currency will be lower than the currency values in countries not experiencing economic turmoil.

When the dollar is strong—that is, relatively high in value—more units of foreign currency are required to purchase each dollar, a situation that tends to depress U.S. exports and stimulate U.S. imports. Conversely, a weak dollar stimulates exports and depresses imports. Between 1980 and 1985, the value of the dollar rose sharply. America's trading partners were not happy about the strong dollar, even though it boosted their exports. The problem was that in addition to attracting exports, the United States was also draining investment capital from those eager to take advantage of the high U.S. interest rates. Foreign trading partners were forced to keep interest rates high in their own countries—which tended to squelch their economic growth. Meanwhile, U.S. companies were

foreign exchange Foreign currency that is traded for domestic currency of equal value

exchange rate Rate at which the money of one country is traded for the money of another

floating exchange rate system World economic system in which the values of all currencies are determined by supply and demand

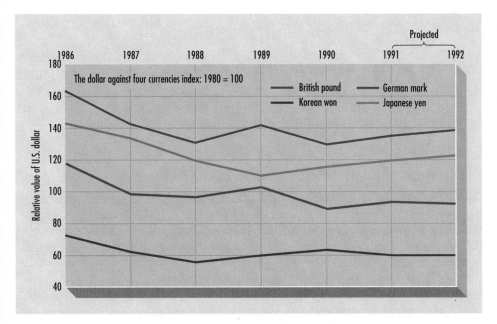

EXHIBIT 5.4

The Value of the Dollar
This chart indexes the dollar's value against the currencies of leading trade competitors. After increasing dramatically between 1980 and 1985, the dollar declined rapidly.

complaining about the difficulty of selling products abroad, and the U.S. balance of payments deficit was widening.

Because of the problems posed by the strong dollar, the federal government decided to bring down its value. The exchange rate for a currency declines when demand for that currency declines or when the supply increases. Given economic conditions in the mid-1980s, the government decided that the best approach was to increase the amount of dollars in circulation, which it did—with the help of Japan, Germany, France, and Britain, which flooded the market with several billion dollars they had in reserve. The value of the dollar began to drop and, for various reasons, remained relatively low for the rest of the decade. However, early in 1991, the dollar's value began to climb again, prompting government officials to keep a cautious eye on its fluctuations. The officials pledged to intervene in the financial markets by buying or selling currencies if the dollar soars too rapidly.

▶ THE GLOBAL CORPORATION FROM THE EMPLOYEE'S PERSPECTIVE

Although government policies have set the stage for the expansion of world trade, the real action has occurred because thousands of companies and individuals acting independently have realized that operating on a global basis is both necessary and beneficial. As more and more U.S. companies compete in the global arena, the odds are increasing that you will be involved in international business at some point in your career. If you work for a U.S. manufacturer, the chances are three out of four that some of your toughest competitors will be foreign companies.[28] The chances are also good that your employer will be selling or producing at least some products abroad, particularly if you work for a large corporation. At last count, some 100,000 U.S. firms were involved in international business in one way or another.[29] Dozens of the Fortune 500 are investing heavily in overseas operations and relying increasingly on foreign markets for sales and profit growth (Exhibit 5.5). Yet another possibility is waking up one morning to discover that the firm you work for has been acquired by a foreign company.

Forms of International Business Activity

As an employee of a company doing business abroad, you might become involved in several forms of international business activity: importing and exporting, licensing, franchising, joint ventures, and wholly owned facilities.

Importing and Exporting

One of the most common forms of international business is importing or exporting merchandise. Importing is particularly prevalent in the retailing industry. Companies like K mart have legions of buyers who scour the world for merchandise to import. Smaller companies, like the gift shop on the corner, also handle imported goods, although they may purchase them through wholesalers in the United States rather than directly from suppliers abroad.

Companies that want to export their products may do so directly by calling on potential customers overseas, or they may rely on intermediaries here or abroad. Working through someone with connections in the target country is particularly attractive to smaller companies and to those with little experience in international business. But many countries now have foreign trade offices that help importers and exporters interested in doing business within their borders. In addition, the International Trade Administration of the U.S. Department of Commerce offers a variety of services, including political and credit-risk analysis, advice on market-entry strategy, and tips on sources of financing. It also introduces U.S. companies to foreign business and to government contacts, and to potential importers, buyers, and agents.

Licensing

Another relatively low-risk approach to international business is **licensing,** where an agreement entitles one firm to produce or market another firm's product in return for a royalty or fee. A U.S. firm might obtain the rights to manufacture and sell a Scandinavian skin lotion in the United States, using the Scandinavian formula and packaging design. The U.S. company would be responsible for maintaining the quality of the product and for advertising, promoting, and distributing the item. In exchange for the rights to the product, the U.S. firm would pay the Scandinavian firm a percentage of its income from sales of the product.

Licensing deals may also work the other way, with the U.S. company acting as the licensor and the foreign company as the licensee. The U.S. firm would avoid the shipping costs, trade barriers, and uncertainties associated with trying to enter a foreign market but would still receive a portion of the revenue from foreign sales.

Franchising

Expanding through franchise arrangements is similar in many ways to licensing. The franchisee obtains the rights to duplicate a product—perhaps a restaurant, photocopy shop, or videotape rental store—and the franchiser obtains a royalty

licensing Agreement to produce and market another company's product in exchange for a royalty or fee

EXHIBIT 5.5

U.S. Involvement in International Business
These charts show the areas of the world that have attracted the most investment dollars and the U.S. companies that derived a large portion of their revenues from operations in foreign countries.

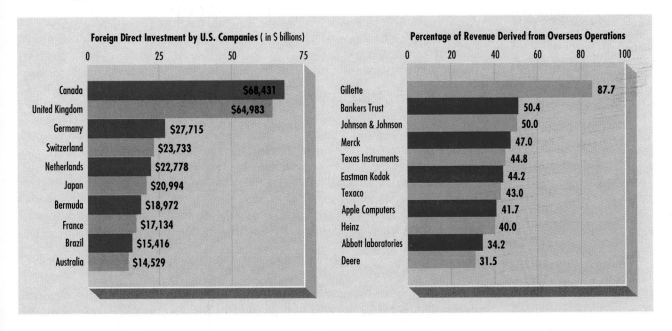

Foreign Direct Investment by U.S. Companies (in $ billions)

Canada	$68,431
United Kingdom	$64,983
Germany	$27,715
Switzerland	$23,733
Netherlands	$22,778
Japan	$20,994
Bermuda	$18,972
France	$17,134
Brazil	$15,416
Australia	$14,529

Percentage of Revenue Derived from Overseas Operations

Company	Percentage
Gillette	87.7
Bankers Trust	50.4
Johnson & Johnson	50.0
Merck	47.0
Texas Instruments	44.8
Eastman Kodak	44.2
Texaco	43.0
Apple Computers	41.7
Heinz	40.0
Abbott laboratories	34.2
Deere	31.5

Avon Products' new joint venture with the Guangzhou Cosmetics Factory may soon bring the sound of *ya fang dao fang* ("Avon calling") to over 500 million women living in communist China (more women than live in the United States and Europe combined). Beginning with a handful of locally produced Avon cosmetics priced to suit the limited Chinese income, Avon predicts that China will eventually become its largest market, providing new earnings potential for over 2 million sales representatives. The venture has already made Chinese history: Avon is the first manufacturer, domestic or foreign, allowed to sell directly to consumers.

fee in exchange. McDonald's and Kentucky Fried Chicken have used this approach to reach consumers overseas, and smaller companies are following suit. Among the hundreds of U.S. franchisers with foreign outlets are Fantastic Sam's haircutting shops, Molly Maid International home-cleaning service, and Zack's Famous Frozen Yogurt.[30] By franchising its operations, a firm can minimize the costs and risks of foreign expansion and avoid violating trade restrictions.

Joint Ventures and Strategic Alliances

Joint ventures offer another practical approach to international business. Two or more companies share the investment costs as well as the profits of the venture, and each brings necessary skills to the business. Often the partnership implies a broad commitment to cooperate on future projects. One such strategic alliance was recently arranged between IBM and Siemans, a large German electronics company. The initial agreement involves construction of a factory in France to produce sophisticated computer memory chips. By teaming up, IBM and Siemans will share the costs of the plant and each will benefit from the other's skills and resources.[31]

In some countries, a joint venture may be the only logical form of business because of local restrictions on direct investment. Many countries will not allow foreign companies to own facilities outright, so to do business at all, you must have a local partner. This was the case when Pizza Hut opened in Moscow. Since private ownership of any business was forbidden in the Soviet Union at that time, Pizza Hut's local partner was the City of Moscow.

Wholly Owned Facilities

The most comprehensive form of international business is a wholly owned operation run on foreign soil, that is, without the financial participation of a local partner. Many U.S. firms currently do business this way, although the operations vary in form, size, and purpose. Some are started from scratch; others are acquired from local owners. Some are small sales offices; others are full-scale manufacturing facilities. Some are set up to exploit the availability of raw materials; others take advantage of low wage rates or provide the most direct access to foreign markets. In almost all cases, at least part of the work force is drawn from the local population.

Take Levi Strauss, the world's most famous brand of blue jeans. Levi's global network of wholly owned manufacturing and distribution facilities provides 40 percent of the company's sales and 60 percent of its profits. Although Levi's San Francisco headquarters maintains tight control of its international operations, the company relies heavily on local managers to find the right approach to meeting the tastes of home markets. Interestingly enough, though, what works in one market can often be translated into another. The Dockers line of chino pants, which provides $550 million in annual sales in North America, combines ideas from Levi's Argentinian and Japanese units. The British operation came up with the popular commercial featuring a young man who throws his jeans into a washing machine along with some rocks to get the stone-washed look.[32]

Foreign Employers Operating in the United States

While U.S. companies are opening facilities overseas, overseas rivals are moving into the United States. In 1991 foreign companies with operations in the United

EXHIBIT 5.6 ▶ **Foreign Employers in the United States**

Many foreign employers have been around for years. The Bank of Tokyo opened its first U.S. office in 1886. Today, it employs 5,000 U.S. workers. Lever Brothers, a Dutch company that opened shop in the United States in 1898, currently has a U.S. work force of 6,000. Swiss-owned Nestlé has been producing jobs for U.S. workers since 1900.

THE FOREIGN PAYROLL

HOME OFFICE	PERCENTAGE OF U.S. EMPLOYEES (1988)
Great Britain	20%
Canada	19%
Japan	11%
Germany	10%
Netherlands	8%
France	7%
Other countries	25%

A SAMPLER OF THE LARGEST FOREIGN EMPLOYERS IN THE UNITED STATES

FOREIGN PARENT	HOME OFFICE	U.S. SUBSIDIARY	U.S. EMPLOYMENT
Tengelmann	Mulheim, Germany	Great Atlantic & Pacific Tea Co.	74,000
Hanson	London	Hanson Industries	50,000
Nestlé	Vevey, Switzerland	Nestlé Enterprises Alcon Laboratories Carnation	48,027
Honda Motor	Tokyo	American Honda Motor	46,238
ABB-ASEA Brown Boveri	Zurich	ASEA Brown Boveri	40,000
British Petroleum	London	BP America	37,000
Royal Dutch/Shell Group	The Hague	Shell Oil	32,434
Siemens	Munich	Siemens	31,000
Bridgestone	Tokyo	Bridgestone/Firestone	28,000
Sony	Tokyo	Sony Corp. of America	20,000
Toyota Motor	Toyota City, Japan	Toyota Motor Sales, U.S.A. Toyota Motor Manufacturing	8,070*

*Does not include 2,800 employees of New United Motor Manufacturing, a joint venture between Toyota and General Motors

States employed some 4.6 million people, and the number of U.S. workers on foreign payrolls is growing by nearly one million each year.[33] Although many people assume the Japanese are doing most of the hiring, in fact Britain, Canada, and Germany all employ more U.S. workers than the Japanese (Exhibit 5.6).

What is it like to work for the U.S. unit of a foreign corporation? If a company headquartered abroad offered you a job tomorrow, should you take it? The answer depends, in large part, on your expectations and on your skill in relating to people from other cultures. Although foreign companies vary widely in their operating styles, U.S. employees tend to agree on a couple of general points about their experiences:

1. Foreign employers are especially good at managing blue-collar workers. Both Japanese and European firms tend to pay their hourly workers somewhat higher wages than U.S.-owned companies do, and they spend more money on training. In addition, foreign-owned companies tend to give employees on the factory floor more say in how to do their work. Job security may also be better with a foreign company, particularly if it is Japanese.

2. White-collar workers are often dissatisfied with the compensation they receive from foreign employers. Although they might have more job security with a foreign-owned firm than they would with a U.S. company, the pay tends to be substantially lower. A high-level executive might make 30 to 40 percent less than someone on a similar level in a U.S. operation.

3. A person's chances of reaching the upper management ranks in a foreign-owned company are limited, particularly if the company is Japanese. Although both Japanese and European firms usually appoint an executive from the home country to the top U.S. spot, Europeans generally hire U.S. managers to fill middle and upper-middle positions. The Japanese, on the other hand, typically reserve the top three levels for Japanese executives. If U.S. managers do hold these jobs, they generally have to clear important decisions with their superiors in Japan.

4. Some U.S. employees have a hard time adjusting to the Japanese emphasis on consensus, seniority, loyalty, dedication, and patience. Adjusting to European management styles is somewhat less difficult because the cultural differences are less pronounced.[34]

If you're seriously considering a career with a foreign-owned company, bear in mind that these observations are generalizations. Each company is unique.

EXPLORING INTERNATIONAL BUSINESS
How to Avoid Business Blunders Abroad

Doing business in another country can be extremely tricky. Companies run the risk of failing spectacularly if any detail is overlooked. For example, merely asking the right question is sometimes crucial. In one reported case, a paper-manufacturing firm neglected to inspect some wooded land for sale in Sicily prior to its purchase. Only after the company had bought the land, built a plant, and hired a labor force did it realize that the trees were only knee-high and not suitable for making paper. The plant had to import logs.

THE IMPORTANCE OF PACKAGING

Numerous problems result from the failure to adapt packaging for various cultures. Sometimes only the color of the package needs to be altered to enhance a product's sales. White, for instance, symbolizes death in Japan and much of Asia; green represents danger or disease in Malaysia. Obviously, using the wrong color in these countries might produce negative reactions.

THE LANGUAGE BARRIER

Some product names travel poorly. American Motors's Matador car might conjure up images of virility and strength in America, but in Puerto Rico its name means "killer," a notably unfavorable connotation in a place with a high traffic fatality rate. When the gasoline company Esso realized that its name means "stalled car" in Japan, it understood why it had had difficulties in that market.

However, some company names have traveled well. Kodak may be the most famous example. A research team deliberately developed this name after searching for a word that was pronounceable everywhere but had no specific meaning anywhere. Exxon is another name that was reportedly accepted only after a lengthy and expensive computer-assisted search.

PROBLEMS WITH PROMOTIONS

In its U.S. promotion, one company had effectively used the phrase "You can use no finer napkin at your

Your best bet is to keep an open mind and base your decision on a careful investigation of the firm's record in handling U.S. employees.

Cultural Differences and How to Handle Them

Regardless of where you work, the growing importance of international business makes it essential to develop skills in dealing with people from other countries. Philosophically, the best approach is to recognize and value the differences that distinguish members of other cultures.

One of the biggest mistakes is to assume that "people are the same all over." In fact, people from other cultures differ in their religion and values, their ideas of status, their decision-making habits, their attitude toward time, their use of space, their body language, and their manners. These differences can lead to misunderstandings in international business relationships, particularly if language differences exist as well. In many countries, for example, women still do not play a prominent role in business. As a result, female executives from U.S. firms may find themselves left out of important decisions when they deal with foreign businessmen.

Although cultural differences pose significant barriers to communication, these problems can be resolved if people maintain an open mind. The best way

VIDEO EXERCISE

dinner table." The U.S. company decided to use the same commercials in England because, after all, the British do speak English. To the British, however, the word "napkin" or "nappy" actually means "diaper." The ad could hardly be expected to boost sales.

LOCAL CUSTOMS

Because social norms vary greatly from country to country, it is difficult for any outsider to be knowledgeable about all of them. Therefore, local input is vital. Many promotional errors could have been averted had this warning been heeded. For example, a marketer of eyeglasses promoted spectacles in Thailand with commercials featuring animals wearing glasses. It was an unfortunate decision, however, because in Thailand animals are considered a low form of life; humans would never wear anything worn by an animal.

TRANSLATION PROBLEMS

Many international advertising errors are due to faulty translations. The best translations embody the general theme and concept of the original ad campaign but do not attempt to be precise duplicates of the original slogan. PepsiCo learned this lesson when it reportedly discovered that its slogan "Come alive with Pepsi" was literally translated into German as "Come alive out of the grave with Pepsi." And in Asia, it was translated as "Bring your ancestors back from the dead." General Motors encountered problems in Belgium, where "Body by Fisher" was translated as "Corpse by Fisher."

THE REASON FOR RESEARCH

Proper market research may reduce or eliminate most international business blunders. Market researchers can uncover needs for product adaptations, potential name problems, promotional requirements, and proper market strategies. Good research techniques may even uncover potential translation problems.

Many blunders have already been made by international marketers, but they need not be repeated by others. Awareness of differences, consultation with local people, and concern for host-country feelings reduce problems and save money.

to prepare yourself to do business with people from another culture is to study their culture in advance. Learn everything you can about the culture's history, religion, politics, and customs—especially its business customs. Who makes decisions? How are negotiations usually conducted? Is gift giving expected? What is the appropriate attire for attending a business meeting? In general, seasoned international businesspeople suggest the following general techniques for improving intercultural interaction:

▶ *Keep an open mind.* Don't stereotype the other person or react with preconceived ideas. Regard the person as an individual first, not as a representative of another culture.

▶ *Be alert to the other person's customs.* Expect him or her to have differing values, beliefs, expectations, and mannerisms.

▶ *Be aware that gestures and expressions mean different things in various cultures.* The other person's body language may mislead you, and he or she may read unintentional meanings into your message. Clarify your true intent by repetition and examples. Ask questions and listen carefully. Rely more on words than on nonverbal communication.

▶ *Adapt your style to the other person's.* If the other person appears to be direct and straightforward, follow suit. If not, adjust your behavior to match.

SUMMARY OF LEARNING OBJECTIVES

1 Differentiate between an absolute advantage and a comparative advantage in international trade.

A country with an absolute advantage can produce a particular product with fewer resources than any other nation. A country with a comparative advantage can produce a particular product at a lower opportunity cost than its trading partners.

2 Distinguish between the balance of trade and the balance of payments.

The balance of trade is the total value of exports minus the value of imports over a specific period. The balance of payments is the total flow of money into the country minus the flow of money out of the country.

3 List and describe three international trade pacts.

The General Agreement on Tariffs and Trade (GATT) is a large-scale agreement among many nations seeking to reduce certain trade barriers. The agreement among members of the European Community is aimed at eliminating virtually all trading barri-

ers among the members, and some see it culminating in political and economic unity. The trade agreement between Canada and the United States represents the first step in a free-trade zone that may eventually encompass all of North and South America.

4 Identify five techniques that countries use to protect their domestic industries.

Five of the most common forms of protectionism are tariffs, quotas, subsidies, restrictive standards, and retaliatory measures.

5 Cite five drawbacks to protectionism.

Protectionism increases prices for consumers, saves jobs at great expense, may cause jobs to be lost in other sectors of the economy, hurts domestic companies that import equipment or components, and is often weakened by loopholes.

6 Discuss the impact of a weaker dollar on U.S. companies.

When the dollar falls in value rela-

tive to other currencies, U.S. products become cheaper on the world market, and its export industries expand to meet the demand. At the same time, imports become expensive, which further boosts demand for U.S. products. Profits also increase when earnings in other currencies are converted to dollars.

7 List five common forms of international business activity.

Importing and exporting, licensing, franchising, joint ventures, and wholly owned facilities are five of the most common forms of international business activity.

8 Cite five things you can do to facilitate international business relationships.

Learn as much as you can about the other person's culture; keep an open mind and avoid stereotyping; be sensitive to the other person's customs; anticipate misunderstandings and guard against them; adapt your style to match the other person's style.

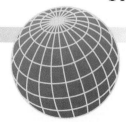

Meeting a Business Challenge at Pizza Hut

When PepsiCo decided to get into the pizza business in the Soviet Union, it established some long-term goals to guide the effort. The company set a basic objective of blanketing the country with Pizza Huts; running a couple of isolated restaurants in Moscow simply wouldn't be profitable enough to justify the effort. Given this ambitious plan, the first two restaurants represented a chance to establish a model that could be duplicated in other parts of the country.

Andrew Rafalat's job, then, was not only to get the two Moscow Pizza Huts up and running, but also to lay the foundation for building a significant presence in the rest of the country. His plan was to set things up, iron out the wrinkles, and train Soviet managers to open similar facilities in other cities. "If we don't develop a construction, supply, and management infrastructure here in Moscow, then we don't have a future in this market," Rafalat explained.

Rafalat started with the Moscow City government. Under Soviet law at the time, foreign companies could not hold a majority interest in a Soviet business, and ownership of private property by Soviet citizens was still restricted. So Pizza Hut had to operate through joint ventures with government entities—in this case, the City of Moscow, which owns 51 percent of the two restaurants.

Rafalat had to pick sites for the first two Pizza Huts. Government officials, who weren't quite sure what a profit *is* and who had doubts about the morality of making one, offered to donate two cellars on the outskirts of Moscow. Rafalat pointed out that succeeding in the restaurant business generally involves putting the outlets where the people are. He eventually wrangled two reasonably decent spots, one with the capacity to seat 325 people; the other, 120 people. After an initial rush of heavy business, the two restaurants were expected to serve between 3,000 and 5,000 cus-

Andrew Rafalat (standing) of Pepsi-Co's Pizza Hut

tomers per day. The typical U.S. Pizza Hut serves approximately 1,200 customers, whereas the European average is 2,000 per day.

Although Rafalat originally planned to rely on local supplies to equip, furnish, and stock the restaurants, he quickly discovered that this was not practical. Nothing was available. He had to import virtually everything from the West, from building materials to tomato concentrate to pizza ovens and restaurant furniture. Eventually, he hopes to develop local sources, particularly for pizza ingredients.

Initially, though, he had to arrange to ship 45 different 20-foot containers from a collection point in London to Moscow. He tried at first to use an all-Soviet transportation route, but the initial shipments were lost for several weeks. Rafalat switched to a London-based shipping company that routed the containers through the port of Helsinki, Finland, and then transferred them to East European and Finnish trucks for the trip south to the Pizza Hut warehouse in Moscow. The warehouse soon had more food than the average Moscow supermarket, including 20 tons of mozzarella and 20 tons of meat toppings.

Rafalat needed to hire and train roughly 300 people—managers, chefs, and other kitchen and restaurant

help. He needed to teach them to make pizza, of course, but more important, he had to teach them about customer service. He hired teenagers rather than more experienced workers because it's easier to teach young people to smile. (At a typical state-owned restaurant in Moscow, customers wait an hour and a half to get seated, wait again for menus, and again to place an order. Then they wait a little longer to be told the kitchen is out of what they want—and no one smiles much.)

Rafalat tackled the training problem by importing five Pizza Hut managers from the West. They spent almost two months giving the Moscow employees a crash course in how to operate a restaurant. They discovered that competition excited the employees; everything from folding pizza boxes to sprinkling on the cheese topping became a team sport, a game to win. Rafalat also sent some of the management-level Soviet employees to London for on-the-job training in existing Pizza Huts. By the time the restaurants opened, the esprit de corps among the staff was incredible; the employees were having *fun,* and so were the customers, who had never seen a cheerful restaurant employee before.

Too bad the government officials weren't as cooperative as the new work force. Rafalat's biggest problem was coping with the many layers of government bureaucracy. Although some members of the government were eager to encourage capitalism and foreign investment, many traditionalists still clung to the communist doctrine and were extremely suspicious of Westerners. Rafalat eventually discovered that many of his problems with the government could be solved with a slice or two of "complementary" pizza.

Finally, after three years of planning and preparation, Rafalat opened Moscow's first two Pizza Huts on September 11, 1990. When he saw hundreds of people lined up to get in, he worried whether the restaurants would make it through the week. Eventually the line wound down, there was plenty of pizza to go around, and everyone survived the initial crush. But Rafalat's troubles had just begun. He had to survive the Russian winter.

Your Mission: When Rafalat took the assignment in Moscow, he asked you to come along as his aide. "You have a knack for figuring out how to get things done, and that will come in handy in the Soviet Union," he said. "I'm counting on you to help me cut through the red tape and develop a reliable network of local people." Handle the following assignments, using your common sense and the principles discussed in this chapter.

1. Andrew Rafalat shakes his head in dismay as he looks at the accounting numbers. "We can't go on importing everything we need," he says. "It's just too expensive, particularly since most of our revenues are in rubles. We can't use them to buy supplies from the West. We have to start living off the land, so to speak, developing local sources. All we really need is the ingredients for dough, cheese, tomato sauce, and vegetable and meat toppings. Surely *somebody* in the country is producing those things. See what you can do." How should you proceed?

   a. Call the manager of the McDonald's that opened in Moscow shortly before the Pizza Huts opened and ask how they're handling the problem of obtaining ingredients.
   b. Seek help from the officials in the City of Moscow who are your joint venture partners. Perhaps they can use their connections to obtain

the necessary ingredients through official channels.
   c. Pass the word among your Muscovite employees that you are eager to line up local sources of ingredients; make it clear that you are prepared to buy through unofficial channels and pay a premium over the state prices in order to obtain consistent quality and delivery.
   d. Look in the Moscow equivalent of *The Yellow Pages* for wholesale food vendors.

2. Although officials with the pro-capitalist Moscow City Council are extremely helpful, officials with the District Council are making life difficult. In fact, a few days after your grand opening, a sanitation inspector closes both Pizza Huts, claiming that you have failed to file the required papers, that your employees have not been properly tested for disease, and that you are using dirty vegetables in your pizza. Rafalat asks for your advice about how to cope with the mess. What should you tell him?

   a. Defy the officials and reopen the restaurants.
   b. Invite the official who ordered the restaurants closed to return for a closer look at the situation. While the inspector is there, subtly indicate that you believe friendly officials should be rewarded with Western currency.
   c. Attempt to comply with all of the requirements as quickly as possible.
   d. Use PepsiCo's influence with highly placed officials to get the restaurants reopened immediately.

3. You accept both rubles and hard currencies from the West as payment at your restaurants. However, since you opened, the value of the ruble has been dropping dramatically as a result of economic changes. As long as you buy ingredients from the West

with Western money and sell pizza in Moscow for rubles, your profits are at the mercy of fluctuations in the value of the ruble. As the ruble falls, so do your profits. Until you can buy more of your ingredients locally, what is the best way to handle the problem?

   a. Raise prices across the board.
   b. Raise prices on all transactions conducted in rubles.
   c. Accept only rubles.
   d. Accept only Western money.

4. Among the many problems that Andrew Rafalat faces, adjusting to Moscow living conditions looms large. He has asked you to help him obtain an apartment before his wife and two children arrive from London, where they have been living while Rafalat checks things out. You have worked with your contacts in the Moscow City government, and they have pulled many strings to get a three-bedroom apartment with a private bath for Mr. Rafalat and his family. However, when you inspect the place you discover that it has no light bulbs, no medicine chest or mirror in the bathroom, no stove, and no drainpipe under the kitchen sink. Large mosquitoes are emerging from the heating vents. What should you do?

   a. Complain to the city officials and ask them to fix all of the problems.
   b. Thank the city officials for their help in finding such a nice apartment for Mr. Rafalat and ask for their advice on correcting these few "minor" things.
   c. Tell Mr. Rafalat that you think he should encourage his wife and children to remain in London indefinitely.
   d. Ask the people at the American embassy to get the names of reliable service people and sources of household appliances and supplies.[35]

KEY TERMS

absolute advantage (125)	exporting (127)	multinational corporations (126)
balance of payments (129)	floating exchange rate system (139)	opportunity cost (125)
balance of trade (127)	foreign exchange (139)	protectionism (132)
comparative advantage (125)	foreign sales corporations (138)	quotas (132)
dumping (133)	free trade (135)	tariffs (132)
embargo (133)	importing (127)	trade deficit (127)
exchange rate (139)	licensing (141)	trading blocs (136)

REVIEW QUESTIONS

1. Why did the United States become so heavily involved in foreign trade after World War II?

2. What is a multinational corporation?

3. What industrial sectors are not currently covered by GATT?

4. What is dumping, and how does the United States respond to this practice?

5. What is the difference among the International Monetary Fund, the World Bank, and the Export-Import Bank?

6. What is a floating exchange rate?

7. What is a licensing agreement?

8. What is an example of a cultural barrier to international business?

A CASE FOR CRITICAL THINKING

Making History in Hungary—Almost

As Paul Panitz watched with amazement the sweeping events that dismantled communist rule throughout Eastern Europe, something inside began to stir. He wanted to join in this tide of change, to become a part of history. His first move was to team up with Fred Martin, president of a Washington, D.C., consulting firm for corporations doing business overseas. In addition to a loan-equity arrangement with a large Hungarian daily newspaper, Martin suggested that Panitz open a small copy shop in Budapest, Hungary.

At the time, international business advisors were predicting that Hungary would make the fastest and easiest transition to a market-driven economy. Economic liberalization had already begun, even before the new democratic government was elected. Free enterprise had been steadily encouraged in limited form, and the new government was the result of peaceful change, with no mass demonstrations or violence. Laws were being rewritten, tax incentives were being offered, and the country's low-paid work force was considered highly skilled in math and science.

Panitz formed a partnership with Martin and Dirck Holscher, a friend who was half-owner of a copy shop chain in the Washington area. The three drew up a business plan and prepared to invest an initial $200,000 in the democratic future of Hungary. Their first need was a storefront in the central business district of Budapest. After considerable effort, Martin located a site through a real estate

agent, and Panitz flew in to take a look. But the deal soured when the Hungarians decided that Panitz was a con man. He didn't wear a suit and tie, and when they asked for a $200,000 "user's fee" in addition to the monthly rent, Panitz gave a flat no rather than negotiating, thus offending the Hungarian sense of taste and diplomacy. After so many years of socialism, U.S. entrepreneurial instincts were regarded with suspicion. Money-changers and black marketeers were the first capitalists on the scene, so the Hungarians seemed to equate all money-making with the lower echelons of life. But such subtleties weren't the only problems.

Panitz's pushy U.S. style was a flop in Hungary, where every business meeting is a dignified occasion, often followed by lengthy meals in which the negotiating parties toast one another with ample glasses of Tokay wine. Moreover, transportation was difficult, few Hungarians possessed telephones, and what phones they had frequently failed. Twice, joint-venture negotiations with state-owned companies were halted while the new democracy undertook extensive reviews of all government-controlled businesses to weed out stagnation and corruption.

Panitz and Martin signed a deal with the elderly manager of one such company, only to learn a few days later that he'd been suddenly pensioned off by the government (apparently designated as a nonproducer).

Another promising intermediary kept changing the subject to other

opportunities: a castle-turned-spa, an import-export business. When he finally did negotiate a lease for Panitz's copy shop, the partners discovered that he was setting up his own jewelry store in the space, leaving them with nothing.

As the new government stopped subsidizing company losses, storefront after storefront was boarded up. But Panitz and his partners were foiled in every attempt to rent the space. The country was in a state of chaos. The old bureaucracy was being taken apart, but new laws and business customs weren't developing fast enough to accommodate free enterprise.

Nevertheless, Panitz and his partners have persisted. At last report, they were negotiating a joint-venture agreement with yet another state-controlled company. The U.S. partners are to supply money and management; the Hungarians are to provide space, employees, and (Panitz hopes) plenty of savvy about the Hungarian way of doing business.[36]

1. How could Paul Panitz and his partners have better prepared themselves for doing business in Hungary? What would your first approach have been?

2. Do you think the partners are wise to continue their efforts to establish a copy shop in Budapest? Why or why not? How do you feel about Panitz's idealistic motivation for the venture?

3. What current events might affect a business venture such as Paul Panitz's copy shop?

BUILDING YOUR COMMUNICATION SKILLS

As directed by your instructor (either in a group of three or four students or on your own), select a U.S.-made good or service that you think might be appropriate for use outside the United States. Next, choose a country that you believe would be a good place to market that product. Finally, develop a strategy for marketing your selected product in the country of your choice.

▶ Using the library as a resource, write a brief profile of your chosen country, and include its geographical location, population, form of government, monetary unit, language, literacy rate, per capita income, and status of communication (number of television sets, radios, newspapers, and magazines).

▶ In addition to the information in your profile, identify other factors that would influence the marketing of your selected product in your chosen country. Such factors might include color, name, potential applications, and social customs.

▶ Prepare a brief presentation outlining how you would present this product in your chosen country. What cultural, political, or legal barriers might impede your business? Would any changes need to be made in the product? Would advertising aimed at the U.S. audience be appropriate in the country you've chosen?

KEEPING CURRENT USING *THE WALL STREET JOURNAL*

Find a *Wall Street Journal* article describing an experience either of a U.S. company or division operating outside the United States or of a foreign company or division operating inside the United States.

1. Describe in your own words the company's experience. Was it positive, negative, or mixed? Why?

2. What cultural or business differences did the company encounter?

What problems did these differences create for the company? What did the company do to overcome the obstacles?

3. Did the company achieve its objectives? What, if any, major changes did it have to make in its plans? What conclusions can you draw from this company's particular experience with international trade?

PART TWO

Operating a Business

CHAPTER 6

LEARNING OBJECTIVES
After studying this chapter, you will be able to

1 Discuss the three categories of managerial roles.

2 Describe the three levels of management.

3 Distinguish among the three types of managerial skills.

4 List the four steps in the management process.

5 Distinguish strategic, tactical, and operational plans, and list at least two components of each.

6 Define staffing as a key component of the organizing function.

7 Cite three leadership styles, and explain why no one style is best.

8 Enumerate the four steps in the control cycle.

9 List five measures that companies can take to better manage crises.

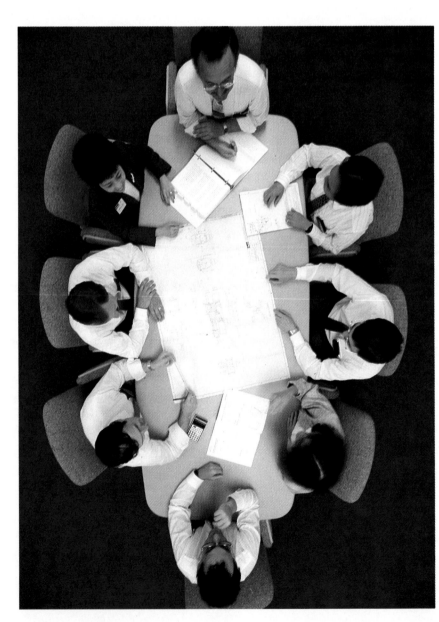

The Fundamentals
of Management

*Facing a Business Challenge
at Microsoft*
STRUGGLING TO SURVIVE SUCCESS

Success brought its own management problems to Microsoft. Shrewd
business deals and sheer luck had propelled the pioneering software
company into a leading role at the center of the volatile, hotly competitive computer industry. But spectacular 50 percent annual growth left Microsoft
unwieldy and disorganized as software companies such as Lotus and Ashton-
Tate were taking aim at its revenues. Computer technology continued to evolve
at a rapid pace, consumers grew more demanding, and rival programmers
worked around the clock to create new and better applications. For founder and
chief executive officer Bill Gates, managing Microsoft required heroic effort.

Gates's visionary leadership was largely the reason for Microsoft's wild success. When Gates dropped out of Harvard to found the company in 1975, personal computers were toys for the "hard-core technoid," as he once described
himself. But Gates envisioned a nation with a computer in every home and in
every office, and a piece of Microsoft software in every computer. An early alliance with computer giant IBM put Microsoft's basic operating program into
80 percent of the nation's 50 million personal computers. Gates boldly led
Microsoft into Europe and Asia too. Motivated by his charisma and technical
knowledge, Microsoft employees investigated new data storage technologies and
broadened software offerings for home and office. In the future, Gates foresaw
handwriting recognition programs, word processing with animation and stereo
sound, modular software that lets anyone combine program features, and more.

But good ideas weren't enough anymore. Gates found he was so swamped by
new business that he could hardly handle day-to-day operational details, much
less develop the vision he needed to beat the competition in the twenty-first
century. Organization was lacking, and planning became an afterthought. Time
after time his company targeted a new market only to introduce a mediocre
product the first time out. Gates put himself in charge of five important product
lines but then couldn't find time to adequately tailor them to client needs. Projects died. Customers got angry.

Gates was also worried about something that threatened his leadership: He feared losing touch with his employees, the people who put his vision into action. In the relaxed atmosphere of Microsoft, talking shop with the CEO was an important morale booster and method of indoctrination. Gates still relished personal contact with employees, but their number had grown past 1,000, and they were spread around the world.

Gates had always made the big decisions at Microsoft, but more decisions were needed and he was already working 65 or more hours a week. How could he both plan for the long haul and effectively manage daily affairs? What could he do to reach the staff and spread his vision? What could he do about control problems? How could he ensure Microsoft's success through the 1990s and beyond?[1]

▶ THE SCOPE OF MANAGEMENT

management Process of coordinating resources to meet an objective

Microsoft's Bill Gates would be the first to admit that management is universally necessary in organizations. It is the force that holds everything in a business enterprise together and that sets everything in motion. **Management** is the coordination of an organization's resources (land, labor, and capital) to meet a goal. Certain basic principles of coordination can be applied to virtually every type of organization, whatever its size or purpose. An auto plant, a city government, a baseball team, a typing service—all require management. Whenever people work together to achieve a goal, someone must make decisions about who will do what, when they will do it, and what resources they will use.

Managerial Roles

roles Behavior patterns

Managers have authority over others, and they gain status from that authority. They maintain relationships with superiors, peers, and subordinates that can be described as **roles**, or behavioral patterns. These managerial roles fall into three categories:

▶ *Interpersonal roles.* As *figureheads* managers represent the firm by performing ceremonial duties such as officiating at company functions, attending employee weddings, and greeting visitors. As *leaders* they hire, train, motivate, and encourage employees while guiding them toward achieving organizational goals. As *liaisons* managers link groups and individuals both inside and outside the company (such as suppliers, competitors, government agencies, consumers, special-interest groups, and interrelated work groups).

▶ *Informational roles.* Among the most important roles managers play are informational roles. As *monitors* they seek useful information, questioning employees and network contacts to obtain as much of the best information as possible. As *disseminators* managers distribute information to employees as well as to supervising managers. And as *spokespeople,* managers transmit information to outsiders, whether through board meetings, mail, or outside contacts.

▶ *Decision-making roles.* Managers use the information they gather to make better decisions. As *entrepreneurs* managers try to improve their units by seeking new ways of using resources and technologies. As *disturbance handlers* they resolve unexpected problems that threaten organizational goals (whether reacting to an economic crisis or disciplining an errant employee). As *resource allocators* they decide how organizational resources will be used to meet planned objectives. And as *negotiators* managers bargain with a great many individuals and groups, including suppliers, employees, consumers, and unions.[2]

McDonnell Douglas managers fulfill their interpersonal roles as figureheads by officiating at the certification ceremony for their MD-11 transport aircraft.

Managers continually change roles as they cope with daily challenges and unexpected situations. However, certain roles may be emphasized more than others, depending on a manager's organizational level.

Managerial Hierarchy

In all but the smallest organizations, more than one manager is necessary to oversee the activities of other employees. Conventionally, companies form a management **hierarchy**—a structure with a top, middle, and bottom. More managers are at the bottom than at the top, as illustrated by the pyramid in Exhibit 6.1. **Top managers** are the upper-level managers who have the most power and who take overall responsibility for the organization. An example is the chief executive officer (CEO), who sets the organization's goals, makes long-range plans, establishes policies, and represents the company to the outside world. Although top managers in similar corporations have various titles—senior vice president, executive vice president, chairman—they may perform the same job within their companies. **Middle managers** develop plans for implementing the broad goals set by top management, and they coordinate the work of first-line managers. At the middle level are plant managers, division managers, branch managers, and their numerous subdivisions. At the bottom of the management hierarchy are **first-line managers** (or supervisory managers). These managers oversee the work of operating employees and put into action the plans developed at higher levels. Positions at this level include supervisor, foreman, department head, and office manager. As more and more companies cut costs and decentralize, middle-management jobs are being eliminated, and greater authority is being given to first-line managers. This increased responsibility is forcing many managers at lower levels to improve their education and increase their managerial skills.[3]

Managerial Skills

Whatever the type or size of the organization, managers employ three basic kinds of skills: technical, human relations, and conceptual. But how they use

hierarchy Pyramidlike organizational structure comprising top, middle, and lower management

top managers Those at the top of an organization's management hierarchy, having the most power and responsibility in the organization

middle managers Those in the middle of the management hierarchy who serve as a conduit between top and first-line management, implementing the goals of top managers and coordinating the work of first-line managers

first-line managers Those at the bottom of the management hierarchy whose power and responsibility are limited to a narrow segment of the organization's activities; also called **supervisory managers**

EXHIBIT 6.1

The Management Hierarchy
Separate job titles are used to designate the three basic levels in the management hierarchy.

Top managers
President
Vice president
General
Pope
College chancellor

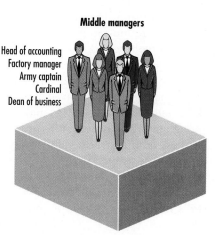

Middle managers
Head of accounting
Factory manager
Army captain
Cardinal
Dean of business

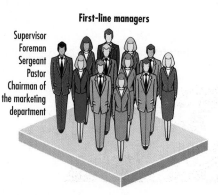

First-line managers
Supervisor
Foreman
Sergeant
Pastor
Chairman of the marketing department

these skills varies according to management level. Because managers accomplish their goals primarily through others, all levels of management need human relations skills. Conceptual skills are needed more in upper-level management, and technical skills are needed more in lower-level management.

An upper-level manager, such as a company president or board chairman, spends a lot of time analyzing information—say, about industry trends and the economic climate—and making decisions based on that information. In addition, top managers spend considerable time communicating with people—eliciting information and conveying decisions. Thus, top managers rely heavily on both conceptual and human relations skills, and they rely less on technical skills.

The middle manager serves as a communication conduit between top management and supervisory management. Planning, decision making, and problem solving are also part of the middle manager's efforts to implement directives from top management and to cope with problems from first-line managers. Thus middle managers rely heavily on human relations; they rely somewhat more on technical skills and somewhat less on conceptual skills.

The first-line manager directly supervises and communicates with employees who are doing the technical work of the organization. For instance, the shift supervisor of a large restaurant would spend most of her time working alongside the serving staff and the kitchen staff, showing them what to do, motivating them, and conveying the wishes of the owner (top management) and the manager (middle management). Thus, lower managers rely most heavily on technical and human relations skills, and they rely much less on conceptual skills.

Fortunately, although some people may start out with a deficit in one or more of the three kinds of management skills—technical, human relations, or conceptual—all of these skills can be acquired with some degree of success.[4] However, some skills can be more difficult to learn than others. For example, some authorities assume that human relations skills are the most difficult to acquire.

Technical Skills

technical skills Ability to perform the mechanics of a particular job

A person who knows how to operate a machine, prepare a financial statement, program a computer, or pass a football has **technical skills;** that is, he or she is able to perform the mechanics of a particular job. First-line managers, such as production supervisors, must often understand a technical skill well enough to train employees in their jobs and to keep higher-level managers informed about problems in the production process. But in certain companies, managers without the relevant technical skills may supervise such highly trained employees as computer programmers, engineers, and accountants.

administrative skills Technical skills in information gathering, data analysis, planning, organizing, and other aspects of managerial work

Regardless of whether they have the technical skills to perform the jobs they supervise, all managers must have some technical managerial skills, or **administrative skills,** such as the ability to make schedules and to read computer printouts. Although many technical skills are not readily transferable from one industry to another, administrative skills may often be applied in a wide range of industries. If you're trained to operate textile-cutting machines, you would probably be unable to use your skills in the restaurant business. But if you're an executive who runs a garment business, you might be able to use your administrative skills in another type of manufacturing business.

Human Relations Skills

All the skills required to understand other people, to interact effectively with them, and to get them working together as a team are **human relations skills.** Managers need human relations skills in countless situations, because their main job is getting things done through people. One human relations skill needed by all managers is **communication,** exchanging information. Communication keeps internal operations running smoothly and fosters good relations with people outside the organization. Of course, successful communication is a two-way street. Effective managers are always attuned to the way people are reacting to what's being said, and most of all, they always listen to what other people have to say.

Effective managers also know how to choose the most appropriate **communication media,** or channels of communication. They understand that the form of communication shapes the message to be communicated. Thus their choice of whether to use oral communication (face-to-face conversation, group meetings, interactive media such as telephones and teleconferencing, or videotapes) or written communication (letters, memos, or electronic mail) depends on the nature of the message. Communication media can be thought of as lying along a continuum from rich to lean, depending on how well they (1) simultaneously handle multiple information cues (such as vocal intensity and facial expression, as well as verbal context), (2) facilitate rapid feedback, and (3) establish a personal focus. Complex, nonroutine messages are best communicated through the richest media (face-to-face or telephone conversations), whereas simpler, routine messages are more likely to be generally understood and so do not require as rich an information exchange.[5]

ORAL COMMUNICATION Speaking and listening—oral communication—generally take up a substantial part of any business day. Within the firm, managers participate in meetings, presentations, conferences, and informal chats with employees at all levels. In fact, some executives use a technique known as **management by walking around** (MBWA) to mingle, develop positive relationships with employees, and learn firsthand what is actually going on. Outside the firm, sales talks, interviews, speeches, and press conferences require managers to use oral communication to achieve organizational goals. Managers often choose oral over written communication because of the nonroutine nature of their work. Face-to-face conversations allow participants to see each other's expressions, hear each other's voices, and understand each other's intensity. Even telephone conversations provide rapid feedback and voice intensity; however, they lack the eye contact, head nods, posture, and other body signals inherent in face-to-face conversations. The more important and unusual the message, the more managers choose oral communication media. However, some volatile situations are best handled through written communication to keep things on an unemotional level.[6]

WRITTEN COMMUNICATION Effective managers choose written communication for routine and simple messages as well as for more complicated and volatile ones. Within an organization—especially a large one—memos, letters, progress reports, policy statements, job descriptions, and other forms of written communication circulate constantly. A company's plans must be recorded in the form of policy statements, summaries of high-level meetings, budget state-

human relations skills Skills required to understand other people and to interact effectively with them

communication Exchange of information

communication media Channels of communication

management by walking around A communication technique used by managers to talk directly to employees and learn what's going on

At Montgomery Ward's distributing center in Baltimore, Maryland, managers often choose to communicate with employees face-to-face, thereby using the richest communication medium to transmit nonroutine messages.

ments, rule books, and any number of other written documents. At the same time, written communication is essential for presenting an organization to the outside world. Letters, press releases, annual reports, sales brochures, advertisements—all play a direct role in shaping a company's public image.

The ability to communicate effectively in writing is a valuable skill at all levels of management. Here are a few basic suggestions:

▶ *Gear your message to your audience.* When explaining how a windmill works, for instance, you would use one style of writing for an elementary-school magazine and quite a different one for a sales brochure directed to potential buyers.

▶ *Write simply and clearly.* Long, needlessly complex sentences will only slow the reader and camouflage the message you're trying to put across.

▶ *Be objective.* If you are not careful about balancing the message, the reader may easily reject it as biased and unreliable.

Conceptual Skills

Managers must be able to think—to see the organization as a whole and to understand the relationships among its parts. Managers like Microsoft's Bill

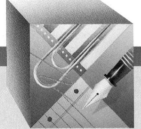

CHECKLIST FOR BUSINESS TODAY

Would You Make a Good Manager?

Assume the role of a manager. Check the statement indicating your probable response to each situation below.

1. If there's an unpleasant job at work that has to be done, I would
A. do it myself. ____
B. give it as punishment to someone who's been goofing off. ____
C. hesitate to ask a lower-level employee to do it. ____
D. ask someone to do it. ____

2. If my boss criticized me, I would
A. feel bad. ____
B. show the boss where she or he is wrong. ____
C. try to learn from the criticism. ____
D. apologize for being stupid. ____

3. If an employee wasn't working out, I would
A. give him or her room to make a big mistake. ____
B. do everything I could to help the employee work out before I had to fire the person. ____
C. put off firing the employee as long as possible. ____
D. get rid of the employee as quickly as possible if the person wasn't any good. ____

4. If my salary increase wasn't as large as I thought it should be, I would
A. tell the boss in no uncertain terms what to do with it. ____
B. keep quiet. ____
C. say nothing but show my dissatisfaction to the boss in other ways. ____
D. ask the boss why it wasn't larger. ____

5. If a lower-level employee continued to ignore instructions after I had told the person something for the third time, I would
A. try to give him or her something else to do. ____
B. keep telling the employee until the job was done right. ____
C. tell the employee that if he or she doesn't do the job right the next time, there won't be a next time. ____
D. try to explain what I want in a different way. ____

6. If the boss rejected a good idea of mine, I would
A. ask why. ____
B. walk away and feel bad. ____
C. try to bring up the idea again later. ____
D. think about joining the competition. ____

Gates use their **conceptual skills** to gain perspective, acquire and interpret information, analyze the information, infer the underlying principles, see relationships, find both problems and opportunities, come to conclusions, formulate plans, and make decisions.

conceptual skills Ability to understand the relationship of parts to the whole

Decision making is a key managerial activity that requires conceptual skill. Many researchers have closely observed decision making and broken it down into six steps:

1. Recognize the need for a decision. Managers continually scan the organization's internal and external environments for changes that may present problems to solve or opportunities to pursue.

2. Analyze and define the problem or opportunity. Managers diagnose causes and specifically define the decision requirements.

3. Develop alternatives. Managers generate a number of possible solutions or courses of action.

4. Select desired alternatives. After considering the advantages and disadvantages of each alternative, managers select the most promising course of action (which may be a combination of several of the alternatives considered).

---

7. If a co-worker criticized me, I would

A. give the co-worker back twice the dose she or he gave me. _____

B. avoid the co-worker in the future. _____

C. try to determine whether the criticism had merit. _____

D. worry that the co-worker didn't like me. _____

8. If someone told a joke that I didn't understand, I would

A. laugh with the rest of the group. _____

B. tell the person that it was a lousy joke. _____

C. tell the person that I didn't understand. _____

D. feel stupid. _____

9. If someone points out a mistake I've made, I

A. sometimes deny it. _____

B. feel very guilty. _____

C. figure it's only human to make mistakes now and then. _____

D. dislike the person. _____

10. If someone working for me were to foul up a job, I would

A. blow up. _____

B. hate to tell him or her about it. _____

C. discuss with that person the proper way to do the job and hope that he or she would do it right the next time. _____

D. not give that person the job again. _____

11. If I had to talk to a top executive, I

A. couldn't look the person in the eye. _____

B. would feel uncomfortable. _____

C. would get a little nervous. _____

D. would enjoy the interchange. _____

12. If a lower-level employee asked me for a favor, I would

A. sometimes grant it, sometimes not. _____

B. feel uncomfortable if I didn't grant it. _____

C. avoid granting favors, since that might set a bad precedent. _____

D. always give in. _____

How did you rate? Give yourself a point for selecting the following answers:

1. a	5. d	9. c
2. c	6. a	10. c
3. b	7. c	11. d
4. d	8. c	12. a

Here's how to score your potential as a manager:

10–12	Excellent
8–9	Good
6–7	Fair
6 or less	Poor

Managers at Westmoreland Coal Sales review potential market opportunities to plan for the decade ahead. Planning is the first function of management and the one on which all other aspects of management depend.

5. Implement the chosen alternative. Through careful planning and sensitivity for those implementing and those affected by the decision, managers translate the chosen alternative into action.

6. Evaluate the results. Managers monitor the results of decisions to see whether the alternative fulfills its purpose, whether any new problem or opportunity arises because of the decision, and whether a new decision must be made.[7]

However, the decision process alone does not guarantee the right decision. For example, when Quaker Oats managers decided to acquire the company that owned Gaines Foods (pet food), Quaker had one of its worst fiscal years in a decade. Even though the logic behind the decision was compelling, the results were a nightmare. Quaker managers made the mistake of overestimating the benefits they would derive from acquiring Gaines, and they did not predict that becoming No. 2 in pet food would make them the No. 1 target in the industry. Competitors intensified aggressive strategies, forcing Quaker to spend against its acquisition rather than manage it for profit, and Quaker's pet food business was badly injured. Nevertheless, executives are planning for the long term and hope to turn the business around.[8]

Managers' decisions are of two types. *Programmed decisions* are routine, recurring decisions made according to a predetermined system of decision rules. *Nonprogrammed decisions* are unique and often nonrecurring, so they cannot be made according to any set procedures or rules. Managers make decisions based on varying amounts of information, so their decisions have varying degrees of possible success or failure. There are four conditions for decision making: (1) When managers have all the information necessary, they feel confident about the success of those decisions, so they make decisions with *certainty*. (2) When managers have good information but not all the information necessary, their decisions have a greater possibility of failure, so they make decisions with some *risk*. (3) When managers have incomplete information, they are required to make assumptions that might be wrong, so they make decisions with *uncertainty*. (4) When managers have unclear objectives, poorly defined alternatives, and little or no information, the possibility that their decision will fail is the greatest, so they make decisions with *ambiguity*—the most difficult and riskiest condition for decision making.[9]

▶ THE MANAGEMENT PROCESS

Managers, whoever they may be, tend to have the same set of functions in an organization. Even managers of the smallest organizations go through the same steps in starting and maintaining a business: planning, organizing, directing, and controlling. As you read the following descriptions of the management process, keep in mind that various levels of management have different responsibilities in each phase of the process.

The Planning Function

Without a doubt, planning is the first management function, the one on which all others depend. Managers engaged in **planning** establish goals for the organization and try to determine the best ways to accomplish them. They consider budgets, schedules, data about the industry and the general economy, the company's existing resources, and resources that may realistically be obtained. An

planning Establishing objectives for an organization and determining the best ways to accomplish them

important aspect of planning is the careful evaluation of basic assumptions. Just because an enterprise has developed along certain lines in response to previous conditions doesn't mean that another way might not be appropriate, given today's conditions. The planning function strongly utilizes a manager's conceptual skills.

Goals and Objectives

An organization's **mission** is its overall purpose. It answers the question "What is the organization supposed to do?" A **mission statement** sets the organization's purpose into words and defines the organization's scope of operations, allowing

mission Overall purpose of an organization

mission statement Putting the organization's mission into words

FOCUS ON ETHICS

When Decisions Are More Than Right or Wrong

When you have all the facts, your information is clear-cut, and your choice is right or wrong, ethical decisions are easy. But situations can be clouded by conflicting responsibilities, incomplete information, and multiple points of view. Large ethical problems arise when a brokerage firm pays huge bonuses to top managers just before declaring bankruptcy, a government contractor hides the truth from customers, and a lawyer trades inside information. Less newsworthy issues include a boss who lies at your expense, a co-worker who pads her expense account, or a supervisor who uses the company's phone for personal calls. The way you handle such everyday ethical decisions shapes the overall ethics of your company, and handling them ethically may help you avoid the sort of front-page scandals that have been in the news lately.

Assume you are leaving your employer to start your own company. Is it ethical to take one or two co-workers with you? Is it ethical to take your employer's accounts with you? If you need to borrow money to make a go of your new business, is it ethical to withhold information from your banker? Three businesspeople faced these questions and made their own decisions.

▶ Andy Friesch founded Heartland Adhesives & Coatings in Germantown, Wisconsin. But before starting his own company, he was still a top sales producer for a very large company in the industrial adhesives industry. He believed that two co-workers would be assets to his own firm, so he asked them to join him in his new enterprise.

Says Friesch, "When it comes to corporate America, individuals have to do what's in their own best interest.

Corporations look out for themselves first and employees second." As it turned out, Friesch's co-workers did not go with him. "They were willing to talk about going off with me, but when it came right down to it they didn't want to make the sacrifice."

▶ John G. McCurdy founded Sunny States Seafood in Oxford, Mississippi. But he was still working for another Mississippi seafood distributor when several of his employer's customers asked to go with him. He believed taking his employer's customers was unethical, so he refused.

Says McCurdy, "I'm only 24 years old, I've got another 40 years left in business, and if I do somebody like that, somebody's going to do me like that." McCurdy is succeeding, but his former employer "got into debt and had to sell out to a big catfish company."

▶ W. Mark Baty, Jr., founded Accredited Business Services, a metals recycling business in Cleveland, Ohio. When approached by a big customer, he needed to purchase a $60,000 specialized truck with hydraulic lift in order to land the account. He asked his bank for a loan, knowing that his finances were a little shaky—he owed his parents and in-laws, his credit cards were stretched thin, and he was juggling his receivables and payables to keep his head above water. He did not lie to his banker, but neither did he reveal the amount of money he owed to relatives and on credit cards. He got the loan.

Says Baty, "You don't lie to a bank—but I certainly don't believe in offering them more information than they ask for." Baty paid off his loan, and his banker never learned of his overextended finances.

1. Given the same circumstances, what would you have done? Did these businesspeople make the right choices?

2. In this sort of ethical dilemma, is there ever a choice that is absolutely correct?

everyone to channel energies in the same direction.[10] For example, the following excerpt is from Motorola:

> The purpose of Motorola is to honourably serve the needs of the community by providing products and services of superior quality at a fair price to our customers.[11]

Through the planning process, the company's mission must be supported by *goals* and *objectives*. Although these terms are often used interchangeably, a **goal** is a broad, long-range target of the organization, and an **objective** is a specific short-range target. A **plan** is the system designed to achieve goals and objectives. Goals and plans have various corresponding levels.

Levels of Goals

To be effective, managers set organizational goals that are specific, measurable, relevant, challenging, attainable, and time-limited. Setting effective goals increases motivation, provides standards of performance, guides action, and clarifies expectations.

Top managers set **strategic goals,** which focus on broad issues and apply to the company as a whole. These goals should encompass eight major areas of concern: market standing, innovation, human resources, financial resources, physical resources, productivity, social responsibility, and profit.[12] Middle managers set **tactical objectives,** which focus on departmental issues and describe the results necessary to achieve the organization's strategic goals. First-line managers set **operational objectives,** which focus on short-term issues and describe the results necessary to achieve the organization's tactical objectives and strategic goals.

Remember, goals are not ends in themselves but the means to ends; that is, you may accomplish your goals, but what is important is whether your accomplishments help your supervisors accomplish their goals. Achieving operational objectives helps achieve tactical objectives, which helps achieve strategic goals.

Levels of Plans

By establishing organizational goals, managers set the stage for the actions needed to achieve those goals. Without planning such actions, the chances of reaching company goals are slim. Each level of goals has a corresponding level of plans for how those goals will actually be achieved.[13]

Strategic plans are the actions designed to achieve strategic goals. Strategic plans are usually long term, defining actions over a period of two to five years. They are laid out by top managers who consult with board members and middle managers. **Tactical plans** are the actions designed to achieve tactical objectives and to support strategic plans. Tactical plans are usually for one to three years. They are developed by middle managers who consult with first-line managers before committing to top management. **Operational plans** are the actions designed to achieve operational objectives and to support tactical plans. Operational plans are usually for less than one year. They are developed by first-line managers who consult with middle managers.

---

goal Broad, long-term target or aim

objective Specific, short-range target or aim

plan The system designed to achieve goals and objectives

strategic goals Goals focusing on broad issues

tactical objectives Objectives focusing on departmental issues, set by middle managers, and describing the outcomes necessary to achieve the results required by the organization's strategic goals

operational objectives Objectives that focus on short-term issues, are set by first-line managers, and describe the outcomes necessary to achieve tactical objectives and strategic goals

strategic plans The actions designed to accomplish strategic goals, usually defined for periods of two to five years and developed by top managers

tactical plans The actions designed to achieve tactical objectives and to support strategic plans, usually defined for a period of one to three years and developed by middle managers

operational plans The actions designed to achieve operational objectives and to support tactical plans, usually defined for less than one year and developed by first-line managers

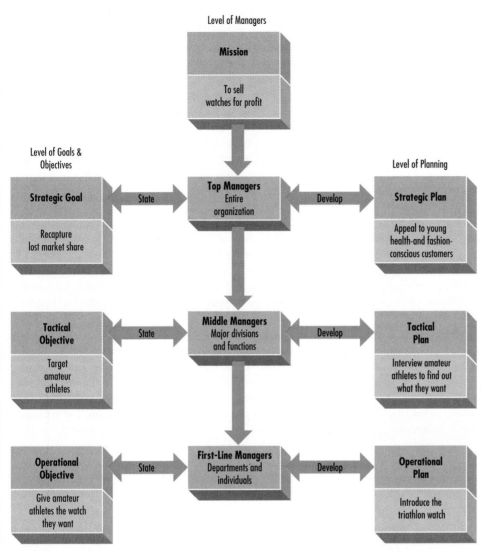

Level of Managers

Mission

To sell watches for profit

Level of Goals & Objectives

Level of Planning

Strategic Goal

Recapture lost market share

State

Top Managers
Entire organization

Develop

Strategic Plan

Appeal to young health-and fashion-conscious customers

Tactical Objective

Target amateur athletes

State

Middle Managers
Major divisions and functions

Develop

Tactical Plan

Interview amateur athletes to find out what they want

Operational Objective

Give amateur athletes the watch they want

State

First-Line Managers
Departments and individuals

Develop

Operational Plan

Introduce the triathlon watch

EXHIBIT 6.2

Managerial Planning at Timex

When managers at Timex responded to hot competition from companies such as Swatch, they stated their goals and objectives clearly and then carefully developed the plans to achieve them. The result was the Triathlon watch, offering sport-chic style as well as the ability to clock activities, including swimming, biking, and running.

When Timex realized that consumers were more interested in style than in durability, top managers defined a bold new direction for the company. They set a strategic goal of regaining the market share they had lost to such hot competitors as Swatch, and they developed a strategic plan to target health- and fashion-conscious consumers. Timex managers set a tactical objective of targeting amateur athletes, and the tactical plan was to interview amateur athletes to find out what these consumers wanted. Managers set their operational objective as giving consumers what they wanted, and the operational plan was to introduce a watch that could clock swimming, biking, and running: the Triathlon watch. The company was so successful with the planning for the Triathlon watch that it developed a watch for skiers, aerobics enthusiasts, sailors, and fishers. Timex's clear mission and planning were directly responsible for the success of its new sport-chic watches.[14] Exhibit 6.2 shows the relationship among the three levels of management, the goals and objectives set by each level, and the plans developed by each level.

The Organizing Function

organizing Process of arranging resources to carry out the organization's plans

Like the planning function, the organizing function makes strong use of a manager's conceptual skills. **Organizing** is the process of arranging resources to carry out the organization's plans. At this stage, the manager must think through all the activities that employees carry out—from programming the organization's computers through driving its trucks to mailing its letters—and all the facilities and equipment that employees need to carry out those activities.

staffing Process of matching the right people with the right jobs

The main problem managers face in organizing is figuring out the division of labor best suited to the goals and objectives of the organization and then **staffing** the various positions, or finding and selecting people who can do what needs to be done. Figuring out how to compensate employees, helping them develop their skills, and evaluating their performance are other important parts of the job.

team Two or more people working together to achieve a specific objective

More and more companies are replacing individuals with teams as the building blocks of organizations. A **team** is two or more people working together to achieve a specific objective. Teams may be found at any level of the organization. They may be formal and permanent (created as part of an organization's permanent structure), they may be informal and temporary (created to increase employee participation), or they may be anything in between. Teams are a powerful management tool: They directly involve employees in decision making and feedback, increasing the power that employees have in the company while increasing the information that management receives from employees. Thus teams appear to increase employee satisfaction, organizational productivity, and product quality. In addition, the broadening of employee tasks makes the organization more flexible.[15] Some authorities cite the success of "egoless" corporations (firms based on team spirit rather than on the ingenuity of one top executive), believing teams should be valued more than maverick geniuses.[16]

Generally, the top managers establish the organizational structure for the enterprise as a whole and staff upper-level positions. Middle managers do the same thing, but usually for just one division. Supervisors seldom set up organizational structure, but they may have important responsibilities in the organizing area, such as hiring and training new employees.

Organizing is particularly challenging because any organization is likely to undergo constant change. Longtime staff members leave, and new employees arrive. Equipment breaks down or becomes obsolete, and replacements are introduced. The public's tastes and interests change, and the organization has to change its objectives. Shifting political and economic trends can cause cutbacks, rearrangements, or perhaps expansion. Every month (perhaps every week), the organization presents a new picture, and so management's organizing tasks are never finished.

The Directing Function

directing Process of getting people to work effectively and willingly

Into the positions and relationships determined by the organizing process come individuals from differing backgrounds with unique interests, aspirations, and personal goals. To meld the staff and the organization into an effective and efficient work team, the manager must also be proficient in a third type of management activity: **directing** is a complex function aimed at getting people to work effectively and willingly. While directing employees, managers may assign work, demonstrate how to do the job, issue orders, and evaluate and correct work. The directing function uses a manager's human relations skills.

Directing consists of two related processes. First, it involves **motivating,** giving employees a reason to do the job and to put forth their best performance. Second, it involves **leading,** showing employees how to do the job, both through demonstration of specific tasks and through the manager's own behavior and attitude. It is this second aspect of the directing function that is focused on here (motivation is the subject of Chapter 9).

motivating Aspect of directing that involves giving employees a reason to do the job and to put forth their best performance

leading Aspect of directing that involves guiding employees in a job

Leadership Traits

When researchers first began studying leadership, they looked for specific characteristics, or *traits,* common to all good leaders, but they were unable to prove any link between specific traits and leadership ability. In fact, whether a particular person will be a successful leader appears to depend primarily on the situation.[17] Even so, researchers have made some conclusions about leadership in general.

Leadership has traditionally been viewed as (1) motivating employees to perform at *expected* levels, (2) providing the structure necessary to clarify employee roles and tasks, and (3) linking reward (self-interest) with goal achievement. This traditional view is called **transactional leadership.** But leaders who are effective seem to go beyond the traditional view. The most effective leaders motivate employees to perform *better than expected,* inspire employees to concern themselves with issues *beyond* their own self-interest, and instill confidence in their employees' ability to achieve their lofty visions of the future. This latest view is called **transformational leadership,** and it includes such traits as charisma, individualized consideration, and intellectual stimulation.[18]

To be an effective leader, you need both transactional skills and transformational traits.[19] Some studies suggest that effective leaders focus their energies on a concrete, original objective and draw inspiration from visualizing that goal in great detail. The effective leader is able to share this vision with others and, by doing so, to inspire them too. Employees perform better when working for a leader who has a lofty ideal than when working for a leader who has no sense of purpose. Finally, effective leaders are able to tolerate failure, and they feel free to explore possibilities that ultimately may not work. Failure is less threatening to effective leaders because they are less likely to assign blame.

transactional leadership Traditional function of management involving motivating employees to perform at expected levels, structuring employee roles and tasks, and linking rewards with goal achievement

transformational leadership Beyond the scope of the traditional management function, involving motivating performance above expected levels, inspiring employee concern for broader issues, and instilling in employees confidence in their ability to achieve the leader's lofty visions of the future

Leadership Styles

Leadership style is the way authority is used by a manager to lead others. Every manager, from the brawling, cursing baseball manager to the urbane, soft-spoken university chancellor, has a definite style. But even though leaders have their own individual characteristics, three broad categories of leadership have been identified: autocratic, democratic, and laissez-faire:

▶ *The autocratic style.* **Autocratic leaders** centralize authority and do not involve others in decision making. These managers use authority in a straightforward manner and simply issue orders. This preference for making decisions without consulting others is highly effective when quick decisions are critical—if the leader indeed has the power to enforce those decisions—because the leader has the necessary information. The autocratic style does have drawbacks, however. In some instances, managers could be more objective,

autocratic leaders Managers who centralize authority and do not involve others in decision making

democratic leaders Managers who delegate authority and involve employees in decision making

laissez-faire leaders Managers who lead by taking the role of consultant, leaving the actual decision making up to employees

situational management Management style that emphasizes adapting general principles to the specific objectives of one's own business

contingency leadership Leadership style promoting flexibility and adoption of the style most appropriate to current conditions

participative management System for involving employees in a company's decision making

Business Around the World

Semco became Brazil's largest manufacturer of marine and food-processing machinery by embracing democracy, profit sharing, and information sharing. By moving beyond participative management, Semco avoids decisions, rules, and executive authority altogether. Says President Ricardo Semler, "It's up to them [employees] to see the connection between productivity and profit and act on it."

could motivate employees better, and could be more open to input from others. This style was the norm for quite a while and is still favored by some managers.

▶ *The democratic style.* **Democratic leaders** delegate authority, involve employees in decision making, and encourage both employee participation and unrestricted communication—all the time making it clear that the leader has the final say. Democratic leaders offer relatively little supervision and are most effective when the employees are highly skilled professionals. But this style has weaknesses: the group may be slow to arrive at decisions, and the leader may end up having little control over employees. The democratic style is coming into use more and more.

▶ *The laissez-faire style.* The French term *laissez faire* can be translated as "leave it alone," or, more roughly, as "hands off." **Laissez-faire leaders** take the role of consultant, provide encouragement for employees' ideas, and offer insights or opinions when asked. These leaders encourage group members to express themselves creatively, but the laissez-faire style may fail if the group pursues goals that do not match the organization's. Although the laissez-faire style was thought to be inadequate for many years, today this approach is seeing a resurgence under such names as self-leadership and employee empowerment.

According to Ronald Pilenzo, president of the Society for Human Resource Management, the move away from autocratic styles and toward more democratic and laissez-faire styles is occurring because "workers of today are different. They have more education, are more self-directed or want to be, and want to control their working conditions. This requires a more participatory or nondirective approach for the manager who wants to get results."[20] As Microsoft's Bill Gates knows, no leadership style works every time. But all three styles work sometimes. In fact, leadership styles can be thought of as existing along a continuum or range of possible leadership behaviors, as suggested by Exhibit 6.3.

Approaches to Management

One manager may use all three leadership styles, but at different times. In fact, each situation may call for a different style. The best approach depends on the leader's personality, the employees' skills and backgrounds, and the problems that the company is facing at any particular moment. A number of contingencies (possible events) may cause the situation to change. For example, the firm may start making new products, or it may begin making old products in a new way. Adapting management principles to the actual needs of one's own business is called **situational management** or **contingency leadership**. Such an approach is more effective than sticking to any one leadership style.

A company that has a regular system for involving its employees in decision making is using **participative management**. Rather than being a particular manager's style, participative management is an overall approach adopted by the organization. It has been widely and successfully used in Japan, and some U.S. companies have practiced it for many years.

The participative approach to management is considered an important tool for today's companies. Participative management works when employees have knowledge and experience that can make a positive contribution to the decision-making process. The success of participative management depends on managers who are willing to involve others and lead them in productive meetings and group problem-solving sessions. It is up to the manager to solicit ideas and encourage discussion and debate. Although participative management does improve human relations, its major value is in improving productivity and quality while reducing costs.[21]

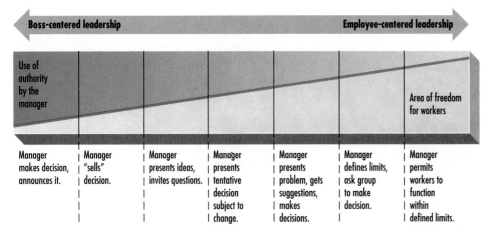

Boss-centered leadership						Employee-centered leadership
Manager makes decision, announces it.	Manager "sells" decision.	Manager presents ideas, invites questions.	Manager presents tentative decision subject to change.	Manager presents problem, gets suggestions, makes decisions.	Manager defines limits, ask group to make decision.	Manager permits workers to function within defined limits.

Use of authority by the manager

Area of freedom for workers

EXHIBIT 6.3

Continuum of Leadership Behavior

Leadership style is a continuum, ranging from boss-centered to employee-centered. Some situations require the exercise of greater authority by a manager and thus fall toward the boss-centered end of the continuum. Other situations call for a manager to give workers leeway to function more independently.

For example, Max Depree, chairman of Herman Miller (HMI), believes in participative management. Every employee of the business-furniture manufacturer is well informed about the company's successes and problems—from factory employees to the chairman himself. Open communication is stressed, and each employee has the ability to go over supervisors and straight to the top with complaints and ideas. HMI managers believe they owe their employees a sense of equality, so they protect *all* employees from hostile takeovers, and they limit top executives' salaries to specific multiples of their average employees' pay. Employees participate in profits, and all are appraised quarterly. The results of HMI's participative management include low absenteeism, low turnover, reduced costs, and increased profits (even during recessionary times).[22]

The Controlling Function

In management, **controlling** means monitoring progress toward organizational goals, resetting the course (if goals or objectives change in response to changing conditions), and correcting deviations (if goals or objectives are not being attained) Managers use their technical skills for the controlling function, comparing where they are with where they should be. If everything is operating smoothly, controls permit managers to repeat acceptable performance. If outcomes are below expectations, controls help managers take any necessary corrective action.

Managers determine where they are by getting reports from other people in the company and from outside sources. They determine where they should be by referring to the goals and objectives that they have drawn up during the planning function. When necessary, they take corrective action by replanning, reorganizing, or redirecting. Thus controlling ties everything together by pinpointing flaws in the other three management functions.

Controlling is strongly tied to the planning function. Strategic plans reflect changes both inside and outside the organization, and the control process tells managers whether the current strategy is working or not. If an organization maintains a continuous control process, mistakes are usually noticed early, and steps can often be taken to correct the problem before any serious injury to the organization occurs.

controlling Process of ensuring that organizational objectives are being attained and of correcting deviations if those objectives are not being reached

At Wilbur Chocolate Factory's cocoa warehouse in Lititz, Pennsylvania, managers monitor employee performance as part of the control function. Controlling links all management functions because it allows managers to repeat acceptable performance and correct inadequate performance by replanning, reorganizing, or redirecting.

EXHIBIT 6.4

The Control Cycle

The control cycle has four basic steps involving all levels of management: (1) based on strategic goals, top management sets the standards by which the organization's overall performance will be measured; (2) all levels of management measure performance; (3) actual performance is compared to the established standards; (4) appropriate corrective action is taken (if performance meets standards, nothing other than encouragement is needed; if performance falls below standards, corrective action may include improving performance, establishing new standards, replanning, reorganizing, or redirecting).

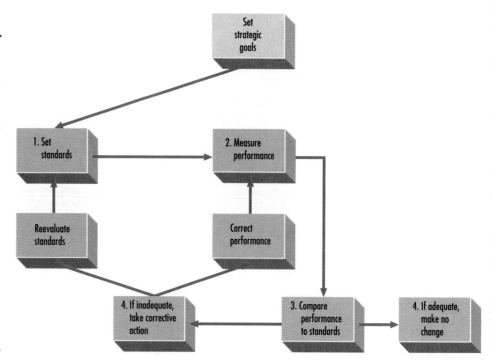

Controlling is a continuous cycle that involves all levels of management, and the control cycle has four steps (see Exhibit 6.4). In the first step, top managers set **standards,** criteria for measuring the performance of the organization as a whole. Control standards must be strongly linked to strategic goals, or else the company may end up strictly controlling the wrong task. Examples of specific standards include

▶ Profits for 1993 will increase from 17 percent to 20 percent.

▶ This unit will produce 1,500 circuit boards monthly with fewer than 1 percent board failures.

▶ Salespeople will contact 20 new prospects each week.

James E. Casey built six messengers and two bicycles into the giant United Parcel Service. He did so by setting customer service as a goal and by maintaining performance standards for delivery people. Some of the 138 rules include emotional stability and neat appearance. Drivers are not to scuffle, engage in loud talk, splash pedestrians with mud, drive on people's lawns, or smoke on a deliveree's premises.[23]

In the second step of the control cycle, performance is measured at all levels throughout the company. Most companies use both quantitative (specific, numerical) and qualitative (subjective) measures. In the third step, performance is compared to established standards. Managers are responsible for discovering the cause of any discrepancies. If the performance meets the standards adequately, the fourth step is to make no changes. However, if the performance falls short of standards for some reason, the fourth step is to take corrective action, which may be done either by adjusting performance or by reevaluating standards.

Another particularly well-known method of controlling is **management by**

standards *Criteria against which performance may be measured*

management by objectives *Control tool in which managers are given the opportunity to structure their personal objectives and work procedures to mesh with the organization's goals*

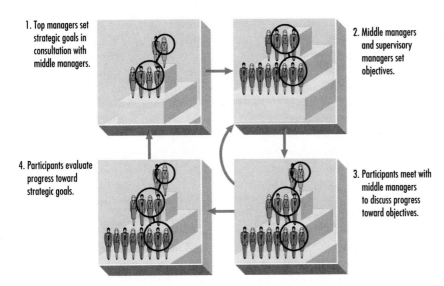

1. Top managers set strategic goals in consultation with middle managers.

2. Middle managers and supervisory managers set objectives.

4. Participants evaluate progress toward strategic goals.

3. Participants meet with middle managers to discuss progress toward objectives.

EXHIBIT 6.5

Management by Objectives
The MBO system of planning has four phases. This cycle is refined and repeated as workers and managers try to mesh personal work goals with the organization's objectives.

objectives (MBO), which uses the goal- and objective-setting ideas discussed earlier in the chapter. This technique, introduced during the 1950s, stresses goal setting at all management levels. An MBO program has four phases (see Exhibit 6.5):

1. The overall strategic goals of the organization are clearly communicated to everyone in the program. These goals are set by top managers, who consult with middle managers.

2. Middle managers meet with first-line managers (and sometimes nonmanagers) to develop objectives. After this discussion, each participant works out measurable plans of action that mesh with the goals of the organization. The new objectives are written up for later review.

3. At frequent intervals, middle managers meet with participants to discuss the participants' performance in relation to the previously established objectives.

4. All participants hold periodic (annual, semiannual, or quarterly) meetings to judge whether strategic goals are being met. The cycle is then refined and repeated.

▶ CRISIS MANAGEMENT

The most important goal of any business is to survive. But any number of problems may arise, some threatening the very existence of the company. An ugly fight for control of a company, a product failure (such as Microsoft's first two versions of the Windows program), breakdowns in an organization's routine operations (as a result of fire, for example)—any surprising event may develop into a serious and crippling crisis. **Crisis management,** the handling of such unusual and serious problems, goes a long way toward determining the company's future. For example, Johnson & Johnson is widely thought to have done a good job of coping with the two Tylenol poisoning scares, moving quickly to remove capsules from the shelves and to publicize the problem. As a result, the effects of the first scare had been almost completely overcome by the time the second hit.

In contrast, H. J. Heinz so badly handled a crisis that the future of its Canadian subsidiary of StarKist Foods was in doubt. StarKist was accused of shipping 1 million cans of "rancid and decomposing" tuna, which were first rejected by Canadian inspectors but later passed by a high government official. Under the

crisis management System for minimizing the harm that might result from some unusually threatening situations

Exxon management has been criticized for its handling of the *Exxon Valdez* oil spill in Alaska. First the company denied the serious nature of the crisis, and then its attempts to clean up the mess were too little too late. Crisis management must be planned to be effective.

prodding of Canadian news media, the prime minister finally had the tainted tuna seized. All along, Heinz and StarKist maintained a stony silence over "Tunagate," and their mishandling of the crisis cost plenty: The company that once controlled half of the Canadian tuna market watched its revenues fall 90 percent. After being closed for almost three years, the StarKist plant reopened in August 1988.[24] Due to the economic downturn in 1979, StarKist closed the plant for good.

Companies that experience a crisis for which they are ill prepared seem to make a series of mistakes. First, warnings about possible problems are ignored at one or several management levels. Then the crisis hits. Under pressure, the company does the worst thing it could do: It denies the severity of the problem, or it denies its own role in the problem. Finally, when the company is forced to face reality, it takes hasty, poorly conceived action.

A better way does exist. Management experts caution that the first 24 hours of a crisis are critical. The first move is to explain the problem—both to the public and to the company's employees. Simultaneously, the offending product is removed from store shelves, and the offending action is stopped, or the source of the problem (whatever it is) is brought under control to the extent possible.

All this is much easier when management has prepared for crises in advance. Many farsighted companies have set up crisis teams composed of people who respond well under stress. These teams identify where their companies are most vulnerable, studying past mistakes committed by their own companies and others. Next, they plan ways to deal with the most serious threats paying particular attention to communication and keeping their companies' strategic goals in mind. The best-prepared companies hold drills, simulating crisis conditions. During the 1992 Los Angeles riots (after a jury acquitted four police officers of beating Rodney King), Arco's crisis team knew what to do for their 132 stations in the area because procedures had been spelled out in the company's crisis management plan. Although developed for disasters such as refinery fires, gas explosions, and earthquakes, the plan was methodically executed by Arco's crisis team, effectively controlling the extent of damage, injury, and loss of life.[25]

SUMMARY OF LEARNING OBJECTIVES

1 Discuss the three categories of managerial roles.

A manager's roles fall into three categories. Interpersonal roles include dealing with people as figurehead, leader, and liaison. Informational roles include handling information as monitor, disseminator, and spokesperson. And decision-making roles include analyzing and making choices as entrepreneur, disturbance handler, resource allocator, and negotiator.

2 Describe the three levels of management.

Top management, or upper-level managers, takes overall responsibility for the organization. Middle management has the task of implementing the broad goals set by top management. Supervisory management, or operating managers, coordinates the work of all who are not managers.

3 Distinguish among the three types of managerial skills.

Managers make use of technical skills, including administrative skills, which are the mechanics of a specific job; human relations skills. which include communication; and conceptual skills, including such intellectual skills as decision making.

4 List the four steps in the management process.

The four steps in the management process are planning, organizing, directing, and controlling.

5 Distinguish strategic, tactical, and operational plans, and list at least two components of each.

Strategic plans are usually designed by top managers to cover two to five years. Tactical plans are then laid out to achieve tactical objectives and to support strategic plans. They are usually made for one to three years by middle managers, who consult with first-line managers before reporting to top management. Operational plans are laid out to achieve operational objectives and to support tactical plans. They cover a period of less than one year and are designed by first-line managers, who consult with middle managers.

6 Define staffing as a key component of the organizing function.

Staffing is the process of finding and hiring the people required to carry out the organization's work. It encompasses compensation, employee training, and performance evaluation.

7 Cite three leadership styles, and explain why no one style is best.

The three leadership styles are autocratic, democratic, and laissez-faire. Each may be best in a different situation: authoritative when quick decisions are necessary, democratic when employee participation in decision making is desirable, and laissez-faire when creativity must be fostered. However, leaders should be flexible enough to respond with the best approach for the situation.

8 Enumerate the four steps in the control cycle.

The control cycle includes (1) setting standards based on the strategic goals of the organization, (2) measuring performance, (3) comparing actual performance to established standards, and (4) taking corrective action if necessary (providing encouragement if performance meets standards, correcting performance if performance falls short of standards, or reevaluating standards if they exceed acceptable performance).

9 List five measures that companies can take to better manage crises.

During a crisis, an organization should (1) explain the problem to the public and to the company's employees and (2) control the source of the problem to the extent possible. Before the crisis occurs, the company may (3) set up a crisis team of people who react well under stress, (4) plan ways to deal with the most serious threats, and (5) hold drills under simulated crisis conditions.

Meeting a Business Challenge at Microsoft

As his much-anticipated Windows program slipped behind schedule, Microsoft chief executive officer Bill Gates knew he had to take himself out of day-to-day operations. Microsoft had great ideas, but it was failing to plan and implement effectively. The new Windows program was supposed to make personal computers easier to use, but it took Microsoft engineers a year to realize that the software needed more memory than most PCs had. When Windows was finally released—almost two years after it had been announced—mediocre reviews told Gates he had a control problem. Other projects had similar woes. Microsoft's reputation was on the line.

So Gates got help. He turned over daily operations to his new president, which freed Gates for more creative work: envisioning products for the twenty-first century and planning for the company's long-term future. Then he got organized. He split the company into two divisions (basic operating systems that control a computer's low-level functions, and applications such as spreadsheets) and eventually into 12 business units, each in charge of a separate type of software.

The new organization improved

Bill Gates, CEO of Microsoft.

both planning and control. The two vice presidents of each new division started holding regular meetings to review progress on product development. And business unit managers began to compare their products to the competition by every conceivable measure of effectiveness and efficiency, from the technical sophistication of a program to the amount of labor that went into creating it. Gates got the same information and called managers directly if he spotted problems. The new organization let Gates stay involved with managers and projects without having to handle daily operational details.

But even though Gates could now effectively lead his managers, he was still concerned that his growing staff might lose touch with him and his strategic goals. He didn't have to look far for the solution: Microsoft established a computer network for its new corporate headquarters, adding an electronic mail system that lets virtually any employee communicate directly with the CEO. Dozens do daily, and Gates tries to respond the same day he receives a message. Employees feel they have direct access to the top. They say Gates's messages are blunt and sometimes sarcastic—but always entertaining. By staying in touch with every level and every employee at Microsoft, Gates ensures that his vision is acknowledged and understood by everyone at Microsoft.

When the third version of the Windows program was finally released, it was a huge hit, energizing the entire computer industry. The program sold 2.8 million copies in less than a year—bringing in more money than the company's total sales of all products five years earlier. Current companywide sales have swelled past

$1 billion, and the staff has grown past 5,000. But with his more enlightened approach to management, Gates is in a better position than ever to handle the complexities of the job.

Your Mission: You're a BUM, one of Microsoft's 12 business unit managers in charge of a particular type of software. Each unit has its own programmers and marketing specialists. Your unit is trying to develop complex software that lets companies tie all their computers together into one network. Although you started as a programmer, you have been a manager for several years and are no longer an expert on the latest technical developments. You report directly to the vice president in charge of business programs, but it's not rare for you to see Gates himself, who sometimes drops by to brainstorm with your engineers. In the following situations, choose the best responses.

1. You're nearing a critical deadline and a subordinate keeps missing his objectives. He promises to do too much and then winds up pleading for more time and resources. He's a recent college graduate with lots of theory but little practical experience. How do you react?

a. You have already distributed a memo stressing the importance of deadlines. You should privately reprimand the sluggish employee and inspire better performance.

b. The subordinate clearly has enthusiasm and technical skills but may lack the analytical and conceptual skills needed to understand his problems and place in the company. Try to lead him out of the morass by talking with him and sharing your experience and perspective.

c. Conduct an efficiency and effectiveness review to see where the problem is. Ask the employee to quantify and justify the hours and resources he has spent as well as the methods he has used. Then

have him pinpoint his least effective and least efficient areas.

d. You hire workers to work, not to make excuses. Simply give the worker what he asks for one more time, then fire him if he fails again.

2. Gates has just left a meeting with your programmers and seems more agitated than usual. During the meeting, one programmer flipped a football, another nonchalantly paged through a magazine, and a third directly rebutted the CEO's criticism with little show of respect. In response, Gates called parts of one program "stupid." You're already behind schedule, and you don't need the CEO breathing down your neck. What should you do?

a. You were intimidated at the meeting because you didn't understand all the technical talk. Bone up on the art and science of programming so that you can better understand and defend your people.

b. Problems are bad enough without your employees showing a lack of respect. Insist that your people adopt a professional air by wearing ties and showing deference to higher managers.

c. Try to get Gates to go through you instead of going straight to your programmers. This would give you more control.

d. Good bosses encourage employees to speak their mind. That's what Gates was doing, and that's what you should do. Talk with your programmers about what they thought of the meeting.

3. Your boss calls and tells you to speak to a magazine reporter about your upcoming PC network program. You know you'll be grilled about product development delays in your unit and in Microsoft as a whole. What is your single best response?

a. Don't deny that you've put extra time into your product, but explain that the company has shifted from a focus solely on innovation to one that also stresses quality and customer satisfaction. Express confi-

dence that your product will be a winner from the start.

b. Don't worry about a thing. If reporters sense that you are too prepared, they'll think you are trying to cover something up.

c. You have the information the reporter needs, so you are in charge of the interview. Prepare responses that promote your products. Avoid answering questions that are embarrassing.

d. Develop a friendly relationship with the reporter to ensure that he or she sees things from a favorable point of view. Suggest that you meet for lunch, and be sure to pick up the tab. Try to avoid talking about product specifics.

4. Your vice president wants you to set up a computer-networking program for company headquarters. You know your current program isn't as good as it could be, and the one you are still developing hasn't been tested in the field. Other companies also offer networking software, and it is possible to combine products from several companies to create your system. You don't want to embarrass yourself—and perhaps the whole company—by installing a system that doesn't work well or by relying on a rival company's software. What's your best response?

a. Your job is to install a networking program, so do it. Use the best available resources, and if Microsoft can provide part of the system, so much the better.

b. Use this opportunity to hone your own software. If problems crop up in the system, fixing them will improve your own product.

c. Seek a delay in installing the networking program until you can work the bugs out of the software you are developing.

d. Announce that you'll use your own software; then tell your programmers to drop everything else until they've perfected the new program. If you succeed, everyone will be a winner.[26]

KEY TERMS

administrative skills (156)
autocratic leaders (165)
communication (157)
communication media (157)
conceptual skills (159)
contingency leadership (166)
controlling (167)
crisis management (169)
democratic leaders (166)
directing (164)
first-line managers (155)
goal (162)
hierarchy (155)
human relations skills (157)
laissez-faire leaders (166)
leading (165)

management (154)
management by objectives (168)
management by walking around
  (157)
middle managers (155)
mission (161)
mission statement (161)
motivating (165)
objective (162)
operational objectives (162)
operational plans (162)
organizing (164)
participative management (166)
plan (162)
planning (161)

roles (154)
situational management (166)
staffing (164)
standards (168)
strategic goals (162)
strategic plans (162)
tactical objectives (162)
tactical plans (162)
team (164)
technical skills (156)
top managers (155)
transactional leadership (165)
transformational leadership (165)

REVIEW QUESTIONS

1. What is management? Why is it so important?

2. Why are human relations important to managers at all levels?

3. Why are communication skills so important in business?

4. What are the elements of decision making?

5. How do goals and objectives differ?

6. What does the control cycle do for businesses?

7. What is situational management?

8. What is the goal of crisis management?

A CASE FOR CRITICAL THINKING

Conquering the Market by Consensus

Considering Compaq Computer's first-year revenues, no one can fault its business style. The company chalked up $111 million in 1983, making it the fastest growing corporation in business history. In 1985, with $503 million in sales, it became the first U.S. company to reach the Fortune 500 in less than four years. The Houston-based computer manufacturer experienced an equally flashy success overseas, boosting worldwide sales close to the $3 billion mark by 1989.

Behind these figures was a "consensus management" technique developed by CEO Rod Canion and two other former Texas Instruments employees (when the three left TI to found Compaq in 1982). Canion

wanted to work at a place that kept him constantly challenged; he cared less about how much money he made than about whether he was enjoying his work, and he figured others would feel the same way. The teamwork management style emphasized at Compaq was based on discipline, balance, continuity, and consensus, and it was backed by a healthy respect for employees.

Canion says his basic philosophy was "to create an environment where people could stay enthused about the company and not be frustrated by red tape and unnecessary burdens," like filling out endless forms and reports, or burning up their creative energy on negative in-fighting. As early as that first year of unexpected growth,

Canion and his top managers did everything they could to avoid developing an entrenched corporate bureaucracy and to maintain a small-company atmosphere. They held company meetings in which all employees got together to talk about the company's progress, problems, and potential.

Most significantly, Canion and his associates developed what they called the "process." Every corporate decision was filtered through a series of meetings among top personnel who formed a product strategy team. The group relentlessly pursued the facts needed to make a good decision, reviewing data on the latest technology, marketing research, and the competition. Two executives would argue opposite sides of an issue to draw out more information, and no one could sway a decision based on their position within the company—not even Canion. Each participant was encouraged to speak up, argue, dispute, question, and eventually (perhaps after many meetings over the course of several months) dig up enough information for the group to reach a consensus. It worked, says Canion, because they took the time to reach "the right decision" by dismantling the industry's conventional wisdom (particularly those conventions that say something is impossible). Once the decision was made, everyone supported it, in true team fashion.

This slow-moving process might seem contradictory to Compaq's reputation for beating the competition to market with new innovations. (When the company introduced its 386 desktop PC, Compaq made business history by being the first competitor ever to get the jump on IBM.) But according to Canion, Compaq's methodological approach was more successful than "speeding along and making mis-

takes that slow you down or permanently derail you."

The company always preferred long-term planning. Shunning such short-term tactics as shifting suppliers or dealers, Compaq defined directions rather than specific goals. As Canion points out, if the company had set out to hit a certain sales figure that first year, they probably would have slowed down in the third quarter at $50 million. No analyst could have dreamed the phenomenal numbers Compaq actually hit, and ever since, the company has resisted the impulse to set targets and shoot for them.

But Compaq's distinctive corporate philosophy is now being put to the test. Its competitors in the PC market are mimicking Compaq's first-to-market style, and Compaq's domestic and overseas sales have slowed dramatically. In 1991 the company's share of the market dropped from 20 percent to 16 percent, and in the third quarter, Compaq reported its first quarterly loss of $70.3 million. Canion was forced to lay off 12 percent of the firm's work force, and a

price war broke out in personal computers.

Canion wanted to wait out the industry slump, keeping Compaq's reputation as an industry leader that can charge higher prices because of product advantages. But the board of directors wanted him to cut costs and prices even more. When Canion refused to share his duties with the European operations chief, the board voted him out. No one knows yet whether Compaq's consensus management will survive the changing business environment.

1. What are the strengths of consensus management?

2. Do you think Compaq's management style is responsible for its financial success? Why or why not?

3. Suppose you were working for Compaq today and felt you had a workable idea for a new product. Given the parameters of "the process," how would you present your suggestion?

BUILDING YOUR COMMUNICATION SKILLS

Examine the managerial hierarchy of a local business. Either interview a member of the business's management team or locate an article that describes the managerial hierarchy of a specific business.

▶ In addition to the job responsibilities of managers at various levels of the hierarchy, consider (1) their roles (interpersonal and informational) within the structure of the business and (2) the skills (technical, human relations, conceptual) required for that position.

▶ Examine how managers are involved in the functions of organizing, directing, and controlling.

▶ Prepare a brief presentation describing the managerial hierarchy you examined. Compare that management system with the systems examined by other members of your class.

KEEPING CURRENT USING *THE WALL STREET JOURNAL*

Find two articles in *The Wall Street Journal* that profile two business or industry leaders.

1. What experience, skills, and business background do the two leaders have? Are there any striking differences in their backgrounds or leadership strengths?

2. What kinds of business challenges have these two leaders faced? What actions did they take to deal with these challenges?

3. Describe the leadership strengths of these two as they are presented in the articles you selected. Is either leader known for his or her ability as a team builder? Long-term strategist? Shrewd negotiator? What are their greatest areas of strength? Financial planning and control? Marketing strategy? Motivating and communicating the company's mission to employees? Or some other aspect of the management function?

CHAPTER 7

LEARNING OBJECTIVES
After studying this chapter, you will be able to

1 Discuss the three purposes of organization structure.

2 Describe the problems associated with specialization.

3 Explain how departmentalization facilitates goal achievement.

4 List five types of departmentalization.

5 Discuss how horizontal organization differs from vertical organization.

6 Explain three methods of horizontal organization.

7 Discuss the positive and negative aspects of the informal organization.

8 List six ways to define the culture of a company.

Organizing for Business

*Facing a Business Challenge
at Campbell Soup*

ORGANIZING A NATIONAL KITCHEN

T he company was a household name. Its chicken noodle, tomato, and cream of mushroom soups were consumed in 94 percent of U.S. homes, and its annual sales topped $4 billion. Most people would forecast a bright future for any company with a track record like that. But former CEO R. Gordon McGovern knew there was something fundamentally wrong at Campbell Soup.

Despite its reputation, the firm was beginning to lose market share. Over the years, smaller firms had developed products that better met the regional tastes of consumers, but Campbell had stayed with its one-taste-fits-all approach, selling the same can of soup coast to coast. It was up to McGovern to examine the company's organization structure to see whether anything could be done.

Campbell Soup's organization structure was composed of teams of experts in functional divisions such as marketing, finance, research, and operations. Within each function was a hierarchy of supervisors, culminating with a functional head who reported to a corporate manager. Top managers coordinated all functional activities, and decisions were centralized to allow the company to meet its goals. Resources such as plants, technology, and advertising were allocated efficiently by function, rather than by duplicating these resources across departments.

For decades, this structure worked well. The management designed successful strategies for rolling out products and promotions like a great carpet from one coast to the other. But the market environment was undergoing profound change. Because of new immigration patterns, people in the United States were becoming more diverse, and Campbell would have to adopt a new strategy; the company had to start thinking regionally, but McGovern saw nothing in Campbell's organization structure that would allow the company to respond to regional differences. He believed that the company's organization had to be redesigned to decentralize decision making, to allow the divisions to be sensitive to (and able to respond to) local tastes. Moreover, he wanted a structure that would allow decisions to be made more quickly.

McGovern recognized that change would not come easily. Such reorganization was not common in the food industry, and certainly not in such a large corporation. How could he restructure the company to be more responsive to its customers? What changes would allow for more efficient coordination? How could he group people and departments to impose a regional focus? How could he decentralize decision making and push it further down the hierarchy? How could he allocate resources more efficiently?[1]

▶ DEFINING ORGANIZATION STRUCTURE

organization Group of people whose interactions are structured into goal-directed activities

organization structure Formal patterns designed by managers to divide labor and assign formal tasks, to define the span of management and the lines of authority, and to coordinate all organizational tasks

As R. Gordon McGovern knows well, a company's strategy is supported by its organization. Whereas strategic planning (Chapter 6) defines *what* a company will do, organization structure defines *how* a company's tasks are divided and *how* its resources are deployed. An **organization** is a group of people whose activities and interactions are structured into goal-directed activities. Whether their activity is playing a sport to win or producing computers to sell, group members work together to achieve the organization's goals.

Organization structure is the formal patterns designed by managers as they (1) divide labor and assign formal tasks to individuals and groups, (2) define managers' span of control and the organization's lines of authority, and (3) coordinate all tasks so that the organization can act as a unit. To be able to talk about organization structures, managers use visual representations known as *organization charts,* which show how employees and tasks are grouped and where the lines of communication and authority flow (see Exhibit 7.1).

Organization structure is important because it lets employees know where and how they fit into an organization, enabling them to work together toward company goals and to feel satisfied with their contributions to the organization. Structure is also the only way to turn strategic plans into action. Without some kind of structure, coordination among employees would not exist, and the best-laid plans would never be executed. Like Campbell Soup, companies around the world are realizing that sound organization structure can be a true competitive advantage.[2]

Technical expertise isn't the only factor in the success of Wood Brothers' Race Shop. Sound organization structure lets everyone know what they are supposed to do, how their tasks fit into the organization as a whole, who makes which decisions, and how everyone can work together to reach company goals.

Consider Glenn and Leonard Wood's small but successful business, Wood Brothers' Race Shop, in Stuart, Virginia. The company is home for three Thunderbirds that are used to race (at over 200 miles per hour) on the professional stock-car circuit. Wood Brothers' has been producing championship racing cars since 1950, and that kind of success doesn't happen by chance. In part, such an accomplishment comes from technical skill and mechanical know-how. But it also comes from good organization.

In the organization Glenn designed, his younger brother Leonard serves as chief mechanic. Under Leonard's direction, Glenn's sons Eddie and Len regularly take the cars apart and rebuild them from the inside out; then Leonard fine-tunes things until he's satisfied. Eddie is also responsible for sealing and smoothing the cars' sheet-metal exteriors (after Leonard has gone over every inch in his never-ending battle with wind resistance). Len works with Leonard on the engines, once they've been built or rebuilt to Leonard's precise specifications by Tommy Turner (who lives in a town nearby). The company's books are kept by Kim Wood, Glenn's daughter.

When explaining the success of his shop, Glenn Wood says, "There ain't no

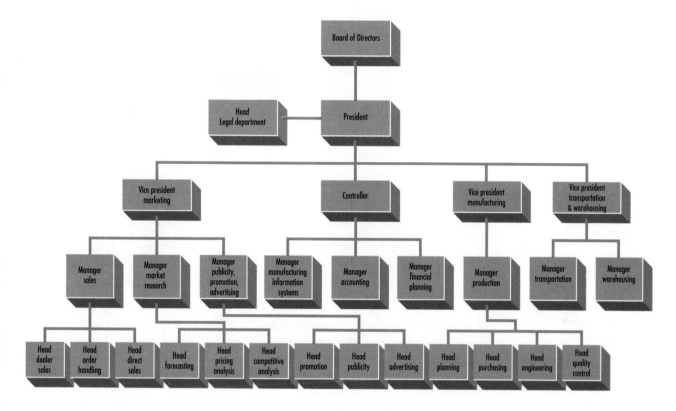

secret. Everybody always does the best they can."[3] But Glenn's too modest about his family business. His organization works: It assigns everyone a specific job, and they all know how and where their jobs fit. It clearly shows who makes the decisions, and it coordinates each task so that everybody can work toward reaching their company's goals.

The organization chart for Wood Brothers' Race Shop shows all the jobs necessary to produce a championship racing car, as well as showing who does each job and who has authority over whom (see Exhibit 7.2). For larger businesses, many of the boxes in the organization chart represent groups of workers performing the same function, as in Exhibit 7.1.

Of course, no one structure will fit every organization, but all companies have one, and each company designs its structure to accomplish its organizational goals. Many companies design relatively rigid structures, with a broad base of employees supervised by several levels of managers. But many other organizations design structures that have fewer levels and are much less rigid.

▶ DESIGNING THE FORMAL ORGANIZATION

The term *formal* means that the organization structure is specifically designed by management to accomplish strategic goals. Thus the formal organization is the official design for accomplishing tasks that lead to goal achievement.[4] (An informal organization structure also exists in every organization and is discussed later in the chapter.) When management writes a description of the way a company is supposed to work and draws up an organization chart, the organiza-

EXHIBIT 7.1

Organization Chart for a Large Consumer-Products Company

At first glance, organization charts may look very similar. In fact, the traditional model of an organization is a triangle or pyramid in which numerous boxes form the base and lead up to fewer and fewer boxes on higher levels, ultimately arriving at one box at the top. A glance at a company's organization chart reveals who has authority over whom, who is responsible for whose work, and who is accountable for whom.

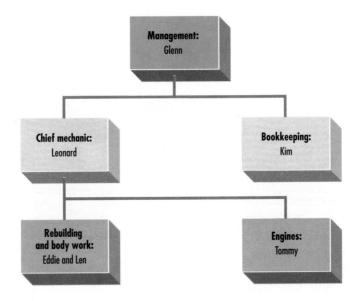

vertical organization Structure linking activities at the top of the organization with those at the middle and lower levels

division of labor Specialization in or responsibility for some portion of an organization's overall task

Business Around the World

To return dignity to employees, Sweden's Volvo abandoned work specialization to run its Uddevalla car-assembly plant without an assembly line, using small teams to build an entire car. However, the company is having trouble competing with the more specialized (and more efficient) assembly-line plants.

tional plan has been *formalized*; that is, the structure is recorded in a form that can be seen by other people and passed from one generation of managers to the next.

To design a company's organization structure, managers must consider three phases: (1) vertical organization (creating jobs out of the tasks necessary to accomplish the planned work), (2) departmentalization (grouping jobs into departments and larger units), and (3) horizontal organization (coordinating all tasks so that the company can operate as a single unit). Neglecting any of these phases would doom even the best-planned company to failure. From president to assembly-line workers, every employee must understand who will make the decisions, how the organization's work is divided, and how everyone can work together to achieve strategic goals.

Vertical Organization

Vertical organization links activities at the top of the organization with those at the middle and lower levels in order to achieve organizational goals.[5] After top managers define the mission and organizational goals, they define the specific tasks necessary to achieve those goals. To perform the tasks, they hire people who can help them achieve their goals.

Division of Labor

Modern business organizations must perform a wide variety of tasks, which must be subdivided into distinct jobs to be accomplished efficiently. This process is called **division of labor**. In 1776 Scottish economist Adam Smith found that if each of 10 workers went through every step needed to make a pin, the entire group could make 200 pins a day. But if each worker performed only a few steps and no one made a pin from start to finish, the same 10 workers could make 48,000 pins a day. Because few employees have the skills to perform every task a company needs, division of labor (or *work specialization*) allows organizations to function.

Dividing labor improves organization efficiency because each worker performs tasks that are well defined and that require specific skills. When employees repeatedly perform the same specialized tasks, their skills are perfected, and they are able to perform the task more quickly. Also, managers can select employees with the specific skills needed, and by not asking employees to shift from task to task, managers can shorten the learning curve.

However, organizations can overdo specialization. If a task is defined too narrowly, employees become bored with performing the same tiny, repetitive job over and over. Also, they feel unchallenged and alienated. All organizational managers must be concerned about how specialized or how broad each task should be.[6] In fact, more and more organizations are attempting to balance specialization and employee motivation by encouraging employees and work teams to share responsibility for the final product and to decide for themselves how to break down a complex task.

An organization functions more smoothly if employees know not only what to do and when to do it but also who is monitoring them to make sure they do it right. So when planners work out divisions of labor for an organization, they must be sure to grant the right amount of authority to those who will need it to do the job.

Specialization helps improve efficiency and perfect skill. Thus Cabeltron uses an assembly line to produce circuit boards in Rochester, New Hampshire. However, too much specialization alienates employees by trapping them in repetitive jobs that offer no challenge.

Authority, Responsibility, and Accountability

In organizations, employees are assigned **responsibility** for their positions; that is, they are obligated to perform those duties and to achieve those goals and objectives associated with their positions. As employees work toward organizational goals, they report their results to supervisors and justify any outcomes that fall below expectations. This reporting is called **accountability.** Managers ensure that employees do their jobs by exercising **authority,** the right to make decisions, issue orders, carry out actions, and allocate resources to achieve organizational goals. A glance at a company's organization chart reveals who has authority over whom, who is responsible for which tasks, and who is accountable to whom.

The organization chart in Exhibit 7.2 shows authority, responsibility, and accountability in Wood Brothers' Race Shop. The boxes representing Eddie, Len, and Tommy are on the same row, indicating that these people are equals in the Wood Brothers' organization. The lines going up from their boxes to Leonard's indicate that Leonard gives them instructions and oversees their work. Although Kim's box is on the same row as Leonard's, the fact that she, as bookkeeper, has no authority over Eddie, Len, and Tommy is indicated by the absence of any lines from their boxes to hers. The placement of Glenn's box at the top of the chart and the lines leading from it show that he has ultimate authority and responsibility. He directly supervises both Kim and Leonard and, through Leonard, indirectly supervises Eddie, Len, and Tommy. Thus vertical structure helps managers delegate authority through the chain of command, it defines each manager's span of control, and it dictates whether decision making will be centralized or decentralized.

responsibility The obligation to perform the duties and to achieve the goals and objectives associated with a position in the organization

accountability The necessity to report results to supervisors and justify outcomes that fall below expectations

authority Power granted by the organization and acknowledged by the employees

Delegation

Except in the smallest businesses, no one person can oversee and control all the work. **Delegation** is the assignment of work and of the authority, responsibility,

delegation Assignment of authority, responsibility, and accountability to lower-level employees

and accountability to do that work. On paper, delegating authority is a fairly simple, straightforward matter. In practice, however, it can be far more complicated. First, planners have to decide the degree to which those at the top of the hierarchy will be held accountable for the performance of those at the bottom. Consider, for example, Joseph Hazelwood, captain of the *Exxon Valdez*, who was forced to stand trial for his ship's oil spill off Alaska, even though he wasn't at the helm when the accident happened.

Second, planners must determine how much authority to give employees in order to allow them to do their jobs properly:

1. If workers are told to drill a hole, they must be given the authority to get a drill from the company's equipment room.

EXPLORING INTERNATIONAL BUSINESS

The ABCs of ABB's Organization Structure

What kind of organization structure is appropriate for a corporation with 1,300 subsidiaries and 215,000 employees spread around the world? Percy Barnevik faced this challenge when he engineered the merger of Sweden's Asea and Switzerland's Brown Boveri into Zurich-based ABB Asea Brown Boveri. ABB is a global organization producing electrical power equipment, robots, locomotives, and other industrial goods. Barnevik needed an organization design that would allow all ABB subsidiaries to concentrate on meeting customer needs. At the same time, the organization structure would have to enhance corporate performance in diverse global environments.

To start, Barnevik embraced decentralization with a vengeance. He quickly pushed responsibility, authority, and accountability as far down the hierarchy as possible to put decision making in the hands of the ABB people closest to the customers they served. Next he created an organization design he calls a "multidomestic corporation." In addition to departmentalizing by function and by division (based on product), he carved out a series of 100 national companies. The top managers of each national company were directed to act as though they managed a domestic company, and they assumed the responsibility for dealing with their own local governments, unions, and customers. Manufacturing was also decentralized so that products would be manufactured in the customer's country whenever possible.

Barnevik's unique multidomestic corporate structure has allowed each national company to develop a local identity that attracts domestic orders as well as export orders. For example, ABB's Combustion Engineering unit (headquartered in the United States) serves many U.S. customers but also serves customers abroad. In South Korea, Combustion Engineering is building nuclear power plants. The subsidiary operates as a U.S. company, so it must comply with U.S. legal and regulatory guidelines. Moreover, despite its Swiss ownership, Combustion Engineering also enjoys the support of the U.S. government, which can be particularly helpful in trade negotiations.

Thanks to this organization design, ABB subsidiaries have been able to reap the benefits of acting locally while taking advantage of the parent company's resources. Although decentralization has helped subsidiaries focus on executing customer-oriented strategy, Barnevik has also applied centralization to coordinate activities that cut across company (and country) lines. He has designated key research-and-development labs in Germany, Switzerland, and Sweden as "centers of excellence." Rather than duplicate research activities in individual subsidiaries, Barnevik has assigned these labs to conduct basic research in support of innovation throughout the corporation. The money he saves as a result of such efficiencies is plowed right back into research so that overall R&D expenditures remain sufficiently high to fuel long-term growth.

Barnevik developed his organization structure in record time, announcing the new design some five months after the merger was announced. He hasn't slowed since, and his subsequent acquisitions and joint ventures have only contributed to ABB's explosive growth.

2. If salespeople are responsible for keeping customers happy, they shouldn't have to go through an elaborate procedure to handle an exchange of merchandise.

3. If managers are made responsible for increasing production, they must be given the authority to hire and fire employees, to raise salaries, or to rearrange work.

Delegation will not work unless responsibility matches authority.

Third, authority can only be delegated to *willing* recipients. If an employee does not accept the authority, there can be no delegation. Of course, people join organizations to achieve certain benefits, and the cost of those benefits is the acceptance of a certain amount of authority and responsibility as determined by the organization. As long as authority is delegated within these bounds, most employees accept them.

Fourth, the planners themselves must also accept the idea of delegation. When planners delegate, they are giving up a portion of their control over people, tasks, and results. Unlike Campbell's McGovern, some managers find it difficult to give up authority.

CHAIN OF COMMAND   Every vertical structure has an identifiable flow of authority and communication. By assigning tasks, authority, and responsibility, the vertical structure establishes the **chain of command,** the unbroken line of authority that connects each level of employee to the next. The chain of command establishes who has the authority to give directions and who reports to whom. Two basic principles are associated with the chain of command: (1) each employee is held accountable to only one supervisor, and (2) the line of authority in an organization includes every employee and is clearly defined.

LINE AND STAFF ORGANIZATION   The simplest and most common chain-of-command system is known as **line organization** because it establishes a clear line of authority flowing from the top down. Everyone knows who is responsible to whom, and the ultimate authority is easily identified. The organization chart in Exhibit 7.2 represents this pattern.

Enterprises structured according to line organization enjoy a number of practical advantages. Because managers know when and where they can make decisions, line authority tends to speed decision making, simplify discipline, and clarify the channels for communication. In addition, the simplicity of line organization sometimes results in lower expenses.

On the other hand, line organization also carries at least three important disadvantages. First, since it concentrates most decision-making power at the upper levels of management, lower-level employees may have trouble learning the skills needed to move into top positions. Second, the technical complexity of a firm's activities may require specialized knowledge that its top management does not have and cannot easily tap. Third, growth may extend the chain of command to the point that communication and decision making take too long.

A more elaborate system, known as **line-and-staff organization,** has developed out of the need to combine specialization with management control. This form of organization has a clear chain of command from the top down but also includes functional groupings of people who come under the heading of staff. Traditionally, the line organization manages the primary activities of the organization. The **staff** supplements the line organization by providing advice and specialized services. Persons in the staff organization are not in the line organization's chain of command (see Exhibit 7.3). The main advantage of line-and-

As in every company, the chain of command at Whiting-Turner Contracting makes it clear who reports to whom.

chain of command Pathway for the flow of authority from one level of an organization's employees to the next

line organization Chain-of-command system that establishes a clear line of authority flowing from the top down to subordinates

line-and-staff organization Organization system that has a clear chain of command from the top down but that also includes functional groups of people who come under the heading of staff

staff Those who supplement the line organization by providing advice and specialized services

EXHIBIT 7.3

Simplified Line-and-Staff Structure

A line-and-staff organization divides employees into those who are in the direct line of command (from the top level of the hierarchy to the bottom) and those who provide staff (or support) services to line managers at various levels but who report directly to top management.

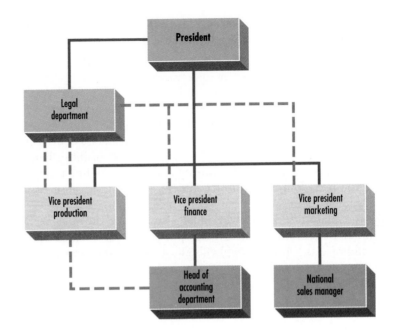

staff organization is that it can incorporate experts in specific areas into the formal chain of command.

Span of Management

span of management Breadth of a manager's authority; also known as **span of control**

The number of people a manager directly supervises is called a **span of management** or *span of control*. When a large number of people report directly to a manager, he or she has a wide span of management. When only a few people report, the span is narrow. Fewer managers are required when each has a wide

At Detroit area's Tech Center, General Motors Automotive Design director Charles Jordan oversees the redesign of a futuristic prototype. When only three or four people report to a manager, the span of management is fairly narrow.

span of control. The question, however, is how many people a manager can effectively oversee.

No formula exists for determining the ideal span of management. How well people work together is more important than the number of people reporting to one person. Nevertheless, several factors affect the number of people a manager can effectively supervise, including the manager's personal skill and leadership ability, the skill of the workers, the motivation of the workers, and the nature of the job. In general, highly skilled employees don't require as much supervision as less-skilled employees. The manager of an organization made up almost exclusively of professionals or scientists may, therefore, have a wide span of management.[7]

The span of management determines the number of hierarchical levels in a company, or whether the vertical structure is tall or flat. A **tall structure** has a narrower span and more hierarchical levels. A **flat structure** has a wide span of management and fewer hierarchical levels (see Exhibit 7.4). Tall structures cost more because more managers must be paid. Their many hierarchical levels delay communication and decision making. They make it harder to pinpoint responsibility for various tasks, and they promote the creation of dull, routine jobs.[8]

To counteract the problems inherent in tall structures and to improve effectiveness, companies have recently been **downsizing**, reducing the layers of middle management, expanding spans of control, and shrinking the size of the work force. At General Electric a decade ago, as many as ten layers of people separated top management from employees on the shop floor, but today only five levels separate CEO Jack Welch from the front lines.[9]

tall structure Structure having a narrower span of management and more hierarchical levels

flat structure Structure having a wider span of management and fewer hierarchical levels

downsizing Laying off employees in an effort to become more profitable

centralization Concentration of authority and responsibility at the top

decentralization Delegation of authority and responsibility to employees in lower positions

Centralization Versus Decentralization

The hierarchical level at which decisions are made is determined by how centralized or decentralized the authority is. **Centralization** focuses decision authority near the top of the organization. **Decentralization** pushes decision authority down to lower organization levels.

EXHIBIT 7.4

Tall Versus Flat Organizations

A tall organization has many levels and a narrow span of management at each level, with relatively few people reporting to each manager on the level above them. In contrast, a flat organization has relatively few levels and a wide span of management, with more people reporting to each manager.

United States Army

General
Colonels
Majors
Captains, Lieutenant
Warrent officers
Sergeants
Corporals
Privates

Roman Catholic Church

Pope
Cardinals
Archbishops and bishops
Priests

Centralization has several advantages: it simplifies vertical coordination (since decisions essentially trickle down from above), it utilizes top management's richer experience and broader view of organizational goals, and by focusing power at the top of the vertical structure, it encourages strong leadership. But decentralization has advantages also: by pushing decision making down to lower levels of management, decentralization eases the burden on top executives and offers lower-level employees more challenge. Also, because decisions are less likely to be referred up the hierarchy, decision making in a decentralized organization tends to be faster.[10] At Campbell Soup, decentralization helps keep regional managers in touch with their local customers.

So which is better? The most recent trend has been toward decentralization in order to improve effectiveness by speeding decision making, freeing top management, and accelerating assessments of the changing environment. However, this trend does not mean that all companies should decentralize. McDonald's has clearly shown how size and centralization can be a competitive advantage.[11]

BEHIND THE SCENES

Managing the Changing Organization

Unprecedented change is challenging U.S. businesses. Companies are trying to adapt to deregulation, disinflation, rapid technological change, takeover threats, and intense competition from abroad. On the other hand, change is itself being sought by some companies as a way to compete. PepsiCo has a passion for change. CEO Wayne Calloway's biggest worry is complacency, and he forces change by moving managers back and forth across company divisions. Whether reacting to change or seeking it out, companies have several organizational techniques for managing it. Among the most common are restructuring and downsizing, but managers are also using intrapreneurs, new ventures, and corporate culture to manage change.

RESTRUCTURING

In attempts to deal with and inspire change, numerous companies are reorganizing. Frances Hesselbein, recently retired head of the Girl Scouts, restructured her organization to get better results by making people feel important and included. She accomplished this by creating an organizational chart that is circular. Called a bubble chart, it placed Hesselbein in the center with all other jobs radiating out from her. Repeated reorganization, however, can hurt product quality, alienate customers, and actually cut pro-

ductivity growth. Apple Computer's CEO John Sculley believes, like other top managers, that a good company should constantly be stretching, so he purposefully provokes change. But Sculley may have been provoking too much change lately. Many Apple employees are confused by the company's repeated reorganizations, finding themselves unsure of the company's future direction.

But other companies are restructuring successfully. By viewing restructuring as a continuing process, managers are carefully examining the activities performed by various departments (rather than just looking at the arrangement of boxes on an organization chart), so that changes are no longer made only in a crisis atmosphere. These companies are beginning to see restructuring not as a short-term fix for some specific problem but as a long-term method of dealing with and instilling change.

DOWNSIZING

To manage change, companies are also trying to reduce the number of their employees. Downsizing is traditionally aimed at cost reduction, but unless managers eliminate work before eliminating people, the side effects of downsizing can lead to an organization so bent on cost reduction and so nervous about who will be laid off next that employees begin to think only of themselves and become unwilling to take risks.

The correct hierarchical level of decision making must be arrived at by each organization, depending on each situation.

Departmentalization

Departmentalization groups people into departments and then groups departments into larger units to achieve goals. By specifying how people will be grouped, departmentalization influences how the organization operates; for example, it dictates the number of supervisors needed to link each department with the levels above and below on the management hierarchy. Because people in one department might share office space, equipment, and budget resources, departmentalization dictates how resources are distributed. And by encouraging a shared view (or group perspective), departmentalization tends to facilitate individual efforts within each department. Of course, this group perspective can make it harder for people in one department to work effectively with people in

departmentalization Grouping people within an organization according to function, division, teams, matrix, or network

Some companies go through agony to downsize, only to end up hiring back people once the pressure is off. AT&T laid off 100,000 employees recently, but according to AT&T spokesman Burke Stinson, "Managers will hire back people who actually do the work in order for full-time people to attend meetings." Chrysler made painful cutbacks a decade ago only to see its staffing levels balloon during the better times, until levels were even higher than they had been before.

But downsizing doesn't have to have uncomfortable side effects. To achieve that lean, mean structure everyone is looking for, companies are downsizing with forethought by (1) cutting unnecessary work, (2) putting quality first, (3) questioning long-held assumptions, (4) empowering people, (5) communicating, and (6) taking care of survivors.

OTHER APPROACHES

Companies that believe in developing new products swiftly (or quickly improving the old ones) need the flexibility of *intrapreneurs*, entrepreneurs within the organization. Intrapreneurs use corporate resources to start their own product line under the corporate umbrella. S. C. Johnson & Son (maker of Johnson wax and Raid bug spray) has set up a $250,000 seed fund available to anyone at the company with a promising new product idea.

In a variation on intrapreneurship, some companies try to accomplish the same things using new ventures. Colgate-Palmolive's new venture is working on such specialized products as a deodorizing pad for cat litter boxes and a cleaning solution for teenagers' retainers. General Foods's Culinova Group is leading its parent into the refrigerated take-out food business. And Scott Paper has set up a special venture group to sell products for the handyman.

Finally, as competitive companies constantly look for ways to change every aspect of their business, they create corporate cultures to support it. They emphasize the value of better performance above everything else, and they structure the organization to permit innovative ideas to rise above the demands of running the business. Hewlett-Packard (HP) provides a culture with just that sense of freedom. Engineers have access to company labs around the clock, and HP encourages researchers to devote 10 percent of company time to exploring their own ideas, without fear of penalty for failure. The constant goal at HP is to encourage scientists to mingle and swap ideas.

Tom Peters sees future business organizations managing change by evolving structures that are flexible. He sees them as purposeful chaos, as confusion that is somewhat ordered, and above all as bastions of adaptiveness and action-taking. Change is constant, and so is the need to react to it. Using these methods and more, successful companies are those that successfully manage change.

other departments, so management must encourage cross-unit coordination (discussed later in this chapter under "Horizontal Organization").[12]

Departments can be organized by function (what people do), by division (such as product, process, customer, or geography), according to teams (including project managers), into a matrix (combining both function and division), and by network (electronically connecting organizations that perform vital functions). Such groupings are not mutually exclusive; more than one of them may be used by a single organization.

Function

departmentalization by function Grouping workers according to their similar skills, resource use, and expertise

Organizing departments according to what people do is **departmentalization by function.** Workers are grouped according to their similar skills, resource use, and expertise. Common functional departments include operations, marketing, human resources, finance, research and development, and accounting.[13] Before reorganizing, Campbell Soup relied heavily on a functional structure.

Companies develop their own patterns to suit the particular functions they must carry out. As seen in Exhibit 7.5, *Time* magazine has four main functional departments: editorial, advertising, production, and circulation. Each department works more or less independently, having its own managers and personnel, budget, work schedules, and so on. The contact among departments is only on certain levels and for specific purposes. For instance, the director of advertising might consult with the production director on the number of four-color advertising pages, but an individual ad salesperson would be unlikely to have direct dealings with anyone on the production staff.

Functional departmentalization offers distinct advantages. It allows efficient use of resources, encourages the development of in-depth skills, provides a clear career path, centralizes decision making so that top management can provide unified direction, and enhances communication and coordination within departments (since all activities are basically related). Disadvantages of functional departmentalization include the barriers that grow between departments, the slow response to environmental change (because innovation and change require

EXHIBIT 7.5

Departmentalization by Function

Departmentalization by function divides employees into groups according to their job functions, allowing specialists to have direct authority in their area of expertise. For example, instead of assigning a word-processing operator to each department head, a company might have a word-processing pool under the supervision of an expert in office automation.

| Editorial | Advertising | Production | Circulation |

the involvement of several departments), and the possibility of overstressing specialization and division of labor (thus alienating employees).[14]

departmentalization by division Grouping departments according to similarities in product, process, customer, or geography

Division

Departmentalization by division groups departments according to similarities in product, process, customer, or geography. In a divisional structure, each division is a self-contained unit with all the major functional resources it requires to achieve its goals (see Exhibit 7.6). Thus it has little need to rely on other divisions. For example, a functional structure would group all accountants in one department and all engineers in another. However, a divisional structure would provide engineering groups and accounting groups for each division.[15]

One difference between functional and divisional structure is the level at which decisions are made. In a functional structure, differences between engineering and accounting would have to be solved by top management. In a divisional structure, the solution comes lower in the hierarchy, at the divisional level.[16]

As already mentioned, *Time* magazine (Exhibit 7.5) has a functional structure that groups people into four departments according to their skills and resources. However, *Time* is itself one division of Time Inc., which also has divi-

VIDEO EXERCISE

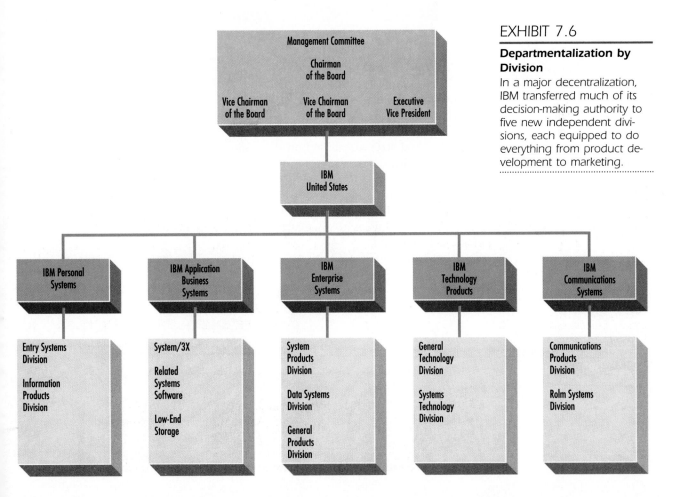

EXHIBIT 7.6

Departmentalization by Division

In a major decentralization, IBM transferred much of its decision-making authority to five new independent divisions, each equipped to do everything from product development to marketing.

EXHIBIT 7.7

Product Divisions

At Time Inc., employees are grouped according to what they produce, which brings together people of diverse skills to produce a specific product or service. Each division has its own editorial, advertising, production, and circulation departments.

product divisions *A divisional structure based on products*

process divisions *A divisional structure based on the major steps of a production process*

sions for *Life, Sports Illustrated, Money, Fortune,* and *People* magazines (see Exhibit 7.7). Time Inc. is a divisional structure based on product, and its **product divisions** are self-supporting, stand-alone units that put out separate products (magazines). Each of Time's product divisions has its own editorial, advertising, production, and circulation departments.

A divisional structure based on the major steps of a production process has **process divisions.** For example, a table manufacturing company might have three divisions, one for each phase of manufacturing a table. Division 1 would size and shape the wood; Division 2 would drill and rough-finish the pieces; and Division 3 would assemble and finish the table (see Exhibit 7.8). Process divisions allow employees to specialize in particular tasks, thus leading to more efficient production.

EXHIBIT 7.8

Process Divisions

Because ·process divisions allow employees to specialize in particular tasks, the production overall is more efficient.

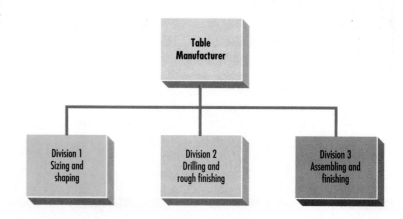

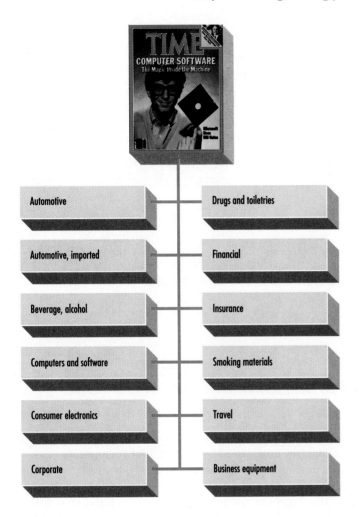

Customer Divisions
Customer divisions lead employees to focus on customer needs and customer service.

Some organizations structure their departments to concentrate on customers. These **customer divisions** are used mainly when there are major differences between customers. For example, at *Time* magazine, a salesperson in the advertising department might specialize in selling space to insurance companies or airlines or tobacco companies (see Exhibit 7.9). Or a company that manufactures parts for Chrysler autos and General Electric refrigerators might create two divisions—one for each major customer. Customer divisions allow employees to focus on customer needs.

When a company is spread over a national or international area and differences from region to region are important enough to merit special attention, departments can be grouped by geographic location. **Geographic divisions** allow companies like Campbell Soup greater responsiveness to local customs, styles, product preferences, and the like. Note, however, that a company doesn't have to use geographic divisions just because it does business across a large geographic area. Today's facilities for high-speed communication allow executives at corporate headquarters to oversee the operations of far-flung branch offices with an efficiency that was impossible a generation ago.

Some of *Time* magazine's editorial and advertising operations have geographic divisions (see Exhibit 7.10). *Time* has several divisional advertising managers for most major U.S. cities, and the magazine maintains a totally sepa-

customer divisions A divisional structure that focuses on customers or clients

geographic divisions A divisional structure based on location

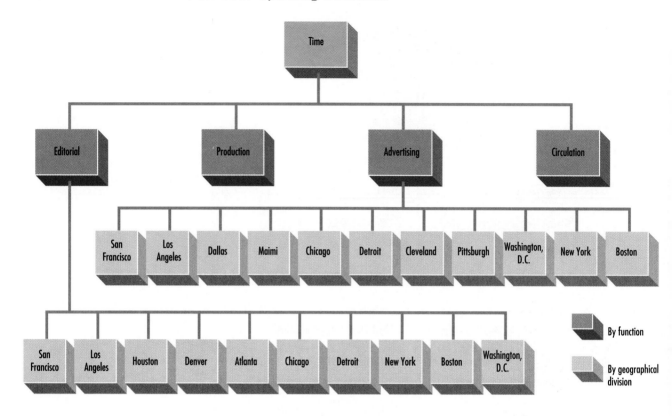

EXHIBIT 7.10

Geographic Divisions
Geographic divisions allow employees to concern themselves with local and regional issues.

rate editorial network, with offices across the country. These geographic divisions are particularly concerned with local and regional issues.

Divisional departmentalization offers several advantages. Divisions can react quickly to change because they don't need to coordinate with other divisions, which makes the organization more flexible. Divisional structure tends to encourage customer service because each division focuses on a limited number of products, customers, or locations. It helps top management focus on problem areas more easily, and it provides a broader experience for developing managers (giving them the opportunity to deal with various functions in their divisions).[17]

Divisional departmentalization also offers distinct disadvantages. It can lead to the duplication of resources, thereby increasing costs. Also, the coordination between one division and others can be poor: employees within a division may focus too narrowly on divisional goals and end up neglecting the overall goals of the organization. Finally, divisions may compete with one another for employees, money, and other resources, causing rivalries that are unhealthy for the organization as a whole.[18]

Teams

departmentalization by teams Assigning employees to functional departments but also assigning them to teams either permanently or temporarily

Because companies today are trying to push decision making to lower levels, the most widespread trend is toward **departmentalization by teams,** assigning employees to functional departments but also assigning them either permanently or temporarily to teams for resolving mutual problems. Teams allow organizations to be more flexible and responsive. They also motivate employees to be more creative, to develop a broader view of goals, and to coordinate across functions.

To improve its services to policyholders, Aid Association for Lutherans (AAL) transformed its huge insurance organization from a functional bureaucracy into streamlined, all-purpose teams. The transformation eliminated three layers of supervisory managers and cut personnel by 10 percent. At the same time, the new teams handled 10 percent more transactions, achieving AAL's goal of speeding up the processing of insurance cases.[19]

However, teams do have disadvantages. Team members may have to endure conflicts and dual loyalties. Because of the time needed for meetings, teams may actually reduce production efficiency. And finally, teams may decentralize decision making too much, causing functional managers to feel out of control and leading members to lose sight of corporate goals as they focus on team goals.[20]

Matrix

Departmentalization by matrix permanently assigns employees to both a functional group and a project team (see Exhibit 7.11), using functional and divisional patterns simultaneously. Organizations use matrix departmentalization when in-depth skills are needed in functional departments at the same time that flexibility is needed to adapt to changing environmental demands.[21]

One convert to the matrix approach is Procter & Gamble, headquartered in Cincinnati, Ohio. Since the 1930s Procter & Gamble had assigned brand managers to oversee the development and marketing of such well-known products as Tide detergent, Crest toothpaste, and Pampers disposable diapers. But problems developed. The smallest details (even the color of the Folgers coffee jar lid) were decided by top managers after a seemingly endless exchange of memos. Moreover, brand managers competed more with one another than with outsiders.

departmentalization by matrix Permanently assigning employees to both a functional group and a project team (thus using functional and divisional patterns simultaneously)

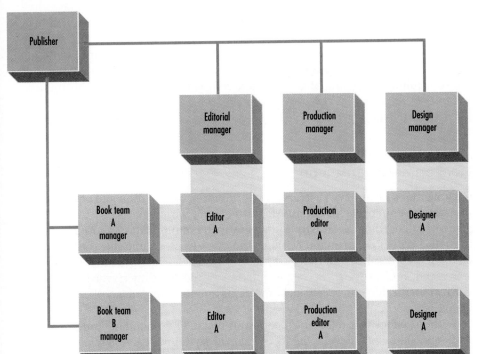

EXHIBIT 7.11

Departmentalization by Matrix

In a matrix structure, each employee is assigned to both a functional group (with a defined set of basic functions, such as production manager) and a project team (which consists of members of various functional groups working together on a project, such as bringing out a new consumer product).

However, by designing the new matrix departments, Procter & Gamble reduced some of these problems. Now competing brand managers plan activities and schedules together.[22]

project management Assigning employees to a functional group but also temporarily assigning them to a specific project

Under **project management,** employees are assigned to a functional group but temporarily abandon their position in the organization's permanent hierarchy when they are assigned to a specific project. Project teams disband when their tasks are completed. For example, one of the most successful U.S. pharmaceutical houses has a system that guarantees good ideas won't be lost during the long product development process. Merck assigns a project manager to each promising research effort. This manager must guide the product through the entire process and across innumerable departments from research to final government approval. It is the project manager who convinces scientists from diverse disciplines to commit their time and budget to each project, which increases loyalty for the product and encourages unity among team members.[23]

Network

departmentalization by network Breaking major functions into separate companies that are electronically connected to a small headquarters organization

Departmentalization by network is a more recent development, essentially breaking major functions into separate companies that are electronically connected to a small headquarters organization. Engineering, marketing, research, and accounting are no longer part of one organization; they are separate organizations working under contract. The network approach is especially appropriate for international operations, allowing them to draw on resources worldwide.

When Digital Equipment Corporation (DEC) tried to build a new processor board for one of its computers, it was able to assemble a team from all over the United States and Europe: circuitry design was done in Ireland, system design in Massachusetts, physical layout in England, design archiving in New Hampshire, and manufacturing in Scotland. In spite of their far-flung locations, groups were able to communicate and share work using DEC's vast computer network.[24]

Network structure is extremely flexible because of the ability to hire whatever services are needed and then change them after a short time. The organization can continually redefine itself, and employees have greater job variety and job satisfaction. However, this approach lacks hands-on control, since the functions are so far-flung. Also, one of the network companies may go out of business or fail to deliver, which may cause severe problems for the central organization. Finally, employee loyalty and team spirit are less likely to develop.[25]

Horizontal Organization

horizontal organization Structure to coordinate activity by facilitating communication and information exchange across departments

Organizations must have systems for coordinating information and communication among employees in various departments at various levels. **Horizontal organization** coordinates activity by facilitating communication and information exchange across departments without the need to go up and down the vertical chain of command. Without horizontal organization, every problem, every decision need, and every piece of information would have to travel through the vertical hierarchy, effectively isolating departments from one another and paralyzing companies.

Without effective global coordination in place, ITT floundered amid conflict and confusion while developing its System 12 switching equipment. Because of its difficulty transferring vital technology across its own unit boundaries, ITT was disastrously late introducing its System 12, and the coordination problems ultimately forced the company to sell its core communications business to a competitor.[26]

The coordination performed by horizontal organization promotes innovation. More views are shared, employee awareness is broadened, and willingness to support and implement ideas is strengthened (by involving more employees in their development). Three common methods of achieving horizontal coordination are information systems, task forces and teams, and managerial integrators.[27]

▶ *Information systems.* All written and electronic forms of sharing information, processing data, and communicating ideas are **information systems.** These include all internal written communication forms (reports, bulletins, and memos) as well as all electronic communication devices (computers, electronic mail, and teleconferences).[28] Electronic systems offer the ability to quickly process and communicate vast amounts of information, thus greatly enhancing horizontal coordination. Digital Equipment Corporation, for example, has an internal network that links 95,000 users and 35,000 computers spanning 33 countries. Any DEC employee can send a message to any other employee at any time, regardless of geographic or organization location.[29] (Electronic technology and information systems are discussed further in Chapter 16.)

information systems All written and electronic forms of sharing information, processing data, and communicating ideas

▶ *Teams and task forces.* A **task force** is a group of people from several departments who are temporarily brought together to address a specific issue or problem. At Oryx Energy (an independent Dallas gas producer), massive efforts to change the corporation's character were carried out by teams who unearthed problems and brainstormed solutions. Each team had between eight and ten members, and only two or three were from the department being studied. Oryx's teams not only succeeded in changing the company from a paper-swamped operation to a dynamic organization, but they also saved the company $75 million a year.[30] Task force recommendations may or may not be implemented by the organization, because such recommendations are usually considered advisory, not mandatory. Members of task forces and teams share information with their departments and thus facilitate coordination.[31]

task force Group of people from several departments who are temporarily brought together to address a specific issue

▶ *Managerial integrators.* A **managerial integrator** is a manager who coordinates the activities of several functional departments but who is a member of none of them. These managers often have titles such as project manager, product manager, brand manager, program manager, or branch manager. The functional department managers retain line authority over their employees, so even though integrating managers have authority over the project, product, brand, or branch, they have no authority over the employees working on it. Nevertheless, integrating managers enhance the horizontal coordination of the departments involved with any given project.[32]

managerial integrator Manager who coordinates activities of several functional departments but belongs to none

The amount of vertical and horizontal organization defines the character of a company. Emphasizing vertical structure gives a company tight control over hierarchical levels, leads to routine jobs that are rigidly defined, requires numerous and exacting organizational rules, centralizes authority, and limits communication to the vertical path. However, emphasizing horizontal structure loosens the control, allowing tasks to be redefined to fit employee or environmental needs. Authority and decision making are decentralized (based on expertise rather than on hierarchy), and communication is horizontal. Many organizations try to strike a balance between vertical and horizontal structures so that they can benefit from the best features of both.[33]

▶ UNDERSTANDING THE INFORMAL ORGANIZATION

In addition to the formal vertical and horizontal organizations, a network of relationships exists that doesn't appear on any official chart. Every company has an **informal organization,** the network of interactions that develop on a personal level among the workers (see Exhibit 7.12). Although the relationships among people in the formal and informal organizations may be the same, they often aren't. Sometimes an individual relates informally as a peer with someone working at a higher or lower level. Sometimes employees who do not work together in a formal sense may informally develop personal relationships. One impact of informal organization comes from natural leaders who get things done. Whether the power of natural leaders is granted to them by their peers or by their influence with management, it benefits the organization.[34]

The informal organization has positive aspects: it provides employees with an opportunity for social interaction, and it provides an outlet for stress, tension, and anxiety. It facilitates organizational communication and provides information that managers may use in decision making. And as mentioned, it showcases future leaders. Negative aspects of the informal organization are also numerous. It can create conflicting loyalties and rumors that lead to the spread of false

informal organization Organizational characteristics and relationships that are not part of the formal structure but that influence how the organization accomplishes its goals

EXHIBIT 7.12

Informal Organization

In addition to its formal organization structure, every company has an informal organization. These networks of social connections are often formed without regard for hierarchy or departmentalization.

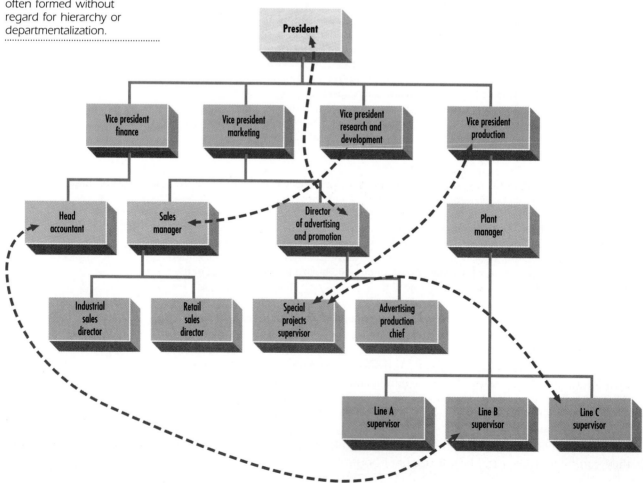

information. It can counteract company values if the informal group does not share those values, and it can encourage resistance to management plans. The informal organization can also encourage complaints, poor-quality work, and absenteeism. Certain aspects of the informal organization have attracted considerable attention lately.

Grapevines

The **grapevine** is the communication network of the informal organization. An unofficial way of relaying news, grapevines bypass the formal chain of command. They may convey either personal or business information, although mostly they consist of personal gossip. Grapevines also exist among companies and within industries. Employees with personal connections to someone in a competing or client company may spread information before it is publicized. In many cases, such gossip simply makes work less boring. Sometimes, however, it contributes to the spread of damaging rumors.

grapevine The communication network of the informal organization

Smart managers make good use of the grapevine, which sometimes provides factual tips that aid decision making, in regard to both internal and external matters. Grapevines also provide feedback on employee attitudes and on outsiders' perceptions of the company. The challenge is to discern when information transmitted via the grapevine is accurate and when it is misleading.

Office Politics

The phrase "office politics" is a trendy way of describing the complex struggle for dominance that takes place in any organization. Every group of human beings develops a social hierarchy. Certain individuals take control, others are low in the social hierarchy, but most fall somewhere in between. Since today's workers care very much about advancement and opportunities for new challenges and rewards, they actively seek ways to make their abilities and achievements known. One of their chief means is through office politics.

To some people, office politics means the ruthless manipulation of other people in an attempt to gain power. To the extent that this sort of behavior is encouraged by the organization's climate, office politics may be stressful. But office politics can also be useful. Highly motivated workers tend to be very productive, and the fact that so many employees are scrambling for recognition means that quite a few of them are producing at a high level. In addition, although ruthlessness and power struggles are one aspect of office politics, simple courtesy and leadership are another. In the long run, those who can demonstrate the ability to work productively with others are most likely to get ahead. Developing productive working relationships is the purpose of two time-honored processes: networking and mentorship.

Networking

It is human nature to prefer doing business with those we know and like. That fact is the basis of **networking,** the art of making and using contacts. Networking is the way people find out about jobs that aren't advertised in the newspaper; it is the way they learn about valuable new developments in their field before the crowd does. And for many managers, networking is the key to fast promotions.[35]

networking Seeking to broaden one's effectiveness in an organization or industry by forming relationships with others in the same and related fields

Networking has three main elements. The first is *visibility,* making your presence known. The more people who meet you, the more you are likely to be remembered. The second element is *familiarity,* letting people get to know you. It takes courage to expose your skills, attitudes, and opinions, but people are more likely to deal with you if they have some idea of how you think and react. The third element, *image,* means giving people the impression that you are competent and pleasant to deal with. An optimistic, enthusiastic approach to business—and to life—is magnetic.[36]

Mentors

mentor Experienced member of an organization who serves as a guide and protector to a lower-level employee

One frequently recommended technique for getting a career on track is to acquire a **mentor,** an experienced employee who can guide you through the corporate maze. Mentors have deep knowledge of the business and a useful network of industry colleagues. In addition, they are familiar with office politics in their own company. A mentor is not typically a person's boss, although such a relationship is certainly possible.

Relationships with mentors are usually set up informally; however, some companies have set up programs for assigning young employees to more experienced ones. Jewel Companies, a Salt Lake City food-store corporation that is now known as American Stores Company, set up a mentor program to help young people fit in. Says Donald S. Perkins, former chairman and chief executive officer of Jewel (and himself a beneficiary of the "sponsorship" program): "I don't know that anyone has ever succeeded in any business without having some unselfish sponsorship or mentorship."[37]

corporate culture Organizational climate or set of values that guides and colors the atmosphere within a company

Corporate Culture

One final element of the informal organization encompasses everything else. **Corporate culture** is the organizational climate—in informal terms, the "feel" of the place. It serves as a guidepost by which employees may judge what the company wants from them, how they should approach problems, and what types of solutions will be acceptable. Corporate culture encompasses the organization's internal environment, its values (its definition of employee success), its heroes, its day-to-day routines, and its method of communicating values.[38]

Corporate culture may permit an informal atmosphere with employees dressing and interacting casually (as here at Texaco), or it may impose a formal environment with more rigid standards of dress and with most business interaction taking place in scheduled meetings.

For example, General Electric is working hard to create an environment in which employees can make a connection between what they do each day and winning in the marketplace. But changing the 112-year-old bureaucracy from a closed culture that discouraged questioning of any kind to an open, empowering atmosphere that nurtures creativity and challenge is a long process that requires years of education and conditioning.[39]

To determine the culture of a company, try the following:

1. Study the physical setting for clues to the company's attitude toward various divisions, departments, and classes of employees.

2. Look for company slogans in annual reports and press releases.

3. Observe the receptionist and reception area.

4. See whether people spend their time on internal matters, such as paperwork and office politics, or on outside matters affecting the company.

5. Observe who gets ahead and why.

6. For a clue to the company's focus on short-term or long-term goals, watch how long people stay in any one position in the company before being promoted.[40]

Someone who does not understand an organization's vital characteristics may experience dissatisfaction or failure. But someone who understands the corporate culture has an extremely powerful tool for getting results. Knowing a company's culture makes it easier (and faster) to get things done and may also provide a sense of stability. An organization is more likely to be successful if it has a strong, well-defined culture.

SUMMARY OF LEARNING OBJECTIVES

1 Discuss the three purposes of organization structure.

Managers use organization structure to divide labor and assign formal tasks to individuals and groups, to define the span of management and the lines of authority, and to coordinate all organizational tasks.

2 Describe the problems associated with specialization.

Specializing too much can alienate employees by giving them small, repetitious tasks so that they become bored and unchallenged.

3 Explain how departmentalization facilitates goal achievement.

Departmentalization breaks work into smaller tasks, grouping people into departments and departments into larger units to achieve goals. It dictates how the organization will operate and how resources are distributed. It also facilitates individual efforts within each department.

4 List five types of departmentalization.

The five types of departmentalization are (1) by function, (2) by division, (3) according to teams, (4) into a matrix, and (5) by network.

5 Discuss how horizontal organization differs from vertical organization.

Emphasizing vertical structure imposes tight control over hierarchical levels, leads to routine jobs that are rigidly defined, requires exacting organizational rules, centralizes authority, and limits communication to the vertical path. Emphasizing horizontal structure loosens control, leads to varied jobs that can be redefined to fit employees or environmental needs, decentralizes authority, pushes decision making down the hierarchy, and coordinates communication and information exchange across departments.

6 Explain three methods of horizontal organization.

The three most common methods of horizontal organization include information systems, teams and task forces, and managerial integrators. All three methods facilitate communication and information exchange across departmental boundaries.

7 Discuss the positive and negative aspects of the informal organization.

The positive aspects of informal organization include providing employees with an opportunity for social interaction; providing an outlet for stress, tension, and anxiety; facilitating organization communication; providing managers with information; and showcasing future leaders. The negative aspects of informal organization include creating conflicting loyalties, encouraging rumors that lead to the dissemination of false information, counteracting company values, and encouraging resistance to management plans.

8 List six ways to define the culture of a company.

A company's culture can be determined by (1) studying the physical setting for clues to the company's attitude toward various divisions, departments, and classes of employees; (2) looking for company slogans in annual reports and press releases; (3) observing the receptionist and reception area; (4) seeing whether people spend their time on internal matters, such as paperwork and office politics, or on outside matters affecting the company; (5) observing who gets ahead and why; and (6) tracking how long people stay in any one position in the company before being promoted.

Meeting a Business Challenge at Campbell Soup

Campbell Soup was facing a crisis of organization structure. The U.S. marketplace was undergoing dynamic change, and Campbell could no longer sell uniform goods nationwide. Former CEO R. Gordon McGovern took his cues from smaller competitors that were succeeding on a regional basis, serving up food with the distinct local tastes consumers wanted.

To play this new game, Campbell had to change its strategy. Management at all levels had to get closer to the customer, understand regional differences, and react more quickly to regional change. To support the new strategy, McGovern had to redesign Campbell Soup's organization structure from functional to divisional, and the divisions had to be geographic. Before the restructuring, Campbell had a separate national sales force for each product category (such as frozen foods and soup). But McGovern decentralized sales efforts by dividing the organization into 22 regions. He assigned a brand sales manager to each geographic region, and he gave each region the autonomy to develop its own marketing strategies.

Sales reps who had once been assigned specific brands were now instructed to sell all Campbell products. This meant that each rep could call on 10 stores rather than the usual 100, giving them time to learn more about their territories. Reps passed their knowledge on to brand sales managers, who used it to develop regional products. To facilitate communication, McGovern added four new managers at headquarters to coordinate the efforts of the regional brand sales managers, and he supplied the regional offices with computers.

To better allocate production resources, McGovern assigned each of the company's domestic manufacturing plants to serve one of five regions. Such regional dedication meant that the plants were better prepared to produce the recipes required. Also, they were expected to come up with their own ideas for new products,

Campbell Soup Company.

which they shared with the regional staffs. Under the company's previous functional structure, manufacturing, sales, advertising, and other departments held separate meetings to plot strategy. But the new divisional structure encouraged coordination by having representatives from all of the formerly separate functions attend the same meetings.

Overall, these structural changes have allowed Campbell Soup to think like its competitors and compete with strong food items that appeal to local tastes. In the years following the restructuring, Campbell reported a 12 percent increase in operating earnings on sales increases of 7 percent. The reorganization helped push Campbell's nine-year sales growth over the 9 percent mark to $6 billion annually. The Campbell experience shows that a company can achieve more profit and sales when it tailors its organization structure to meet the demands of a changing environment.

Your Mission: As Campbell's vice president of human resources, you are responsible for advising current president and CEO David W. Johnson about how the company can fine-tune its organizational design to operate efficiently in a dynamic environment. For each of the following situations, select the best solution.

1. The new geographic divisions have helped Campbell immensely. However, one regional manager has contacted Johnson, requesting permission to reinstate a functional organization within her division. The functional structure is more familiar to her, and she believes she can cut costs by grouping functions along the traditional lines of sales, marketing, accounting, operations, and so forth. Johnson has asked for your opinion.

a. Advise Johnson to refuse this manager's request outright. Reinstituting a functional structure at the regional level would defeat several advantages already realized by the company, especially the new coordination among manufacturing, sales, and advertising people who currently plan strategy in cross-functional meetings.

b. Advise Johnson to accept the manager's proposal. As long as the regional office is a part of the geographic divisions, it doesn't matter how each division is itself organized.

c. Advise Johnson to request more information from this manager. If the regional manager has worked out a way to coordinate the functional departments so that communication and information can still flow freely from one department to another without getting delayed in the functional hierarchy, then her proposal may have merit.

d. Advise Johnson to leave all such decisions to the regional managers. He has decentralized authority to allow regional offices to make this kind of decision. If he starts making decisions for the region now, he will defeat the original purpose.

2. Johnson has received messages from several regional managers, asking his advice on how to solve various and sundry problems, few of which bear any similarity from one geographic division to another. One division wants to use a different advertising agency, another wants to use new quality-control methods, and still another wants to develop new vacation policies. Johnson has asked for your suggestions.

a. Because the problems are so varied, you believe Johnson should handle each one on an individual basis. This is the only way to make sure the problem solution is uniform.

b. Because the problems are so varied, you believe Johnson should leave such decisions to the regional offices. You suggest using teams made up of people within each division to analyze the problem and suggest solutions.

c. Because the problems are so varied, you believe Johnson should depend heavily on information systems and computer networks so that he will learn of the problems quickly and thus be able to communicate his solutions to each geographic division faster.

d. Because the problems are so varied, you believe Johnson should stay out of the solution process completely. It is up to the regional offices to use their own authority to solve such problems now.

3. One of the new managers at headquarters has pulled you aside for a chat. He's a young man with little experience in coordinating geographic divisions, and he feels "thrown to the wolves," making decisions he's unsure of and not knowing the right way to approach some problems. He is well qualified for his position, and you would hate to lose him because of his present (and you believe temporary) lack of confidence. What should you advise him to do?

a. As hard as it may seem, you must get him to fly on his own as quickly as possible. Explain to him that he is an adult in the real world and that he has to cope with decision making or change careers.

b. You believe a word from you at this time will go a long way, so you describe how this manager should begin networking with colleagues and supervisors—building contacts with professionals both inside and outside the company. Networking is the fastest way for this young manager to learn the ropes of his position and come to grips with the philosophy of geographic divisions.

c. You explain to the young manager that uncertainty is often a part of the job but that you will contact a senior colleague who might just be willing to act as his mentor. With a little guidance, you believe this new manager will blossom into an irreplaceable asset for the company, and you sense relief from him when you mention the possibility.

d. You suggest that the young manager form a special advisory team from the employees who work for him. The team can advise him about the pros and cons of each situation and can even suggest alternative solutions. The young man

may never have to make a decision alone again.

4. As with all organizations, Campbell headquarters has an active grapevine through which all sorts of information passes. For the past few days, however, misleading rumors have been spreading through the grapevine like wildfire. The talk is of a new restructuring that will focus on downsizing, and innumerable employees are beginning to worry about their jobs. You don't have a clue about how the rumor got started, but it is false. What should Johnson do?

a. Most rumors are only half true, if not entirely false. Johnson can't concern himself with every whisper in the organization. He should ignore the entire matter and wait for the scare to pass—as all unfounded scares eventually do.

b. Johnson should do whatever he can to quash the grapevine and stop the rumors. This kind of scare is nonproductive and can even be dangerous.

c. Johnson should prepare a statement that flatly denies the rumored downsizing and that wastes no time with muddying detail. A reassuring word from the CEO is all that's needed to set the rumor mongers straight.

d. Johnson should prepare a straightforward message about the facts of the situation, clearly stating the company's intent in the foreseeable future. Then he should make sure that every employee in the organization receives it, whether by memo, by face-to-face meetings, or by electronic mail.[41]

KEY TERMS

accountability (181)
authority (181)
centralization (185)
chain of command (183)
corporate culture (198)
customer divisions (191)
decentralization (185)
delegation (181)
departmentalization (187)
departmentalization by division (189)

departmentalization by function (188)
departmentalization by matrix (193)
departmentalization by network (194)
departmentalization by teams (192)
division of labor (180)
downsizing (185)
flat structure (185)
geographic divisions (191)

grapevine (197)
horizontal organization (194)
informal organization (196)
information systems (195)
line-and-staff organization (183)
line organization (183)
managerial integrator (195)
mentor (198)
networking (197)
organization (178)

organization structure (178)   responsibility (181)   task force (195)
process divisions (190)   span of management (184)   vertical organization (180)
product divisions (190)   staff (183)
project management (194)   tall structure (185)

REVIEW QUESTIONS

1. Why is organization structure important?

2. Discuss the three phases of organization structure.

3. Under what circumstances would it be best for an organization to set up geographic divisions?

4. Why would you expect a manager of a group of nuclear physicists to have a wide span of management?

5. What are the characteristics of tall organizations and flat organizations? Is the U.S. Navy a tall organization or a flat one? What about the Roman Catholic church?

6. Why would horizontal organization promote innovation?

7. Is it better to emphasize horizontal or vertical organization?

8. How might a manager use the informal organization to good effect?

A CASE FOR CRITICAL THINKING

Intrapreneurship: How Does It Work at 3M?

3M Corporation, renowned for innovation, has a decentralized organization that works. As a matter of fact, 3M was practicing intrapreneurship before Gifford Pinchot III (author of *Intrapreneuring*) coined the word in 1985. In fact, 3M's goal has been for 25 percent of its sales to come from products that did not exist five years before. And using intrapreneurship to achieve this goal has certainly worked well for the company.

Art Fry, a 3M corporate scientist, is an ideal person to talk about as an example of the company's encouragement of individual enterprise. As the inventor of 3M's Post-it Notes, he epitomizes the intrapreneur. Post-it Notes are self-sticking pieces of colored paper that allow you to write notes, stick them just about anywhere, then remove them with ease. When you get used to Post-it Notes, you can't imagine how you ever got along without them.

The idea for Post-it Notes came to Fry in 1974, while he was singing in his church choir. He had used scraps of paper to mark his hymnal. As he watched the bookmarks fall out of the book, he envisioned a piece of paper that would stick but be movable. Then he remembered an adhesive that had been discovered at 3M by Spencer Silver. While Silver had been

developing superstrong adhesives, he accidentally made one that could be easily removed. Although the adhesive didn't suit his purpose, Silver took it to his colleagues, hoping they could find a use for it. Several years later, Art Fry thought of a way to use Silver's temporarily permanent adhesive. As Fry said, "At 3M, we never throw ideas away, because you never know when someone else may need it." Although half of the new ideas at 3M are never developed as products, the management accepts these risks as the price of innovation.

To develop his self-sticking pieces of paper, Fry took advantage of the 3M policy that allows scientists to spend up to 15 percent of their time on projects of their own choosing. This policy dates back to 1923, when 3M's chief executive William McKnight discovered Dick Drew working on a tape project that he'd been ordered to abandon. Recognizing that people do their best work on projects that interest them, McKnight didn't stop Drew. How wise he was! The project Drew wouldn't give up produced the transparent tape that most of us know as Scotch tape. Since then, 3M has established a corporate culture that encourages teamwork but also stresses individuality.

Fry's lab director became his

champion, and Fry scrounged the necessary materials to continue his experimentation. After a year of solving technical problems, Fry was ready to present his prototype pads to the 3M business-development people. The core problem for an intrapreneur is communicating his or her vision to the company and to a team of people who can turn that vision into reality. Fry succeeded in getting a little more money and was able to put together teams of laboratory, engineering, cost-accounting, production, packaging, and marketing people. Fry's lab director passed out samples of the Post-it Notes to 3M secretaries, and the little yellow notes were a hit. In 1977 the vice president and technical director of Fry's division took samples into the field. They discovered that once people had the little yellow notes in their hands, they created all kinds of uses for them. So giving away samples became the key to marketing strategy. When Post-it Notes were marketed nationwide in 1980, sales took off and Fry's project became a dramatic success.

In keeping with 3M's dual-career-ladder policy, Fry was promoted to corporate scientist. As he explained, "The 3M dual ladder system allows people to advance on the technical side of the ladder, assuming additional responsibility for technologies instead of people and budgets. That means that people who are happiest working in the lab can remain there without losing pay raises or recognition." In addition, Fry expressed his personal feeling of achievement: "As an inventor, developing a successful new product is about as close as you can come to achieving immortality."[42]

1. If you want to develop intrapreneurship within a company you are managing, would you want to have a tightly run organization? Why or why not?

2. You are managing a corporation that encourages intrapreneurship. One of your scientists has developed a substance that, at first glance, doesn't seem to have any market value. What do you do?

3. One of the intrapreneurial scientists in your company has invented a top-selling product. Should you promote him to vice president of research and development? Why or why not?

BUILDING YOUR COMMUNICATION SKILLS

Either as an individual or as part of a small group, examine the formal organizational structure of a business or institution (such as a hospital, college, public service agency). If you are unable to obtain an organization chart for this business or institution, you might find it useful to create one using the information you can gather by observing operations.

▶ Using information from the text as a resource, determine the division of labor, the form of departmentalization, and the centralization of your chosen business or institution.

▶ Describe the organization in a written or oral presentation. Compare the structure with that of businesses or organizations examined by other class members.

KEEPING CURRENT USING *THE WALL STREET JOURNAL*

Choose an article from *The Wall Street Journal* that describes a company restructuring.

1. What changes took place in the company's organization, structure, and corporate culture?

2. What reasons are given for the changes? If no reasons are given,

what is your best guess about the reasons for the change?

3. What impact have the organizational changes had on the company, its markets, and its products? Or, if the changes are just now being implemented or announced, what results does the company expect the restructuring to have?

CHAPTER 8

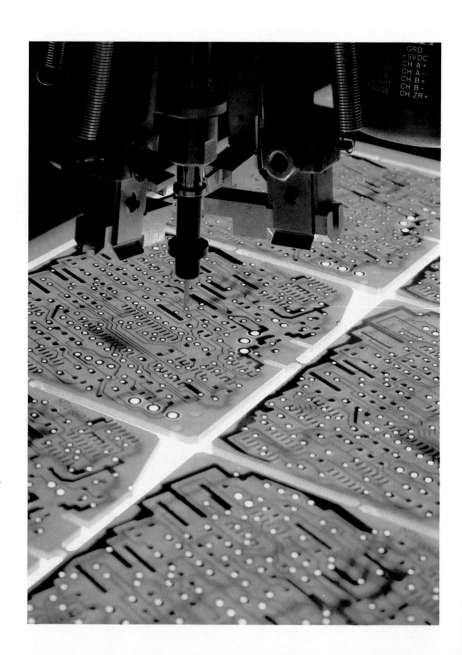

LEARNING OBJECTIVES

After studying this chapter, you will be able to

1 Diagram the conversion process.

2 Define the goal of most advances in production technology.

3 Cite the four technological advances that made mass production possible.

4 Explain three innovations in materials management.

5 Differentiate between quality control and quality assurance.

6 Define the five basic steps in production control.

7 Identify the three main production layouts.

8 Describe three techniques for improving scheduling.

The Production of Goods and Services

*Facing a Business Challenge
at Harley-Davidson*

GETTING HARLEY BACK ON THE ROAD

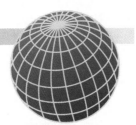

When Japanese companies began selling heavyweight motorcycles in the United States, Harley-Davidson management remained calm. They controlled 99.7 percent of the market, and they had few doubts that they would retain much of it. After all, they argued, customers who tattoo our logo on their chest will be loyal. However, Harley management was mistaken. Newly appointed chairman Vaughn Beals had never ridden a motorcycle, but he recognized a company with a serious production problem.

The Harley was no longer the superb machine that Marlon Brando drove across the screen in *The Wild One*. Harleys leaked puddles of engine oil, vibrated like jackhammers, and broke down frequently. Although longtime Harley customers patiently pulled them apart and rebuilt them correctly, the new generation of motorcyclists were not tinkerers. They gravitated toward the trouble-free, smooth-riding motorcycles that Honda, Yamaha, Suzuki, and Kawasaki imported. By the time Harley's market share had slipped to 23 percent, it had begun to leak red ink along with engine oil. If the company couldn't make its existing line of bikes correctly, how was it going to introduce new, well-built models to compete with Japanese cycles?

At the heart of Harley's difficulties were its outmoded production systems, which were devised during the era when Harley was a small, close-knit, family company. When Harley tried to increase production to meet the Japanese threat, its production systems collapsed, and quality skidded off the road.

One source of trouble was bloated, disorganized inventory. Parts at Harley's assembly plant in York, Pennsylvania, were made in large batches for long production runs, stored until needed, and then loaded onto the 3.5 mile conveyor that clattered endlessly around the plant. In Harley's cavernous inventory warehouse, it sometimes took hours to find necessary components, and when they were found, they were often rusty or damaged. Even though Harley spent $25 million a year to maintain its inventory, over half its cycles came off the line missing parts.

Harley had to maintain an extensive work-in-progress inventory because it took so long to adjust its machine tools that short runs were just not feasible. When one machine broke down, hundreds of parts piled up behind it. To make matters worse, Harley plants were labyrinths of work stations. To build a single motorcycle frame, Harley workers had to cart components from one corner of the plant to the other, logging miles of travel in the process.

When Beals introduced the Cafe Racer, a new model meant to signal Harley's return to quality, he established an ad hoc team to inspect the first hundred bikes off the assembly line. The news was terrible. The group uncovered $100,000 worth of defects. Beals expanded his inspection teams to cover all Harley cycles, and the quality of cycles leaving the factory improved. But Beals realized that the Quality Audit Program was an expensive, time-consuming Band-Aid that simply identified defects after they were made.

Beals's experience with the Cafe Racer convinced him that the only way to save Harley was to stop mistakes before they occurred. But where should he start? How could Beals reduce the time it took to set up machinery for production runs, cut back on costly inventory, and streamline the factory layout? How could he revamp the entire production system without adding to the mounting losses that Harley was already facing?[1]

▶ THE QUEST FOR COMPETITIVENESS

production Transformation of resources into forms that people need or want

The managers at Harley-Davidson recognize that **production,** the transformation of resources into goods or services that people want, is the foundation of any business. A great deal of attention has been focused on the production function in recent years, as companies around the world try to increase their competitive strengths through higher quality, greater efficiency, faster production, and lower costs.

conversion process Sequence of events (input → transformation → output) for transforming materials into goods and services

At the core of production is the **conversion process,** the sequence of events in which resources are converted into products. It can be simply diagrammed: input → transformation → output (see Exhibit 8.1). This formula applies to both intangible services and tangible goods. For example, a consultant's knowledge

EXHIBIT 8.1

The Conversion Process
Production of goods or services is basically a process of conversion. Input (the basic ingredients or skills) is transformed (by the application of labor, equipment, and capital) into output (the desired product).

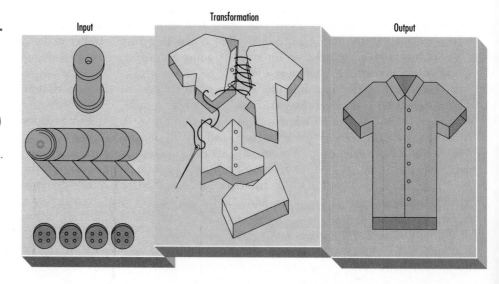

about a company and ability to communicate (input) can be transformed through analysis into specific advice about running a company (output). For a shirtmaker to produce a shirt, the resources that are converted—cloth, thread, and buttons—are tangible; the form that people want, the shirt, is tangible, too.

Two basic types of conversion exist. One type, called an **analytic system,** breaks raw materials into one or more distinct products, which may or may not resemble the original material in form and function. In meat packing, for example, a steer is divided into hide, bone, steaks, and so on. The second type of conversion, the **synthetic system,** combines two or more materials to form a single product. In steel manufacturing, iron is combined with small quantities of other minerals at high temperatures to make steel.

The ultimate goal of production, as in all business endeavors, is to make a profit. When competition is fierce and the price cannot readily be raised to increase profits, smart businesspeople seek production **effectiveness,** increasing competitiveness by emphasizing not only efficiency but quality and human relations as well.

analytic system A production process that breaks incoming materials into various component products

synthetic system A production process that combines two or more materials or components to create finished products; the reverse of an analytic system

effectiveness Increasing competitiveness through efficiency, quality, and improved human relations

The Industrial Revolution

Throughout most of human history, people have sought ways of improving production **efficiency**—they have tried to lower costs by getting the optimum output from each resource used in the production process. For example, the feudal system provided a more efficient division of labor than nomadic life or small tribal settlements. Then a series of technological advances began in England more than 200 years ago (known as the industrial revolution), which brought about even more efficient production.

The first of these technological advances was **mechanization,** the use of machines to do work previously done by people. Adding to mechanization's efficiency was **standardization,** or the production of uniform, interchangeable parts. Henry Ford introduced the technological advance with the most wide-ranging influence, the **assembly line,** where an item is put together as it progresses past a number of work stations, with each worker performing a specific task.

As manufacturers became more adept at integrating mechanization, standardization, and the assembly line into the production process, they turned their attention toward eliminating as much costly manual labor as possible through **automation,** the process of performing a mechanical operation with the absolute minimum of human intervention. In automated production, people put machines into operation and monitor or regulate them and inspect their output. Beyond that, the machines do the work.

These advances in production efficiency were part of the development of **mass production.** Manufacturing uniform goods in great quantities has cut prices, made products available to more people, and contributed significantly to the high standard of living in countries where mass production has been implemented.

efficiency Minimizing cost by maximizing the level of output from each resource

mechanization Use of machines to do work previously done by people

standardization Uniformity in goods or parts, making them interchangeable

assembly line Series of work stations at which each worker performs a specific task in the production process

automation Process of performing a mechanical operation with the absolute minimum of human intervention

mass production Manufacture of uniform products in great quantities

The Second Industrial Revolution

At Deere & Company's tractor plant in Waterloo, Iowa, a conveyor belt sends freshly cut gears humming toward another assembly area. At one point, a mech-

The hallmarks of the industrial revolution were mechanization and the standardization of parts, which together made possible assembly lines such as this one at Ford Motor.

anized arm seizes a roughly cut cogwheel, swings away from the belt, and inserts the gear into a device that polishes it smooth. At the other end of the device, another arm retrieves a finished gear and replaces it on the conveyor belt. Before this plant opened, several workers would have polished the unfinished gears. Today, however, the polishing job is done more cheaply and precisely by computer-controlled machines and robots.[2]

What do developments like these mean? Many experts have compared them to the industrial revolution because recent advances in production technology and processes are dramatically increasing efficiency. But the second industrial revolution includes more than the efficiency of improved technology. Forward-looking companies now consider the structure and process of manufacturing to be strategic weapons, not merely ways to decrease cost and increase efficiency.[3] Thus, they are pursuing effectiveness through efficiency in production technology, in process design, and in materials management, as well as through quality assurance and improved human relations.

In addition, operations effectiveness yields another powerful competitive strength: time. Companies such as Xerox, Wal-Mart, Toyota, and Ford, which have learned to design and produce new products faster or to perform the on-going functions of business faster, have a big advantage over their slower competitors.[4]

Advances in Production Technology

To date, a minority of U.S. companies have refitted and reorganized their factories to take advantage of these improvements. But the trend is clear, and industries that want to remain competitive are doing what they can to join the revolution. Computers and robots have been the most visible advances in production technology. This is *not* to say that their use is *always* desirable. At Apple Computer's factory, for instance, five automated guided vehicles (AGVs) have been replaced by an even more efficient system called an HGV—the human-guided vehicle—because continually rerouting the AGVs to keep up with changes in the factory's layout was a problem.[5] The use of advanced technology helps improve efficiency under certain conditions:

▶ When there is high concentration of manual operations in one area

▶ When a job is so difficult or tedious that no one wants to do it

▶ When many injuries occur in one area of the factory[6]

VIDEO EXERCISE

As Vaughn Beals learned at Harley-Davidson, one of the worst mistakes a company can make is converting manual processing to automatic without first examining the underlying process. If the basic process creates the wrong products or involves needless steps, there is no sense in automating it without cleaning it up first. In fact, just fixing the manual process can often lead to impressive productivity gains. When Corning Glass examined the manufacturing process at two of its factories, it discovered that 115 of the 235 processing steps were no longer necessary. It eliminated the steps, which cut production time from four weeks to three days—without automating the plants.[7]

computer-aided design Use of computer graphics in the development of products or processes

COMPUTER-AIDED DESIGN AND ENGINEERING   The starting point for the production of anything—by any means—is designing the product. Computers are becoming an important part of the design phase. **Computer-aided design**

(CAD), for example, is the use of computer graphics in the design of products; a related term is **computer-aided engineering** (CAE). Computer-generated three-dimensional images and calculations performed on the computer allow engineers to test products without ever building preliminary models. With CAD and CAE, new ideas can be subjected electronically to temperature variations, various stresses, and even simulated accidents, leading to great savings in time and money. Quality improves, too. For example, as Boeing engineers design and build their new 777 widebody transport plane, they can get the details right without building anything. Bugs can be ironed out and new ideas can be tested on video screens rather than on life-sized models.[8] So products can now be perfected—or a bad idea abandoned—before they're put into production.

In Raleigh, North Carolina, Landmark G.I.S. designs topographical maps of commercial and residential areas. To simplify the process, a CAD system is being used here to digitize an aerial photo.

COMPUTER-AIDED MANUFACTURING   The use of computers to control production machines (robots, inspection devices, AGVs, and the like) is called CAM, or **computer-aided manufacturing.** Good CAM systems increase the output, speed, accuracy, and dependability of assembly lines. Combinations of CAD and CAM are rapidly becoming significant factors at all sorts of companies. For instance, Hasbro Bradley designs toy parts on its CAD/CAM system. And Oneida uses CAD/CAM to design and produce forks, knives, and spoons. What used to take the company 70 weeks to do now takes about half as long and sometimes even less.[9]

computer-aided engineering Use of computers for engineering

computer-aided manufacturing Use of computers to control production machines

COMPUTER-INTEGRATED MANUFACTURING   The highest level of computerization in operations management is **computer-integrated manufacturing** (CIM), in which all of the elements of design, engineering, and production, including CAD and CAM, are integrated in computer networks that communicate across departments.[10] For many companies, CIM is proving to be a better route to competitive success than the massive automation schemes attempted in the last several decades.[11]

CIM is a key component of "the factory of the future." The Fanuc plant in Japan, for example, has a small crew working with machines by day to manufacture parts for robots and machine tools. But by night, the factory works alone. AGVs whiz along preprogrammed routes in the twilight. Some robots unload raw materials, and others work them into simple shapes that can be used by the computer-controlled machining center—a machine that can change its tools, reposition the part, and cut away unwanted portions of the workpiece like a sculptor forming a figure. One person monitors the plant's activity on closed-circuit television screens and is able to correct production problems simply by typing commands on a computer keyboard.[12]

computer-integrated manufacturing Computer-based systems that coordinate and control all the elements of design and production, including CAD and CAM

New Process Designs

Advances in production technology have been accompanied by changes in the way the production process is organized. The industrial revolution encouraged a trend toward large factories with several assembly lines, each producing a single product. Today, however, two new trends have emerged: flexible manufacturing and the focused factory.

FLEXIBLE MANUFACTURING   One of the most recent changes in the production process has been the development of an alternative to **hard manufacturing,** the use of specialized production equipment that is locked into place. Generally,

hard manufacturing Use of specialized production equipment that cannot readily be moved

repetitive manufacturing
Repeated, steady production of identical goods or services

setup costs Expenses incurred each time a producer organizes resources to begin producing goods or services

flexible manufacturing
Production use of computer-controlled machines that can adapt to various versions of the same operation; also called **soft manufacturing**

job shop Firm that produces dissimilar items or that produces its goods or services at intervals

focused factory Manufacturing facility that deals with only one narrow set of products

hard manufacturing is associated with **repetitive manufacturing,** in which the same thing is done over and over. It is economical only if similar items are produced at a steady rate. The mass production of everything from televisions to garden tools can fall into this category. If hard manufacturing is repetitive, it may benefit from long-term savings on **setup costs,** the expenses incurred each time a manufacturer begins a production run of a different type of item. However, because hard manufacturing usually involves producing one unchangeable product design in large volume, its applications in many of today's markets are limited. In addition, the initial investment is high, because hard manufacturing requires specialized equipment for each of the operations involved in making a single item. Only after much production on a massive scale is the cost of that specialized equipment recouped.

The alternative is **flexible manufacturing** (also called *soft manufacturing* or FMS, for flexible manufacturing system), in which computer-controlled machines such as a machining center adapt to differing versions of similar operations (see Exhibit 8.2). With flexible manufacturing, changing from one product design to another requires only a few signals from the computer, not a complete refitting of the machinery. Thanks to flexible manufacturing, a General Electric plant that produces over 1 million electric meters a year can easily be reprogrammed to produce any one of 2,000 variations.[13] With such flexibility, producers can outmaneuver less-agile competitors by moving swiftly into profitable new fields, by moving out when those fields begin to decline, and by quickly adapting product innovations to improve their products.

A flexible manufacturing layout is particularly desirable for a **job shop,** which makes dissimilar items or produces at so irregular a rate that repetitive operations are not feasible. Most small machine shops are examples. The specialized equipment they produce is not churned out in any great quantity, and their customers often require customized features. The flexibility provided by computerization is also making some repetitive manufacturers more like job shops. For example, although Deere has a long tradition of repetitive manufacturing, in its new plant it can actually turn out some 5,000 types of tractors—including one with a 15-gear transmission, one with fewer gears, one with a stereo tape deck, and one without so much as a radio.[14] The result is the flexibility of a job shop combined with the lower setup costs of repetitive manufacturing.

Flexible manufacturing does have its limitations, however. In fact, fewer than 20 percent of U.S. factories currently employ FMS.[15] The products made by any one system require similarly sized machines, accuracy, power, and tolerance. Therefore, part designs may have to be standardized. Also, developing an integrated system requires long planning and long development cycles before any payoff is realized. Managers with an eye on short-term profit might be tempted to avoid the investment required by flexible manufacturing systems.[16]

THE FOCUSED FACTORY One advantage of flexible manufacturing is that plants can be smaller, more specialized, and closer to important markets, which are also key characteristics of the **focused factory.** Instead of trying to produce in one location everything that the market may desire, the focused factory concentrates on a narrower set of products for a particular market.

Two important concepts underlie the idea of focused factories. First, it is difficult for a factory to do *everything* well. Management must decide what it needs to do particularly well—say, cut delivery time—and trade that against something that is not so important. Second, competence comes from simplicity and repetition. A focused factory with clear objectives and support from top

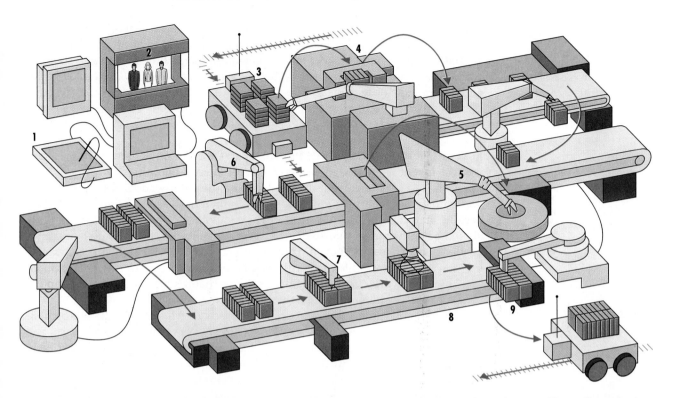

1. A fully automated flexible manufacturing system begins with an electronic drafting board that transmits data to the electronic "foreman" of the system.

2. Managers keep track of the robots' work simply by consulting remote terminals for daily output data.

3. In response to a computer command, an AGV is loaded automatically in the storage area and brings the parts to the assembly line. A wire under the floor sends low-frequency radio signals that establish the carrier's path.

4. A programmed pick-and-place robot picks up pieces from the carrier, fits them into the lathe, and places them on the conveyor belt.

5. The various machining tools needed for this operation are supplied by a revolving holder. The central controller directs the lathe to choose the appropriate tool for each cutting step.

6. An assembly robot joins the parts together. Because assembly operations are often quite complex, robots of this type are more difficult to develop than some of the other kinds.

7. A welding robot, which fixes the parts in place, is a good example of flexible automation in action: The robot has been programmed to make all the different welds required on this product.

8. An inspection device, a camera plus a semiconductor chip, checks the finished item against standards.

9. Another pick-and-place robot puts the finished products on an AGV, which will bring them to shipping.

management as well as sufficient experience is likely to be efficient and therefore competitive.[17]

Materials Management

Modern companies like Harley-Davidson are also attempting to become more efficient and profitable by taking a closer look at the way they handle **inventory,** the goods and materials they stock for the production process and for sales to final customers. Every company needs a system of **inventory control,** some way of determining the right quantities of supplies and products to have on hand and some way of keeping track of their location. Inventory control is also concerned with protecting inventories. Taking pains to purchase materials efficiently or to stockpile finished products is pointless if the materials or products become lost or damaged in storage.

One of the main issues in materials management is inventory size. Large inventories take advantage of economies of scale and allow customer demand to be met quickly, but they also tie up the company's capital. That's why more and more companies are trying to limit inventories—sometimes to practically noth-

EXHIBIT 8.2

Fully Automated Flexible Manufacturing System
A flexible manufacturing system uses computer-controlled robots throughout the production process. It is capable of switching rapidly from production of one item to production of another.

inventory Goods held on hand for the production process or for sales to final customers

inventory control Method of determining the right quantity of various items to have on hand and of keeping track of their location, use, and condition

ing. However, whittling down supplies too much carries its own dangers. It is just as costly, if not more so, to stop the production process to await the delivery of supplies. Thus, a major goal of materials management is to shorten and stabilize **lead times,** the periods that elapse between the placement of a purchase order and the receipt of materials. The challenge is to maintain an inventory large enough to keep production going at full bore yet small enough to keep costs at a minimum.

lead times Periods that elapse between placement of a purchase order and receipt of materials from the supplier

MATERIAL REQUIREMENTS PLANNING   One technique now widely used to control inventory is called **material requirements planning** (MRP). Its basic function is to get the correct materials where they are needed, doing so on time and without unnecessary stockpiling. A computer is used to determine when certain materials are needed, when they should be ordered, and when they should be delivered so that they won't cost too much to store. Some companies produce only those products already ordered and have little difficulty determining how much inventory they will need throughout production. Other companies, however, cannot predict as precisely, so their estimation of inventory materials becomes more complicated.[18]

material requirements planning Method of getting the correct materials where they are needed for production and doing it on time and without unnecessary stockpiling

The companies most likely to use MRP are those whose products are complicated. For example, a job shop's products are always changing, so the parts and materials required for production are always changing. But each part must be in the right place at the right time. What's more, there may be subassemblies such as motors or circuit boards that also require careful scheduling in order to be in the right place when required. Computer-based MRP is valuable in coordinating the delivery of various materials, each subassembly, and finished products.

JUST-IN-TIME SYSTEMS   A newer approach to inventory control is the **just-in-time system** (JIT). It is another method of achieving the goal sought through MRP—having only the right amounts of materials arrive at precisely the times they are needed—but it adds the human element by involving everyone in the production process. The purpose of JIT is to eliminate waste by utilizing small inventories that require less storage space, less accounting, and less investment. Moreover, JIT is geared for continual and constant improvement. The JIT system grew out of the Japanese *kanban* system, in which cards are used to keep various operations informed about what they should be doing to maintain a smooth production flow.[19]

just-in-time system A continuous process of inventory control that, through teamwork, seeks to deliver a small quantity of materials to where they are needed precisely when they are needed

As Harley-Davidson's managers learned, a JIT system requires careful pre-planning, which has some indirect benefits. For instance, reducing stockpiles to practically nothing ("zero inventory") requires managers who can keep production flowing smoothly from beginning to end without any holdups. In addition, workers have an opportunity to see where the bottlenecks are, so management should communicate with them in a friendly, cooperative way—which lowers tensions, improves morale, and increases productivity. The result is a spirit of teamwork: No one wants to be caught slowing the flow or standing out as the weak link in the chain. On the other hand, JIT places a tremendous burden on suppliers, such as the steel companies that supply an auto factory, because they must be able to meet the production schedules of their customers. With JIT systems, suppliers no longer have the luxury of shipping massive quantities at infrequent intervals; they must stay in close, regular contact with their customers.

Organizations that use JIT report enormous returns on their investment. St. Luke's Episcopal Hospital in Houston saved $1.5 million over three years when it closed its enormous supplies warehouse and set up "stockless distribution." Rather than storing and handling thousands of items, the hospital receives daily deliveries from Baxter International (the nation's largest hospital supplier), whose computers communicate directly with St. Luke's inventory management system. Each day, Baxter pulls together the materials needed and delivers them directly to each area inside the hospital.[20]

MANUFACTURING RESOURCE PLANNING   Advanced inventory-control methods such as MRP and JIT have caused some dramatic shifts in corporate management. For example, in the past, employees spent hours maintaining inventory records, some of which were only 60 percent accurate.[21] However, plants that have installed **manufacturing resource planning** (MRP II) are less likely to experience such inefficiencies if employees are able to maintain the necessary discipline and commitment at every level of the organization.

MRP II is a comprehensive computer-based system that supports management with information for decision making. However, unless every employee

manufacturing resource planning Companywide computer system that coordinates data from all departments in order to maintain minimum but sufficient inventories and a smooth production process

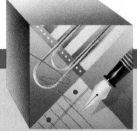

CHECKLIST FOR BUSINESS TODAY

Taking the Steps Toward Successful JIT Implementation

Just-in-time (JIT) inventory management is an increasingly popular method used to manage inventory levels. JIT is a fairly simple concept: Rather than holding massive inventories of parts and materials, manufacturers and service providers have suppliers deliver items right before they are needed. However, it isn't all that easy to implement. A company might have millions of dollars tied up in warehouses, transportation networks, and inventories that are incompatible with the JIT philosophy. In addition, the company may have been using its old methods for decades, and getting people inside and outside the company to change can be a big challenge. However, the cost and time benefits of JIT are encouraging more and more managers to make the switch, in spite of the short-term turmoil.

To successfully implement JIT, managers need to make sure that the following elements are in place:

▶ *Close communication between suppliers and customers.* Suppliers must have sufficient time to deliver needed items. For example, AAA Trucking is a major supplier to Harley-Davidson's assembly plant in York, Pennsylvania. AAA set up an electronic communication system with the Harley plant to allow production schedulers to communicate directly and immediately with the delivery company. This ensures that the JIT process flows without interruption.

▶ *Attention to quality.* No backup stocks exist to replace items found to be defective. Tektronix, an Oregon manufacturer of electronic instruments, dropped its number of suppliers from 100 to 36. The suppliers who made the grade all passed a rigorous certification program to make sure they would provide quality parts.

▶ *Adequate storage facilities and transportation options.* Suppliers must be able to supply items quickly. The Volvo GM Truck plant in Dublin, Virginia, was experiencing unacceptable delays in the delivery of some parts, which were trucked in after being flown to the Roanoke Airport, 65 miles away. After moving the air freight drop-off point to an airport only 5 miles away, Volvo GM reduced the delay enough to run a successful JIT operation.

▶ *Reliable service from suppliers.* Customers have to shut down their production lines if JIT suppliers don't come through. Toyota runs its production lines with only a few hours' parts inventory, so it requires its suppliers to meet down-to-the-minute delivery schedules.

For those companies that can get all the pieces in place, JIT provides an attractive technique for keeping inventory costs down and productivity up. Suppliers of all sizes and shapes need to pay attention to JIT because more and more of their organizational customers will be demanding it.

EXHIBIT 8.3

MRP II
An MRP II computer system gives managers in every department easy access to data from all other departments, which in turn makes it easier to generate—and adhere to—the organization's overall plans, forecasts, and schedules.

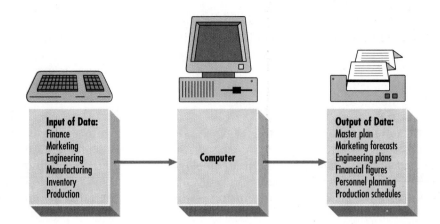

Input of Data:
Finance
Marketing
Engineering
Manufacturing
Inventory
Production

Computer

Output of Data:
Master plan
Marketing forecasts
Engineering plans
Financial figures
Personnel planning
Production schedules

conscientiously feeds updates into the system, errors may accumulate so that the information becomes invalid and the system falters. Handled with painstaking discipline, the software can simulate what might happen in the plant under various conditions, thus allowing managers to perform "what if" analyses.[22] MRP II can also integrate a company's activities, both in the plant and in the office (see Exhibit 8.3). With MRP II, every department works from the same data. Moreover, the system can schedule each step of production, thus allowing managers in various branches of the company to consult other managers' inventories, schedules, and plans. An MRP II system linked with computer-aided design can automatically begin the process of ordering the parts and materials needed to produce a new product. MRP II can provide middle managers with an information base that helps them do their jobs better, freeing them for planning, forecasting, and personnel management. With MRP II operating effectively, even people on the factory floor spend time at the computer keyboard, drawing on data once reserved for executives, such as inventory levels, back orders, and unpaid bills.

Quality Assurance

U.S. companies are beginning to realize that efficiency and productivity alone are not enough to ensure their competitive standing. An emphasis on quality is also required. During the 1970s, some major U.S. industries let quality levels slip drastically, seemingly convinced that advertising and sheer presence in the market could sell anything. But they soon discovered how wrong they were. For example, as much as one-third of the market share for U.S. automobile sales went to Japanese firms during this time. Experts in Detroit said that the average sticker price of a U.S.-built car was once inflated by as much as 25 percent to pay for costs directly related to low quality, including surplus scrap, rejected parts, inspections, repairs, and warranties.[23] As a matter of fact, just to make up for poor quality, the typical U.S. company spent 10 to 20 percent of its revenue on everything from product testing to defending itself against product-liability suits.[24]

Recently, however, some U.S. industries, including the automobile industry, have greatly improved their attention to quality. The traditional means for doing so is **quality control,** measuring quality against some standard after the good or

quality control Routine checking and testing of a product or process for quality against some standard

service has been produced. With some quality-control systems, output is checked and tested at random—every tenth item, every hundredth, and so on—and a report is prepared on all the "rejects," telling how many there were in a given period and why they were thrown out or reworked. But quality control is only part of the picture.

The new watchword is **quality assurance**—a companywide system of practices and procedures to assure that the company's products satisfy customers. Quality assurance includes quality control as well as doing the job right the first time by designing tools and machinery well in the first place, demanding quality components from suppliers, training workers better, and encouraging workers to take pride in their work. Henry J. Heinz, founder of the food products giant, described the essence of this effort years ago: "Doing common things uncommonly well."[25]

Quality assurance also includes the now widely used concept of **statistical process control,** in which the *process* of production is monitored through the use of control charts so that management can see whether production is proceeding as planned or whether the quality of performance is backsliding.[26] Quality assurance demands management's complete cooperation; responsibility for quality cannot be relegated to production workers while management pushes them to produce more and produce faster. With cooperation, high quality and high production are both possible, and the payoffs are worth the effort. Says a general manager at Hewlett-Packard:

> The earlier you detect and prevent a defect, the more you can save. If you throw away a defective 2-cent resistor before you use it, you lose 2 cents. If you don't find it until it has been soldered into a computer component, it may cost $10 to repair the part. If you don't catch the component until it is in the computer user's hands, the repair will cost hundreds of dollars. Indeed, if a $5,000 computer has to be repaired in the field, the expense may exceed the manufacturing cost.[27]

Early in the history of modern industry, companies started keeping track of defective products and analyzing the sources of problems. About 30 years ago, however, statistician W. Edwards Deming began helping companies institute **statistical quality control** (SQC), a system designed to solve the types of quality problems that crop up in industries where the production process is so complex that thousands of tests have to be conducted to ensure quality at all levels. Statistical quality control applies the same method that Gallup polls use to determine popular opinion: If you carefully select a handful of representative parts, you can figure out an approximate truth about the whole.

Companies that institute statistical quality control experience increased efficiency. Inventories decline, work moves more smoothly, and costs drop. Moreover, managers may also learn of other problems when they focus on quality. Not long ago, Deming suggested that workers at Pontiac Engine Plant No. 18 track problems that were cropping up with some connecting-rod bolts. Sure enough, they discovered that all the defects originated from one supplier, and that contract was immediately terminated. At this one plant, statistical quality control increased the proportion of acceptable products coming off the production line from 60 percent to 96 percent, and scrap rates and inventories fell.[28]

The highest level of quality awareness is the concept of **total quality management** (TQM), which is a philosophy or style of management that places quality at the center of everything the company does. With TQM, quality is more than a

A quality-control device checks for defects in Scripto ballpoint pens.

quality assurance *A companywide system of practices and procedures to assure that company products satisfy customers*

statistical process control *Monitoring the production process using control charts*

statistical quality control *Use of random sampling to test the quality of production output*

total quality management *An all-encompassing philosophy of management based on a vision of quality and customer satisfaction*

product attribute; it is the very reason a company exists. Leading manufacturers such as Hewlett-Packard and Motorola employ TQM, and the concept applies equally well to service businesses and nonprofit organizations and government agencies.[29]

Improving Human Relations

Companies today are seeking to improve their effectiveness by improving human relations so that employees will approach their work more intelligently, will be happier, and will work harder.[30] **Methods improvement** is an effort to examine jobs with an eye to improving the level of efficiency.[31] It includes such considerations as changing operation sequences, balancing work loads, training workers, simplifying materials handling, and utilizing **ergonomics,** the study of human characteristics in designing and arranging the most effective and safest tasks, equipment, and environments.[32]

In addition to improved efficiency, companies should be interested in the workers themselves. Various theories have been proposed for helping workers stay happy and motivated. Job rotation may provide challenges for workers and increase personal esteem as they develop new skills. Job enlargement, expanding a worker's tasks, may be the answer to oversimplification. Similarly, job enrichment expands tasks as well as responsibility, providing a sense of achievement, recognition, and growth.[33]

Another way of providing more job satisfaction is by using **quality circles,** in which about five to fifteen workers meet regularly to identify and find solutions to quality, safety, and production problems. Then, with management's approval, they implement those solutions. When properly structured, quality circles and similar problem-solving teams not only improve the final product but also help create a sense of unity among all the employees of the company.

For example, as part of its well-publicized "Quality Is Job One" campaign, Ford Motor Company set up quality circles at its Louisville, Kentucky, plant. Trucks from the plant had consistently rated lowest on Ford's quality scale. But workers and managers, under threat of a permanent plant shutdown, agreed on a series of changes, some directly related to production issues. One assembly-line worker suggested turning some bolts to face up instead of down so that the bolts could be tightened easily from above. And plant management added the new position of "quality upgrader," which carries the responsibility of paying attention to such problems as loose bolts and poorly fitting parts, while other workers keep the assembly line running. Other issues at the Ford plant also involved the human dimension. To begin with, the plant was spruced up and kept spotless, and workers who once had to sit on spare parts to eat lunch found picnic tables throughout the plant. Morale improved to the point that absenteeism dropped to 1 percent from a high on some days of more than 6 percent. Most important, however, Ford halved warranty costs and the number of defects per truck, and it began closing in on foreign competition.[34]

Quality circles have been more successful in Japan than they have been in the United States, however. Management professor Peter Drucker attributes this to the fact that U.S. companies haven't adopted statistical quality control to the extent that Japanese firms have. Without the constant monitoring and feedback that statistical quality control provides, the efforts and contributions of quality circles would be difficult to measure, and the lack of such feedback would lead to frustration among both employees and managers.[35]

methods improvement Examining all aspects of a job or task in order to improve efficiency levels

ergonomics Study of human performance in relation to the tasks performed, the equipment used, and the environment

quality circles Regularly scheduled meetings of about five to fifteen workers to identify and suggest solutions to quality, safety, and production problems

During a meeting of a quality circle at GM's Saturn plant, members give management the benefit of their expertise by recommending improvements in production techniques.

Competitiveness in Service Operations

Although efficiency has received stronger emphasis in the goods-producing sector of U.S. industry, its potential has not been lost on the service industries. Some services, though, may never be suited to such products of the industrial revolution as mass production. The mind shrinks from the image of a patient on a hospital assembly line, with robot-doctors performing the segmented steps of a standardized appendectomy. But service industries such as fast-food chains, hotels, accounting firms, car-rental agencies, and even some real estate firms use mass-production principles ingeniously. Like in a Model T factory, each step and procedure is standardized, and equipment performs each task efficiently.

Quality, both of product and of human relations, is also an issue outside assembly-line industries. Darla Mendales, vice president of corporate quality management at Fidelity Investments, is working to ensure that the services her company provides meet customer expectations. This ranges from fast, courteous phone service to simpler application forms. Her task is far from simple; one of her colleagues notes that a shift to customer satisfaction is difficult for a system that has always emphasized speed and efficiency, where the "customer was always the bad guy." However, Mendales is making impressive strides as she gradually convinces other managers to define quality in terms of customer satisfaction.[36]

Toward World-Class Manufacturing

Companies like Harley-Davidson now realize they are competing in a global economy; some have to sell products in other countries in order to keep growing, and most must compete with companies from other countries that increasingly look to the huge U.S. market for their growth. To compete at the global level, such companies are increasingly pursuing *world-class manufacturing,* a term used to describe a level of quality and operational effectiveness that puts a company among the top performers worldwide. As an executive at Convex Computer puts it, "If you are in a worldwide business, you had better be world-class."[37]

Compare the performance of Nucor, an upstart steel producer, with that of Bethlehem Steel, one of the country's oldest and largest producers. An innovative Nucor plant in Crawfordsville, Indiana, produces roughly 1 million tons of steel a year with about 400 employees. In contrast, the Burns Harbor Bethlehem Steel plant, also in Indiana, produces 4½ times as much steel, but needs 15 times as many employees to do so. Not surprisingly, Nucor's efficiency and effective use of resources has helped it stay financially healthy while Bethlehem and other "Big Steel" companies are hurting.[38]

Production and the Natural Environment

Today's production managers spend a significant amount of time on environmental concerns. Virtually every aspect of a company's operations has the potential to pollute. Factories can generate air pollution, water pollution, solid waste disposal problems, excessive noise, and other undesirable elements. Service businesses can't escape the environmental issue either; even if their processes don't generate pollution, just the conglomeration of hundreds of people in an office building can create problems.

Business Around the World

Many people equate "made in Taiwan" with low quality. However, the country now boasts state-of-the-art manufacturing technology and is highly respected among industry insiders. In fact, some of the biggest U.S. computer companies, including IBM and Apple, use Taiwanese components in their own products.

Union Carbide's plastics recycling plant is one of the largest in the Northeast. Carbide's concern for the natural environment is an integral part of the company's life.

Since pollution control is often expensive, many of these environmental problems pit nature against the bottom line. However, an increasing number of manufacturers are discovering that they can win on both counts. Reynolds Metals saved $30 million in pollution control equipment and reduced emissions by 65 percent when it switched to water-based inks in its packaging plants. And Clairol, which used to flush production pipes with water, now cleans them with foam balls. This change netted $240,000 a year in reduced disposal costs and cut wastewater discharge by 70 percent.[39]

▶ PRODUCTION AND OPERATIONS MANAGEMENT

Despite all the recent advances in production technology and methods, someone must still take overall responsibility for this important aspect of a company's existence. **Production and operations management** (POM) is the coordination of an organization's resources in order to manufacture its goods or produce its services. Like other types of management, POM involves the basic functions of planning, organizing, directing, and controlling. In addition, the production and operations manager must see to the creation of the good or service.

POM is growing as one of the business world's most dynamic areas of speciali-

production and operations management Coordination of an organization's resources in order to manufacture its goods or produce its services

BEHIND THE SCENES

World-Class Manufacturing at Next

Steve Jobs, co-founder of Apple Computer, is widely recognized as a visionary designer of new products. However, visit him at his current company, Next, and he'll tell you that he's as proud of the factory as he is of the innovative Next computer system.

Jobs and his team were determined from the beginning to build a world-class manufacturing facility. However, they didn't just blindly apply the latest high-tech automation. They started by designing a fast, efficient process and an easy-to-build product, then they judiciously applied automation technologies where such technologies made sense.

The results are indeed impressive. A Next computer grows from start to finish in about 20 minutes, compared to the days or even weeks that products can take in old-style manufacturing facilities. The manufacturing time is so short that engineers can make design changes and implement them almost instantly, which has made the Next product quite free of the patches and fixes found in many electronic products. In addition, the Next factory is surprisingly small, because it doesn't have to store vast supplies of parts or collections of half-finished computers. And no less important than the manufacturing speed, defect rates in Next computers are one-tenth the industry average.

Why does the Next system work so well when so many advanced automation projects haven't lived up to their promises? For several reasons. First, as a relatively new company, Next had the advantage of not being tied down to decades-old factories and embedded methods and mindsets. It created the system from the ground up, taking advantage of the industry's accumulated knowledge and experience. Second, Jobs gave manufacturing a higher priority than it often gets in U.S. companies. At one point, more Ph.D.s worked in production than on the team working on the next product design. Third, the Next computers are designed for fast, easy manufacturing; no unpleasant surprises are found when a new product moves from design into production. And finally, machines and people do the work that each is best suited for; the machines take care of the repetitive, boring assembly work, and the people monitor the process, analyze results, and make adjustments as necessary, all the while applying generous doses of creativity and ingenuity.

zation. For one thing, it is becoming the focus of many companies' efforts to become more competitive and profitable. POM is a challenging subject for several other reasons: the field is undergoing rapid change; it involves many activities, from interpreting market research (determining what kinds of goods and services should be produced) to production planning and control of the production process; and it applies to all kinds of companies, regardless of their size or whether they produce goods or services. Once regarded as a second-class career track for business-school graduates, production management is enjoying a surge in popularity. Leading schools such as MIT, Northwestern, Cornell, and Purdue have added or upgraded courses and degree programs in manufacturing.[40]

Efficient production is no accident. Thus POM, like all other types of management, requires careful thought beforehand about the company's goals, the strategies for attaining those goals, and the standards against which the outcome will be measured. Someone must consider how much demand there is likely to be for the company's products in the future, what product changes will probably be required to maintain market share, whether the company has the resources to implement those changes, and, if not, how the company can pull together the required resources.

One of the earliest long-term issues that must be resolved is the location of production facilities. Although being near low-cost resources and transportation was once of overriding importance, today such considerations as local living standards and the qualifications and values of the local work force enter into the decision (see Exhibit 8.4). Take the labor question, for instance. Firms that need highly trained accountants, engineers, or computer scientists often sink roots near university communities such as Boston and the Silicon Valley area of California. If, on the other hand, most of the jobs can be filled by unskilled or semiskilled workers, managers can choose locations where this type of labor is available at a relatively low cost. Or take the question of access to transportation and resources. For a company that needs to transport bulky materials into a plant or cumbersome products out, proximity to such facilities as highways and rail lines has long been critical. But advanced telecommunications now make it possible for some service industries and service components of manufacturing industries to operate from such out-of-the-way places as Greenwood, South Carolina, where the George W. Park Seed Company is based. If information is all that needs to be transported, telephone lines can easily do the job.

In the shorter term, top managers must clarify exactly what is expected of those responsible for production and operations. To do so, they must first engage in **production forecasting,** which deals specifically with the question of how much to produce in a certain time span. Using past sales figures and educated guesses about the future behavior of the economy and of competitors, management estimates future demand for the company's products. (When a company is beginning to produce new products and has no history to rely on, managers must adapt information about related products and markets as best they can.) These estimates are used in turn to plan, budget, and schedule the use of resources.

production forecasting Estimating how much of a company's goods and services must be produced in order to meet future demand

▶ PRODUCTION CONTROL

For an idea of the wide range of activities involved in one part of POM, consider **production control,** a set of steps leading to the efficient production of a high-

production control Production planning, routing, scheduling, dispatching, and follow-up and control in an effort to achieve efficiency and high quality

EXHIBIT 8.4

Important Factors in Site Selection

This chart shows the results of a survey measuring the importance of various factors in site selection. Shown is the percentage of 1,000 executives who rated a given factor "vitally important."

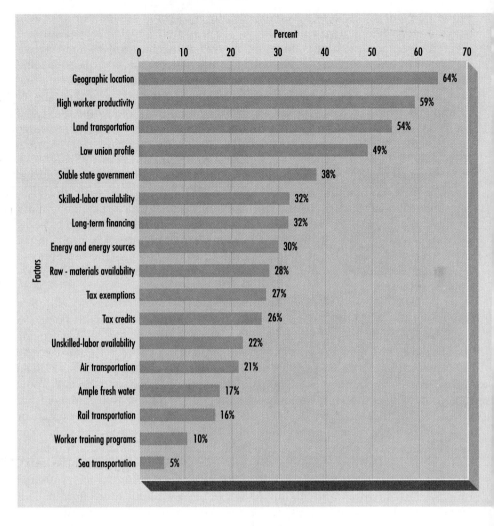

quality product. The manufacture of complex goods is not simply a matter of adding part *A* to part *B* to part *C* and so forth until a product emerges ready to ship. Automobiles, for example, are assembled from subunits that vary from car to car. A system is needed to ensure that the correct engine, the right tires, and the proper chrome trim reach each car at the precise point in the assembly process at which they are to be added. In the production of complex services, too, someone needs to keep track of the various elements and workers involved. For example, in the development of computer software, someone has to make sure that parts of the program written by various people mesh well and that the handbook accompanying the software is accurate too.

Production-control procedures vary from company to company. Most manufacturing processes, however, have five steps: planning, routing, scheduling, dispatching, and follow-up and control. When many resources and complex procedures are involved, production control may become complicated. To help illustrate, follow the five steps taken by an imaginary small company as it makes a simple product, wooden tables. The company has just received a rush order for 500 white and 500 unpainted tables.

Production Planning

Once the larger goals have been set, the production process itself can be planned. This is no small task either, as the imaginary table company illustrates. From industrial and design engineers, the production manager receives lists of all the labor, machinery, and materials needed to make the 1,000 tables that have been ordered. A **bill of materials** lists all the required parts and materials and specifies whether they are to be made or purchased:

bill of materials Listing of all parts and materials in a product that are to be made or purchased

MAKE	PURCHASE
1,000 table tops	4,000 dowels (one to fasten each leg)
4,000 table legs	50 gallons of white paint

The next step is to determine the quantity of these materials already on hand. The production manager discovers that the company has enough wood and paint but only 2,000 dowels. So an order for an additional 2,000 dowels must be placed with a supplier who can get them there in time.

Routing

Routing, the second step in production control, is the task of specifying the sequence of operations and the path through the facility that work will take. The way production is routed depends on the type of product and the layout of the plant (see Exhibit 8.5). The three main classifications are process, assembly-line, and fixed-position layouts.[41] They apply to both the manufacture of goods and the production of services.

routing Specifying the sequence of operations and the path the work will take through the production facility

Process Layout

The table-manufacturing company has three departments, each handling a different phase of the table's manufacture and each equipped with specialized tools, machines, and workers. Department 1 cuts wood into desired sizes and shapes. Department 2 does drilling and rough finishing. Department 3 assembles and finishes. This is a **process layout,** because it concentrates in one place everything needed to carry out a specific phase of the process. The table tops and legs are routed from Department 1, where they are made, to Department 2 to have the dowel holes drilled and to be rough-finished, then to Department 3 for assembly, finishing, and painting.

process layout Method of arranging equipment so that production tasks are carried out in discrete locations containing specialized equipment and personnel

Although the production process is straightforward under this system, materials handling is not. The table tops and legs are routed first to Department 1 and then to Department 2, but the dowels and paint are routed directly from inventory to Department 3 (see Exhibit 8.5A). There, all 1,000 tables are assembled, but only 500 are painted.

Process layout is frequently used in service industries as well. A college, for example, may have a language department, a business department, a science department, and so on, each with its own supply of professors and classrooms. As students are processed into college graduates, they travel from one department to the next for exposure to a specific set of ideas.

EXHIBIT 8.5

Routing and Production Layouts

The way a company routes the sequence of operations and the path the work will take (see Figure A) depends on the layout of the plant (see Figures A, B, and C).

(A) Process Layout (producing two batches of tables)

Department 1

Department 2

Department 3

Routing: Steps in the sequence of operations

1. Wood is dispatched from the storeroom to Department 1 to be cut into tops and legs.
2. The dowels are sent directly to Department 3, because they won't be needed until the tables are assembled.
3. Paint is also moved to Department 3 to await the arrival of the 500 assembled tables that are to be painted.
4. Cut tops and legs are moved to Department 2 for drilling.

5. The table pieces receive their first rough finishing—sanding—in Department 2 before being passed along to Department 3.
6. The tables are assembled and finished.
7. Those not being painted are dispatched for shipping.
8. The 500 tables designated for painting are moved to another area in Department 3.
9. Once they have received their coats of paint, they too are dispatched for shipping.

Assembly-Line Layout

assembly-line layout Method of arranging equipment in which production is a flow of work proceeding along a line of work stations

An alternative to process layout is the **assembly-line layout,** in which the main production process occurs along a line, and developing products flow smoothly from one work station to the next. Materials and subassemblies of component parts may feed into the main line at several points, but still the flow of production is continuous. Automobile and personal-computer manufacturers are just two of the many goods-producing industries that typically use this layout.

Some production of services is also organized this way. When students register for college classes in person, for example, the various clerks and registrars are stationed in some sort of line. Students proceed from one station to the next, smoothly (it is hoped) accumulating the various documents that enable them to put together a schedule. Some colleges, however, such as the University of Washington in Seattle, have taken this production process into the high-tech age

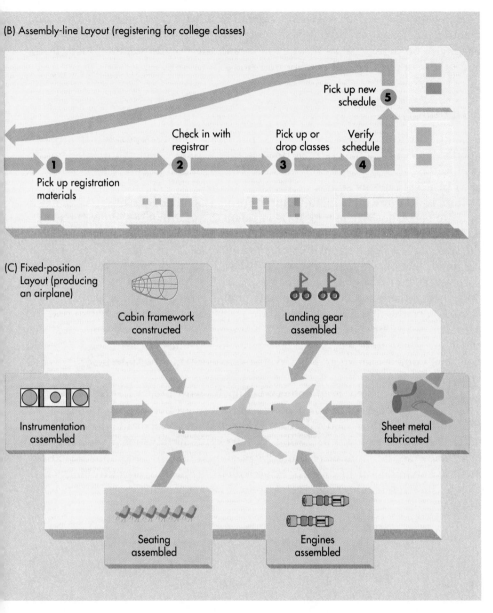

(B) Assembly-line Layout (registering for college classes)

1 — Pick up registration materials
2 — Check in with registrar
3 — Pick up or drop classes
4 — Verify schedule
5 — Pick up new schedule

(C) Fixed-position Layout (producing an airplane)

- Cabin framework constructed
- Landing gear assembled
- Instrumentation assembled
- Sheet metal fabricated
- Seating assembled
- Engines assembled

Production layouts:
The type of production layout that a company chooses depends on the goods or services it is producing.
(A) A process layout is arranged according to the specialized workers and materials involved in various phases of the production process.
(B) In an assembly-line layout, the developing product moves in a continuous sequence from one work station to the next.
(C) A fixed-position layout requires workers and materials to be brought to the product.

by allowing students to register for class by phone. Piles of paper are replaced by the school's computer system, which guides callers through the registration process.

Fixed-Position Layout

Companies that produce such hard-to-move products as large aircraft and buildings use a **fixed-position layout**. In contrast to process and assembly-line layouts, the product stays in one place as it develops, and the workers and production equipment come to it. This approach saves the considerable expense of moving the product and the danger of damaging it. But it also means that scheduling workers and equipment is more difficult. A building contractor, for example, must plan carefully to avoid bringing in the cement trucks needed to pour the foundation before the bulldozers have finished grading the site.

fixed-position layout Method of arranging equipment in which the product is stationary and equipment and personnel come to it

Many services use fixed-position production as well. Home and landscape maintenance requires a fixed-position layout, and so does intensive care in a hospital. The patient stays in one place, and the nurses, doctors, food, drugs, and other supplies are all transported there.

Scheduling

It is not only in fixed-position layouts that scheduling is important. In any production process, managers must incorporate a time element into the routing plan, setting up a time for each operation to begin and to end. This is not easy, even in businesses as simple as the imaginary table company.

Here is what the table manufacturer's production manager has to consider in order to construct a schedule: If Department 2 can drill 4,000 dowel holes in a day, then all 4,000 legs and all 1,000 table tops should arrive in Department 2 on the same day. If Department 1 can make 1,000 table tops and 1,000 legs a week, it should start on the legs three weeks before it starts to cut the tops, or all the parts won't be ready for Departments 2 and 3 at the same time. If the entire order is to be shipped at the same time and as soon as possible, Department 3 should paint the first 500 tables as they are assembled and finished so that the paint will be dry by the time the last 500 are completed. The schedule must also show how much time will elapse before the job reaches Department 3—that is, how much time Department 3 has available to work on other jobs before this one arrives.

Although this project is complicated enough, many are far more complicated. Thus, making a chart of the project's various steps is often of great value. Earlier this century, Henry L. Gantt developed a technique for charting the steps to be taken and the time required. Exhibit 8.6 is a **Gantt chart,** which is basically a bar chart showing the amount of time that it should take to accomplish each element of a manufacturing process. Such a chart is one way of controlling schedules by showing managers where they are with respect to where they planned to be.

Gantt chart Bar chart used to control schedules by showing how long each part of a production process should take and when it should take place

EXHIBIT 8.6

A Gantt Chart: Scheduling a Complicated Table Order
A chart like this enables a production manager to see immediately the dates on which production steps must be started and completed if goods are to be delivered on schedule. Some steps may overlap to save time. For instance, after three weeks of cutting table legs, cutting table tops begins. This overlap ensures that the necessary legs and tops are completed at the same time and can move on together to the next stage in the manufacturing process.

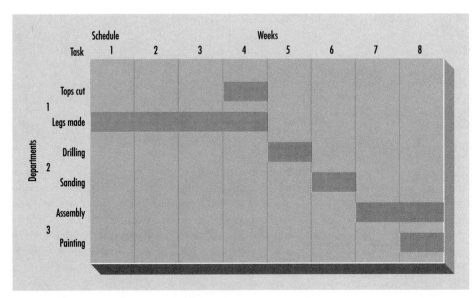

In every process or project, there is one combination of tasks that affects the elapsed time more than any other. For instance, at the table factory, producing the legs is one of the tasks in this sequence; if the legs take longer than expected, they will slow down the entire operation. On the other hand, the production schedule for the table tops is less critical—the tops could slip by up to two weeks and still be done by the time the legs are all done. The legs, then, are said to be on the *critical path,* whereas the tops aren't. Identifying the critical path is a vital step in efficient production because it shows managers where the highest-priority tasks are. Scheduling based on the critical path is called the **critical path method** (CPM) because it focuses on the particular sequence of tasks that is expected to take the longest time, thus determining when the project can be completed.

Consider the manufacture of shoes in Exhibit 8.7. At the beginning of the process, three parallel paths deal with heels, soles, and tops. All three processes must be finished before the next phase (sewing tops to soles and heels) can be started. However, one of the three paths—the tops—takes 33 days, whereas the other two take only 18 and 12 days. The shoe tops, then, are on the critical path because they will delay the entire operation if they fall behind schedule. Compare this with the soles, for example; these components could start up to 21 days after starting the tops, without slowing down production. (This free time in the soles schedule is called *slack time;* managers can choose to produce the soles anytime during the 33-day period required by the tops.)

The production manager uses CPM to estimate the least possible amount of time in which the whole project can be completed, basing this estimate on the projection of the time needed for completion of the critical path. CPM can also help managers balance work loads. For instance, the shoe manager might have the sole people finish their work as soon as possible and then help the tops people with their work, which would speed up the entire process.

Another scheduling method, the **program evaluation and review technique** (PERT), is similar to CPM but is better suited to processes and projects in which managers can't predict task durations with complete confidence. Like CPM, PERT also focuses on the order in which tasks must occur. However, in place of the single duration figure for each task, PERT uses four figures: an *optimistic* estimate (if things go well), a *pessimistic* estimate (if they don't go well), a *most likely* estimate (how long the task usually takes), and an *expected* time estimate, which is an average of the other three estimates.[42]

critical path method Scheduling method that estimates the smallest amount of time in which a whole project can be completed by projecting the time needed for completion of the longest sequence of tasks (the critical path)

program evaluation and review technique Scheduling method similar to the critical path method but relying on statistical estimates of how long each task should take

EXHIBIT 8.7

A CPM Chart: Manufacture of Shoes
In the manufacture of shoes, the critical path involves receiving, cutting the pattern, dyeing the leather, sewing the tops, sewing the tops to soles and heels, finishing, packaging, and shipping—a total of 62 time units.

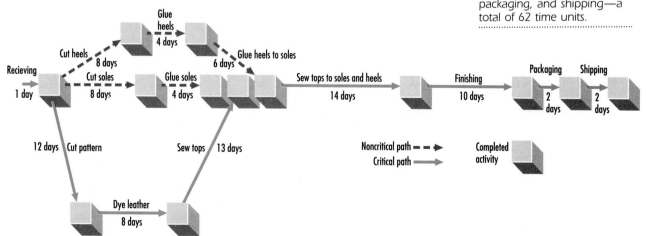

Dispatching

Dispatching is the issuing of work orders and the distribution of papers to department supervisors. These orders specify the work to be done and the schedule for its completion. In the case of the table manufacturer, the production manager would dispatch orders to the storeroom, requesting delivery of the needed materials (wood, dowels, paint) to the appropriate departments and machines before the scheduled starting time. Dispatching is considerably more difficult in industries employing fixed-position layouts. In hospitals, for example, dispatching is of central importance.

Follow-Up and Control

Once the schedule has been set up and the orders dispatched, a production manager cannot just sit back and assume that the work will automatically get done correctly and on time. Even the best scheduler may misjudge the time needed to complete an operation, and production may be delayed by accidents, mechanical breakdowns, or supplier failures. Thus, the production manager must have a system for handling delays and preventing a minor disruption from growing into chaos. A successful system is based on good communication between the workers and the production manager.

Suppose a machine breakdown causes Department 2 of the table company to lose half a day of drilling time. If the schedule is not altered to direct other work to Department 3, the workers and equipment in Department 3 will be unnecessarily idle for a while. So Department 2 must inform the production manager of its machine problem right away, and the production manager must immediately reschedule some fill-in work for Department 3.

In addition to such a follow-up system, production managers must set up a control system for making sure the company's products meet quality standards. Traditionally, this has been done by checking and testing completed components and products. Today, however, there's more emphasis on making sure that quality components are used in the first place and that the process itself is designed to minimize flaws. All sorts of businesses have come to realize that paying careful attention to every phase of production is what improves effectiveness and, therefore, competitiveness and profits.

SUMMARY OF LEARNING OBJECTIVES

1 Diagram the conversion process.
The conversion process is input → transformation → output.

2 Define the goal of most advances in production technology.
Competitiveness, or maximizing the efficiency and the quality of the production process, is the goal of most advances in production technology.

3 Cite the four technological advances that made mass production possible.
Mass production became possible after the development of mechanization, standardization, the assembly line, and automation.

4 Explain three innovations in materials management.
Material requirements planning

(MRP) determines when materials are needed, when they should be ordered, and when they should be delivered. Just-in-time (JIT) is the practice of limiting the quantity of materials on hand by making them available only when they are actually required for the production process. Manufacturing resource planning (MRP II) is a computerized system that brings together data from all parts of a company (including financial and design departments) to automatically produce inventory-control information; this process simulates "what if" analysis.

5 Differentiate between quality control and quality assurance.

Quality control focuses on measuring products or processes against some standard. Quality assurance, on the other hand, includes all activities performed to be sure that quality is built into the product.

6 Define the five basic steps in production control.

Planning is the analysis of what to produce and how much to produce, as well as where and how to produce it. Routing is figuring out how production will proceed. Scheduling adds the time element to the production process. Dispatching is sending production orders. And follow-up and control is seeing that everything proceeds according to plan, as well as figuring out how to cope with problems as they arise.

7 Identify the three main production layouts.

In a process layout, the developing product is sent from one department to another for a certain type of processing; specialized equipment and workers are stationed in each department. In an assembly-line layout, the developing product proceeds along a continuous line of work stations at which some small task is performed. In a fixed-position layout, the product stays in one place, and the workers and equipment are brought to it.

8 Describe three techniques for improving scheduling.

Scheduling may be improved with the use of (1) the Gantt chart, which is a bar chart indicating the expected duration of specific tasks; (2) the critical path method (CPM), which identifies the sequence of tasks expected to take the longest in order to control the project completion time; and (3) the program evaluation and review technique (PERT), which is much like CPM but which is based on statistical estimates of how long tasks can be expected to take.

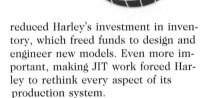

Meeting a Business Challenge at Harley-Davidson

Harley-Davidson saw its commanding lead in heavyweight motorcycles falter when powerful Japanese bikes appeared in the U.S. market. If Harley was to stay on the road, CEO Vaughn Beals had to uncover the key elements of Japanese success and put them to work in his own company. Initially, he was baffled. Honda's motorcycle plant in Marysville, Ohio, was staffed by U.S. workers, just as Harley's plant was. It bought parts from U.S. suppliers, just as Harley did. And it had no clear technological advantage that Beals could identify. In fact, Honda didn't own a PC, whereas Harley used a complex, computerized MRP system.

Gathering his senior managers and engineers together, Beals toured Honda's Marysville plant, and there he found his answer. Honda turned out better motorcycles because it used Japanese production systems. If Harley was to make a comeback, it would have to adopt some of those systems.

Beals set his staff to work installing a version of Japanese just-in-time inventory control. Switching to JIT was

Vaughn Beals, Chairman of Harley-Davidson.

not easy. Some workers laughed when Tom Gelb, senior vice president for operations, announced that Harley was replacing its computer-based control system, overhead conveyors, and high-rise part storage with a system that uses pushcarts. But within two months, the employees were converts. Switching to JIT almost immediately

reduced Harley's investment in inventory, which freed funds to design and engineer new models. Even more important, making JIT work forced Harley to rethink every aspect of its production system.

Harley was forced to change its purchasing practices. Suppliers were no longer adversaries; they were partners. Harley forged cooperative relationships with a select group of suppliers who could deliver high-quality parts according to Harley's demanding JIT schedule. Paradoxically, this approach allowed Harley to cut costs as well as increase quality. Because Harley used fewer suppliers, it could place larger orders and qualify for bulk discounts.

To keep its own work-in-progress stocks low, the company reduced machine-tool setup times so that components could be made in smaller quantities. One way it cut setup time was to standardize components for various product lines. For instance, working closely with production engineers, Harley's designers reworked the crankpins used in two models, thus saving the time it took to switch from making one crankpin to making the other.

This reduction of setup time improved productivity. It also enabled Harley to switch from a product layout to a process layout, which is better suited to the small production runs that Harley needed in order to keep inventory down. Small runs also helped Harley introduce upgrades more quickly, and they have boosted quality. With small runs, defects are limited to fewer parts.

These changes helped Harley roar back into the motorcycle business. With 66 percent of the market, it has beaten back Japanese competition while demonstrating that it's possible for a U.S. firm to be a low-cost, high-quality producer. Harley no longer has stockrooms; all the materials are on the floor. It no longer relies on inspection programs such as Quality Audit, so production-control staff has been slashed from 22 to 2. It no longer buys parts from 820 companies; the number of suppliers has been reduced more than 50 percent. Revamping its operations management systems has even positioned Harley to turn the tables on Japanese companies: Harley-Davidson is now the best-selling imported motorcycle in Japan.

Your Mission: Since 1986 Harley-Davidson's sales have nearly doubled, and its earnings have grown at an annual rate of 57 percent. Such success, critics say, has bred complacency. Sensing that there might be some truth in these remarks, Tom Gelb, senior vice president of operations, has hired you as an operations consultant to evaluate the company's manufacturing systems and to help plot its strategy for the future. For each of the following situations, choose the best response.

1. Harley-Davidson's approach to automation has changed a great deal in recent years, switching from automating without evaluating the underlying processes to fixing the processes first and then automating where it makes sense. At a recent quarterly meeting with the entire production staff, you asked the various work groups to submit proposals for automating tasks that are still done manually. You currently have enough money to implement only one of these. Based on the following descriptions, which of these four areas would be the most appropriate to automate?

a. A machining area where employees make a wide variety of unique tools and fixtures for use on the production line

b. The assembly area where gas tanks are attached to the cycle frames and where employees are complaining that they have to do the same simple job over and over again

c. The parts-receiving department where incoming parts (some of which are quite heavy and hard to handle) are unpacked and directed to the appropriate locations on the production line

d. The warranty-claims-processing department where employees have to process the same basic form over and over again

2. The company's employees continually offer suggestions on improving quality and customer satisfaction. However, some of these ideas are better than others, and you have to choose which ones to implement. Based on the notions of quality control and quality assurance, which of the following suggestions is best?

a. Have an inspector measure the time it takes to start the engines on finished motorcycles when the bikes are driven off the assembly line.

b. Find out why the stitching in some leather seat covers is breaking after only a few months of use; then ask the manufacturer concerned to fix the problem.

c. Survey dealers to find out how often the factory ships the wrong owner's manual with the various motorcycle models; ask them if this error rate is acceptable.

d. Survey owners to see whether the traditional Harley-Davidson problems of oil leaks and vibrations have begun to crop up again.

3. The management team at Harley-Davidson is well aware of the impact that employee attitudes and motivation have on product quality and manufacturing productivity. In studying several other manufacturing firms, Harley-Davidson uncovered a number of approaches to getting employees involved and making sure they are satisfied with their work. Considering both cost and effectiveness, which of the following involvement/motivation programs do you think Harley-Davidson should adopt?

a. Rotate all employees through all the jobs in the factory, from engineering and design all the way through shipping, clerical work, and even janitorial work. Employees who move to new jobs will better appreciate the challenges each job entails, and the result will be a more cohesive work force with a greater sense of teamwork.

b. Get rid of job classifications entirely and empower every employee to tackle whatever tasks he or she thinks is necessary to produce motorcycles effectively. For instance, if the people responsible for painting the cycles see a problem with the design of the frame, they would redesign the frame themselves, rather than trying to convince somebody else to do it.

c. Encourage employees to start quality circles throughout the plant, and make sure they link their efforts to the company procedures for statistical quality control.

d. Adapt (c) so that employees start quality circles, but do not require the statistical reporting element; too much attention to tracking and monitoring will demotivate employees who feel that their every move is being watched and criticized.

4. One phase of the motorcycle assembly process is split into four parallel task groups, each taking care of one general area of the motorcycle. The assembly line continues in a single line after the four parallel tasks are done (similar to the three parallel task groups in Exhibit 8.7). Considering the individual task times and critical path analysis, where should you assign several people whose old jobs in another factory have been eliminated?[43]

TASK	TIME REQUIRED
Preparing stereo	15 minutes
Preparing saddle bags	5 minutes
Preparing mirrors	6 minutes
Preparing fog lights	10 minutes
Installing inner tubes	3 minutes

TASK	TIME REQUIRED	TASK	TIME REQUIRED
Installing tires	5 minutes	Installing connectors	18 minutes
Inflating tires	1 minute	Testing for continuity	10 minutes
Testing for pressure/ leaks	5 minutes		
Inspecting paint job quality	45 minutes		
Cutting wires to length	9 minutes		

a. Preparing accessories, which includes testing the stereo, inspecting the saddle bags, getting the mirrors ready to attach, and installing bulbs in the fog lights.

b. Inspecting paint, which is done entirely by an automated electro-optical inspection robot.

c. Assembling the tires, which includes installing the inner tubes and tires, inflating, and checking for correct pressure and leaks.

d. Assembling the electrical harness, which includes cutting wires to length, adding connectors, and testing for electrical continuity.[43]

KEY TERMS

analytic system (207)
assembly line (207)
assembly-line layout (222)
automation (207)
bill of materials (221)
computer-aided design (208)
computer-aided engineering (209)
computer-aided manufacturing (209)
computer-integrated manufacturing (209)
conversion process (206)
critical path method (225)
dispatching (226)
effectiveness (207)
efficiency (207)
ergonomics (216)
fixed-position layout (223)

flexible manufacturing (210)
focused factory (210)
Gantt chart (224)
hard manufacturing (209)
inventory (211)
inventory control (211)
job shop (210)
just-in-time system (212)
lead times (212)
manufacturing resource planning (213)
mass production (207)
material requirements planning (212)
mechanization (207)
methods improvement (216)
process layout (221)
production (206)

production and operations management (218)
production control (219)
production forecasting (219)
program evaluation and review technique (225)
quality assurance (215)
quality circles (216)
quality control (214)
repetitive manufacturing (210)
routing (221)
setup costs (210)
standardization (207)
statistical process control (215)
statistical quality control (215)
synthetic system (207)
total quality management (215)

REVIEW QUESTIONS

1. How has the computer revolutionized production?

2. Why is an effective system of inventory control important to every producer?

3. What are the benefits of JIT systems?

4. Why has quality become an important issue for U.S. manufacturers, and what is being done to improve it?

5. What contributes to effectiveness in service operations?

6. Why is production and operations management particularly important today?

7. What is involved in each step of production control?

8. What factors need to be considered when selecting a site for a production facility?

A CASE FOR CRITICAL THINKING

Profit Formulas Include People

At many companies, production problems arise when top management tries to impose changes from above. Workers refuse to operate machinery or intentionally slow down the work, def-

initions of occupational roles are confused, and systems are designed without consideration for the people who will run them. But none of this has to happen. From conception of

change through implementation, a policy of frank and open communication among top executives, managers, and workers will smooth the road for all concerned.

James Lewis, president of Continental Container Systems (a division of Continental Can Company in Chicago), is credited with making the company profitable by installing process technology and by using effective people management. "To explain Continental's commitment to a future in manufacturing, we started 'communication circles,' which have gradually evolved into quality circles. To further show management's resolve, we established a no layoff policy for the shop. We treat shop-floor workers as fixed assets." The result was an older work force adapting to process changes quickly and easily.

Employee involvement is having positive effects at General Motors and Ford as well. "Although GM is not yet the lowest-cost producer of motor vehicles, CIM [computer-integrated manufacturing] coupled with HIM [human-integrated manufacturing] will bring this about," predicts Gerald L. Elson, executive director of artificial intelligence. HIM emphasizes training; and while old machinery is being torn out, employees are being trained to use the new tools being installed. During the planning phase of the new Taurus sedan at Ford, management asked assembly-line workers for advice and was overwhelmed with helpful suggestions. Sales of the Taurus have boosted Ford's profits by 40 percent.

At Consolidated Edison Company of New York, there is an Employee Suggestion Awards Program. Employees can be awarded as much as $15,000, based on how much money is actually saved as a result of the suggestion. "Most ideas are really solutions to problems that employees encounter regularly in the process of doing their jobs," says Laurie Hanson, Con Ed spokesperson. "How often have we all said, 'there's got to be a better way to do this'? But if we find a better way, no one—except maybe a nearby co-worker doing the same job—hears about it. Certainly supervisors or managers don't hear about it.

This program helps correct that oversight."

If workers are treated with respect and are provided a good working environment, they respond. "Declining productivity was never a blue-collar problem," said Bruce Bumpus, vice president of Zymark Corporation, which makes robotic systems in the Boston area. Thus, executives are beginning to brief workers (even on financial and sales information), and management is beginning to listen to workers—to the benefit of all.[44]

1. How does improving human relations contribute to the goal of most advances in production technology?

2. Besides increasing employee involvement, what can be done to improve human relations?

3. In any attempt to improve human relations, is it possible for management to involve employees too much?

BUILDING YOUR COMMUNICATION SKILLS

Many phases of production, from design to inspection, have become computerized. With your class, or in small groups of three or four students, discuss the personnel issues that have arisen as a result of this technological revolution in business. You might wish to create a chart that depicts the positive and negative results of technology on human resources. Develop a consensus opinion (or a written summary) regarding the various issues discussed.

▶ How has technology affected the job market? Are jobs being enhanced or replaced by computers?

▶ Consider pride in process. Has computerized production created a feeling of distance from the end product for some employees?

▶ How have companies involved workers in an effort to improve morale and make them feel more involved?

KEEPING CURRENT USING *THE WALL STREET JOURNAL*

Find an article in *The Wall Street Journal* that describes a problem or an innovation in one of the following areas:

▶ Quality assurance

▶ Production control

▶ Technology in manufacturing

▶ Manufacturing layout

▶ Manufacturing cost or time

1. What are the causes of the problem or reasons for the innovation?

2. How will the problem or innovation affect the company's employees? Costs? Competitive position?

3. What career opportunities or problems are suggested by this development?

PART THREE

Managing Human Resources

CHAPTER 9

LEARNING OBJECTIVES
After studying this chapter, you will be able to

1 List the three main components of good human relations within an organization.

2 Explain the five steps in Maslow's hierarchy of needs as they relate to worker motivation.

3 Identify the two factors affecting worker motivation in Herzberg's motivational-hygiene theory.

4 List three basic assumptions of expectancy theory.

5 Describe three concepts linking motivation and management style.

6 Discuss the impact of three major trends in the work force.

7 Identify three approaches to motivating individual employees.

8 Name four job-oriented techniques for improving the motivation of workers.

Human Relations

Facing a Business Challenge at Nucor

PUTTING THE BACKBONE BACK INTO STEEL

Skeptics laughed when they heard that F. Kenneth Iverson wanted to beat the system by opening his own steel mill. How could a tiny firm named Nucor produce material more cheaply than so-called Big Steel? Since the end of World War II, the American steel industry had boomed until it was larger than all the other nations' steel industries put together. These skeptics pointed out that expensive labor alone would prevent Iverson from cutting costs enough for Nucor to compete. Union contracts guaranteed steelworkers wages that were half again higher than those in other industries.

But Iverson had to act, and act fast. His company was a successful maker of steel roof joists. But the firm's main supplier, United States Steel (now known as USX), was raising prices so that it was charging more for steel than Iverson could get for his finished joists. His firm was faced with extinction.

Besides, Iverson saw things the skeptics didn't. He looked closely at Big Steel and saw complacent operations trapped in webs of bureaucracy. He saw management rewarding itself with favorable employment contracts while ignoring the needs of shop workers. He saw the workers' resentment toward managers who insulate themselves from mill operations with layers of supervision, who rule by decree rather than by inspiration, and who enjoy special perks such as country club memberships, exclusive cafeterias, and separate rest rooms.

On the other hand, Iverson saw Big Steel managers accusing unions of pampering workers and accusing workers of being more concerned about racking up their paid sick leave than about the quality of the product coming out the factory doors. He also saw management accusing unions of enforcing restrictive work rules that serve only to increase production costs so that the customer has to pay for the resulting high price of steel.

Iverson concluded that the problem with Big Steel wasn't the high cost of labor; it was the declining productivity of an alienated work force. If employees could only be motivated by managers sensitive to their needs, they would perform with enthusiasm and produce steel in fewer worker-hours. That would enable Iverson's company to make its own steel at a cost that would allow Nucor to sell roof joists at a profit. Furthermore, Iverson believed that by motivating workers with the right techniques he could keep unions out of his shop.

Iverson had to attract workers to his new mill with nothing more than a promise, and he had to convince them he was sincere. Was he just a dreamer? How could he get workers to stay with his company when they could get juicy guarantees at union shops? How could he motivate them to produce steel at rock-bottom cost when they traditionally viewed such efforts as benefiting management only? [1]

▶ HUMAN RELATIONS WITHIN AN ORGANIZATION

human relations The way two or more people interact with one another

As F. Kenneth Iverson knows well, motivation is just one part of human relations. The term **human relations** refers to the ways people interact with one another. This chapter is mainly concerned with the ways in which they interact within a business organization. In that setting, human relations are determined by the organization's culture and management practices as well as by other, more general forces.

The Roles of the Organization and Management

Most organizations and their managers realize the importance of maintaining good human relations. A climate of openness and trust can stimulate performance and foster loyalty. For example, everyone at Walt Disney Productions—including the president—wears a name tag with first name only, and at IBM the chairman of the board personally answers employee complaints.[2] This kind of atmosphere can only have a positive effect on human relations.

Although many managers get a lift from knowing that they're treating their workers right, there are practical benefits as well. When workers are satisfied with the interpersonal component of their jobs, they are usually more productive. They are also less likely to resign or to file a complaint with the personnel office, the union, or some other agency—both actions that could create additional expense and effort for the company.

leadership The ability to motivate someone to do something

The Components of Good Human Relations

Rockwell managers know that communicating with employees is an essential aspect of good human relations.

How can managers ensure good human relations? Three components are particularly important: leadership, communication, and motivation. **Leadership** is the ability to influence people to work toward accomplishing a goal. A leader's approach is determined by the demands of the situation, by the needs and personalities of the followers, and by the culture of the organization. The manager who inspires enthusiasm and who works hard alongside employees is usually more effective than the boss who invokes authority and takes all the credit for the group's accomplishments. Managers must learn to distinguish between authority—the ability to *make* someone do something—and leadership—the ability to *inspire* someone to do something. A true leader, one who inspires people to tap their own potential, is usually more likely to foster productivity and profitability.

A second component of good organizational human relations is **communication.** Through speaking, listening, writing, and reading, managers and lower-level employees not only share crucial job-related information but also build interpersonal networks and patterns of interaction. Effective business communication should be clear and should avoid subtlety and ambiguity. At the same time, it must incorporate courtesy and respect to help keep lines of communication open and effective. One study found that 90 percent of the people who report good communication with their bosses are satisfied with their jobs.[3]

A third factor contributing to good organizational human relations is **motivation,** the goal of which is to increase worker productivity. Motivation is sometimes defined as getting people to do what you want them to do. But that definition doesn't go far enough. Fear of management or of job loss may motivate people, but it is much less effective than encouraging the employee's own sense of direction and creativity. Consider managers who motivate workers by penalizing them for any deviation from company standards. Now think of managers who encourage workers to feel pride in doing the job well. In which case would human relations be more positive? In which case would the quality of work be better? Motivation that successfully activates, directs, and maintains employee behavior leads to worker performance significantly beyond the level that can be required or enforced. In short, effective managers take into account workers' individual needs and persuade them that those needs can be satisfied within the organization's framework (see Exhibit 9.1).

A concept closely related to motivation is **morale,** a person's attitude toward both the job and the organization. Employee perception of the workplace affects morale. Traditionally, managers believed that performance was determined by real conditions, such as sufficient resources, competent employees, efficient systems, and clear goals. Today, managers realize that *perceived* conditions—fairness, clarity, appreciation, responsiveness, involvement—significantly affect performance as well. Employees work best when they feel positive about perceived conditions. Positive conditions include the following:

Fairness. The environment is nonpolitical and free of patronage; promotions are based on merit.

communication Transmitting information from one person to another

motivation Giving employees a reason to do their jobs and to perform at their best

morale General outlook in regard to a job or an organization

EXHIBIT 9.1

The Motivation Process
The key to effective motivation is to demonstrate to workers that their individual needs dovetail with the needs of the organization.

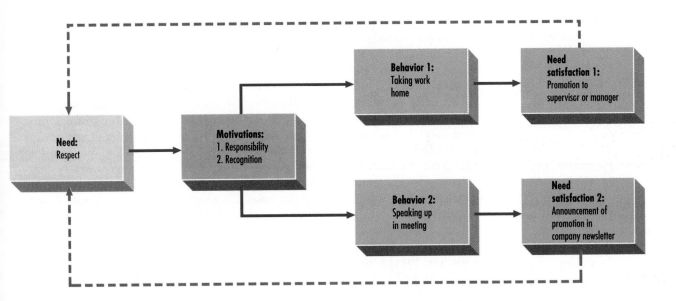

Clarity. Organizational, work-group, and individual goals are clearly defined.

Appreciation. Employees believe that they are of value to the organization.

Responsiveness. Employees feel that their needs and problems are of concern to management.

Involvement. Employees feel that they are contributing to organizational goals.[4]

A worker who has good morale is more likely to be cheerful, enthusiastic, and loyal. The morale of a department or of an organization as a whole may be characterized in similar fashion. A manager who wants to boost morale tries to find ways to encourage people to work more enthusiastically and to perform at maximum capacity. To understand all the variables involved in motivating workers, it is helpful to know something about motivation theory and about the specific motivational challenges that today's work force presents.

▶ MOTIVATION THEORY

By today's standards, nineteenth-century working conditions were barbaric: 12- to 14-hour workdays; six- and seven-day workweeks; cramped, unsafe factories; marginal wages; and no legal protection. Yet employers seldom had problems motivating their workers; poverty and unemployment were so widespread that any job was welcome.

One of the few exceptions to the neglect of employees was Robert Owen, a Scottish industrialist of the early nineteenth century who pioneered such modern business practices as the merit system. Owen thought of his textile-mill employees as "vital machines"—in contrast to the factory's "inanimate machines"—and considered their upkeep as important as that of the mechanical equipment. Owen's views were not widely shared, however, and it was not until the end of the century that social pressures forced industrialists to consider the wisdom of motivating workers.

The Classical Theory of Motivation

classical theory of motivation The view that money is the sole motivator in the workplace

The **classical theory of motivation** can be stated simply: Money is the sole motivator in the workplace. In this view, human beings are economic creatures who work only to pay for food, clothing, and shelter (and whatever luxuries they may be able to afford beyond that). To motivate workers, then, a manager has only to show them that they'll earn more money by doing things the company way.

The chief spokesperson for the classical theory was Frederick W. Taylor (1856–1915). A firm believer in the division of labor, Taylor broke work into small units that were both efficient and easy to measure. He then determined a reasonable level of productivity for each task and established a quota, or minimum goal, that he expected each worker to reach. Under this **piecework system,** workers who just met or fell short of the quota were paid a certain amount for each unit produced. Those who surpassed it were paid at a higher rate for *all* units produced, not just for those that exceeded the quota. Needless to say, his system gave workers a strong incentive to increase productivity.

piecework system The practice of paying workers a certain amount for each unit produced and paying those who surpass a stated quota at a higher rate for **all** units produced

About 1900 Taylor's system, called *scientific management,* was introduced at Bethlehem Steel with impressive results. The average steel handler's wage rose from $1.15 to $1.85 a day, and productivity increased so sharply that handling costs were cut by more than half. The experiment had a profitable outcome for everyone.

The classical theory of motivation worked well in the early part of this century for a good reason: Most workers were very poor. Today, however, classical theory fails to explain why a person whose spouse makes a good living will still want to work or why a Wall Street lawyer will take a hefty pay cut to serve in government. Clearly, money is not the only thing that motivates people to work (as Taylor was quite aware—he also did pioneer work in job design and worker health).

The Hawthorne Studies

Between 1927 and 1932, researchers conducted landmark motivation studies at Western Electric's Hawthorne plant in Cicero, Illinois. The researchers had initially intended to examine the relationship between work environment—lighting, temperature, pay scale—and productivity. They found that altering the environment had an impact that differed from what they expected. Only extreme changes seemed to have a significant effect; otherwise, workers apparently produced at the same pace, regardless of changes in the physical surroundings.[5]

Investigators were baffled. Was there some offsetting force that made the workers either ignore the change or, if that was impossible, do their best to make up for it? Further research revealed that there was, indeed, such a motivating force: social pressure. The workers had established their own **group norms,** or standards of behavior, for what the correct output should be. The group sneered at overproducers as "rate busters" and underproducers as "chiselers." And the pressure was effective; the workers were more concerned with the approval of their peers than with earning higher wages.

group norms Standards of behavior that all members of a given group accept

The Hawthorne studies show that the informal organization has at least as much power to motivate workers as the formal organization. The studies also reveal another important phenomenon. Even though no changes in work methods or equipment had been introduced, the productivity of the workers rose 30 percent during the course of the project. The researchers concluded that this increased productivity was simply a result of participating in the research—of being asked for opinions and ideas, of being listened to. This phenomenon came to be known as the **Hawthorne effect.** The mere fact that someone was paying attention to them made the workers more productive.

Hawthorne effect Improvement in performance as a by-product of attention, revealed in the Hawthorne studies of worker productivity

Maslow's Hierarchy of Needs

In 1943 psychologist Abraham Maslow proposed that behavior is determined by a wide variety of needs. He organized these needs into five categories (see Exhibit 9.2). Maslow arranged these categories in a hierarchy, with the most basic needs (food, water, shelter) at the bottom and more advanced needs (esteem, self-actualization) toward the top. A human being, according to Maslow, is a "perpetually wanting animal." When needs on a lower level have been satisfied, at least in part, a person strives to achieve those on the next level.[6]

All the requirements for sustaining life—food, clothing, shelter—fall into the category of *physiological needs.* These basic needs must be satisfied before the person can pursue other objectives. Today, physiological needs are so readily fulfilled by most wage earners that more advanced needs tend to be more moti-

EXHIBIT 9.2

Maslow's Hierarchy of Needs

According to Maslow, needs on the lower levels of the hierarchy must be satisfied before higher needs can be addressed.

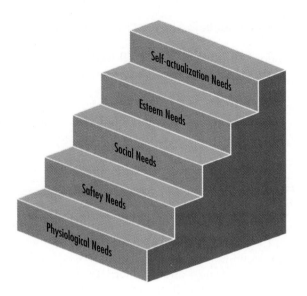

vating. For example, when the bare essentials have been taken care of, the person is motivated to fulfill the need for security, for a cushion against misfortune. Such *safety needs* may be satisfied through wages high enough to allow saving, as well as by health insurance, pension plans, guaranteed job security, and Social Security benefits.

Beyond safety needs, human beings have a powerful need to associate with others, to give and receive love, and to feel a sense of belonging. As the Hawthorne studies showed, these *social needs* may be more important to the worker than financial considerations. People also have *esteem needs*—they need a sense of personal worth and integrity. They also need the respect of others, a respect based on competence and achievement. These needs are closely related to the idea of status, which is one's rank or importance in the eyes of others. The opportunity to fill these needs can serve as a powerful motivator on the job.

Maslow defined the need for *self-actualization* as "the desire to become more what one is, to become everything one is capable of." This need is the highest and most difficult to fulfill; workers who reach this point work not simply to make money or to impress others but also because they feel their work is worthwhile and satisfying in itself.

Although Maslow's hierarchy is a convenient way to classify human needs, it would be a mistake to view it as a rigid sequence. Each level of needs does not have to be completely satisfied (which may in itself be impossible) before a person can be motivated by a higher need. Indeed, at any one time, most people are motivated by a combination of needs.

Motivational-Hygiene Theory

In the 1960s, Frederick Herzberg and his associates undertook their own study of human needs. They asked workers to describe specific aspects on the job that made them feel satisfied or dissatisfied and then analyzed the results. What they found is that two entirely different sets of factors are associated with satisfying and dissatisfying experiences (see Exhibit 9.3). What Herzberg called **hygiene factors** were associated with dissatisfying experiences. Company policy, work-

hygiene factors Aspects of the work environment that are demotivating only if deficient

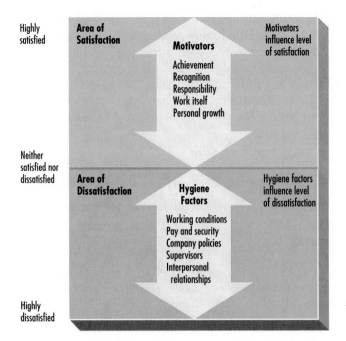

Highly satisfied

Area of Satisfaction

Motivators

Achievement
Recognition
Responsibility
Work itself
Personal growth

Motivators influence level of satisfaction

Neither satisfied nor dissatisfied

Area of Dissatisfaction

Hygiene Factors

Working conditions
Pay and security
Company policies
Supervisors
Interpersonal
   relationships

Hygiene factors influence level of dissatisfaction

Highly dissatisfied

EXHIBIT 9.3

Herzberg's Two-Factor Theory

Hygiene factors—environmental influences such as company policies and working conditions—can produce worker dissatisfaction, but only if they are inadequate in some way. Beyond them is a category called motivators—human relations factors such as possibilities for achievement and recognition—that can increase productivity, assuming hygiene factors are adequate.

ing conditions, and job security are potential sources of work dissatisfaction only if they are deficient. Nor can management motivate employees solely by improving hygiene factors that are already perceived as adequate. On the other hand, **motivators** such as achievement, recognition, responsibility, and other personally rewarding factors may be used to increase productivity. Herzberg's theory is an obvious outgrowth of Maslow's: The motivators closely resemble Maslow's higher-level needs, and the hygiene factors resemble the lower-level needs.

Should managers such as Nucor's Iverson concentrate on motivators or on hygiene factors? It depends. A skilled, well-paid, middle-class, middle-aged worker may be motivated to perform better if motivators are supplied. But a young or elderly unskilled worker who earns low wages or a worker who is insecure will probably still need the support of strong hygiene factors before the motivators can be effective.[7]

motivators Factors of human relations in business that may increase motivation

Expectancy Theory

Another theoretical approach to motivation that has been influential in recent years was developed by David Nadler and Edward Lawler.[8] According to their **expectancy theory,** the amount of effort that individuals will expend on a task depends on the expected outcomes. Workers take into account (1) how well they think they will do on the task ("Can I do it?"), (2) whether they think they will be rewarded for that performance ("If I do it, what will I get?"), and (3) whether the reward will be worth the amount of effort required ("Will it be worth my while?"). An important aspect of this theory is that it sees motivation as varying from individual to individual. Each worker may perceive the difficulty of a task differently, the value of the reward differently, and the connection between the two differently.

Based on their model of expectancy, Nadler and Lawler suggest that managers

expectancy theory The idea that the amount of effort a worker expends will depend on the expected outcome

can improve employee performance by (1) determining the rewards valued by each worker, (2) determining the desired level of performance from each worker, (3) making performance levels attainable, (4) linking rewards to performance, and (5) making sure the reward is adequate.

Walter Newsome amplified on expectancy theory by introducing what he calls the "nine Cs." These characteristics capture the theory's significant aspects and summarize the main issues that effective managers address to implement the theory:

▶ *Capability.* Does the individual have the capability to perform the job well?

▶ *Confidence.* Does the individual believe he or she can do the job well?

▶ *Challenge.* Does he or she have to work hard to perform the job well?

▶ *Criteria.* Does he or she know the difference between good and bad performance?

▶ *Credibility.* Does he or she believe the manager will deliver on promises?

▶ *Consistency.* Does he or she believe that all individuals receive similar preferred outcomes for good performance and similar less preferred outcomes for poor performance?

▶ *Compensation.* Do the outcomes associated with good performance reward the individual?

▶ *Cost.* What does it cost the individual—in effort and outcome forgone—to perform well?

▶ *Communication.* Does the manager communicate with the employee? (This is an underlying factor in the entire process.)[9]

Exhibit 9.4 shows how the first eight Cs relate to the basic model of expectancy theory.

EXHIBIT 9.4

Expectancy Theory
According to expectancy theory, employee motivation depends on each worker's evaluation of whether the desired effort is possible, whether the effort (performance) will lead to rewards, and whether the expected rewards (outcomes) will be worth the effort. The worker takes several factors (the first eight "Cs") into account when evaluating each aspect.

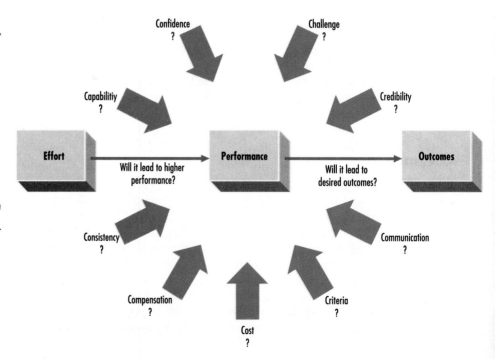

Motivation and Management Style

The motivation of workers is highly related to the attitudes of managers toward them. Over the years, a number of management styles have come into and gone out of vogue.

Theory X and Theory Y

In the 1960s psychologist Douglas McGregor identified a certain set of assumptions as underlying most management thinking. He labeled this set of assumptions **Theory X:**

1. The average person dislikes work and will avoid it if possible.

2. Because of the dislike for work, the average person must be forced, controlled, directed, or threatened with punishment in order to be motivated to expend enough effort to achieve organization objectives.

3. The average person prefers to be directed, wishes to avoid responsibility, has relatively little ambition, and wants security.

In other words, Theory X–oriented managers believe that workers can be motivated only by fear of losing their jobs or by external rewards. This management style emphasizes physiological and safety needs and tends to ignore the higher-level needs in Maslow's hierarchy.

To counteract this sort of thinking, McGregor proposed another set of assumptions for managers to focus on. He termed these assumptions **Theory Y:**

1. The average person does not dislike work. It is as natural as play or rest.

2. External control and the threat of punishment are not the only ways to motivate people to meet organization goals. The average person naturally works toward goals to which she or he is committed.

3. How deeply a person is committed to organization objectives depends on the rewards for achieving them.

4. Under favorable conditions the average person learns not only to accept responsibility but also to seek it.

5. Many people are capable of using imagination, cleverness, and creativity to solve problems that arise within an organization.

6. Especially in modern industrial life, the average person's intellectual potential is only partially realized.

Theory Y–oriented managers believe that workers can be motivated by the opportunity to be creative, to work hard for a cause they believe in, and to satisfy needs beyond the basic need to pay the rent.

The assumptions behind Theory X emphasize authority; the assumptions behind Theory Y emphasize growth and self-direction. It was McGregor's belief that although some workers need the strong direction demanded by Theory X, those who are ready to realize their social, esteem, and self-actualization needs will not continue working well under Theory X assumptions.[10]

Theory X Set of managerial assumptions about workers' motivations that coincide with an authoritarian management style

Theory Y Set of managerial assumptions about workers' motivations that coincide with a participative management style

Theory Z

Theory Z Human relations approach that seeks to encourage worker involvement by satisfying a wide range of needs

Today, a third "alphabet" theory has entered the management vocabulary. A perspective on human relations developed by William Ouchi, **Theory Z** assumes that the best management involves workers at all levels and treats employees like family. As in the ideal family, everyone works harmoniously toward the same goal. Managers who adopt Theory Z believe that employees with a sense of identity and belonging are more likely to perform their jobs conscientiously and will try more enthusiastically to achieve a perfect final product.

Theory Z satisfies the lower-level needs in Maslow's hierarchy by looking after worker welfare. It also satisfies middle-level needs by utilizing the group process. And it satisfies higher-level needs by letting workers take responsibility and participate in decisions. Theory Z works effectively because it tries to satisfy needs on all levels.

Theory Z is often called Japanese management, because it usually refers to techniques used by U.S. companies that have adopted a Japanese approach to business. In Japanese firms, everyone participates in decision making, and duties are rotated to avoid boredom, extreme specialization, and rigidity. Does this group-oriented approach work in the United States? Surviving in a small, densely populated, resource-poor land has made teamwork and compromise essential for the Japanese. People in the United States, on the other hand, have a tradition of individualism and self-reliance. Even so, some U.S. firms are already using Theory Z. Some Procter & Gamble plants, for example, have instituted partially self-governing work groups, and Hewlett-Packard keeps worker turnover down during economic slumps by making sure all employees—not just those in the lowest-paid positions—work shorter hours and give up certain privileges.[11]

▶ THE CHALLENGE OF MOTIVATING WORKERS IN THE 1990S

Nucor's F. Kenneth Iverson isn't the only one concerned with motivating employees. Managers trying to motivate employees today are faced with a number of challenges that make their task especially difficult. These challenges relate to the changing nature of the work force, the changing economy, and the changing organizational culture.

The Changing Work Force

VIDEO EXERCISE

The work force in North America is undergoing significant changes that over the next decade will require major alterations in how managers keep employees happy and productive on the job. Some of the most significant trends affecting the makeup of the work force include the following:

The population and the labor force will grow very slowly over the next decade. By the year 2000, the work force will increase by only 1 percent annually.

The pool of young workers entering the labor market will shrink. In 1985, workers aged 16 to 24 accounted for 20 percent of the work force; that number will decline to 16 percent by the year 2000.

The average age of the work force will rise from 35 to 39.

More women will enter the labor market. By the year 2000, some 80 percent of women aged 25 to 44 will be working.

Immigrants will represent the largest share of the increase in both population and work force since World War I—4 million to 7 million by the year 2000.

Women, minorities, and immigrants will form more than 80 percent of the net additions to the labor force between now and the year 2000.[12]

Three of the most significant trends include the aging of the work force, the swelling ranks of women into the work force, and the increasing cultural diversity in the work force.

The Aging of the Work Force

The baby boomers—people born between 1946 and 1964—are so numerous that they tend to distort most statistics. When they first entered the work force, the average age of U.S. workers fell. Now that they are approaching mid-career, the average age is again rising (see Exhibit 9.5). This aging labor pool and the declining number of young workers are largely due to baby boomers' decisions to marry later, to postpone or forgo starting a family, and to have fewer children— about half as many children as their parents did.

Because of their sheer numbers, competition for jobs and promotions among baby boomers is likely to remain strong. The current tendency toward corporate restructuring and downsizing limits opportunities still further, so management may be severely challenged to help baby boomers feel satisfied with their jobs in the face of decreasing promotion possibilities. How companies manage to do so, according to analyst Anne Fisher, "could make the difference between ending up leaner and more competitive or just ending up leaner."[13]

Boomers who are in their 30s and 40s want more from their jobs than just a good paycheck and satisfying work. Most are in dual-worker families and are trying to balance their careers and family lives. They want employers to offer them flexible work schedules and a choice of career paths to help them in this balancing act. And as the baby boomers enter their 50s, they will be viewing

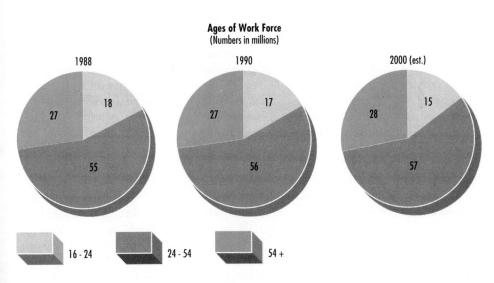

Ages of Work Force
(Numbers in millions)

1988 — 18, 27, 55

1990 — 17, 27, 56

2000 (est.) — 15, 28, 57

16 - 24   24 - 54   54 +

EXHIBIT 9.5
─────────────
The Aging of the Work Force
As the baby-boom generation gets older, so does the work force as a whole.

Employees must adjust to the changing composition of the work force, including the fact that more and more women are filling traditionally male jobs. At Weyerhaeuser's plywood and lumber operations in Millport, Alabama, team coordinator Mike Logan and green chain puller Annie Wright work together to achieve company goals.

Business Around the World

Changes in work force composition are occurring throughout the world. In Mexico, for example, only 8 percent of women aged 15 to 64 were working in 1950. That percentage had more than doubled, to 17 percent, in 1980, and today nearly 30 percent of Mexican women work.

their jobs and work environment differently. They'll expect to be treated with respect and to have more of a say in the company. They'll be particularly interested in employee stock-ownership plans and other means for giving them more involvement in the company as well as a comfortable retirement to look forward to.[14]

Women in the Work Force

The consequences of increasing numbers of women workers are even broader. Because of the increase in the number of two-career households, it is no longer easy to transfer a worker to another part of the country. Nor can employers assume that workers of either gender will be willing—or able—to sacrifice family needs in order to work overtime. Child care, for example, has become a critical issue. By 1995, women will make up some 63 percent of the total work force (see Exhibit 9.6).[15]

Employment decisions must increasingly take into account the needs of *all* family members. By acknowledging current family situations, business can offer solutions such as child-care assistance, maternity/paternity leave, flexible work schedules, telecommuting (home-based employees linked to the office by computer), and flexible benefit plans. These and other solutions are explored later in this chapter.

Cultural Diversity

A growing percentage of the work force is made up of members from diverse cultural and ethnic backgrounds (see Exhibit 9.7 on page 246). These workers bring with them a wide range of skills, varying attitudes toward work, and a wealth of customs and traditions that can affect their work behavior. Some come from indigenous American groups, while others are recently arrived immigrants. The challenge for managers is to communicate with this diverse work force and facilitate cooperation and harmony among employees.

Some companies have tackled the situation head-on by instituting management-training programs for dealing with cultural diversity. Hundreds of companies have used a series of seven 30-minute videotapes titled "Valuing Diversity" (produced by Copeland Griggs with funding from major corporations) to sensitize managers to stereotypes, introduce them to typical types of misunderstandings, and give them suggestions for making the most of what employees from varying backgrounds have to offer. The program encompasses not only ethnicity and culture but also gender, age, race, disability, and sexual orientation. In addition, many companies are instituting programs to encourage workers to be tolerant of cultural and language differences.

At Digital Equipment Corporation, a program called "Valuing Differences" has been in place for several years. It is based on the philosophy that "people work best when they feel valued, and that people feel more valued when their differences—their unique attributes—are taken into account."[16] A staff of 26 people at corporate headquarters, plus managers at DEC facilities around the country, offer training programs, produce materials on various themes, and run resource centers. Among other companies that have made a major commitment to diversity management are Apple Computer, Avon, Corning, Du Pont, Hewlett-Packard, Honeywell, Pacific Bell, Procter & Gamble, Security Pacific Bank,

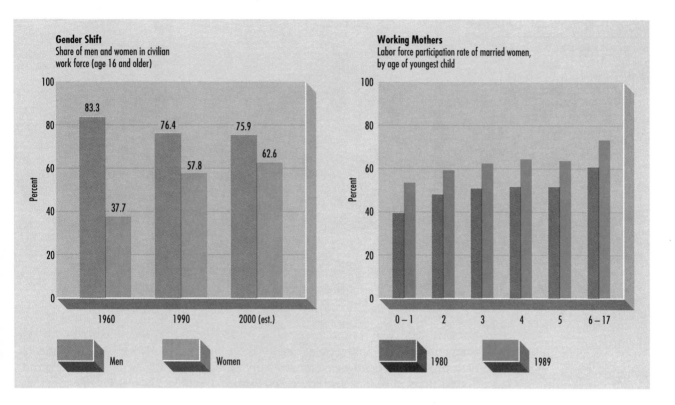

Gender Shift
Share of men and women in civilian work force (age 16 and older)

Percent

83.3
76.4
75.9
37.7
57.8
62.6

1960 1990 2000 (est.)

Men Women

Working Mothers
Labor force participation rate of married women, by age of youngest child

Percent

0–1 2 3 4 5 6–17

1980 1989

US West, and Xerox.[17] Many of these companies have orientation programs for new minority employees, encourage the formation of cultural support groups or networks, and sponsor cultural awareness activities.

The Changing Economy

The way business is conducted in the United States is evolving daily. Managers are confronting comprehensive changes throughout their organizations. Changes in work-force demographics, technology, markets, competition, organization, management, and ideas and beliefs are transforming all aspects of business life.

In the past, most employees and the companies they worked for were reciprocally loyal. Now, instead of providing lifetime employment, companies are much more likely to lay off workers because of takeovers, mergers, and recessions. In the past, the average person worked for two companies during a lifetime; today, the average person changes jobs every three to seven years.[18]

The shift from an industry-based economy to a service-based economy has displaced many manufacturing employees, leading to increased unemployment and job turnover in this sector. At the same time, technology is upgrading skill requirements, making it difficult for former industrial workers and less-skilled workers to qualify for jobs. Less-educated American workers are competing more and more with incoming foreign workers (especially Asian and Hispanic) for entry-level jobs.

Baby boomers compete for increasingly limited advancement opportunities as companies downsize, causing job plateauing (the attainment of the highest level on one's career ladder) and discontent. Massive layoffs even in high-tech

EXHIBIT 9.6

Women and Mothers in the Work Force

The participation of women in the work force is expected to pass 62 percent by 2000, and more and more of those women are mothers with children at home.

EXHIBIT 9.7

Minorities in the Work Force

African-Americans, Hispanics, Asian-Americans, and other minorities are making up a greater proportion of the work force.

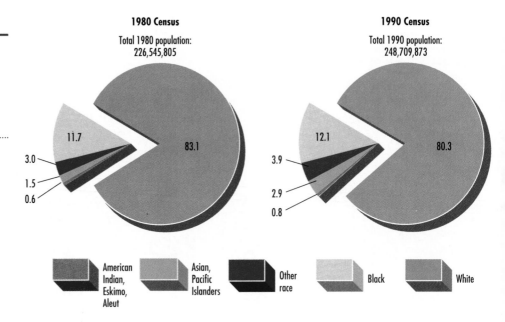

1980 Census
Total 1980 population: 226,545,805

11.7 83.1
3.0
1.5
0.6

1990 Census
Total 1990 population: 248,709,873

12.1 80.3
3.9
2.9
0.8

American Indian, Eskimo, Aleut   Asian, Pacific Islanders   Other race   Black   White

companies have employees fearing for their jobs. Certainly such anxiety affects their productivity and weakens company loyalty. In fact, a Time/CNN poll found that 57 percent of those surveyed believed companies to be less loyal to employees today than they were 10 years ago, and 63 percent said that employees are less loyal to their companies.[19]

FOCUS ON ETHICS

Should Employees Speak English on the Job?

When Frances Arreola read the memo announcing that she and her co-workers should speak only English during work hours, she was outraged. Arreola, a lens inspector for Signet Amoralite, a lens-manufacturing firm in southern California, remembers having been punished and humiliated by elementary school teachers for speaking in her native Spanish. She is now fluent in both English and Spanish but feels the English-only rule constitutes discrimination.

Signet Amoralite defends the English-only rule on the grounds that "speaking in another language that friends and associates cannot fully understand can lead to misunderstandings, is impolite, and can even be unsafe." The company claims that the English-only requirement is not written policy, just a guideline, and violating it carries no punishment.

Nevertheless, this policy—and ones like it at hundreds of companies throughout the United States—is

considered by civil libertarians to violate federal laws against discrimination on the basis of national origin. According to Equal Employment Opportunity Commission rules, employers can establish language restrictions only when such restrictions are required by valid business necessities.

The main reason that businesses institute English-only rules is in response to complaints from employees who feel that they are being gossiped about or excluded. A Chinese-American employee at a Sears, Roebuck billing office in Los Angeles, for example, complained that other workers were talking about her in Spanish during office hours. (The English-only rule subsequently enforced in that office is now being challenged in court by one of the Hispanic workers.) The number of such complaints is escalating as workplaces become more culturally diverse. At Signet Amoralite, for example, over half the 900 employees are Asian, Filipino, or Hispanic.

Managers are being caught in the middle of this

Despite the difficulty some workers are having in finding desirable jobs, many companies, especially small businesses, are scrambling to find qualified workers. With the shrinking labor pool, employers are having to sweeten the pot, wooing applicants with hiring bonuses, flexible work schedules, free trips, job training, and other incentives. Business is being challenged to assume responsibility for ensuring that employees are trained and retrained to meet the needs of the changing workplace. And to compete effectively, more corporations are recognizing the relevance of an investment in human capital.

The Changing Organizational Culture

In light of the changes in both the work force and the economy, organizational cultures themselves must change. When plateauing rather than promotion becomes the norm, organizational culture will need to downplay the importance of job advancement as the main source of job satisfaction. Otherwise, turnover will become an even more crucial problem as employees change jobs in a continuing effort to climb to the top. J. Alan Ofner, president of Managing Change, a management-consulting firm, offers several solutions for keeping employees motivated, including training them in new skills, assigning them to corporate task forces or special projects, and restructuring jobs to be more personally fulfilling.[20]

Organizational culture will also have to become more open. Honest communication during restructuring, for example, can keep rumors from getting out of control, improve morale, and allow workers to concentrate on performance. Organizations will have to communicate to employees that change is a natural

cultural clash over language. On the one side are employees who are disturbed by co-workers speaking to each other in a language they don't understand and who consider this behavior rude. On the other side are employees who feel they have a right to speak to each other in a more familiar language as long as it doesn't affect their work. Instituting English-only rules can be divisive as well as illegal. What is a manager to do?

The best solution, according to experts on cultural diversity management, is to offer cultural sensitivity training to workers. The purpose is to eliminate misconceptions on both sides. Native English speakers often assume that non-natives simply don't want to make the effort to learn and use English. But more commonly, non-native speakers are highly motivated to learn English because they believe it will improve their chances for advancing in the work world. "They tend to speak English as often as they can," says Michael Adams, who is involved in running cultural sensitivity programs for employees at the University of California at San Francisco. "When

they speak another language, it's done in order to help a fellow worker understand something."

Such workers need to become aware, however, that they may be alienating fellow employees when they converse in a different language on the job. "Most people aren't inherently rude," says Kathy Imahara of the Asian-Pacific American Legal Center in Los Angeles, "and they know what it's like to feel excluded. Usually it just takes a little discussion to take care of this problem."

English speakers may empathize if they are in the non-native speaker's shoes. They can be asked to imagine traveling in a foreign country and encountering another American. What language would they converse in? Would that be rude, or would it simply be more comfortable? Training sessions can go a long way toward increasing understanding and reducing tensions between culturally diverse workers. So far, however, such programs remain rare in U.S. companies.

and normal process. If employees are too concerned about job security, they will be less willing to take risks. Thus organizations will need to find ways of supporting and encouraging creativity and risk taking.

Given the changing work force, the changing economy, and the changing organizational culture, and taking into account theories of motivation, how can companies motivate employees to be their most productive and to want to stay with the firm? The remainder of this chapter addresses this question.

▶ MOTIVATIONAL TECHNIQUES

How do managers motivate workers? If employees had their way, they would choose the techniques in the proportions shown in Exhibit 9.8. Nucor is known around the world for its financial motivation. However, employees today are motivated by more than just good pay; satisfaction of higher-level needs is equally important. For example, more and more of the in-demand educated young people now entering the job market—the "baby-buster" generation—are less driven toward success and more concerned with personal fulfillment. To them, leisure, family, lifestyle, and nonmaterial satisfactions are as important as work.[21] To motivate such workers, employers must go beyond traditional incentives. Motivational techniques can focus on motivating the individual worker, on enhancing the job or the workplace, or on involving the employees in the fate of the organization as a whole.

Employee-Oriented Techniques

Sometimes motivation is a problem only for certain workers. If an organization is doing well and most of its employees are productive and satisfied, management may find that the best course is to work individually with the unmotivated employee. Someone with physical or emotional problems needs professional

EXHIBIT 9.8

Motivating Forces for Today's Workers
This graph shows the results of a survey of workers who were asked to identify the motivators that were most important to them.

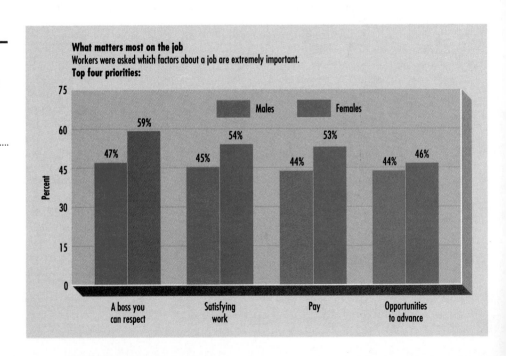

What matters most on the job
Workers were asked which factors about a job are extremely important.
Top four priorities:

Males · Females

A boss you can respect: 47% · 59%
Satisfying work: 45% · 54%
Pay: 44% · 53%
Opportunities to advance: 44% · 46%

Percent

help. But for the healthy worker, a variety of techniques are available to bring him or her closer to productive potential. These techniques include goal setting, behavior modification, and retraining.

Goal Setting

Some workers are highly motivated by clear and achievable goals. Just as managers are better able to attain success if they know exactly what success consists of, so too are individuals. Nucor utilizes goal setting by paying production bonuses to employees who produce more than the standard amount of steel. The individual's goals are different from the organization's goals, however:

Individual goals are fewer in number.

They are narrower in scope.

They involve shorter time spans.

They involve less uncertainty and risk.[22]

The secret to using goal setting as a motivational technique is to let workers participate in setting their own goals. If goals are imposed from above, the advantage of this technique—bringing the workers' higher-level needs into play—will be lost, and workers will feel manipulated. Furthermore, it is important to build feedback into the system so that workers know whether they are in fact meeting their goals.

Behavior Modification

The idea behind **behavior modification** is simple: Encourage actions that are desirable and discourage those that are not. Studies have found that in order to obtain desired results, praise and recognition for efforts are superior to disapproval (whether in the form of reprimand, ridicule, or sarcasm).

behavior modification Application of punishments and rewards, with the aim of improving human behavior

Praise as a simple means of behavior modification has been used successfully by several companies. When Emery Air Freight announced the goal of answering all customer inquiries within 90 minutes, each customer-service representative was asked to record, on a log sheet, the actual time it took to answer each inquiry. If an employee's performance improved, he or she was praised by the supervisor. Those who didn't improve performance were praised for their honesty and accuracy in filling out their log sheets and were then reminded of the 90-minute goal. After a few days of such feedback, customer-service reps were meeting the 90-minute deadline 90 percent of the time.[23] Similar successful reward programs have been introduced at 3M, Ford, AT&T, PepsiCo, and numerous other large corporations.

Michael LeBoeuf, a management expert who teaches at the University of New Orleans, has these suggestions for managers who want to take advantage of what he calls "The Greatest Management Principle in the World" (rewarding people):

1. Reward solid solutions instead of quick fixes.

2. Reward risk taking instead of risk avoidance.

3. Reward applied creativity instead of mindless conformity.

4. Reward decisive action, not paralysis by analysis.

At UNUM, the campaign to link employee self-interest with company goals and performance has been successful. Each year that the company meets its profit goals, employees are paid cash bonuses as high as 14 percent of their salary.

5. Reward smart work instead of busywork.

6. Reward simplification instead of needless complication.

7. Reward quietly effective people instead of "squeaky wheels" (people who create their own crises).

8. Reward quality work instead of fast work.

9. Reward loyalty.[24]

A number of companies use rewards of various kinds to single out hardworking employees. These rewards may take the form of gifts, certificates or medals, dinners, trips, and other forms of recognition. For example, Omni Hotels confers on-the-spot commendations to employees who go above and beyond the call of duty to help guests. Accumulation of such commendations earns an employee medals, cash prizes, and the chance to attend a gala celebration for Omni Service Champions.[25]

Retraining

In today's changing economy, workers in some sectors feel threatened by the loss of a basic source of security—the jobs that help feed their families. Workers who are worried about losing their jobs may be poorly motivated to produce at even their usual level. They may also experience more family problems, alcoholism, mental disturbance, and other personal difficulties that ultimately affect their work.

A variety of approaches may be used to solve problems related to employee cutbacks and layoffs. One is to offer company-sponsored training that will teach workers new skills. Workers in industry may learn to operate robots and other computerized equipment; workers in the service sector may learn to sell instead of manage. Although some people find it difficult to adjust to any change, most appreciate the opportunity to become useful again—to their company or to the

Borden is constructing new plants, expanding, and consolidating to become more efficient in every business. Here, employees work with machines to produce single-portion strawberry preserves. With suitable preparation and retraining, workers accept automation more readily, even in traditionally labor-intensive manufacturing industries.

economy as a whole. After the slump in productivity that is a natural accompaniment to learning new skills, they are soon motivated to perform again at the peak of their powers.

Job-Oriented Techniques

If many workers in a department or in a certain type of job are having motivational problems, chances are that the jobs themselves are at fault. In this case the best way to improve performance is to find ways of changing the job structure rather than the workers' behavior. And that usually means soft-pedaling the authoritarian aspect of management in order to allow workers to feel that they are part of the team. Quality circles (discussed in Chapter 8) are one way of accomplishing this goal. Allowing workers and managers to pool ideas may release some of the productive energy that can develop when people work together. Other methods—such as job enrichment and redesign, flextime, telecommuting, work sharing, and job sharing—can be used as well. The key factor is whether alternative work schedules and job arrangements serve the needs of both the organization and the workers.

Job Enrichment and Redesign

Although the extreme division of labor was successful with the uneducated workers of the early twentieth century, it doesn't make as much sense today. For one thing, highly specialized jobs rarely satisfy today's better-educated and more sophisticated workers, many of whom know more about the technical aspects of their work than their supervisors do. Moreover, machines have taken over some of the specialized tasks previously performed by workers. Faced with these changes, many companies are attempting to boost productivity by reorganizing the way jobs are done. One type of job reorganization is **job enrichment**—giving workers a more vivid sense of where they fit into the organization by making their jobs less specialized and giving them more meaningful work to do.

For example, managers at a Cadillac plant in Livonia, Michigan, tapped the power of groups to make dull jobs more interesting. Workers were given the opportunity to make more money by learning new skills, which in turn motivated them to make their jobs less specialized. In weekly meetings, these "paid for knowledge" business teams then used their expanded awareness of factory operations to make decisions in areas that had once been the sole responsibility of management—from safety precautions to housekeeping to redistributing tasks on the assembly line for greater efficiency.[26]

A Bethlehem Steel mill in Sparrows Point, Maryland, has taken a different approach to job enrichment. A weekly business-news roundup is distributed throughout the plant so that employees can gain a better understanding of the economic forces affecting the steel business. Furthermore, some line operators are sent to visit Bethlehem customers. "We know what we're doing now," says one of the steelworkers. "Before we were just rolling steel."[27]

How do workers feel when their jobs are restructured to include new duties? One man who had been a boilermaker with Gulf Oil for 28 years was unhappy when he was reassigned to help workers in other crafts. He resented the change because he could not take pride in performing unfamiliar tasks such as pipe fitting or welding. "When you're not doing the thing you've been trained to do," he says, "it has to affect your identity."[28] At the other extreme is a woman who

job enrichment Dividing work in an organization so that workers have more responsibility for the total process

spent 17 years performing one tedious step on a check-processing line at a Chicago bank and was then given a new, less-specialized job. Making use of recent advances in office automation, the bank assigned her to a computer terminal, where she could perform most of the steps necessary to process and deposit checks. "I like it because you see the package from beginning to end," she says. "It's better to be part of the whole thing. Everyone should have change in their life."[29]

Flextime

flextime A scheduling system in which workers are given certain options regarding time of arrival and departure

The changing work force has changing lifestyles and needs. Two-career couples with children must perform miracles of scheduling and routing to make sure that the kids get to school or to the baby-sitter and still get themselves to work on time; single parents have half the resources and twice the problem. And more workers are going back to school or taking a second job in order to afford housing and cars. No wonder many workers have found **flextime** a desirable option. Instead of working the standard nine-to-five day, five days a week, they choose their own hours within certain limits. For instance, a company may stipulate that everyone has to be at work between 10:00 A.M. and 2:00 P.M., but workers may arrive or depart whenever they want as long as they work a total of eight hours. Such flexibility helps people arrange their complicated lives. When they don't have outside problems to worry about, they are more likely to work productively and happily on the job. The sense of control they get from arranging their own schedules is in itself motivating for many people.

One national poll found that 78 percent of adult workers would prefer to have flexible hours, even if it meant slower career advancement, in order to spend more time with their families.[30] In response to this employee need, more and more companies are offering flextime. In fact, a survey of 259 major employers found that 42 percent already offered flextime.[31]

Flextime is more widespread in white-collar businesses that do not have to maintain customer-service hours. Flextime is not usually an option for blue-collar and "pink-collar" workers on production teams or for workers in retail stores and in many offices who have to be on hand to wait on customers or answer calls. Among other drawbacks to flextime are (1) supervisors often feeling uncomfortable and less in control when employees are coming and going, and (2) co-workers possibly resenting flextimers and assuming they take their jobs less seriously.

Telecommuting and Home Offices

telecommuting Working from a home office, commuting via telephone, computer modem, and fax

In congested urban areas, rush-hour traffic makes the commute to work an unbearable ordeal for some. That time can often be more productively spent in a home office, linked by computer to the main office. The advantages of such **telecommuting** are many. The employee increases production 15 to 20 percent, office space costs are reduced, an employee who might otherwise leave is retained, and disabled workers can be employed more easily.[32] Employees like this option because they can set their own hours, reduce job-related expenses, and have more time with their families. Of course, only certain types of jobs lend themselves to telecommuting, and documentation of hours worked can be difficult. Furthermore, setting up home-based workstations can be expensive, especially if they include fax machines, teleconferencing equipment, and the like.

Elaine Garzarelli, an executive vice president with Shearson Lehman Brothers, worked for the New York brokerage firm out of her Greenwich Village apartment for three years. To her, the main advantage of working at home was that she actually got things done; there were no office chats, meetings, and lunches to distract her. She finally returned to the office because she missed the hustle and bustle.[33] Other executives working at home have found that they actually put in longer hours or that they encounter too many distractions, such as young children requiring attention. Most telecommuters, however, see the arrangement as having more benefits than drawbacks.

Work Sharing and Job Sharing

Two techniques are used to improve morale when there is a mismatch between the amount of work available and the amount of work desired by the employee. **Work sharing,** which is more common in an economic downturn, balances the hardships among a company's entire work force by slicing a few hours off everybody's workweek and pay. **Job sharing** lets two workers share a single full-time job and split the salary and benefits.

When a company adopts work sharing instead of laying off workers, nearly everyone stands to gain. Workers are less anxious about being unemployed and are thus willing to spend more money, which helps local merchants stay in business. Because most employees keep their jobs rather than being "bumped" from one job to another by those workers with seniority, quality remains high. When business surges forward again, companies that have instituted work sharing are better equipped to meet the stepped-up demand because they do not have to call back old workers or train new ones. In addition, when times get brighter, workers are more willing to put in long hours for a company that helped them through a tough spell.

Job sharing, by contrast, is a voluntary solution to the needs of working parents, employees pursuing a degree, and the like. It is usually offered to people who already work for the company but need to cut back their hours; rather than lose a good employee or go to the trouble of finding and training someone new, the company finds a way to split responsibilities.

At Steelcase, the giant office furniture manufacturer in Grand Rapids, Michigan, a job-sharing program has been in place since 1982. There, job sharers must have been full-time employees with the company for at least one year, and the job must not have any supervisory or budgetary responsibilities. The two people sharing a job must put in a combined 40-hour workweek, and each receives 50 percent of the job's benefits. For instance, two women who share a recruiting position in the marketing department each work two and a half days a week; they meet for lunch on Wednesdays to compare notes.[34]

At present, job sharing is more common in government agencies and universities than in private industry. In 1984, for the first time, the federal government's personnel manual devoted an entire section to job sharing. Otherwise, few rules exist for implementing this technique—with one exception. Andrea Hoffman (who shares her job as budget examiner in the federal Office of Management and Budget with Carol Dennis) advises that "chemistry between the two is crucial."[35]

Hiller Real Estate Associates is a company in Norwalk, Connecticut, specializing in commercial, business, and property management. Paul Hiller Jr., telecommutes (works from his home) at least four days a week, communicating with his office and with clients via computer, fax, and telephone.

work sharing Slicing a few hours off everybody's workweek and pay in order to minimize layoffs

job sharing Splitting a single full-time job between two workers for their convenience

At the construction equipment division of Westinghouse in Greenwood, South Carolina, members of a quality team are responsible for improving switchgear and bus duct products.

empowerment Giving employees greater involvement in the day-to-day workings of a company

gain sharing Earning short-term monetary rewards based on team performance

Organization-Oriented Techniques

When a company is having persistent and pervasive motivation problems such as overall declining productivity or high employee turnover, more drastic measures are required. Top management may have to revamp organization objectives, strategies, or culture in order to get the company back on track. Such changes are not to be initiated lightly. They are likely to affect everyone in the company, and there is no guarantee that they will work. But if they do work, everyone who survives the changes will have a renewed sense of purpose and belonging, which is a strong motivator indeed.

Most organization-oriented motivators fall under the category of employee **empowerment,** or getting employees more involved in the actual workings of the company, usually by offering them greater decision-making power. Empowerment gives employees greater responsibility and greater accountability for the company's performance.

Federal Express has been a pioneer in the field of employee empowerment, also referred to as "participative management." Fed Ex employees are involved in hiring and advancement decisions within their area, serve on quality assurance teams, elect representatives to work closely with management on operations and human resources issues, and can take grievances to a review board of their own choosing. These and other means of inviting worker participation help forge a team spirit at the company and increase company loyalty.[36]

The basic on-the-job approach to empowerment is the idea of self-directed work teams. Such teams consist of groups of workers who set their own goals, brainstorm new ways to solve problems, and in essence manage their own work. A survey of companies using the work-team concept found that such teams are set up in a variety of ways, in sizes ranging from 6 to 32 members. The most successful programs have resulted in reduced labor costs, increased quality and productivity, and improved morale. The main problems reported by workers and managers have been inadequate training in using such a system, worker distrust of management, and resistance of supervisors.[37]

The work-team approach is unlikely to be successful unless it is accompanied by an appropriate compensation plan. One such approach is **gain sharing,** in which dollar rewards are tied to team performance. Gain-sharing bonuses are usually given on a monthly basis (as opposed to long-term profit sharing) and are tied to goals in areas that employees can directly influence, such as sales, payroll costs, customer satisfaction, and material costs.[38]

Employee stock options are another monetary incentive for increasing employee involvement. The goal of such plans is to demonstrate to employees the connection between performance and financial reward. This kind of monetary incentive is discussed in greater detail in Chapter 10.

In some cases, companies go so far as to seek new owners—their own employees. *Employee-owned businesses* may sometimes be the best bet if the alternative is a shutdown. For example, Manco in Westlake, Ohio, is an employee-owned company that manufactures consumer mailing materials, duct tape, and office supplies. Everyone in the firm keeps track of the company's daily sales, shipments, and billings via large charts posted in the company cafeteria. Workers enjoy the satisfaction of directly controlling their company, and they benefit from the most effective of all motivational techniques: a stake in their own success.[39]

SUMMARY OF LEARNING OBJECTIVES

1 List the three main components of good human relations within an organization.

Leadership, communication, and motivation are the major elements that contribute to good human relations.

2 Explain the five steps in Maslow's hierarchy of needs as they relate to worker motivation.

Physiological needs, the most basic requirements for human life, are seldom strong motivators for modern wage earners. Safety (or security) needs can be met through job security and pension plans. Social needs, which drive people to seek membership in informal groups, may be more important than financial considerations. Esteem needs, which relate to feelings of self-worth and respect from others, are met by motivational techniques of recognition. Self-actualization needs may be met by giving workers the opportunity to expand their skills and take on additional responsibility.

3 Identify the two factors affecting worker motivation in Herzberg's motivational-hygiene theory.

Hygiene factors—such as company policy, working conditions, and job security—have a bad effect on motivation only if they are deficient. Motivators—achievement, recognition, and responsibility—are positively related to increases in productivity.

4 List three basic assumptions of expectancy theory.

The three basic assumptions of expectancy theory are (1) the worker's perception of task difficulty ("Can I do it?"), (2) the worker's perception of the reward ("If I do it, what will I get?"), and (3) the worker's perception of the connection between the two ("Will it be worth my while?").

5 Describe three concepts linking motivation and management style.

Theory X and Theory Y describe two opposite sets of assumptions about workers' motives for working; Theory X emphasizes authority, and Theory Y emphasizes growth and self-direction. Theory Z, which describes human relations within U.S. companies that have adopted certain Japanese management techniques, assumes that workers are part of a

family and that their needs therefore deserve consideration.

6 Discuss the impact of three major trends in the work force.

The surge of baby boomers into the work force has accelerated employee demands for satisfaction and participation. The influx of women has created a need for more flexible arrangements to accommodate family requirements outside the job. The increasing cultural diversity has begun to create a sensitivity in managers toward ethnicity, cultural background, gender, age, race, disability, and sexual orientation.

7 Identify three approaches to motivating individual employees.

Goal setting, behavior modification, and retraining may all be used to improve the productivity of individual employees.

8 Name four job-oriented techniques for improving the motivation of workers.

Job enrichment and redesign, flextime, telecommuting, and work sharing/job sharing are all techniques for making jobs more motivating.

Meeting a Business Challenge at Nucor

As critics shook their heads, F. Kenneth Iverson opened a tiny steel mill to challenge Big Steel's domination of the marketplace. Cynics said Iverson's company, Nucor, would collapse under the weight of the industry's sky-high wage scale. But Iverson believed he could pull off his nervy scheme by motivating workers properly.

Iverson opened his first mills in rural areas where industry was still largely nonunion. He hired farm youths with more determination than

knowledge of steel. Then he introduced a series of motivational programs. He assigned each employee to a small work group dedicated to a specific task in the steelmaking process.

Iverson encouraged employees to think of their work groups as small businesses of their own. The financial reward for each worker included hefty bonuses scaled to production achieved by the work groups. Even though the base pay for a typical plant might be $8 an hour, workers in teams that

produced more than the standard amount of steel could earn twice the going wage through performance bonuses. These production bonuses were posted daily on bulletin boards and paid weekly to stimulate goal-oriented individuals.

Workers also received bonuses based on return-on-assets-employed. And 10 percent of all the pretax earnings were paid to employees in a profit-sharing plan. Nucor took attitude surveys to develop personnel policies, hospitalized workers got benefits from the first day, and the company offered tuition assistance for children of employees.

But Nucor also introduced punishments. A worker who arrived 15 minutes late lost a whole day's production bonus. The whole week's bonus was lost if the worker was a half hour late. Moreover, workers were not paid if their group's machinery broke down. Employees supported such rules because they helped groups earn their maximum bonuses.

Management layers were minimized. Nucor had four in an industry that traditionally has eight. Iverson empowered workers with the ability to communicate ideas to managers. As supervisors walked through plants they solicited ideas, and managers called group meetings to hash out problems. Management pay dropped faster than the workers' when times were slow. Managers and workers had the same vacation time, had the same insurance program, and even wore the same color hard hat.

Subsequent events proved Iverson correct in his approach to motivation. Today his $1.4 billion company produces 980 tons of steel per employee per year, far better than the industry average of 420. Including bonuses, Nucor's average worker compensation of $32,000 is higher than the going rate for union steel labor. Iverson's views on the vulnerability of Big Steel have also proven correct. Nucor remained highly profitable while larger steel companies underwent painful downsizing. During the 1980s Nucor doubled in size while Big Steel laid off 70 percent of its work force and reduced its annual capacity by 50 million tons.

From one small North Carolina mill in 1968 Iverson built Nucor into the nation's ninth largest steel producer. The company is known around the world for its system of financial motivation. Nucor's success proves that motivated workers make a difference.

Your Mission: You have joined Nucor as the vice president for human resources. You must suggest solutions for the following problems and suggest how company policies might be altered to avoid conflicts that result from rapid growth.

F. Kenneth Iverson, CEO, Nucor.

1. Although workers are basically pleased with Nucor's bonus structure, they are still powerless to alter the structure to fit specific situations at specific plants. You have been asked to come up with a way to empower the employees in this area. What would you suggest?

a. Let workers know they already have it a lot better than their counterparts in other companies, and be sure they understand that anyone making trouble over this issue will be fired immediately.

b. Have managers empower employees by organizing quality circles made up of shop workers who meet regularly and who can make suggestions to higher management about modifying the bonus structure.

c. Let workers, on an individual basis, submit suggestions in writing to upper management so that every employee will feel included and empowered.

d. When managers stroll through the plant and talk with employees, have them solicit suggestions from workers and then choose the best one to be submitted to higher management.

2. In one of Nucor's attitude surveys, a large number of employees complained about growing boredom on the job. You suspect this may be related to the narrowness and repetitiveness of the tasks assigned. Moreover, you fear there may be a connection between this boredom and the lower productivity figures you've been hearing about lately. What should Nucor do?

a. Alert managers to the growing boredom problem and have them severely dock the bonuses of any workers who appear to be slacking off.

b. Have managers immediately redesign tasks and institute job enrichment programs to combat the boredom problem.

c. Increase rewards to those who maintain the highest productivity figures, thus motivating all employees to overcome their boredom and produce more.

d. Appoint a team of managers and workers to determine whether narrow, repetitive tasks are at the core of the problem. If so, the team might investigate ways the current tasks can be enriched or redesigned to combat boredom.

3. One employee has been consistently late to work in the morning, usually one-half to one hour. He never complains about losing anywhere from half to all his week's bonus, and once he arrives, he is one of the most highly motivated and productive workers in all of Nucor. You decide to inquire about his habitual tardiness, and he explains that he is a widower with three young children. By the time he feeds and clothes them each morning, and by the time he drives one to school, one to preschool, and the youngest to the babysitter, he has a hard time making the 8:00 deadline at work. What should you do?

a. Leave it alone. The man's kids are his problem, not Nucor's. And since the worker is abiding by the rules and not complaining about losing his bonuses, things are working out fine as they are.

b. Tell the employee that in his case, it's okay for him to be as much as one hour late. He won't lose any more bonuses unless he comes in after 9:00.

c. Inform the employee's supervisor of the problem, and suggest that he hold a meeting to discuss the possibilities of using flextime with the work teams that are already in place.

d. Appoint a team to investigate

further to see how many other employees might benefit from flextime. If the numbers warrant it, have the team look into how flextime might be used with the work teams already in place.

4. A dozen or so employees have been talking avidly with union organizers who have started showing up at the gates of one of your plants. According to reports from other workers, these dozen employees are angry that Nucor has not explained the necessity for the latest technological investments, which are having a negative impact on company earnings and therefore on the profit-sharing plan.

This discontent has arisen despite the fact that Nucor management has said that such information, if revealed, could be used by competitors. Other workers are afraid that if the union moves in, it will destroy the financial incentive system they have grown to trust, and they have twice gotten into shoving matches with the dozen workers who've been talking with union organizers. How should management respond?

a. Set up open meetings to discuss the issue of corporate secrecy about sensitive technology. Allow all employees and managers to have a say. Then have workers vote on

whether the details of the technological investment should be revealed.
b. Send a letter to all of the employees. Signed by the company president, it should detail how well the company treats its workers.
c. Explain that a company can't be run as a democracy and that some decisions must simply be made by management alone.
d. Award bonuses to workers who speak out against unions. This should motivate the complainers to calm down and see things management's way.[40]

KEY TERMS

behavior modification (249)
classical theory of motivation (236)
communication (235)
empowerment (254)
expectancy theory (239)
flextime (252)
gain sharing (254)
group norms (237)

Hawthorne effect (237)
human relations (234)
hygiene factors (238)
job enrichment (251)
job sharing (253)
leadership (234)
morale (235)
motivation (235)

motivators (239)
piecework system (236)
telecommuting (252)
Theory X (241)
Theory Y (241)
Theory Z (242)
work sharing (253)

REVIEW QUESTIONS

1. Why did the classical theory of motivation work well when it was first proposed? How well does it work today?

2. What did the Hawthorne studies reveal? What effect did they have on worker productivity? Why?

3. What are the practical implications of Maslow's hierarchy? What are its limitations?

4. How do Theories X and Y relate to Theory Z?

5. What are the major challenges of managing a diverse work force?

6. What effect does downsizing have on employee motivation?

7. What large-scale organizational approaches to motivation are being implemented today?

8. What is employee empowerment, and how is it related to self-directed work teams?

A CASE FOR CRITICAL THINKING

The Pizza Olympics: A Question of Dough . . .

. . . the kind you spend as well as the kind you knead and spread in a pizza pan. Domino's Pizza Olympics, management's brainstorm for providing recognition and ensuring high, uniform standards at the same time, take place every July and feature competition in events ranging from forming dough balls to driving pizza trucks to balancing a ledger.

The Olympics began as a way of recognizing the essential, but as yet unsung, efforts of Domino's subsidiary, the Distribution Corporation, which services Domino's retail stores worldwide with vegetables, toppings, napkins, uniforms—and, of course, dough. Although its performance was critical to Domino's success, maintaining morale was difficult, partly because the unit was virtually unknown outside the company. Valerie

Russell, an accountant at company headquarters, believed participation in the Olympics not only would stress the importance of every individual's job but also would act as a means of monitoring and improving standards of performance by making performance competitive.

The three-day event is now companywide. More than half the work force is flown to headquarters to compete for cash, rings, and vacations. Management meets with the winners to discuss procedures, methods, and techniques to help improve everyone's job performance. The dough event, for example, yielded unexpected dividends. Observing that contestants were using a number of techniques and achieving varying results in preparing that crucial product, Domino's picked the brains of the best dough-

makers to create a manual detailing the specifics of dough production. Also rising to the occasion was the Florida-based truckdriver—and the many others like him who were galvanized into special effort by special recognition—who now times himself whenever he loads his truck.[41]

1. Domino's budgets more than $1 million yearly for the games. What does the company gain in return?

2. What effect does the pooling of expertise have on employee morale and performance?

3. The games improved the quality and speed of almost every job function in the company. How do those results bear out the Hawthorne findings?

BUILDING YOUR COMMUNICATION SKILLS

With a small group of three or four students (preferably students you don't know well), select a ready-made assembly project that can be completed in one or two hours. This can be a jigsaw puzzle, a plastic model, or some other similar craft project. As

you work, consider the process that your group goes through to complete the project. How did you decide on the project? Did your group select a leader, or was leadership a shared responsibility? How did you delegate responsibilities in the project? After

you complete the project, write a brief summary of the activities of your group as they relate to the following factors: human relations, leadership, communication, motivation, and morale. As a class, share and discuss the experiences of each group.

KEEPING CURRENT USING *THE WALL STREET JOURNAL*

Select one or two articles from recent issues of *The Wall Street Journal* that relate to employee motivation or morale.

1. What is the problem, solution, or trend described in the article(s)?

2. Is it relevant to just one company's experience, or does it have broader implications? Who is affected by it now, and who do you think might be affected by it in the future?

3. What challenges and opportunities does this development offer management in this company or industry? The employees?

CHAPTER *10*

LEARNING OBJECTIVES

After studying this chapter, you will be able to

1 State the six main functions of human resource departments.

2 Identify six stages in the hiring process.

3 List at least three types of training programs.

4 Identify two general ways of compensating workers.

5 Describe the two possible components of employee pay.

6 Explain at least four standard employee benefits and services.

7 Describe three ways an employee's status may change.

8 Distinguish between the two reasons that employment may be terminated.

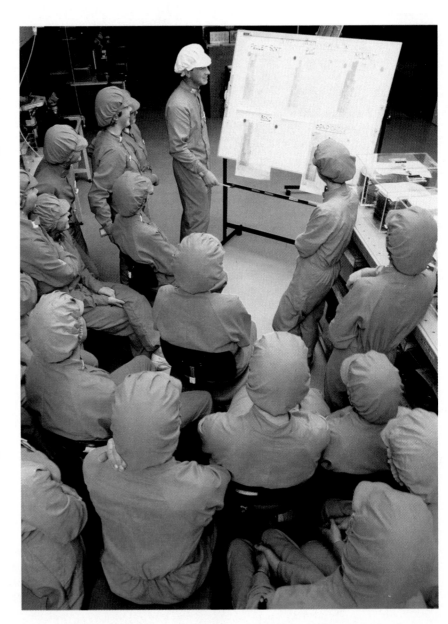

Human Resource Management

KEEPING EMPLOYEES IN THE PINK AND THE COMPANY IN THE BLACK

B y the time James E. Burke took over as chairman and CEO of Johnson & Johnson, the baby-boom generation had matured—and with it the company's baby products business. Burke knew that for J&J to continue to prosper, it must follow the aging baby boomers into new, more sophisticated markets, and in four years he acquired 25 companies, many of them in high-tech fields. But Burke also knew that successful entry into new markets required a committed and enthusiastic work force. To support J&J's new-product diversity, Burke faced the challenge of developing satisfied and productive employees by successfully managing the company's human resources.

One major issue Burke addressed was employee health. For example, studies showed that over 30 percent of Johnson & Johnson's employees were smokers, and an internal report revealed that smokers had a 45 percent greater rate of absenteeism than nonsmokers. Smokers also contributed disproportionately to the company's major medical expenses (30 percent higher than nonsmokers), an ominous statistic at a time when health-care costs were rising at nearly twice the rate of inflation.

Another problem that Burke had to confront was the effect of changing demographics on employees. Johnson & Johnson employees increasingly fell into one of three groups: they were part of two-career couples with children; they were responsible for an aging parent; or they were single mothers or fathers. A survey of 10,000 J&J employees revealed that they were increasingly frustrated by their inability to meet all their obligations, both to their families and to their employer. Many stated that they had difficulty finding day care, especially sick child and infant care, and almost 20 percent responded that they could not afford day care even if they could have located a suitable provider. Furthermore, most stated that their managers were unsympathetic about their dilemma. Balancing their work and family obligations took its toll on employees who reported higher levels of stress, greater absenteeism, and lower job satisfaction.

For guidance, Burke turned to Johnson & Johnson's operating document, the corporate credo written by Robert Wood Johnson, son of a founding Johnson brother and chairman of the company for 25 years. Johnson ranked the company's obligation to its employees ahead of its responsibility to its shareholders and second only to its commitment to its customers. Burke believed the credo could serve as a blueprint for successful human resource management.

But how could Burke promote health in the workplace? How could he help employees balance family and career obligations? What programs could he establish to meet the needs of his employees?[1]

▶ THE PROCESS OF HUMAN RESOURCE MANAGEMENT

As James E. Burke knows, employees are an important component of every business. More and more companies consider employees their most valuable asset, and such attitudes have fueled the rising emphasis on obtaining the people a company needs and then overseeing their training, evaluation, and compensation. This specialized function, formerly referred to as *personnel management,* is now termed **human resource management** to reflect the importance of a well-chosen and well-managed work force in achieving company goals.

human resource management The specialized function of planning how to obtain employees, oversee their training, evaluate them, and compensate them

Human resource management is becoming more complex in the 1990s, and its role is increasingly viewed as a strategic one. The work force, the economy, and consequently organizational culture are being transformed at an accelerating pace; changes in technology alone have already created crucial mismatches between workers' skills and employers' needs. And these changes are taking place within a social environment in which workers' rights, privacy, and health risks are but a few of the factors at stake.

Human resource managers must figure out how to attract qualified workers from a shrinking pool of entry-level employees; how to train less-educated, poorly skilled young and minority workers; how to keep experienced workers when they have fewer opportunities for advancement; and how to lay off workers equitably in an era of downsizing and economic recession. They must also retrain workers to enable them to cope with increasing automation and computerization, manage increasingly complex (and expensive) employee benefits programs, fit workplace policies to changing work-force demographics and employee needs, and cope with the challenge of meeting government regulations in hiring practices and equal opportunity in employment. In addition, human resource executives are increasingly required to take a global perspective, providing for employees who travel to and work in other countries. For example, Fluor, a California-based engineering and construction firm with more than 22,000 employees worldwide, has some 500 international human resource professionals who administer payroll, benefits, and training programs and coordinate recruiting and staffing at operations in 80 countries.[2] Given the growing importance and complexity of human resource problems, it is scarcely surprising that all but the smallest businesses employ specialists to deal with them.

What exactly do human resource departments do? Every human resource staff member is involved in planning to meet a company's human resource needs, recruiting and selecting employees, training and developing workers, and appraising employee performance. The staff also administers pay and employee benefits and oversees changes in employment status (promotion, reassignment, termination, retirement). This chapter explores each of these human resource responsibilities, beginning with planning.

Human Resource Planning

The first step in staffing business organizations, as in any other management endeavor, is to plan (see Exhibit 10.1). As one human resource staff director explains, a company must have "people on hand at the right time and in the right place to make a thing go."[3]

Planning is a critical step. A miscalculation could leave a company without enough workers to keep production up to the level of demand, resulting in lost business because customers or clients go elsewhere. Yet if a company expands its staff too rapidly, profits may disappear into the payroll. Or the firm may have to lay off the very people it just recruited and trained at considerable expense. Some of the most spectacular surges and slumps in staffing have occurred in the electronics industry. When Silicon Valley firms anticipated greatly increased demand for electronic components, they hired inordinate numbers of new workers, only to lay them off shortly thereafter because expected business upturns failed to materialize.

Forecasting

Supply and demand are factors in human resource planning, just as they are in more general business planning. Forecasting begins with estimates of *demand,* the numbers and kinds of workers that will be needed at various times. For example, a boutique chain that is planning to open another store within six months would estimate that it needs an additional store manager and an assistant manager as well as part-time salesclerks. Although the chain might start looking immediately for someone as highly placed as the manager, hiring salesclerks could wait until just before the store opens.

The next task is to estimate the *supply* of available workers. In many cases, that supply is within the company already—perhaps just needing training to fill future requirements. For example, the boutique chain may well find that the

The human resource department at Apple Computer must plan carefully to have the right number of production employees to meet the demand for its 2E machines and other products.

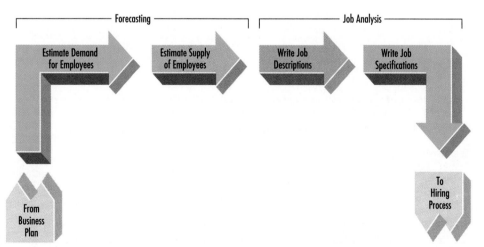

EXHIBIT 10.1

Steps in Human Resource Planning

Careful attention to each phase of this sequence helps ensure that a company will have the right human resources when it needs them.

assistant manager at an existing store can be promoted to manager of the new store and that current salesclerks can be made assistant managers. If existing workers in the company cannot be tapped for new positions, the human resource manager must figure out how difficult it will be to find people in the general work force who have the necessary skills. The boutique chain may have to look outside for the new manager, assistant managers, and additional clerks, which would mean training them in the store's operations.

THE CHANGING LABOR MARKET   Every business needs to know whether enough people with the required skills are available in the general work force. Keeping track of the job market is a particularly arduous undertaking these days, because it is undergoing substantial change. Although fewer jobs are available for factory workers in troubled "smokestack" industries, the demand for people with skills in engineering, nursing, paralegal work, electronic data processing, and many other technical areas is mushrooming. Nurses are particularly hard to come by. National Medical Enterprises, a major U.S. hospital company, has gone so far as to recruit nurses from Ireland, Scandinavia, and China.[4] And there is a nationwide shortage of tool and die makers, despite pay that can reach as high as $80,000 a year.[5] Companies are having difficulty finding qualified people to fill jobs in a wide range of categories (see Exhibit 10.2).

The gap is widening between what employers will require of new workers in the years ahead and the actual skills of these workers. Nearly all new jobs created in this country in the next 10 years will require college graduates to fill them. Yet it is estimated that by the year 2000, the largest share of new workers will consist of young people, minorities, and immigrants with relatively low levels of education. Many businesses complain that the U.S. educational system is turning out graduates ill prepared to enter the work world. Many simply lack

EXHIBIT 10.2 ▶ **Labor Shortages**

Employers are having difficulty finding qualified applicants in a wide variety of job categories.

Job Categories Experiencing Labor Shortages Today
Percentage of Companies Reporting Difficulty Recruiting Now

	SOME DIFFICULTY	GREAT DIFFICULTY
Secretarial/clerical	39%	9%
Skilled crafts	35	9
Technical	51	13
Professional	50	11
Sales	29	3
Administrative	31	2
Supervisory/management	45	3

Job Categories Where Labor Shortages Are Expected in Five Years
Percentage of Companies Expecting Difficulty in Future Recruiting

	SOME DIFFICULTY	GREAT DIFFICULTY
Secretarial/clerical	32%	21%
Skilled crafts	28	18
Technical	36	27
Professional	41	22
Sales	27	8
Administrative	35	6
Supervisory/management	42	11

good "work habits": They show up late or not at all, their output is of low quality, and they lack a work-oriented attitude. To make matters worse, a distressing number of high school graduates are functionally illiterate. Faced with this drop in both the quantity and quality of available workers, companies must either revise their plans for growth or hire unqualified people and train them—often an unavoidable but expensive option, as discussed later in this chapter.

STRATEGIC STAFFING TECHNIQUES   Human resource planners must also take into account today's fluid business conditions. To avoid drastic overstaffing or understaffing, many companies are turning to part-time and temporary workers, who are easily added when business picks up and easily let go when it slows down again.

The part-time labor force has been increasing by leaps and bounds in recent years, particularly the segment made up of "involuntary" part-timers. These are people who want full-time jobs but who are forced to settle for part-time. Between 1970 and 1990, the number of such involuntary part-timers grew by 121 percent; they now make up about 6 percent of all workers. The number of voluntary part-timers increased by 69 percent during the same period. A burgeoning number of businesses trying to save money and increase flexibility have built their work forces around part-time workers, whose schedules can be rearranged to suit the company's needs.[6]

A large percentage of the work force is also made up of temporary workers. Some 85 percent of American firms enlist the services of temporary agencies. "Temps" can perform tasks ranging from the repetitive and boring to the highly technical and demanding. In fact, some 20 percent of temps are highly skilled professionals, constituting the fastest growing segment.[7] Although one of the benefits of using temps has been that they are given no company benefits, even that is changing. In an effort to attract high-quality temporary workers, many companies are providing at least some benefits.[8]

Retailers such as the Wet Seal clothing chain hire part-time and temporary employees during seasons when business is brisk. When business slows down again, these employees are usually laid off.

Job Analysis

If you were the owner of a small business, it might make sense for you to hire employees on an informal basis, since you would be in a good position to know the requirements of all the jobs in your company. However, in large organizations like Johnson & Johnson, where hundreds or thousands of employees are performing a wide variety of jobs, management needs a more formal and objective method of evaluating job requirements. That method is called **job analysis.**

Several questions must be asked in job analysis: What tasks are involved in the job (what does the person do all day)? What qualifications and skills are needed to do the job? What kind of setting does the job take place in? (Some jobs, such as sales, require extensive public contact; others, such as factory work, do not.) Does the job entail much time pressure (such as newspaper reporting) or little time pressure (such as attending to children in a day-care center)?

To obtain the information needed for a job analysis, human resource experts simply ask employees or supervisors for information. They also observe employees directly, perhaps using a stopwatch or videotape to monitor someone's work activities. Some employers even ask employees to keep daily diaries describing exactly what they do during the workday.

After job analysis has been completed, the human resource manager develops

job analysis *Process by which jobs are studied to determine the tasks and dynamics involved in performing them*

EXHIBIT 10.3

Sample Job Description and Job Specification

A job description lists the tasks the job involves and the conditions under which those tasks are performed. A job specification spells out the characteristics—skills, education, and experience—of the ideal candidate for the job.

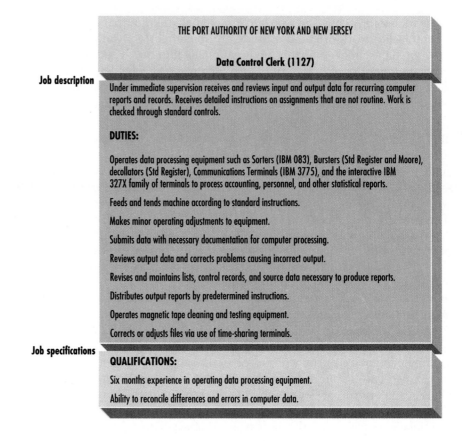

THE PORT AUTHORITY OF NEW YORK AND NEW JERSEY

Data Control Clerk (1127)

Job description

Under immediate supervision receives and reviews input and output data for recurring computer reports and records. Receives detailed instructions on assignments that are not routine. Work is checked through standard controls.

DUTIES:

Operates data processing equipment such as Sorters (IBM 083), Bursters (Std Register and Moore), decollators (Std Register), Communications Terminals (IBM 3775), and the interactive IBM 327X family of terminals to process accounting, personnel, and other statistical reports.

Feeds and tends machine according to standard instructions.

Makes minor operating adjustments to equipment.

Submits data with necessary documentation for computer processing.

Reviews output data and corrects problems causing incorrect output.

Revises and maintains lists, control records, and source data necessary to produce reports.

Distributes output reports by predetermined instructions.

Operates magnetic tape cleaning and testing equipment.

Corrects or adjusts files via use of time-sharing terminals.

Job specifications

QUALIFICATIONS:

Six months experience in operating data processing equipment.

Ability to reconcile differences and errors in computer data.

---

job description Statement of the tasks involved in a given job and the conditions under which the holder of the job will work

job specification Statement describing the kind of person who would be best for a given job—including the skills, education, and previous experience that the job requires

recruiters Members of the human resource staff who are responsible for obtaining new job candidates

a **job description,** a specific statement of the tasks involved in the job and the conditions under which the holder of the job will work. The manager may also develop a **job specification,** a statement describing the skills, education, and previous experience that the job requires. Exhibit 10.3 presents a job description and a job specification of the same job.

Recruiting and Selecting New Employees

The next step is to match the job specification with an actual person or selection of people. **Recruiters** are specialists on the human resource staff who are responsible for obtaining candidates. They consider people already working for the company; they seek referrals from employees or colleagues in the industry; they advertise in newspapers and work through public and private employment agencies; they visit union hiring halls or college campuses; they sometimes even resort to pirating key employees from other companies.

As it becomes more and more difficult to find qualified candidates in the immediate area, recruiters are becoming more creative in their efforts. They may advertise in areas where a similar business has recently closed or downsized, make an effort to seek out older workers and the disabled, or enter into cooperative arrangements with vocational schools that offer training in desired skills.

Stages in the Hiring Process

After exploring at least one—but usually more—of these recruitment channels to assemble a pool of applicants, the human resource department may spend weeks and sometimes months on the selection process. Most companies go through the same basic steps in sifting through applications to come up with the person or people they want.

First, a small number of qualified candidates are selected from the total number of applicants. A person may be chosen on the basis of a standard application form that all candidates are required to fill out or on the basis of a **résumé**, a summary of education, experience, and personal data compiled by the applicant. Sometimes both sources of information are used.

résumé Summary of education, experience, and personal data compiled by the applicant for a job

The next step in the hiring process is to interview each candidate to clarify her or his qualifications and to fill in any missing information. Another goal of the interview is to get an idea of the applicant's personality. Depending on the type of job at stake, candidates may also be asked to take a test or a series of tests. After the initial interviews, the best candidates may be subjected to another, more probing interview by someone in the human resource department. These candidates are then interviewed by the person who will be the new worker's immediate supervisor. The supervisor, sometimes in consultation with her or his boss, then picks the most suitable person. The search is over—provided the candidate accepts the offer and is all he or she appears to be. Reference checks and sometimes a physical examination may be used to make sure.

The following sections look a bit more closely at two of these steps, interviewing and testing. Both can play a crucial role in hiring decisions, and testing in particular is highly controversial. Then the text explores some of the legal land mines that human resource managers must avoid in the course of screening job applicants and making hiring decisions.

Interviewing

For interviews to be useful, they should follow established, standardized procedures tailored to the company's needs. An often overlooked aspect of the interview process is advance preparation. The interviewer should provide a comfortable, private environment for the meeting, should allot sufficient time, and should develop basic questions in light of the applicant's résumé and application.

Whirlpool, in Oxford, Mississippi, not only makes sure the candidate is right for the job but also makes sure the candidate is right for co-workers. Any candidate seeking employment at Whirlpool is interviewed by the employees who would be working with and for that applicant.

During the course of the interview, the interviewer should keep the conversation focused on job-related issues in order to determine whether the person is right for the job and whether the job is right for the person. Questions should cover the applicant's background and work experience, professional goals, and related skills and interests. The questions in Exhibit 10.4 are typical.

Good interviewers have mastered the skills of building trust and rapport. They create a relaxed atmosphere that puts applicants at ease and encourages communication. They also realize the importance of careful listening and of being nonjudgmental. These interviewing skills help in gathering the important information on which hiring decisions can be made.[9]

Testing

One much-debated aspect of the hiring process is testing—not just the tests that prospective employers give job applicants, but any devices that they may use to

EXHIBIT 10.4 ▶ **Interview Questions**

These are some of the most important questions that should be asked during a job interview.

EMPLOYMENT HISTORY

▶ Why do you wish to change employment?

▶ What do you like the least about your position?

▶ What goals do you expect to achieve in this job that you have not already accomplished?

THE NEW POSITION

▶ What are your expectations of this position?

▶ What do you anticipate being the most challenging aspects of this job?

▶ What can you contribute to this position?

▶ What would be your first goal in this position?

▶ How would you handle a 10 percent budget cut in your area of responsibility?

CAREER GOALS

▶ What are your long-term goals?

▶ How have you moved from each stage in your career to the next?

▶ What factors are most important to you in terms of job satisfaction?

▶ When do you anticipate a promotion?

COMPANY "FIT"

▶ Do you consider yourself amicable?

▶ Are you a team player or are you more satisfied working alone?

▶ Do you praise the contributions of others?

▶ What characteristics do you believe an outstanding subordinate should possess? Peer? Superior?

▶ How would you handle a "problem" employee?

▶ How would you deal with a colleague who has competed with you for a position, feels better qualified than you, and is now your subordinate?

categorize people when making job decisions. Tests are used to gauge abilities, aptitude, intelligence, interests, and sometimes even physical condition and personality.

More and more companies are relying on preemployment testing to determine whether applicants are suited to the job and will be worth the expense of hiring and training. Companies use three main procedures: job-skills testing, psychological testing, and drug testing.

The most common types of tests are job-skills tests designed to assess competency or specific abilities needed to perform a job. Thus, secretaries might be given a word-processing test, and people applying for jobs requiring physical dexterity might be given an eye-hand coordination test.

Psychological tests usually take the form of pencil-and-paper questionnaires filled out by job applicants. These tests can be used to assess overall intellectual ability, attitudes toward work, interests, managerial potential, or personality characteristics. Advocates of psychological testing claim that it can provide accurate and useful information, highly predictive of how well people will actually perform on the job. Critics say that psychological tests are ineffective and potentially discriminatory. The best course of action for human resource managers who use preemployment testing is to choose well-validated tests, administer them equally to all candidates for the same position, and never rely on test results as the sole basis for hiring decisions.

A different type of testing, testing for the presence of illegal substances, is being used by an increasing number of employers in the private sector. Studies have shown that drug users have greater absenteeism rates, are involved in significantly more on-the-job accidents, and incur much higher medical costs than non–drug-using employees. To avoid the increased costs and reduced productivity associated with illegal drug use in the workplace (estimated to cost industry some $100 billion a year), employers are more frequently requiring applicants to submit to drug testing. According to a survey by the American Management Association, more than 60 percent of U.S. firms conduct drug testing; of those, 96 percent will not hire applicants who test positive.[10] Because drug testing is surrounded by legal controversy, it is one of the issues addressed in the next section.

Hiring and the Law

Federal and state laws and regulations govern many aspects of the hiring process. In particular, employers must be careful to avoid discrimination in the wording of their application forms, in interviewing, and in testing. They must also worry about obtaining sufficient information about employees to avoid becoming the target of a negligent-hiring lawsuit. For example, a trucking company would check applicants' driving records to prevent the risks involved in hiring a new driver with poor driving skills.

Application forms typically include questions about a person's job experience and may also include questions about matters that are not strictly job-related (outside activities and so on). Questions about unrelated factors (marital status, age, religion, credit status) violate EEOC regulations because they are potential channels for discrimination in hiring. The exception is when such information relates to a bona fide occupational qualification (BFOQ) that arises out of the nature of the specific job. Despite restrictions on questions that are unrelated to job requirements, some standard application forms ordered from business stationers still include them; companies that use these forms may, therefore, unwittingly be violating the law.[11] Since the Immigration Reform and Control Act was passed in 1986, employers must also be wary of asking too few questions. Almost all companies are forbidden to hire illegal aliens and must verify that the newly hired are legally eligible to work. At the same time, the act prohibits discrimination in hiring on the basis of national origin or citizenship status, resulting in a sticky situation for many employers trying to determine their applicants' citizenship.

Interviewers, too, must avoid asking questions unrelated to the job. For instance, even though the Family Support Act of 1988 requires employers to withhold child support from wages, employers are prohibited from inquiring about an applicant's child-support obligations. And doing so could result in state and federal penalties.[12] In addition, questions about whether the person is married or has children, whether he or she owns or rents a home, what caused a physical disability, whether the person belongs to a union, whether he or she has ever been arrested, and when the applicant attended school (because the answer would indicate the applicant's age) are prohibited. People who conduct employment interviews should be aware of these restrictions, since breaching them may invite expensive lawsuits.

Although some psychological tests provide necessary job-related information with a degree of accuracy, not all do. Furthermore, testing has the potential for abuse. As the result of a 1982 Supreme Court ruling that tests are unlawful if they discriminate, employers have had to scrutinize their testing programs to ensure that tests accurately measure qualities related to job performance and that test scores are not relied on as the principal basis for hiring decisions. Since these are difficult determinations, many employers avoid the issue by not testing at all.

The legal aspects of drug testing vary from state to state and continue to change. Some states prohibit drug testing by private employers, whereas others severely limit the situations in which testing can be used. The U.S. government mandates that certain government employees and employees of federal contrac-

FOCUS ON ETHICS

The Right to Privacy Versus the Right to Know

Companies have the right—and, to some extent, the obligation—to protect themselves against litigation and theft, their employees against unsafe conditions, and their customers against unhealthy and faulty products. No one will argue with these goals. But some have criticized the methods by which companies have begun trying to protect that right, particularly the large-scale testing of job applicants and employees to ensure that they will not expose companies to undue risk. Critics believe that companies' right to know is offset by workers' "right to be let alone," in the now-historic words of U.S. Supreme Court Justice Louis D. Brandeis. The growing concern is over invasion of privacy, especially in regard to workers' activities off the job.

The privacy issue getting the biggest headlines these days is employee use of substances such as drugs and alcohol, which may impair productivity and pose a safety hazard to others. Despite the legislation in some states that restricts drug testing, an increasing number of companies insist on testing urine specimens from prospective and sometimes current employees for the presence of mind-altering substances. Use of such screening poses two important questions: Does an employer have any right to be concerned with an employee's behavior off the job? Are the tests valid—that is, do they reveal information that is relevant to the problem? Although the

tests are increasingly accurate, they still cannot distinguish between the alcohol from a cough syrup and the alcohol from a cocktail. Furthermore, tests may detect marijuana as long as 30 days after its use, and eating three poppy-seed bagels can produce enough morphine in the body to result in a positive test. In short, someone who is not under the influence of a substance may test positive for it, and that "positive test" may reflect only legitimate medicinal use. Finally, the Centers for Disease Control have found that some laboratories erroneously find drugs and alcohol present as much as 66 percent of the time. Even the testing firms recommend confirmation by more expensive tests, and they warn against the poor operating procedures and poor quality control at some labs.

Another newsworthy privacy issue pertains to AIDS (acquired immune deficiency syndrome). Although medical experts have repeatedly emphasized that AIDS cannot be transmitted by food handling or casual contact, many people remain fearful. Workers who are found to have AIDS or related conditions are now covered by laws protecting the handicapped, but they have little or no insulation against discrimination by co-workers. Employers are becoming more aware of the scientific realities of AIDS transmission, calling for education and for confidentiality of medical records, but many employees still refuse to work with AIDS-infected colleagues.

It is one thing to test employees for physical con-

tors undergo drug screening. It is important to make sure that applicants sign a waiver consenting to the testing, that the testing be conducted reliably and accurately, and that the results be kept confidential. Those who test positive should be given an opportunity for a retest. Employers also have the right to test job applicants for contagious diseases, including AIDS, but only on a voluntary basis. Before instituting any kind of physical test, a company should determine whether such testing is really necessary.

Despite the pitfalls businesses encounter in gleaning information about potential employees, they are facing greater accountability for the actions of employees on the job resulting from what has been called "negligent hiring." In one case, McDonald's was ordered to pay damages to a mother and her three-year-old son who had been assaulted by a McDonald's employee in one of the company's fast-food outlets in Denver. It was discovered that the employee, who had been hired as part of a special employment program for the mentally and physically disabled, had a previous conviction for child molestation. McDonald's was held negligent for having failed to fully investigate the man's past—despite the fact that he had been recommended by the state Department of Social Services,

ditions that may affect their work; it is another to determine such nebulous personality characteristics as honesty. Many employers, especially in the retail industry, claim that lie-detector tests are a valuable weapon in the war against theft and embezzlement, and the use of such tests has been widespread. However, in December 1988, the Employee Polygraph Protection Act placed major restrictions on the use of polygraph testing by private industry, especially for preemployment screening and random use—though federal, state, and local governments are exempt from its provisions.

These three issues are currently the most visible aspect of the controversy over employees' right to privacy versus employers' right to know. The following are other areas of concern:

▶ Do psychological tests demonstrate an employee's suitability for a job, or are they a gratuitous invasion of privacy?

▶ Has a company the right to check for "goldbricking" by monitoring a restroom or lounge?

▶ Is it appropriate for companies to use "computer surveillance" to keep track of employees' every action?

▶ Does a company have the right to listen in on phone calls to find out whether they relate to the job or are being made for private purposes or for passing on company secrets?

▶ Does a company have the right to fire workers who smoke, even when the smoking is done only off the job?

▶ Is it an invasion of privacy for a company to check applicants' or employees' credit records?

▶ Can a company perform genetic screening for the purpose of denying employment or of pinpointing future health problems that might increase the company's health costs?

▶ How far should a company go in determining whether an employee's dinner with a colleague from a competing firm is a date, a professional friendship, or industrial spying?

▶ Does a company have the right to fire employees because it disapproves of their sexual lifestyles (such as cohabiting)?

It is difficult to fault companies for trying to make their products safer and their work sites more secure. However, few companies have adopted formal policies regarding employee privacy, which leaves room for abuse. Furthermore, many of these issues have yet to be put to the test in court. And the laws that do exist vary considerably from state to state. At this point, therefore, only one thing is clear: Finding a balance between employer and employee rights is likely to be one of the most debated issues of the 1990s.

which had withheld the information about the conviction.[13] This and similar cases emphasize the need for employers to conduct thorough background checks on job applicants, including verifying all educational credentials and previous jobs, accounting for any large time gaps between jobs, and checking references. This type of background check is particularly important for jobs that will put workers in a position where they can do harm to others. The human resource department must balance this need to know with a respect for the privacy of applicants.

Training and Development

In one way or another, every new employee needs training. Each company has its own way of doing even routine procedures. Accounting, for example, requires the same skills and procedures everywhere. But one company's accountants may need to focus on one aspect of the job, whereas another company's accountants may need to focus on different job aspects; the accounting work may be divided up differently; and, if nothing else, a new accountant needs to know such mundane things as how long the lunch breaks are.

To make sure that all new employees have a clear idea of the company's goals, policies, and procedures, most large firms and many small ones have well-defined **orientation** programs. Although they vary, such programs tend to include these topics:

orientation Session or procedure for acclimating a new employee to the organization

Company background and structure, including the chain of command

Employment policies, including overtime requirements, paydays, termination procedures, and the like

Standards of employee conduct, such as dress codes and smoking policies

Benefit programs, including insurance benefits and vacation policies

Job duties and responsibilities[14]

The new employee's supervisor typically spends time making her or him feel comfortable, introducing co-workers, and giving a tour of the facilities. Time spent helping an employee get acquainted is worthwhile because it helps reduce anxiety and sets the newcomer on the right track from the beginning.

Many companies also devote considerable resources to training and retraining workers because worker competence has a direct effect on company profits. Johnson & Johnson retrained its managers to be more sensitive toward employees' conflicting obligations to work and to family. Training employees may take place at the work site (where an experienced worker oversees the trainee's on-the-job efforts) or in a classroom (where an expert lectures groups of employees). Often a training program simply teaches the nuts-and-bolts skills of a particular job. In an electronics plant, for example, workers may spend a few weeks becoming familiar with the components they'll be putting together, learning to attach components to a board, and so on. And such training increasingly goes beyond the basics, helping employees acquire polish, confidence, and specialized talents.

As the pool of qualified entry-level workers continues to shrink, employers are also finding it necessary to provide remedial education in language and arithmetic to new workers. According to one source, every fifth person now hired by U.S. industry lacks basic reading and math skills, and functional illiteracy costs

Business Around the World

In Germany, training is still deeply rooted in the apprenticeship tradition and is highly regarded. Vocational schools have rigorous academic programs, and their graduates are highly sought after by businesses. Many attribute Germany's continuing productive growth to this vocational training tradition.

business over $6 billion annually in lost productivity.[15] The literacy problem is so pervasive that 93 percent of large corporations surveyed are offering or plan to offer some form of basic skills courses to employees.[16]

Some companies are tackling the training problem in a different way: by contributing to or working with the public schools. A recent poll of Fortune 500 companies found that 78 percent of those responding contribute money to schools, 64 percent offer materials or equipment, and 50 percent encourage their employees to tutor or teach at schools.[17] IBM, for example, gives more than $10 million a year to elementary and secondary education, and even more to

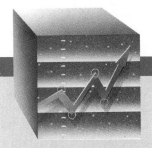

TECHNIQUES FOR BUSINESS SUCCESS

What Your Boss Really Wants from You

In the first few days of a new job, you are likely to discover that your boss expects you to know a host of things that she or he hasn't taken the time or trouble to tell you. Here's a remedy for the sinking feeling that you've failed before you've even begun: a list of 15 things your boss expects from Day 1. Of course, every boss has an idiosyncratic way of doing things, which you will learn in time by watching and probing. For those first hectic weeks, however, rely on this list to help you start off on the right foot and stay there.

1. *Do more than you're asked to do.* What you have been hired to do is the minimum expected. You won't be fired for not doing more, but you won't be promoted either. Follow up on work you've completed. If you can handle more work, let your boss know. Be willing to work late or take work home when necessary.

2. *Don't give alibis.* If a project isn't ready on time, it really doesn't matter why.

3. *Troubleshoot your own problems.* On each project, anticipate potential problems, and take steps to prevent them. If you depend on assistance from others, make sure they know exactly what you want and when you need it; then check up on them before the work is due. Solve your own problems whenever possible. If you must bring a problem to your boss, also bring suggestions for solving it and a rundown of what you've already done.

4. *Be familiar with what other employees do.* It's easy to get so caught up in your own job that you lose sight of the company's goals. Knowledge of how your job and the jobs of others relate to those goals helps you understand much of their behavior and enables you to set priorities.

5. *Have respect for your job.* Treat your job as the most important thing you do. Show up on time every day, ready to work.

6. *Be flexible.* No one knows what the future holds, so don't cut your options by refusing to relocate, to learn new skills, or to explore new job areas within the company.

7. *Encourage those above and below you.* As they move up in the organization, so do you.

8. *Don't gripe or fight.* A negative attitude shuts off communication. Before you get into a battle, make sure your winnings will be worth the cost in time, energy, and allies. Making concessions to keep peace could win you more in the long run.

9. *Respect your competition.* Win or lose, when the battle is over, you still have to work with your opponents. Bear no grudges.

10. *Be truthful.* No situation is so bad that it cannot be made worse by lying.

11. *Don't make too many assumptions.* It's better to ask what someone means or wants than to find yourself on the far end of a limb.

12. *Be a professional.* Keep abreast of what is happening in your field or industry through professional associations and trade journals. Get to know others in your field and in your industry.

13. *Be fluent in the boss's language.* "Would you please" means "Do it"; "I don't want to rush you" means "Step on it"; "If you wouldn't mind" means "I need it as soon as I can get it."

14. *Watch your timing.* Make your requests when they are most likely to be granted. Ask for more responsibility when your boss compliments you on a major project. Request a raise when department sales are up.

15. *Show discretion.* When in public, never discuss your firm, its business, or people you work with. Even in private, don't discuss the firm's problems or politics with someone outside the organization.

To increase quality, Motorola University in Schamburg, Illinois, trains and retrains employees in courses ranging from basic reading and writing skills to advanced engineering.

colleges and universities. An increasing number of businesses are entering into school partnerships, in which they adopt local schools. Phoenix Mutual Life Insurance, for example, has adopted schools in Hartford, Connecticut, where company employees tutor children and provide other services. Another approach being tried is to work with vocational schools to provide necessary training. Near Seattle, the Applied Technology Center operated by two community colleges routinely contracts with companies such as Honeywell and Boeing to train employees in specific skills, such as electronics assembly.[18]

The company that has perhaps taken the biggest plunge into all aspects of training is Motorola, which has established what it calls Motorola University. Its mandate includes not only training and retraining 100,000 worldwide employees but also playing a role in public and private education. The ambitious program ranges from basic skills training (to ensure that all employees can read and write English at a seventh-grade level, at least) to advanced engineering programs. The courses are taught at facilities at the company's headquarters in Schamburg, Illinois, and at four other locations around the world. "The purpose of MU is to help our employees exceed the challenges of the 1990s, and we feel to this end that it is a competitive investment," says MU's president A. William Wiggenhorn. The $60 million a year Motorola has committed to the program is already paying off in increased product quality.[19]

Appraising Employee Performance

When should an employee be given a raise? When should someone be promoted, demoted, or transferred? Under what circumstances should a worker be let go? The answers to such questions can be obtained only by evaluating the employee's work.

But how should an employee's performance be evaluated? All too often, evaluations are subjective responses that accumulate haphazardly. To correct for the arbitrary nature of such evaluations, many companies are developing highly structured **performance appraisal** systems designed to allow objective evaluations. Such systems promote fairness because their standards are usually job-related ("Rhonda turns in weekly reports on time" rather than "Rhonda's always bustling around the office, so she must be doing an efficient job"). When performance appraisals are used, the standards are written down so that both employee and supervisor understand what is expected and are therefore able to determine whether the work is being done adequately. Most formal systems also require regular evaluations of each employee's work—in writing (see Exhibit 10.5)—thereby providing a record of the employee's performance. (Such a record may protect the company in cases of disputed terminations.) Finally, many performance appraisal systems require the employee to be rated by several people (including more than one supervisor and perhaps several co-workers). This practice further promotes fairness by correcting for the possible bias that might color one person's appraisal.

The biggest problem with appraisal systems is finding a way to measure performance. Productivity is the ultimate criterion, but it is not always easy to measure. In a production job, the person who types the most pages of acceptable copy or who assembles the most defect-free microprocessors in a given amount of time is clearly the most productive. But how does an employer evaluate the productivity of the registration clerk at a hotel or the middle manager at a large television station? Although the organization's overall productivity can be mea-

performance appraisal Evaluation of an employee's work according to specific criteria

EXHIBIT 10.5

**Sample Performance
Appraisal Form**
Many companies use printed
forms like this to make sure
performance appraisals are as
objective as possible.

Name _____	Title _____	Service Date _____	Date _____
Location _____	Division _____	Department _____	
Length of Time in Present Position _____	Period of Review From: _____ To: _____	Appraised by _____ Title of Appraisor _____	

Area of Performance	Comment	Rating
Job Knowledge and Skill Understands responsibilities and utilizes background for job. Adapts to new methods/techniques. Plans and organizes work. Recognizes errors and problems.		5 4 3 2 1
Volume of Work Amount of work output, adherence to standards and schedules, effective use of time.		5 4 3 2 1
Quality of Work Degree of accuracy–lack of errors; thoroughness of work; ability to exercise good judgment.		5 4 3 2 1
Initiative and Creativity Self motivation in seeking responsibility and work that needs to be done; ability to apply original ideas and concepts.		5 4 3 2 1
Communication Ability to exchange thoughts or information in a clear, concise manner. Dealing with different organizational levels and clientele.		5 4 3 2 1
Dependability Ability to follow instructions and directions correctly; performs under pressure; reliable work habits.		5 4 3 2 1
Leadership Ability/Potential Ability to guide others to the succesful accomplishment of a given task; potential for developing subordinate employees.		5 4 3 2 1

5. **Outstanding**	Employee who consistently exceeds established standards and expectations of the job.
4. **Above Average**	Employee who consistently meets established standards and expectations of the job. Often exceeds and rarely falls short of desired results.
3. **Satisfactory**	Generally qualified employee who meets job standards and expectations. Sometimes exceeds and may occasionally fall short of desired expectations. Performs duties in a normally expected manner.
2. **Improvement Needed**	Not quite meeting standards and expectations. An employee at this level of performance is not quite meeting all of the standard job requirements.
1. **Unsatisfactory**	Employee who fails to meet the minimum standards and expectations of the job.

I have had the opportunity to read this performance appraisal.	How long has this employee been under your supervision?
Signature of Employee Date	Signature of Supervisor Date

sured (number of rooms booked per night, number of viewers per hour), often no direct correlation exists between the tasks performed by service employees and those performed by white-collar workers. Thus, additional criteria, such as rating of the organization by customers, the behavior of the worker toward co-workers and customers, job knowledge, motivation, and skills, are needed to help judge worker performance.

► COMPENSATION

In return for their services, employees receive **compensation,** a combination of payments, benefits, and employer services. Although it isn't the only factor in motivating employees, proper compensation is crucial. Few people will work for

compensation Payment to employees for their work

nothing, and many people use compensation as a yardstick for measuring their success in the world of work.

Wage and Salary Administration

On what basis should workers be paid? How much should they be paid? And when should they be paid? Such questions are prime concerns of the human resource department.

Wages Versus Salaries

wages Cash payment based on a calculation of the number of hours the employee has worked or the number of units the employee has produced

Many blue-collar and some white-collar workers receive compensation in the form of **wages,** which are based on a calculation of the number of hours the employee has worked or the number of units he or she has produced. Sometimes compensation is based on a combination of both time and productivity. Wages provide a direct incentive to a worker: The more hours worked or the more pieces completed, the higher the worker's pay.

salaries Weekly, monthly, or yearly cash compensation for work

Workers whose output is not always directly related to the number of hours they put in or the number of pieces produced are paid **salaries.** Salaries, like wages, base compensation on time, but the unit of time is a week, two weeks, a month, or a year. Salaried workers such as managers and professionals normally receive no pay for the extra hours they sometimes put in; overtime is simply part of their obligation. However, they do get a certain amount of leeway in their working time.

Both wages and salaries are, in principle, based on the contribution of a particular job to the company. Thus, the marketing director gets higher pay than her or his secretary. Another basis for pay is the market value or "going rate" for the job. An executive secretary can command better pay in New York City than in San Diego, for example.

In 1990 the average U.S. worker received pay of $23,602.[20] Pay varies widely by position and industry. Among the best-paid workers in the world are chairmen of the boards of large American corporations. In 1990 CEOs at midsized firms received an average of more than $2.1 million (including stock options and other long-term compensation); for billion-dollar companies, the average was more than $3.3 million.[21] Over the decade of the 1980s, CEO pay jumped 212 percent, compared to a mere 78 percent increase in earnings per share of Standard & Poor's 500 companies.[22] Employees are baffled and angry that, in a time when they are being asked to tighten their belts because company earnings are down, their chief executives are actually making even more money. Increasingly, critics are asking for a reassessment of how CEO compensation is set and are demanding that the fortunes of the people on top be more closely tied to the successes and failures of the company itself.

Incentive Programs

incentives Cash payments to workers who produce at a desired level or whose unit (often the company as a whole) produces at a desired level

Johnson & Johnson isn't the only business concerned with productivity. To encourage employees to be more productive, companies often provide CEOs, managers, sales representatives, and other types of workers with **incentives** linked to reaching certain personal or company levels of production or profitability. In other words, achievements, not just activities, are made the basis for payment.

BONUSES AND COMMISSIONS   For both salaried and wage-earning workers, one type of incentive compensation is the **bonus**—a payment in addition to the regular wage or salary. Some firms pay an annual year-end bonus (amounting to a certain percentage of each employee's earnings) as an incentive to reduce turnover during the year. Other cash bonuses are tied to company goal attainment. Although such bonuses used to be reserved for the executive and management levels, they are becoming increasingly available to lower-level employees as well.

Commissions are payments based on sales made. Used mainly for sales staff, they may be the sole compensation or may be an incentive payment in addition to a regular salary.

bonus Cash payment in addition to the regular wage or salary, which serves as a reward for achievement

commissions Payments to workers who achieve a certain level of sales

PROFIT SHARING AND GOAL SHARING   Employees may be rewarded for staying with a company and encouraged to work harder through **profit sharing,** a system whereby employees receive a portion of the company's profits. Depending on the company, profits may be distributed quarterly, semiannually, or annually. Or payment may be put off until the employee retires, is disabled, or leaves the company—provided the employee has worked the minimum number of years called for in the plan. With deferred payments like these, the company pools and invests funds for the employees until they are ready to collect their share.

profit sharing System for distributing a portion of the company's profits to employees

Goal sharing is similar to profit sharing but with one significant difference. The rewards to employees are tied not to overall profits but to cost savings resulting from meeting goals for quality, safety, and customer service. For example, at AT&T Universal Card Services, incentive payments are based on how quickly and accurately employees process credit-card requests and handle other tasks.[23] The success of such programs often depends on how closely incentives are linked to actions within the worker's control.

goal sharing Plan for rewarding employees not on the basis of overall profits but in relation to cost savings resulting from increased output

One approach to goal sharing, often referred to as **pay for performance,** entails some risk for employees. They accept a lower base pay but are well rewarded if they reach production targets or other goals. When such a plan was launched at Long John Silver's 1,000 company-owned fast-food restaurants, hourly wages actually increased by more than $.75 in the first quarter.[24] Other companies that have had success with pay-for-performance programs include Corning, Nordstrom, and Monsanto. Yet similar programs have failed elsewhere. Most notably, Du Pont had to scrap the plan it set up for its fibers group when employees balked at taking a 6 percent decrease in base pay and the federal government would not allow Du Pont to give workers a choice of whether or not to participate.[25]

pay for performance Accepting a lower base pay in exchange for bonuses based on meeting production or other goals

KNOWLEDGE-BASED PAY   An approach to compensation being explored by some companies is **knowledge-based pay,** or skill-based pay, which is keyed to employees' knowledge and abilities rather than to their job per se. Alcoa, Polaroid, TRW, Chrysler, and Westinghouse are just a few of the companies that have developed knowledge-based pay programs. Typically, the pay level at which a person is hired is pegged to his or her current level of skills; as the employee acquires new skills, the pay level goes up. Advocates of knowledge-based pay say it can reduce staffing requirements, increase teamwork, increase flexibility (because a single employee may have the skills to perform a variety of jobs), and decrease overall labor costs.[26] Such programs also motivate "flat-line" employees, who have little opportunity for promotion. Critics are skeptical of the poten-

knowledge-based pay Pay keyed to an employee's acquisition of skills

EXHIBIT 10.6 ▶ **Executive Perks**

Here are the top ten perks offered by companies to their CEOs and company presidents.

OVERALL RANKING	PERCENTAGE OF ALL COMPANIES
1. Company car/limousine for business use	64%
2. Disability coverage	58
3. Entertainment expense account	56
4. Telephone credit cards	55
5. Company car for personal use	47
6. Supplemental life insurance	46
7. Car telephone	36
8. Physical exams	35
9. Tax preparation assistance	29
10. Club membership (dining/social)	27

tial for knowledge-based pay to lower labor costs, and they point out that such programs can be complicated to administer.

Employee Benefits and Services

fringe benefits Compensation other than wages, salaries, and incentive programs

perks Special class of fringe benefits made available to a company's most valuable employees

Companies regularly provide their employees with **fringe benefits,** financial benefits other than wages, salaries, and incentives. Executives often receive a special set of additional fringe benefits referred to as **perks,** or perquisites, which include such niceties as company cars and club memberships. Exhibit 10.6 lists some of the most popular executive perks. Companies also provide health and safety programs for all workers, which can be expensive.

Actually, the term *fringe benefits* is somewhat misleading; the amount of money allotted for "fringes" is far from negligible and has been rising steadily (see Exhibit 10.7). According to U.S. Chamber of Commerce statistics, in 1990 companies paying an average annual wage of $32,299 spent $12,402 on fringe benefits, well over a third of the total pay.[27] Benefits and services for salaried employees typically cost even more. Still, companies provide benefits because benefits encourage employees to stay.

EXHIBIT 10.7

The Benefits Package
An employee whose hourly salary is $10.84 typically receives additional benefits worth over $4.12.

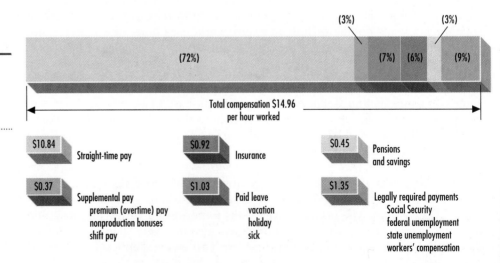

Many types of benefits and services are provided. Some, such as Social Security and unemployment insurance, are mandatory; others, such as health coverage, are optional. Only the benefits most commonly provided by an employer are described here. Be aware, however, that this aspect of the business world is undergoing considerable change to meet the shifting needs of the work force and to take into consideration the requirements of various types of workers. In an earlier era, the typical worker was a middle-aged, family-oriented, blue-collar man who intended to stay with the same employer for most, if not all, of his working life. Today's workers are much less homogeneous, and the two-career family has far different needs for benefits. Instead of two sets of insurance benefits, for example, such a family may prefer one spouse to receive insurance and the other to receive day-care assistance.

Insurance Plans and Unemployment Benefits

Although it is entirely optional, insurance is the most popular fringe benefit. Most businesses offer substantial compensation in the form of life and health insurance; dental plans, disability insurance, and long-term-care insurance are also gaining in popularity. A company will negotiate a group insurance plan for its employees and pay all or most of the premium costs (see Exhibit 10.8). Faced with exploding health-care costs, however, many companies now require workers to pay part of their insurance premiums or more of the actual doctor bills.

Unemployment is a misfortune that can befall any worker. Under the terms of the Social Security Act of 1935, employers in all 50 states finance special **unemployment insurance** to benefit workers who are laid off or (to a lesser extent)

unemployment insurance
Government-sponsored program for assisting workers who are laid off or, to a lesser extent, who quit their jobs

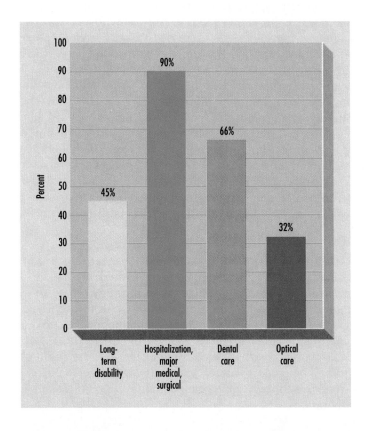

EXHIBIT 10.8

Types of Insurance That Companies Pay For
Ninety-two percent of U.S. firms offer workers at least some medical benefits. The graph shows the percentages of firms that pay in full for various types of employee medical insurance.

who quit their jobs. Each employer pays into a state fund a tax corresponding to the number of people in the industry who have been on the unemployment rolls. A worker who becomes unemployed for reasons not related to performance is entitled to collect benefits. The amount of the benefit is usually tied to the employee's total earnings during the previous year, but both the amount of the payment and the length of time it is available vary from state to state. Workers in certain industries—notably automobile, steel, rubber, and glass—receive additional benefits (called supplemental unemployment benefits) from either the company or the union.

Retirement Benefits

In the past, few people were able to save enough money in the course of their working years to be financially independent when they retired. The main purpose of the Social Security Act was to provide those who could not accumulate enough retirement money with the basic support they would need in their old age. However, over the years nearly everyone who works regularly has become eligible for Social Security payments during retirement, whether or not she or he needs the money. This income is paid for by the Social Security tax, which is withheld by the employer from employees' wages and matched by a more or less equal contribution from the employer.

Few workers can rely on Social Security payments to support more than a minimal standard of living. The average monthly Social Security payment to retired workers in January 1990 was $720; the average monthly payment to couples was $1,074. But many retirees collected the maximum monthly benefit: about $975 for a single worker and $1,706 for a family.[28]

pension plans Company-sponsored programs for providing retirees with income

A variety of company-sponsored **pension plans** have sprung up over the past few decades as a way of providing additional retirement security. The number of workers covered by pension plans increased steadily over the years, reaching 48.3 percent coverage in 1979. But the cost and complexity of such plans increased so dramatically that some employers began canceling them. By 1988 the number of workers covered had dropped to 43.2 percent, and in 1990 more pension plans were canceled than were started.[29]

Under some company pension plans, retired employees are paid out of the business's current income. More often, pension plans are funded—that is, money is set aside on a regular basis to provide retirement benefits in the future. In the most popular type of plan, workers make regular contributions out of their paychecks, and the company matches some portion (usually 50 percent) of the amount. Although employers are not required by law to provide pensions for their employees, many choose to do so as a way of attracting and keeping good workers.

PENSION GUARANTEES   Despite their pensions, retirees are often in tight economic circumstances. If their pensions were suddenly cut off—if a former employer went out of business or declared bankruptcy, or if the pension fund ran out of money—many of these people would be destitute. Recognizing this fact, Congress passed the Employee Retirement Income Security Act of 1974 (ERISA), which established a federal agency to insure the assets of pension plans. This act guarantees that, with some exceptions and limitations, retirement benefits will be paid no matter what happens to the company or the plan. It also sets standards for managing pension funds and requires public disclosure of a plan's operations.

Although this law has meant a new degree of security for retirees, it has also meant trouble for companies with pension plans. With rising salary rates and people living longer after retirement, many companies are finding that their pension claims for the foreseeable future have grown nearly as large as their total assets.

CURRENT PENSION ISSUES In the uncertain economic climate of the 1990s, companies have become creative about substituting other assets for cash payments to retirees. Despite ERISA rulings that companies must pay at least 75 percent of pension funds in cash, companies sometimes ignore these requirements. Some employees are offered the option of stocks and bonds instead of cash. United States Steel (now USX), for example, met pension-plan obligations in 1984 with a special type of stock that can't be sold, thereby saving itself $333 million in cash and linking its pension plan to the corporation's future success. As helpful as this tactic may be to a company that has suffered considerably in recent years, it threatens the arm's-length relationship that companies are supposed to have with their retirement funds.[30]

As companies scramble to keep pension funds from drying up, legislation prohibiting gender-based discrimination threatens to strain pension programs further. In 1983 the Supreme Court ruled against companies that paid women smaller monthly amounts than men on the grounds that women tend to live longer. Legislators and women's groups argued that treating women as members of a class was a violation of their civil rights; they said that this was not unlike the discrimination suffered by African-Americans, who at one time were charged 50 percent more than whites for life insurance because they died at a younger age.

Employee Stock-Ownership Plans

Another fringe-benefit program being offered by a number of companies is the **employee stock-ownership plan,** or ESOP. In an ESOP, a company places a certain amount of its stock in trust for all or some of its employees, with each employee entitled to a certain share. If the company does well, the ESOP may be a substantial employee benefit. An additional advantage of the ESOP is that it's free to the employee and nearly so to the employer (because it is financed by a federal tax credit).

employee stock-ownership plan Program enabling employees to become owners or part owners of a company

ESOPs work well for some companies, less well for others. When W. L. Gore & Associates (a chemical-fabrication company in Newark, Delaware) instituted its ESOP, 5,000 employees (called "associates") owned company stock. The company was growing 25 percent a year, and associates felt like part of the management team. As one worker explained: "I want to make sure this company works, and I feel I'm a part owner because I have a lot to say about my area of expertise." At the other end of the spectrum, when Dan River (a textile manufacturer in Danville, Virginia) established its ESOP, about 8,000 employees owned 70 percent of the stock. But the company was firmly in the hands of the managers and outside investors (who owned 30 percent of the company) because the ESOP plan was instituted for its tax advantages, and employee involvement in operations was ignored. "The company stamps its cartons with a big 'D' and 'employee-owned.' But most of the people realize that they don't own anything. They're just paying the bill for these big management people to own the company," complained one employee. The ESOPs were meant to give employees

VIDEO EXERCISE

more of a stake in the companies they work for, but abuse of such plans causes employees to be disillusioned and angry.[31]

The intergeneration day-care center at Stride-Rite in Cambridge, Massachusetts, serves low-income people from the community as well as relatives of employees.

Family Benefits

More and more working parents are looking for such benefits as unpaid leave to take care of a new baby and day-care assistance once the parent returns to work. Johnson & Johnson provides on-site child care at two of its facilities, and it provides family-care leave of up to one year. Such family benefits are proving helpful (not only to employees but also to companies) in the form of higher employee morale and productivity as well as lower absenteeism. Although gaining momentum, the concept of family benefits is only getting started. Now, one out of ten companies provides child-care assistance of some sort, from handing out lists of local community services to providing day-care facilities on the premises; a few, such as the American Bankers Insurance Group in Miami and Target Stores in Minneapolis, have even built satellite schools for children of employees. About 40 percent of U.S. firms offer some form of maternity leave, and a growing number are expanding their programs to give fathers paternity leave (although few men are taking advantage of such leave, primarily out of concern over damage to their careers).[32]

A related family issue, especially among baby boomers, is care for aging parents. An estimated 20 percent of large corporations offer some form of elder-care assistance, ranging from referral services that help find care providers to dependent-care allowances.[33] An innovative program at Stride-Rite headquarters in Cambridge, Massachusetts, combines child care and elder care in an "intergenerational center." Children learn and play in four classrooms in one wing, while the older people engage in a variety of activities in their own wing. Both age groups share a common area that contains a dining room and library. In addition to the relatives of Stride-Rite employees, low-income elderly people from the community also use the center.[34]

Other Fringe Benefits

Although sometimes overlooked, paid holidays, sick pay, premium pay for working overtime or unusual hours, and paid vacations are important fringe benefits. In 1989 employers provided each employee an average of 9.1 paid vacation days per year after 1 year of service, 16.5 paid vacation days after 10 years of service, and 9.2 paid holidays.[35] Companies have various policies as to how many days they consider legitimate holidays; a company with a liberal policy on holidays usually emphasizes this fact in its employment advertising. Sick-day allowances also vary from company to company, although sick days are usually limited to curb excessive absenteeism. To provide incentives for employee loyalty, most companies grant employees longer paid vacations if the workers have been with the organization for a prescribed number of years.

Among the many other benefits that companies are beginning to offer are sabbaticals and tuition loans, personal computers and company cars, financial counseling and legal services, club and association memberships, assistance with buying a home, and paid expenses for spouses who travel with employees.

Flexible Benefits

Until recently, most fringe benefits came as a package with a particular job. Once hired, the employee got whatever insurance, paid holidays, pension plan, and other benefits the company had set up. But a newer approach allows employees to pick their benefits—up to a certain dollar amount—to meet their particular needs. A worker with a young family might want extra life or health insurance, for example, and might feel no need for a pension plan. A single worker might choose to forgo life insurance for a tax-deferred retirement plan. Another worker might "buy" an extra week or two of vacation time by giving up some other benefit.

About 25 percent of large companies have taken this flexible "cafeteria" approach to fringe benefits, and it seems to be gaining in popularity, even among small businesses. The type of company that might best adopt it would be one experiencing rapid growth, one with few skilled employees, one in an industry where the competition for employees is strong, one that already has generous benefits, or one with a diverse group of employees.[36]

Health and Safety Programs

Health and safety programs reduce potential suffering and keep health-related losses to a minimum. Thus they are, or should be, a major concern of every human resource manager. By educating employees in safety procedures, establishing and enforcing safety regulations, and redesigning work environments to minimize the potential for death, injury, and illness, businesses have often succeeded in cutting their health-related losses sharply. And they also have happier, healthier, and usually more productive employees.

Some two-thirds of companies with at least 50 workers are taking a more active role in maintaining employee health. Wellness and fitness programs encourage employees to eat sensibly, stop smoking, control stress, and exercise. The results have been impressive. Mutual Benefit Life Insurance found that employees who used the fitness center at its Newark, New Jersey, headquarters missed an average of 2.5 workdays a year (compared to 4.25 missed days for employees who don't use the facilities), and their medical claims average $313 a year (compared to $1,086 for nonusers).[37] Johnson & Johnson has had similar success with a program it calls Live for Life, which is available to all 35,000 employees in the United States. Participants receive an individualized health-risk profile and are encouraged to watch their diets, exercise, and give up smoking. On-site gyms and "healthy heart" foods in the cafeteria help workers with their wellness programs. As a result of this program, J&J says it has saved $378 a year per employee by lowering absenteeism and reducing health-care costs.[38] Some large companies have gone so far as to provide in-house medical care for employees. Southern California Edison, for example, has eight primary-care clinics, two first-aid stations, and a corporate pharmacy for its 57,000 employees. Using in-house doctors and buying drugs at wholesale rates helps keep Edison's health-care costs under control.[39]

A number of companies have also instituted **employee assistance programs** (EAPs) for employees with personal problems, especially drug or alcohol dependence. Such programs have been reported (on the average) to reduce absenteeism by 66 percent, health-care costs by 86 percent, sickness benefits by

employee assistance programs Company-sponsored counseling or referrals for employees with personal problems

Shaklee employees take advantage of their company's on-site fitness program.

33 percent, and work-related accidents by 65 percent.[40] Participation in EAPs is voluntary and confidential. Employees are given in-house counseling or are referred to outside therapists or treatment programs.

▶ CHANGES IN EMPLOYMENT STATUS

Sometimes, despite the most rigorous planning, recruiting, selecting, and training, a worker leaves the job for which she or he was hired. The worker may choose to quit because the job proves unsatisfying or because a better opportunity arises. Or the company may take the initiative in making the change—either reassigning the worker or letting the worker go. Exhibit 10.9 shows the top five reasons people leave their jobs. Whatever the reason, losing an employee usually means going to the trouble and expense of finding a replacement, whether from outside or from within the company.

Promoting and Reassigning Workers

Partly to avoid the expense of recruiting new employees, companies often fill jobs with people already working for them. If nothing else, these candidates have already incorporated the company's culture into their own outlook and are familiar with its policies and procedures. Also, morale is usually better when the company promotes from within because others see that they have a chance for advancement.

A potential pitfall of promotion is that a person may be given a job beyond his or her competence. It is not uncommon for someone who is good at one kind of job to be made a manager, a position that requires a completely different set of

EXHIBIT 10.9

Why People Leave Their Jobs

In a recent exit survey of federal government employees, young professionals identified these reasons as the single most important in their decision to leave.

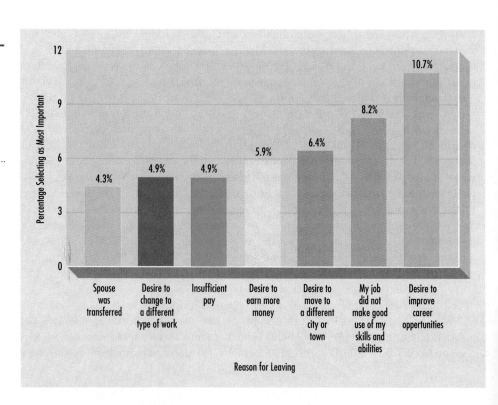

skills. Someone who consistently racks up the best sales in the company, for example, is not necessarily the person who should be promoted to sales manager. If the promotion is a mistake, the company not only loses its sales leader but also risks losing the employee altogether. People who aren't performing well generally become demoralized and lose confidence in the abilities they do have.

One big issue these days for companies that are promoting and reassigning workers is *relocation.* In the past, companies transferred some employees often, especially those being groomed for management positions. Now, however, fewer and fewer workers are willing to accept transfers. One reason is that many more couples have two careers; if one of them is transferred, either the other has to give up what may be a good job or the couple has to accept a "commuter" marriage, in which they see each other only on weekends and vacations. Changing values are another factor; many workers today are as committed to community activities and quality of life as to their career advancement. And economics is often a factor as well. It is expensive to sell and buy houses (especially if real estate values in the new location are higher than in the old one), and the cost of one spouse quitting a job and being unemployed for a few months may not be offset by the raise that typically accompanies a transfer.[41]

Companies have traditionally helped in transfers by providing house-hunting trips; temporary living expenses; and moving, storage, and transportation expenses. In addition, many corporations are now helping spouses find good jobs in new locations, assisting transferees with home sales, and sometimes reimbursing transferees for spouses' lost wages and for financial losses arising from selling and buying houses. Many companies are even reconsidering their transfer policies and reducing the number to those transfers that are absolutely necessary.

In today's corporate climate of flatter organizational structure, fewer middle managers are seeing opportunities for advancement; instead, many are stuck at plateaus. One of the challenges of human resource managers is to keep these talented people on staff. One approach used by such companies as PepsiCo and Hughes Aircraft is the "lateral transfer," such as from electrical engineering to quality control. Other companies offer stalled employees challenging tasks in unfamiliar areas to help broaden their experience. Overseas assignments, academic sabbaticals, and career-development programs are among the other approaches being used to motivate those on the "slow track."[42]

Terminating Employment

A company invests time, effort, and money in each new employee it recruits and trains. This investment is lost when a reliable employee is removed by **termination**—laying the employee off because of cutbacks or firing the employee for poor performance. Many companies facing a downturn in business have avoided wholesale layoffs by **restructuring**—cutting administrative costs (curtailing travel, seminars, and other frills), freezing wages, postponing new hiring, or encouraging early retirement. Sometimes, however, a company has no alternative but to **downsize,** or reduce the size of its work force. In December 1991, pounded by the recession and by foreign rivals, General Motors announced its three-year program to close 25 North American plants and lay off 74,000 employees.[43] Also, acquisitions, mergers, and leveraged buyouts have forced many companies to downsize, leaving the human resource department with the task of handling layoffs and their resulting effects on both the terminated and remaining employees.

termination *Act of getting rid of a worker*

restructuring *Process of changing the nature of a company by reordering its ownership, composition, operation, or work force*

downsize *Reduce the size of a company's work force*

Layoffs

seniority Longevity in a position or company, frequently used as a basis for making human resource decisions (compensation, termination, and so on)

Companies were once free to lay off whomever they pleased. Recently, however, some laid-off employees have sued, charging that they were unfairly singled out because of age, gender, religion, or race. Even employers that have a supposedly discrimination-free system of layoffs based on **seniority**, or length of time with the company, have found themselves in court. The reason? The so-called last-hired, first-fired principle (that is, the workers most recently hired are the first to be laid off) means that women and minorities are more likely to be the ones laid off, since in most cases they have only recently been hired in significant numbers.

An alternative is a "valuableness" system that evaluates each worker according to criteria (reliability, communication skills, and so on) picked by both workers and supervisors. Each worker accumulates a certain number of points under this system, and those with the fewest points are laid off. This method has been used in a number of large industrial companies, and to date it has not been successfully challenged in court.[44]

outplacement Job-hunting and other assistance that a company provides to laid-off workers

To help ease the pain of layoff, many companies are now providing laid-off workers with job-hunting assistance. Although **outplacement** aids such as résumé-writing courses, career counseling, office space, and secretarial help are most often offered to executives, even middle managers and blue-collar workers are beginning to receive this type of help. When McDonnell Douglas reduced its St. Louis headquarters work force by 5,000, its human resource department not only provided outplacement support centers equipped with computers, phones, and career advisers but also sponsored a job fair and even ran radio ads touting the high quality of laid-off workers to potential employers.[45]

Nevertheless, layoffs affect both the morale and the productivity of employees who are staying, as well as affecting those who have been notified that they will be leaving. Says L. Marshall Stellfox, partner in a top Manhattan human resource consulting firm, "Companies can help bolster sagging morale if they tell their remaining employees truthfully about the status of job security and their opportunity for promotion."[46]

Some companies have adopted no-layoff, or guaranteed employment, policies. Employees may still be fired for not doing their job, but in an economic downturn they may be shifted to other types of jobs, perhaps at reduced pay, or given the chance to participate in work-sharing programs. At Honda's plant in Marysville, Ohio, layoffs have been avoided by slowing down the production lines. Ethically, such policies are a good idea, but they have practical benefits as well: Employees tend to be more loyal to the company and more motivated because they know they will not work themselves out of a job. Cleveland's Lincoln Electric discovered such benefits in its guaranteed-employment policy. Its factory workers (dubbed "Lincoln's leopards") volunteered to go out on sales calls and to pay their own expenses to get the company through hard times. They brought in $10 million in sales.[47] Delta Air Lines, Federal Express, Hallmark, and Polaroid are among other companies well known for their no-layoff policies, and they believe their "lifetime-employment" approach pays off in the long run. Hallmark's CEO Irving Hockaday, Jr., put it this way: "We believe that we have to manage for the long term, protect our people from cyclical, changing markets, and if they know we're going to do that, they will help us solve the problem."[48]

Firings and "Employment at Will"

It has long been illegal for a company to fire an employee because he or she is a would-be union organizer, has filed a job-safety complaint, or is of an "undesirable" race, religion, gender, or age. Beyond this, the courts have traditionally held that any employee not covered by a contract may be fired "at will." In other words, because the employee may quit whenever he or she pleases, the employer should be able to return the favor. Recently, however, a number of legal decisions have begun to alter this doctrine. The most far-reaching decisions have held that there may be an implied contract between employer and employee requiring that any firing be done "fairly." Some commentators on the subject have called this notion "the right to a job."

Employees have won **wrongful discharge** suits against former employers by arguing that documents issued by the company (employee handbooks, for example) state that no employee may be fired without proper warning and an opportunity to remedy whatever problems may exist. Some fired workers have even argued that their being called "permanent" employees by the company should protect them from firing—or at least from unfair firing. The question of fairness is difficult to pin down, but most companies losing court cases did so because they fired the employee with inadequate warning that the employee's job was on the line and with little or no explanation of why. Therefore, before they fire anyone, managers should ask themselves: "Has this worker been properly warned and notified? Have both the warning and the grounds for dismissal been clearly noted in the worker's record?"

Wrongful discharge cases have been plentiful in light of the massive layoffs in recent years. Analysts say that a former employee has an 86 percent chance of winning a wrongful discharge suit brought against a private business, with an average damage award of $650,000.[49] To avoid such suits, many companies are requiring employees to sign an "employment at will" statement acknowledging that they may be fired at any time at the company's discretion. Some companies are also now including statements in application forms or company handbooks that affirm the employment at will doctrine. Blue Cross and Blue Shield of Michigan, for example, pulls no punches when it says that any employee "can be terminated at any time without reason." It avoids implied promises by referring to employees as "regular" or "full-time" rather than "permanent."[50] Whether the courts will continue to hand down decisions supporting the "right to a job" remains to be seen. But for now, an official disclaimer would seem to protect a company's right to fire a worker, even though it might be offensive to employees.

wrongful discharge Firing an employee with inadequate advance notice or explanation

Retiring Workers

The U.S. population is aging rapidly. For the business community, an aging population presents two challenges. The first is to give job opportunities to people who are willing and able to work but who happen to be past the traditional retirement age. Many older citizens are horrified by the prospect of future inflation eating up fixed retirement incomes. Others simply prefer work over the alternatives available to them. The second challenge is to encourage some older workers to retire early. As the baby-boom generation ages, it will be pushing hard for higher-level jobs held by older executives.

Mandatory Retirement

mandatory retirement Required dismissal of an employee who reaches a certain age

For several decades now, our society has accepted the idea of a widespread, arbitrary cutoff point for the normal work life. Many companies and industries had **mandatory retirement** policies that made it necessary for people to quit working as soon as they turned a certain age. The Federal Age Discrimination Act, passed in 1967, made it illegal to discriminate against anyone between the ages of 40 and 65. Despite the law, some workers have involuntarily been retired. They are beginning to seek relief in the courts, and they are winning. For example, Chase Manhattan Bank was ordered to pay more than half a million dollars in back pay and fringe benefits to three former executives. The employees, who were between the ages of 49 and 55 when they were forced to retire, had been replaced by younger, lower-paid employees.[51] More than 13,000 such cases are being filed with the EEOC each year.

In 1986 Congress amended the Age Discrimination in Employment Act to prohibit mandatory retirement for most workers. As a corollary, employers are also prohibited from stopping benefit contributions or accruals because of age. Under federal law, those who complain of age discrimination are also granted the right to a jury trial. This right means that many more cases will probably be decided in the workers' favor; juries are usually sympathetic to the problems of workers who have been asked to go because they are "too old." As a result nine out of ten age discrimination cases are settled out of court.[52]

Early Retirement

worker buyout Distribution of financial incentives to workers who voluntarily depart, usually undertaken in order to shrink the payroll

One method a company may use to trim its work force is simply to offer its employees (often those nearing retirement) financial incentives to resign, such as enhanced retirement benefits or one-time cash payments. Inducing workers to depart by offering them financial incentives is known as a **worker buyout.** Although this method is more expensive than firing or laying off workers, it has several advantages. The morale of the remaining workers is preserved, because they feel less threatened about their own security. Also, because those who participate in the buyout are usually senior staff members, younger employees see their chances for promotion rise.

Nevertheless, inducement for early retirement can create substantial long-term financial burdens for a company. It is interesting to note that despite the law forbidding mandatory retirement, early retirements are on the rise. One survey found that two-thirds of U.S. workers now retire before age 65.[53] It seems that many people who are eligible for early retirement often take advantage of it in order to pursue new interests or to start a new business.

SUMMARY OF LEARNING OBJECTIVES

1 State the six main functions of human resource departments.

Human resource departments engage in planning, recruiting and selecting new employees, training and developing employees, appraising employee performance, compensating employees, and accommodating changes in employment status.

2 Identify six stages in the hiring process.

The stages in the hiring process include soliciting applicants, collecting application forms or résumés, interviewing, administering employment tests (optional), conducting reference checks, evaluating candidates, and selecting one candidate for the job.

3 List at least three types of training programs.

One type of training program is orientation, which helps new employees become acclimated to the new environment. Two other types are job-skills training and basic-skills training.

4 Identify two general ways of compensating workers.

Employees are compensated through cash payments and through benefits and services.

5 Describe the two possible components of employee pay.

Wages (for hourly workers) and salaries (for nonhourly workers) are the most typical component of employee pay. Some employees also receive incentive payments (bonuses, commissions, profit sharing, and goal sharing), which are cash payments tied to employee or company performance in order to encourage productivity and accountability.

6 Explain at least four standard employee benefits and services.

Insurance plans, including unemployment benefits, are the most popular type of benefit; they help protect workers who lose their income through illness or changing economic conditions, and they provide for survivors if a worker dies. Retirement benefits, including Social Security, are also popular as a means of guaranteeing working people a comfortable old age. Employee stock-ownership plans, in which employees receive shares of the company's stock, give workers a say in its management. Family-benefit programs include maternity/paternity leave, child-care assistance, and elder-care assistance. Flexible benefit plans give employees the unique combination of benefits that suit their needs. Health and safety programs, including fitness and wellness programs, help keep employees at peak productivity.

7 Describe three ways an employee's status may change.

An employee's status may change through promotion to a higher-level position or reassignment to a similar or lower-level position; through termination (removal from the company's payroll); or through retirement at the end of the employee's work life.

8 Distinguish between the two reasons that employment may be terminated.

Employment may be terminated through layoffs or firings. Layoffs occur because the company is restructuring, has changed management or ownership, or is in distress, and they may be temporary. Firings, however, are permanent removals of employees because of their inadequacy.

Meeting a Business Challenge at Johnson & Johnson

James E. Burke's drive to move Johnson & Johnson into new high-tech markets succeeded. Relinquishing its position as the world's largest baby-products producer, the company entered such grown-up businesses as painkillers, surgical sutures, contraceptives, and feminine-hygiene products. With this new strategy, Burke quadrupled sales in 12 years.

One reason for J&J's success is the attention Burke gave to effective human resource management, which resulted in a satisfied and highly productive work force. Burke boosted productivity by sponsoring several initiatives that helped employees meet their dual responsibilities to family and job. The company opened an on-site child-care center at its corporate headquarters in New Brunswick, New Jersey, and a second center at its nearby Somerset office. Child-care costs at these centers are limited to 10 percent of an employee's disposable income. Another component of J&J's work/family initiative is a liberal policy on family-care leave. Employ-

James E. Burke, former chairman and CEO of Johnson & Johnson.

ees may take family-care leave of up to one year after the arrival of a newborn or adopted child and may arrange a flexible work schedule to attend an ailing family member.

To ensure the success of these initiatives, J&J's human resource executives sent the company's managers to a training program to sensitize them to work and family issues. Moreover, human resource managers underscored the company's commitment to family care by adding a new sentence to the company credo: "We must be mindful of ways to help our employees with their family responsibilities." This commitment to helping employees become better family members boosted productivity by reducing absenteeism, tardiness, and stress. In addition, the company's work/family initiative helped attract and keep qualified employees in a tightening labor market.

Burke increased productivity further by establishing a wellness program, Live for Life, which emphasizes steps employees can take to maintain and improve their health. The program sets four straightforward goals for employees: they should quit smoking, eat more fruit and fewer fatty foods, exercise regularly, and buckle their seatbelts. At J&J headquarters, employees work out in a first-floor gym, select "healthy heart" foods in the cafeteria, and check their weight in rest rooms. Live for Life programs are promoted by signs in the hallways and by brochures sent to employees, and participants win prizes for meeting their goals. Over 35 J&J locations have fitness centers and wellness programs.

The results are impressive. Smoking among employees has been reduced to less than 20 percent, a decline of more than one-third. Live for Life costs J&J $200 a year for each employee, but lower absenteeism and decreasing health costs have saved $378 per employee. For example, employees who participate in Live for Life have hospitalization costs that are 40 percent lower than those of employees who don't participate.

Live for Life was so successful that J&J formed a new company to market it: Johnson & Johnson Health Management. In addition to the Live for Life program, the new company assists with fitness center design and management, and it orchestrates health-promotion campaigns in such areas as smoking cessation, nutrition, and stress management. Live for Life is available at 60 leading corporations and medical centers that together employ more than 850,000 people.

Your Mission: Ralph S. Larsen, Johnson & Johnson's new chairman and CEO, is determined to reduce costs while improving quality. He sold the company's mail-order toy business because its sales were mediocre, and he consolidated the Baby, Health Care, and Dental Care companies into a single operating unit, eliminating 300 jobs in the process.

As vice president for human resources, your mission is to create employee programs that reflect Larsen's vision of a leaner, more streamlined Johnson & Johnson by maintaining the loyalty, well-being, and productivity of employees. How would you handle the following situations?

1. Larsen's biggest challenge is revitalizing J&J's consumer goods operations in the United States. To boost sales, J&J introduced a series of new products and line extensions, including No More Tears Baby Sunblock, Tylenol Cold Night Time, Tylenol Chewables, Sesame Street Adhesive Bandages, and Johnson's Creamy Baby Oil. Because it is the consumer products sales team that will ultimately place these items on supermarket shelves, Larsen has asked you to use human resource methods to increase the effectiveness of the sales force. You devise a list of four steps that you should take. Which should you implement first?

a. Johnson & Johnson currently offers double commissions to sales representatives who exceed their sales projections. Energize the sales force by offering triple commissions to top producers.

b. Conduct a job analysis of the sales department to ensure that the various components needed for a well-coordinated, effective sales effort are in place.

c. Have all members of the sales team participate in an intensive one-week training program to refamiliarize them with J&J products and to boost their assertiveness.

d. Review the sales force's employee performance appraisals and conduct new appraisals if necessary. Weed out weak employees and promote those who have demonstrated their ability to sell.

2. In the two years since they were introduced, Johnson & Johnson's Acuvue disposable contact lenses have become the leading soft contact lens in the United States for new patients and for those switching from other lenses. So successful are they that Johnson & Johnson Vision Products is going to double the size of its facility in Jacksonville, Florida.

B. W. Walsh, president of Johnson & Johnson Vision Products, asks you for advice on evaluating applicants for new manufacturing positions. Walsh is looking for employees with a high degree of manual dexterity who have experience working on an assembly line. He gives you a list of the four selection methods he intends to use, but he is uncertain about weighting

them. Walsh asks you to advise him about which method should be given highest priority in the decision-making process.

a. Job applications
b. Interviews
c. Reference checks
d. Performance tests

3. Acuvue lenses emerge from the assembly line in a soft, wet state. They must be produced in a sterile environment in order to protect the customer from infection. Reports that some assembly-line employees abuse drugs and alcohol have raised concerns that they might inadvertently contaminate the work area, jeopardizing the health of customers and undermining the reputation of the Acuvue brand. Walsh wants to institute drug testing and asks you for suggestions about how tests might be administered. What do you recommend?

a. Test only those employees who are suspected of substance abuse.

b. You sympathize with people who resent having to take a drug test. Test only those assembly-line employees whose carelessness could harm the customer.

c. The only fair way to administer a drug test is to test everyone at Johnson & Johnson Vision Products. You suggest that Walsh set an example and volunteer to take the first test.

d. Whatever the risk, you find drug testing offensive. You recommend that Walsh abandon the idea.

4. An important priority for Larsen is cutting costs. He asks you to review the Live for Life program and the Johnson & Johnson work/family initiative to determine whether there are any areas where savings can be realized. You draw up a preliminary list of suggestions. After reviewing them, you forward one to Larsen's office. Which one do you choose?

a. Statistics show that the voluntary Live for Life program saves J&J $178 net for each person enrolled. Make the program compulsory for every employee and realize even greater savings.

b. Raise the percentage that employees pay for child care to 25 percent of their disposable income.

c. During the hiring process, ask female candidates whether they intend to have children. Give preference to those who have decided to postpone childbirth; their medical expenses and absentee rate will be lower than those who don't.
d. Offer employees on family-care leave the option of working at least 15 hours a week. Install phone lines and computer terminals so that they can work at home on a flexible schedule.[54]

KEY TERMS

bonus (277)
commissions (277)
compensation (275)
downsize (285)
employee assistance programs (283)
employee stock-ownership plan (281)
fringe benefits (278)
goal sharing (277)
human resource management (262)
incentives (276)
job analysis (265)

job description (266)
job specification (266)
knowledge-based pay (277)
mandatory retirement (288)
orientation (272)
outplacement (286)
pay for performance (277)
pension plans (280)
performance appraisal (274)
perks (278)
profit sharing (277)

recruiters (266)
restructuring (285)
résumé (267)
salaries (276)
seniority (286)
termination (285)
unemployment insurance (279)
wages (276)
worker buyout (288)
wrongful discharge (287)

REVIEW QUESTIONS

1. What are the major forecasting challenges for human resource managers?

2. What is the purpose of conducting job analysis? What are some of the techniques used for gathering information?

3. What are the major legal pitfalls in the hiring process?

4. What methods are companies using to deal with the lack of basic skills in the employee pool?

5. What is the purpose of using incentive programs as part of the compensation package?

6. Why are more companies offering family benefits and flexible benefits?

7. What effect has downsizing had on promotion and reassignment of workers? On termination procedures?

8. What are some of the problems facing workers who are nearing retirement?

A CASE FOR CRITICAL THINKING

A Furnace Named Amanda

John Scheel watches proudly as orange molten iron is heated to precisely 3,700 degrees and rushes down a brick-lined path to the waiting torpedo tank car. "A cast in a blast furnace is like a religious experience," says Scheel, senior blast-furnace engineer for Armco. It is Scheel who must ensure that the raw materials—iron ore, limestone, and coke—combine at exactly the right temperature to be converted into pig iron, the main ingredient of steel. And it is because of

Scheel that, since 1982, Armco's fuel costs have dropped 17 percent and the production cost of a ton of iron has decreased more than 25 percent. For Armco, Scheel is a pivotal worker.

Symbolized by silicon chips and robots, manufacturing is becoming more and more impersonal, but there are still a few people whose unique skills mean success for their employers—even though their number is dwindling as technology advances. Pivotal personnel are found on factory

floors rather than in boardrooms, and their knowledge comes more often from experience than from education. Given that CEOs and management teams are needed for critical decisions, "once those decisions are made, the crucial part of accomplishing a project comes with the pivotal jobs," says Tsun-yan Hsieh, who studied the role of pivotal jobs for the management-consulting firm of McKinsey & Company.

In addition to his engineering degree, Scheel has an MBA in finance and international business, and he writes poetry—not exactly your basic steel man. Nevertheless, he is single-mindedly devoted to Armco's blast furnace, which is named Amanda. He keeps photographs of Amanda both in his apartment and in the local restaurant he owns a piece of. Already working 12-hour days, Scheel is often found at the furnace late at night (even at two o'clock in the morning on Christmas). "The process runs you, you don't run the process," says Scheel. But he also says his work is like "being an orchestra conductor." Not only has he created a computer system to monitor the makeup of the

iron Amanda produces, but he has devised a computer warning system that can detect potential problems before any damage can be done, and he has developed a process for accurately regulating the amount of coal slurry that goes into Amanda (which Armco has patented and now sells to other steelmakers). In addition, he tracks late coal shipments by phone, he bangs jammed ore dumpers with a shovel, and he convinces fellow workers to accept new technology.

"With his background and ability, John could be working in several places other than a steel mill," says Glenn D. Easterling, one of Scheel's supervisors. But lucky for Armco,

John Scheel is filling a pivotal role working with a furnace named Amanda.[55]

1. Do you think it will be easy for present employers to replace their pivotal workers? Will employers of the future be able to find pivotal workers in the first place? Explain.

2. How important do you think salary and bonuses are to such specially skilled workers as John Scheel?

3. Do you suppose that low visibility is a problem for pivotal workers such as Scheel? Are such workers likely to resent the high-profile executives in the boardroom?

BUILDING YOUR COMMUNICATION SKILLS

Use job analysis to evaluate the specific requirements of a career you aspire to. Develop a job description and a job specification. With the members of your class, generate a list

of items that should be included in the job analysis. To obtain information about the career you have chosen, you might interview a person working in that field, interview a per-

sonnel director with a company who employs people in that field, or use reference books pertaining to that career.

KEEPING CURRENT USING *THE WALL STREET JOURNAL*

Locate one or more articles in *The Wall Street Journal* that illustrate how a company or industry is adapting to changes in its work force. (Examples include job-enrichment and job-redesign programs, retraining, literacy or basic-skills training, flextime, and benefits aimed at working parents.)

1. What employee needs or changes in the work force is the company (or industry) adapting to?

2. Was the company (industry) forced to change for some financial or legal reason, or did it move voluntarily to meet the need or adapt to the change? Why?

3. What other changes in the work force or employee needs do you think this company or industry is likely to face in the next few years? What are your reasons for making this prediction?

CHAPTER *11*

LEARNING OBJECTIVES
After studying this chapter, you will be able to

1 Identify two main types of labor unions.

2 Outline the organizational structure of unions.

3 Identify the two main steps unions take to become the bargaining agent for a group of workers.

4 Describe the four main stages in collective bargaining.

5 Identify four options that unions have if negotiations with management break down.

6 Identify five options that management has if negotiations with the union break down.

7 List five general issues that may be addressed in a labor contract.

8 Describe four major practices that management and unions are using to respond to changes in the structure of the economy.

Union-Management Relations

Facing a Business Challenge at Saturn

NEGOTIATING A RADICALLY NEW CONTRACT

G eneral Motors's Richard LeFauve and United Auto Workers's Donald Ephlin had been adversaries for years. LeFauve represented management (white collars, planners, order-givers) and Ephlin represented labor (blue collars, strong backs, order-takers) as they faced one another from opposite sides of the negotiating table. But when LeFauve became president of Saturn, GM's newest nameplate, both men saw that a drastic change was necessary in the relationship between management and labor. Facing aggressive Japanese automakers, both men believed that management *and* labor had a lot to lose unless an altogether new relationship could be forged.

LeFauve saw GM facing further erosion of its business. Honda, Toyota, and Nissan had carved their way into the U.S. market, reducing GM's share to about 35 percent. Customers believed that buying GM meant they were getting less car for their money, and GM was finding it increasingly difficult to compete on the cost issue alone. For one thing, Japanese companies could build a car in about 100 hours, including suppliers' labor. General Motors took twice as long, and LeFauve could point his finger directly at archaic union work rules as one major cause of GM's low productivity. At some plants, union jobs were divided into more than 100 classifications, compartmentalizing assembly workers to such a degree that an entire line might be shut down while a lone electrician rewired a faulty outlet. Workers' seniority rights, job security, and wage increases continued to drag out successive contract negotiations as GM tried in vain to streamline production rules. LeFauve believed that without changes, the union would drain the prosperity of the company in favor of its own interests.

Yet Ephlin saw union members facing more than the possibility of losing market share; employees were concerned with personal security: More than 230,000 union jobs had already disappeared because of the onslaught of foreign cars, and at least 83,000 more were projected to vanish as Japanese manufacturers transferred more of their production to U.S. nonunion factories. But beyond job security lay a much deeper issue: pride. Auto plants in the United States were averaging 82 defects for every 100 cars, whereas plants in Japan averaged only 65. Union autoworkers were increasingly seen as poor craftsmen turning out shoddy products, and they blamed the problem on managers who were more interested in production schedules and quotas than in raising worker proficiency. Ephlin could point to a telling statistic as proof: Japanese autoworkers received an average of 370 hours of job training, whereas their U.S. counterparts received somewhere around 46 hours of training. Ephlin realized that the skills and security of his union members would continue to falter unless something was done to reverse the trends.

Both LeFauve and Ephlin were facing some of the most crucial questions in their long careers, and a lot was riding on the answers they would come up with. How could management convince labor to streamline production rules for the good of the company? How could labor convince management to look beyond purely financial goals? But the most basic question loomed largest: Was it possible to negotiate a completely new agreement between management and labor so that they would be teammates instead of adversaries?[1]

▶ LABOR ORGANIZATIONS IN THE U.S. ECONOMY

As Saturn's Richard LeFauve and the UAW's Donald Ephlin are well aware, certain unavoidable differences of interest exist between workers and the employers who pay them. On the one hand, owners and managers of businesses have a right to use their resources as they see fit in order to increase productivity and profits. On the other hand, workers feel that they should have job security, safe and comfortable working conditions, and rewards commensurate with their contributions to the organization. In the best of times and in the most enlightened companies, these two sets of needs can often be met simultaneously. But in uncertain times, when the economy slows down and competition speeds up, the desires of workers and management tend to conflict. Because of this potential for conflict, workers form **labor unions,** organizations that seek to protect workers' interests when they conflict with those of management.

labor unions Organizations of workers formed to protect and advance their members' interests

One thing workers have in common with management is that both have something to sell: management a product and workers their own labor, the services they can perform for the employer. Naturally, both want to get the best possible price. And just as the price that a company charges for a product is affected by the forces of supply and demand, so is the price that workers charge for their services. A labor union alters the supply-and-demand equation by representing most or all of the workers—the supply of labor—that the company needs. In that sense, a labor union is monopolistic. By using their combined bargaining strength, workers can put more pressure on management than they could as individuals. An individual worker can easily be replaced, but the whole group cannot.

A History of Unions

In 1792 a group of shoemakers held a meeting in Philadelphia to discuss matters of common interest. The result of their modest assembly was the formation of the first known union in the United States. During the next several decades, other unions appeared. They were chiefly local **craft unions,** made up of skilled artisans belonging to a single profession or craft and concerned only with trade-related matters.

craft unions *Unions made up of skilled artisans belonging to a single profession or practicing a single craft*

In the 1840s and 1850s, as improved transportation cut shipping costs, created a national market, and made workers more mobile, local craft unions banded together into national craft unions. And in 1869, several national craft unions joined forces as the Knights of Labor. Over the next two decades, membership in this national union reached 700,000. However, several member unions became dissatisfied with the leadership's emphasis on moral betterment instead of improvements in wages and working conditions. Furthermore, the 1886 Haymarket Riot—during which a bomb exploded among Chicago police trying to break up a labor rally—turned public opinion against the labor movement, of which the Knights were the most visible symbol. By 1890 control of the union movement had passed to a rival group, the American Federation of Labor (AFL), founded in 1886. The AFL dominated the labor movement for the next 40 years.

During the 1930s, labor unions expanded their membership enormously, especially among unskilled workers. They benefited greatly from legislation passed during President Franklin D. Roosevelt's four terms in office. (The most significant laws relating to unions, many dating from this era, are described in Exhibit 11.1.) They also benefited from the work of an unofficial Committee for Industrial Organization, which was set up within the AFL in 1935. Its goal was to organize **industrial unions** representing both skilled and unskilled workers from all phases of a particular industry.

industrial unions *Unions representing both skilled and unskilled workers from all phases of a particular industry*

The committee organized the auto and steel industries, boosting AFL membership to over 4 million. But three years later, the AFL formally expelled the committee. The craft unionists who controlled the AFL viewed the industrial unions as a threat. The committee thus became a fully independent federation of industrial unions and changed its name to the Congress of Industrial Organizations (CIO).

During World War II, full employment helped unions grow even more. In exchange for a no-strike pledge, unions were able to win many concessions from management. After the war, labor's demands for wage increases erupted into a series of severe strikes. In 1947 pro-industry legislators in Washington responded by enacting legislation that restricted some of the practices used by labor to force its demands on industry, such as making union membership a condition of employment.

From 1955, when the AFL and the CIO merged their 16 million members, union growth began to level off. In the late 1950s, disclosures of corruption and links to organized crime further tarnished labor's image, and to curb abuses, Congress imposed stiff new regulations on unions' internal affairs in 1959. Since then, union membership has declined for a number of reasons, but up through the late 1970s, unions continued to enjoy considerable clout in the U.S. economy.

White Consolidated Industries makes Tappan ranges and other kitchen appliances. When hundreds of its production and maintenance workers said they wanted to become union members, some 50 organizers from USWA visited 900 potential members in one weekend—describing the union and asking workers to sign union authorization cards. Known as an organizing "blitz," this tactic is designed to build quick organizing momentum.

The Labor Movement Today

Labor leaders today are rethinking their methods. That adjustment is a response to some distressing trends in union participation. Exhibit 11.2 shows how badly union strength has eroded, particularly in the past decade. A tarnished image, a leadership out of touch with the concerns of a changing work force, a trend

EXHIBIT 11.1 ▶ **Key Legislation Relating to Unions**

Most major labor legislation was enacted in the 1930s and 1940s.

LEGISLATION	PROVISIONS
Norris–La Guardia Act of 1932	Limits companies' ability to obtain injunctions against union strikes, picketing, membership drives, and other activities
National Labor Relations Act of 1935 (Wagner Act)	Prohibits employers from interfering with employees' right to form, join, or assist labor organizations; from interfering with labor organizations by dominating them or by making financial contributions to them; from discouraging membership in labor organizations by discriminating against members in employment or by requiring promises not to join union as condition of employment; from refusing to bargain collectively with the labor organization chosen by employees to represent them; from discharging employees because they have testified or filed charges against employer under act
Taft-Hartley Labor Act of 1947	Amends Wagner Act to restrict unions (declares closed shop illegal, requires 60-day notice before strike or lockout, empowers federal government to issue injunctions to prevent strikes that would endanger national interest); declares jurisdictional strikes (in disputes between unions), featherbedding, refusal to bargain in good faith, and secondary boycotts illegal; requires union officers to certify that they are not Communists; requires unions to submit financial reports to secretary of labor; allows unions to sue employers for contract violations; permits employers to petition National Labor Relations Board for elections under certain circumstances
Landrum-Griffin Act of 1959	Aims to control union corruption by penalizing bribery of union officials by employers; closing loopholes in law forbidding secondary boycotts; prohibiting hot-cargo clauses in employment contracts, which give unions right not to handle goods of company whose employees are on strike; requiring all unions to file constitutions and bylaws with secretary of labor; requiring all unions to publish financial records open to inspection by members; making union officials more personally responsible for unions' financial affairs, making embezzlement of union funds a federal offense, and forbidding union loans of more than $2,000 to officers; denying convicted felons right to hold union office for five years following release from prison; giving every member of union equal rights to vote on issues, attend meetings, and speak freely; forbidding unions from raising dues unless majority of members vote for increase by secret ballot; giving union members right to sue unions; requiring that members be formally charged and given fair hearing before being fired, expelled, or punished in any way by union

toward more and more deregulation, and an unsympathetic administration—these are some of the causes for the dramatic decrease in union membership in the last decade. Unions now represent only 16 percent of nonfarm workers in the United States, down from a peak of over 35.5 percent in 1945.

Another reason for the overall decline is a massive shift in U.S. industry. Older, less efficient industries are falling victim to more efficient, lower-cost foreign competitors. During the last decade a fifth of large unionized companies have gone bankrupt, unable to compete against companies with lower wage expenditures.[2] Furthermore, even though heavy industry is on the decline, high-tech and service industries are on the rise. Some of these new industries are much harder to unionize than the blue-collar "smokestack" industries, where the unions have a long tradition. In fact, the labor movement worldwide appears to be in an irreversible decline. English trade unions, for example, lost a quarter of their members in the last decade. Japan's most powerful union split in half following its failure to prevent the privatization of the Japanese National Rail-

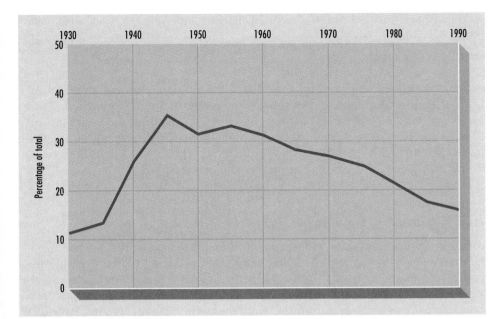

EXHIBIT 11.2

Union Membership Among Nonagricultural Workers
The influence of labor unions has declined since they first gained strength in the 1930s and peaked in the 1940s and 1950s. By 2000, membership is expected to be 7 percent.

way. Union membership and power are also declining in Italy, France, and Germany.[3]

But unions are by no means giving up the fight. Instead, they are seeking members among professionals, white-collar workers, women, and youth—groups that they have traditionally ignored but that are rising to prominence as the economy shifts from heavy industry to services. Union membership has increased in a few of these areas, despite the general decrease in the number of unionized workers. One of the major growth areas has been among government employees. Whereas the proportion of nonfarm private-sector workers in unions is only 12 percent, the percentage of unionized public employees has grown to roughly 37 percent in the past decade.[4]

Another example of union commitment to a new era is the 1991 election of Ronald Carey as president of the International Brotherhood of Teamsters. The largest private-sector union in the United States, the Teamsters union has been noted as the most mob influenced (three of its five presidents were sentenced to prison). But Carey has vowed to clean house, to rid his union of the Mafia-controlled "Old Guard," and to stop the erosion of union wages by ending union wages by ending union concessions to employers.[5]

Why Workers Join

Polls have found that most of today's workers believe that unions stifle individual initiative and are not necessary to ensure fair treatment from employers; about half believe that unions make it harder for companies to stay in business.[6] The companies that have most successfully resisted unionization seem to have adopted participative management styles and an enhanced sense of responsibility toward employees. Nevertheless, many employees in today's work force still see unionization as a positive move. These workers are likely to express a preference for unionizing if the following conditions are present:

▶ They are deeply dissatisfied with their current job and employment conditions.

▶ They believe that unionization can be helpful in improving those job conditions.

▶ They are willing to overlook the generally negative stereotype of unions held by the population as a whole.[7]

And just who are the workers most likely to express an interest in unionization? Recent studies have shown them to be primarily women, minorities, and low-wage workers.[8] At Farris Fashions in Brinkley, Arkansas, for example, employees receive relatively low pay and minimal benefits. So, when the Amalgamated Clothing and Textile Workers Union approached them about unionizing, 70 percent signed the cards required to hold an election.[9]

How Unions Are Structured

national union Nationwide organization representing workers in a particular craft or industry

locals Relatively small union groups, usually part of a national union or a labor federation, composed of those who work in a single facility or in a certain geographic area

A **national union** is a nationwide organization representing workers in a particular craft or industry; examples include Ephlin's United Auto Workers of America (which negotiated a revolutionary contract with GM's Saturn), the United Steelworkers, and the Service Employees International Union. The national union is typically composed of several **locals,** or local unions, each representing workers in a specific geographic area or facility. A national union is responsible for such activities as organizing new areas or industries, negotiating industrywide contracts, assisting locals with negotiations, administering benefits, lobbying Congress, and lending assistance in the event of a strike. In return, local unions send representatives to the national delegate convention, submit negotiated contracts to the national union for approval, and provide financial support in the form of dues. They have the power to negotiate with individual companies and to undertake their own membership activities.

labor federations Umbrella organizations of national unions and unaffiliated local unions that undertake large-scale activities on behalf of their members and that resolve conflicts between unions

The AFL-CIO is a **labor federation** consisting of a variety of national unions and of local unions that are not associated with any other national union. The AFL-CIO's two primary roles are to promote the political objectives of the labor movement and to provide assistance to member unions in their collective-bargaining efforts.[10] In addition, the AFL-CIO provides research and technical support to members and will arbitrate disputes between competing unions.

shop steward Union member and worker who is elected to represent other union members and who attempts to resolve employee grievances with management

business agent Full-time union staffer who negotiates with management and attempts to resolve grievances brought up by union members

Each local union is a hierarchy with a broad base of "rank and file" members, the workers the union represents. These members elect a president. Each department or facility also has or elects a **shop steward,** who works in the facility as a regular employee and serves as a go-between with supervisors when a problem arises. In large locals and in locals that represent workers at several locations, an elected full-time **business agent** visits the various work sites and handles member problems.

National unions and federations have a full complement of officers and often a sizable staff of experts. The organizers who go out seeking to set up new locals are an essential element at this level. Delegates elected by the locals attend regularly scheduled national conventions to elect the officers and approve changes to the umbrella organization's constitution.

How Unions Organize

For unions seeking to survive the 1990s, organizing is an ongoing activity (see Exhibit 11.3). The main goal is to find a group of dissatisfied employees and convince them that unionization is the solution to their problems. Sometimes

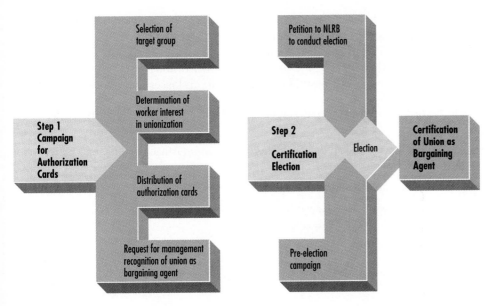

EXHIBIT 11.3

The Union-Organizing Process

This diagram summarizes the steps a labor union takes when organizing a group of workers and becoming certified to represent them in negotiations with management.

the employees must also be convinced that they are dissatisfied. Union organizers conduct surveys by calling the employees of a company and asking such questions as "Have you ever been treated unfairly by your supervisor?" Employees who seem ripe for unionization are sent information about the union along with **authorization cards,** which designate the union as their bargaining agent. If 30 percent or more of the employees in the group sign the union's authorization cards, the union may ask management to recognize it. Usually, however, unions do not seek to become the group's bargaining agent unless a majority of the employees sign.

Management is generally unwilling to recognize the union at this stage, so the union asks the National Labor Relations Board (NLRB) to supervise a **certification** election. If a majority of the affected workers choose to make the union their bargaining agent, the union becomes certified. If not, that union and all other unions have to wait a year before trying again.

Why Unions Are Challenged or Removed

In recent years companies have become much more aggressive about challenging unionization. Their primary motivation is to avoid the associated costs and labor-management conflicts that often occur in unionized industries. To keep workers satisfied and unions out, management offers higher wages and pleasant working conditions. If it becomes aware that a union is seeking a certification election, management may mount an active campaign to point up the disadvantages of unionization. A company is not allowed, however, to make specific threats or promises about how it will respond to the outcome of the election, and it is not allowed to change general wages or working conditions until the election has been concluded.

Even though a union wins a certification election, there's no guarantee that it will be able to represent a particular group of employees forever. Sometimes employees become dissatisfied with their union and no longer wish to be represented by it. When this happens, the union members can take a **decertification**

authorization cards Sign-up cards designating a union as the signer's preferred bargaining agent

certification Process by which a union is officially recognized by the National Labor Relations Board as the bargaining agent for a group of workers

decertification Process workers use to take away a union's right to represent them

vote. If a majority votes for decertification, the union is removed as bargaining agent. Although still infrequent, decertification elections have increased since the mid-1970s, accounting for 20 percent of all representation elections (as opposed to half that in 1977). During the 1980s, unions lost 75 percent of all decertification elections. Possible reasons for union losses include the following:

▶ The increase in foreign competition has forced management to emphasize productivity.

▶ The unions have failed to deliver higher wages, more fringe benefits, and better job security.

▶ The National Labor Relations Board has shown more concern for employee interests.

▶ The nature of work has changed; workers are better educated, and the percentage of women and part-timers has increased.

▶ Nonunion industries have grown.

▶ The relationship between employer and employees has improved.[11]

BEHIND THE SCENES

The Challenge of Organizing Today's Work Force

It's not easy being a union organizer these days—not that it ever was. But with today's diverse work force and declining interest in union membership, union organizers have to be even more creative when it comes to recruiting members. Some organizers work patiently behind the scenes to attract members over the long term. Others try to quickly rally support before management finds out what's going on.

The International Ladies Garment Workers Union (ILGWU), for example, uses the long-term approach to attract the more than 100,000 immigrants who work in garment shops in Los Angeles, El Paso, and New York City. Such workers speak little English, usually do not understand their legal rights, and are afraid to do anything that might jeopardize their jobs. So ILGWU organizers get involved with community groups where they can patiently counsel workers on their rights under immigration and labor law. They also teach the workers English as a second language. The union then offers "associate membership" with dues often as low as $1 a month. Eventually some of the associate members win formal union representation at their shops.

Organizers for the United Steelworkers, on the other hand, use a different tactic for reaching beyond their manufacturing base and attracting office workers. Of course, observers note that organizing office workers can be a tough transition for some of the "good old boys" used to dealing with disgruntled laborers in steel mills. And that's exactly why the Steelworkers hired Katie Gohn. One of the union's newest organizers, Gohn is a 41-year-old former secretary with a business degree. She'd never even set foot in a steel mill, but more important to Gohn's success was learning union organizing strategies. To accomplish that she spent four months at the AFL-CIO's Organizing Institute and served as apprentice on half a dozen organizing campaigns before going it alone. Unlike the ILGWU's long-term approach to new immigrant workers in the garment industry, Gohn pursues office workers with intense campaigns that last only a few days.

Gohn often puts in 14-hour days, eats in her room at the Holiday Inn, and surveys workers to find issues appealing to them. She calls on other women and on ethnic organizers to help her reach the diverse work force. During one year with the Steelworkers, Gohn spent only six weeks at home, and on some campaigns she's gone without sleep for three days at a time. Even so, her 17-year-old daughter and her husband (who's a member of the Teamsters) support her work as an organizer. Winning over today's work force may not be easy, but union organizers are still convinced the challenge is worthwhile.

▶ THE COLLECTIVE-BARGAINING PROCESS

As long as a union has been certified as the bargaining agent for a group of workers, its main job is to negotiate employment contracts with management in a process known as **collective bargaining.** Together, union and management negotiators forge the human resource policies that will apply to the unionized workers—and other workers covered by the contract—for a certain length of time.

collective bargaining Process used by unions and management to negotiate work contracts

Most labor contracts are a compromise between the desires of union members and of management. The union tries to guess how far management can afford to go, and management tries to guess at what point the union will call off negotiations and vote for a strike. Because neither side really wants a strike, it is in the best interests of both to bargain to a reasonable compromise. Exhibit 11.4 illustrates the process described here.

Preparing to Meet

Before meeting with management, the union negotiating team must thoroughly understand the key needs of its members. The management side, meanwhile, tries to anticipate the union's demands and calculates the point at which labor's proposals are likely to cost the company more than a strike will.

These realistic estimates are often withheld from the other side at the beginning of negotiations, because each side is trying to outguess the other. Both may come to the bargaining table with extreme positions from which they can fall back during actual bargaining. Management may offer a contract with no wage gains, for instance, and the union may demand an outrageous pay increase. Neither expects these demands to be met.

Before or during negotiations, the union may flex its muscle by calling a strike vote. This vote does not signal an actual strike; it is called merely to show management that the members are solidly behind their negotiating team and to remind management that a strike is possible when the current contract expires.

Company representatives from Alcoa and Reynolds recently met in Cincinnati with union representatives from USWA local unions to negotiate contract terms.

Meeting and Reaching an Agreement

When the negotiating teams actually sit down together, management's chief negotiator may be the vice president in charge of industrial relations or someone hired from the outside. The union's chief negotiator may be the local's business agent or a negotiator supplied by national headquarters. Although insiders might

EXHIBIT 11.4

The Collective-Bargaining Process
Contract negotiations go through the four basic steps shown here.

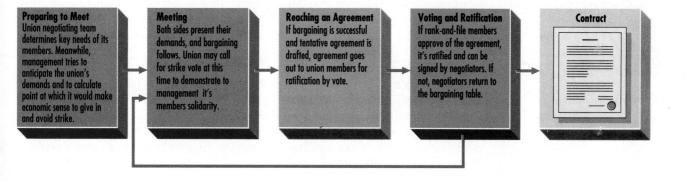

Preparing to Meet	Meeting	Reaching an Agreement	Voting and Ratification	Contract
Union negotiating team determines key needs of its members. Meanwhile, management tries to anticipate the union's demands and to calculate point at which it would make economic sense to give in and avoid strike.	Both sides present their demands, and bargaining follows. Union may call for strike vote at this time to demonstrate to management it's members solidarity.	If bargaining is successful and tentative agreement is drafted, agreement goes out to union members for ratification by vote.	If rank-and-file members approve of the agreement, it's ratified and can be signed by negotiators. If not, negotiators return to the bargaining table.	

be expected to know more about their side's needs, outsiders often do a better job in tough negotiations because their nerves are less likely to become frayed in grueling bargaining sessions. Near the end of negotiations, meetings may last 12 to 15 hours—and calm discussion may give way to personal insults. But labor and management negotiators generally try to remain calm and reasonable, especially in an era when cooperation between management and labor is necessary to combat foreign competition.

Once the negotiating teams have assembled, they state their opening positions, and each side discusses them point by point. Labor usually wants additions to the current contract. Management counters with the changes it wants, sometimes including givebacks. In a cooperative atmosphere, the real issues behind the demands gradually come to light. For example, management may begin by demanding the right to determine the sizes of work crews when all it really wants is smaller crews; the union is unlikely to give up total control over crew sizes, which is a key element of its power, but may agree to specific reductions. After many stages of bargaining, each party presents its package of terms. Any gaps between what labor wants and what management is willing to concede are then dealt with.

What if one side or the other simply refuses to discuss a point? If one side is unwilling even to talk, the other side can ask the NLRB to rule on whether the topic is one that can be omitted (a **permissive subject**)—such as health insurance for retired employees—or one that must be discussed (a **mandatory subject**)—such as wages, hours, pension benefits, and medical insurance.

If negotiations reach an impasse, outside help may be needed. The most common alternative is **mediation**—bringing in an impartial third party to study the situation and make recommendations for resolution of the differences. Mediators are generally well-respected community leaders whom both sides will listen to. However, the mediator can only offer suggestions—his or her solutions are not binding. For a binding decision to be made by a third party, the negotiators may resort to **arbitration**. In this case, union and management bring in an impartial arbitrator who listens to both sides and then makes a judgment by accepting one side's view. The arbitrator cannot compromise, but the decision reached by an arbitrator is binding to both parties.

permissive subject Topic that may be omitted from collective bargaining

mandatory subject Topic that must be discussed in collective bargaining

mediation Process for resolving a labor-contract dispute in which a neutral third party meets with both sides and attempts to steer them toward a solution

arbitration Process for resolving a labor-contract dispute in which an impartial third party studies the issues and makes a binding decision

Voting and Ratifying a Contract

The contract constructed and agreed to during the collective-bargaining sessions then goes to the union members for **ratification,** a vote by the majority to accept or reject the contract in its entirety. If the contract is rejected, the negotiators return to the bargaining table to try to bring the contract more in line with the workers' wishes.

Ratification procedures vary substantially among unions. Some unions use representatives of different groups of workers with special interests to help secure ratification from their constituents. When a companywide agreement is negotiated, many unions first send a proposed agreement to a council of lower-level union officers. However, union constitutions usually require that all workers covered by an agreement have an opportunity to approve contract settlements.[12]

ratification Process by which union members accept or reject a contract negotiated by union leaders

► WHEN NEGOTIATIONS BREAK DOWN

The vast majority of management–union negotiations are settled quickly, easily, and in a businesslike manner. This was not always the case. In the early days of unionism, conflicts often arose over such basic issues as money and working conditions, and both sides used pressure tactics that are now illegal. To defy management, the unions used threats of property damage, violence against workers siding with management, and sabotage of plants and equipment. To try to prevent the spread of unionism, management used the **yellow-dog contract,** an agreement that forced workers to promise not to join or remain in a union, and the **blacklist,** a secret list circulated among employers to keep union organizers from getting jobs. These tactics were outlawed in the 1930s. Today, both sides are able to draw on an arsenal of powerful options when negotiations or mediation procedures break down.

yellow-dog contract Agreement forcing workers to promise, as a condition of employment, not to join or remain in a union

blacklist Secret list circulated among employers to keep union organizers from getting jobs

Labor's Options

Strikes and picket lines are perhaps labor's best-known tactics, but a number of others are also used. In a **slowdown,** for example, workers continue to do their jobs, but at a snail's pace. However, employees who participate in slowdowns are not protected under the National Labor Relations Act and thus may be disciplined by management. Other tactics include boycotts and the judicious use of financial influence, political influence, and publicity.

slowdown Decreasing worker productivity to pressure management

Strikes and Picket Lines

The most powerful weapon that organized labor can use is the **strike,** a temporary work stoppage aimed at forcing management to accept union demands. The basic idea behind the strike is that, in the long run, it costs management more in lost earnings to resist union demands than to give in. An essential part of the strike is **picketing:** Union members positioned at entrances to company premises march back and forth with signs and leaflets, trying to persuade nonstriking workers to join them and to persuade customers and others to cease doing business with the company. In most instances, one union will honor another's picket line, so that even a relatively small union can shut down an employer. For example, striking department-store employees can close down a business if union truckers won't cross their picket line to make deliveries.

strike Temporary work stoppage aimed at forcing management to accept union demands

picketing Strike activity in which union members march before company entrances to persuade nonstriking workers to walk off the job and to persuade customers and others to cease doing business with the company

Since the early 1980s, the number of strikes in the United States has dropped dramatically. One reason for the decline in use of this tactic is that many companies are able to continue operating throughout a strike, either because they are highly automated or because union jobs can be performed by management and temporary hirees. Companies can usually hold out longer than the strikers can. And nonstriking workers seem to have little respect for picket lines, perhaps because of the uncertain outlook for jobs, perhaps because of the general decline in union popularity.

Boycotts

A less direct but equally powerful weapon is the **boycott,** in which union members and sympathizers refuse to buy or handle the product of a target company.

boycott Union activity in which members and sympathizers refuse to buy or handle the product of a target company

Millions of union members form an enormous bloc of purchasing power, which may be able to pressure management into making concessions. One of the best-known boycotts of the past couple of decades was the grape boycott organized by César Chávez in the early 1970s. In order to pressure California growers into accepting the United Farm Workers as the bargaining agent for previously unorganized farm laborers, he and his colleagues persuaded an estimated 17 million people in the United States to stop buying grapes. Eventually, the California legislature passed the country's first law guaranteeing farmworkers the right to hold union elections, and today the UFW has about 100,000 members.[13]

A 1988 Supreme Court decision paved the way for more aggressive boycotting activities by clarifying the legality of *secondary boycotts,* or boycotts of companies that do business with the targeted union employer. Such boycotts are now legal if they do not involve coercive tactics or picketing. One of the first unions to take advantage of this ruling was the United Paper Workers International. Already embroiled in a year-long strike against International Paper, the union immediately began boycotts against two banks that finance International Paper.

FOCUS ON ETHICS

Should Workers Strike When the Public Welfare Is at Stake?

Striking workers often make the headlines, cause a ruckus, and sometimes even get what they want—or something close to it. But even though they create difficulties for management, most of the time they cause only minor inconveniences for the public in general. In some industries, however, a massive strike can have devastating effects on large segments of the population. Workers who must vote whether or not to strike face the dilemma of choosing between their own needs and the needs of thousands of innocent bystanders.

Consider, for example, the 6,000 Greyhound bus drivers who walked off the job in early 1990. Greyhound is the only nationwide bus company, and nearly 10,000 communities depend on it to meet their public transportation needs. In nearly half of those communities, the strike halted bus service altogether. Even though Greyhound eventually replaced most of the striking drivers, it could no longer afford to service many small communities where routes were marginally profitable. For people like Geneva Fisher, a 66-year-old widow who lives in Tipton, Missouri, the strike's effect was discouraging to say the least. Fisher doesn't drive and has always relied on Greyhound for frequent trips to visit her sister in Sedalia. Without Greyhound, she is forced to do most of her visiting by phone.

Railroad workers faced a dilemma similar to that of Greyhound drivers when they voted to strike in 1991. However, in an effort to minimize public anger over a strike, union leaders decided to refrain from striking rail-commuter operations. But even in the age of the space shuttle, U.S. industry is still highly dependent on the railroad's stodgier technology. A lengthy coast-to-coast rail strike would have stranded thousands of passengers, stopped the flow of one-third of U.S. goods, and idled as many as a half-million non-railroad workers.

This latest railroad strike didn't have a chance to inflict long-term damage. Eighteen hours after the strike began, Congress ordered the strikers back to work. Fortunately, the strike's effect on consumers was minimal; however, it did cost $1 billion in lost production and wages.

Perhaps the people who face the greatest dilemma when deciding whether or not to strike are hospital workers. Currently, fewer than 20 percent of the country's 3.6 million hospital workers belong to unions. But that percentage may soon increase. A recent Supreme Court ruling makes it much easier for labor unions to organize hospital employees, including doctors and clerical workers. So only time will tell whether hospital workers will ever have to face the dilemma of voting for a nationwide strike or taking care of their patients.

Members handed out leaflets in front of the banks, urging customers not to do business there. For International Paper employees, the ploy was ultimately unsuccessful.[14]

Financial and Political Influence

Many unions have huge financial assets, including the more than $500 billion in their members' pension funds, which they may use to exert influence. In the International Paper strike, for example, union organizers threatened to withdraw union funds from banks that shared directors with International Paper. They were also able to convince other unions, such as the American Federation of State, County and Municipal Employees, to make similar threats.[15] But the threats didn't work at International Paper—the strike ended with 2,300 union members being permanently replaced.

Unions may also exercise significant political power by endorsing candidates and (theoretically, at least) delivering the votes of union members. They often raise funds for candidates as well. For example, the Committee on Political Education (COPE), founded by the AFL-CIO in 1955, solicits funds from union members for distribution to candidates favorable to labor's positions. In 1987–1988, eight union political action committees each contributed more than $500,000 to candidates; the Teamsters PAC alone gave $5.5 million. The direct participation of union members in the electoral process may be even more effective. In 1988, more than a fifth of the delegates to the Democratic presidential nominating convention were union members.[16]

Publicity

One of the newer tactics that labor has used is the publicity attack, a concerted "corporate campaign" of news and promotion mounted not only against the target company but also against all companies affiliated with it. After J. P. Stevens had fought 20 years (both legally and illegally) to prevent any direct effort toward organizing its workers, the Amalgamated Clothing and Textile Workers Union unleashed ads, letters, phone calls, and news releases about the company's lenders, major stockholders, and outside board members. At long last, even though J. P. Stevens had become the number one anti-union employer in the United States (perpetuating illegal activities and demeaning behavior among its managers), the company relented under the pressure of the corporate campaign.[17]

Management's Options

Companies are not helpless when it comes to fighting unions. Management can resort to a number of legal methods to pressure unions when negotiations break down.

Strikebreakers and Management-Run Operations

When union members walk off their jobs, management can legally replace them with **strikebreakers,** people who cross the picket line to work. (Union members brand them as "scabs.") Management is even allowed to hire permanent replace-

Business Around the World

When Canadian government workers launched their first national strike in 1991, they slowed tax collection, snarled airports, disrupted grain exports, and jammed traffic. The workers want job security and higher pay, and the government wants to reduce its budget deficit—a common predicament worldwide.

strikebreakers People who cross a picket line to work

ments for strikers if necessary to keep a business operating. Greyhound Lines, for example, kept its nationwide bus system rolling by hiring 3,000 permanent replacements for the 6,000 unionized drivers who walked off the job in 1990. Other companies that took on permanent replacements in recent years include Colt Industries, Eastern Airlines, Continental Airlines, the *Chicago Tribune*, and the New York *Daily News*.[18] Organized labor has become increasingly angered by this practice and is waging an all-out battle in Congress to have it outlawed. But even if Congress approves pending legislation, a presidential veto is expected.

Another way for management to put pressure on unions when negotiations break down is to substitute white-collar and supervisory personnel for the striking workers. In some industries, management is able to hold out during strikes by depending on their computers. At AT&T, for example, the computer has shifted the ratio of workers to supervisors from 5:1 to 2:1 over the past 20 years, making it easier for supervisors to take over during a strike. But this type of victory comes at a price. During one strike at AT&T, more than 2,000 cases of vandalism were reported as workers took out their frustration on the new electronic "scabs."[19]

Lockouts

lockout Management activity in which union members are prevented from entering a business during a strike, to force union acceptance of management's last contract proposal

The United States Supreme Court has upheld the use of **lockouts,** in which management locks out union workers in order to pressure a union to accept a contract proposal. A lockout is legal only if union and management have come to an impasse in negotiations. During a lockout, the company may hire temporary replacements as long as it has no anti-union motivation and negotiations have been amicable.[20]

Greyhound strikers met at a one-year rally to protest "scabs" crossing picket lines to fill their jobs.

Although the lockout is rarely used in major industries today, some instances still occur. For example, during the Wheeling-Pittsburgh steel strike, state officials in Ohio identified the labor dispute as a lockout and approved unemployment-compensation payments to the idled workers. Pennsylvania authorities also agreed when the company canceled the last year of the labor contract as part of bankruptcy proceedings, effectively locking out workers.

Injunctions

An **injunction** is a court order directing someone to do something or to refrain from doing it. Management used this weapon without restriction in the early days of unionism, when companies typically sought injunctions to order striking workers back to work on the grounds that the strikers were interfering with business. Today, injunctions are legal only in certain cases. For example, the president of the United States has the right, under the Taft-Hartley Act, to obtain a temporary injunction to halt a strike deemed harmful to the national interest. When Jimmy Carter was president, he invoked the Taft-Hartley Act to get striking miners in the bituminous coal industry back to work, stating that coal production was in the national interest. However, coal workers disobeyed the court, so the judge lifted his order.

injunction Court order directing someone to do something or to refrain from doing it

Industry Pacts and Organizations

Some industries have copied the united-front strategy of the AFL-CIO by forging mutual-assistance pacts: They temporarily agree to abandon competition in order to assist a competitor singled out for a strike. Such agreements provide a form of strike insurance to help the company hold out against union demands. Certain industries have also formed national organizations such as the National Association of Manufacturers to counterbalance the powerful national unions. These organizations try to coordinate industrywide strategy and to keep wage and benefit levels even among companies. They also lobby for legislation to protect management against union demands.

▶ THE COLLECTIVE-BARGAINING AGREEMENT

Signing a collective-bargaining agreement (or contract) between union and management doesn't mark the end of negotiations. Rather, it lays the groundwork for discussions that will continue throughout the life of the contract to iron out unspecified details of the various contract issues.

Basic Contract Issues

As Saturn's LeFauve and the UAW's Ephlin know well, most contracts cover similar issues. Whether a union represents teachers, hospital workers, miners, or assembly workers, the issues of common concern are union security and management rights, compensation, job security, work rules, and worker safety and health.

closed shop Workplace in which union membership is a condition of employment

union shop Workplace in which the employer may hire new people at will but only for a probationary period, after which they must join the union

agency shop Workplace requiring nonunion workers who are covered by agreements negotiated by the union to pay service fees to that union

open shop Workplace in which nonunion workers pay no dues

right-to-work laws Laws giving employees the explicit right to keep a job without joining a union

EXHIBIT 11.5

Right-to-Work States
Twenty-one states have laws that give workers the right to get a job without joining a union.

Union Security and Management Rights

Once a union has been established, the contracts it negotiates begin with a provision guaranteeing the security of the union. This provision is included because unions want a firm institutional base from which to work.

Ideally, a union would like to see all workers under its jurisdiction, but such a **closed shop,** compelling workers to join the union as a condition of being hired, was outlawed by the Taft-Hartley Act. The next best alternative for labor is the **union shop,** which allows an employer to hire new people at will, but after a probationary period—usually 30 days—the workers must join the union. Another alternative is the **agency shop,** which requires nonunion workers who benefit from agreements negotiated by the union to pay service fees to that union. Least desirable to unions is the **open shop,** in which nonunion workers pay no dues. Certain states, mostly in the Sunbelt, have passed **right-to-work laws,** which give employees the explicit right to keep a job without joining a union (see Exhibit 11.5).

Compensation

A collective-bargaining agreement addresses several issues relating to employee compensation. The most common issues are wage rates, cost-of-living adjustments, profit sharing, and employee benefits.

WAGE RATES   Until recently, unions negotiated similar wages for members working for all companies in a particular industry or at all plants within a partic-

States with right-to-work laws

ular company. This practice is referred to as **pattern bargaining**. For example, up until 1980, union assemblers at all General Motors, Ford, Chrysler, and American Motors plants earned within 3 cents an hour of each other.[21] But many companies began breaking away from patterns in their industries and negotiating separately with the unions. In particular, the major steel companies have abandoned pattern bargaining, as have several of the largest railroads, coal companies, and meat packers.[22]

Two primary factors have prompted the recent changes in the way unions negotiate wage rates: economic recessions and tough foreign competition. Many unions have even entered into "concession bargaining," agreeing to contracts freezing wages at current levels or even to wage cuts. Such givebacks are usually accepted in return for job-security guarantees of various types in the belief that it is better to have a job at a lower wage than to have no job at all.

During the recession-ridden early 1980s, some unions agreed to **two-tier wage plans,** in which the pay scale of new employees differed from that of senior employees. Although this strategy was widely used by industries struggling to compete, it later came under fire because of the morale problems it created for lower-paid newcomers. As a result of such wage concessions, givebacks, and otherwise small wage increases negotiated over the past decade, union wages have sometimes increased at a slower rate than nonunion wages—and sometimes more slowly than the cost of living (see Exhibit 11.6). Today, union wage gains are at the lowest point in the past few decades, although union workers still average 23 percent higher wages than nonunion workers.[23]

COLAs   In 1950 the United Auto Workers and General Motors adopted an innovative policy. To guarantee that workers' pay would keep pace with inflation, their contract adopted a **cost-of-living adjustment** (COLA) clause. During the term of the contract, workers' wages would automatically be increased in proportion to inflation in the general economy. By 1976 over 60 percent of workers covered by labor contracts benefited from COLA provisions.[24]

COLAs remain popular because they seem to maintain workers' buying power without any particular effort in negotiating contracts or raising productiv-

pattern bargaining Negotiating similar wages and benefits for all companies within a particular industry

two-tier wage plans Compensation agreements in which new employees are put on a wage scale lower than that of veteran employees

cost-of-living adjustment Clause in a union contract ensuring that wages will rise in proportion to inflation

EXHIBIT 11.6

Wages, Inflation, and Unions

In recent years, union wage increases have been smaller than nonunion wage increases and in many cases have not even kept pace with inflation.

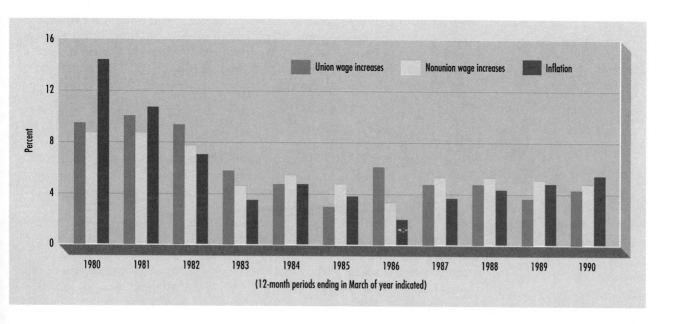

ity. In reality, however, some analysts have found major flaws in them. For one thing, COLAs are believed to magnify the effects of inflation in the general economy, especially when inflation jumps suddenly, as in the oil crises of the 1970s. The cost of COLAs is also less predictable than standard wage agreements and therefore complicates management's strategic planning. In the climate of the mid-1980s, when unions and management began trying to work together to save industries and when the inflation rate remained low, COLAs lost some of their appeal. By 1991, only 34 percent of workers covered by labor contracts benefited from COLAs.[25]

PROFIT SHARING　Although profit sharing is not a new idea, it has attracted increased attention in recent years. Today approximately 16 percent of all full-time employees in medium and large private companies are included in profit-sharing plans.[26] Some plans provide employees with deferred income they may claim on retirement as an incentive to produce more in the present. Others provide cash payments to employees each time the company's profits are determined.

Both management and unions are increasingly looking at profit sharing as a means of reducing wage inflation and increasing productivity. However, labor has some apprehension about the income risks associated with profit sharing. In fact, the AFL-CIO recently advised its affiliates to make profit sharing the smallest part of any total economic package they negotiate.[27] In addition, union negotiators are developing innovative bargaining strategies to protect employees when profits are down. The United Steelworkers, for example, agreed to a wage-cut–profit-sharing arrangement with LTV Steel, with the wage cuts treated as loans to be repaid from future profits. And just in case future profits turn out to be insufficient to satisfy the debt, the contract requires LTV to issue interest-bearing stock to employees for the unpaid balance.[28]

EMPLOYEE BENEFITS　Management can also avoid increasing basic wage rates in labor contracts by providing additional benefits. In particular, unions have been stressing higher pensions. But employers are fighting these demands because in the past few years they have had to absorb large increases in Social Security taxes and unemployment compensation rates. Employers have also been trying to persuade workers to pay more of the $100 billion that medical insurance costs companies every year. Unfortunately, the skyrocketing costs of medical insurance have made employee benefits a prime area of union-management contention in recent years.

Job Security

In the face of continuing corporate cutbacks, deregulation, and competition from importers and nonunionized domestic companies, unions have been stressing job security over wage increases. In fact, job security is *the* issue of the 1990s. Unions often demand **lifetime security,** protection for workers against temporary layoffs due to economic slowdowns and against permanent layoffs due to closing outmoded plants or expanded subcontracting (getting another company to do work previously done in house).

Automation is a special source of discomfort for unions. They are demanding that management give them advance notice of any attempts to introduce new equipment that would cost their members jobs, and they are demanding that

lifetime security Arrangement that gives workers some protection against temporary layoffs during an economic slowdown and against job loss during a downsizing or plant closing

those workers already on the job not be laid off because of the introduction of automated equipment. Two unions acutely aware of the potential of automation for reducing the number of jobs have been the Communications Workers of America (CWA) and the International Brotherhood of Electrical Workers (IBEW), which represent nearly 90 percent of the telephone work force. Both unions negotiated the creation of labor-management "technology committees" at American Telephone & Telegraph (AT&T), through which both unions and management discuss the introduction of new equipment. The CWA has also been arranging retraining programs for its members so that they can learn high-technology skills ranging from computer programming to the repair of electronic equipment.[29]

In large industries often plagued by job insecurity, such as the automotive industry, unions tend to focus on job guarantees. However, with the U.S. auto industry bracing for tough economic times and intense competition, unions are more willing to accept "income" guarantees and better retirement packages in lieu of jobs. In 1990, for example, the United Auto Workers won unprecedented job-security provisions in a contract with the Big Three automakers. Under the pact, many of the companies' 450,000 blue-collar workers will receive 85 percent of their regular take-home pay for three years if they take "preretirement leave" or are laid off. A decade ago, those same workers could expect only one year of benefits.[30]

Thanks to the unparalleled job-security program that UAW leaders negotiated with General Motors, many workers will receive 85 percent of their pay for three years after recently being laid off.

Work Rules and Job Descriptions

High on the list that Saturn's LeFauve and the UAW's Ephlin had to scrutinize were traditional work rules and restrictive job classifications, both of which tend to reduce productivity. **Work rules** are definitions of the types of work that covered workers may do and of the working conditions they must have. In the past, unions seized on narrow work rules as a means of preserving jobs. For example, if there was too much work for one carpenter, another had to be hired—even if an electrician already on the payroll was sitting idly by (this practice was called *featherbedding*). But in the late 1970s and early 1980s, management and unions both began to realize that for productivity to be increased, some fundamental changes had to be made in work rules. For example, after tough negotiations, unions at Chrysler Corporation agreed to change many job definitions. A welder who had been kept on the payroll for many years to handle occasional welding jobs was dismissed, and one of the maintenance workers was trained to handle the welding jobs. Under the old rules, only an electrician could unplug one of the plant's sewing machines; now anyone can do that. The result of the joint union-management effort has been the rescue of a doomed plant, increased production, and savings of $6.4 million a year—even without automation.[31]

work rules *Policies set during collective bargaining that govern what type of work union members will do and the conditions under which they will work*

Worker Safety and Health

Union negotiators are concerned with maintaining a safe and pleasant working environment for their members. Thus, the great majority of today's union contracts have provisions covering workers' safety and health, although the contracts rarely do more than restate federal regulations already in force. But the combination of escalating health-care costs and greater awareness of environmental hazards has given rise to important new demands in labor negotiations.

Administration of the Agreement

grievances Employee complaints about management violating some aspect of a labor contract

Once a collective-bargaining agreement goes into effect, it is up to management and union representatives to make it work. **Grievances,** or complaints of management violation of some aspect of the contract, will inevitably arise. Grievances typically come up when workers feel that they have been passed over for promotion, aren't getting a fair share of overtime, or are being asked to work too much overtime.

due process System of procedures and mechanisms for ensuring equity and justice on the job

A contract's grievance procedures protect the employees' right to **due process,** which is a system of procedures and mechanisms for ensuring equity and justice on the job. Under the Fifth Amendment, "No person shall . . . be deprived of life, liberty, or property, without due process of law." Since most employees covered by a collective-bargaining agreement have a "property interest" in their employment, they can't be disciplined or terminated without an explanation and an opportunity to present their side of the story.

Although grievance procedures vary somewhat from contract to contract, grievances are usually referred first to the shop steward, who discusses them with the employee's immediate supervisor. If these discussions fail, the problem may then be discussed by the chief steward and the department head. The next step in the process brings together the union grievance committee and the human resource (or personnel) manager. If they fail to solve the grievance, it is then up to the union business agent and the plant manager to try to resolve the issue.

If the worker's complaint still cannot be satisfied, it goes to an *arbitrator,* whose powers are defined in the contract and whose ruling is usually final. Arbitration is generally considered a last resort because it removes control from both union and management, and it may be complicated and expensive. As a result, there has been a shift to *grievance mediation,* in which a neutral third party meets with both sides and attempts to steer them toward a solution to the problem.

Although grievance procedures are still an important aspect of contract administration, today's competitive environment has caused labor to focus less on grievance and more on cooperation and teamwork. GM's Saturn division is just one example of a team effort between labor and management that should minimize conflicts and make contract administration less costly.

▶ UNION-MANAGEMENT RELATIONS IN A CHANGING ENVIRONMENT

Economic pressures have brought new approaches to the twin goals of maintaining the health of U.S. companies and protecting the rights of workers. To survive against foreign competition, whose labor costs are often much lower, unions and management alike have had to develop some new strategies.

Plant Shutdowns and Bankruptcy

Companies sometimes decide to close an inefficient factory so that they can institute sweeping improvements in a new one, and sometimes they are forced to close a factory because business is bad. Regardless of the reason, a factory closing may cause a wide variety of problems. Some are foreseeable, such as unemployment and economic problems for the local area. Less obvious problems are alcoholism, drug abuse, depression, marital stress, and other psychological difficulties among laid-off workers. Most plants close with little advance notice, and workers bear the brunt of the problems.

In 1989 a new law went into effect requiring companies to give workers at least 60 days' notice of impending plant closings or layoffs. But unions are concerned that even 60 days is not enough for most workers to look for new jobs, since a big plant is often the primary employer in a town.

If business is bad enough, a company may file for bankruptcy in order to relieve some of the pressure from creditors. Most companies prefer not to take such a drastic step, but some employers have discovered that filing for bankruptcy may have its advantages. When Texas Air acquired Continental Airlines, it declared Continental bankrupt and then reopened the company as a nonunion carrier with much lower wages. Other companies used this tactic as well, which led to passage of federal legislation that limits the use of bankruptcy in labor relations.

Still other employers have sought to rid themselves of unions by shutting down a plant and then selling it to a supposedly independent company that is actually under the control of the old employer. Or the parent company—which may be fully unionized—solicits work that it then passes off to a nonunion entity it controls.

Employee Rights Without Unions

In the effort to reduce union influence and power, management has resorted to another approach: granting its nonunionized employees many of the same benefits enjoyed by union members. These benefits include salaries competitive with those earned by union members, liberal work rules, and seniority privileges. One study showed that 30 percent of all nonunion employers even had formal grievance procedures in place. Employees who enjoy benefits like these frequently feel that it is unnecessary to join a union.[32]

Another factor in the changing balance of power between labor and management is the changing role of government. In recent years, no new legislation has been passed to protect the unions' right to organize, despite union efforts. But there has been legislation that directly guides and controls the actions of management without unions having to step in. Laws now mandate health and safety standards on the job, and a variety of federal and local laws prohibit discrimination on the basis of race, gender, or age (see Exhibit 11.7). New legislation has also clarified employers' responsibility for pension plans, and the minimum-wage law has been steadily expanded to include all workers. Unions once had to fight for these items; now government regulates them.

Worker Ownership

Faced with the increasing occurrence of mergers and plant closings, concern about mounting job losses has led unions to pursue a number of innovative means for ensuring that union companies stay in business. These options have ranged from placing union representatives on company boards to increasing employee stock ownership to actually engineering leveraged buyouts.

In many cases, unions have granted givebacks in exchange for enhanced employee-ownership programs that give workers a bigger say in how a company is run. Labor representatives now sit on the boards of Pan Am, Kaiser Alumi-

The Weirton steel mill in West Virginia is an example of successful conversion to employee ownership.

EXHIBIT 11.7 ▶ **Recent Guarantees of Employee Rights**

Nonunion as well as union employees have benefited from a number of state and federal legislative actions.

ISSUE	LEGISLATION/COURT RULINGS	SOURCE
Privacy	Limits on employee data that government may disclose to employers	Federal Privacy Act of 1974, 10 states
	Limits on use of lie-detector tests for job applicants	20 states
	Employee rights to access personnel files	9 states
	Limits on use of arrest records in hiring	12 states
Safety/health	Broad requirements for guaranteeing a safe and healthful workplace	Occupational Safety & Health Act of 1970, 24 states
	Protections for mine workers	Federal Mine Safety & Health Act of 1977
Discrimination	Broad protection against discrimination in hiring, promotion, and discharge	Civil Rights Act of 1964
	Protection for older workers against age discrimination	Age Discrimination in Employment Act of 1967
	Prohibition of any mandatory retirement age	19 states
	Prohibition of policies mandating retirement before age 70	1978 amendment to Age Discrimination in Employment Act
	Limits on discrimination on the basis of marital status and sexual orientation	Various states and localities
	Limits on gender discrimination in pay	Equal Pay Act of 1963
	Requirements of equal pay for comparable work	Some federal court decisions
	Increased protection against bias and harassment, allowing trials by jury and increasing cash awards for damages and reimbursement costs	Civil Rights Act of 1991
Pension and other benefit plans	Funding, vesting, and other standards	Employee Retirement Income Security Act of 1974, various states
Wages and working conditions	Provisions for national minimum wage, 40-hour workweek for regular pay, and other working conditions	Fair Labor Standards Act of 1938, state wage and hour laws (all states)
Union security	Limits on employers' ability to discharge and discipline employees for union activity	National Labor Relations Act of 1935
	Protection of union security in railroad industry	Railway Labor Act of 1926
Right to know	Requirement that companies divulge information on hazardous substances used in workplace	25 states
Whistle-blowers	Protection for corporate and government employees who expose wrongdoing	21 states
Employment at will	Limits on employment-at-will doctrine, which holds that employees may be fired at any time without cause	Court decisions in 30 states
Plant shutdowns	Requirement that workers receive 60 days' advance notice of plant shutdowns or massive layoffs	Worker Adjustment and Retraining Notification Act of 1988

num, Wheeling-Pittsburgh Steel, and many smaller companies. Unions are encouraging workers to learn more about the business end of their industry and are fighting for greater employee access to companies' financial records. According to one steel industry labor expert, "Being an effective union today is having an understanding of the core business the union is in, and communicating that understanding to members."[33]

The primary means that unions have used to keep businesses in operation is the employee stock-ownership plan (ESOP), described in Chapter 10. In 1990 some 10,000 companies had such plans. With ESOPs, employees have been able to gain partial or complete ownership of some 1,500 companies. One of the more visible conversions to employee ownership was the Weirton steel mill in West Virginia, once owned by National Steel. The mill was the largest employer in the state, with 7,000 employees, and the economy of the entire region depended on it. National had announced plans to scale back operations and ultimately phase out the plant. But closing would have been expensive because the steelmaker had pension liabilities of $400 million. Giving employees an opportunity to buy the mill solved this problem; moreover, it gave them a chance to save their own jobs and help support the local economy. Also, once they acquired the mill, the workers were able to do things that National's management couldn't. For example, the workers voted to take a 32 percent pay cut, which reduced operating costs by $128 million a year. After being acquired by its employees, Weirton Steel emerged as one of the 10 largest steel mills in the United States.[34]

Unions have also tried to buy companies outright; the Air Line Pilots Association attempted to buy United Airlines, and the rail unions bid $1 billion on Southern Pacific. Most such buyout attempts have been unsuccessful, but the machinist union did succeed in purchasing Chase Brass & Copper from Standard Oil, and the maritime unions successfully purchased WFI Industries, a family-owned tugboat company, thus paving the way for more such actions in the future.[35]

New Directions for Unions

In light of declining memberships and increasing nonunion employee rights, unions are beginning to pursue new issues and different workers, and they are doing so in new and different ways. For example, in high-tech companies, unions are making headway with workers who face layoffs and delays in pay increases when employers get caught in an old-fashioned economic squeeze. Unions are also actively seeking women by offering them more leadership roles and by emphasizing such concerns as child care, pregnancy leave, and the minimum wage.[36]

Unions are also beginning to realize that if they are to remain relevant in today's economy, they will have to make changes in their basic approach. One analyst believes that unions must do the following in order to stay healthy between now and the end of the century:

▶ Win job guarantees—perhaps not lifetime jobs but at least guarantees that workers will get another job in the company before being laid off.

▶ Make imaginative pay deals that exchange a piece of the profits for traditional wages and benefits.

▶ Communicate with members to find out how they feel and to let them know the facts of economic life.

▶ Accept new technology that will make employers more competitive and therefore more stable sources of jobs.

▶ Attract new members from the service industries, perhaps by hiring more female union executives and organizers.[37]

VIDEO EXERCISE

Some unions, like the National Union of Hospital and Health Care Employees, have already begun experimenting. For example, they are finding that hard facts may be more persuasive with today's workers than rallies and pep talks. They are using union pension funds to finance projects that use organized labor. And they are offering insurance to selected groups of workers who sign up as associate members, with the hope that the associate members will someday become full-fledged unionists.

More fundamentally, faced with a basic change in the relationship between management and labor, unions have started reconsidering their position and have begun emphasizing the benefits that they can provide to employers as well as to workers. For one thing, unions can provide skilled workers who are less likely to quit; they offer a source of responsible labor.[38] Unions have also been stressing their ability to help train people and upgrade their skills. And they have tried to expand their appeal to members by offering such nontraditional services as free legal advice and low-interest MasterCards.[39] These are new directions, but union officials are proving that they can adjust to changing realities.

SUMMARY OF LEARNING OBJECTIVES

1 Identify two main types of labor unions.

Craft unions, which developed first, are composed of people who perform a particular type of work. Industrial unions organize people who perform different types of work within a single industry, such as the automobile and steel industries.

2 Outline the organizational structure of unions.

National unions are composed of local unions; labor federations are composed of national unions and unaffiliated local unions. Each local has a hierarchy consisting of rank-and-file members, an elected president, elected shop stewards, and perhaps a business agent. National unions and federations consist of delegates elected by the local unions, who in turn elect officers; staff experts and organizers are hired to carry out the unions' programs.

3 Identify the two main steps unions take to become the bargaining agent for a group of workers.

First, unions distribute authorization cards, which designate the union as bargaining agent. If at least 30 percent (but usually a majority) of the target group sign the cards, the union asks the National Labor Relations Board to sponsor a certification election. If a majority of the workers vote in favor of being represented by the union, the union wins.

4 Describe the four main stages in collective bargaining.

The first stage is preparing to meet. The second stage is actually negotiating. The third stage is forming a tentative agreement. And the fourth stage is ratifying the proposed contract.

5 Identify four options that unions

have if negotiations with management break down.

Unions conduct strikes, organize boycotts, exercise financial and political influence, and use publicity to pressure management into complying with union proposals.

6 Identify five options that management has if negotiations with the union break down.

To pressure a union into accepting its proposals, management may continue running the business with strikebreakers and managers, institute a lockout of union members, seek an injunction against a strike or other union activity, seek a pact with other companies in the industry, or undertake lobbying and public relations campaigns.

7 List five general issues that may be addressed in a labor contract.

Among the issues that may be sub-

ject to negotiation are union security and management rights, compensation, job security, work rules, and worker safety and health.

8 Describe four major practices that management and unions are using to respond to changes in the structure of the economy.

First, management has tried using plant shutdowns and bankruptcy to void burdensome labor contracts. Second, as a result of legislation, court rulings, and changing management philosophies, companies have given nonunionized employees most of the same rights and benefits that unions demanded in the past. Third, employ-

ees sometimes become owners of a company to safeguard their jobs. Fourth, unions have experimented with new organizing tactics designed to make them more appealing to groups of workers who have not traditionally belonged to unions.

Meeting a Business Challenge at Saturn

Saturn could be viewed as one of the most expensive and risky experiments in the history of U.S. manufacturing: $5 billion for a mile-long factory to produce a car that, as one dealer said, "drives and feels like a Honda." But Saturn is more than just a new car and factory; it is the beginning of a radical relationship between management and labor. Although parts of the agreement between General Motors and the United Auto Workers have been implemented in other industries, Saturn's was the first attempt to bring so many ideas together into one pact between former adversaries. For Richard LeFauve and Donald Ephlin, Saturn is the culmination of their desire to get management and labor working for a common purpose.

The cornerstone of the agreement is their belief that people are the most valuable asset of an organization. So instead of the traditional boss-worker structure, white-collar and blue-collar employees are joined together into units and committees to make decisions by consensus. These groups decide everything about Saturn's operation, including who does what job, who goes on vacation when, how to engineer component parts for the car, how to market it, and even the long-range strategy of the company. For the first time, labor is integrally involved in every decision concerning product, personnel, and profits. Union representatives even helped choose an advertising agency and helped select which GM dealers would be allowed to sell the new

Richard LeFauve, president of Saturn.

Donald Ephlin, former vice president of the United Auto Workers.

car. The arrangement is not just symbolic. Union workers are paid a salary instead of an hourly wage, and 80 percent of them—determined by seniority—cannot be laid off, except in the case of some catastrophic event. Even then, the joint management-labor committees can decide to reduce hours of operation or even to stop production to prevent any layoffs at all.

In return for these accommodations to union members, the UAW agreed to GM's desire to streamline the production process. The key change here was a reduction in job classifications from more than 100 to a maximum of six: one for production workers and up to five for skilled workers. This point, combined with state-of-the-art production processes and factory design, should help raise Saturn's productivity to world-class levels. Ephlin's union also agreed to an initial 20 percent cut in compensation in exchange for the salaries and management-style bonuses they now receive. Future salary levels are decided by consensus of the Strategic Advisory Committee (the highest group of decision makers under the new hierarchy), and these levels are based on the average hourly rates at all domestic manufacturing plants, including those owned by Mazda. Finally, in an effort to tear down all walls between management and labor, all employees park in the same parking lots and eat in the same cafeterias, regardless of how much they're paid or how dirty their job may be.

This landmark agreement between GM and the UAW, between LeFauve's managers and Ephlin's union members, is unlike any other contract in the U.S. auto industry. Known as a living document, it never expires. Instead, the agreement can be altered at any time, as long as all parties agree on the change. Formal negotiations between GM and the UAW can still be conducted if agreement cannot be reached on a proposed alteration, and labor still has the right to strike in extreme circumstances, but most observers who have studied the agreement doubt that the relationship between management and labor at Saturn will ever return to its old adversarial state. In fact, in November 1991, Saturn workers voted to alter the landmark contract, moving it a bit closer to the conventional contract that prevails at other GM plants. Even though relations between managers and employees have been smooth at Saturn, the lack of profits has led to dissention among workers (especially those who took a pay cut to transfer to the Saturn plant). The altered contract increases wages and calls for a slow phase in the plan to base 20 percent of employee pay on company profits. Also, Saturn workers who transferred from other GM plants and who have 10 years of service can now withdraw from Saturn's pension plan (which predicts no specific benefits) and go back to the GM pension plan (which does promise specific benefits).

Many people inside and outside the auto industry think this agreement may be the beginning of a completely new chapter in U.S. labor relations. The Saturn agreement goes beyond the arrangements of Japanese automakers and their employees. It is a progressive agreement between management and labor, based on a concept that has been alien to both parties throughout history: cooperation.

Your Mission: You have been a labor relations consultant to the United Auto Workers for several years, helping union strategists with long-term planning. You have never been involved in specific negotiations, but you're aware of the terms of all negotiated contracts, and you help guide UAW leaders in negotiation strategies.

How would you handle the following situations?

1. Management-labor relations are going well at Saturn, apparently justifying the company's sweeping changes. But the factory is selling only 75 percent of the cars it originally estimated, giving Saturn less profit than expected. Given these ambivalent circumstances, what would be the best approach for the UAW to pursue when negotiating at other GM plants?

a. Press for a Saturn-type agreement at all GM plants.

b. Negotiate a more traditional, one-year pact at other GM plants, and wait for the Saturn agreement to prove its viability.

c. Negotiate for certain parts of the Saturn agreement that the UAW thinks would be good for all employees, regardless of what happens at Saturn.

d. Ignore Saturn altogether. It's an experiment and really has no applicability to GM's other plants, mainly because no other plant among all domestic automakers incorporates the state-of-the-art design and manufacturing processes found at Saturn.

2. A few of the decisions made by various committees at Saturn have turned out to be bad ones. Some of the groups have been discussing whether the consensus process itself might be to blame. Some management employees are saying that the poor decisions result from the poorly trained union representatives on those committees. But union representatives have rebuffed these criticisms, observing that management team members agreed to the proposals made by union members and that all decisions from those committees were reached by consensus. What should the UAW do?

a. Try to force changes in the consensus process so that union members can't be blamed for poor group decisions.

b. Ignore the matter and think of it as a tempest in a teapot.

c. Press for better business-management education for union representatives on applicable committees so that they will be better able to handle complex business problems.

d. Gain greater representation on all committees. This has been suggested by some UAW members who believe that the poor decisions were a result of the disproportionate influence of managers on the committees.

3. Relations between Saturn managers and the production-line employees have been so successful that some employees are starting to question the value of staying with the union. A small group has approached you, explaining how they feel and asking you to help them build support for a decertification vote. Considering the time and effort you've spent fostering a positive relationship with union leadership, the group's request leaves you in an uncomfortable position. How should you respond?

a. As a manager, this is great news for you. If you can get the union out of the way, you'll be free to run the factory as you wish. Tell the group to go for it, and tell them you'll do everything possible to help.

b. You would certainly like to manage without the constraints placed on you by the union, but you don't want the union leadership to think that you're undercutting their efforts. The best alternative is to tell the group to go for it and to explain that you can't offer any support.

c. Explain to the employees that the newfound cooperation between management and the union is critical to Saturn's success and that a decertification attempt at this point would jeopardize the entire venture. Suggest that the group approach the union leaders and explain why group members are dissatisfied. Offer to talk to the union leaders yourself if the group is unsuccessful on its own.

d. Chastise the employees for trying to undo the progress of several years' worth of negotiating and building trust. Tell them that the union is committed to their success and that they should remain loyal to it.

4. Saturn and the union have achieved a harmonious arrangement for the day-in, day-out operation of the plant. However, you know that it is crucial to have a crisis-management plan in place for emergency situations—a fire at the plant, flooding, and so on. Which of the following would be the best approach to take?

a. During a crisis, fast, decisive action is absolutely necessary. Consequently, there simply isn't time to get employees or the union leadership involved. Management should have free rein to act according to their own instincts in the event of an emergency.

b. It's true that fast action is often necessary in a crisis, and there isn't always time to get input from everyone concerned. But this doesn't mean that the union should be shut out completely. The best idea would be to get the union involved before any crisis actually happens. Together with union leaders, you can plan escape routes, shut-down procedures, and other actions that will have to be taken in an emergency. Then when something does happen, management is free to act quickly.

c. Since employees will be justifiably concerned about their personal safety during an emergency, they should be allowed to form a crisis management team, independent of both management and the union.

d. The union watches out for the safety of the employees during normal times, so they should have the opportunity and the responsibility to do so during the crisis as well. Let union leaders handle any problems that arise.[40]

KEY TERMS

agency shop (310)
arbitration (304)
authorization cards (301)
blacklist (305)
boycott (305)
business agent (300)
certification (301)
closed shop (310)
collective bargaining (303)
cost-of-living adjustment (311)
craft unions (297)
decertification (301)
due process (314)

grievances (314)
industrial unions (297)
injunction (309)
labor federations (300)
labor unions (296)
lifetime security (312)
locals (300)
lockout (308)
mandatory subject (304)
mediation (304)
national union (300)
open shop (310)
pattern bargaining (311)

permissive subject (304)
picketing (305)
ratification (304)
right-to-work laws (310)
shop steward (300)
slowdown (305)
strike (305)
strikebreakers (307)
two-tier wage plans (311)
union shop (310)
work rules (313)
yellow-dog contract (305)

REVIEW QUESTIONS

1. Why do workers join labor unions? Why don't they join labor unions?

2. What factors have contributed to the current decline in union power?

3. What are grievances, and how are they resolved?

4. What is the conflict between union security and management rights?

5. In an era when wage increases are moderating, what sorts of compensation plans are being adopted?

6. What is the relationship between automation and job security?

7. How do unions attempt to improve the quality of members' work lives?

8. What new groups of workers are unions trying to reach, and what strategies are the unions using?

A CASE FOR CRITICAL THINKING

A Nightmare at Nordstrom

For more than 60 years United Food and Commercial Workers Local 1001 represented employees at Nordstrom's Seattle-area department stores. Although the classy retail chain boasts 64 stores in nine states and is staffed by some 30,000 employees, fewer than 2,000 salespeople are union members. Only the Seattle-area stores are unionized, which didn't create any major problems—until the summer of 1989.

During contract negotiations that summer, management proposed optional union membership in response to employee complaints about mandatory union dues. When Seattle Local 1001 put the proposal to a vote, the

250 or so members who showed up voted overwhelmingly to reject the idea. But Nordstrom stood its ground, causing negotiations to break down.

Joe Peterson, head of the local, was convinced that management was bent on throwing out his union. So he struck back by putting up the fight of his life, stirring dissension in Washington as well as in nonunionized stores as far away as southern California and Virginia. It didn't take long for Peterson to show that a little-known union leader described as a nice guy can play tough against a major league corporation with an unblemished record. "The company vastly underestimated our resolve to protect not only this contract but the other retail contracts" in the area, Peterson insisted.

In a surprise move, the union decided not to go on strike but to fight with negative publicity. To acquire ammunition, the union set up an 800 phone number for employee complaints. The common gripe was about being pressured to work "off the clock" when attending store meetings, writing thank-you notes to customers, and delivering merchandise to customers' homes and offices. A union inquiry eventually uncovered 825 current and former salespeople who claimed the company owed them more than $5.3 million in back wages. Peterson informed the press, which eagerly followed the story.

The state of Washington's Department of Labor and Industries (DLI) investigated the claims and ordered Nordstrom to change its practices and pay back wages. But Joe Demarte, Nordstrom's vice president of personnel, claimed the union used its inquiry as a publicity stunt: "For the DLI, it was a routine audit and a routine report, but the union had the press there."

In the meantime, anti-union salespeople at Nordstrom began organizing a move to decertify the union. They felt the union had slandered the company and the integrity of the people who work for it. "All the salespeople here operate as entrepreneurs," said John Rockwood, a shoe salesman in one of the Seattle stores. As for the DLI's report, he said: "It's petty little timekeeping stuff. We make twice as much money as anybody else in the industry. We just haven't kept meticulous records as to the time we have actually spent working for the company."

Still, Nordstrom tried to resolve the troublesome off-the-clock issue. The company's solution was to mail a settlement form to current sales employees so that they could enter detailed information that would substantiate the amount of time they worked. All in all, the company paid out just under $3 million in claims. The union, however, calculated that Nordstrom owed its employees as much as $300 million in back pay.

In addition, the union charged Nordstrom with drumming up anti-union sentiment and aiding the anti-union forces. For example, during the decertification campaign the company ran a 24-hour telephone hotline and produced three anti-union videos. In one video, actors portrayed pro-company and pro-union employees discussing the decertification vote with a new employee. The union charged that the actor playing the pro-company worker was attractive and well-dressed, whereas the burly pro-union worker had a wart on his face. Nordstrom insisted the actors weren't intentionally typecast. Nevertheless, as long as the company faced charges of unfair labor practices, the National Labor Relations Board wouldn't authorize a decertification election.

In August 1990 Nordstrom finally agreed to settle with the NLRB all charges of unfair labor practices. Yet its battle with the union raged on. More charges were filed, but this time the NLRB cleared Nordstrom of allegations of unfair labor practices. By early 1991, a group called Nordstrom Employees Opposed to Union Representation had collected the necessary signatures to petition the NLRB for an election to decertify the union as bargaining agent for the Seattle-area employees. When the election was held, workers at the five unionized stores voted 1,022 to 407 against union representation; 171 ballots were challenged, but not enough to affect the outcome.

Nordstrom hailed the victory as confirmation of its contention that employees no longer wanted union representation. After all, union members received the same wages and benefits as the store's nonunion salespeople elsewhere. Local union head Joe Peterson was disappointed by the vote but hadn't decided whether to file a formal objection with the NLRB.[41]

1. When negotiations between Nordstrom's management and union leaders broke down over the optional union-membership issue, why do you think the union chose to fight back with negative publicity instead of with a strike?

2. What do you think the union could have done to make membership more attractive to the employees in Nordstrom's Seattle-area stores?

3. What effect do you think the union decertification will have on Nordstrom and its employees?

BUILDING YOUR COMMUNICATION SKILLS

Debate the pros and cons of union membership with a small group of no more than three or four students. Consider the relevance of unionism at a time when legislation is becoming more protective of workers' rights. Are unions necessary when participatory management and employee involvement in decision making are becoming more commonplace? What about the role of unions in occupations considered professional? Are unions more relevant in specific types of industry or business?

▶ If possible, develop a consensus opinion about unions, and draft a position statement regarding the various issues discussed by the group.

▶ Compare the attitudes of your group with those held by other class members. Is there agreement on any of the issues discussed?

KEEPING CURRENT USING *THE WALL STREET JOURNAL*

Choose one or two articles from *The Wall Street Journal* illustrating one of the following aspects of labor-management relations:

▶ Union organizing

▶ Collective-bargaining negotiations

▶ Strikebreakers or lockouts

▶ Worker layoffs and plant closings

▶ Union givebacks and concessions

▶ Government-mandated labor practices

1. What are the major issues described in the article?

2. From the information presented in the article, what seem to be the major sources of disagreement between management and labor, the major reasons behind a drive to unionize, or the major issues surrounding the government-mandated labor practices?

3. Are the issues or problems still unresolved, or has some kind of agreement or solution been reached? If so, what are the terms of the agreement? What did each side gain? What did each side concede?

PART FOUR

Marketing

CHAPTER 12

LEARNING OBJECTIVES
After studying this chapter, you will be able to

1 Explain what marketing is.

2 Describe the four forms of utility created by marketing.

3 Discuss the three major eras in the evolution of marketing.

4 Identify and contrast the two basic types of markets.

5 Specify the four basic components of the marketing mix.

6 Outline the four steps in the strategic planning process.

7 Describe the five steps in the buyer's decision process.

8 Define market segmentation and list the four bases most often used to segment markets.

Marketing and Consumer Behavior

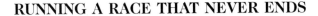

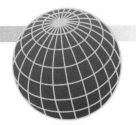

Facing a Business Challenge at Nike

RUNNING A RACE THAT NEVER ENDS

Manufacturers of athletic shoes are running a race that never seems to end. One of those manufacturers was named Nike, after the Greek goddess of victory, and for a good reason: The company has no intention of letting the competition run away. Started by former collegiate sprinter Phillip Knight and his University of Oregon coach, Bill Bowerman, Nike stressed technology and high-performance products from the very beginning. An experiment with urethane rubber and a waffle iron got it all started, and serious runners loved the new waffle-soled shoes. By 1981 Knight and his company had about half the U.S. athletic shoe market, outpacing established overseas competitors such as Adidas and Puma.

By 1980 Nike offered over 140 models of shoes. As the running boom of the 1970s faded, Knight knew he had to look beyond high-performance running shoes to expand the company's sales. He identified target segments in the sports market, including basketball and tennis. And with products designed specifically for those athletes, Nike continued to prosper.

The 1980s brought a new twist to the market, however. Serious athletes weren't the only people interested in athletic shoes. Capitalizing on the aerobic exercise boom, younger rival Reebok boldly poured on the speed, taking the lead by 1986 on the strength of its innovative aerobics shoes. Two years later, Reebok's share of the market was 27 percent, and Nike's share had tumbled from around 50 percent to 23 percent. Then the aerobics fad was followed by another important change in the U.S. shoe market. Athletic shoes became fashionable footwear. People who had no intention of being serious athletes, or even serious exercisers, adopted athletic shoes as their favorite shoes. And again, Reebok was ahead of Nike in responding to this shift. First, actress Cybill Shepherd arrived at the Emmy Awards wearing an elegant evening gown and blazing orange Reeboks. Then, on a poster for his hit movie *Back to the Future,* Michael J. Fox dashed through time wearing Reeboks. What had begun as a product for dedicated runners had turned into a product for dedicated followers of fashion.

Despite impressive technology, its own series of celebrity endorsements, and award-winning advertising, Nike lost its footing in 1986, and Reebok streaked ahead. By 1988 Reebok was selling 75 million pairs of shoes annually, compared with Nike's 50 million. But the scrappy Knight fought back with new products and an emphasis on style and fashion.

Going into 1990, Nike led the pack once again, with a 26 percent share, just topping Reebok's 23 percent. Reebok has stayed right behind, pushing hard with an advertising budget of over $70 million a year and a new roster of famous players and coaches to promote its peak performance model, The Pump. L.A. Gear, a winner in women's fashion-oriented athletic shoes, is number three, showing signs of slipping, and Converse is getting itself back on track with aggressive marketing.

The race continues. If you were Phillip Knight, what would you do to keep Nike on top while defending against competitors? How would you help Nike meet the ever-changing demands of consumer tastes and advances in shoe technology? How would you define your market and identify segments for potential growth? How would you get your message to potential customers? And how would you make your shoes available to more diverse groups of customers?[1]

▶ MARKETING FUNDAMENTALS

Nike's Phillip Knight knows how important marketing is. And by this point in your life, you already know quite a bit about marketing. People have been trying to sell you things for years, and you've learned something about their techniques—advertisements, price markdowns, special contests, tantalizing displays of merchandise. But despite marketing's high visibility, the term is difficult to define. The American Marketing Association (AMA) recently evaluated 25 definitions before agreeing on the meaning of the word. According to AMA's definition, **marketing** is planning and executing the conception, pricing, promotion, and distribution of ideas, goods, and services to create exchanges that satisfy individual and organizational objectives.[2]

marketing *Process of planning and executing the conception, pricing, promotion, and distribution of ideas, goods, and services to create exchanges that satisfy individual and organizational objectives*

As this definition implies, marketing encompasses a wide range of activities. If you set out to handle all of a firm's marketing functions, you would be very busy indeed. In fact, in most large organizations, each division has its own marketing department, staffed by a legion of specialists. Some of them conduct research to determine what consumers want to buy; some use that research to design new products and services; others make decisions on how to price the firm's offerings; still others handle the transportation, storage, and distribution of the goods; and, finally, some are responsible for advertising, sales promotion, publicity, and personal selling. Marketing is involved in all decisions related to determining a product's characteristics, price, production quantities, market entry date, sales, and customer service.

Although we generally think of marketing in connection with selling tangible products for a profit, the AMA definition applies to services and ideas as well. Social activists, religious leaders, politicians, universities, and charities of all types rely on the principles of marketing to "sell" themselves and their causes to the public. The term *product* is used in this text to refer to both goods and services.

The Role of Marketing in Society

Take another look at the AMA definition of marketing. Notice that it involves an exchange between two parties—the buyer and the selling organization—both of whom obtain satisfaction from the transaction. This suggests that marketing plays an important role in society by helping people satisfy their needs and wants and by helping organizations determine what to produce.

Needs and Wants

Think about what you really need: food, water, shelter, clothing, companionship, affection, knowledge, achievement. **Needs** are the basic elements that are essential to your physical, psychological, and social well-being. When your needs are not met, you feel deprived and are highly motivated to change the situation.

Your **wants** are based on your needs, but they are more specific. Producers do not create needs, but they do shape your wants by exposing you to alternatives. For instance, when you *need* some food, you may *want* a Wendy's hamburger. A fundamental goal of marketing is to direct the customer's basic need for various products into the desire to purchase specific brands.

Exchanges and Transactions

When you participate in the **exchange process,** you trade something of value (usually money) for something else of value, whether you're buying dinner, a car, or a college education. When you make a purchase, you cast your vote for that item and encourage the producer of that item to make more of it. In this way, supply and demand are balanced, and society obtains the goods and services that are most satisfying.

When the exchange actually occurs, it takes the form of a **transaction.** Party A gives party B 69 cents and gets a medium Coke in return. A trade of values takes place. Most transactions in an advanced society involve money, but money is not necessarily required. When you were a child, perhaps you traded your peanut butter sandwich for bologna and cheese in a barter transaction.

The Four Utilities

To encourage the exchange process, marketers enhance the appeal of their products and services by adding four types of **utility,** or value to the customer (see Exhibit 12.1). **Form utility** refers to the characteristics of the product—its shape, size, color, function, and style. The producers of Softsoap, for example, enhanced the appeal of hand soap by producing it in liquid form and dispensing it through a pump, making it more pleasant to use and thereby increasing its form utility. In other cases, marketers try to make their products available when and where customers want to buy them, creating **time utility** and **place utility.** The final form of utility is **possession utility**—the satisfaction that buyers get when they actually possess a product, both legally and physically.

needs Things that are necessary for a person's physical, psychological, and social well-being

wants Things that are desirable in light of a person's experiences, culture, and personality

exchange process Act of obtaining a desired object from another party by offering something in return

transaction Exchange between parties

utility Power of a good or service to satisfy a human need

form utility Consumer value created when a product's characteristics are made more satisfying

time utility Consumer value added by making a product available at a convenient time

place utility Consumer value added by making a product available in a convenient location

possession utility Consumer value created when someone takes ownership of a product

By delivering its pizza, Domino's has increased the place utility of its product.

EXHIBIT 12.1 ► **Examples of the Four Utilities**

The utility of a good or service has four aspects, each of which enhances the product's value to the consumer.

TYPES OF UTILITY	EXAMPLE OF UTILITY
Form utility	Sunkist Fun Fruits appeal to youngsters because of their imaginative shapes—numbers, dinosaurs, letters, spooks, animals. The bite-sized fruit snacks are both functionally and psychologically satisfying.
Time utility	Lens Crafters has captured a big chunk of the market for eyeglasses by providing on-the-spot, one-hour service.
Place utility	By offering home delivery, Domino's has achieved a major position in the pizza market and prompted competitors to follow suit.
Possession utility	TEST, Inc., a manufacturer of materials testing equipment for the aerospace industry, allows customers to try its $100,000 machine free of charge on a 90-day trial basis.

The Evolution of Marketing

Marketing has changed dramatically since the turn of the century, when a firm could rely on a good, solid product to sell itself. Increasing competition, shifts in consumer attitudes, and the growth of mass media have all contributed to the evolution of marketing (see Exhibit 12.2).

The Production Era

Until the 1930s, many business executives viewed marketing simply as an off-shoot of production. Product design was based more on the demands of mass-production techniques than on customer wants and needs. Manufacturers were generally able to sell all that they produced; they could comfortably limit their marketing efforts to taking orders and shipping goods. Henry Ford, for example, focused on ways to produce automobiles more quickly and inexpensively, confi-

EXHIBIT 12.2

The Evolution of Marketing
Marketing has changed dramatically, evolving from the old-fashioned concept of simply producing the merchandise and making it available for customers to today's highly competitive marketing strategies, which involve aggressively seeking market niches and consumer needs to fill.

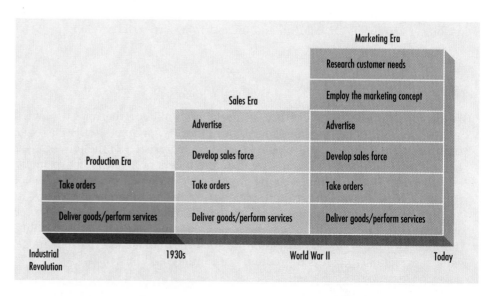

dent that people would buy them. When customers asked for a choice of color, Ford reportedly replied: "They can have any color they want, as long as it's black." Ford wasn't necessarily ignoring customer demands; he simply knew that a single color made car production much more efficient.

The Sales Era

As production capacity increased in the late 1920s, the markets for manufactured goods became more competitive. Business leaders, realizing that they would have to persuade people to buy all the goods they could make, expanded their marketing activities. To stimulate demand for their products, they spent more on advertising. They also began to develop trained sales forces that could seek out and sell to the thousands of potential customers across the country.

In spite of their increasing marketing sophistication, most companies were still overlooking the needs of the marketplace during this era. Instead of asking what the consumer wanted, they were producing what the company could make and getting their sales force to create demand. They were thinking primarily in terms of the company and its abilities rather than in terms of the consumer's needs.

The Marketing Era

The 1950s were the start of the marketing era, during which companies began to practice marketing in its current form. The development of efficient production techniques earlier in the century laid the groundwork for plentiful supplies of most products. The method of achieving business success shifted from pushing products on customers to finding out what buyers wanted and then filling that need.

The notion of marketing continued to evolve, and businesspeople started talking about the **marketing concept,** stressing customer needs and wants that lead to long-term profitability and the integration of marketing with other parts of the company (see Exhibit 12.3).[3] The marketing concept came into existence in the 1960s and continues to develop and expand, although its application is not universal. Many companies continue to operate in the sales era, and some even operate with production-era values.

marketing concept Belief that a business must determine and satisfy customer needs in order to make a profit

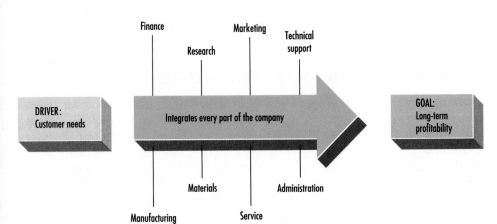

EXHIBIT 12.3

The Marketing Concept
The marketing concept integrates every part of the company while placing emphasis on customer satisfaction and long-term profitability.

With the marketing concept, the emphasis on *long-term* profitability is key. If your only interest is making a fast buck, it doesn't make sense for you to invest in research laboratories, support personnel, service facilities, and the other elements often needed to satisfy customers. But if you want to be financially healthy 5, 10, or 20 years from now, it is perfectly sensible to make these investments.

Competitive Marketing

competitive advantage Quality that makes a product more desirable than similar products offered by the competition

In addition to paying more attention to customers, companies have also been giving more thought to the competition. Just as Nike must keep tabs on Reebok, companies can no longer succeed simply by satisfying customers if competitors are satisfying them just as well. What companies seek is a **competitive advantage,** something that sets them apart from their rivals and makes their product more appealing to customers.

A competitive advantage may be established in two ways: (1) by offering a lower price for a similar product or (2) by offering a product that does a better job of meeting customer needs.[4] With the first approach, the key to success lies in driving down costs so that a company can produce and sell its product less expensively than its competitors can. Wal-Mart has become the nation's largest retailer with a strategy based on everyday low costs, and traditional retailers such as Sears have had a hard time responding because they don't have the cost advantages that Wal-Mart enjoys. For example, Wal-Mart spends 16 percent of sales on overhead costs, whereas Sears spends 29 percent and K Mart spends 23 percent.[5]

product differentiation Features that distinguish one company's product from another company's similar product

A company pursuing the second approach must analyze existing and potential customers to determine what matters most to them—delivery, service, style, image, reliability. Then the company must create and communicate that quality better than competitors do, an approach known as **product differentiation.**[6] IBM, Nordstrom, Mercedes-Benz, Honda, and L. L. Bean are some of the many companies that choose to compete primarily by trying to satisfy customers better than their competitors can.

Establishing a competitive advantage is complicated by the fact that conditions shift: Competitors get better at producing and marketing; consumers change their minds about what they want. A company has to stay one jump ahead of the market and the competition in order to maintain its lead. The increase in foreign competition and the growing importance of export markets have added to the challenge. The growth of Japanese and Korean car manufacturers is a good example of the dynamic nature of international competition.

▶ MARKETING MANAGEMENT AND PLANNING

marketing strategy Overall plan for marketing a product

Because marketing is so complicated and so central to an organization's success, a business should develop an overall plan—a **marketing strategy**—for its goods and services. The first step in plotting a strategy is to identify the particular group of customers the firm will attempt to satisfy. The second step is to settle on the combination of ingredients to be used in the marketing program. To accomplish these steps, the organization must study the environment, analyze its own capabilities, and decide on a plan that maximizes its strengths.

Types of Markets

A central concern in marketing is the **market**—the group of customers who might need or want your product and who could afford to buy it. Markets may be classified in two broad categories. The **consumer market** consists of individuals or households that purchase goods and services for personal use. The **organizational market** is made up of three main subgroups: the industrial/commercial market (companies that buy goods and services to produce their own goods and services), the reseller market (wholesalers and retailers), and the government market (federal, state, and local agencies).[7]

Consumer and organizational customers approach their purchases in different ways; as a consequence, differing techniques are required to reach them. Say that you recently opened a stationery store and are wondering whether to focus on the consumer or organizational market. The products you sell, the hours you are open, and many other basic decisions will depend on which type of market you decide to serve.

In analyzing the situation, you find that both the consumer and the organizational markets for stationery are large and diverse, composed of many **market segments,** or subgroups with distinctive needs, interests, and behaviors. To avoid spreading your resources too thin, you decide to focus on specific **target markets.** You want to learn what kinds of office supplies they are currently buying and why, what these customers might want in the future, and how your company could satisfy their needs. You also want to know what your competitors have to offer this target group and how you can achieve a competitive advantage. This type of research will help you make better decisions about what items to stock in your store and how to promote and price them.

market People who need or want a product and who have the money to buy it

consumer market Individuals who buy goods or services for personal use

organizational market Customers who buy goods or services for resale or for use in conducting their own operations

market segments Groups of individuals or organizations within a market that share certain common characteristics

target markets Specific groups of customers to whom a company wants to sell a particular product

The Marketing Mix

As you make decisions about how to satisfy your customers, you are creating a **marketing mix,** a combination of four major ingredients: product (ideas, goods, or services), price, place (distribution), and promotion. A marketer creates a blend of these ingredients—also known as the **four Ps**—to respond to the needs of the intended customers or audience (see Exhibit 12.4):

marketing mix Blend of elements satisfying a chosen market

four Ps Marketing elements—product, price, place, and promotion

Product. A businessperson's first marketing task is to decide on the goods or services that will attract customers. The key is to determine the needs and wants of customers and then translate those needs and wants into desirable products. Social trends often provide a clue to the types of products that consumers will want. Rising crime rates, for example, have created a growing need among small businesses for security services. Similarly, the rapid increase in the number of working women has inspired clothing manufacturers to produce more women's suits.

Price. Having made basic decisions about its products, the company must decide on how to price them. Sometimes low prices maximize profits, as the discussion of supply and demand in Chapter 1 demonstrated. On the other hand, the desirability of some products—like Nike shoes—depends on a high-quality image, which a high price helps to confer.

Place. The third element in the marketing mix is place (or distribution): how products get to customers. Transportation comes into play here, but place also entails decisions about distribution outlets. Many alternatives are possible. For example, E. T. Wright, a shoe manufacturer, boosted sales by distributing a catalog to augment its traditional

VIDEO EXERCISE

EXHIBIT 12.4 ▶ **The Marketing Mix**

The right decisions about product, price, place, and promotion yield the marketing mix that best meets the needs of the customers.

DECISION AREA	COMPONENTS	DEFINITION
Product	The product	The set of tangible and intangible attributes of the good, service, person, or idea that is being exchanged
	Brand name	Words, letters, or numbers that may be spoken
	Packaging	The activities that involve designing and producing the container or wrapper for a product
	Services	Activities, benefits, or satisfactions that are offered for sale or are provided in connection with the sale of goods
	Warranty	A manufacturer's promise that the product is fit for the purpose intended
	Postexchange servicing	Activities, such as warranty services, that ensure customer satisfaction
Price	Pricing	Activities concerned with setting the price of a product
	Discount	A reduction from the asked price of a product
Place (distribution)	Channels of distribution	The route taken by a product as it moves from the producer to the final consumer
	Physical distribution	The physical movement of goods from the point of production to the point of consumption
Promotion	Advertising	Nonpersonal communication that is paid for by an identified marketer to promote a product or service
	Personal selling	Person-to-person communication between a marketer and members of the market
	Public relations	Any communication created primarily to build prestige or goodwill for an individual or an organization
	Sales promotion	Promotional activities other than advertising, personal selling, and publicity that stimulate consumer purchases and dealer effectiveness

retail outlets. Tupperware distributes directly to the consumer through its party approach. Most clothing manufacturers sell to retailers, who resell to consumers.

Promotion. Often, the most important decision a company makes is how it should inform prospective customers about its products. The alternatives are many, and the choice may determine the success of a marketing effort. Some companies, such as Avon and Mary Kay Cosmetics, emphasize direct selling and spend most of their promotion dollars training and paying salespeople. Others, including the many producers of soap and headache remedies, promote their products through advertising, mainly on television. Department stores also spend heavily on advertising, but they choose local newspapers as the most effective medium.

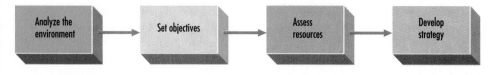

| Analyze the environment | → | Set objectives | → | Assess resources | → | Develop strategy |

The Marketing Planning Process

Companies that live by the marketing concept realize that marketing efforts are more successful when they are carefully planned. *Strategic marketing planning* examines a company's market opportunities, allocates resources to capitalize on those opportunities, and predicts the market and financial performance that is likely to occur.[8] The marketing planning process starts with analyzing the external environment (see Exhibit 12.5).

Analyzing the External Environment

Current economic conditions, social trends, technology, competition, the legal and regulatory climate, and the natural environment all have a profound impact on a firm's marketing options. The external environment can create entirely new markets, destroy old markets, and generally present an endless parade of problems and opportunities for marketers.

ECONOMIC FORCES　Marketers are keenly aware of the importance of such broad economic trends as gross national product, interest rates, inflation, unemployment, personal income, and savings rates. In tough times, consumers postpone the purchase of expensive items like major appliances, automobiles, and homes. They cut back on travel, entertainment, and luxury goods. Conversely, when the economy is good, consumers open their pocketbooks and satisfy their pent-up demand for higher-priced products and services.

By being aware of these trends, marketers can adjust the firm's inventory levels and juggle the elements of the marketing mix to respond to the customer's buying mood. During recessions, for example, a firm might reduce prices or offer favorable credit terms to lure customers.

SOCIAL TRENDS　Planners also study the social and cultural environment to determine shifts in consumer values. If social trends are running against a product, the producer might need to increase its advertising budget to educate consumers about the product's benefits. Alternatively, it might modify the product to respond to changing tastes, as UltraBeef Ranches has done. Recognizing the trend toward healthier eating habits, the firm is raising a leaner breed of cattle.[9] Ski resorts around the United States are getting hit at the cash register by another social trend—the aging of the U.S. population. As more people slide into middle age and cut down on skiing, fewer younger people come along to take their places on the slopes. As a result, the number of visits to ski areas has dropped by 8 percent from the peak winter of 1987–1988.[10]

TECHNOLOGY　Technology is a double-edged sword, providing both risks and opportunities. When technology changes, marketing approaches must often be revised to cope with new competitors, new market segments, and new product features.

EXHIBIT 12.5

The Marketing Planning Process

By analyzing the environment, setting objectives, and assessing its own capabilities, the organization is able to develop a marketing strategy that will give it a competitive advantage when approaching the customer.

One of the ways Toyota promotes its name is by sponsoring special events such as this auto race in Long Beach, California. Marketers have a wide range of creative promotion options at their disposal, including skywriting and having a professional athlete wear brand-name products.

Discount retailers and off-price retailers have been one of the few healthy segments in the retail industry in recent years. As more and more consumers abandon free-spending ways and start looking for better values, they turn to discount stores such as this Wal-Mart in Bentonville, Arkansas.

Aspirin provides an interesting example of the "good news, bad news" aspects of technology. When ibuprofen became available without prescription in 1984, aspirin sales began to slip as customers switched to pain relievers such as Advil and Nuprin. But in 1988, technology came to aspirin's rescue when researchers reported that taking an aspirin every other day could reduce the risk of heart attack in men by almost half. Buoyed by the good news, aspirin makers geared up to launch advertising campaigns linking aspirin with the prevention of heart disease.[11]

COMPETITION   Knowing the competition is an essential ingredient in any marketing plan. If you own a Burger King franchise, for instance, your success obviously depends on what McDonald's and Wendy's do. And to some extent, you are at the mercy of Taco Bell, Kentucky Fried Chicken, and Pizza Hut as well. On any given day, your customers might decide to satisfy their hunger in any number of ways—they might even fix themselves a sandwich.

LEGAL AND REGULATORY CLIMATE   Marketers must also respond to changes in the legal and regulatory climate. In recent years, the airline, banking, trucking, telecommunications, and securities industries have all scrambled to adjust to deregulation. Firms have lowered their prices, increased their advertising, and developed a host of new products and services to respond to these changes.

NATURAL ENVIRONMENT   In addition to coping with changes in the political environment, marketers must deal with natural forces. Interruptions in the supply of raw materials can upset even the most carefully conceived marketing plans. For example, the drought in the Midwest during the summer of 1988 damaged the wheat, corn, and soybean crops, boosting the cost of raw materials required by many food companies. These cost increases prompted many manufacturers to adjust their prices for such end products as bread, cereal, and cake mix. Although it is often impossible to predict the occurrence of natural events, companies must be prepared to react to circumstances.

Setting Objectives

Once the marketer has a basic understanding of the external environment, the next step is setting marketing objectives. These objectives define the firm's operating targets for the future and are generally stated in terms of sales growth, profitability, return on investment, research and development, and the like. The marketing objectives are derived from the organizational objectives. Generally, they establish a projected level of sales growth by product line, geographical area, or customer group. Often, they are directed at increasing the firm's **market share,** the percentage of the market served by the company. Although there are exceptions, the company with the largest market share is generally the most profitable competitor in an industry, since higher sales volume leads to economies of scale and lower production costs.

market share Percentage of total industry sales that are made by a particular company

Assessing Resources

In addition to surveying external factors, marketers must look within their own companies to determine their strengths and weaknesses. Various marketing strategies require differing financial resources, production capabilities, distribution networks, and promotion capabilities. For example, the manufacturer with the lowest production costs is in a better position to compete on the basis of price than a competitor with high production costs, whereas a company with wide distribution has a natural advantage in promoting products through mass advertising.

Developing Strategy

Having analyzed both the external environment and the firm's internal capabilities, the planner can select a strategy designed to achieve the organization's marketing objectives. Generally speaking, the proper strategy depends on the organization's relative position in the marketplace. The dominant firm in the industry has the advantage. It's up to the challengers to figure out a way to capture additional sales, which is one reason Nike and Reebok strive so hard to be first in athletic shoes. The key lies in maximizing the firm's strengths and capitalizing on the opponent's weaknesses.

THE LEADER'S OPTIONS   Firms like IBM, Procter & Gamble, McDonald's, and Coca-Cola generally have one primary goal: to stay on top. They attempt to accomplish this in one of two basic ways: by defending against their attackers or by trying to strengthen their advantage.

The defensive strategy involves matching all challengers move for move. If rivals introduce new products, the market leader counterattacks with an even better product. If an upstart initiates a price war, the leader responds by cutting prices even further. If the attack involves advertising, promotion, or distribution, the leader retaliates by outspending and overpowering the challengers. Because the dominant firm generally has superior resources, it can often defend itself successfully. By and large, holding on to customers is easier than luring them away.[12]

Although most market leaders employ defensive strategies to one degree or another, some also attempt to expand their market share. They do this by appealing to new users, encouraging customers to use the product more frequently, and promoting new uses for existing products.[13]

THE CHALLENGER'S OPTIONS   The challengers in an industry have three basic options: (1) They can assault the leader directly, as Pepsi has done with Coke; (2) they can play a "me too" game, riding along in the leader's wake, as Royal Crown Cola has done; or (3) they can carve out a special niche, offering a lower price, better service, different product features, or higher quality than the leader.[14] The Dundee, Scotland, division of NCR chose the first route in the automated teller machine (ATM) market, taking on market leader IBM head-on. Once a minor player in ATMs, NCR set out to build more reliable machines with the features that customers wanted; it was so successful that it became the top ATM maker in the world, with 63 percent more market share than IBM. In fact, NCR's success eventually forced IBM to form a joint venture with a third company in order to stay in the business.[15] Successful frontal assaults against a company as big as IBM are uncommon, but NCR proved that with attention to quality and customer, it is indeed possible.

As the dominant producer of adhesive tape, 3M has a distinct marketing advantage.

The Role of Market Research

✖**marketing research** Process
of gathering information about
marketing problems and
opportunities

As you can see, developing a modern marketing program is not a simple matter.
To aid in the process, more and more firms are employing **marketing research.**
Every year U.S. companies spend over $2 billion in an attempt to find out such
things as

▶ What products consumers want

▶ What forms, colors, packaging, price ranges, and retail outlets consumers prefer

▶ What types of advertising, public relations, and selling practices are most likely to
appeal to consumers[16]

By analyzing this sort of information, companies can decide who its best prospects are and how to appeal to them most effectively.

For example, when the U.S. Travel and Tourism Administration, a division of
the U.S. Department of Commerce, wanted to stimulate pleasure travel to the
United States, it commissioned descriptive research to survey vacationers in
Great Britain, Germany, and France. The purpose was to identify the characteristics of people who travel internationally for pleasure, to estimate the U.S. market share of international vacation travel, and to learn how potential travelers
view the United States and its attractions relative to competing destinations.
From this research, the USTTA learned that tourists from various countries

FOCUS ON ETHICS

Your Right to Privacy Versus the Marketing Databases

Right now, even as
you're reading this, your name and your life are part
of dozens and dozens of databases. Your school
knows the courses you take, the grades you get, and
your home address. Your bank knows your account
balance, where you used to bank, probably even
your mother's maiden name (it's requested on
most account applications). Your government knows
how much money you made last year, the kind of
car you own, and how many speeding tickets you've
gotten. The list goes on and on: video stores, libraries, doctors, dentists, insurance companies, and
many others keep records on your behavior and
activities.

There's nothing unethical about maintaining a
database, and there's certainly nothing unethical
about using a computer to manage the database. The
ethical dilemmas arise when marketers buy, borrow,
rent, or exchange information, usually without your
knowledge or permission. Computers make it so fast

and simple to mix and match databases that the process is usually invisible. Most of the time, you won't
even know that your records are being seen or used
by others, people you never imagined would or
should be able to put together a big file on your life.

That's dilemma number one: Who should have
the right to see your records? Should the government have the right to ask your employer to turn
over your employment records? Should a marketer
selling low-cost long-distance telephone service be
allowed to look at your telephone records? In the
1980s, the Selective Service Administration wanted
to find men of draft age who hadn't yet registered.
Among other databases, they bought a list of names
and birthdays from an ice cream parlor, a list developed as a promotion to recognize children's birthdays in some special way. In the outcry that followed, the Selective Service gave back the list. But
the dilemma remains: Who should see your records?

Dilemma number two: Should you have the right

generally have differing views of America as a travel destination, and they also tend to have differing priorities when planning vacations. Moreover, the research showed the USTTA that it needed to vary its marketing mix on a country-by-country basis because of these varying perceptions and interests.[17]

Broadly speaking, marketing research has two basic approaches: (1) the interview or survey methods, which attempt to analyze the consumer's thought processes; and (2) the observational methods, which analyze the consumer's current behavior in an attempt to predict future buying patterns. Both methods have advantages and disadvantages. Interviews and surveys can provide valuable clues to why people behave in certain ways. However, critics argue that people can say one thing when polled but behave differently in practice. Observational methods, on the other hand, provide little insight into the consumer's motives, but they are relatively objective.[18] Recent technological advances, including checkout scanners and grocery-cart tracking systems inside stores, have made it much easier to collect massive amounts of data directly on consumer behavior.

Many companies combine the two methods, getting the best of both the attitudinal and observational techniques. Before opening a new Italian restaurant, the first phase of General Mills's research was focused on determining consumers' likes and dislikes in terms of food and decor. A team of two dozen interviewers discovered a host of interesting facts from their conversations with over 5,000 consumers. For example, people consistently complained that Italian food has too much garlic and basil and that the spaghetti sauce runs all over the plate—two problems you'll never run into at an Olive Garden restaurant.

to know who wants your records and be able to refuse access? Say you've been getting all kinds of unsolicited mailings lately, and you're tired of having your mailbox filled with offers to buy magazine subscriptions, computer software, or ski parkas. You can ask that mailers not use your name and address by writing to the Direct Marketing Association. But that's the easy part. What happens when you apply for health insurance and you're asked to sign a statement that allows the insurer to search a medical records database for your history and to provide information on you to others? In some cases, such as when the government wants to verify your eligibility for welfare, you must be contacted for a response before the government can move on a negative decision. Should you have the right to know when people want your records? Should you have the right to allow some people to see your records and to refuse others?

Dilemma number three: What information should or should not be disclosed? The United States has passed at least five major federal laws on privacy, dealing with credit data, governmental data, bank files, videotape movie rentals, and computerized matching of government data. Despite some state laws, a lot of personal information about Americans can still be disclosed, information that may embarrass people or in some other way have a negative impact on their lives. Denmark has strict laws that prohibit marketers from exchanging information about substance abuse, criminal activities, or sexual inclinations. But who decides what should or should not be allowed to be disclosed?

A debate is raging between marketers and those who are concerned about privacy. On the one hand, privacy advocates argue that people should have the right to be left alone. On the other, marketers argue that they should have the right to freedom of speech, the right to inform customers about their offers. Thus the ultimate dilemma: Does a marketer's freedom of speech outweigh the consumer's right to privacy? Some argue that although the freedom of speech is guaranteed in the U.S. Constitution, the right to privacy is not. As the number of comprehensive databases continues to grow, this issue promises to be a central topic in marketing.

By carefully researching consumer needs, PepsiCo has succeeded in targeting Hispanic consumers, who drink one-third more soft drinks than the U.S. population as a whole. At Carnaval Miami's "Calle Ocho" street festival, PepsiCo unveiled the world's largest piñata, thrilling Hispanic youngsters and appealing to Hispanic parents, who tend to be strongly family-oriented.

After almost two years of attitudinal research, General Mills opened an experimental restaurant where researchers could observe the consumer's reaction to various recipes and service features. Customers were invited to give their opinions on everything from the food to the decor.

After operating the prototype restaurant for three years, General Mills opened seven additional restaurants designed to give the customers what they wanted. When all seven of the new restaurants succeeded, management decided to launch a major expansion effort.[19] The careful planning is paying off handsomely; Olive Garden is now one of the largest restaurant chains in the United States, with several hundred locations and sales well over a half-billion dollars a year.[20]

It takes sizable financial resources to conduct marketing research on the same scale as General Mills, but even the smallest companies can gather useful information to guide their marketing decisions. One of the best and least-expensive sources of information is a company's existing customers. By talking with customers, a firm can identify marketing problems, fine-tune its products, learn about the competition, and analyze alternative marketing strategies.[21]

▶ BUYING BEHAVIOR

Organizations put a great deal of effort into analyzing their markets for one basic reason: They want to know why the customer selects one product and rejects another (or one store or restaurant, in the case of retailing). Armed with this information, companies can tailor their marketing efforts to appeal to the buyer's motives. The motives of individual consumers generally differ from those of organizational buyers.

Consumer Buying Behavior

Many theories attempt to explain what it is that induces individuals to buy products. One way to look at the psychology of buying is in terms of how consumers make decisions. A simple formula sums up the decision-making process that nearly everyone goes through when making a purchase:

Choice = want + ability to buy + attitude toward the brand

The following sections take a closer look at this process and at the factors that influence it.

The Buyer's Decision Process

The consumer buying process begins when you become aware of a problem. Your next step is to look for a solution. Possibilities occur to you based on your past experience (your prior use of certain products) and on your exposure to marketing messages. If none of the obvious solutions seems satisfying, you gather additional information. The more complex the problem, the more information you are likely to seek. You may turn to friends or relatives for advice, read articles in magazines, talk with salespeople, compare products and prices in stores, and study sales literature and advertisements.

After satisfying your information needs, you are ready to make a choice. You may select one of the alternatives, postpone the decision, or decide against making any purchase at all, depending on the magnitude of your desire, the outside pressure to buy, and your financial resources.

Once you have made your purchase decision, you will evaluate the wisdom of your choice. If the item you bought is satisfying, you will tend to buy the same thing again under similar circumstances, thus developing a loyalty to the brand. If not, you will probably not repeat the purchase. Often, if the purchase was a major one, you will suffer from **cognitive dissonance,** commonly known as buyer's remorse. You will think about all of the alternatives you rejected and wonder whether one of them might have been a better choice. At this stage, you are likely to seek reassurance that you have done the right thing. Realizing this, many marketers try to reinforce their sales with guarantees, phone calls to check on the customer's satisfaction, user hot lines, follow-up letters, and so on. For instance, when Infiniti (the luxury car division of Nissan) tied for first place (with Lexus) in the 1991 J. D. Powers Car Customer Satisfaction Index Study, it sent a letter to owners announcing the fact, trying to reinforce the notion that they had made a smart choice.[22] Such efforts help pave the way for repeat business.

cognitive dissonance Anxiety following a purchase that prompts buyers to seek reassurance about the purchase

Factors That Influence Buyer Behavior

Throughout the buying process, various factors may influence the buyer. A person's culture, social class, reference group, and self-image all have a bearing on the purchase decision, as do situational factors like the presentation of the product, the events in the buyer's life, and the person's mood at the time of the purchase.

CULTURE   We are all members of particular cultures and subcultures. As residents of the United States, for example, we attend school and study certain subjects. We learn to admire people such as George Washington, Abraham Lincoln, and Martin Luther King. Because of our cultural heritage, we share certain values, attitudes, and beliefs that shape our response to the world around us. For example, in the past few years we have seen a shift toward healthier lifestyles. People are "saying no" to drugs, cigarettes, and alcoholic beverages. They are exercising and eating properly. By responding to such trends, marketers enhance the appeal of their products.

SOCIAL CLASS   In addition to being members of a particular culture, we also belong to a certain social class that affects our attitudes and buying behavior. Membership in a particular class—be it upper, middle, lower, or something in between—is based primarily on educational level, occupation, and family history. In general, the members of the various classes enjoy different activities, buy different goods, shop in different places, and react to different media. Take sports. Upscale consumers prefer golf, tennis, skiing, and sailing, whereas downscale buyers go bowling, hunting, fishing, and waterskiing.[23] An awareness of these likes and dislikes enables companies to tailor the elements of the marketing mix to appeal to the group most likely to respond to its products or services.

REFERENCE GROUPS   Although culture and social class exert an important influence on purchasing patterns, reference groups carry perhaps an even greater weight. A reference group consists of people who have a good deal in common—family members, friends, co-workers, fellow students, teenagers, sports enthusiasts, music lovers, computer buffs. We are all members of many such reference groups, and we use the opinions of the appropriate group as a benchmark when we buy certain types of products or services. For example, our friends influence our choice of clothes, books, music, and movies. We consult our families in choosing cars, homes, food, investments, and furniture.

In every reference group, one or two people are especially important. These are the "influentials," the 10 percent of the population who are the first to try new products and embrace new ideas and who then share their opinions with everyone else. They tend to be more assertive than the average person and are an important source of advice on everything from hairstyles to financial investments. Because their opinions carry so much weight, these are the people that marketers especially want to reach.[24]

SELF-IMAGE   Our picture of ourselves is also a key determinant of our purchasing behavior. We all have an image of who we are, and we reinforce this image through our purchases. The tendency to believe that "you are what you buy" is especially prevalent among young people. In a recent study on the meaning of possessions, researchers discovered that students consider possessions the most important aspect of their lives. They attach personal meaning to such objects as stereos, cars, and clothing.[25] Marketers capitalize on our need to express our identity through our purchases by emphasizing the image value of products and services. That's why professional athletes and musicians are used so frequently as product endorsers; we want to incorporate part of their public image into our own self-image.

SITUATIONAL FACTORS   Every purchase decision is influenced by a person's cultural, social, and personal identity, but factors of a more circumstantial nature also come into play. When we shop for bread, for example, we may choose one brand instead of another because we have a coupon or because one variety is displayed more prominently than another. A special sale may entice us to buy something that we would ordinarily resist. Important events in our lives, such as weddings, birthdays, and Valentine's Day, also trigger buying decisions.

Even our mood has a bearing on what we buy and how we make our choices. We turn to sweets, alcohol, and cigarettes when we are depressed.[26] We shop to alleviate boredom, dispel loneliness, escape reality, and fulfill our fantasies. For many people, shopping is a leading form of recreation, although in recent years more and more people have found shopping to be more stressful and less enjoyable, and many have become "shopping dropouts."[27]

Organizational Buying Behavior

Although Nike is concerned with the buying behavior of consumers, Nike itself is an organizational customer with a buying behavior all its own. Organizational buying behavior is similar in some ways to consumer buying behavior, but it is quite different in other ways. These differences fall into two general categories: (1) the kinds of products marketed and how they are purchased and (2) the nature of the buyer-seller relationship.

Differences in Products and Purchasing

The products sold to organizational markets include both raw materials (grain, steel, fabric) and highly technical and complex products (printing presses, telecommunications systems, management consulting). Between these two extremes, organizations buy many products also found in consumer markets; food, paper products, cleaning supplies, and landscaping services are some examples. Federal Express, for instance, sells its services to both organizational customers and individual consumers. However, even though the products may look the same, the quantities purchased and the buying processes are different.

Many organizational products are designed specifically for individual customers, especially production machinery and component parts for the customer's own products. For example, Sonoco Products, an industrial and consumer packaging supplier in Hartsville, South Carolina, actively surveys its customers to learn of specialized needs. When one customer expressed a need for more innovative packaging to differentiate a consumer product, Sonoco came up with a reclosable cap, a plunger system for dispensing the package, and improved print quality on the label so that the package would look more vibrant.[28]

Many industrial products are purchased in massive quantities—often by the ton or truckload. And also in contrast to consumer buying, organizational purchases tend to have large dollar values. Even the average consumer's biggest purchases, such as a home, can pale in comparison to the sorts of purchases that industrial giants make, from blast furnaces to skyscrapers.

Because orders are large, organizations tend to make purchases less often than consumers do. In addition, the purchase-planning period is longer. A consumer who decides to buy a new toaster simply goes to the store and picks one up, but an organizational buyer in need of machine tools usually has to get input from various departments, select both product and supplier, negotiate the deal, place a purchase order, arrange for delivery, and so on. In complicated situations, the buying process can stretch out over several years.

The motivations behind consumer and organizational purchases are also different. In a general sense, consumer purchases are driven by a desire for personal satisfaction, whereas organizational purchases are driven by economic motives. As a consumer, you purchase airline tickets to visit relatives or to escape to the beach during spring break. As a businessperson, you purchase airline tickets so that you can make sales calls, service customers' equipment, negotiate with suppliers, or perform a variety of other business functions—all of which are motivated by money.

Finally, many organizational purchases entail much greater risks to the buyer than consumer purchases do. Choosing the wrong equipment or suppliers can cripple a business. Critical purchase decisions involve the commitment of huge amounts of money, affect the daily operations of the company, and influence the long-term profitability and survival of the business. For instance, if you choose a United Airlines flight that turns out to be late, the consequences aren't usually disastrous. But if United chooses the wrong computers for its reservations and ticketing system, it could lose millions of dollars. Because of this risk, organizational buyers make more of a commitment to the important products and suppliers they select.[29]

Differences in the Buyer-Seller Relationship

Unlike consumer households, many organizations have people specially trained to make informed purchases. They have titles such as purchasing agent, and they may be certified by a professional organization. Because organizational buyers number far fewer than consumer buyers, they are often approached individually, rather than through mass marketing. These buyers are constrained by standardized purchasing procedures and by company guidelines concerning suppliers, prices, and negotiations.

Once established, relationships between organizational buyers and their suppliers tend to be stable and long term. Most buyers will choose two or three suppliers for a frequently purchased item. That way, the buyer ensures a smooth, regular supply and price competition while preventing overdependence.[30] Buyers prefer to stick with tried-and-true sources—if those sources continue to perform to expectations. This *source loyalty* results in part from the amount of time and effort spent choosing the supplier, especially if the buyer has had to make a major commitment by modifying plant equipment in order to use the supplier's product, by training employees on the equipment, or by taking other risks. Source loyalty may also stem from the fear of taking new risks or from lack of desire to make the effort to locate new sources.[31] Source loyalty benefits the buyer by improving communication flow, providing better customization (adapting a product to fit a single customer's needs) of products, and giving preferred status in case of shortages or other crises.[32]

A final significant difference between organizational buying and consumer buying is that many more people are involved in the organizational decision process. Whereas consumers make decisions by themselves or with the input of a few other household members, as many as 50 organizational members may contribute to a single buying decision. This *multiple buying influence* is perhaps the most important aspect of organizational purchasing behavior.

▶ MARKET SEGMENTATION

How does it feel to be a target market? Because you're a college student, you're part of a major market that many companies want to reach. The college market holds as much as $45 billion in disposable income—and an increasing number of marketers want to grab a chunk of that change. Textbooks are at the top of the collegiate shopping list, followed by clothes and then health and beauty aids. But American Express, Sony, Plymouth, PepsiCo, Coppertone, and lots of other firms are also wooing you, as you can tell from the marketing materials at your campus bookstore, in your mailbox, on bulletin boards, and even at the beach during spring break.[33]

College students are only one example of a group that can be identified for marketing purposes. Marketers must target specific markets because too many differences exist between people and organizations to treat the whole world as a single market. After all, college students are certainly different from high school students, who are different from junior high school students. Each group has its own unique needs and wants, so each will respond to marketing efforts differently. **Market segmentation** is the process of dividing a large market into smaller subsets of consumers or organizations that are similar in characteristics, behavior, wants, or needs. Each of these marketing segments can then be targeted using variations of the marketing mix.

market segmentation Division of a market into subgroups

Bases of Segmentation

The four most common bases for segmenting the consumer market are demographic, geographic, behavioral, and psychographic (see Exhibit 12.6). To some extent, these same approaches can also be applied in industrial markets.[34]

EXHIBIT 12.6 ▶ **Common Bases for Segmenting Markets**

The purpose of segmenting a market is to identify a group of customers who are likely to value the same things in a particular product or service.

CATEGORY	SEGMENTATION VARIABLE	
Demographic	Age Sex Buying power Occupation	Education Race and nationality Family life cycle
Geographic	Global regions Nations National regions States Counties Cities Neighborhoods Climate	Terrain Population density Market density
Behavioral	Amount of usage Type of usage Brand loyalty Benefits sought	
Psychographic	Social class Personality Lifestyle	

Demographic Segmentation

For many products, considerations such as the buyer's age, gender, income, occupation, or education are the most useful clues to market segmentation. Such factors are the subject of **demographics,** or the statistical analysis of population. The cosmetics industry lends itself to this form of segmentation because gender, age, and income all influence a consumer's purchases of skin care and beauty products. Noxell, one of the most successful companies in the industry, created the Cover Girl line for young working women interested in inexpensive, no-nonsense cosmetics. It recently added a new medium-priced line, Clarion, aimed at women over 30 who have sensitive skin.[35]

One demographic group is becoming increasingly attractive to U.S. marketers: Asian-Americans. Once virtually ignored, Asian-Americans spend $38 billion a year on retail items. In San Francisco (where 30 percent of the residents are Asian-American), the Chinese- and Vietnamese-language Yellow Pages sell more than $2 million a year in ads.[36]

demographics Study of the statistical characteristics of a population

Geographic Segmentation

Potential customers in various locations often have special needs or tastes. When differences result from location, it makes sense to use **geographic segmentation.** More snow shovels are bought in Detroit than in Miami, and more surfboards in Honolulu than in Manhattan. Campbell Soup manufactures two

geographic segmentation Categorization of customers according to their geographic location

EXHIBIT 12.7 ▶ **Geographic Markets for Selected Products**

Regional differences in tastes and needs provide a useful basis for segmenting the market for many products.

MERCHANDISE PURCHASED	THE BEST MARKET	THE WORST MARKET
Beer and ale (percentage of drinkers who consume)	Milwaukee (67.9)	Dallas/Fort Worth (44.2)
Canned chili (percentage of homemakers who use)	Dallas/Fort Worth (72.7)	Boston (6.0)
Insecticides (percentage of homemakers who use at least once a month)	Houston (61.9)	New York (26.4)
Life insurance (percentage of adults who currently have)	Pittsburgh (80.3)	Miami (53.4)
Lipstick (percentage of women using at least twice a day)	Seattle/Tacoma (58.2)	Cincinnati (35.6)
Panty hose (percentage of women who bought in past month)	Houston (61.1)	Miami (39.7)
Popcorn (percentage of adults who buy for home use)	Minneapolis/St. Paul (54.3)	Miami (26.5)
Scotch whiskey (percentage of drinkers who consume)	New York (35.9)	Cincinnati (9.6)

types of nacho cheese sauce—a spicy one for customers in the Southwest and West, and a mild one for everyone else.[37] Many other products can also be segmented geographically (see Exhibit 12.7). Geographic segmentation is an important issue in global marketing; companies that venture into other countries should always ask themselves whether each new country would be best served by a unique marketing mix.

Many industrial products also lend themselves to geographic segmentation because certain types of industrial customers tend to be clustered in the same area—electronics companies in Silicon Valley, aerospace companies in southern California, lumber companies in the Pacific Northwest, and so on. International markets are defined in part by geography. For instance, Japan, Korea, Taiwan, and Germany are major manufacturing centers, whereas London is a major financial center.

Behavioral Segmentation

behavioral segmentation
Categorization of customers according to their relationship with products or response to product characteristics

Another way to segment a market is to classify customers on the basis of their knowledge of, attitude toward, use of, or response to products or product characteristics. This approach is known as **behavioral segmentation**. Imagine that you are in the hotel business. You might classify potential customers according to when and why they stay in hotels, making a distinction between business travelers and vacationers. You could then tailor your services and promotion for one group or the other. The business traveler might be attracted by ads in *The Wall Street Journal,* and the tourist might respond to ads in *Condé Nast Traveler* magazine.

You could also think in terms of the benefits your customers might seek. Some travelers, for example, might be interested in price, others in status, service, location, or dependability. You could gear your hotel marketing plan to appeal to each group.

Measurement of the extent to which a product is used provides another behavioral approach to segmenting both consumer and industrial markets. With this approach, a company divides its market into nonusers, former users, potential users, occasional users, and frequent users. As a rule of thumb, marketers expect 80 percent of a product's sales to come from the 20 percent of the customers who are frequent users. By focusing on these customers, the company gets "more bang for its marketing buck." Another approach is to classify potential customers according to whether they use your product or your competitor's product. This enables you to develop a marketing approach aimed at your competitor's possible weaknesses.

Psychographic Segmentation

Psychographics is a relatively new specialty that characterizes consumers in terms of psychological makeup—their social roles, activities, attitudes, interests, opinions, and lifestyle. Psychographic analysis focuses on why people behave the way they do. In segmenting a market psychographically, you would examine a person's brand preferences, favorite radio and TV programs, reading habits, values, and self-concept.

A common psychographic model used to segment consumer markets is called Values and Life-Styles (VALS). The latest version, VALS 2, identifies consumer segments based on two dimensions: self-orientation (how one views oneself in relation to the world in general) and resources (one's income, employment, education, and so on).[38]

Target-Marketing Alternatives

The market-segmentation process helps a company identify which target customers to serve and how to appeal to them. There are basically four alternative approaches to target marketing: undifferentiated, concentrated, differentiated, and customized (see Exhibit 12.8).

Undifferentiated Marketing

When a company engages in **undifferentiated marketing** (commonly known as *mass marketing*), it does not subdivide the market at all. Rather, it concludes that all of the buyers have similar wants and can be served with the same standardized product. This approach is commonly used with basic products such as sugar and salt, which are physically and chemically identical regardless of who produces them.

Undifferentiated marketing has one big advantage: It enables a company to

Business Around the World

Researchers identified five psychographic segments among Dutch women, based on their attitudes toward traditional and nontraditional roles for women. The segments range from "Conservatives," who are satisfied with their traditional roles and who reject nontraditional roles, to "Pioneers," whose attitudes are just the opposite.

psychographics Classification of customers on the basis of their psychological makeup

undifferentiated marketing Marketing program that offers a single standard product to all consumers

EXHIBIT 12.8 ▶ **Comparison of the Four Basic Segmentation Strategies**

Various types of products and markets lend themselves to different segmentation strategies.

TARGET CUSTOMERS	MARKETING APPROACH	ADVANTAGES	DISADVANTAGES
Undifferentiated (Entire market)	Sell single product to everyone, using same pricing, promotion, and distribution	Minimizes costs	Makes company vulnerable to competitors who focus on specific niches
Concentrated (One homogeneous group)	Tailor marketing mix to needs of specific group	Gives company competitive advantage in serving target segment; is relatively economical	Limits growth potential; makes company vulnerable to shifting tastes of segment and competitive attack
Differentiated (Several distinct customer groups)	Create separate mix of product, price, distribution, and promotion to serve each of the distinct customer groups	Enables company to achieve competitive advantage in several segments in order to maximize its market share	Increases production and marketing costs
Customized (Individual buyer)	Tailor elements of marketing mix to needs of each individual buyer	Enables company to satisfy each customer's needs	Increases production and marketing costs

minimize its production and marketing costs. With only one basic product to manufacture and promote, the firm achieves economies of scale. However, firms that follow this approach are vulnerable to competitors who use a more targeted approach. For example, Morton's plain table salt has lost ground to flavored salts produced by rivals like Lawry's and McCormick.

Concentrated Marketing

concentrated marketing Marketing program aimed at a single market segment

A **concentrated marketing** approach is aimed at a single market segment. All of the organization's efforts are directed toward satisfying the specific needs of the target customer group. Carnival Cruise typifies those companies that have made their mark using a concentrated marketing approach. Until Carnival came along, most cruises were designed for the wealthy. But Carnival saw an opportunity to sell cruise vacations to people in other income brackets. The firm's formula was to offer all-inclusive air-and-sea packages priced about 20 percent below the competition and to schedule relatively casual four-day and seven-day cruises that were more compatible with the average person's budget and vacation schedule. The strategy has enabled Carnival to achieve a dominant position in the cruise industry.[39]

For all its attractions, the concentrated strategy has several disadvantages. The organization's sales are limited by the size of the segment, and business tends to fluctuate according to the changing tastes and fortunes of a particular

Can Universal Appeal Overcome Cultural Differences?

You've got a great product that's been selling like hotcakes in the United States. Now you want to market it in other countries. How do you go about it? Do you go into each country and conduct extensive market research so that you can adapt—or even create—the product, the packaging, and the promotion specifically for that culture? Or do you keep everything essentially the same for all countries, changing only the language on the package and in the advertising? In other words, do you go local or do you go global?

According to Harvard marketing professor Theodore Levitt, global is the only way to go. He argues that, thanks to telecommunications and cheap, easy travel, consumers the world over are becoming more and more alike. People everywhere share certain needs and desires, which allows marketers to sell standardized products at low prices the same way around the world. He points to Coca-Cola as the perfect example of a global product. In Levitt's view, adopting a global marketing perspective not only saves time and money in production and advertising outlays but also helps a company clarify its focus and objectives, making operations easier to manage and coordinate.

When Levitt's controversial ideas were first published in the early 1980s, many companies thought he made a lot of sense and jumped on the global bandwagon. But many more were wary of the whole idea. They saw numerous barriers to worldwide product standardization, including problems in technology (disparate electrical systems), packaging (colors, for example, can have different meanings in different cultures), consumer habits (it's difficult to sell cereal to Brazilians, who tend not to eat breakfast), and even physical characteristics of consumers (Japanese, on average, have smaller frames than Western people, and some products are too big or heavy for them).

Of course, some products are certainly global. On the streets of any major city in the world, you'll be able to stop for a snack at McDonald's, Pizza Hut, or Kentucky Fried Chicken. You'll see people wearing Levi's jeans and Swatch watches, carrying Gucci bags. They'll be driving Hondas and Volkswagens, shooting pictures with Canon cameras containing Kodak film, and then heading home to watch "Dallas" on their Sony TVs.

The market for such products, according to consultant Kenichi Ohmae, is primarily in what he calls the "Triad": the United States, Europe, and Japan. In his book *Triad Power: The Coming Shape of Global Competition,* Ohmae suggests that what many consider to be "global" products—those with a universal appeal—have their greatest demand within the Triad because of the increasing homogeneity of consumers in these three major world areas. He notes that high educational levels, exposure to television, and high levels of purchasing power lead to a similar lifestyle in these areas, setting them off from the rest of the world. Ohmae does believe, however, that some modifications should be made to adapt to each market. Manufacturers should strive to make the "insides" of a product the same for all countries but modify the exteriors to meet specific consumer desires. For example, pianos can have the same basic design and components, but people in the United States prefer a woodgrain exterior (as a fine piece of furniture), whereas people in Japan want black enamel (as an educational tool for children).

Along these same lines, other experts have suggested that *products* can be standardized globally but that *brands* need to reflect local conditions in terms of positioning and promotion. One marketing authority has summarized this approach as "thinking global, acting local." Thinking global refers to looking for something that people in many countries have in common and appealing to that common need with a universal product or service or one that is easily modified. Acting local means basing marketing strategies on knowledge of consumer behavior and desires in specific target areas. Ohmae gives the example of Mister Donut's entry into Japan. The U.S. fast-food chain found that the Japanese weren't fond of cinnamon, a key ingredient in doughnuts. So for this particular market the amount of cinnamon was drastically reduced. However, over a five-year period the ingredient was gradually increased, and today the doughnuts in Japan have as much cinnamon as they do in the United States.

It seems, then, that global marketing is a great idea if (1) your product is one that lends itself to standardization and has universal appeal, and (2) you take local cultural conditions into account when it comes to the specifics of branding and promotion.

Levitt himself has clarified his position by stating that he is not against some modifications on a local basis. Whether all products can be marketed like Coke remains to be seen.

customer group. Furthermore, the organization has all of its eggs in one basket, and if competitors move in, sales can plummet.

Differentiated Marketing

differentiated marketing
Marketing program aimed at several market segments, each of which receives a unique marketing mix

With a **differentiated marketing** approach, the organization avoids some of the problems associated with concentrated marketing. Instead of focusing on a single segment, the firm selects several target customer groups then varies the elements of the marketing mix to appeal specifically to each segment. This is the approach Nike takes when it designs shoes for basketball, running, aerobics, and other segments. In fact, adding new market segments is a logical way to build a business. Carnival Cruises is currently moving in this direction with the addition of higher- and lower-priced cruises aimed at groups it had not previously served.[40]

Differentiated marketing is probably the most popular segmentation approach, particularly for consumer products. However, it requires substantial resources because the organization incurs additional costs in tailoring its products, prices, promotional efforts, and distribution arrangements for each segment.

Customized Marketing

customized marketing A marketing program in which each individual customer is treated as a separate segment

Companies that use a **customized marketing** approach view each customer as a separate segment and tailor the marketing mix to that individual's specific requirements. This approach is necessary in certain types of industrial markets where the product cannot be standardized. Civil-engineering firms, for example, must design each bridge, road, or sewer system to meet the specific requirements of the customer. This approach is also used for many consumer services such as interior design, home repairs, and custom tailoring.

Increasingly, customized marketing is showing up in some surprising places. You wouldn't think that a consumer-goods marketer selling relatively inexpensive products over wide market areas could possibly build relationships with individual customers, but more and more of them are doing just that. The basic tool they use is *database marketing,* collecting information about customers and using it to fine-tune marketing programs. In the baby food market in France, for instance, Sopad Nestlé's sales have grown dramatically because it records every contact with customers (through letters and phone calls to the company's four dieticians) and uses the information gained during these contacts to send birthday cards and Mother's Day cards, which are a customized form of promotion and which help cement strong customer relationships.[41]

SUMMARY OF LEARNING OBJECTIVES

1 Explain what marketing is.

Marketing is the process of planning and executing the conception, pricing, promotion, and distribution of ideas, goods, and services to create exchanges that satisfy individual and organizational objectives.

2 Describe the four forms of utility created by marketing.

Form utility is created when the characteristics of a product or service are made more functionally and psychologically satisfying. Place utility is created when a product is made avail-

able at a location that is convenient for the consumer. Time utility is created by making the product available when the consumer wants to buy it. Possession utility is created by facilitating the transfer of ownership from seller to buyer.

3 Discuss the three major eras in the evolution of marketing.

Marketing initially had a production orientation; companies concentrated on producing products, taking orders, and distributing goods. As competition increased, companies began to adopt a sales orientation, aimed at stimulating demand for existing products. Today, most companies are part of the marketing era, which emphasizes trying to meet customers' wants and needs, rather than simply trying to sell whatever a company makes.

4 Identify and contrast the two basic types of markets.

The two basic types of markets are consumer markets and organizational markets, which include industrial/commercial customers, resellers

(wholesalers and retailers), and government agencies. In consumer markets, the individual buys goods or services for personal use. In organizational markets, the buyer purchases goods or services for resale or for use in conducting its own internal operations.

5 Specify the four basic components of the marketing mix.

The marketing mix consists of the four P's: product, price, place (distribution), and promotion.

6 Outline the four steps in the strategic planning process.

The first step is to analyze the external environment. The next step is to establish overall corporate goals and translate them into marketing goals. The third step is to assess re-

sources. The final step is to develop a marketing strategy.

7 Describe the five steps in the buyer's decision process.

The buyer recognizes a need, searches for solutions, gathers information, makes a decision, and then evaluates that decision.

8 Define market segmentation and list the four bases most often used to segment markets.

Market segmentation is the process of subdividing a market into homogeneous groups in order to identify potential customers and to devise marketing approaches geared to their needs and interests. The most common types of segmentation are demographic, geographic, behavioral, and psychographic.

Meeting a Business Challenge at Nike

Phil Knight's company was facing a formidable challenge launched by an upstart company in a newly emerging market segment. Aerobic exercise and the new world of athletic shoe fashion that it helped create were quite a departure from the millions of high-performance athletic shoes sold by Nike each year. Reebok's chairman, Paul Fireman, was among the first to spot the trend, and he had his designers create a unique shoe for aerobic workouts. But even Fireman wasn't prepared for what happened next. As running and sport shoes became fashionable footwear, Reebok's sales shot past those of its older competitor.

The result was that Nike slipped into the runner-up position in 1986, and Knight knew he had to act. Using marketing research, Nike marketers learned more about customer needs. To boost Nike's appeal, the company introduced stylish accents and colors. Now the company could compete more effectively against Reebok and L.A. Gear, both successful in combining fashion and active footwear.

Phillip Knight, CEO of Nike.

But Nike—and the industry—was built on performance, and that remained a high priority for many customers. Knight poured money into research and development, resulting in the new Nike Air technology. Soon many Nike shoes featured Nike Air,

and the firm built a special model with a small window on each side of the heel, revealing the air sac inside. Shoe stores were encouraged to show this Visible Air model to help sell all the shoes in the Nike line.

Knight had always been adept at exploiting advertising. Even before Reebok stole the show with aerobics shoes, Knight was using aggressive marketing and advertising approaches to keep the public's feet in Nike shoes. For the 1984 Olympics in Los Angeles, the company brought out a daring new billboard ad campaign, featuring colorful, dramatic pictures of athletes performing at their peak. The Nike name and logo appeared only in one corner, without any headline or sales message. In the race with Reebok, this award-winning Olympics series was followed by other high-profile ad campaigns, including "Just Do It," running from 1989 to 1990.

Knight also raised the stakes on celebrity endorsements, the industry's major marketing technique. Ever since Adidas and Puma pioneered the concept, success in the athletic footwear industry has depended on attaching the image of a sports star to a line of products. In 1984 Nike signed Michael Jordan (captain of the U.S. Olympic basketball team and a rising star with the Chicago Bulls) to a multiyear, multimillion-dollar deal. Other sports celebrities in the Nike lineup include John McEnroe, Jim Everett, Joan Benoit Samuelson, Bo Jackson, and Wayne Gretzky.

New products and new ads drew new customers, making distribution a key element in Nike's strategy. And Nike learned how important it is to maintain good relations with the distribution channel. Back when aerobics shoes were all the rage, Nike had mountains of unsold running shoes. The company turned to discount stores to empty its warehouses, which alienated the 12,000 sporting goods dealers and department stores that carried Nike's regularly priced shoes. Fortunately for Knight, he was able to win the retailers back with Nike Air.

Looking at the competition, Reebok is now neck-and-neck with Nike. Reebok introduced its answer to Nike Air: The Pump, a $170 shoe with a built-in pump to force air into the heel and midfoot. And this new technology seemed such a threat that Nike's stock price declined on the news of its introduction. In addition, Reebok has caught up with Nike's expenditures for its annual ad budget. For 1990, Reebok's budget topped $70 million—$10 million spent on The Pump alone.

Clearly, performance is the key to succeeding in today's athletic shoe market. But Phil Knight is also expanding Nike into apparel and children's shoes to capitalize on today's fitness and fashion partnership for all ages. The latest results look promising, and the race goes on.

Your Mission: You have been hired as a student marketing assistant at Nike headquarters in Beaverton, Oregon. You are assigned to the staff of Jody Rubin, children's marketing manager, to make a special four-week study of the children's shoe industry. This is a relatively new market segment for Nike, and Rubin must strengthen the firm's position. Use your knowledge of the marketing mix and your experience as a consumer to help identify potential winning strategies, to suggest effective competitive approaches, and to plan creative marketing programs.

1. Another competitor entering the children's shoe market is KangaROOS USA, best known for the pockets in its adult sports shoes. The first ad used by KangaROOS in the kids market was "ROOS: Shoes for your feet, pockets for your stuff." Although Nike has no pockets in its kids' shoes, you feel the high-performance fashion statement made by Nike shoes will attract kids. You know you need to open up your thinking and consider all kinds of product possibilities, however. Evaluate the following new product ideas. Which one has the greatest chance of success?

a. Develop a longer-lasting sports-style shoe for kids, with double soles and reinforced toes to keep the shoes intact long after competitive products have worn out. Don't worry if they look a little goofy; the important thing is to make sure they last a long time.

b. Manufacture current top sellers from the adult line in smaller sizes for kids, making adjustments for differences in children's feet. This will work because younger kids like to copy the styles worn by adults, and they'll feel grown-up in their miniature Nikes.

c. For dress-up occasions, create a new line of fancier Nike athletic shoes in leather with fashion accents. These shoes would meet the parent's desire to have their children looking halfway presentable and the child's need to be comfortable and fashionable.

d. Just wait and copy whatever KangaROOS USA does. Let them spend all their money on marketing research and product design. After they introduce new shoes, wait and see whether the shoes are successful. If a particular model of shoe does take off, copy the design and come out with your own version. Of course, you'll have to make sure you don't violate any trademarks or patents, but this strategy eliminates all the risk.

2. As part of the marketing plan for this year, Rubin wants to expand the distribution channels for the Nike children's shoe line. She has asked you to examine all feasible choices and make recommendations, based on Nike's image as a high-performance, fashion-oriented shoe interpreted for children. Which of the following types of stores would be the best choice for Nike?

a. Full-price department stores such as Bloomingdale's and Nordstrom would be the best choice for selling Nike shoes. Parents will like the fact that they can buy all their kids' clothing and shoes in one place. And Nikes "belong" in upscale department stores; they're too expensive to fit in other types of stores.

b. Discount department stores such as K Mart or Wal-Mart would be a better choice because parents like to save as much money as they can on their kids' clothes and shoes.

c. You need to have specialized outlets, and sporting goods dealers would work best. After all, Nike started out as a shoe for serious athletes, so it only makes sense that customers should come to buy them at a place that sells athletic products.

d. The best choice would be to sell the shoes through mail-order catalogs. Parents don't have to fight traffic or drag their kids through the mall. They simply make a phone call, and the shoes show up on the doorstep in several weeks.

3. You are attending a meeting at which Nike executives are considering how to make the product more attractive to consumers without changing the shoe itself. One executive suggests offering a lifetime warranty, guaranteeing that the shoes will last until outgrown by the children. Another proposes a money-back 30-day trial period, to give mothers an opportunity to see whether the shoes perform as well as expected. You are asked for your opinion. Which of the following ideas would you present as the strongest product enhancement?

a. Give customers a trade-in allowance with their next purchase of Nike kids' shoes. They would take advantage of this offer when buying a replacement for the original Nike pair, and they would be asked to bring in one of the original shoes to get the trade-in allowance.

b. Package a permanent color marker with each pair of Nike kids' shoes sold. The marker can be used to write the owner's name inside each shoe, and it might even be used to decorate the shoe to suit the wearer.

c. Prepare a wallet-sized card showing five or more new ways to thread shoelaces, as a fashion aid for kids. Tuck the card inside the shoebox, and print updated cards every six months or so, as needed.

d. Package the shoes in an inexpensive plastic carrying case with the Nike logo, which can be used to bring shoes to school or along on a trip.

4. To get new products out in front of adult audiences, Nike uses a network of professionals, such as aerobics trainers, who are given shoes in exchange for appearing in trade shows and for fulfilling other promotional duties. These professionals are frequently asked for advice on athletic apparel and shoes. You would like to have a similar panel of people who are in a position to recommend Nike kids' shoes to purchasers. Which of the following groups of people would have the most influence on children's shoe purchasers?

a. Podiatrists, doctors who specialize in care and treatment of foot problems, would be your best choice. They understand feet, and parents will trust their opinions.

b. Scholarship winners from local schools would make the best spokespersons. They will be respected for their scholastic achievements, so parents and children will put faith in what these students have to say.

c. Nobody knows more about Nike's children's shoes than the children of Nike employees. They could appear in ads explaining how their parents design and manufacture quality shoes that are the best available for young people.

d. Young celebrities would make the best representatives because children look up to them. Young athletes, musical performers, and television and movie stars will have the visibility to grab the children's attention and get their loyalty.[42]

KEY TERMS

behavioral segmentation (346)
cognitive dissonance (341)
competitive advantage (332)
concentrated marketing (348)
consumer market (333)
customized marketing (350)
demographics (345)
differentiated marketing (350)
exchange process (329)
form utility (329)
four Ps (333)

geographic segmentation (345)
market (333)
market segmentation (344)
market segments (333)
market share (336)
marketing (328)
marketing concept (331)
marketing mix (333)
marketing research (338)
marketing strategy (332)
needs (329)

organizational market (333)
place utility (329)
possession utility (329)
product differentiation (332)
psychographics (347)
target markets (333)
time utility (329)
transaction (329)
undifferentiated marketing (347)
utility (329)
wants (329)

REVIEW QUESTIONS

1. What is marketing, and why is it important to the U.S. economy?

2. How has marketing evolved over time?

3. How does organizational buying differ from consumer buying?

4. What are the main ingredients in the marketing mix?

5. What are the strategic options available to the market leader, and how do they differ from the strategies available to challengers?

6. What factors influence the consumer in making purchasing decisions?

7. What factors are considered in a demographic approach to market segmentation?

8. How does an undifferentiated approach to market segmentation differ from a concentrated approach?

A CASE FOR CRITICAL THINKING

What Color Are Your Spark Plugs?

You have discovered that you can afford to buy a new car after all, and you opt to order one from an American automobile manufacturer. Having made that relatively simple decision, you must now consider the available options. First there's body style: two-door or four-door? Then there's the engine: four, six, or eight cylinders? Automatic or manual transmission? Power steering? Air conditioning? Central locking system? Tinted glass? Power windows? Defoggers? Defrosters? By the time you actually place an order for a car, you will effectively have ruled out some 30,000 alternative versions of your particular vehicle. But you can take pleasure in the knowledge that the car will truly be yours—one of a kind. You may be less pleased to know that this "uniqueness" has added more than $1,000 to the car's price, because that's what it costs the manufacturer to build the required flexibility into assembly operations.

When Henry Ford started out, he simply built the best cars he could, and they were all pretty much alike. At that time, Ford's buyers—who outnumbered the cars—were happy to snap them up as they rolled off the assembly line. Today's automakers, however, offer an enormous variety, a result of the industry's greatly enlarged output, its apparent shortage of buyers, and its consequent determination, in the words of a former General Motors chairman, to build a car "for every purse and purpose." This is a logical approach to a buyers' market. That is, if there are many more cars than buyers, it makes sense to try to attract as many of those buyers as possible by finding out exactly what each one would like to have in a car and then providing exactly that.

Now it's becoming obvious to many companies that this strategy does not always work. Apart from the fact that variety costs the manufacturers a great deal, they have found that it may not pay to focus on a very small market; the potential buyers may be so few that it would not be possible to recover the costs of design, manufacture, promotion, and distribution, let alone make a profit. Therefore, Detroit has already begun following the lead of the Japanese, who—with plants halfway around the world—have not been able to offer so many options. Instead, they have carefully researched the U.S. market and broken it into several large segments. By offering only 20 or 30 versions of a popular model, the Japanese are able to engineer and manufacture a higher-quality car, distribute it more efficiently, and sell it for less than the price of a comparable American car. It's a formula that has paid off nicely.

Automakers in the United States would like to find a reasonable compromise between standardization and variety. As one General Motors executive says, "The challenge for all of us is to figure out what product differences the consumer is willing to pay for and which ones are spurious and too expensive."[43]

1. How do you think U.S. consumers would react if Detroit no longer offered an extensive array of options on cars? Explain your answer.

2. How do automakers that focus on a limited number of market segments figure out what kinds of cars to produce?

3. If total marketing means catering to the consumer, then why have the standardized Japanese cars outsold the more customized American cars?

4. New manufacturing techniques may reduce the cost of doing small runs, thus making small runs cheaper than mass production. How might this development change Detroit's marketing strategy? Explain your answer.

BUILDING YOUR COMMUNICATION SKILLS

Either individually or in a small group of three or four, select a consumer product with which you are familiar, and identify the elements that make up the marketing mix: product, price, place, and promotion. Use personal observation of print ads, television commercials, radio spots, and information from periodicals and books (available in the library) that focus on advertising and marketing.

▶ Describe how the elements of the marketing mix create a marketable product.

▶ Compare your product with similar products to determine which elements of the marketing mix make one product more successful than others.

▶ Share your findings with the members of your class in a brief presentation. To support your findings, include examples such as print ads and information obtained as a result of your library search.

KEEPING CURRENT USING *THE WALL STREET JOURNAL*

From recent issues of *The Wall Street Journal,* select an article that describes in some detail a particular company's marketing strategy (either in general or for a particular product or product line).

1. Describe the company's market. What geographic, demographic, behavioral, or psychographic segments of the market is the company targeting?

2. What factors influenced the company's decisions about its marketing strategy?

3. According to the article, how successful has this strategy been? What marketing problems or opportunities can you foresee if the company continues to follow this strategy?

CHAPTER *13*

LEARNING OBJECTIVES
After studying this chapter, you will be able to

1 List three types of consumer products and two types of organizational products.

2 Cite the three levels of brand loyalty and explain the concept of brand equity.

3 Discuss the functions of packaging.

4 Describe the five stages of product development.

5 Specify the four stages in the life cycle of a product.

6 Identify four ways of expanding a product line.

7 List seven common pricing objectives.

8 Distinguish between two methods for setting prices.

Product and Pricing Decisions

PERSONALITY WITH A POP

I t's a funny name for a food product, but Orville Redenbacher has been laughing all the way to the bank since 1970. In just five years, his Orville Redenbacher Gourmet Popping Corn surpassed 82 brands to become the market leader. Before Orville Redenbacher, there was no such thing as "gourmet" popcorn. In fact, before Redenbacher energized the entire category, popcorn production in the United States languished under 350 million pounds a year. Only after Redenbacher's product became a hit did production pop up past 675 million pounds. But it was a long way from the corn crib to the store shelf.

As a boy, Redenbacher had grown corn for popping as part of a 4-H project to devise a better strain. He majored in agronomy (soil management and field crops) at Purdue University in the 1920s, and after graduation he served as an agricultural agent. Then he managed a large Indiana farm where he became involved in growing hybrid corn and processing popcorn seed. That's when Redenbacher met Charlie Bowman, who ran a seed program at Purdue. In 1951 the two entrepreneurs bought a small company that raised and sold corn seed, renamed it Chester Inc., and started to experiment with popcorn seed.

Bowman handled grain storage and irrigation systems for the company, and Redenbacher worked with corn-breeding experts on a new corn hybrid. By 1965 he had crossbred 40 generations of corn and come up with what he considered the consummate corn for popping. The new corn popped up fluffier than other varieties, and a higher percentage of individual kernels popped. Redenbacher's secret? He harvested and stored the hybrid corn on the cob, drying it at a controlled temperature to maintain a specific moisture level in each kernel.

Redenbacher now faced the challenge of producing and marketing his newfangled snack. Farmers weren't exactly lining up to grow the new corn. It cost more to harvest than other popping corns, and crop yields were lower per acre than with traditional corns. Nor were retailers eager to stock the new popcorn, which had been dubbed Red Bow. Over and over again, merchants told Reden-

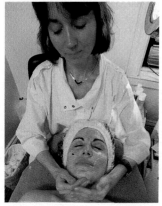

When we think of products, we generally think in terms of tangible goods such as perfume or paint. But the term *product* also encompasses services such as haircuts, accounting advice, medical treatment, taxi rides, and home repairs. At April's, a hair and nail salon in New York City, facials are one of the products customers can purchase.

product Good or service used as the basis of commerce

bacher that people just wouldn't pay more for a new popcorn, even popcorn that was of higher quality.

By 1970 Redenbacher realized he needed a new approach. He traveled to Chicago to meet with a team of marketing specialists, and he spent hours talking about popcorn. At a cost of $13,000, Redenbacher was staking a great deal on these specialists. He came back a week later to hear their recommendations and was astonished when they advised calling the product Orville Redenbacher's Gourmet Popping Corn. Moreover, the marketers wanted Redenbacher to put his own picture on the label. Finally, they suggested the new popcorn be positioned as unabashedly upscale, packaged appropriately, and tagged with a premium price.

Although he was skeptical, Redenbacher decided to get his money's worth and try these marketing ideas. Put yourself in Redenbacher's shoes: How would you create and support the new brand? What packaging and labeling decisions would you have to make as you introduce the new product? How would you encourage people to try your popcorn, and then buy it again? And how would you sustain sales after the product was established?[1]

▶ PRODUCTS: THE BASIS OF COMMERCE

Orville Redenbacher's Gourmet Popping Corn has been a highly successful product. If you were asked to name three other popular products off the top of your head you might think of Snickers, Levi's, and Pepsi—or three similar products. But you might not think of the Boston Celtics, Disneyland, or the television show "60 Minutes." That's because when we're on the buying side of an exchange, we tend to think of products as *tangible* objects that we can actually touch and possess. Basketball teams, amusement parks, and TV programs provide an *intangible* service for our use or enjoyment, not for our ownership; nevertheless, they are products just the same. From a marketing standpoint, a **product** is anything that is offered for the purpose of satisfying a want or need in a marketing exchange.

Types of Products

Marketers have a variety of ways to categorize products as they develop marketing strategy. You wouldn't market a garden tractor the same way you'd market accounting services; the buyer behavior, product characteristics, market expectations, competition, and other elements of the equation are all different. The two most significant categorizations involve the degree of tangibility and the nature of the customer.

Tangible and Intangible Products

It's convenient to group products as tangible goods or intangible services and ideas, but in reality, things aren't quite so simple. Nearly all products are combinations of tangible and intangible components. Some products are predominantly tangible, others are mostly intangible; most products fall somewhere between these two extremes. The *product continuum* graphically indicates the relative amounts of tangible and intangible components in a product (see Exhibit 13.1). Political ideas are an example of products at the intangible extreme,

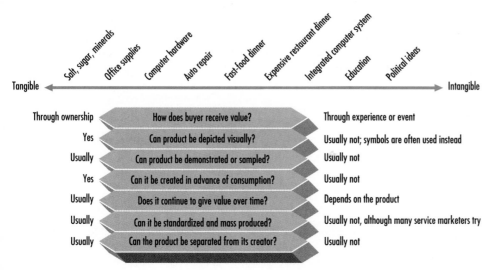

EXHIBIT 13.1

The Product Continuum
All products are made up of both tangible and intangible components, and the particular mix in a given product has a lot to do with the way it should be marketed.

whereas salt and sugar represent the tangible extreme. Dinner in a restaurant falls somewhere in the middle because customers get both tangible components (food and beverages) and intangible components (the food is cooked and served, the dishes are washed, etc.). Dinner in an expensive restaurant, where you're likely to have several servers, live music, and so on, has a greater degree of intangibility than dinner at McDonald's or Burger King. Auto repair, on the other hand, can range all over the continuum, depending on the particular problem being repaired.

As the product continuum indicates, service products have some special characteristics that affect the way they are marketed. The most important of these is the fundamental intangibility of services. You can't usually show a service in an ad, demonstrate it for customers before they buy it, or give customers anything tangible to show for their purchase. Successful services marketers often compensate for intangibility by using tangible symbols or by adding tangible components to their products. Prudential Insurance uses the Rock of Gibraltar in its logo and talks about having "a piece of the rock." Gibraltar is a symbol of solid stability, and Prudential wants you to think the same about its services.

Another unique aspect of service products is that they can't usually be created in advance and stored until people want to buy them. This presents big challenges in terms of staffing, pricing, and other management issues. For example, it is this *perishability* of services that leads movie theaters to offer cheaper tickets during the day. The theaters want to shift some of the customer demand from the busy evening and weekend times, and they want to use their service capacity as much as possible.

Because services are performances or experiences, the people providing the service are an important part of the equation. For instance, if a computer company received orders for more computers than it could build, it could pay someone else to build the extra computers; customers who received those particular products would never know the difference and would probably not care if they did. On the other hand, you can't separate a service such as live music from its provider. Robert Cray can't put on a B. B. King concert, for instance, even though both are blues guitarists. If King were unable to perform due to illness, the concert would have to be canceled.

In addition to considering the tangible and intangible makeup of a product, marketers need to take into account the intended buyer of the product. As discussed in Chapter 12, consumers and organizations have different purchasing patterns, and these differences have important implications for companies trying to optimize their marketing mixes.

Consumer Products

Although some products are sold to both consumer and organizational markets, many are sold exclusively to consumers. Most marketing specialists divide the

FOCUS ON ETHICS

Is Product Liability Getting Out of Hand?

An Illinois man, Robert Loitz, injured a thumb when his 12-gauge shotgun exploded during a trap-shooting contest. He sued the gun manufacturer, Remington Arms Company, and a state jury awarded him $1.5 million in punitive damages. For Loitz, who had incurred only $5,000 in expenses for medical bills and lost wages, the award was like winning the state lottery. Fortunately for Remington, the Illinois Supreme Court rescinded the award, leaving Loitz with a more reasonable award of $75,000.

In the last decade, the number of product-liability claims in the United States has tripled, with increasing numbers of consumers seeking the kind of riches initially bestowed upon Loitz. Between 1975 and 1986, the number of million-dollar damage awards rose 85 percent, with the average award quadrupling to $1.8 million. The result is that insurance costs for U.S. businesses have skyrocketed and consumers have a smaller range of product choices at higher prices. In fact, in one survey of 500 CEOs, 39 percent reported deciding against introducing new products and 47 percent discontinued product lines altogether because of adverse impacts of liability experience (both actual and anticipated).

On the other side of the coin, however, the same survey revealed equal numbers of CEOs who redesigned product lines and improved product usage and warnings because of litigation experience. When it comes to safety innovation, consumer advocates are convinced that the fear of litigation forces manufacturers to think safety first, thereby creating mechanisms previously ignored. Thanks to product-liability suits we now have air bags, explosive-resistant fuel tanks, roll bars, and thousands of other safety features on all types of products that otherwise might never have been introduced.

But the bottom line is that our current product-liability system is costing all of us a bundle in one way or another, and the penalties get worse from year to year. Who's to blame? Greedy consumers who take advantage of deep-pocketed corporations? Greedy attorneys who encourage their clients to file outrageous claims? Greedy businesspeople who cut corners to make bigger profits? Or naive business-people who unknowingly market defective or unsafe products?

Congress may finally get its arms around this issue when it considers a new product-liability bill that would provide uniform liability standards, a pro-consumer statute of limitations, uniform standards for punitive damage awards, and expedited product-liability settlements. In the meantime, companies cannot escape being sued. And even if we manage someday to improve our product-liability system, businesses will always be vulnerable to a lawsuit.

Although no defense is infallible, there are ways to reduce the likelihood of facing a product-liability lawsuit, and especially of losing one. Some of the most important steps include thinking of everything that could possibly go wrong when someone uses the product, striving for zero defects, providing specific instructions and warnings, advising distributors to sell only to targeted consumers, testing component parts manufactured elsewhere, testing the finished product under the toughest conditions it is likely to encounter, and documenting your testing efforts. According to Leonard M. Ring, former president of the Association of Trial Lawyers of America, "The law doesn't require a perfect product—the idea is to make it as safe as can reasonably be done for the foreseeable use."

broad category of consumer products into three subgroups according to the approach people take when shopping for them.

CONVENIENCE PRODUCTS   The goods and services that people buy frequently, without much conscious thought, are called **convenience products**—inexpensive items such as toothpaste, soda, and razor blades. Routine personal services like dry cleaning, film developing, and photocopying are convenience products, too. Because the buyer is already familiar with these products, habit is a strong influence in the purchase decision. People buy the same brand or go to the same shop because it is easy to do so. Unless something has made them particularly conscious of price, they don't often even think about the relative cost of alternatives that could serve their purpose just about as well.

> **convenience products** Products that are readily available, low priced, and heavily advertised and that consumers buy quickly and often

To cultivate these strong buying habits, many sellers of convenience products use advertising and packaging to create an easily recognizable image. Special pricing and promotion tools may also be important elements in the marketing mix. But personal selling efforts generally aren't important, because most convenience products are familiar items sold in self-serve outlets.

Services that qualify as "conveniences" are typically sold on the basis of location and personal rapport between buyer and seller. A person will generally go to the closest dry cleaner, for example, unless the price is outrageous and the service is dreadful. If the service is adequate, the convenience of the location will probably outweigh particularly friendly or cheap service at a more distant location.

SHOPPING PRODUCTS   Purchases that require more thought fall into the category of **shopping products.** These are fairly important goods and services that a person doesn't buy every day: a stereo, a washing machine, a suit, an interior decorator, a tax service, or a college. Such purchases require more thought about the brand differences like price, features, quality, or reputation. These brand differences prompt comparison shopping. Thus the shopping process is a form of education; the more unusual and expensive the product, the more the buyer checks around to compare models, features, and prices. Various sources of information are consulted, including advertisements, salespeople, friends, and relatives.

> **shopping products** Products for which a consumer spends a lot of time shopping in order to compare prices, quality, and style

SPECIALTY PRODUCTS   People use a different approach when they are shopping for **specialty products,** items that have been mentally chosen in advance and for which there is no acceptable substitute to the consumer. These are things like Chanel perfume, Brooks Brothers suits, and Suzuki violin lessons—particular brands that the buyer especially wants and will seek out, regardless of location or price. The buyer is attracted mainly by the features of the product, although advertising may have helped create an aura of special value. Not all specialty products are expensive, however. Consider your own shopping behavior when you purchase a six-pack of soda: If you're like many people, you want only your favorite brand, and you won't readily accept a substitute.

> **specialty products** Products that a consumer will make a special effort to locate

Organizational Products

Organizational buyers tend to base their selection of goods and services on objective criteria such as performance, support services, warranty, and *cost of ownership,* the total cost of buying and owning a product. However, buying

expense items Relatively inexpensive organizational products that are generally consumed within a year of their purchase

capital items Relatively expensive organizational products that have a long life and are used in the operations of a business

approaches vary, depending on the purpose and price of the item being procured. Organizational products fall into two general categories (which are based on cost and life span). **Expense items** are relatively inexpensive goods and services that are generally used within a year of purchase. Those that are more expensive and have a longer useful life are considered **capital items.** Most organizations, in fact, have a specified purchase amount, above which a product is classified as a capital item.

Buying behavior can be quite different for these two classes of products. The purchase of most capital items is planned over many months or years, and specific items are often identified in the buyer's budget. In purchasing these items, organizational buyers behave much like consumers who are purchasing shopping products. They educate themselves about the alternatives before making a decision. A person-to-person explanation of the product's features is generally an important part of the education process. If a capital item is particularly complicated or expensive, the purchase decision is often based on written, competitive bids. These bids are evaluated by a team of top managers and technical people who carefully weigh product features and price. Frequently, the selection process takes several months and requires a strong personal-selling effort on the part of competing vendors. A similar purchasing process is used when companies sign contracts for long-term services such as accounting, consulting, and legal services.

Expense items, on the other hand, might be purchased with relatively little advance notice, and companies may have a general budget category of "supplies" or "raw materials" (as opposed to every purchase being specifically identified). Expense items are often purchased by lower-level managers and nonmanagers, and many are ordered automatically by computers that monitor inventory and supply levels. Organizational buyers shop for expense items in much the same way that consumers shop for convenience products. Habit has a lot to do with their choices. The most important factors in the buying decision are generally availability, familiarity, and special promotions.

Aside from dividing products into expense and capital items, organizational buyers and sellers often classify products according to their intended usage as well:

▶ *Raw materials.* Manufacturing and processing companies have to buy a variety of raw materials, ranging from iron ore and crude petroleum to lumber and chemicals.

▶ *Components.* In addition to raw materials, most manufacturers also buy components, which are parts that go into the manufacturers' final products.

▶ *Supplies.* Organizational customers of all types need supplies to keep their operations going. A common term for supplies is **MRO items,** which refers to maintenance, repair, and operating items. Depending on the customer, supplies can mean anything from pencils to nails to floor wax.

MRO items A common term for supply products purchased by organizational customers; it stands for maintenance, repair, and operating items

▶ *Equipment.* Even if it's only a desk and a telephone, organizational customers need equipment. For a small service provider, such as an independent consultant, the equipment needs are fairly modest. At the other extreme, the U.S. government, Citicorp, and General Motors have mammoth equipment needs, including robots, computers, vehicles, and thousands of pieces of office furniture. The largest pieces of equipment are often considered installations, the next organizational product category.

▶ *Installations.* Installations are among the most complicated organizational goods. They are composed of buildings and large, stationary equipment such as production lines, milling machines, and semiconductor fabrication machinery. Some examples of complete installations include factories, power plants, airports, and mainframe computer systems. Such purchases hold a great deal of risk for the buyer because there are so many ways things can go wrong with major projects such as these. In addition, the location itself is an important part of an installation. Various cities, states, and countries promote themselves as ideal places to build factories and other business facilities. For instance, the French Industrial Development Agency advertises in U.S. magazines, hoping to catch the attention of companies looking to expand their European operations.[2]

▶ *Business services.* Business services range from simple and fairly risk-free services such as landscaping and cleaning to complex services such as management consulting and auditing, which can strongly affect an organization's success or failure.

Product Brands and Trademarks

Regardless of what type of product a company sells, it usually wants to create a **brand** identity by using a unique name or design that sets the product apart from those offered by competitors. Tide, Oldsmobile, and Bic are *brand names;* McDonald's golden arches, the Jolly Green Giant, the Pillsbury doughboy, and the Prudential rock are *brand symbols.*

Brand names may be owned by wholesalers, by retailers, and by producers of a product. Macy's, for example, buys merchandise from many manufacturers, which it then sells under some 50 in-house private labels.[3] A & P, the supermarket chain, purchases canned fruits, jellies, rice, household cleaning products, and frozen foods from hundreds of suppliers and offers them under the Jane Parker, A & P, and Ann Page brand names. Brands owned by national manufacturers are called **national brands.** Brands owned by wholesalers and retailers, such as Macy's and A & P, are **private brands.**

As an alternative to branded products, some retailers also offer **generic products,** which are packaged in plain containers that bear only the name of the product. These products are most often standard rather than first quality. They cost up to 40 percent less than brand-name products because of uneven quality, plain packaging, and lack of promotion. Generic goods have found a definite market niche, as a look at your local supermarket shelves will demonstrate. However, sales of generics have declined in recent years, partly because inflation has moderated, partly because consumers are disappointed with the uneven quality, and partly because brand-name producers have fought back with cents-off coupons that reduce the generics' cost advantage.[4]

Brand names and brand symbols may be registered with the Patent and Trademark Office as trademarks. A **trademark** is a brand that has been given legal protection so that its owner has exclusive rights to its use. Because a well-known name is a valuable asset and generates more sales than an unknown name, manufacturers zealously protect their trademarks. White-Westinghouse, for example, runs advertisements to remind people that Laundromat and Frigidaire are registered trademarks, not generic terms. When a name becomes too widely used, it no longer qualifies for protection under trademark laws. Cellophane, kerosene, linoleum, escalator, zipper, shredded wheat, trampoline, and raisin bran are just a few of the many brand names that have passed into the public domain, much to their creators' dismay.

Brand Loyalty

Of the 25 consumer brands with leading market shares in 1923, 20 are still number one in their market, providing convincing evidence of the strength of

The emotional appeals that move consumer goods won't sell products like Philips Medical's BV29 X-ray system. The magnetic resonance equipment is marketed directly to hospitals, whose purchasing agents base their decisions on cost, reliability, efficiency, availability, or even familiarity and habit.

brand Any name, term, sign, symbol, design, or combination used to identify the products of a firm and to differentiate them from competing products

national brands Brands owned by a manufacturer and distributed nationally

private brands Brands that carry the label of a retailer or wholesaler rather than a manufacturer

generic products Products in plain packaging that bears only the name of the item, not of its producer

trademark Brand that has been given legal protection so that its owner has exclusive rights to its use

EXHIBIT 13.2

Brand Loyalty and Product Type

Some types of products inspire more brand loyalty than others. A study conducted by J. Walter Thompson ad agency found that consumers were relatively unwilling to switch brands of products that they associated with their self-image—even when they were offered an alternative brand at half-price.

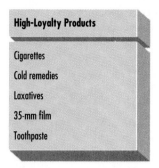

High-Loyalty Products

Cigarettes

Cold remedies

Laxatives

35-mm film

Toothpaste

Medium-Loyalty Products

Cola drinks

Furniture polish

Hand lotion

Margarine

Shampoo

Low-Loyalty Products

Crackers

Facial tissues

Paper towels

Plastic trash bags

Scouring powder

brand loyalty.[5] Nevertheless, a company has to think carefully about the benefits before spending $20 million to $40 million or more on a huge promotion campaign to establish a national brand name.[6] The cost of such a campaign may drive up the price of the product, making it possible for other companies to sell unbranded or lesser-known brand products at a substantially lower price. And just because consumers recognize the brand name is no guarantee they will buy the product. Surveys have shown that some of the best-known brands are among the least-respected products.[7]

Before deciding to build a brand, marketers evaluate whether the payoff will be worth the investment. Often the answer depends on the type of product. People are more loyal to some types of branded products than others (see Exhibit 13.2). Mundane products designed to handle tedious chores are less likely to inspire loyalty than products associated with an individual's personal image.[8]

Brand loyalty can be measured in degrees. The first level is *brand recognition,* which means that people are familiar with the product; they are likely to buy it because they recognize it. The next level is *brand preference.* At this level, people habitually buy the product if it is available. However, they may be willing to experiment with alternatives if they have some incentive to do so. The ultimate in brand loyalty is *brand insistence,* the stage at which buyers accept no substitute.

One of the most intriguing examples of brand loyalty was seen when the Coca-Cola Company attempted to discontinue traditional Coke and replace it with a new formula. Although a $4 million taste test of 200,000 consumers demonstrated that people preferred the new flavor, the company was deluged with protests when it made the switch. People were incensed that anyone would tamper with Coke, which had become an American institution in its 99 years. Within months, the company admitted that it had goofed and brought back the old formula, calling it Coca-Cola Classic and selling it alongside the new Coke.[9] As it turned out, the incident worked to Coke's advantage. With two main products, it now has almost twice the shelf space in supermarkets.

Brand Equity

A brand is often an organization's most valuable asset because it provides customers with a way of recognizing and specifying a particular product so that they can choose it again or recommend it to others. A brand also enables marketers to develop specific images and interrelated marketing strategies for a particular product. In addition, a brand can command a premium price in the marketplace, and it is often the only element of a product competitors can't copy—although sometimes they try. Agricultural specialists may eventually be able to duplicate Orville Redenbacher's popcorn, but they'll have to search far and wide for a name that could match his. Rather than building brands from scratch, some firms simply buy established brand names. Highly successful brands can be worth millions of dollars in the acquisition marketplace. Cadbury Schweppes, for example, calculated that the $220 million it paid for Hires and Crush included $20 million for physical assets and $200 million for "brand value."[10] This notion of the value of a brand is also called **brand equity**, which indicates a brand's overall strength in the marketplace.[11]

brand equity *The overall strength of a brand in the marketplace and its value to the company that owns it; increasingly, companies are trying to assign financial value to brand equity*

Brand Strategies

Companies take various approaches to building brands. The traditional approach is to create a separate identity for each product a company sells so that if a problem develops with that product, the other items in the line will not suffer. This approach has the added advantage of allowing a company to create separate product images for various market segments. Take the U.S. automobile companies, for example, with their varied product lines aimed at various types of buyers. The person who likes a Corvette and the person who wants a Cadillac are looking for completely different things, even though both want a General Motors car. Among more recent car introductions, Nissan, Toyota, and Honda all opted to create separate brand names for their luxury car divisions (Infiniti, Lexus, and Acura, respectively). Mitsubishi, on the other hand, decided to keep the company brand name for its first luxury model, the Diamante.

Although individual branding has its advantages, in the past few years an increasing number of companies have been using **family branding** (or using a brand name on a variety of related products) to add to their product lines. Frito-Lay, for example, launched Cool Ranch Doritos and Cajun Spice Ruffles, extending the brand by building on the reputations of regular Doritos Tortilla Chips and Ruffles potato chips. Of course, Frito-Lay isn't alone. Between 90 and 97 percent of the new products recently introduced by five of the largest consumer food companies were brand extensions.[12] Building on the name recognition of an existing brand enables companies to cut both costs and risks associated with introducing new products. However, there are limits to how far a brand name can be stretched to accommodate new products. Snickers ice cream bars, Rubbermaid feed bins (for farm use), and Dr. Scholl's socks and shoes worked as brand extensions, but Bic perfume, Rubbermaid computer accessories, and Playboy men's suits did not. The secret is in extending with products that fit the buyer's perception of what the brand stands for.[13]

family branding *Using a brand name on a variety of related products*

Another way to reduce the cost of building a new brand is to buy the rights to specific names and symbols that are already well known and then to use these licensed labels to help sell products. **Licensing** is common among manufacturers of children's products, who license popular cartoon or movie characters and affix them to everything from toys to clothing and breakfast cereals. However, the approach may backfire if the popularity of the licensed property declines, as Pepperidge Farm learned when it launched Star Wars cookies. Despite this risk, however, licensing is on a roll. Retail sales of licensed goods have soared to $17 billion.[14]

licensing *Giving rights to a company to use a well-known name or symbol in marketing its products*

Packaging

With annual sales of $55 billion, the packaging business is the third largest industry in the United States, providing everything from tin cans to airtight

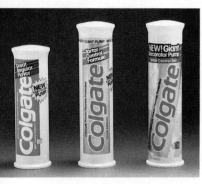

In many purchasing decisions, customers pay as much attention to the package as they do to the contents.

boxes.[15] But because 80 percent of all buying decisions are made in the store, product manufacturers consider the money they pay for packaging well spent.[16] Effective packaging not only protects products from damage or tampering but also promotes a product's benefits through shape, composition, and design.

Packages serve other purposes as well. They make products easier to display, attract customers' attention, and reduce the temptation to steal small products. Also, packages provide convenience. For example, more and more frozen foods are being packaged in cardboard rather than aluminum so that they can be used in microwave ovens. In addition, clever packaging can give a manufacturer a real cost advantage against competitors. The packaging for The Budget Gourmet, a popular line of frozen foods, is 30 to 40 percent cheaper than traditional frozen-dinner packaging, allowing the firm to offer a low price on its entrées without skimping on the quality of the food.[17] In many cases, packaging is an essential part of the product itself. Consider microwave popcorn or toothpaste in pump dispensers. Innovative packages like these may give a company a powerful marketing boost, whereas a poor package may drive consumers away (see Exhibit 13.3).

Apart from performing practical functions, packaging also acts as a form of communication. Consumers see certain colors and draw conclusions about a product even before they read the label. A red soft-drink can means cola; green means lemon-lime. Dishwashing liquid in a yellow container is lemony; a household cleaner in a green package is associated with pine. Many things packaged in black project an image of elegance.[18]

Labeling

Labeling is an integral part of packaging. Whether the label is a separate element attached to the package or a printed part of the container, it serves to identify a brand. Sometimes the label also gives grading information about the product or information about ingredients, operating procedures, shelf life, or risks.

The labeling of foods, drugs, cosmetics, and many health products is regulated under the federal Food, Drug and Cosmetic Act of 1938. This act gives the Food and Drug Administration the authority to monitor the accuracy of the list of ingredients on labels. For example, a fruit drink cannot be labeled and sold as

---

EXHIBIT 13.3 ▶ **The Packages That Irk People the Most**

In a recent survey, consumers identified packaging they don't like. Could producers get a marketing boost by developing innovative packaging for items such as the staples listed here?

PRODUCT	PERCENTAGE OF CONSUMERS WHO DISLIKE PACKAGE
Lunch meat	77
Bacon	76
Flour	65
Sugar	63
Ice cream	57
Snack chips	53
Cookies	51
Detergents	50
Fresh meat	50
Noodles	49

a fruit *juice* unless it contains an established minimum fruit content. Labels are also regulated by the Fair Packaging and Labeling Act of 1966, which mandates that every label must carry the product name as well as the name and address of the manufacturer or distributor, and it must conspicuously show the net quantity.

In addition to communicating with consumers, labels may also be used by manufacturers and retailers as a tool for monitoring product performance. Electronic bar codes give companies a cost-effective method of tracking the move-

BEHIND THE SCENES

The Mysteries of Product Packaging

The Nabisco Brands executive put her foot down. "We can't tell you something like that," she snapped. "We'd have to go into our whole marketing strategy, how we target consumers and so on. That's all highly confidential information." The question the snack-foods executive had been asked: Why do Oreo cookies come 42 to a pack?

As this incident demonstrates, product-packaging decisions are somewhat impenetrable. Why do hot dogs come in packages of 10 while hot dog buns come in bags of 8 or 12? How do the makers of Kleenex know exactly how many tissues to put in a box? These and other manufacturers apparently have their ways. For instance, to determine the proper package size for its candy bars, M & M/Mars recently conducted a 12-month test in 150 stores. It kept the price of its product constant but altered its size from one outlet to the next. In stores where dimensions were increased, sales went up 20 to 30 percent almost overnight. As a result, M & M decided to change almost its entire product line. On the other hand, take the example of Bohemia beer. In a now-classic marketing experiment, the brewers of the Mexican brand lowered the quantity in each bottle to 11 ounces from the standard 12. They then applied some of the cost savings toward a fancier container and a bigger ad budget. The result: Sales nearly doubled.

Essentially, a company has three choices when determining the size of a package. It can attempt to outdo its rivals by offering more for the money. It can try scratching out a better profit by offering less. Or it can simply go along on size and do battle over other characteristics of the product. What the company decides to do often depends on the consumer. If shoppers aren't likely to notice a small difference, it might pay to skimp. Campbell Soup Company believes it is better off selling its pork and beans in a 20¾-ounce can, but rival Stokely Van Camp merrily goes on selling its brand in 21-ounce cans.

Other decisions are more clear-cut. When Kimberly-Clark recently brought out a new version of Kleenex, its marketing experts had little doubt that the company should put 60 tissues in each pack. Why? Because that's the average number of times people blow their nose during a cold. Kimberly-Clark's researchers asked hundreds of customers to keep count of their Kleenex use in diaries.

Sometimes the consumer seems just plain irrational. Oscar Mayer says it routinely gets complaints from customers who want hot dogs sold in packs of 8 or 12 to match the number of buns they get to a bag. But an official laments that whenever the company has tried to comply by selling wieners in those quantities, hardly anyone has bought them. "We can't explain it," an official says with a sigh.

Regional preferences may also affect the popularity of a size. In the bathroom-tissue business, for instance, manufacturers must balance the trade-off between the thickness of sheets and the number on a roll. But not all parts of the country agree on the proper balance. Californians go for more sheets. Southerners like thicker sheets. And as a rule, people in big cities prefer smaller packages, whereas suburbanites, with station wagons and bigger cupboards, like larger packages.

Consumer preferences may have a lot to do with psychology. One packaging expert says that a number of his clients have elaborate theories about the subconscious thinking of their customers. A candy-bar maker, for example, has decided never to put more than one piece of chocolate in a pack because, it believes, people secretly hate to share their candy with anyone else.

ment of goods. The lines on the code, which are read by laser scanners, identify the product and allow a computer to record what happens to it. In addition to simply recording sales, scanner data can help measure the effectiveness of promotional efforts, such as coupon programs and sale prices.

▶ PRODUCT DEVELOPMENT AND THE PRODUCT LIFE CYCLE

When you buy a package of laundry soap, you get more than a detergent—you get the results of hundreds of small decisions about brand image, packaging, pricing, distribution, and promotion. And although the soap you buy next year may look and smell just like the soap you buy today, over time the product will evolve as the manufacturer adjusts these decisions to respond to changing circumstances.

The Product-Development Process

The possibility of developing a big winner is so alluring that U.S. companies spend billions of dollars a year trying to create new products or improve old ones.[19] Over 10,000 new consumer products are introduced every year.[20] Foods, drugs, beverages, and cosmetics account for the lion's share of "new" products. Actually, some of these products are not really new; only about 5 percent are true innovations.[21] The rest are variations on familiar products, created by changing the packaging, improving the formula, or modifying the form or flavor.

How many of the new products created every year will endure? Nobody knows for sure, but the odds are that most will disappear within a few years. According to one authority on new products, "To be a real success, a product should be both better and different—a lot better and a little different."[22]

Coming up with a winning product requires both research and creativity. The **product-development process** involves analysis of the marketplace, the buyer, the company's capabilities, and the economic potential of new product ideas. This process (see Exhibit 13.4) may be both expensive and time-consuming. To accelerate the process, many companies create multidisciplinary teams so that manufacturing and marketing plans can be developed in tandem while the product is being designed.

product-development process Stages through which a product idea passes—from initial conceptualization to actual appearance in the marketplace

EXHIBIT 13.4

The Product-Development Process

For every hundred ideas generated, only one or two salable products may emerge from the lengthy and expensive process of product development.

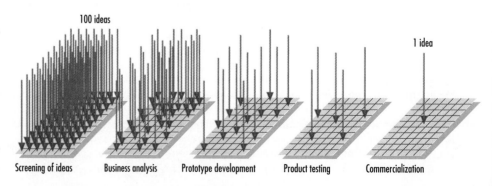

100 ideas   1 idea

Screening of ideas   Business analysis   Prototype development   Product testing   Commercialization

Generation and Screening of Ideas

The first step is to come up with ideas that will satisfy unmet needs. A producer may get new product ideas from its own employees or from outside consultants, it may simply adapt a competitor's idea, or it may buy the rights to someone else's invention. Customers are often the best source of new product ideas. Smith & Hawken, a world-famous supplier of gardening tools, once received a suggestion for a new rake design from a customer named Alan Rothenberg. The company took him up on the idea and even named its new product the "Rothenberg Rake."[23]

Often, good luck plays a role in new products. Aspartame, the artificial sweetener in NutraSweet, was "discovered" when a researcher at G. D. Searle spilled some experimental liquid, wiped it up, licked his finger, and noticed the sweet taste.[24]

From the mass of ideas suggested, the company culls a few that appear to be worthy of further development, applying broad criteria such as whether or not the product can use existing production facilities and the amount of technical and marketing risks involved. In the case of industrial or technical products, this phase is often referred to as a "feasibility study," in which the product's features are defined and its workability is tested. In the case of consumer products, marketing consultants and advertising agencies are often called in to help evaluate new ideas. In fact, a new-products industry is growing, made up of consultants who handle all aspects of product development. In some cases, potential customers are asked what they think of a new product idea—a process known as **concept testing.**

concept testing Process of getting reactions about a proposed product from potential customers

Business Analysis

A product idea that survives the screening stage is subjected to a business analysis. At this point the question is: Can the company make enough money on the product to justify the investment? To answer this question, companies forecast the probable sales of the product, assuming various pricing strategies. In addition, they estimate the costs associated with various levels of production. Given these projections, the company calculates the potential cash flow and return on investment that will be achieved if the product is introduced.

Prototype Development

The next step is generally to create and test a few samples, or **prototypes,** of the product, including its packaging. During this stage, the various elements of the marketing mix are put together. In addition, the company evaluates the feasibility of large-scale production and specifies the resources required to bring the product to market.

prototypes Working samples of a proposed product

Product Testing

During the product-testing stage, a small group of consumers actually use the product, often in comparison tests with existing products. If the results are good, the next step is **test marketing,** introducing the product in selected areas of the country and monitoring consumer reactions. This is expensive and time-consuming. Testing a new product in a supermarket may cost $1 million and

test marketing Product-development stage in which a product is sold on a limited basis

take nine months or more. In addition, the test may give competitors a chance to find out about a company's newest ideas.[25] Test marketing makes the most sense in cases where the cost of marketing a product far exceeds the cost of developing it.

One way to reduce the cost of test marketing is to test the product in a so-called electronic minimarket, which consists of several thousand consumers monitored by computers that are operated by market-research companies. Each consumer has a plastic identification card that she or he uses to make purchases in local stores. Computers in the stores track their purchases. In addition, each household's television set is equipped with a meter so that the market-research company can monitor the family's TV viewing habits and record the commercials they are exposed to. Using all these data, companies can evaluate consumer responses to new products and to pricing and promotion alternatives. Many argue that computer simulations are less reliable than traditional test marketing. But simulations cost only about half as much.[26]

Commercialization

commercialization Large-scale production and distribution of a product

The final stage of development is **commercialization,** the large-scale production and distribution of those products that have survived the testing process. This phase requires the coordination of many activities—manufacturing, packaging, distribution, pricing, and promotion. A classic mistake is letting marketing get out of phase with production so that the consumer is primed to buy the product before the company can supply it in adequate quantity. A mistake of this sort can be costly, because competitors may be able to jump in quickly. Many companies roll out their new products gradually, going from one geographic area to the next. This enables them to spread the costs of launching the product over a longer period and to refine their strategy as the rollout proceeds.

The Product Life Cycle

product life cycle Stages of growth and decline in sales and earnings

After launching a new product, the company is naturally eager for it to have a long and profitable life. But few products last forever. Most go through a **product life cycle,** passing through four distinct stages in sales and earnings: introduction, growth, maturity, and decline (see Exhibit 13.5). As the product passes from stage to stage, various marketing approaches become appropriate.

The amount of time that elapses during any one of the stages depends on customer needs and preferences, economic conditions, the nature of the product, and the manufacturer's marketing strategy, among other factors. A basic product that serves a real need is likely to show steady growth for quite a few years before leveling off. In contrast, some high-technology items and many fashions and fads generally have relatively short life cycles. Electric hot dog cookers may sell for a season or two, then fall out of favor. But baking soda and safety pins have been around for a long time.

Introduction

The first stage in the product life cycle is the *introductory stage,* during which the producer tries to stimulate demand. Typically, this stage involves an expensive advertising and promotional campaign, plus research and development

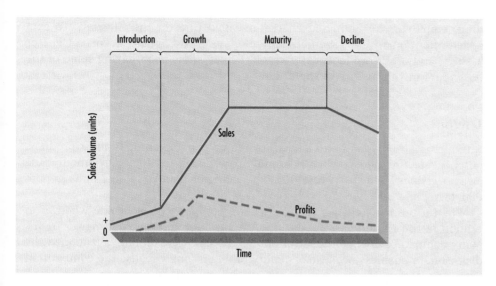

EXHIBIT 13.5

Stages in the Product Life Cycle

Almost all products and product categories have a life cycle like the one shown by the curve in this diagram. However, the duration of the life cycle varies widely from product to product. A business must introduce new products periodically to balance sales losses as older products decline.

costs. Products in the introductory phase generally require large investments to cover the costs of developing the product, building distribution systems, and educating the public about the product's benefits. The producer isn't likely to make a great deal of profit during this phase and, in many cases, won't make any profit for some time to come. Still, these costs are a necessary investment if a product is to succeed.

Growth

Next comes the *growth stage,* marked by a rapid jump in sales—and, usually, in the number of competitors—as the introductory effort starts paying off. As the product enters the growth phase, competition increases and the struggle for market share begins, creating pressure to maintain large promotional budgets and reduce prices. This competitive warfare is expensive, and often the small, weak firms do not survive. For the remaining participants, prices stabilize, and as sales volume increases, per-unit costs decline. The combination of stable prices and lower costs creates better profits, and producers begin to reap the reward of their investment.

Maturity

During the *maturity stage,* sales begin to level off or show a slight decline. This slowdown may result in overcapacity in the industry, prompting producers to cut prices to fill their plants. The maturity phase is typically the longest phase in the product life cycle, and the costs of introduction and growth have diminished. Companies count on the profits generated by mature-phase products to fund development of new products, so they work hard to keep products competitive.

One key to success in the maturity phase is to stimulate consumption of the existing product by broadening its appeal or making minor improvements. This is what Frito-Lay recently did with Cheetos corn curls. The company pared down the Cheetos product line and revamped its advertising to appeal to chil-

The life cycle of a best-seller is relatively brief—six to eight months, on the average.

dren, employing an animated character called Chester the Cheetah. To gain added attention without spending any money, Frito-Lay also licensed Cheetos T-shirts and other products. As a result, Cheetos has been having some of the best years in the history of the brand.[27]

Decline

Although maturity can be extended for many years, eventually most products enter the *decline phase,* when sales and profits begin to slip and eventually fade away. Declines occur for several reasons: changing demographics, shifts in popular taste, and advances in technology.

When a product reaches this phase, the company must decide whether to remain in the game or to discontinue the product and focus on newer items. Many companies choose the latter course. Kodak, for example, abandoned the disk-camera business because of quality problems and because the competition from easy-to-use 35mm cameras ate into its market. At about the same time, Kodak branched into a variety of new areas such as consumer batteries.[28]

Nevertheless, the decline phase can be profitable for a few producers. As Kathryn Harrigan, a Columbia University business professor, points out, "The last surviving player makes money serving the last bit of demand, when the competitors drop away." Hence, Liquid Paper is turning a nice profit selling correction fluid to firms that cannot afford to junk their typewriters and switch to word processors.[29]

▶ PRODUCT MIX AND LINE DECISIONS

Anticipating the impact of product life cycles, most companies continually add and drop products to ensure that declining items will be replaced by growth products. In this way, they develop a **product mix,** a collection of goods or services offered for sale. The broad product groups within the product mix are called **product lines,** which consist of groups of products that are similar in terms of use or characteristics (see Exhibit 13.6).

product mix Complete list of all products that a company offers for sale

product lines Groups of products that are physically similar or that are intended for similar markets

Width and Depth of Product Mix

Product mixes vary in terms of their width and depth. The simplest product mix is not really a mix at all, but rather a single product. The WD-40 Company, for example, has thrived for over 30 years by producing only one item—WD-40, an all-purpose lubricant. Although WD-40's success is impressive, its product mix is unusual. Most major companies find that they need more than one product to sustain their sales growth. Sears sells a huge variety of products in its retail outlets and also offers real estate, investment, insurance, and credit services.

When deciding on the width of its product mix, a company weighs the risks and rewards associated with various approaches. Some companies limit their product offerings because this method is economical: They can keep production costs per unit down and also limit selling expenses to a single sales force. Other companies follow the philosophy that a broad product mix is insurance against shifts in technology, taste, and economic conditions.

Width of Product Mix

Ready-to-Eat Cereals	Convenience Foods	Snack Foods	Baking Products	Dairy Products
Clusters	Betty Crocker Cake Mixes	Pop Secret Popcorn	Gold Medal Flour	Yoplait Yogurt
Total	Creamy Deluxe Frosting	The Berry Bears	Bisquick	
Wheaties	MicroRave Dessert Mixes	Shark Bites	Bac-Os	
Raisin Nut Bran	Hamburger Helper	Fruit Roll-Ups		
Oatmeal Raisin Crisp	Potato Medleys Side Dishes	Fruit Wrinkles		
Oatmeal Swirlers	Suddenly Salad	Squeezit Fruit Drink		
Cinnamon Toast Crunch		Nature Valley Granola Bars		
Cheerios		Bugles Corn Snacks		
Kix				
Benefit				

Depth of Product Mix

Product-Line Strategies

Within each product line, a company once again confronts decisions about the number of goods and services to offer. How many sizes and flavors of popcorn products should Orville Redenbacher offer? A full-line strategy involves selling a wide number and variety of products, whereas a limited-line strategy focuses on selling a few selected items.

Product lines have a tendency to grow over time as companies look for new ways to boost sales. A line can be expanded in a number of ways:

▶ *Line filling* is developing items to fill gaps in the market that have been overlooked by competitors or that have emerged as consumers' tastes and needs shift.

▶ *Line extensions* are new variations of a basic product, such as Tartar Control Crest.

▶ *Brand extensions* occur when the brand name for an existing product category is extended to a new category, like Jell-O Pudding Pops.

▶ *Line stretching* involves the addition of higher- or lower-priced items at either end of the current product line, thus extending its appeal to new economic groups.

▶ PRICING

Once a company has developed a product, it has to decide how to price it. Unfortunately, there are no easy answers. Deciding on a price is tricky, and the stakes are high. If the company charges too much, it will make fewer sales; if it charges too little, it will sacrifice profits that it might have gained. But how much is just right?

Factors That Affect Pricing Decisions

A company's pricing decisions are influenced by a variety of internal and external factors. The firm's marketing objectives and costs provide a rough indication

EXHIBIT 13.6

The Product Mix at General Mills

Selected products from General Mills show a product mix that is fairly wide but is of varying depth inside each product line.

Rolex reinforces its quality image with a premium price.

return on investment Profit equal to a certain percentage of a business's invested capital

skimming Charging a high price for a new product during the introductory stage and lowering the price later

of what it should charge for its goods or services. But before establishing a final price, the firm also considers government regulations, the level of demand, the nature of the competition, and the needs of wholesalers and retailers who distribute the product to the final customer.

Marketing Objectives

The first step in setting a price is to decide what you are trying to accomplish with a particular good or service. Some of the most common objectives are

▶ To achieve a certain overall profit target

▶ To increase sales

▶ To get a bigger share of the market

▶ To achieve high profits on a particular product

▶ To discourage competition

▶ To promote a particular product image

▶ To accomplish social or ethical goals[30]

Sometimes more than one of these objectives are pursued simultaneously.

A major goal for most companies is to reach overall profit targets. To measure their success in hitting those targets, companies use **return on investment** (ROI), which is profit expressed as a percentage of capital investment. General Motors, for example, which pioneered this concept in the 1920s, traditionally sets an ROI goal of 20 percent per year. Once a target ROI figure has been established, a complex formula (and a degree of guesswork) is then applied to come up with appropriate prices for all products in the line.

In addition to its general pricing policy, a company may also have specific objectives for individual products. For example, it may want to maximize sales or gain market share. Or it may want to achieve high returns on each unit sold, although this objective may conflict with the desire to build sales volume, because the price required to earn a high return may be so high that it discourages customers.

Other objectives might relate to the competitive environment. To eliminate competition or discourage new companies from becoming competitors, a company might charge an extremely low price for its product. Later, when the company has established control of the market, it might then raise the price to improve its own profits.

Some pricing decisions are based on a desire to achieve a particular image or reputation. Rolex watches, for example, are priced at a premium partly to convey the message that they are superior products and partly to cover the higher costs associated with high-quality materials. An organization's pricing objective might also be related to public relations or to social and ethical considerations. Many hospitals adjust their prices to accommodate people who are unable to pay the full rate.

Often a company's pricing goals for a product vary over time, depending on the product's stage in its life cycle. During the introductory phase, the objective might be to recover development costs as quickly as possible. To achieve this goal, the manufacturer might charge a high initial price—a practice known as **skimming**—then drop the price later, when the product is no longer a novelty and competition heats up. Alternatively, a company might try to build sales volume by charging a low initial price, a practice known as **penetration pricing**. The objective would be to reach a high volume of sales quickly in order to achieve economies of scale and reduce per-unit costs. This approach might have the added advantage of discouraging competitors, because the low price (which the competition would be pressured to match) limits the profit potential for everyone.

penetration pricing Introducing a new product at a low price in hopes of building sales volume quickly

Later, during the maturity phase, the goal might be to attract additional customers or to maximize the cash provided by the product. As the product enters its decline, the company's objective might be to get out of the business quickly. To accomplish this, it might establish a low price that will clear out the inventory.

Costs

Every company must translate its own particular objectives into specific prices for specific products. To do so, it must first analyze its costs, since costs establish the minimum acceptable price. To survive over the long term, the company must charge a price that will cover the costs incurred in producing and selling the product.

Two types of costs are associated with producing a product: fixed costs and variable costs. **Fixed costs**—including rent payments, utility bills, insurance premiums, and administrative expenses—are not affected by the number of products sold. Regardless of whether a company sells 10 units or 100 units, the rent on the building must be paid on time. **Variable costs**, on the other hand, do depend on the volume sold. They include raw materials, labor used in production, and supplies consumed during production. The total cost of operating the business is the sum of the fixed and variable costs.

fixed costs Business costs that must be covered no matter how many units of a product a company sells

variable costs Business costs that increase with the number of units produced

Businesses have differing cost structures. Airlines, for example, have high fixed costs and low variable costs. The cost of flying a plane is the same whether 3 or 300 passengers are traveling (aside from meals and other service items). So the more seats the airline fills, the more money it makes. Businesses of this type are said to be "volume sensitive," because their profits depend heavily on how much is sold. Businesses with low fixed costs and high variable costs are said to be "price sensitive." Their profits depend more on price than on volume. Department stores, for example, can increase or decrease the stock they keep on the racks to match trends in demand. Although they have a certain amount of overhead to support, they are most concerned with getting a good price for their merchandise.

In general, costs decline as volume increases. The more units you produce, the lower the cost per unit tends to be, since the fixed costs are spread over a larger number of units. In addition, as you produce more units, you achieve economies of scale in production, distribution, and promotion. Also, as employees become more skilled at their jobs, production and marketing costs decline even more. This phenomenon, referred to as the **experience curve**, gives companies an incentive to price their products relatively low in order to build volume.

experience curve Predictable decline of all costs associated with a product as the total number of units produced increases

Government Regulations

The U.S. government plays a big role in pricing, as do the governments of many other countries. In an effort to protect consumers and encourage fair competition, the government has enacted various price-related laws over the years, and all marketers need to be aware of their ramifications. Three important classes of price regulations are price fixing, price discrimination, and deceptive pricing.

PRICE FIXING   When two or more companies supplying the same type of products agree on the prices they charge or on the formulas they use to set prices, they are engaging in a practice known as **price fixing.** In nearly all cases, price fixing is illegal; two exceptions are when the government itself fixes prices or when regulated public utilities set prices for their services (which they can do only after government approval).[31]

price fixing The illegal cooperation between two or more companies that agree on prices in order to reduce competition

PRICE DISCRIMINATION   One of the most important pieces of pricing-related legislation in the United States is the Robinson-Patman Act. A key part of this legislation outlaws **price discrimination,** the practice of unfairly offering attractive discounts to some customers but not to others. Price discrimination applies only to tangible goods of the same grade and quality; it doesn't apply to services. Furthermore, the difference in prices must be proven to adversely affect competition. Robinson-Patman was originally passed to protect small retailers who weren't able to command the same discounts from food producers as their large chain-store competitors could; nearly all the defendants in Robinson-Patman cases are large companies.[32]

price discrimination Offering a discount to one customer but not to another, with the intention of restraining competition

DECEPTIVE PRICING   The Federal Trade Commission (FTC) has the authority to investigate and stop pricing schemes that it considers misleading; the term normally used in such cases is **deceptive pricing.** The problem being addressed is not so much a pricing issue; rather it's the way prices are promoted. The FTC's guidelines describe several practices considered deceptive pricing, including (1) comparisons with old prices that weren't in effect for a substantial length of time, (2) comparisons with competitive prices that aren't really being charged by competitors, (3) comparisons with manufacturers' suggested retail prices, and (4) bargains with strings attached.[33]

deceptive pricing A range of pricing and promotion practices that are considered misleading by government regulators

Laws against deceptive pricing are common throughout the world. Germany, France, Japan, Finland, New Zealand, Norway, Sweden, Switzerland, the United Kingdom, and other countries all have laws that regulate the promotion of prices. Concern is growing in many countries about the way prices are advertised, so all marketers operating internationally must learn about the price regulations of each country in which they do business.[34]

Business Around the World

A survey conducted in Norway and several neighboring countries revealed that many shoppers were confused by sale-price promotions. In response to such problems, Norway and a number of other countries around the world have enacted restrictions on the way that marketers can promote sale prices.

Price and Demand

While a company's costs establish a floor for prices, demand for the product establishes a ceiling. Theoretically, if the price for an item is too high, demand falls and the producers reduce their prices to stimulate demand. As prices fall, profits decline, thereby discouraging further production. Conversely, if the price for an item is too low, demand increases and the producers are motivated to raise prices. As prices climb and profits improve, producers boost their output until supply and demand are in balance and prices stabilize.

The relationship between price and demand isn't always this clear-cut, however. Some goods and services are relatively insensitive to changes in price.

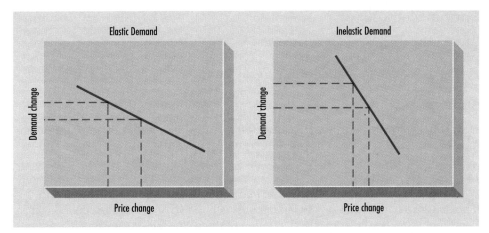

Elastic Demand | Inelastic Demand

Demand change / Price change

EXHIBIT 13.7

Price Elasticity
The two general categories of price-demand relationships are elastic demand, in which a given change in price creates a disproportionately larger change in demand, and inelastic demand, in which a price change generates a proportionately smaller demand change. In other words, when prices are elastic, customers are more sensitive to price changes.

Marketers refer to this as **inelastic demand**—meaning that demand does not stretch or contract with changes in price. Conversely, a market that is highly responsive to price changes exhibits **elastic demand.** Undifferentiated goods and services typically fall into this category (see Exhibit 13.7).

Generally speaking, when people go shopping, they have a rough price range in mind. If the item they seek is available within that range, they are likely to buy it. But if the price is either too low or too high, they hesitate.[35] An unexpectedly low price triggers fear that the item is inferior in quality, whereas an unexpectedly high price makes buyers question whether the product is worth the money.

inelastic demand Situation in which a percentage change in price produces a smaller percentage change in the quantity sold

elastic demand Situation in which a percentage change in price produces a greater percentage change in the quantity sold

Competitive Conditions

Because many customers compare prices before buying, companies need to consider the competition when making their pricing decisions. Orville Redenbacher wants his popcorn to be perceived as top quality, so it is generally priced above the market—that is, at prices higher than those of competitors. His choice is appropriate because he wants consumers to perceive a price-quality relationship. A premium price is also appropriate when the producer wants to appeal to a status-conscious buyer. The expense of owning a Rolls-Royce is part of its appeal.

Other firms follow the practice of pricing below the market. Sometimes this policy of underselling the competition is used as a way of breaking into an established market. Volkswagen initially priced its automobiles in this manner. Some firms rely totally on lower prices to attract customers. Discount stores use this approach. Pricing below the market is a particularly effective way to capture a larger share of the market.

A third alternative is pricing with the market. Generally, this means following the pricing policy of a major company in the industry. This company is known as the **price leader.** By pricing with the market, companies avoid the effort required to find out what the consumer would actually pay. Instead, they assume that the price leader has done this research and has established the right price. In this way, they also avoid the unpleasantness of price competition. Companies almost always prefer to compete by attracting customers with their product's features rather than by waging a pricing war.

price leader Major producer in an industry that tends to set the pace in establishing prices

Pricing Methods

After considering all of the internal and external factors that have a bearing on price, the company must establish a specific price for its goods or services. Two common methods for setting prices are markup pricing and break-even analysis.

Markup Pricing

Department stores and other retailers often use this method of setting prices. **Markup** is usually defined as the difference between the cost of an item and its selling price. In modern merchandising, firms generally express this difference in terms of the **markup percentage.** For example, if an item costs a firm $50 and is sold for $75, the markup is $25; the markup is $33\frac{1}{3}$ percent of the selling price. This markup percentage has two purposes: It must cover all the expenses of the firm (including both the cost of the item and the cost of selling it), and it must be high enough to allow some profit.

Many businesses offer a large number of products; Macy's department stores, for example, reportedly handle over 100,000 items. In cases like this, calculating the markup percentage for each single item is difficult. Thus, many businesses use an **average markup** when setting prices—that is, the same markup percentage is used for each item in a given product line.

Markups vary by type of store. Take an item costing retailers 50 cents. The markup might range from a low of 22 percent for a supermarket to a high of 55 percent for a florist, and thus the retail price might vary from a low of 61 cents to a high of $1.11. Florists have a high markup percentage because they deal in extremely perishable goods that are sold to a relatively small market. Another factor in the wide range of markup percentages is **turnover,** the number of times the firm's average inventory is sold during a given period. If a firm's average inventory is $1,000 and sales for a month amount to $3,000, the firm can surmise that the average inventory has turned over three times. The slower the rate of turnover, the higher the markup must be to yield a given amount of profit.

markup Amount added to the cost of an item to create a selling price that produces a profit

markup percentage Difference in percentage between the cost of an item and its selling price

average markup Constant markup percentage used in setting prices for all products in a product line

turnover Number of times that average inventory is sold during a given period

When Sears shifted its policy to everyday low prices, it had to reconsider its average markup when setting those prices.

Break-Even Analysis

Another approach to pricing involves the use of **break-even analysis**, which enables a company to determine how many units of a product it would have to sell at a given price in order to cover all costs, or break even. The **break-even point** is the minimum sales volume the company needs in order to keep from losing money. Sales above that point produce a profit; sales below that point result in a loss. You can determine the break-even point with this simple calculation:

$$\text{Break-even point (in units)} = \frac{\text{fixed costs}}{\text{selling price per unit} - \text{variable costs per unit}}$$

If you wanted to price haircuts at $20, you would need to sell 4,000 of them to break even:

$$\text{Break-even point} = \frac{\$60,000}{\$20 - \$5} = 4,000 \text{ units}$$

But $20 isn't your only pricing option. Why not charge $30 instead? When you charge the higher price, you need to give only 2,400 haircuts to break even (see Exhibit 13.8). However, before you raise your haircut prices to $30, bear in mind that the lower price may attract more customers and enable you to make more money in the long run.

Break-even analysis by itself won't indicate exactly what price a company should charge, but it will provide some insight into the number of units that will have to be sold at a given price to make a profit. This form of analysis is also useful if the price of an item may be set at various levels. The airlines, for example, offer a variety of fares. Once a certain number of seats are filled at the standard price, the airline breaks even. Beyond that point, any additional ticket sales are pure profit. The airline can afford to offer super-low fares for these seats because filling them doesn't cost the airline anything extra. Any revenue earned from these discount seats translates directly into profit.

break-even analysis Method of calculating the minimum volume of sales needed at a given price to cover all costs

break-even point Sales volume at a given price that will cover all of a company's costs

VIDEO EXERCISE

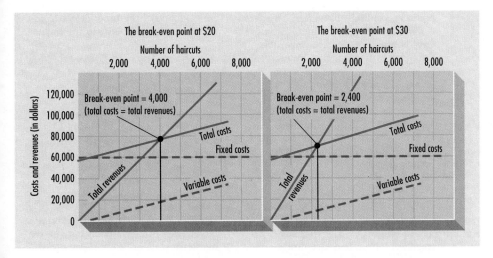

EXHIBIT 13.8

Break-Even Analysis
The break-even point is the point at which revenues will just cover costs. After fixed costs and variable costs are met, any additional income represents profit. The chart shows that at $20 per haircut, the break-even point is reached at 4,000 haircuts; charging $30 per haircut yields a break-even point at only 2,400 haircuts.

Pricing Strategies

Fine-tuning the price of a product may mean the difference between success and failure in a business. Companies use a variety of techniques to optimize their pricing decisions, three of which are described here: price lining, odd pricing, and discount pricing.

price lining *Offering merchandise at a limited number of set prices*

Many companies follow a policy called **price lining,** offering their products at a limited number of set prices. For instance, companies marketing audio cassettes may offer a $6 line, a $9 line, and a $12 line. Price lining has two advantages: It simplifies the job of selling the products, and it makes the consumer's choice easier by limiting the number of alternatives.

odd-even pricing *Setting a price at an odd amount slightly below the next highest dollar figure*

In many industries, prices tend to end in numbers slightly below the next dollar figure, such as $3.95, $4.98, or $7.99. This method is known as **odd-even pricing.** The assumption here is that a customer sees $3.98 as being significantly lower than $4.00; thus, the company will sell more at only 2 cents less. Another rationale for this kind of pricing is that customers set price limits for themselves, defining how much they will pay for a given product. For example, a man may decide that $25.00 is the maximum that he will spend on a dress shirt. According to this reasoning, a price tag of $24.99 will appear to be safely within his range, whereas one of $25.00 may give him pause. Few studies have tested the effectiveness of such pricing, but those that have been done suggest that customers are more rational than odd-even pricing assumes.

discount pricing *Offering a reduction in price*

trade discount *Discount offered to a wholesaler or retailer*

quantity discount *Discount offered to buyers of large quantities*

cash discount *Discount offered to buyers who use cash instead of credit*

With **discount pricing,** companies offer various types of temporary price reductions, depending on the type of customer and the type of item being offered. A **trade discount** is offered by the producer to the wholesaler or retailer. An interior decorator, for example, may buy furniture from a manufacturer at a discount and then resell it to a client. A **quantity discount** is offered to buyers who order large quantities of a product. Theoretically, these buyers deserve a price break because they are cheaper to serve; they reduce the cost of selling, storing, and shipping products and of billing customers. A **cash discount** is a price reduction offered to people who pay in cash or who pay promptly.

SUMMARY OF LEARNING OBJECTIVES

1 List three types of consumer products and two types of organizational products.

Consumer products may be subdivided into convenience products, shopping products, and specialty products, depending on the approach that the buyer uses when shopping for the item. Organizational products may be subdivided into expense items, which are lower-cost products normally consumed within a year of purchase, and capital items, which cost more and typically last longer.

2 Cite the three levels of brand loyalty and explain the concept of brand equity.

The first level of brand loyalty is

brand recognition, in which the buyer is familiar with the product. The next level is brand preference, in which the buyer will select the product if it is available. The final level is brand insistence, in which the buyer will accept no substitute. Brand equity is a measure of the value a brand represents to the company that owns it; more and more companies are trying to assign financial values to their brands, just as they do to their tangible assets.

3 Discuss the functions of packaging.

Packaging provides protection, makes products easier to display, attracts attention, and discourages theft. In addition, packaging enhances the

convenience of the product and communicates its attributes to the buyer.

4 Describe the five stages of product development.

The first stage of product development involves generating and screening ideas to isolate those with the most potential. The promising ideas are analyzed to determine their likely profitability. Those that appear worthwhile enter the prototype-development stage, in which a limited number of the products are created. In the next stage, the product is subjected to a market test to determine buyer response. Products that survive market testing are then commercialized.

5 Specify the four stages in the life cycle of a product.

Products move from the introductory phase through a growth phase then pass into maturity and eventually decline.

6 Identify four ways of expanding a product line.

A product line can be expanded by filling gaps in the market, by extending the line to include new varieties of existing products, by extending the brand to new product categories, and by stretching the line to include lower- or higher-priced items.

7 List seven common pricing objectives.

Through their pricing tactics, companies attempt to achieve a particular return on investment, increase sales, gain market share, earn a high profit on a product, discourage competition, promote a particular image, or accomplish social or ethical goals.

8 Distinguish between two methods for setting prices.

In setting prices, companies often apply a markup percentage that sets the price at some level above costs. Another approach is to conduct a break-even analysis that indicates how many units of a product a company would have to sell at a given price in order to cover its costs.

Meeting a Business Challenge at Orville Redenbacher

Popcorn marketers divide time into two distinct eras: pre-Redenbacher and post-Redenbacher. The pre-Redenbacher period in the United States stretches back centuries. At the first Thanksgiving celebration in Plymouth, the Indians treated the colonists to the taste of corn popped over the fire. In the years to come, people sometimes popped corn in a wire basket held over the fire in the fireplace, but popcorn never even came close to being a food fad.

The popcorn business started to heat up late in the nineteenth century, when agricultural experts discovered how to grow hybrid corns that produced better-tasting, fluffier popcorn. By the turn of the century, the industry had its first brand-name product. The pioneer was Cracker Jack, the caramel-covered popcorn and peanut confection packaged with a prize inside. In the twentieth century, unflavored pop-at-home corn products appeared regionally on store shelves, primarily in the South and the Midwest. Products such as Jolly Time employed modest advertising claims. Then Orville Redenbacher arrived in 1970 with his hybrid gourmet brand, Orville Redenbacher's Gourmet Popping Corn, and the post-Redenbacher period was set to begin.

Even after changing the name from Red Bow (a combination of his and partner Charlie Bowman's names),

Orville Redenbacher.

Redenbacher wasn't sure his product would be a hit. Consumers still thought of popcorn as a commodity good. The challenge was to encourage people to sample his popcorn and to begin thinking of it as a specialty product so that they would ask for it by name and pay a premium price. Redenbacher differentiated his product in a variety of ways. Whereas competitors packaged their corn kernels in cans or in plastic bags, Redenbacher packaged his corn in glass jars

that were vacuum-sealed to keep the kernels fresh. Another twist was in the labeling. The label sported a picture of Redenbacher himself, portraying the co-founder as the sincere popping corn expert and enthusiast he is.

Redenbacher also went to work on distribution and promotion. He decided that Marshall Field's, the illustrious Chicago department store, would be an appropriate retail outlet. So he sent a case of his popcorn to the manager of the gourmet food department, waited a month, then called to ask if he liked it. The manager was very enthusiastic and placed an order immediately. Redenbacher drove his truck to the store's loading dock and hung around, offering to autograph jars for purchasers. That was the start of a promotional strategy that worked wonders for the fledgling product. Marshall Field's ran newspaper ads about the product and the offer, Redenbacher signed countless jars over the course of three days, and television reporters recounted the story of "the popcorn with a personality."

Next, Redenbacher drove a shipment up to Byerly's, an upscale Minnesota supermarket, and looked for other retailers who wanted fancier foods. By this time, the product was catching on, bolstered by the personal promotion. Redenbacher and his partner Charlie Bowman could barely keep up with the flood of orders. In late 1971, Redenbacher turned over distribution in the South and the Southeast to Blue Plate Foods, a subsidiary of Hunt-Wesson Foods. The following year, when Blue Plate launched Orville Redenbacher's Gourmet Popping Corn across the country, Redenbacher traveled almost nonstop for six months to promote his product on radio, on television, in newspapers, and in magazines.

Redenbacher's strategy was paying off: More people were buying the notion of a gourmet popcorn and buying his brand. The product sold 365,000 pounds in 1970–1971, 1 million pounds in 1972–1973, and more than 5 million pounds in 1975–1976. In 1976, Redenbacher and Bowman sold their business to Hunt-Wesson, and Redenbacher agreed to continue his popcorn pilgrimages as brand spokesperson. New parent Hunt-Wesson promptly plunked down several million dollars to promote its popcorn sensation, a figure that was reportedly 10 times larger than the annual ad budgets of all competitors combined. This advertising onslaught sealed Redenbacher's fate as the most famous name—and face—in popcorn.

Of course, it didn't hurt that the product was top quality and hit the market at the right time. In an increasingly weight-conscious, health-conscious society, a snack low in calories and high in fiber was appealing. Other brands began to chime in with their own claims, some stressing quality, some stressing economy, all riding the crest of the popcorn revolution that Redenbacher had spawned.

The post-Redenbacher boom continues, with new popcorn products (the most successful being microwavable popcorn) capturing the imagination and the pocketbooks of consumers everywhere. The Orville Redenbacher brand is still the best-selling popcorn brand in the world, and Hunt-Wesson intends to keep it that way, no matter how competitors try to turn up the heat.

Your Mission: You're the product manager for Orville Redenbacher's Gourmet Popping Corn. You've been delighted with the sales results of the Orville Redenbacher brand to date, but you've noticed that the number of competitors in the gourmet popcorn market has multiplied. Also, you're concerned that premium popcorn is losing its appeal as a specialty product. Hunt-Wesson wants you to consider additional ways to increase the product's appeal, based on the product life cycle and the product's own elements. In the following situations, use your knowledge of product concepts to select the answers that will best support your product.

1. As the product manager, you are responsible for recommending new product ideas. Marketing research tells you that the Orville Redenbacher brand is the best-known name in the popcorn business, thanks to your extensive advertising and the personal promotion efforts of Redenbacher himself. You are thinking about using the brand loyalty your customers feel for Orville Redenbacher's Gourmet Popping Corn to create new products under the same brand name. You've checked out your competitors, and you've also gone into the field to take a look at other snacks and related products. Of the brand extension ideas you got when you were doing your research, which of these would you recommend?

a. A line of Orville Redenbacher salty snacks, including pretzels and potato chips.

b. A line of Orville Redenbacher popcorn accessories, including popcorn popping oil, popcorn butter, and popcorn salt.

c. A line of Orville Redenbacher popcorn appliances, such as hot-air poppers.

d. A line of Orville Redenbacher baked corn products, such as corn muffins and cornbread.

2. There's no doubt that the supermarket shelves are overflowing with premium home-popping competitors such as Borden's Cracker Jack Extra Fresh Popping Corn, Old Capital Popcorn, and Yoder's T. T. Popcorn. Although Orville Redenbacher sales have been going up steadily, the pace of growth has slowed. You suspect that the rate of adoption for all gourmet popcorns has increased as consumers learn more about this type of product, but that increased competition is cutting into the sales momentum for your own product. In effect, gourmet popcorns have become a convenience product again because the novelty has worn off. How can you persuade consumers to see the Orville Redenbacher product as a shopping product (or even as a specialty product) so that they will purchase by brand? At the same time, how can you keep competitors in the convenience product category?

a. Remove Orville Redenbacher popcorn from supermarkets and distribute the product only through gourmet food shops, mail-order fancy-food catalogs, and upscale department stores.

b. Hold in-store demonstrations of Orville Redenbacher popcorn being popped alongside the leading brands. Prove to consumers that your brand pops up fluffier, tastes better, and produces more popcorn per jar than any competitor.

c. Change the packaging and the label. Use a classier looking label in black and gold foil that emphasizes the premium nature of the product, and put the popcorn into a jar that's shaped like a champagne glass. This will convey upscale quality to the consumer.

d. Don't remove Orville Redenbacher from supermarket shelves, but add the other distribution channels mentioned in (a). However, for these distribution channels, change the packaging and label as in (c). This will give the new distributors a more elegant product to sell.

3. Now that your product is in the mature stage of the product life cycle and has attracted a bucketful of competitors, it may be time to rethink the premium-pricing aspect. Even the consumers who are laggards have probably tried gourmet popcorn by now. It may not be feasible to continue promoting Orville Redenbacher as an expensive but high-quality popcorn product when other brands are making similar quality claims. However, you know that your brand is differentiated from nongourmet products by a variety of elements, including higher price. Which of these price-related actions can you take (1) to keep customers coming back for more and (2) to maintain the image of a gourmet popcorn product?

a. Offer a limited-time two-for-one promotion that encourages customers to stock up on Orville Redenbacher. When they have two jars of your product, customers are less likely to buy another package of a competing product.

b. Offer a rebate coupon. When consumers send in two labels from Orville Redenbacher products, send them a coupon good for $1.00 off their next Orville Redenbacher purchase.

c. Place 25-cent coupons for Orville Redenbacher in upscale newspapers and magazines (such as *Money*). Emphasize the gourmet taste and encourage trial and comparison against other brands.

d. Cut your wholesale price and allow distributors to pass the savings along to consumers in the form of lower retail prices for Orville Redenbacher products. Pay for in-store promotional materials such as shelf and window signs to alert shoppers to the price break, which should be for a limited time.

4. Another way to boost sales in the maturity phase is to stimulate additional sales to current customers. At this point, you believe that all the consumers who plan to adopt your product have already given it a try and made a decision. But popcorn's status as a healthy snack has been underexploited and you think that people who like gourmet popcorn will buy and eat more if they become aware of the nutritional benefits of the product. You can approach this challenge from many angles. Of the following ideas, which do you think will help sell more Orville Redenbacher Gourmet Popping Corn to current customers?

a. Enhance the product by adding nutritional flavorings to the popcorn. For example, use vitamin-fortified flavorings to boost the level of nutrients. Then advertise the extra nutritional value in a special campaign, and develop new labels that highlight the added nutritional value.

b. Have Weight Watchers endorse Orville Redenbacher popcorn as the perfect snack for people on a diet or for anyone who cares about nutrition. Give Weight Watchers a free supply of your popcorn to serve during meetings, and provide them with a sign that reinforces the Orville Redenbacher name as the official popcorn of the Weight Watcher program.

c. Write articles for nutritional journals and health magazines. The articles should explain why popcorn is nutritious, comparing Orville Redenbacher's nutritional value with that of other snacks such as pretzels and chocolate bars.

d. Offer a free booklet about the nutritional value of Orville Redenbacher's Gourmet Popping Corn, and include recipes that show how to use popcorn as an ingredient in healthier snacks. Ask customers to send a self-addressed, stamped envelope so that they can receive the booklet.[36]

KEY TERMS

average markup (378)
brand (363)
brand equity (365)
break-even analysis (379)
break-even point (379)
capital items (362)
cash discount (380)
commercialization (370)
concept testing (369)
convenience products (361)
deceptive pricing (376)
discount pricing (380)
elastic demand (377)
expense items (362)
experience curve (375)
family branding (365)

fixed costs (375)
generic products (363)
inelastic demand (377)
licensing (365)
markup (378)
markup percentage (378)
MRO items (362)
national brands (363)
odd-even pricing (380)
penetration pricing (375)
price discrimination (376)
price fixing (376)
price leader (377)
price lining (380)
private brands (363)
product (358)

product-development process (368)
product life cycle (370)
product lines (372)
product mix (372)
prototypes (369)
quantity discount (380)
return on investment (374)
shopping products (361)
skimming (374)
specialty products (361)
test marketing (369)
trade discount (380)
trademark (363)
turnover (378)
variable costs (375)

REVIEW QUESTIONS

1. What is the difference between expense items and capital items?

2. What are the advantages and disadvantages of establishing a brand name?

3. Why would a marketer want to use a licensed label?

4. Why do businesses continually introduce new products, given the risks

and high rate of failure of new products?

5. What function do mature products play in a company's product mix?

6. What are the advantages and disadvantages of having a wide product mix as opposed to a narrow product mix?

7. What role does the government play in pricing?

8. What three alternatives are available to companies that take a market-based approach to pricing?

A CASE FOR CRITICAL THINKING

The Sweet Smell of Success

"Don't tell me how it smells; tell me how it sells," proclaims one executive in the fragrance industry. It may sell very well indeed. A highly successful perfume such as the heady Oriental scent Giorgio may produce as much as $60 million in annual sales. But if you were about to spend $150 an ounce for this fragrance, you'd probably be interested in how it smells. No worry there, either. It has been said that the distinctive scent of Giorgio wafting across a room filled with glitterati advertises the wearer who can afford "the very best-selling fragrance in Beverly Hills, U.S.A."

Browsing at a cosmetics counter, you may have wondered why perfume is so expensive. Such popular perfumes as L'Air du Temps and Joy are routinely priced from $100 to $200 per ounce. But aren't they just basically nice-smelling liquids in little glass bottles? Maybe manufacturers charge such exorbitant prices because they think the cost will add prestige to their products. Certainly a woman does create a special aura when people know that she can spend $200 for an ounce of floral-scented Joy.

Although prestige is an element in perfume pricing, fixed and variable costs also account for the high prices. When a cosmetics company like Revlon wants to market a new fragrance, it will call on the services of a perfumer—called a "nose" in the trade. A nose who has turned out several popular scents can earn around $100,000 a year.

Then there are the ingredients. A perfumer chooses among some 400 natural scents and 4,000 or so synthetic ones, and the resulting perfume may contain as many as 800 ingredients. Some are costly and rare. For example, the fragrant oil of jasmine absolute, extracted from jasmine petals through a time-consuming process, costs $3,500 for a mere pound. Even more expensive is attar of rose ($4,500 a pound), which is extracted from the rare Rose de Mai. Animal oils, which produce a leathery or musky scent and give perfumes their staying power, are also very costly, partly because they are so hard to obtain. For example, civet oil is a fatty substance that comes from a large East African cat, and musk is a spray given off by musk deer of central Asia only during certain times of the year. It doesn't take much imagination to see how difficult and expensive it would be to harvest either of these ingredients.

If only natural oils were used to manufacture perfume, the retail price of $200 per ounce would be an impossible bargain. Tincture of musk costs around $6,000 a pound, although it can be synthesized in a laboratory for a fraction of that price. Likewise, synthetic civet oil costs only $100 a pound, but it lacks the finesse and warmth of the real thing. Still, it is regularly used because real civet oil is rare.

Perfume pricing reflects other factors, too. Say that you have purchased an ounce of a fragrance like Shalimar, which runs about $130 a bottle. Ingredients, shipping, and box each cost $10. Promotion and a fancy glass bottle each cost $20. Finally, $50 goes to the department store or other retailer, and $10 goes to the designer or perfume company. But the price must also account for the cost of developing and launching a new product, a sum that averages between $8 million and $10 million. Launching Obsession, a Calvin Klein perfume, cost nearly $15 million.

And finally there's the risk: It often takes at least four years for a fragrance to turn a profit, and only one out of five perfumes makes any money at all. As you can see, pricing perfume is a tricky business.[37]

1. What role does supply and demand play in the perfume business?

2. Say that you work with a newly popular clothing designer who has decided that her label needs to be represented at the perfume counter, right along with Calvin Klein's and Gloria Vanderbilt's. Would you advise that she aim for the low, middle, or top price range? What would be the pros and cons for aiming at each range? What factors, in addition to those described, could affect your pricing formula?

3. Launching a new perfume is exceptionally expensive. How might you use pricing to take advantage of the surrounding hype to increase sales at the outset?

BUILDING YOUR COMMUNICATION SKILLS

Examine the life cycle of a product with which you are familiar. Locate an article in a magazine or book that describes the life cycle of that product. Note the factors affecting its introduction, its growth, and the strategies that have been used to maintain sales as it reached maturity. If this product has experienced a decline, identify the causes, and describe the manufacturer's attempts to revive the product.

▶ As directed by your instructor, prepare a brief presentation describing the life cycle of the product.

▶ In a class discussion, identify the factors contributing to the various stages in your chosen product's life cycle, and compare them with those of products examined by other students. Identify common elements in the life cycles of all the products evaluated by class members.

KEEPING CURRENT USING *THE WALL STREET JOURNAL*

Scan recent issues of *The Wall Street Journal* for an article related to one of the following:

▶ New-product development

▶ The product life cycle

▶ Pricing strategies

▶ Packaging

1. Does this article report on a development in a particular company,

several companies, or an entire industry? Which companies or industries are specifically mentioned?

2. If you were a marketing manager in this industry, what concerns would you have as a result of reading the article? What questions do you think companies in this industry (or related ones) should be asking? What would you want to know?

3. In what ways do you think this industry, other industries, or the public might be affected by this trend or development in the next five years? Why?

CHAPTER *14*

LEARNING OBJECTIVES
After studying this chapter, you will be able to

1 List nine functions performed by marketing intermediaries.

2 Name the alternative distribution channels for consumer goods, organizational goods, and services.

3 Differentiate among intensive, selective, and exclusive market-coverage strategies.

4 Describe the three types of wholesalers.

5 Identify at least 10 types of retailers.

6 Explain what is meant by the "wheel of retailing."

7 Specify the activities included in physical distribution.

8 List the five most common ways of transporting goods.

Distribution

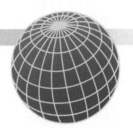

POWER TOOL MAKER HAS A
REMODELING PROJECT OF ITS OWN

Nolan Archibald had a bit of a mess on his hands. He had recently been promoted to chairman and CEO of Black & Decker, an octogenarian power tool manufacturer that was having profit problems, losing market share, and generally annoying many of the wholesalers and retailers it relied on to sell products to consumers and construction professionals.

The problem with wholesalers and retailers was particularly acute. The company was considered rather arrogant, to put it mildly. In the words of a former Black & Decker employee referring to Archibald's predecessors, "Management seemed to think it had the answer to every question and would generously impart its wisdom to the masses." Such an attitude nearly got Black & Decker kicked out of Wal-Mart, the largest retailer in the United States. Not the best plan for selling products, to say the least.

Inventory shortages plagued retailers. If a Black & Decker product turned out to be popular with the public, there was a pretty good chance that retailers would run out of it because Black & Decker put a lot of emphasis on meeting its internal financial goals. The company restrained production toward the end of its fiscal year to make sure its inventory levels dropped quite low. This practice made Black & Decker's balance sheet look good, but it was driving retailers away.

To complicate matters, Archibald's predecessors had recently purchased General Electric's entire line of small household appliances (at the time, the biggest brand transfer in history). But although the new line of products provided a strong stream of revenue, it gave Black & Decker yet another distribution headache. Before the acquisition, most Black & Decker products were sold through hardware stores, home-improvement centers, mail-order retailers, and discount stores. But to be successful, small appliances had to be sold through department stores as well, and Black & Decker had little experience in this area.

Unfortunately, the company tried to use the same approach it had used with power tools, which only served to alienate the department stores that had grown used to good treatment from General Electric.

Finally, back in the power tool division, the very foundation of the company, Black & Decker continued to pursue its traditional segments of low-cost home-owner tools and high-cost professional tools. Yet a new market segment had developed in between. Serious amateur woodworkers and semiprofessionals wanted higher quality than was being offered by the homeowner tools, but they didn't need the built-like-a-tank reliability of the professional tools, nor were they prepared to pay that much. Into this growing gap jumped several competitors, led by Japan's Makita. Because it worked hard to fill a product gap that worried retailers, Makita earned more and more shelf space. And in the retail world, shelf space is absolutely vital; without adequate shelf space, manufacturers can't survive.

So this was the challenge faced by Nolan Archibald. How could he repair the bad reputation that Black & Decker had gained with wholesalers and retailers? How could he combat the pressure from competitors who were trying to push Black & Decker off the shelf? How could he handle the new small appliances, given the company's lack of experience? In short, what steps could he take to ensure Black & Decker's survival and continued success?[1]

▶ THE DISTRIBUTION MIX

distribution channels Systems for moving goods and services from producers to customers

distribution mix Combination of intermediaries and channels that a producer uses to get a product to end users

Black & Decker's Nolan Archibald had to figure out some way to balance inventory while regaining the support of wholesalers and retailers. Whether the product is a power tool, a haircut, toothpaste, or insurance, it needs to be conveyed from the producer to the ultimate user. The systems used to move goods and services from producers to customers are called **distribution channels,** or *marketing channels.* Some channels are short and simple; others are complex and involve many people and organizations. An organization's decisions about which combination of channels to use—the **distribution mix**—play a major role in the firm's success.

The Role of Marketing Intermediaries

marketing intermediaries Businesspeople and organizations who channel goods and services from producers to consumers

Stop and think about all the products you buy: food, cosmetics, toiletries, clothing, sports equipment, airplane tickets, haircuts, gasoline, stationery, appliances, cassettes, videotapes, books, magazines, and all the rest. How many of these products do you buy directly from the producer? If you're like most people, the answer is probably less than 3 percent.[2] For the other 97 percent of your purchases, you rely on **marketing intermediaries** to simplify the transactions between you and the original producers.

Without these intermediaries, the buying and selling process would be an expensive, time-consuming experience (see Exhibit 14.1). Intermediaries are instrumental in creating three forms of utility mentioned in Chapter 12: place utility, time utility, and possession utility. By transferring products from the producer to the customer, intermediaries ensure that goods and services are available at a convenient time and place. They also simplify the exchange process.

In addition, intermediaries perform a number of specific functions that make life easier for both producers and customers:

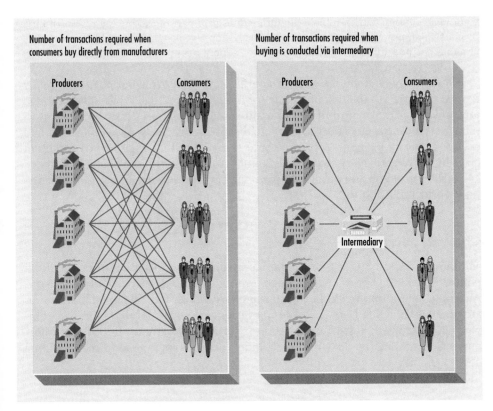

Number of transactions required when consumers buy directly from manufacturers

Producers   Consumers

Number of transactions required when buying is conducted via intermediary

Producers   Consumers

Intermediary

EXHIBIT 14.1

How Intermediaries Simplify Commerce
Despite the common assumption that buying directly from the producer saves money, intermediaries actually reduce the price we pay for many goods and services. Intermediaries eliminate many of the contacts between producers and consumers that would otherwise be necessary. At the same time, they create place, time, and possession utility.

1. *Providing a sales force.* Many producers, like Black & Decker, would find it expensive and inefficient to employ their own salespeople to sell directly to final customers. Instead, they rely on intermediaries to perform this function.

2. *Providing market information.* Intermediaries often sell dozens of competing or complementary lines to hundreds of buyers. Thus, they are in an ideal position to give producers useful marketing information such as which products are currently popular.

3. *Providing promotional support.* Intermediaries often help a producer by advertising certain product lines to boost their own sales. Intermediaries also design and distribute eye-catching store displays and other promotional devices for some products.

4. *Sorting, standardizing, and dividing.* Intermediaries break large shipments from producers into more convenient units, sorting bulk quantities into smaller packages and grading products for quality and uniformity.

5. *Carrying stock.* Most intermediaries maintain an inventory of merchandise, which they buy from a manufacturer in the hope of eventually selling it to other intermediaries or final customers. Without the intermediary, a manufacturer would have to provide storage space and wait for payment until goods were ordered.

6. *Delivering the product.* By keeping stock on hand in convenient locations, intermediaries can speed up deliveries to customers. Some intermediaries assume complete responsibility for transporting the producer's goods to widely scattered buyers.

7. *Assuming risks.* By transferring goods to intermediaries, manufacturers can avoid the risks associated with damage, theft, product perishability, and obsolescence.

8. *Providing financing.* Sometimes an intermediary that is much larger than the producers it represents can provide them with loans.

VIDEO EXERCISE

Vermont American relies on retailers to help sell its power tool accessories through attractive store displays.

EXHIBIT 14.2

Alternative Channels of Distribution

Consumer goods, organizational goods, and services each have characteristic types of distribution channels. Consumer-goods channels tend to require the most intermediaries, and channels for services tend to require the fewest.

9. Buying. Intermediaries relieve the ultimate user of part of the buying responsibility. By consolidating a variety of goods in one place, they save people the trouble and expense of going out and finding separate sources of supply for every product they purchase.

Interestingly enough, the services performed by intermediaries may actually reduce the price that consumers pay for many goods and services, even though intermediaries make a profit (or are paid a fee) on the items they handle. Intermediaries exist because they are able to distribute products more efficiently and economically than manufacturers could (see Exhibit 14.1). Every transaction costs money, and by reducing the number of transactions required to move goods and services from producers to end users, intermediaries often reduce the total cost of distribution.

Channel Alternatives

The number and type of intermediaries involved in a distribution channel depend on the kind of product and the marketing practices of a particular industry. An arrangement that might be appropriate for a power tool and appliance manufacturer like Black & Decker would not necessarily work for an insurance company, a restaurant, a steel manufacturer, or a movie studio. Important differences exist among the distribution channels for consumer goods, organizational goods, and services (see Exhibit 14.2).

Channels for Consumer Goods

Channels for consumer goods are generally the most complex distribution channels, although they can be quite simple:

▶ *Producer to consumer.* The most direct way to market a product is for the producer to sell directly to the consumer. Artisans who sell their leather goods or jewelry at crafts fairs or on the street are using this simple distribution channel. Large companies may also prefer to sell directly to the consumer, because this approach gives them more

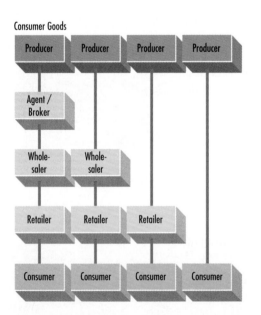

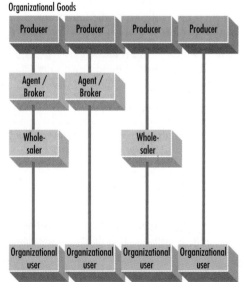

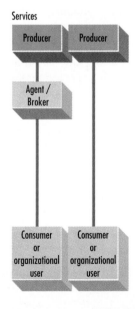

control over sales and eliminates the intermediary's cut of the profit. The problem with direct distribution is that it forces a producer to assume many marketing functions. Hiring a marketing and sales staff, setting up a marketing budget, and distributing goods may be costly, so many producers choose alternatives that involve intermediaries.

▶ *Producer to retailer to consumer.* Some producers sell their products to retailers, who then resell them to consumers. Automobiles, paint, gasoline, and clothing are typical of the many products distributed in this way.

▶ *Producer to wholesaler to retailer to consumer.* The most common channel for consumer products is for the producer to sell to a wholesaler who in turn sells to a retailer. This approach is generally the most advantageous alternative for small producers who cannot afford to employ their own sales forces.

▶ *Producer to agent/broker to wholesaler to retailer to consumer.* Another wholesaling level is typical in certain industries, such as agriculture, where specialists are required to negotiate transactions or perform such functions as sorting, grading, or subdividing the merchandise.

Channels for Organizational Goods

The most common approach for organizational products is direct distribution from producer to user. However, in industries composed of many small producers or many widely scattered buyers, one or more levels of intermediaries may be required to simplify the distribution process. The more fragmented the industry, the more likely it is to rely on the services of intermediaries.

Channels for Services

Most services are distributed directly by the producer to the user because the nature of the service usually requires direct contact between the customer and the service provider. A hairstylist or lawyer, for example, would not be likely to use an intermediary to deal with clients. In addition, because of the intangible nature of many services, such functions as storing, sorting, grading, and transporting goods are needed less frequently.

Some service businesses, however, do employ intermediaries. The travel industry, for example, relies on agents to package vacations and sell tickets. Insurance companies market their policies through insurance brokers, and entertainers book engagements through agents who negotiate deals for them.

Reverse Channels

Although most marketing channels move products from producers to customers, **reverse channels** move in the opposite direction. The two most common reverse channels are those used for recycling and for product recalls and repairs. Recycling channels continue to grow in importance as consumers and businesses become more sensitive to solid-waste–disposal problems. Local, state, and federal government agencies also contribute to the growth of recycling channels as they pass tighter and tighter restrictions on disposal of glass, paper products, plastics, and recyclable organic material such as grass clippings and Christmas trees.

The channels for some recycled goods use traditional intermediaries, which is the case for returnable soft drink bottles, for which retailers and bottlers form

Business Around the World

Marketing channels in Japan are usually very complex; goods often pass through a number of intermediaries, including as many as four levels of wholesalers, before reaching consumers.

reverse channels Distribution channels designed to move products from the customer back to the producer

the reverse channel. In other cases, recycling collection centers have been established to funnel material from consumers back to processors. More and more, local governments are creating recycling channels, often in cooperation with waste-management companies.

Another common reverse channel is used for product repairs and recalls. Any firm selling products that need maintenance or repair should establish a channel to direct goods from customers back to an appropriate service facility. Depending on the complexity of the products involved and the financial return on the repair business, companies can establish their own service centers or rely on independent repair and maintenance centers. Reverse channels are also needed for product recalls, which can be massive undertakings in some cases. For instance, in February 1990, U.S. government inspectors found traces of the chemical benzene in Perrier bottled water, and Perrier recalled all its inventory in North America, some 72 million bottles.[3] Such a wide-scale recall requires close communication with retailers and other marketing intermediaries to ensure that products are removed from store shelves as quickly as possible.

Channel Selection

Should a producer sell directly to end users or rely on intermediaries? Which intermediaries should be selected? Should the company try to sell its products in every available outlet or limit its distribution to a few exclusive shops? Should more than one channel be employed? Should distribution be revised over time?

The answers to these questions depend on a number of factors, some related to the product and the market, others to the company—its strengths, weaknesses, and objectives. In general, however, choosing one channel over another is a matter of making trade-offs among three factors: the number of outlets where the product is available, the cost of distribution, and the control of the product as it moves through the pipeline to the final customer. With a short distribution chain, the producer gets the most control but generally gets thinner market coverage and bears more of the expense of warehousing, transportation, and marketing. A longer chain increases market coverage and minimizes the producer's costs but introduces more complexity and thus less control.

intensive distribution Approach to distribution that involves placing the product in as many outlets as possible

selective distribution Approach to distribution that relies on a limited number of outlets

Market Coverage

The question of market coverage has to do with the availability of a product. Should a manufacturer blanket the market so that people can find the item anywhere, or should distribution be limited to create an exclusive image? The answer depends primarily on the type of product. Inexpensive convenience goods or organizational supplies—such as bread, toothpaste, cleaning products, and typing paper—sell best if they are available in as many outlets as possible. To achieve this type of **intensive distribution,** where the market is saturated with a product, a producer will almost certainly need a long distribution chain. Trying to cover each and every outlet without intermediaries would be a major undertaking, one that only the largest, best-financed producers could handle.

A different approach to market coverage might work better for a producer that specializes in shopping goods such as apparel, appliances, or certain types of organizational products. When the buyer is likely to compare features and prices, the best strategy is usually **selective distribution,** in which a limited number of outlets are capable of giving the product adequate support. With

The Dial Corporation tries to reach a wide audience with convenience products such as its Purex bleach, so the company opts for intensive distribution, which seeks to put products in customers' hands whenever and wherever possible.

fewer outlets, the distribution chain for shopping goods is generally shorter than it is for convenience goods.

When a company produces expensive specialty or technical products, it may opt for direct sales or **exclusive distribution,** in which the product is available in only one outlet in each market area. Here again, exclusive distribution normally involves simpler and shorter distribution systems.

exclusive distribution Approach to distribution in which intermediaries are given the exclusive right to sell a product within a given market

Cost

Costs play a major role in determining a firm's distribution mix. It takes money to perform all the functions that are handled by intermediaries. Small or new companies cannot often afford to hire a sales force large enough to sell directly to end users or to call on a host of retail outlets. Neither can they afford to build large warehouses and distribution centers or buy trucks to ship their goods. These firms need the help of intermediaries who can spread the cost of these activities across a number of noncompeting products. With time and a larger sales base, a producer may build enough strength to take over some of these functions and reduce the length of the distribution chain.

Control

Another important issue to consider when selecting distribution channels is control. As soon as dealers buy the product, they own it; they can do anything they want with it. A manufacturer cannot force the intermediaries to promote the product aggressively. The longer the distribution chain, the bigger the problem, since the manufacturer becomes increasingly distant from the ultimate seller.

For certain types of products, control is particularly important because the product can be cheapened if it falls into the wrong hands. A designer of high-priced clothing, for example, might want to limit distribution to exclusive boutiques, since the clothing would lose some of its appeal if it were available in discount stores. The company's entire merchandising strategy could be undercut if an intermediary sold some of the fashions to the wrong retailers. Similarly, producers of complex technical products don't want their products handled by unqualified intermediaries who can't provide adequate customer service.

Other Factors

Coverage, cost, and control are the three big issues to consider when selecting a distribution channel, but they aren't the only issues involved. Manufacturers must also take into account a host of other factors, including the dollar value of the item, the market's growth rate, the geographic concentration of the customers, the buyer's need for service, and the importance of rapid delivery (see Exhibit 14.3).

Often, the best solution is to use multiple channels to reach various target markets. Say that you have invented a new board game. You might sell your product through department stores, discount outlets, specialty stores, direct-mail catalogs, or some combination of these outlets.

Over time, the optimum distribution arrangement for a product is likely to change. When a product is introduced, buyers may need help making a purchase

EXHIBIT 14.3 ▶ **Factors Involved in Selecting Distribution Channels**

The choice of distribution channel depends on the product, the customer, and the company's capabilities.

FACTOR	EXPLANATION
Number of transactions	When many transactions are likely, the channel should provide for many outlets, which suggests that several levels of intermediaries will be required. If only a few transactions are likely, the number of outlets can be limited, and the channel can be relatively short.
Value of transactions	If the value of each transaction is high, the channel can be relatively short and direct, since the producer can better absorb the cost of making firsthand contact with each customer. If each transaction has a low value, a long channel is used to spread the cost of distribution over many products and outlets.
Market growth rate	In a rapidly growing market, many outlets and a long channel of distribution may be required to meet demand. In a shrinking market, fewer outlets are required.
Geographic concentration of market	If customers are clustered in a limited geographic area, the channel can be short, since the cost of reaching each account is relatively low. But if customers are widely scattered, a multilevel channel with many outlets is preferable.
Need for service and sales support	Complex, innovative, or specialized products require sophisticated outlets where customers can receive information and service support; short, relatively direct channels are generally used. If the product is familiar and uncomplicated, the consumer requires little assistance; long channels with many self-serve outlets can be used.
Speed of delivery	Perishable products or products that must be delivered quickly to the customer generally require relatively short channels, which are quicker than long channels.

decision, particularly if the item is technical or unusual. At this stage, the most efficient channel consists of a few highly specialized dealers who can spot trends and identify leading-edge customers. As the product enters the growth stage, distribution must be expanded to handle higher sales volume, but dealers should continue to provide extensive selling support. When the product reaches maturity, the distribution emphasis should shift from service and support to economy, since most customers will already be familiar with the item and will be interested in getting the best price. At this point, producers can rely on advertising as opposed to dealer support to convince the consumer to buy. During the product's decline phase, cost becomes an even more important issue in the distribution decision, since the manufacturer's objective is usually to extract the maximum profit from the item before phasing it out entirely.[4]

Channel Conflicts

In an ideal world, merchandise would move smoothly through the various distribution channels. After all, success in each phase of the process depends on success in the phase before. A retailer can't make money unless it gets a steady supply of merchandise from wholesalers, and the wholesalers rely on producers to deliver goods for resale. But the business world doesn't always operate so simply. Sometimes the various members of the distribution chain have conflict-

FOCUS ON ETHICS

When Does Healthy Competition Become Unhealthy Control?

Roses are red
Violets are blue
Go after our market share
And we'll destroy you

Greeting card companies send some awfully sweet messages to their customers, but they're more likely to send angry letters and aggressive lawyers to each other. The $3.7 billion card market is essentially flat, and competitors can increase sales only by taking market share from each other. Three giants, Hallmark Cards, American Greetings, and Gibson Greetings, control this market, with a combined share of about 80 percent. A host of smaller companies vie for share, frequently with alternative cards ranging from New Age sentiment to explicit sexual humor.

These smaller companies struggle to stay in the battle, a battle that increasingly centers around control of the distribution channel. Greeting cards are sold through a variety of retail outlets, including grocery, drug, discount, and specialty stores. None of the producers has a commanding legal authority over the channel; for instance, most of the 21,000 stores that carry Hallmark cards and sometimes bear the Hallmark name are ostensibly free to carry anybody's products. Lacking any legal power over retailers, producers use a mixture of sweet talk and strong arm to move their goods through the channel.

Sometimes the struggle for control gets downright nasty. In a highly publicized case, Blue Mountain Arts accused Hallmark of copying the look of its cards, pressuring retailers into dropping (and in some cases allegedly destroying) Blue Mountain cards, and then filling the vacant shelf space with products from its new Personal Touch line, which looked nearly identical to Blue Mountain cards. Blue Mountain won the first round of the legal battle when a federal judge ordered Hallmark to stop selling 83 designs until a trial could be held to sort things out. In a related bit of legal action, the prestigious Society of Illustrators recommended to a federal court that

specific card styles shouldn't be monopolized, but their recommendation was tossed out when Blue Mountain lawyers discovered that Hallmark paid for the Society's legal expenses and contributed a sizable amount to its scholarship fund.

In an amendment to its filing, Blue Mountain accused Hallmark of several other channel control measures that present intriguing legal and ethical issues. Prominent among the allegations: Greeting card dealers were pressured to pull Blue Mountain cards if they wanted to maintain a "beneficial business relationship" with Hallmark. Also, the smaller company alleges that Hallmark leases shopping center stores to dealers only if they pledge not to sell Blue Mountain products. Hallmark denied all the charges Blue Mountain leveled against it. The case was settled when Hallmark promised not to exert pressure on retailers and to redesign the product line that was similar to Blue Mountain's.

Some people complain that such power struggles hurt consumers as well because they place a greater emphasis on profit margins and shelf space than on creativity and originality. Perri Ardman of Maine Line (specializing in humorous cards for women—and the first card company owned by a woman) says that smaller companies with creative offerings just don't have the financial muscle to get their cards on the retailers' shelves. Ardman and her partner, Joyce Boaz, wound up selling Maine Line to a large novelty gift company with the hopes that greater financial power would let them expand their product offering and break into international markets.

Card makers continue to get some unpleasant greetings about control in marketing channels. In any industry in which the competitors are clawing for shares of stagnant or slow-growth markets, fights over channel control seem inevitable. As these fights heat up, ethical issues such as shelf space control and slotting allowances are likely to consume a greater share of the marketer's time.

ing objectives, as Black & Decker's retailers experienced before Nolan Archibald took over.

Channel conflicts are of two basic types: vertical and horizontal. **Vertical conflict** occurs between channel members at different levels in the distribution chain—say, between producers and wholesalers or wholesalers and retailers. A recent example involves a conflict between small publishers and B. Dalton Bookseller, the nation's number two retail bookstore chain. Dalton announced that it would no longer deal directly with publishers that sell less than $100,000 a year through Dalton's stores. This decision reduces Dalton's costs for ordering, shipping, and returning books. But it also diminishes the small publishers' ability to get exposure for their books.[5] In this case, the retailer's clout works against the producer. But in other businesses, producers may call the shots, making life tough for intermediaries.

The second type of channel conflict, **horizontal conflict,** occurs between channel members at the same level in the distribution chain, such as two or more retailers or two or more wholesalers. Consider the consumer electronics field. The emergence of giant discount stores like Circuit City, Federated, and Silo has created a brutal environment for smaller electronics retailers. In most areas, the population base is large enough to support only one or two superstores, each of which can meet the needs of about 350,000 people. If several giants invade the same territory, they generally resort to price wars to attract business, thus driving down profit margins for both themselves and smaller competitors.[6]

Vertical Marketing Systems

One way to reduce conflicts in the distribution system is to plan and control it more carefully. Thus **vertical marketing systems** have evolved in which members work together to conduct distribution activities.

Vertical marketing systems vary in their level of formality. The most controlled form is the *corporate vertical marketing system,* in which both production and distribution operations are owned by the same organization. In some cases, the entire distribution chain is controlled by a single firm, but often the channel contains a mix of independently owned and corporate-controlled operations. For example, approximately 10 percent of the nation's movie screens are owned by major movie studios such as Columbia Pictures, Paramount, Warner Brothers, and MCA.[7] This assures the studios of an outlet for their films, but to reach significant ticket sales, they must also reach the vast number of independent theaters.

An *administered vertical marketing system* is a less formal arrangement in which one member of the distribution chain has enough power to influence the behavior of the others. The dominant company, known as the **channel captain,** performs functions that work to the mutual benefit of the entire chain. Toys 'R' Us, for instance, has developed computer software that spots emerging trends in toy sales. By passing on this information to toy manufacturers, Toys 'R' Us helps the industry balance its production volume.[8] Often, the channel captain is the manufacturer as opposed to the retailer. Companies like Procter & Gamble, Kraft General Foods, and Gillette are the dominant forces in the distribution of their products.

A *contractual vertical marketing system* is a compromise between a corpo-

---

vertical conflict Conflict between channel members at different levels in the distribution chain

horizontal conflict Conflict between channel members at the same level in the distribution chain

vertical marketing systems Planned distribution channels in which members coordinate their efforts to optimize distribution activities

channel captain Channel member that is able to influence the activities of the other members of the distribution channel

rate system and an administered system. With this approach, the members of the channel are legally bound by a contractual agreement that spells out their respective responsibilities. Franchising is the most common form of contractual vertical marketing system.

International Distribution

International distribution adds its own set of complexities to the management of marketing channels. If a U.S. company wants to market its goods in Austria, for example, it has to (1) abide by the export laws of the United States, (2) abide by the import and general business laws of Austria, and (3) abide by the applicable laws of any countries the goods pass through on their way. Such legal requirements and constraints add to the differences inherent in doing business in foreign countries, ranging from language barriers to diverse government policies to local customs.

Franchises such as this Mail Boxes Etc. are the most common form of contractual vertical marketing.

Sometimes even the simplest assumption doesn't apply when a company considers international distribution. For instance, Doubleday Book and Music Clubs uses an extensive magazinelike catalog to promote books, CDs, and other items to its members. In France, customers order through the mail, just as they do with clubs such as the History Book Club here in the United States. However, in Spain, Portugal, and Italy, Doubleday relies on a door-to-door direct-sales force to hand out catalogs, take orders, and deliver products. Why the different channel? The company considers the postal services in these three countries to be too unreliable to support mail-order sales.[9]

When Kodak introduced a line of copier/duplicators in Europe, it faced a complex international distribution channel. The company chose a marketing region that encompassed 18 countries, 400 million people, and numerous languages and cultures. Furthermore, Kodak knew it would be competing with IBM, Xerox, and a number of European and Japanese firms. To deal with all the issues of currency, regulations, localized competition, and other market aspects, Kodak wound up establishing 13 separate companies, each with its own management and marketing channels.[10]

▶ TYPES OF INTERMEDIARIES

Basically, intermediaries are of two main types: wholesalers and retailers. **Wholesalers** sell primarily to retailers, other wholesalers, and organizational users such as governments, institutions, and commercial operations (all of which either resell the product or use it in making products of their own). **Retailers** sell to individuals who buy products for ultimate consumption.

wholesalers Firms that sell products to other firms for resale or for organizational use

retailers Firms that sell directly to the public

Wholesalers

Because wholesalers seldom deal directly with consumers, many people are unfamiliar with this link in the distribution chain. However, despite their low profile, the 300,000 wholesalers in the United States are a vital force in the economy.[11] The recent trend has been toward consolidation among distributors, so the number of firms is declining, but the average sales volume per firm is increasing.[12]

Merchant Wholesalers

merchant wholesalers Independent wholesalers that take legal title to products

Roughly 80 percent of all wholesalers are **merchant wholesalers,** independently owned businesses that take title to merchandise (become the owners of it) and then resell it to retailers or organizational buyers. Some merchant wholesalers provide a wide variety of services to their customers, such as storage, delivery, and marketing support. **Rack jobbers,** for example, set up displays in retail outlets, stock inventory, and mark prices on merchandise displayed in a particular section of a store. Other merchant wholesalers provide fewer services.

rack jobbers Merchant wholesalers that are responsible for setting up and maintaining displays in a particular store area

Agents and Brokers

manufacturer's agents Wholesalers that do not take title to products but that receive a commission for selling products

The big difference between merchant wholesalers and **manufacturer's agents** is that agents never actually own the merchandise they sell. Producers retain title to the product and pay the agents a commission (a percentage of the money received) for any transaction they handle. One of the most common types of agent is the manufacturer's representative. The rep calls on customers in a specific territory, takes orders, and arranges for delivery of the products. By representing several products at once, the sales rep can achieve enough volume to justify the cost of a direct sales call.

brokers Agents that specialize in a particular commodity

Brokers are special types of agents who concentrate on selling a particular commodity, such as soybean oil or coffee. Commodity brokers arrange sales for clients who grow the commodity, and they receive a commission for this service. Brokers also operate in the financial field. Real estate brokers, insurance brokers, and securities brokers all are paid a commission for providing information and arranging transactions—sometimes by the seller, sometimes by the buyer, and sometimes by both. Another unique attribute of brokers is that they usually work for the seller for a short period of time, often only for a single transaction.

Producer-Owned Wholesalers

branch office Producer-owned operation that carries stock and sells it

Two types of wholesale businesses are owned by the producer. The first is the **branch office,** an establishment that carries inventory and performs a full range of marketing and business activities. The second type is the **sales office,** which often conducts the same range of marketing and business functions but doesn't carry inventory.

sales office Producer-owned operation that markets products but doesn't carry any stock

Retailers

In contrast to wholesalers, retailers are a visible element in the distribution chain—too visible, according to some. As the chairman of K Mart recently pointed out, the United States is in "a very, very overstored situation." Over a recent 12-year period, the amount of retail space in suburban malls almost doubled; at the same time, the population increased by only 13 percent. This country currently has 40 percent more retail capacity than the population needs.[13] And the resulting turmoil has been dramatic. As a reporter for *Fortune* put it, "You need to check every week to see who's in and who's out of business."[14]

On average, each of us spends over $6,500 per year in retail establishments that sell everything from safety pins to Rolls-Royces and from hot dogs to haute cuisine. Although large multiunit chain stores account for over half of all retail

EXHIBIT 14.4 ▶ **Retailing Strategies**

Instead of trying to be all things to all people, retailers have begun to create special identities to respond to various target markets. Here are some of the most successful strategies.

STRATEGY	EXPLANATION
Value	Retailer offers greater overall value, lower prices than competitors. Holds down costs by eliminating alterations, delivery, exchanges, credit, gift wrapping. Stores are spartan; service is minimal.
Efficiency	Retailer caters to customers who have little time for shopping. Convenience stores are situated in handy locations, remain open long hours. Superstores offer one-stop shopping. Mail-order shopping, telemarketing, and TV shopping all allow customers to shop at home.
Service	Retailer emphasizes personal contact, expert assistance with purchase, postsale service.
Ambience	Retailer creates exciting shopping environment, caters to customer's fantasies with special effects such as theme décor, music, special events, imaginative architecture.
Portfolio	Retailer has a mix of several outlets, each of which caters to specific segment.

sales, about one-third of all retail establishments are small operations with no paid employees other than the owner.[15]

If you've been shopping lately, you know that retailing is undergoing major changes. New, highly specialized stores are cropping up to cater to every taste. At the same time, distinctions between one type of retailer and another are blurring. You can order videotapes along with your pizza or buy clothes at the grocery store. Department stores, bargain stores, specialty shops, supermarkets, convenience stores, and nonstore retailers are all experimenting with new ways to appeal to the consumer (see Exhibit 14.4).

Department Stores

Department stores are large retail establishments that bring together a vast variety of merchandise under one roof and departmentalize both their merchandising activities and their operating functions. Department stores usually enjoy a reputation for the highest quality, fashion, and service, providing such amenities as credit, delivery, personal service, and in most cases a pleasant atmosphere. Some, like Sears and J. C. Penney, operate coast to coast; others, like Marshall Field's and Nordstrom, focus on narrower geographic territories.

Until the end of World War II, when they expanded into suburban shopping malls, most department stores were in downtown locations. In the last several decades, many chains enjoyed steady growth as they opened outlet after outlet in malls across the country. Today, however, the rush to build new malls is slowing, and department-store chains are focusing on increasing the profitability of their current locations.

In the 1990s, many department stores are struggling. For one thing, the same merchandise is generally available in other types of outlets, which has encouraged consumers to shop around for the best price. Sears, once the nation's largest retailer, is in a double squeeze between discounters on the low end and upscale department stores like Nordstrom on the high end. In order to compete,

department stores Large retail stores that carry a wide variety of merchandise retailers have taken to having more and more sales, which cut into profit margins. Consumers, meanwhile, have learned to expect to get everything at reduced prices, and they often wait for markdowns before buying.

Department stores are dealing with competitors in a variety of ways. Selling merchandise not available anywhere else is one approach. In many cities, department stores are the fashion leaders. They are usually the first retailers to carry a variety of the newest merchandise, and some, like Bloomingdale's and Neiman-Marcus, offer unusual and one-of-a-kind items as well as goods bearing their own labels. Many are also attempting to build traffic via **scrambled merchandising,** stocking goods that are ordinarily handled by another type of retailer. Many big department stores, for example, now sell food items.

Another approach is to maximize the profit that the store makes per square foot of selling space by focusing sales efforts in the areas where they will be most successful. Some department stores have eliminated major appliances and furniture from their inventories, concentrating instead on fashion goods. Technology is also helping stores reduce costs and improve operations. When redesigning its stores recently, Sears installed computerized checkout points similar to those used in supermarkets, which enable the company to monitor sales more closely. Such systems are also important in helping control costs.

Department stores are also emphasizing service to lure customers. Chicago's Carson Pirie Scott, for example, has created a new "store-within-a-store" called the Corporate Level, aimed at professional women with plenty of money but very little spare time for shopping. At the Corporate Level, everything the customer might need is available in one convenient place—clothes, accessories, and such services as hairstyling, dry cleaning, and photocopying. For a $50 annual fee, the customer may also obtain the services of a personal shopping consultant, not to mention check-cashing privileges and the use of meeting rooms.[16]

Bargain Stores

Extras like these are generally not available in retail outlets that offer bargain prices. By keeping their facilities lean and their services at a minimum, these retailers are able to offer a variety of nationally advertised and private-brand goods at prices significantly below traditional department-store prices. Sales growth in these outlets is outpacing that of department stores.

DISCOUNT STORES   **Discount stores** like Zayre, K Mart, and Wal-Mart initiated the movement toward cut-rate pricing after World War II by opening bare-bones facilities in inexpensive locations. They offer a mix of merchandise that is weighted toward relatively inexpensive items but also carry nationally advertised brands that are sold at a discount.

Gradually, many discounters have upgraded their operations and become more like department stores in appearance, merchandise, and price. This process of store evolution, known as the **wheel of retailing,** follows a predictable pattern: An innovative company with low operating costs attracts a following by offering low prices and limited service (see Exhibit 14.5). Over time, management adds more services to broaden the appeal of the store. But in the process, prices creep upward, opening the door to lower-priced competitors. Eventually, these competitors also upgrade their operations and are replaced by still other lower-priced stores.

---

scrambled merchandising
Policy of carrying merchandise that is ordinarily sold in a different type of outlet

discount stores Retailers that sell a variety of goods below the market price by keeping their overhead low

wheel of retailing Evolutionary process by which stores that feature low prices are gradually upgraded until they forfeit their appeal to price-sensitive shoppers and are replaced by new competitors

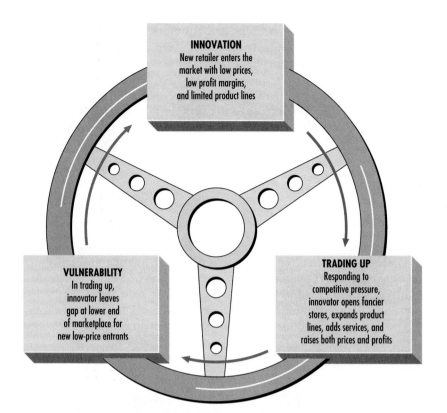

EXHIBIT 14.5

The Wheel of Retailing
The wheel of retailing is one of several theories explaining the continuous evolution in the world of retailing.

OFF-PRICE STORES   Like discounters, **off-price stores** sell name-brand merchandise at prices below those in department stores; unlike discounters, however, off-price retailers buy their goods at below-wholesale prices. They are able to do this by taking advantage of other people's mistakes—buying overstocked merchandise, irregulars, end-of-season items, and production overruns. In addition, they obtain merchandise at cut rates directly from manufacturers by agreeing to do without some of the privileges accorded to department stores, such as help with promotions, extended payment terms, and return privileges.[17] An off-price store such as T. J. Maxx or Burlington Coat Factory features the same merchandise typically found in more luxurious department stores but sells it for 20 to 60 percent less.

The off-price phenomenon poses dilemmas for businesses in many parts of the clothing industry. Manufacturers enjoy increased sales through the popular new off-price outlets, but some fear that their carefully nurtured brand-name image will be ruined by association with a discounter. Meanwhile, department stores, which have been losing business to the off-price competition, have threatened to stop buying from manufacturers that sell to these outlets. Some lawyers contend that these measures may violate antitrust laws if they are aimed at keeping retail prices high. Yet even as they try to isolate the off-pricers from their suppliers, department stores themselves are entering the game by acquiring or creating their own off-price subsidiaries.[18]

WAREHOUSE CLUBS   The latest thing in bargain shopping is **warehouse clubs,** big, bare outlets similar to storage warehouses with merchandise stacked to the ceiling on steel shelving and moved around by forklift trucks. The typical

off-price stores Retailers that offer bargain prices by maintaining low overhead and acquiring merchandise at below-wholesale costs

warehouse clubs Low-priced stores that sell memberships to small retailers and consumer members

warehouse sells annual memberships to customers, who get low prices on the goods sold. Shoppers are flocking to take advantage of the bargains. Sales generated by warehouse clubs are currently running over $20 billion per year, up from $1 billion in 1983.[19]

FACTORY OUTLETS   In contrast to the other types of bargain stores, factory outlets are owned and operated by manufacturers and sell only the manufacturer's goods. Facilities are generally spartan, but the prices are attractive because manufacturers rely on these outlets to rid themselves of closeouts, discontinued merchandise, irregulars, and canceled orders.

Specialty Shops

At the same time that shoppers are hunting for bargains, they are also hunting for other things—excitement, ambience, unusual merchandise, personalized service, convenience. (Looking for lessons from a golf pro while you get fitted for a new suit? Visit the Bergdorf Goodman Men shop in New York City.)[20] In many cases, customers are finding what they want in **specialty shops**, which carry only particular types of goods. The basic merchandising strategy of a specialty

specialty shops Stores that carry only particular types of goods

EXPLORING INTERNATIONAL BUSINESS

Toys 'R' Us Stores Play Santa Internationally

Imagine 18,000 toys in a 45,000 - square - foot toy store—sounds more like Santa's distribution center at the North Pole than a toy store here in town. But Charles Lazarus has put Santa-sized Toys 'R' Us stores in over 400 locations around the world. With a marketing strategy that translates into any language, cash registers are jingling 12 months of the year.

As Toys 'R' Us founder and chairman, Lazarus started with a single discount store in 1957, building the chain into an international juggernaut selling over $4 billion worth of toys each year. His first expansion beyond American borders was into Canada in 1984, followed by Great Britain in 1985. Today, shoppers in Singapore, Hong Kong, Germany, and France can also wheel their shopping carts through cavernous Toys 'R' Us stores and buy dolls, trucks, video games, even disposable diapers at discount prices. In 1991 foreign sales alone were estimated to exceed $900 million.

The Toys 'R' Us international marketing strategy combines a clearly defined target market (parents) with unambiguous positioning (the largest possible year-round selection of toys, offered self-service style in a convenient location at discount prices).

Toys 'R' Us buyers buy in quantity from manufacturers around the world and tailor the merchandise assortment in each store to local market tastes, which is an important advantage Lazarus uses as he expands globally. Each country's merchandise assortment is fine-tuned individually, with as much as 20 percent of the merchandise geared toward local preferences. In Great Britain, cricket bats are sold alongside Louisville Sluggers. But just because local kids aren't familiar with a particular item doesn't mean it won't sell. Singapore children have learned to play street hockey, thanks to the hockey sticks and pucks available in Toys 'R' Us stores. And when Toys 'R' Us buyers toured Germany to research local toy tastes before opening the first stores there, they found wooden toys, trains, and blocks that were so appealing they're now part of the Toys 'R' Us merchandise assortment in America.

Toys 'R' Us faces various competitors in each foreign market. Generally, the competition is similar to that in the United States: small neighborhood mom-and-pop toy stores, department stores, and discount and variety chains. But as the toy superstore concept catches on outside America, foreign competitors are challenging Toys 'R' Us head-on. In Canada, for example, Toy City is a tough opponent. Toy City intro-

shop is to offer a limited number of product lines but an extensive selection of brands, styles, sizes, models, colors, materials, and prices within each line that is stocked. Specialty shops are particularly strong in certain product categories—books, children's clothing, fast food, and sporting goods.

Although many specialty stores are individually owned and operated, a significant number are chain operations with several outlets, such as Crown Books, The Limited, B. Dalton, PlayCo, and Baskin-Robbins. Franchising is a common format for specialty stores, particularly those in the restaurant business.

Supermarkets

The large departmentalized food stores known as **supermarkets** vary in size from those with annual sales of less than half a million dollars to giant, block-long stores with annual sales of several million dollars. Regardless of size, they rely on high values to stay in business; the average supermarket has a profit margin of less than 1 percent.[21] Supermarkets carry nationally branded merchandise, private brands, and generic products. Self-service is an important characteristic, but the latest trend is toward separate delicatessen or bakery departments employing their own salespeople.

supermarkets Large departmentalized food stores

---

duced the toy superstore concept to Canada in 1978 and now has a chain of 20,000-square-foot outlets in 11 cities from Vancouver to Quebec City. Like Toys 'R' Us, Toy City builds its reputation on gigantic product selection. Although neither Toys 'R' Us nor Toy City guarantees the absolute lowest prices, their price tags are competitive. In fact, prices are so low that smaller competitors as well as department stores find their profit margins evaporating when they try to compete. Unless these competitors find a way to boost efficiency for improved margins, the market share battle between Toys 'R' Us and Toy City will probably claim some Canadian casualties. But Toys 'R' Us is counting on its immense buying power to give the firm the profit edge it needs to stay ahead of all Canadian competitors.

In Britain, the major competitors are Boots Company, a national drugstore chain, and F. W. Woolworth PLC, a variety store chain. Both are keenly aware of the Toys 'R' Us invasion, and both have developed very different competitive strategies. As the country's leading toy retailer, Woolworth launched a new chain called Kidstore in 1987. Located in urban areas rather than the suburban free-standing locations that Toys 'R' Us prefers, Kidstore stocks toys in addition to a wide variety of children's goods. On the other hand, Boots positioned its Children's World as full-price, with higher-quality mer-

chandise and with stores that are located away from downtown areas. Each store is divided into boutiques dedicated to a particular product line or service, such as children's apparel, shoes, toys, and haircutting. Compared with these two competitors, the Toys 'R' Us concept of a discount superstore devoted exclusively to toys is a strong differentiator.

Now Charles Lazarus wants to set up shop in Japan. Under a joint-venture agreement with McDonald's (Japan), Toys 'R' Us plans in time to open 100 stores throughout Japan. However, the Japanese market is anything but child's play. Large retailers are subject to Japan's "large-scale retail law," which holds that merchants planning to open stores larger than 5,400 square feet must first obtain approval from nearby retailers. Because the $5.5 billion toy market in Japan is split among thousands of small, family-owned stores and department stores, local retailers are up in arms and prepared to stall the Toys 'R' Us debut as long as possible.

Faced with legal obstacles, Toys 'R' Us has become a high-profile test case for access to the thriving retail market in Japan. Lazarus has already proven that Toys 'R' Us can adapt and flourish in a global retailing environment. And if he has his way, Japanese shoppers will soon find Go (their traditional board game) on the shelves of a 54,000-square-foot Toys 'R' Us store in Niigata City.

In recent years, competitive pressures have forced supermarkets to adopt many changes. The *hypermarket* takes one new approach: It combines the merchandise of a typical discount store with a full range of grocery products. Slightly smaller variations, known as superstores or combo stores, also stock an assortment of nonfood items, ranging from children's pajamas to small appliances. Note that the term "superstore" is also commonly applied to very large specialty discounters like Toys 'R' Us.

Convenience Stores

Convenience stores such as the 7-Eleven chain represent the rebirth of the traditional mom-and-pop store. As the name implies, these are food stores whose chief stock in trade is time and place utilities. They are typically open 24 hours a day, seven days a week. They can operate in fringe locations that do not have an adequate population base for a supermarket. They control expenses and profits by carrying only a limited selection of brands and sizes and charging higher prices to their customers—who may be too late to get to the supermarket or may simply want to pick up some milk, soft drinks, or bread without standing in a long checkout line.

Nonstore Retailers

Nonstore retailers do not sell in the traditional store setting. The latest innovation is retailing via computers and cable TV. But telephone marketing, mail-order catalogs, vending machines, automated teller machines, and door-to-door sales forces are more familiar to most consumers.

TELEMARKETING   You are probably familiar with telephone retailing, or **telemarketing.** No doubt you have been called by insurance agents, newspaper circulation departments, real estate brokers, and assorted nonprofit organizations, all trying to interest you in their goods, services, and causes. Advances in telephone technology are partly responsible for the barrage. With low-cost WATS lines and computer dialing systems, firms can economically deliver their sales message to a large, dispersed audience.

MAIL-ORDER FIRMS   **Mail-order firms** provide customers with a wide variety of goods ordered from catalogs and shipped by mail. Many of the most successful mail-order firms are more like specialty stores, focusing on a narrow range of merchandise; they include J. Crew, L. L. Bean, Lands' End, and Banana Republic, to name a few. Some companies use mail order to supplement and promote their base business, which is conducted primarily through retail stores. Others, such as Harry and David's Fruit-of-the-Month Club, rely almost entirely on mail-order sales. Still others, including J. Crew, view retail stores as a logical expansion from their mail-order businesses.[22]

VENDING MACHINES   For certain types of products, vending machines are an important retail outlet. This is particularly true in Japan, where a wide variety of products are available from vending machines. Soda pop, coffee, candy, sandwiches, and cigarettes are all commonly sold this way. From the consumer's point of view, the chief attraction of vending machines is their convenience: They are open 24 hours a day and may be found in a variety of handy locations

Automated teller machines, such as this cash station in Chicago, have revolutionized retail banking by increasing the time and place utility of banking services.

convenience stores Food stores that offer convenient locations and hours but stock a limited selection of goods

telemarketing Sale of goods and services by telephone

mail-order firms Companies that sell products through catalogs and ship them directly to customers

such as college dormitories. On the other hand, vending-machine prices are usually no bargain. Because the cost of servicing the machines is relatively high and vandalism is a factor, high prices are required to provide the vending-machine company and the product manufacturer with a reasonable profit.

DOOR-TO-DOOR RETAILERS   A door-to-door retailer relies on a large sales force to call directly on customers in their homes or offices, demonstrate merchandise, take orders, and make deliveries. The famous names in door-to-door selling—and its variant, the party plan—include Tupperware, Fuller Brush, Avon, and Electrolux. With more and more women working outside the home, this method of retailing is diminishing in importance.

▶ PHYSICAL DISTRIBUTION

Whatever channel a producer chooses, the goods or services must be physically transferred to the customer. In order for that new computer or three-speed hair dryer to reach the customer, the seller must resolve the practical, sometimes difficult question of how to get it there. For a producer with goods to move, there is a great deal more involved than loading cartons onto a truck and waving good-bye. Technically, **physical distribution** encompasses all the activities required to move finished products from the producer to the consumer (see Exhibit 14.6).

physical distribution All the activities required to move finished products from the producer to the consumer

From both a technical and an administrative standpoint, physical distribution is a complicated activity. In many goods-producing businesses, certain aspects of the physical distribution function are controlled by the production department, which also handles the movement of raw materials into the plant and the flow of work in process. This organizational arrangement sometimes creates tension between the marketing people, who are eager to please the customer with outstanding distribution service, and the production people, who are concerned with optimizing internal efficiency and achieving the lowest overall distribution cost.

To further complicate the picture, in many industries the producer and the intermediary share the distribution function. A manufacturer of potato chips, for example, might transport the product to a grocery wholesaler, who would then truck it to individual supermarkets or warehouses owned by supermarket chains. When responsibility for the shipping process is shared, nobody is completely in charge of meeting the delivery schedule.

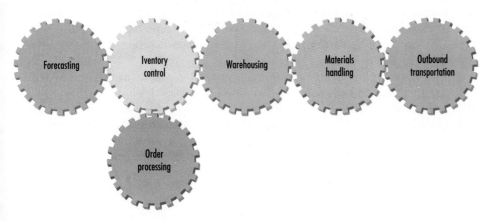

EXHIBIT 14.6

Steps in the Physical Distribution Process
The phases of a distribution system should mesh as smoothly as the cogs in a machine. Because the steps are interrelated, a change in one phase can affect the other phases. The objective of the process is to provide a target level of customer service at the lowest overall cost.

Distribution managers at Hitachi go over orders and work behind the scenes to get the product to the customer on time and in good condition.

The key to success in managing physical distribution is to coordinate the activities of everyone involved. The overriding objective of all concerned should be to achieve an acceptable level of distribution service at the lowest total cost. Generally speaking, as the level of service improves, the cost of distribution increases. A producer must analyze whether it is worthwhile to deliver the product in, say, three days as opposed to five, if doing so increases the price of the item by 5 or 10 percent.

This type of trade-off can be difficult to make because the steps in the distribution process are all interrelated. A change in one affects the others. For example, if you use slower forms of transportation, you reduce your shipping costs, but you probably increase your storage costs. Similarly, if you reduce the level of inventory to cut your storage costs, you run the risk of being unable to fill orders in a timely fashion. The trick is to optimize the *total* cost of achieving the desired level of service. This requires a careful analysis of each step in the distribution process in relation to every other step.

In-House Operations

The steps in the distribution process can be divided into in-house operations and transportation. The in-house steps in the process include forecasting, order processing, inventory control, warehousing, and materials handling.

Forecasting

To control the flow of products through the distribution system, a firm must have an accurate estimate of demand. To some degree, historical data can be used to project future sales; however, the firm must also consider the impact of unusual events such as special promotions that might temporarily boost demand. For example, if Black & Decker decided to offer a special discount price on electric drills during the month of September, management would need to ship additional drills to the dealers during the latter part of August to satisfy the extra demand.

Order Processing

order processing Functions involved in receiving and handling an order

Order processing involves a number of activities such as checking the customer's credit, recording the sale, making the appropriate accounting entries, arranging for the item to be shipped, adjusting the inventory records, and billing the customer. Because order processing involves direct interaction with the customer, it affects a company's reputation for customer service. Most companies establish standards for filling orders within a specific time period. For example, a company might attempt to ship 90 percent of its orders within 72 hours after they are received.

Computers are playing an increasingly important role in processing orders. Consider the case of McKesson, a San Francisco–based wholesaler that sells pharmaceuticals to drugstores. The company provides its customers with specially coded labels for their shelves. A clerk in a drugstore can order more of McKesson's cough medicine or sinus pills simply by waving a hand-held scanner over the label on the shelf. The signal is picked up by a computer at the drugstore and then transmitted immediately to another computer at McKesson's facilities.[23]

Inventory Control

In an ideal world, a company would always have just the right amount of goods on hand to fill the orders it receives. In reality, however, inventory and sales are seldom in perfect balance. Most firms like to build a supply of finished goods so that they can fill orders in a timely fashion. The question is, How much inventory is enough? If your inventory is too large, you incur extra expenses for storage space, handling, insurance, and taxes; you also run the risk of product obsolescence. On the other hand, if your inventory is too low, you may lose sales when the product is not in stock. The objective of **inventory control** is to resolve these issues. Inventory managers decide how much product to keep on hand and when to replenish the supply of goods in inventory. They also decide how to allocate products to customers if orders exceed supply.

inventory control *The process of maintaining inventories at a level that prevents stockouts and minimizes holding costs*

Warehousing

Products held in inventory are physically stored in a **warehouse.** Warehouses may be owned by the manufacturer, by an intermediary, or by a private company that leases warehouses.

Some warehouses are almost purely holding facilities in which goods are stored for relatively long periods. Others, known as **distribution centers,** serve as command posts for moving products to customers. In a typical distribution center, goods produced at a company's various locations are collected, sorted, coded, and redistributed to fill customer orders.

You might suppose that one warehouse is more or less like another and that warehousing decisions are relatively unimportant in the context of a company's overall business. But Sam Walton has demonstrated otherwise. Warehouses have actually played a major role in Wal-Mart's remarkable track record. Walton's distribution costs are about half those of his competitors, largely because the stores are stocked from company-owned warehouses. As Walton says, when Wal-Mart was relatively young, "we didn't have distributors falling over themselves to serve us like our competitors did in larger towns. Our only alternative was to build our own warehouse so we could buy in volume at attractive prices and store the merchandise." Walton's distribution centers are equipped with optical scanning devices, automated materials-handling equipment, and satellite communications equipment that provides immediate communication with individual stores.[24]

warehouse *Facility for storing backup stocks of supplies or finished products*

distribution centers *Warehouse facilities that specialize in collecting and shipping merchandise*

materials handling *Activities involved in moving, packing, storing, and inventorying goods*

Wal-Mart distribution centers such as this one in Bentonville, Arkansas, increase warehouse efficiency with automated materials-handling equipment such as optical scanning devices.

Materials Handling

Materials handling, the movement of goods within and between physical distribution facilities, is an important part of warehousing activities. One of its main areas of concern is storage methods—whether to keep supplies and finished goods in individual packages, large boxes, or sealed shipping containers. The choice of storage method depends on how the product is shipped, in what quantities, and to which location; a firm that typically sends small quantities of goods to widely scattered customers, for example, probably wouldn't want to use large containers. Materials handling also involves keeping track of inventory so that the company knows where in the distribution process its goods are located and when they need to be moved.

EXHIBIT 14.7

Physical Distribution Costs
Although the cost of physical distribution varies widely by product, in some cases it adds as much as 20 percent to the retail price of an item. Transportation is the single biggest factor in physical distribution costs.

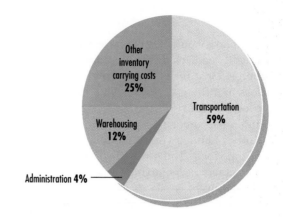

Transportation

For any business, the cost of transportation is normally the largest single item in the overall cost of physical distribution (see Exhibit 14.7). It doesn't necessarily follow, however, that a manufacturer should simply pick the cheapest available form of transportation. When a firm chooses a type of transportation, it has to bear in mind its other marketing concerns—storage, financing, sales, inventory size, and the like. The trick is to maximize the efficiency of the entire distribution process while minimizing its cost. Transportation, in fact, may be an especially important sales tool. If the firm can supply its customers' needs more quickly and reliably than its competitors do, it will have a vital advantage. Thus, it may be more profitable in the long run to pay higher transportation costs rather than risk the loss of future sales.

Modes of Transportation

Each mode of transportation has distinct advantages and disadvantages:

▶ *Trucking.* Trucks are the most frequently used form of transportation for two reasons: convenient door-to-door delivery and operation on public highways that do not require an expensive terminal or right of way, as airlines and railroads do. The main drawback of trucks is that they cannot carry all types of cargo cost-effectively, for example, bulky commodities such as steel or coal.

▶ *Rail.* Railroads can carry heavier and more diverse cargoes and in fact carry a larger volume of goods than any other mode of transportation. But they have the big disadvantage of being constrained to railroad tracks, so they can seldom deliver directly to the customer.

▶ *Water.* The cheapest form of transportation, water is widely used for such low-cost bulk items as oil, coal, ore, cotton, and lumber. But the disadvantages make it unsuitable for most businesses. Ships are slow, and service to any given location is infrequent. Furthermore, like rail, another form of transportation is usually needed to complete delivery; reloading may add substantial cost because of theft, extra handling, and spoilage caused by weather.

▶ *Air.* Although airplanes offer the fastest form of transportation, they have numerous disadvantages. Many areas of the country are still not served by conveniently located airports. Airplanes can carry only certain types of cargo because of size and shape limitations. Furthermore, airplanes are the least dependable and most expensive form of transportation. Weather may cause flight cancellations, and even minor repairs may lead to serious delays. However, when speed is paramount, air is usually the only way to go.

▶ *Pipelines.* For certain types of products, such as gasoline, natural gas, and coal and wood chips (suspended in liquid), pipelines are quite useful. Although they are expensive to build, they are extremely economical to operate and maintain. On the other hand, transportation via pipeline is surprisingly slow (three to four miles per hour), and the route is not flexible.

Environmental Impact of Transportation

Transportation has an undeniable effect on the natural and human environments. Its effects range from the noise of aircraft to the wildlife hazards posed by railways in remote areas. We were all given a grim reminder of transportation's potential environmental damage when the *Exxon Valdez* spilled millions of gallons of crude oil in Alaska's Prince William Sound. Activists responded by calling for tighter regulations on shipping companies, and they requested double-hulled tankers, which provides a good example of the total cost concept. Double-hulled tankers are less vulnerable to the sort of punctures that caused the *Valdez* disaster, but they cost substantially more to build. The oil companies would have to pass all or part of this cost on to consumers. How many consumers are ready to pay higher gas prices in order to decrease the risk of oil spills?

There is a sizable cloud on the horizon for trucking as well. Trucks rely heavily on the nation's 42,798-mile interstate highway system, and that system is in bad shape. In some states, as much as 30 or 40 percent of the interstate miles are considered deficient. Potholes and other problems plague a system that was designed more than 30 years ago to last only 20 years and to carry only one-third the traffic. Trucking surely suffers from bad roads, but it is also a big part of the problem. The U.S. Transportation Department estimates that one 80,000-pound truck causes as much damage to an interstate as 9,600 automobiles. It's not surprising that proposals to increase the size of truck-trailer combinations are meeting with stiff opposition. Railroads are joining the antitruck protests, and their position is supported by the fact the trucks generate four times as much pollution per ton hauled as railroads.[25]

SUMMARY OF LEARNING OBJECTIVES

1 List nine functions performed by marketing intermediaries.

Intermediaries provide a sales force, market information, and promotional support. They also sort, standardize, and divide merchandise; carry stock; and deliver products. In addition, they assume risks and provide financing for producers. Finally, they perform a preliminary buying function for users.

2 Name the alternative distribution channels for consumer goods, organizational goods, and services.

Four distribution channels are used for consumer goods: from producer to consumer, from producer to retailer to consumer, from producer to wholesaler to retailer to consumer, and from producer to agent/broker to wholesaler to retailer to consumer. For organizational goods, the channels may be from producer to user, from producer to one or more agent/ brokers or wholesalers to user, or from producer to agent/broker to wholesaler to user. Most services are distributed directly from the producer to the user; however, in a few cases an agent or a broker intervenes.

3 Differentiate among intensive, selective, and exclusive market-coverage strategies.

With an intensive distribution strategy, a company attempts to saturate the market with its products by offering them in every available outlet. Companies that use a more selective approach to distribution choose a limited number of retailers that can adequately support the product. Firms that use exclusive distribution grant a single wholesaler or retailer the exclusive right to sell the product within a given geographic area.

4 Describe the three types of wholesalers.

The three types of wholesalers are merchant wholesalers, agents and brokers, and producer-owned wholesalers. Merchant wholesalers take title to the goods they sell; agents and brokers do not. Producer-owned wholesalers include branch offices and sales offices.

5 Identify at least 10 types of retailers.

Some of the most common types of retail stores are department stores, discount stores, off-price stores, warehouse clubs, factory outlets, specialty stores, supermarkets, and convenience stores. Nonstore retailers include electronic shopping services, telemarketers, mail-order firms, vending machines, and door-to-door retailers.

6 Explain what is meant by the "wheel of retailing."

The "wheel of retailing" is a term used to describe the evolution of stores from low-priced, limited-service establishments to higher-priced outlets that provide more services. As stores are upgraded, lower-priced competitors move in to fill the gap.

7 Specify the activities included in physical distribution.

Physical distribution encompasses not only transportation but also such in-house operations as forecasting, order processing, inventory control, warehousing, and materials handling.

8 List the five most common ways of transporting goods.

Trucks, railroads, airplanes, ships, and pipelines are the most common methods of moving goods.

Meeting a Business Challenge at Black & Decker

It's hard to say which is more impressive: the speed at which Nolan Archibald and his colleagues turned around the corporate culture, or the thoroughness of the results. Black & Decker used to be a manufacturer driven by financial measurements; it is now well on its way to being Archibald's vision of a worldwide marketing powerhouse. And the company's approach to managing its marketing channels is a central component of the new Black & Decker.

The change started with strategic planning, as it should. In Archibald's own words, "You analyze the problems that are unique to the company and the industry and then determine what the strengths and weaknesses are. Then you develop a plan to leverage the strengths and correct the weaknesses." Archibald and his colleagues made sure that marketing channels were a part of that strategic plan. Moreover, the new approach manages channels as a vital marketing resource, rather than simply as a pipeline for pumping products to customers.

The analysts who have observed Black & Decker's remarkable turnaround point out several aspects of channel management that have been

Nolan Archibald, chairman and CEO of Black & Decker.

a vital part of the success. The first change was simple but most important: more respect for marketing intermediaries. Black & Decker had a tough act to follow when it acquired General Electric's small household appliance line. Known as "Generous Electric" in some circles, GE went out of its way to be a good supplier. This

included ample support of retailer promotions, deep inventories to ensure no shortage of products in the stores, and a general level of respect for the people and organizations on the front line. Black & Decker's efforts to improve relations started by emulating this regard for retailers.

Out of this new respect flowed assistance. Black & Decker made several important moves to help its channel partners. One of these was a segmented channel strategy that focuses specialized sales assistance on the company's two major groups of customers: industrial/professional and retailers. This allows Black & Decker to give each kind of intermediary the unique help it needs. Another key move was to train its sales force thoroughly, not only in terms of product performance but also in helping retailers with inventory management, purchasing, and in-store product displays. Also, the promotional budget was beefed up to help pull customers into retail stores.

The assistance is mutual. Black & Decker established a number of dealer advisory panels, which retailers can use to give the company feedback on new products customers would like to see. By using its channel as a source of marketing-research information, Black & Decker benefits by getting a better picture of customer needs, and the retailers benefit by being able to deliver the right products.

Coordinated physical distribution is another change that helps both the company and its intermediaries. To better mesh its delivery systems with the needs of distributors and retailers, Black & Decker changed virtually every aspect of its physical distribution. This included new locations for distribution centers, modified transportation policies, and more powerful systems for managing and coordinating information.

Increasing the number of products held in inventory was another important step. This gives retailers the confidence that they'll be able to keep up with demand, particularly during the Christmas shopping season, when many tools and small appliances are purchased.

A final key element in Black & Decker's strategic plan is growth through acquisition, which has been tied closely to marketing channel management. The recent $2.8 billion purchase of Emhart is a good example. Some observers criticized the move, which gave Black & Decker a big presence in hardware. But the logic was clear after a second look: Some of Emhart's products fit in perfectly with Black & Decker's existing consumer goods channels, and others mesh well with the industrial channels. The units of Emhart that don't align with the existing marketing channels were put up for sale.

Black & Decker's dramatic turnaround is convincing evidence of the importance of effectively managing marketing channels. Its sales are growing in every channel of distribution it uses. And the company is starting to be praised as a strong marketing organization that helps create demand for retailers.

Your Mission: Nolan Archibald faces some tough issues in the selection and management of Black & Decker's marketing channels. But he knows he can rely on you for help. In your role as the manager in charge of marketing channels, examine the following situations and make your recommendations from the available choices.

1. Archibald knows that marketing channels can perform a wide array of functions, ranging from gathering marketing information to providing physical distribution. He also knows that Black & Decker should identify the most crucial functions that the company would like to see its intermediaries perform. He's asked you to identify these crucial functions. Which of the following combinations of marketing intermediary functions would be most important to Black & Decker?

a. Most of the vital channel functions required of intermediaries by Black & Decker occur after the sale. Keeping customers satisfied is an absolute necessity, and to do that you need to be in direct contact. Black & Decker can't be there for every single customer. The functions of most interest here are providing product service and helping customers use products successfully.

b. Black & Decker's products are not terribly complicated, so customers don't need much help. The most important channel functions are at the beginning of the sales process, not at the end. Providing feedback from customers is the best place to start because market information like this is necessary if the company is going to design and manufacture the right products for its customers. With that information in place, the intermediaries should all have a say in Black & Decker's strategic planning process; after all, they are quite dependent on the decisions made during the company's planning process.

c. Alleviating discrepancies and matching buyers and sellers are definitely the most important tasks Black & Decker should ask of its channel partners. It simply isn't economical for the company to deliver individual products to each customer; marketing intermediaries need to fill the gap by rearranging quantities and assortments so that customers can get the right number and selection of products. Also, Black & Decker wouldn't necessarily know where to go to find potential customers, so it must rely on retailers to get the products to customers. And standardized transac-

tions wouldn't hurt, either.

d. Black & Decker needs help before and after the sale. The most important combination of functions would start with providing feedback from customers and suggesting products that should be developed. Promotion is also vital, particularly cooperative promotions that combine the power of Black & Decker's international presence and big ad budget with the retailers' individual feel for local markets. Physical distribution is important as well; you can't sell products if you can't put them in front of customers. After the sale, both customer support and product service will be needed to ensure satisfied buyers of Black & Decker tools, appliances, and hardware.

2. Customer service is, of course, a vital ingredient in all successful marketing transactions. Archibald knows this and also realizes that customer service is not all that easy to define and execute in a multichannel system like the one Black & Decker relies on. Which of the following definitions of and approaches to customer service best fits the company's situation?

a. Customer service efforts should focus on the final purchasers of the product. Black & Decker can do this in several ways. The first is simply to make it easier to be successful with Black & Decker products. This includes designing for ease of use, providing helpful user guides, and perhaps offering a toll-free number that customers can call with specific questions about using products. A second way to help customers might be to sponsor seminars at places like woodworking shows (for the power tool and hardware lines) and home shows (for all three lines). And for organizational customers in the power tool segment, another way to help would be to send Black & Decker specialists to customer sites to help them solve specific problems.

b. Black & Decker's real customers are the thousands of marketing intermediaries that buy and then resell its tools, appliances, and hardware. These are the customers that the company should worry about servicing. The intermediaries will, in turn, satisfy the final customers. Black & Decker can help the intermediaries in a number of ways, including promotions, pricing advice, product selection, and display help.

c. The best answer would be a combination of (a) and (b). Although it is true that the intermediaries are Black & Decker's most immediate customers, the sales process really isn't complete until final customers purchase and are satisfied with the product. Therefore, Black & Decker has to pay attention to serving the intermediaries directly *and* serving final customers indirectly through the intermediaries. All of the elements suggested for (a) and (b) could apply here.

d. The concept of customer service is irrelevant in this case because Black & Decker doesn't sell to final customers. It is the job of intermediaries to satisfy customers. That is, after all, the number one purpose of intermediaries and the reason they make money on the products manufactured by Black & Decker.

3. Black & Decker's engineers have developed a new tool that cuts concrete. Unfortunately, it doesn't really fit in the marketing channels that you already have in place, so it's time for you to design a new channel. Here are some important variables you'll need to consider:

Customer type: Organizational, ranging in size from one-person contractors to multinational construction firms

Geography: Customers are all over the place; the geographic distribution roughly mirrors the population distribution, with concentrations in large cities and widely dispersed customers elsewhere

Market size: Big; the saw costs around $2,000, and Black & Decker expects to sell thousands every month; it makes sense to put a sizable investment into the distribution channel

Life cycle: Somewhere between the growth and maturity phases; most customers have a pretty good idea of how to use them and what they're all about

Support needs: These customers don't need a lot of help, but they do need to be assured of fast service when things go wrong; downtime is critical, and customers would prefer on-site delivery of loaner units in the event of a breakdown

Based on these variables, what's the best channel system for this product?

a. Consider the purchase habits of the people likely to use these products. Even though they are industrial customers, they are human beings after all. As such, they need to do personal shopping as much as the rest of us. Because of that, the retail stores where they do their other shopping remain a good choice. That way they can combine their personal shopping with their business shopping.

b. The market is large and geographically diverse, and customers don't need much in the way of support. Therefore, mail order would be the perfect channel for this new product. It reaches every corner of the country, and it costs less because retail store space and salespeople are not needed.

c. This new product should be restricted to tool stores and masonry supply stores that cater exclusively to professionals. These stores should be able to deliver superior customer service, including on-site delivery of replacement and loaner units. The biggest drawback of using this channel is that these outlets are not as widespread as homeowner-oriented retail stores, but professional builders in out-of-the way locations are accustomed to a little travel time when it comes to shopping for tools and supplies.

d. A combination of all three channels would be the best bet. Not all organizations will purchase products in the same manner, so you can maximize your chances of reaching all potential customers when you open as many channels as possible.

4. A new product has just been designed by the small home appliance division. This new device is a combination coffee bean grinder and espresso machine. What is the best channel system for this product? Here are some factors to consider, and this time consider the problem of product and brand image.

Customer type: Consumer

Geography: Again, customers are all over the place, but they are concentrated primarily in and around large cities and, for the time being, are found mostly on the West Coast

Market size: Not terribly large because of the price, which is around $700; many people like espresso made from freshly ground coffee beans, but only the most avid connoisseurs are willing to pay that much for the quality and convenience of the combination grinder/maker

Life cycle: Espresso machines have been around for years, but their move into consumer markets is fairly new; in the past most were sold to restaurants

Support needs: The machine is fairly easy to use and clean, and you don't expect much in the way of repair trouble, but some customers will initially need help and advice in order to brew the perfect demitasse of espresso

a. Specialty kitchen stores, particularly those that cater to upscale urban consumers, would be the best choice. These stores carry other kitchen and household products of similar quality and price, so it's a natural that the new espresso machine will fit in here as well. The customers who frequent stores like this enjoy buying quality products, and some like to boast that they purchase such goods only from specialty stores, never from department or discount stores.

b. Because this is a fundamentally new direction for Black & Decker, asking customers to buy direct from the company itself is a sensible choice. If you put the new machine on the retail shelves next to $19 Black & Decker toasters, its image will be tarnished beyond retrieval. To maintain a premium image for this product, you've got to separate it from the company's other products. The only sure way to do this is to have customers buy direct from the factory.

c. No self-respecting connoisseur is going to buy an espresso machine from a manufacturer of power drills. Even the most astute channel selection isn't going to rescue this project; recommend to your managers that they abandon the product entirely or sell the design to another company. You'll need more than just a good marketing channel to make this miracle happen.

d. The existing channels are fine. A $700 coffee maker might look a little out of place in K Mart, but its presence will raise the image of the entire Black & Decker product family.[26]

KEY TERMS

branch office (398)
brokers (398)
channel captain (396)
convenience stores (404)
department stores (399)
discount stores (400)
distribution centers (407)
distribution channels (388)
distribution mix (388)
exclusive distribution (393)
horizontal conflict (396)
intensive distribution (392)

inventory control (407)
mail-order firms (404)
manufacturer's agents (398)
marketing intermediaries (388)
materials handling (407)
merchant wholesalers (398)
off-price stores (401)
order processing (406)
physical distribution (405)
rack jobbers (398)
retailers (397)
reverse channels (391)

sales office (398)
scrambled merchandising (400)
selective distribution (392)
specialty shops (402)
supermarkets (403)
telemarketing (404)
vertical conflict (396)
vertical marketing systems (396)
warehouse (407)
warehouse clubs (401)
wheel of retailing (400)
wholesalers (397)

REVIEW QUESTIONS

1. What forms of utility do intermediaries create?

2. How does the presence of intermediaries affect the price of products?

3. How does the length of the distribution chain tend to vary for convenience goods, shopping goods, and specialty goods?

4. What is the difference between a merchant wholesaler and an agent?

5. What are some of the strategies that department stores have begun using to compete with stores that offer lower prices?

6. How do off-price stores function, and what are the advantages they offer?

7. What is the goal of inventory management?

8. What are the advantages and disadvantages of truck, rail, air, ship, and pipeline transportation?

A CASE FOR CRITICAL THINKING

Hub-and-Spoke Is Wheel of Fortune for Federal Express

Back in the 1960s, Frederick W. Smith was sure that his innovative physical distribution ideas could increase efficiency and decrease the cost of moving packages around the United States. Against the advice of numerous skeptics, he implemented the radical concept of hub-and-spoke distribution, and by 1988 he was flying high with $4 billion in revenues. But as he continued to expand, Smith faced obstacles that hub-and-spoke couldn't solve: air transport regula-

tions and the challenge of international operations.

The air express industry that Smith envisioned would fly packages from around the country to a central location to be sorted and then shipped to their final destinations. He reasoned that a company using this system would be able to optimize its airplane and trucking resources and provide fast and efficient package handling for shippers anywhere in the country.

Smith chose his hometown, Memphis, as the hub; it is centrally located and the airport is rarely closed by bad weather. Despite his high hopes, the first night of service was anything but encouraging. Federal Express handled a grand total of eight shipments, seven of which were sent by its own employees to employees in other locations.

One year later, the fledgling company was losing $1 million a month and Smith realized that he needed a new marketing approach to reach organizational buyers. After a couple of false starts, Federal Express aired an ad campaign based on the slogan, "When it absolutely, positively has to be there overnight," and sales soared.

By the mid-1980s, Federal Express was delivering nearly half of the overnight packages sent within the United States. However, because he knew the market was maturing, Smith began to look beyond U.S. borders for additional growth. In 1985 Federal Express crossed the oceans with a new international service and quickly got caught in the mire of overseas competitors and foreign aviation regulations.

Over a three-year period, Smith lost about $74 million trying to compete internationally. Finally, in 1989 he won government approval to purchase Tiger International, which gave Federal Express access to the Flying Tiger Line air cargo organization, with its 40 years of international experience and well-established routes. Moreover, Smith could now use Tiger's fleet of long-range planes and become a player in the international heavy-freight market. Combining Tiger's strengths with Federal Express's expertise in door-to-door delivery, Smith forged a formidable weapon to shake up the global cargo market.

Another international roadblock Smith faced was a bewildering maze of aviation and customs regulations in various countries. Bilateral trade treaties in some countries restrict the pricing and market entry of goods transported by air. In other countries, antiquated customs systems hinder Federal Express's ability to expedite packages.

Smith tackled these regulations through a combination of lobbying efforts and technology. For example, he set out to educate the authorities in other countries about the problems that aviation regulations cause in the global economy. To make the customs procedure more efficient, Federal Express relies on its ability to identify and track every shipment according to its origin and destination. Seeing the benefits of more modern customs procedures, an increasing number of countries are adopting new, faster methods to speed goods transport.

1. Although Federal Express has taken on the burden of warehousing inventory for clients of its Business Logistics Services (BLS) division, Smith believes he can improve this service by expanding its functions. As a new service, should he offer to accept inventory returns to the BLS warehouse from his clients' customers, or should he offer to prepare customers' goods with price tags, instruction sheets, and packaging?

2. Because there are so many competitors in the air express business, imagine that Smith wants to expand into a new area. Which of these two options should he implement: (1) a chain of state-of-the-art public warehouses that rent space to numerous companies near the airport in cities with heavy commercial air traffic, or (2) an international water transportation service that would speed containerized goods between major port cities around the world?

3. The Federal Express hub at Memphis airport is virtually unused starting about 4:30 each morning (when planes leave loaded with packages for destinations around the country) until about 11:30 each night (when the planes arrive bearing packages to be sorted for delivery the next day). Smith might want to make the hub more productive during its idle hours. Would you suggest that he make the hub available to passenger airlines during the daytime hours? Or would you suggest that he utilize the hub during daytime hours to offer a two-day freight consolidation and forwarding service, a lower-cost shipping option that combines packages going to the same general location?

BUILDING YOUR COMMUNICATION SKILLS

In a group of three or four students, select a consumer product with which you are familiar, and trace its channel of distribution. The product might be fresh foods, processed foods, cosmetics, clothing, or manufactured goods (ranging from something as simple as a fork to something as complex as a personal computer).

▶ For information, you might contact a business involved in the manufacture or distribution of the product, either by letter or by telephone. Or you could locate an article in a trade periodical that describes the channel of distribution for your chosen product.

▶ Examine the various factors involved in the distribution of the product, and prepare a brief summary of your findings. Consider the following:

The role of the middleman in distribution

The type of distribution: intensive, selective, or exclusive

The amount of control the manufacturer has over the distribution process

The type of channel used in the distribution process and its influence on the cost of the product

KEEPING CURRENT USING *THE WALL STREET JOURNAL*

Find an article in *The Wall Street Journal* describing changes in methods of distribution or distribution policies used by a company or several companies in the same industry. For example, have they changed from using an in-house sales force to using manufacturers' reps? Have they added local warehouses or centralized their distribution? Eliminated wholesalers and gone directly to dealers? Opened more company stores or eliminated independent retailers? Added a mail-order division to a retail operation or a retail operation to a mail-order firm? Changed discount policies or shipping methods? Closed stores in downtown areas and moved to malls? Added on-line ordering capabilities?

1. What changes in distribution have taken place? What additional changes, if any, are planned?

2. What were the reasons for the changes? How have population, lifestyle, financial, or other factors affected distribution in this industry?

3. If you were a stockholder in a company in this industry, would you be concerned about distribution-related changes hurting the company in the next five years? Why or why not?

CHAPTER *15*

LEARNING OBJECTIVES

After studying this chapter, you will be able to

1 Describe the four basic categories of promotion.

2 Distinguish between push and pull strategies of promotion.

3 Explain the concept of positioning.

4 List the seven steps in the personal-selling process.

5 Define institutional, product, and competitive advertising.

6 List the five main types of advertising media and at least three less well-known types.

7 Explain the role of public relations in marketing.

8 Distinguish between the two main types of sales promotion, and give at least two examples of each type.

Promotion

CAN SUCCESSFUL PROMOTIONS HURT?

H ow can promotions be successful and still hurt the company? It can happen if the right people get the wrong message, or even if the wrong people get the right message. Apple Computer learned that clever promotional strategies can be dangerous: Sometimes they work in ways you don't expect.

When Steven Jobs and Steve Wozniak pieced together the first Apple, they envisioned a computer for all of us. Apple's first computers, the Apple and Apple II, were easy to learn and easy to live with. They started popping up in homes and classrooms all over.

But back at the office, the longtime king of computers, IBM, agreed that the personal computer might be a pretty good idea. So Big Blue made one of its own, the IBM PC. Unlike Apple, however, IBM walked past the home and education markets to knock on the doors of its existing mainframe computer customers. The IBM PC became a fixture in well-groomed offices.

Life was good: Apple targeted the home and education segments, and IBM took care of the business world. But Apple's leaders soon discovered that the home market wasn't quite as big as they had originally thought. Gradually, they realized that the serious personal computer action really was in the business market, so they set their sights on IBM's turf.

Apple's weapon was the Macintosh. People who wanted to use a computer but weren't "computer types" fell in love with the Mac. Unlike the IBM PC, just about anybody could use it. The Mac also had a vague counterculture appeal; it looked different, and using it didn't require the blessing of the computer wizards in the back room. Moreover, the company selling it was different too, from its whimsical name to its brash young executives.

These two themes became central messages in Apple's promotional strategy: Here was a computer for ordinary people, and it didn't come from some old corporate codger. One Apple TV commercial likened IBM to George Orwell's Big

417

Brother, and another implied that IBM customers were like silly lemmings, blindly following each other into the sea. Another emphasized friendliness, contrasting the slim Macintosh user's booklet with the massive three-ring binder that came with the IBM PC.

Was this strategy successful? Yes . . . and no. Apple did get a message across. The world was convinced that Apple products were friendly, even safe enough for young children. Unfortunately, many business buyers were also convinced that a machine so friendly could never be powerful enough for the office. Clearly, the right people got the wrong message. And the Big Brother and lemming commercials turned off some of the very people Apple needed to turn on: corporate computing managers who had been IBM customers for years. They didn't appreciate some upstart company telling them they were fools for staying with IBM. Apple got its message across all right. Corporations were convinced that Apple was not the computer company for them.

This was the situation facing John Sculley, Apple's chief. Too many corporate buyers considered the Mac an amusing toy; it was fine for artists and kids but not for businesspeople. And Apple the company didn't fit in the corporate environment any better than the computer did. How could Sculley win over the corporate buyers? What would it take to reposition Apple as a viable business partner? Finally, how could Apple show the world that even though the Mac was as friendly as ever, it really was powerful enough for corporate work?[1]

▶ THE PROMOTIONAL MIX

Apple's John Sculley needed the right kind of promotion to change his company's image. Of the four ingredients in the marketing mix—product, price, distribution, and promotion—promotion is perhaps the one most often associated with marketing. And although it is no guarantee of success, promotion does have a profound impact on a product's performance in the marketplace.

promotion *A wide variety of persuasive techniques used by companies to communicate with their target markets and the general public*

What exactly is **promotion**? Although the term is defined in many ways, it is basically persuasive communication that motivates people to buy whatever an organization is selling—goods, services, or ideas. Promotion may take the form of direct, face-to-face communication or indirect communication through such media as television, radio, magazines, newspapers, direct mail, billboards, and other channels.

Promotional Goals

Promotional activities have three basic goals: to inform, to persuade, and to remind. *Informing* is the first promotional priority, since people cannot buy something until they are aware of it and understand what it will do for them. Potential customers need to know where the item can be found, how much it will cost, and how to use it. *Persuading* is also an important priority, since most people need to be motivated to satisfy their wants in a particular way. If customers have never used the item before, they must be convinced that doing so will be beneficial. If they are using a competing brand, they must be persuaded to switch. *Reminding* the customer of the product's availability and benefits is also important, since such reminders stimulate additional purchases.

Informing, persuading, and reminding are the main goals of promotion, but a good promotional effort also seeks to achieve specific objectives. These include attracting new customers, increasing usage among existing customers, aiding

Creative promoters at Breyers, Chevron, and Westin use the visibility of hot air balloons to get in touch with consumers and to get their messages across.

distributors, stabilizing sales, boosting brand-name recognition, creating sales leads, and influencing decision makers.

Promotional Ethics

Although promotion serves many useful functions, critics argue that its goals are self-serving. Some contend that sellers use promotional tools to convince people to buy unnecessary or potentially harmful goods like anti-aging creams, baldness "cures," sweetened cereals, liquor, and cigarettes. Others argue that promotion encourages materialism at the expense of more worthwhile values, that it exploits stereotypes, and that it manipulates the consumer on a subconscious level. Still others argue that the money spent on promotion could be put to better use inventing new products or improving the quality of existing items.

Public concern about potential misuse of promotion has led to the passage of government regulations that limit promotional abuses. The federal government's primary advertising watchdog is the Federal Trade Commission (FTC), which has developed some ground rules for promotion. One rule is that *all statements of fact must be supported by evidence.* This includes words ("Lipton. The Only Naturally Decaffeinated Tea Bags.") and demonstrations. Thus, companies cannot use whipped cream in a shaving-cream commercial to create an impression of a firm, heavy lather. Another rule is that *sellers must not create an overall impression that is incorrect.* In other words, they cannot claim that doctors recommend a product if doctors do not; nor can they present an actor who delivers the message dressed in a doctor's white jacket. Most states also regulate promotional practices by individual industries such as liquor stores, stock brokerages, employment agencies, and small loan companies.

In response to growing concern and confusion among consumers and health professionals, the Food and Drug Administration and the U.S. Department of Agriculture recently developed sweeping guidelines and policies for advertising claims and product-label wording. For instance, the word *light* can now be used to describe a product only if it contains at least one-third fewer calories than the regular version of the product; *low calorie* means no more than 40 calories per standard-sized serving.[2]

Self-regulation by businesses provides still another vehicle for the restraint of false and misleading promotion. The National Advertising Review Board, whose members include advertisers, agencies, and the general public, has a full-time professional staff that investigates complaints of deceptive advertising. If the complaint appears justified, the board uses both its persuasive power and the threat of referral to governmental agencies to try to get the offending company to stop. Many individual companies and agencies also practice self-regulation.

Four Elements of Promotion

Within the framework of these ethical guidelines, marketers use a mix of four activities to achieve their promotional objectives. The activities are personal selling, advertising, public relations, and sales promotion (see Exhibit 15.1). These elements can be combined in various ways to create a **promotional mix** for a particular product or idea.

Personal selling involves direct, person-to-person communication, either face-to-face or by phone. It is the only form of promotion that allows for immediate interaction between the buyer and seller. It is also the only form that enables the seller to adjust the message to the specific needs and interests of the individual customer. The chief disadvantage of personal selling is its relatively high cost.

Advertising consists of messages paid for by an identified sponsor and transmitted through a mass communication medium. As we shall see later in the chapter, advertising can take many forms. Its chief advantage lies in its ability to reach a large audience economically. Advertising has several disadvantages,

promotional mix The particular blend of personal selling, advertising, public relations, and sales promotion that a company uses to reach potential customers

personal selling In-person communication between a seller and one or more potential buyers

advertising Paid, nonpersonal communication to a target market from an identified sponsor utilizing mass communications channels

EXHIBIT 15.1 ▶ **The Four Elements of Promotion**

The promotional mix typically includes a blend of various elements. The "right" mix depends on the nature of the market and the characteristics of the item being sold. Over time, the mix for a particular product may change.

CONTACT MODE	TIMING	FLEXIBILITY	CONTROL	COST/EXPOSURE
Personal selling (Direct, personal interaction)	Regular recurrent contact	Message tailored to customer and adjusted to reflect feedback	Sender controls content of message	Relatively high
Advertising (Indirect, no personal interaction)	Regular, recurrent contact	Standard, unvarying message	Seller controls content of message	Low to moderate
Public relations (Indirect, no personal interaction)	Intermittent as newsworthy events occur	Standard, unvarying message	Medium usually controls content of message	No direct cost
Sales promotion (Indirect, no personal interaction)	Intermittent based on short-term sales objectives	Standard and unvarying	Seller controls content of message	Varies

however, starting with the expense of creating an advertising campaign. Second, advertising can't provide direct feedback, as personal selling can, and advertising is also difficult to personalize. Finally, advertising can't always motivate customers to action as effectively as personal selling can.

Public relations encompasses all the nonsales communications that businesses have with their various audiences. Part of the public relations effort covers general topics such as responding to journalists' requests for information and helping local schools with educational projects. The other side of the public relations effort seeks to generate significant news coverage about the company and its products and tries to encourage favorable reviews of products in newspapers and magazines and on radio and television programs.

Sales promotion is the final element in the promotional mix, and it is the most difficult to define. It includes a wide range of events and activities designed to stimulate interest in the product. Coupons, rebates, contests, in-store demonstrations, free samples, trade shows, and point-of-purchase displays all fall into this category.

public relations Nonsales communication that businesses have with their various audiences (includes both communication with the general public and press relations)

sales promotion A wide range of events and activities (including coupons, rebates, contests, in-store demonstrations, free samples, trade shows, and point-of-purchase displays) designed to stimulate interest in a product

Promotional Strategies

How do you decide on the right blend of personal selling, advertising, public relations, and sales promotion? That's not an easy question to answer because so many factors must be taken into account. When marketing a product, the seller combines the various elements of the promotional mix, depending on the characteristics of the product and of the market.

Product-Related Factors

Various types of products lend themselves to differing forms of promotion. Simple, familiar items like laundry detergent can be explained adequately through advertising, but personal selling is generally required to communicate the features of unfamiliar and sophisticated goods and services such as office automation equipment or municipal waste-treatment facilities. Direct, personal contact is particularly important in promoting customized services such as interior design, financial advice, or legal counsel. In general, consumer and organizational goods usually require differing promotional mixes.

The product's price is also a factor in the selection of the promotional mix. Inexpensive items sold to a mass market are well suited to advertising and sales promotion, which have a relatively low per-unit cost. At the other extreme, products with a high unit price lend themselves to personal selling because the high cost of a sales call is justified by the size of the order. Furthermore, the nature of the selling process often demands face-to-face interaction between the buyer and seller.

Another factor that influences both the level and mix of promotional activity is the product's position in its life cycle. Early on, when the seller is trying to inform the customer about the product and build the distribution network, promotional efforts are in high gear. Selective advertising, sales promotion, and public relations are used to build awareness and to encourage early adopters to try the product; personal selling is used to gain the cooperation of intermediaries. As the market expands during the growth phase, the seller broadens the advertising and sales promotion activities to reach a wider audience and continues to use personal selling to expand the distribution network. When the product reaches maturity and competition is at its peak, the seller's primary goal is to differentiate the product from rival brands. Advertising generally dominates the promotional mix during this phase, but sales promotion is an important supplemental tool, particularly for low-priced consumer products. As the product begins to decline, the level of promotion generally tapers off. Advertising and selling efforts are carefully targeted toward loyal, steady customers.

Market-Related Factors

push strategy Promotional approach designed to motivate wholesalers and retailers to push a producer's products to end users

pull strategy Promotional strategy that stimulates consumer demand, which then exerts pressure on wholesalers and retailers to carry a product

To some extent, the promotional mix depends on whether the seller plans to focus the marketing effort on intermediaries or final customers. If the focus is on intermediaries, the producer uses a **push strategy** to persuade wholesalers and retailers to carry the item. Personal selling and sales promotions aimed at intermediaries dominate the promotional mix. If the marketing focus is on end users, the producer uses a **pull strategy** to appeal directly to the ultimate customer, using advertising, direct mail, contests, discount coupons, and so on. With this approach, consumers learn of the product through promotion and request it from retailers, who respond by asking their wholesalers for it or by going directly to the producer.

The promotional mix is also influenced by the size and concentration of the market. In markets with many widely dispersed buyers, advertising is generally the most economical way of communicating the product's features. In markets with relatively few customers clustered in a limited area, personal selling is a practical promotional alternative.

Positioning

positioning The process of achieving a desired position in the minds of potential customers

As a consumer, you have a place in your mind for each product category that you are aware of, and in each place, you rank individual products. Think of the pair of basketball shoes that you consider to be the best on the market. If this product represents the ultimate basketball shoe to you, it occupies the primary *position* in the basketball shoe category in your mind. When you think of basketball shoes, you tend to compare all other products with this one. The companies and products that hold these primary positions have a powerful advantage over their competitors.

Not surprisingly, smart marketers do everything possible to achieve the top position in your mind. Think of business newspapers and you probably think of *The Wall Street Journal*; for traveler's checks, it's probably American Express; for pianos, it might be Steinway. These products achieved their positions through a careful combination of product qualities, advertising, public relations, and other aspects of the marketing mix. The process of achieving a desired position in the mind of the market is called **positioning**.[3]

Although promotion is just one aspect of the positioning process, it is certainly one of the most important. Consequently, positioning strategies should play a key role in the design of every company's promotional mix. The nature of a company's advertising, the type of salespeople it hires, its policy regarding coupons, its support for cultural events—decisions like these have a dramatic effect on the position that a company and its products will occupy in the minds of potential customers. For instance, Apple Computer's Big Brother commercial enhanced the company's position in the minds of some computer users, but it offended other computer users. People are still talking about the commercial, even though it aired only once nearly a decade ago.

▶ PERSONAL SELLING

By almost any measure, personal selling is the dominant form of promotional activity. Nearly one out of every ten workers in the United States is a salesperson.[4] And most companies spend twice as much on personal selling as they do on all other marketing activities combined.[5] The roles these salespeople play can vary widely, however, depending on the product and the market.

Salespeople working in retail, such as at Brooks Brothers in San Francisco, often have more than one area of responsibility. They act as order getters and order takers, and they often support sales efforts by educating customers, building goodwill, and providing service to customers after the sale.

Types of Sales Personnel

From the general public's perspective, salespeople are salespeople. However, from a business perspective, salespeople play various roles depending on the size and organization of the company, the type of product it sells, and the nature of its customer base. In general, salespeople can be categorized according to three broad areas of responsibility: (1) order getting, (2) order taking, and (3) sales support services. Although some salespeople focus primarily on one area of responsibility, others may have broader responsibilities that span several areas.

Order Getters

Order getters are responsible for generating new sales and for increasing sales to existing customers. Order getters can range from telemarketers selling bottled water and stockbrokers selling securities to engineers selling computers and nuclear physicists selling consulting services. Order getting is sometimes referred to as **creative selling,** particularly if the salesperson must invest a significant amount of time in determining what the customer needs, devising a strategy to explain how the product can meet those needs, and persuading the customer to buy. This type of creative selling requires a high degree of empathy, and the salesperson takes on the role of consultant in a long-term relationship with the customer.

order getters Salespeople who are responsible for generating new sales and for increasing sales to existing customers

creative selling The selling process used by order getters, which involves determining customer needs, devising strategies to explain product benefits, and persuading customers to buy

Order Takers

Order takers do little creative selling; they primarily process orders. Unfortunately, the term *order taker* has assumed negative overtones in recent years because salespeople often use it to refer to someone too lazy to prospect or actively close orders, or they use it to refer to someone whose territory is so attractive that he or she can just sit by the phone and wait for orders to roll in. But regardless of how salespeople use the term, order takers in the true sense play an important role in the sales function.

order takers Salespeople who generally process incoming orders without engaging in creative selling

With the aim of generating additional sales, many companies are beginning to train their order takers to think more like order getters. You've probably noticed, for example, that nearly every time you order a hamburger at McDonald's, the person at the counter will ask, "Would you like an order of fries to go with that?" Such suggestions can prompt customers to buy something they may not otherwise order.

Sales Support Personnel

Sales support personnel generally don't sell products, but they facilitate the overall selling effort by providing a variety of services. Their responsibilities can

sales support personnel Salespeople who facilitate the selling effort by providing such services as prospecting, customer education, and customer service

missionary salespeople Salespeople who support existing customers, usually wholesalers and retailers

technical salespeople Specialists who contribute technical expertise and other sales assistance

trade salespeople Salespeople who sell to and support marketing intermediaries by giving in-store demonstrations, offering samples, and so on

telemarketing Selling or supporting the sales process over the telephone

Telemarketers at Fidelity Investments in Boston can cover far more sales territory, find more leads, qualify more prospects, and close more sales than a team of traveling salespeople. However, many products need the face-to-face interaction that personal selling provides.

include prospecting, educating prospects and customers, building goodwill, and providing service to customers after the sale. The three most common types of sales support personnel are missionary, technical, and trade salespeople.

Missionary salespeople are employed by manufacturers to disseminate information about new products to existing customers (usually wholesalers and retailers) and to motivate them to sell the product to their customers. Manufacturers of pharmaceuticals and medical supplies, for instance, use missionary salespeople to call on doctors and pharmacists. They leave samples and information, answer questions, and persuade doctors to prescribe their products.

Technical salespeople contribute technical expertise and assistance to the selling function. They are usually engineers and scientists or have received specialized technical training. In addition to providing support services to existing customers, they may also participate in sales calls to prospective customers. Companies that manufacture computers, industrial equipment, and sophisticated medical equipment use technical salespeople to sell their products as well as to provide support services to existing customers.

Trade salespeople sell to and support marketing intermediaries. Hormel, Nabisco, and Sara Lee use trade salespeople to give in-store demonstrations, offer samples to customers, set up displays, restock shelves, and obtain more shelf space. Increasingly, producers work to establish lasting, mutually beneficial relationships with their channel partners, and trade salespeople are responsible for building these relationships.

Telemarketing

As the cost of personal sales calls continues to increase, many companies and nonprofit organizations are trying to keep costs down by turning to **telemarketing**—selling over the telephone. Businesses like telemarketing because they can reach a great number of customers, and many customers like it because it saves them time. Telemarketers now sell everything from investment services to computer systems.[6] Sometimes telemarketing is used by itself; in other cases, it is used to supplement door-to-door and other selling methods.

Telemarketing can be broken down into two classes: *Outbound telemarketing* occurs when companies make cold calls to potential customers that have not requested a sales call; *inbound telemarketing* establishes phone lines for customers to call in to place orders. Many consumers and organizational customers enjoy the convenience of inbound telemarketing. However, using costly 900 numbers can alienate consumers. Many 900 numbers abuse inbound telemarketing by charging outrageous prices for shady, sleazy, or misleading gimmicks. Responsible marketers make sure their 900 numbers provide value to their customers (offering useful information or something tangible such as a coupon or a booklet) so that potential customers see the price of the call as a legitimate trade-off.[7]

Outbound telemarketing can generate a lot of criticism because it interrupts family or business activities and can even pose a threat to safety by tying up a phone line needed in an emergency. If you've been bothered during dinner or roused from a deep sleep just to answer the phone and listen to someone's sales pitch, you understand the criticism. Perhaps the worst abuse comes from computerized dialing systems that call numbers automatically and send a recorded message. Public pressure is leading some states to consider legislation that would regulate or even ban outbound telemarketing.[8]

The Creative Selling Process

Although it may look easy, creative selling is not a simple task. Of course, some sales are made in a matter of minutes. But others, particularly for large organizational purchases, can take years to complete. Salespeople should follow a carefully planned process from start to finish (see Exhibit 15.2).

Step 1: Prospecting

Prospecting is the process of finding and qualifying potential customers. This involves three activities:

▶ *Generating sales leads.* Sales leads are names of individuals and organizations that *might* be likely prospects for the company's product.

▶ *Identifying prospects.* A prospect is a potential customer who indicates a need or a desire for the seller's product.

▶ *Qualifying prospects.* Not all prospects are worth investing sales time in. Some may not have the authority to buy, and others won't have enough money. The ones who do have both the authority and the available money are called **qualified prospects**.

qualified prospects Potential buyers who have both the money needed to make the purchase and the authority to make the purchase decision

Step 2: Preparing

With a list of hot prospects in hand, the salesperson's next step is to prepare for the sales call. Without this preparation, the chances of success are greatly re-

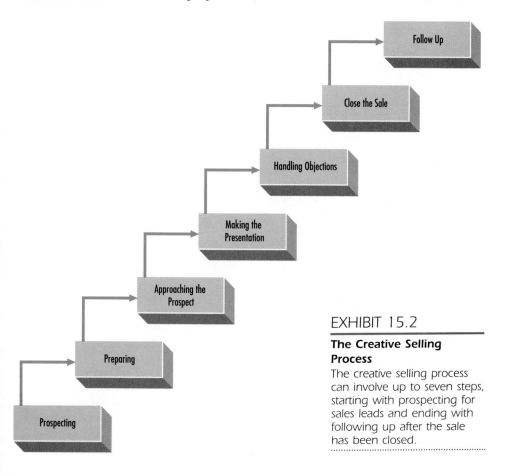

EXHIBIT 15.2

The Creative Selling Process
The creative selling process can involve up to seven steps, starting with prospecting for sales leads and ending with following up after the sale has been closed.

duced. Preparation starts with creating a prospect profile, which includes the names of key people, their role in the decision-making process, and other relevant information such as the prospect's buying needs, motive for buying, current suppliers, income/revenue level, and so on.

Next, the salesperson decides how to approach the prospect. Possible options for a first contact include sending a letter or *cold calling* in person or by telephone. For an existing customer, the salesperson can either drop by un-

TECHNIQUES FOR BUSINESS SUCCESS

Steps to an Effective Sales Presentation

In personal selling, the sales representative has an opportunity to build rapport—a sense of psychological connection—with the prospect. Skillful sales reps constantly use body language and verbal directions to get a message to and from the prospect. Here are some hints on how it's done.

ESTABLISHING A BOND

Prospects are much more inclined to buy from people who make them feel good and with whom they have developed a personal bond.

▶ *Try to make yourself seem compatible with the prospect.* Be similar (or seem so) in dress, speaking patterns, and interests.

▶ *Be sure to set aside a preliminary period to build a feeling of agreement.* Don't plunge into the presentation immediately.

▶ *Pace your statements and gestures to mirror the customer's observations, experience, or behavior.* "It's been awfully hot these last few days, hasn't it?" "You said you were going to graduate in June."

▶ *Be sure to use a "probing" period during which you draw out information and identify the prospect's real needs and problems.* A consumer may want status from a car as much as performance; the organizational buyer wants to avoid looking bad to management. Good sales reps are excellent listeners at the probing stage.

DESCRIBING AND DEMONSTRATING THE PRODUCT

Once the prospect's needs have been identified, you should concentrate on relating product features to benefits that may meet the buyer's needs or solve a problem.

▶ *Focus on benefits.* "This drill will help you make holes faster and more cheaply" is better than a statement about product features ("This drill engine delivers *x* foot-pounds of torque").

▶ *Use product demonstrations that the prospect can easily see and comprehend.* Say that you have won an appointment with Ms. McCormick to discuss your company's cash-management account. You could show Ms. McCormick a sample statement of the type she would receive every month, outlining the activity of an imaginary account and showing how her money will keep earning interest.

USING A TRIAL CLOSE

Your purpose is ultimately to close the sale by obtaining an order or by getting some other commitment.

▶ *Try using a "yes" technique.* Use a series of questions or statements that get the prospect to nod or say yes over and over. By the time you finally ask for the order, the prospect may be in the mood to say yes just one more time.

Experienced sales reps know that most prospects won't be entirely satisfied until they've asked questions or posed objections to the sales points. To deal with this very human trait, you may want to launch a trial balloon known as the *trial close*—a maneuver that may not get the order then and there but that will draw out whatever may be standing between the prospect and the sale. The following is a typical trial close:

announced or call ahead for an appointment, which is generally preferred.

Before meeting with the prospect, the salesperson establishes specific objectives to achieve during the sales call. Depending on the situation, objectives can range anywhere from "getting the order today" to simply "convincing prospects to accept the company as a potential supplier." Following that, the salesperson prepares the actual presentation, which can be as basic as a list of points to discuss or as elaborate as a product demonstration or multimedia presentation.

Salesperson: Would you agree that your money works harder to earn you interest in a cash-management account than in the money-market fund you're using now?

Customer: I suppose it does.

Salesperson: Then we can open an account for you this week with as little as $1,000 . . . and I can sign you up today with your signature on this acceptance.

Customer: Yes, but what about getting my money if I need it in an emergency? I don't want to tie up my funds or pay a penalty for taking them out.

Now you have a bona fide objection on the table, and you know where the buyer's resistance lies.

HANDLING OBJECTIONS

The way to answer objections is *not* to argue with the customer. If you do, you may prove how smart you are by winning the argument, but you will probably lose the sale.

▶ *Recognize the nature of the objection.* Some objections are rational and product-oriented. Others are psychological: They have more to do with the buyer's "hidden agenda" of needs. For instance, the prospect may be afraid of trying something new or may dislike the sales rep.

▶ *Register agreement.* No matter what the buyer says, the skillful sales rep usually agrees courteously and then shifts the derailed prospect back on the right track. Instead of blurting out, "Oh, no, our service is better than you'd get from your supplier," it's smarter to begin, "I can understand why you're concerned about service. These days, you have to be. That's why we offer a seven-point service contract." In other words, answer with a statement that proves your service is better.

▶ *Probe with a new trial close.* Once the objection has been handled, you may use another trial close to extract new objections. You handle these objections one by one, and eventually you exhaust the buyer's doubts and problems so that you can go to a final close. For instance, a sales rep might say, "I can appreciate your need for 24-hour access to your cash without paying a penalty. That's why we give you this special American Express Gold Card (pulls the card out of portfolio) that lets you get cash from any participating bank whenever you need it."

MOVING TO THE FINAL CLOSE

The most striking characteristic of a great sales rep is her or his ability to close the sale and walk away with the prospect's signature on an order blank. For some sales reps, the final close is a frightening or an embarrassing moment: It always entails the risk of rejection. Some sales reps botch the sale because they can't stop talking—they effectively sell the product and then buy it back. So be sure that when you end the presentation stage and go for the final close, you are able to keep quiet while the customer orders. Here are some useful closing techniques:

▶ *Summarize the presentation.* Use a simple anecdotal statement that clearly positions the need for the product in the buyer's mind.

▶ *Make the offer available for a limited time only.* This approach often gets immediate action.

▶ *Ask for a small "trial" order.* You can reduce the customer's risk this way.

▶ *Turn the buyer's last objection into a close.* Say, "Then you'd order if I could guarantee a one-year warranty in writing?" This way, you leave the buyer in the position of having run out of valid objections.

Step 3: Approaching the Prospect

Perhaps you've heard the saying "You never get a second chance to make a first impression." It certainly holds true when approaching a prospective customer—whether the approach is by telephone, by letter, or in person. Positive first impressions result from three elements. The first is an appropriate *appearance*—you wouldn't wear blue jeans to call on a banker, and you probably wouldn't wear a business suit to call on a farmer. Appearance also covers the things that represent you, including business cards, letters, and automobiles. Second, a salesperson's *attitude and behavior* can make or break a sale. A salesperson should come across as professional, courteous, and considerate. Third, a salesperson's *opening lines* should include a brief greeting and introduction, followed by a few carefully chosen words that get the prospect's attention and generate interest. The best way to accomplish this is to focus on a benefit to the customer rather than on the product itself.

Step 4: Making the Presentation

canned approach A selling method based on a fixed, memorized presentation

need-satisfaction approach A selling method that starts with identifying the customer's needs and then creating a presentation that addresses those needs; this is the approach used by most professional salespeople

The most crucial step in the selling process is the presentation. It can take many forms, but its purpose never varies: to personally communicate a product message that will convince a prospect to buy. Most sellers use one of two methods: The **canned approach** is a memorized presentation (easier for inexperienced sellers, but inefficient for complex products or for sellers who don't know customer's needs). The **need-satisfaction approach** (now used by most professionals) identifies the customer's needs and creates a presentation to specifically address them.

Virtual-reality technology adds a new dimension to presentations. Japan Inc. uses the three-dimensional computer graphics system (with goggles and controller) to give customers the fullest sense of spatial relationships in kitchen displays. The company sees virtual reality as a great leap beyond the old sales pitch.

Step 5: Handling Objections

No matter how well a presentation is delivered, it doesn't always conclude with an immediate offer that might move the prospect to buy. Often, the prospect will express various types of objections and concerns throughout the presentation. In fact, the absence of objections is often an indication that the prospect is not very interested in what the salesperson is selling. Many successful salespeople look at objections as a sign of the prospect's interest and as an opportunity to develop new ideas that will strengthen future presentations.

Three basic approaches to overcoming objections include asking the prospect a question, giving a response to the objection, or telling the prospect that you will need to look into the matter and address it later. For example, if a prospect objects to the price, you might ask, "Why do you feel the price is too high?" The prospect may then point out underlying problems or objections that you can address, such as perceived shortcomings the product may have in comparison to a competing product.

Step 6: Closing

So far, you haven't made a dime. You may have spent weeks or months—years in some cases—to bring the customer to this point, but you don't make any money until the prospect decides to buy. This stage of the selling process, when you persuade the customer to place an order, is referred to as **closing**.

closing The point at which a sale is completed

How should you ask for the order? Closing techniques are numerous; here are some of the more popular. The *alternative proposal close* asks the prospect to choose between some minor details, such as method of shipment. With the *assumptive close,* you simply proceed with processing the order, assuming that the prospect has already decided to buy. Another alternative is the *silent close,* in which you finish your presentation and sit quietly, waiting for the customer to respond with his or her buying decision. Finally, many salespeople prefer the *direct close,* where you just come right out and ask for the order.

These closing techniques might strike you as tricks, and in the hands of unethical salespeople, some closing approaches certainly can be. But the professional salesperson uses these techniques to make the selling process effective and efficient—not to trick people into buying when they aren't ready.

Step 7: Following Up

Most salespeople depend on repeat sales, so it's important that they follow up on all sales and not ignore the customer once the first sale is made. During this follow-up stage of the selling process, you need to make sure that the product has been delivered properly and that the customer is satisfied. Inexperienced salespeople may avoid the follow-up stage because they fear facing an unhappy customer. However, an important part of a salesperson's job is to ensure customer satisfaction and to build goodwill.

US West Cellular, for example, has its service representatives place "Welcome Aboard" calls to new subscribers to thank them for their business and to answer questions. The company has learned that when representatives call customers periodically, the customers perceive improvements in their cellular telephone service—even if there were no improvements.[9]

In order to improve the odds of keeping a satisfied customer after the sale, salespeople should remember to

▶ Handle complaints promptly and pleasantly

▶ Maintain contact with customers

▶ Keep serving the customer

▶ Show appreciation[10]

▶ ADVERTISING

The average person in this country is exposed to hundreds of advertising messages, perhaps as many as several thousand, every day.[11] The prevalence of advertising underscores its many advantages. Of the various forms of promotion, it is the best for reaching mass audiences quickly at a low per-person cost. It is also the form of promotion over which the organization has the greatest control. In an advertisement, you can say whatever you want, as long as you stay within the boundaries of the law and conform to the moral and ethical standards of the advertising medium and trade associations. You can promote goods, services, or ideas, using a full range of creative approaches and media to convey your message.

Little wonder then that businesses of all kinds spend large amounts of money on advertising—more than $400 for every woman, man, and child in the coun-

EXHIBIT 15.3

The Growth of Advertising Expenditures
Money spent on advertising of all types has more than doubled in the past decade.

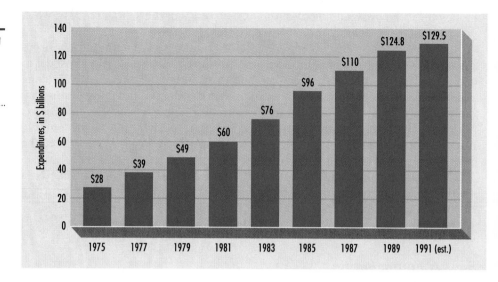

try (see Exhibit 15.3).[12] As you might expect, large companies like Procter & Gamble, Philip Morris, Sears, and General Motors are the heaviest advertisers.

The percentage of income that a company spends on advertising varies according to the product and the market. A cosmetics company like Estée Lauder, for example, may spend 30 percent of total earnings to promote its products in a highly competitive market; a company that manufactures heavy industrial machinery may spend less than 1 percent. In most small businesses, the typical advertising budget is 2 to 5 percent of income.[13]

Types of Advertising

product advertising Advertising that tries to sell specific goods or services, generally by describing features, benefits, and occasionally price

Advertising can be divided into several categories. The most familiar type of advertising is **product advertising,** which tries to sell specific goods or services, such as Kellogg's cereals, California raisins, or Estée Lauder cosmetics. Product advertising generally describes the product's features and may mention its price.

institutional advertising Advertising that seeks to create goodwill and to build a desired image for a company rather than to sell specific products

Institutional advertising, on the other hand, is designed to create goodwill and build a desired image for a company rather than to sell specific products. For example, many companies are now spending large sums for institutional advertising that focuses on *green marketing,* creating an image of companies as corporate conservationists. Businesses tout their actions, contributions, and philosophies not only as supporting the environmental movement but as leading the way. Also known as *corporate advertising,* institutional advertising is often used by corporations to promote an entire line of products. At the same time, institutional ads serve to remind investors that the company is doing well. Institutional ads that address hotly debated public issues are called **advocacy advertising.** W. R. Grace & Co., a diversified chemical company, has used such ads since the 1970s to influence public opinion. Grace's ads, which appear in business publications, deal with such issues as the capital gains tax, productivity, and the federal deficit.

advocacy advertising Ads that present a company's opinions on public issues such as education and health

competitive advertising Ads that specifically highlight how a product is better than its competitors

You can argue that all advertising is competitive in nature, but the term **competitive advertising** is applied to those ads that specifically highlight how a product is better than its competitors. When two or more products are directly contrasted in an ad (as when Apple likened IBM to Orwell's Big Brother), the

Product advertising, such as this ad for North Beach Leather, sells specific goods or services.

technique being used is **comparative advertising.** In some countries, comparative ads are tightly regulated and in some cases banned, but that is clearly not the case in the United States. Indeed, the Federal Trade Commission started the ball rolling by encouraging advertisers to use direct product comparisons with the intent of better informing customers; 35 to 40 percent of all advertising in this country is comparative.[14]

Comparative advertising is frequently used by competitors vying with the market leader, but it is useful whenever you believe you have some specific

comparative advertising An advertising technique in which two or more products are explicitly compared

Advocacy advertising, such as this ad from Amoco Chemical, addresses public issues in an attempt to influence public opinion.

Business Around the World

Belgium has some of the strictest advertising regulations in the world. For instance, comparative advertising is not allowed if it is denigrating, and no advertising of any type or style may be directed toward children.

national advertising Advertising sponsored by companies that sell products on a nationwide basis; refers to the geographic reach of the advertiser, not the geographic coverage of the ad

local advertising Advertising sponsored by a local merchant

cooperative advertising Joint efforts between local and national advertisers, in which producers of nationally sold products share the costs of local advertising with local merchants and wholesalers

product strengths that are important to customers. Burger King used it on McDonald's, Pepsi used it on Coke, and Ford finally got tired of getting slammed by Chevrolet truck advertising and decided to fight back with comparative ads. This is bare-knuckle marketing, and when done well, it is effective. However, comparative advertising sometimes ends up getting neutralized by look-alike campaigns from the competition. Analgesics (pain killers) is one category cited as an example of comparative advertising taken too far. There are so many claims and counterclaims in this "ad war" that consumers can't keep it all straight anymore.[15]

Comparative ads can cross legal and ethical boundaries in two ways. First, some ads tout a product's strengths, but they do so selectively, talking about only those areas in which the product beats the competition and ignoring the rest. In the analgesics category, for example, Johnson & Johnson distributed a "safety profile" to doctors, showing that its Tylenol brand exhibited fewer side effects than three of its competitors. However, the company didn't list some other possible side effects, including potential liver damage and greater risk of overdose, in which it lost out to the competition. Second, some comparative ads simply overstep the bounds of truth and embellish claims of superiority. For instance, Jartran, a truck-rental firm, claimed in its ads that it could "save consumers big money" compared to U-Haul. However, Jartran was promoting a temporary, introductory price, not its normal price. The court determined that the company deliberately tried to deceive customers.[16]

Another potential problem with comparative advertising is unfair portrayal of the quality or characteristics of competitors' products. To help bring an end to this, Congress enacted a law in late 1989 making such unfair comparisons illegal. This new law will undoubtedly make advertisers more careful and will probably encourage more victims of unfair ads to sue for damages.[17]

Finally, advertising can be classified according to the sponsor. **National advertising** is sponsored by companies that sell products on a nationwide basis. The term *national* refers to the level of the advertiser, not the geographic coverage of the ad. If a national manufacturer places an ad in only one city, the ad is still classified as a national ad. **Local advertising,** on the other hand, is sponsored by a local merchant. Its objective is to provide details about where a product can be found, at what price, and in what quantity. The grocery store ads in the local newspaper are a good example. **Cooperative advertising** is a cross between local and national advertising in which producers of nationally sold products share the costs of local advertising with local merchants and wholesalers.

Advertising Appeals

Well-designed ads use a carefully planned appeal to whatever it is that motivates the target audience. Naturally, the best appeal to use depends largely on the target audience. By segmenting along life-styles and other variables, advertisers try to identify which groups of people can be reached with various kinds of appeals.

Logic and Emotion

One of the most important decisions to make in this regard is whether the ad uses an appeal that is predominantly rational or predominantly emotional.

Some ads try to convince you with data, and others try to tug at your emotions to get their point across. Even with the most unemotional sort of product, however, emotions play a very big role. When selling to engineers and other technical people, some industrial and high-technology marketers assume that logic is the only way to go. But people are people, and they all have hopes, fears, desires, and dreams, regardless of the job they have or the products they're buying.

These emotional pulls range from the most syrupy and sentimental to the downright terrifying. Fear has been used to sell a variety of products, from AT&T's phone systems (fear about losing your job if you don't buy an AT&T system) to Campbell's bean and pea soups (fear of getting cancer if you don't eat enough fiber). Personal-care products are often marketed on the basis of fear; after all, you don't want to be rejected because you have dandruff or because you don't smell quite right. Appeals to fear have to be managed carefully, however. Laying it on too thick can anger the audience or even cause them to block out the message entirely.[18]

On the other hand, reducing someone's fear or anxiety, rather than artificially increasing it, can also be effective. Before bottled water became a common beverage in this country, Perrier recognized that some people felt compelled to drink alcoholic beverages in social situations, out of fear of being rejected. To get people to start drinking Perrier in public, the company used advertising that reduced those fears of rejection and sent the message that it's acceptable not to drink alcohol.[19]

Anger can be a strong emotional pull, particularly for nonprofit organizations. For example, Handgun Control recently sent out an appeal for money to fight the National Rifle Association's congressional lobbying efforts. Here was the message on the outside of the envelope: "Enclosed: Your first real chance to tell the National Rifle Association to go to hell!" If you hated the NRA to start with, you probably ripped the envelope open. And if you loved the NRA, you probably ripped the envelope open too.

On the lighter side, some companies try to convince you of how good it will feel to use their products. Hal Riney, one of the modern masters of feel-good advertising, heads an advertising agency that creates tender, sometimes humorous moments that reach out to human emotions. For example, one of his commercials for California-based Security Pacific Bank (since merged with BankAmerica) shows a boy coming home from school with what must be a very disappointing report card. His father is due home any minute. But when Dad arrives, he doesn't get mad; he takes his son up to the attic and pulls out one of his own report cards, showing that even Dads can get bad grades. And the narrator says, "Understanding is the ability to look at life through someone else's eyes." This commercial doesn't have anything at all to do with the facts, figures, and features of the bank; it is trying to convince viewers that Security Pacific understands the needs of banking customers.[20]

Celebrity Appeal

A popular ad approach is the use of celebrities. The theory behind these ads is that people will be more inclined to use products that celebrities use themselves, and that some of the star's image will rub off on the products they're holding. Bill Cosby seemed to like the taste of Jell-O, Michael J. Fox would stop at nothing to get a Pepsi for a woman he wanted to impress, and former New York Mets ace Tom Seaver pitched the American Express card. Celebrity endorsements are extremely popular in Japan, particularly when they feature American stars. And American stars who generally refuse to endorse products here, including Sylvester Stallone, Paul Newman, and Woody Allen, have shown up in Japanese television commercials.[21]

Celebrity ads do have potential problems, however. First, consumers don't always find them convincing. In fact, one survey on the power of various advertising appeals ranked celebrity endorsements as the least convincing, as cited by 70 percent of the respondents. Some companies avoid this by carefully matching products with celebrities. For example, Adidas researched public perception of the personalities of Ivan Lendl and Boris Becker and concluded that Lendl's image was the best fit for the company. Another big problem is that the public's image of the celebrity can get tangled up with their image of the product, and if the star gets in trouble, the brand can get in trouble too. This is one of the reasons animated cartoon characters remain popular as "celebrity" endorsers. Take Bart Simpson, for instance. An executive at Fox Television (producers of "The Simpsons") put it this way: "Bart will never get caught doing crack."[22]

Sex Appeal

Another old standby in the advertising world is selling with sex. The classic technique is to have an attractive, scantily attired model share the page or TV screen with the product. If the model's looks and pose somehow make sense, fine; if they don't, fine. The point is to have the audience associate the product with pleasure. In the United States, this technique went about as far as it could go with such advertisers as Georges Marciano's Guess Jeans and Calvin Klein's Obsession perfume. But advertisers seem to be pulling away from such extreme measures. A more popular approach today is to keep the clothes on the models and just hint about sex. As *Forbes* magazine put it, advertisers are switching to "fantasy, not flesh." And women are being shown in less passive roles, another big change from previous years. For example, a commercial for Sansabelt men's slacks featured a woman saying, "I always lower my eyes when a man passes to see if he's worth following."[23]

The Power of Novelty

An approach that has taken hold in recent years is trying to catch the audience's attention by making ads really strange. Honda used this technique with some success when it tried to expand scooter sales in the United States. One of its stranger commercials had questions like this appearing in scrawled white handwriting against a black background: "Who am I? Can dogs think? Am I ugly? Is there truth? Is there any pizza left? Should I buy a vowel?" The commercial concludes with "The new Honda Elite 50. If it's not the answer, at least it's not another question."[24]

Simply making an advertisement "off the wall" doesn't ensure success, however. Advertising critics and some retailers often berate the stranger ads. The "Reeboks Let U.B.U." campaign was definitely different, with a cast of characters that included a three-legged man and a fairy godmother with a briefcase, and it left some people cold. Nissan's Infiniti division introduced the Infiniti cars with ads that never showed the car but featured landscapes, seascapes, and other soothing pictures accompanied by an announcer talking about completely unrelated topics. The Infiniti brand scored well in audience recall tests, but sales didn't exactly skyrocket. Getting people to remember your name doesn't mean they'll buy your product.[25] Infiniti sales did start to pick up after the ad strategy was changed to a more traditional approach.

The Elements of an Advertisement

All ads feature two basic elements. The first is **copy,** which is the verbal part of the ad, and the second is **artwork,** which is the visual part of the ad. For a magazine ad, the copy is the words you see on the page. For a radio or TV commercial, the copy is spoken by the actors.

copy The verbal (spoken or written) part of an ad

artwork The visual, graphic part of the ad

Ever look at an ad that has two sentences of copy and then think to yourself, "That looks easy. Anybody could crank out a couple of sentences"? Alas, looks are deceiving. Writing ad copy is part art, part science, and part luck, and few people can do it well. Top copywriters are rewarded handsomely for their ability to create effective copy.

Ad copy has five fundamental purposes:

▶ Getting the prospect's attention

▶ Stimulating the prospect's interest

▶ Building credibility for the product and the company

▶ Heightening the prospect's desire for the product

▶ Motivating the prospect toward action[26]

Crafting words that can accomplish all these goals is no easy task. It requires good communications skills, a flair for language, and a thorough knowledge of both the product and the customer.

As powerful as good copy can be, it is usually enhanced by creative artwork. In fact, the artwork is sometimes much more prominent than the copy, with the visual images conveying most or all of the message. The arrangement of copy and artwork in an ad is referred to as the *layout.* Visual elements can be based on a variety of themes, including the product's own package, the product in use, product features, humor, before-and-after comparisons, visual comparisons with other products, and testimonials from users or celebrities.

Advertising Media

To get the message to potential customers, suitable **media,** or channels of communication, must be chosen. The **media plan** specifies the advertising budget, establishes how the money will be divided among the various media, and indicates exactly when the advertisements will appear. The goal of the media plan is to make the most effective use of the company's advertising dollar.

media Communications channels, such as newspapers, radio, and television

media plan A written plan that outlines how a company will spend its media budget, including how the money will be divided among the various media and when the advertisements will appear

The Media Mix

The critical task in media planning is to select a **media mix,** the combination of print, broadcast, and other media for the advertising campaign. In selecting the media mix, the first step is to determine the characteristics of the target audience and the types of media that will reach the greatest audience at the lowest

media mix The combination of various media options that a company uses in an advertising campaign

cost. The choice is also based on what the medium is expected to do (show the product in use, list numerous sale items and prices, and so on). An increasingly popular approach to creating the media mix is the "concentration" strategy, which channels most of the budget into one media type, such as full-page newspaper ads or prime-time TV spots. This strategy allows the advertiser's message to dominate a particular medium in its product class and may help the advertiser obtain better prices on advertising space. The second step in choosing the media mix is to pick specific vehicles in each of the chosen media categories, such as individual magazines (*Time, People, Sports Illustrated*) or individual radio stations (a rock station, a classical station).

Media Buying

Sorting through all the media is a challenging task. In fact, many advertisers rely on professional media planners to find the best combinations of media and to negotiate attractive terms. These planners use four important types of data in selecting their media buys. The first is **cost per thousand,** a standardized ratio that converts the total cost of advertising space to the more meaningful cost of reaching 1,000 people with the ad. Cost per thousand is especially useful for comparing media that reach similar audiences.

Two other decision tools are reach and frequency, which represent the trade-off between breadth and depth of communication. **Reach** refers to the total number of audience members that will be exposed to a message at least once in a given time period; it is usually expressed as a percentage of the total number of audience members in a particular population. **Frequency** is the average number of times that each audience member is exposed to the message; it is calculated by dividing the total number of exposures by the total audience population.

The fourth decision tool is **continuity,** which refers to the period spanned by the media schedule and the timing of ad messages—evenly spread over the schedule or heavily concentrated in some periods. Obviously, within a fixed budget, a media plan cannot do everything: If it is important to reach a high percentage of a target group with significant frequency, the cost of doing so on a continuous basis may be prohibitive. Media planners often resort to airing messages in "waves" or "flights"—short periods of high reach and frequency that sacrifice continuity. This strategy is common in the travel industry, which crowds much of its annual media spending into the peak vacation seasons.

Advertising media fall into eight categories (see Exhibit 15.4). Newspapers and television each account for roughly one-quarter of total media spending;

cost per thousand The cost of reaching 1,000 people with an ad

reach The total number of audience members who will be exposed to a message at least once in a given period

frequency The average number of times that each audience member is exposed to the message (equal to the total number of exposures divided by the total audience population)

continuity The pattern according to which an ad appears in the media; it can be spread evenly over time or concentrated during selected periods

EXHIBIT 15.4

How the Advertising Dollar Is Allocated

This chart shows the amounts and percentages of advertising purchased in various media. Despite the prevalence of television in U.S. homes, newspapers remain the most popular advertising medium.

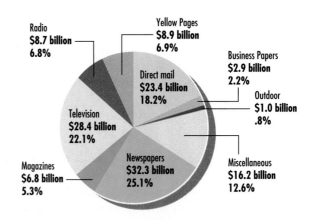

Radio
$8.7 billion
6.8%

Yellow Pages
$8.9 billion
6.9%

Business Papers
$2.9 billion
2.2%

Direct mail
$23.4 billion
18.2%

Outdoor
$1.0 billion
.8%

Television
$28.4 billion
22.1%

Magazines
$6.8 billion
5.3%

Newspapers
$32.3 billion
25.1%

Miscellaneous
$16.2 billion
12.6%

EXHIBIT 15.5 ▶ **Advantages and Disadvantages of Major Advertising Media**

When selecting the media mix, marketers attempt to match the characteristics of the media audience with the characteristics of the potential buyers. A typical advertising campaign involves the use of several media.

MEDIUM	ADVANTAGES	DISADVANTAGES
Newspapers	Geographic selectivity and flexibility Broad reach possible Advertising permanence Readership not seasonal Quick response to orders for ads	Limited color availability with variable quality Short life span, often with hasty reading Cluttered pages Little demographic selectivity Little secondary readership
Television	Broad reach Frequent messages Creative opportunities for demonstration Appeal to senses of sight and hearing Entertainment carryover	High cost for production and air time Commercial clutter Decreased viewing in summer Short life for message Long time for preparation
Direct mail	Ability to saturate specific area Advertising permanence Ability to target selected prospects Great flexibility in format and style Excellent control over circulation and quality of message	High cost per exposure Delivery delays No editorial matter to support content Difficulty of obtaining desired mailing list Consumer resistance
Radio	Low cost High frequency Short notice for scheduling Little seasonal change in audience Highly portable	No visual possibilities Short life for message Commercial clutter Tendency for people to use for background sound and ignore commercials
Magazines	Good reproduction Permanence of message Demographic selectivity Local and regional market selectivity Authority and believability	Limited demonstration possibilities Less compelling than other major media Long advance preparation High cost

direct mail, radio, and magazines together account for about one-third of the total. Other media, including yellow pages, business papers, and outdoor advertising, account for the remaining one-fifth. Each medium has its own strengths and weaknesses for various advertising applications (see Exhibit 15.5).

In the past few years, the distribution of media spending has shifted. Marketers are putting an increasing percentage of their advertising budgets into specialized media directed at selected audiences. The three major TV networks and the national magazines are losing ground to cable stations and to magazines aimed at narrow interest groups. At the same time, alternative media are gaining ground as companies look for fresh ways to get their message through the clutter of competing advertisements.[27] Next time you're out and about, keep your eyes open for advertisements in unexpected places—in elevators and on shopping carts, for example.

NEWSPAPERS   Newspapers offer some definite strengths, including extensive market coverage, low cost, selection of topic areas in which to place ads (sports, home, etc.), and short lead time for placing ads. The downside of newspaper advertising includes short life span, lots of visual competition from other ads, and poor graphic quality.[28]

VIDEO EXERCISE

TELEVISION   TV commercials have numerous advantages, starting with the combined impact of sight, sound, and motion. Other strong points include prestige (relative to other media) and the ability to catch people's attention. In addition, television reaches a massive audience—virtually every U.S. home has at least one TV set, and the average set is turned on for six hours a day. The average viewer is exposed to as many as 30,000 commercials a year.[29] The downsides include high cost (both initial and ongoing), short message life, general lack of selectivity, and vulnerability to getting zapped by viewers' remote controls. According to some estimates, viewers zap past 10 to 40 percent of TV commercials that air while they're watching (depending on the time of day and programming), although network executives tend to dispute these numbers.[30] Look for continued changes in television advertising, as syndication, cable, and pay-per-view systems grow. And look for the continuing growth of new types of TV advertising, including program-length commercials modeled after talk shows, cooking shows, and other established formats.[31]

Another new type of television advertising is being developed at iPlus (sister company of VCR Plus, the gadget that automatically programs VCRs to record shows based on code numbers appearing in TV listings). Also using code numbers, iPlus would program VCRs to record commercials that would be aired on little-used cable channels during late-night hours, delivering video "brochures" to consumers who request them. The cost to advertisers would be as low as $1 or $2, and because consumers request the commercials, advertisers would reach highly qualified prospects.[32]

direct mail Advertising sent directly to potential customers, usually through the U.S. Postal Service

database marketing Direct marketing in which advertisers take advantage of comprehensive information on customers, including purchase behavior, demographics, and lifestyle

DIRECT MAIL   The third largest advertising medium, after newspapers and television, is **direct mail,** which includes both catalog sales and sales of single items marketed through the U.S. Postal Service and private carriers. Its biggest advantage is the ability to deliver large amounts of information to narrowly selected audiences. A promising development in audience selection is **database marketing,** in which the advertiser collects, stores, and uses data about each customer's needs, purchase habits, and so on. This should allow precise targeting of advertising messages.[33] The biggest drawbacks to direct mail are high cost per contact, a generally poor image ("junk mail"), and competition from all the other direct-mail pieces in everyone's mailbox.

RADIO   Radio advertising has recently experienced a great boost from the renaissance of network radio. Although network TV audiences have begun to shrink, network radio audiences have increased. Yet the cost of network radio advertising has grown more slowly than that of advertising on network TV.[34] One of the main advantages of radio advertising is its large potential audience: More than 500 million radios are in use in the United States, and the average U.S. resident over the age of 12 spends three hours a day tuned in.[35] But radio advertising is not without disadvantages. Among them is the fact that listeners, like TV viewers, can easily switch stations to avoid listening to commercials. Most advertisers regard radio primarily as a reminder tool to stimulate the use of already familiar products.

MAGAZINES Magazines offer some strong benefits, including highly targeted audiences in many cases. Magazines such as *Sound & Vibration* and *Hog Farm Management* are targeted for narrow market niches and are thus efficient ways to reach specialized audiences. Magazines also provide high-quality production, long message life, and the opportunity to reach multiple readers. The biggest drawbacks for magazines are the long lead time between placing and publishing ads (up to several months in some cases) and the absence of motion and sound.[36]

Billboards like this one from Johnson's Jewelers work well in reaching potential customers within a limited geographic area, but the image must have a lot of impact to make a point quickly.

OTHER MEDIA Although newspapers, television, direct mail, radio, and magazines account for the lion's share of all advertising dollars spent, other media are also effective in reaching certain kinds of customers. Advertisers spend billions of dollars on the familiar yellow pages, for example.[37] A variety of outdoor and transit advertising options (from billboards to ads in subway trains) reach people while they are on the move. Other ways of bringing advertising messages to the public are limited only by the imagination. Free movie magazines are distributed in theater lobbies, commercial airlines carry in-flight advertising, and supermarkets run ads on their shopping bags and shopping carts. A growing trend in food-marketing is ADDvantage's shopping-cart calculator. Advertisers pay for the calculators and place ads next to them on the handles of shopping carts. Grocers are also now operating in-store radio networks that broadcast ads interspersed with music, and they are giving away electronic coupons, which are issued by check-out scanners based on what shoppers buy, not cut from newspapers. Companies are increasingly taking advantage of electronic media, marketing their products through CompuServe, Prodigy, and other on-line services. Moreover, technological advancements such as in-home video carried by fiber optic lines promise advertisers entirely new channels of communication.[38]

▶ PUBLIC RELATIONS

Public relations plays a vital role in the success of most companies, and this applies to more than just the marketing of goods and services. Like Sculley's Apple computers, smart businesses know they need to maintain positive relations with their communities, investors, industry analysts, government agencies and officials, and the news media. All of these activities fall under the umbrella of public relations. For many companies, public relations is the fastest-growing element of the promotional mix.[39]

A good reputation is one of a business's most important assets. A recent study showed that companies with a good public image have a big edge over less respected companies. Consumers are more than twice as likely to buy new products from companies they admire. Investors are willing to invest 50 percent more in "good" companies than in "bad" ones. Highly regarded companies have a three-to-one advantage in attracting talented employees, and their chances are much better of winning community support for new plant construction.[40]

To build and maintain good reputations, many businesses place heavy emphasis on the coverage they receive in the media, both in general news media and in specialized media that cover specific industries. **Press relations** is the process of communicating with newspapers, magazines, and broadcast media. In

press relations The process of communicating with reporters and editors from newspapers, magazines, and radio and television networks and stations

the personal computer industry, for example, manufacturers know that many people look to *PC/Computing, PC, Byte,* and other computer publications as influential sources of information about new products. Editors and reporters often review new products and then make recommendations to their readers, pointing out both strengths and weaknesses. Companies roll out the proverbial red carpet for these media figures, treating them to hospitality suites at conventions, factory tours, and interviews with company leaders. When introducing products, manufacturers often send samples to reporters and editors for review, or they visit the media offices themselves.

The standard tools of press relations are the press release, or news release as it is sometimes called, and the press conference, or press briefing. A **press release** is a short memo sent to the media covering topics that are of potential news interest; some companies send video press releases to television stations.[41] Companies send press releases in the hope of getting favorable news coverage about themselves and their products. A **press conference** is arranged when companies have significant news to announce. They are used in addition to press releases when the news is of widespread interest, when products need to be demonstrated, or when the company wants to be able to answer reporters' questions.

> ### ▶ SALES PROMOTION

The fourth element of promotion, sales promotion, covers a wide variety of activities, including coupons, discounts, samples, contests, sweepstakes, and frequent-flyer programs. Sales promotion can be broken down into two basic categories: consumer promotion and trade promotion. Consumer promotion is aimed directly at final users of the product, whereas trade promotion is aimed at retailers and wholesalers. Although shoppers are more aware of consumer promotion, trade promotion actually accounts for a larger share of promotional spending.

Consumer Promotion

Consumer promotions include coupons, specialty advertising, premiums, point-of-purchase advertising, rebates, games and sweepstakes, special events, and other incentives. Such promotions are used to stimulate repeat purchases and to entice new users.

The biggest category of consumer promotion, **couponing**, aims to spur sales by offering a discount through redeemable coupons. In the United States, companies distribute over 200 billion coupons every year. That's nearly 1,000 coupons for every woman, man, and child every year. Coupons work well in several situations, including stimulating trial of new products, reaching out to nonusers of mature products, encouraging repeat purchases, and reducing the price of products without having to enlist the cooperation of retailers. Coupons have several drawbacks, however. The first is encouraging delayed purchases; some customers won't purchase a product until a coupon is available. The second is wasted advertising and lost profits resulting from delivering coupons to people who would buy the product anyway. Third, coupons have been accused of instilling a bargain-hunting mentality in many consumers, which emphasizes the

---

press release A brief statement or video program released to the press announcing new products, management changes, sales performance, and other potential news items; also called a news release

press conference Gathering of media representatives at which companies announce new information; also called a press briefing

consumer promotions Sales promotions aimed at final consumers

couponing Distribution of certificates that offer discounts on particular items

importance of low prices. And fourth, coupons have a tendency to tarnish the brand's image by making it appear cheap.[42]

A **point-of-purchase display** is a device for showing a product in a way that stimulates immediate sales. It may be simple, such as the end-of-aisle stacks of soda pop in a supermarket or the racks of gum and mints at checkout counters. Or it may be more elaborate, like the "computers" Estée Lauder uses to encourage consumers to buy the Clinique line. Potential buyers enter facts about their skin and makeup problems into a "data bank." Based on this information, the Clinique "computer" recommends a complete cosmetics program tailored to the woman's specific needs.

Special-event sponsorship has become one of the most popular sales promotion tactics. Thousands of companies spend a total of over $1 billion to sponsor events ranging from golf to opera. For example, Federal Express paid $8 million to link its name to the Orange Bowl football game for three years. In addition to having its name splashed over everything, a Federal Express marketing manager got to address the crowd in the stadium and 20 million TV viewers at home.[43]

Other sales promotion techniques include rebates, free samples, and **premiums,** which are free or bargain-priced items offered to encourage the consumer to buy a product. Contests and sweepstakes are also quite popular in some industries. Particularly when valuable or unusual prizes are offered, contests and sweepstakes can generate a great deal of public attention. And **specialty advertising,** advertising on coffee mugs, pens, calendars, and so on, helps keep a company's name in front of customers for a long period of time. Advertisers constantly search for ways to display their names and logos. Need boxer shorts with the Domino's Pizza logo, ads made of chocolate, or Christmas ornaments with corporate logos? They're all available from specialty advertising firms.[44]

Trade Promotion

Sales promotion efforts aimed at inducing distributors or retailers to push a producer's products are known as **trade promotions.** The usual lure is a discount on the price of the merchandise—a **trade allowance**—which enables the distributor or retailer to pass on a price cut to the ultimate consumer.

Many producers would like to see fewer trade allowances because they cut into producers' profit margins. But according to one specialist: "Trade allowances are like opium." Once retailers and distributors get used to receiving such allowances, they become addicted. In some product categories, up to 100 percent of all merchandise sold to retailers is sold on a trade deal.[45] Because the first producer to stop offering trade allowances is likely to lose market share, they all grit their teeth and continue the practice.

Trade allowances also create the controversial practice of **forward buying,** in which the retailer takes advantage of a trade allowance by stocking up while the price is low. For instance, say the producer of Bumble Bee tuna offers retailers a 20 percent discount for a period of six weeks. A retailer might choose, however, to buy enough tuna to last eight or ten weeks, which cuts into the producer's profit and increases the retailer's profit.

One of the best promotional tools for many industrial products is the **trade show,** a gathering where producers display their wares to potential buyers. Most of those who attend trade shows are hot prospects. According to one estimate, the average industrial exhibitor can reach 60 percent of all its prospects at a

point-of-purchase display Advertising or other display materials set up at retail locations to promote products to potential customers as they are making their purchase decisions

premiums Free or bargain-priced items offered to encourage consumers to buy a product

specialty advertising Advertising that appears on various items such as coffee mugs, pens, and calendars, designed to help keep a company's name in front of customers

trade promotions Sales promotion efforts aimed at inducing distributors or retailers to push a producer's products

trade allowance A discount offered by producers to wholesalers and retailers

forward buying Retailers taking advantage of trade allowances by buying more products at discounted prices than they hope to sell

trade show A gathering where producers display their wares to potential buyers; nearly every industry has one or more trade shows focused on particular types of products

trade show, and some exhibitors do 25 percent or more of annual sales at a single show. Apart from attracting likely buyers, trade shows have the advantage of enabling a producer to demonstrate and explain the product and to compile information about prospects.[46]

In addition to trade allowances and trade shows, producers use several other trade promotion techniques, including display premiums, dealer contests or sweepstakes, and travel bonus programs, all designed to motivate the distributor or retailer to push the producer's merchandise.

SUMMARY OF LEARNING OBJECTIVES

1 Describe the four basic categories of promotion.

The four basic categories of promotion are personal selling, advertising, public relations, and sales promotion.

2 Distinguish between push and pull strategies of promotion.

In the push strategy, the producer "pushes" an item to distributors, which in turn promotes the product to end users. The pull approach depends on stimulating enough consumer demand to "pull" a product through the distribution channel. Consumer products are more likely to rely on pull strategies; organizational products are more often pushed.

3 Explain the concept of positioning.

As a consumer, your mind has a place for each product category that you are aware of, and in each place, you rank individual products. The most desirable product in each product category occupies the primary position in your mind, and you tend to compare all other products with this one. The companies and products that hold these primary positions have a powerful advantage over their competitors. Positioning is the process of achieving a desired position in the mind of the market; it includes every-

thing from product design to store design.

4 List the seven steps in the personal-selling process.

The seven steps are prospecting (finding prospects and qualifying them), preparing, approaching the prospects, making the sales presentation, handling objections, closing, and following up after the sale has been made.

5 Define institutional, product, and competitive advertising.

Institutional advertising promotes a company's overall image, not any particular products. Product advertising, on the other hand, doesn't emphasize the company but the actual products themselves. Competitive advertising is the class of ads that emphasize the differences between a product and its competitors.

6 List the five main types of advertising media and at least three less well-known types.

Of the total media budget, the largest percentage goes to newspapers. Most of the rest goes to television, direct mail, radio, and magazines. Other media include yellow pages, billboards, signs, hot-air balloons, and signs on shopping carts.

7 Explain the role of public relations in marketing.

Public relations falls into two general categories. The first is general communication with people on the outside, including government officials, labor unions, community groups, and anyone seeking information about the company. The second category is more active; businesses try to generate media coverage of the company and its products through press releases and press conferences.

8 Distinguish between the two main types of sales promotion, and give at least two examples of each.

The two main types of sales promotion are trade promotion and consumer promotion. Trade promotions are designed to induce wholesalers and retailers to stimulate sales of a producer's products. Examples include trade allowances, trade shows, display premiums, dealer contests, and travel bonus programs. Consumer promotions are intended to motivate the final consumer to try new products or to experiment with the company's brands. Examples include coupons, free samples, specialty advertising, premiums, point-of-purchase displays, and special events.

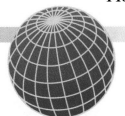

Meeting a Business Challenge at Apple

John Sculley faced a big test as Apple tried to shift its emphasis from the home and education markets to a combination of education and business markets. First, the Macintosh was perceived by many in the business market as a novelty, an interesting toy unfit for real business computing. Second, Apple didn't fit the mold expected by corporate customers; it was brash, at times to the point of arrogance, and slightly off-center when compared to IBM. Finally, Apple simply had a size problem. At the time, IBM maintained a direct sales force in the United States of 6,000 to 7,000 people; Apple had about 300.

Sculley needed a "hook," some high-visibility phenomenon that Apple could use to catch the attention of business users. He found just the answer in desktop publishing. This new capability was called PageMaker. Created by Aldus Software, it allowed personal computers to perform the page layout functions that had previously required lots of time-consuming manual labor from graphic artists and technical illustrators. What used to be a laborious process of cutting and pasting bits of paper to create a newspaper or brochure became a fairly painless procedure on the computer screen. Most important, desktop publishing put this capability in the hands of businesses that couldn't afford the expensive phototypesetting and design talent required by traditional methods.

Businesses of all sizes took a quick liking to desktop publishing. And best of all (at least from Apple's perspective), PageMaker was available only on the Apple Macintosh. Sculley had his hook: Business users would fall in love with PageMaker and buy Macs just so they could run the software. The Mac found a chink in business's armor, the desktop software package made the Mac shine, and corporate customers began to view the Apple machine as a viable business solution.

John Sculley, CEO of Apple Computer.

Aldus eventually made PageMaker available on IBM-compatible machines, but the Macintosh was well entrenched by that time.

In a telling metaphor, Sculley later called desktop publishing his "Trojan horse." Apple used desktop publishing to get Macintoshes past the corporate computer guards. Once inside, Macs were used for spreadsheets, word processing, and other common business applications—the traditional home turf of IBM computers.

Sculley's next step was to polish Apple's image as a business partner for corporate customers. But he didn't concentrate solely on recruiting and training an army of salespeople to send into executive suites around the world. He went himself. Sending the chairman of the board out on the road to sell computers had four positive effects. First, it caught the attention of corporate managers; this wasn't just some Apple salesperson, this was John Sculley, the former president of Pepsi, the guy they read about in *Business Week* and in *The Wall Street Journal*. Second, it showed buyers that Apple was serious

about getting their business. Sculley sent the message that spending time with potential customers was as important as staying home managing his company. Third, Sculley's visits took some of the edge off Apple's reputation for arrogance. He wasn't sitting on the beach in California making brash claims about the superiority of Apple computers; he was on the road proving it. And fourth, Sculley listened to criticisms about the original Macintosh, and he made changes. The result was the Macintosh II, which does a better job of meeting business users' technical needs.

Apple also toned down its aggressive statements about conquering IBM in the personal computer market. Once it realized that IBM was there to stay, and had in fact become a standard in many companies, Apple began to preach peaceful coexistence. Promotional messages and personal statements from Sculley talked about "building bridges to the IBM world." This new stance helped calm the fears of large corporations that had viewed Apple as too arrogant and out of touch with the new realities of personal computing.

To help overcome its small size, Apple became a master at big, splashy special events. New products were introduced with huge press conferences and flashy, high-tech shows. Apple's promotions became news events in themselves, thereby generating far more awareness than Apple could buy with its promotional dollars alone.

To gain further credibility, Apple's promotional plan combined "showcase accounts" and strategic alliances with highly visible, established corporations. Sculley focused his small sales team on selected corporate accounts that they could show off to the rest of the world. He knew that other corporate customers would see these showcase accounts as a validation of Apple and its products. One of the earliest such customers was Seattle-based Seafirst Bank, which purchased 1,000

Apple computers, enough to draw the attention of *Fortune* magazine. An alliance with General Electric Information Services made Apple computers a visible part of GE's telecommunications network. Every time GE's sales staff shows its system to a potential customer, Apple products are part of the picture. Moreover, by linking itself with GE, one of the most respected large companies in the world, Apple's credibility with other large companies got a big boost.

Finally, Apple's new, improved marketing wasn't confined to the United States. New leadership at Apple Japan and Apple Europe adopted the strategies and are well on the way toward reversing sales problems in both regions. By combining clever promotions with a strong dose of reality, John Sculley was able to reverse Apple's position as a smug outsider and make serious inroads into large corporations.

Your Mission: As vice president of marketing at Apple, your job is to lead a team that develops and implements promotional mixes. You're well aware of Apple's position in the market as an innovative company that doesn't quite fit the traditional corporate mold. However, you also realize that many of the businesses you're marketing computers to are run by traditionalists, so you need to conform to their expectations. Consider the following business situations and determine the best response from the perspective of promotions.

1. Apple is about to introduce a portable computer, and your staff needs to define the promotional mix. The target customers for this new product are architects and building contractors who frequently need computing capability at the job site. Most of the architects are familiar with computers and their benefits, but this is not the case with building contractors. Which of the following promotional mixes would be most effective at generating sales as soon as possible?

a. Devise two advertising campaigns, one for the leading architectural magazines and the other for the leading construction magazines. Follow up with splashy exhibits at national trade shows that appeal to these two professions. At these shows, offer a discount if customers place orders before they leave the show, and sponsor these exhibits jointly with local dealers, allowing them to share in the profits from all sales made as a result of the show.

b. Design an aggressive personal sales campaign that allows you to demonstrate the product to potential customers, either in their offices or at construction sites. Run television and radio commercials that encourage prospects to call for a free demonstration.

c. Focus on the larger issue of Apple's relationship with technical professions across the United States and in other industrialized countries. Include public relations announcements highlighting educational support for architectural and construction studies.

d. Place advertisements in leading national magazines, such as *Time* and *Newsweek,* and offer a discount if the computer is purchased within one week of the magazine's cover date. In the ads, try to convince potential customers to call a toll-free number to get more information and place orders.

2. After establishing its computers in some large corporate accounts, Apple wants to go after small-business owners. These people are busy, and most are not computer experts. However, they all recognize that a bad decision on a computer system could cripple their businesses. Which of these promotional mixes would best address the attitudes and motives of this group?

a. Compose a logical message that shows how much money and time small businesses can save by computerizing their accounting and marketing activities. Present this message in free half-day seminars that explore in some detail how computers can deliver on the promise of saving time and money. After the seminars, have salespeople mingle with business owners to answer questions and close orders.

b. Compose an emotional message that appeals to the sense of fear these businesspeople have about computerization. Run TV and radio ads that focus on the fears and the relief that comes from a well-implemented computer system. Send a message of emotional security. Present Apple as a company that cares deeply about its customers, perhaps with some real-life examples of Apple employees going the extra mile to help customers out of troublesome situations.

c. Design ads that feature successful business owners who have improved productivity and profits by using personal computers. Have these businesspeople discuss the technical and administrative aspects of computerization, but have them summarize their experiences on a personal note, such as "And buying the Macintosh not only increased my profits, it increased the time I can spend with my family."

d. Modify choice (c) so that you don't focus on Apple products but on the benefits of personal computers in general. You need to convince these people to buy computers first, then you can worry about steering them to Apple once they've made the decision to computerize.

3. John Sculley wants to increase Apple's sales to the U.S. government. Here's what you know about government customers. They use computers for the same purposes as commercial customers, such as budgeting, writing, and graphic design. The government buys in volume, several hundred computers at a time, and the purchase process takes a year or more. Unlike commercial customers, individual users have little or no influence on the purchase decision; high-level officials make the call. The biggest purchase factor is cost of ownership (a combination of initial price and all support, training, and maintenance costs). Finally, you know the government uses a competitive bidding process, which will be monitored by certain members of Congress. Your assignment: Pick the promotional mix for this market that will do the best job of positioning Apple effectively as you wait for the chance to submit a bid.

a. Because government users buy computers for the same reasons as their commercial counterparts, you should rely on your general marketing programs to reach this audience. An accountant in the General Accounting Office of the federal government has the same requirements and reads the same magazines as private industry accountants. You can save a bundle of money by using your existing marketing programs.

b. Place ads in media that Congress is likely to read, such as the *New Republic* and the *Washington Post*; use these ads to position Apple as a leading high-tech company that sells reliable, cost-effective computers for organizations throughout the country. Support this with strong lobbying efforts to make sure Apple gets its fair share of attention from key members of the House and Senate.

c. Provide key decision makers at the relevant government agencies with comparative cost-of-ownership data, showing how Apple's ease of use contributes to lower training and support costs. Support this with ads in media that Congress is likely to read, such as the *New Republic* and the *Washington Post*; these ads position Apple as a leading high-tech company that sells reliable, cost-effective computers for organizations throughout the country.

d. As in (c), provide key decision makers at the relevant government agencies with comparative cost-of-ownership data, showing how Apple's ease of use contributes to lower training and support costs. Support this with a personal sales campaign that gets the attention of these individuals. Finally, run ads in local media around Washington, D.C., to reinforce your message.

4. Apple has been effective at selling to individuals but needs to improve its performance with organizational customers. Two aspects clearly distinguish organizational customers from other consumers: computers are purchased by committees, not by individuals; and computers are often purchased several dozen or several hundred at a time. A typical purchase committee is made up of four people: a computer specialist who has to implement the new systems, a purchasing agent who needs to negotiate contracts, a computer user who represents other users throughout the company, and an executive who needs to ensure that any computer purchase contributes to the bottom line. Although the decision isn't democratic, all members have strong influence.

You are preparing a sales presentation to be delivered at large companies. Which of the following presentations would be most effective?

a. Design a presentation that focuses on the needs of end users, stressing the friendliness of Apple's computers and the wide range of software available for the various tasks these users need to accomplish.

b. Design a presentation that focuses on the financial benefits customers will receive if they purchase Apple computers, including lower training costs, higher productivity, and lower employee turnover.

c. Design a presentation that focuses on the technical capabilities of Apple computers, such as data storage, networking, and peripherals. This would concentrate on how to put the Apples to work so that new customers will be able to get their systems up and running in a hurry.

d. Design a presentation that attempts to address the needs of all buying influences, even if it has to send an abbreviated message to each group.[47]

KEY TERMS

advertising (420)
advocacy advertising (430)
artwork (435)
canned approach (428)
closing (429)
comparative advertising (431)
competitive advertising (430)
consumer promotions (440)
continuity (436)
cooperative advertising (432)
copy (435)
cost per thousand (436)
couponing (440)
creative selling (423)
database marketing (438)
direct mail (438)
forward buying (441)
frequency (436)

institutional advertising (430)
local advertising (432)
media (435)
media mix (435)
media plan (435)
missionary salespeople (424)
national advertising (432)
need-satisfaction approach (428)
order getters (423)
order takers (423)
personal selling (420)
point-of-purchase display (441)
positioning (422)
premiums (441)
press conference (440)
press relations (439)
press release (440)
product advertising (430)

promotion (418)
promotional mix (420)
public relations (421)
pull strategy (422)
push strategy (422)
qualified prospects (425)
reach (436)
sales promotion (421)
sales support personnel (423)
specialty advertising (441)
technical salespeople (424)
telemarketing (424)
trade allowance (441)
trade promotions (441)
trade salespeople (424)
trade show (441)

REVIEW QUESTIONS

1. What is promotion?

2. What is the biggest advantage of personal selling over other forms of promotion?

3. What techniques do skilled salespeople employ when closing a sale?

4. What are the advantages and disadvantages of the major advertising media?

5. What are the four chief criteria used in media buying?

6. Why and how do companies seek to foster positive relationships with the general public?

7. What are some common types of consumer promotion?

8. What is the biggest problem with trade allowances, from the producer's perspective?

A CASE FOR CRITICAL THINKING

Viva! Metropolitan Life Goes Latin

Looking for foreign sales? Look around. Right here in the United States are almost 19 million Hispanics, enough to constitute a country within a country. And with an average family income of $22,900, they are ready, willing, and able to buy a wide range of products. Furthermore, their ranks are growing at five times the national average.

But tapping the Hispanic market is not easy. You can't just translate your ads into Spanish and let it go at that. For one thing, the Hispanic market consists of several subcultures: people of Mexican, Puerto Rican, South/Central American, and Cuban descent; longtime residents and recent immigrants; affluent, well-educated people and those with very little money or education. Each subculture has its own values and customs, different from one another and different from the mainstream Anglo community. As pointed out by Marge Landrau, a New York marketing consultant, "When marketing to Hispanics, you absolutely must take into consideration their tradition, religion, and family orientation."

When Metropolitan Life Insurance Company decided to target the Hispanic market, it assigned Ruben P. Lopez, marketing director of personal insurance, to the project. He and his co-workers approached the job gradually, using market research to develop preliminary plans. Based on this research, Metropolitan launched market tests in San Antonio and Miami, where Metropolitan had a nucleus of Spanish-speaking insurance agents. Lopez placed advertisements in Spanish-language media, urging people to call a toll-free number for more information. The calls, which were answered by bilingual operators, were an excellent source of leads for the insurance agents.

Buoyed by results in the test markets, Metropolitan began a city-by-city expansion into Los Angeles, New York, San Francisco, Houston, and Dallas. Next on the agenda: the Rio Grande Valley, Albuquerque/Santa Fe, El Paso, and Chicago. Before moving into each city, Metropolitan builds up its Hispanic sales force and support staff.

The company's entrance into each new market is accompanied by an advertising campaign crafted by a firm that specializes in marketing to Hispanics. The ads are playful and indirect since, as Lopez points out, "The one thing Hispanics don't want to discuss is death."

The campaign features a combination of print and broadcast ads that show a genie rising from a disaster and saying, "I am a genie. I am all powerful so I don't need insurance. If you're not a genie, maybe you do." The ads involve a subtle play on words, since *genie* means "genius" in Spanish. Follow-up tests suggest that the ads are delivering the desired message: More than 50 percent of Hispanics associate the genie with Metropolitan Life. By addressing Hispanic values in their promotional efforts, Lopez and the Metropolitan team are earning the loyalty of their customers.[48]

1. Suppose you are involved in Metropolitan's entry into the Albuquerque/Santa Fe area. What sort of sales promotion might you use?

2. Assume that you work for a rival insurance company that is trying to tap the Hispanic market. Your company is eager to catch up with Metropolitan Life and is contemplating a national campaign aimed at capturing a significant portion of the market within 12 months. What would you advise management to do first to promote its services?

PART FIVE

Tools of Business

CHAPTER *16*

LEARNING OBJECTIVES
After studying this chapter, you will be able to

1 Distinguish between data and information and explain the characteristics of useful information.

2 List the five generations of computer hardware.

3 Describe the five classes of computers.

4 Identify the major elements of a computer system.

5 Name the main categories of application software.

6 Describe the four generations of computer languages.

7 Explain the purpose of computer networks.

8 Discuss the social and business concerns about extensive computerization.

Computers and Information Technology

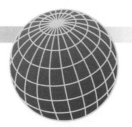

Facing a Business Challenge at American Express

INFORMATION HAS ITS PRIVILEGES

D ay after day, week after week, more than 30 million people around the world told James D. Robinson III all about themselves: what they ate, where they traveled, when they were likely to buy luxuries, how busy their lifestyles were, and a host of other facts. And that was the problem. They were giving him facts—tons of them. More than 3 million charge card receipts were arriving each day, so much paper that American Express was having a difficult time managing the bulk data, let alone capitalizing on the information that could be derived from those receipts. Robinson pushed every employee to provide high-quality service to customers, but he was also watching his company being buried beneath a mountain of paper. In a hotly competitive market, he couldn't afford to lose customer loyalty because of the inefficient management of information.

American Express did have a microfiche system for storing images of the receipts, but processing the millions of pieces of paper for their return to cardholders was cumbersome and was causing inaccuracies. Hundreds of employees were required to film receipts for storage, to enter charge amounts into a mainframe computer for billing, to sort receipts and match them with others in the same accounts, to process billing statements, and to insert the receipts and their corresponding statements into envelopes for mailing. Mistakes were made; time was wasted. Some receipts were mangled. Account numbers were misread. Receipts were inserted into the wrong envelopes, so some customers received no receipts while others received those of strangers. Nearly 200 people were employed just to resolve errors that had been made during the initial processing— and these employees also had to shuffle piles of paper. Answering a cardholder's query about a single transaction could take hours while employees searched through long cartridges of film for a record of the appropriate receipt.

The cost of doing business this way was more than excess wages and low productivity. American Express did not grant credit for partial or late payment, so a "float" of cash had to be maintained to pay merchants for purchases while awaiting payment from cardholders. The longer it took to process receipts and to bill customers, the longer it took for American Express to get paid, which forced the company to keep more money in its float. If handling the receipts could be made more efficient and accurate, the company would get paid sooner and be able to reduce the float.

One solution to these problems was to stop returning receipts to cardholders with their statements, a step already taken by Visa and MasterCard. But Robinson demanded a high level of service for his customers. American Express cardholders, most of whom used their cards for business purposes, needed their receipts for business and tax records.

Moreover, even if the paper mountain could be flattened with a more efficient system, that would still leave the question of how to manage all of those data describing the wants and behaviors of American Express cardholders. Robinson's goal was to make American Express into a service-industry giant by offering a wide variety of services, from charge cards to financial planning to travel to entertainment. Those 30 million customers were telling Robinson a lot about themselves, and he had to use their data to gain a competitive advantage, build customer loyalty, and enter new markets. How could Robinson get a grip on the mountain of paper? How could he transform the data into useful business information?[1]

▶ COMPUTERS IN TODAY'S BUSINESS ENVIRONMENT

James Robinson and his management team at American Express recognize two vital aspects of contemporary business: the importance of information and the usefulness of computers. Most businesses rely on computers and information technology to at least a small degree; many simply couldn't get by without them. In addition to computers, other information technologies play important roles, including fax machines, voice mail (phone systems that can store messages and route calls), and videoconferencing (communicating with television images between two or more locations). AT&T hopes its new VideoPhone will catch on; if business views it as a less-expensive alternative to videoconferencing, the VideoPhone could turn out to be popular in tomorrow's offices. But before exploring computers in greater detail, however, it is important to understand the difference between data and information and to grasp information's role in business management.

data *Recorded statistics, facts, predictions, and opinions; data need to be converted to information before they can help people solve business problems*

database *A collection of related computer files that can be cross referenced in order to extract information*

information *A specific collection of data that pertain to a particular decision or problem*

From Data to Information to Insight

The receipts that pour into American Express offices every day are an example of **data,** which are recorded statistics, facts, predictions, and opinions. A **database** is a collection of data (usually computerized). However, without further analysis, such data have little meaning. A stack of receipts from restaurants in Boise won't tell James Robinson very much. What he needs is **information,** a specific collection of data that are relevant to a particular decision or problem. For instance, on January 12 of this year, American Express customers in Boise charged $22,000 worth of meals on their cards, and this fact represents one data point—by itself, not terribly useful. But if Robinson also knew that on the same date last year customers charged $19,000, and the year before that they charged

$13,000, he would have some useful information—namely, that American Express's restaurant business is increasing in Boise.

With enough useful information at hand, managers can develop insight into the business challenges their companies face. What if James Robinson knew that over the last three years, Boise restaurant charges on the Discover card for January 12 had increased from $5,000 to $12,000 to $22,000? He could tell that he's running even with this competitor this year, but that Discover is increasing at a faster rate. Unless circumstances change, he can reasonably expect Discover to be ahead of him by January 12 next year.

Information is such an important strategic resource for most companies that many of them now have a top-level executive, often called the **chief information officer** (CIO), who focuses on information and information systems. And these executives do a lot more than just keep an eye on computers. James Marsten, CIO of American President Companies, manages a wide variety of projects and systems for the California-based shipping company. For instance, one of American President's competitive advantages is its ability to let customers on both sides of the Pacific monitor the progress of their shipments. To deliver this capability, the company uses a sophisticated satellite communications system that constantly tracks the location and progress of each ship on its way across the ocean. Customers can tap into the system and find out exactly where their shipments are and when they are expected in port. It is the CIO's job to manage the design and operation of this and many other advanced information systems.[2] Even companies that don't operate over vast geographic areas have prodigious amounts of data and information to manage (see Exhibit 16.1).

Every aspect of a business operation depends on the successful collection, storage, and application of data and information. The marketing department

chief information officer A top corporate executive with responsibility for information and information systems

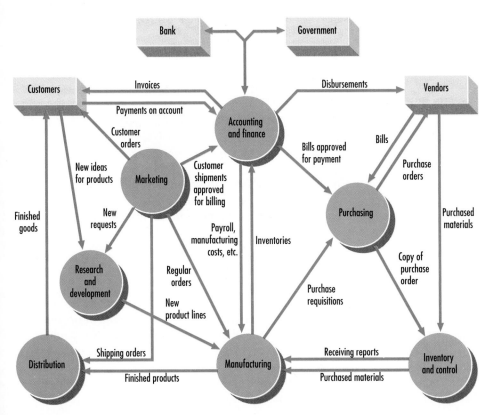

EXHIBIT 16.1

Information Flow in a Typical Manufacturing Company
Many kinds of manipulations and transfers of information support daily operations and decision making in a manufacturing company.

needs to know about customers and their needs; the accounting department needs to know how much products cost to make and how much they are selling for; the human resources department needs to keep track of employees and their salaries, benefits, and performance—every department needs particular data and information.

Making Information Useful

As James Robinson, James Marsten, and other managers concerned with information can attest, information is valuable only if it is useful. You can have a never-ending supply of interesting, amusing, and even shocking information, but if it's not useful, it won't help you manage better. And for information to be useful, it must meet five criteria:[3]

▶ *It must be accurate.* Just how accurate information needs to be depends on the situation. If you're trying to size up the market for toothpaste in North America, a population figure within a few hundred thousand people would probably be just fine. On the other hand, if your checkbook balance is getting down toward zero, you need to know the exact amount you have left in the bank, down to the last cent.

▶ *It must be timely.* Any manager will tell you that decisions must be made, with or without "necessary" information. Most business decisions need to be made within a finite period, and if the information that sheds light on the decision comes a week or a month later, it is of little use. Similarly, unless a manager has a good storage and retrieval system, giving him or her information months ahead of time probably won't be much help either.

▶ *It must be complete.* A manager facing a decision needs information that covers all areas affecting that decision. If you're studying the records of your employees in order to choose a new production supervisor, you need to see the records of all qualified employees, or you won't be able to make an optimum decision.

▶ *It must be relevant.* Have you ever taken an exam and discovered that some of the clues apply to the question asked whereas some clues don't? One of the most difficult aspects of information management is deciding what is relevant, deciding what isn't, and then providing the relevant information only.

▶ *It must be concise.* Finally, information must be in a form that is efficient for the decision maker to use. Handing your boss a 50-page report when he or she asks for a single figure is an inefficient way to convey the information.

Of course, information in the real world is rarely perfect, and managers must often make do with whatever information they can get. But the closer information comes to meeting these five criteria, the more it will improve the management process.

Information Systems

If you've spent any time at all around computers, you know that data and information can pile up fast. If you're not organized, you'll be swimming in printouts, disks, notes, programs, and all the other elements of computing. Now imagine the mess American Express would be in if it didn't have information systems to help it take care of business.

Information systems can be classified according to the type of information they handle and according to the people in the organization they serve. Informa-

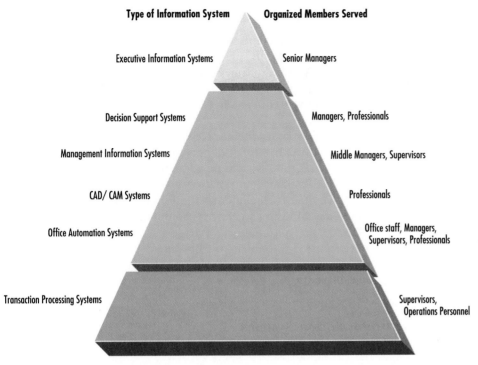

Type of Information System   **Organized Members Served**

Executive Information Systems — Senior Managers

Decision Support Systems — Managers, Professionals

Management Information Systems — Middle Managers, Supervisors

CAD/ CAM Systems — Professionals

Office Automation Systems — Office staff, Managers, Supervisors, Professionals

Transaction Processing Systems — Supervisors, Operations Personnel

EXHIBIT 16.2

Types of Information Systems
Information systems fall into six general categories. The transaction processing systems serve people on the front line of the organization, and the executive information systems help top managers make decisions.

tion systems are grouped into six general classes: transaction processing systems, office automation systems, CAD/CAM systems, management information systems, decision support systems, and executive information systems (see Exhibit 16.2).[4]

Transaction Processing Systems

Much of the daily flow of data into and out of the typical business organization is handled by a **transaction processing system** (TPS), which takes care of customer orders, billing, employee payroll, and other essential transactions. Sometimes a TPS interacts directly with another computer system, as when a drugstore's computers transmit orders to a drug wholesaler's computers. In most cases, however, human beings are involved. When you check in for a flight and the airline representative checks with the computer to assign you a seat, a TPS is the type of system at work. When you get a seat assignment, the computer updates its database by taking that seat off the available list and confirming your name on the passenger log.

transaction processing system A computerized information system that processes the daily flow of customer, supplier, and employee transactions, including inventory, sales, and payroll records

Office Automation Systems

Office automation systems (OAS) help people execute typical office tasks more efficiently, whether the job is producing a report or calculating next year's budget. Office automation systems range from a single personal computer with word-processing software to networks of computers that allow people to communicate using electronic mail to share work among computers. Important recent advances in office automation include "groupware," which lets a team of people work on a single document without getting in each other's way or enables them to schedule meetings by checking everyone's electronic calendars.

office automation systems Computer systems that assist with the tasks that people in a typical business office face regularly, such as drawing graphs or processing documents

CAD and CAM Systems

Business can also use computers to automate the work of architects, engineers, and other technical professionals. In many instances, computer-aided design (CAD) systems are replacing the drafting boards and mechanical instruments that engineers and architects traditionaly used to lay out designs for new products and projects. Instead of sketching a circle with a compass, for example, an engineer using a CAD system can tell the computer to draw a circle with a certain diameter at a certain spot on the drawing. Advanced systems let designers perform such tasks as creating three-dimensional models or estimating a product's response to shock and vibration. Computer-aided manufacturing (CAM) systems, on the other hand, automate a wide variety of tasks on the factory floor. Applications of CAM include robotic welders, hazardous material handling, and precision machining of steel parts. Some manufacturers have successfully linked CAD and CAM, automatically transferring product specifications from the engineering department to the manufacturing department. These combined CAD/CAM systems can be of great help in a company's efforts to get new products on the market faster.

Management Information Systems

management information systems Systems that supply periodic, predefined reports to assist in managerial decision making

Management information systems (MIS) typically serve middle management, although they can help anyone in an organization. An MIS usually supplies reports and statistics, such as monthly sales figures, employee records, and production schedules for factories. In doing so, an MIS often takes data from a transaction processing system and transforms them into useful information. In addition, in cases involving routine decision making (such as how many tires to order to build a certain number of cars), an MIS can sometimes go beyond simple report generation and provide answers to management questions.

Decision Support Systems

decision support systems Extensions of management information systems that provide managers with the tools and data they need for decision making

Whereas management information systems provide structured, routine information for managerial decision making, **decision support systems** (DSS) assist managers in solving highly unstructured and nonroutine problems. In other words, a DSS gives managers the tools they need to create their own information. Note that DSSs *support* managerial decisions; the systems don't make decisions on their own. Compared to an MIS, a DSS is more interactive (allows the user to interact with the system, as opposed to simply receiving information) and usually relies on both internal and external information (marketing conditions, competitive activity, and so on).[5]

Executive Information Systems

executive information systems Similar to decision support systems, but customized to the strategic needs of executives

In the top ranks of the organization, **executive information systems** (EIS) help executives make the decisions they need to make to keep the organization moving forward. Although an EIS is similar in concept to a DSS, it usually has a more strategic focus to handle the decisions executives face. The EIS used by Hertz, the international car-rental company, helps executives make such decisions as whether or not to add cars at a certain location, what sort of discount promotion is needed to build business at a certain time of the year, and even how to respond to changes in the weather. The EIS operates on the vast database Hertz has compiled, a database that includes information about cities, climates, holidays, and business cycles, as well as information about past marketing efforts and forecasts.[6] If managers in Florida want to know whether a discount will help build sales during the slow season, they can query the DSS about the company's experience with discounting programs.

Other Information Systems

In addition to these general classes of information systems, businesses and organizations occasionally design specialized information to solve specialized problems. For instance, companies whose business success depends on an understanding of geographic information can turn to *geographic information systems*. These are essentially computerized maps that help companies with tasks ranging from identifying target markets to analyzing the petrochemical potential of geological formations. A movie distribution company uses a geographic information system to see how well films do in various neighborhoods. Banks can use similar systems to get a geographic profile of their mortgage businesses. Although these specialized systems seem different from other information systems, they are in fact just another way that managers are using technology to help them manage information more successfully.[7]

Can Computer Systems Really Think?

Powerful systems raise an interesting question: Can computers really think like managers do? Efforts to create computers that mimic human thought processes fall under the heading of **artificial intelligence**.[8] Although the question about whether computers can truly duplicate human thought processes is likely to be debated for many years, artificial intelligence has yielded some important advances that are already making an impact on the business world.

One of these is the **expert system**, a computer system that mimics the thought processes of a human expert who is adept at solving particular problems.[9] Executives at Ocean Spray, the company known for its cranberry drinks, use an expert system called CoverStory, which analyzes market data and offers explanations for such occurrences as changes in sales volumes.[10]

Expert systems are typically built to solve fairly narrow problems in which the knowledge of one expert can benefit less experienced employees. For instance, the troubleshooting methods used by an experienced auto mechanic could be programmed into an expert system. A beginning mechanic could describe a sick engine's symptoms to the system, which would then apply the expert mechanic's facts and rules to suggest which troubleshooting methods might reveal the cause of the problem. American Express, for instance, uses an expert system to help with credit card authorizations, a risky and time-consuming part of the credit card business.

A second advance in artificial intelligence to make its way into business is the **natural-language processor**, which lets a user communicate with a computer using his or her own "natural" language (English, French, etc.) rather than using a computer language.[11] Even on a simple level, natural-language processing can be a boon to computer users. Say that you have a sales meeting on alternate Monday mornings at 10:00. Using a paper calendar, you'd have to turn to every other Monday and write down a reminder about the meeting. If you wanted to

artificial intelligence Use of computers to mimic human thought processes

expert system A computer system that mimics the thought processes of a human expert who is adept at solving particular problems

natural-language processor A system or software program that converts a natural language to a computer language; natural-language processing is the primary feature of fourth-generation languages

automate your to-do list with a typical computer setup, you'd have to write a computer program using BASIC or some other language. However, with Lotus Agenda, an information-management program that features a modest degree of natural-language processing, you would literally type into your computer the exact words: "sales meeting every other Monday at 10:00 a.m." Then on alternate Monday mornings, you'll see on your computer screen a reminder to go to the meeting. Natural-language processing like this promises to make many kinds of computer tasks much easier, particularly when you combine them with voice-input and other user-friendly technologies.

▶ INFORMATION-PROCESSING TECHNOLOGY

With an idea of the scope of computers in business, it's time to take a closer look at computers themselves. This section considers the major elements of information-processing technology, starting with a look at how computers evolved into the machines that have become so important to contemporary business.

The Evolution of Computer Systems

How far have computers come in the last four decades? If automobiles had advanced as much, you would be able to buy a Rolls-Royce for less than $3, and it would get something like 3 million miles to a gallon of gas.[12] This is more than just an amusing piece of trivia. If computers hadn't made such mind-boggling advances since the 1950s, they wouldn't be much of a force in business today. Few companies would have the budget—or the patience—for a computer that would fill a large room, dim city lights when it was operating, last an average of only a few hours between failures, and have less computing power than today's cheapest pocket calculator.[13]

Five Generations of Computer Technology

The brief life history of commercial computing can be divided into five generations:[14]

▶ *First-generation systems.* Some of the fundamental concepts behind today's computers can be traced back to the 1640s and perhaps even to the Chinese abacus (invented 4,000 years ago).[15] The first electronic computer, the ENIAC, appeared in 1946. The first computer sold to businesses and other organizations, the UNIVAC, appeared around 1950 and was used to tabulate the U.S. census. These first-generation computers relied on *vacuum tubes,* early electronic components that had the unfortunate habit of burning out frequently, generating considerable heat, and consuming massive amounts of electricity. Another shortcoming of these early machines was the method of **programming,** the steps involved in giving a computer the instructions necessary to perform a desired task. You couldn't tell one of these computers to "add 2 plus 2." You had to communicate using long strings of 1's and 0's because that was the only "language" the machines understood.

programming Process of creating the sets of instructions that direct computers to perform desired tasks

▶ *Second-generation systems.* In the 1950s, the transistor, a solid-state replacement for the vacuum tube, ushered in a new generation of computers that were cheaper, smaller, and more reliable. Programming became easier because these new machines used a language that could be read by human beings. Instead of sending a command such as 0111 0110 1101 001, programmers could now send commands such as CLR and MUL. They still couldn't come right out and say "add 2 plus 2," but they were getting closer.

Today's users of handheld miracles and superfast supercomputers can trace the roots of their technological wonders back to cumbersome, auditorium-sized machines such as this ENIAC (from Unisys).

▶ *Third-generation systems.* By the early 1960s, computers had evolved into yet another phase. Third-generation systems continued the advance in power and affordability, but just as important, they introduced languages that accomplished much more with much less effort. Now programmers could finally tell a computer to "add 2 plus 2" and it would be smart enough to do it. Moreover, these computers sported **integrated circuits,** collections of transistors on a single chip of silicon, which reduced size and heat generation. Computers were starting to look like real business machines, and they began to show up in accounting offices, warehouses, laboratories, and factories around the world.

▶ *Fourth-generation systems.* In 1971 computers began to resemble the machines we use on desktops today. Many began to incorporate **microprocessors,** advanced integrated circuits that combine most of the basic functions of a computer onto a single chip. It was the microprocessor that shrank computers far enough to put them on your desk, on your lap, and even in your hand. The fourth-generation systems gave rise to the Apple I and

integrated circuits Electronic components that contain thousands of transistors and can therefore perform complicated tasks, such as arithmetic and data storage

microprocessors Advanced integrated circuits that combine most of the basic functions of a computer onto a single chip; sometimes called "computers on a chip"

Today's mainframe computer systems have their roots in the third-generation developments of the 1960s.

the IBM Personal Computer. From the compact units you can hold in your hand to some of the most powerful business systems, most computers in use today are fourth-generation computers.

▶ *Fifth-generation systems.* This class of machine, the state of the art in computer technology, is the focus of attention for artificial intelligence and other advanced uses. One of the most significant aspects of these computers is their use of **parallel processing,** in which multiple processors divide complex tasks, with each processor taking one part of the problem—rather like 10 students working on 10 parts of a homework problem at the same time. The computational speed of these fifth-generation computers is finally offering hope for the most ambitious projects, such as modeling the world's weather patterns.

parallel processing The use of multiple processors in a single computer unit, with the intention of increasing the speed at which complex calculations can be completed

From Batch Processing to Real Time

As computers have evolved in the last several decades, so have the ways that businesses approach information processing. Up until the 1960s (and for many years after that in some organizations), one didn't just walk up to the computer and go to work. Computer use at the time was characterized by **batch processing,** in which users prepared data and programs, then submitted their "jobs" to the computer center, where operators collected the jobs and fed them to the computer in "batches" at regular intervals. Users had no choice but to sit and wait for the results. It isn't hard to imagine the impact that such delays would have on organizational performance.

batch processing A computing method in which "jobs" are submitted to the computer in "batches" at regular intervals, so users must wait for their results

Batch processing is still the appropriate choice for many computing applications, including payrolls, customer billings, and marketing research. In many data processing situations, however, anything more than a modest amount of delay in intolerable. What if a bank's customers tried to get cash from an ATM, and the machine reponded with the message, "I'm working on your request; please come back tomorrow for your cash"? Or what if the computers processing radar data for an air traffic control system were so slow that they couldn't keep up with the movement of all the planes? In cases such as these, the computer has to respond nearly instantaneously in order for the information it provides to be useful. This leads to the idea of **real-time processing,** in which the computer's files are updated as soon as new information arrives.[16]

real-time processing A method of information processing in which the computer's files are updated as soon as new information arrives

microcomputer The smallest and least expensive class of computers, such as the Apple Macintosh and the IBM PS/2

Types of Computer Systems

Some computer applications absolutely need real-time processing, such as traffic control at Pearson International Airport in Toronto, Canada. The definition of *real time* depends on the situation.

The work of the last few decades has produced quite a range of computer types, from micro units you can hold in your hand to blindingly fast supercomputers. In increasing order of processing power, today's computers can be grouped into five classes: microcomputers, workstations, minicomputers, mainframes, and supercomputers. Keep in mind that lines between the various classes aren't always clear; as technology continues to advance, the computers in one class can start to behave like their higher-performing cousins in the next category.

Microcomputers

Microcomputers are the machines that most people are familiar with; the Apple Macintosh and the IBM Personal Computer (PC) are among the best known. A **microcomputer,** often referred to generically as a *personal computer,* represents the smallest and least-expensive class of computers. A microcomputer is built around a single microprocessor. In fact, you might hear terms such as *286, 386,* or *486* used to describe a microcomputer's power. These numerical terms are actually derived from the manufacturer's part number of the microprocessor used inside. Computers in this category are now available in several sizes, designated by *desktop, laptop, notebook,* and even *palmtop* (for computers that fit in your hand). The leading manufacturers of microcomputers include IBM, Apple, and Compaq, but there are hundreds of companies fighting for a share of this market.

Workstations

The **workstation** is a relatively recent development that marries the speed of minicomputers with the desktop convenience of microcomputers. Workstations are used primarily by designers, engineers, scientists, and others who need fast computing and powerful graphics capabilities to solve mathematically intense problems. A typical application in this segment is the *computer-aided design* (CAD) function already discussed. An engineer for Rockwell International, for instance, might use a CAD system to design a part for the space shuttle; the system could perform such tasks as predicting responses to stress and calculating the amount of steel required to make the part. Three of the leading manufacturers of workstations are Sun Microsystems, Hewlett-Packard, and Digital Equipment Corporation (DEC).

Workstations are just as "personal" as microcomputers, in that they are typically used by a single person. But the term *workstation* is used to separate this more powerful class of computers from microcomputers. Traditionally, the term *workstation* was applied to any terminal at which a computer user works, but the computer industry is increasingly using the term to describe this particular class of computers.

workstation A recently developed class of computers with the basic size and shape of microcomputers but with the speed of traditional minicomputers (traditionally, the term was applied to any terminal at which computer users work)

Minicomputers

Emerging in the 1960s (at the same time as the modern mainframe), **minicomputers** have the same general capabilities as mainframes (such as supporting multiple users simultaneously), but they are smaller, cheaper, and less powerful. Typical applications of minicomputers include controlling a manufacturing process in a factory, managing a company's payroll, and helping a wholesaler keep track of sales and inventory. Some important applications that were once handled by minicomputers (particularly in scientific research and engineering) are now handled by workstations, whose power has increased in recent years. Leading makers of minicomputers include Hewlett-Packard, DEC, and IBM.

minicomputers Computers that fall between workstations and mainframes in terms of cost, size, and performance

Mainframe Computers

Until the arrival of the microcomputer in the late 1970s and early 1980s, the most common image of a computer was the **mainframe computer,** a large and powerful system capable of handling vast amounts of data. Those refrigerator-sized units that you've seen whirring away in computer rooms and on movie sets are mainframes. They handle a variety of trans-processing tasks, particularly finance and accounting activities, which require a lot of repetitive calculations. The traditional way for users to gain access to mainframe computing power is

mainframe computers With the exception of supercomputers, the largest and most powerful computers

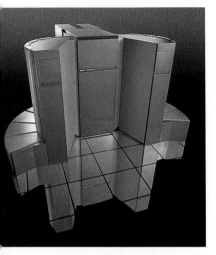

Supercomputers, like this Cray Y-MP, have the processing power to tackle the most complex computing tasks, such as modeling weather patterns or molecular chemistry.

supercomputers Computers with the highest level of performance, often boasting speeds greater than a billion calculations per second

hardware The physical components of a computer system, including integrated circuits, keyboards, and disk drives

software The instructions that drive computers

programs Organized sets of instructions, written in a computer language, that perform designated tasks such as word processing

through *dumb terminals,* devices that look like desktop computers but that don't have the processing power to operate on their own. Today's major mainframe manufacturers include IBM, Control Data, Hitachi, Siemens, Unisys, and Amdahl.[17]

Supercomputers

Supercomputers represent the leading edge in computer performance. A **supercomputer** is capable of handling the most complex processing tasks, with speeds in excess of a billion calculations per second. A Cray Research Y-MP, one of the best-known supercomputers, can process in one minute the work that a typical mainframe would take several hours to accomplish. It carries an equally breathtaking price tag, in the neighborhood of $20 to $25 million.[18]

For a certain class of engineering and scientific problems, a supercomputer is the only tool that can do the job. Seismic analysis, weather forecasting, complex engineering modeling, and genetic research are among the common uses of supercomputers. As you might expect, only a handful of companies are in this market, including leader Cray Research, IBM, Fujitsu, Hitachi, NEC, and two companies with roots in Cray Research, Cray Computer Corporation and Supercomputer Systems.[19]

Hardware

To understand what makes all these computers tick, the first step is to distinguish hardware from software. **Hardware** represents the physical equipment used in a computer system—the integrated circuits, keyboards, disk drives, and so on. **Software,** on the other hand, encompasses the instructions, or **programs,** that direct the activity of the hardware.

Whether it's a palmtop computer keeping track of your appointment schedule or a supercomputer modeling the structure of a DNA molecule, every computer is made up of a basic set of hardware components. Of course, the hardware in a Cray Y-MP differs greatly from the hardware in a hand-held unit, but the concepts are similar. Hardware can be divided into four basic groups: input devices, the central processing unit, output devices, and storage (see Exhibit 16.3).

EXHIBIT 16.3

Hardware Elements in a Computer System

The primary elements of computer hardware are the central processing unit, input devices, output devices, and storage; software is divided into operating systems and applications software.

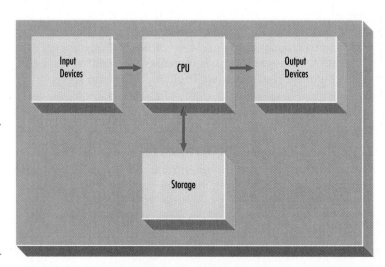

Input Devices

Before it can perform any calculations, a computer needs data, and it gets those data from one or more input devices. The *keyboard* is the most obvious input device, but other devices used to feed data to computers include the *mouse,* which can be used to select commands based on a pointer's position on the computer screen; the *computer pen,* which lets you write on special tablets that translate your handwriting into computer-compatible data; the *scanner,* which essentially takes a picture of a piece of paper and sends the computer either a graphic image or an interpretation of the text on the page; and the *bar code reader,* which reads the black and white Uniform Product Codes you see on packages in the supermarket.

Central Processing Unit

A computer's calculations are made in the **central processing unit** (CPU), which performs the three basic functions of arithmetic, logic, and control/communication.[20] Actually, computer arithmetic is nothing more than addition; subtraction

central processing unit The core of the computer, performing the three basic functions of arithmetic (addition, etc.), logic (comparing numbers), and control/communication (managing the computer)

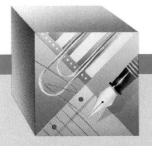

CHECKLIST FOR BUSINESS TODAY

Buying a Computer

Buying a computer has its perils, but you can sidestep difficulties by asking yourself these questions before you shop:

1. What am I going to do with a computer? You need to have a clear idea of your main goal. Otherwise, you may end up either paying for extras you don't really need or owning a computer model that doesn't do enough.

2. How much money am I willing to spend? The cost of a microcomputer system varies considerably. Sometimes the lowest price translates into the shoddiest service. If you think you might like advice or other help from the dealer after you buy the computer, be prepared to spend 5 to 10 percent more.

3. How am I going to educate myself about what the computer can do and what software is available? Product reviews in computer magazines are a good place to start. Most bookstores also sell guides to buying computers.

4. Where should I shop for a computer? Before you start visiting stores, ask friends or business associates where they bought their computers and whether they were satisfied with the advice and the service they received. How was your friend treated after buying the computer and going back to the store with questions or complaints? The answer will tell you a great deal about how reputable the firm is.

5. What options do I need? Computers come with a variety of features. Check to be sure that the ones you need come with the machine you're buying.

6. What kind of software—and how much—is available for the computer I prefer? Some models have more than 10,000 software programs available. For others, only a few dozen are available. In fact, many experts suggest that you start your purchase process by picking out the software you want and then look for the computers that will run that software.

7. What kind of training and support will I get after I buy the computer? Who will be available when you're stuck and need someone to talk you through a program? Are there free classes on using your computer?

8. What kind of warranty exists? In addition to the standard manufacturer's warranty, the dealer may be able to offer service contracts that provide on-site maintenance and repairs by factory-trained specialists. Ask for references so that you can find out how other customers were treated when something went wrong with their computers.

9. Is the computer I prefer one that can grow with me? Don't buy a computer just for your immediate needs. Find one you will be able to do more with as your abilities grow and your needs change.

Decimal	Binary Equivalent
5	0 0 0 0 0 1 0 1
10	0 0 0 0 1 0 1 0
46	0 0 1 0 1 1 0 0
73	0 1 0 0 1 0 0 1
127	0 1 1 1 1 1 1 1

EXHIBIT 16.4

Binary Representations of Data

Various combinations of the binary digits 0 and 1 make it possible for a computer to process and store any type of information that can be represented as, or converted into, numbers, letters, or symbols. This example shows how various decimal numbers are represented in binary format.

bit A single unit of information; can consist of either a 1 or a 0

byte A collection of eight data bits

is performed through negative addition, multiplication is repetitive addition, and division is repetitive negative addition.[21] Computer logic is also a simple operation, nothing more than comparing two numbers. For instance, when a person calls PaperDirect, a New Jersey paper-supply company, the salesperson first asks for the caller's phone number so that the company's computer system can compare that phone number with those it has on file to see whether the caller is already a customer. The control/communication function of the CPU keeps the computer working in a rational fashion. This includes deciding when to accept data from the keyboard, when to perform arithmetic and logic operations, and when to display characters or graphics on the screen.

In microcomputers and workstations, the CPU is composed of a single microprocessor (and some associated support circuitry). In minicomputers, mainframes, and supercomputers, the CPU can be either a single processing unit made of multiple integrated circuits or multiple processing units operating in parallel (in fact, some designs use multiple microprocessors, the *parallel processing* referred to earlier).

In a sense, even the most complex electronic circuit is nothing more than a collection of switches. Each switch can be either on or off, representing either a 1 or a 0. This represents one **bit** of information, which is shorthand for *binary digit*. The binary number system uses strings of 1's and 0's to represent all numbers (see Exhibit 16.4). For example, the "regular" number 1 is expressed in binary as 1, the number 2 is expressed as 10, 3 is 11, 4 is 100, 5 is 101, and so on. Bits are usually packaged in groups of eight, which make up a **byte** of information. The number 5, for instance, would be expressed in a byte of information as 00000101.

Every CPU is designed around a certain number of bits simultaneously. The original IBM PC, for instance, could handle 8 at a time, its successor could handle 16 at a time, and current top-end microcomputers can handle 32 bits at a time. Why would a businessperson care about this technical detail? Because the number of CPU bits has a big influence on the speed of the computer. If you ask an 8-bit computer to do something with the number 300, you may be surprised to find out how long it takes. When converted to binary, the number 300 needs nine bits (1 0010 1100), but your 8-bit CPU can't handle the entire number at once, so it has to deal with half the number at a time. The process of shuffling parts of numbers back and forth is time-consuming, and the result is lower performance. (The total picture of computer performance is a lot more complicated than this, but this example addresses one of the fundamental issues.) To get an instant impression of the importance of CPU bits, just ask microcomputer users with 32-bit machines to trade them for 16- or 8-bit machines. They will probably chase you out of the room.

Output Devices

Once the data have been successfully entered and the CPU has successfully processed them, they won't be of any use unless they are sent back to the outside world. The first place a computer's output usually goes is the *display*, or monitor, as it is often called. The display acts in the same basic manner as a television and provides the user with text, graphics, or a combination of both.

When you need a permanent record or when you need to share output with someone, you usually need a *printer*. Laser printers have become the output device of choice in many offices, since they provide sharp, clear reports, memos, and graphs. Newer laser printers can even print in color. An alternative often used by engineers and scientists is a *plotter,* a device that uses pens to reproduce a displayed image by drawing it on paper.

As with input devices, specialized equipment can provide output for particular applications. For instance, North Carolina attorney John DeLucia hasn't let blindness stop him from being a computer user. His microcomputer is equipped with a voice synthesizer that reads the displayed text to him. To help with input, the system also reads aloud as DeLucia types at the keyboard, letting him know if his typing is on the mark.[22] Systems such as these have gone a long way toward helping physically challenged people integrate smoothly into the business environment.

Storage

Input, processing, and output complete the basic computing cycle, but this can't happen without some form of storage for the data being processed and for the software that is in charge of the operation. A **primary storage device** stores data and programs while they are being used in the computer. This usually involves a set of semiconductor devices known as **random access memory** (RAM), so called because the computer can access any piece of data in such memory at random. Computers use RAM for temporary storage of programs and data during input, processing, and output operations. Unless it is provided with special back-up circuitry, RAM is erased when electrical power is removed from the computer. (That's why you hear cries of anguish from computer users when the electricity goes out.) RAM's counterpart is called **read only memory** (ROM), which keeps its contents even when power is cut off. ROM is used for programs such as the start-up routines that computers go through when they are first turned on, which involves checking for problems and getting ready to go to work.

Secondary storage takes care of data and programs that aren't needed at the moment, and it also provides a permanent record of those data and programs. For instance, if you've finished work on a report that you might need to modify in a month, you put it in secondary storage, which gets it out of the CPU's way and keeps it until you need to go back to work. The most common mechanism for secondary storage is the **disk drive,** which can be of two types. *Hard disk drives* are usually enclosed inside the computer and can store data internally on rigid magnetic disks. *Floppy disk drives,* on the other hand, are accessible to the user and store data externally on removable magnetic disks. These removable disks are called *floppy* disks because they are flexible: Some are encased in light cardboard (5¼-inch disks), and other are encased in stiff plastic (3½-inch disks). Floppy disks are easily portable, but they can store far less information than hard disks.

Software

The hardware components just described can be assembled to create impressive computer systems. However, the hardware isn't much good without software telling it what to do and how to behave. Software can be divided into two general categories. *Systems software* is the most important category because it includes

primary storage devices Storage for data and programs while they are being processed by the computer; also called RAM

random access memory Primary storage devices in a computer

read only memory Special circuits that store data and programs permanently but don't allow users to record their own data or programs; a common use of ROM is for the programs that activate start-up routines when the computer is turned on

secondary storage Computer storage for data and programs that aren't needed at the moment

disk drive The most common mechanism for secondary storage; includes both hard disk drives and floppy disk drives

operating systems The class of software that controls the computer's hardware components

application software Programs that perform specific functions for users, such as word processing or spreadsheet analysis

operating systems, which control the computer's most basic overall functions. For example, an operating system controls such fundamental actions as storing data on disk drives and displaying text or graphics on monitors. **Application software** encompasses programs that perform specific user functions such as word processing, drawing, organizing, scheduling, and so on.

Systems Software

As mentioned, operating systems make up the most important category of systems software. Other major categories are utilities, shells, and languages. The following material briefly describes the first three types of systems software; languages are discussed later in the chapter.

▶ *Operating Systems.* As already stated, languages and applications need operating systems to accomplish their designated tasks. A word-processing program can't read the disk or write text to the display by itself; it relies on the operating system to direct the computer's hardware and to manage the flow of data into, around, and out of the system. Operating systems that are unique to one particular computer are usually called **proprietary operating systems.** Others, called **open systems,** will run on computers from various manufacturers. Proprietary operating systems often have the advantage of better performance since the software can be "tuned" to take maximum advantage of a particular hardware configuration. On the other hand, these proprietary systems force customers to choose from a narrower range of hardware and software options. In recent years, customers have become less willing to limit themselves to proprietary systems.

proprietary operating systems Operating systems that run on only one brand of computer; they offer users a limited selection of hardware and software choices

open systems Operating systems (such as UNIX) that run on a wide variety of computers and don't restrict users to a single company's hardware

Proprietary operating systems have long been the norm in the computer world. The VMS operating system from Digital Equipment Corporation, for example, runs only on DEC computers. If you want to buy a word-processing program that runs only on the Macintosh operating system, you have no choice but to buy a Macintosh computer. And if you want everyone in your company to use this word-processing program, every person needs access to a Macintosh.

UNIX The most prominent open operating system; it can run on a wide variety of machines from microcomputers to supercomputers

At the other extreme is the most prominent open system, **UNIX,** which can run on a wide variety of machines from microcomputers all the way up to mainframes and supercomputers.[23] This means that programs can be moved from computer to computer and that a business can have several brands and classes of computers all running the same software package.

disk operating system The most common operating system for microcomputers

Somewhere between these two extremes lies Microsoft's **disk operating system** (DOS), the operating system used on the vast majority of microcomputers. Microsoft's operating system product is called MS-DOS, and it can run on any brand of computer that is compatible with IBM's line of personal computers, of which there are now hundreds. So MS-DOS doesn't tie you to a particular brand of computer, as proprietary systems do, but it doesn't give you the tremendous range of hardware and software options that an open system such as UNIX does. For instance, a DOS application package can't run on a minicomputer or mainframe—at least not without significant modification.

For the first time, traditionally proprietary companies are sharing technologies. IBM and Apple will be collaborating on a new operating system for their personal computers. Apple's future Macintosh computers will be using a processor licensed from IBM, and the two firms will form a separate company to explore the possibilities for multimedia products (combining video or still pictures with text and sound).[24]

▶ *Utilities.* Composing one of the biggest software categories are utilities, which help computer users take care of the daily business of being in business. Many of these packages focus on the computer itself, helping users manage the files on hard disks or running performance checks to make sure everything is working properly. For example, the Norton Utilities, a popular utility product for personal computers, provides such capabilities as "unerasing" files that a user accidentally deletes and reorganizing data on a hard disk to speed access.

▶ *Shells.* One of the frustrations many computer users experience is dealing with operating systems. Even if a person's only intention is to use a word processor, for example, he or she still has to use some basic operating system commands to start the word-processing program, to copy files to other disks, and even to find the word-processing program in order to get it running. Even though application software has become increasingly user-friendly in recent years, no one will accuse the typical operating system of being overly nice. To insulate users from operating systems and to make their computing lives easier, programmers have created a variety of *shells,* which essentially work between the operating system and the application software. One of the best-known shells is Microsoft Windows, a package that runs on microcomputers. Windows lets you point a mouse at a picture of an application program, and it will find the program and get it running for you. Windows also assists with transferring data between application packages, and perhaps its biggest contribution is providing a graphic display (one in which pictures can be used) as opposed to the text-only displays typically available with computers.

Application Software

Application software performs the business tasks that people need to do their jobs. (The term *application* refers both to an application software product, such as a word processor, and to the actual task for which the software is used, such as preparing reports and memos.) Application software can be either *custom* (developed specifically for a single user or set of users and not sold to other users) or *general purpose* (developed with the goal of selling it to multiple users). Commercially available general purpose software products are commonly referred to as *packages,* as in a "word-processing package."

In today's business software market, the array of software packages is vast, including products that can prepare books and newspapers, monitor the stock market, produce full-color 35mm slides and overhead transparencies, track employee records, and produce sales reports, to name just a few. Here's a quick look at the major categories of application software:

▶ *Accounting/finance.* Computers got their start in business doing accounting and financial tasks, and these remain a fundamental business application. In fact, nearly all the activities discussed in the next four chapters—on accounting, money and banking, financial management, and securities markets—can be managed faster and more effectively with software.

▶ *Spreadsheets.* A **spreadsheet** is a program designed to let users organize and manipulate data in a row-column matrix (see Exhibit 16.5). The intersection of each row and

spreadsheet A program that organizes and manipulates data in a row-column matrix

EXHIBIT 16.5

Sample Spreadsheet Analysis

Setting up a spreadsheet by hand takes time—especially to do the calculations. A spreadsheet program prepares the computer to accept values in preestablished spreadsheet cells. Paula Chang's hourly wage, for example, is entered in the cell where the "Paula Chang" row intersects the "wage" column. A spreadsheet program also performs basic mathematical operations, given the proper instructions. To compute an employee's regular pay (**X**), the computer must multiply that employee's wage (**W**) by his or her regular hours worked (**R**).

EMPLOYEE'S NAME	WAGE (W)	REGULAR HOURS (R)	OVERTIME HOURS (O)	REGULAR PAY (X = WR)	OVERTIME PAY [Y = 1.5(WO)]	TOTAL PAY (Z = X + Y)
Paula Chang	$10.00	40	6	$400.00	$90.00	$490.00
Lewis Bond	$7.50	32	5	$240.00	$56.25	$296.25

Employees name	Wage	Reg. Hours	OT Hours	Reg. Pay	OT Pay	Total Pay
	W	R	O	X=WR	Y=1.5 (WO)	Z=X+Y
Paula Chang	10.00	40	6	400.00	90.00	490.00
Lewis Bond	7.50	35	5	240.00	56.25	296.25

column pair is called a *cell,* and every cell can contain a number, a mathematical formula, or text used as a label. Among the spreadsheet's biggest strengths is the ability to quickly update masses of calculations when conditions change. For instance, if you have a spreadsheet that calculates profit sharing for your employees, and the profit-sharing percentage changes, you don't have to go through each employee's record and change the number by hand. You simply update the percentage in one place, and the spreadsheet will do all the updating for you (assuming you've programmed it to do so). Although spreadsheets were originally designed to replace the ledger books of accountants, business-people now use them to solve a wide variety of problems, ranging from statistical analysis to simulation models used in decision support systems.

▶ *Word processing.* Word processing is another fundamental business application of computers. Although word processing is frequently described as an enhanced alternative to the typewriter, today's word processors go far beyond anything imaginable on a typewriter. For instance, you've probably received a promotional letter that had your name inserted into it to give the appearance that it wasn't a form letter. Word-processing programs can do this with a function called *mail merge,* in which a single generic letter is merged with a list of names at printing time. When each letter is printed, the software picks a name from the list and inserts it into the letter.

▶ *Publishing.* Publishing software goes a step beyond typical word processors by helping designers lay out printer-ready pages that incorporate artwork, photos, and a large variety of typographic elements. Together with scanners and other specialized input devices, publishing programs let businesspeople create sophisticated documents in a fraction of the time it once took. Publishing software that runs specifically on microcomputers, such as Aldus Pagemaker, gives rise to the term **desktop publishing** (DTP).

desktop publishing The ability to prepare documents using computerized typesetting and graphics processing capabilities

▶ *Business graphics.* Businesspeople need to produce quite a variety of graphic materials, including charts, graphs, and diagrams. Together with specialized output devices such as plotters and color printers, business graphics software can produce overhead transparencies, 35mm slides, posters, and signs. In addition, the graphic images created with these packages can be fed into publishing programs for incorporation into books and reports.

▶ *Communications.* With communications software, a computer can exchange information with other computers. This opens up an entirely new spectrum of business capabilities, including **electronic mail**, the transmission of written messages in electronic format between computers, and **bulletin board systems** (BBS), electronic versions of traditional bulletin boards, which allow users to exchange ideas, news, and other information. Communications software also gives business users access to an eye-popping array of business information services. Dialog Information Services, for instance, gives users access to nearly 400 databases, containing a total of more than 260 million records ranging from government statistics to newspaper articles.[25]

electronic mail The transmission of written messages in electronic format between computers

bulletin board systems The electronic equivalents of traditional bulletin boards; users can "post" messages, data, and programs for other people to access

▶ *Drafting and CAD.* Drafting and CAD are the technical counterparts of business graphics. Included in this category are programs that help architects prepare blueprints, programs that let technical illustrators create schematic drawings, and CAD programs that help engineers design new products.

▶ *Production and process control.* These packages, typically running on minicomputers and mainframes, help manage the production of goods and services by controlling production lines, robots, and other machinery and equipment. In some cases, *computer-aided manufacturing* (CAM) software is linked with CAD software to automate the entire design and production cycle. For instance, an engineer designing a new component for a car engine can electronically transfer the design from his or her CAD package to a CAM package, which will then control a milling machine that automatically carves the part from a block of steel.

▶ *Project management.* The Gantt and PERT charts (introduced in Chapter 8) are often computerized in today's business environment. This helps businesspeople in two important ways. First, it helps them create and update schedules much more quickly than could be done by hand. Some scheduling packages, for instance, can automatically adjust each employee's work load to make sure no one works more than eight hours a day. Second, scheduling software helps businesspeople communicate with their employees, peers, and managers. Most programs can create attractive printouts that can be used in reports or on overhead transparencies.

▶ *Database management.* As the American Express example at the beginning of the chapter pointed out, businesses often have massive amounts of data on their hands. This represents two important challenges: first, how to store all that information in a way that is safe while still making it accessible to the employees who need it, and second, how to transform the data from a database into useful information when such information is needed. It is the job of **database management software** to create, store, maintain, rearrange, and retrieve the contents of databases.[26] Almost anywhere you find a sizable amount of data in electronic format, you'll find a database management package at work, whether it's on a microcomputer or a supercomputer. Such software helps users produce useful information through its ability to look at data from various perspectives. For instance, say that your business class has quizzes every week, that the class has 100 students, and that a helpful assistant logs all the quiz results into the computer every week, along with some basic data about each student. If your instructor wants to know how the class did on the last quiz, he or she can *query* the database for a printout of all 100 scores or for a simple average of the scores. Or, to show how the class has done throughout the course, the instructor could "look back through time" and get a list of the weekly averages since the course began. The same could be done for a single student. If enough data were in the database, the instructor could look only at the scores of students who've taken courses in business before or of those students who are majoring in journalism. Alternatively, if the scores on one quiz were unexpectedly low, the instructor could compare your class's performance on this quiz with the performance of previous classes to see whether the quiz was too difficult. Even in this simple example, you can see that database management can provide a great deal of information from a single stack of data.

database management software Programs designed to create, store, maintain, rearrange, and retrieve the contents of databases

VIDEO EXERCISE

▶ *Industry-specific solutions.* The application categories just described can be used in many industries. In addition to these, many application packages have been designed to meet the needs of specific industries and types of businesses. For example, a package called Associate helps real estate agents track sales leads, property listings, escrow companies, inspectors, and other important information.[27] Specialized packages are used to help manage dentists' offices, retail stores, law firms, hospitals, and just about every other business institution in existence.

▶ *Integrated software.* Finally, the category of integrated software contains programs that perform multiple functions. For instance, the Works product from Microsoft combines spreadsheet, business graphics, word processing, and other capabilities into one package. Doing so makes it easier to take care of multiple business tasks, and it also simplifies the job of moving data back and forth between applications.

In addition to these major categories, software developers have produced packages for a wide array of specialized business applications, ranging from marketing research to math solvers. The *Business Software Database,* which provides information on application software available for business, currently lists over 10,000 products.[28]

Computer Languages

The final category of information technology covered in this chapter concerns the way software is created. All software is created by another special class of

computer languages *Sets of programmable rules and conventions for communicating with computers*

software, **computer languages,** which are sets of rules and conventions for communicating with a computer. Just as human beings communicate with each other using designated languages, so too do human beings communicate with computers using designated languages.

Like computer hardware, languages have evolved over several generations. Unlike hardware, however, each new generation of language hasn't replaced the existing generation. Instead, each generation builds on the previous generation. The four language generations are machine language, assembly language, high-level languages, and fourth-generation languages.[29]

Machine Language

machine language *The "lowest" level of computer language, consisting entirely of 1's and 0's; the only level of computer language that hardware understands*

No matter how sophisticated or powerful, every computer communicates in machine language at its lowest level for the simple reason that computer hardware understands only 1's and 0's, and that is the stuff of **machine language.** A machine language program consists of pages and pages of nothing but 1's and 0's. Every CPU has a unique machine language, unless the CPU is designed specifically to be compatible with another CPU. Machine language was the only programming option available on the first-generation computers introduced in the 1940s and early 1950s.

Assembly Language

assembly language *One level above machine language; it consists of fairly cryptic low-level commands that initiate CPU commands*

Although machine language is absolutely necessary for a computer to operate, it is not something that humans are naturally conversant in. One of the most significant advances introduced with the second-generation computers of the 1950s was **assembly language,** which still didn't look like any language people spoke but was at least composed of mnemonic code words that people could read and write more easily. Instead of the 1's and 0's of machine language, programmers could write programs using commands such as "ST" (for "store") and "M" (for "multiply"). Keep in mind that even when assembly language is used to develop a program, the computer still operates using machine language. To make this happen, programmers need to convert their assembly-language program to machine language, which is done automatically with a special software tool called an *assembler*.

High-Level Languages

high-level languages *The computer languages most people are familiar with, such as BASIC, Logo, and C; single commands accomplish the equivalent of several assembly-language commands, and the language is easier for humans to read and write*

Assembly language was a big advance over machine language, but it still had two big drawbacks: It required a lot of instructions to accomplish even simple tasks, and each CPU had its own assembly language, which meant that you couldn't write a program for one computer then run it unmodified on another computer. To solve these problems, high-level languages were introduced during the third generation of computers in the late 1950s and 1960s. Using **high-level languages,** programmers could use a single command to accomplish the equivalent of several assembly-language commands. Moreover, these new languages were not restricted to a single model of computer, so programmers could move their programs from machine to machine much more easily. Once again, high-level languages didn't replace assembly or machine languages but merely provided an easier way to write programs. High-level languages must first be converted to assembly language before they can be run, which is done with either a *compiler* (if the entire program is converted before it is run) or an *interpreter* (if each line in the program is converted and then run before the next line is converted). Chances are you've already heard the names of some of the more popular high-level languages: BASIC, FORTRAN, Ada, Pascal, and C.

Fourth-Generation Languages

High-level languages helped make the computer revolution fast and pervasive, but they also have some disadvantages. One of the most significant (in the eyes of many computer users) is that people still have to learn a computer language. It may be easier to read and write than assembly language was, but it is another language nonetheless. Also, high-level languages still focus on what the computer should do, rather than focusing on what the user wants done. For instance, you can't use a high-level language to tell a computer to "summarize travel expenses for last month." You have to walk through the process step by step, telling the computer where to get the relevant data, how to process them, and what to do with the results.

In response to these limitations, computer scientists have begun to develop so-called **fourth-generation languages** (4GLs), which is a collective name applied to languages designed to make it easier for people to interact with computers. In many instances, users can give instructions to computers in a language that is remarkably similar to English, French, or another natural language (the natural-language–processing capability referred to earlier in the chapter). It is hard to define 4GLs precisely because various manufacturers have taken unique approaches to the problem, so no industrywide standards or conventions exist for 4GLs, as they do for high-level languages. However, 4GLs are still attractive. In the hypothetical example presented in Exhibit 16.6, a manager wants a list of her employees, together with their performance ranking and current monthly salary. Rather than writing a lengthy program, she merely provides the instructions shown, and the table is generated without a hitch.[30] Such 4GL capabilities have become common in database management software.

Computer Networks

The brief discussion of communications software hinted at one of the most important issues in business computing: connecting multiple computers in one fashion or another and allowing them to send data back and forth, a process

Business Around the World

The development of software has become an increasingly important part of India's economy. India has traditionally emphasized higher education, so it has an ample supply of trained technical specialists who are conversant in today's software technologies.

fourth-generation languages
A collective name applied to a variety of software tools that ease the task of interacting with computers; some let users give instructions in natural languages such as English

EXHIBIT 16.6

Benefits of Fourth-Generation Languages
If the manager in this hypothetical example wants an employee list that compares performance rankings and current monthly salaries, she doesn't have to write a program (as she would have to do with a high-level language); she can use a fourth-generation language to query the employee database.

Manager Inputs: Select from employee_database all records. Display last_name, first_name, ranking, salary

Resulting output:

Last_Name	First_Name	Ranking	Salary
Anderson	Jack	7.7	$3420
Josephson	Hank	6.4	$2850
Maalik	Sally	8.8	$4200
Zephry	Zelda	9.5	$4125

data communications The process of connecting computers and allowing them to send data back and forth

known as **data communications.** Data communications systems allow users not only to communicate with each other but also to gain access to centralized databases and expensive resources such as supercomputers and high-speed laser printers.

Data communication is quite complex and involves many variations in hardware and software. However, it can be divided into three general categories:

network A collection of computer, communications software, and transmission media line (such as a telephone) that allows computers to communicate

▶ *Long-distance networks.* In general, a **network** is a collection of hardware, software, and communication media that allow computers to communicate. The primary components are the computers themselves, communications software, and some sort of transmission medium. In a *wide area network,* computers at different geographic locations are linked through regular telephone lines, private telephone lines established just for data communication purposes, or radio-frequency connections such as microwave stations or satellites.[31] To communicate over telephone lines, a computer must be equipped with a **modem** (<u>mo</u>dulator-<u>dem</u>odulator), which can be either a stand-alone unit or a circuit board that is plugged into the computer.

modem A hardware device that allows a computer to communicate over a regular telephone line

local area network A computer network that encompasses a small area, such as an office or a university campus

▶ *Local area networks.* A **local area network** (LAN), as its name implies, meets data communications needs within a small area, such as an office or university campus. LANs can consist entirely of microcomputers or workstations communicating with one another, or they can have a special computer called a *file server.* The file server can provide common data storage facilities, electronic mail, access to laser printers, and other resources that all the LAN users can share. The proliferation of LANs has created the opportunity for **workgroup computing,** in which teams of employees can more easily work together on projects such as writing books or developing software.

workgroup computing A computing arrangement in which teams can easily work together on projects

BEHIND THE SCENES

Fidelity Invests in Information Technology

Strong customer service and the excellent performance of its investment products have made Fidelity Investments the largest mutual fund company in the world. Companies such as Fidelity pool money from investors to buy stocks, bonds, and other investment products. Investors can choose from more than 100 Fidelity funds, with options that include retirement accounts, company pension plans, college savings plans, and general investing. Chairman and CEO Edward C. Johnson III focuses on technology to keep Fidelity ahead of its competitors—in fact, the company maintains its own technology research department to look for ways that emerging technologies (such as talking workstations) can help it grow and serve its customers better.

Recent Fidelity information-management innovations include Fidelity On-line Xpress (FOX), a microcomputer software package. FOX connects individual investors directly to the financial markets, and it

supplies them with research reports, statistics, and other information needed to make informed investment decisions. Another innovation is Fidelity TouchTone Trader. This phone system doesn't offer the additional information services of FOX, but it does allow customers to buy and sell from any touchtone telephone.

Johnson knows that information management is more than hi-tech breakthroughs. The basic transaction-processing and customer-service systems that handle the flow of data into and out of the company must be accurate and reliable. For Fidelity, this includes a telephone system that can handle the millions of calls the company gets every year. The firm maintains more than 20 toll-free numbers for current and potential customers to access accounts, ask questions, and request information.

Johnson is intimately familiar with the consequences of inadequate information management capabilities; the company's systems were strained

▶ *Micro-to-mainframe links.* Many business offices have a central mainframe computer (to handle important databases such as customer records and employee records) along with an array of microcomputers (used by individual employees). Some of the computing tasks that employees do can be handled entirely on their microcomputers, such as word processing and preparing charts and graphs. In other cases, however, such as analyzing sales trends or accessing some electronic mail systems, the employee needs to tap into the central mainframe system. To accomplish this, each microcomputer is wired directly to the mainframe, and employees activate special communications software that makes their micros act like the dumb terminals traditionally associated with mainframes. When the employee is finished accessing the mainframe, he or she signs off the communications software and returns to normal microcomputer operation.

Communications networks can be centralized or decentralized in much the same way as business organizations themselves can be. In a traditional system, the mainframe has all the processing power, and the terminals merely act as communication ports to give users access to the mainframe. This mirrors a centralized organization in which top management makes all the decisions and employees simply do as they're told.

The alternative is **distributed processing,** in which some, occasionally all, of the processing power is spread out among the various computers attached to the network. In a LAN, for instance, users have complete computing capabilities on their own, and the network is more of a support system to help them work efficiently. This resembles a decentralized organization in which various teams

distributed processing An approach to computer network design in which processing power is spread out among the various computers attached to the network

---

past the limit when the stock market crashed in 1987. Fidelity, like every investment firm, was flooded with calls from customers who wanted to sell. Disconcerted by their inability to handle the calling volume, Fidelity redesigned its information systems to boost capacity. A combination of hardware, software, well-organized data, motivated people, and efficient procedures ensures that Fidelity will never be caught short again.

Fidelity's first step was to replace its limited-capacity phone system. Handling 672 callers simultaneously on its toll-free lines, the upgraded system allows Fidelity operators to leave customers on hold no more than 15 seconds. A master console in Boston routes calls throughout the country to the first available operator. The system typically handles 120,000 calls a day. Realizing that its 1,000 operators are personally responsible for much of the information transmitted to customers, Fidelity gives them an extensive amount of training in the company's product lines. The college-educated operators spend

60 hours in initial study and attend more training sessions when new products are introduced.

The next step was to develop a computer-based information system to give operators immediate access to customer account information. The computer workstations access six separate mainframe computers to display customer account information on one screen. Says Fidelity's John Cook, "Fidelity has spent more on developing systems in the last five years than anyone else—and probably more on enhancing systems than most firms spend to develop them."

Fidelity is aware of its dependence on computers and manages its vulnerability carefully. It has five backup generators to keep its systems running during any electrical blackout, and its own system protects Fidelity from problems with local telephone service. By carefully maintaining its existing information systems and constantly looking for ways to apply new technologies, Fidelity plans to keep its customers satisfied and its competitors on the run.

Distributed processing spreads the computing power around the system, giving users enough power to accomplish many of their tasks but still giving them access to other computers.

manage their own affairs, and the central organization exists mainly to support the more or less independent teams.

Computer networks can dramatically change the way a company operates. Mrs. Fields Cookies uses its network to feed data back and forth between corporate headquarters and each store. Aside from required government forms, the system has virtually eliminated paperwork. In addition, Debbi and Randy Fields encourage their employees to use the electronic mail system made possible by the network to send complaints and suggestions directly to top management. Using the network for transmission of business data and electronic mail has significantly reduced the number of employees needed at headquarters, kept the layers of management in the organization to a minimum, and allowed top management to react immediately to problems and new ideas.[32]

Electronic data interchange (EDI) is another important change made possible by computer networks. EDI allows the computers in one business to communicate directly with computers in other businesses, accomplishing such tasks as placing orders and tracking shipments.[33] Because the computers transmit data directly to other computers, without much human interaction, EDI cuts down on processing costs and decreases transaction times. For instance, the textile company Milliken buys fibers from suppliers such as Du Pont and then weaves the fabric for delivery to customers such as Levi Strauss. By using EDI to transmit orders, shipment dates, and inventory data, Milliken has linked its 55 plants and warehouses with its suppliers and customers, reducing its order turnaround time from 6 weeks to 1 week.[34]

▶ COMPUTERS AND SOCIETY

Computers are machines, and most machines can be used either well or poorly. Just as automobiles are both convenient and dangerous, computers can be both a help and a hindrance. Thanks to computers, a retired couple may receive Social Security checks rapidly, but they may also get 50 pieces of computer-generated direct mail that they don't want. A computer can enable a criminal to break into a bank and steal thousands of dollars while safely sitting at a terminal miles away. Also, an amazing amount of information will become part of your permanent file, and you can only hope it will be entered correctly: Mistakes such as typos and transposed numbers are far easier to make than to find and fix.

One of computerization's most dangerous drawbacks is the unethical use of data processing and databases, which may lead to invasion of privacy. Never before have so many organizations known so much about so many individuals. Nothing is inherently wrong with this; your credit card company has a right to know what you've charged and whether you're late in paying your bills. (You gave them that right when you accepted the card.)

However, two questions are cause for concern: (1) Do organizations know more about you than they need to? (2) Are they telling anyone else? If you apply for a loan, it makes sense for creditors to check your bank balance or credit history. But what if, like some organizations, they also interview your neighbors in an attempt to determine your character? Is it relevant to your financial affairs that you once threw a party that kept your next-door neighbor awake or that you have frequent domestic disputes? Once the information is in place, relevant or not, a great many people will be able to read it, from the bored worker or prankster who reads people's files at lunchtime to the companies that sell their databases to, or share them with, other institutions—companies that you may never have heard of or that have no legitimate right to know everything about you.

Even firms that don't share their databases are subject to lack of data security. Besides everything else, companies with sensitive information stored in a computer worry about competitors raiding the database simply by dialing in through a modem. Several well-publicized incidents of teenage "hackers" breaking into bank, hospital, and government computer systems have dramatized the danger. Computer "viruses," programs that can work their way into computer systems and erase or corrupt data and programs, present another critical security challenge. The problem is that security often conflicts with convenient, decentralized computer use. Safer systems are possible, but a Pentagon-style system with passwords that change daily and special keys for hardware and peripheral devices would bring business to a stop—an ironic turn for a technology that became popular because of the increased convenience and access it offered.

SUMMARY OF LEARNING OBJECTIVES

1 Distinguish between data and information and explain the characteristics of useful information.

Data are recorded statistics, facts, predictions, and opinions; information is created when data are arranged in such a manner as to be meaningful in a particular problem or situation. In order to be useful, information needs to be accurate, timely, relevant, complete, and concise.

2 List the five generations of computer hardware.

The first generation included the ENIAC and UNIVAC; among other problems, these machines were huge, electrically unreliable, and difficult to program. Second-generation machines addressed the programming difficulty problem, partially solving it with assembly languages, and they reduced size and increased reliability by switching from vacuum tubes to transistors. Third-generation machines introduced integrated circuits and high-level languages. The fourth generation introduced microprocessors, and fifth-generation machines focus on supercomputer-level performance.

3 Describe the five classes of computers.

Microcomputers, such as the Apple Macintosh and the IBM PS/2 and PC, are the smallest and cheapest computers. Workstations are a step up in price and performance; similar in size and shape to microcomputers, they approach or equal the performance of minicomputers. Minicomputers are a price and performance compromise

between the lower-end micros and workstations and the higher-end mainframes; they aren't as powerful as mainframes, but they don't cost as much either. Mainframes represent the traditional notion of big computers, and they are the largest and most powerful, with the exception of supercomputers. This final class contains the fastest and most expensive computers available today.

4 Identify the major elements of a computer system.

Hardware and software are the two major aspects of a computer. Hardware includes input devices (such as keyboards), central processing units, output devices (such as printers), and primary and secondary storage. Software is divided into operating systems, application software, and computer languages.

5 Name the main categories of application software.

The categories mentioned in the chapter are accounting/finance, spreadsheets, word processing, publishing, business graphics, communications, drafting and CAD, production and process control, project management, database management, industry-specific solutions, and integrated software packages.

6 Describe the four generations of computer languages.

Unlike computer hardware, each new generation of languages did not replace the previous generation. Instead, new generations made programming easier. The four generations

start with machine language, which consists of the 1's and 0's that actually drive the hardware; assembly language, the next level up, which consists of simple instructions that can be read by humans; high-level languages that do more with fewer commands than assembly language and that are much easier for humans to read and write; and fourth-generation languages that attempt to let users communicate in their natural languages as much as possible.

7 Explain the purpose of computer networks.

Networks provide computer users with two important benefits: (1) the ability to share data, programs, messages, and so on; and (2) common access to centralized resources such as databases, printers, mainframes, and supercomputers. Computer networks can dramatically change the way a company operates by reducing paperwork and administrative tasks, allowing employees to communicate electronically, and allowing managers to keep in closer contact with their organizations.

8 Discuss the social and business concerns about extensive computerization.

Many people are concerned that businesses may know too much about consumers and may share their data and information illegitimately; for businesses, maintaining computer security (including guarding against hackers and viruses) poses an important problem.

Meeting a Business Challenge at American Express

James D. Robinson III is a manager who doesn't shrink from innovation—indeed, he encourages it. So when confronted with an avalanche of paper charge receipts threatening to bury his company's efficiency and growth, he chose to have a management information system designed that would copy, store, analyze, sort, and mail the millions of receipts the company received every day. He wanted a system that would reduce costs, increase productivity, enhance customer service, and give American Express a competitive edge by using the information derived from the data contained on those receipts. He got what he wanted—six years and $80 million later.

Today more than 3 million charge receipts are received every day at American Express, and they are sent through a unique transaction processing system that converts paper into digitized images stored on optical disks. All of those pieces of paper are shredded and buried in secret locations (for security), so American Express processes images of receipts. Computers index and sort the images according to billing cycle and zip code, collate the images with their appropriate billing statements, print more readable and useful copies of the images on perforated paper, and insert those sheets of paper along with billing statements into envelopes, which are then presorted for mailing. All of this is done so quickly that 100,000 pages of billing statements are printed in only one hour at two processing sites in the United States. Customer queries can be processed within minutes now that the images are stored on optical disks.

Nearly 400 people were once employed only to process, correct, and retrieve the millions of paper receipts received each day, but they have been replaced by the transaction processing system, which is operated by three people who are able to do more work in less time and with greater accuracy. Billing costs have

James D. Robinson III, CEO of American Express.

been reduced by 25 percent, with nearly half of that saving coming from a reduction in the cash American Express needs to have available to pay merchants for charged purchases.

The system has enabled the company to gain a competitive advantage in two ways. First, of the three major card companies, American Express is the only one that still returns copies of receipts to its customers for recordkeeping—a service that is especially useful for businesspeople. Second, Robinson now knows his customers very well because the purchasing data on each receipt are transformed into useful information. Each cardholder is categorized and profiled according to 450 attributes derived from his or her purchasing patterns, age, sex, and other data. These continually updated portraits are augmented with surveys that are targeted to that cardholder's income and lifestyle.

All these data, and the information that can be derived from them, have allowed American Express to enter a booming business: direct-mail merchandising, its fastest-growing subsidiary. This information has also prevented the company from providing costly services to the wrong cardholders; for example, only holders of platinum cards are greeted at airports with limousine service. The information is also used to find new subscribers to magazines owned by the

company's publishing subsidiary—periodicals that, again, are appropriate to each cardholder's lifestyle.

What began with a transaction processing system has been utilized to help Robinson make better strategic decisions. He has a wealth of information useful in making decisions about new products, new services, new markets, and new ways to further innovate for a competitive advantage.

Your Mission: American Express is considered an industry leader in its use of technology, as evidenced by its unique transaction processing system. You are the CIO, responsible for considering tactical and strategic issues to ensure the best use of information throughout American Express subsidiaries, which include Shearson Lehman (the second largest securities company on Wall Street), IDS Financial Services (a financial-planning firm), and Travel Related Services (American Express's best-known business, which includes the green, gold, and platinum cards).

1. You know that organizing the right data is crucial to providing useful information to decision makers in the company. Assume that each of the following pieces of data is available to the people who make approval decisions for new customers for the classic green American Express card. In addition to providing the right data, you don't want to overload the decision makers with irrelevant or unnecessary data. Which of the following pieces of data would be most useful for the card-approval decision?

a. The applicant's past history with credit, specifically whether or not the applicant pays bills on time

b. The applicant's income, since people with more income are likely to use their cards more often, which increases American Express's revenue

c. The applicant's age, since older people are likely to make more money

d. The applicant's educational background, so that you can pick the people who've graduated from the best universities

2. Suppose that several dozen customers called to complain about the new system that delivers processed images of their receipts, not the actual receipts themselves. Your customer service staff tried to convince them the processed images contain the same data and information as the original, and in fact they offer even more. These customers are adamant, however; if they can't get the receipts back, they'll cancel their cards. What should you do?

a. Explain to the customers that American Express needs to use the new system in order to stay competitive.
b. Explain to the customers that the new system is better for them because it provides better records of their transaction, and keep trying to convince them of that fact.
c. For these customers only, circumvent the new system and provide them with their actual receipts.
d. You hate to lose customers, but your calculations show that circumventing the system for these few customers will cost you more than the revenue that these customers represent. Thank them graciously for their past use of American Express cards, and explain that you won't be able to cater to their particular needs, that you hope they'll reconsider, and that you understand if they want to go ahead and turn in their cards.

3. Like nearly all credit customers, American Express cardholders are concerned about database privacy. They worry that hackers will get access to their card numbers, and they fear that companies are building profiles of them that say more than they are comfortable revealing, such as what kind of videos they like to rent or which hotels they prefer to stay in. How could American Express best calm the fears of its customers?

a. The company should institute security measures to minimize the risk of people breaking into its databases, but it can't restrict access so much that employees are unable to access the data; in addition, the company should give customers control over how their personal data are used and by whom.
b. To be completely secure, the company should never use any of the data it collects, should never sell data to anyone, and should restrict access to a handful of top executives.
c. The problem is much larger than American Express; thousands of companies build databases, so American Express can do little to allay the fears of its customers.
d. Simply by using their cards, American Express customers forfeit their right to privacy, since there is no way to process a transaction without the customer's name being involved; if customers are worried about their privacy, they should use cash instead.

4. Since being bought by American Express, IDS Financial Services and Shearson Lehman have differing modes of operation and histories. IDS charges fees for financial services and sells relatively conservative financial products primarily to middle-income households. As a result, its revenues and profits do not fluctuate wildly with varying economic cycles, and its natural market has provided a solid growth potential for American Express. Shearson, on the other hand, charges transaction fees on the sale of stocks and bonds, as well as underwriting fees on large stock offerings. Its clients are major corporations, pension funds, and wealthier individuals whose investment decisions are greatly affected by market cycles. As a result, Shearson's revenues and profits can rise and fall rapidly, having a major impact on American Express's bottom line. What would be the best way to use the information available to American Express for IDS and Shearson?

a. Use it as client prospecting lists for both companies, regardless of cardholders' profiles.
b. Use it to match young couples and middle-class cardholders with IDS and to match businesspeople and wealthy cardholders with Shearson.
c. Add a financial magazine to the publications subsidiary and then build subscribers with current cardholders and clients of IDS and Shearson.
d. Use it as client prospecting lists for IDS only, to avoid subjecting cardholders to the high-pressure sales techniques of a stock brokerage and to introduce them to the fee-based relationship IDS representatives have with clients.[35]

KEY TERMS

application software (466)
artificial intelligence (457)
assembly language (470)
batch processing (460)
bit (464)
bulletin board systems (468)
byte (464)
central processing unit (463)
chief information officer (453)
computer languages (470)
data (452)
data communications (472)
database (452)

database management software (469)
decision support systems (456)
desktop publishing (468)
disk drive (465)
disk operating system (466)
distributed processing (473)
electronic mail (468)
executive information systems (456)
expert system (457)
fourth-generation languages (471)
hardware (462)
high-level languages (470)
information (452)

integrated circuits (459)
local area network (472)
machine language (470)
mainframe computers (461)
management information systems (456)
microcomputer (460)
microprocessors (459)
minicomputers (461)
modem (472)
natural-language processor (457)
network (472)
office automation systems (455)

open systems (466)
operating systems (466)
parallel processing (460)
primary storage devices (465)
programming (458)
programs (462)

proprietary operating systems (466)
random access memory (465)
read only memory (465)
real-time processing (460)
secondary storage (465)
software (462)

spreadsheet (467)
supercomputers (462)
transaction processing system (455)
UNIX (466)
workgroup computing (472)
workstation (461)

REVIEW QUESTIONS

1. Would employee records be considered data or information? Explain your answer.

2. How do transaction processing systems, management information systems, and executive information systems differ?

3. How has artificial intelligence been applied to business?

4. What does real-time processing mean, and when is it important?

5. How do workstations differ from microcomputers and minicomputers?

6. What are the functions of a central processing unit?

7. How do the purposes of primary and secondary storage differ?

8. Why are operating systems necessary?

A CASE FOR CRITICAL THINKING

High-Tech Time Bomb: The Spread of Computer "Viruses"—And Their Prevention

A competitor's raid on a database is only one security problem faced by information managers. Another potential nightmare is a wipeout of their data due to some unforeseen natural disaster such as an earthquake or flood. But losses from this kind of catastrophe stand to be overshadowed by damage from computer "viruses." Viruses are small fragments of software that make copies of themselves and spread those copies from computer to computer. Some viruses carry program instructions that can destroy data, damage computer hardware, or monopolize computer communications lines.

According to Philip McKinney of Thumb Scan, a computer security firm in Illinois, the first viruses were devised in the 1970s by software companies trying to protect their profits. Like most published books, most commercial software is copyrighted. The copyright holder has the right to sell the software or give it away free. The first viruses were used to track the spread of programs being copied illegally in violation of copyright. The viruses never showed their presence. They just kept track of what computer systems they had passed through. Software authors who knew

how to read them hoped that the virus programs could be used to trace the routes of the piracy.

Today viruses are often created by pranksters or vandals. Some amateur programmers ("hackers") enjoy introducing viruses just to show how vulnerable computer systems are. Disgruntled employees or former employees, competitors, and creditors could also introduce viruses. Some viruses are designed to act as "time bombs," sitting quietly until a specified time and then activating themselves and wreaking havoc.

The wide-open exchange of data and ideas promised by the information age is threatened by viruses. Because so many computers are interconnected, viruses can spread quickly. They can infect all the computers linked on a local area network and then spread over telephone lines to other computers linked in national and even international networks. One virus infected 350,000 computers in the United States and Europe.

Even viruses created accidentally or with no intent of harm can interfere with business by tying up computers and operators. Some viruses use a computer's CPU to copy themselves without restraint. The normal

information-processing operations of a business slow as more and more of the computer's processing capacity and memory are used by the renegade programs. Operators must spend time removing viruses, checking to see whether programs or data have been destroyed, and rechecking to make sure that no new infections have taken hold.

One unintentional infection was caused by a Christmas message naively sent over a local network by a German student. The message automatically forwarded itself to everyone on each recipient's regular outgoing electronic mail list. The message swamped the local network and eventually moved through interconnecting links to IBM's international network, attaching itself to every mailing list it contacted.

Besides originating in business networks, viruses sometimes spread through the electronic bulletin boards that allow computer users to share public-domain (noncopyrighted) programs. To protect users of his Manhattan-based electronic bulletin board, Ross Greenberg carefully screens for computer viruses before he posts any new programs. Besides contaminating their own microcomputers at home, users who download a virus along with useful public-domain programs might carry them into the office on disk. Such a virus could quickly infect a corporate network.

Just as with biological diseases, experts are scrambling to devise preventives for computer viruses. Greenberg uses these "vaccines" to spot invading viruses and to render them harmless. In an attempt to protect computer systems, vaccines are used by all kinds of businesses from home-based sole proprietorships to IBM and the Internal Revenue Service.

Although some experts downplay the danger of viruses, others consider them a serious threat. Suppose that a vandal learned how to confuse the computers that manufacturers use to set specifications or those of a country's military, banking system, or air traffic control. Michael Peckman, systems analyst at George Washington University, recommends a combination of computer security tools and safeguard practices that can limit the risk of virus infection. For example, using a write-protect tab on program disks prevents the addition of anything, including viruses, to a disk while it's being used in a disk drive. Regularly backing up (copying) data and programs to disks or tapes that are safely stored at a distance provides a fallback if some virus causes destruction within the computer system.

Requiring users to enter a password limits access to the computer system by unauthorized personnel. An audit system allows a computer-system manager to track who accessed data, when it was accessed, and what kinds of things were done to it. Policies that limit and control the movement of data, programs, and hardware among microcomputers within an organization can help control the spread of viruses. Restricting the use of public-domain software, bulletin boards, and on-line services can also reduce the risk of infection. Finally, using a vaccine program regularly can help detect viruses that have slipped through other lines of defense.[36]

1. Like the viruses that cause biological diseases, computer viruses come in many varieties with many "disease" strategies. They can be designed to seek out various sites in the computer. What are some of the problems inherent in "vaccinating" computer systems against viruses?

2. What sorts of business information stored in computers would be most painful to lose?

3. Why do you think a bank might go under after a computer disaster? If you were a bank president, how would you plan for such a disaster?

4. Some computer experts say that media coverage of computer viruses should be toned down or stopped because it only encourages publicity-seeking hackers to generate more viruses. What are some advantages and disadvantages of press reports about viruses?

BUILDING YOUR COMMUNICATION SKILLS

Select a local business that uses computers in its management operations, and examine how those operations are affected by technology. Contact a member of the management team, and ask about the applications of computers in that business. If this is not possible, locate an article in a periodical that describes the implementation of computer technology in a particular business.

► Consider any changes or improvements in the efficiency of information processing that were made possible by computer technology, including management information systems, data processing, and desktop publishing. Have jobs been enhanced or eliminated by computers?

► Prepare a written or oral summary of your investigation, as directed by your instructor. Compare the applications of computer technology in the business you examined with those in businesses examined by other students.

KEEPING CURRENT USING *THE WALL STREET JOURNAL*

Scan recent issues of *The Wall Street Journal* for an article showing how computers or other office technology advances have helped a company improve its competitive advantage or its profitability.

1. What advantage did technology give the company? Are other companies in the same industry using the same technology as effectively?

If the information is available, comment on why or why not.

2. Did the article mention any problems the company had implementing its new technology? What were they? Do you think the problems could have been avoided? How?

3. How do you think employees feel about this technology? How would you feel if your job required you to use it?

CHAPTER 17

LEARNING OBJECTIVES

After studying this chapter, you will be able to

1 Describe the importance of accounting to managers, investors, creditors, and government.

2 Distinguish between public and private accountants.

3 State the basic accounting equation.

4 Explain the purpose of the balance sheet and identify its three main sections.

5 Explain the purpose of an income statement and identify its three main components.

6 Explain the purpose of the statement of cash flows.

7 Identify five areas in which accountants may exercise considerable discretion in their methods and assumptions.

8 List the four main categories of financial ratios.

Accounting

COMPANY ACCOUNTANTS—FRIENDS OR FOES?

W hen people get together to make business decisions about their company, their products, and their costs, they need information they can trust and rely on. But at Roseville Networks Division (RND) of Hewlett-Packard, such meetings often ended in heated arguments and emotional discord. During decision-making sessions, representatives from marketing, manufacturing, product design, and accounting could not agree on the right way to find a product's "real" cost. Each department would come up with a different cost, would defend the method used to determine that cost, and would argue about which number was right.

Hewlett-Packard's RND produces about 250 products, mostly printed-circuit assemblies and mechanical devices used with central processing units (the brains of computers). Debbie Berlant is cost accounting supervisor, and she recalls that people began to resent the accounting department, because no matter how individual departments calculated costs, the "official" accounting department numbers were invariably the numbers used for the company's internal cost accounting. Production people were especially sensitive, looking at accountants as opponents, not as team members. Moreover, it seemed that many of the measurements required by accounting were wasteful.

Every time an assembly worker inserted a part on a circuit board manually, the amount of time spent on the task had to be recorded. Technicians had to keep track of the time they spent on each test, and they had to charge that time to a particular work order. Manufacturing (and other departments such as product design) tracked a lot of information just for accounting and then used different data to estimate production costs for themselves. Clearly, the figures from accounting were not providing the various departments with the figures they needed.

Procurement people complained that accounting's estimated cost of purchasing and handling inexpensive parts was not realistic. Product designers complained that because of accounting, they were being forced to design products that could be assembled without direct labor, even when manufacturing those products would be more difficult without it. Production people complained that direct labor hours did not reflect the number of manufacturing resources actually consumed by a product. And marketing accused accounting of systematically overestimating the costs of commodity-type products.

What was wrong? RND's traditional system for internal cost accounting had been working for years. The accounting department still had to make sure that cost data met the provisions laid out by generally accepted accounting principles. And as Berlant points out, accounting still had to "set standard costs, track actuals against standards, verify and value inventory, and determine our sales discounts and cost of sales."

If you were the cost accounting supervisor at RND, what could you suggest to bring the various departments to agreement? Is accounting so inflexible and narrowly defined that it cannot adapt to the information needs of other departments? Should the people from product design, manufacturing, and marketing be more reasonable and simply accept the guidelines and information from accounting? How does accounting actually affect the business decisions that must be made by companies?[1]

▶ THE NATURE OF ACCOUNTING

accounting Process of recording, classifying, and summarizing the financial activities of an organization

Accounting is the system a business uses to measure its financial performance by recording and classifying sales, purchases, and other transactions. Accounting also summarizes this information in statements that make it possible to evaluate a company's past performance, present condition, and future prospects. Exhibit 17.1 presents the process for putting all of a company's financial data into standardized formats that can be used for analysis and planning.

Functional Areas of Accounting

Accounting is important to business for two reasons. First, it helps managers plan and control a company's operations, as it did at Hewlett-Packard's RND. Second, it helps outsiders evaluate the business. Because these two audiences use accounting information in different ways, accounting has two distinct facets. **Financial accounting** is concerned with preparing information for the outside world; **management accounting** is concerned with preparing information for internal use.

financial accounting Area of accounting concerned with preparing financial information for users outside the organization

management accounting Area of accounting concerned with preparing data for use by managers within the organization

Financial Accounting

The outsiders who use accounting information have a variety of interests. Suppliers, banks, and other lenders want to know whether the business is creditworthy; investors and shareholders are concerned with the company's profit potential; government agencies are mainly interested in regulating the business and collecting taxes. These users need information that is objective, consistent over time, and comparable to information supplied by other companies. Thus, financial accounting statements adhere to certain standard formats and are pre-

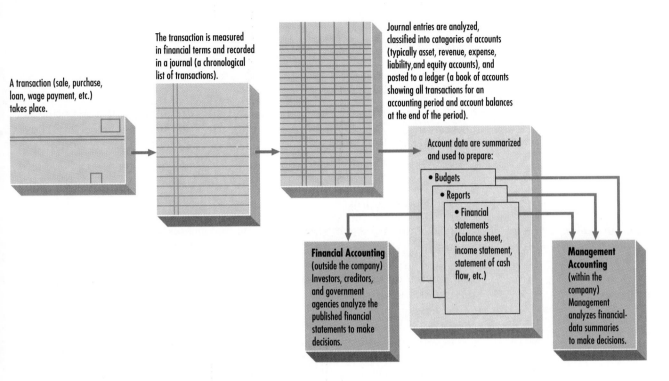

A transaction (sale, purchase, loan, wage payment, etc.) takes place.

The transaction is measured in financial terms and recorded in a journal (a chronological list of transactions).

Journal entries are analyzed, classified into catagories of accounts (typically asset, revenue, expense, liability, and equity accounts), and posted to a ledger (a book of accounts showing all transactions for an accounting period and account balances at the end of the period).

Account data are summarized and used to prepare:
• Budgets
• Reports
• Financial statements (balance sheet, income statement, statement of cash flow, etc.)

Financial Accounting (outside the company) Investors, creditors, and government agencies analyze the published financial statements to make decisions.

Management Accounting (within the company) Management analyzes financial-data summaries to make decisions.

pared according to **generally accepted accounting principles** (GAAP) that have been established and agreed on by the accounting profession over many years.

Management Accounting

Management accounting, in contrast, is tailored to the needs of managers in a particular company. Its overall purpose is to help the managers evaluate results and make informed decisions. In a typical company such as Hewlett-Packard's RND, the management-accounting system covers a wide range of financial activities, from recording sales and sending out invoices to helping top management evaluate expenditures on buildings, equipment, and labor.

The employees of a typical firm's accounting department perform many functions. One of their biggest jobs is financial planning, which involves forecasting sales, costs, expenses, and profits. These forecasts enable management to spot problems and opportunities and to allocate resources intelligently. Part of the process includes developing a **budget,** a financial blueprint for a given period (often one year) that structures financial plans in a framework of estimated revenues, expenses, and cash flows. Because working out a budget forces a company to determine how much money will be coming in and how much will be going out, budgeting simultaneously becomes a controlling as well as a planning operation. The master (or operating) budget—the overall estimate of revenues, costs, expenses, and cash flow—is based on several component budgets, including the sales budget and the production budget.

In addition to preparing a budget, company accountants are involved in analyzing production costs so that management will know what the company spends to produce a given product; for example, Debbie Berlant was on the team that developed a new cost accounting system at Hewlett-Packard's RND. Man-

EXHIBIT 17.1

The Accounting Process
The traditional printed accounting forms are shown here. Today, most medium-sized and large firms use the computer equivalents of these forms.

generally accepted accounting principles Professionally approved standards used by the accounting profession in preparing financial statements

budget Financial plan for company's future activities that estimates revenues and proposed expenditures and that forecasts how expenditures will be financed

agement uses this information to control expenses and to make pricing and product decisions.

Types of Accountants

The distinction between financial accounting and management accounting is reflected in the professional orientation of the accountants themselves. They may be divided into two groups: public accountants and private, or corporate, accountants (see Exhibit 17.2).

Public Accountants

public accountants Independent outsiders who provide accounting services for businesses and other organizations

audit Accountant's evaluation of the fairness and reliability of a client's financial statements

Public accountants are independent of the businesses, organizations, and individuals they serve. They are retained to prepare financial statements, prepare taxes, and provide consultation for individuals and organizations. For larger companies they are also retained to prepare reports on the fairness of those statements. Sometimes such a report is based on an **audit,** a formal evaluation of the fairness and reliability of financial statements. The report accompanies the client's published financial statements and indicates (1) whether the statements have been prepared in accordance with GAAP and (2) whether it's necessary to include any disclosures about uncertainties that would materially affect the client's financial position.

Public accountants' detached position obligates them to be objective and, when necessary, critical. Thus they are of value to anyone who must have an unbiased picture of the financial standing of a particular business, such as creditors, shareholders, investors, and even government agencies.

EXHIBIT 17.2 ▶ **Public Versus Private Accounting**

Accountants who sell their services to a variety of individuals and businesses have responsibilities that are different from those of accountants who are employed privately.

PUBLIC ACCOUNTANTS' RESPONSIBILITIES	PRIVATE ACCOUNTANTS' RESPONSIBILITIES
Auditing: Provide independent analysis of financial statements, which is used in reports to shareholders, investors, and purchasers of businesses	General Accounting: Record all business transactions and prepare reports and financial statements
Management Consulting: Provide objective evaluations of decisions in such areas as finance, marketing, and manufacturing for large and small businesses; offer advice on meeting special requirements for accounting, taxes, and reporting in other countries	Management Accounting: Use reported data to help managers plan operations, price new products, select alternative methods of financing, and make other decisions
	Internal Auditing: Check the accuracy of company records and accounting methods; police errors and possible employee larceny
Tax Accounting: Provide tax planning, tax preparation, and representation in case of tax audit	Cost Accounting: Provide information to help management control the cost of manufactured products and their distribution; help management estimate future costs
	Installing Accounting Systems: Design systems for recording and reporting financial data and for cross-checking record keeping

Public accountants become **certified public accountants** (CPAs) by meeting a state's requirements for education and experience and by passing an examination prepared by the American Institute of Certified Public Accountants. In 1991 the total number of CPAs in the United States was 370,000. Some analysts estimate that every year another 33,000 people complete and pass all parts of the CPA examination.[2]

Some 44 percent of the CPAs in the United States are in private practice, working in accounting firms that range in size from one-person shops to large partnerships employing hundreds of CPAs. The profession is dominated by a small number of firms that together audit more than 95 percent of the Fortune 500 companies and take in a good portion of the profession's annual revenues.[3]

The trend in the past few years has been toward mergers among the largest companies. Accounting firms merge to cut costs through lower overhead, to increase revenues by eliminating a competitor, and to try to become number one. Moreover, firms are encouraged by the success of huge KPMG Peat Marwick, whose revenues have increased 44 percent to $3.9 billion since the 1986 merger of Peat Marwick International with Klynveld Main Goerdeler. Through such mergers, the accounting firms known in 1990 as the "Big Eight" reduced their number to six by 1991. Ernst & Whinney merged with Arthur Young & Company, and Deloitte Haskins & Sells merged with Touche Ross & Company.

The six firms currently at the top are Arthur Andersen and Company, Coopers & Lybrand, Deloitte & Touche, Ernst and Young, KPMG Peat Marwick, and Price Waterhouse & Company. These new megafirms are able to reach global customers, offer broader services, and provide both auditing and consultation in one convenient location. However, competition for clients is increasing, and these megafirms are making it more difficult for smaller firms to compete. In addition, critics are concerned that higher prices will be passed along to consumers, that clients will have more difficulty switching auditors, and that more competitors will share the same accountant.[4]

Some of the "Big Six" have been in the news recently in connection with business failures. Coopers & Lybrand was recently sanctioned by the Office of Thrift Supervision for charges relating to the failure of Denver-based Silverado Banking, Savings & Loan Association. The Federal Deposit Insurance Corporation (FDIC) is seeking damages of $560 million from Ernst and Young for the failure of Texas-based Western Savings Association. The FDIC also filed other claims against Ernst and Young for an additional $281 million, against KPMG Peat Marwick for $76 million, and against Deloitte & Touche for $892 million. This litigation against public accounting firms has focused attention on the accounting profession's responsibility for identifying client fraud during their audits.[5]

As a member of the subcommittee on oversight and investigations of the House Energy and Commerce Committee, Congressman Ron Wyden has attended hearings since 1985 on whether accountants are protecting the public against financial fraud. Wyden is pushing for legislation that would force auditors to report fraud to regulators. Accountants, on the other hand, maintain that such a role would cause their clients to mistrust them, possibly resulting in client suits for libel, negligence, or misrepresentation. Thus, the accounting profession favors voluntary internal controls, and it recently proposed guidelines to help businesses prevent management fraud. But critics such as Wyden believe the guidelines fall far short of what is needed, and Wyden is promising legislation that will mandate reporting by auditors.[6]

certified public accountants
Professionally licensed accountants who meet certain requirements for education and experience, and who pass an examination

Private accountants are responsible for all aspects of a firm's financial planning and record keeping. Here, members of the Checkers, Simon & Rosner accounting firm review figures during a breakfast meeting.

private accountants In-house accountants employed by organizations and businesses

certified management accountants Accountants who have fulfilled the requirements for certification as specialists in management accounting

bookkeeping Record keeping, clerical phase of accounting

controller Highest-ranking accountant in a firm, responsible for overseeing all accounting functions

These developments, along with increased competition resulting from the shrinking pool of clients as more and more companies merge, have prompted many large accounting firms to diversify into other areas. As consultants, accountants are designing computer systems for businesses, giving financial advice, and setting up personnel plans. These activities, often referred to as *management advisory services* (MAS), have been especially valuable for small and midsized businesses. For example, the accounting firm of Friedman & Fuller in Rockville, Maryland, offers its clients services in three subsidiary areas: profit improvement, risk management, and systems training. As a logical outgrowth of MAS, accountants are also expanding their services to include *personal financial planning* (PFP). In fact, they were already performing a number of these services when involved in income tax planning, estate tax planning, retirement planning, and profit sharing.[7] Congressman Wyden and others are concerned that as accountants become more involved in their clients' businesses, they may lose some of the objectivity they need as independent auditors.

Private Accountants

Private accountants, sometimes called corporate accountants, are those employed by a business (like Debbie Berlant of Hewlett-Packard's RND), a government agency, or a nonprofit corporation to supervise the accounting system and the bookkeeping staff. They are also responsible for generating and interpreting financial reports. Many private accountants are CPAs; however, a growing number are **certified management accountants** (CMAs), a relatively new designation that indicates they have passed a test comparable in difficulty to the CPA exam.

The work of an in-house accounting staff is varied, ranging from routine **bookkeeping,** the clerical function of recording transactions, to high-level decision making. The highest-ranking private accountants typically have the title of **controller** or financial vice president. They oversee virtually every aspect of a company's financial operations and usually report directly to the president. The controller of a medium or large corporation monitors and cross-checks all financial data, usually with the help of a computer, in order to evaluate the company's financial health at any given point. The controller also supervises the preparation of financial analyses, budgets, forecasts, internal audits, and tax returns.

The Reliability of Accounting Information

Accounting is not an exact science. Using the same financial data, honest accountants may legitimately develop a wide range of results, depending on the assumptions they make and the way they interpret the accounting rules. For example, many companies keep two sets of financial records—one for external reporting purposes and one for income-tax–assessment purposes. Accountants present shareholders with a fair picture of the company's financial position and the results of operations. However, for the tax collector, accountants use all the legal options the tax code allows to minimize the income subject to taxes.

The "creativity" an accountant can exercise is limited by generally accepted accounting principles. Although these principles are not legally binding on non-public companies, most accountants adhere to their provisions for all financial statements and report any deviations from GAAP in published financial statements. Moreover, financial statements that do not conform to current GAAP are not acceptable to the Securities and Exchange Commission in the filings required for issuing and trading stock. Nevertheless, it is important to realize that to a considerable extent, accounting numbers represent human judgment.

▶ KEY ACCOUNTING CONCEPTS

In all their work with financial data, accountants are guided by two fundamental concepts: the accounting equation and double-entry bookkeeping. Both were developed centuries ago but remain central to the accounting process.

The Accounting Equation

For thousands of years, businesses and governments have kept records of their **assets**—valuable things they own, like gold and wheat—and their **liabilities**—what they owe to others. When it was said of ancient princes that they were "as rich as Croesus" (a wealthy king of Lydia), it was not just because they had stored away much gold and grain. It was because they owned these treasures almost outright and had few debts or creditors' claims on their assets. In other words, wealth does not consist of assets alone; it is what remains after liabilities have been deducted from assets. That remainder is called **owners' equity**:

Assets	*$100,000*
Liabilities	*−30,000*
Owners' Equity	*$ 70,000*

This simple observation is the basis for the all-important **accounting equation**:

$$Assets\ =\ Liabilities + Owners'\ Equity$$
$$\$100,000 =\ \$30,000\ +\ \ \ \ \$70,000$$

The company's liabilities are placed before owners' equity in the accounting equation because creditors have first claim on assets. After liabilities are paid, anything left over belongs to the owners or, in the case of a corporation, to the shareholders. However, to emphasize the amount of owners' equity, the accounting equation may be written as

$$Assets\ -\ Liabilities = Owners'\ Equity$$
$$\$100,000 -\ \ \$30,000\ \ =\ \ \ \ \$70,000$$

Whichever form is used, the relationship of assets, liabilities, and owners' equity remains in balance; in other words, one side of the equation always equals the other side.

Double-Entry Bookkeeping

To keep the accounting equation in balance, companies use a double-entry system that records every transaction affecting assets, liabilities, or owners' equity. This system dates back to 1494 and an Italian monk, Fra Luca Pacioli, who immediately caught the attention of the merchants and princes of his day. Fra Luca explained that every transaction—a sale, a payment, a collection—had

Business Around the World

General Electric bought a 50 percent stake in Tungsram, the Hungarian light-bulb maker, only to realize it was doing business in the dark. Hungary's lack of proper accounting systems makes it impossible for Western companies (or anyone else) to track costs, assets, or profits.

assets Physical objects and intangible rights that have economic value to the owner

liabilities Debts or obligations a company or government owes to other individuals or organizations

owners' equity Portion of a company's assets that belongs to the owners after obligations to all creditors have been met

accounting equation Assets equal liabilities plus owners' equity

double-entry bookkeeping
Way of recording financial transactions that requires two entries for every transaction so that the accounting equation is always kept in balance

two offsetting sides. No matter what kinds of transactions are made, the accounting equation remains in balance if the transactions are properly recorded. **Double-entry bookkeeping** requires a two-part, "give-and-get" entry for every transaction.

Say that you decide to open a videocassette rental shop. You need to stock 1,000 cassettes, costing you $30 each, or a total of $30,000 in capital. If you have $20,000 of your own to invest, your accounting equation would show

$$Assets \quad = Liabilities + Owners' \ Equity$$
$$\$20,000 \ (cash) = \quad 0 \quad + \quad \$20,000$$

In other words, $20,000 in cash is equal to your owners' equity of $20,000. As yet, your business has no liabilities.

Next, say that you do three things:

1. You borrow from the bank the additional $10,000 you need. That $10,000 is added both to your cash account under "assets" and to your bank-loan account under "liabilities." Thus, your accounting equation is kept in balance.

retained earnings Net increase in assets (cash and outstanding receivables) for an accounting period; part of owners' equity

2. You go videocassette shopping and spend $30,000 on the inventory you need. Your assets are thus converted from cash into videocassettes, $10,000 worth of which your creditor, the bank, has a claim on. The other $20,000 worth of cassettes represents owners' equity. The right side of the accounting equation is not affected by the conversion of assets from one form (cash) into another (cassettes).

3. In the first month, you rent each of the 1,000 cassettes once, charging $2 per rental, for a total revenue of $2,000. You find that it costs you $1,500 to run your store, including salaries, rent, and $400 in wear and tear on your cassettes. The $500 excess (rental revenues minus expenses), which is your profit, is plowed back into the business, becoming **retained earnings** and thus part of your owners' equity. Earnings retained by the firm consist of the increase in assets (cash and amounts due from others) for an accounting period.

These transactions might be recorded as shown in Exhibit 17.3. Note that the two sides of the accounting equation are—and must always be—equal.

EXHIBIT 17.3

An Example of Double-Entry Bookkeeping
In double-entry bookkeeping, the sum of the numbers on both sides of the equal sign must always be in balance. In this example, the equation in each row balances, as does the "bottom-line" equation.

| | ASSETS | | = LIABILITIES + | | OWNERS' EQUITY | |
TRANSACTION	CASH	INVENTORY (CASSETTES)	BANK LOAN	STOCK		PROFIT (RETAINED EARNINGS)
Investment	20,000	—	= —	+ 20,000		—
Loan	+ 10,000	—	= + 10,000	+ —		—
	30,000	—	= 10,000	+ 20,000		—
Inventory purchase	− 30,000	+ 30,000	= —	+ —		—
	—	30,000	= 10,000	+ 20,000		—
Rental revenue	+ 2,000	—	= —	+ —		+ 2,000
Expenses	− 1,100	− 400	= —	+ —		− 1,500
	900	29,600	= 10,000	+ 20,000		500

| 30,500 | | 30,500 |

▶ FINANCIAL STATEMENTS

After a few months, the transactions recorded by a bookkeeper will accumulate, making it difficult for management to sort out what is going on. To simplify the picture, accountants prepare financial statements that summarize the transactions. Three of the most important are the balance sheet, the income statement, and the statement of cash flows.

The Balance Sheet

A **balance sheet**, also known as a statement of financial position, is a kind of "snapshot" of where a company is, financially speaking, at one moment in time. It includes all the elements in the accounting equation, showing the balance between assets on the one hand and liabilities and owners' equity on the other. Exhibit 17.4 is a balance sheet for Sweet Dreams Ice Cream, a small corporation that makes ice cream and sells it through its own shop. Most detailed balance sheets classify assets, liabilities, and owners' equity into categories like those shown in Sweet Dreams's balance sheet.

balance sheet Financial statement that shows assets, liabilities, and owners' equity on a given date

But no business can stand still while its financial condition is being examined. A business may make hundreds of transactions of various kinds every working day. Even during a holiday, office fixtures grow older and decrease in value, and interest on savings accounts accumulates. Yet the accountant must set up a balance sheet so that managers and other interested parties can evaluate the business's financial position as if it were static.

Accordingly, every company prepares a balance sheet at least once a year, most often at the end of the **calendar year,** covering from January 1 to December 31. However, many business and government bodies use a **fiscal year,** which may be any 12 consecutive months. For example, a business may choose a fiscal year that runs from June 1 to May 31 because its peak selling season ends in May. Its fiscal year would then correspond to its full annual cycle of manufacturing and selling. Some companies prepare a balance sheet more often than once a year, perhaps at the end of each month or quarter. Thus, every balance sheet is dated to show when the financial "snapshot" was taken.

calendar year Twelve-month accounting period that begins on January 1 and ends on December 31

fiscal year Any 12 consecutive months used as an accounting period

Assets

Most often, the asset section of the balance sheet is divided into three types of assets—current, fixed, and intangible—listed in order of the ease with which the assets can be turned into cash. The balance sheet gives a subtotal for each type of asset and then a grand total for all assets.

CURRENT ASSETS   **Current assets,** which include cash and other items that will or can become cash within the following year, are always listed first.

current assets Cash and other items that can be turned back into cash within one year

▶ *Cash:* Funds on hand in checking and savings accounts. Not included are funds in special deposits or in any other form not readily available for use.

▶ *Marketable securities:* Stocks, bonds, and similar investments that can quickly be turned into cash when needed. Such investments are temporary and do not represent any sort of long-term control over the company that issued the securities.

EXHIBIT 17.4

A Sample Balance Sheet
The categories used on Sweet Dreams Ice Cream's year-end balance sheet are typical.

SWEET DREAMS ICE CREAM, INC.
Balance Sheet
December 31, 1993

ASSETS

Current Assets

Cash		$22,790	
Marketable securities		4,200	
Accounts receivable	$19,780		
Less: Allowance for uncollectable accounts	430	19,350	
Notes receivable		21,500	
Merchandise inventory		12,685	
Prepaid expenses		4,400	
TOTAL CURRENT ASSETS			$ 84,925

Fixed Assets

Factory equipment	$64,919		
Less: Accumulated depreciation	11,706	$53,213	
Leasehold improvements			
Less: Accumulated amortization	$77,030		
	14,308	$62,722	
TOTAL FIXED ASSETS			115,935

Intangible Assets

Organization costs		$ 420	
Trademark		6,405	
Goodwill		5,000	
TOTAL INTANGIBLE ASSETS			11,825
TOTAL ASSETS			$212,685

LIABILITIES AND SHAREHOLDERS' EQUITY

Current Liabilities

Accounts payable		$23,790	
Note payable (short-term)		15,115	
Salaries payable		7,452	
Taxes payable		6,318	
TOTAL CURRENT LIABILITIES			$52,675

Long-Term Liabilities

Long-term note payable @ 12%			53,750
TOTAL LIABILITIES			$106,425

Shareholders' Equity

Common stock, 10,000 shares		$43,000	
Retained earnings		63,260	
TOTAL SHAREHOLDERS' EQUITY			$106,260
TOTAL LIABILITIES AND SHAREHOLDERS' EQUITY			$212,685

▶ *Accounts receivable:* Amounts due from customers. Often accountants deduct from accounts receivable an allowance for bad debts (uncollectible accounts). This deduction notifies creditors and shareholders that some of the receivables may not be collectible.

▶ *Notes receivable:* Written and signed promises by customers to pay a definite sum, plus interest, usually on a certain date and at a certain place. They are generally collected routinely through customers' banks.

▶ *Inventories:* Usually merchandise on hand. Manufacturing companies may have inventories of raw materials, goods in process, and finished goods ready for sale.

▶ *Prepaid expenses:* Supplies on hand and services paid for but not yet used. An example is prepaid insurance, the unexpired portion of insurance purchased by a business. It is classified as a current asset because it can be turned into cash if canceled or because it will be used and thus reduce cash outlay in the next year.

FIXED ASSETS   Fixed assets—sometimes referred to as property, plant, and equipment—are long-term investments in buildings, equipment, furniture and fixtures, transportation equipment, land, and any other tangible property used in running the business. They have a useful life of more than one year and are not expected to be directly converted into cash.

A long-lived asset such as a machine or a truck slowly wears out or becomes obsolete and at some point will become useless. The accounting procedure for systematically spreading out the cost of such an asset over its estimated useful life is known as **depreciation** if the asset involved is a tangible asset such as a building or **amortization** if the asset involved is an intangible asset such as a patent. Depreciation (or amortization) allocates the cost of a long-lived asset to those accounting periods in which it is used to produce revenue. When the balance sheet is prepared, the accountant records the depreciation for the period. Of the various kinds of fixed assets, only land does not depreciate.

INTANGIBLE ASSETS   Intangible assets include the costs of organizing the business, obtaining patents on a process or invention, obtaining copyrights on written or reproducible material, and registering trademarks. Even though patents, copyrights, and trademarks are not physical assets like chairs or desks, they are valuable because they can be licensed or sold outright to others. For example, the song "Happy Birthday to You," one of the most popular songs in the English language, was sold in 1988 for $25 million.

Least tangible of all but no less valuable is **goodwill,** which consists mainly of a company's reputation, especially in its relations with customers. Goodwill is not entered as an asset unless the business has been purchased. In that case, the purchaser records goodwill as the difference between the cost of the purchased company as reflected in its financial statements and the price that the purchaser is willing to pay. This goodwill premium paid by the purchaser may range from a single token dollar to several million dollars.

Liabilities

The debts that a business has incurred represent claims against the assets, and they come next on the balance sheet. Liabilities may be current or long term, and they are listed in the order in which they will come due. The balance sheet gives subtotals for current and long-term liabilities and then a grand total for all liabilities.

CURRENT LIABILITIES   Obligations that will have to be met within a year of the date of the balance sheet are known as **current liabilities.**

▶ *Accounts payable:* Generally due in 30 days or less and thus frequently listed first. Such liabilities usually result from buying goods or services on credit.

▶ *Notes payable:* Written and signed promises to pay a certain sum plus interest at a definite time and place. Unlike notes receivable, these liabilities represent money owed rather than money coming in. Notes payable generally come due after a much longer time than accounts payable. Because notes usually require payment of interest as well as repayment of the principal, this item in the balance sheet represents both.

▶ *Accrued expenses:* Expenses that have been incurred but for which bills have not yet been received. Wages, interest, and taxes are examples of expenses that will be payable in the near future. If such expenses and their associated liabilities were not recorded, the

---

fixed assets Assets retained for long-term use, such as land, buildings, machinery, and equipment

depreciation Accounting procedure for systematically spreading the cost of a tangible asset over its estimated useful life

amortization Accounting procedure for systematically spreading the cost of an intangible asset over its estimated useful life

intangible assets Assets having no physical existence but having value because of the rights they confer on the owner

goodwill Value assigned to a business's reputation, calculated as the difference between the price paid for the business and the underlying value of its assets

current liabilities Obligations that must be met within a year

financial statements of the business would be misleading because some debts and costs of earning revenue would not be shown.

long-term liabilities Obligations that fall due more than a year from the date of the balance sheet

LONG-TERM LIABILITIES   Obligations that fall due a year or more after the date of the balance sheet are categorized as **long-term liabilities.** They are similar to owners' equity because they are claims on the business that may go unpaid for a long time (though interest on such debts must be paid when due). When a company goes out of business, the claims of long-term creditors are normally paid before those of the owners.

Other liabilities may fall into the long-term category, including many types of leases (agreements that enable their holders to use assets without legally owning them) and mortgages (agreements that pledge property owned by a business—such as land, buildings, or machines—to creditors as security).

Owners' Equity

The owners' investment in a business is listed on the balance sheet under owners' equity. Sole proprietorships list owner's equity under the owner's name with the amount (assets minus liabilities). Small partnerships list each partner's share of the business separately, and large partnerships list the total of all partners' shares. Owners' equity for a corporation (referred to as shareholders' equity, as in Exhibit 17.4) is presented in terms of the amount of common stock that is outstanding, meaning the amount that is in the hands of shareholders. The amount shown represents the investment that was paid into the corporation by the shareholders when the stock was issued. This is also the section that shows a corporation's retained earnings—the total earnings of all previous periods minus the amount distributed as dividends.

The Income Statement

income statement Financial statement showing how a business's revenues compare with expenses for a given period of time

revenues Amount of sales of goods or services and inflow from miscellaneous sources such as interest, rent, and royalties

expenses Costs created in the process of generating revenues

net income Profit or loss of a company, determined by subtracting expenses from revenues

The **income statement** reflects the results of operations over a period of time, typically one year. If the balance sheet is a snapshot, the income statement is a movie. It summarizes all **revenues** (or sales), the amounts that have been or are to be received from customers for goods or services delivered to them, and all **expenses,** the costs that have arisen in generating revenues. Expenses are then subtracted from revenues to show the actual profit or loss of a company, a figure known as **net income**—profit or the "bottom line." Exhibit 17.5 is an income statement for Sweet Dreams Ice Cream.

Revenues

The revenues of a business usually come from sales to customers, fees for services, or both. Other kinds of revenue include rents, commissions, interest, and fees paid by other firms to use the company's patents.

TWO METHODS OF RECORDING REVENUES   In an ice cream store like Sweet Dreams, the shopkeeper receives revenue the moment a customer hands over a dollar for a cone. But in a business that sells more expensive products—business computers, for example—a certain amount of time elapses between the moment the salesperson and the customer make a deal and the day the cus-

EXHIBIT 17.5

A Sample Income Statement
An income statement summarizes the company's financial operations over a period of time, usually a year.

SWEET DREAMS ICE CREAM, INC.
Income Statement
For The Year Ended December 31, 1993

Revenues		
Gross sales	$478,293	
Less: Returns and allowances	3,079	
Less: Discounts	1,200	
NET SALES		$474,014
Cost of Goods Sold		
Beginning inventory	$ 10,473	
Purchases for the year	$198,267	
Less: Purchase discounts	5,300	
Net purchases	192,967	
Cost of goods available for sale	$203,440	
Less: Ending inventory	12,685	
COST OF GOODS SOLD		190,755
Gross Profit		$283,259
Operating Expenses		
Selling expenses		
Wages	$101,700	
Advertising	18,075	
Store supplies	24,016	
Payroll taxes	10,170	
Rent	31,142	
Repairs and maintenance	7,418	
Auto and truck	11,697	
Insurance	4,068	
Utilities	8,700	
Depreciation and amortization	13,245	
Miscellaneous	400	
TOTAL SELLING EXPENSES	$230,631	
General expenses		
Professional services	$ 3,916	
Office supplies	1,354	
Miscellaneous	300	
TOTAL GENERAL EXPENSES	$ 5,570	
TOTAL OPERATING EXPENSES		236,201
OPERATING INCOME		$ 47,058
Other Income and Expenses		
Interest expense	$ 4,750	
Interest income	(986)	
TOTAL OTHER INCOME AND EXPENSES		3,764
INCOME BEFORE TAXES		$ 43,294
INCOME TAXES		6,494
NET INCOME		$ 36,800

tomer pays for the merchandise. At what point has the vendor actually made a sale? If a company records its sales on an **accrual basis,** the company puts the revenue on its books as soon as the deal is made and the product is delivered, even if the customer does not pay until the following year. If a business is run on a **cash basis,** however, the company records revenue only when money from the sale is actually received.

Although most companies use the accrual method, some small companies prefer to avoid that method of recording revenue because it usually generates

accrual basis Accounting method in which revenue is recorded when a sale is made and expense is recorded when incurred

cash basis Accounting method in which revenue is recorded when payment is received and expense is recorded when cash is paid

tax obligations before the cash has been collected. For businesses that have to borrow money just to pay their tax bills, the advantages of cash-based accounting are obvious. But accrual-based accounting benefits the government, because the Internal Revenue Service gets its tax money sooner. In fact, since 1982 the IRS has required manufacturers and retailers to use the accrual method and has allowed only farmers and certain service businesses to use the cash method. The Tax Reform Act of 1986 further limits the use of the cash method.

GROSS SALES VERSUS NET SALES   **Gross sales,** the total dollar amount of products sold, doesn't give the entire revenue picture. In the normal course of business, deductions are made from gross sales, and these deductions may be considerable. For example, customers may return the goods they have bought and get full refunds. Cash discounts, offered to customers who pay early, also reduce gross sales. After such discounts are deducted from gross sales, the remaining amount is called **net sales.** Exhibit 17.5 shows the impact of returns and discounts on Sweet Dreams's gross sales.

Expenses

Expenses, the costs of doing business, include both the costs directly associated with creating products and general operating expenses.

COST OF GOODS SOLD   For any products that a producer or distributor sells, it must pay certain costs. For instance, a manufacturer like Hewlett-Packard's RND must take into account the expense of producing its goods, whereas a retailer must allow for the expense of buying merchandise. **Cost of goods sold** is calculated differently for these two kinds of businesses.

Manufacturers must first total the costs of producing goods, including expenses for labor, raw materials, and factory operations. These costs are then added to the value of the inventory of finished goods on hand at the beginning of the year. The value of the inventory (finished goods not sold) at the end of the year is then subtracted, yielding the cost of goods sold.

In contrast, wholesalers and retailers start by evaluating inventory on hand at the beginning of the year. Purchases made during the year (less discounts) are then added to this figure. These sums make up the total cost of goods available for sale. To find out the cost of goods sold, the cost of inventory still on hand at the end of the period is deducted. As shown for Sweet Dreams in Exhibit 17.5, cost of goods sold is then deducted from net sales to arrive at gross profit.

OPERATING EXPENSES   In addition to the costs directly associated with producing their goods or services, companies must account for two types of **operating expenses. Selling expenses** are operating expenses incurred through marketing and distributing the products that the company offers for sale. They include wages or salaries of salespeople, advertising, supplies, insurance for the sales operation, depreciation of the store and other sales equipment, and all miscellaneous sales-department expenses such as utilities and maintenance. **General expenses** are operating expenses incurred in the overall administration of a business. They include professional services (accounting and legal fees), office salaries, depreciation of office equipment, insurance covering office operations, supplies, and so on.

---

gross sales All revenues received from the sale of goods or services

net sales Amount remaining after cash discounts, refunds, and other allowances are deducted from gross sales

cost of goods sold Cost of producing or acquiring a company's products for sale during a given period

operating expenses All costs of operation that are not included under cost of goods sold

selling expenses All the operating expenses associated with marketing goods or services

general expenses Operating expenses such as office and administrative expenses not directly associated with creating or marketing a good or service

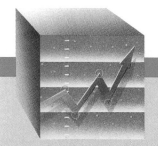

TECHNIQUES FOR BUSINESS SUCCESS

What's Your Net Worth?

How much do you think you are really worth? Take a guess. Now get ready for what may be a pleasant surprise. At the very least, filling out the personal balance sheet included here will help you evaluate your resources and plan for the future. Wouldn't you like to know whether you're too deeply in debt? Whether you have enough insurance? Whether you're accumulating the trappings of material success?

Net worth is simply the difference between assets and liabilities. The first step in calculating your net worth, then, is to assess your assets. How much would you receive for your investments, your home, and your automobile if you were to liquidate them today? Be realistic. For personal property, be especially conservative; it's easy to let sentiment inflate the value of your prized possessions. Now write down only a quarter of the amount you have estimated as the value of your personal property, because it is not easy to liquidate used goods like these. Be similarly tough-minded about money other people owe you: How much are you really likely to collect?

The liabilities section of your personal balance sheet includes all your current financial obligations: what you owe on your home, car, credit cards, furniture, college education, and so on. It also includes any taxes you owe for which money has not already been withheld.

Once you're sure you haven't overlooked any of your assets or liabilities, total each column. Then subtract your liabilities from your assets. The result is your net worth today. But a year from now—even a month from now—that figure will be different. So to keep abreast of your financial status, you must plan to revise your personal balance sheet a year from now and every year thereafter.

ASSETS		LIABILITIES	
Checking account	$_____	Installment loans (include interest charges)	$_____
Savings account	_____	Other loans (include interest charges)	_____
Money-market fund	_____	Charge accounts (include interest charges)	_____
Time deposits and certificates	_____	Mortgage	_____
House (market value)	_____	Current bills outstanding	_____
Other real estate	_____	Taxes due	_____
Securities (bonds, stocks, other)	_____	Other debts	_____
Life insurance cash value	_____	TOTAL	$_____
Investments	_____		
Annuities	_____	NET WORTH	
Company or union pension	_____	Subtract your total liabilities from your total assets to find your net worth.	
Individual Retirement Account or Keogh Plan	_____	TOTAL ASSETS	$_____
Interest in business	_____	−TOTAL LIABILITIES	−$_____
Automobile	_____	NET WORTH	$_____
Personal property (clothing, jewelry, furniture, cameras, and the like)	_____		
Loans receivable (debts owed to you)	_____		
Other	_____		
TOTAL	$_____		

Net Income or Loss

Net income is figured using revenues and expenses. The first step is to deduct the cost of goods sold from net sales (gross sales minus returns and allowances and discounts) to obtain the **gross profit** (or gross margin).

The next step is to deduct the total operating expenses from gross profit. The remainder is the **operating income.** Other revenues received by the business (such as interest income) are added to operating income, and other expenses (such as income taxes) are deducted. The balance is *net income,* the company's profit or loss for a particular period. Owners, creditors, and investors can form judgments about the firm's past performance and future prospects by comparing net income for one year with net income for previous years.

The Statement of Cash Flows

In addition to preparing a balance sheet and an income statement, all public companies and many privately owned firms prepare a **statement of cash flows.** The Financial Accounting Standards Board (FASB, the chief rule-making body for accountants) requires public companies to include this statement among its annual financial statements.[8] The statement of cash flows summarizes receipts and disbursals of cash in three areas: operations, investments, and financing. An analysis of cash flows provides a good idea of a company's *liquidity,* or ability to pay its short-term obligations when they become due; the cash-flow status is thus one good indicator of financial health.

VIDEO EXERCISE

▶ FINANCIAL ANALYSIS

Organizations and individuals use financial statements—balance sheets, income statements, statements of cash flows, and others—to spot problems and opportunities. When analyzing financial statements, managers and outsiders try to evaluate a company's performance in relation to the economy as a whole and to the company's competitors, taking into account the methods the company has used to make various accounting disclosures. To perform this analysis, most users look at historical trends and certain key ratios that indicate how the company is performing.

Reviewing the Economic and Competitive Context

The state of the economy as a whole has a big impact on most industries and companies. Consider the housing industry. When times are tough, people tend to put off buying a new house, and home builders' sales drop. Hard times may make even the best-run companies look weak. The converse is also true: Good times are likely to improve the earnings of even the worst-run businesses.

When gauging the quality of a company, it is important to take into account these uncontrollable economic forces and then examine how the company has responded compared to its competitors. For example, sales growth may slow during a recession for all companies in an industry. But a company that maintains healthy profit margins while its competitors struggle may be assumed to be doing well.

Allowing for Different Accounting Methods

Comparing one company to another may be tricky because of the subjectivity involved in accounting techniques. Some accountants—like some professors—are tough graders, taking the most conservative approach to everything. Others allow a more liberal interpretation of the rules. Thus, a company that gets the equivalent of a B on its financial report card may well be better managed than a competitor that gets an A using less rigorous accounting methods. To be sure you aren't comparing apples to oranges, you must question how various accounting matters have been handled.

When Are Revenues Recorded?

Companies have some discretion in deciding when to record a sale on their books. Therefore, when evaluating an income statement, you would have to ask, "Are these sales really firm?" Some manufacturers load up their distributors with supplies well before payments are due and create the impression that sales are booming. In fact, these producers have not generated revenue but have merely transferred inventory to their wholesalers. If the product does not sell well, the producer may have to accept sizable returns from distributors; at this point, the producer will have to revise the sales figures downward. The conservative accounting approach is to record revenues only after all potential returns can reasonably be projected.

Which Depreciation Method Is Used?

Accountants may use any of several methods of calculating depreciation expenses. But various depreciation methods require different procedures. All the methods are based on the accountant's estimate of the useful life of each fixed asset. Estimates of useful life may vary—can a delivery truck be expected to last ten years, or is five years more realistic? But GAAP forbid the deliberate overestimation of a fixed asset's useful life, so users of financial statements may assume that such estimates are within reasonable limits. The method chosen to depict the pattern of a fixed asset's depreciation, however, can make financial statements trickier to analyze. One commonly used method, for example, allocates an equal amount of depreciation expense to every year of the asset's estimated useful life, whereas another method permits more depreciation expense to be deducted in the early years of the asset's life than in its later years. Thus, the depreciation method used can make a company look more or less profitable.

How Is Cost of Goods Sold Calculated?

A company can also raise or lower its earnings by changing the way it calculates the cost of goods sold. Say that you are in the retail motorcycle business, buying bikes from the manufacturer and reselling them to customers. Over a year or two, the manufacturer might raise its prices, so your inventory would consist of machines that had cost you different amounts. You might have five motorcycles that you bought several months ago for $2,000 each and five that you just bought for $2,200 apiece. If you sell five bikes for $3,000 each, you'll have revenues of $15,000. But which five bikes did you sell? If you assume that you sold the oldest

FIFO First in, first out: method of pricing inventory under which the costs of the first goods acquired are the first ones charged to the cost of goods sold

bikes first, your gross profit will be $5,000 ($15,000 in revenues less $10,000, or five bikes at $2,000 each). But if you assume that you sold the newest bikes first, your gross profit will be only $4,000 ($15,000 less $11,000, or five bikes at $2,200 each).

Whether your gross profit is $4,000 or $5,000 depends on which method you use to determine the cost of inventory. The "first in, first out" method, or **FIFO**, treats inventory costs as if they were on a conveyor belt traveling through the balance sheet to the income statement. The costs you enter in your books as the

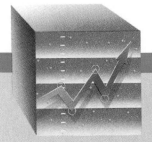

TECHNIQUES FOR BUSINESS SUCCESS

How to Read an Annual Report

Spring is the time of year for bluebirds to sing, flowers to bloom, pro baseball players to take the field, and annual reports to pour off the printing presses. The nation's 10,000 publicly traded corporations "tell all" in these financial reports to shareholders, but finding the important information in them isn't easy. More and more companies are turning out glossy magazine-style reports filled with color photos and glowing accounts of the company's accomplishments. The real story about the company's financial health is often buried in footnotes and dense tables. You'll need to know how to read annual reports in your career, whether you're thinking of investing in companies, becoming a supplier for them, or applying for a job with them. Thus, it's worth your while to consider the advice of Newsweek columnist Jane Bryant Quinn, who provided the following pointers in an ad created for International Paper Company as part of its "The Power of the Printed Word" campaign. Using as her example the annual report of the fictional Galactic Industries, Quinn tells you how to find the important information.

START AT THE BACK

First, turn back to the report of the Certified Public Accountant. This third-party auditor will tell you right off the bat if Galactic's report conforms with "generally accepted accounting principles."

What else should you know before you check the numbers?

Stay in the back of the book and go to the footnotes. Yep! The whole profits story is sometimes in the footnotes.

Are earnings down? If it's only because of a change in accounting, maybe that's good! The com-

pany owes less tax and has more money in its pocket. Are earnings up? Maybe that's bad. They may be up because of a special windfall that won't happen again next year. The footnotes know.

FOR WHAT HAPPENED AND WHY

Now turn to the letter from the chairman. Usually addressed "to our shareholders," it's up front—and should be in more ways than one. The chairman's tone reflects the personality, the well-being of the company.

In this letter, the chairman should tell you how the company fared this year. But more important, the letter should tell you why. Keep an eye out for sentences that start with "Except for . . ." and "Despite the . . ." They're clues to problems.

INSIGHTS INTO THE FUTURE

On the positive side, a chairman's letter should give you insights into the company's future and its stance on economic or political trends that may affect it.

While you're up front, look for what's new in each line of business. Is management getting the company in good shape to weather the tough and competitive [years ahead]?

Now—and no sooner—should you dig into the numbers!

One source is the balance sheet. It is a snapshot of how the company stands at a single point in time. On the top are assets—everything the company owns. Things that can quickly be turned into cash are current assets. On the bottom are liabilities—everything the company owes. Current liabilities are the debts due in one year, which are paid out of current assets.

units are purchased are assigned in the same order to the units as they are sold. This is the method you are using if you figure that you have sold the five $2,000 "old" bikes. The "last in, first out" method, or **LIFO,** is like stacking inventory costs in a box. When a layer of costs is at the bottom, it can't be reached until all the layers above it are removed. This is the method you are using if you figure that you have sold the five $2,200 "new" bikes.

In times of high inflation, the LIFO method produces a higher cost of goods sold, a lower value for remaining inventory, and lower profits. This arrangement

LIFO *Last in, first out: method of pricing inventory under which the costs of the last goods acquired are the first ones charged to the cost of goods sold*

The difference between current assets and current liabilities is working capital, a key figure to watch from one annual (and quarterly) report to another. If working capital shrinks, it could mean trouble. One possibility: The company may not be able to keep dividends growing rapidly.

LOOK FOR GROWTH HERE

Owners' or shareholders' equity is the difference between total assets and liabilities. It is the presumed dollar value of what the owners or shareholders own. You want it to grow.

Another important number to watch is long-term debt. High and rising debt, relative to equity, may be no problem for a growing business. But it shows weakness in a company that's leveling out. (More on that later.)

The second basic source of numbers is the income statement. It shows how much money Galactic made or lost over the year.

Most people look at one figure first. It's in the income statement at the bottom: earnings per share. Watch out. It can fool you. Galactic's management could boost earnings by selling off a plant. Or by cutting the budget for research and advertising. (See the footnotes!) So don't be smug about earnings until you've found out how they happened—and how they might happen next year.

CHECK NET SALES FIRST

The number you should look at first in the income statement is net sales. Ask yourself: Are sales going up at a faster rate than the last time around? When sales increases start to slow, the company may be in trouble. Also ask: Have sales gone up faster than inflation? If not, the company's real sales may be behind. And ask yourself once more: Have sales gone

down because the company is selling off a losing business? If so, profits may be soaring.

(I never promised you that figuring out an annual report was going to be easy!)

GET OUT YOUR CALCULATOR

Another important thing to study is the company's debt. Get out your pocket calculator, and turn to the balance sheet. Divide long-term liabilities by owners' or shareholders' equity. That's the debt-to-equity ratio.

A high ratio means the company borrows a lot of money to spark its growth. That's okay—if sales grow, too, and if there's enough cash on hand to meet the payments. A company doing well on borrowed money can earn big profits for its shareholders. But if sales fall, watch out. The whole enterprise may slowly sink. Some companies can handle high ratios, others can't.

YOU HAVE TO COMPARE

That brings up the most important thing of all: One annual report, one chairman's letter, one ratio won't tell you much. You have to compare. Is the company's debt-to-equity ratio better or worse than it used to be? Better or worse than the industry norms? Better or worse, after this recession, than it was after the last recession? In company-watching, comparisons are all. They tell you if management is staying on top of things.

Financial analysts work out many other ratios to tell them how the company is doing. You can learn more about them from books on the subject. Ask your librarian.

Each year, companies give you more and more information in their annual reports. Profiting from that information is up to you. I hope you profit from mine.

EXHIBIT 17.6

How Different Methods of Costing Inventory Affect Taxes

Note that in this example, the tax is 25 percent higher with the FIFO method than with the LIFO method.

	FIFO	LIFO
Sales	$15,000	$15,000
Cost of goods sold	10,000	11,000
Gross profit	$ 5,000	$ 4,000
Taxes (at 30 percent)	1,500	1,200
Net income	$ 3,500	$ 2,800

usually results in lower taxes, as Exhibit 17.6 shows. In contrast, FIFO produces a higher value for ending inventory and a lower cost of goods sold. Because the profit—the difference between that lower cost and the inflated selling price—is greater, taxes are higher. Many executives believe that FIFO taxes their firms on "phantom" profits—earnings that are not really profits but that merely represent money needed to restock the shelves at tomorrow's prices. In inflationary times, executives often opt for LIFO to lower their paper profits and thus their cash tax payments.

In general, however, neither FIFO nor LIFO is necessarily better. The point to remember is that during periods of price changes in an industry, two firms (doing equally well in most respects) could legitimately report differing levels of profit. After a superficial look at the financial statements, a person unfamiliar with accounting might conclude that the firm using FIFO was more profitable. But the firm using LIFO might actually be better managed because its use of that method would reduce its tax bill. Because the inventory costing method has such a powerful impact on net income, a company must state in the footnotes to its financial statements which method it used.

Making Allowances

Whatever the business, certain debts are uncollectible, some loans incur losses, or company pension funds must be provided for retiring employees. Preparing for the inevitable is a business practice that some companies ignore; however, other companies make allowances for various inevitable contingencies. To the casual observer, the conservative companies that make allowances look less profitable, but if things go wrong, these companies will be better off than their less cautious competitors.

Consider uncollectible accounts receivable. For almost every company, some accounts receivable will be uncollectible. But which ones, and how much will the bad debts amount to? Accountants may allow for uncollectible accounts by basing their estimates either on a percentage of credit sales or on a percentage of outstanding accounts receivable. Both of these percentages are determined on the basis of the company's past experience with uncollectible accounts and on its expectations about future uncollectibles. Again, depending on what percentage is used, the company will look more or less profitable.

Savings and loan companies must allow for loan losses, but insufficient reserves have been cited as one factor in the recent closing and bankruptcy of many S&Ls. In fact, creative accounting procedures and overestimated real estate appraisals allowed S&Ls to ignore the inevitable while their executives grew rich on high salaries and on fees for doling out more and more S&L money. Two of the most publicized figures in the S&L failures are Charles H. Keating, Jr. (for his part in the downfall of Lincoln Savings) and Neil Bush (for his part in the closure of Silverado Bank, Savings and Loan).[9]

Investment funds for pensions are another type of allowance that may be handled in various ways. How much will companies need in order to pay employees when they retire? This is a difficult question because no one is sure how long a retired employee will actually draw a pension. Nevertheless, many people feel that if readers of a balance sheet are to get a true and total picture of the firm's financial position, it is important to include **unfunded pension liabilities,** the difference between how much a company estimates its pension obligations will be and how much it has already allowed for that expense. Recent rule changes now require unfunded pension liabilities to be displayed in the liability section of the balance sheet, which doesn't materially affect a company's cash flow but does make its liabilities look larger.

unfunded pension liabilities Amount by which a company's estimated future pension obligations exceed the funds set aside to cover those obligations

What Are the Effects of Extraordinary or Unusual Items?

Some companies make money the old-fashioned way—they earn it through their basic operations. Other companies resort to "extraordinary" or unusual measures—selling off assets, for example, or changing the way they account for various items. Consider Prime Motor Inns, once the world's second largest hotel operator. In 1989 Prime's bottom line showed a net income of $77 million (up nearly 15 percent from the year before). But much of Prime's reported income came from selling hotels, not from operating them. When financing for those sales dried up, Prime was suddenly short of cash and unable to pay its debts. In September 1990, Prime Motor Inns filed for Chapter 11 bankruptcy.[10]

Although there is nothing wrong with making money on a one-time transaction, there is generally a limit on how long a company can sustain a record of earnings growth through such unusual means. A "healthy" track record may be an illusion if it is based on liquidation of assets or on a switch in accounting methods from one accounting period to the next.

Calculating Trends and Ratios

Besides summarizing business transactions, financial statements provide information that can be analyzed for further clues to the present health and future prospects of a business. Information in financial statements is most often analyzed in terms of trends and ratios.

Trend Analysis

The process of comparing financial data from year to year in order to see how they have changed is known as **trend analysis.** It points up shifts in the nature of the business over time and may also be used to compare the company with others in its industry or with the economy as a whole. Most large companies

trend analysis Comparison of a company's financial data from year to year to see how they have changed

Trend and ratio analyses help accountants at ISC Educational Systems track where they've been in order to get a better idea of where they want to go.

provide data for trend analysis in their annual reports. Their balance sheets and income statements typically show three to five years of data (making comparative statement analysis possible); changes in other key items—such as revenues, income, earnings per share, and dividends per share—are usually shown in tables and graphs.

When analyzing trends, it is important to ask whether the results have been distorted by changes in the value of the dollar. During the late 1970s, when the inflation rate was in double digits, every company in the United States could automatically increase its sales revenue by at least 10 percent annually without achieving any real improvement in its basic business. By simply raising prices to keep up with inflation, a company could give at least a superficial appearance of growth. When inflation slowed in the 1980s, many companies' sales growth slowed as well—not because their business was bad, but because the built-in inflation kicker had diminished.

To correct for this potential distortion, in 1979 the Securities and Exchange Commission began to require the largest public companies to supplement their financial statements with footnotes showing what their historical costs would look like when adjusted for inflation. Now that inflation has abated, the accounting profession has put this sort of inflation-adjusted accounting on the back burner. Accountants may return to it, however, if inflation starts to rise again.

Ratio Analysis

ratio analysis Comparison of two elements from the same year's financial results, stated as a percentage or a ratio

In **ratio analysis,** two elements from the same year's financial figures are compared. For example, sales might be compared to assets or to income. The result of such a comparison is stated as a percentage or a ratio, which can be compared to the firm's past ratios or to those of competitors.

Like trend analysis, ratio analysis reveals how the firm is performing relative to similar companies in its industry, but it focuses on certain key areas of current performance instead of on comparisons of performance over time. Every industry tends to have its own "normal" ratios, which act as a yardstick for individual firms. The average statistics for various industries, grouped by company size, are available in published sources. One such report is published by Dun & Bradstreet, a credit-rating firm.

PROFITABILITY RATIOS   One way to tell how well a company is conducting its ongoing operations is to compute **profitability ratios.** Three of the most common profitability ratios are return on investment, return on sales, and earnings per share.

Return on investment (ROI), also known as return on equity, is the income a business generates per dollar of owner or stockholder investment. Consider Sweet Dreams Ice Cream, which made $43,294 in income before taxes on an equity base of $106,260. (These amounts and those used in calculating the following ratios are taken from Exhibits 17.4 and 17.5.) The ratio (expressed as a percentage) would be

$$\frac{Income\ Before\ Taxes}{Owners'\ Equity} = \frac{\$43,294}{\$106,260} = 40.74\%$$

In other words, for every dollar of equity, the company made about 40 cents in income before taxes in 1993. How good is this particular return on investment? Very high, although there is no agreed-on ideal. For the most part, managers and investors evaluate return on investment by comparing it to the ratios for similar businesses and to the company's own past ratios.

Return on sales, or net profit margin—the before-tax income a business makes per unit of sales—is another important indicator of profitability. It is determined by comparing before-tax income to net sales. For Sweet Dreams, the ratio would be set up as follows:

$$\frac{Income\ Before\ Taxes}{Net\ Sales} = \frac{\$43,294}{\$474,014} = 9.13\%$$

Sweet Dreams's return on sales of 9.13 percent indicates that just over 9 cents of every dollar earned is profit. When compared to the percentages of other companies in the same business, this figure may give a potential investor a valuable warning of inefficiency—or reassurance that the business is doing well. In this case, Sweet Dreams is above average. Most companies in the ice cream business average a return on sales of only 2.0 to 3.5 percent.[11]

Earnings per share is a measure of how much profit a company earns for each share of stock outstanding. Managers and investors are particularly interested in this ratio because it sheds light on the company's ability to build up the business and pay dividends. The earnings per share for Sweet Dreams is calculated as follows:

$$\frac{Net\ Income}{Number\ of\ Shares\ of\ Common\ Stock\ Outstanding} = \frac{\$36,800}{10,000\ shares} = \$3.68\ per\ share$$

In other words, if the company were to distribute all of its earnings to shareholders, each one would get $3.68 per share for 1993.

One company's earnings per share is difficult to compare with another's because the figure depends on both net income and the number of shares of stock

profitability ratios   Financial ratios that indicate to what extent a company is making a profit

return on investment   Ratio between the income earned by a firm and total owners' equity

return on sales   Ratio between income before taxes and net sales

earnings per share   Measure of a firm's profitability for each share of outstanding stock, calculated by dividing net income by shares of stock outstanding

outstanding. The best way to compare is to look at the growth in the two companies' earnings per share over the past five years or so. If company A's earnings per share have grown at an annual rate of 10 percent and company B's have grown by only 6 percent, you may conclude that company A's profit growth is superior, even if company B's earnings per share show a higher absolute number.

LIQUIDITY RATIOS A company's ability to pay its bills as they come due is indicated by **liquidity ratios.** As you might expect, liquidity measures are of particular interest to lenders and creditors. Liquidity can be judged on the basis of working capital, the current ratio, and the quick ratio.

A company's **working capital**—current assets minus current liabilities—reflects the resources (provided by investors and long-term creditors) that the company has invested in its current assets. Because it represents current assets remaining after payment of all current liabilities, working capital is an indicator of liquidity. The dollar amount of working capital can be misleading, however. For example, it may include the value of slow-moving inventory items that could not be used to enable the firm to pay its short-term debts.

A different picture of the company's liquidity is provided by the **current ratio**—current assets divided by current liabilities. On December 31, 1993, Sweet Dreams had current assets of $84,925 and current liabilities of $52,675. The current ratio would be calculated as follows:

$$\frac{\text{Current Assets}}{\text{Current Liabilities}} = \frac{\$84{,}925}{\$52{,}675} = 1.61$$

Sweet Dreams has $1.61 of current assets to meet every dollar of short-term liabilities. How safe is this ratio? To answer the question, analysts compare a company's current ratio with the average for the particular type of business. As a rule, however, a company with a current ratio of at least 2.0 is considered a safe risk for short-term credit. If the ratio is less than 1.5, a company may have to stretch so far to pay its debts that it won't have anything left to reinvest in the business.

The **quick ratio,** also called the acid-test ratio, is another more conservative measure of a company's ability to meet its short-term debts with its cash, marketable securities, and receivables. Some analysts consider it a better indicator of ability to pay immediate debts than the current ratio because the quick ratio leaves out inventories. The quick ratio for Sweet Dreams would be calculated as follows:

$$\frac{\text{Cash} + \text{Marketable Securities} + \text{Accounts Receivable} + \text{Notes Receivable}}{\text{Current Liabilities}}$$

$$= \frac{\$22{,}790 + \$4{,}200 + \$19{,}350 + \$21{,}500}{\$52{,}675} = \frac{\$67{,}840}{\$52{,}675} = 1.29$$

Analysts consider a quick ratio of 1.0 to be reasonable, so Sweet Dreams is in good shape. If the company became pressed for cash and inventory were moving sluggishly, it would still have $1.29 in quick assets to meet each dollar of current liabilities.

liquidity ratios Financial ratios that indicate how quickly a company can repay obligations

working capital Current assets minus current liabilities

current ratio Measure of a company's short-term liquidity, calculated by dividing current assets by current liabilities

quick ratio Measure of a company's short-term liquidity, calculated by adding cash, marketable securities, and receivables, then dividing that sum by current liabilities

ACTIVITY RATIOS   A number of **activity ratios** may be used to analyze how well a company is managing its assets. The most commonly used is the **inventory turnover ratio,** which tells potential investors how fast the company's inventory is turned into sales. The quicker the better is the general rule.

The **inventory turnover ratio** is computed by dividing the cost of goods sold by the average value of inventory for a period. Where inventories are fairly constant, an average of the beginning inventory and the ending inventory would be accurate enough. But if inventories fluctuate widely during the year, all month-end inventories for the year should be averaged. Sweet Dreams's inventory is more or less constant, so its turnover ratio is calculated as follows:

$$\frac{Cost\ of\ Goods\ Sold}{(Beginning\ Inventory + Ending\ Inventory)/2}$$

$$= \frac{\$190{,}755}{(\$10{,}473 + \$12{,}685)/2} = \frac{\$190{,}755}{\$11{,}579} = 16.47$$

This ratio means that Sweet Dreams's average inventory is converted (turned over) into sales 16.47 times per year, or approximately once every 22 days (365 days divided by 16.47). A potential investor would be interested in this information because it demonstrates that the company converts its average monthly inventory into receivables every 22 days. This information, combined with the turnover ratio for accounts receivable, enables users of financial statements to analyze the company's cash-flow (liquidity) status and its managerial efficiency. The "ideal" turnover ratio varies with the type of operation. A grocery store's turnover ratio, for example, would be around 16. A yarn shop, in contrast, would turn over its inventory only about 3.0 to 3.5 times per year.

DEBT RATIOS   To measure a company's ability to pay its long-term debts, **debt ratios,** or coverage ratios, are calculated. Lenders look at these ratios to determine whether the potential debtor has put enough money into the business to serve as a protective cushion for the loan.

The **debt-to-equity ratio** indicates the extent to which a business is financed by debt as opposed to invested capital (equity). From the lender's standpoint, the lower this ratio, the safer the company, because the company has less existing debt and may be able to support more. But a company that is conservative in its long-term borrowing is not necessarily well managed; often a low level of debt is associated with a low growth rate. The debt-to-equity ratio for Sweet Dreams is

$$\frac{Total\ Liabilities}{Stockholders'\ (Owners')\ Equity} = \frac{\$106{,}425}{\$106{,}260} = 1.00$$

In other words, creditors have lent the company one dollar for each dollar of equity. A debt-to-equity ratio above 1.0 indicates that debts exceed equity and thus the business may be relying too heavily on debt.

The **debt-to-total-assets ratio** also serves as a simple measure of a company's ability to carry long-term debt. As a rule of thumb, the amount of debt should not exceed 50 percent of the value of total assets. For Sweet Dreams, this ratio is

$$\frac{Total\ Liabilities}{Total\ Assets} = \frac{\$106{,}425}{\$212{,}685} = 0.50$$

---

activity ratios Financial ratios that indicate the amount of business a company is doing

inventory turnover ratio Measure of the time a company takes to turn its inventory into sales, calculated by dividing cost of goods sold by the average value of inventory for a period

debt ratios Financial ratios (sometimes called coverage ratios) that indicate the extent of a company's burden of long-term debt

debt-to-equity ratio Measure of the extent to which a business is financed by debt as opposed to invested capital, calculated by dividing the company's total liabilities by owners' equity

debt-to-total-assets ratio Measure of a company's ability to carry long-term debt, calculated by dividing total liabilities by total assets

For every dollar of assets, then, the company is only 50 cents in debt—which matches the 50 percent debt-to-assets guideline.

But this ratio, like the others, is not a magic formula. Even companies whose financial ratios indicate straight A's may suddenly develop unexpected problems. Like grades on a report card, ratios are clues to performance. Managers, creditors, lenders, and investors can use them to get a fairly accurate idea of how a company is doing.

SUMMARY OF LEARNING OBJECTIVES

1 Describe the importance of accounting to managers, investors, creditors, and government.

The financial reports developed by accountants help managers spot problems and opportunities; they provide investors, suppliers, and creditors with the means to analyze a business; and they facilitate the government's efforts to collect taxes and regulate business.

2 Distinguish between public and private accountants.

Public accountants operate independently of the businesses they serve, and they monitor the businesses' financial statements. Private accountants serve a single business in one of a number of specialized areas.

3 State the basic accounting equation.

The basic accounting equation is Assets = Liabilities + Owners' Equity.

4 Explain the purpose of the balance sheet and identify its three main sections.

The balance sheet provides a snapshot of the business at a particular point in time. Its main sections are assets, liabilities, and owners' equity.

5 Explain the purpose of an income statement and identify its three main components.

The income statement reflects the results of operations over a period of time. Its main components are revenues, expenses, and net income or loss.

6 Explain the purpose of the statement of cash flows.

The statement of cash flows summarizes receipts and disbursals of cash (and cash equivalents) in three areas: operations, investments, and financing.

7 Identify five areas in which accountants may exercise considerable discretion in their methods and assumptions.

The five areas where accountants have the most latitude are in the timing of revenue recognition, the choice of a depreciation method, the choice of an inventory valuation method, the determination of allowance amounts, and the method of disclosing extraordinary or unusual items. The choices made in these areas may greatly affect a company's earnings picture.

8 List the four main categories of financial ratios.

Most of the important ratios fall into one of four categories: profitability ratios, liquidity ratios, activity ratios, and debt ratios.

Meeting a Business Challenge at Hewlett-Packard

When people at Roseville Networks Division of Hewlett-Packard began resenting the accounting department, it was because they weren't getting the information from accounting that they needed and because they had to give so much seemingly useless information back to accounting. But Debbie Berlant and RND's cost accounting manager, Reese Browning, refused to let things stay as they were. Initially motivated to eliminate unnecessary measurements, Berlant and Browning decided to rethink their internal cost accounting system to provide the other departments with information that would be useful.

They agreed on three goals. They wanted their new system to (1) reflect manufacturing costs accurately, (2) use data that manufacturing and other departments could collect easily, and (3) meet the legal and practical needs of the accounting function. The key was learning what truly drives costs.

First they had to decide which costs to trace. Eventually, they eliminated direct labor as a separate category and combined it with overhead.

They discovered that direct labor was making up only 2 percent of total manufacturing costs, but the old system had spent a lot of time tracking it. They also found that they didn't really need production to track and charge its time on every task. They had to decide which categories of manufacturing overhead they would use, ending up with procurement overhead, production overhead, and support overhead. Then, within these categories, they separated the important activities and, with the help of people in every department, they narrowly defined each activity. Finally, they had to decide what factors were actually driving the costs for the various activities they had defined, which was "really just a matter of talking to the people on the factory floor," say Berlant and Browning. "We recognize that costs cannot be traced with surgical precision. But we're convinced that at least for now, we have found cost drivers that produce more accurate product costs than before."

The results of the new accounting system are important ones. People can think in more physical terms, understanding more fully the processes of manufacturing as well as what drives the related costs. People no longer argue about how the cost is determined, which allows them to speak the same language and thus make sensible trade-offs. And people continue to suggest ways for improving the accounting system, which means it just gets better and better. In RND's competitive computer market, accurate and timely cost information is crucial. Finally, accounting and every other department at RND are getting numbers and information they can trust.

Your Mission: As a member of Roseville Networks Division accounting department, you are expected to contribute your own ideas on how to continue fine-tuning the cost accounting system and all activities of your department.

1. RND is considering a new line of semicustomized software products, and division management wants to find the best way to record the revenues from these products. The marketing department proposes that

Debbie Berlant, cost accounting supervisor of Hewlett-Packard's RND.

customers shouldn't have to pay for their customized software until they are completely satisfied that it will meet their needs. Moreover, if it turns out that the software can't meet their needs, customers don't have to pay for it at all. This raises the question of timing: When should you record the revenue from these sales? Which of the following proposals makes the most sense to you?

a. It's your job to make the financial picture look as bright as possible. As soon as the salesperson indicates that a customer is likely to order some software, you should log the sale. If the customer then decides not to order, you can just go back and erase that sale.
b. You should wait until after the customer has ordered and the software installation team is confident that the product is going to work. There is still some risk in this method, but it is less risky than (a), and you can always set aside a small reserve to cover those situations that don't work out.
c. It shouldn't be a question of timing; a balanced work load for the accounting department is more important. You should set aside a certain amount of time each week to log all new orders, regardless of their status.
d. You don't want to mislead management or stockholders at all; you should therefore refrain from re-

cording a sale until you actually have money in the bank. If you try to record sales earlier, there is too much risk of accounting errors caused by customers who decide not to pay.

2. In the course of her financial analysis of RND, Berlant notes some problems with the way the accounting department is calculating the cost of goods sold. In an effort to optimize the effect of inventory on cost, Berlant is considering changing the way the cost of goods is currently calculated. She asks you to evaluate the FIFO and LIFO methods, and she instructs you to give her a recommendation of the method RND should use.

a. If Berlant is going to change the method of calculating cost of goods sold, then she must see a pressing need to lower the company's earnings in order to save tax dollars. So after considering each method carefully, you recommend using the LIFO method because it results in less profit and thus saves taxes.
b. Berlant's interest in changing the method of pricing inventory must mean that she's worried about showing the highest profits possible. You realize that inflation is down during the current recession, so you don't really have to worry about RND being taxed on "phantom" profits. You conclude that since the FIFO method results in higher profits, RND should be using FIFO so that profits will look the best they can.
c. Your research into both methods reveals that neither FIFO nor LIFO is really better. However, using one or the other can affect what profits look like and how much RND must pay in taxes. You recommend that Berlant use LIFO if she believes that saving money in taxes is more important than showing the highest profit possible. However, if Berlant believes that profits are more important than saving money on taxes, you recommend that FIFO be used.
d. You realize that either method would serve RND equally well. Your recommendation to Berlant is that it doesn't really make that much difference whether RND uses LIFO or FIFO.

3. RND is considering the purchase of a small company to help fill some holes in its technology base. The division's strategic planners have identified four companies that have the necessary technology, and now they want you to add a financial perspective to the selection process. You've reviewed their annual reports for the past few years, and you've uncovered some interesting points about each company. Here is the most significant negative information you've uncovered in each case. Which company do you think is in the *worst* financial shape?

a. Company A didn't grow at all in the last year. The chairman explained that this was caused by a short-term recession in its major markets. On the positive side, she noted, the company didn't lose any market share and was able to hold its own throughout the recession.

b. Company B did grow in the last year, even though it competes in the same recessionary markets as Company A. The reason for its apparent success was aggressive price-cutting that dropped its prices 10 percent below those of the competition. The report points out, however, that this price-cutting caused the company to operate at a

loss for the year. You get curious and dig back several years, only to discover that the company has always operated at a loss, even when its prices were higher than the market average.

c. Company C doesn't present a very exciting financial picture. Its sales grew slightly faster than inflation, and its market share grew slightly as well. However, you note that both of these resulted from a key competitor's bankruptcy a year and a half earlier.

d. Company D's profit picture looks very strong in the last couple of years, but you dig through its annual report and learn that the company has eliminated nearly all of its research-and-development work in order to make its short-term profits look better.

4. The accounting department is always interested in analyzing information for more clues to the company's current condition and future prospects. Berlant has asked you to analyze current financial records to discover how efficiently RND is utilizing its assets. Which of the following methods should you use?

a. Trend analysis would be the best method to use because it allows you to compare your figures over time. If you are careful to allow for corresponding changes in the value of the dollar, you should come up with a pretty accurate picture of how RND utilizes its assets.

b. Return on investment would be the best method because it will tell you the income RND is generating per dollar of investment. By comparing your figures with those of other companies, you will be able to estimate how well RND is utilizing its assets.

c. Liquidity ratios would be the best method to use because they yield the amount of working capital RND has. By calculating how well the company can pay its bills, you will generate a picture of how efficiently assets are being utilized at RND.

d. The inventory turnover ratio would be the best method to use because it shows how fast the company's inventory is turned into sales. Depending on how inventories fluctuate, you can either average the beginning and ending inventory or average all month-end inventories for the year.[12]

KEY TERMS

accounting (482)
accounting equation (487)
accrual basis (493)
activity ratios (505)
amortization (491)
assets (487)
audit (484)
balance sheet (489)
bookkeeping (486)
budget (483)
calendar year (489)
cash basis (493)
certified management accountants (486)
certified public accountants (485)
controller (486)
cost of goods sold (494)
current assets (489)
current liabilities (491)
current ratio (504)
debt ratios (505)
debt-to-equity ratio (505)

debt-to-total-assets ratio (505)
depreciation (491)
double-entry bookkeeping (488)
earnings per share (503)
expenses (492)
FIFO (498)
financial accounting (482)
fiscal year (489)
fixed assets (491)
general expenses (494)
generally accepted accounting principles (483)
goodwill (491)
gross profit (496)
gross sales (494)
income statement (492)
intangible assets (491)
inventory turnover ratio (505)
liabilities (487)
LIFO (499)
liquidity ratios (504)
long-term liabilities (492)

management accounting (482)
net income (492)
net sales (494)
operating expenses (494)
operating income (496)
owners' equity (487)
private accountants (486)
profitability ratios (503)
public accountants (484)
quick ratio (504)
ratio analysis (502)
retained earnings (488)
return on investment (503)
return on sales (503)
revenues (492)
selling expenses (494)
statement of cash flows (496)
trend analysis (501)
unfunded pension liabilities (501)
working capital (504)

REVIEW QUESTIONS

1. What is the difference between financial accounting and management accounting? Between a public accountant and a private accountant?

2. What factors affect the reliability of accounting information?

3. Why is it important that the two sides of the accounting equation be kept in balance?

4. What are the three types of assets and the two types of liabilities listed on a balance sheet?

5. What is the difference between an income statement and a balance sheet?

6. How is net income calculated?

7. What is the difference between FIFO and LIFO, and which produces the lower profit figure in times of high inflation?

8. What are the three main profitability ratios, and how is each calculated?

A CASE FOR CRITICAL THINKING

Going to the Cleaners

Obsessed with the idea of owning a business, you decide that a dry-cleaning business is just the thing. Luckily for you, two establishments happen to be for sale—at the same price and in equally attractive locations. You manage to get enough financial data to compare the year-end condition of the two companies, as shown in Exhibit 17.7. Study the numbers carefully; your livelihood depends on choosing wisely between the two.[13]

1. What factors should you consider before deciding which company to buy? What additional data might be helpful to you? (Note that net income is implied.)

2. On the basis of the data provided, which company would you purchase? Detail the process you use to make your decision.

EXHIBIT 17.7

Financial Data for Two Companies

December 31, 1993, year-end balance sheet.

	Ajax Services, Inc.	Mallard Cleaners, Inc.
ASSETS		
Cash	$10,000	$ 25,000
Accounts receivable	2,000	4,000
Cleaning equipment	50,000	80,000
Office equipment	11,000	18,000
Supplies	22,000	34,000
TOTAL ASSETS	$95,000	$161,000
LIABILITIES AND OWNER'S EQUITY		
Accounts payable	$21,000	$ 38,000
Bank loans payable	49,000	68,000
Owner's equity	25,000	55,000
TOTAL LIABILITIES AND OWNER'S EQUITY	$95,000	$161,000
Personal withdrawals from cash during 1993	$40,000	$ 38,000
Owner's investments in business during 1993	$16,000	$ 32,000
Capital balances for each business on January 1, 1993	$30,000	$ 12,000

BUILDING YOUR COMMUNICATION SKILLS

Obtain a copy of the annual report of a business and, with a group of three or four other students, examine it to learn about the finances and most recent operations of that business. In addition to other chapter material, use the information in "How to Read an Annual Report" on pages 498–499 as a guideline for understanding its content.

► Consider the statements made by the CEO regarding the past year: Did the company do well, or are changes in operations necessary to its future well-being? What are the projections for future growth or for maintenance of assets?

▶ Examine the financial summaries for information about the fiscal condition of the company: Did the company show a profit?

▶ If possible, obtain a copy of the company's annual report from the previous year, and compare it with the current report to determine whether past projections were accurate.

▶ Prepare a brief written summary of your conclusions.

KEEPING CURRENT USING *THE WALL STREET JOURNAL*

Select an article from *The Wall Street Journal* detailing the quarterly or year-end performance of a company that industry analysts consider notable for either positive or negative reasons.

1. Did the company report a profit or a loss for this accounting period? What other performance indicators were reported? Did the company's

performance represent an improvement over previous accounting periods?

2. What, according to the article, was the significance of this performance? Did it match industry analysts' expectations, or was it a surprise?

3. What reasons were given for the company's improvement or decline in performance?

PART SIX

Finance

CHAPTER *18*

LEARNING OBJECTIVES

After studying this chapter, you will be able to

1 Name three functions of money.

2 Distinguish M1 from the total money supply.

3 Differentiate between demand deposits and time deposits.

4 Identify nine members of the banking system.

5 Explain how deregulation has affected the financial system.

6 Explain the responsibilities and insurance methods of the FDIC.

7 Describe the organization of the Federal Reserve System.

8 Cite the four ways the Federal Reserve System regulates the money supply.

Money and Banking

Facing a Business Challenge at NCNB

LEADING THE CHARGE INTO BANKING'S NEW AGE

anking was a sleepy business for a long time, as was the whole financial-services industry. Federal and state laws and regulations provided neat, profitable cubbyholes in which everyone enjoyed success: Savings and loans made home loans, commercial banks made business and consumer loans, investment banks financed the stock offerings of public companies, and securities brokerages sold stocks and bonds. They were all regulated, with ceilings on interest paid and fees charged, and in return they were safe from competition. It was a mild-mannered business managed during "bankers' hours." But this comfortable little world was suddenly thrown into chaos. Deregulation, inflation, globalization, and technological innovation forced everyone to compete. One banker unafraid of the new climate was Hugh L. McColl, Jr., a brusque ex-Marine who loved a good fight and approached his job as chairman and CEO of North Carolina–based NCNB as if he were leading troops into battle.

McColl had once said, "I like growth; I like change; I like excitement." He faced all three now, for the battle that was shaping up on banking's horizon was guaranteed to be "winner take all." Once the smoke cleared, McColl was sure the industry would be dominated by a few superlarge banks with branch systems spread coast to coast. These superbanks, he believed, would make money by reducing costs through economies of scale and by providing a wide array of services to customers of all types. They would conduct banking and securities business with foreign corporations, mom-and-pop businesses, wealthy individuals, and blue-collar families alike. McColl's challenge was to make NCNB into one of those superbanks.

The prospect of NCNB becoming a superlarge bank seemed unlikely, even though it was a strong regional bank with branches in North Carolina, South Carolina, and Florida. McColl tried for years to acquire crosstown rival Citizens and Southern (C&S), but his attempts were frustrated. Citizens and Southern rushed into a merger with Sovran Financial Corporation of Virginia—a merger that, as much as anything, was a result of C&S executives' desire to escape McColl's tough, take-no-prisoners management style. So despite years of buying up small banks throughout the South, McColl still had not improved NCNB's net worth enough to make a major acquisition, let alone to achieve the status of a national bank.

The matter was becoming urgent for McColl. Banks of all sizes were failing, including many of the nation's savings and loans (particularly in the Southwest). These institutions were ideal takeover targets for stronger institutions. But even though they offered opportunities for growth and expansion, these failing banks and thrifts presented great risks as well. They all carried large numbers of bad real estate loans. Overbuilt markets caused borrowers to default on their loans, which in turn plunged the banks and thrifts into a financial abyss. The larger the failing bank or thrift, the larger the number of bad loans it carried. Thus any bank wanting to grow rapidly by acquiring a failing institution would risk its own financial strength by taking on so many bad loans. This situation caused the federal government to step in with the largest taxpayer-financed bailout in U.S. history. Although McColl's bank was one of the healthiest in the country, it still wasn't large enough to assume a sizable and insolvent institution.

The challenge for McColl was straightforward: Either find a way to make NCNB into one of the nation's largest banks or watch it disappear into the structure of an even more aggressive competitor during the next major wave of mergers and acquisitions. How could he change NCNB from a southern regional bank into a national institution? Would he be able to take advantage of the tumultuous times to buy a troubled bank or thrift cheaply? And how could he capitalize on the desperate position of federal and state regulators, who wanted the banking industry to avoid the disastrous insolvency and failure of the savings and loan industry?[1]

▶ THE NATURE OF MONEY

money Anything used by a society as a token of value in buying and selling goods and services

NCNB is only one bank that is changing with the times. As never before, the business of money has entered a new era. **Money** is anything generally accepted as a means of paying for goods and services. Before it was invented, people "bought" what they needed by trading their services or possessions; in some primitive societies, the barter system still prevails. However, barter is inconvenient and impractical in a modern industrial society, where many of the things we want are intangible or require the combined work of many people. For example, think about trying to buy an airplane ticket if all you had to offer in exchange was milk from the family cow. How much milk would the ticket cost? Of the many people involved in running an airline, whom would you pay? What if none of them liked milk? And what if the milk spoiled before you saved enough to pay for the ticket?

Functions and Characteristics of Money

Problems like these are solved when you have money, a token of wealth that performs three main functions. First, money is a *medium of exchange,* a tool for simplifying transactions between buyers and sellers. With money in your pocket, you can go to a travel agent and get a ticket; the travel agent can give the money to the airline, which uses it to meet expenses. Second, money also functions as a *measure of value,* so you don't have to negotiate the relative worth of dissimilar items every time you buy something, as you would if you were bartering milk for airline tickets. The value of the ticket is stated in dollars, and your resources are measured in the same terms. Because of this common denominator, you can easily compare your ability to pay with the price of the item. Third, money serves as a *store of value.* Unlike many goods, it will keep. You can put it in your pocket until you need it, or you can deposit it in a bank.

Any object can be used as money, but some items serve better than others. For example, societies using cattle as money have had problems with purchases costing half a cow and with savings being wiped out by hoof-and-mouth disease. Salt served well as money for the Romans because it was hard to come by in those times (the word *salary* comes from the Latin word for salt). But most societies have tended to choose substances that are relatively durable, easy to divide, and easy to carry. In addition, most societies have designed and produced money so that it is hard to copy or counterfeit. One of the reasons money is valuable is that it is scarce (it would lose value if people could fabricate more of it whenever they wanted), and making it hard to counterfeit helps assure the money's legitimacy. Also, money has the characteristic of liquidity: It can be converted into other forms of wealth relatively quickly.

The Money Supply

In the United States today, money comes in various forms: currency, demand deposits, time deposits, and plastic. Oddly enough, nobody knows precisely how much money there is, although the federal government has a rough idea. When it measures the money supply, it looks at various combinations of currency, demand deposits, and time deposits (see Exhibit 18.1). The narrowest commonly used measure of money, known as **M1,** consists of currency and demand deposits. All the money defined as M1 can be used as a medium of exchange. **M2,** a broader measure of the money supply, includes time deposits as well. As discussed later in the chapter, the money supply is regulated by the Federal Reserve Board.

M1 That portion of the money supply consisting of currency and demand deposits

M2 That portion of the money supply consisting of currency, demand deposits, and time deposits

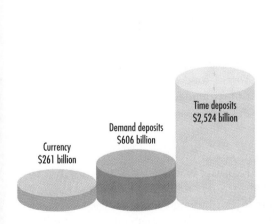

Currency
$261 billion

Demand deposits
$606 billion

Time deposits
$2,524 billion

Currency
$261 billion
+
Demand deposits
$606 billion
=
Total M1
$867 billion

Total M1
$867 billion
+
Time deposits
$2,524 billion
=
Total M2
$3,391 billion

EXHIBIT 18.1

The Total Money Supply
M1 is a measure of the U.S. money supply that includes currency and demand deposits. M2 is a broader measure that also includes time deposits.

Until the start of the Civil War, the United States lacked a uniform national currency. Individual banks printed up their own bank notes, and thousands of different "dollars" were in circulation. Today, the Bureau of Engraving and Printing prints all U.S. money—some $71 billion per year.

currency Bills and coins that make up the cash money of a society

payee Person or business a check is made out to

demand deposit Money in a checking account that can be used by the owner at any time

time deposits Bank accounts that pay interest and restrict withdrawals to a specified time

Currency

The most obvious form of money is **currency**—bills and coins. A recent study estimates that about $171 billion in currency is floating around somewhere, although exactly where is a mystery. At any given time, most adults have about $100 in cash, for a total of $18 billion, or about 10 percent of all the currency supposedly in circulation. Businesses also keep cash on hand, and children hoard some in their piggy banks. But the rest of the currency—about 75 percent—is officially unaccounted for. Undoubtedly, part of it is circulating in the underground economy. And some of it—perhaps as much as $100 billion—has made its way overseas.[2]

Cashier's checks, money orders, and traveler's checks are also considered currency. They may be purchased from a bank for their face value plus a small fee. These checks differ from a customer's business or personal checks because checks purchased from a bank are payable from the funds of the bank itself, rather than from a business or personal account.

Demand Deposits

Although cash has its advantages, it is difficult to imagine businesses functioning without the convenience of checks. The idea of checks originated in the Middle Ages when gold was the only widely accepted form of currency. Because traveling merchants found gold bulky and dangerous to carry, banks emerged to issue documents that would be honored abroad against a gold deposit that would remain at home.

With the checking accounts of today, a customer deposits money in an account and is given a book of checks. Each check the customer writes and signs is, in effect, an order to the bank to release on demand the specified amount from the account and give it to the **payee**, the business or person indicated. (However, the bank may refuse to honor the check if the account is overdrawn—that is, if the customer's account lacks sufficient funds.) Thus, the origin of the term **demand deposit.**

Checks are the most common medium of exchange, more popular than either cash or credit cards as a form of payment. Eighty-three percent of all households have checking accounts, and the average family uses checks for 57 percent of its purchases.[3]

Time Deposits

Most of the money supply is held in **time deposits,** accounts that pay interest and restrict the owner's right to withdraw funds on short notice. They include savings accounts, certificates of deposit (CDs), and money-market funds. The rate of interest for CDs is fixed for specified periods, whereas money-market funds pay interest that fluctuates daily for as long as the money remains on deposit. A time deposit is not a medium of exchange.

Plastic Money

The typical adult generally carries about seven credit cards—national cards such as Visa, MasterCard, and American Express, as well as gasoline and department-store cards.[4] Although credit cards are not officially considered money, they do function as a medium of exchange. For buying things, they are every bit as handy as cash or checks, except that they are more expensive. Some institutions issue credit cards for free, but many charge an annual fee ranging from $25 to $250. In addition, an interest charge is imposed on bills that aren't paid within a specified time.[5]

Consumer use of credit cards has increased considerably in recent years as more and more people run up bigger and bigger bills on more and more cards. This growth in credit card volume is partly due to lending institutions pushing these profitable devices. The combination of fat annual fees and high interest rates makes credit cards extremely attractive from the banks' standpoint, even if some credit card holders are unable to pay their bills. Citicorp, the leading issuer of bank cards, earns more than $700 million per year from its credit card operations.[6]

▶ THE BANKING SYSTEM

Credit cards are one of the newer services offered by banks and related financial institutions. In addition to the introduction of new services, the competition for traditional bank customers has increased since deregulation of the banking industry. The result is a series of changes in the banking environment.

Members of the System

Money goes round and round: Individuals receive money in the form of salaries and wages, which they spend on goods and services. This process of moving money from person to person and business to business is facilitated by a network of financial institutions. Exhibit 18.2 shows the members of that network and summarizes their services. The main source of banking services for business, however, remains commercial banks.

Commercial Banks

Commercial banks are profit-making businesses that accept deposits and use these funds to make loans. As long as the return on loans exceeds both expenses and the interest paid on deposits, banks make a profit. Commercial banks have traditionally been a key source of capital for businesses, but deregulation and competition, particularly from finance companies, have reduced their market share of short-term business loans.[7] Commercial banks also provide loans, checking, time deposit, and credit card accounts to individuals.

Commercial banks are of two types: **national banks** chartered by the federal government and **state banks** chartered by state governments. Competitive pressures have been reducing the number of both types, but there are currently some 4,065 national banks and 8,445 state banks. All national banks are members of the Federal Reserve System, whereas about 90 percent of state banks are members.[8]

> **commercial banks** Traditional banks offering savings, checking, and loan services

> **national banks** Banks chartered by the federal government

> **state banks** Banks chartered by a state government

Thrift Institutions

Thrifts such as **savings banks** (located mostly in New England) and **savings and loan associations** have historically been the primary source of home loans. But changes in banking laws and the S&L crisis of the late 1980s provoked a large-scale consolidation of the industry that continues today. Experts agree that most, if not all, thrifts will merge into banks within this decade. Only about 2,950 thrifts remain in business today.[9] Like banks, they provide checking and savings accounts and make consumer loans.

> **savings banks** Mostly in New England, banks offering interest-bearing checking, savings, and mortgages

> **savings and loan associations** Banks offering savings, interest-bearing checking, and mortgages

EXHIBIT 18.2 ▶ **Banking Institutions and Services**

Despite their differences, all financial institutions are in the business of buying and selling money.

SERVICE	COMMERCIAL BANKS	THRIFT INSTITUTIONS	CREDIT UNIONS
Checking accounts	Regular checking plus interest-bearing NOW and super NOW accounts, automatic teller machines	NOW and super NOW accounts, automatic teller machines	Interest-bearing share-draft accounts that resemble conventional checking accounts, automatic teller machines
Savings accounts	Passbook and statement savings, certificates of deposit, and money-market deposit accounts	Passbook and statement savings, certificates of deposit, and money-market deposit accounts	Passbook savings, certificates of deposit, money-market deposit accounts, and vacation and Christmas Club accounts
Loans	Personal secured and unsecured loans, automobile and home-improvement loans, first and second mortgages, and home-equity lines of credit	Personal secured and unsecured loans, automobile and home-improvement loans, first and second mortgages, and home-equity lines of credit	Small personal secured and unsecured loans, automobile and home-improvement loans, and first and second mortgages
Brokerage services	Discount and full-service stock and bond brokerage; direct investment advice; banks may lease space to brokers	Discount and full-service stock and bond brokerage	Discount stock and bond brokerage at a few larger credit unions
Insurance services	Credit life and credit disability insurance; travel, accident, life, and health policies through credit cards; banks may also lease space to independent insurance companies	Credit life and credit disability insurance, property and casualty insurance, life insurance, and health insurance	Credit life and credit disability insurance, group life and auto insurance
Credit cards	American Express Gold Card, MasterCard, and Visa	MasterCard and Visa	Visa and sometimes MasterCard
Other services	Investment management and counseling, estate planning, and tax planning, usually through trust department or private banking division; financial-planning services on a fee basis at some banks or through leasing space to independent advisers; bond trading to raise money for corporations	Investment counseling, estate planning, retirement planning, and tax preparation	Budget counseling, investment counseling, and retirement planning

Credit Unions

credit unions Cooperative financial institutions that provide loan and savings services to their members

Credit unions are nonprofit, member-owned cooperatives that offer checking accounts, savings accounts, credit cards, and consumer loans. All 15,600 credit unions were formed by people with a "common bond," usually an employer, union, or similar organization.[10] Some of these institutions are able to provide credit on favorable terms, mainly because of their nonprofit status.

Finance Companies

finance companies Unregulated companies that specialize in making loans

Finance companies offer short-term loans to businesses or individuals. They do not accept deposits. In general, finance companies charge high rates of interest because they are willing to provide loans to high-risk customers who are unable to obtain financing elsewhere. Led by General Motors Acceptance Corporation

FINANCE COMPANIES	BROKERAGE HOUSES	LIMITED-SERVICE BANKS
Not offered in finance-company offices, but parent corporations may own consumer banks	Checking as part of an asset-management account at full-service and a few discount firms; some offer automatic teller machines	Regular checking plus interest-bearing NOW and super NOW accounts
Not offered in finance-company offices, but parent corporations may own consumer banks	Money-market funds and certificates of deposit from full-service and some discount firms	Savings accounts, certificates of deposit, and money-market deposit accounts through asset-management accounts
Personal secured and unsecured loans, automobile and home-improvement loans, and second mortgages	Home-equity lines of credit at full-service firms and margin loans at both full-service and discount firms	Personal secured and unsecured loans, automobile and home-improvement loans, first and second mortgages, home-equity lines of credit
Not offered	Full-service and discount stock and bond brokerage	Full-service brokerage or discount brokerage
Credit life and credit disability insurance	Fixed and variable annuities and single-premium life insurance at full-service firms	Life, health, and property and casualty insurance, fixed and variable annuities, and single-premium life insurance
MasterCard and Visa through consumer-bank subsidiaries of parent corporations	American Express Gold Card, Gold MasterCard, and Visa debit card through asset-management accounts	MasterCard, Visa, and Discover; Visa debit card through asset-management accounts
Tax preparation	Investment counseling and management, estate planning, and retirement planning at full-service firms	Investment counseling and management, real estate brokerage, and tax preparation

(GMAC), GE Capital, Ford Motor Credit, and IBM Credit, finance companies have increasingly taken market share from banks. Although they began with consumer loans for new cars, their portfolios have expanded to include major corporate loans, mortgages, and even insurance. Finance companies now provide a quarter of all commercial business loans.[11]

Other Financial Institutions

A variety of other institutions provide selected banking services to businesses and individuals:

▶ *Limited-service banks,* also known as nonbank banks, are hybrid organizations that mix other businesses with certain banking functions. Despite their name, they are anything but limited, often offering a mix of stock-brokerage, insurance, real estate, mortgage, banking, and credit services. They are limited in only one respect: They may make commercial loans or they may accept demand deposits, but they may not do both.

▶ *Large brokerage houses* such as Merrill Lynch have joined the club by expanding beyond the business of selling securities and moving into related financial services. Many now offer personal loans as well as combination savings and checking accounts at attractive interest rates.

▶ *Insurance companies* use part of the money they receive in premiums from policyholders to provide long-term financing for corporations and commercial real estate developers.

▶ *Pension funds* are large pools of money created to provide retirement income for an organization's members. Pension-fund managers invest the money in various ways: business loans, commercial real estate mortgages, government bonds, and corporate securities.

investment banks *Financial institutions that specialize in helping companies or government agencies raise funds*

▶ **Investment banks,** also known as underwriters, are specialized institutions that help corporations raise capital. When a company decides to issue new stocks or bonds, the investment bank buys the entire issue and then resells the securities to the public.

What Banks Do

Although financial institutions differ in the specific services they provide, most do two things: They attract deposits and then lend some of the money to other customers. In addition to accepting deposits and making loans, many offer other money-handling services, for which customers usually pay a fee.

Deposit Functions

Banks have two ways of attracting depositors. First, they can offer interest. Second, they can offer such services as deposit insurance, convenient local branches, free or low-cost checking, long hours, and gifts for new accounts. In the past decade or so, the need to balance costs and income has introduced some unaccustomed flexibility into two major areas of bank operations: interest rates and customer accounts.

INTEREST RATES In the past, the federal government said that banks could pay interest only on savings accounts, and it controlled the interest rates banks could offer. The ceilings were 5.25 percent for commercial banks and 5.50 percent for thrifts. Because banks could not compete on interest rates, they competed on services.

But in the late 1970s, when the annual rate of inflation exceeded 5.50 percent, depositors' savings began losing value; people started depositing less of their money in banks. Hurt by the withdrawal of funds, banks began to press for relief from regulation. In response, the government began to lift interest-rate ceilings. Now competition among financial institutions is partly based on interest rates.

CUSTOMER ACCOUNTS Because of deregulation, the line between checking and savings accounts has blurred. Banks and thrifts now vie for depositors by offering a bewildering array of options featuring various combinations of privileges, fees, and interest rates. And even though banks are under increasing com-

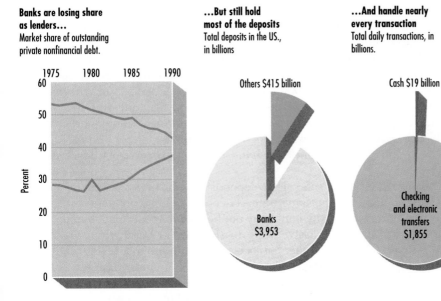

Banks are losing share as lenders...
Market share of outstanding private nonfinancial debt.

...But still hold most of the deposits
Total deposits in the US., in billions

...And handle nearly every transaction
Total daily transactions, in billions.

Others $415 billion

Banks $3,953

Cash $19 billion

Checking and electronic transfers $1,855

EXHIBIT 18.3

The State of U.S. Banking
Banks are losing competitive ground to nonbank lenders. Yet they still hold more than 90 percent of the total number of deposit accounts and handle 99 percent of all monetary transactions in the United States.

petition from nonbanks for loan business, they still hold nearly all deposits in the United States, as indicated in Exhibit 18.3.

Regular checking accounts pay little or no interest, and there is generally a monthly fee as well as a per-check cost. Basic savings accounts, which used to be called passbook accounts, pay a modest interest rate and do not allow check writing. Several types of hybrid accounts combine features of these two traditional accounts. To earn interest on a checking account, for example, you may open a **NOW account,** or negotiable-order-of-withdrawal account, which allows unlimited check writing and pays interest but requires a minimum balance of $2500. A variation, known as the **Super NOW account,** requires an even larger minimum balance but pays higher interest. **Money-market accounts** earn the highest interest of all but often limit the number of checks that may be written.

Checking and savings accounts have one big advantage: They give you immediate, unrestricted access to your money. On the other hand, they pay relatively low interest. If you are willing to invest at least $500 and sacrifice some liquidity, you may earn higher interest by buying a **certificate of deposit,** or CD, a type of time deposit that requires you to leave your money in the bank for a specified period. Banks may offer any interest rates they wish on CDs.

You may also invest up to $2,000 a year ($2,250 for married, single-income couples) in an **individual retirement account,** or IRA, which earns interest that is not taxed until you retire. Some people (depending on their income and pension coverage) can deduct all or part of their IRA contribution from their income taxes. A similar account for self-employed people—a **Keogh account**—has a ceiling of $30,000 a year. Both accounts pay relatively high interest and have certain tax advantages. However, there is a financial penalty if you withdraw your money from an IRA or a Keogh plan prematurely.

Loan Functions

Once the banks have your money, they do not simply put it in a nice little pile in the vault with your name on it. On the contrary, they combine it with all their

NOW account Interest-bearing checking account with a minimum-balance requirement

super NOW account Interest-bearing checking account with a relatively high minimum-balance requirement

money-market accounts Bank accounts that pay money-market interest rates and permit the depositor to write a limited number of checks

certificate of deposit Note issued by a bank that guarantees to pay the depositor a relatively high interest rate for a fixed period of time

individual retirement account Type of savings account that provides tax and interest-rate advantages to depositors who are building a fund for retirement

Keogh account Type of retirement savings account for the self-employed that provides tax and interest-rate advantages

When deciding whether to make loans, bankers look for the three Cs: the *character* of the loan applicant, the applicant's *capacity* to repay the debt, and the *collateral* used to back up the loan. In Glendale, Arizona, First Interstate Bank's loan officer helps a couple apply for a loan.

other deposits and use it to make loans. Because banks know that all their depositors will not withdraw their funds simultaneously, they feel free to lend a majority of those funds to borrowers. The smaller the percentage of total deposits a bank keeps on reserve, the more new loans it can make.

In the process of making loans, banks literally create new money. Say that you apply to your bank for a $1,000 business loan. If the bank grants the loan, it permits you to withdraw up to $1,000 from a reserve account into which you haven't made any deposits. This reserve is in a sense "new" money created by the bank. The government allows banks to create money in this fashion as long as they keep enough real money on hand to meet expected withdrawals by depositors.

What level of reserves is safe? That depends on how many people decide to draw on their accounts at the same time. If depositors lose confidence and rush en masse to withdraw cash, the bank may not be able to meet the demand. Such bank runs occurred on a massive scale in the early 1930s. When President Franklin D. Roosevelt decreed that banks close their doors to forestall panic, he euphemistically called the crisis a "bank holiday." Some individual banks have experienced runs since then, but the federal government has guarded against another national catastrophe by requiring banks to hold in reserve a specified portion of their deposits. The reserve requirement for demand deposits varies from 3 to 12 percent, depending on the total amount of demand deposits that a particular bank has.

The impact of the reserve requirement is greater than meets the eye. Imagine an island with only one bank, which has a 20 percent reserve requirement. Someone deposits $100 in the bank. The bank could make a loan of $80 from that deposit. Now say that the borrower of that $80 deposits it in a checking account at the bank (see Exhibit 18.4). The bank would be required to reserve 20 percent of that new account, or $16, but could lend the other $64. If the second borrower deposited the full $64 in the bank, once again 80 percent of that amount, or $51.20, could be lent. If the process continues, the bank will

EXHIBIT 18.4

How Banks Create Money
Banks stay in business by earning more on interest from loans than they pay out in the form of interest on deposits; they can increase their earnings by "creating" money. When customer A deposits $100, the bank must keep some in reserve but can lend, say, $80 to customer B (and earn interest on that loan). If customer B deposits the borrowed $80 in the same bank, the bank can lend 80 percent of **that** amount to borrower C. The initial $100 deposit, therefore, creates a much larger pool of funds from which customer loans may be made.

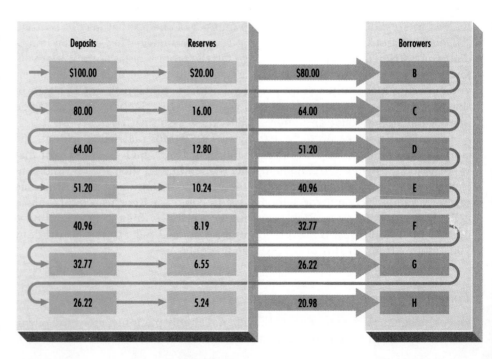

Deposits	Reserves		Borrowers
$100.00	$20.00	$80.00	B
80.00	16.00	64.00	C
64.00	12.80	51.20	D
51.20	10.24	40.96	E
40.96	8.19	32.77	F
32.77	6.55	26.22	G
26.22	5.24	20.98	H

lend about three times the original amount by the time it makes six loans—assuming that all the borrowers eventually deposit their loans in the bank.

Other Services

Although taking deposits and making loans are the main activities of most financial institutions, banks such as NCNB also offer other services, for which they charge a fee. For example, most banks operate a trust department that handles money on behalf of people who are unable to do so directly (such as children or the mentally impaired). Many banks also provide safe deposit boxes for their customers, issue traveler's checks, wire funds around the globe, exchange currency, and issue credit cards—among other things.

One way banks are attepting to increase customer service is by sending customers computer-generated images of canceled checks with monthly statements (rather than returning the checks themselves) One banker says that the new system saves customers having to store check records in shoeboxes or shopping bags. The computerized system also saves a portion of the $45 billion banks spend annually on check processing.[12]

DISCOUNT BROKERAGE   In the early 1980s, many banks added discount brokerage to their service package. The Glass-Steagall Act of 1933 explicitly prohibits banks from underwriting stocks and from giving customers advice on stocks, but discount brokers do neither of these things (the main reason they are able to charge lower fees than full-service brokers). Although the securities industry challenged this invasion of its turf, the Supreme Court ruled in 1986 that banks are within their rights to expand into discount brokerage.[13] NCNB is one bank that has obtained approval to go beyond discount-brokerage services and offer its customers investment advice.

ELECTRONIC BANKING   Banking with the aid of computerized equipment is one of the financial industry's newest and most controversial "services." It takes many forms, some of which are popular with bank customers and some of which are not. Theoretically, at least, **electronic funds transfer systems** (EFTs) offer something for everyone: convenience for customers and cost savings for financial institutions. One of the most popular electronic-banking options allows employers to transfer wages directly from the company bank account to employee accounts. This service saves both employer and employee the inconvenience of handling large amounts of cash.

Convenience is also a major attraction of **automated teller machines** (ATMs), which are freestanding self-service terminals that can do about 60 percent of a teller's job 24 hours a day at less than half the cost of a human teller.[14] To use an ATM, you insert a plastic card into the terminal and then enter an identification code. The machine responds by cashing checks, taking deposits, or handling other simple banking transactions.

A more complex variation of electronic banking involves the use of point-of-sale terminals located at merchants' checkout counters and tied electronically to a bank computer. When a store customer presents a **debit card,** the point-of-sale terminal automatically transfers the money for the purchase from the customer's account to the store's account. Yet another variation enables a person to pay bills automatically by using a personal computer, which is linked by telephone to the bank computer. When the customer types in the required information, the bank computer transfers money from the customer's account to the biller's account.

Automated teller machines cannot provide the human touch, but they are convenient for customers and economical for banks.

electronic funds transfer systems Computerized systems for performing financial transactions

automated teller machines Electronic terminals that permit people to perform simple banking transactions without the aid of a human teller

debit card Form of plastic money that automatically decreases a person's bank account when used

Today's Banking Environment

Technological advances are but a small part of the revolution occurring in U.S. banks; the entire financial system is undergoing a sea change not seen since the Great Depression. From 1980 through 1990, 1,228 banks failed, much of the thrift industry had to be salvaged by the largest taxpayer-financed bailout in history, the loan-deposit insurance fund for savings and loan associations collapsed, and the similar fund for banks floundered on the verge of insolvency. By 1990 banks' after-tax profits had dropped to a meager $20 billion, and the total amount of bad loans had soared to $418 billion. But a look at the world's 30 largest banks may provide the most ominous indication of how far U.S. banks have fallen: in 1969, nine were in the United States, including the top three; by 1989, only Citibank was on the list, and it was in 27th place.[15]

The financial system's plight was caused by a combination of inflation and its subsequent easing, deregulation, growth in commercial building, and competition both within the United States and from foreign banks. Since the Depression, banking had been a highly regulated industry, part of a fragmented financial system: Commercial banks made business loans, thrifts lent money for home mortgages, investment banks underwrote corporate stock and bond issues, brokerages sold those securities, and insurance companies insured businesses and individuals.

This segmented approach worked well until double-digit inflation hit the U.S. economy in the late 1970s. Its effect on financial institutions was pernicious. First, major depositors increasingly moved their money out of banks and thrifts and into money-market accounts, which could offer higher market rates of interest because they were not regulated. In turn, banks and thrifts convinced Congress to deregulate their industries so that they could compete for depositors. As a result, financial institutions made decisions that, in noninflationary and less competitive times, might not have been made.

Banks and thrifts invested heavily in real estate, particularly large-scale projects like office towers and shopping malls. The majority of these loans were questionable, if not blatantly risky and, in some cases, fraudulent. Congress unwittingly contributed to the problem when it decided in 1982 to raise the ceiling on all insured deposits at banks and thrifts to $100,000. This enabled institutions to raise the interest they paid on deposits to unrealistic levels, while allowing them to lend money on overly liberal terms. So a commercial building boom swept the United States, eventually producing more than 500 million square feet of vacant office space. The glut took its toll: The U.S. real estate market crashed with a devastating impact on all banks and thrifts, large or small.[16]

Simultaneously, deregulation was blurring the lines between various kinds of financial institutions. Many large banks now have subsidiaries that sell stocks and bonds, just as major brokerages now offer checking and credit card accounts. Real estate services can be found at banks and brokerages, and banks in states that allow it are entering the insurance business for the first time since the Depression. But probably the biggest change has been in banks' cornerstone business: short-term commercial lending. Rising inflation hurt U.S. businesses that relied on short-term loans from major banks. As inflation rose, businesses paid increasingly higher interest rates on debt financing.

However, the situation did not reverse itself when inflation began falling; banks kept rates high to raise profits during difficult times. This caused an increasing number of U.S. businesses to turn to foreign banks, which charged

In the wake of deregulation, financial institutions such as this Manhattan branch of First Federal Savings and Loan are competing more aggressively for business.

lower interest rates, and it caused corporations to issue **commercial paper,** an IOU from corporations to raise short-term capital.

As banks became increasingly reluctant to make commercial loans, businesses found buyers willing to purchase corporate paper in finance companies, particularly companies like General Motors Acceptance Corporation (GMAC) and GE Credit, a subsidiary of General Electric. Finance companies thrived on the commercial-paper market, which grew 500 percent during the 1980s. The losers were the banks, which saw a key part of their business slip away to unregulated companies. By 1989, GMAC and Ford Motor Credit had become the largest corporate lenders in the United States.[17]

But private companies weren't the only competitors; foreign banks took a larger share of the U.S. market for corporate business. And it was the largest U.S. corporations that were going offshore for capital: By the end of the 1980s, 40 percent of corporations with at least $5 billion in sales were using Japanese banks.[18]

commercial paper An IOU issued by corporations to raise short-term capital

VIDEO EXERCISE

Banks

All of these factors together meant that by the beginning of the 1990s, the U.S. banking system was in its worst condition since the Depression. The decade opened with the federal government rescuing one of the nation's largest banks and Congress debating sweeping reform proposals. The 1990s promise to be a time of consolidation in the industry; some experts predict that the top 125 banks will be reduced to 15 nationwide institutions.[19]

The federal rescue of the Bank of New England (BNE) was a landmark event. On the morning following the bank's announcement that it would lose $450 million in one quarter alone, depositors made a run for their money. Nearly $1 billion was withdrawn, much of it electronically by pension fund and insurance companies that pulled out multimillion-dollar deposits. By Sunday the Federal Deposit Insurance Corporation (FDIC) took over the failing institution, and calm was restored, albeit at an estimated cost of $3 billion.

But the dramatic episode made bankers everywhere nervous. BNE's collapse began when the value of its loan portfolio did a freefall along with the region's real estate market—the same situation faced by most of the nation's large banks. Moreover, the declining value of real estate loan portfolios was only the latest problem faced by the large banks, which were still struggling with problem loans to Third World nations.[20]

So it was no wonder that the largest U.S. banks enthusiastically supported the sweeping reforms before Congress. The heart of the program, introduced by the Bush administration only 12 days before BNE's rescue, appeared as three proposals that would dismantle the archaically segmented financial system:

▶ *Interstate banking.* Long considered a necessity if U.S. banks were to operate efficiently, this proposal would allow banks to open branches anywhere in the United States (nullifying the McFadden Act of 1927).

▶ *Financial services.* Bankers had complained for years that regulations prevented them from competing with nonbanks, so this proposal would allow commercial banks to merge with investment banks, sell stocks and bonds, and give investment advice (thereby annulling the Glass-Steagall Act of 1933).

▶ *Industrial ownership.* Considered one of the most radical proposals, this would allow industrial corporations to own banks (effectively canceling the Bank Holding Act of 1956).[21]

Business Around the World

Wielkopolski Bank Kredytowy is leading Poland into a market-based, private banking system. WBK is the first commercial bank in Poland to be sold by the government to private interests. It has 46 branches, 3,000 employees, and $124 million in assets.

Lawmakers and industry leaders agreed that these changes were necessary if the U.S. banking system was to compete globally into the twenty-first century. Bankers didn't waste their time preparing for the inevitable changes. A wave of consolidations began throughout the industry, mergers that are likely to continue until most of the excess capacity has been squeezed out of the system. Hugh L. McColl's NCNB is only one bank that has gone on the hunt; its mergers with First RepublicBank and C&S–Sovran are only two of the early consolidations.

Only three days before NCNB decided to merge with C&S–Sovran, Wachovia Bank and Trust announced its merger with South Carolina National Bank. Meanwhile, Fleet-Norstar Financial Group acquired the untroubled assets of BNE, and scores of smaller consolidations turned once medium-sized banks into superregionals such as Banc One in Columbus, Ohio. By acquiring smaller, troubled banks and thrifts, Banc One grew in a relatively short period to more than 850 branches in seven states, with assets of just under $100 billion. Among the largest banks, New York City rivals Chemical Bank and Manufacturers Hanover agreed to merge into the nation's second largest bank with $135 billion in assets, but that status lasted a scant three weeks before California behemoths BankAmerica and Security Pacific announced they would join in a $4.5 billion deal, taking over second place with $194 billion in assets.[22]

Estimates predict that the creation of megabanks with an interstate market could trim $10 billion a year from the industry's operating costs (since mergers and acquisitions always cause layoffs and other cost-cutting steps). Even banks that remain independent are cutting the fat by combining departments, closing branches, and expanding low-cost, high-revenue financial services such as credit card operations. But not everyone thinks consolidation is necessarily

EXPLORING INTERNATIONAL BUSINESS

Japan's Banking Empire: Changing Strategies to Retain World Lender Leadership

Not one Japanese bank was listed among the world's top five banks in 1980. But by 1988 the top 12 banks were all Japanese (ranked by deposits). The largest Japanese banks grew not only domestically but internationally, opening branches in the United States, in Europe, and throughout Asia. Now winds of change are blowing, and Japanese banks are facing an end to their expansionist days.

Japanese banks were able to expand during the 1980s because the country's economy was growing rapidly, financed by a high rate of domestic savings and a low rate of interest (which was deliberately kept low by the government to fuel industrial development). Japanese banks were so profitable that they invested heavily in domestic and foreign real estate and in the securities of Japanese corporations, which also owned large amounts of real estate. More-

over, their high-flying success allowed them to pursue a long-term strategy of gaining market share in foreign markets. This was particularly true in the United States, where interest charged on commercial loans was much higher and, therefore, less competitive than the rates offered by Japanese banks.

But the 1980s came to an end, and so did the easy profits for Japanese banks. Early 1990 brought a wave of changes that are still sweeping across the Japanese banking industry:

▶ A dramatic devaluation of Japanese securities and the beginning of what appears to be a long-term slide in domestic real estate values. The Tokyo stock market took a sudden plunge in 1990, and values have remained lower for longer than expected. At the same time, Japanese real estate values began their own fall from once-lofty heights.

▶ A drop in value (drastic, in some cases) of foreign real estate holdings held by Japanese banks. This was princi-

good, despite its inevitability. Economists at the Federal Reserve have found that depositors earn less interest and that borrowers pay more interest in states having highly concentrated banks.[23]

The institutions that could fare the best during the industry's consolidation are small community banks. They have a characteristic that larger banks are striving to duplicate: personal relationships with customers. This is particularly true with small businesses, which have found it increasingly difficult to obtain loans from banks squeezed by competition and regulation. In many communities around the United States, small businesses have even acted as the catalyst for start-up banks. Although most community banks, particularly the weaker ones, will be swallowed up in the wave of consolidation, many are expected to remain viable institutions with less than $100 million in assets.[24]

Thrifts

The institutions facing an even more questionable future are thrifts. In the wake of the S&L debacle and a bailout that is likely to cost taxpayers $500 billion (and take until 2020 to be paid off), many in the financial-services industry wonder whether savings and loan associations are even necessary anymore.

The thrift industry was created in the 1930s for the sole purpose of providing inexpensive home loans. S&Ls did nothing but finance mortgages for decades. But when inflation caused their costs to go up as regulations capped their earnings, Congress passed a series of deregulatory measures. The one that inevitably caused the industry's fall was a provision allowing S&Ls to invest directly in real estate. With the government insuring all deposits up to $100,000, thrift manag-

pally because the banks bought at the top of the U.S. and European markets. Real estate in the United States took an especially sudden and sharp plunge, leaving Japanese owners with the prospect either of holding property for years at less than purchase price or of losing money by selling out.

▶ A gradual deregulation of both the Japanese banking industry and the Japanese interest rates. This reform was instituted by the Japanese Finance Ministry, and it is expected to be complete by 1993. The goal of deregulation is to make nearly all Japanese banks equal in terms of what kinds of business services they can offer to what types of clients. With interest rates rising to market levels (unfettered by government regulations), Japanese banks are already seeing their profit margins being squeezed.

▶ A requirement for all Japanese banks to have enough capital on hand to cover 8 percent of risk-adjusted assets. The Bank for International Settlements, which sets rules for all banks doing international business, is changing a key guideline, to take effect in 1993. For example, Sanwa Bank, the fourth largest bank in Japan, saw its capital ratio drop to 7.7 percent because it had invested so heavily in Japanese equity markets. The result is that Sanwa and most Japanese banks must now raise fresh capital.

Because of such market and regulatory changes, the profits of Japanese banks are being squeezed by falling asset values, corporate clients who are finding competitive loan rates overseas, retail clients who are saving less than in the past, and increased reserve requirements. Thus, Japanese banks have changed their business strategies from gaining long-term market share and asset growth to a shorter-term concern for profits. And this shift has caused the Japanese banking industry to undergo its own consolidation.

The rest of the world's banking community is wary, even when it might be expected to rejoice: Larger Japanese banks will likely be even more fearsome competitors. An eye-opening example came in late 1989, when the largest bank merger in history was announced. Mitsui and Taiyo Kobe banks agreed to create the second largest bank in the world, with $348 billion in assets, $9.02 billion in capital, and 611 branches worldwide.

In Patterson, New Jersey, hundreds of investors waited in line to collect their money from United Savings Bank, a savings and loan that recently failed.

ers sought out increasingly speculative deals. So when real estate markets crashed, taxpayers were forced to bail out the industry.

But the rescue had a steep price. The sweeping bailout bill passed by Congress in 1989 authorized interested banks to immediately buy thrifts and merge their branch systems. It also required thrifts to meet more stringent financial requirements—so rigorous that many of the nation's thrifts are expected to go out of business because of this measure alone.

Ironically, the most restrictive part of the legislation required 70 percent of thrifts' assets to be in mortgage-related investments. Essentially, Congress took the industry back to its roots: lending to homebuyers. But mortgage finance has changed drastically since the 1930s. Today, mortgages are packaged into securities, which are then sold to institutional investors such as pension funds and insurance companies. Increasingly, commercial banks and finance companies underwrite these securities. So the question is whether thrifts can remain viable as distinct financial institutions.

Thrifts are regulated by the Office of Thrift Supervision, which is supervised by the Treasury Department, and their deposits are insured by the FDIC. The Federal Savings and Loan Insurance Corporation (FSLIC), which once insured thrift deposits, does not exist today.[25]

Bank Safety

Concern over the S&L industry has been surpassed by worries about the U.S. banking system and deposit insurance, which has become enormously important. As former FDIC Chairman L. William Seidman said, "Our whole financial system runs on confidence and not much else when you get down to it."[26] And

FOCUS ON ETHICS

BCCI Trips Up a Statesman

As an elder statesman who embodied Washington respectability, Clark Clifford had advised such presidents as Harry Truman, John F. Kennedy, Lyndon B. Johnson, and Jimmy Carter during his historic career. But in 1991, his reputation was ruined in the largest banking scandal in history. As one old friend said, he took "one of the 'grand falls.'" Whether he broke federal banking laws or not, Clifford's ethical lapse, his decade-old failure to do the right thing, destroyed all he had worked hard to build.

The story erupted when 62 nations shut down branch operations of the Bank of Credit & Commerce (BCCI) of Pakistan. It was discovered that BCCI was running a $20 billion Ponzi scheme. In a typical Ponzi scheme, "investors" are paid "gains" out of money taken from new investors, a process that requires ever-larger amounts of money to be taken from an increasing number of investors. BCCI's scheme relied on fictitious loans created from deposits, a process that could last only as long as additional deposits were brought into the bank and its subsidiaries.

BCCI bought First American Bankshares, a holding company for the third largest bank in the District of Columbia, Maryland, and Virginia. Clifford was BCCI's secret intermediary in this transaction, and he was later installed as First American's chairman. BCCI's true ownership of the bank was not registered with bank regulators, who thought the money had come from Clifford and an associate. Later, when Clifford sold his shares in First American, he received $6 million in profit. And during the decade that he served as an intermediary for BCCI, he defended BCCI against money-laundering charges involving a Florida bank that was owned by BCCI but that had no association with First American.

confidence is in short supply, even in the industry. One survey found that 47 percent of the American Bankers Association doubted the FDIC could insure all deposits.[27]

The controversy surrounding the FDIC focuses on three points:

▶ Solvency of the so-called fund that insures deposits in FDIC banks

▶ The unwritten "too-big-to-fail" doctrine

▶ The amount of insurance available on each deposit

The idea that the FDIC is in charge of a pool of money is a myth; in fact, no fund exists. The FDIC collects insurance premiums from banks only to send the money to the Treasury, where it is put in the general fund to finance everything from defense needs to highway construction. When a bank fails, the Treasury borrows money in the financial markets on behalf of the FDIC, which actually keeps a balance at all times of how much money it's collected and how much it's spent. Therefore, the fund is nothing more than a balance sheet.[28]

The FDIC was in black ink by about $2 billion at the end of 1990 and expected to be in the red by 1992. Proposals for how to keep the FDIC solvent have focused on increasing the agency's authority to borrow from the Treasury (raising amounts from $5 billion to $70 billion). In question is who would pay for the higher borrowing needs. Insurance premiums paid by banks already skyrocketed 277 percent between 1989 and 1991 alone, and bankers warned that further increases would only cause more failures.[29]

Everyone from members of Congress to members of the financial community is most concerned about the FDIC having to bail out a money-center bank, which by itself would bankrupt the "fund." For decades everyone believed that

The legal questions were obvious. Foremost was whether Clifford had deliberately misrepresented ownership of First American to U.S. regulators; the Federal Reserve was unaware of the bank's true owners for 10 years. Beyond the legalities, however, were serious ethical questions. Did Clifford lie to regulators and other shareholders of the bank? Why had he kept the true owners of First American a secret for a decade? Was the $6 million profit his or someone else's? Did he misrepresent himself when he sold those shares of stock? Why would he represent BCCI in the Florida money-laundering case when it wasn't his bank that was under indictment?

Clifford summed up his dilemma himself: "I have a choice of either seeming stupid or venal." Harry McPherson, former aid to President Johnson and friend of Clifford, said that if the stories were true, "this required either a failure of intellect or a failure of ethical reasoning."

Clifford protested publicly that he had been deceived by BCCI's ringleaders. But the damage was done. A fallen man whose ethics were being questioned on all sides, Clifford found himself at the center of investigations by the Federal Reserve Board, the Justice Department, and the Manhattan district attorney's office. Instead of giving advice, as he had so often done in years past, Clifford was forced to seek it. But all he could get was legal counsel; it was too late for ethical advice.

In December 1991, BCCI pleaded guilty to federal and state charges of racketeering, fraud, and money laundering. The bank surrendered all U.S. assets, some $550 million, making BCCI's settlement the largest criminal forfeiture in history. The bank is shut down in most countries but still operates in Pakistan, Switzerland, Zambia, and Zimbabwe.

the federal government would never let a major bank fail. Hence, the FDIC had stepped in immediately when the Bank of New England was threatened with collapse. BNE was an institution considered too large to let fail, so all deposits, even those of more than $100,000, were protected. In reality, though, the "too-big-to-fail" doctrine has been extended to all but the smallest community banks, which is the primary reason for the FDIC's financial problems. As one observer described it, deposit insurance "is like an auto-insurance fund where 16-year-old drunks and Sunday drivers pay the same premium, and everybody gets fully paid off in an accident."[30]

The debate about reforming the entire banking system has included suggestions for changing deposit insurance. The Bush administration's bank reform package included a proposal to limit the number of insured accounts to two, each with a $100,000 ceiling. But the most far-reaching reform idea is to insure only some deposits. Banks would essentially have two types of deposit "windows." At one window, depositors would receive a lower rate of interest but would have the confidence that their deposit was insured by the federal government. If, on the other hand, depositors wanted to receive a higher rate of interest, they could go to the other window. In return for a higher rate of interest, the deposit would not be insured. This would allow banks to make a variety of loans, from conservative to speculative ones. Thus they would be better able to compete with nonbank banks, strengthening the banking system and the U.S. financial system.[31]

▶ THE FEDERAL RESERVE SYSTEM

The Federal Reserve System was created in 1913 and is commonly known as the Fed. It is the nation's most powerful financial institution, serving as the country's central bank. The Fed's primary role is to supply us with the "right" amount of money so that we avoid both recession and inflation. It also supervises and regulates banks and serves as a clearinghouse for checks.

The Federal Reserve's Structure and Mission

The Fed is a network of 12 regional banks that controls the country's banking system. Each bank serves as a central bank for its district and is owned by the participating commercial banks within its region. Almost 5,500 banks are members of the system, including all the national banks and 90 percent of the state banks. (The rest of the state banks are regulated chiefly by state governments, which tend to have more liberal policies than the Fed.)[32]

The Fed's regulatory authority was strengthened in 1980 by the Depository Institutions Deregulation and Monetary Control Act, which, among other things, extended some of the Fed's regulatory powers to cover nonmember banks, savings banks, and savings and loan associations. In addition, the Fed can often persuade nonmember banks to follow its policies simply by "jawboning," or threatening to use its considerable power.

The overall policy of the Fed is established by a seven-member board of governors in Washington, D.C. To preserve their political independence, the members are appointed by the president to 14-year terms, staggered at 2-year intervals. This board is so influential that the chairman is considered by some to be the second most powerful person in the United States.

The Federal Reserve's Functions

The Fed's main job is to establish and implement **monetary policy,** which is a set of guidelines for handling the nation's economy and the money supply. It aims to make certain that enough money and credit are available to allow the economy to expand, thus giving the country an ever-increasing supply of goods, services, and jobs. It must also be careful not to release too much money and credit into the economy at any one time because a surplus has historically produced inflation. In attempting to foster steady and stable economic growth, the Fed works with the president and Congress, who are responsible for fiscal policy, or government spending and taxation.

The Federal Reserve System has three major functions: regulating the money supply, supplying currency, and clearing checks. The most important of these is regulating the money supply.

Regulating the Money Supply

The Fed uses monetary policy in an attempt to stimulate growth and employment while keeping inflation down. However, complications may arise. For example, when the money supply increases and there is more money to go around, banks can charge lower interest to borrowers. But an increased money supply may lead to more spending and thus more inflation. During inflationary periods, the dollars that borrowers repay to lenders have less purchasing power than they had when the loan was made. To offset this loss of purchasing power, lenders must add a certain percentage—corresponding to the rate of inflation—to the interest rates they would otherwise charge. So a growth in the money supply, if it fans inflation, may actually lead to higher interest rates.

The Federal Reserve has an additional responsibility: The Fed is the official banker of the federal government—specifically, the U.S. Department of the Treasury. When the federal budget is running a deficit, the Treasury must raise money to fill the gap. If the Treasury borrows from the public, it competes with consumer and business borrowing, which may push up interest rates. To avoid such pressure on interest rates, the Fed might choose to lend money to the Treasury itself. But the cash (or demand deposits) that the Fed supplies to the Treasury is new money pumped into the economy. This increase in the money supply may lead to inflation, thus conflicting with other aspects of monetary policy.

To implement its monetary policy, the Fed has four basic tools: It can change reserve requirements; it can change the interest rate that member banks must pay to borrow from the Fed (the discount rate); it can buy or sell government securities (open-market operations); and it can set the terms of credit for certain types of loans (selective credit controls). Exhibit 18.5 summarizes the effects of using these tools.

RESERVE REQUIREMENTS   The Fed requires all member banks and financial institutions to set aside **reserves,** sums of money equal to a certain percentage of their deposits. The percentage of deposits that banks must set aside is called the **reserve requirement.** The bank keeps this money on deposit with the Federal Reserve Bank in its district.

Changing the reserve requirement is a powerful tool that is used for occasional gross adjustments to the money supply. If the Federal Reserve believes

monetary policy Tactics for expanding or contracting the money supply as a means of influencing the economy

reserves Funds a financial institution keeps on tap to meet projected withdrawals

reserve requirement Percentage of a bank's deposits that must be kept on hand

EXHIBIT 18.5

How the Fed Controls the Money Supply

The Fed manipulates the money supply in various ways in its efforts to keep both inflation and interest rates at acceptable levels.

To increase the money supply		To decrease the money supply
Decrease	**Reserve requirements**	Increase
Lower	**Discount rate**	Raise
Buy	**Open-market operations**	Sell
Fewer	**Selective credit controls**	More

that consumers and businesses are buying too much and that inflation is heating up, the Fed increases reserve requirements. When reserve requirements increase, banks cannot lend as much to their customers, so less is spent in the economy. Conversely, the Fed may reduce reserve requirements if its economists feel that stimulating business would benefit the economy. Theoretically, banks will make more loans to businesses and consumers when reserve requirements are reduced; businesses and consumers, in turn, will spend more. The desired result is more sales for business and more jobs for everyone.

Some banks invariably find that they have more reserves on deposit at the Fed than they need for the short term; others find that their reserves are insufficient for the short term and that they must make up the difference. If a bank with a surplus wishes to lend its excess reserves to a bank with a deficit, the Fed conveniently makes the bookkeeping entries for the two banks so that the funds never actually need to be moved around. The interest rate that banks charge each other for overnight loans is called the **Fed funds rate**.

Fed funds rate Interest rate charged for overnight loans between banks

THE DISCOUNT RATE Banks can obtain extra funds to lend to their customers by borrowing from their regional Federal Reserve Bank, which in a sense is banker to the banks. The interest rate that the Fed charges member banks for loans is called the **discount rate.** Discounting is often attractive to commercial banks because they can charge their customers a substantially higher rate for the loans made from the funds that they themselves have borrowed from the Fed, thereby earning a nice profit. But discounting has disadvantages too: When a bank borrows from the Fed, the Fed typically imposes conditions on the bank's operations.

discount rate Interest rate charged by the Federal Reserve on loans to member banks

Here again is a way in which the Fed can control the economy. If the Fed wishes to encourage member banks to make loans to customers, it lowers the discount rate. And if the Fed wants to discourage loans, it raises the discount rate. These actions may indirectly affect the **prime interest rate**—the lowest rate at which banks will make loans to their most creditworthy business customers. The prime interest rate is also directly affected by supply and demand for loans.

prime interest rate Lowest rate of interest charged by banks for loans to their most creditworthy customers

The power of interest rates to affect the economy may be significant. Overall, each percentage-point drop in average interest rates adds about one-third of a percentage point to the nation's annual economic growth.

OPEN-MARKET OPERATIONS   The tool that the Fed uses most frequently to carry out monetary policy is its power to buy and sell government bonds (which are promises to repay a debt, with interest). Because anyone can buy these government bonds on the open market, this tool is known as **open-market operations.** The bonds are attractive purchases because lending to the government is considered a risk-free way of earning interest.

If the Fed is concerned about inflation and wants to reduce the amount of money available, it sells government bonds to the public and to banks. The money paid for the bonds immediately goes out of circulation. Conversely, when the Fed wants to get the economy moving again, the government buys back its bonds, thus putting additional cash back into the economy. Because the money supply increases, interest rates drop, so businesses borrow more money at a lower cost and expand their opportunities for growth and competition.

open-market operations Activity of the Federal Reserve in buying and selling government bonds on the open market

SELECTIVE CREDIT CONTROLS   The Fed also has the power to set credit terms for various kinds of loans. By exercising this power, known as **selective credit controls,** it can exert great influence on business activity.

For example, the Fed may set **margin requirements,** which limit the amount of money that stockbrokers and banks may lend a customer for buying stocks. When government economists feel that there is too much stock-market speculation for the economy's good, the Fed simply sets margin requirements at levels that will prevent financial institutions from lending much money for stock purchases.

selective credit controls Federal Reserve's power to set credit terms on various types of loans

margin requirements Limits set by the Federal Reserve on the amount of money that stockbrokers and banks may lend customers for the purpose of buying stocks

Supplying Currency

In addition to regulating the money supply, the Fed performs other functions that help keep the financial system running smoothly. For example, individual Federal Reserve Banks are responsible for providing member banks with adequate amounts of currency.

The demand for coins and paper money is seasonal. As you might expect, many people withdraw some of their savings from the banks in the form of cash during the winter holidays. The Federal Reserve has to supply the extra currency that banks need at such times.

Clearing Checks

Another function of the Fed is to act as a clearinghouse for checks. Banks use the Fed's check-processing system to clear checks drawn on banks outside their Federal Reserve districts (see Exhibit 18.6). For example, a check written against an account in a Chicago bank may be deposited in a bank in Atlanta. The Atlanta bank forwards the check to the Federal Reserve Bank in Atlanta, which collects the funds from the Chicago Federal Reserve Bank and credits the account of the local bank. For a high-value check, the Atlanta bank may do a "direct send"—that is, it may forward the check to the Federal Reserve Bank in Chicago.

Not all checks are sent to the Fed for clearance. Many rural banks simply pay larger banks to perform this service for them. And transactions among banks in the same area are handled locally and then reported to the Federal Reserve, which charges and credits the appropriate accounts. Imagine that, on a particu-

EXHIBIT 18.6

How a Check Clears
The Fed has been processing more than 55 billion checks per year.

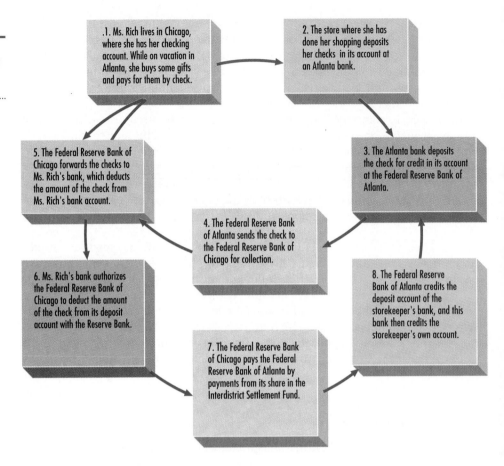

.1. Ms. Rich lives in Chicago, where she has her checking account. While on vacation in Atlanta, she buys some gifts and pays for them by check.

2. The store where she has done her shopping deposits her checks in its account at an Atlanta bank.

3. The Atlanta bank deposits the check for credit in its account at the Federal Reserve Bank of Atlanta.

4. The Federal Reserve Bank of Atlanta sends the check to the Federal Reserve Bank of Chicago for collection.

5. The Federal Reserve Bank of Chicago forwards the checks to Ms. Rich's bank, which deducts the amount of the check from Ms. Rich's bank account.

6. Ms. Rich's bank authorizes the Federal Reserve Bank of Chicago to deduct the amount of the check from its deposit account with the Reserve Bank.

7. The Federal Reserve Bank of Chicago pays the Federal Reserve Bank of Atlanta by payments from its share in the Interdistrict Settlement Fund.

8. The Federal Reserve Bank of Atlanta credits the deposit account of the storekeeper's bank, and this bank then credits the storekeeper's own account.

lar day, checks written on accounts at the Tallahassee National Bank total $550 and have been deposited in accounts at the First Miami Bank. At the same time, the Federal Reserve Bank in Atlanta notes that First Miami's depositors have written $400 worth of checks that have been deposited at Tallahassee. The Federal Reserve Bank balances out the difference, crediting First Miami with $150 and subtracting the same amount from Tallahassee National's account. But the checks written by the customers of Tallahassee National and First Miami are actually deposited in banks all over the district during the normal course of business. In actuality, all the debits and credits from all the banks in the district have to be added up before the proper amounts can be added to or subtracted from Tallahassee National's and First Miami's accounts with their Federal Reserve district bank.

SUMMARY OF LEARNING OBJECTIVES

1 Name three functions of money.
Money functions as a medium of exchange, a measure of value, and a store of value.

2 Distinguish M1 from the total money supply.

The total money supply comprises currency, demand deposits, and time deposits. M1 is that part of the money supply slated to be spent fairly soon, and it consists of currency and demand deposits.

3 Differentiate between demand deposits and time deposits.
Demand deposits are more liquid than time deposits. A demand deposit, such as a checking account or NOW account, may be used as a medium of exchange; time deposits (savings ac-

counts, money-market funds, certificates of deposit) may not.

4 Identify nine members of the banking system.

The participants in the banking system include commercial banks, thrift institutions, credit unions, finance companies, limited-service banks, brokerage houses, insurance companies, pension funds, and investment banks.

5 Explain how deregulation has affected the financial system.

By enabling banks and thrifts to compete on the basis of interest rates, deregulation has increased the cost of money and depressed banks' profits.

At the same time, deregulation has enabled banks to diversify their activities and expand their geographic base of operations. Banking has become a more competitive business.

6 Explain the responsibilities and insurance methods of the FDIC.

The Federal Deposit Insurance Corporation is a federal insurance program that protects depositors in member banks. It insures depositors for up to $100,000 per account if a bank should fail. Banks pay premiums to the FDIC, so it can keep banks solvent by borrowing from the Treasury Department.

7 Describe the organization of the Federal Reserve System.

The Federal Reserve System consists of almost 5,500 member banks and 12 regional banks, which are owned by participating banks in each district. The overall system is administered by a seven-member board of governors whose members are appointed to 14-year terms, at 2-year intervals.

8 Cite the four ways the Federal Reserve System regulates the money supply.

The Fed regulates the money supply by changing reserve requirements, changing the discount rate, carrying out open-market operations, and setting selective credit controls.

Meeting a Business Challenge at NCNB

Hugh L. McColl, Jr., had spent years extending his bank's presence throughout the Southeast, first in NCNB's home state of North Carolina and then into South Carolina and Florida. McColl had brought NCNB to superregional status, but he knew that the time had come to take some huge steps: Either NCNB would become one of the nation's largest and most powerful banks by making major acquisitions, or it would be gobbled up by an even more aggressive national competitor.

McColl's first big chance came in the Southwest, where ailing banks and thrifts were ripe for picking. He pulled off a buyout that critics and admirers alike called the deal of the century. He was headlined as the banker who had bought Texas after he engineered the acquisition of First RepublicBank, the largest and most financially troubled bank in the Lone Star State. What made it so remarkable was that NCNB acquired a bank that was larger than itself, thus gaining precious market share in four of the five largest cities in Texas. Moreover, NCNB did so without assuming any of the bad

Hugh L. McColl, Jr., chairman of NCNB.

real estate loans that had caused First RepublicBank's downfall. About $10 billion in nonperforming loans was taken over by the Federal Deposit Insurance Corporation (FDIC), which was desperate to keep First RepublicBank afloat. With the government essentially assuming the risk of the bad loans, McColl's NCNB was able to buy the solid assets of the troubled institution for a song:

$210 million for a 20 percent stake in First RepublicBank, with a five-year option to purchase the remaining 80 percent from the FDIC (which had recapitalized the ailing bank with $840 million). The only shortcoming to First RepublicBank was its small branch system, a problem McColl rectified by buying 18 other failing banks and thrifts across Texas. Almost overnight NCNB went from having no presence in Texas to being that state's largest bank.

The acquisition made NCNB a bank to watch and McColl a banker to fear. He wasn't fooling when he said, "Once you stop growing, you start dying." The question was, Which bank would fall prey to his empire-building grasp next? As it turned out, it was an old adversary, C&S–Sovran, itself the product of a merger between North Carolina's Citizens and Southern (which McColl had unsuccessfully tried to acquire years earlier) and Virginia's Sovran Financial Corporation. Citizens and Southern had fled NCNB's takeover attempt and run right into the arms of Sovran, an institution that carried a sizable load of bad real estate loans, many of them in the overbuilt commercial real estate market around Washington, D.C. Unable to manage those bad loans, C&S–Sovran now had to find its own white knight, which brought McColl riding in at full gallop. NCNB's acquisition of C&S–Sovran was actually made possible by its buyout of First RepublicBank: Because the FDIC had assumed the risk of the Texas bank's bad loans, NCNB was financially large enough to withstand the risks it would encounter by taking over C&S–Sovran's sickly real estate loans. The $26 billion deal resulted in the creation of a $116 billion (assets) institution, eclipsed only by Citicorp, BankAmerica, and Chemical Banking Corporation. McColl named his new institution after the vision of prominence he had clung to for years: NationsBank.

In less than five years, McColl had changed his superregional southeastern bank into the country's fourth largest bank with branches stretching from the Chesapeake Bay to the Rio Grande, from the Blue Ridge of Virginia to the swaying palms of Miami Beach. McColl set a stunning example for the future of U.S. banking: Large-scale, service-oriented institutions can make money by using economies of scale to reduce costs and by providing customers of all types with a wide array of services, thereby avoiding the traps of speculative loans. It is a new age of banking in the United States, one that will likely continue evolving as the twentieth century draws to an end.

Your Mission: NCNB is now NationsBank. Hugh L. McColl, Jr., has appointed you his special assistant in charge of growth strategy. It is your job to work with McColl on issues facing NationsBank as it grows ever larger. You are less concerned with operational issues and more concerned with the overall direction of the company and its major policies. You report directly to McColl.

1. The Senate Committee on Banking, Housing and Urban Affairs has invited McColl to testify at hearings concerning the future of banking and financial services in the United States. Some senators want to reregulate the industry to prevent a repetition of the S&L scandal and subsequent bailout; others want to deregulate the industry even more, paving the way for complete interstate banking so that any bank would be allowed to operate in all 50 states. Given NationsBank's history and McColl's experience and outlook, what should McColl recommend?

a. Reregulate the industry to return it to the sensibly safe and profitable business it once was.

b. Retain just enough regulation to protect depositors and institutions alike during the industry's drive to merge and consolidate.

c. Strip away all remaining regulations that make distinctions between commercial banks, investment banks, and securities brokerages so that there would be competition among all types of financial services in all types of companies.

d. Assign a larger role to the federal government—and hence to the U.S. taxpayer—in helping banks merge and consolidate, principally by assuming the bad loans of failing institutions.

2. One of the problems NationsBank is experiencing in its aggressive growth strategy is having enough qualified managers to oversee the increasing number of branches and services. What should NationsBank do?

a. Hire managers whose jobs have been eliminated by the merging and consolidation of other institutions.

b. Improve NationsBank's training program for midlevel managers so that the company's culture won't be diffused by managers who have grown used to other, and possibly less aggressive, management styles.

c. Raid Citicorp, BankAmerica, and Chemical banks for experienced managers, even though they would be coming from money-center banks and would be less versed in managing the problems that accompany mergers and acquisitions.

d. Combine answers (a) and (b).

3. Small-business customers have fled a number of the larger banks participating in mergers and acquisitions because they feel lost in the shuffle. They often lose a long-established personal relationship with one banker, seeing that person replaced by a succession of less-interested managers and loan officers. Moreover, the problem has been exacerbated by the traditional debate within many banks over who should serve the small-business community—commercial divisions that are usually housed in centralized locations, or branch managers who are closer to their communities but who don't always have the experience or support necessary for serving the small-business community. How should NationsBank prevent small-business owners from moving their accounts to smaller competitors?

a. Add small-business loan officers to each branch, regardless of the added cost and loss of centralization.

b. Establish small-business services units that would be attached to branches based on geographical areas so that branch managers would have direct support in their banking relations with the small-business community.

c. Let branch managers handle small-business services.

d. Centralize all small-business services through the commercial banking division.

4. Of Citicorp, BankAmerica, Chemical, and NationsBank, only McColl's NationsBank is not a true money-center bank, because (1) it doesn't offer major institutional services to the world's largest corporations, and (2) it doesn't offer a complete line of financial products to consumers through its retail banking division. But NationsBank has an advantage over Citicorp, BankAmerica, and Chemical: It isn't burdened with a large percentage of Third World and bad real estate loans. McColl wants NationsBank eventually to become a major money-center bank. What is the most important step he can take to do just that?

a. Develop NationsBank's international presence through loans to Eastern European and Pacific Rim businesses and nations.

b. Increase NationsBank's investment activities by underwriting more of the United States's corporate equity financing.

c. Diversify into even more financial services such as credit cards, traveler's checks, and insurance services in order to compete directly with Citicorp.

d. Postpone any such move until NationsBank has reduced the percentage of all bad and troubled loans it assumed in its various mergers and acquisitions, thus mak-

ing it a much stronger bank when it finally begins to pursue money-center status.[33]

KEY TERMS

automated teller machines (523)
certificate of deposit (521)
commercial banks (517)
commercial paper (525)
credit unions (518)
currency (516)
debit card (523)
demand deposit (516)
discount rate (532)
electronic funds transfer systems (523)
Fed funds rate (532)
finance companies (518)

individual retirement account (521)
investment banks (520)
Keogh account (521)
M1 (515)
M2 (515)
margin requirements (533)
monetary policy (531)
money (514)
money-market accounts (521)
national banks (517)
NOW account (521)

open-market operations (533)
payee (516)
prime interest rate (532)
reserve requirement (531)
reserves (531)
savings and loan associations (517)
savings banks (517)
selective credit controls (533)
state banks (517)
super NOW account (521)
time deposits (516)

REVIEW QUESTIONS

1. What is the difference between M1 and M2?

2. How are demand deposits created?

3. How does a limited-service bank differ from a commercial bank?

4. What advantages do electronic funds transfer systems offer banks and consumers?

5. How did changes in federal regulations partially cause the collapse of the thrift industry?

6. What is the main objective of the Federal Reserve System?

7. What are three of the Federal Reserve's functions?

8. What role do the 12 Federal Reserve Banks play in clearing checks drawn on commercial banks?

A CASE FOR CRITICAL THINKING

Can an Inner-City Community Bank Survive?

When four community activists decided to start an inner-city bank on Chicago's South Side, they purchased South Shore Bank by raising only $800,000 from two individual investors, some foundations, and a church. Experienced employees could not be enlisted because no one believed the bank would survive. South Shore was a community with worsening poverty, a sense of despair, and dysfunctional

market forces that seemingly doomed the community to its plight.

But by 1991, the four community activists had built South Shore Bank into a successful local institution, and their efforts had so revitalized the community that today it is a model for community banking. The reason is that the group of activists believes that "banks have local areas, and that they owe those areas service."

During the same period that South Shore Bank was succeeding, most U.S. banks were concerning themselves with branch-system growth, profit margins on transactions, and fending off or managing mergers. So how was an inner-city bank able to make itself profitable *and* reverse the downward spiral of its community? Essentially, by redirecting capital the way all banks do, only with a twist.

A bank's depositors don't necessarily see their savings reinvested in their communities. This is particularly true of national banks. Citibank depositors in Arizona might be helping to finance a business in New York, and BankAmerica depositors in Redding, California, might be helping a corporation based in Los Angeles. Loans are made where the risk is least.

The new owners of South Shore Bank decided to redirect capital also, but *into* South Shore instead of out of it. They created "Development Deposits"—savings, money-market accounts, certificates of deposit, and even checking accounts that had one thing in common: The deposits came from people and institutions who wanted their money to help revitalize an inner-city community.

By 1982 South Shore Bank had raised $20 million through Development Deposits. That amount has grown today to more than $94 million, representing better than half of the bank's deposits. Customers making the deposits are diverse; they include a New York institutional investor and a Pacific Northwest forester.

The capital has been used to make some fundamental and dramatic changes to the community the bank serves. And here, too, the new owners

have put a twist on how a bank traditionally conducts business. Even though South Shore Bank led the financing of a shopping mall—the first large commercial venture in the area for 25 years—the bank's managers realized that the community's primary business market was housing itself.

So the bank's officers made housing loans a top priority. Most important, no loan was approved unless the borrower made a commitment to renovating the property. The requirement has resulted in a snowballing of housing redevelopment and entrepreneurship and in the reestablishment of vital market forces in the community. Individual home owners have renovated their properties to fulfill the condition put on their loans. And they aren't the only ones—more than 6,000 rental units have been purchased and renovated, the buyers becoming successful landlords proud of their investments. Moreover, once other landlords realized that the best tenants would live only in rehabilitated houses, they became motivated to renovate their own properties. In other words, the market, not just the bank, became the driving force.

All of this activity has begun transforming the entire South Shore community and has even prompted banks from outside the area to once again make home loans there. South Shore

Bank has shown how important a local bank can be to its community, and its owners believe that the pursuit of community service should be reinstilled in all banks, especially money-center banks. It's a philosophy that will probably help many small banks across the United States remain viable during the industry's consolidation.[34]

1. If you were an officer of a major money-center bank who agreed with South Shore's philosophy of banking, how would you change your institution's policies to better aid in community development?

2. Does the federal government have a role, through its laws and regulations, in encouraging the duplication of the South Shore Bank's experience, or should such efforts be left to the marketplace? If the government's influence is necessary, what would you recommend it do?

3. Is it realistic to believe that community banks can continue to be a viable part of today's commercial banking system, especially given the drive toward consolidation that is occurring in the United States and around the world?

BUILDING YOUR COMMUNICATION SKILLS

Examine a financial institution and its services by interviewing a member of the management team. If this is not possible, write the public information office of the institution to get a description, or locate an article in a periodical or book that describes a specific institution. Using your text as a resource, consider the type of institution and its target clientele, its deposit and loan functions, other services (such as EFTs and discount brokerage), and the promotions and special services it offers consumers as incentives to use that institution.

▶ Prepare a brief report (as directed by your instructor) describing the institution you have investigated.

▶ Compare the institution you have investigated with those examined by other students in your class. Discuss the advantages and disadvantages of each, particularly the services offered to consumer and commercial accounts.

KEEPING CURRENT USING *THE WALL STREET JOURNAL*

From recent issues of *The Wall Street Journal,* choose an article that explains in some detail problems facing a particular bank or an entire class of banks (such as thrift institutions).

1. What are the problems faced by the bank or group of banks? Be as specific as possible.

2. To what degree are these problems related to specific current economic developments? To the pressures of deregulation and competition? List all the major reasons given in the article.

3. What efforts are bank officials making to deal with these problems? Have regulatory agencies or officials either taken or threatened to take action? What are they doing or proposing to do?

CHAPTER *19*

LEARNING OBJECTIVES
After studying this chapter, you will be able to

1 List the five steps involved in the financial-planning process.

2 State the matching principle.

3 Explain the chief advantage of debt versus equity.

4 Define the objective of the capital-budgeting process.

5 Name three major types of short-term debt.

6 List four major long-term financing options.

7 Explain the guiding principle of cash management.

8 State the financial manager's primary goal in handling receivables and payables.

Financial Management

Facing a Business Challenge at Emerald Homes

PAYING FOR THE BURDENS OF LEVERAGE

O nce a leading builder of single-family homes in the Southwest, Emerald Homes was on the verge of being forced into bankruptcy—perhaps forced out of business altogether. Even after selling its California and Texas divisions to raise much-needed capital, the company's outlook was grim. Upon being named president and CEO of the Arizona-based builder, Lewis J. Wright faced a crisis unlike any he had ever seen. It was Wright's job to save the troubled company through financial management—by finding the money to keep Emerald in business.

Every company finances itself with debt or equity—taking out loans with banks, finance companies, and investors; selling ownership positions to investors by issuing company stock; or using a combination of both. As with most homebuilders, Emerald relied mostly on construction loans, or debt. Then, when the real estate market crashed, the company couldn't sell enough houses to pay operating expenses or to meet principal and interest payments on $50 million worth of bank and thrift loans.

The builder owed about $32 million to four savings and loan associations. During the thrift bailout, these S&Ls were taken over by the Resolution Trust Corporation, or RTC (the government agency running the savings and loan cleanup), which quickly foreclosed on four Emerald subdivisions. Emerald owed the remaining $18 million to four commercial banks. Although they weren't likely to foreclose, Wright faced the real possibility that the company's line of credit would be discontinued. Of course, besides paying off loans and maintaining credit, Wright also had to find enough additional financing to continue building houses. Wright's task was threefold: pay off the debt owed to the RTC in order to avoid bankruptcy, save Emerald's commercial line of credit, and find the extra financing needed to keep the company going.

To settle with the RTC, Emerald had to find an institution or individual to pay off $32 million worth of debt. Of course, in return for bailing out the company, the investor would own a large portion of Emerald, and such a major shareholder could certainly affect how Emerald would be operated over the long term. But at least the company would still be in business; that is, Emerald would be in business *if* Wright could retain Emerald's line of credit with the banks and locate new sources of construction loans.

Emerald's financial sources had traditionally been thrifts and banks, but these institutions were virtually useless to the builder now: After a decade of loose credit for real estate loans, federal regulators were clamping down on all loans to real estate–related businesses. What made it even more difficult for Emerald to keep its lines of credit open and to find new loans was the company's negative cash flow: More money was going out than was coming in each month. This situation didn't help Wright when he tried to negotiate with his bankers and with other possible sources of financing. Most of Emerald's revenues were barely covering interest payments on old bank loans. The rest, an important part of the company's revenues, was used to pay operating expenses, mainly salaries and marketing costs, important expenses for homebuilders.

How could Wright cut expenses and increase revenues to improve Emerald's cash flow? Where would he find new financing in such a tight credit market? And where would he find the money to pay off the RTC?[1]

▶ FINANCE: A COMPANY'S LIFEBLOOD

Lewis Wright is trying to save Emerald Homes from going out of business. His predecessor was intent on making the company grow. The key to both of these efforts is money. Every company, from the little shop on the corner to General Motors, worries about money—how to get it and how to use it. This area of concern, known as **financial management,** or finance, is tremendously complex.

The Goals of Financial Management

All companies need to pay their bills and still have some money left over to improve the business. But the ultimate objective is to increase a business's value to its owners by making it grow. Maximizing the owners' wealth sounds simple enough. Just sell a good product or service for more than it costs to produce. But before you can earn any sales revenue, you need money to get started. And once the business is off the ground, your need for outside funds continues—whether it's to tide you over a slack season or to build or renovate facilities and equipment.

Because it takes money to make money, companies often need to borrow additional funds. The use of borrowed money to make more money is called **leverage** because the loan acts like a lever: It magnifies the power of the borrower to generate profits. If you combine your own funds (your equity) with borrowed money, you have a bigger pool of capital to work with. As long as you earn a greater rate of return on the borrowed money than the interest you pay, you stay ahead (see Exhibit 19.1). However, leverage works both ways: Borrowing may magnify your losses as well as your gains.

Borrowing is complicated by the fact that many sources of funding exist, each with advantages and disadvantages, costs and benefits. The financial manager's task is to find the combination of funding sources with the lowest cost. This

---

financial management Effective acquisition and use of money

leverage Use of borrowed funds to finance a portion of an investment

Like all companies, Minga's Restaurant in Phoenix, Arizona, must pay its bills to stay in business. Minga's business manager, Patsie Garcia, understands that borrowing money, or leveraging, can create the advantage of increasing her company's capital and, at the same time, create the disadvantage of increasing her company's debt.

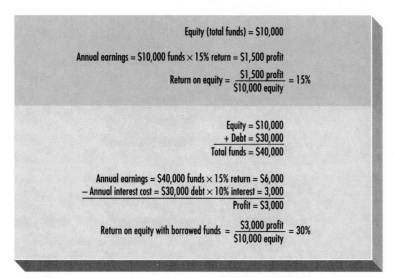

EXHIBIT 19.1

How Leverage Works
If you invest $10,000 of your own money in a business venture and it yields 15 percent (or $1,500), your return on equity is 15 percent. However, if you borrow an additional $30,000 at 10 percent interest and invest a total of $40,000 with the same 15 percent yield, the ultimate return on your $10,000 equity is 30 percent (or $3,000). The key to using leverage successfully is to try to make sure that your profit on the total funds is greater than the interest you must pay on the portion of it that is borrowed.

process is dynamic because changing economic conditions affect the cost of borrowing.

In addition to obtaining funds, the financial manager needs to make sure those funds are used efficiently. In most companies, the number of potential expenditures is large, but the amount of capital is limited. To choose the best expenditures, the financial manager needs a selection process that highlights the options that are best able to meet the company's objectives.

The Process of Financial Management

Developing a financial plan for a company is done with two objectives in mind: achieving positive cash flow and efficiently investing excess cash flow to make the company grow. The process consists of five basic steps:

1. Estimate the month-by-month flow of funds into the business from all sources, including gains on external investments.

2. Estimate the month-by-month flow of funds out of the business, including both operating expenses and capital investments.

3. Compare inflows and outflows. If cash flow is negative, determine how to make it positive, either by reducing outflows or increasing inflows. If cash flow is positive, determine how to invest excess funds most productively.

4. Choose which capital investments should be made for continued growth. Determine the most cost-effective combination of inside and outside sources of financing.

5. Establish a system for tracking the flow of funds and measuring the return on investment.

Because of the extraordinary conditions at Emerald Homes, Wright and his top lieutenants coordinate financial management. But in larger operations, financial planning is the responsibility of a department that reports to a vice president of finance. In addition to overseeing the inflow and outflow of money, the financial manager often handles a number of related functions (see Exhibit 19.2).

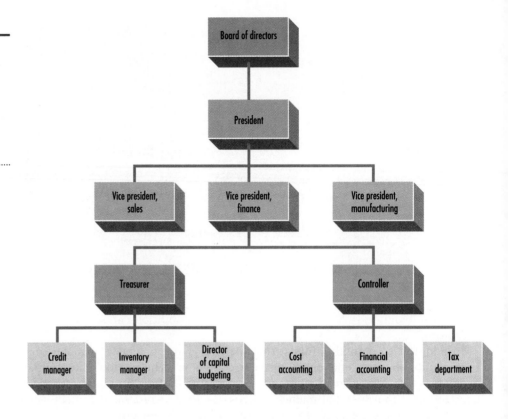

The Sources and Uses of Funds

Where can a firm obtain the money it needs? The most obvious source would be revenues—cash received from sales, rentals of property, interest on short-term investments, and so on. Another likely source would be suppliers who may be willing to do business on credit, thus enabling the company to postpone payment. Most firms also obtain money in the form of loans from banks, insurance companies, or other commercial lenders. In addition, public companies sell stocks, and large corporations sell bonds.

The money obtained from these sources is used to cover the expenses of the business and to acquire new assets (see Exhibit 19.3). Some financing needs are related to day-to-day operations—for example, meeting the payroll and buying inventory. More important, though, is the need for money to buy land, production facilities, and equipment. As you might imagine, finding money to take care of next month's payroll is different from arranging the financing for a new manufacturing plant that won't be in production for three years. For this reason, financial matters are often discussed in terms of time periods: short-term (less than one year) and long-term (anything over one year).

The Cost of Capital

Generally speaking, the goal of a company is to obtain money at the least cost and risk, whereas the goal of lenders and investors is to receive the highest possible return on their investment at the least risk. Therefore, a company's **cost of capital,** the price it must pay to raise money, depends on the risk associated

cost of capital The average rate of interest a firm pays on its combination of debt and equity

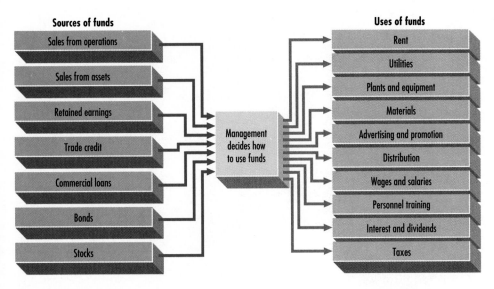

Sources of funds
- Sales from operations
- Sales from assets
- Retained earnings
- Trade credit
- Commercial loans
- Bonds
- Stocks

Management decides how to use funds

Uses of funds
- Rent
- Utilities
- Plants and equipment
- Materials
- Advertising and promotion
- Distribution
- Wages and salaries
- Personnel training
- Interest and dividends
- Taxes

EXHIBIT 19.3

The Flow of a Company's Funds

Financial management involves both finding suitable sources of funds and deciding on the most appropriate uses for those funds.

with the company, the prevailing level of interest rates, and management's selection of funding vehicles.

Risk

Lenders and investors who provide money to businesses expect to be rewarded on a scale that's commensurate with the risk they incur. They face two types of risk: the quality of the venture and time. Obviously, the more financially solid a company is, the less risk investors face. But time plays a key role. The longer it takes for a lender or investor to receive an expected return, the greater the risk; a dollar is worth less tomorrow than it is today. For this reason, long-term loans or investments cost a company more than short-term loans or investments.

Generally speaking, those companies with the soundest financial position that are seeking capital for short-term needs can obtain money more cheaply than their less secure rivals. Companies that are considered financial risks and that are seeking capital for long-term needs (for example, a state-of-the-art manufacturing plant for a small semiconductor products company) pay more for their capital.

Interest Rates

Regardless of how solid a company is, its cost of money will vary over time because interest rates fluctuate. The prime rate is the lowest interest rate offered on bank loans to preferred borrowers. The prime changes irregularly and, at times, quite frequently (see Exhibit 19.4). For example, a financial manager planning a project in March 1988 (when the prime rate was 8.5 percent) probably had to reevaluate the project just six months later (when the prime rose to 10 percent). Nor would his or her concern have eased shortly afterward, for the prime climbed even more before topping out at 11.5 percent in March 1989.

Financial managers try to time their borrowing to take advantage of drops in interest rates, but this is not always possible; a firm's need for money may not coincide with a period of favorable rates. A company may be forced to borrow when rates are high and then renegotiate the loan when rates drop.

EXHIBIT 19.4

Variations in Interest Rates
The prime is the rate of interest charged on loans that banks make to their largest, most creditworthy commercial and industrial customers. Because fluctuations in the prime rate are tied closely to the interest rates banks pay the Federal Reserve, the prime is "set" by the handful of U.S. money-center banks.

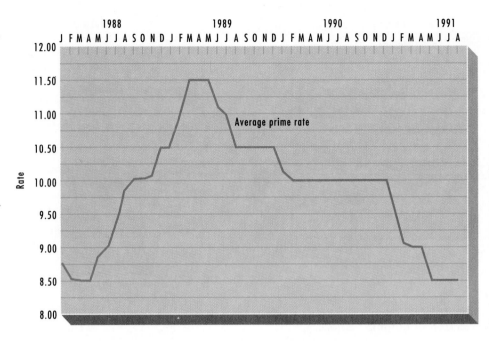

capital structure Financing mix of a firm

matching principle Concept that long-term projects should be funded with long-term sources of capital, whereas short-term expenditures should be funded from current income

Business Around the World

One way companies raise money is by selling assets. By the end of 1991, Citibank Italia, the Italian subsidiary in Citicorp's global empire, was quietly put up for sale. With 52 branches and $2 billion in assets, Citibank Italia's sale could help the cash-poor parent corporation.

Mix of Funding Vehicles

Apart from timing their borrowing properly, financial managers must choose from an array of funding vehicles. When deciding how to balance these options, financial managers analyze the pros and cons of internal versus external financing, short- versus long-term funding, and debt versus equity.

INTERNAL VERSUS EXTERNAL FINANCING   Using a company's own money to finance its growth has one chief attraction: No interest payments are required. For this reason, many companies utilize *retained profits,* the money kept by the firm after meeting its expenses and taxes. Some companies also raise capital internally by *selling assets.* But internal financing is not free; this money has an opportunity cost. That is, a company might be better off by investing retained profits in external opportunities rather than using it as internal financing. Most companies depend on some degree of external financing. The issue is not so much *whether* to use outside money; rather, it's a question of how much should be raised, by what means, and when. The answers to such questions determine the firm's **capital structure,** its mix of debt and equity.

SHORT- VERSUS LONG-TERM FUNDING   When choosing between short- and long-term financing, companies are guided by the **matching principle**—the concept that the timing of a company's borrowing should roughly match the timing of its spending. If you borrow money for short-term purposes, you should plan to pay it back in that time frame so that the flow of money into and out of the business is balanced. At the same time, when you undertake a project that will last for some time, you should fund it with long-term financing that will stretch your repayment schedule over an extended period.

DEBT VERSUS EQUITY   When choosing between debt and equity, companies consider various factors (see Exhibit 19.5). Generally speaking, debt is cheaper

EXHIBIT 19.5 ▶ Debt Versus Equity

The cost of debt is generally lower than the cost of equity, largely because the interest paid on debt is tax deductible. However, too much debt can increase the risk that a company will be unable to meet its interest and principal payments.

CHARACTERISTIC	DEBT	EQUITY
Claim on income	Company must pay interest on debt held by bondholders and lenders before paying any dividends to shareholders. Interest payments must be met regardless of operating results.	Shareholders may receive dividends after creditors have received interest payments; however, company is not required to pay dividends.
Claim on assets	If company fails, bondholders and lenders have a claim on company assets, which are sold and used to reimburse the creditors.	After all creditors have been paid, shareholders can claim any remaining assets.
Repayment terms	Company must repay lenders and retire bonds on a specific schedule.	Company is not required to repay shareholders for their investment in the enterprise.
Tax treatment	Company can deduct interest payments from its corporate income tax.	Company must pay dividends from after-tax income.
Influence over management	Creditors can impose limits on management only if interest payments are not received.	As owners of the company, shareholders can vote on some aspects of corporate operations. Shareholder influence varies, depending on whether stock is widely distributed or closely held.

than equity for two reasons: (1) companies can deduct the interest on debt from their taxes, whereas dividend payments on stock (earnings distributed to shareholders) are not deductible; (2) bondholders and lenders must always be paid before shareholders, and because they assume less risk than stockholders, the company can pay them a lower rate of return over time.

Although debt has its advantages, it also has one major disadvantage: Too much of it causes a high degree of risk. A company that sells stock can survive rough times by omitting dividends, but one that can't meet its loan and bond commitments could be forced into bankruptcy. Emerald Homes got into its financial bind because it had too much debt outstanding when the market for its homes became depressed.

But Emerald wasn't the only U.S. company that took on too much debt during the 1980s—the majority of them did. The result was that by 1990, debt as a percentage of total capital for nonfinancial companies had soared to 49 percent, from 34 percent a decade earlier, and interest payments ate into profits (see Exhibit 19.6). Corporate debt became so widespread that it was a major cause of the economic recession and anemic recovery at the beginning of the 1990s. Bonds are rated according to their investment quality, and they generally became less safe because of the amount of debt carried by corporations. Moody's Investors Service, one of three major rating agencies, downgraded far more bonds than it upgraded throughout the 1980s, and it reported a higher number of companies that defaulted on their bond payments (see Exhibit 19.7). All this

EXHIBIT 19.6

Corporate Debt

U.S. corporations took on so much debt during the 1980s that the cost of paying that debt had an increasingly negative effect on profits. In 1990, interest payments by nonfinancial corporations accounted for 28.1 percent of cash flow.

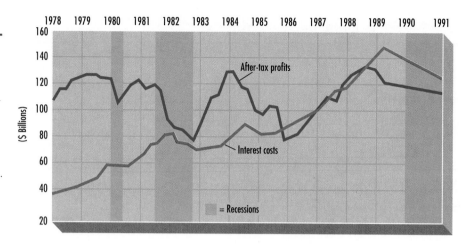

EXHIBIT 19.7

Bonds Downgraded and Issuers in Default

When a company issues bonds, the issue is rated by at least two of three major rating agencies. The more financially solid the company, the higher the rating. As the company takes on excessive debt and its financial condition worsens, the rating on all of its bond issues will be downgraded. If a company can no longer make the interest payments on a bond issue, then that issue goes into default.

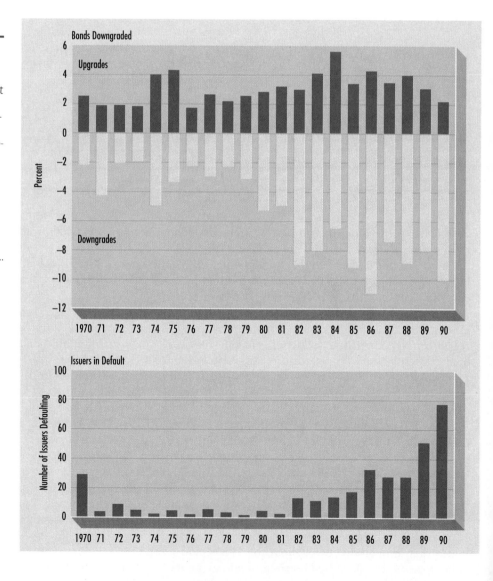

debt effectively canceled out the tax advantages of leveraging, and the financial condition of many companies became so weak that they paid higher interest on new debt, whether bank loans or corporate bonds.[2]

Issuing stock has its own set of pros and cons. Dividend payments can be omitted and, unlike creditors, stockholders do not have to be repaid at some future date. Equity financing is a more expensive way of raising money because dividends are paid with dollars that remain after the company has paid income tax. In addition, when common stock is sold, the original owners of the company are forced to share both their control of the company and their rights to future earnings. Nevertheless, given the debt binge of the 1980s, businesses have returned to equity financing.

Capital Budgeting

Stockholders, of course, invest in public companies for more than just dividends. They're speculating on a company's ability to grow and compete. For that to happen, a company makes **capital investments** such as new or renovated plant, new equipment, or even major personnel training programs. But before any move can be made, each company faces crucial questions, including which of the many possible capital investments should be made, how to finance those that are undertaken, and even whether to make any capital investments at all. This process is called **capital budgeting.**

All divisions within a company might issue capital requests—essentially "wish lists" of investments that would make the company more profitable and thus more valuable to its owners over time. The financial manager first decides which investments need evaluation and which don't. The routine replacement of old equipment probably wouldn't need evaluation; however, a new manufacturing facility would. The purpose of a financial evaluation is to determine whether

capital investments Money paid to acquire something of permanent value in a business

capital budgeting Process for evaluating proposed investments in select projects that provide the best long-term financial return

Mead Corporation used capital budgeting when deciding to make a capital investment in constructing a new plant in Phenix City, Alabama.

the amount of money required for a particular investment will be greater than, equal to, or less than the amount of revenue it will generate. If the present value of its future cost is greater than or equal to the present value of its projected rate of return, the investment shouldn't be made. If its cost will be less than its projected rate of return, then *perhaps* the investment should be made.

Possible capital investments are not only evaluated but are ranked according to whatever criterion is considered most important to the company. For example, if the strategy of the firm is to grow, then those projects that would produce the greatest growth rates would receive highest priority. On the other hand, if the company is trying to reduce costs, those projects that enhance the company's efficiency and productivity would be ranked toward the top. Money can be spent only on appropriate investments because only so much money exists.

In fact, the financial manager may decide that, given the company's strategy, the financial risks of all proposed investments are much greater than alternative uses for that money. So instead of buying new equipment, a company may choose to invest in short-term certificates of deposit, or it may even choose to repurchase shares of stock from investors. That's why some companies increase their capital spending more than others, even though economic conditions are the same for both.

During the mid-1980s, General Motors spent more than twice as much as Ford on capital investments—some critics say to little effect. Instead, Ford put its money into ways of reducing costs and gaining efficiency. The result was that by 1989 Ford manufacturing plants were the most efficient of the Big Three automakers. Ford was ready to make larger capital investments only after its break-even point had been reduced by 40 percent and its manufacturing plants were stretched to capacity.[3]

▶ SHORT-TERM FINANCING

short-term debt Borrowed funds used to cover current expenses (generally repaid within a year)

Short-term debt is any debt that will be repaid within one year. The three primary categories of short-term debt are

▶ Trade credit from suppliers

▶ Loans from a commercial bank or some other type of short-term lending institution

▶ Money from the sale of commercial paper to outside investors or other businesses

Exhibit 19.8 gives an overview of these three sources.

Trade Credit

trade credit Credit obtained by the purchaser directly from the supplier

Trade credit is the most widespread source of short-term financing for business. Rather than borrowing money to pay for products or supplies, a company buys on credit from the supplier. The degree of formality in such arrangements ranges from a simple handshake to an ironclad written agreement. Two of the most common forms of trade credit are open-book credit and promissory notes.

Open-Book Credit

open-book credit Payment terms that allow the purchaser to take possession of goods and pay for them later

A majority of all business transactions involving merchandise are financed through **open-book credit**, sometimes referred to as an "open account." This is

EXHIBIT 19.8 ▶ **Major Sources of Short-Term Funds**

Although companies of all types and sizes use short-term debt, these financing vehicles are particularly important for small businesses, which typically do not have the option of selling bonds or stock.

ARRANGEMENT	EXAMPLE
TRADE CREDIT	
Open-book account	EverFresh Grocery Store buys display racks from Reliable Retail Equipment and agrees to pay the debt in full in 30 days or with a discount in 10 days.
Promissory note	EverFresh signs a note promising payment in 30 days.
LOANS FROM FINANCIAL INSTITUTIONS	
Unsecured bank loan	EverFresh borrows from First National Bank on its good name and repays with interest.
Secured loan	
Pledge of accounts receivable	EverFresh borrows from a bank or commercial finance company on the bills owed it and repays with interest.
Pledge of inventory	EverFresh borrows from a bank or finance company on its marketable groceries and repays with interest.
Pledge of other property	EverFresh borrows from a commercial lender on its delivery truck and repays with interest.
Sales of accounts receivable	EverFresh sells what is owed it for less than the amount owed.
LOANS FROM INVESTORS	
Commercial paper	EverFresh borrows money from First National and Reliable at a lower interest rate solely on the promise to repay.

an informal arrangement whereby a purchaser may obtain products before paying for them. Say that you own a sportswear store. You place an order for swimsuits with the manufacturer, who agrees to let you have them on credit. Later, when you begin to sell the suits, you pay the manufacturer's bill. This arrangement enables you to minimize the mismatch between cash outflows and inflows.

The swimsuit manufacturer also benefits. By offering you 60 days to pay your bills, as opposed to the more customary 30 days, the manufacturer convinces you to buy from him or her rather than from a rival supplier.

Promissory Notes

Not all businesspeople are comfortable with the relative informality of open-book credit. They prefer the security of a written agreement to repay, signed in advance by the customer they're supplying. One such agreement is a **promissory note,** an unconditional written commitment drawn up by the borrower, who promises to pay the creditor a fixed sum of money on a specified date in return for immediate credit. Promissory notes often include an interest rate, which is indicated on the note itself.

promissory note Unconditional written promise to repay a certain sum of money on a specified date

Loans

As important as trade credit may be to a business, a time may come when other sources of short-term funding are required. Perhaps the business finds itself

A promissory note gives the creditor a written guarantee of payment for goods obtained on credit.

Promissory Note

$ 10,000 $\frac{00}{100}$ Date July, 1   19 93

Abbott Steel   after date 10/1/93 promise to pay to the order of Gray Manufacturing Corporation

Ten Thousand $\frac{00}{100}$ — Dollars

Payable at 29th Pine Street New York, New York

for value received with interest at 9.5 per cent per annum.

John Simpson
Abbott Steel

Witness
Cameron Winston
Gray Manufacturing Corp

No. 297   Due Oct. 1   19 93

P607—PRINTED BY JULIUS BLUMBERG, INC., NYC 10013

unable to pay its own debts because customers have not yet paid theirs. Or the managers of the business may want to make a purchase for which they have to pay cash. In either case, the business may turn to a commercial bank or other financial institution for short-term credit.

Commercial bank loans account for 28 percent of all short-term financing.[4] The interest charged on a short-term loan may be either fixed or floating. With a fixed-rate loan, interest payments are constant throughout the life of the loan. With a variable-rate loan, interest payments fluctuate, depending on increases and decreases in prevailing rates. Regardless, the level of interest depends on the customer's creditworthiness. The largest corporate customers at major banks are charged the most favorable rate—the prime rate. All other businesses are charged the prime plus a given number of percentage points.

secured loans Loans backed up with something of value that the lender can claim in case of default, such as a piece of property

collateral Tangible asset a lender can claim if a borrower defaults on a loan

Secured Loans

Secured loans are those backed by something of value, known as **collateral,** which may be seized by the lender should the borrower fail to repay the loan. The three main types of collateral are accounts receivable, inventories, and other property.

When a business loan is secured with *accounts receivable,* its customers' outstanding balances on open-book accounts are used as collateral. Suppose the Global Gadget Company has sold $100,000 worth of gadgets to various customers on open-book credit. Global may borrow about $75,000 from its bank by promising that all open-book credit payments will be paid to the bank.

A less attractive alternative for most businesses is to sell accounts receivable to a finance company instead of using them for collateral. This procedure is known as **factoring** accounts receivable. Customers are directed to pay their bills directly to the factor, a firm that specializes in this type of loan.

factoring *Sale of a firm's accounts receivable to a finance company, known as a factor*

Companies that borrow against their receivables are often desperate for cash, so this form of financing is expensive. The factor charges a discount, which means that a percentage of the monthly payment on *each* invoice goes to the factor. If an invoice isn't paid on time, the discount to the factor is raised on that invoice.[5] As an example, suppose Global Gadget Company sells $100,000 of its accounts receivable to a factor, which charges a 5 percent discount on each invoice each month. That's $5,000 a month that goes to the factor. Multiply that by 12 months, and it's obvious how expensive factoring can be: Gadget is paying the equivalent of a 60 percent interest rate ($60,000 is 60 percent of $100,000).

In some businesses, it is common to borrow by pledging *inventories* (generally finished goods rather than raw materials) as security for a loan. If a firm has an excellent credit rating and valuable inventories, its bank or finance company may simply accept the firm's signed statement that the inventories are pledged to the lender in the event of nonpayment. More often, the lender insists that the borrower place the inventory in a separate warehouse for safekeeping.

Many other forms of collateral are used to secure loans. If something has value, chances are that some bank or financial institution will lend on it. Short-term loans are commonly made against *movable property,* including automobiles, trucks, and agricultural machines. When a business takes out a loan to buy such an item, the bank or finance company will sometimes require the borrower to sign a **chattel mortgage** agreement in addition to a loan agreement. Under the terms of the chattel mortgage, the movable property—along with the risk of loss—belongs to the borrower, but the lender can take possession of the property if payments are not made as specified in the loan agreement.

chattel mortgage *Agreement that the movable property purchased through a loan belongs to the borrower, although the lender has a legal right to the property if payments are not made as specified in the loan agreement*

Unsecured Loans

An **unsecured loan** is one that requires no collateral. Instead, the lender relies on the general credit record and the earning power of the borrower. To increase their returns on such loans and to obtain some protection in case of default, most lenders insist that the borrower maintain some minimum amount of money at the bank—a **compensating balance**—while the loan is outstanding. Although the borrower pays interest on the full amount of the loan, a substantial portion of it remains on deposit in the bank.

unsecured loan *Loan requiring no collateral but a good credit rating*

compensating balance *Portion of an unsecured loan that is kept on deposit at the lending institution to protect the lender and increase the lender's return*

Another important type of unsecured loan eliminates the need to negotiate with the bank each time a business needs to borrow. The **line of credit** is an agreed-on maximum amount of money the bank is willing to lend the business during a specific period of time, usually a year. Emerald Homes struggled hard to maintain its line of credit with its four commercial banks. Once a line of credit has been established, the business may obtain unsecured loans for any amount up to that limit, provided the bank has funds. However, a line of credit does not guarantee that the loan will be available. If you want an ironclad agreement, you

line of credit *Agreement stating the amount of unsecured short-term loans that the lender will make available to the borrower, provided the lender has the funds*

revolving line of credit Guaranteed line of credit

need a **revolving line of credit,** which guarantees that the bank will honor the line of credit up to the stated amount. An extra fee is usually charged for this guarantee.

Commercial Paper

A short-term financing option that has become increasingly popular is to borrow from other businesses and investors. The company borrowing money issues **commercial paper,** which represents a promise to pay back a stated amount of money within a stated number of days (legally, 1 to 270 days). The business or investor generally buys commercial paper at a price lower than the face value; then at the end of the period, the buyer receives the face value. The difference between the discounted price and the face value is the equivalent of interest on a loan. For example, a 90-day, $1 million offering of Exxon commercial paper is

commercial paper Short-term note issued by a company and backed by the company's good name

TECHNIQUES FOR BUSINESS SUCCESS

How to Plan and Negotiate a Business Loan

You have an idea for a product or a service that you are convinced has a market just waiting to be tapped. But you need money—perhaps to get started, to purchase inventory, to train employees, or to build a plant. The following steps may help you obtain a loan.

DEFINE YOUR PROJECT

Be as specific and as accurate as possible. Ask why you need the money. Be sure it is money (and not some sort of management action) that is needed. Once your project is clearly defined, prepare a forecast of what will happen as a result of your loan. This forecast must include precisely where the money will go, how it will affect your business, when it will show a return, how much of a return can reasonably be expected, and when and how you will repay the loan. Three formats for this information include the profit-and-loss statement, the balance sheet, and the cash flow. If you cannot do these forecasts yourself, hire an accountant.

TARGET POSSIBLE LENDERS

Choose a variety of lenders with whom to discuss your plans—for example, a commercial bank, a savings and loan association, a finance company, and an equity investor. Survey neighbors and local busi-

nesspersons or your own suppliers, major customers, and business colleagues for the names of both lenders and particular loan officers. You are looking not only for competitive services from institutions but also for a loan officer who is competent and easy to work with.

Once you have an idea about the institution and the person you would like to work with, contact that person and request an initial interview. At your first meeting, it is best to present a nuts-and-bolts oral summary of your project, including your background, your experience, and an indication of the amount and duration of the credit you are seeking. Let the person know you have done your homework by mentioning some of the research pertinent to the need for your product or service in that area. Ask what papers you will need to prepare, which documents must accompany those papers, and what terms the bank will offer on your type of loan. If the bank asks about collateral, postpone that discussion as well as any discussion of existing debts, mortgages, or personal assets. You are there to gather information, not actually to apply for the loan.

Get an idea of the lending institution's approval process—how long it will take and what mechanics are involved. Take precise notes, keeping separate files for each lender you contact. If you ever feel uneasy or vague about anything discussed, call that lender for clarification (being sure to make note of the time, the date, and the person who gives you the information).

a promise by Exxon to repay $1 million to the holder of the paper 90 days from the date of the loan. The buyer would give Exxon less than $1 million, perhaps $970,000. The $30,000 difference is the interest earned by the holder during the 90 days.

The market for commercial paper grew dramatically during the 1980s (see Exhibit 19.9), mainly because of increased competition with commercial banks. The total number of companies issuing commercial paper increased 70 percent in the second half of the 1980s. Incredibly, the number of nonbank financial companies issuing commercial paper increased 115 percent during the same period, and even the number of nonfinancial companies involved in this market increased nearly 90 percent.

The appeal of commercial paper is threefold: (1) it doesn't require a compensating balance, as unsecured loans do; (2) it allows a borrower to lock in an acceptable interest rate for up to 270 days; and (3) it's easier for a company to

PREPARE A PERSUASIVE APPLICATION

This is the time to sell yourself, your project, and your loan to the bank. Even a weak balance sheet may be overlooked if the bank has confidence in you and in your project. Do not use the bank's preprinted form to present your figures; your own statement will highlight the information key to your application.

Above all, your project must be creditworthy. There must be adequate equity and unencumbered assets to back up the enterprise. (If you are not sure how much of an equity base you will need, make a comparison with similar existing businesses.) Show earning power or cash flow sufficient to repay the loan (preferably both), and provide a wide margin of safety. Most important, project confidence in the business ability of the management of your company.

NEGOTIATE THE BEST TERMS AND CONDITIONS POSSIBLE

Negotiating your loan involves two areas: terms and conditions. *Terms* refer to the rate of interest for your loan and the maturity schedule—when and how much you will pay the lender on a regular basis in order to repay the loan. Request a "skip-payment" plan so that, if needed, payments can be suspended for a time. If the lender will not accept a repayment schedule that you know you can make, go elsewhere.

Conditions involve the lender asking for collateral in the business, additional equity, or other covenants (meaning any other restrictions the lender wants to attach to your loan). Resist pledging more collateral than necessary, and in case things should go awry, beware of too short a notice period. Fifteen business days should be the minimum notice period. Read everything in the loan papers. Better yet, have an attorney review them as well.

LEARN FROM REJECTION

If your application is rejected, get a clear statement of exactly what the lender needs for approval, and ask for suggestions about alternative ways to finance your project. If that fails, take all that you have learned and go to another creditor.

MAINTAIN A POSITIVE RELATIONSHIP WITH YOUR LENDER

Pay on time, not one day late. If you realize that you are unable to comply with any condition or payment schedule, call the lender immediately and follow that up with a letter. Periodic reports to the bank should be timely and should be presented in person now and then. If you have any setbacks, make sure to explain the circumstances in person, and take a detailed written report with you. The annual review of your loan presents an opportunity for requesting a lower rate and better loan conditions. If after a time you are dissatisfied with the relationship between you and your bank, you may want to find an additional bank to handle part of your business. This rekindles the competitive spirit and provides you with another source of credit.

EXHIBIT 19.9

The Market for Commercial Paper

As competition for loan services grew during the last decade, the market for commercial paper enjoyed tremendous growth. U.S. corporations found it easier to find buyers for their commercial paper than to go to a bank for a traditional short-term loan.

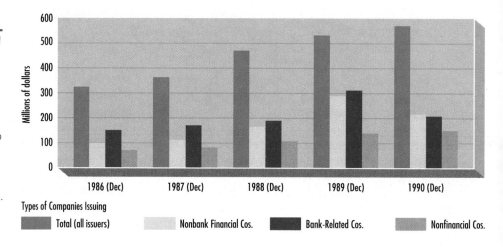

Commercial paper is bought at a discount from the face value.

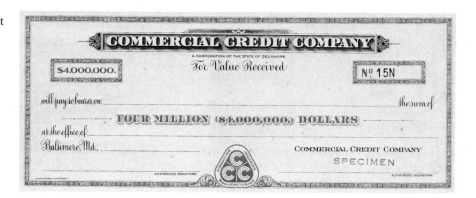

sell commercial paper for short-term financing than to receive a commercial loan at a bank (because companies don't have to "qualify" to sell commercial paper). More than any other, this last feature is what made commercial paper increasingly popular during the 1980s.

▶ LONG-TERM FINANCING

When it comes to financing long-term projects—such as major construction, acquisition of other companies, and research and development—most companies rely on a combination of internal and external funding sources (see Exhibit 19.10). The four main sources of external funding are loans, leases, bonds, and equity.

Long-Term Loans and Leases

long-term loans Debt that must be repaid over a period of more than a year

Long-term loans are repaid over a period of one year or more and may be either secured or unsecured. The most common type of secured loan is a mortgage, in which a piece of property is used as collateral. Commercial banks have traditionally made most long-term loans, but pension funds and insurance companies have increased the number of long-term corporate loans they make. Interest

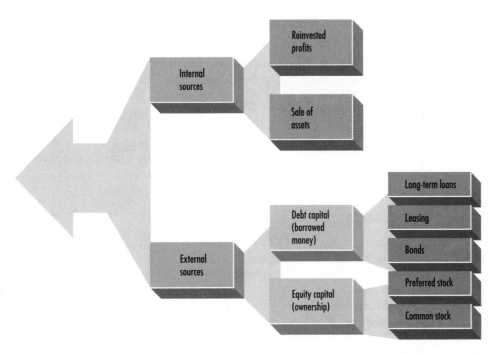

EXHIBIT 19.10

Sources of Long-Term Funds
To finance long-term projects, financial managers rely on both internal and external sources of capital.

rates on long-term loans are generally higher than those on short-term loans because the extended time horizon increases the risk that the borrower will be unable to repay the money.

Rather than borrowing from a commercial lender to buy a piece of property or equipment, a firm may enter into a **lease,** under which the owner of an item allows another party to use it in exchange for regular payments. Under certain conditions, leasing provides tax advantages for both lessor and lessee. Leasing may also be a good alternative for a company that has difficulty obtaining loans because of a poor credit rating. Creditors are more willing to provide a lease than a loan because, should the company fail, the lessor need not worry about a default on loan payments; it can simply repossess equipment it legally owns. Some firms use leases to finance up to 35 percent of their total assets, particularly in industries such as airlines, where assets are mostly large pieces of equipment.

lease Legal agreement that obligates the user of an asset to make payments to the owner of the asset in exchange for using it

Bonds

When a company needs to borrow a large sum of money, it may not be able to get the entire amount from a single source. Under such circumstances, it may borrow from many individual investors by issuing bonds. A **bond** is a corporate IOU that obligates the company to repay a certain sum, plus interest, to the bondholder.

A bond is like a loan certificate indicating that its issuer has borrowed a sum of money from the bondholder. Each bond has a **denomination,** the amount of the loan represented by one bond. Bonds sold by corporations are usually available in $1,000 denominations, but they also come in denominations of $5,000, $10,000, $50,000, and $100,000. A bond usually shows the date when the full amount of the bond, or the **principal,** must be repaid. Bonds typically have maturity dates of 10 years or more.

bond Certificate of indebtedness that is sold to raise funds

denomination Face value of a single bond

principal Amount of a debt, excluding any interest

Secured and Unsecured Bonds

secured bonds Bonds backed by specific assets

unsecured bonds Bonds backed only by the reputation of the issuer

debentures Bonds not backed by specific assets

Like loans, bonds may be either secured or unsecured. **Secured bonds** are backed by specific property of one kind or another that will pass to the bondholders if the issuer does not live up to the terms of the agreement. The security may be a mortgage on a piece of real estate or a claim to other assets, such as freight cars, airplanes, or plant equipment owned by a company. **Unsecured bonds,** also called **debentures,** are backed not by collateral but by the general good name of the issuing company. If the bond-issuing company fails, the bondholders have a claim on the assets—but only after creditors with specific collateral have been paid.

Bond Interest Rates

A bond also provides interest, stated in terms of an annual percentage rate but paid at six-month intervals. For example, the holder of a $1,000 bond that pays 8 percent interest due January 15 and July 15 could expect to receive $40 on each of these dates.

A look at the financial section of any newspaper will show that some corporations sell new bonds at an interest rate two or three percentage points higher than that offered by other companies. Yet the terms of the bonds seem similar. These variations in interest rates reflect the level of risk associated with the bond. A corporation with excellent prospects of earning enough money in future years to pay both the interest on the bonds and the principal at maturity can afford to offer a relatively low interest rate. A less secure borrower has to offer a higher interest rate in order to attract buyers. Bond-rating agencies rate bonds based on the financial stability of issuing companies. Bonds that are rated investment grade are considered the safest bonds for investors. Bonds rated below investment grade became popularly known as **junk bonds** in the 1980s.

junk bonds Bonds that pay high interest because they are below investment grade

Retirement of Debt

A company that sells bonds must repay its debt to the bondholders. Normally, this is done when the bonds mature—say, 10, 15, or 20 years after the bond is issued. The cost of retiring the debt can be staggering because bonds are generally issued in quantity—perhaps thousands of individual bonds in a single issue. To ease the burden of redeeming its bonds, companies sometimes issue **serial bonds,** which mature at various times, as opposed to **term bonds,** which all mature at the same time.

serial bonds Bonds from a single issue that must be repaid at intervals

term bonds Bonds from a single issue that must be repaid simultaneously

sinking fund Account into which a company makes annual payments for use in redeeming its bonds in the future

callable bonds Bonds that a company can redeem before the stated maturity date

Another way of relieving the financial strain of retiring many bonds all at once is to set up a **sinking fund.** When a corporation issues a bond payable by a sinking fund, it must set aside a certain sum of money each year to pay the debt. This money is either used to retire a few bonds each year or set aside to accumulate until the issue matures.

With most bond issues, a corporation retains the right to pay off the bonds before maturity. Bonds containing this provision are known as **callable bonds,** or redeemable bonds. If a company issues bonds when interest rates are high and interest rates fall later on, it may want to pay off its high-interest bonds and sell a new issue at a lower rate. But this feature carries a price tag: Investors must be offered a higher interest rate to encourage them to buy callable bonds. The portion of the percentage rate that is above market rates is actually a "call premium."

Bonds are transferable long-term securities that pay interest regularly for the term of the loan.

Another way for a company to pay off bonds is to repay them with stock rather than with money. Bonds that may be paid off with stock are called **convertible bonds.** The actual decision to accept stock or money is left up to the bondholder. Suppose a company sold an issue of $1,000 convertible bonds with an interest rate of 10 percent and a maturity date of 1999. A purchaser would receive $100 a year and get back the original $1,000 in 1999. But at any time before 1999, the bondholder could exchange each bond for an agreed-on number of shares of common stock in the company. If the value of the stock rose appreciably after the date on which the bonds were first issued, the investor might decide to convert the bond to common stock. Because investors have two options for making money with them, convertible bonds generally carry lower interest rates—a feature that reduces the company's costs.

convertible bonds Bonds that offer the buyer the option of converting them into a stated number of shares of common stock

Equity

Unlike debt, which must be repaid, equity represents a "piece of the action." When a company raises capital by increasing equity, it expands the ownership of the business. Each investor becomes a part owner of the company, with the expectation of sharing in its profits through dividends and the capital gain that results when the stock is sold at a price higher than its purchase price. In a small company, the source of equity is generally a single individual or a limited number of investors. For example, the owner might personally invest more money in the business or might seek outside funding through a venture capitalist. If the firm is a partnership, a new partner might be brought in. In a larger business, when the need for funds exceeds the resources of a few people, equity may be obtained by selling stock to many individual investors on the open market.

Stocks are simply shares of ownership in a company, and the **stock certificate** that a shareholder receives is evidence of ownership. Each certificate shows the name of the shareholder, the number of shares of stock owned, and the special characteristics of the stock. Many stock certificates also bear a **par value,** an arbitrary face value that is usually less than the stock's estimated market value and that may be used (for certain kinds of stock) as the basis for figuring dividends.

stock certificate Document that proves stock ownership

par value Arbitrary value assigned to a stock

authorized stock Shares that a corporation's board of directors has decided to sell eventually

issued stock Authorized shares that have been released to the market

unissued stock Authorized shares that are to be released in the future

dividends Payments to shareholders from a company's earnings

The number of stock shares a company sells depends on the amount of equity capital the company will require and on the price of each share it sells. But a corporation's board of directors sets a maximum number of shares into which the business can be divided. In theory, all these shares—called **authorized stock**—may be sold at once. What often happens, however, is that the company sells only part of its authorized stock. The part sold and held by shareholders is called **issued stock;** as yet unsold stock is called **unissued stock.**

Well-established companies distribute part of their profits to shareholders in the form of **dividends.** Dividends may be paid in cash, but rapidly growing companies often issue dividends in the form of stock. By doing so, they conserve the firm's cash for capital investment, research and development, and similar types of expenditures.

Preferred Stock

preferred stock Shares that give their owners first claim on a company's dividends and assets

A company may issue two classes of stock. **Preferred stock** gives its holders certain preferences or special privileges that holders of common stock do not have:

▶ *They are preferred as to dividends.* Dividends on preferred stocks must be paid before any dividends are paid on common stocks.

▶ *They are preferred as to assets.* If a company fails, preferred shareholders have the right to receive their share of whatever assets are left (after the company's debts have been paid) before common shareholders receive anything.

The amount of the dividend on preferred stock is shown on the stock certificate. It may be expressed either as a percentage of the par value or as a dollar amount. Most preferred stock accumulates dividends if the corporation does not pay them in a given period. The company must pay this accumulation before it can pay any dividends on its common stock.

Generally, preferred shareholders play a smaller role in company affairs than do the common shareholders. In some companies, preferred shareholders have no voting power at all. More commonly they receive limited voting privileges, usually on matters that directly concern their rights, such as a decision to sell off a major part of the company or to change a provision of the charter that involves the preferred stock.

Common Stock

common stock Shares whose owners have the last claim on distributed profits and assets

In spite of its name, preferred stock is far less popular than **common stock** as a vehicle for raising money. In fact, many corporations issue only common stock, which entitles shareholders to participate in the selection of the company's board of directors and to speak out on other issues such as mergers, acquisitions, and takeovers. But common shareholders enjoy no special privileges as far as dividends or assets are concerned. The claims of preferred shareholders and bondholders take precedence over those of common shareholders. Also, common stock never carries a stated dividend, nor are its dividends cumulative.

Why do people buy common stock when they could have more security with preferred stock? Because, in addition to receiving dividends, the owners of common stock can profit if they sell their shares for more than the purchase price.

Preferred stock is dependable and stable; dividends are assured, but the value of the shares does not usually change much. Common stock, on the other hand, is less predictable but potentially more valuable.

COMMON-STOCK DIVIDENDS   There is no law that requires a corporation to pay dividends on common stock. The decision is up to the board of directors, who may decide—for good reasons—to omit the dividend or keep it to a minimum. In the case of a small, young company, for instance, the best course is usually to put all the profits back into the business. This enables the company to grow without using expensive outside financing. In the long run, the shareholders benefit more from the growth of the company and the resulting increase in the value of their stock than they do solely from the dividend.

In addition to paying a dividend, another option for increasing shareholder value is to repurchase outstanding common stock. This reduces the amount of issued stock, thus increasing the value of each share.

When large, well-established companies cut or omit dividends, the reason is usually a decline in profits. Dividends theoretically represent a share of the profits; when profits fall, there is less to share. The company hangs on to its cash in order to cover operating expenses. Unfortunately, shareholders not only lose out on their dividends in such situations but also frequently lose out on the value of the stock as well. When a big company cuts its dividend, the price of its stock generally falls—at least temporarily.

STOCK SPLITS   A dividend is not the only benefit a company can offer its common shareholders. Another alternative is a **stock split,** a procedure whereby the company doubles (or triples, or whatever) the number of shares that each stock certificate represents. In a 2-for-1 stock split, for example, a company whose stock was selling for $50 per share would double the number of shares outstanding, giving each shareholder two shares instead of one. Initially, these shares would each be worth only $25, but as the market price of the stock increased, the shareholder could realize a handsome profit. A stock split is different from a stock dividend in that a dividend is paid on existing stock, whereas a split involves the authorization of new stock.

VIDEO EXERCISE

stock split Increase in the number of shares of ownership that each stock certificate represents

Stock certificates represent a share of the ownership of a company.

New Issues and the Secondary Market

When a company issues new stock, it is offering more slices of the profit pie, and the amount of money a company can raise for each new slice depends on what the market expects the size of the total earnings pie to be. Not surprisingly, corporations often react to a rise in share prices by deciding to issue new stock.

stock exchanges Facilities where shares of stock are bought and sold

Most stocks are purchased from other investors rather than directly from corporations. After stock has been issued, it is bought and sold in secondary markets known as **stock exchanges,** where investors trade their individual shares. As shares are traded back and forth, any gain or loss in value goes to the shareholders—not to the companies that issued the stock. But even though corporations do not make any money on stock traded in the secondary market, they are concerned about the fluctuations in the price of their shares, because the "going rate" establishes what a company can raise through a new issue. Companies try to buoy their stock price by paying dividends, achieving ambitious performance goals, promoting the company's reputation with investors, and buying back their shares when the price is low.

► INTERNAL FINANCIAL PLANNING AND CONTROL

Although raising money is important, using that money wisely is an equally vital task. Thus, financial managers spend a good deal of their time managing the firm's working capital. The ultimate goal in managing working capital is to minimize the amount of money that is tied up in excess cash, uncollected bills (receivables), and inventory. The trick is to synchronize the amount of money flowing out of the business with the amount flowing in. Success depends on shortening the period between the purchase of raw materials and services from vendors and the collection of cash from sales to customers.

Managing Cash and Marketable Securities

How much cash do you carry in your wallet? If you have more than you need to cover your immediate expenses, you lack the instincts of an aggressive financial manager. Although excess cash might make you feel secure, it isn't earning any interest for you. An underlying concept of financial management is that all money should be productively employed.

Still, companies occasionally find themselves with more cash on hand than they need. In a seasonal business, a quiet period may ensue between the time when revenues are collected from the last busy season and the time when suppliers' bills are due. Department stores, for example, may have excess cash during a few weeks in January and February. A firm may also have excess cash if it is holding funds to meet a large commitment in the near future. It may be about to reach the next stage in the construction of a new plant, or it may be waiting for a special bargain on supplies. Finally, every firm keeps some surplus cash on hand as a cushion in case its needs are greater than expected.

marketable securities Stocks, bonds, and other investments that can be turned into cash quickly

Part of the financial manager's job is to make sure that this cash is invested so that it earns interest. The task is to find a good "parking place" for the funds, some sort of investment that will yield the highest possible return but will create no problem if the firm needs to liquidate the investment for instant cash. A number of short-term investments, called **marketable securities,** meet these needs. They are said to be "marketable" because they are relatively low in risk and can easily be converted back to cash.

The financial manager has many varieties of marketable securities to choose from. Banks sell large-denomination *certificates of deposit,* which are essentially time deposits at that bank. The federal government issues *Treasury bills,* which work like commercial paper; they are bought at a discount and redeemed by the U.S. Treasury for the face value on a specific maturity date (the date on which they must be repaid—in this case, less than a year from the date of purchase). Many federal agencies issue similar securities—such as Fannie Maes, Freddie Macs, Ginnie Maes, and Sallie Maes (all abbreviations of lengthy agency names)—to finance housing and student loans. And other businesses offer commercial paper.

When selecting a portfolio of marketable securities, financial managers must make trade-offs between safety/liquidity and maximum rate of return. Because marketable securities are generally viewed as contingency funds, most financial managers take a reasonably conservative approach to the management of these securities.

Managing Receivables and Payables

One of the big problems in managing working capital is that a company's revenues don't always come in at exactly the same rate that bills have to be paid. Financial managers such as Emerald Homes's Lewis J. Wright must therefore carefully monitor cash flow, the total amount of money acquired and spent to keep the business running.

One important aspect of this task is to keep a sharp eye on accounts receivable—the money owed to the firm by its customers. The volume of receivables

BEHIND THE SCENES

Tactics for Smart Cash Management

Instead of borrowing on a short-term basis, more and more companies are tapping fluid cash, the money that companies temporarily gather in the course of their business. Some ways of using fluid cash are perfectly legal; some are in a "gray area," ethically speaking; and some are both illegal and unethical. The following tactics are legal:

▶ *Take possession of cash as quickly as you can.* To get their money as soon as they're entitled to it, many corporations establish a network of post-office boxes in strategically selected locales with good mail delivery. Companies instruct customers to mail payments to these addresses, arranging to have a local bank pick up and deposit the checks to the firm's credit.

▶ *Put off paying bills as long as possible.* A corporation can rely on the shortcomings of the U.S. Postal Service in certain areas to make sure that checks go out as slowly as possible. But the simplest way to increase available cash is to pay bills only at the very last minute.

▶ *Use controlled disbursement accounts.* By choosing a bank offering controlled disbursement accounts, a company might write its checks on a remote bank and not cover them with funds until they are presented for collection. Every morning the bank tells the firm which checks will clear that day, leaving the firm enough time to transfer the funds. The Federal Reserve Bank is doing all it can to eliminate this ploy because the practice absorbs much of the Fed's costs.

depends on the financial manager's decisions regarding several issues. For example, who qualifies for credit and who does not? How long do customers have to pay their bills? How tough is the firm in collecting its debts? In addition to answering questions of this type, the financial manager analyzes the firm's receivables to identify patterns that might indicate problems.

The flip side of managing receivables is managing payables—the bills that the company owes to its creditors. Here the objective is generally to postpone paying bills until the last moment, since accounts payable represent interest-free loans from suppliers. However, the financial manager also needs to weigh the advantages of paying promptly, if doing so entitles the firm to cash discounts.

Managing Inventory

Inventory is another area where financial managers can fine-tune the firm's cash flow. Inventory sitting on the shelf represents capital that is tied up without earning interest. Furthermore, the firm incurs expenses for storage and handling, insurance, and taxes. And there is always a risk that the inventory will become obsolete before it can be converted into finished goods and sold.

economic order quantity The optimal, or least-cost, quantity of inventory that should be ordered

The firm's goal is to maintain enough inventory to fill orders in a timely fashion at the lowest cost. To achieve this goal, the financial manager tries to determine the **economic order quantity** (EOQ), or quantity of raw materials that, when ordered regularly, results in the lowest ordering and storage costs. The problem is complicated by the fact that minimizing ordering costs tends to increase storage costs and vice versa. The best way to cut ordering costs is to place one big order for parts and materials once a year, while the best way to cut storage costs is to order small amounts of inventory frequently. The challenge facing the financial manager is to find a compromise that minimizes total costs.

just-in-time inventory control A computerized system of managing inventory

That's why many businesses today are turning to **just-in-time inventory control**. Businesses—and even divisions within companies—link up through computers with their customers and suppliers, thereby automatically ordering only as much as is necessary for a given period of time. For example, Wal-Mart uses computers to track the inventory and sales of retail products. After a certain number of a given product, say toasters, have been sold off the shelf, the store automatically orders from its warehouse the necessary number of toasters to restock its shelf space. The warehouse, in turn, is linked by computer with the toaster supplier, so that when a certain number of toasters have been shipped to stores, a new order is automatically requested from the supplier via computer. In this way, Wal-Mart ensures that the optimal amount of toasters is shipped either to its warehouse or its stores "just in time." The financial manager's objective hasn't changed, it's just that the job of inventory control has been made a little easier.[6]

SUMMARY OF LEARNING OBJECTIVES

1 List the five steps involved in the financial-planning process.

When developing a financial plan, the financial manager estimates the monthly inflow of funds, estimates the monthly outflow of funds, compares them to determine whether they are negative or positive and how to use or create excess funds, chooses which capital investments should be made, and establishes a system for monitoring cash flows and return on investments.

2 State the matching principle.

The timing of a company's borrowing should roughly match the timing of its spending so that the flow of cash out of the company balances the flow of cash into the company.

3 Explain the chief advantage of debt versus equity.

Debt is cheaper than equity because debt payments can be deducted from a company's income tax and because dividend payments on stock are paid with after-tax dollars.

4 Define the objective of the capital-budgeting process.

The objective of the capital-budgeting process is to choose long-term investments that provide a satisfactory cash flow and rate of return.

5 Name three major types of short-term debt.

The three major types of short-term debt are trade credit, loans, and commercial paper.

6 List four major long-term financing options.

The four major long-term financing options are loans, leases, bonds, and equity.

7 Explain the guiding principle of cash management.

The guiding principle of cash management is to limit the amount of cash on hand to the minimum necessary to cover immediate expenses so that all available money is productively employed.

8 State the financial manager's primary goal in handling receivables and payables.

The financial manager's goal is to shorten the cycle between the collection of receivables and the payment of payables.

Meeting a Business Challenge at Emerald Homes

The financial management of Emerald Homes was such an immense job that Lewis J. Wright didn't have the luxury of avoiding any of the problems; they all had to be solved as quickly as possible, from paying off old debts and finding new financing to cutting back expenses so that the company would operate profitably. Wright started by convincing his commercial bankers to extend Emerald's line of credit. He was completely open about the probabilities for success of both the company and his own reorganization plans. As Wright observed: "It's crucial that your relationship with the bank be aboveboard." Maintaining that line of credit kept six critical subdivisions open, which created the revenue to help make principal and interest payments on bank loans. At the same time, Wright raised additional money by selling some of the company's assets (undeveloped land) to competitors, thus reducing the amount of construction loans Emerald had to pay off.

Wright cut operating costs by consolidating subdivisions under fewer construction superintendents and marketing managers, by reducing office space, and by eliminating all philanthropic expenses from the budget.

Lewis J. Wright, president and CEO of Emerald Homes.

And he made two other drastic, short-term cutbacks: He eliminated all marketing expenses, benefiting from competitor advertising by building homes in nearby areas, and he laid off high-salaried employees, including

Emerald's chief financial officer and controller. Financial duties were handled by Wright and three vice presidents who "ran the company out of the checkbook."

Finding new short-term construction loans (in order to keep building homes while he managed other financial problems) wasn't easy. Traditional loan sources (banks and savings and loans) had dried up, so Wright was forced to borrow small amounts from mortgage brokers, companies that normally provide financing to home buyers. Each loan was good for about four months, the time it took to build a house. But this capital wasn't cheap; not only did each loan carry an interest rate that was two percentage points above the prime rate, but Emerald had to pay 3 percent of the loan up front. Nevertheless, even though Emerald had to pay a steep price, houses could be built without having to turn to banks for the cash.

Still, the largest problem was the $32 million that Emerald owed the Resolution Trust Corporation. Wright's plan was to try to convince the RTC that the debt Emerald owed it could be sold to investors at a discount. In other words, instead of the RTC receiving the full $32 million, it might receive only $22 million. Then, in return for paying Emerald's debt to the RTC, investors would become part owners of the company, each owning a certain number of shares of Emerald's common stock. Even though the RTC would ultimately receive less than it was owed, Wright's plan would save the RTC from gaining nothing more than a bankrupt company. That, observed Wright, would be in no one's best interest.

If Wright could turn the troubled company away from bankruptcy and insolvency, he had no intention of ever leveraging the company to such an extent again. Wright had become CEO to save Emerald Homes. Once he succeeded, he intended to keep the company healthy through more careful management of the company's finances.

Your Mission: You are the general manager at Emerald Homes, second only to Wright in the company's management hierarchy. Until the chief financial officer and controller were laid off, your duties were concerned solely with home construction and subdivision development. Now you must help in the financial management of Emerald. Because you are new to this area of responsibility, Wright has asked that you discuss all financial decisions with him.

1. Before you begin your new duties in financial management, Wright has asked that you think about the situation Emerald is in and how it got there. To help guide you in making the best financial decisions in the future, Wright has asked you to ponder the lessons that should be learned from Emerald's story. What is the most important lesson you could learn?

a. Emerald should rely solely on equity financing.
b. Overleveraging the company can be dangerous.
c. Managing cash flow is the most important financial issue for the company.

d. Emerald should be more careful about who it borrows money from. If the savings and loan companies had conducted their business correctly in the first place, the RTC would never have foreclosed so quickly on Emerald's construction loans.

2. The four commercial banks that Emerald continues to work with have placed the company's accounts in what are called *B banks,* divisions of each bank overseeing loans that are either in default or in danger of default. Companies with accounts in these B banks have major credit problems and generally cannot receive new loans until the problem loans have been paid off. Once Emerald has a positive cash flow and is able to make principal and interest payments on all loans, the company's credit status should be restored to its former standing. At that time, what should Emerald's debt strategy be?

a. Seek construction loans from banks and curtail all short-term, high-cost loans from third parties, such as mortgage brokers.
b. Seek construction loans from banks while continuing to use short-term, high-cost loans from third parties.
c. Reduce the number of commercial banks with which Emerald does business.
d. Forgo bank loans altogether and use short-term loans as needed to build houses, despite the higher cost of capital associated with these loans.

3. Homebuilders have traditionally bought undeveloped land and kept it in inventory until market conditions are right for building a housing development. But the cost of keeping land in inventory has climbed dramatically. Purchase price and annual taxes are part of this cost, but the highest part is the opportunity cost; that is, the money cannot be used in other, perhaps more productive, ways. What is Emerald's best approach to this problem?

a. Despite the cost of doing so, keep only very large sections of land in inventory. Larger sections of land are more easily sold to competitors who need to develop subdivisions and planned communities.
b. Keep only very small sections of land in inventory so that costs remain low. Even though smaller sections of land are more difficult to sell and bring in less money, the cost savings make up for such shortcomings.
c. Keep land in inventory, but decide how much should be kept by balancing its costs with (1) the opportunity of using the money in some other way and (2) the opportunity of using the land. Whether the land can be used as an asset to sell in case additional cash is needed should be a secondary consideration.
d. Keep no land in inventory so that all funds can be used most productively at all times.

Your Mission: You are a loan officer at a commercial bank that does a lot of business with homebuilders, not just Emerald. In this position, you are expected to make the best decisions regarding loans and lines of credit, based on the financial information you receive from your customers.

4. What would be the most important financial information for you to obtain when doing business with homebuilders?

a. How much of each company's revenue is devoted to repaying loans and how much is devoted to current operations
b. Whether each company's cash flow is positive or negative, and if it's negative, what each company is doing to remedy the situation
c. Understanding current market conditions and the probability of each company's future success
d. All of the above[7]

KEY TERMS

authorized stock (560)
bond (557)
callable bonds (558)
capital budgeting (549)
capital investments (549)
capital structure (546)
chattel mortgage (553)
collateral (552)
commercial paper (554)
common stock (560)
compensating balance (553)
convertible bonds (559)
cost of capital (544)
debentures (558)
denomination (557)
dividends (560)

economic order quantity (564)
factoring (553)
financial management (542)
issued stock (560)
junk bonds (558)
just-in-time inventory control (564)
lease (557)
leverage (542)
line of credit (553)
long-term loans (556)
marketable securities (562)
matching principle (546)
open-book credit (550)
par value (559)
preferred stock (560)
principal (557)

promissory note (551)
revolving line of credit (554)
secured bonds (558)
secured loans (552)
serial bonds (558)
short-term debt (550)
sinking fund (558)
stock certificate (559)
stock exchanges (562)
stock split (561)
term bonds (558)
trade credit (550)
unissued stock (560)
unsecured bonds (558)
unsecured loan (553)

REVIEW QUESTIONS

1. What is the primary goal of financial management?

2. What are the two main types of trade credit?

3. What are some of the assets a business can pledge as collateral for a loan?

4. What is the function of commercial paper?

5. What are the four ways to pay back the debt that bonds incur?

6. What is the difference between the new-issues market and the secondary market?

7. What are marketable securities, and what purpose do they serve?

8. What types of projects are typically considered in the capital-budgeting process?

A CASE FOR CRITICAL THINKING

Financing the Most Expensive Motion Picture

Making a blockbuster motion picture is not a normal business. It's one of the riskiest ventures possible, and it requires enormous amounts of money. A lot can be lost. Or a lot can be gained, especially if the star is an international idol, the director is a celebrity in his or her own right, and the movie is a science fiction /action /adventure that's packed with the latest special effects. Carolco hoped to gain a lot when it decided to make *Terminator 2: Judgment Day,* starring Arnold Schwarzenegger.

How much would *T2* cost? For starters, Carolco had to buy the rights to the picture from Hemdale Film Corporation, which had produced the

original *Terminator.* That alone would cost Carolco $10 million—enough to finance a small independent film by a new director. Schwarzenegger, who by then was one of the highest paid actors in the world, would star in the sequel for at least $12 million. James Cameron, who had written and directed other profitable sci-fi movies, would write the script and direct *T2* for at least $5 million. Production costs, including state-of-the-art special effects, set designs, costumes, cast, and crew, were budgeted to exceed $51 million. Then would come at least $10 million of indirect production costs like travel, lodging, and miscellaneous overhead.

The grand total to produce *T2* was somewhere in the neighborhood of $90 million—by far the most expensive motion picture made to date. Why would Carolco or anyone else be willing to invest in a movie that could turn out to be a flop in the United States and internationally? Because the combination of Carolco, Schwarzenegger, and Cameron made the odds of spectacular success pretty good.

Carolco is a public company whose shares have been traded on the New York Stock Exchange since 1986. But its shareholders, although providing equity capital for the business, do not finance motion picture production in a strict sense. That's done in a manner peculiar to Hollywood, and particularly so for Carolco: through the sale of distribution rights.

Most motion picture production companies distribute their own movies. The costs of distribution include marketing. Advertising alone for a motion picture like *T2* can run into millions of dollars. For a production company that distributes its own movies, the rewards are great if the picture is a box-office hit; but if it flops, the entire venture can end in the red because of distribution costs. A string of flops makes it more difficult for a production company to raise money from investors willing to speculate on a future movie. That can spell doom for the production company and, in turn, drive down the value of the company's stock.

Carolco has managed the financial side of its business differently from the start. Instead of owning its distribution system, Carolco sells distribution rights to motion picture distributors in the United States and internationally, and to video distributors, cable television companies, and television networks the world over. These companies pay Carolco a percentage of the rights fee up front, which provides financing for the motion picture. The remainder is

paid after the movie is made and revenues begin flowing from the box office, video rentals, and television advertising sales. If the movie is a flop, Carolco has protected itself by placing more financial risk in the hands of distributors.

Also, Carolco has positioned itself to take advantage of international distribution by producing the kinds of action-adventure movies that attract big audiences around the world. The company made its start by producing the *Rambo* motion pictures, which were global successes in the early 1980s. Carolco's signing Schwarzenegger for the sequel to his hit *Terminator* was a boon for the sale of distribution rights.

Carolco received a $61 million advance for the film's international distribution. A $4 million advance came from Tri-Star Pictures, a unit of Columbia Pictures Entertainment, for distribution of the movie to U.S. theaters. Live Entertainment, a Carolco affiliate, paid a $10 million advance for video rights in the United States and Canada. Showtime, a unit of Viacom International, paid a $9 million advance for the cable television rights, and the sale of broadcast television rights brought another $7 million. So the advances on distribution rights to *T2* totaled $91 million—

enough to meet the movie's budget.

But Carolco had written the distribution contracts to make even more money if the movie was a runaway hit. Once the distributors' costs were covered, and if the film's box-office revenues were greater than a certain amount, Carolco's take would increase. Carolco executives estimated that $260 million worth of worldwide box-office receipts—the amount another Schwarzenegger movie, *Total Recall,* had made—would produce a $30 million profit for the company. As it turned out, *T2* was a great investment. Only four months after release, it had grossed $400 million worldwide.[8]

1. If you were a video distributor, what factors would you want to consider before agreeing to any distribution-rights contract with Carolco on *T2*?

2. Why would any institutional or individual investor buy shares in Carolco, given the uncertain nature of its business?

3. Why doesn't Carolco (or any other motion picture production company) use bank loans or commercial paper to finance production of its movies?

BUILDING YOUR COMMUNICATION SKILLS

It is common for start-up businesses to defray initial expenses by obtaining a business loan. Interview the loan officer of a financial institution to determine what is required for a small-business loan. If this is not possible, obtain information from a financial institution by writing a letter to its loan department, or locate information in the reference section of the library. Even if you don't have an idea for a specific business, you can find out what is required by the financial

institution. As you acquire information, you might wish to consider the following:

▶ The advance business and financial planning required to start a business

▶ Your personal credentials

▶ Other sources of income or indicators of financial solvency

▶ The various terms and conditions of the loan

As directed by your instructor, prepare a brief summary of the information you have obtained regarding the small-business loan policies of that financial institution. Compare your findings with the information obtained by other students. Which institutions are most responsive to small-businesses? Are the terms and conditions of the various institutions similar?

KEEPING CURRENT USING *THE WALL STREET JOURNAL*

Choose a recent article from *The Wall Street Journal* that deals with the financing arrangements or strategies of a particular company.

1. What form of financing did the company choose? Did the article indicate why the company selected this form of financing?

2. Who provided the financing for the company? Was this arrangement considered unusual, or was it routine?

3. What does the company intend to do with the arranged financing—purchase equipment or other assets, finance a construction project, finance growth and expansion, or something else?

CHAPTER 20

LEARNING OBJECTIVES

After studying this chapter, you will be able to

1 List five objectives that should be considered when choosing investments.

2 List five investment options available to the investor and compare them in terms of safety and potential rate of return.

3 Describe asset allocation and how it's used during changing economic conditions.

4 Explain the efficient market hypothesis and its importance to institutional investors.

5 Describe two types of securities marketplaces.

6 Characterize six indexes that provide a broad indication of how the stock market is performing.

7 List at least four sources of information about investments.

8 Name two federal agencies involved in regulating the investment industry.

Securities Markets

SEARCHING FOR GROWTH BENEATH A
MOUNTAIN OF DEBT

I t was a heavy responsibility: managing millions of dollars invested by clients so that their wealth would continue to grow. Moreover, clients expected their wealth to grow regardless of prevailing economic or stock market conditions. As a vice president at Landes Associates (a Delaware-based investment management firm), William A. Francis could choose from a wide array of investment vehicles, including commodities futures, common and preferred stock, corporate and government bonds, and mutual funds. The challenge was knowing when to buy which products, how long to hold them, and when to sell them.

His challenge was made more difficult by the investment needs of his clients. Primarily wealthy individuals, these investors didn't need extra income. They wanted their wealth to grow steadily, and they were unwilling to invest in anything with a high degree of risk. Francis decided to avoid commodities, the riskiest of available investments. He also decided against preferred stock, corporate bonds, and government bonds, primarily because such investments are usually designed to produce reliable income (something his clients didn't need). Finally, he ruled out mutual funds, mainly because such funds are intended for small investors who lack the financial means to create their own portfolios. So Francis was left with common stocks.

To pick the right companies to invest his clients' money in, Francis had to know three things: (1) the major forces at work in the economy that could affect a particular industry or company, (2) the general investment climate of the securities markets, and (3) the performance of particular companies. As Francis observed, purchasing stock isn't like buying products in a store where prices are clearly marked and where value is relatively easy to recognize. Investors buy expectations. They are always asking: "What's going to attract other investors to this stock? Why should somebody else be willing to pay a higher price for this stock than I'm paying now?" The answer to both questions is the company's expected growth.

But the economic climate had changed drastically in less than a decade. It hadn't been difficult at all for investors to realize capital gains during most of the 1980s: The Dow Jones Industrial Average shot up 250 percent during that decade, so even a conservative investor could have averaged 10 to 13 percent interest compounded annually. But at the same time, most U.S. corporations failed to reinvest adequately in their own long-term growth. Thus corporate growth stagnated as the 1990s got under way, and Francis found it more difficult to make investment decisions for his clients. Because fewer companies had solid growth potential, fewer stocks were available to provide the sort of low-risk capital gains his clients wanted.

With the slowing economy of the early 1990s and the decrease in companies having solid growth potential, Francis faced a tremendous challenge. He had to find the few companies worth investing in. Then he had to decide the best time to invest in them: immediately, after the economy improved, or once Wall Street showed clear signs of beginning another bull market. Finally, he had to determine the best time to sell stocks—both those his clients were currently invested in and those he would recommend. Where would Francis find the information he needed to make these decisions? How could he determine which companies his clients could invest in to make their wealth grow without undue risk? And how would he know when to sell a client's stock?[1]

▶ INVESTORS AND INVESTING

As an investment adviser and broker, William A. Francis is part of a multitrillion-dollar industry that spans the globe. Investments are the foundation of most of the world's financial systems, whether in the United States, in Europe, in Japan, or in any of the Third World nations that have their own stock exchanges. Profit-oriented businesses, nonprofit institutions, and individuals make investments so that governments and businesses can raise the capital necessary to finance their operations and so that investors can earn interest, dividends, and capital gains.

Institutional and Private Investors

marketable securities Securities that can be bought and sold easily in an organized market

institutional investors Companies that invest money entrusted to them by others

Marketable securities are financial assets for which organized markets exist. Two types of investors buy and sell marketable securities: institutions and individuals. **Institutional investors**—such as pension funds, insurance companies, investment companies, and colleges and universities—dominate U.S. securities markets. A study by the Securities Industry Association found that institutions and large securities firms constitute nearly 82 percent of all trading on the New York Stock Exchange, whereas individual investors account for only 18 percent.[2] Institutions hire professional money managers to handle their accounts, and these managers increasingly use computers to make instantaneous trades based on hundreds of financial and economic factors. Because institutions have such large pools of money to work with, their investment decisions have a major impact on the market, increasingly in the form of *volatility*—that is, the securities markets tend to gain or lose more in shorter periods of time than in the past.

Individuals can invest either directly (in securities) or indirectly (through mutual funds, insurance products, or employee pension plans). Because of the security market's increasing volatility, individual investors are turning to indirect investments. Individual investors are changing from direct investments (such as common stocks) to indirect investments (such as mutual funds). Although the migration is a 20-year-old trend, it has intensified dramatically since the stock market crash of October 19, 1987.[3]

Investment Objectives

If institutional and individual investors seem at odds with each other, it may be because their objectives are generally different. Institutions tend to seek the highest return in the quickest period possible, so they trade large amounts of securities frequently. On the other hand, the majority of individual investors have traditionally made long-term investments, trading their securities only when they felt it necessary to do so, whether because of market conditions or changes in their personal lives. In general, people make investment decisions based on five criteria: *income, growth, safety, liquidity,* and *tax consequences.*

If a steady, reasonably predictable flow of cash is sought, income is the chief concern. Fixed-income investments include certificates of deposit, government securities, corporate bonds, and preferred stocks. A retired person wanting to supplement Social Security or pension benefits would be a customer for this type of investment.

Many investors are concerned with wealth accumulation, or growth. Their objective is to maximize **capital gains**—the return made by selling a security for a price that is higher than its purchase price. Common stock is generally known as *equity* because it represents an ownership position in a company and because common stock is the primary investment instrument for achieving growth. Other instruments include options, futures contracts, and commodities. Some nonfinancial assets such as fine art, horses, and real estate can achieve the same goal, but usually a much longer period is needed.

Safety is another concern. Generally, the higher the potential for income or growth, the greater the risk of the investment. **Speculators** are investors who accept high risks in order to realize large capital gains. Of course, every investor must make such a trade-off to some extent. This is true for all investments. Government bonds are safer than corporate bonds, which are safer than common stocks, which are safer than futures contracts, which are safer than commodities. But even within the bond and stock markets, an investor will face varying degrees of risk. For example, investment-grade corporate bonds are safer than speculative-grade corporate bonds, commonly known as junk bonds. Likewise, the common stock of a major, established corporation such as Wal-Mart is safer than that of a technology company that's less than six months old. This doesn't mean that Wal-Mart's stock will never decline in value, but it does mean that Wal-Mart's stock is more likely to climb in price and provide dividends over a longer period of time than the stock of a small technology company with an unproven product or service.

Two final factors that investors take into consideration are liquidity and tax consequences. Liquidity is the measure of how quickly an investor can change an investment into cash. For example, common stock is more liquid than real estate; most financial assets can be changed into cash within a day. Some, like certificates of deposit, can be cashed in before maturity, but only after the investor has paid a penalty.

All investors must consider the tax consequences of their decisions. Historically, dividend and interest income have been taxed heavily, and capital gains

Money managers at Fidelity Stock Investment Center in Boston, Massachusetts, handle investment accounts and use computers to make instantaneous stock trades.

capital gains *Difference between the price at which a financial asset is sold and its original cost (assuming the price has gone up)*

speculators *Investors who seek large capital gains through relatively risky investments*

have been taxed relatively lightly. But in 1986 Congress eliminated the tax advantage associated with long-term gains. Individuals in the highest tax bracket have another decision to make: whether they want to be taxed on the income they receive from their investments. The income from some government securities is not taxed at the federal or state levels.

The Investment Portfolio

investment portfolios Assortment of investment instruments

No single investment instrument will provide income, growth, and a high degree of safety. For this reason, all investors—whether institutions or individuals—build **investment portfolios,** or collections of various types of investments. Money managers and financial advisers, like William Francis, are employed (1) to determine which investments should be in an investor's portfolio and (2) to buy and sell securities and maintain the client's portfolio. A major concern for them is **diversification**—reducing the risk of loss in a client's total portfolio by investing funds in several different securities, so a loss experienced by any one will not affect the entire portfolio.

diversification Assembling investment portfolios in such a way that a sudden loss in one investment won't affect the value of the entire portfolio

A portion of a portfolio might be in investment-grade corporate bonds, and a portion might be in common stocks. Likewise, owning stock in ten large corporations provides greater safety through diversification than owning the stock of only one small technology company. The loss of one stock might be offset by one or more other stocks. A portfolio might also be structured to provide a desired **rate of return,** the percentage gain or interest yield on investments. For example, an investment-grade corporate bond might pay 7 percent interest but provide an expected capital gain of only 2 percent, whereas a growth stock might be expected to return a capital gain of 14 percent but pay no dividend.

rate of return Percentage increase in the value of an investment

Asset Allocation

asset allocation Method of shifting investments within a portfolio to adapt them to the current investment environment

Managing a portfolio to gain the highest rates of return while reducing risk as much as possible is known as **asset allocation.** A portion of the portfolio might be devoted to cash instruments such as money-market mutual funds, a portion to income instruments such as government and corporate bonds, and a portion to equities (mainly common stock). The money manager then determines how much each portion should be, based on economic and market conditions. For example, if the economy is booming and the stock market is performing well, the money manager might shift 75 percent of the total portfolio into stocks, 20 percent into bonds, and 5 percent into cash to take advantage of the good times. If the economy turns bad, the stock market heads downward, and inflation heats up, the money manager might readjust the portfolio and put 30 percent of its assets in stocks, 40 percent in short-term government securities, and 30 percent in cash. This way the value of the portfolio is protected during poor investment conditions.[4]

Efficient Market Theory

efficient market hypothesis Theory that the market finds its true value quickly and efficiently

Modern portfolio management has been influenced heavily by a controversial theory known as the **efficient market hypothesis** (EMH), which holds that all securities are appropriately valued at all times because securities markets make quick and efficient price adjustments. These adjustments are based on all available information about individual securities and about the economy as a whole. For example, IBM's stock may rise one day and fall the next. That's because the buyers and sellers of IBM stock have quickly taken into account the thousands of bits of information concerning the company, its stock, and the economy (everything from IBM's revenues and profits to interest rates and currency exchange rates). Because it implies that no individual money manager or investor can "beat" the market, the EMH has held a powerful place in market theory; indeed, EMH supporters would maintain that a chimpanzee randomly pointing at stocks in the newspaper will be as successful in choosing the right investments as Wall Street's smartest money manager.

Investors who believe in the EMH believe they can rarely beat the market by continually changing investments. So institutional investors are trying to do at least as well as the market itself. **Market indexes** such as Standard & Poor's 500 use a selection of securities as a model to gauge the activity of the market as a whole. To avoid wasting time trying to beat the market, many institutional investors are tying the performance of their investments to the performance of the market. They do this by **indexing,** that is, by building a portfolio of securities that are selected because together they reflect the profile of the market as a whole.

But the EMH fell on hard times with the market's crash on October 19, 1987, when the Dow Jones Industrial Average dropped 22.6 percent, wiping out more than $500 billion in market value. Critics of the EMH say that if the market is as efficient as claimed, then stocks were priced too high before the crash, which means that the market failed to reflect their true value. Moreover, the critics assert that the EMH can't explain the crash itself. They contend that because the market isn't as efficient as once thought, it can be influenced at any time by the mass psychological behavior of investors—what is commonly known as the "herd instinct." This view implies that it's possible to beat the market with careful analysis of corporations, of their stock's performance, and of economic factors.

The verdict is still out on the EMH. Its followers believe that the market was operating efficiently on the day of the crash, but critics still abound. In general, most analysts believe the market is efficient to a great degree. So like Landes Associates' William Francis, most money managers encourage individual investors to hold onto a good portfolio for the long term, rather than trying to beat the market, and institutional investors are increasing their use of indexing. It is estimated that a third of all institutional portfolios are indexed to follow the ups and downs of major markets. Additionally, institutional money managers are developing strategies for indexing foreign security investments.[5]

market indexes Measures of security markets calculated from the prices of a selection of securities

indexing Assembling investment portfolios by selecting securities that together reflect the profile of the market as a whole

Money managers at Fidelity Investments encourage investors to hold onto a good portfolio for the long term. The investment firm even talks about its commonsense approach to long-term results when advertising in *The Wall Street Journal.*

▶ INVESTMENT CHOICES

As William Francis knows well, various investment instruments serve different purposes. Government securities raise money for federal, state, and local governments to fund public expenses, from national defense to road improvements. Corporate bonds finance business operations and are debt obligations of the issuing companies. Stocks also finance business operations, but they are certificates of ownership that let the investor reap the benefits—and suffer the losses—of the issuing companies. These and other securities are all traded in organized markets, which are cyclical in their performance: Sometimes they rise in value, sometimes they fall.

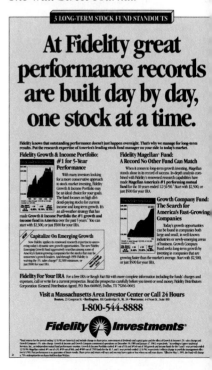

Government Securities

The most risk-free investments possible are U.S. government securities, which are of two basic types: those backed by the U.S. Treasury and those backed by agencies of the government. State and local governments also raise money through bond issues. Although government securities pay less interest than corporate bonds, they do provide advantages in terms of safety and tax consequences.

Federal Government Issues

The three principal types of U.S. government issues are **Treasury bills** for short-term debt, **Treasury notes** for debt obligations of 1 to 10 years, and **Treasury bonds** for long-term debt. All three are generally the most liquid investments available and are traded in an organized market. Investors trade government securities with each other, except for savings bonds, which are redeemed directly back to the government.

Treasury bills come in maturities of 13 weeks, 26 weeks, or 52 weeks. Unlike many income-oriented investments, T-bills do not pay interest. Instead, they are sold at a discount from their face value and then redeemed at full face value when they mature. The difference between the purchase price and the redemption price is, in effect, interest. T-bills require a minimum investment of $10,000. Treasury notes and Treasury bonds, which have maturities of 10 to 30 years, are available for a minimum investment of $1,000. Twice a year they pay a fixed amount of interest, which is exempt from state and local income taxes.

Small investors are particularly fond of **U.S. savings bonds,** because they are available in denominations ranging from $50 to $10,000. Like T-bills, they are sold at a discount from their face value; if held to maturity, they pay the face value on the savings bond plus interest.

Some 20 other government agencies also issue debt, including the Student Loan Marketing Association and the Farm Credit System. The two largest and most important are the Government National Mortgage Association (Ginnie Mae) and the Federal National Mortgage Association (Fannie Mae). These agencies raise money to help finance mortgages for U.S. homeowners, so they issue mortgage-backed securities. Ginnie Maes require a $25,000 investment and are guaranteed by the issuing agency (they are backed by the full faith and credit of the U.S. government). Fannie Maes do not enjoy such a guarantee; however, the agency does have a line of credit with the federal government, making these issues safe investments. They are also highly liquid; the market for these securities is huge and active.

Municipal Bonds

Municipal bonds are issued by states, cities, and special government agencies such as the Tennessee Valley Authority, port authorities, and airports to finance public services. They come in two forms, general obligation bonds and revenue bonds. Governments pay off their principal and interest obligations to the buyers of **general obligation bonds** through tax receipts. The principal and interest on **revenue bonds** are paid from the revenues raised by the issuer. For example, bonds issued by a city airport are paid from revenues raised by the airport's operation.

Treasury bills Short-term debt issued by the federal government

Treasury notes Debt securities issued by the federal government that mature within 1 to 10 years

Treasury bonds Debt securities issued by the federal government that mature in 10 to 30 years

U.S. savings bonds Debt instruments in small denominations sold by the federal government

municipal bonds Debt issued by a state or a local agency; interest earned on municipal bonds is exempt from federal income tax and from taxes in the issuing jurisdiction

general obligation bonds Municipal bonds backed by the issuing agency's general taxing authority

revenue bonds Municipal bonds backed by revenue generated from the projects financed with the bonds

U.S. savings bonds are popular among people who want to invest smaller amounts of money, anywhere from $50 to $10,000.

U.S. SAVINGS BONDS

Making American Dreams a Reality

The interest received from municipal bonds is not taxed by the federal government. Also many states do not tax the interest paid on bonds issued by governments within those states. Capital gains made on the sale of municipal bonds are taxed at the federal and state levels.

Corporate Bonds

The stock market gets most of the attention in financial news, but the bond market is actually several times larger. Furthermore, nearly as many individual investors own bonds as own common stock.[6] Perhaps the bond market has been ignored out of habit; for years bonds just quietly earned interest for investors. But that changed during the 1980s when the junk bond market ballooned and then burst. Corporations all across the United States found themselves in **default** on their bond issues—that is, they didn't have enough money on hand to meet their interest payments.

Corporations issue three principal types of bonds. **Mortgage bonds** are backed by real property owned by the issuing corporation so that if the corporation goes bankrupt, the investor has a greater chance of recouping a portion of the original investment. **Debentures** aren't secured by anything other than the promise of the corporation to pay. Because debentures are riskier than bonds, they pay higher interest to the investor. **Convertible bonds** can be exchanged, at the investor's discretion, for a certain number of shares of the corporation's common stock.

Corporate bonds are rated for their safety by Standard & Poor's Corporation and by Moody's Investors Service. Exhibit 20.1 shows how these two companies rate bonds. The higher the rating on a bond, the safer it is considered, so the less interest it pays; the lower the rating, the riskier it is, so it pays a higher rate of interest.

Michael Milken is the man credited with singlehandedly making the junk bond market into the phenomenon of the 1980s. Milken convinced thousands of institutional and individual investors to put their money into high-risk junk bonds in return for high rates of interest.

default *Failure of issuers to meet their contractual principal and interest obligations*

mortgage bonds *Corporate bonds backed by real property, not by mortgages*

debentures *Corporate bonds backed by the company's good faith*

convertible bonds *Corporate bonds that can be exchanged at the owner's discretion into common stock of the issuing company*

EXHIBIT 20.1 ▶ Corporate Bond Ratings

Standard & Poor's Corporation and Moody's Investors Service are the two primary companies that rate the safety of corporate bonds. As ratings decline, investors take on more risk, so they are compensated with higher interest rates.

S&P	MOODY'S	RATING EXPLANATION
AAA	Aaa	Highest rating; strongest capacity to pay principal and interest
AA +	Aa1	
AA	Aa2	Very strong capacity to pay principal and interest
AA−	Aa3	
A +	A1	
A	A2	Strong capacity to pay principal and interest, but more susceptible to the adverse effects of changing business and economic conditions
A−	A3	
BBB +	Baa1	
BBB	Baa2	Adequate capacity to pay principal and interest; any changes in business or economic conditions will likely lead to weakened financial status
BBB−	Baa3	Speculative investment grade; "junk bonds"

In addition to receiving interest, bondholders can also realize capital gains on bonds by taking advantage of shifts in interest rates, which trigger increases or decreases in the face value of the bonds. For example, a $1,000 bond with an interest rate of 8 percent will sell for more than $1,000 if interest rates fall to 7 percent, because new bonds will pay annual interest of $70 instead of $80. If investors can sell the 8 percent bond for more than $1,000, they realize a capital gain. In fact, interest rates move up and down every day, and so do the prices at which bonds are traded, but in the opposite direction. The degree of movement in a particular bond depends on its maturity date. In general, the longer the maturity of the bond, the more it will fluctuate.

Stocks

shareholder An owner of equities

An investor in a company's stock owns a portion of that company and is known as a **shareholder.** As a part owner, the shareholder gets to vote on the members of the company's board of directors as well as on any major policies that will affect ownership. The shareholder also has an opportunity to share in the company's profits or losses in two ways, through capital gains (or losses) and through dividends (or the cancellation of dividends). After a company has paid all expenses and taxes out of revenues, its board of directors can pay a portion of what remains—its earnings—to investors in the form of **dividends.** The board decides whether to make dividend payments; no law mandates that a company do so. Therefore, a board may decide either to reduce the dividend or to suspend its payment altogether (if the company needs the money to continue operating).

dividends Payments to shareholders from a company's earnings

Common Stocks

common stock Equities issued by corporations, generally carrying no special privileges and usually paid off last if a firm liquidates

Most stock issued by corporations is **common stock,** which generally carries no special privileges and which is the last to be paid off (if any funds remain) when the company liquidates to go out of business. **Blue-chip stocks** are the stocks of established corporations that have paid sizable dividends consistently for years and that have periodically raised their dividends as profits increased. These are considered to be conservative equity investments because, in addition to the dividends they pay, their prices tend to rise slowly over longer periods, and they are generally less susceptible to sudden drops in the market. To put this in perspective, **growth stocks** are issued by younger and smaller companies that have strong growth potential. They normally don't pay dividends because they reinvest earnings in the company to expand operations. Their stock prices tend to rise more quickly, but they can fall just as quickly. For this reason, growth stocks are considered aggressive investments; the investor is hoping to make a capital gain more quickly.

blue-chip stocks Equities issued by large, well-established companies with consistent records of price increases and dividend payments

growth stocks Equities issued by small companies with unproven products or services

Most shareholders are looking for growth, some for the income provided by dividends. But an investor might also want to own common stock because of special situations regarding the issuing companies. Three specific examples are turnarounds, cyclicals, and plays. In a *turnaround,* the investor thinks a company that has been close to, or even in, bankruptcy court is going to turn itself around and become profitable. The shareholder expects the stock's price to increase as a result. A *cyclical stock* is one issued by a company whose business reflects the cycles of the economy. Automakers are an example; consumers buy more cars when the economy booms. If the economy is showing signs of coming out of a recession, an investor might want to invest in cyclical stocks to take advantage of the growing economy. *Plays* often involve the merger of two companies or the acquisition of one by another. Generally, when a company is "in play," rumors or published reports indicate that it will be acquired by another, and the price of the stock temporarily spurts upward. Also, companies that are in financial trouble and yet hold large salable assets can become plays even without the threat of takeover; the shareholder believes the company will sell assets to become "leaner and meaner," often to avoid a takeover, thereby driving up the price of the stock.

Preferred Stocks

Investors who buy preferred stocks do so primarily for the dividends they pay. **Preferred stock** offers two advantages over common stock: (1) shareholders of preferred stock are guaranteed to receive their dividends before shareholders of common stock and (2) if the issuing company liquidates its assets to go out of business, holders of preferred stock will be paid off after bondholders and before holders of common stock. For these reasons, preferred stocks are a hybrid of fixed-income securities and equities. Their prices tend to react more to changes in interest rates than to changes in the prices of the issuing company's common stock.

preferred stocks Shares that give their owners first claim on a company's dividends and assets

Cumulative preferred stock has an additional advantage: If the issuing company suspends dividends, the dividends on these shares will accumulate until shareholders have been paid in full. *Convertible preferred stock* can be exchanged at the shareholder's discretion for a certain number of shares of common stock issued by the company.

Corporations are some of the largest buyers of preferred stock because they receive a 70 percent tax break. So if $100,000 in dividend income is received in a year by the investing corporation, it pays taxes on only $30,000 of that income.

Short Selling

Short selling is selling stock that is borrowed from a broker in the hope of buying it back later at a lower price. When the borrowed stock is returned to the broker, the investor keeps the difference between what it sold for and what it was bought back for. Although "shorting" has traditionally been done by specialists, individual investors are increasingly using this method in search of gains. About $30 billion in stock is sold short these days, compared with $3 trillion of stocks that are owned the common way.[7]

short selling Selling stock borrowed from a broker with the intention of buying it back later at a lower price, repaying the broker, and pocketing the profit

Selling a stock short is something done by an investor who is pessimistic. For example, suppose you think a company's stock will decline in the near future. You borrow shares of the stock that are selling for $30 per share and then sell short, pledging to deliver the shares you do not own back to the broker from whom you borrowed them. When the stock's price has sunk to $15 per share, you buy the stock on the open market and make $15 a share profit (minus transaction costs).

Selling short is not without its risks. If you had not covered your short position at $15 a share but instead had held out in hope of seeing the stock's price go even lower, you might have been left owing your broker money. For instance, if the stock had gone back up to $30 a share, you would have had to buy it at the same price you sold it for; paying the broker's commissions and interest charges would have left you in the hole.

Mutual Funds

mutual funds Pools of money raised by investment companies and invested in stocks, bonds, or other marketable securities

Investment companies such as Landes Associates have traditionally provided a solution for individual investors without enough money to own individual securities. They operate **mutual funds,** pooling money from small investors to buy stocks, bonds, government securities, gold, or other marketable securities. Various funds have different investment priorities. Some target income, some growth. Some invest in companies that make up particular industries, and others balance their investment portfolios with both fixed-income securities and equities. Among the more popular mutual funds are **money-market funds,** which are invested entirely in short-term securities such as commercial paper, certificates of deposit, Treasury bills, and other liquid investments. Mutual funds are particularly suited to small investors who do not have the time or experience to search for investment opportunities. However, small institutional investors are increasingly putting money in mutual finds, seeking the same diversification and liquidity realized by individual investors.

money-market funds Mutual funds that invest in short-term securities

Investment companies offer two types of funds. An *open-end fund* invests on behalf of as many investors as want to be in it; its size increases or decreases as investors put their money into, or take their money out of, the fund. In essence, the fund's books remain open and never close. Shares in an open-end fund aren't traded in a separate market; investors receive shares in the fund when they put money into it, and they can redeem those shares for cash only with the investment company.

Closed-end funds invest on behalf of a fixed number of investors; as soon as a certain number of shares are sold, the fund closes its books. The shares in a closed-end fund are then bought and sold in the same markets in which other securities are traded. Other than this major distinction, they offer the same diversification as open-end funds.

Other Investments

Stocks, bonds, and mutual funds are the most common marketable securities available for investors. But other securities have been developed. For the most part, these securities—including options, futures, and their variations—are used by money managers and savvy traders. In recent years, some of these securities, particularly options, have been used more by individual investors.

Options

stock option Contract allowing the holder to buy or sell a given number of shares of a particular stock at a given price by a certain date

A **stock option** is the purchased right—but not the obligation—to buy or sell a specified number of shares of a stock at a predetermined price during a specified period. By trading options, the investor doesn't have to own shares of stock in a company—only an option to buy or sell those shares. The cost of buying an option on shares of stock is significantly less than the cost of purchasing the stock itself. And option sellers receive a premium for the transactions they complete.

call option The right to buy shares at a specified price and sell at a market price

A **call option** is the right to buy stock at a specified price and sell at market price. An investor who buys a call option believes the price of the underlying stock will increase, thus making the call more valuable. The investor who sells that call believes just the opposite—that the price of the underlying stock will decline. If the buyer of a call is correct and exercises the right to purchase those shares of stock before the right expires, he or she can buy the stock from the option seller at the option's exercise price and then sell the stock for a capital gain.

On the other hand, a **put option** is the right to buy stock at market price and sell at a specified price. An investor who buys a put option believes the price of the underlying stock will decline, thus making the put more valuable. The buyer usually already owns shares of the underlying stock. The investor who sells that put believes the price of the underlying stock will rise. If the buyer of a put is correct and exercises the right to sell the stock before the right expires, then he or she can sell the shares of stock to the seller of the put option at the higher exercise price.

put option The right to buy shares at market price and sell at a specified price

Options can be used for wild speculation, or they can be used as a way of making an investor's stock portfolio a little safer. For example, investors can **hedge** their position—that is, they can partially protect against a sudden loss— by selling a call option at the price of the underlying stock that is in the investor's portfolio. This way, the seller receives the premium to help offset a loss if the price of the stock suddenly falls.

hedge An investment that protects the investor from suffering loss on another investment

Financial Futures

Financial futures are similar to options, but they are *legally binding* contracts to buy or sell a financial instrument (stocks, Treasury bonds, foreign currencies) for a set price at a future date. Like options traders, investors in financial futures are betting that the price of a financial instrument will either rise or fall. Most financial futures are traded on margin—borrowing a portion of the money needed to purchase a security—which magnifies both the potential risks and the potential rewards. In addition, investors can borrow more money to margin options and futures than they can to option stocks.

financial futures Legally binding agreements to buy or sell financial instruments at a future date

STOCK INDEX FUTURES   One of the newest types of financial futures is also one of the most popular: stock market index futures. With this financial instrument, traders speculate on the behavior of a certain group of stocks. The cumulative or average prices of the stocks in that group tend to rise and fall with the stock market as a whole. In effect, those who trade stock market index futures are speculating on the behavior of the stock market and the economy. Investing in stock index futures is consistent with the implications of the efficient market hypothesis: If you can't beat the market, you can at least do as well as the market.

STOCK INDEX OPTIONS   As if investing in financial futures wasn't complicated enough, investors now have stock index options, the right to buy or sell a hypothetical portfolio of stocks at a particular price and time. A small initial cash outlay buys command over stocks worth much more, so the options can provide a quick, cheap capital gain. The seller of these options incurs a greater risk because small downward changes in an index easily produce large dollar losses.

Commodities

For the investor who enjoys a risky market, nothing compares with speculating in **commodities**—raw materials and agricultural products such as petroleum,

commodities Raw materials used in producing other goods

When investing in commodities markets, speculators buy contracts rather than the actual items being sold. The rancher who owns this herd of cattle near Austin, Texas, might sell contracts calling for delivery of the cattle at some time in the future.

spot trading Trading in commodities that will be delivered immediately

commodities futures Contracts for commodities that will be delivered at a future date

VIDEO EXERCISE

auction exchange A centralized marketplace where securities are traded by specialists on behalf of investors in auctions

stock specialists Intermediaries who trade in particular securities on the floors of auction exchanges; "buyers of last resort"

dealer exchanges Decentralized marketplaces where securities are bought and sold by dealers out of their own inventories

gold, coffee beans, pork bellies, beef, and coconut oil. Commodities markets originally sprang up as a convenience for buyers and sellers interested in trading the actual commodities. A manufacturer of breakfast cereals, for example, must buy wheat, rye, oats, and sugar from hundreds of farmers. The easiest way to arrange these transactions is to meet in a forum where many buyers and sellers come to trade. Since the commodities are too bulky to bring to the marketplace, the traders buy and sell contracts for delivery of a given amount of these raw materials at a given time.

Trading contracts for immediate delivery of a commodity is called **spot trading,** or cash trading. Most commodity trading is for future delivery, usually months in advance, sometimes a year or more; this is called trading **commodities futures.** The original purpose of futures trading was to allow producers and consumers of commodities to hedge their position, or protect themselves against violent price swings. For example, farmers might sell futures contracts calling for delivery of some of the wheat they expect to have grown by harvest time to bakers who expect to use the flour milled from that wheat to bake bread. By selling before the crop is in, farmers get operating capital—as well as the assurance that they'll get a certain fixed price for their crops, even if prices collapse later. The bakers, on the other hand, can buy some of the supplies they expect to use and be assured that no matter how bad the crop is or how high the price goes, they'll have enough wheat to stay in business.

Today, speculators play an important role in the commodities markets, doing the lion's share of the trading and increasing the liquidity of the market. Hoping to profit as prices rise and fall, they voluntarily assume the risk that the hedger tries to avoid. In reality, however, 75 percent of the people who speculate in commodities lose money in the long run.[8] Even seasoned veterans have been known to lose literally millions of dollars within a few days.

▶ THE MECHANISMS OF INVESTING

When Wall Street was in its infancy, investors could buy stocks "over the counter," as though they had walked into a store for a loaf of bread. Around 1817, the New York Stock Exchange board organized an indoor market for trading securities. Investors must work through a broker, who places the order with a central clearinghouse for trading in that type of security. After 200 years of dominance by the New York Stock Exchange, technology promises to restore some of that "over-the-counter" feeling from the past by letting investors trade through their brokers on-screen (via computer). In the next few years, the mechanisms of investing will change as much as the types of investments have changed in the past two decades.

Securities Marketplaces

Two types of marketplaces exist for trading securities: auction exchanges (the traditional marketplace) and dealer exchanges. In an **auction exchange,** all buy and sell orders (and all information concerning companies traded on that exchange) are funneled onto an auction floor. There, buyers and sellers are matched by a **stock specialist,** a member of a brokerage firm who occupies a post on the trading floor and conducts all the trades in a particular stock. The process is different in **dealer exchanges,** primarily because no central place exists for making transactions. Instead, all buy and sell orders are executed through computers by **market makers,** registered stock and bond representatives who sell securities out of their own inventories and who are spread out across the country—in some cases, even around the world.

The differences have profound implications for the future of securities trading. Advances in computerized trading are occurring so quickly, and its practice is becoming so widespread, that the New York Stock Exchange (NYSE), the world's most famous auction exchange, is under threat of losing its preeminent place in global capitalism. A senior Wall Street executive has gone so far as to pronounce: "Time is running out for the New York Stock Exchange."[9]

Auction Exchanges

The NYSE, also known as the "Big Board," is one of nine stock exchanges in the United States (see Exhibit 20.2), and it dwarfs the other eight. The stocks and bonds of more than 1,600 companies, whose market values exceed $2.6 trillion, are traded on the exchange's floor.[10] Options, futures, and closed-end funds are also traded there. For all of its importance, however, the NYSE is battling a rising tide of critics.

The primary problem that the NYSE and other auction exchanges confront is that the auction process itself is rapidly becoming antiquated. In an auction exchange transaction, the stock specialist occupies a post on the trading floor and conducts all the trades in a particular stock. When brokers send their buy and sell orders to the exchange, the specialist matches them up by acting as an auctioneer. The specialist must fill small public orders before handling large institutional trades, thus ensuring that the small trader gets a fair shake.

Probably the most important duty of the specialist is to act as the buyer or seller if one can't be found. Thus the specialist keeps his or her own inventory of stocks. During the market's crash on October 19, 1987—when 608 million shares were traded on the NYSE—specialists were forced to buy countless stocks for which there were no buyers. As good as this may sound for investors who want to bail out of a freefalling stock, the specialist's role is one reason for the NYSE's problems. The system worked fine when individual investors accounted for most of the NYSE's business, but matters have changed. Twenty years ago, individual investors held 80 percent of equities in the United States, but today they hold only 55 percent. Institutions trade such huge quantities of securities that some specialists can no longer serve as "buyers of last resort."[11]

PROGRAM TRADING   The inability of specialists to cover all stock sales could become a major problem because of **program trading,** in which institutional investors use computer programs to buy and sell diversified collections, or "baskets," of shares. Program trading has a number of variations, but the most common approach involves **arbitrage,** the age-old practice of buying something in one market and simultaneously selling its equivalent in another market at a higher price (and pocketing the difference). For example, when the price of a futures contract on the Standard & Poor's 500 rises above the prices of the actual stocks, an institutional investor might sell the futures (which are expensive), buy the actual stocks (which are cheaper), and make a tidy little profit on the transaction.

Institutional investors use computers to make program trades. For the trades to work best, large blocks of stock must be traded instantaneously without causing stock prices to fluctuate sharply. If prices change too much too quickly, the

Exchange	1990 Average Daily Volume (In millions of shares)	Percentage of Total
New York	156.8	48
NASDAQ	131.9	41
American	11.6	4
Midwest	9.6	3
Pacific	6.4	2
Philadelphia	3.7	1
Boston	3.2	1
Cincinnati	1.5	0.5
Spokane	0.03	

Note: Doesn't include off-exchange stock trading, such as Instinet

EXHIBIT 20.2

Average Volume of National, Regional, and Dealer Exchanges
The New York Stock Exchange and the American Stock Exchange (both in New York) are known as the national exchanges. Both are auction exchanges (as are the six regional exchanges). NASDAQ is a dealer exchange and is larger than all other exchanges except the NYSE. The regionals are so small that, although they are taking some business away from the NYSE and the AMEX, they frequently consider merging. Spokane's exchange is so small that it still uses a chalkboard to track trades.

market makers Dealers in dealer exchanges who sell securities out of their own inventories so that a market is always available for buyers and sellers

program trading Investment strategy using computer programs to buy or sell large numbers of securities, thereby taking advantage of price discrepancies between stock index futures or options and the actual stocks represented in those indexes

arbitrage Simultaneous purchase in one market and sale in a different market with a profitable price or yield differential

The New York Stock Exchange is the biggest—and often the busiest—of the nine American stock exchanges. This is the trading floor, where the action is heaviest.

commodity exchanges Marketplaces where contracts for raw materials are bought and sold

over-the-counter market Network of dealers who trade securities that are not listed on an exchange

gains that program traders expect may not materialize. By serving as buyers and sellers of last resort, specialists have traditionally prevented prices from making sharp swings. But institutional investors doubt that specialists will be able to continue doing so as program trading becomes more common. Conceivably, if stock prices fall too much, specialists could run out of capital and be unable to buy stocks from program traders in a rush to sell.

COMMODITY EXCHANGES   Not all auction exchanges face such problems. Commodity exchanges continue to operate much as they always have—even though their operations can seem quite confusing. **Commodity exchanges** use their own variation of the auction: Crowds of dealers (who work for companies that are members of the exchanges) stand in auction "pits," buying and selling commodity contracts in a frenzy of activity. Of course, products do not actually change hands at the exchange; contracts are bought and sold to deliver goods at future dates.

Various goods are traded on each exchange. The Chicago Board of Trade handles corn, soybeans, wheat, oats, and plywood as well as gold, silver, and financial futures. At the Chicago Mercantile Exchange, traders deal in cattle, hogs, pork bellies, lumber, potatoes, Treasury bills, gold, foreign currency, and stock market futures. Other exchanges include the Chicago Board Options Exchange; the New York Futures Exchange; the New York Mercantile Exchange; the Commodity Exchange (COMEX); the New York Cotton Exchange; the Minneapolis Grain Exchange; the Kansas City Board of Trade; the Mid-America Commodity Exchange; and the Coffee, Sugar, and Cocoa Exchange.

Dealer Exchanges

Despite its central position in the U.S. financial system, the NYSE is feeling competitive pressures from many directions. The regional exchanges handle the stocks of many large corporations, as does the NYSE. Because it costs less to trade on the regionals, institutional investors often use them to trade stocks listed on the Big Board.

However, the biggest threat to all auction exchanges comes from dealer exchanges, decentralized marketplaces where securities are bought and sold by dealers out of their own inventories. They come in many forms, the largest and most important of which is the **over-the-counter market** (OTC). Instead of a single trading floor where transactions occur, the OTC market consists of a network of about 415,000 registered stock and bond representatives across the country. Some 420 of these brokers are market makers—meaning they buy and sell securities held in inventory—and they are linked by a nationwide computer network called NASDAQ (National Association of Securities Dealers Automated Quotations).

NASDAQ has grown so much that it now represents a total market value of $462 billion—second only to the NYSE (see Exhibit 20.2). Because it has been a computerized trading system from the beginning, it enjoys a head start in creating a global, 24-hour securities exchange—which is what many market experts expect will be common in the next decade. NASDAQ became the first intercontinental exchange in January 1992 by opening a branch in Great Britain. Called NASDAQ International, its trading hours are between 3:30 a.m. and 9 a.m. (eastern standard time) each trading day. Through NASDAQ market makers, U.S. investors can trade the equities of foreign companies listed on NASDAQ International, and foreign investors can trade the equities of U.S. companies.[12]

But NASDAQ must compete with rivals in the computerized securities trading industry. Reuters Holdings PLC, a British media conglomerate, operates Instinet Crossing Network, and U.S. brokerage Jefferies & Company has teamed up with a California consulting firm to offer Posit. Both of these companies are national services that match buyers and sellers at certain times of the day for trades based on closing NYSE prices. Reuters has also joined with the Chicago Mercantile Exchange to develop Globex, a computerized night-trading system that allows traders to buy and sell securities listed on foreign exchanges.

Technology isn't the only advantage dealer exchanges have over auction exchanges; they cost less, too. On auction exchanges, all buy and sell orders are funneled to specialists, who match the closest bidding and asking prices. Therefore, these markets are driven by the volume of orders that are placed. Exchanges charge commissions—sometimes very expensive ones—for every trade that is made. In contrast, dealer exchanges are so named because dealers buy and sell out of their own inventory; they don't match buyers and sellers as much as they provide a service for buyers and sellers, and that service is less expensive than the commission structure at auction exchanges.[13]

Foreign Exchanges

New York was once the center of the financial world; today the Tokyo Stock Market is second only to the NYSE, followed closely by stock exchanges in London, Frankfurt, Paris, Toronto, and Montreal. And in recent years, companies listed on exchanges in Mexico, Spain, and Hong Kong have produced large gains for investors around the world.

As might be expected, U.S. institutional investors are the main players in foreign stock markets. Pension funds alone increased their investments abroad from $400 million in 1980 to $28 billion in 1990.[14] But individual investors can easily invest in foreign stocks and bonds through mutual funds. *Global funds* invest in foreign and U.S. securities, whereas *international funds* invest strictly in foreign securities. Many investment advisers recommend global and international funds for individual investors, so these funds are becoming more popular. By the end of October 1991, U.S. investors had put $34.8 billion into global and international equity funds, and they were doing so at a 27 percent growth rate.[15]

For the more serious investor, it's possible to buy foreign securities either through major U.S. brokerages or through brokerages in any country the investor chooses. It is more difficult to invest in foreign equities, however, because most exchanges around the world require less information from listed companies than U.S. exchanges do. Moreover, regulatory standards are looser in all foreign markets.[16]

Trading Procedures

The first step for an investor trading securities on an exchange is to select a brokerage firm such as Landes Associates to handle the transaction. Next, the investor chooses, or is assigned, a commodities broker or a stockbroker, depending on the type of investment the individual is planning to make. A **broker** is an expert who has studied the intricacies of the market and has passed a series of examinations on buying and selling securities. Landes Associates' William Francis is a broker and investment adviser.

broker Individual registered to sell securities

The Order to Buy or Sell

market order Authorization for a broker to buy or sell securities at the best price that can be negotiated at the moment

limit order Market order that stipulates the highest or lowest price at which the customer is willing to trade securities

open order Limit order that does not expire at the end of a trading day

discretionary order Market order that allows the broker to decide when to trade a security

Brokers need specific instructions. A **market order** gives the broker the go-ahead to make the trade at the best price that can be negotiated at the moment. A **limit order** specifies the highest price at which the investor is willing to buy, or the lowest price at which the investor is willing to sell. Limit orders are good for one day only. An investor can also place an **open order,** which instructs the broker to leave the order open until canceled by the investor.

An investor may have special confidence in a stockbroker's ability to judge the trend of market prices and may place a **discretionary order,** which gives the broker the right to buy or sell the security at his or her discretion. In some cases, discretionary orders can save the customer from taking a loss, because the broker may have a better sense of when to sell a stock. If the broker's judgment proves wrong, however, he or she cannot be held legally responsible.

Margin Trading

An investor can leverage an investment to magnify the potential for capital gains through **margin trading.** Instead of paying for the stock in full, the investor

TECHNIQUES FOR BUSINESS SUCCESS

How to Make a Stock Purchase

Nancy Richards, who lives in Chattanooga, Tennessee, wants to buy some shares of Eli Lilly common stock because she believes that growth prospects for drug companies are good. She has read the listings of New York Stock Exchange transactions that appear daily in her Chattanooga newspaper, and she knows that Lilly is selling at around $79 a share. She calls her local stock-brokerage firm, Jones & Company, and enters a market order with her broker to buy 100 shares of Lilly.

The order is telephoned to the Jones & Company clerk on the floor of the New York Stock Exchange. The clerk hands it to the New York Stock Exchange member who is a partner in Jones & Company. This member goes to the Lilly trading post (the specific location on the floor where that particular stock is traded) and calls out, "How's Lilly?" A specialist in Lilly stock answers, "Seventy-nine to a quarter," meaning that someone is currently bidding $79 a share for 100 shares (or more) of the stock and that someone else is willing to sell at $79.25. The Jones & Company member could buy the stock immediately for Nancy Richards at $79.25 a share, because hers was a market order. More likely, however, the member will bid 79⅛ for a few minutes, hoping to save a little money.

The broker receives a call from the customer, who requests that a market order be entered.

In Palo Alto, California, meanwhile, Doug Andrews has decided to sell his 100 shares of Lilly stock in order to pay his son's college bills for the year. He has phoned his broker and given him an order to sell 100 shares of Lilly at 79⅛. The exchange member representing Andrews's brokerage firm reaches the trading post in time to hear the interchange between the Lilly specialist and the Jones & Company mem-

borrows money from his or her stockbroker, paying interest on the borrowed money and leaving the stock with the broker as collateral. The Federal Reserve Board sets margin requirements, dictating the percentage of the stock's purchase price that the customer must place on deposit with the broker. For many years, the margin on most stock trades has been set at 50 percent.

margin trading Borrowing money from brokers to buy stock, paying interest on the borrowed money, and leaving the stock with the broker as collateral

Here's how margin works: With $1,000, only 100 shares could be bought of a stock selling at $10 a share. But with a 50 percent margin, $2,000 worth of stock can be controlled with $1,000 ($2,000 × 50% = $1,000). Suppose the interest on the amount borrowed from the broker is 10 percent annually, or $100 a year. And suppose that, by the end of the year, the stock doubles in price to $20 per share. The investor receives $4,000 if all 200 shares are sold. Subtracting $1,000 for the original investment, and subtracting $1,100 in interest and principal on the loan, the investor has a capital gain of $1,900. Had the investment not been margined, the gain would have been only $1,000 (100 shares × $20 = $2,000 − $1,000 for the original investment).

However, buying on margin increases risk. If the price of a stock falls, investors have to give the broker more money to increase collateral—which increases the probability that the investors will lose more money than if they had simply bought the stock without margin.

A clerk calls in an order to a member firm as a broker checks on incoming orders and an ITS operator receives incoming orders from the Intermarket Trading System.

ber. He hears the Jones & Company member bid $79\frac{1}{8}$ for the stock and shouts out, "Sold at seventy-nine and an eighth." The two exchange members initial each other's order slips. A stock exchange employee, known as a reporter, makes a note of the trade. Within minutes, the transaction is reported back to the brokerage houses and to the two customers.

The trading procedures for over-the-counter stocks are different. Say that Nancy Richards wanted to buy 100 shares of American Greetings, which is not listed on any stock exchange. Her stockbroker would check the NASDAQ quotes via computer to determine the current bidding and asking prices offered by each of the broker-dealers who trade in the stock. Nancy's broker would then consummate the trade at the best price, using the computer to complete the transaction instantaneously.

Brokers trade with each other.

The Cost of Trading

transaction costs Costs of trading securities, including broker's commission and taxes

Investors pay **transaction costs** for every buy or sell to cover the broker's commission and the taxes on a sale. Commissions vary with the size of the trade: The fewer the shares traded, the more it costs; the more the shares traded, the less it costs. Trades must be executed in *round lots* of 100s. Fewer than 100 shares are traded in *odd lots*. So if an investor wants to sell 150 shares of a stock, the brokerage actually makes two trades, one of 100 shares and another of 50 shares. Trading in odd lots is more expensive for the broker and the investor.

full-service brokerages Financial services companies with a full range of services, including investment advice, securities research, and investment products

discount brokerages Financial-services companies that sell securities but give no advice

The nature of the brokerage house also affects transaction costs. **Full-service brokerages,** like Merrill Lynch, provide research and a variety of proprietary products, such as their own mutual funds. As a result, the commissions they charge are higher than those charged by **discount brokerages,** which provide nothing more than a service to buy or sell. At many discount brokerages, brokers give no investment advice.

▶ ANALYSIS OF THE FINANCIAL NEWS

The serious investor continually researches financial markets. No single source of information is the best, but a good start is with the daily reports on stocks, bonds, mutual funds, government securities, commodities, and financial futures in major city newspapers.

Other sources of financial information include newspapers aimed specifically at investors (such as *Investor's Daily* and *Barron's*) and general-interest business newspapers and magazines that not only follow corporate developments but report news and give hints about investing (such as *The Wall Street Journal, Forbes, Fortune,* and *Business Week*). Standard & Poor's, Moody's Investor Service, and Value Line continually publish newsletters and special reports on equities, bonds, and mutual funds. These publications can often be found in large libraries.

Investors with personal computers have even more alternatives, including the Dow Jones News Retrieval Service, Investor's Express, and The Source. These services provide the investor with up-to-the-minute data on financial markets and on the world events that may affect markets.

Broad Market Indicators

Equity investors always want to know whether now is the time to buy or sell. The most closely watched market is the NYSE, where the performance of stocks generally sets the tone for investor sentiment on all other exchanges. If investors are buying low and selling high, that is, if they are counting on making a profit from rising prices because they are optimistic and believe business is improving,

bull market Rising stock market

then Wall Street is said to be in a **bull market,** one characterized by a long-term trend of rising prices. Conversely, if investors are selling short, that is, if they are counting on making profits from falling prices because they are pessimistic and believe business is getting worse, then Wall Street is said to be a **bear market,**

bear market Falling stock market

one characterized by a long-term trend of falling prices.

How might you determine whether you should be bullish or bearish? First, look at the broad movements in the markets (see Exhibit 20.3). Has a bull market gone on maybe too long, which would suggest that stocks are overvalued

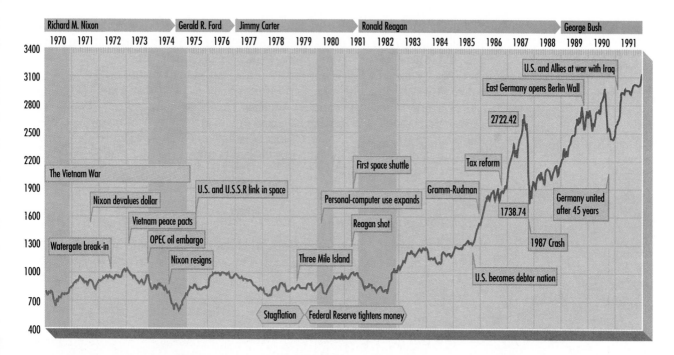

and a *correction* might be imminent? If so, the market will correct itself downward, sometimes slowly and other times quickly, as it did in the crash of October 19, 1987. Second, pay attention to the volume of shares traded each day. If the stock market is down on heavy volume (that is, if prices are moving downward and a lot of trading is going on), you might conclude that investors are trying to sell before prices go down further—a strong bearish sign.

The most common way investors determine whether the market is bullish or bearish is to watch indexes and averages, which use the performance of a representative sampling of stocks, bonds, or commodities as a gauge of activity in the market as a whole. The most famous is the Dow Jones Industrial Average (DJIA), which tracks the prices of 30 blue-chip stocks traded on the NYSE. The DJIA is the barometer that captures the headlines. But money managers and most professional investors are critical of its usefulness; it consists of relatively few stocks, so they prefer to follow the Standard & Poor's 500 Stock Average (S&P 500).

Other averages and indexes include the Dow Jones Utility Average of 15 utility stocks; Dow Jones Transportation Average of 20 transportation stocks; the New York Stock Exchange Index, which covers 1,614 common and preferred stocks listed on the exchange; the NASDAQ Index; and the Wilshire Index, which includes 5,000 stocks and gives the broadest indication of stock market trends.

The most widely followed indicators for commodities are the Dow Jones commodity indexes, which cover spot and futures trading. Dow Jones also publishes a bond average, and movements in the Treasury bond market are tracked by the Shearson Lehman Treasury Bond Index.

Daily Price Quotations

Once you have some insight into underlying market trends, you can begin to identify specific investments that meet your objectives. This is an important

EXHIBIT 20.3

The Stock Market's Ups and Downs
The performance of the stock market is affected by the state of the economy and other world events. The peaks and valleys on this chart represent swings in the Dow Jones Industrial Average, the most widely used indicator of stock prices.

step because the mix of investments you select will have more impact on your overall success than any other factor. Indeed, one consulting firm estimates that deciding where to put your money—in stocks, bonds, cash, or whatever—accounts for about 85 percent of the return on your investment.[17]

Because it is difficult to be well informed about everything, some investors focus on one type of investment such as stocks or commodities. They often narrow their focus even further, specializing in a particular industry or type of commodity. You might decide to specialize in consumer-products companies, for example, because as a consumer you are familiar with the relative strengths of some of those companies.

Stock Exchange Listings

Once you have narrowed your focus, the search for specific stocks becomes easier. You might pick 20 companies that appeal to you and begin to track their

CHECKLIST FOR BUSINESS TODAY

Stock Analysis: Calculating Prospects for Growth

Inexperienced investors may use some of the same techniques that professional analysts employ when deciding whether a stock is worth buying. One tried-and-true method is "fundamental analysis," an approach to stock selection that involves careful examination of a company's history, current financial position, and prospects for the future. Fundamental analysis emerged shortly after the stock market crash of 1929; until then, the most common means of stock selection could have been called the "grapevine method."

Analyzing a company's fundamentals requires careful evaluation of its balance sheet and income statement, making comparisons with benchmarks established by that company in earlier years and by other firms in the industry. The worksheet here is designed to help you make the key comparisons that will tell you whether a stock deserves further consideration. You'll find the basic numbers you need in the stock market listings of your newspaper or *The Wall Street Journal* and in the Value Line Investment Survey, available in well-stocked libraries. Value Line makes earnings estimates and compiles some of the industry averages; the others can be calculated from Value Line reports on companies in specific industries. You'll also have to work out the percentage change in earnings. To determine whether the stock is widely held by financial institu-

tions, divide the number of shares they own (listed in Value Line under "Institutional Decisions") by total shares outstanding (found under "Capital Structure"). Check your newspaper to make sure the stock price that Value Line used for such data as the price-earnings ratio is not out of date.

In addition to earnings growth, a company's financial strength shows up in its net profit margin (which is the rate of return on sales), in its return on net worth (another gauge of profit), and in its cash flow per share (which indicates how much money the company is generating to finance further growth). This information is available in Value Line as well. Give the company a plus for each of these values if it is higher than the industry average. The last three measures on the worksheet give you an idea of the relative value of the stock. Give the stock a plus if any of these ratios are below average. When you've scored the company on each item, tally the pluses and minuses. Plus three or better is encouraging.

Once you've isolated a promising stock, more work needs to be done. Dig energetically for clues about the future prospects for the firm's industry and the quality of the firm's management. And just before you place an order, check with your broker for late news about the company. Although the company looks rock solid from your perspective, its stock price may be down for an important reason.

daily performance in the newspaper. Exhibit 20.4 is a sample of a stock exchange report in a daily newspaper, showing high and low prices for the past 52 weeks, the number of shares traded (volume), and the change from the closing price of the day before.

One item of information also included in stock listings for the major exchanges is the **price-earnings ratio,** or *p/e* ratio (also known as the price-earnings multiple), which is computed by dividing a stock's market price by its earnings per share. Say that Acme stock sold for $20 a share last year and earned $2 per share. The price-earnings ratio would be 10:

price-earnings ratio Comparison of a stock's market price with its earnings per share

$$\frac{\$20 \text{ Market Price}}{\$2 \text{ Earnings per Share}} = 10$$

Stocks in the same industry tend to have *p/e* ratios that are roughly the same. You might expect to see a *p/e* ratio of 20 in a high-tech area like genetic engineering and a *p/e* ratio closer to 5 in the electric utilities industry. Price-

Example: SmithKline Beckman
Industry: Drugs

Ticker symbol:	SKB	Your stock		SKB	Your stock
Latest price	$63.75	Last year's per-share earnings		$5.51	
52-week range	$57–$77.	This year's estimated earnings		$6.40	
Annual dividend	$2.60	Estimated change		+15.6%	

The Financial Analysis

The following should be above the industry average:	SKB	INDUSTRY AVERAGE	ABOVE OR BELOW AVERAGE	SCORE	YOUR STOCK	INDUSTRY AVERAGE	ABOVE OR BELOW AVERAGE	SCORE
Five-year average annual earnings growth	33%	17%	above	+				
Net profit margin	15.3%	11.4%	above	+				
Return on net worth	24.7%	18%	above	+				
Cash flow per share	$6.58	$3.51	above	+				

The following should be below the industry average:	SKB	INDUSTRY AVERAGE	ABOVE OR BELOW AVERAGE	SCORE	YOUR STOCK	INDUSTRY AVERAGE	ABOVE OR BELOW AVERAGE	SCORE
Price/earnings ratio	11.5	24	below	+				
Ratio of price to book value	311%	474%	below	+				
Institutional stockholdings	61%	46%	above	—				
			Net score:	+5			Net score:	

EXHIBIT 20.4

How to Read a Newspaper Stock Quotation

To the uninitiated, the daily stock quotations in the newspapers look like a mysterious code. But the code, when broken, yields a great deal of information on the performance of a particular stock.

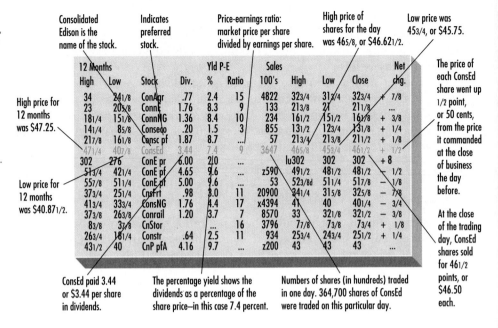

Consolidated Edison is the name of the stock.

Indicates preferred stock.

Price-earnings ratio: market price per share divided by earnings per share.

High price of shares for the day was 46 5/8, or $46.62 1/2.

Low price was 45 3/4, or $45.75.

High price for 12 months was $47.25.

Low price for 12 months was $40.87 1/2.

12 Months High	Low	Stock	Div.	Yld %	P-E Ratio	Sales 100's	High	Low	Close	Net chg.
34	24 1/8	ConAgr	.77	2.4	15	4822	32 3/4	31 3/4	32 3/4	+ 7/8
23	20 5/8	ConnE	1.76	8.3	9	133	21 3/8	21	21 1/8	...
18 1/4	15 1/8	ConnNG	1.36	8.4	10	234	16 1/2	15 1/2	16 1/8	+ 3/8
14 1/4	8 5/8	Conseco	.20	1.5	3	855	13 1/2	12 3/4	13 1/8	+ 1/4
21 7/8	16 1/8	Consc pf	1.87	8.7	...	57	21 3/4	21 3/8	21 1/2	+ 1/8
47 1/4	40 7/8	ConsEd	3.44	7.4	9	3647	46 5/8	45 3/4	46 1/2	+ 1/2
302	276	ConE pr	6.00	2.0	...		lu302	302	302	+ 8
51 3/4	42 1/4	ConE pf	4.65	9.6	...	z590	49 1/2	48 1/2	48 1/2	− 1/2
55 7/8	51 1/4	ConE pf	5.00	9.6	...	53	52 3/8d	51 1/4	51 7/8	− 1/8
37 3/4	25 1/4	CnsFrt	.98	3.0	11	20900	34 1/4	31 5/8	32 5/8	− 7/8
41 3/4	33 3/4	ConsNG	1.76	4.4	17	x4394	41	40	40 1/4	− 3/4
37 3/8	26 3/8	Conrail	1.20	3.7	7	8570	33	32 1/8	32 1/2	− 3/8
8 3/8	3 7/8	CnStor		...	16	3796	7 7/8	7 3/8	7 3/4	+ 1/8
26 3/4	18 1/4	Constr	.64	2.5	11	934	25 3/4	24 3/4	25 1/2	+ 1/4
43 1/2	40	CnP pfA	4.16	9.7	...	z200	43	43	43	...

The price of each ConsEd share went up 1/2 point, or 50 cents, from the price it commanded at the close of business the day before.

At the close of the trading day, ConsEd shares sold for 46 1/2 points, or $46.50 each.

ConsEd paid 3.44 or $3.44 per share in dividends.

The percentage yield shows the dividends as a percentage of the share price—in this case 7.4 percent.

Numbers of shares (in hundreds) traded in one day. 364,700 shares of ConsEd were traded on this particular day.

earnings ratios also vary from year to year, depending on corporate profitability and the performance of the stock market. Over the past 10 years, the average *p/e* ratio for all companies has ranged from 8 to 16.[18]

A high or low *p/e* ratio is not necessarily good or bad. The important thing is a company's ratio relative to those of other companies in its industry. If the *p/e* ratio is significantly below the industry norm, you may conclude either that the company is having problems or that it is an undiscovered gem that may soon go up in price.

Listings of Other Investments

Many newspapers carry a report of trading in bonds on the major exchanges (see Exhibit 20.5). When reading bond prices, remember that the high and low are given as a percentage of the bond's face value. For example, a $1,000 bond shown closing at 65 actually sold at $650.

Price quotations for mutual funds, commodities, options, and government securities may also be found in the major newspapers. Exhibit 20.6 illustrates a mutual-fund listing, and Exhibit 20.7 is a listing of spot prices on the commodities market.

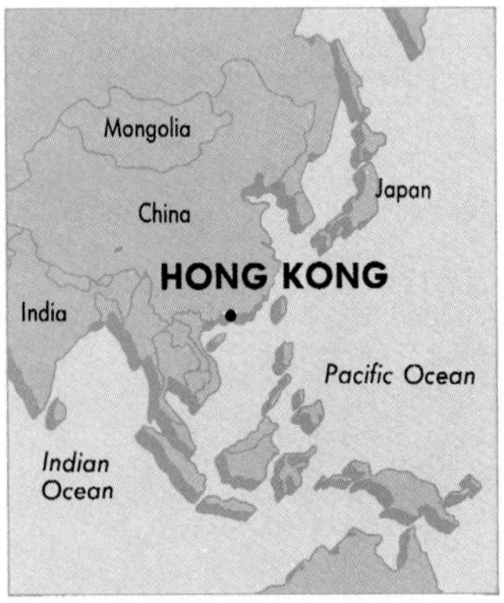

Business Around the World

In the Far East, many investors are still watching the Hang Seng index. Despite the fact that Hong Kong will be swallowed up by mainland China by 1997, investors haven't given up looking for undervalued gems on the tiny colony's stock exchange.

▶ REGULATION OF SECURITIES TRADING

Since the early days of stock trading, state governments have tried to control the way stocks are bought and sold. But even though almost every state has its own laws governing securities trading, the federal government has the leading role in investment regulation (see Exhibit 20.8). Today, trading in stocks and bonds is monitored by the Securities and Exchange Commission (SEC), and trading in commodities is supervised by the Commodity Futures Trading Commission (CFTC).

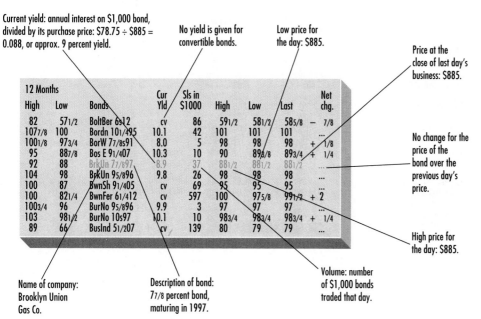

Current yield: annual interest on $1,000 bond, divided by its purchase price: $78.75 ÷ $885 = 0.088, or approx. 9 percent yield.

No yield is given for convertible bonds.

Low price for the day: $885.

Price at the close of last day's business: $885.

No change for the price of the bond over the previous day's price.

High price for the day: $885.

12 Months									
High	Low	Bonds	Cur Yld	Sls in $1000	High	Low	Last	Net chg.	
82	57 1/2	BoltBer 6s12	cv	86	59 1/2	58 1/2	58 5/8	−	7/8
107 7/8	100	Bordn 101/495	10.1	42	101	101	101	...	
100 1/8	97 3/4	BorW 77/8s91	8.0	5	98	98	98	+	1/8
95	88 7/8	Bos E 91/407	10.3	10	90	89 3/8	89 3/4	+	1/4
92	88	BrkUn 77/897	8.9	37	88 1/2	88 1/2	88 1/2	...	
104	98	BrkUn 95/896	9.8	26	98	98	98	...	
100	87	BwnSh 91/405	cv	69	95	95	95	...	
100	82 1/4	BwnFer 61/412	cv	597	100	97 5/8	99 1/2	+	2
100 3/4	96	BurNo 95/896	9.9	3	97	97	97	...	
103	98 1/2	BurNo 10s97	10.1	10	98 3/4	98 3/4	98 3/4	+	1/4
89	66	BusInd 51/207	cv	139	80	79	79	...	

Name of company: Brooklyn Union Gas Co.

Description of bond: 7 7/8 percent bond, maturing in 1997.

Volume: number of $1,000 bonds traded that day.

EXHIBIT 20.5

How to Read a Newspaper Bond Quotation

Many newspapers carry bond quotations in addition to stock quotations. Prices represent a percentage of a bond's face value, which is typically $1,000.

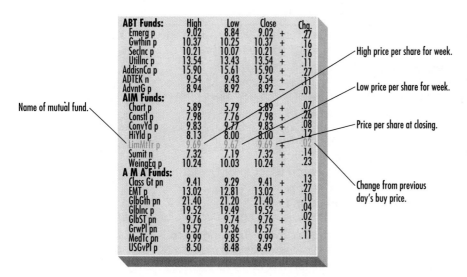

ABT Funds:	High	Low	Close	Chg.	
Emerg p	9.02	8.84	9.02	+	.27
Gwthin p	10.37	10.25	10.37	+	.16
SecInc p	10.21	10.07	10.21	+	.16
UtilInc p	13.54	13.43	13.54	+	.11
AddisnCa p	15.90	15.61	15.90	+	.27
ADTEK n	9.54	9.43	9.54	+	.11
AdvntG p	8.94	8.92	8.92	−	.01
AIM Funds:					
Chart p	5.89	5.79	5.89	+	.07
ConstI p	7.98	7.76	7.98	+	.26
ConvYd p	9.83	9.77	9.83	+	.08
HiYld p	8.13	8.00	8.00	−	.12
LimMtTr p	9.69	9.67	9.69	+	.02
Sumit n	7.32	7.19	7.32	+	.14
WeingEq p	10.24	10.03	10.24	+	.23
A M A Funds:					
Class Gt pn	9.41	9.29	9.41	+	.13
EMT p	13.02	12.81	13.02	+	.27
GlbGth pn	21.40	21.20	21.40	+	.10
GlbInc p	19.52	19.49	19.52	+	.04
GlbST pn	9.76	9.74	9.76	+	.02
GrwPl pn	19.57	19.36	19.57	+	.19
MedTc pn	9.99	9.85	9.99	+	.11
USGvPl p	8.50	8.48	8.49		

Name of mutual fund.

High price per share for week.

Low price per share for week.

Price per share at closing.

Change from previous day's buy price.

EXHIBIT 20.6

How to Read a Newspaper Mutual-Fund Quotation

A mutual-fund listing shows the net asset value of one share (the price at which one share is trading) and the change in trading price from one day to the next.

Of the two federal agencies, the SEC is the older and stronger. Its 2,450 staff members are busy supervising the stock exchanges, over-the-counter markets, 10,500 brokerage houses, 417,000 registered representatives, 17,385 investment advisers, and 21 public-utility holding companies. Every year, it screens 14,000 prospectuses, 6,500 proxy statements, 15,200 annual reports, and 40,000 investor complaints. Although the securities industry has mushroomed in the past 10 years, the SEC has barely added to its staff, and it has an annual budget of about $187 million.[19]

Like many regulatory agencies with a heavy work load and a limited staff, the SEC tries to focus its efforts where they will do the most good. It concentrates on a few big cases and urges brokerage houses and securities exchanges to police themselves. One of the SEC's top priorities is to crack down on *insider trading,*

EXHIBIT 20.7

Newspaper Listing of Cash Trading Prices on the Commodities Market

The basic information in a listing about the performance of an item on the commodities market—in this case, eggs—is its price per unit today and yesterday.

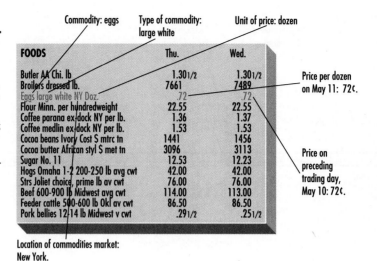

Commodity: eggs
Type of commodity: large white
Unit of price: dozen

FOODS	Thu.	Wed.
Butler AA Chi. lb	1.30 1/2	1.30 1/2
Broilers dressed lb.	7661	7489
Eggs large white NY Doz.	.72	.72
Flour Minn. per hundredweight	22.55	22.55
Coffee parana ex-dock NY per lb.	1.36	1.37
Coffee medlin ex-dock NY per lb.	1.53	1.53
Cocoa beans Ivory Cost $ mtrc tn	1441	1456
Cocoa butter African styl $ met tn	3096	3113
Sugar No. 11	12.53	12.23
Hogs Omaha 1-2 200-250 lb avg cwt	42.00	42.00
Strs Joliet choice, prime lb av cwt	76.00	76.00
Beef 600-900 lb Midwest avg cwt	114.00	113.00
Feeder cattle 500-600 lb Okl av cwt	86.50	86.50
Pork bellies 12-14 lb Midwest v cwt	.29 1/2	.25 1/2

Price per dozen on May 11: 72¢.

Price on preceding trading day, May 10: 72¢.

Location of commodities market: New York.

EXHIBIT 20.8 ▶ Major Federal Legislation Governing the Securities Industry

Although there are no guarantees that you'll make money on your investments, you are protected by laws against unfair trading practices.

Securities Act of 1933
Known as the Truth in Securities Act; requires full disclosure of relevant financial information from companies that want to sell new stock or bond issues to the general public

Securities Exchange Act of 1934
Created the Securities and Exchange Commission (SEC) to regulate the national stock exchanges and to establish trading rules

Maloney Act of 1938
Created the National Association of Securities Dealers to regulate over-the-counter securities trading

Investment Company Act of 1940
Extended the SEC's authority to cover the regulation of mutual funds

1964 Amendment to the Securities Exchange Act
Extended the SEC's authority to cover the over-the-counter market

Securities Investor Protection Act of 1970
Created the Securities Investor Protection Corporation to insure individual investors against losses in the event of dealer fraud or insolvency

Commodity Futures Trading Commission Act of 1974
Created the Commodity Futures Trading Commission (CFTC) to establish and enforce regulations governing futures trading

Insider Trading and Securities Fraud Enforcement Act of 1988
Toughened penalties, authorized bounties for information, required brokerages to establish written policies to prevent employee violations, and made it easier for investors to bring legal action against violators

Securities Market Reform Act of 1990
Increased SEC market control by granting additional authority to suspend trading in any security for 10 days, to restore order in the event of a major disturbance, to establish a national system for settlement and clearance of securities transactions, to adopt rules for actions affecting market volatility, and to require more detailed record keeping and reporting of brokers and dealers

in which a few people with access to nonpublic information (say, a pending merger) buy or sell a company's stock before the information can become public and before the price can change in reaction to the news.

The stock exchanges also play a role in monitoring the securities industry. For example, to be listed on an exchange, a company must file registration papers and fulfill certain requirements. In addition, traders must conform to the rules of the exchange, many of which are designed to protect investors. Generally speaking, the New York Stock Exchange and the American Stock Exchange enforce more stringent rules than the over-the-counter market. Yet all over-the-counter companies with assets of more than $1 million and having at least 500 shareholders must file comprehensive annual financial reports with the SEC, just as listed companies must do.

How are investors protected if their brokerage fails? Since 1970, 228 brokerages have gone bankrupt. To cope with such collapses, Congress established the Securities Investor Protection Corporation. The SIPC is not a part of the federal government; its operations and insurance fund are financed by the securities industry. It provides up to $500,000 worth of insurance against fraud or bankruptcy for each investor who buys and leaves securities for safekeeping with a brokerage house, and it provides up to $100,000 worth of insurance for cash left with a brokerage house. The SIPC does not cover commodities contracts or limited-partnership investments. Nor does it protect investors against losses from declines in the price of their securities. Of the 330,000 claims filed with the SIPC since 1970, all but 293 have been fully covered by insurance.[20]

SUMMARY OF LEARNING OBJECTIVES

1 List five objectives that should be considered when choosing investments.

Investors should consider the income, growth, safety, liquidity, and tax consequences of alternative investments.

2 List five investment options available to the investor and compare them in terms of safety and potential rate of return.

Investors may choose stocks, corporate bonds, government securities, mutual funds, and commodities. Although the performance of these investments varies from year to year and depends on the specific issue selected, they can be characterized in terms of safety and potential rate of return. Government securities are considered the safest investment, followed by corporate bonds, mutual funds, stocks, and commodities, in that order. In terms of potential rate of return, commodities and stocks lead the pack, followed by mutual funds, corporate bonds, and government securities.

3 Describe asset allocation and how it's used during changing economic conditions.

Asset allocation is a method of shifting investable assets within a portfolio to maximize income and growth while minimizing loss. If economic conditions are good, the majority of a portfolio tends to be invested in equities, whereas if economic conditions are poor, the majority of a portfolio will be invested in fixed-income instruments, such as long-term bonds and cash instruments.

4 Explain the efficient market hypothesis and its importance to institutional investors.

The efficient market hypothesis (EMH) states that all securities are appropriately valued at all times because the markets make quick and efficient adjustments to new information. It is an important theory because institutional investors are using it as a basis for their computer trading strategies. According to EMH, no one can ever beat the market because of its efficiency. Instead of trying to beat the market, these investors try to make gains that are at least as good as the market in general.

5 Describe two types of securities marketplaces.

Auction exchanges funnel all buy and sell orders, and all information regarding the traded stocks, into one centralized location. There, specialists match buy and sell orders to get the best price for both parties on a given security. Specialists also act as "buyers of last resort" if no investor is willing to buy a security that has been offered for sale. Dealer exchanges are decentralized marketplaces in which dealers are connected electronically, usually by computer. Dealers, also known as market makers, carry their own inventory of securities, so they perform a service for buyers and sellers by completing the transactions, instead of by trying to match buyers and sellers to a market price.

6 Characterize six indexes that provide a broad indication of how the stock market is performing.

The Dow Jones Industrial Average is the most widely recognized market indicator; it is limited to 30 blue-chip stocks traded on the New York Stock Exchange. The Standard & Poor's 500 Stock Average and the New York

Stock Exchange Index cover a wider cross section of stocks traded on the NYSE. The Dow Jones Utility Average covers 15 utility stocks, and the NASDAQ Index covers shares traded on the over-the-counter market. The Wilshire Index, which covers 5,000 NYSE, AMEX, and OTC stocks, is the broadest market indicator.

7 List at least four sources of information about investments.

Investors may obtain information on investments from newspapers,

business magazines, investment-rating services, and electronic-data services (as well as from television shows, brokerage houses, financial planners, and corporations).

8 Name two federal agencies involved in regulating the investment industry.

The Securities and Exchange Commission oversees trading on the stock markets, and the Commodity Futures Trading Commission oversees trading on the commodities exchanges.

Meeting a Business Challenge at Landes Associates

William A. Francis had to understand the economic trends that affected the stock market. But no matter how well the economy fared, no matter whether the stock market was bullish or bearish, his objective remained the same: to steadily increase the wealth of his clients over time; speculating for a quick gain could lead to an even quicker loss.

Therefore, Francis had to know how *not* to invest. He didn't want to invest in companies just because they were fascinating or just because they were big. Biotechnology might be exciting, but it had yet to realize its promise. Until it did, investing in biotechnology companies carried a heavy risk. As for big firms, a $60 billion giant has less growth potential than a company worth $6 million (a 10 percent gain would be $6 billion for the giant firm, but only $600,000 for the smaller one). Neither did Francis want to invest in companies that were unsure of their business. Corporations that garner a lot of headlines tend to be those that are continually changing focus, management structure, or business plans, and their potential is generally uncertain. Well-managed companies that stick to their business might attract less press, but the news is usually much better.

So just what was Francis looking

William A. Francis, vice president at Landes Associates.

for in a company? Most important, Francis wanted to see companies developing a particular advantage. Whether they developed it through their product, their customer service, or their market share wasn't important, as long as the advantage gave the company a sustainable growth potential. A software firm might specialize in the types of products that businesses are expected to need in the coming years, or a major retailer might be steadily increasing its market share. In addition, Francis wanted to see companies that had positive track records: at least two years of

rising productivity, falling costs, low debt, and consistent spending for research and development.

Francis was in search of the few companies that were still pursuing long-term growth. He needed information about products and services that were relatively new. He wanted to know about companies that held great promise. And he needed information about which companies were satisfying their customers and increasing sales. Even though the times had changed, his methods of searching had not. He turned to business publications such as *The Wall Street Journal, Investor's Daily, Barron's, Business Week, Fortune,* and *Forbes.* He also read industry publications and studied statistical profiles found in *Standard & Poor's Stock Guide* and in *Value Line.*

To determine when to sell a stock, Francis needed the same information. The only difference was that instead of looking for growth potential, he looked for the likelihood that growth would slow down enough to affect stock prices. Before selling a stock, he asked three questions: (1) Are the stocks, in general, overvalued? (2) Are the profit margins ("the blood pressure of the company") beginning to drop? (3) Is the company making any unnecessary strategic changes?

A *yes* to all three questions signaled Francis to consider selling. After all, he invests his clients' money in common stock to realize capital gains, not capital losses.

Your Mission: You have just been hired as an investment adviser at Landes Associates. In addition to your assignment to cultivate new business on your own, a certain number of existing accounts have been handed to you. They include investors who are interested in both growth and income, who are more conservative and less conservative, and who all seek good value investments. Your job is to manage these accounts.

1. A new client has come to you seeking safe income from her investments. Which of the following would be the best investment for her needs?
a. Buying below-investment-grade corporate bonds
b. Buying U.S. Treasury bonds
c. Short selling common stocks
d. Buying pork belly futures

2. One of your best clients is thinking about buying stock in General Motors.

He asks for your opinion. Before you give him an answer, you need to find out for yourself whether it's a good investment. What source would you use to find the latest, most accurate, and least biased information about GM's current business and future prospects?
a. Automotive industry reports
b. *Standard & Poor's Stock Guide*
c. Both (a) and (b)
d. GM's annual and quarterly reports

3. A friend has asked you for some advice. She has a small amount of money to invest and is looking for a diverse portfolio of stocks and bonds, mainly for long-term capital gains. Which would be the best investment?
a. A mutual stock fund of common stocks and a mutual bond fund of corporate and government bonds
b. A mutual stock fund of common stocks and individual corporate bonds
c. Individual common stocks and a mutual bond fund of corporate bonds
d. Individual common stocks and individual corporate bonds

4. You have to buy a new battery for your car one Saturday, so you decide to visit the new auto parts store that just opened on the corner. When you enter the store, you notice how busy the store is, how large the store's selection of auto parts is, and how well customers (including you) are being served. As you're paying for your battery, you recall reading about the company that owns and operates this chain of auto parts stores—an article that complimented the company's management and its business strategy. You also believe that, with the economy in its current downturn, more people will be repairing their old cars rather than buying new ones. Based on these quick observations, you think this company might make a good investment, but you aren't sure. What would be the best way for you to find out?
a. Study the company's annual and quarterly reports
b. Research the company in general business and industry publications
c. Research the future prospects for new and used car sales and for the auto parts market
d. All of the above[21]

KEY TERMS

arbitrage (583)
asset allocation (574)
auction exchanges (582)
bear market (588)
blue-chip stocks (578)
broker (585)
bull market (588)
call option (580)
capital gains (573)
commodities (581)
commodities futures (582)
commodity exchanges (584)
common stock (578)
convertible bonds (577)
dealer exchanges (582)
debentures (577)
default (577)
discount brokerages (588)
discretionary order (586)
diversification (574)

dividends (578)
efficient market hypothesis (574)
financial futures (581)
full-service brokerages (588)
general obligation bonds (576)
growth stocks (578)
hedge (581)
indexing (575)
institutional investors (572)
investment portfolios (574)
limit order (586)
margin trading (587)
market indexes (575)
market makers (583)
market order (586)
marketable securities (572)
money-market funds (580)
mortgage bonds (577)
municipal bonds (576)
mutual funds (580)

open order (586)
over-the-counter market (584)
preferred stocks (579)
price-earnings ratio (591)
program trading (583)
put option (581)
rate of return (574)
revenue bonds (576)
shareholder (578)
short selling (579)
speculators (573)
spot trading (582)
stock option (580)
stock specialists (582)
transaction costs (588)
Treasury bills (576)
Treasury bonds (576)
Treasury notes (576)
U.S. savings bonds (576)

REVIEW QUESTIONS

1. What is an institutional investor?

2. When might an investor sell stock short? What risks are involved in selling short?

3. What are the differences among a Treasury bill, a Treasury note or bond, and a U.S. savings bond?

4. What is the difference between a general obligation bond and a revenue bond?

5. What factors account for the popularity of mutual funds?

6. What are the limitations of the Dow Jones Industrial Average?

7. What is a *p/e* ratio, and what does it signify to an investor?

8. What is the function of the Securities Investor Protection Corporation?

A CASE FOR CRITICAL THINKING

A Legendary Investor Now Prefers Preferreds

Probably the greatest investor of the late twentieth century is Warren Buffett, a short, soft-spoken Nebraskan who characterizes his investment strategy as "lethargy bordering on sloth"—meaning that he's perfectly willing to keep a quality investment for years. Buffett is not one to continually buy and sell equities in an attempt to beat the market at every turn. But even Buffett admits that it's not as easy as it used to be, and he sometimes finds himself in situations he never expected.

Buffett gained his reputation as chairman of Berkshire Hathaway, a Massachusetts textile manufacturer that he essentially transformed into an investment company. He acquired about a dozen insurance companies, organized them into one group under the Berkshire umbrella, and used the continuous flow of insurance premiums to make investments. About 80 percent of Berkshire's investments are held by the insurance group. Buffett's investment strategies have increased the value of Berkshire's common stock from a 1980 low of $240 per share to a 1991 high of $9,000. That's a 3,650 percent increase in 11 years.

He began his string of successful investments by looking for companies whose assets were undervalued by the market—that is, companies whose stock prices reflected little more than operating profits. In time, the market saw the same value in those companies as Buffett did, and it bid the stock prices up, increasing the wealth

of Berkshire Hathaway and of Buffett, who owns 45 percent of Berkshire common stock.

In the 1970s, Buffett believed media companies were undervalued, so he invested in several, including the Washington Post Company. The Post Company has done well for Buffett: Berkshire paid an average of $5.63 per share in 1973, and by 1991, the stock had reached a high of $251. The 1980s were a time of corporate takeovers, leveraged buyouts, and reorganizations, all of which increased stock prices, at least for the short term. Buffett invested in General Foods, Beatrice, and RJR Nabisco. True to his foresight, all three were takeover plays, and the prices of their common stocks reached dizzying heights. Such deals alone netted Buffett a 35 percent return in 1988, a time when the S&P 500 gained only 17.07 percent.

By the late 1980s, though, Buffett found it increasingly difficult to identify undervalued stocks or to make quick gains on takeovers. So he tried an unorthodox strategy: buying convertible preferred stock in companies that were threatened with hostile takeovers. If converted into common shares, the investments were large enough to thwart the intentions of corporate raiders, so Buffett was called a "white knight." Even so, Buffett's strategy was unusual because preferred stock doesn't usually produce significant capital gains. Moreover, Buffett doesn't consider his strategy aggressive; he calls it "lending

money, plus an equity kicker."

Buffett invested $2 billion using this strategy. Berkshire bought preferred stock of Champion International, USAir Group, Gillette, and Salomon Brothers. The first two investments have underperformed, but Buffett won big on Gillette. Berkshire's $600 million investment in Gillette convertible preferred stock was changed into common stock for a 50 percent gain after only two years. Here's how his strategy worked in the case of Salomon.

Berkshire invested $700 million in Salomon preferred stock, which could be converted after three years into Salomon common stock at $38 a share. Until the stock was converted, though, Berkshire would receive a 9 percent dividend yield. Because Berkshire got a 70 percent tax break on dividend income from the Salomon preferred stock, Buffett's company received an 8 percent yield after taxes—which at the time was better than the after-tax yield on high-quality corporate bonds. If the preferred stock was converted into common, Berkshire would then own 14 percent of Salomon, more than any other single investor. This investment resulted in Buffett's being named chairman of the company.

The appointment came after Salomon admitted to illegal bidding in the $2.2 trillion U.S. Treasury-securities market. Salomon's board of directors named Buffett in an effort to restore the company's credibility, keep it out of the criminal courts, and most important, retain Salomon's status as a major player in the Treasury-securities market.

Berkshire has yet to realize any capital gain on Salomon, whose stock dropped into the low-$20 range after the firm admitted guilt in the Treasury-securities trading scandal. Berkshire can't make a capital gain until the preferred shares are converted into common shares—at $38 per share—and then sold. But even if that never happens, it's unlikely Berkshire will lose on the deal, either.

First, it's still receiving dividend income. Second, if Buffett decides against converting the preferred into common shares, Salomon must begin buying the stock back between 1995 and 1999.[22]

1. Buffett prefers to buy and hold investments for long periods. Why do you think he has been called the investor's investor?

2. What do you think is the most important factor in deciding whether to invest in a company's convertible preferred stock: the stock's dividend yield computed on an after-tax basis, the price at which the preferred stock can be converted into common, or whether you need income or growth in your portfolio?

3. Do you think the small investor can really learn anything practical from Buffett? Or is it impossible because he's such a big investor?

BUILDING YOUR COMMUNICATION SKILLS

Using this chapter as a resource, investigate the world of securities markets by interviewing a stockbroker. The interview may be conducted either by phone or in person. Prepare for the interview by drafting a list of eight to ten questions. Then, as requested by your instructor, write a brief report describing the results of your interview, or give a three-minute oral report to the class.

KEEPING CURRENT USING *THE WALL STREET JOURNAL*

You have $10,000 to invest. Using as much information as your instructor recommends, select a well-known company traded on the New York Stock Exchange, American Stock Exchange, or NASDAQ. Assignment: Begin a stock-transaction journal. On the first page, record the company's name, the stock exchange abbreviation, the exchange on which it is traded, the 52-week high and low, the price/earnings ratio, and your reasons for selecting this stock.

▶ **Buying:** On the first day of the project, record the number of shares purchased (whole shares only), the price per share, the total purchase price (number of shares × price/share), the commission paid on your purchase (assume 1 percent of the purchase price), and today's Dow Jones Industrial Average. Now add the commission paid to the purchase price to get your *total purchase cost.*

▶ **Monitoring:** Record and chart the closing price of your stock each day, and plot it on a graph. Scan *The Wall Street Journal* regularly for articles on your company to include in your journal. Note any major developments that may affect your stock.

▶ **Selling:** In this exercise, you select the best time to sell—as long as it meets two requirements: You must sell on or before the day designated by your instructor, and (if your instructor wishes) you must notify your instructor on the day you sell your stock. (This means that you'll probably need to sell on a day that your class meets—unless your instructor posts a sign-up sheet that you can use on other days.) On the day you sell your stock, record the following information: the selling price (the closing price/share that day), the number of shares sold, the total sales price (the number of shares × selling price/share), the commission paid on the sale (assume 1 percent of the total sales price), and today's Dow Jones Industrial Average. Now subtract the commission paid from the total sales price to arrive at your *sales proceeds.*

▶ **Analysis:** Subtract your total purchase cost from your sales proceeds to arrive at your *net gain* or *net loss.*

How well did your investment do? How did it compare to gains or losses in the Dow Jones Industrial Average during this period? How close was the selling price to the stock's 52-week high or low? Use the articles you collected during this project to relate recent developments to the performance of your stock.

The Environment of Business

CHAPTER *21*

LEARNING OBJECTIVES
After studying this chapter, you will be able to

1 List three roles of government that affect business.

2 Name two general areas in which government regulates business.

3 List five revenue-raising taxes and two regulatory taxes.

4 Explain how business influences government.

5 Describe the three sources of law.

6 Name six areas of law related to business.

7 State the seven elements of a valid contract.

8 Distinguish among real, personal, and intellectual property.

Government Regulation and Business Law

Facing a Business Challenge at Disney

MICKEY MOUSE ENTERS POLITICS

Mickey Mouse, the squeaky-voiced cartoon character, is a mouse with clout, a distinction that derived from Disney's transformation of nearly 7,000 swampy acres in central Florida into Disney World, the nation's number one tourist destination, attracting more than 30 million visitors a year and generating more than 32,000 jobs. That economic potential impressed Florida legislators enough to grant Disney the power to levy taxes to pay for its own police force, fire department, and infrastructure. But when Michael D. Eisner, CEO of Disney, wanted to build another huge park near the original Disneyland, he needed political clout in southern California.

A mere 80 acres of citrus groves had been developed into Disneyland in the mid-1950s, and developers had flocked to the area, surrounding the Magic Kingdom with a garish assortment of hotels, motels, and restaurants—businesses that siphoned off much of Disney's potential profits. But Eisner had learned an important lesson from Disney World: internalize profits and externalize costs. Expanding Disneyland into a Disney World–type park would prevent profits from leaking to so many nearby businesses, but Eisner knew the costs of doing so would be steep.

Eisner's company would have to buy properties in a highly developed commercial district, land that was selling for more than $1.6 million an acre. Real estate purchases alone could exceed $600 million for a project that would cost around $3 billion and take at least five years to complete. However, real estate costs would only be the beginning; infrastructure costs would be staggering, and unless the California legislature empowered Disney as Florida lawmakers had done—a wholly unrealistic prospect—local governments would have to pick up the tab. If they balked, Eisner's dream of an ultramodern destination theme park would be reduced to nothing more than a renovation of Disneyland.

Much of the infrastructure issue centered on the automobile. The new park would attract an additional 13 million visitors every year, all of whom would arrive by car or bus. The Santa Ana Freeway, the principal artery to Disneyland, was already carrying over 159,000 vehicles a day, more than 6,000 of which were traveling to the park. Disneyland's expansion would more than double the number of vehicles destined for the park. A planned widening of the Santa Ana Freeway would help increase business volume at the larger park, but in addition, more and better entrance and exit ramps would be crucial. Such extensive transportation improvements would have to be paid for by local taxpayers. Moreover, in order to externalize costs wherever possible, Eisner believed the public should also pay for the huge parking garages that would be an integral part of Disney's plan to reduce air pollution in the entire area, including the park.

Another issue Eisner concerned himself with was water usage. Always a precious commodity in southern California, water threatened to become a major political issue in two ways: (1) an expanded park would increase the demand for water, and (2) a marketing study showed that a water theme park would be more profitable than a traditional amusement theme park.

In all, Eisner understood that the famous mouse would have to work closely with city councils, air and water quality boards, zoning panels, environmental regulators, and even the California legislature. How could Eisner present the most appealing case to the city of Anaheim? How could he ensure the city government's participation in the project? How could he create a situation that would benefit both Disney and the surrounding community?[1]

▶ BUSINESS AND GOVERNMENT

Over the years, the United States has accumulated laws and regulations that help resolve disputes such as those Disney faces with environmental regulators, city councils, and zoning panels. Although the United States is philosophically committed to the free-enterprise system and its economy is shaped primarily by market forces, the government has often stepped in to solve specific problems. In many ways, therefore, a company's success hinges on its ability to understand the law and to manage its relations with the government.

The process of managing government relations is complicated by the fact that more than one government must be dealt with. In addition to worrying about Uncle Sam, a business has to consider local, county, state, and possibly foreign governments, all of which impose specific and sometimes conflicting laws and restrictions. Furthermore, each government body interacts with business in a variety of ways. On Monday, a business may approach the government as a friend, partner, or customer; on Tuesday, it may clash with the government over standards and regulations; on Wednesday, the company may interact with the government on a tax matter; and on Thursday, it may be involved in legal actions of a criminal or civil nature, as defined by the government.

Government as Friend, Partner, and Customer

Although it often seems that business and government are adversaries, the opposite is true. One of government's chief objectives is to foster business prosperity; a nation's, state's, or locality's economic health depends on the success of individual companies. When business is making a profit and creating jobs, citizens benefit. Government support for business takes several forms:

Promoting economic growth. The federal government tries to keep the economy growing at a steady pace by adjusting monetary (money supply) policy; all governments affect the economy through their fiscal (taxing and spending) policies. Theoretically, these actions help the economy avoid high inflation and severe recessions, both of which are harmful to business. By smoothing out the economic cycle, the government creates a climate that is good for business.

Supporting and subsidizing business. Governments operate countless programs that are specifically designed to help businesses. One of governments' most valuable functions is simply providing information and training through agencies such as the federal Department of Commerce. Governments also provide direct loans, loan guarantees, and subsidies of various types. Occasionally, governments come to the aid of specific companies that are in trouble. For example, the federal government bailed out the Continental Bank and Lockheed and will spend hundreds of billions of dollars bailing out failed savings and loan institutions.

Maintaining the infrastructure. By building roads, bridges, dams, airports, harbors, and the like, governments indirectly help businesses distribute their products. In addition, governments own and operate power plants that provide energy for business operations. Public schools provide companies with a supply of educated labor.

Buying industry's products. In 1991 federal, state, and local governments spent an estimated $1.2 trillion for goods and services provided by private industry, accounting for roughly 21 percent of the gross national product.[2] Government procurements range from army uniforms and delivery trucks to consulting services and computers; such products involve companies of every size and description.

Government as Watchdog and Regulator

Despite government's underlying support for business, the interests of business and society have frequently clashed. When business's actions have jeopardized the public welfare, people have protested, prompting government to pass laws and adopt regulations that curb the abusive practices. The following sections discuss just two types of business activities that government has sought to regulate: those that reduce competition and those that may endanger the rest of society.

Government Regulation of Noncompetitive Practices

In the U.S. free-market system, government's main role in regulating business is to establish the rules of the game so that all competitors have an equal chance of producing a product, reaching the market, and making a profit. By setting ground rules and establishing basic standards of proper business behavior, government helps prevent conflicts and facilitates the workings of the system.

INTERSTATE COMMERCE ACT The federal government's regulation of harmful business practices began during the period of rapid industrialization after the Civil War, when railroad tycoons were forging their empires. During this period, railroad management gave relatively little thought to what was good for the public and focused instead on maximizing profits. Eventually, the railroads' cavalier attitude provoked enough public outrage to prompt government action. In 1887 the Interstate Commerce Act was passed, creating the first independent regulatory body in the United States. Over the years, the once-limited activities of the Interstate Commerce Commission (ICC) expanded to include

During the Gulf war, employees of the Sac and Fox manufacturing company in Idabel, Oklahoma, were kept busy producing uniforms that would help protect soldiers against Iraq's chemical weapons.

the control of interstate trucking rates and the establishment of standards for interstate commerce. However, with passage of the Motor Carrier Act of 1980, the ICC no longer sets trucking rates, although it has the power to reject or suspend operating authorities, and it continues to monitor compliance with various interstate commerce guidelines.

SHERMAN ANTITRUST ACT   Following passage of the Interstate Commerce Act, the federal government expanded its attempts to control unfair business practices. Its principal target was the **trust**, originally an arrangement whereby people who owned stock in several companies gave control to trustees who then gained control of and managed the companies. In return, the stock owners received a specified share of these companies' earnings. Some companies used trusts to buy up or drive out smaller competitors. The economic powerhouses that remained could then monopolize markets, fix prices, and freely engage in other unfair business practices. With competition stifled and prices artificially high, the monopolies made huge profits. In 1890 a new law, the Sherman Antitrust Act, declared that trusts and conspiracies "in restraint of trade or commerce" were illegal.[3] Over the years, it has been up to the courts to interpret the vague language of the Sherman Act in order to clarify the intended goals.[4]

CLAYTON ANTITRUST ACT   The Clayton Antitrust Act was enacted in 1914 (1) because of public concern that the Supreme Court would not enforce the vague Sherman Act and (2) to clarify which specific practices were illegal.[5] The forbidden practices were **tying contracts,** or forcing buyers to purchase unwanted goods along with goods actually desired; using **interlocking directorates,** or boards of directors made up of board members from competing firms; acquiring large blocks of competitors' stock; and setting discriminatory prices other than the discounts given "in good faith." These practices were illegal if they substantially lessened competition or tended to create a monopoly.

FEDERAL TRADE COMMISSION ACT   The Sherman and Clayton acts were both a step in the right direction, but they failed to stop many abuses of the market system. Therefore, the federal government tried another approach: to outlaw unfair trade practices in very general laws and then establish a powerful federal commission that would continue to look for specific abuses. The result was the Federal Trade Commission Act of 1914. This act, with its deliberately vague wording, states that "unfair methods of competition in commerce are hereby declared illegal." It also set up a five-member commission empowered to define, detect, and enforce compliance with this act and the Clayton Act.

The Federal Trade Commission (FTC) is still much in evidence. It can act on complaints made by business or by the public, or it can act on its own initiative, whether merely on a suspicion that the law is being violated or just to ensure that no violation exists. However, the effectiveness of the FTC depends on the five people running it. Consequently, over the years enforcement has ranged from very tough to not tough enough.

ROBINSON-PATMAN ACT   Following the Great Depression of the 1930s, the rise of giant retailing firms prompted small retailers to turn to the federal government for protection against the chains, which were able to negotiate big price discounts from suppliers. The government responded in 1936 by passing the Robinson-Patman Act, which outlaws discrimination against buyers as well as sellers. One provision of the act that applies primarily to wholesalers selling to

trust Arrangement in which people owning stock in several companies give control of their securities to trustees who then gain control of and manage the companies; sometimes used to buy up or drive out smaller companies, thus giving monopolistic powers to the trusts

tying contracts Contracts forcing buyers to purchase unwanted goods along with goods actually desired

interlocking directorates Situation in which members of the board of one firm sit on the board of a competing firm

retailers states in effect that no seller can make a price concession—that is, mark down its prices—to any one buyer without giving competing buyers the same concession. Promotional assistance must be available on proportionally equal terms as well. For example, providing retailers with television advertisements about a product would be more helpful to a large chain than to a small, local store; proportionally equal assistance to the smaller store might be point-of-purchase displays or newspaper advertisements about the product. The act also forbids suppliers to offer any quantity discounts that might tend to lessen competition. The only permissible quantity discounts are those that reflect decreased costs or the need to meet competitors' prices.

WHEELER-LEA AMENDMENT   In 1938 the Wheeler-Lea Amendment expanded Federal Trade Commission jurisdiction to include practices that injure the public generally, in addition to those that specifically harm competitors. It also declared illegal the false advertising of foods, drugs, cosmetics, and therapeutic devices. And it gave the FTC authority to increase the fines it imposes if its orders aren't obeyed within 60 days.

CELLER-KEFAUVER AMENDMENT   In 1950 the Celler-Kefauver Amendment finally closed one of the most glaring loopholes in the Clayton Act, which had prohibited only certain kinds of anticompetitive mergers and only if they were made by stock acquisition. The new act forbade additional types of anticompetitive mergers, including those made by acquisition of assets.

ANTITRUST IN THE 1970s AND 1980s   Two more major antitrust laws were enacted in the 1970s. The first was the Antitrust Procedures and Penalties Act of 1974, which increased the fines for violation of Sherman Act provisions to $100,000 for individuals and to $1 million for corporations. It also made violation of the law a more serious crime, increasing the penalty from a misdemeanor to a felony punishable by a maximum jail sentence of three years. In 1976 the Antitrust Improvements Act made it necessary for companies to notify the FTC of their merger plans before the mergers take place; it also empowered state attorneys general to bring suit on behalf of injured consumers in their states.

In 1982 and 1984, the Department of Justice issued new guidelines for determining the legality of mergers. Whereas previous guidelines based merger legality simply on market share as measured by sales or assets, the new guidelines advocated a more sophisticated evaluation in terms of a merger's economic impact.[6] During the Reagan administration, antitrust enforcers challenged few large mergers because they were thought to enhance efficiency and benefit consumers.[7] However, when Coke proposed the acquisition of Dr. Pepper, and when Pepsi proposed the acquisition of Seven-Up, the government blocked both because the newly combined companies would control 80 percent of the soft-drink market in the United States.[8] The government did, however, allow Pepsi to buy Seven-Up's European operation.

ANTITRUST NOW   Following a decade of limited antitrust activity, Congress passed the Anti-Trust Amendments Act of 1990, which raised the ceiling on antitrust fines from $1 million to $10 million.[9] In addition, the Bush administration is boosting its antitrust enforcement efforts, particularly when it comes to helping U.S. firms compete in the global marketplace. The Federal Trade Commission, for example, investigated whether Japanese automakers were violating antitrust laws by favoring Japanese parts suppliers for cars made in their

U.S. plants.[10] Soon after, Nissan announced plans to increase its purchases of U.S.-made vehicle parts and materials by 40 percent over a two-year period. Toyota and Mazda took similar action.[11]

Government Regulation to Protect the Public

VIDEO EXERCISE

In addition to seeing that the free-market system works smoothly and that competition has a chance to flourish, governments look out for the public's interests in other ways. For instance, because individual companies often lack the perspective and the incentive to consider the common welfare, governments establish regulations that protect society. The federal government protects the rights of consumers, employees, minorities, investors, and the environment through administrative agencies such as the Consumer Product Safety Commission, Occupational Safety and Health Administration (OSHA), Equal Employment Opportunity Commission, Securities and Exchange Commission, and Environmental Protection Agency. State and local governments have similar agencies. In his plans to expand Disneyland, Michael Eisner must deal with environmental regulators on air- and water-quality issues at both the state and the federal levels. The extent of government's role as watchdog is exemplified in Exhibit 21.1, which shows how regulations relating to food quality affect fast-food hamburgers.

EXHIBIT 21.1

Government Regulations Affecting Fast-Food Hamburgers

Each of the government-imposed specifications shown here is intended to ensure that fast-food burgers are both nutritious and safe to eat.

Enriched bun: Must contain at least 1.8 mg. of thiamine, at least 1.1 mg. of riboflavin, and at least 8.0 but no more than 12.5 mg. of iron

Meat: Must be fresh or frozen chopped beef without added water, binders, or extenders; must be inspected before and after slaughter and at boning, grinding, fabrication, and packaging stages

Growth promoters: Must not be used beyond the time specified by law

Pesticides: No more than 5 parts of the pesticide DDT per million parts of fat in the meat

Fat: No more than 30 percent fat content

Pickle slices: Must be between 1/8 and 3/8 inch thick

Tomatoes: Must be mature but not overripe or soft

Lettuce: Must be fresh, not soft, overgrown, burst, or "ribby"; no sulfites may be used to preserve a fresh appearance

Cheese: Must contain at least 50 percent milk fat and, if made with milk that is not pasteurized, must be cured for 60 or more days at a temperature of at least 35°F

Ketchup: To be considered grade A fancy, must flow no more than 14 cm in 30 seconds at 20°C (69°F)

Mayonnaise: May be seasoned or flavored as long as the substances do not color it to look like egg yolk

Government regulators appear to be taking a stronger stand as business watchdogs. The Supreme Court, for example, has increasingly upheld state decisions against business with regard to punitive damages, litigation rules, and sex discrimination. With regard to worker safety, a major reform proposal was recently introduced in Congress that would (1) give a state 6 months to improve weak safety plans before OSHA takes over, (2) require companies to involve employees in safety by setting up management-employee committees, and (3) strengthen employee rights to refuse hazardous work. Perhaps the most evident backlash against business is the Bush administration's war on polluters. For example, John Borowski, president of metal-finisher Borjohn Optical Technology in Burlington, Massachusetts, is the first person ever to be convicted under the "knowing endangerment" provision of the Clean Water Act. Having ordered his employees to dump toxic wastes down a sewer, Borowski was sentenced to two years in jail and fined $400,000.[12]

Deregulation

Government regulation of business is beneficial—up to a point. Many people believe that some of the restrictions on business are poorly conceived and poorly enforced. Critics argue that government regulation increases the costs of doing business, creates delays and frustrations, produces unexpected burdens on certain groups, impedes innovation, and distorts economic incentives.

A move toward **deregulation,** the abandonment or relaxation of existing regulations, began during Richard Nixon's administration and gained momentum with Jimmy Carter's election. In addition to pressing for regulatory simplification in general, the federal government began taking steps to deregulate specific, tightly controlled industries on the theory that market forces are more efficient than government intervention (see Exhibit 21.2).

But deregulation produced some problems. In the airline industry, for example, which was deregulated during the Carter administration, competition intensified when the Civil Aeronautics Board stopped setting fares and allocating airline routes. New air carriers took wing in heavily traveled corridors, and several major carriers cut prices to attract passengers and dropped less popular air routes. As a result, some smaller cities lost air service entirely, and some established airlines began to teeter on the edge of bankruptcy. Of the 22 major airlines that began operating after deregulation, only 4 survived. And of the eight airlines left controlling 90 percent of the market, three failed in 1991. Some people are asking for reregulation, but others are convinced the problems lie in not completely deregulating in the first place. They suggest privatizing airports and auctioning landing slots to achieve the full benefits of unhampered competition.[13]

The Reagan administration continued the trend toward deregulation and created a Task Force on Regulatory Relief to review all existing and proposed regulations.[14] Following a two-year study, the group (chaired by Vice President Bush) issued a report recommending simplifications that it claimed would save the economy $150 billion over a decade. In its evaluation of regulations, the administration focused on the use of **cost-benefit analysis**—comparing the cost of all regulations to their benefit. For example, the administration argued that before requiring factories to install smokestack scrubbers costing $100 million or more, regulators should first measure those costs (and the costs of people losing their jobs) against the benefits of cleaner air. But others argued that although the benefits of cleaner air are intangible and therefore harder to measure

deregulation Removal or relaxation of rules and restrictions affecting business

cost-benefit analysis Comparison of the costs and benefits of a particular action for the purpose of assessing its desirability

EXHIBIT 21.2

The Steps in Deregulation
The move toward deregulation started slowly in the late 1960s and gained momentum in the 1970s and 1980s. Advocates of deregulation claimed it would revitalize the affected industries and give the overall economy a boost. However, the results have been mixed, ranging from a telecommunications industry that's thriving to a savings and loan industry in ruins and an economy struggling to recover from another recession.

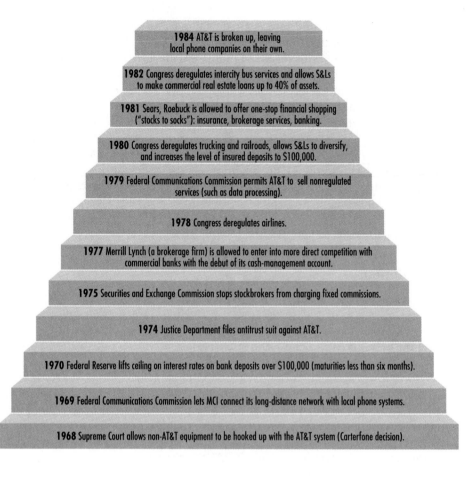

1984 AT&T is broken up, leaving local phone companies on their own.

1982 Congress deregulates intercity bus services and allows S&Ls to make commercial real estate loans up to 40% of assets.

1981 Sears, Roebuck is allowed to offer one-stop financial shopping ("stocks to socks"): insurance, brokerage services, banking.

1980 Congress deregulates trucking and railroads, allows S&Ls to diversify, and increases the level of insured deposits to $100,000.

1979 Federal Communications Commission permits AT&T to sell nonregulated services (such as data processing).

1978 Congress deregulates airlines.

1977 Merrill Lynch (a brokerage firm) is allowed to enter into more direct competition with commercial banks with the debut of its cash-management account.

1975 Securities and Exchange Commission stops stockbrokers from charging fixed commissions.

1974 Justice Department files antitrust suit against AT&T.

1970 Federal Reserve lifts ceiling on interest rates on bank deposits over $100,000 (maturities less than six months).

1969 Federal Communications Commission lets MCI connect its long-distance network with local phone systems.

1968 Supreme Court allows non-AT&T equipment to be hooked up with the AT&T system (Carterfone decision).

than costs, they are nevertheless significant. Cost-benefit analysis is mandated by executive order for all executive agencies; however, some independent agencies voluntarily perform such analyses.[15]

The Reagan administration also tried to control some regulatory agencies by cutting their budgets. Strapped for cash to pay personnel, these agencies had to limit their activities. As a result, there was insufficient oversight in many areas that led to problems later—such as the fraud and risky investing that occurred within the savings and loan industry.

When the Bush administration took over, the glowing optimism about deregulation gave way to alternating calls for regulatory laxity and toughness. The new administration focused on making government regulations more acceptable to business, with "regulatory reform" the favored terminology. To help achieve his hoped-for reforms, President Bush appointed Vice President Quayle chairman of the Council on Competitiveness, with the responsibility of overseeing every regulation proposed by the government. Within months the council had killed a major recycling regulation, attempted to weaken costly clean air laws, and redefined wetlands in a way that could open millions of acres to commercial development.[16] As the federal government tries to minimize its regulatory control, many state governments are increasing theirs. The result is that more business owners are pushing for federal reregulation so that they won't have to deal with a multitude of differing state regulations.

With the 1991 confirmation of Clarence Thomas as associate justice of the Supreme Court, the Bush administration believed it was ensuring judicial backing through the 1990s for its pro-business approach toward government regulations.

Government as Tax Collector

Taxes have historically been used for two purposes in the United States. The most obvious purpose is to raise revenue for government. In addition, taxes are used to provide incentives or disincentives for certain types of behavior. A **tax credit** is an amount deducted from the income on which a person or a business is taxed. The investment tax credit, for example, was designed to encourage companies to invest in capital equipment; the special tax rates for capital gains (profits made on investments) were instituted to provide incentives for investing in securities. In order to obtain special tax breaks like these, individuals and companies often made decisions they wouldn't otherwise have made.

Although many groups benefit from tax incentives, the public in general came to believe that the tax laws contained too many loopholes. Recognizing that the use of tax breaks had gotten out of hand, the federal government passed a tax-reform bill that was intended to simplify the federal tax code. One thrust of the legislation was to reduce the burden on individual taxpayers and to extract more tax revenues from businesses. In addition, the new tax package eliminated many loopholes in order to encourage both businesses and individuals to base their investment decisions less on tax considerations and more on economic merits. However, many people now question the wisdom of the tax changes, which resulted in individuals paying an increasingly bigger share of the tax bill.[17] Moreover, the onslaught of higher state taxes is hurting the business community. In California, New York, Pennsylvania, Connecticut, New Jersey, and North Carolina, the increased state taxes have so soured the economy that businesses are taking jobs elsewhere. For example, one in four California companies is now considering moving some or all of its operations out of the state.[18]

The major taxes that affect businesses include those assessed to provide revenue for the operation of government—personal and corporate income taxes, property taxes, sales taxes, value-added taxes—and those assessed to regulate

tax credit Amount deducted from the income on which a person or business is taxed

EXHIBIT 21.3

Sources of Tax Revenues
The two charts at the right show the sources of tax revenues collected by the federal government (left) and by state and local governments (right). The federal government receives 57 percent of all revenues collected.

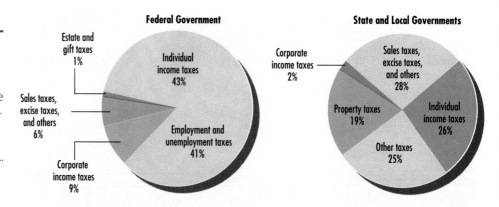

Federal Government

Estate and gift taxes 1%
Sales taxes, excise taxes, and others 6%
Corporate income taxes 9%
Individual income taxes 43%
Employment and unemployment taxes 41%

State and Local Governments

Corporate income taxes 2%
Sales taxes, excise taxes, and others 28%
Property taxes 19%
Individual income taxes 26%
Other taxes 25%

and restrict certain business activities—excise taxes and customs duties. Some of these taxes are levied by the federal government, some by state and local governments, and some by foreign governments (see Exhibit 21.3).

Personal Income Taxes

Personal income taxes have been the federal government's largest single source of revenue, accounting for $499.5 billion in 1991, and a major source of state revenues as well.[19] On the federal level, the personal income tax is a graduated tax, which means that as you make more money, the tax you pay is a higher percentage of your income.

Although the personal income tax is assessed on individual income, it does affect businesses. In partnerships and sole proprietorships, profits are considered the personal income of the owners and are therefore taxable at personal-income-tax rates. Corporations are also affected by personal income taxes because all companies are required to withhold a percentage of employees' earnings to be forwarded to the government. Although the money collected is taken out of employee earnings, the company pays all expenses of administering the pay deductions, which add up rapidly for a large company. Furthermore, companies are affected by personal income taxes because the money that individuals pay in taxes might otherwise have been invested in stocks and bonds or deposited in savings accounts, thereby making money available for business expansion rather than bureaucratic or military growth.

Corporate Income Taxes

Corporations pay taxes on their profits, much as individuals pay taxes on their income. Under tax-reform measures passed in 1986, the top tax rate for corporations was reduced from 46 percent to 34 percent, and a minimum corporate tax rate of 20 percent was imposed. In the past, such well-known corporations as General Electric and Boeing sometimes paid little or no tax by taking advantage of various special tax breaks.[20] The minimum tax on corporate income was designed to prevent large, prosperous companies from avoiding their fair share of the tax burden, which would otherwise end up being shifted to other companies and to individuals.

Many state and local governments also impose corporate income taxes—but at lower rates. And because most of this country's large corporations also operate abroad, they must pay income taxes in foreign countries as well. (It should be noted that the federal government allows U.S. corporations a tax credit for taxes paid to a foreign government.) The tax system and corporate income tax rate of a state or country typically influence a business's decision to operate there.

When California started charging sales tax on candy and certain snack foods, the new tax became known as the "Twinkie tax." Although it provides an additional source of revenue for the state, the new sales tax means more administrative work for businesses that sell snack foods. Moreover, the Twinkie tax has been widely protested by those who believe that the definition of *snack* is unclear and that its selective application to food categories is unfair.

Property Taxes

Businesses pay property taxes on the land and the structures they own. In some communities, taxes are assessed on the basis of the value of buildings. A 20-story office tower, for instance, is worth far more on the tax rolls than a fast-food restaurant. In addition, commercial property is usually taxed at a higher rate than houses and farms, so businesses often pay a large portion of a community's property tax.

Sales Taxes

In many states and in some localities, merchandise sold at the retail level is subject to a sales tax. An item marked for, say, $10 in a place with a 6 percent sales tax would actually cost $10.60. Although businesses are exempt from paying a sales tax on merchandise they buy for resale, the sales tax does affect business: It increases the prices customers have to pay. Also, as with personal income taxes, businesses are required to collect the sales tax from their customers and forward it to the government, which involves administrative expense.

Value-Added Taxes

From time to time, policymakers in this country have espoused **value-added taxes** (VATs), which are assessed all along the chain of distribution on the difference in value between the cost of the goods and services used in production (inputs) and the price that the end products (outputs) are sold for. VATs have not yet been adopted in this country, but they do exist in other countries. In the European Economic Community, for instance, they are the main type of tax on sales of goods and services. U.S. companies operating overseas may therefore be subject to VATs.

value-added taxes Taxes paid at each step in the distribution chain on the difference between the cost of inputs and the price obtained for outputs at that step

Excise Taxes

A number of items are subject to **excise taxes,** taxes intended to help control potentially harmful practices ("sin taxes") or to help pay for services used only by certain people. The United States imposes excise taxes on products such as gasoline, tobacco, and liquor. Federal excise taxes are also levied on certain services of national scope, such as air travel and telephone calls.

Income from federal excise taxes must be used for a purpose related to the tax. The gasoline tax, for example, goes toward funding road-building projects. Thus, the burden of paying for the roads is in large part borne by those who use them most.

Excise taxes are imposed on the manufacturer, the retailer, or both. Ultimately, however, the consumer pays these taxes, because they are often fac-

excise taxes Taxes intended to help control potentially harmful practices or to help pay for government services used only by certain people or businesses

tored into the prices of products. Because products with these hidden taxes are frequently subject to a general sales tax as well, those who consume the products may be hit twice.

Customs Duties

customs duties Fees imposed on goods brought into the country

Products brought into this country are often subject to import taxes, or **customs duties.** These taxes are selective; they vary with the product and its country of origin. Designed to protect U.S. businesses against foreign competition, customs duties have the effect of raising the price of imports to a level comparable to similar U.S.-made merchandise. Customs duties have been used with increasing frequency as a weapon in foreign policy: The products of friendly nations are often taxed at lower rates than those of indifferent or openly hostile countries.

Business's Influence on Government

lobbies Groups who try to persuade legislators to vote according to the groups' interests

Given the impact that government has on business, it is not surprising that business has responded by trying to influence government in various ways. One of the most common approaches is to create **lobbies,** groups of people who try to persuade legislators to vote according to the groups' interests. Industry associations such as the American Bankers Association, the Chamber of Commerce of the United States, and the American Medical Association are typically involved in lobbying. Although the members of such associations are competitors, they often have common objectives when it comes to government action. In its efforts to expand Disneyland, Disney has begun actively lobbying to influence city and county officials, coastline regulators, and state legislatures.

In many quarters, lobbyists have a poor reputation; they are perceived as "fat cats" who spend their days wining and dining legislators on an expense account. But others see lobbyists as hard-working, ethical people who perform a genuine service to government. By providing information on the needs and interests of business and other groups, they help legislators make informed decisions about complex issues.

political action committees Groups formed under federal election laws to raise money for candidates

Businesses also try to influence government by donating money to politicians. Campaign laws strictly limit businesses' ability to donate money directly to candidates; however, they may funnel contributions through **political action committees** (PACs). Through a PAC, a company can solicit contributions from its employees and then allocate the money to various campaigns. In addition to operating company PACs, many companies also work through trade-association PACs. Opponents of PACs complain that these committees corrupt the democratic process, favor incumbents, and drive up the cost of campaigning for everyone. Some employees dislike PACs because they feel pressured to contribute yet have little say in how their money will be allocated. The Senate recently considered a bill that would eliminate PACs, but it appears they may still be around for a while.[21]

PACs control large sums collectively. For example, the PAC sponsored by the National Association of Realtors donated $3.1 million to various candidates in 1990.[22] To keep the influence of PACs from corrupting politicians, the law limits the amount a PAC can give to any one candidate to $3,000. However, no federal law limits the amount of money corporations can give to state or local parties. So many corporations make large contributions to political parties (earmarked for specific congressional campaigns) as well as smaller contributions to individual candidates. ARCO, the giant gas, oil, and chemical company, gave over $290,000 to the Republican party and $12,000 to the Democratic party in 1990.[23]

▶ THE U.S. LEGAL SYSTEM

One of the most pervasive ways that government affects business is through the legal system. The law protects both individuals and businesses against those who threaten society. It also spells out accepted ways of performing many essential business functions—along with the penalties for failure to comply. In other words, like the average person, companies must obey the law or face the consequences. Although this fact limits a company's freedom, it also provides protection from wrongdoers.

Sources of Law

The U.S. Constitution, including the Bill of Rights, is the foundation for our laws. Since most of the drafters of the Constitution were men who owned property, they naturally were concerned about creating a document that protected their own interests. They were also influenced by the philosopher John Locke, who believed that governed individuals must retain certain rights (including the rights of life, liberty, and property) in order to prevent their government from being oppressive. The property rights that are protected under the U.S. Constitution extend to business owners' interests as well.[24]

Because the Constitution is a general document, laws offering specific answers to specific problems are constantly embellishing its basic principles. However, law is not static; it develops in response to changing conditions and social standards. Individual laws originate in various ways: through legislative action (statutory law), through administrative rulings (administrative law), and through customs and judicial precedents (common law). To one degree or another, all three forms of law affect businesses.

Statutory Law

Without Congress, there would be no federal **statutory law,** which is law written by legislative bodies. The Constitution, in fact, specifically grants the Senate and the House of Representatives the right "to regulate [interstate] commerce." Because of the many steps involved in passing a bill, most statutory law reflects a broad consensus of opinion. In some cases, however, laws benefiting narrow interests are sometimes pushed through Congress by senators or representatives friendly to those interests. Nevertheless, all statutes must be constitutional to be legal.

States also have legislative bodies that write statutory laws applicable within their boundaries. But state laws can vary considerably, presenting problems for companies that do business in several states. The problem would be much worse, however, without the **Uniform Commercial Code** (UCC), which provides a nationwide standard in many areas of commercial law such as the writing of sales contracts and warranties. The UCC has been adopted in its entirety in 49 states and the District of Columbia, and about half of it has been adopted in Louisiana.

statutory law *Statute, or law, created by a legislature*

Uniform Commercial Code *Set of standardized laws that govern business transactions and that have been adopted by most states*

Administrative Law

administrative law Rules, regulations, and interpretations of statutory law set forth by administrative agencies and commissions

Once laws have been passed by a legislature or Congress, an administrative agency or commission typically takes responsibility for enforcing them. That agency may be called on to clarify a regulation's intent, often by consulting representatives of the affected industry. The administrative agency may then write more specific regulations, which are considered **administrative law.** For example, the Federal Trade Commission issues regulations and enforces statutory laws concerning such deceptive trade practices as unfair debt collection and false advertising. Governmental agencies cannot, however, create regulations out of thin air—they must be linked to specific statutes to be legal.

consent order Settlement in which an individual or organization promises to discontinue some illegal activity without admitting guilt

Administrative agencies also have the power to investigate corporations suspected of breaking administrative laws. A corporation found to be misbehaving may agree to a **consent order,** which allows the company to promise to stop doing something without actually admitting to any illegal behavior. As an alternative, the administrative agency may start legal proceedings against the company in a hearing presided over by an administrative law judge. During the hearing, witnesses are called and evidence is presented to determine the facts of the situation. The judge then issues a decision, which may impose corrective actions on the company. If either party objects to the decision, it may file an appeal to the appropriate federal court.[25]

Common Law

common law Law based on the precedents established by judges' decisions

Common law, the sort of law that comes out of courtrooms and judges' decisions, began in England many centuries ago and was transported to America by the colonists. It is applied in all states except Louisiana, which has a French heritage and therefore follows some of the principles of the Napoleonic Code. Common law is sometimes called the "unwritten law" to distinguish it from legislative acts and administrative agency regulations, which are written documents. Instead, common law is established through custom and the precedents set in courtroom proceedings.

stare decisis Concept of using previous judicial decisions as the basis for deciding similar court cases

Despite its "unwritten" nature, common law has great continuity, which derives from the doctrine of **stare decisis** (Latin for "to stand by decisions"). What the stare decisis doctrine means is that judges' decisions establish a precedent for deciding future cases of a similar nature. Because common law is based on what has gone before, the legal framework develops gradually.

In the United States, common law is applied and interpreted in the system of courts (see Exhibit 21.4). Common law thus develops through the decisions in trial courts, special courts, and appellate courts. The Supreme Court (or the highest court of a state when state laws are involved) sets precedents for entire legal systems; lower courts must then abide by those precedents as they pertain to similar cases.

In legal proceedings, common law, administrative law, and statutory law may all be applicable. If they conflict, statutory law generally prevails. But the three forms of law overlap to such an extent that the difference among them is often indistinguishable. For instance, if you bought what you thought was a goose-down coat and then found out that it was actually filled with reprocessed polyester, you could sue the coat manufacturer for misrepresentation. Although the basis for this suit is an old concept in common law, it has also been incorporated in state and federal legislation against fraudulent and misleading advertising, which is further interpreted and enforced by the Federal Trade Commission.

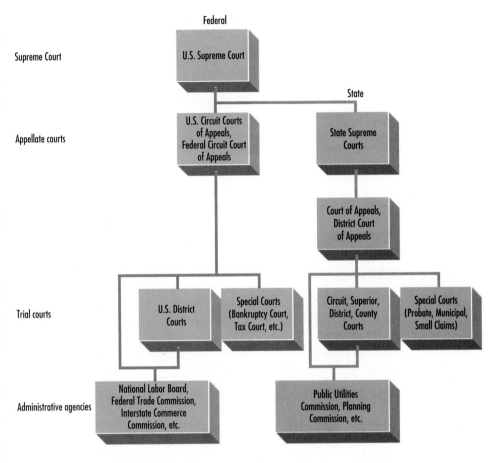

Federal

Supreme Court — U.S. Supreme Court

State

Appellate courts — U.S. Circuit Courts of Appeals, Federal Circuit Court of Appeals | State Supreme Courts

Court of Appeals, District Court of Appeals

Trial courts — U.S. District Courts | Special Courts (Bankruptcy Court, Tax Court, etc.) | Circuit, Superior, District, County Courts | Special Courts (Probate, Municipal, Small Claims)

Administrative agencies — National Labor Board, Federal Trade Commission, Interstate Commerce Commission, etc. | Public Utilities Commission, Planning Commission, etc.

EXHIBIT 21.4

The U.S. Court System
A legal proceeding may begin in a trial court or an administrative agency (examples of each are given here). An unfavorable decision may be appealed to a higher court at the federal or state level. (The court of appeals is the highest court in states that have no state supreme court; some other states have no intermediate appellate court.) The U.S. Supreme Court, the country's highest court, is the court of final appeal.

Business-Related Law

Regardless of its source, law can also be classified as either public or private. **Private law** concerns itself with relationships between individuals, between an individual and a business, or between two businesses. **Public law** concerns itself with the relationships between the government and individual citizens.[26] For example, insider trading on Wall Street, forgery of signatures on checks and other documents, unauthorized access to computer data banks, negligence in regard to worker safety, and other "white-collar" crimes are covered by public law. One company infringing on another company's trademark or copyright is covered by private law.

private law Law that concerns itself with relationships between individuals, between an individual and a business, or between two businesses

public law Law that concerns itself with relationships between the government and individual citizens

Torts

A **tort** is a noncriminal act (other than breach of contract) that results in injury to person or property.[27] The victim of a tort is legally entitled to some form of compensation (a compensatory damage award). In some cases the victim may also receive a punitive damage award to punish the wrongdoer if the misdeed was glaringly bad. For example, in an Alabama case involving insurance fraud, the Supreme Court upheld a punitive damage award of $840,000 to a victim cheated out of $3,800 in medical coverage.[28] Tort law covers intentional torts, negligence, and strict liability.

tort Noncriminal act (other than breach of contract) that results in injury to a person or to property

intentional tort Willful act that results in injury

INTENTIONAL TORTS   An **intentional tort** is a willful act that results in injury. For example, accidentally knocking a ball through someone's window while you're playing softball is a tort, but purposely knocking down someone's tree because it obscures your view is an intentional tort.

Intent does not mean the intent to cause harm; it is the intent to commit a specific physical act. The most common intentional torts include assault, or intentionally placing someone in fear of immediate, offensive bodily contact; battery, or making intentional bodily contact that is unwanted and offensive; and defamation, or intentionally communicating a false statement that is harm-

FOCUS ON ETHICS

Should Companies Be Allowed to Withhold Information About Potentially Harmful Products?

Business owners and executives often face the dilemma of choosing between what's best for business and what's best for everyone else—employees, customers, investors, and the general public. The ideal situation would benefit everyone. But, of course, then there would be no dilemma.

Potential health and safety hazards have created especially troubling dilemmas for a number of companies. Most of us would like to think that a business would put the public welfare ahead of profits when it comes to a potential health hazard. On the other hand, if unsubstantiated information turns out to be of little or no concern, it could be too late for a business already devastated by unwarranted fears. If the business can't recover, its employees, customers, investors, and suppliers all lose.

In many cases, however, potential hazards become real hazards. But some companies go so far as to keep a lid on potentially dangerous products even when there is strong evidence that people have been injured. For example, when lawsuits were filed alleging that Bic lighters were blowing up, burning, maiming, and killing consumers, the manufacturer settled an estimated 20 damage cases under a veil of secrecy. Eli Lilly sought protective orders to withhold information about Oraflex, an arthritis treatment hailed as a "wonder drug" but later linked to 49 deaths and 1,000 injuries. And Ford tried to have records sealed involving a child who died in the crash of his parents' Ford Escort, which was not equipped with rear shoulder harness restraints. Although the child's parents would not agree to confidentiality, Ford settled the case for $6 million.

State senator William Lockyer, chairman of the

California Senate Judiciary Committee, is sponsoring a bill that would require California courts to discourage the sealing of damage-suit documents that could warn the public of hazards to safety and health. But lobbyists for big business "have pulled out all the stops" to defeat the bill. They say it would prove too costly to business and ultimately consumers. Trial lawyers, they say, will swarm over newly disclosed trade secrets and generate a tidal wave of product-liability lawsuits. Companies will become more reluctant to settle cases out of fear that they will be sitting ducks for even more litigation. Other groups counter that the social cost of secrecy is far higher. They also believe that companies must take the initiative in getting the word out when products are potentially harmful.

In one of the worst medical-device disasters ever, Pfizer waited years before attempting to identify patients who had received one of its faulty mechanical heart valves. Pfizer did notify doctors, but not until several years after the valves were manufactured. The valves in question had failed the company's quality-control tests when production first started, but according to Pfizer they were repaired before being sold. Unfortunately, however, many of the valves fractured, causing 261 deaths and untold anxiety. A Washington-based watchdog group, Public Citizen, filed a lawsuit asking that Pfizer be required not only to notify all valve recipients of the possible problems but also to provide free medical checkups and psychological counseling on request. Yet Pfizer did not try to identify the remaining valve recipients most at risk until just before the FDA ordered it to do so.

ful to another's reputation (if the communication is in writing or on television, it is libel; if it is spoken, it is slander).[29]

NEGLIGENCE   These days, one of the most controversial areas of tort law is **negligence,** a failure to use a reasonable amount of care necessary to protect others from unreasonable risk of injury.[30] The tort of negligence bases liability on some degree of fault, and to prove a case of negligence, five elements must be established:

1. Duty of care. The defendant must be obligated to follow a reasonable standard of care.

2. Breach of duty. The defendant must fail to perform that duty of care.

3. Injury. An injury must result from the breach of duty.

4. Cause. The defendant must cause the injury.

5. Proximate cause. The injury must be a foreseeable consequence of the defendant's breach of duty.[31]

Clorox, for example, was sued for negligence when it masked the offensive odor of its bleach. Without its usual odor, a person could mistake a glass of Fresh Scent Clorox for a harmless glass of water, as Rebecca Caruso did. As a result, 14-year-old Rebecca suffered a severely scarred esophagus when she gulped down the bleach.[32]

STRICT LIABILITY   The tort of **strict liability** focuses on liability even when the defendant has used reasonable care and has committed no wrongdoing. If a defendant engages in an inherently dangerous activity, such as blasting for construction purposes or keeping dangerous animals (lions, tigers, poisonous snakes), risk of harm is high no matter how much care is used, and the defendant is strictly liable.[33] In strict liability, then, liability can be assigned without fault.

Product-Liability Law

A classic product-liability case involved the Ford Pinto. Manufactured from 1971 through 1976, Pintos were found by the federal government to have improperly designed fuel systems. Ford responded by recalling the cars for repairs and settling damage suits brought by the families of those who had died in suspicious Pinto accidents. Nevertheless, after a 1980 case in which three young women were burned to death in a Pinto, Ford was charged with "reckless homicide" (a reckless failure to perform an act that one has a duty to perform). Although Ford was eventually found not guilty, the negative publicity emphasized our society's feelings about who is responsible for problems with products. Developing out of tort law, **product-liability law** holds companies responsible for their products on the grounds of negligence, strict liability, and warranty.[34]

NEGLIGENCE   As in tort law, the five elements of negligence must be established for a company to be held liable for injuries caused by such things as a product that is defective because of poor design, improper construction, improper assembly, or negligent advertising. The company must perform reasonable tests and must use reasonable care when inspecting a product. For example, Disney was sued for negligence in inspection and maintenance by a patron whose chair collapsed in a Disney World movie pavillion.[35] Further, companies

negligence Failure to observe a reasonable standard of care in order to protect others from unreasonable risk of injury

strict liability Concept of liability even in cases where the defendant has used reasonable care

product-liability law Law that holds a manufacturer liable for injuries caused by a defective product

must warn people about the possible dangers of using their products properly as well as the foreseeable dangers of using the product improperly.[36]

warranty Guarantee or promise

BREACH OF WARRANTY   A **warranty** is a guarantee or promise and may be either express or implied. Companies may create an *express warranty* by making a promise about the product, by specifically describing the product, or by furnishing a model or a sample of the product. A company is in breach of express warranty if the product does not perform as the company said it would, is not as the company described, or is different from the model or sample. An *implied warranty* is neither written nor spoken but is created by operation of law when a seller enters into a contract. For example, an *implied warranty of merchantability* guarantees that a product is reasonably fit for the ordinary purposes for which the product will be used. An *implied warranty of fitness for a particular purpose* guarantees that the buyer may rely on the seller's skill or judgment in selecting or furnishing goods that are suitable for the buyer's particular expressed need.[37]

strict product liability Concept that assigns product liability even if the company used all reasonable care in the manufacture, distribution, or sale of its product

STRICT PRODUCT LIABILITY   A company may be held liable for injury caused by a defective product even if the company used all reasonable care in the manufacture, distribution, or sale of its product. Such **strict product liability** makes it possible to assign liability without assigning fault. It must only be established that (1) the company is in the business of selling the product, (2) the product reached the customer or user without substantial change in its condition, (3) the product was defective, (4) the defective condition rendered the product unreasonably dangerous, and (5) the defective product caused the injury.[38]

Ace-Chicago Great Dane (a dealer and distributor of trailers) faced a lawsuit based on strict product liability when it allowed a defective trailer to enter the stream of commerce. Although Ace-Chicago wasn't the manufacturer, it was found liable for an injury caused to a mechanic checking a possible leak in the trailer's refrigeration unit. The mechanic worked for the company that serviced the refrigeration unit and was injured when the improperly attached unit fell off and struck him.[39]

market-share liability Concept that extends strict product liability by dividing responsibility for injuries among all manufacturers in an industry according to their market share at the time of the injury

MARKET-SHARE LIABILITY   A new wrinkle in product-liability law exposes manufacturers to even greater potential liability problems. The concept, known as **market-share liability**, makes it possible for a company to be sued even if it did not actually produce the item that caused the injury.

The precedent-setting case, which occurred in California in 1980, involved a 22-year-old woman who had developed cancer. In the early 1950s, her mother had taken a drug called DES to prevent miscarriage during her pregnancy. It was later discovered that DES causes cancer in children exposed to it in the womb. The daughter wanted to sue, and because she could not prove which company produced the particular dose her mother had taken, the court allowed her to sue, as a group, all the companies that had made DES at the time. Each defendant was held liable for a percentage of the damages equal to its share of the market at the time.[40] Thus, a company that had a 30 percent market share was liable for 30 percent of any damages. Market-share liability shifts the burden of proof to the defendant—that is, any company able to prove that it did not manufacture the drug taken by this woman's mother would be relieved of liability.[41]

Although individual victims of harmful products are clearly entitled to some sort of compensation, many people question whether such strict interpretation of product-liability laws is good for society. Because of the increasing frequency and size of compensatory and punitive damage awards, many companies are having trouble obtaining product-liability insurance at a reasonable price. As a consequence, they are withdrawing from high-risk businesses such as drug manufacturing. If each product innovation brings on an innovation in lawsuits, our society could quickly lose the benefits of advancing technology. To forestall that result, some states have instituted reforms designed to control excessive damage awards. Nevertheless, those who support strict interpretation of product liability point out that (1) the cost of losses can best be borne by manufacturers because they can distribute such costs to all users of the product, and (2) it seems more fair for the manufacturer (the party able to make a product safer) to bear the liability rather than the consumer (the party who has no way of knowing whether a product is safe).[42]

New business technology generates new business crimes. This detective is displaying the computer equipment confiscated from a group of young "hackers" in New Jersey who used the machines to make free phone calls all over the world, to obtain the numbers of stolen credit cards, and even to learn some Pentagon codes.

Contracts

Broadly defined, a **contract** is an exchange of promises enforceable by law. Many business and personal transactions—including marriage, estate planning (wills), and credit purchases—involve contracts. As with warranties, contracts may be either express or implied. An **express contract** is derived from the words (either oral or written) of the parties; an **implied contract** is derived from the actions or conduct of the parties.[43]

ELEMENTS OF A CONTRACT   The law of contracts deals largely with identifying the exchanges that can be classified as contracts. Intent is the essence of a contract. In addition, the following factors must usually be present for a contract to be valid and enforceable:

An offer must be made. One party must propose that an agreement be entered into. The offer may be oral or written—for example, a salesperson may telephone or write a prospective client, offering to sell the client materials at a certain price. In either case, the offer must be firm, definite, and specific enough to make it clear that someone intends to be legally bound by the offer. Finally, the offer must be communicated to the intended party or parties.

An offer must be accepted. For an offer to be accepted, there must be clear intent (spoken, written, or by action) to enter into the contract. An implied contract arises when a person requests or accepts something and the other party has indicated that payment is expected. If, for example, your car breaks down on the road and you call a mobile mechanic and ask him to repair it, you are obligated to pay the reasonable value for the services even if you didn't agree to specific charges beforehand. However, when a specific offer is made, the acceptance must satisfy the terms of the offer—that is, if a car salesperson offers to sell you a used Jeep Cherokee for $5,800 and you say you would take it for $5,000, you have not accepted the offer. Your response is a counteroffer, which may or may not be accepted by the salesperson. When both parties to a contract are merchants, the Uniform Commercial Code allows additional or different terms to become part of a contract unless (1) the offer expressly limits acceptance to the terms of the offer, (2) the new terms materially alter the offer, or (3) the party making the offer objects to the new terms within a reasonable amount of time.[44]

Both parties must give consideration. A contract is legally binding only when the parties have bargained with one another and exchanged something. This bargained-for exchange, or **consideration**, does not have to be money, goods, or services. But it must impose a **legal detriment**, the assumption of a duty or the forfeit of a right, to one or both parties. For example, when a business is sold, the buyer incurs a legal detriment by

contract Exchange of promises enforceable by law

express contract Contract derived from words, either oral or written

implied contract Contract derived from actions or conduct

consideration Bargained-for exchange necessary to make a contract legally binding

legal detriment The assumption of a duty or the forfeit of a right that is necessary to make a contract legally binding

> The band entitled "XYZ" agrees to provide entertainment at the Club de Hohenzollern on April 30, 1993 between 8:30 P.M. and 12:30 P.M.
>
> The band will be paid $500.00 for its performance.
>
> Signed on the date of
> *February 19, 1993*
>
> *Violetta Harvey*
> Violetta Harvey,
> Manager,
> Club de Hohenzollern
> and
> *Ralph Perkins*
> Ralph Perkins,
> Manager, XYZ

EXHIBIT 21.5

Elements of a Contract
This simple document contains all the essential elements of a valid contract.

breach of contract Failure to live up to the terms of a contract, with no legal excuse

agreeing to pay a certain amount to the seller. Likewise, the seller incurs a legal detriment by agreeing to give up his or her interest in the business. The relative value of each party's consideration does not generally matter to the courts. Thus, if someone makes what seems later to be a bad deal, it is not the court's concern. Consideration is legally sufficient when there is a bargained-for exchange and legal detriment.[45]

Both parties must give genuine assent. To have a legally enforceable contract, both parties must agree to it voluntarily. The contract must be free of fraud, duress, undue influence, and mutual mistake.[46] If only one party makes a mistake, it ordinarily does not affect the contract. On the other hand, if both parties make a mistake, the agreement would be void. For example, if both the buyer and seller of a business believed it was profitable, when in reality it was operating at a loss, their agreement would be void.

Both parties must be competent. The law gives to certain classes of people only a limited capacity to enter into contracts. Minors, people who are senile or insane, and in some cases those who are intoxicated cannot usually be bound by a contract for anything but the bare necessities: food, clothing, shelter, and medical care.

The contract must not involve an illegal act. The law will not enforce a promise that involves an illegal act. For example, a drug dealer cannot get help from the courts to enforce a contract to deliver illegal drugs at a prearranged price. Nor can a contract be enforced if it is inconsistent with general public policy or is unconscionable.

The contract must be in proper form. Most contracts can be made orally, by an act, or by a casually written document; however, certain contracts are required by law to be in writing. For example, the transfer of goods worth $500 or more must be accompanied by a written document. The written form is also required for all real estate contracts. When the law requires a written document, any change in the agreement must also be written.

A contract need not be long; all these elements of a contract may be contained in a simple document (see Exhibit 21.5). In fact, a check is one type of simple contract.

BREACH OF CONTRACT   Most valid contracts are obeyed by both parties. Each party does what was promised, and the contract is terminated by being carried out or by performance, which discharges both parties. But sometimes a contract will not be fulfilled (or discharged) because both parties agree to end it. A contract may also be discharged because of impossibility of performance—for example, (1) the death or serious illness of a person who has promised personal performance and for whom there is no substitute, (2) the change of a law making performance of the contract illegal, or (3) the destruction of the subject matter of the contract.[47] However, when one party has no legal excuse for failure to live up to the terms of a contract, the other party may claim **breach of contract.**

The essence of a contract is that the law will enforce legal promises. Say that Suzanne Shelby, an interior designer, contracts to buy 50 yards of black wool carpet from The Carpet Center. The contract stipulates that the price for the carpet is to be $26 per yard and that delivery must be made by January 25. But on January 10 the manager of The Carpet Center calls Shelby and tells her that another designer has offered to buy all the store's black wool carpet at $28 per yard. The manager tells Shelby that she must pay the higher price or wait until February 15 for delivery. Shelby has the following options:

Discharge: When one party violates the terms of the agreement, generally the other party is under no obligation to continue with his or her end of the contract. In other words, the second party is discharged from the contract. Shelby is free to buy her carpet from another store. If The Carpet Center goes ahead and delivers the carpet at the later date, Shelby does not have to accept it.

Damages: A party has the right to sue in court for damages that were foreseeable at the time the contract was entered into and that result from the other party's failure to fulfill the contract. The amount of damages awarded usually reflects the amount of profit lost and often includes court costs as well. If Shelby had to pay another store a higher price to get her black carpet, she would be entitled to collect the difference from The Carpet Center.

Specific performance: A party can be compelled to live up to the terms of the contract if money damages would not be adequate. If, for instance, The Carpet Center had agreed to sell Shelby not a standard black wool carpet, but a custom-dyed carpet that is no longer being manufactured, Shelby could demand specific performance of the contract.

In the past, most businesspeople negotiated informally with each other when there were contract problems. In recent years, however, studies show that companies increasingly resort to litigation to solve problems. In fact, contract cases in federal district courts more than quadrupled to 56,300 in 1990 from 13,268 in 1960.[48]

Agency

These days it seems that nearly every celebrity has an agent. Baseball players' agents sign their clients to do cereal commercials and handle their contract negotiations; authors' agents sell manuscripts to the publishers that offer the largest advances; actors' agents try to find choice movie and television roles for their clients. These relationships illustrate a common legal association known as **agency,** which exists when one party, known as the principal, authorizes another party, known as the agent, to act on his or her behalf and when the principal has the right to control the conduct of the agent in whatever activity is delegated. It is this power of control that distinguishes agents from other similar roles such as executors, administrators of estates, and trustees.[49]

All contractual obligations come into play in agency relationships. The principal usually creates this relationship by explicit authorization, either orally or in writing. If, for instance, you telephone a stockbroker and ask her to buy stock for you, she is then empowered to act as your agent (assuming you've already signed a written agreement with her firm). In some cases—where a transfer of property is involved, for example—the authorization must be written in the form of a document called **power of attorney,** which states that one person may legally act for another to the extent of the express written authorization. In some situations, an "implied agency" may be created simply by allowing someone else to act in a principal's behalf; the principal can't subsequently deny that an agency relationship existed, even though no oral or written authorization was ever actually given.

Anita Beck Bosiger, president of Anita Beck Cards & Such, and Shirley Hutton, a national sales director of Mary Kay Cosmetics, agreed that Beck would manufacture calendars and stationery to be sold at Mary Kay conventions. Hutton paid Beck $20,000 to finance the project and was to receive a 15 percent commission on any stationery sold. Unsold goods were to be shipped back to Beck at her expense. When the venture proved to be a dismal failure, Hutton sued Beck for the return of the $20,000, claiming that she was Beck's agent and the money was a loan. Even though Beck never used the term "agent," the court ruled in Hutton's favor based on a signed document indicating that Hutton was to receive a commission and that unsold goods were to be returned to Beck.[50]

Usually, an agency relationship is terminated when the objective of the rela-

agency Business relationship that exists when one party (the principal) authorizes another party (the agent) to act on her or his behalf, while controlling the agent's conduct

power of attorney Written authorization for one party to legally act for another

Some agencies become almost as well known as their famous clients. The William Morris Agency, for example, is renowned for representing big names. As president of William Morris, Jerry Katzman has worked with such celebrated clients as Angela Lansbury, William Shatner, Steve Guttenberg, Andy Griffith, and Joan Van Ark.

When Steven Jobs left Apple Computer to start his own firm (NeXT computers), he took with him intellectual property—a knowledge of Apple's customers and operations—that worried Apple management. Did this intellectual property belong to Jobs? Did it belong to Apple? Although Jobs and Apple reached an agreement about how the intellectual property could be used, any determination of ownership concerning such intangible property can be difficult.

property Rights held regarding any tangible or intangible object

real property Land and everything permanently attached to it

personal property All property that is not real property

intellectual property Intangible personal property such as ideas, songs, or any mental creativity

deed Legal document by which an owner transfers the title to real property to a new owner

lease Legal agreement that temporarily transfers the right to use an asset from the owner to another individual or business

title Legal ownership of property

tionship is met or at the end of a period specified in the contract between agent and principal. But it may also be ended by a change of circumstances, by the agent's breach of duty or loyalty, or by the death of either party.

Property Transactions

Anyone interested in business must know the basics of property law. Most people think of property as some object they own (a book, a car, a house). However, **property** is actually the relationship between the person having rights with regard to any tangible or intangible object and all other persons. The law recognizes two primary types of property: real and personal. **Real property** is land and everything permanently attached to it, such as trees, fences, or mineral deposits. **Personal property** is all property that is not real property; it may be tangible (cars, jewelry, houses, or anything having a physical existence) or intangible (bank accounts, stocks, insurance policies, customer lists). A piece of marble in the earth is real property until it is cut and sold as a block, when it becomes personal property.

Some intangible personal property is called **intellectual property,** such as trademarks, trade secrets, patents, and copyrights.[51] It is sometimes difficult to determine ownership of intellectual property. For example, when Steven Jobs left Apple Computer to start his own firm, Apple management was worried that Jobs would use what he knew about his old company's customers and operations to compete against it. Was Jobs taking information illegally from Apple, or did it belong to him?[52] Eventually, Jobs and Apple came to an understanding and settled without any court action, but the controversy could have led to a lawsuit.

Even when ownership is more clear-cut, property rights are subject to limitations and restrictions. For example, the government monitors the use of real property for the welfare of the public, actually prohibiting some property uses and abuses.[53] Zoning is one example of real-property regulation.

TRANSFER OF REAL PROPERTY   Two types of documents are important in obtaining real property for factory, office, or store space. A **deed** is a legal document by which an owner transfers the title to real property to a new owner. A **lease** is used for a temporary transfer of interest in real property. The party that owns the property is commonly called the landlord; the party that occupies or gains the right to occupy the property is the tenant. The tenant pays the landlord, usually in periodic installments, for the use of the property. Generally, a lease may be granted for any length of time that the two parties agree on.

TRANSFER OF PERSONAL PROPERTY   A permanent transfer of tangible or intangible personal property—such as merchandise or a check—is technically a transfer of **title,** or ownership of the property. Most problems with the transfer of personal property relate to the question of when the sale occurred or who should be responsible for damaged or lost goods. These questions may sound easy to answer, but in a legal sense their solution is sometimes difficult.

When an individual is buying something from a merchant, the time of transfer is usually easily established. In the typical cash-register sale, for example, title passes when the clerk accepts the customer's money and hands over the goods. When property is purchased COD (cash on delivery), the time of transfer is not so easily determined. Although an agreement to sell and buy something has already been struck, title is not transferred until the buyer accepts the goods and pays for them. Installment purchases are even more complicated. Generally, title passes when the buyer takes possession of the property. If, for example, you buy a compact disc player on credit, you have title to it as soon as you take possession. If it is stolen or damaged before you've finished paying for it, you are responsible for paying the full purchase price.

Bankruptcy

Even though the U.S. legal system establishes the rules of fair play and offers protection from the unscrupulous, it can't prevent most businesses from taking on too much debt. The legal system does, however, provide help for businesses that find themselves in deep financial trouble. **Bankruptcy** is the legal means of relief for debtors (either individuals or businesses) who are no longer able to meet their financial obligations. U.S. district courts have jurisdiction over all bankruptcy cases and may refer them to adjunct bankruptcy courts.[54]

Voluntary bankruptcy is initiated by the debtor; **involuntary bankruptcy** is initiated by creditors. Generally, under Chapter 7, the debtor's assets will be liquidated, and the proceeds will be divided equitably among the creditors. Under Chapter 11 (which is usually aimed at businesses but does not exclude individuals other than stockbrokers), a business is allowed to reorganize and to continue functioning while it arranges to pay its debts.[55] For the steps involved in a Chapter 11 bankruptcy, see Exhibit 21.6. By entering Chapter 11, a company gains time to cut costs and streamline operations while, in some cases, stopping regular payments to creditors and delaying lawsuits. Many companies emerge from this sort of bankruptcy as leaner, healthier organizations.

Thanks in part to the debt binge of the 1980s, some 60,000 U.S. businesses declared bankruptcy in 1990.[56] Most of the very small firms that file for bankruptcy do not survive. However, the majority of larger firms manage to survive and even to prosper. Some critics contend that many of these companies did not really need to file for bankruptcy but were using bankruptcy to avoid unpleasant obligations. In one controversial case, Continental Airlines used Chapter 11 to avoid paying wages and benefits agreed to during a collective-bargaining session with a union, claiming that it could not meet those obligations and remain in business; the bankruptcy court sided with Continental. Another case involved materials. Manville claimed that it could not afford to pay the costs of settling an estimated 16,500 lawsuits filed against it by people who had become ill after exposure to asbestos. However, the bankruptcy judge ordered Manville to create a $2.5 billion fund to compensate the victims. Experts believe that the settlement will discourage other companies from resorting to bankruptcy under similar circumstances.[57] This case is another example of how government and business interact to establish the ground rules for commerce.

Business Around the World

U.S. and European manufacturers consider Thailand the capital of counterfeiting. Although Asia has a long tradition of imitative flattery, the Thais are notorious for disregarding copyrights and trademarks. Their nonchalant attitude toward pirating is estimated to cost foreign manufacturers $100 million annually in lost sales.

bankruptcy Legal procedure by which a person or a business that is unable to meet financial obligations is relieved of debt

voluntary bankruptcy Bankruptcy proceedings initiated by the debtor

involuntary bankruptcy Bankruptcy proceedings initiated by a firm's creditors

EXHIBIT 21.6

Steps in Chapter 11 Bankruptcy Proceedings

Chapter 11 bankruptcy may buy a debtor time to reorganize finances and continue operating. But using this device to evade financial obligations is extremely risky from a legal standpoint, and declaring bankruptcy may severely damage the reputation and credit rating of a firm or an individual.

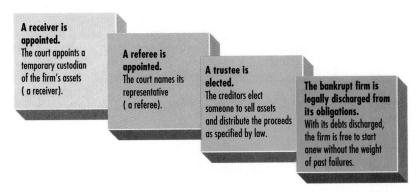

A receiver is appointed. The court appoints a temporary custodian of the firm's assets (a receiver).

A referee is appointed. The court names its representative (a referee).

A trustee is elected. The creditors elect someone to sell assets and distribute the proceeds as specified by law.

The bankrupt firm is legally discharged from its obligations. With its debts discharged, the firm is free to start anew without the weight of past failures.

Three Ways to Protect Your Ideas: Copyrights, Trademarks, and Patents

Several forms of legal protection are available for your creations. Which one you should use depends on what you have created.

COPYRIGHTS

Copyrights protect the creators of literary, dramatic, musical, artistic, and other intellectual works. Any printed, filmed, or recorded material can be copyrighted. The copyright gives its owner the exclusive right to reproduce (copy), sell, or adapt the work he or she has created. Copyright law covers reproduction by photocopying, videotape, and magnetic storage.

The Copyright Office, Library of Congress, will issue a copyright to the creator or to whomever the creator has granted the right to reproduce the work. (A book, for example, may be copyrighted by the author or the publisher.) Copyrights issued after 1977 are valid for the lifetime of the creator plus 50 years. Copyrights issued prior to 1977 are good for 75 years.

Technically, copyright protection exists from the moment you create the material. When you distribute a work, place on the copies a notice that includes the term "copyright" or an abbreviation, the name of the author or creator, and the year of publication or production—for example, "Copyright 1986 Jane Doe." Works can be registered with the Copyright Office for $10. For more information, write to the Copyright Office, Library of Congress, Washington, DC 20559. Ask for Copyright Kit 118, which is available free.

TRADEMARKS

A trademark is any word, name, symbol, or device used to distinguish the product of one manufacturer from those made by others. A service mark is the same thing for services. McDonald's golden arches are one of the most visible of modern trademarks. Brand names can also be registered as trademarks. Examples are Exxon, Polaroid, and Chevrolet.

If properly registered and renewed every 20 years, a trademark generally belongs to its owner forever.

Among the exceptions are popular brand names that have become generic terms, meaning that they describe a whole class of products. A brand-name trademark can become a generic term if the trademark has been allowed to expire, if it has been incorrectly used by its owner (as in the case of Borden's ReaLemon lemon juice, which the Federal Trade Commission ruled was being used by Borden to maintain a monopoly in bottled lemon juice), or if the public comes to equate the name with the class of products (for example, yo-yos).

It is a good idea to have a patent attorney do a "clearance search" before you begin using a mark in order to be sure it isn't already in use. There's a filing fee of $175 for registration with the Patent and Trademark Office. Registration protects your mark for 20 years, and you may renew every 20 years. For more information and registration forms, request a free copy of the booklet *General Information Concerning Trademarks* from the Commissioner of Patents and Trademarks, Patent and Trademark Office, Washington, DC 20231.

PATENTS

A patent protects the invention or discovery of a new and useful process, an article of manufacture, a machine, a chemical substance, or an improvement on any of these. Issued by the U.S. Patent Office, a patent grants the owner the right to exclude others from making, using, or selling the invention for 17 years. After that time, the patent becomes available for common use. On the one hand, patent law guarantees the originator the right to use the discovery exclusively for a relatively long period of time, thus encouraging people to devise new machines, gadgets, and processes. On the other hand, it also ensures that rights to the new item will be released eventually. Other enterprises may be able to make use of it more creatively than its originator.

For more information, get a copy of *Introduction to Patents* from the Small Business Administration, P.O. Box 15434, Fort Worth, TX 76119. *Questions and Answers About Patents* is available free from the Commissioner of Patents and Trademarks, Patent and Trademark Office, Washington, DC 20231.

SUMMARY OF LEARNING OBJECTIVES

1 List three roles of government that affect business.

Government relates to business as a friend, partner, and customer; as a watchdog and regulator; and as a tax collector.

2 Name two general areas in which government regulates business.

Government regulates business activities that might destroy competition or that might harm the public.

3 List five revenue-raising taxes and two regulatory taxes.

Revenue-raising taxes include personal income taxes, corporate income taxes, property taxes, sales taxes, and value-added taxes. Regulatory taxes include excise taxes and customs duties.

4 Explain how business influences government.

Businesses band together to form lobbies that approach politicians in order to influence legislation. They also donate money to political candidates in order to gain access to the legislative process and to help elect those whose attitudes toward their industry or business are favorable.

5 Describe the three sources of law.

Statutory law is developed through the legislative process. Administrative law arises when administrative agencies issue interpretations of statutory law and specific regulations derived from statutory law. Common law is developed in courts on the basis of statutory law, administrative law, and courtroom precedents.

6 Name six areas of law related to business.

Torts, product liability, contracts, agency, property transactions, and bankruptcy are all areas of law related to business.

7 State the seven elements of a valid contract.

A valid contract includes a clear offer, a clear acceptance of the offer, consideration from both parties, genuine assent from both parties, competency, legality, and proper form.

8 Distinguish among real, personal, and intellectual property.

Real property is land and anything that is permanently attached to it, such as trees, buildings, and mineral deposits. Personal property is anything that is not real property. Intellectual property is a type of intangible personal property such as copyrights, trademarks, ideas, songs, or any product of mental creativity.

Meeting a Business Challenge at Disney

Michael D. Eisner, CEO at Disney, knew that if his company had any political clout, it was the economic bonanza Disney could provide to local governments. For an example he had to look no further than Florida, where Disney World had cemented that state's claim as the nation's top tourist mecca: Orlando boasts more hotel rooms than either New York or Los Angeles, and the city's employment growth through the last decade led the country at 73.7 percent. Such a rags-to-riches story greatly helped Eisner in southern California, where he hoped to build a new theme park.

Eisner began by announcing that Disney would build a destination resort and theme park either in Anaheim, home of the original Disneyland, or in Long Beach—essentially pitting the two cities

Michael D. Eisner, CEO of Disney, with Disney characters.

against each other for an economic windfall. The prize for Long Beach would be Port Disney, a $2.8 billion, 360-acre project that would include five new hotels, a shopping and entertainment complex, and a water park with heart-stopping rides and educational exhibits. Long Beach and the surrounding areas would gain about 59,000 construction-related jobs over five years and employment for nearly 50,000 people when the park opened. The projected numbers were about the same for Anaheim, where Eisner suggested he might build Disneyland Resort and WESTCOT Center, in all a $3 billion project with 5,100 new hotel rooms, a shopping and dining district, and a theme park based on Disney World's highly successful EPCOT Center. The announcements themselves were political: Neither city was willing to forgo the impact such a project would bring it, even though both areas were already congested, overdeveloped, and in need of significant overhauls just to accommodate Disney.

The concessions loomed larger for Anaheim officials, who were faced with having to buy real estate and construct huge parking garages before Disney would build its resort park next to Disneyland. The estimated price to the city would be as high as $500 million. And yet city officials still hoped Eisner would pick Anaheim, even as the city struggled to cope with a $20 million deficit—such was the lure of Mickey Mouse. Eisner was able to turn up the political heat by meeting traffic and air pollution criticisms with a detailed transportation plan; Traffic would exit from the Santa Ana Freeway directly into parking garages, from which electric "people movers" would transport tourists into the park without causing any further air pollution. Also, all gasoline-powered motors and generators in Disneyland and in the new park would be replaced with cleaner, more efficient machinery, thus reducing the park's emissions—of course, such changes would be required to gain operations permits from the South Coast Air Quality Management District.

Developing Port Disney in Long Beach required political clout in a different area. Eisner's lawyers and public affairs specialists had legislation introduced in the California legislature that would allow an amusement park to be built on 250 acres of landfill in San Pedro Bay in Long Beach. Politically, Eisner's team of specialists not only helped shepherd the bill through the legislature but also had to overcome objections to it by the Coastal Commission, a separate governmental body whose job is to regulate all commercial activity along California's coastline. Just to lay the groundwork for Port Disney, Eisner's group lobbied city and county officials, coastline regulators, and state legislatures. Indeed, lobbying has become an important part of the company's daily business operations.

Contributions to state and local politicians and to groups supporting ballot initiatives took a sudden jump when Eisner began planning for a new park in southern California. In one year, Disney spent more than $300,000 on local politicians' campaigns, the largest portion earmarked for transportation tax increases in Los Angeles and Orange counties. Even though one local politician said Disney didn't need to make large contributions because "most people have a warm spot in their heart for . . . Mickey Mouse," Eisner wouldn't skimp on his political budget. And the result: Disney decided to build the new theme park in Anaheim. But if Eisner has learned anything from Disney World, it's that his company's success increasingly relies on political clout. Perhaps with that lesson in mind, Disney executives have indicated that some version of Port Disney may eventually be built, so the company may continue working on the plans.

Your Mission: You are a member of Eisner's team of public affairs specialists. Public affairs includes government relations (the political lobbying function of the group) and public relations (a type of lobbying activity aimed at the general public instead of just at the political community). Your duties involve overseeing both areas, which are considered crucial to the success of any new park in southern California.

1. Some current Anaheim property owners (whose parcels around Disneyland will be necessary for a new park) are holding out for even better deals. A couple of them control key pieces of property. Within the Disney corporation, the suggestion has been made to involve public officials or governmental bodies in the company's efforts to obtain those properties. If there is a way to do so, which is the best?

a. Design the park so that the properties in question would be used for public access and infrastructure. Then those parcels might be condemned under eminent domain laws, which would shift the cost to the public.

b. Use political connections, such as state legislators or former national politicians, to pressure the landowners into selling their properties at reasonable prices.

c. Use community connections, such as contiguous landowners, to pressure the landowners into selling their properties at reasonable prices.

d. Do not use political pressure whatsoever; instead continue to negotiate for the properties as the company has been doing.

2. More and better entrance and exit ramps between the park and the Santa Ana Freeway cannot be funded solely by local taxpayers. The costs of undertaking such major transportation renovations are so high that federal money will be necessary. But obtaining the extra funds from Congress would require even greater lobbying efforts, and on a level that Disney is unaccustomed to. What would be the best approach for the company?

a. Let city and county officials (who are already lobbying for extra funding for the freeway-widening project) include the ramps in their efforts within Congress.

b. Send a team of Disney lobbyists to Washington to coordinate lobbying efforts with city and county officials.

c. Hire a Washington lobbying firm to represent the company's interests in the highway-funding legislation.

d. Rely on national advertising to win over the politicians you'll need to obtain federal money.

3. The state landfill legislation that would be necessary to ensure Disney's legal rights to develop a water theme park in Long Beach has reached an impasse in the California legislature. The original sticking point was opposition from the environmentally concerned Coastal Commission, but that group has changed its opinion and supports the legislation. Now the problem is with certain legislators. Time is running out for the company, since the current legislative session is approaching its final gavel. What should the company do?

a. Forget about building the water theme park in Long Beach and continue negotiations with the city of Anaheim for the expansion of Disneyland.

b. Delay choosing a site for the park another year so that lobbying can be continued in hopes of getting the landfill legislation approved in the next legislative session.

c. Build the park in Anaheim and delay a decision on any water theme park in Long Beach for at least the time it takes to build the new park.

d. Increase the company's lobbying efforts within the state legislature, even though such a move could further jeopardize the pending legislation.

4. Convincing elected officials that Disney's resort park should be built is one matter; convincing a skeptical public is another matter altogether. The company's political power in Florida has generated a lot of criticism in that state, which has caused negative publicity nationally and in southern California. What would be the best strategy for selling the new park to southern California's skeptical residents?

a. Do nothing special. React only to negative publicity as is warranted, and as it occurs.

b. Become proactive by arranging for positive publicity through south-ern California newspapers, magazines, and television and radio stations.

c. Become proactive by publishing your own newspaper about the benefits of the proposed park. Distribute that paper to all voters in the affected areas. This would be more costly, but may be more effective.

d. Become proactive by arranging for positive publicity *and* by publishing your own newspaper about the benefits of the proposed park.[58]

KEY TERMS

administrative law (616)
agency (623)
bankruptcy (625)
breach of contract (622)
common law (616)
consent order (616)
consideration (621)
contract (621)
cost-benefit analysis (609)
customs duties (614)
deed (624)
deregulation (609)
excise taxes (613)
express contract (621)
implied contract (621)

intellectual property (624)
intentional tort (618)
interlocking directorates (606)
involuntary bankruptcy (625)
lease (624)
legal detriment (621)
lobbies (614)
market-share liability (620)
negligence (619)
personal property (624)
political action committees (614)
power of attorney (623)
private law (617)
product-liability law (619)
property (624)

public law (617)
real property (624)
stare decisis (616)
statutory law (615)
strict liability (619)
strict product liability (620)
tax credit (611)
title (624)
tort (617)
trust (606)
tying contracts (606)
Uniform Commercial Code (615)
value-added taxes (613)
voluntary bankruptcy (625)
warranty (620)

REVIEW QUESTIONS

1. What is the current trend in antitrust regulation?

2. Why did deregulation become so popular? What are the dangers of deregulation?

3. What is *precedent,* and how does it affect common law?

4. What is the difference between private law and public law?

5. What is the difference between negligence and intentional torts?

6. How is the concept of market-share liability different from the concept of strict product liability?

7. Why is agency important to business?

8. What is the advantage of declaring Chapter 11 bankruptcy? Why is Chapter 11 bankruptcy controversial?

A CASE FOR CRITICAL THINKING

Public Servant or Mailing Monopoly?

The *ka-chunk* of mail passing through a postage meter has become as familiar to business as ledgers and letter openers. In the United States, nearly

every cluster of curbside mailboxes includes one designated "For Metered Mail Only." That's because the U.S. Postal Service loves postage meters;

they save the government over $500 million annually in reduced handling costs. In fact, the Postal Service itself uses nearly 40,000 meters at its service windows, contributing to the $17.4 billion in postage sold each year through postage meters (at 1990 prices, that's half the annual revenue of the Postal Service).

But wait a minute. Aren't those meters made by private manufacturers? Precisely. So just who is reaping the windfall of this love affair with metered mail? According to *The Wall Street Journal,* the thoroughly entrenched champion of the meter business is Pitney Bowes, which commands a full 88 percent of the U.S. market.

The manufacturer's dominance began in 1920, when the U.S. Post Office took a liking to the new device presented by Chicago inventor Arthur H. Pitney and his partner, Walter H. Bowes. In subsequent years, as Pitney Bowes seized and controlled the market for its new meters, the company's near-monopoly did not escape the notice of government officials. The Justice Department filed an antitrust suit against Pitney Bowes in 1959. With no admission of guilt on the part of Pitney, the suit was settled out of court and Pitney agreed to share its patents, royalty-free, with "qualified manufacturers." But a decade later this and other restrictions were lifted, and the Justice Department has since determined that Pitney Bowes is operating within the law.

The problem is that postage meters are so efficient that both government and consumers have come to depend on them. The meters store a large amount of postage bought at one time from the Postal Service (which "sets" the meter according to how much postage is purchased). That postage is

then doled out slowly as each piece of mail is stamped with the appropriate amount. Since this stamping can be done in the consumer's own mail room, it saves time and labor at both ends. And the Postal Service contends that the ultimate benefactor of this cost saving is the mailing public.

Pitney's competitors aren't quite as happy with the chummy relations between the manufacturer and the U.S. government. In recent years, German, French, and Swiss manufacturers have managed to grab 11 percent of Pitney's market share (which used to be 99 percent). Yet because of Pitney's close relations with the Postal Service, competitors complain that they are at an unfair disadvantage. Because the Postal Service tightly regulates meter design in order to protect its postage revenue, competitors must "design around" Pitney's patents, risk patent-infringement suits, or wait until Pitney sells the rights to use its designs (which, of course, Pitney won't do until it has already upgraded its own meters, drawing from its heavy investment in research and development).

To keep its edge, Pitney employs a full-time director of postal regulations in Washington, D.C., just a few steps away from postal headquarters. The director's job is clearly defined: Get all information possible so that Pitney encounters no surprises in terms of new government regulations. When the Postal Service came out with new requirements regarding large-volume mailings, Pitney was ready with a high-tech mailing system designed to help mailers meet those regulations *before* the government specifications had been released to the public. Whether or not the fortuitous timing

was an "absolute fluke," as claimed by a Pitney engineer, Pitney's competitors were left at the starting gate, waiting for the official announcement.

Another technological boon, known as "remote meter reset," allows customers to have their meters reset by telephone rather than having to haul the heavy machines to the post office. Despite some early attempts by the Postal Service to limit Pitney's control of the new technology, the manufacturer managed to delay competitors by haggling over licensing fees. Then Pitney convinced the Postal Service to reword its requirement that Pitney share its patents, in effect giving Pitney a decade-long dominance over the remote reset market.

Meanwhile, the Postal Service has logged some $3.3 million in annual savings from the popular new technology. One postal official admitted that the Postal Service has no stomach to fight Pitney Bowes. "Ours is an extensive and wide-ranging cooperative relationship. We don't want to jeopardize it." And another official explained, "The real loser would be the mailers."[59]

1. How has Pitney Bowes controlled the U.S. market for postage meters?

2. How might the government change its policies to allow freer competition among postage-meter manufacturers?

3. Do you think the Postal Service is correct in its contention that consumers would suffer from any attempt to loosen Pitney Bowes's hold over the postage-meter market?

BUILDING YOUR COMMUNICATION SKILLS

Select a business lobby by consulting the *Encyclopedia of Associations*, and examine the influence of that group on the process of government. Pre-

pare a brief report summarizing the information you have obtained about that lobby. As directed by your instructor, share your report with mem-

bers of your class, and discuss the positive and negative impact of these groups.

KEEPING CURRENT USING *THE WALL STREET JOURNAL*

Choose an article from *The Wall Street Journal* that relates to one of the following topics:

▶ Deregulation

▶ Product liability

▶ Contract disputes

▶ Business taxation

▶ Business lobbying and political action committees (PACs)

1. What is the significance of the event reported in the article? Does it point to a new development in this area or does it relate to a long-standing problem or issue?

2. Who is affected by this development? Is it expected to touch other companies? an entire industry? the general public?

3. Is the local, state, or federal government involved in this situation? If so, what role does government play—watchdog/regulator, tax collector/enforcer, or a combination of these roles?

CHAPTER 22

LEARNING OBJECTIVES

After studying this chapter, you will be able to

1 Explain the difference between pure risk and speculative risk.

2 Discuss the risk-management techniques available to a risk manager.

3 Distinguish uninsurable risks from insurable risks.

4 Clarify how insurance companies decide the amount of income they need to generate from premiums.

5 List the two main government insurance programs.

6 Name four types of business risks that are often insured.

7 Identify the two main types of health-insurance coverage.

8 Describe the five main forms of life insurance.

Risk Management and Insurance

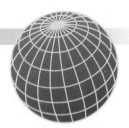

Facing a Business Challenge at Marriott

TAKING THE "HOSPITAL" OUT OF HOSPITALITY

J. W. Marriott, Jr., chairman of the international lodging and hospitality corporation, was not pleased. He expected to encounter some extra and unforeseen costs when he acquired seven companies, introduced two major hotel divisions, and formed a child-care venture over a seven-year period. But he never expected to hear operations managers complain so loudly or so bitterly about runaway insurance costs, and he never expected to see a $10 million increase in the company's reserves for funding its insurance program. Insurance costs had gotten out of hand, and he wanted to know *why:* Why was the corporation charging each operating unit self-insurance premiums that increased in each of five consecutive years, with annual increases of up to 38 percent for some units over a three-year period? Why were workers' compensation claims rising faster than expected during the company's expansion to more than 209,000 employees and to more than 150,000 hotel rooms worldwide? And why was the cost of controlling risks becoming prohibitive?

Insurance costs had become a problem years earlier in ways that Marriott could not control, when catastrophic fires swept through several competing hotels. In the largest single tragedy, 84 people died and another 700 were injured in a fire at the MGM Grand Hotel in Las Vegas. Newsmaking fires at three other hotels killed 44 and injured 240. Although Marriott's hotels passed unscathed through the series of disasters, the company's liability coverage did not: Commercial insurance (once available to all lodging companies) virtually dried up. In one year alone, Marriott's commercial insurance was cut in half—and that coverage had been pieced together like a patchwork quilt.

But Marriott's insurance problems weren't caused solely by the fallout from others' misfortunes; the numbers of workers' compensation claims were rising, and medical costs were escalating more rapidly than the general level of inflation. First, the sudden increase of worker compensation claims from injured employees was coming from companies that Marriott had acquired (such as the Howard Johnson hotel/restaurant chain and Saga, one of the nation's largest food-service companies with sizable operations at major universities and large health-care institutions). Essentially, these companies had poor records for safety before they were acquired, and their lax practices were allowed to continue by Marriott managers, who assumed that the new companies would automatically absorb Marriott's corporate culture. Second, workers' compensation claims were being processed by third-party administrators, which was a common business practice throughout the United States but which was costing more and more as the number of claims increased. Finally, and probably most troublesome, the costs of health care and lost productivity during employee recuperation were increasing. The longer employees were away from work, the more costly their accidents became for the corporation.

Marriott faced a serious and perplexing problem: The number of insurance claims being filed against the corporation was increasing, health-care costs were skyrocketing, and commercial insurance coverage was becoming more difficult—and more expensive—to purchase. How could the company reduce the number of workers' compensation claims? How could it lower health-care costs? How could Marriott obtain commercial insurance coverage more easily and more cheaply?[1]

▶ PROTECTION AGAINST RISK

risk The threat of loss

Like any business, Marriott must protect itself from **risk,** the threat of loss. Reasonable or not, risks are inescapable in business because the possibilities for loss are as real as the prospects for profit. Even though managers do everything they can to ensure that their businesses succeed, they cannot guard against every conceivable form of risk. Consider the experience of Alpine Meadows, a ski resort near Lake Tahoe. During a violent snowstorm, the resort closed its 13 lifts and warned skiers to stay off the slopes. Ironically, an avalanche buried the parking lot and ski-patrol building—not the ski trails. The families of three victims sued Alpine Meadows for $10 million in **damages,** the amount the court awards a plaintiff in a successful lawsuit. Although the jury ruled that the resort was not responsible, Alpine Meadows incurred legal fees of $700,000 defending itself, and its liability premiums doubled to $800,000 per year.[2]

damages Amount a court awards a plaintiff in a successful lawsuit

Pure Risk Versus Speculative Risk

pure risk Risk that involves the chance of loss only

An avalanche represents one kind of risk that no business can predict or escape. **Pure risk** is the threat of a loss without the possibility of gain. In other words, a disaster such as an earthquake or a fire is costly for the business it strikes, but the fact that no disaster occurs contributes nothing to a firm's profit. It is pure risk that insurance primarily deals with.

speculative risk Risk that involves the chance of both loss and profit

Speculative risk, on the other hand, is the type of risk that offers the prospect of making a profit; it prompts people to go into business in the first place. Every business accepts the possibility of losing money in order to make money. Consider Sure-Grip International, a producer of roller skates and skateboards. When roller skating became a sudden craze among teenagers, the 24-year-old son of Sure-Grip's president decided to make himself a pair of skates, using an old pair of Adidas jogging shoes with wheels attached to the soles. The resulting Joggers represented a real departure from the traditional high-top boot styles. There was no guarantee that the public would prefer the new skates, but the company was willing to take a chance. It took a speculative risk in deciding to mass produce the new style, and the risk paid off. Within eight months, Sure-Grip became the leading manufacturer of outdoor skates.[3]

At the same time, Sure-Grip was facing a variety of pure risks: Fires, floods, or earthquakes could have destroyed the factory; inventory might have been stolen from the warehouse; the company's delivery trucks might have been involved in accidents; or someone might have been hurt by defective skates. The company would not have benefited from any of these events. At best, it could try to prevent a loss.

Risk Management

The process of reducing the threat of loss from uncontrollable events is called **risk management.** Those areas of risk in which a potential for loss exists are called **loss exposures,** and they fall under four headings: (1) loss of property (due to destruction or theft of tangible or intangible assets); (2) loss of income (either through decreased revenues or through increased expenses resulting from an accidental event); (3) legal liability to others, including employees; and (4) loss of the services of key personnel (through accidental injury or death).[4]

One event may involve several kinds of losses. For example, when Ashland Oil had a storage tank collapse, 1 million gallons of diesel fuel oil spilled into the Monongahela River and then flowed into the Ohio River. As a result of this one accident, Ashland suffered property loss (destruction of the tank, loss of fuel, and damage to other Ashland equipment and property), income loss (increased expense of cleaning up the spill), and liability loss (damages claimed by property owners, by local businesses, and in class-action suits).[5]

The function of preventing losses is typically performed by the risk manager, whose job has become increasingly complex and critical. Risk managers must be able to implement a program that is cost-effective and that provides maximum risk protection. Thus they must (1) assess the risk, (2) choose the risk-management techniques that provide an appropriate mix of insurance and loss-prevention methods, and (3) implement and monitor those techniques.[6]

Risk Assessment

Consider just one of the many loss exposures that a manufacturer of stuffed toys must face: the product-liability exposure. First, the manufacturer must identify the ways a consumer (most likely a child) can be injured by a stuffed toy. Among numerous possibilities, the child might choke on button eyes, get sick from eating the stuffing, or have an allergic reaction to any material in the toy. Second, the company must identify any possible flaws in the production or marketing of the toys that might lead to one of these injuries; for example, a child may have an allergic reaction to the toy if its materials are not carefully tested for allergenic substances, if impurities enter the toy during manufacture, or if the toy is not properly packaged (allowing foreign substances to reach it). Third, the manufacturer must analyze the possibilities in order to compute possible product-liability losses. Because it is often impossible to identify all the ways a product might cause injury or property damage, and because it is often impossible to calculate an exact value for these losses, the risk manager must often be satisfied with rough estimates.

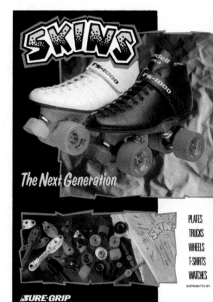

When Sure-Grip International decided to mass produce its new style of skate, the company was taking a speculative risk, seeking the possibility of making larger profits.

risk management Process of evaluating and minimizing the risks faced by a company

loss exposures Areas of risk in which a potential for loss exists

Before Hasbro begins manufacturing stuffed toys in Rhode Island, it must make a risk assessment, considering any and all loss exposures it may encounter, including product liability.

Risk-Management Techniques

Once all risks have been assessed, the risk manager must consider the techniques available to deal with the problems. The two categories of techniques are risk control and risk financing.

risk-control techniques Methods of minimizing losses

RISK CONTROL   Risk managers use **risk-control techniques** to minimize the losses that strike an organization:

▶ *Risk avoidance.* A risk manager might try to completely eliminate the chance of a particular type of loss. With rare exception, such risk avoidance is extremely difficult. The stuffed-toy manufacturer could avoid being sued for a child's allergic reaction by not making stuffed toys, but of course the company would also be out of business.

▶ *Loss prevention.* A risk manager may try to reduce (but not totally eliminate) the chance of a given loss. The toy manufacturer might reduce the risk of children having allergic reactions to the stuffed toys by testing the materials before production, by controlling impurities during manufacture, or by carefully packaging each toy to guard against foreign substances. Steps taken for other kinds of loss exposures typically include installing overhead sprinklers to prevent extensive damage from fire, putting safety locks on doors to prevent theft, and checking equipment to prevent accidents.

▶ *Loss reduction.* A risk manager may try to reduce the severity of the losses that do occur. By adhering to all government regulations, the toy company can avoid the addition of punitive damages to any damages the company may have to pay an injured consumer. Also, by maintaining good relations with consumers whose children do have allergic reactions, and by paying their medical expenses, the toy company can reduce the size of the claims they may have to pay.

▶ *Risk-control transfer.* A risk manager may try to eliminate risk by transferring to some other person or group either (1) the actual property or activity responsible for the risk or (2) the responsibility for the risk. A firm can sell a building to eliminate the risks associated with ownership, or a contractor already commited to a job can eliminate the risk of cost increases by hiring a subcontractor. Such transfers are closely related to risk avoidance. A risk manager may also try to eliminate risk by transferring responsibility, that is, by transferring the risk itself. A tenant may be able to convince a landlord to take any responsibility for damage to the landlord's property. Or a manufacturer may make a retailer take responsibility for any product damage occurring after products leave the manufacturing facility. The idea of transfer also applies in risk-financing techniques, discussed next.

risk-financing techniques Paying to restore losses

RISK FINANCING   Risk managers use **risk-financing techniques** to pay (at the least possible cost) to restore losses that occur despite the organization's risk-control efforts:

▶ *Risk retention.* A risk manager may choose to pay losses with funds that originate within the organization. Many companies draw on current revenues or set aside a "contingency fund" to cover unexpected losses. Some businesses form their own liability-insurance companies. Actually, the risk-retention programs of various businesses and city governments fall along a continuum. Lederle Laboratories decided to **self-insure** with a liability reserve fund, putting aside a certain sum each year to cover possible liability losses. Du Pont, on the other hand, invested $20 million in the creation of two companies that insure not only Du Pont but also 550 other businesses. Together with 50 other firms, Control Data Corporation formed Corporate Officers & Directors Assurance.[7] However, self-insuring differs greatly from "going naked" (having no reserve funds). In a small company, setting aside enough money to cover catastrophes is virtually impossible. If disaster strikes, companies that cannot afford insurance may have to borrow funds to cover the losses, or they could be forced out of business.

self-insurance Arrangement whereby a company insures itself by accumulating funds to pay for any losses, rather than buying insurance from another company

▶ *Risk-financing transfer.* A risk manager may choose to limit risk by paying losses with funds that originate outside the organization. By purchasing **insurance**, companies transfer the risk of loss to an insurance firm, which agrees to pay for certain types of losses. For example, Hardee's Food Systems buys catastrophe insurance for any losses over $2 million. In exchange, the insurance firm collects a fee known as a **premium.**

insurance Written contract that transfers to an insurer the financial responsibility for any losses

premium Fee that the insured pays the insurer for coverage against losses

Proper risk management nearly always requires a combination of at least one risk-control technique and at least one risk-financing technique.

Implementing and Monitoring Risk-Management Techniques

Risk managers implement those techniques that contribute to the total value of the organization, which is best measured through the organization's net cash flows. Thus the stuffed-toy manufacturer must decide whether testing materials, controlling impurities during manufacture, or packaging toys individually would best fit the company's cash flow. Of course, the company may choose all three. Risk managers must also decide whether purchasing conventional insurance or establishing some form of self-insurance would have the least impact on the company while providing the best coverage. In the end, the best choice may be a combination of several options.

Monitoring the risk-management program determines whether the original choice of techniques was correct and, if so, whether conditions have changed enough to warrant choosing new techniques. Effective monitoring has three aspects: (1) setting standards for defining acceptable performance, (2) comparing actual results with these standards, and (3) correcting any technique to comply more fully with the standards.

Insurable and Uninsurable Risks

Risk managers must distinguish between insurable and uninsurable risks (see Exhibit 22.1). Outside insurers are unwilling to promise they will pay for losses unless they can reasonably expect that they won't have to. Most (but not all) pure risks are insurable; in general, speculative risks are not insurable.

Uninsurable Risks

An **uninsurable risk** is one that no insurance company will agree to cover. It is possible to purchase disaster insurance against such calamities as floods (available from the federal government), hurricanes, tornadoes, and earthquakes. But insurers are reluctant or unwilling to consider covering potential government actions and general economic conditions. Such uncertainties as changes in the law and economic fluctuations are beyond the realm of insurance.

uninsurable risk Risk that few, if any, insurance companies will assume because of the difficulty of calculating the probability of loss

Sometimes uninsurable risks become insurable when enough data become available to permit accurate estimation of future losses. Insurers were once reluctant to cover passengers on airplanes, but decades of experience have made these risks predictable. Similarly, companies can now buy insurance against the prospect of a foreign country seizing their overseas factories, mines, or offices.

EXHIBIT 22.1

Insurable and Uninsurable Risks

Insurance companies consider some pure risks insurable. They usually view speculative risks as uninsurable. (Some pure risks such as flood and strike are also considered uninsurable.)

Insurable	Uninsurable
Property risks: Uncertainty surrounding the occurrence of loss from perils that cause 1. Direct loss of property 2. Indirect loss of property	**Market risks:** Factors that may result in loss of property or income, such as 1. Price changes, seasonal or cyclical 2. Consumer indifference 3. Style changes 4. Competition offered by a better product
Personal risks; Uncertainty surrounding the occurrence of loss due to 1. Premature death 2. Physical disability 3. Old age	**Political risks:** Uncertainty surrounding the occurrence of 1. Overthrow of the government or war 2. Restrictions imposed on free trade 3. Unreasonable or punitive taxation 4. Restrictions on free exchange of currencies
Legal liability risks: Uncertainty surrounding the occurrence of loss arising out of 1. Use of automobiles 2. Occupancy of buildings 3. Employment 4. Manufacture of products 5. Professional misconduct	**Production risks:** Uncertainties surrounding the occurrence of 1. Failure of machinary to function economically 2. Failure to solve technical problems 3. Exhaustion of raw-material resources 4. Strikes, absenteeism, labor unrest
	Personal risks: Uncertainty surrounding the occurrence of 1. Unemployment 2. Poverty from factors such as divorce, lack of education or opportunity, loss of health from military service

---

insurable risk Risk for which an acceptable probability of loss may be calculated and that an insurance company might therefore be willing to cover

Earthquakes such as the one that caused such devastation at Coalinga, California, are insurable risks—unlike potential government actions and general economic conditions.

Insurable Risks

An **insurable risk,** one that an insurance company will cover, generally meets the following requirements:

▶ *The peril covered must not result from deliberate actions of the insured.* Insurers do not pay for losses that are intentionally caused by the insured, at the insured's direction, or with the insured's collusion. For example, a fire-insurance policy excludes loss caused by the insured's own arson. However, the same policy does cover losses caused by an employee's arson.

▶ *Losses must be calculable, and the cost of insuring must be economically feasible.* To operate profitably, insurance companies must have data on the frequency and severity of losses caused by a given peril. If this information covers a long period of time and is based on a large number of cases, insurance companies can usually predict how many losses will occur in the future. For example, the death rate per 1,000 people in the United States has been calculated with great precision, and insurance companies use this information to set policyholders' life-insurance premiums.

▶ *A large number of similar cases must be subject to the same peril.* The more cases there are in a given category, the more likely it is that future experience will reflect insurance-company predictions. Insurance companies are therefore more willing to issue insurance for risks that many businesses or individuals face. For example, fire is a common danger that threatens virtually all buildings, so insurance for loss by fire is usually easy to come by. Even though Marriott hotels had trouble getting affordable fire insurance, the opportunity to obtain coverage was always there. However, the possibility that Monica Seles will fracture her serving arm and miss several lucrative tennis matches is an unusual risk because there is only one Monica Seles. Most insurance companies would not consider issuing this sort of insurance.

▶ *The peril must be unlikely to affect all insured simultaneously.* Unless an insurance company spreads its coverage over large geographic areas or a broad population base, a single disaster might force it to pay out on all its policies at once.

▶ *The possible loss must be financially serious to the insured.* An insurance company could not afford the paperwork involved in handling numerous small **claims** (demands by the insured that the insurance company pay for a loss) of a few dollars each, nor would a business be likely to insure such a small loss. As a result, many policies have a clause specifying that the insurance company will pay only that part of a loss greater than an amount stated in the policy. This amount, the **deductible**, represents small losses that the insured has agreed to absorb. Your health insurer, for example, may require you to pay the first $100 of your physician's fees, and the company that insures your car may require you to pay the first $200 of any needed repairs.

claims Demands for payment by an insurance company due to some loss by the insured

deductible Amount of loss that must be paid by the insured before the insurer will pay for the rest

▶ THE INSURANCE INDUSTRY

In its simplest form, the idea of insurance is probably as old as humankind. Since the days of the cave dweller, groups of people have banded together to help one another in times of trouble. They have stored food in years of plenty so that they would have something to draw on during years of famine. If their neighbor's house burned, they helped rebuild it, with the tacit understanding that the favor would be returned if they were ever in need. Over the years, the informal cooperation between neighbors gradually became institutionalized. Mutual-aid societies were formed, and dues were collected from the members for use in emergencies. Ultimately, modern insurance companies emerged, with professional management.

Basic Insurance Concepts

Private insurance companies are businesses. The product they sell is financial protection. To succeed, they must cover their costs, which include payments to cover the losses of policyholders as well as sales and administrative expenses, dividends, and taxes.

To decide how much income they need to generate from premiums, insurance companies must predict the amount they will probably have to pay in claims over a given period. The amount of the premium for a specific type of risk is based mainly on the probability of loss. For example, because fire is a greater risk for wooden than for brick buildings, insurance premiums tend to be higher for wooden structures. The people who figure out how many deaths, illnesses, fires, accidents, natural disasters, and so on, are likely to occur over the course of a year are called **actuaries;** they develop "actuarial tables" of probabilities for various occurrences that can be used to calculate premiums. **Underwriters,** insurers, then decide which risks to insure and under what terms.

When calculating probabilities, actuaries rely on the **law of large numbers**— that is, the larger the pool of insured parties, the more accurate the predictions of the loss per unit. Insurance companies don't count on making a profit on any particular policy, nor do they count on paying for a single policyholder's losses out of the premium paid by that particular policyholder. Rather, each insurance company pays for a loss by drawing money out of the pool of premiums it has received from all its policyholders (see Exhibit 22.2). In this way, the insurance company redistributes the cost of losses from a single individual to a large number of policyholders.

actuaries Persons employed by an insurance company to compute expected losses and to calculate the cost of premiums

underwriters Insurance company employees who decide which risks to insure, for how much, and for what premiums

law of large numbers Principle that the larger the group on which probabilities are calculated, the more accurate the predictive value

EXHIBIT 22.2

How the Law of Large Numbers Works

An insurance company covers the cost of a policyholder's loss out of the premiums paid by a large pool of policyholders. Thus, if 100 policyholders pay $400 each to insure against fire damage, the insurance company can afford to compensate one policyholder who actually suffers fire damage with $40,000.

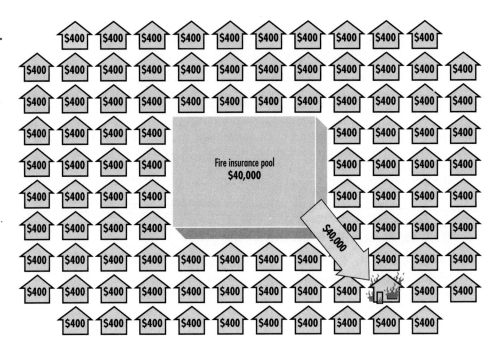

Insurance Providers

When most people think of insurance, they think of private insurance—the kind purchased from an insurance company. Actually, the largest single source of insurance in the United States is the government, which accounts for nearly half of the total insurance premiums collected for all types of coverage combined. Some 29 percent of the federal government's budget dollar comes from social insurance receipts.[8]

Government Insurance Programs

Most government insurance programs are designed to protect people from loss of income, either because they have reached retirement age or because they have lost their job or become disabled. Unlike private insurance, which is voluntarily chosen by the insured, government-sponsored programs are compulsory. The largest of the public insurance programs is Social Security, which was created by the federal government during the Great Depression of the 1930s. Officially known as Old-Age, Survivors, Disability, and Health Insurance, this program covers 9 out of 10 workers.

The basic purpose of the Social Security program is to provide a minimum level of income for retirees, their survivors, and their dependents, as well as for the permanently disabled. The program also provides hospital and medical payments—known as Medicare—for people age 65 and over. Social Security benefits vary, depending on how long a worker has contributed to the system. In 1991, some 40.1 million people received Social Security benefits.[9] The program is funded by a tax paid by workers and their employers. In most cases, these taxes are automatically deducted from each paycheck. Currently, there are three workers for every beneficiary, but by the year 2000, the ratio of workers to retirees will be 2 to 1.[10]

The Social Security Act of 1935 also provided for federal and state cooperation to insure workers against unemployment. The cost is borne by employers. A worker who becomes unemployed for reasons not related to performance is entitled to collect benefits. The amount of the benefit is usually tied to the employee's total earnings during the previous year, but both the amount and the length of time the benefit is available vary from state to state.

Private Insurance Companies

About 5,800 private insurance companies are currently doing business in the United States; most are either stock or mutual companies.[11] A **stock company** is a profit-making corporation with shareholders who expect to receive dividends on their investment in the company. A **mutual company** is a nonprofit cooperative owned by the policyholders; excess income may be returned to the policyholders, either in the form of dividends or as a reduction in their insurance premiums. In terms of premium volume, a firm such as Marriott would probably go to stock companies for property and liability insurance, and it would probably go to mutual companies for medical and life insurance.

INTERNATIONAL INSURERS   The most famous international insurer is Lloyd's of London, an association of individuals who issue insurance as members of syndicates within the Lloyd's organization. Lloyd's is one of a handful of companies that take on unusual risks, such as insuring racehorses, athletes, movie stars, and oil tankers operating in a war zone. Some insurance companies provide various types of coverage for fledgling exporters. When companies start to send people and products overseas, they expose themselves to a wide range of risks, such as workers' compensation claims, product-liability suits, and kidnapping. CIGNA Property and Casualty Group, the Chubb Group of Insurance Companies, and American International Global are three international insurers that offer special insurance packages tailored to the needs of small exporters.[12]

ENVIRONMENTAL INSURERS   The insurer's role in certain types of environmental damage is still being debated—particularly in the area of toxic waste damage. Insurers argue that the typical property policy was never intended to cover the kinds of damage resulting from long-term waste disposal by businesses. However, in California the state supreme court recently ruled that the cost of cleaning up toxic pollution at waste dumps can indeed be charged to the polluters' insurance companies under standard coverage for property damage.[13] Even a small amount of toxic waste can expose a company to substantial risk. For example, a small manufacturer in California neglected to repair a leaky gasoline storage tank that it kept on the property for its delivery trucks. When the owner tried to refinance the property, the appraiser noted the oily patch of dirt, which put the refinance on hold and created a costly cleanup project.

Insurance-Industry Problems

Historically, the insurance industry has gone through cycles of profit and loss that depend on financial markets. When interest rates are high, insurance companies make extra money from investment income, and premiums go down. When interest rates fall, investment income diminishes, and companies must rely more heavily on premiums, which then go up. The length of these cycles is

stock company Profit-making insurance company owned by shareholders

mutual company Nonprofit insurance company owned by the policyholders

Business Around the World

Lloyd's of London is changing a 300-year-old policy, limiting the liability of its wealthy investors who traditionally pay off claims—down to their last penny. Major disasters such as Hurricane Hugo and the *Exxon Valdez* oil spill have raised doubts about the company's ability to continue providing worldwide high-risk insurance.

usually three years up and three years down, but in the last decade a seven-year downturn was followed by only two years of upturn before profits began dipping again. Some analysts worry that if rates and premiums drop too sharply or for too long, insurance companies will become insolvent.[14]

People in the United States are already paying some $500 billion to rescue the insolvent firms in the savings and loan industry. But these failing thrifts weren't the only companies to invest in inflated real estate and shaky junk bonds. Insurance companies are seeing similar investments plummet. Although the insurance industry in general remains healthy, the number of individual companies having difficulty is increasing.

For example, thousands of West Virginians were left to face $50 million in unpaid medical bills when Blue Cross & Blue Shield of West Virginia collapsed in 1991.[15] That same year, Executive Life Insurance failed its 400,000 customers nationwide when California and New York state regulators seized the troubled company.[16]

Other insurers experiencing losses or shrinking profits are cutting back on or pulling out of whole areas of insurance. Once insurers such as Aetna, Travelers, and Continental attempted to sell all things to all people: life policies to newly-weds, fire insurance to homeowners, and liability coverage to corporations. But Aetna, Travelers, and Cigna are now making major pushes in group health insurance. Chubb is focusing on large companies and wealthy individuals. Continental has sold its life- and health-insurance interests, to concentrate on selling property and casualty insurance. And Crum & Forster (the insurance subsidiary of Xerox) has been shrinking its workers' compensation division.[17]

► TYPES OF BUSINESS INSURANCE

If you were starting a business, what type of insurance would you need? To some extent, the answer to that question would depend on the type of business you were in. In general, however, you would probably want to cover your property against losses and protect assets such as cash and securities from loss due to natural or human causes. In the discussion of risk management, four types of loss exposure are listed: loss of property, loss of income, liability, and loss of services of key personnel. Businesses can purchase insurance to cover each of these four areas (see Exhibit 22.3).

Loss of Property

Property can be lost through a variety of causes, including accidental damage, natural disaster, and theft. Property can also be lost through employee dishonesty and nonperformance.

Loss Due to Destruction or Theft

When a cannery in California ships jars of pizza sauce by truck to New York, the goods face unavoidable risks in transit. One wrong turn could cover a whole hillside with broken glass and sauce, which would represent a sizable loss to the manufacturer. The canning factory itself is vulnerable to fire, flood, and (especially in California) earthquake.

EXHIBIT 22.3 ▶ Business Risks and Protection

Here are some of the more widely purchased types of business insurance available.

RISK	PROTECTION
Loss of property	
Due to destruction or theft	Fire insurance
	Disaster insurance
	Marine insurance
	Automobile insurance
Due to dishonesty or nonperformance	Fidelity bonding
	Surety bonding
	Credit life insurance
	Crime insurance
Loss of income	Business-interruption insurance
	Extra-expense insurance
	Contingent business-interruption insurance
Liability	Comprehensive general liability insurance
	Automobile liability insurance
	Workers' compensation insurance
	Umbrella liability insurance
	Professional liability insurance
Loss of key personnel	Key-person insurance

Property insurance covers the insured for physical damage to or destruction of property and also for its loss by theft. In purchasing property insurance, the buyer has a choice between two options: replacement-cost coverage or depreciated-value coverage (actual cash value insured). **Replacement-cost** coverage is more expensive but provides more protection because it entitles the policyholder to buy new property to replace the old. **Depreciated-value** coverage assumes that the property that was lost or damaged was worth less than new property because the owner had used it for some period of time.

Loss Due to Dishonesty or Nonperformance

Dishonest employees and criminals outside the company pose yet another threat to business property and assets. Various ways exist for dealing with this problem. One is a **fidelity bond,** which protects the insured business against dishonest acts committed by employees, such as embezzlement, forgery, and theft.

Another is a **surety bond,** a three-party contract in which one party agrees to be responsible to a second party for the obligations of a third party. For example, in public construction projects, the law requires surety bonds that guarantee the performance of every contract. The insurance company would pay damages for any uncompleted or incompetent work of its insured (a construction company, for example) that had been awarded a contract by a municipality. Similar bonds are required for municipal contracts for garbage collection and snow removal as well as for elected officials, who must be insured against untrustworthiness while in office. Surety bonds are also commonly used in the private sector. Railroads, for example, permit shippers to defer payment of freight charges with the filing of a bond; corporations reissue lost or destroyed securities if there is a satisfactory bond.[18]

property insurance Insurance that provides coverage for physical damage to, or destruction of, property

replacement cost Cost of replacing a lost or damaged item with a new one

depreciated value Value of something after it has been in use for a time, which is less than its value when new

fidelity bond Coverage that protects employers from dishonesty on the part of employees

surety bond Coverage that protects companies against losses incurred through nonperformance of a contract

credit life insurance Coverage that guarantees repayment of a loan or an installment contract if the borrower dies

crime insurance Insurance against loss from theft

Another form of insurance against loss due to nonperformance is **credit life insurance,** which guarantees repayment of the amount due on a loan or an installment contract if the borrower dies. Yet another is **crime insurance,** which covers loss from theft of any kind, whether it is burglary (forcible entry into the premises) or robbery (taking property from another person by violence or the threat of violence).

Loss of Income

A fire in a supermarket chain's warehouse would result in property loss, but that's only part of the story. Fires also disrupt the business, often costing the company more than repairs or replacement of damaged stock. Expenses continue—salaries, interest payments, rent—but no revenues are coming in. Disruption also results in new expenses: leasing temporary space, paying overtime to meet work schedules with a reduced capacity, or buying additional advertising to assure the public that the business still exists. A prolonged interruption of business could even cause bankruptcy.

business-interruption insurance Insurance that covers losses resulting from temporary business closings

extra-expense insurance Insurance that covers the added expense of operating the business in temporary facilities after an event such as a fire

contingent business-interruption insurance Insurance that protects a business from losses due to an interruption in the delivery of supplies

For this reason many companies carry property insurance protection that goes beyond mere loss of property. Available coverage includes **business-interruption insurance,** which protects the insured against lost profits and continuing expenses when a fire or other disaster causes a company to shut down temporarily; **extra-expense insurance,** which pays the additional costs of maintaining operations in temporary quarters; and **contingent business-interruption insurance,** which protects against loss of profit due to fire or other disaster that interrupts the operations of an important supplier.

Liability

liability insurance Insurance that covers losses arising either from injury to an individual or from damage to other people's property

All licensed drivers are aware that they may be held liable for substantial damages if they cause an auto accident. Similarly, businesses are liable for any injury they cause to a person or to the property of others. **Liability insurance** covers the insured for losses arising from injury to an individual, death due to something the company does, and damage to the property of others. During the liability-insurance crisis of the mid-1980s—when premiums soared and availability plunged—many small businesses found liability insurance unaffordable or impossible to obtain. Now, however, most small businesses find it relatively easy to obtain the coverage they need.[19]

Sources of Liability

What sorts of accidents or corporate practices might make a company liable for damages? The types of accidents that most commonly result in legal action are injuries received on the company's property, injuries caused by the company's products, injuries to the company's own employees, and injuries from professional malpractice. Injuries received on the company's property may affect employees or outsiders; for instance, an elevator accident may involve either, whereas injury resulting from the collapse of metal shelving in a warehouse is likely to affect employees only. Examples of injuries caused by a company's products are food poisoning and choking on a loose toy part. Malpractice includes bodily injury arising from treatment by doctors and dentists and loss of assets due to mishandling by lawyers and accountants.

Types of Liability Insurance

To accommodate these various forms of liability, the insurance industry has created various types of liability policies.

COMPREHENSIVE GENERAL LIABILITY For basic coverage, most companies carry **comprehensive general liability insurance,** which automatically provides protection against all forms of liability not specifically excluded under the terms of the policy. Most comprehensive general liability policies cover liability for operations on the business premises, product liability, completed operations, and operations of independent contractors.[20] **Product-liability** coverage protects insured companies from being threatened financially when someone claims that one of their products caused damage, injury, or death.

When purchasing liability insurance, the buyer can choose between two options. *Occurrence policies* cover losses that occur during the policy period, no matter when the claim is made. *Claims-made policies* cover claims filed during the policy period for losses that occurred on or after some retroactive date, which may be the beginning of the policy period or some earlier date.[21]

AUTOMOBILE LIABILITY Many companies also carry insurance that specifically covers liability connected with any vehicles owned or operated by the company. In states having **no-fault insurance laws,** which limit lawsuits connected with auto accidents, this form of coverage is less important.

WORKERS' COMPENSATION Another form of liability coverage, **workers' compensation insurance,** pays the medical bills of employees who are hurt or become ill as a result of their work. It covers loss of income by occupationally injured or diseased workers plus rehabilitation expenses for these workers, and it provides death benefits to the survivors of any employee killed on the job. In most cases, it covers both full- and part-time employees. Workers' compensation insurance is required by law throughout the United States. It can be obtained through adequate self-insurance in some states, from state funds in some states, and from a private insurer in most states. The cost to employers for workers' compensation coverage totaled almost $70 billion in 1990, and experts predict that figure will double every five years.[22]

An employee who is temporarily disabled receives weekly benefits. If the injury is fatal, dependents receive weekly payments for a specified period. In nearly all states, the weekly benefit rate for an injured worker is normally two-thirds of the employee's weekly wage.

Over the years the courts have interpreted workers' compensation laws broadly, holding employers liable for injuries related even indirectly to an employee's work. In one case, a worker in Rhode Island got angry, punched a coffee machine, and permanently damaged an arm. The worker was awarded $7,500 because the injury was "deemed to have met the requirements for a compensable situation—arising out of and in the course of employment."[23]

The premiums for workers' compensation vary from state to state, depending on the hazards in particular lines of work. Approximately 400 premium rate classifications range from as low as $.48 per $100 of payroll for clerical workers to more than $60 per $100 of payroll for bridge workers. It is important for businesses to monitor their classification to ensure they are not classified at a higher level of risk than necessary. When Kansas City–based Hickerson Cable Installation opened a new branch, its workers' compensation rates jumped from

Companies and government agencies may want to purchase comprehensive general liability insurance to protect themselves against financial claims from injury or death resulting from a variety of services. For example, this low-income housing unit in Baltimore is being decontaminated as part of Maryland's pilot project for lead paint abatement. Although the project is no longer active, future tenants might hold the state of Maryland responsible for any signs of poisoning from remaining lead.

comprehensive general liability insurance *Liability insurance that covers a wide variety of losses, except certain losses specifically mentioned in the policy*

product liability *Company's responsibility for injuries or damages that result from use of a product the company manufactures or distributes*

no-fault insurance laws *Laws limiting lawsuits connected with auto accidents*

workers' compensation insurance *Insurance that partially replaces lost income, medical costs, and rehabilitation expenses for employees who are injured on the job*

Making sure employees have—and use—protective clothing and other safety devices is one way companies can reduce risk.

umbrella policies *Insurance that provides businesses with coverage beyond what is provided by a basic liability policy*

$1.80 per $100 to $3 per $100. After doing some checking, the owner found out his insurance agent had classified Hickerson with companies that string cable lines between telephone poles when he should have classified it with underground cable installers.[24]

Workers' compensation premiums have more than doubled in recent years, for a variety of reasons: Higher benefits are being paid as wages and living costs rise; employees are not encouraged to control costs through cost sharing; the courts have expanded the definition of "work-related injuries," as we have seen; and lawsuits have opened up new areas of coverage. Work-related illness, especially lung ailments from chemicals and fibers encountered on the job, is an area in which workers' compensation claims seem certain to grow.

To find less expensive alternatives, many businesses are turning to self-insurance programs for workers' compensation coverage. Another way to avoid paying high premiums was taken by Marriott: The company cut down on the number of employee claims by reducing injuries and job-related illnesses. With that aim in mind, many companies are examining their safety programs more closely.

UMBRELLA LIABILITY INSURANCE   **Umbrella policies** are designed to give extra protection above and beyond that provided under other liability policies. Because of the unknowns associated with this type of coverage, many insurance companies have recently raised their rates for umbrella coverage by up to 1,000 percent or have refused to issue this form of policy. As a result, some insurance buyers such as Du Pont have set up their own insurance companies to obtain additional coverage.

BEHIND THE SCENES

Risk Management in the Entertainment Industry Is Serious Business

As insurance broker Shel Bachrach tells it, he was sleeping soundly when a client telephoned at 2 a.m. to ask a question about his insurance coverage. It wasn't anything so pedestrian as an automobile policy. Says Bachrach, "They asked if they had coverage in place for a helicopter to fly over and film their concert." As a principal in Albert G. Ruben Company of Beverly Hills, Bachrach sells insurance to rock stars.

Bachrach advised his client that if there was an accident, the people inside the helicopter, their relatives, or their estates could sue under nonowned-aircraft liability. If the stagehands were hurt or killed, the client would need workers' compensation. If one of the backup singers couldn't sing anymore, they would need permanent total disability insurance. If the concert stage and field were damaged, third-party property damages would come in. If they

couldn't get the field ready in time for the football game scheduled there for the next day, they would need extra-expense coverage and more third-party property damage coverage. If the group couldn't appear the next day, they'd need nonappearance insurance. So Bachrach calmly advised his client that he could be at risk for hundreds of millions of dollars if he went ahead with the helicopter filming. Nevertheless, his client wanted to go for it. So Bachrach called around, set up the insurance, and his client filmed the concert three days later.

Rock bands with superstar status pay as much as $1 million a year in premiums to cover big-time mishaps. Lesser-known groups can get by on $100,000 a year in premiums. In his 1988 concert tour, rock star David Lee Roth "surfed" over the audience on an airborne surfboard. Had he fallen and hit someone in the audience, he could have been sued for millions.

PROFESSIONAL LIABILITY INSURANCE   Doctors, lawyers, accountants, architects, stockbrokers, and other professionals usually carry some form of **malpractice insurance**. This type of coverage, which protects professionals from financial ruin if they are sued by dissatisfied clients, is another form of insurance that is becoming increasingly—and prohibitively—expensive. For accounting firms, the cost per partner for professional liability has tripled in only five years. And because of the escalating costs of malpractice insurance, thousands of obstetricians decided to stop delivering babies.[25] Because of the high premiums, estimates are that one in ten CPA firms are going bare (carrying no coverage), and most of these are the smaller firms.[26]

malpractice insurance Insurance that covers losses arising from damages or injuries caused by the insured in the course of performing professional services for clients

Loss of Services of Key Personnel

In some businesses, just one executive or employee has expertise or experience that is crucial to the company's operation. **Key-person insurance** can be purchased by a company to protect itself against the financial impact of the death of such a key employee. The beneficiary is the company, not the executive's survivors.

key-person insurance Insurance that provides a business with funds in compensation for loss of a key employee

▶ TYPES OF EMPLOYEE INSURANCE

Besides insuring their property and assets, most businesses buy coverage for risks to employees. Disease and disability may cost employees huge sums of money unless they are insured. In addition, death carries the threat of financial

Promoters say that of the average ticket price, 8 percent goes to pay the insurance.

Hollywood film producers sometimes face even more unusual risks than rock stars. For *Indiana Jones and the Last Crusade,* Lucasfilm had 2,000 rats specially bred for the scene in which Jones and his sidekick wade through a dank underground chamber. Lucasfilm asked Fireman's Fund to insure the rodents and cover the cost of any delays in filming if the production company lost a large number of the animals. The insurer, however, demanded a "1,000-rat deductible," meaning that it wouldn't pay any claims resulting from the loss of the first 1,000 rats. So as any good risk manager would do, Lucasfilm lined up an extra 1,000 rats as a cushion.

Filming delays are extremely costly in the movie business—as much as $500 a minute, or $250,000 a day. With films today costing an average of $19 million, the insurer of a major picture might have as much as $75 million on the line. The price of such coverage is usually 1 to 3 percent of a movie's budget.

Some observers are concerned that insurers are taking too big a risk in pursuing the entertainment industry. Lloyd's of London, for example, insured MGM's filming of *Brainstorm.* When Natalie Wood died during filming, MGM wanted to abandon the movie and collect from its insurers. But underwriters at Lloyd's thought it would be cheaper to complete the film, using a stand-in for Wood in the scenes that remained. Lloyd's got its way, but it still had to pay about $8 million in claims to cover production delays.

Back in the 1950s, insurance coverage in the entertainment industry was less complex, and it seldom covered much beyond damage to props. Today, however, little can be left to chance, with coverage limited only by the imagination of the people involved.

As part of a companywide wellness program, the Xerox Corporate Fitness Center is provided for employees at headquarters in Stanford, Connecticut.

VIDEO EXERCISE

hospitalization insurance Health insurance that pays for most of the costs of a hospital stay

surgical and medical insurance Insurance that pays for the costs of surgery and physicians' fees while a person is hospitalized or recovering from hospitalization

major-medical insurance Insurance that covers many medical expenses not covered by other health-insurance plans

coinsurance The share of medical costs the patient picks up to supplement the remaining costs paid by the insurer

dental and vision insurance Insurance that covers a portion of the costs of dental and eye care

hardship for an employee's family. Unemployment caused by a slowdown in business threatens even model workers with loss of income.

Federal law requires employers to pay half the cost of employees' Social Security taxes and to help finance state unemployment insurance funds. All 50 states mandate benefits for work-related injury, and a few states even require employers to provide disability income insurance. But beyond these mandatory programs, most businesses also provide employees with substantial additional coverage.

Generally, companies are interested in three kinds of employee protection: health insurance, life insurance, and pension plans (discussed in Chapter 10). This protection is usually provided through group policies, which are sold to the company by the insurer. In some cases, the employer pays for the insurance in full; in other cases, employees pay part or all of the cost through a payroll deduction plan.

Health Insurance

There have traditionally been two main types of health insurance—one covering medical expenses, the other guaranteeing income in the event of a disabling illness or injury. That framework still exists, but today there tends to be more coverage for "ordinary" care as well as for serious medical problems. Dental coverage, for example, is more widespread: Some 85 percent of employers now offer some form of dental insurance.[27] As for group disability protection, benefits now last longer and payments are higher. Waiting periods are longer, however; many policies do not begin paying benefits until six months after the disability occurred.

Medical Coverage

Health insurance covers a variety of medical expenses. Although the types of coverage available have increased in the last few years, the vast majority of programs fall into five general areas:

Hospitalization insurance pays the major portion of the cost of a hospital stay. Coverage varies, but most policies pay all or part of the cost of a semiprivate room and the total cost of drugs and services while the insured is in a hospital.

Surgical and medical insurance pays the costs of surgery and of physicians' in-hospital care. Policies usually specify a maximum payment for each surgical procedure covered.

Major-medical insurance covers all the medical expenses that fall outside the coverage limits of hospitalization insurance and surgical and medical insurance. Frequently, the insured must pay at least $250 to $500 of her or his own medical costs per year. But a typical major-medical policy may pay 80 percent of all medical expenses up to $1 million; after the employee's own co-payment in a given year has passed $1,500, most plans pick up 100 percent of the rest.[28] This arrangement of sharing costs is referred to as **coinsurance.** In recent years a trend has developed toward *comprehensive* medical insurance, which is a variation of major medical.[29]

Dental and vision insurance covers a fixed percentage of an employee's expenses for eyeglasses, medically prescribed contact lenses, and various forms of dental work. The best plans, however, have a "stop-loss" cutoff of about $1,000, after which the insurance company pays the whole tab.[30] These programs are becoming increasingly popular.

Mental-health insurance pays for psychiatric care and psychological counseling. After satisfying the deductible required by the policy, an employee with a mental or nervous disorder is usually eligible for mental-health benefits ranging from 50 to 80 percent of the cost of treatment. However, some companies do not offer mental-health insurance.[31] Substance abuse (drug and alcohol) treatment programs are usually handled on the same terms as mental-health benefits. Many employers today spend up to 30 percent of their health-care dollars on mental health and substance abuse treatment, compared with 6 percent in 1985.[32]

THE COSTS OF MEDICAL CARE More than three-fourths of all employees are covered by employer-provided health insurance.[33] Employers typically pay about 80 percent of the premiums; however, as costs rise employers are shifting more of the cost burden to employees by requiring them to pay a larger portion of their own premiums, larger deductibles, and higher co-payments. Still, it cost employers an average of $3,217 per employee for health care in 1990, and that could rise to a staggering $22,000 by the year 2000 if current trends continue.[34] Exhibit 22.4 illustrates the rapid growth in total employer spending for health-insurance protection during the last several years. In fact, employer spending on health care amounted to 26 percent of corporate profits in 1990.[35] Premiums have climbed faster for small businesses than for large ones. As a result, many small companies have been forced to drop health insurance altogether. The health-care crisis has employers and employees alike clamoring for reform, and the problem is getting more and more attention from Congress, which has entertained no fewer than 14 proposals to revamp the national health-care system.[36] One particularly controversial proposal would require employers to provide health coverage for their workers or pay to support a public program. A plan first discussed in Oregon is medical rationing, or spreading skimpy state funds among the greatest number of people by deciding which illnesses can be treated most cost-effectively and by abandoning payments for costly treatments such as organ transplants. Whether medical rationing is workable or even ethical is the subject of heated debate.[37]

Several factors have led to the escalating cost of health care. Some observers assert that the most significant factor is **cost shifting,** hospitals and doctors boosting their charges to private paying patients to make up for the shortfall in government reimbursements for their Medicare and Medicaid patients.[38] When hospitals and doctors increase their charges, health-insurance premiums go up. Other factors causing the escalation of insurance premiums include the AIDS epidemic (which has put an added burden on the health-care system), the spread of costly surgical procedures such as organ transplants, and the use of expensive high-tech diagnostic equipment such as computed tomography (CT) and magnetic resonance imaging (MRI) scanners. In addition, more doctors are becoming specialists and thus commanding higher fees.

To help employees cope with costs above and beyond the scope of traditional health-insurance policies, some employers include new types of policies in their insurance packages, offer their workers the option of paying for extra coverage through payroll deductions, or, like Marriott, develop their own hybrid programs for managing health-care costs.

COST-CONTAINMENT MEASURES Allied-Signal is one example of a company that developed its own program to help control health-insurance costs. Rather than resort to traditional remedies, such as increasing deductibles and asking employees to pay a larger share of their premiums, the high-tech aero-

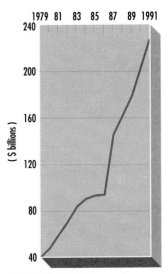

EXHIBIT 22.4

Employer Spending on Group Health Insurance
Employee health-insurance plans are an increasingly expensive part of the compensation package as health-insurance premiums skyrocket along with health-care costs.

mental-health insurance Insurance that covers the costs of psychiatric care, psychological counseling, and substance abuse treatment programs

cost shifting Hospitals and doctors boosting their charges to private paying patients to make up for the shortfall in government reimbursements for their Medicare and Medicaid patients

managed care *Health care set up by employers (usually through an insurance carrier) who provide networks of doctors and hospitals that agree to discount the fees they charge in return for the flow of patients*

space and automotive products company chose a **managed-care** approach. Under managed care, employers (usually through an insurance carrier) set up their own networks of doctors and hospitals that agree to discount the fees they charge in return for the flow of patients.[39] Allied-Signal's managed-care program covers its 70,000 nonunion employees nationwide. At the end of the initial three-year contract, Allied-Signal's annual premium increases were less than 10 percent, the average cost per employee was reduced from $3,200 to $2,700, and the total premium bill was $360 million—substantially less than the $613 million projected had the company stayed with its original program.[40]

Many companies have also instituted worksite disease-prevention programs, referred to as "wellness programs" or "wellcare." Keeping employees healthy reduces absenteeism and lowers health costs. Johnson & Johnson's version of a wellness program is "Live for Life": Employees volunteer for physical checkups to identify health risks, after which they participate in free, professionally run workshops to stop smoking, control weight, improve nutrition, reduce stress, and promote physical fitness. Other companies reward employees for staying well with cash incentives.

health maintenance organizations *Prepaid medical plans in which consumers pay a set fee in order to receive a full range of medical care from a group of medical practitioners*

Some companies use **health maintenance organizations** (HMOs), which are comprehensive, prepaid, group-practice medical plans in which consumers pay a set fee and in return receive all their health care at little or no additional cost. Unlike hospitals and doctors in private practice, who charge on a fee-for-service basis, HMOs charge a fixed annual fee with which they must cover all their expenses. Forced to operate within each year's "subscription income," they have a strong incentive to limit treatment and to avoid costly hospitalization. HMOs are actually the precursor to managed-care programs, which are sometimes called "open HMOs" because members have the option of using hospitals and doctors outside the network. The advantages of an HMO include lower co-payments, coverage for preventive care, and no claim forms to fill out.[41]

preferred-provider organizations *Health-care providers offering reduced-rate contracts to groups that agree to obtain medical care through the providers' organization*

As an alternative to HMOs, some employers are opting for **preferred-provider organizations** (PPOs), health-care providers that contract with employers, insurance companies, or other third-party payers to deliver health-care services to an employee group at a reduced fee. In most companies, employees are not required to use preferred providers, but they are offered incentives to do so: reduced deductibles, lower co-payments, or "wellcare." PPOs not only save the employer money, they allow employers to control the quality and appropriateness of services provided. But critics point out that without cost-control incentives, PPOs may be tempted to make up in quantity of services what they lose in reduced fees. Other disadvantages are the restrictions placed on employees' choice of hospitals and doctors, the additional paperwork required to get approval for some services, and the fact that preventive services are not covered.[42]

Disability Coverage

disability income insurance *Insurance that protects an individual against loss of income while that individual is disabled as the result of an illness or accident*

Workers are protected from loss of income while disabled or partially disabled by **disability income insurance.** The insured employee receives monthly payments while disabled, usually after a specified waiting period. The payment and size of benefits normally depend on whether the disability is partial or total, temporary or permanent. Disabled workers generally receive 50 to 60 percent of their salary until retirement, offset by disability payments from Social Security. Some policies even provide partial payments if an employee is able to return to work but unable to maintain the same pace of career advancement or hours of labor per week.

Life Insurance

Life insurance is the closest thing there is to a universal employee benefit: It is offered to 91 percent of the employees in the United States.[43] Of the nearly $9.4 trillion worth of life insurance in force in the United States in 1990, over $5.4 trillion worth was bought by private individuals on behalf of their **beneficiaries,** who are paid by the insurance company when the individual dies. Another $3.7 trillion worth of life insurance is held as group policies by employers for their employees; typically, these policies guarantee payment of twice or three times an employee's annual salary to beneficiaries in case of death. Nearly $250 billion of the remaining $300 billion worth of life insurance is made up of credit life insurance, required by many lending institutions to guarantee that a mortgage or other large loan will be paid off in case of the borrower's death.[44]

Term insurance, which, as the name implies, covers a person for a specific period of time—the term of the policy. If the insured does not die before the term expires, the policy has no value. Group term insurance usually carries a one-year renewable term but generally cannot be renewed past the age of 65. The older the insured, the higher the insurance premium.

Types of life insurance not usually provided by companies include whole life, endowment, variable, and universal. **Whole life insurance,** which is more expensive than term insurance, provides a combination of insurance and savings. The policy stays in force until the insured dies, provided that the premiums are paid. In addition to paying death benefits, whole life insurance accumulates value, much as a savings account does. A whole life policyholder can take out a low-interest loan against the accumulated value or, when it's time to retire, withdraw the accumulated value either in annual payments or in one lump sum.

Endowment insurance is similar to whole life insurance in that it is a form of savings as well as a form of insurance; however, endowment policies are written for a specific term. If the insured dies before the term expires, the insurance company pays the face value of the policy to the beneficiary. If the insured is still alive when the term expires, the insurance company pays the full face value at that time. These policies have become rare.

Variable life insurance was developed in response to the soaring inflation of the late 1970s and early 1980s. Like whole life insurance, it guarantees benefits until the death of the insured (as long as the policy remains in force) and accumulates cash value. The difference is that variable life insurance is most often associated with an investment portfolio. The insured can decide how to invest the cash value, whether in stocks, bonds, or money-market funds. If the insured's investment decisions are good, the policy's cash value and death benefit will increase. But if the investments do poorly, the cash value and death benefit may also decrease—although usually not below a guaranteed minimum level.

Universal life insurance is also a flexible policy, but it is better than variable life insurance for those who are not comfortable making their own investment decisions. Premiums on a universal life insurance policy are used to fund, in essence, term insurance and a savings account. The interest that accumulates on the savings portion of the policy is pegged to current money-market rates (but generally guaranteed to stay above a certain level). Premium payments may vary too, depending on the insured's preferences, as long as the cash value is large enough to fund the term insurance portion of the policy. Of course, cash value accumulates more slowly when interest rates or premiums decline. This policy has lost popularity during the past few years.

beneficiaries People named in a life-insurance policy who are paid by the insurer when the insured dies

term insurance Life insurance that provides death benefits for a specified period

whole life insurance Insurance that provides both death benefits and savings for the insured's lifetime, provided that premiums are paid

endowment insurance Life insurance that guarantees death benefits for a specified period, after which the face value of the policy is paid to the policyholder

variable life insurance Whole life insurance policy that allows the policyholder to decide how to invest the cash value

universal life insurance Combination of a term life insurance policy and a savings plan with flexible interest rates and flexible premiums

SUMMARY OF LEARNING OBJECTIVES

1 Explain the difference between pure risk and speculative risk.

A pure risk involves only the potential for loss, without any possibility of gain; a speculative risk is one that accompanies the possibility of a profit.

2 Discuss the risk-management techniques available to a risk manager.

Managers use risk-control techniques to minimize organizational losses. These techniques include risk avoidance, loss prevention, and loss reduction. Managers use risk-financing techniques to restore losses that occur. These techniques include risk retention and risk transfer.

3 Distinguish uninsurable risks from insurable risks.

An uninsurable risk is one for which insurance generally is not available, for example, losses due to economic and environmental conditions,

poor management, and changes in government regulations. Insurable risks are relatively calculable, and insurance companies are willing to cover them.

4 Clarify how insurance companies decide the amount of income they need to generate from premiums.

The insurance companies must predict the amount they will probably have to pay in claims over a given period.

5 List two large government insurance programs.

Two large government insurance programs are Social Security and unemployment compensation.

6 Name four types of business risks that are often insured.

Businesses run the risk of property loss, losses due to liability, income loss, and loss of key personnel.

7 Identify the two main types of health-insurance coverage.

Health insurance includes medical coverage (hospitalization insurance, surgical and medical insurance, major-medical insurance, dental and vision insurance, and mental-health insurance) and disability coverage.

8 Describe the five main forms of life insurance.

Term life insurance provides death benefits for a specific period. Whole life insurance provides both savings and death benefits throughout the insured's life, as long as premiums are paid. Endowment life insurance (now rare) provides both savings and death benefits for a specified period. Variable life insurance is similar to whole life, except that it allows the policyholder to manage the investment portion of the policy. Universal life insurance is, in effect, a combination of term insurance and a savings account.

Meeting a Business Challenge at Marriott

Faced with a serious challenge to his company's liability exposure, J. W. Marriott, Jr., found that the best way to hold down costs was to minimize the chances for liability in the first place. In other words, instead of waiting for accidents to happen, he decided to prevent as many accidents as possible. This philosophy guided the company in all its risk-management efforts, from claims processing to medical care. Marriott's managers were so effective that costs were reduced, accident claims were decreased, employee morale was boosted, and the company became a model for other lodging and food-service corporations.

The crucial first step was a multi-million-dollar effort to get as much commercial insurance coverage as possible—beyond the company's own

J. W. Marriott, Jr., chairman of Marriott.

self-insurance program—and to get it at the least possible cost. Coverage had dried up after a series of tragic

hotel fires, so in response, Marriott ordered all hotels managed by his company to be retrofitted with quick-response sprinkler systems. What made this program noteworthy throughout the industry (and what impressed fire-safety officials nationwide) was Marriott's use of plastic pipe instead of the traditional black iron pipe. Retrofitting a hotel with iron pipe was prohibitively expensive in many cases because entire floors had to be shut down while the sprinkler system was installed. Fire-safety officials had always avoided plastic piping because they thought it would melt in a fire. But Marriott managers proved in a $1 million experiment that plastic pipe would do the job. The experiment's success convinced building-safety and fire-safety officials across the country that Marriott's system was more than adequate to prevent major hotel fires. And it convinced insurance companies that Marriott was worthy of receiving more liability coverage than its competitors.

Marriott's next step was to reduce the number and the cost of workers' compensation claims. It started with a companywide safety program, placing special emphasis on those units that had been acquired by Marriott. Safety programs became an integral part of all Marriott businesses. The number of workers' compensation claims was halved in two years at Marriott's Great American amusement park—a remarkable achievement considering that the park's work force swelled by more than 3,000 young employees every summer season. But not only were claims reduced; the costs of processing those claims were slashed by bringing claim administration in-house and designing a computerized system to manage it. A key benefit of that system was a reduction in lost work time for employees recuperating from accidents; these employees were often able to return to work early by filling positions that would not hamper their recovery.

Finally, Marriott took on the problem of rising health-care costs—a problem so vast that it continues to have a major detrimental effect on all businesses in the United States. Marriott hired a staff of highly competent nurses to review all workers' compensation claims and doctors' reports, ensuring that treatment costs wouldn't get out of hand. The nurses also manage a companywide employee-assistance program that helps injured workers select the appropriate doctors, fill out and manage the paperwork, and speed up recuperative periods. In addition, nurses are available at nearly all of Marriott's business sites, including hotels and food-service facilities, to monitor safety standards and working conditions and, when necessary, to administer first aid quickly. The nursing program has helped boost employee morale and has contributed to reducing costs in another interesting way: Legal costs have come down substantially because fewer claims are filed against the corporation—one more benefit of reducing the risks associated with doing business.

Your Mission: You have just been promoted to vice president for risk management and insurance at Marriott. It is your job to monitor all insurance programs, internal and external, and to continue reducing costs wherever possible through risk control.

1. Although Marriott manages hotels, the company doesn't own all the properties. Most are owned by outside investors, which has made some risk-management programs difficult to implement companywide. Extra time and effort were required to convince some owners of the benefits of joining Marriott's self-insurance program and of installing plastic pipe sprinklers in their properties. Now some owners are objecting to the cost of adding nurses to their staffs, saying their operations are not large enough to warrant such expense. Of the following, which would be your best response?

a. Conduct a cost-benefit study for each independently owned property; that is, analyze the cost of adding a nurse and compare it to the amount that having a nurse would save in health-claim costs.
b. Increase the responsibilities of nurses working out of corporate-owned hotels by including independently owned hotels in their service areas.
c. Group hotels according to region, size, and room bookings to determine which properties should have nurses on staff and which should be covered by centralized nursing staffs.
d. Do not include in the nursing program those hotels whose owners are balking at the program's cost.

2. A number of Marriott properties are in high-risk earthquake zones. Assume that earthquake insurance is available at all the properties. The good news is that these insurance options cover replacement costs; in other words, the value of the policy fluctuates with the cost of rebuilding or repairing a hotel. If it costs 25 percent more to replace a hotel in 1997 than it did to build it in 1991, the insurance will pay the additional amount. The bad news is twofold: Earthquake coverage is expensive, and, on average, these coverage options carry a 10 percent deductible

(so Marriott would have to pick up the first 10 percent of the replacement or repair costs). What should you do?

a. Earthquakes are such rare occurrences that it really isn't sensible to waste time or money worrying about them. Don't bother with any kind of earthquake coverage.
b. Yes, earthquakes are rare, but the damage they do is often extensive, and the costs of unexpectedly having to replace a hotel or conduct major repairs could be a big blow to the company's cash flow. It is important to cover all the hotels for earthquake risk, regardless of the expense.
c. Yes, when they do hit, earthquakes are likely to cause serious damage to Marriott properties. However, the risk of earthquakes hitting more than one Marriott property in a given period is rather low, so the company should self-insure for earthquakes, setting aside enough capital to rebuild a hotel quickly if one is damaged or destroyed.
d. The costs associated with earthquakes are simply too great. Marriott should sell all locations that have high earthquake risks.

3. Health-care costs used to be dominated by hospitalization cases. But as employers (including Marriott) have found ways to reduce costs, hospitalization cases have been reduced. Now, however, the problem is with outpatient claims: Their number and costs are rising to unmanageable proportions. Among the following options, which is the best way to reduce corporate medical insurance costs?

a. Contract with a health maintenance organization, a type of prepaid health-care service that keeps outpatient costs low.
b. Increase the deductible paid by all employees on their medical insurance, thereby providing a financial incentive for them to use outpatient services less.
c. Begin a program for health information and education to be administered by company nurses and physicians, teaching employees how to lead healthier lives in the first place.
d. Contract with a preferred-provider organization, a type of pre-

paid health-care service that is similar to an HMO in its objective.

4. Liability claims filed by Marriott hotel guests are another source of insurance concern. These claims range from major catastrophes (such as a building collapsing) to individual incidents (such as people tripping on stairs). What's the best way to reduce the costs of these claims (regardless of whether you cover them with commercial insurance or self-insurance)?

   a. Build an aggressive legal team

that fights every liability claim and does everything possible to reduce the amounts that the company has to pay.
   b. Load up on as much liability insurance as you can get, regardless of the cost. Juries are awarding ever-higher liability damage awards, and there is no end in sight.
   c. Instead of focusing on insurance, focus on the things and situations in Marriott hotels that cause accidents. Require all properties to provide comprehensive reports on all

accidents and then analyze the causes and get to work on fixing the highest-priority problems, which might be anything from poor stairway design to inadequate maintenance.
   d. These problems are much like the earthquake situation; you can't predict them, and you can't control the actions of guests that might lead to accidents. There is no sense trying to worry about liability claims.[45]

KEY TERMS

actuaries (639)
beneficiaries (651)
business-interruption insurance (644)
claims (639)
coinsurance (648)
comprehensive general liability insurance (645)
contingent business-interruption insurance (644)
cost shifting (649)
credit life insurance (644)
crime insurance (644)
damages (634)
deductible (639)
dental and vision insurance (648)
depreciated value (643)
disability income insurance (650)
endowment insurance (651)
extra-expense insurance (644)
fidelity bond (643)

health maintenance organizations (650)
hospitalization insurance (648)
insurable risk (638)
insurance (637)
key-person insurance (647)
law of large numbers (639)
liability insurance (644)
loss exposures (635)
major-medical insurance (648)
malpractice insurance (647)
managed care (650)
mental-health insurance (649)
mutual company (641)
no-fault insurance laws (645)
preferred-provider organizations (650)
premium (637)
product liability (645)
property insurance (643)

pure risk (634)
replacement cost (643)
risk (634)
risk management (635)
risk-control techniques (636)
risk-financing techniques (636)
self-insurance (636)
speculative risk (634)
stock company (641)
surety bond (643)
surgical and medical insurance (648)
term insurance (651)
umbrella policies (646)
underwriters (639)
uninsurable risk (637)
universal life insurance (651)
variable life insurance (651)
whole life insurance (651)
workers' compensation insurance (645)

REVIEW QUESTIONS

1. What are the four types of loss exposure?

2. What is self-insurance, and why is it becoming increasingly popular among large corporations?

3. What are the five characteristics of insurable risks?

4. What is the difference between a stock company and a mutual company?

5. What are the causes of the insurance industry's historical profitability problems?

6. What sorts of business insurance are available to protect against the four main types of business risks?

7. What is the difference between workers' compensation insurance and disability income insurance?

8. How are the insurance companies and the government responding to the soaring costs of liability insurance?

Managing Risk Without a Risk Manager

Many small and midsized companies cannot afford to hire someone whose sole responsibility is managing risk. Without a risk manager, the company's owner, chief executive officer, or controller is likely to inherit the responsibility by default. The main drawback of this arrangement is that the day-to-day responsibilities of running a business leave little or no time for evaluating insurance coverage and developing strategies for controlling losses. And even when there is time, the process is becoming too complex for many managers to handle effectively. Factors contributing to the complexity are inflation, the growth of international operations, more complex technology, and increasing government regulation.

As a result, more companies are turning to outside consultants to help them cost-effectively manage risk. For example, when John Cirigliano became managing director and chief executive of HBSA, a New York–based manufacturer of department-store fixtures, he made overhauling the company's insurance coverage a top priority. But Cirigliano didn't know much about risk management and insurance, so he went to insurance consultant Paul Gregory for a review that is known in the trade as a *conceptual.*

Because consultants are not in the business of selling policies or giving recommendations about specific insurers, they can provide an unbiased perspective on a company's insurance needs. Gregory's conceptual involved analyzing the premiums, claims records, insurance appraisals and adjustments, and coverage descriptions of all HBSA's insurance policies. His conclusion was bleak. "This was a company," says Gregory, "that had stayed with one insurance broker for 40 years and just kept renewing its policies out of inertia. The kinds of coverage and policy options it had chosen didn't make sense anymore."

The conceptual for HBSA pointed to three problem-ridden insurance areas: workers' compensation, property-casualty coverage, and group health insurance. Using the conceptual as a guide, Cirigliano interviewed several insurance brokers, looking not only for lower prices but also for technical support on issues such as improving worker safety. A year after revamping HBSA's coverage, Cirigliano cut costs by 20 percent. Here's how he did it.

▶ *Workers' compensation.* Companies don't often bother to see whether their workers' compensation job classifications are current and accurate. In HBSA's case, clerical workers at one of its southwestern facilities had been incorrectly classified in a costly high-risk manufacturing category for years. Cirigliano applied to the state for a reclassification and not only reduced premiums but earned a retroactive refund as well. In addition, Cirigliano found ways to reduce the frequency and severity of the company's workers' compensation claims. One way was to have HBSA's insurance broker hold employee-safety workshops. Cirigliano also encouraged his managers to consult the broker when they had questions about workers' compensation. The advice was free, and it helped control costs.

▶ *Property-casualty insurance.* HBSA's conceptual revealed some costly blunders in its property-casualty coverage. The most glaring was the continuation of flood-insurance coverage for a manufacturing facility the company had stopped leasing two years earlier. To further reduce the cost of insuring machinery and inventory at its 13 production sites, Cirigliano switched to a blanket loss

policy, which pegs loss limits at the value of the entire company. Since there's virtually no risk that all 13 sites will be damaged simultaneously, premiums remain affordable. In addition, Cirigliano added a 5 percent annual cost-of-living increase to the loss limit to eliminate the need for yearly appraisals. As Cirigliano points out, "If we enter a period of intense growth, we can either raise that figure or start doing some appraisals at that point."

▶ *Group health insurance.* The primary problem with HBSA's group health-insurance coverage was that the company was providing more generous benefits than other companies in its industry. Instead of paying for 100 percent coverage for his employees, Cirigliano set up a coinsurance scheme requiring employees to pay a $250 deductible as well as 20 percent of the price of their annual premium.

HBSA's consultant recommended that the company update its conceptual every three years. Insurance is one area where a little forethought and planning can produce measurable cash flow improvement if not actual savings. In fact, Cirigliano said he saved so much money on insurance during the first year that he can actually afford to start thinking about ways to broaden the company's employee benefits.[46]

1. What types of employee insurance are companies required by law to provide?

2. How do job classifications affect workers' compensation rates?

3. What steps do you think small companies can take to cost-effectively manage risk if they can't afford to hire a consultant or risk manager?

BUILDING YOUR COMMUNICATION SKILLS

Either individually or in a group of three or four students, develop a risk-management plan for a local business (small or large, from beauty salon to manufacturer). Interview a member of the company's management team, develop a profile of the business, and evaluate the risk factors that should be considered. If this is not possible, locate a description of a business in a book or periodical that supplies you with enough information to develop the risk-management plan.

Based on this information, select the types of insurance coverage that would be most appropriate. You might want to contact an insurance broker to help with the selection process.

▶ As you develop a risk-management plan for the business, consider such factors as contingency funds and self-insurance, uninsurable risks, employee insurance needs, types of liability needs, and types of property risks.

▶ Prepare a brief presentation that describes the business, the risk-management plan you developed, and the reasons for your choices.

▶ Discuss the process with other members of your class. Were there any factors that made it more difficult for some and easier for others? What were the major considerations in developing the risk-management plan?

KEEPING CURRENT USING *THE WALL STREET JOURNAL*

Locate a recent article in *The Wall Street Journal* that describes a company's experience with one of the following risks:

▶ Product liability

▶ Professional liability

▶ Casualty losses and other expenses caused by fire or other physical disaster

▶ Losses caused by fraud, theft, or employee dishonesty

▶ Workers' compensation

▶ Employee medical coverage

1. What was the company's experience? If the firm suffered a loss, was it the result of a pure risk (over which it had no control) or a specu-

lative risk (part of the anticipated risks of doing business)? Could the company have done anything to avoid or minimize the risk?

2. Was the company insured by an outside company, self-insured (with a reserve fund), or uninsured? Was this coverage adequate?

3. What was the financial impact of this experience on the company? What, if any, major changes did it bring about in the company's business practices?

APPENDIX I

Careers in Business

CAREERS IN MANAGEMENT

TITLE	JOB DESCRIPTION	REQUIREMENTS	STARTING SALARY*	OUTLOOK THROUGH 2000	COMMENTS
TWO-YEAR PROGRAM					
General Clerk	In small company, writes and types bills, statements, and other documents. Answers inquiries; compiles reports.	High-school diploma minimum. Community-college degree desired. General clerical skills required, plus aptitude for office work.	$11,500	Good	Good starting point for learning and growing with a solid organization.
Bookkeeper	Maintains records of financial transactions for organization; computes and mails statements; operates calculating and bookkeeping machines.	Community-college training. Some accounting and computer courses a plus. Advancement limited without four-year degree.	$12,000	Good	Excellent training for learning about organization.
Management Trainee	Learns many assigned duties. Usually participates in work assignments under close supervision in sales, finance, personnel, production, and similar departments.	Two-year associate degree. Four-year degree may offer greater growth potential.	$19,000	Very good	Usually involves substantial investment by employer, so candidates with "good potential" usually chosen.
Interviewer (employment agency)	Helps job seekers find employment and helps employers find qualified staff.	Four-year or two-year associate degree. Ability to screen people and match them with jobs. Must know requirements of jobs to be filled.	$16,000 (may be on a commission basis)	Excellent	Good entry-level position for personnel work in business or government.
Blue-Collar Worker Supervisor	Trains and manages other employees. Ensures that equipment and materials are used properly. Recommends wage increases. Where necessary, enforces union requirements.	Community-college training a plus. Job knowledge and experience are most important factors, plus ability to work well with others, command respect, and communicate effectively.	$20,000 (usually 20 percent to 40 percent higher than subordinates' salaries)	Fair	Most new jobs found in trade and service sectors because of increased foreign competition in manufacturing areas.

*Salaries may vary from company to company.

657

CAREERS IN MANAGEMENT (continued)

TITLE	JOB DESCRIPTION	REQUIREMENTS	STARTING SALARY*	OUTLOOK THROUGH 2000	COMMENTS
Customer-Service Representative	Interacts with clients, researches problems. May do order processing, usually on computer.	Two-year associate degree. Four-year degree preferred. Must have strong communication skills, both oral and written.	$16,500	Very good	Good starting point for learning and for growing with an organization.
CAM Production Supervisor	In CAM operations, monitors production schedules to maintain appropriate work pace.	Two-year associate degree.	$18,000	Excellent	

FOUR-YEAR PROGRAM

TITLE	JOB DESCRIPTION	REQUIREMENTS	STARTING SALARY*	OUTLOOK THROUGH 2000	COMMENTS
Administrative Assistant	Helps coordinate work of administrator, with varied responsibilities.	Four-year degree or two-year associate degree. Aptitude for office work.	$18,000	Good	Good opportunity for learning administrative function first-hand.
Department Manager	Directs the department's activities within the framework of the organization's overall plan. Strives to achieve the department's goals as rapidly and economically as possible.	Four-year college degree, with major in an area related to the function of the department.	$26,000	Good	Nature of work will vary significantly, depending on the type and size of the organization.
Personnel Representative	Hires and processes hourly and salaried personnel. Participates in recruiting, placement, salary administration, job analysis, and employee counseling and training.	Four-year college degree. Knowledge of many jobs and their requirements. Ability to deal with people.	$17,000	Fair	In larger organizations, many of these responsibilities are handled by specialists.
Public-Relations Specialist	Writes news releases, brochures, and advertising mailings and serves as bridge between companies and public. Communicates customers' needs and ideas to management.	Four-year college degree. Good writing skills essential.	$19,500	Good	More small organizations and professional groups are beginning to use public-relations specialists.
Manufacturing (Production) Supervisor	Takes responsibility for or assists with operations within manufacturing and assembly divisions of company, including cost control, reporting systems, production schedules, work standards, etc.	Four-year college degree, plus summer work experience in manufacturing. Practical work experience, plus ability to handle people, essential.	$18,000	Excellent	One of best starting points for career in manufacturing. Shortage of good people in this field. Leadership ability required.

*Salaries may vary from company to company.

CAREERS IN MANAGEMENT (continued)

TITLE	JOB DESCRIPTION	REQUIREMENTS	STARTING SALARY*	OUTLOOK THROUGH 2000	COMMENTS
Purchasing Manager	Purchases goods, materials, supplies, or services needed by the organization. Uses computers to obtain up-to-date product and price lists and to keep track of inventory levels.	Four-year college degree. Master's in business administration or management a plus.	$21,000	Fair	Complete understanding of the items to be purchased is essential.

GRADUATE PROGRAM

TITLE	JOB DESCRIPTION	REQUIREMENTS	STARTING SALARY*	OUTLOOK THROUGH 2000	COMMENTS
Human Resources Manager	Supervises all personnel departments and all facets of employment. Handles workers' compensation, employee benefits, salaries and wages, labor negotiations, training, and records.	Four-year college degree in management or personnel, with minor in labor relations. MBA in management desirable.	$28,000	Very good	Work experience in as many fields as possible (while attending school) is very good training for personnel work.
Operations Manager	Uses scientific methods to evaluate and improve decisions about a company's alternative methods of operation.	Four-year college degree and master's program in operations research or management science. Strong quantitative background important.	$26,000	Excellent	On-the-job training is important.
International Planning Analyst	Takes responsibility for international management decisions. Utilizes forecasts and budgets to project optimal business success.	Four-year college degree and MBA. Excellent writing skills.	$44,000	Very good	
Computing Systems Director	Develops and schedules work for the computing center according to company needs.	Four-year college degree in computer science. MBA preferred.	$45,000	Excellent	Must have general management skills as well as technical knowledge.

CAREERS IN MARKETING

TITLE	JOB DESCRIPTION	REQUIREMENTS	STARTING SALARY*	OUTLOOK THROUGH 2000	COMMENTS

TWO-YEAR PROGRAM

TITLE	JOB DESCRIPTION	REQUIREMENTS	STARTING SALARY*	OUTLOOK THROUGH 2000	COMMENTS
Travel-Agency Representative	Arranges travel and tours for leisure and company business; coordinates and sometimes accompanies tours. Uses telephone extensively.	Two-year associate degree desirable.	$12,000	Excellent	Good way to combine interest in travel with job.

*Salaries may vary from company to company.

CAREERS IN MARKETING (continued)

TITLE	JOB DESCRIPTION	REQUIREMENTS	STARTING SALARY*	OUTLOOK THROUGH 2000	COMMENTS
Buyer— Retail	Decides on each piece of merchandise to be sold. Checks invoices and return of merchandise, and authorizes payment for merchandise. Keeps abreast of trends in market.	Two-year associate degree in marketing, plus co-op or part-time experience in retail store.	$15,000	Fair	Good base for future career in retailing.
Buyer— Wholesale	Purchase goods from the manufacturer for commercial or retail firms. Searches for lowest prices and quality merchandise.	Two-year associate degree. Four-year degree desired by largest firms.	$15,000	Fair	Must have complete knowledge of merchandise to be purchased.
Assistant Manager— Retail	Assists in all phases of store operations: sales, display, buying, inventory control, accounting.	Two-year associate degree.	$15,000	Very good	Good foundation for managerial position in retailing.
Sales—Real Estate	Lists, sells, and sometimes rents property. Solicits property listings and sells to clients. Draws up contracts such as deeds or leases, and negotiates selling price, loans, and mortgages.	Two-year associate degree.	Commission	Good	Requires tenacity. Good financial opportunity. Supplemental real-estate courses helpful.
Sales— Insurance	Sells insurance, recommending amount and type of coverage based on clients' needs.	Two-year associate degree.	Commission	Good	Requires a C.L.U. (Certified Life Insurance Underwriter) certificate.
Sales— Wholesale	Sells to retail stores or institutions (hospitals, etc.). Provides product information. Evaluates customer needs and makes recommendations. Provides services.	Two-year associate degree. Four-year degree desirable.	$18,500	Very good	In many fields, technical knowledge of product required.
Sales— Computers	Learns and meets requirements of customer. Maintains ongoing relationship, providing service and new information and answering questions.	Two-year associate degree. Four-year degree desirable.	$19,000	Excellent	Specialist training in product line necessary and usually available in training programs.

*Salaries may vary from company to company.

CAREERS IN MARKETING (continued)

TITLE	JOB DESCRIPTION	REQUIREMENTS	STARTING SALARY*	OUTLOOK THROUGH 2000	COMMENTS
FOUR-YEAR PROGRAM					
Sales—Securities	Provides clients with information on stocks, bonds, market conditions, and history and prospects of corporations. Transmits buy and sell orders to trading division as customers wish. Develops portfolios for clients.	Four-year college degree in marketing preferred. Strong academic background in economics helpful. Lengthy training required.	Commission	Very good	Unlimited opportunities for persistent, personable, knowledgeable person. Must have good numerical ability.
Advertising Assistant	Assists in general running of office. Assists in development of advertising campaigns.	Four-year college degree. Good writing and communication skills essential.	$17,000	Excellent	Good entry-level position, where creativity and hard work may pay off.
Assistant Account Executive—Advertising	Acts as the go-between for the client and the various departments of the agency. Recruits new accounts. Handles day-to-day business functions.	Four-year college degree. Good writing and communication skills essential.	$18,000	Very good	Bonuses are awarded for high achievers.
Market Researcher—Interviewer, Editor, Statistician, or Analyst	Performs one or several of the following duties: secures information from consumers; writes and proofreads survey material; analyzes and interprets data; collects secondary data for compilation of final report on project.	Four-year college degree, with emphasis on marketing, math, or advertising. Computer courses desirable.	$21,500	Very good	Mathematical aptitude helpful.
Advertising-Space Sales	Solicits advertisements for newspapers and magazines. Helps potential advertisers match sections of the publication with their target markets.	Four-year college degree preferred. Strong communication skills a must.	$25,000	Very good	Bonus potential for self-starters.
Promotion Assistant	Proofreads copy; helps prepare ads; may display exhibits at conferences; performs other general office work.	Four-year college degree.	$18,000	Good	Opportunity for advancement.
Marketing Manager	Coordinates advertising programs. Communicates information and plans to salespeople. Relays information from sales force to management.	Four-year college degree. Writing skills essential.	$25,000	Very good	Must enjoy working with people.

*Salaries may vary from company to company.

CAREERS IN MARKETING (continued)

TITLE	JOB DESCRIPTION	REQUIREMENTS	STARTING SALARY*	OUTLOOK THROUGH 2000	COMMENTS
GRADUATE PROGRAM					
Advertising Manager	Manages one or more of the following departments; research, production, writing, layout, media sales.	MBA specializing in marketing or advertising.	$27,000	Very good	Competition keen for most jobs. Great potential for those who can make it.
Technical Sales	Sells highly technical equipment such as generators, computers, jet engines, turbines, structural materials to customers, usually involving high-dollar volume.	MBA in marketing, with engineering undergraduate degree.	$32,500	Excellent	Combination of nontechnical (sales) and technical (engineering) abilities required.

CAREERS IN FINANCE

TITLE	JOB DESCRIPTION	REQUIREMENTS	STARTING SALARY*	OUTLOOK THROUGH 2000	COMMENTS
TWO-YEAR PROGRAM					
Bank Teller	Cashes customers' checks; handles deposits and withdrawals and foreign-currency exchanges; issues traveler's checks and sells savings bonds.	Two-year associate degree in finance or accounting. Courses in banking helpful. Ability to handle precise, detailed work.	$9,200	Fair	Good math skills a must.
Bank Clerk	May sort checks and other documents, post and process accounts, keep interest files, handle mortgages, maintain tax records and insurance on customers' property.	Two-year associate degree in finance or accounting.	$12,000	Good	Good entry-level position for career in banking.
Accounting Clerk	In small company, writes and types bills, statements, etc. Answers inquiries; compiles reports; handles payroll; balances accounts.	High-school diploma minimum. Community-college degree desired. General clerical skills required, plus aptitude for office work.	$12,000	Good	Entry into government; good starting point for learning and growing in stable occupation.

*Salaries may vary from company to company.

CAREERS IN FINANCE (continued)

TITLE	JOB DESCRIPTION	REQUIREMENTS	STARTING SALARY*	OUTLOOK THROUGH 2000	COMMENTS
Junior Auditor—County Government	Under county auditor, records deeds and similar legal instruments, keeps record of county accounts, compiles and transfers fiscal records as directed, prepares financial statements.	Minimum of two-year associate degree in finance or accounting.	$13,000	Very good	Responsibilities vary greatly, depending on size of government office.
Claims Adjuster—Insurance	Investigates claims for loss or damages filed with insurance companies. Interviews parties involved. Inspects accident areas and property damaged; negotiates settlements; attends legal hearings.	Two-year associate degree with work experience. Four-year degree desired.	$16,000	Very good	Usually requires some travel.
Loan Counselor	Analyzes loan contracts and attempts to obtain overdue installments; receives and records payments; prepares reports on delinquent accounts; answers loan inquiries. May represent employer in legal proceedings.	Two-year associate degree minimum, specializing in finance or accounting.	$16,000	Very good	

FOUR-YEAR PROGRAM

TITLE	JOB DESCRIPTION	REQUIREMENTS	STARTING SALARY*	OUTLOOK THROUGH 2000	COMMENTS
Actuary	Monitors statistics to create insurance and pension plans. Determines mortality, accident, sickness, disability, and retirement rates. Constructs probability tables; calculates premiums.	Four-year college degree in statistics, actuarial science, or mathematics. MBA in finance or statistics a plus.	$22,000	Excellent	Excellent potential for top people.
Statistician	Interprets numerical results of surveys and market research to help managers make decisions and predict outcomes.	Four-year college degree, with major in statistics or mathematics.	$17,000	Very good	Good grades influence starting salary.
Trust and Estate Administration	Handles day-to-day administration of trusts and estates. Analyzes trust agreements and wills to ensure proper maintenance.	Four-year degree. Experience with trusts and estates desirable.	$29,000	Very good	

*Salaries may vary from company to company.

CAREERS IN FINANCE (continued)

TITLE	JOB DESCRIPTION	REQUIREMENTS	STARTING SALARY*	OUTLOOK THROUGH 2000	COMMENTS
Credit Analyst	Analyzes financial data, provides credit information on customers; transcribes balance sheets into reports. Writes credit reports on customers, providing information on operating, depository, borrowing figures, etc.	Four-year college degree with major in finance or accounting. Internship in accounting desirable.	$26,000	Excellent	High grade-point average helpful.
Accountant (Public)	Provides a variety of accounting services to clients either as individuals or as members of firms.	Four-year college degree in accounting or finance. MBA desired. Additional computer courses a must.	$22,100	Excellent	Affords opportunity for highly diversified experience with many organizations. High grade-point average helpful.
Accountant (Corporate)	Installs and maintains accounting system. Handles bookkeeping; maintains accounting controls over inventories and purchases. Audits contracts, orders, and vouchers. Prepares tax returns.	Four-year college degree in accounting or finance. MBA desired. Additional courses in computers, taxes, economics desirable.	$22,200	Excellent	Excellent opportunity for career path to top management in organization.
Economist	Looks for solutions to economic questions of businesses. Conducts research, prepares reports, develops alternative plans.	Four-year college degree. Graduate work necessary for advancement.	$22,500	Very good	Must keep up with current economic trends.

GRADUATE PROGRAM

TITLE	JOB DESCRIPTION	REQUIREMENTS	STARTING SALARY*	OUTLOOK THROUGH 2000	COMMENTS
Stockbroker	Gives data to clients on stocks, bonds, market conditions, history, and prospects of companies or government bonds. Transmits buy and sell orders on stocks and bonds for clients. Develops portfolio of selected investments for clients.	Four-year college degree in finance or economics. MBA preferred. Must have broker's license for state in which one works. Sales experience desirable.	$19,000, plus commissions	Excellent	High income potential after a year or two in the field.
Operations Analyst	Conducts logical analyses of management problems and formulates mathematical models of problems for solution by computer. Develops proposals to afford maximum probability of profit in relation to risk.	Four-year college degree in finance, operations research, or computer science (nontechnical). Master's degree preferred.	$25,000	Excellent	

*Salaries may vary from company to company.

CAREERS IN FINANCE (continued)

TITLE	JOB DESCRIPTION	REQUIREMENTS	STARTING SALARY*	OUTLOOK THROUGH 2000	COMMENTS
Financial Analyst	Conducts statistical analyses and interprets data on investments, yield, stability, and future trends. Performs analyses of financial institutions such as banks, savings and loan companies, and brokerage houses.	Four-year degree in management, finance, economics, mathematics, statistics, or accounting. MBA preferred. Internship or experience with financial house desirable.	$30,000	Excellent	Dealing with "big money" opens doors for great potential development.
State Bank Examiner	Regulates state-chartered and state-licensed financial institutions to ensure their soundness.	Master's in accounting, auditing, banking, business administration, economics, finance, or computer science.	$27,500	Excellent	

CAREERS IN COMPUTERS AND DATA PROCESSING

TITLE	JOB DESCRIPTION	REQUIREMENTS	STARTING SALARY*	OUTLOOK THROUGH 2000	COMMENTS
TWO-YEAR PROGRAM					
Computer Scheduler	Schedules jobs to be run on computer in order of importance.	Two-year degree or on-the-job experience. Must be able to evaluate time needed for programs to run and to revise schedules in case computer goes down.	$15,000	Excellent	
Data-Processing Clerk	Inputs and accesses information. Creates tabulations, tables, and charts for analysis.	Two-year degree or on-the-job training.	$15,000	Excellent	
Computer Operator	Monitors the functioning of the computer.	Two-year degree in data processing desirable.	$18,000	Very good	Limited potential advancement
Robot Programmer	Reprograms robots to perform additional or new tasks on assembly line.	Two-year degree.	$12,500	Very good	New job made possible by increasing use of high-technology equipment in industry.

*Salaries may vary from company to company.

CAREERS IN COMPUTERS AND DATA PROCESSING (continued)

TITLE	JOB DESCRIPTION	REQUIREMENTS	STARTING SALARY*	OUTLOOK THROUGH 2000	COMMENTS
Support Programmer	Revises and updates existing programs.	Two-year degree.	$15,000	Excellent	Entry-level position.
Applications Programmer	Uses specifications prepared by systems analyst to design programs or expand existing programs that run the computer.	Two-year degree. B.S. in computer science desirable.	$22,000	Very good	Part-time experience a plus.
Computer Service Technician	Keeps computers running smoothly.	Two-year degree.	$19,000	Excellent	Greater salary potential with experience.
Customer-Services Representative	Takes orders, checks inventory on computer. Fills orders if material is in stock, passes purchase order via computer to billing and shipping departments.	Two-year degree.	$16,000	Excellent	
Computer-assisted Graphics-terminal Input Artist	With direction from layout artist, composes typefaces and lettering designs on computer.	Two-year degree.	$18,000	Very good	Applications include marketing brochures, annual reports, packaging.
Graphic Technician	Design charts and graphs on computers for business applications. Works on annual reports, budgets, payroll, etc.	Two-year degree in business or data processing. Knowledge of business procedures preferred.	$20,000	Excellent	

FOUR-YEAR PROGRAM

TITLE	JOB DESCRIPTION	REQUIREMENTS	STARTING SALARY*	OUTLOOK THROUGH 2000	COMMENTS
Systems Programmer	Keeps entire computer system operational.	Four-year college degree in computer science, statistics, or math preferred.	$22,000	Excellent	Highly detailed work that requires location of specific problems within complex system.
Scientific Programmer	Uses mathematical methods to compile data sets to help end users solve problems.	Four-year college degree in computer or information science, math, statistics, or engineering.	$27,000	Excellent	Computer-knowledgeable people are much in demand.
Program Analyst	Analyzes, designs, tests, and implements programs.	Four-year college degree in business, statistics, data processing, or math.	$24,000	Excellent	Must have strong communication skills.

*Salaries may vary from company to company.

CAREERS IN COMPUTERS AND DATA PROCESSING (continued)

TITLE	JOB DESCRIPTION	REQUIREMENTS	STARTING SALARY*	OUTLOOK THROUGH 2000	COMMENTS
Systems Analyst	Researches user needs, develops programs to solve user problems and increase efficiency. Oversees implementation.	Four-year college degree. More complex jobs may require graduate work.	$27,000	Excellent	
Documentation Specialist	Writes marketing brochures and in-house manuals instructing users in what computer systems do and how to use them.	Four-year college degree in business administration or computer science.	$22,000	Excellent	Must be a good communicator, able to translate complex concepts into understandable instruction.
Computer Design	Designs hardware to meet business needs. Creates working model, then writes specification sheet so it can be produced.	Four-year college degree in computer science, electronics, or mechanical engineering. MBA or master's in engineering desirable.	$32,000	Excellent	

GRADUATE PROGRAM

TITLE	JOB DESCRIPTION	REQUIREMENTS	STARTING SALARY*	OUTLOOK THROUGH 2000	COMMENTS
Computer Engineer	Designs, improves, and manufactures hardware to meet needs.	Four-year college degree in electronics, mechanical engineering, or industrial engineering, plus extensive work in computer science. Master's preferred.	$26,500	Excellent	Fast-growing field.
Applications Analyst (Sales)	Provide sales information for marketing. Takes responsibility for software installations and maintenance, programmer consultation, and liaison with customer and employer software groups.	MBA plus BS in computer science (technical), math/statistics, or engineering.	$28,000	Excellent	Good communication skills a must.
Development Manager	Locates and summarizes problems with computer operations and presents forecasts to other managers.	MBA or master's degree in computer science. Requires understanding of technical side of computer operations.	$32,000	Excellent	Top administrative position that requires administrative, supervisory, and technical skills.

*Salaries may vary from company to company.

CAREERS IN COMPUTERS AND DATA PROCESSING (continued)

TITLE	JOB DESCRIPTION	REQUIREMENTS	STARTING SALARY*	OUTLOOK THROUGH 2000	COMMENTS
Computer-Project Manager	Supervises activities of engineers, designers, and technicians in all aspects of building computers from scratch.	Master's degree preferred. Four-year college degree in computer science a minimum. Good organization and communication skills.	$35,000	Excellent	

CAREERS IN THE FEDERAL GOVERNMENT (continued)

TITLE	JOB DESCRIPTION	REQUIREMENTS	STARTING SALARY*	OUTLOOK THROUGH 2000	COMMENTS
TWO-YEAR PROGRAM					
Workers' Compensation Claims Examiner	Processes claims for workers' compensation.	Two-year degree with experience, or four-year degree.	$17,686 (GS5 rating)	Good	
Clerical Stenographer	Performs various clerical duties, including typing, filing, shorthand.	Two-year degree in clerical studies. Shorthand or speed-writing skills required. High-school diploma with two years' experience also acceptable.	$15,808 (GS4 rating)	Very good	Excellent entry position for secretarial career.
Clerk	Acts as receptionist and clerk; assists supervisor in carrying out various assignments.	Associate degree in general studies or one year's minimum work experience.	$14,082 (GS3 rating)	Good	
FOUR-YEAR PROGRAM					
Internal Revenue Agent	Examines and audits records of individuals and businesses to determine their federal tax liabilities.	Four-year college degree, accounting major. Best opportunities for those in top quarter of class. Must be willing to travel. Must be in upper 25 percent of class to start at GS7.	$17,686 (GS5 rating) $21,906 (GS7 rating)	Very good	Highly competitive, but opportunities for promotion make this career a desirable goal.

*Salaries may vary from company to company.

CAREERS IN THE FEDERAL GOVERNMENT (continued)

TITLE	JOB DESCRIPTION	REQUIREMENTS	STARTING SALARY*	OUTLOOK THROUGH 2000	COMMENTS
Special Agent, IRS	Working with the U.S. attorney general, investigates potential criminal violations of federal tax laws; determines whether there is cause for trial; prepares trial documents.	Four-year college degree, accounting major desirable.	$17,686 (GS5 rating) $21,906 (GS7 rating)	Very good	
Personnel-Staffing Specialist	Handles various phases of personnel, including classification, salary analysis, recruiting, and research.	All majors, preferably with degree in personnel or labor relations. Employment experience helpful.	$26,798 (GS9 rating)	Fair	Stable field with substantial competition.
Social Insurance Representative	Handles all facets of social-insurance administration.	All majors, with accounting, management, personnel, and general business having the edge.	$17,686 (GS5 rating)	Good	Positions available nationwide. Especially good for those seeking long-range careers in Social Security.
Accountant (Auditor)	Provides variety of accounting services to various agencies of government. May audit contracts, orders, and vouchers.	Four-year college degree in accounting. Internship in public, industrial, or government accounting highly desirable. Must be at top of class to rate GS7.	$17,686 (GS5 rating) $21,906 (GS7 rating)	Very good	Competition keen. Apply well in advance of graduation.
Economist	Performs various economic analyses of projects in labor, agriculture, industry econometrics, material resources, finance, and transportation.	Four-year college degree in economics; advisable to consider advanced degrees for best long-range career opportunities.	$17,686 (GS5 rating)	Good	Most jobs in Washington, D.C., although some are available nationwide. Highly competitive.

GRADUATE PROGRAM

TITLE	JOB DESCRIPTION	REQUIREMENTS	STARTING SALARY*	OUTLOOK THROUGH 2000	COMMENTS
Accountant	Studies financial data. Develops and installs new accounting systems. Prepares and evaluates financial reports.	MBA in accounting; four-year degree in accounting with experience or CPA certificate.	$26,798 (GS9 rating)	Very good	Excellent experience for later entry into business.
Budget Analyst	Evaluates programs to develop budgets; usually develops alternative budgets as well. Keeps an eye on debts and expenditures.	MBA in business administration, economics, accounting, or related field. Undergraduate degree should be in accounting or finance.	$26,798 (GS9 rating)	Good	

*Salaries may vary from company to company.

CAREERS IN THE FEDERAL GOVERNMENT (continued)

TITLE	JOB DESCRIPTION	REQUIREMENTS	STARTING SALARY*	OUTLOOK THROUGH 2000	COMMENTS
Examiner— Savings and Loan, Farm Credit, or Investment Company	Makes examinations and audits of savings and loan associations, cooperative banks, investment institutions, national banks, and other financial organizations to determine financial soundness, compliance with regulatory laws and provisions, and integrity of accounts.	MBA in business administration, economics, accounting, or related field. Undergraduate degree should be in accounting or finance.	$28,584 (GS9 rating)	Good	Excellent growth potential.
Management Analyst	Using the basics of management science, makes recommendations to improve organizational work flow, structure, and planning.	MBA in business administration or management science.	$28,584 (GS9 rating)	Excellent	Excellent experience for later move into business.
Logistics- Management Specialist	Coordinates logistical support activities to provide financial, physical, and services support needed on various projects.	Graduate degree in business logistics, distribution of logistics management.	$28,584 (GS9 rating)	Very good	Candidates must work well with people.
Financial Analyst	Uses theory and principles of finance to make recommendations for various decisions necessary to government operations. Studies the security filings of corporations to determine financial soundness. Makes loan recommendations for various government ventures. Evaluates potential contractors.	MBA in finance, business administration, economics, or accounting.	$28,584 (GS9 rating)	Very good	Excellent growth potential.
Realty Specialist	Studies and directs purchase and sale of real estate. Manages property for best return.	Two years' graduate work in real estate, regional or city planning, business administration, economics, or other related fields.	$28,584 (GS9 rating)	Good	Candidate must know real-estate regulations and market values.

*Salaries may vary from company to company.

Research, Statistical Analysis, and Reports

B usinesspeople use sophisticated information-gathering methods and interpretation techniques to get a clear view of many factors affecting the efficiency, productivity, and profits of their businesses. Production managers use statistics in quality control. Human resource managers may use statistics to ensure that test scores reflect the ability to do a job. Marketing managers do a lot of research, measuring the size of markets, the effectiveness of various marketing techniques, and the needs and desires of prospective customers. In accounting, audits are often conducted by analyzing in detail a representative group of accounts. Financial managers analyze the performance of their investment portfolios. And risk managers use statistics to determine risks. Without such research, managers might make some very costly errors.

▶ BASIC RESEARCH

The first step in business research is to decide what needs to be studied. What precisely is the problem, and what are the possible answers? For example, a production manager may know that the quality of a finished product is a problem, but she or he needs to make some educated guesses about the specific components or processes that are faulty in order to pursue solutions. The next step is to seek data that will prove or disprove the possible solutions.

Sources of Data

Staff people and all levels of managers need to know where and how to obtain data; it is an important business skill. They must also understand the two main ways to classify data: (1) according to where they are located and (2) according to the reason they were gathered.

Data grouped according to location are either internal data or external data. **Internal data** are those available in the company's own records—invoices, purchase orders, personnel files, and the like. **External data** are those obtained from outside sources, including government agencies—say, the Census Bureau— and nongovernment sources such as trade associations and trade periodicals. Internal data are sometimes easier to obtain and more specific to the company, but outside sources often have better resources for gathering data on broad economic and social trends.

Data grouped by purpose are either primary or secondary. **Primary data** consist of information gathered for the study of a specific problem. **Secondary data** consist of information previously produced or collected for a purpose other than

internal data Facts available in a company's own records

external data Facts obtained from sources outside the records of the business itself

primary data Facts gathered for the study of a specific problem

secondary data Facts previously produced or collected for a purpose other than that of the moment

671

that of the moment. Sometimes the collection of secondary data is characterized as "library research." In business research, government and trade organizations are the major sources of secondary data.

Businesspeople usually examine secondary data first because these data often have three advantages over primary data:

▶ *Speed.* Secondary data sources, such as *A Guide to Consumer Markets,* put out by The Conference Board, provide information at a moment's notice.

▶ *Cost.* Collecting primary data may be an expensive process. But for the cost of membership in an organization, a business can have the results of all the group's research at its disposal.

▶ *Availability.* The owner of a business can hardly expect the owner of a competing firm to make information available. Trade associations and the government, on the other hand, collect information from all firms and make it available to everyone.

Secondary data do have some drawbacks, however. The information may be out of date, or it may not be as relevant as it first seems. And the company or agency that collected the data may not be as impartial as it should be. Furthermore, the source may lack expertise: The survey may not be broad enough to cover the targeted geographic area or income group, or questions may be phrased in such a way that the respondents may guess the "correct answers"—that is, they may say what the researcher wants to hear.

Primary Research Techniques

The best way to overcome the disadvantages of secondary data may be to collect primary data through original research. Although primary data may also be collected ineptly, they are certain to be more relevant to the particular business's needs. To find answers to their problems, businesses of all sizes and types use the following techniques: sampling, observation, surveys, and experimentation.

Sampling

sample Small part of a large group

A **sample** is a small part of a large group of people or items. (In statistical language, the group from which a sample is drawn is known as a *population* or *universe.*) Researchers use data collected from a properly selected sample to draw conclusions or to make forecasts about the population from which the sample was drawn, and they are able to do so because of the laws of probability.

probability Likelihood, over the long run, that a certain event will occur in one way rather than in another way

PROBABILITY   **Probability** is the likelihood, over the long run, that a certain event will occur in one way rather than in another way. For example, if you flip a coin, the likelihood of throwing "heads" is one-half, or 50 percent (because a coin has only two sides), and the likelihood of throwing "tails" is also 50 percent. In a series of 10 tosses, you would expect to throw heads about 5 times. You could throw heads 10 times, but that outcome would be unlikely.

How does a businessperson use probability in everyday operations? Suppose the manager of a department store found that out of every 1,000 letters from customers, about 50 letters, or 5 percent, were complaints. The manager would expect that on any day when 100 letters arrive from customers, about 5 of them will be complaints. Of course, there may be more or fewer complaint letters, but if the number suddenly increases to 20 or 30 and stays at that level for a few days, the manager might suspect a problem: Perhaps someone is tampering with the customer correspondence file; perhaps customers don't like something new or different in the store's operations. In either case, a sudden shift that contradicts probability will alert the manager.

Probability is the principle behind sampling. For instance, if 10 out of 100 finished products sampled Monday are found to be defective, it is probably safe to assume that 10 percent of the whole production run is defective, provided that the sample was selected to represent fairly the universe of finished products.

RANDOM SAMPLING   The most common method of selecting a sample is **random sampling.** A group of items or individuals is chosen from a larger group in a way that gives all items or persons in the group an equal chance of being selected. Simple methods of random selection include drawing names from a hat, taking every hundredth product to come off the production line, and auditing every fifth financial report.

Imagine that a college bookstore in an urban area has ordered 1,000 T-shirts imprinted with the school's name. The T-shirt manufacturer may use sampling to determine whether clothing stores in that city would also like to stock the T-shirts. It is impractical for the manufacturer to call the 200 stores that, according to the yellow pages, carry this kind of merchandise. Instead, the manufacturer may call every twentieth shop listed. The 10 stores that would be called represent a random sample because they are listed alphabetically—not by size, location, type of customer, or any other factor that might affect their interest in the T-shirts. A good response from those 10 stores would indicate that many of the other 190 stores would be interested in the T-shirts, too.

The major limitation of random sampling is that the population to be sampled has to be small enough and sufficiently concentrated geographically so that a list of all the names or items it includes is available or can easily be prepared. To draw a sample from all the clothing stores in the United States would be too large and expensive a task. But other sampling techniques may be used in such instances. For the purposes here, it's sufficient to note that random sampling is most effective when used in limited populations.

random sampling Selecting a sample in a way that gives all items or persons in the larger group an equal chance of being selected

Observation

Observation is the technique of watching or otherwise monitoring incidents of the particular sort that the investigator wants to study. One example of observation would be an employer using cameras and videotape to study the way employees do their work. Another example would be a municipal traffic department utilizing a counting mechanism to record the number of cars that use a given street; the department would then be able to determine whether the street should be widened or whether a traffic light should be installed.

Observation sounds simple enough, but deciding exactly what sort of activity should be measured can be difficult, especially when it comes to observing human behavior. For example, if the purpose of the research is to determine the level of procrastination among office workers, what behavior reveals procrastination? Is gazing into space a sign of procrastination, or is it a necessary pause to reflect and plan? Is someone who makes frequent trips to the water cooler procrastinating? Or is the procrastinator the one who industriously writes 10 relatively pointless memos instead of writing 1 important 10-page report?

observation Technique of watching or otherwise monitoring all incidents of the particular sort that the investigator wants to study

Surveys

Businesses often need to know why employees or potential customers behave the way they do. The simplest way to find out is to ask them, and that's where **surveys** come in. To conduct a survey, investigators may mail a questionnaire (a list of questions) to the respondents (the people who answer the questions), or they may get their answers via face-to-face or telephone interviews. Respondents may be questioned once or a number of times. The biggest problems in doing surveys are selecting an appropriate sample and phrasing questions objectively.

survey Data-collection method in which the subjects are asked questions to determine their attitudes and opinions

Experimentation

In an **experiment,** the investigator tries to find out how one set of conditions will affect another set of conditions by setting up a situation in which all factors may be carefully measured. An experiment differs from ordinary observation because the experimenter can deliberately make changes in the situation to see what effect each change has. The conditions that change are called **variables.** The changes that the experimenter makes deliberately are the **independent variables;** those that change in response are the **dependent variables.** In a taste test, for example, the independent variable would be the various brands sampled; the dependent variable would be the tasters' preferences for particular brands.

Experiments are often conducted in laboratories, where independent variables can be easily controlled. For example, a scientist studying the effects of crowding on mice could, in the laboratory, control the size of the cages, the number of mice in each cage, and so on. But some experiments may be performed in an ordinary social setting.

An experimenter usually tries to observe two separate groups made up of similar individuals who are randomly assigned to one group or the other. One group is exposed to a specific independent variable, and the other is not. (The group that is not exposed to the independent variable is called the control group.) To find out whether employees who undergo a certain type of training do better work, a personnel director might put one group of workers through on-the-job training only, while putting the other group through both on-the-job training and classroom training. After a suitable time in the actual work setting, the performance of the two groups of workers could be compared. If the group that underwent both classroom and on-the-job training was doing a significantly better job, the dual-training approach (the independent variable) might be considered worth the expense. But if the control group (the group that received only on-the-job training) did better or if the two groups did equally well, the dual-training approach would not be considered advantageous.

experiment Data-collection method in which the investigator tries to find out how one set of conditions will affect another set of conditions by setting up a situation in which all factors and events involved may be carefully measured

variables Changeable factors in an experiment

independent variables Events that are controlled by outside factors

dependent variables Events that change as the independent variables change

▶ STATISTICS

Some data obtained through primary and secondary research pertain to people's likes and dislikes, their opinions and feelings; other data are of a more factual nature. Factual data presented in numerical form are referred to as **statistics.** Examples of statistics include the batting averages of ballplayers, the number of highway deaths in a year, and the number of ice cream cones eaten in August. Statistics are often expressed as percentages—an inflation rate of 17 percent, for instance.

statistics Factual data that can be presented in numerical form

Businesspeople rely on statistical information because of its relative precision and analytical value. Although they must be able to understand such statistics, they do not really need to be statisticians. Today, many microcomputer software packages are available that allow even those who have little experience with statistics to analyze and interpret data.

Analyzing Data

Raw data—lists and tables of numbers—are of little practical value by themselves. Instead, they must be manipulated to bring forward certain key numbers such as averages, index numbers, and trends.

Averages

One way to present data in an easily understood way is to find an **average**, a number typical of a group of numbers or quantities. For example, a personnel manager may want to know the average wage of workers in each labor classification in order to make a forecast of future labor costs when a new union contract is negotiated. Or a marketing manager may want to know the average age of potential consumers of a new product in order to slant advertising toward that age group.

The most widely used averages are the mean, the median, and the mode. A single set of data may be used to produce all three. In Exhibit II.1, for example, the mean, median, and mode are different numbers, even though all three have been calculated on one week's performance by a sales force.

THE MEAN The statistic most often thought of as an average is the **mean,** the sum of all the items in a group divided by the number of items in the group. The mean is invaluable when comparing one item or individual with a group.

For example, if a sales manager wants to compare the performance of her salespeople during a certain week, the mean would give a simple figure for comparison. She would begin with the basic data in Exhibit II.1 and then divide total sales by the number of salespeople:

$$\frac{\$63,000}{9} = \$7,000 \text{ Mean Sales for the Week}$$

By this measure, Wimper's sales were average; the three people with sales below $7,000 were below average; the five with sales above $7,000 were above average. If some of the salespeople needed to be cut, the sales manager could base decisions on figures like these.

The advantages of the mean are ease of comprehension and speed of computation. But one disadvantage is that the mean gives a distorted picture when there is an extreme value. For instance, if Caruso's sales for the week were $27,000, the mean for the nine salespeople would be $9,000 ($81,000 divided by 9). Because eight of the nine salespeople would have sold less than the mean, this calculation would be of little help to the sales manager.

THE MEDIAN When items or numbers are arranged from lowest to highest, as in Exhibit II.1, it is possible to find the **median**—the midpoint, or the point at which half the numbers are above and half are below. With an odd number of

average Number typical of a group of numbers or quantities

mean Sum of all the items in a group, divided by the number of items in the group

median Midpoint, or the point in a group of numbers at which half are higher and half are lower

EXHIBIT II.1

Mean, Median, and Mode
The same set of data can be used to produce three kinds of averages, each of which has important business applications.

Salesperson	Sales
Wilson	$3,000
Green	5,000
Carrick	6,000
Wimper	7,000 —— Mean
Keeble	7,500 —— Median
Kemble	8,500
O'Toole	8,500 —— Mode
Mannix	8,500
Caruso	9,000
Total $63,000	

items, the median may be arrived at by inspection. In Exhibit II.1, for example, the median is $7,500. Four figures are above it and four are below. With an even number of items—say, 10 salespeople instead of 9—the midpoint would be the mean of the two central figures. The chief disadvantage of the median is that many people do not understand what it means. Moreover, it is cumbersome to arrange a large number of items in order of size.

But with a limited number of items, the median is easy to find, and when items that are difficult to measure can be arranged in order of size, the median is a great time-saver. It also avoids the distortion caused by extreme values and thus gives a more accurate picture of the data. For example, if Caruso's sales were $27,000 instead of $9,000, the median would not be affected. Or if it were necessary to know the average amount spent on advertising by retail grocers, the figure used would probably be the median because the amounts spent by the big chains would not distort the average. In business, therefore, the median is a useful measure.

mode Number that occurs most often in any series of data or observations

THE MODE   The **mode** is the number that occurs most often in any series of data or observations. The mode answers the question "How frequently?" or "What is the usual size or amount?" In the sales manager's study, the mode is $8,500.

One important use of the mode is to supply marketing information about common sizes of shoes and clothing. If you were the owner of a shoe store, you would not want to stock four pairs of every shoe size in each style. You might find that for every 40 pairs of size 8 sold, only 2 of size 12 were sold.

Like the median, the mode is not influenced by extreme values. The mode should not be used, however, when the total number of observations is small or when a large group is subdivided into many small groups. In such cases, a significantly repeated value may not exist, and there is no mode if a number does not appear more than once.

Index Numbers

In business, it is often important to know how results in one period compare with those of another. To express this comparison conveniently, an index number is used. An **index number** is a percentage that represents the amount of fluctuation between a base figure, such as a price or cost at one period, and the current figure.

index number Percentage used to compare such figures as prices or costs in one period with those in a base or standard period

Say an oil company wants to keep an index on the number of workers it employs. It chooses as a base year 1990, when it employed 5,000 workers. In 1991, employment slipped to 4,900 workers. In 1992, it surged to 5,300. The index numbers for the years 1991 and 1992 are obtained by dividing the base-year figure into the current-year figure and then multiplying by 100 to change the resulting decimal into a percentage:

$$\frac{Current\text{-}Year\ Employment\ (1991)}{Base\text{-}Year\ Employment} = \frac{4{,}900}{5{,}000} = 0.98,\ or\ 98\%$$

$$\frac{Current\text{-}Year\ Employment\ (1992)}{Base\text{-}Year\ Employment} = \frac{5{,}300}{5{,}000} = 1.06,\ or\ 106\%$$

These figures tell us that employment was off 2 percent in 1991 but up 6 percent in 1992.

One of the best-known index numbers is the Consumer Price Index, which is used by economists to track inflation. Others include the Dow Jones Industrial Average (which gauges ups and downs in the stock market), the Index of Industrial Production, and the Wholesale Price Index.

Trend Analysis

Managers must often determine whether the variations in business activity indicated by statistics have any regular pattern. Suppose that a department store's monthly index of sales shows an increase of 6 percent for December. Before the manager can decide whether to increase the number of sales clerks, the amount of inventory, and the advertising budget, he or she must know whether the increase in sales will continue into January and February and beyond.

Trend analysis, also known as time-series analysis, is the examination of data over a sufficiently long time so that regularities and relationships can be detected, interpreted, and used as the basis for forecasts of business activity. Such an analysis generally explains change in terms of three factors: seasonal variations, cyclical variations, and secular (or long-term) trends in business growth.

trend analysis Examination of data over a sufficiently long period so that regularities and relationships may be detected, analyzed, and used as the basis for forecasts

SEASONAL VARIATIONS A **seasonal variation** is a regular, predictable change over the course of a year. For instance, the demand for ice cream is always higher in August than in February. Two other examples are increased store sales before Christmas and the rise in sales of swimsuits when the temperature rises.

seasonal variation Regular, predictable change over a year's time

Businesses can sometimes use knowledge of seasonal variations to open up new markets in slack seasons. Makers of tea, for example, noticed that tea drinking fell off sharply at the end of winter. But they wanted to maintain a constant labor and sales force; they wanted to avoid hiring extra workers in peak seasons and laying off workers in slack periods. So they successfully promoted iced tea to keep sales (and thus production) more evenly distributed throughout the year.

CYCLICAL VARIATIONS Over a period of several years (often four), the economy goes through a fluctuation known as the business cycle, which is a familiar example of medium-term **cyclical variation.** The business cycle begins with prosperity, a period of high income and employment in which businesses grow and construction activity is high. Then follows a recession, during which income, employment, and production all fall. If sufficient corrective measures (usually by government regulation) are not taken, depression sets in. A depression is a radical drop in business activity with consequent high unemployment and frequent business failures. Generally, a depression is followed by recovery, which is characterized by a rise in production, construction, and employment. The cycle usually begins again. Government spending, wars, and inflation may temporarily disrupt this pattern, but eventually the cycle's phases are likely to return to normal.

cyclical variation Change that occurs in a regularly repeating pattern

An understanding of this cycle is important in financial management because investments yield various results in various economic climates. Cycles are also important in manufacturing and other capital-intensive businesses. Building an expensive new plant just before the economy hits a recession phase is dangerous because orders for the goods produced in it may not reach necessary levels for several years. If the plant is built at the tail end of a recession, however, the manufacturer will be ready to take advantage of the surge in demand that accompanies the recovery phase.

secular trend *Pattern of growth or decline in a particular business, industry, or economy that occurs over a long period of time—say, 20 or 30 years*

SECULAR TRENDS   A **secular trend** (or *long-term trend*) is a pattern of growth or decline in a particular industry or in a national economy over a long period, usually 20 or 30 years. Secular trends may result from changes in population, availability of capital, new technology and production methods, consumer habits and spending patterns, and so on. One familiar secular trend has been the decline in the demand for rail travel since the development of the automobile and airplane. Another is the upward trend the drug companies have been enjoying because of increased interest in health care. Managers study secular trends to plan for the future, to compare their company's growth with that of other firms in the same industry, and to set standards for their own performance.

Interpreting Data

As useful as key numbers are in making business decisions, more sophisticated techniques may produce even more valuable statistics. Further calculations can reveal relationships between sets of data, suggest predictions, and help uncover the underlying factors that contribute to a wider range of findings. In effect, data analysis yields a picture; data interpretation yields a story.

correlation *Statistical relationship between two or more variables*

One of the most common types of data interpretation is the calculation of a **correlation,** which is a relationship between two or more variables (changeable factors in a situation or experiment). Imagine that analysis has shown a decrease in worker productivity over the past year. It is possible, but not efficient, to think of all the variables that might have caused the change and then, one by one, construct experiments to test their relationship to the decrease. It costs far less and takes far less time to statistically compare the trends for all those variables with the trend in productivity to see whether any of them exhibit a similar pattern.

positive correlation *Statistical relationship in which an increase or decrease in one variable is associated with another variable's change in the same direction*

negative correlation *Statistical relationship in which a change in one variable is associated with the other variable's change in the opposite direction*

Correlations may be positive or negative. A **positive correlation** is one in which the trends travel in the same direction simultaneously. The decrease in productivity, for instance, may be positively correlated with workers' experience levels or with incentive pay scales; in other words, as experience levels or incentive pay scales go down, so does productivity. A **negative correlation,** on the other hand, is like a mirror image: The trends travel in opposite directions. If productivity goes down as the number of accidents goes up, the two variables are negatively correlated.

Correlations may point the way toward solutions, but remember that correlations do not indicate cause-and-effect relationships. They merely show that two variables change at the same time, not that change in one actually causes change in the other. Even though productivity drops when the number of accidents goes up, for instance, there is no evidence that accidents cause productivity declines or vice versa.

To predict or control business activity, it may be foolish to rely on a correlation without further interpretation. For example, a large department store noticed that its sales seemed to be positively correlated with the Dow Jones Industrial Average: An increase in the stock price index was regularly followed by a similar increase in the store's sales. After several years, however, the correlation suddenly turned negative: When the stock price index went up, store sales went down. Statisticians soon found the reason. The Dow Jones Industrial Average and the store's sales were both dependent variables related to a third variable, the state of the economy as a whole. When the economy started to decline, so did the store's sales (a positive correlation). But the economy's health and stock prices were not so clearly correlated. Stock prices sometimes rose temporarily during periods of low prosperity. So the store managers realized that watching stock prices would not help them predict how well the business would do; there was no real cause-and-effect relationship between the two.

▶ REPORTS

Even the most carefully planned and painstakingly prepared statistical research project may be a waste of time if the information is poorly presented. Written reports that highlight key research results must be clear and easy to follow. Tables and graphs help, and such visual aids may even be crucial to giving readers a clear picture of the situation.

Business-Report Format

A good business report has six parts:

▶ The *title* should be a brief description of the report as a whole rather than a catchy headline. The names of the authors and the date go under the title.

▶ The *introduction* should briefly state the subject of the report, the research techniques used, and the nature of the specific problem to be solved.

▶ The *conclusions*—the answers to the problem outlined in the introduction—should be presented concisely.

▶ *Recommendations*—suggestions on how the company might deal with the problem— should be practical, specific, and derived from the conclusions.

▶ The *body of the report* should present data to back up the conclusions and recommendations.

▶ *Appendixes* (which contain data not directly related to the problem), *notes* (which give additional information on points made in the body), and *sources* (which tell the reader where the information in the report was obtained) all go at the end of the report.

Sometimes the conclusions and recommendations follow the body of the report.

Tables and Diagrams

With all the graphics software available for computers, there is little reason not to present data in a form that has visual impact. Several types of diagrams are used to display relationships among data (see Exhibit II.2):

▶ A *line graph* is a line connecting points. Line graphs show trends, such as an increase in profits.

▶ A *bar chart* uses either vertical or horizontal bars to compare information. Because of its simplicity, the bar chart is frequently used in business reports.

▶ A *pictograph* is a variation of the bar chart, with symbols or pictures instead of bars used to represent data. Pictographs are good attention-getters, but using them can often mean sacrificing some accuracy.

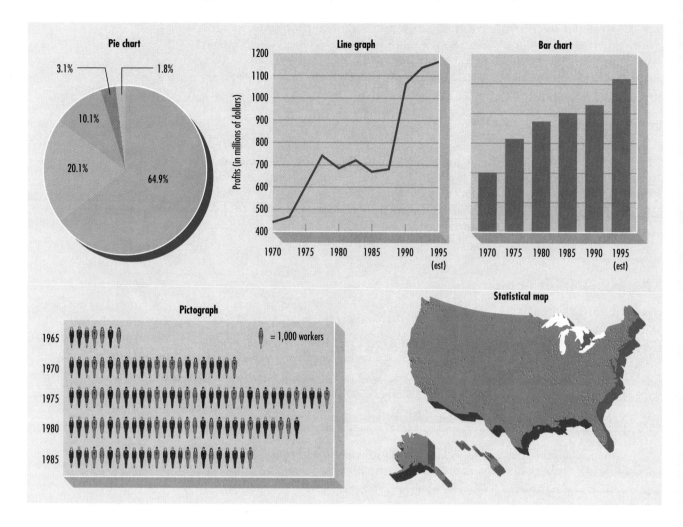

EXHIBIT II.2

Diagrams Used in Business Reports

These types of diagrams—line graph, bar chart, pictograph, pie chart, and statistical map—are most often used in presenting business data.

table Grid for displaying relationships among words and numbers, particularly many precise numbers

▶ A *pie chart* is a circle divided into slices. The slices are labeled as percentages of the whole circle, or 100 percent. A pie chart provides a vivid picture of relationships, but it is not good for showing precise data.

▶ A *statistical map* shows both locations and quantities by variations in color, texture, or shading or by a concentration of dots. Like the pie chart, it shows general relationships better than it shows specifics.

A **table,** a grid of words and numbers, is commonly used to present data when there is a large amount of precise numerical information to convey. Exhibit II.3 shows the standard parts of a table.

Statistics and Honesty

Numbers don't lie, as the saying goes. But it's also true that the people who collect and present numbers are not always as straightforward as they might be. Statistical findings are sometimes manipulated or juggled to make them appear in the best possible light. One of many such tactics is the use of precise, impressive-sounding statistics that may actually prove very little. For instance, an ad-

EXHIBIT II.3 ▶ **The Parts of a Table**

All tables, whether long or short, simple or complicated, contain a title, column heads (across the top), line heads (down the side), and entries in the "cells" of the grid. They may also include footnotes and a source note.

GROSS REVENUES BY SOURCE (in thousands of dollars)				
	1989*	1990	1991	1992
Entertainment and recreation	445,165	508,444	571,079	643,380
Motion pictures	118,058	152,135	134,785	161,400
Consumer products and other	66,602	80,564	90,909	109,725
TOTAL REVENUES	629,825	741,143	796,773	914,505

*Reclassified for comparative purposes and to comply with reporting requirements adopted in 1989.
Source: Company Annual Reports, 1989, 1990, 1991, 1992.

vertising agency may claim that half an ounce of an antiseptic killed 31,108 germs in a test tube in 11 seconds. But an antiseptic that kills germs in a test tube may not in fact work in the human body. Or there may be so many thousands of germs in a comparable portion of the human anatomy that the ability to kill 31,108 is woefully inadequate.

Another juggling technique is the "shifting base." Suppose a store offers $10 Christmas gifts in October and urges customers to buy right away to save 50 percent. Save 50 percent of what? The store plans to increase the price to $20 in November, so the saving would be 50 percent of the coming markup, not of the advertised price. In neglecting to say what base the percentage was figured on, the store is being less than honest.

The people who misuse statistics cannot take all the blame, however. There are so many ways to analyze, interpret, and report numbers that judgment naturally becomes a big factor. Anyone in business (and, for that matter, any consumer) should therefore take some responsibility for understanding what the numbers are saying before making decisions based on those numbers.

KEY TERMS

average (675)
correlation (678)
cyclical variation (677)
dependent variables (674)
experiment (674)
external data (671)
independent variables (674)
index number (676)
internal data (671)

mean (675)
median (675)
mode (676)
negative correlation (678)
observation (673)
positive correlation (678)
primary data (671)
probability (672)
random sampling (673)

sample (672)
seasonal variation (677)
secondary data (671)
secular trend (678)
statistics (674)
survey (674)
table (680)
trend analysis (677)
variables (674)

REFERENCES

CHAPTER 1

1. Adapted from John H. Johnson, with Lerone Bennett, Jr., *Succeeding Against the Odds* (New York: Warner Books, 1989), 114, 115, 118, 119, 156, 174, 175; John H. Johnson, "The Untold Story of How Publisher Made Millions with a $500 Loan," *Ebony*, June 1989, 48–57; Dennis Kimbro, "Dreamers: Black Sales Heroes and Their Secrets," *Success*, May 1990, 40; Gloria Gordon, "EXCEL Award Winner John H. Johnson Communicates Success," *IABC Communication World*, May 1989, 18–20; Marcia Froelke Coburn, "Inside the *Ebony* Empire," *Savvy Woman*, December 1989, 55–57; Lois Therrien, "A Nice Graduation Present: Johnson Publishing," *Business Week*, 13 July 1987, 40. **2.** U.S. Department of Commerce, *Survey of Current Business*, 71, no. 8 (Washington, D.C.: GPO, August 1991), 9. **3.** Robert L. Heilbroner and Lester C. Thurow, *Economics Explained*, updated ed. (New York: Simon & Schuster, 1987), 27. **4.** David Satter, "End of the Road in Magnitogorsk," *The Wall Street Journal*, 6 May 1991, A12. **5.** Francis X. Clines, "11 Soviet States Form Commonwealth without Clearly Defining Its Powers," *New York Times*, National Edition, 22 December 1991, 1. **6.** Lynn Curry and Dinah Lee, "For China's Free Marketers, a String of Small Victories," *Business Week*, 8 July 1991, 49; Serge Schmemann, (Revolution Dies of Old Age at 74," *San Diego Union*, 26 December 1991, A-1. **7.** William C. Symonds, Dori Jones Yang, and Larry Zuckerman, "Hong Kong Hustle Is Heating Up Canada," *Business Week*, 23 September 1991, 50–51; Eric Ransdell and David Bartal, "China Casts a Long Shadow over Elections in Hong Kong," *U.S. News & World Report*, 16 September 1991, 44. **8.** Christopher Knowlton, "The Triumph of the Market," *Fortune*, 14 January 1991, 14; Jeremy Main, "How Latin America Is Opening Up," *Fortune*, 6 April 1991, 84–88; Miriam Bensman, "Latin America's Year of the Deal," *Institutional Investor*, March 1992, 67–76. **9.** Kathy Brown, "59 Cent Burrito Lesson: Fast-Food Chains Trade Image for Price," *Adweek*, 11 March 1991, 10; Rajan Chaudhry, "Fast-Food Seafood Chains Sell Health, Variety," *Restaurants & Institutions*, 26 February 1992, 12–13. **10.** Paulette Thomas, "Commercial Buildings, in a Huge Oversupply, May Hobble Recovery," *The Wall Street Journal*, 17 May 1991, A1; Ivan Faggen, "Survey 1992: Recovery Could Take Three to Five Years, 50% of Survey Respondents Believe," *National Real Estate Investor*, February 1992, AA3–AA16. **11.** "A Global Overcapacity Hurts Many Industries: No Easy Cure Seen," *The Wall Street Journal*, 9 March 1987, 1; Stephen Kindel, "Trade: Reshaping the Global Economy," *Financial World*, 3 March 1992, 26–33. **12.** Robert F. Black, Don L. Boroughs, Sara Collins, and Kenneth Sheets, "Heavy Lifting," *U.S. News & World Report*, 6 May 1991, 54–55. **13.** Robert Pear, "In Bush Presidency, the Regulators Ride Again," *The New York Times*, 28 April 1991, sec. 4, 5; "Bush Declares Regulatory Moratorium," *SCRIP World Pharmaceutical News*, 7 February 1992, 18; Michael Russo, "Bureaucracy, Economic Regulation, and the Incentive Limits of the Firm," *Strategic Management Journal*, February 1992, 103–118; "American Survey: Reregulation Frenzy," *The Economist*, 15 February

1992, 25–26. **14.** Alfred L. Malabre, Jr., "Business-Cycle Lens Helps Focus Slump," *The Wall Street Journal*, 20 May 1991, A1. **15.** Stephen L. Mangum, "Impending Skill Shortages: Where Is the Crisis," *Challenge*, September–October 1990, 7, 8; Jonathan Weisman, "Skills and Schools; Is Education Reform Just a Business Excuse," *The Washington Post*, 29 March 1992, C1+. **16.** Black, Boroughs, Collins, and Sheets, "Heavy Lifting," 52–61. **17.** See note 1. **18.** Adapted from James Sterngold, "New Doubts on Uniting 2 Koreas," *The New York Times*, 30 May 1991, sec. c, 1, 6; Karen Elliot House, "Where Communism Still Thrives—For Now," *The Wall Street Journal*, 6 June 1991, A16; Ford S. Worthy, "Can the Koreas Get Together," *Fortune*, 11 February 1991, 126–132; Jack Lowenstein, "Won-Schluss: The Economics of Korean Unification," *Euromoney*, September 1990, 43–48; Robert Neff, Laxmi Nakarmi, Amy Borrus, and Rose Brady, "How Chung Ju-Yung Is Trying to Reunite Korea," *Business Week*, 13 May 1991, 110–111.

CHAPTER 2

1. Adapted from Alison Leigh Cowan, "The Partners Revolt at Peat Marwick," *The New York Times*, 18 November 1990, sec. 3, 1, 10; Albert B. Crenshaw, "KPMG to Fire 300 Partners," *Washington Post*, 15 January 1991, D1; Robert Daniels, "Peat Marwick's Horner to Leave Top Position," *The Wall Street Journal*, 9 August 1990, B4; "Peat Marwick Partner Cuts," *The New York Times*, 1 February 1991, D2; Alison Leigh, "Marwick's Chairman Leaving Post," *The New York Times*, 9 August 1990, C4; Lee Berton, "Peat Marwick Pegs Severance Costs at $52 Million," *The Wall Street Journal*, 1 February 1991, A6; Lee Burton, "Peat Marwick's Madonna Will Dismiss About 300 of Firm's Partners in U.S.," *The Wall Street Journal*, 15 January 1991, B6; Alison Leigh Cowan, "Peat Says It Will Cut 300 Partners," *The New York Times*, 14 January 1991, C1; "One Hundred Peat Partners Volunteer for Severance," *The Wall Street Journal*, 31 January 1991, C9; Rachel Alterman, "A Keen Sense of Priorities," *Business Atlanta*, March 1992, 70; Alan Breznick, "Big Six Consultants Called to Account," *Crain's New York Business*, 17 February 1992, 3+; "Peat Marwick to Advise Russians," *The Wall Street Journal*, 25 March 1992, A8+. **2.** John S. McClenahen and Perry Pascarella, "America's New Economy," *Industry Week*, 26 January 1987, 30. **3.** John W. Wright, ed., *The Universal Almanac, 1991* (Kansas City, Mo.: Andrews and McMeel, 1990), 227; Sylvia Nasar, "American Revival in Manufacturing Seen in U.S. Report," *The New York Times* 5 February 1991, A1. **4.** Sylvia Nasar, "Unexplored Territory: A Recession in Services," *The New York Times*, 3 February 1991, B1. **5.** Nasar, "American Revival in Manufacturing," D8. **6.** Sylvia Nasar, "Employment in Service Industry, Engine for Boom of 80s, Falters," *The New York Times*, 2 January 1992, sec. a, 1, sec. c, 5. **7.** Nasar, "Unexplored Territory," 20. **8.** Nasar, "Unexplored Territory," 20. **9.** Steven Solomon, *Small Business USA* (New York: Crown, 1986), 28. **10.** Nasar, "Unexplored Territory," 20. **11.** Fe-

licity Barringer, "What America Did After the War: A Tale Told by the Census," *The New York Times*, 2 September 1990, sec. 4, 5. **12.** Nasar, "American Revival in Manufacturing," D8; Thomas J. Lueck, "Rural, Rusted New York County Stages an Unexpected Manufacturing Revival," *The New York Times*, 16 March 1992, B12+. **13.** Steve Lohr, "U.S. Industry's New Global Power," *The New York Times*, 4 March 1991, C1. **14.** Sylvia Nasar, "It's Gloves-Off Time," *U.S. News & World Report*, 1 January 1990, 40–42; Sylvia Nasar, "America Still Reigns in Services," *Fortune*, 5 June 1989, 64–68. **15.** Walter Guzzardi, "Big Can Still Be Beautiful," *Fortune*, 25 April 1988, 50. **16.** Solomon, *Small Business USA*, 27. **17.** Lamar James, "Farmers Appear to Be Dwindling," *The Arkansas Gazette*, 4 August 1991, 10F. **18.** *Statistical Abstract of the United States: 1990* (Washington, D.C.: GPO, 1990), 521. **19.** Nina Barnett, "All Set to Bounce Back," *Fortune*, 22 April 1991, 281; *Census and You* (Washington, D.C.: GPO, March 1991), 3. **20.** Brain L. Schorr, "LLCs: A New Form of Ownership," *Small Business Reports*, October 1991, 43–46. **21.** Brett Duval Fromson, "The Big Owners Roar," *Fortune*, 30 July 1990, 67. **22.** Judith H. Dobrzynski, Michael Schroeder, Gregory L. Miles, and Joseph Weber, "Taking Charge," *Business Week*, 3 July 1989, 66. **23.** Michael Galen, "A Seat on the Board Is Getting Hotter," *Business Week*, 3 July 1989, 72; "Boards Should Get Their Hands Dirty," *Business Week*, 20 April 1992, 126; Robert J. McCartney, "GM Shift May Signal Surge of Outside Director Activism," *The Washington Post*, 8 April 1992, C1+. **24.** Dobrzynski, Schroeder, Miles, and Weber, "Taking Charge," 66. **25.** John Forbis and William Adams, "Corporate Victims of the Eighties," *Across the Board*, December 1990, 16. **26.** John S. McClenahen, "Alliances for Competitive Advantage," *Industry Week*, 24 August 1987, 34; Brian C. Twiss, "Innovate: How to Gain and Sustain Competitive Advantage," *R & D Management*, January 1992, 100+; Sue Gibson, "Leading the Team Organization: How to Create an Enduring Competitive Advantage," *Industry Week*, 16 March 1992, 43; Samuel Eilon, "On Competitiveness," *Omega*, January 1992, I+. **27.** Lawrence M. Fisher, "New Venture for Compaq Called Near," *The New York Times*, 7 March 1991, C1; Lisa L. Spiegelman, "Low-End RISC Workstations Expected Before Year End," *Computer Reseller News*, 1 July 1991, 1; Mark Ivey, "Does Compaq's Formula Still Compute?" *Business Week*, 13 May 1991, 100, 104; Michael W. Miller, "Race to Develop HDTV Narrows to Five Plans," *The Wall Street Journal*, 24 March 1992, B1; Philip Elmer-Dewitt, "The Picture Suddenly Gets Clearer," *Time*, 30 March 1992, 54–55. **28.** Robert England, "The Takeover Tug-of-War Continues," *Insight*, 28 December–4 January 1988, 40. **29.** Thomas McCarroll and William McWhirter, "The Proxy Punch-Out," *Time*, 16 April 1990, 41. **30.** Michael Oneal, Brian Bremner, Jonathan B. Levine, Todd Vogel, Zachary Schiller, and David Woodruff, "The Best and Worst Deals of the '80s," *Business Week*, 15 January 1990, 52. **31.** Jaclyn Fierman, "Deals of the Year," *Fortune*, 28 January 1991, 90–92. **32.** See note 1. **33.** Adapted from Richard W. Stevens, "Battling for Shareholder Rights," *The New York*

Times, 6 June 1991, sec. c, 1; Jayne Levin, "The Clout of Calpers," *Investment Dealers' Digest,* 27 May 1991, 16–17; "CalPERS Outlines Investment Philosophy," *Employee Benefit Plan Review,* February 1991, 40–42; Stuart Silverstein, "CalPERS Backs Activist for Seat on Sears Board," *Los Angeles Times,* 18 April 1991, D2; John Greenwald and David E. Thigpen, "Whose Company Is This?" *Time,* 6 May 1991, 48; Teresa Carson and Jonathan B. Levine, "California's New Crusader for Shareholder Rights," *Business Week,* 30 January 1989, 72-73; Randall Smith and Laura Landro, "California Pension Plan Hires Law Firm to Quiz Time Warner on Rights Plan," *The Wall Street Journal,* 21 June 1991, A4; Marcia Parker, "Looking Over the Shoulder: Sears, Avon the Targets of Fund's Governance Efforts," *Pensions & Investments,* 26 November 1990, 3, 38.

CHAPTER 3

1. Adapted from Steven Flax, "Perils of the Paper Clip Trade," *The New York Times Magazine,* 11 June 1989, 65; "Staples Inc.," *Boston Business Journal,* 8 October 1990, 26; Stephen D. Solomon, "Born to Be Big," *Inc.,* June 1989, 94; Michael Barrier, "Tom Stemberg Calls the Office," *Nation's Business,* July 1990, 42; David Rottenberg, "Staple's Top Gun," *Boston Magazine,* December 1987, 91–97; "Staples Inc.," *The New York Times,* 25 February 1992, C4; "Staples Moves to Purchase 10 Workplace Stores in Fla," *HFD-The Weekly Home Furnishings Newspaper,* 2 March 1992, 6; "Staples Inc.," *The Wall Street Journal,* 3 February 1992, B4. **2.** "Matters of Fact," *Inc.,* April 1985, 32. **3.** John Case, "The Market Makers," *Inc.,* December 1990, 55; "The 500 Quiz," *Inc.,* December 1990, 63–65; "The 1990 Inc. 500," *Inc.,* December 1990, 71. **4.** Louis Uchitelle, "The New Surge in Self-Employed," *The New York Times,* 15 January 1991, C2; John F. Sutphen, "Forming a New Business? First, Choose Its Form," *CNY Business Journal,* 10 February 1992, 8. **5.** Steven Solomon, *Small Business USA* (New York: Crown, 1986), 18. **6.** Web Bryant, "More Women Mean Business," *USA Today,* 21 June 1989, 4B; Sharon Nelton, "The Age of the Woman Entrepreneur," *Nation's Business,* May 1989, 22, 23; Nancy Myers, "The Woman Entrepreneur," *Library Journal,* 1 February 1992, 106+; Andris Straumanis, "The Not-So-Programmed Life of an Entrepreneur," *Corporate Report-Minnesota,* January 1992, 19+; Jenny McCune, "Champions of Change," *Success,* April 1992, 29–35; James S. Howard, "Supporting Roles," *D & B Reports,* March/April 1992, 28–30; Genevieve Soter Capowski, "Be Your Own Boss? Millions of Women Get Down to Business," *Management Review,* March 1992, 24–30. **7.** Small Business Administration, *The State of Small Business,* 43. **8.** David E. Gumpert, "Each Year, a Million New Businesses," *The New York Times,* 17 April 1988, D17. **9.** Brent Bowers, "Business Failure Rate Grows, Fueling Recession Worries," *The Wall Street Journal,* 4 September 1990, B2. **10.** John R. Wilke, "New Hampshire Firms Struggle as Bank Crisis Dries Up Their Credit," *The Wall Street Journal,* 21 February 1991, A10; Douglas E. Donsky, "SBA's New Hampshire Plan Has Democrats Crying Foul," *American Banker,* 24 February 1992, 7; Lewis Koflowitz, "Reverse LBOs: Time, Conditions Right for Going Public," *Corporate Cash-*

flow, March 1992, 47–48. **11.** "The 1990 Guide to Small Business," *U.S. News & World Report,* 23 October 1989, 72. **12.** Lisa J. Moore and Sharon F. Golden, "You Can Plan to Expand or Just Let It Happen," *U.S. News & World Report,* 23 October 1989, 78; John Case, "The Origins of Entrepreneurship," *Inc.,* June 1989, 56. **13.** Mark Robichaux, "Business First, Family Second," *The Wall Street Journal,* 12 May 1989, B1. **14.** Roger Ricklefs, "Road to Success Becomes Less Littered with Failures," *The Wall Street Journal,* 10 November 1989, B2. **15.** Case, "The Origins of Entrepreneurship," 54, 62. **16.** Bryant, "More Women Mean Business," 4B; Small Business Administration, *The State of Small Business,* 41–42. **17.** Ricklefs, "Road to Success Becomes Less Littered with Failures," B2. **18.** Small Business Administration, *The State of Small Business,* 43–45. **19.** Patricia O'Toole, "Battle of the Beauty Counter," *The New York Times Magazine, Part 2: The Business World,* 3 December 1989, 28–36. **20.** David Wessel and Buck Brown, "The Hyping of Small-Firm Job Growth," *The Wall Street Journal,* 8 November 1988, B1. **21.** Small Business Administration, *The State of Small Business,* 38. **22.** John Case, "The Disciples of David Birch," *Inc.,* January 1989, 41. **23.** Solomon, *Small Business USA,* 74–75. **24.** Janice Castro, "Big Vs. Small," *Time,* 5 September 1988, 49; Solomon, *Small Business USA,* 124. **25.** Stuart Gannes, "America's Fastest-growing Companies," *Fortune,* 23 May 1988, 30. **26.** Advertisement in *The New Yorker,* 18 February 1991, 75. **27.** Ricklefs, "Road to Success Becomes Less Littered with Failures," B2; "The 1990 Guide to Small Business," 72–73. **28.** Case, "The Origins of Entrepreneurship," 52. **29.** Case, "The Origins of Entrepreneurship," 54. **30.** Ricklefs, "Road to Success Becomes Less Littered with Failures," B2. **31.** "The 1990 Guide to Small Business," 78. **32.** Case, "The Origins of Entrepreneurship," 58. **33.** Ronaleen R. Roha, "Raising Money for Your Small Business," *Changing Times,* May 1990, 47. **34.** Ronaleen R. Roha, "Big Loans for Small Businesses," *Changing Times,* April 1989, 105–109. **35.** Roha, "Big Loans for Small Businesses," 105. **36.** Monua Janah, "'Angels' Find Financing Start-Ups Isn't So Heavenly," *The Wall Street Journal,* 4 June 1990, B2. **37.** Roha, "Raising Money for Your Small Business," 48. **38.** Udayan Gupta, "How Big Companies Are Joining Forces with Little Ones for Mutual Advantage," *The Wall Street Journal,* 25 February 1991, B1. **39.** Martha E. Mangelsdorf, "Inc.'s Guide to 'Smart' Government Money," *Inc.,* August 1989, 51. **40.** David Riggle, "Great Places to Grow a Business," *In Business,* September–October 1990, 20–22. **41.** Data provided by the National Incubation Association, 153 South Hanover Street, Carlisle, PA 17013. **42.** David L. James, "When the Going Gets Public," *Small Business Reports,* October 1989, 26. **43.** James, "When the Going Gets Public," 31; Moore and Golden, "You Can Plan to Expand," 77; Udayan Gupta, "The Art of Going Public," *Black Enterprise,* June 1985, 191; "Going Public—Watch for the Pitfalls," *PR Newswire,* 10 April 1992, 0410A7128; George Anders, "Cyclical Firms with LBO Ties Hit IPO Market," *The Wall Street Journal,* 5 March 1992, C1+. **44.** William M. Bulkeley, "It Needn't Always Cost a Bundle to Get Consumers to Notice Unfamiliar Brands," *The Wall Street Journal,* 14 February 1991, B1. **45.** Moore and Golden, "You Can Plan to Expand," 77. **46.** Jeremy Main, "Why Franchising

Is Taking Off," *Fortune,* 12 February 1990, 124; Meg Whittemore, "Four Paths to Franchising," *Nation's Business,* October 1989, 1; Meg Whittemore, "Franchising Beats the Recession," *Nation's Business,* March 1992, 55–64; Greg Matusky and Joan Delaney, "Back to Basics: Master the Fundamentals and Overcome Any Obstacle; Incredible Growth! There's No Depression in Franchise Land; Franchising: Know Your Enemy," *Success,* March 1992, 51–63; Paul M. Forbes, "Acquiring a Company or a Franchise," *NPN: National Petroleum News,* January 1992, 60+; John Jesitus, "Franchises to Feel Financial Crunch in 1992," *Hotel & Motel Management,* 13 January 1992, 21–22, 24; Andrew J. Sherman, "The Long Arm of Franchising," *Small Business Reports,* January 1992, 44–48; Philip F. Zeidman, "International Franchising: It Works Both Ways," *Franchising World,* January/February 1992, 46–47. **47.** Nancy Croft Baker, "Franchising into the '90s," *Nation's Business,* March 1990, 61. **48.** Meg Whittemore, *Growth Opportunities in Franchising* (Washington, D.C.: International Franchise Association). **49.** Carol Steinberg, "The Path to Franchise Gold," *Venture,* July 1987, 60; conversation with I Can't Believe It's Yogurt Corporate Office, 1 March 1991. **50.** Buck Brown, "Franchisers Now Offer Direct Financial Aid," *The Wall Street Journal,* 6 February 1989, B1. **51.** Janice Castro, "Franchising Fever," *Time,* 31 August 1987, 37. **52.** Constance Mitchell, "Franchising Fever Spreads," *USA Today,* 13 September 1985, 4B. **53.** John R. Wilke, "Fraudulent Franchisers Are Growing," *The Wall Street Journal,* 21 September 1990, B1. **54.** See note 1. **55.** 1991 Mail Boxes Etc. annual report.

CHAPTER 4

1. Adapted from Erik Larson, "Forever Young," *Inc.,* July 1988, 50; Steven S. Ross, "Green Groceries," *Mother Jones,* February–March 1989, 48; Mark Bittman, "Ben & Jerry's Caring Capitalism," *Restaurant Business,* 20 November 1990, 132; Jim Castelli, "Management Styles: Finding the Right Fit," *HRMagazine,* September 1990, 38; Bill Kelley, "The Cause Effect," *Food and Beverage Marketing,* 9 (2 March 1990): 20; Ellie Winninghoff, "Citizen Cohen," *Mother Jones,* January 1990, 12; Jeanne Wegner, "This Season, Sharp-Dressed Dairy Products Are Wearing Green," *Dairy Foods,* September 1990, 72; "Soda, Milk Bottles Lead the Way: State Mandates Spur Creation of Alliances That Will Focus Initially on the Easiest Plastics to Recycle," *Plastics World,* 22 April 1990, 7; Therese R. Welter, "Industry and the Environment: A Farewell to Arms," *Industry Week,* 20 August 1990, 36; Ben Announces Sabbatical, Stock Falls," *Dairy Foods Newsletter,* 30 March 1992, 2; "Ben & Jerry's, Dari Farms Ink Distribution Agreement," *Dairy Foods Newsletter,* 23 March 1992, 2; Fleming Meeks, "We All Scream for Rice and Beans," *Forbes,* 30 March 1992, 20; Daniel F. Cuff, "Big Scoop: Ben Will Be Back with Jerry," *The New York Times,* 5 April 1992, sec. 3, F14+; "Ben & Jerry's Recognized for Environmental Innovations," *Dairy Foods Newsletter,* 24 February 1992, 2; Ben and Jerry's Turns Off the Light," *Dairy Foods Newsletter,* 3 February 1992, 3. **2.** See letters in *The New York Times,* 25 August 1918, and *New York Herald,* 1 October 1918. **3.** Louis Harris, *Inside America* (New

York: Vintage, 1987), 235. **4.** Timothy D. Schellhardt, "What Bosses Think About Corporate Ethics," *The Wall Street Journal,* 6 April 1988, B25; S. Andrew Ostapski and Camille N. Isaacs, "Corporate Moral Responsibility and the Moral Audit: Challenges for Refuse Relief Inc.," *Journal of Business Ethics,* March 1992, 231–239; John A. Byrne, "The Best-Laid Ethics Programs. . . ," *Business Week,* 9 March 1992, 67–69; Simcha B. Werner, "The Movement for Reforming American Business Ethics: A Twenty-Year Perspective," *Journal of Business Ethics,* January 1992, 61–70. **5.** Manuel Velasquez, Dennis J. Mober, and Gerald F. Cavanagh, "Organizational Statesmanship and Dirty Politics: Ethical Guidelines for the Organizational Politician," *Organizational Dynamics,* Autumn 1983, 67–74. **6.** Amal Kumar Naj, "Can $100 Billion Have 'No Material Effect' on Balance Sheets?" *The Wall Street Journal,* 11 May 1988, A1. **7.** Gregg Easterbrook, "Cleaning Up," *Newsweek,* 24 July 1989, 27–42. **8.** Rose Gutfeld, "For Each Dollar Spent on Clean Air Someone Stands to Make a Buck," *The Wall Street Journal,* 29 October 1990, A1. **9.** Sam Atwood, "Superfund: Boon or Bust? Debate Rages On," *USA Today,* 22 April 1991, 9E; Kimberly C. Harris, "The Hazards of Environmental Crime," *Security Management,* February 1992, 26–32; John Dobson, "Ethics in the Transnational Corporation. The 'Moral Buck' Stops Where?" *Journal of Business Ethics,* January 1992, 21–27. **10.** *The World Almanac and Book of Facts 1991* (New York: Pharos Books, 1990), 249. **11.** Jeremy Main, "The Big Cleanup Gets It Wrong," *Fortune,* 20 May 1991, 95–96, 100–101. **12.** Barbara Rosewicz, "Americans Are Willing to Sacrifice to Reduce Pollution, They Say," *The Wall Street Journal,* 20 April 1990, A1; John H. Sheridan, "Pollution Prevention Picks Up Steam," *Industry Week,* 17 February 1992, 36–43; David J. Hanson, "Pollution Prevention Becoming Watchword for Government, Industry," *Chemical & Engineering News,* 6 January 1992, 21–22; "Strategies for Pollution Prevention in Small Companies," *Environmental Manager,* January 1992, 10, 14. **13.** Dick Thompson, "Giving Greed a Chance," *Time,* 12 February 1990, 67–68. **14.** David Kirkpatrick, "Environmentalism: The New Crusade," *Fortune,* 12 February 1990, 44–53; Bradford A. McKee, "Environmental Activists Inc.," *Nation's Business,* August 1990, 27–29. **15.** Philip Shabecoff, "In Search of a Better Law," *The New York Times,* 14 May 1989, sec. 4, 1, 5. **16.** Barbara Rosewicz, "Price Tag Is Producing Groans Already," *The Wall Street Journal,* 29 October 1990, A6. **17.** Scott McMurray, "Chemical Firms Find That It Pays to Reduce Pollution at Source," *The Wall Street Journal,* 11 June 1991, A1, A6. **18.** Easterbrook, "Cleaning Up," 27–42. **19.** Gutfeld, "For Each Dollar Spent on Clean Air Someone Stands to Make a Buck," A1, A6. **20.** Easterbrook, "Cleaning Up," 27–42. **21.** Easterbrook, "Cleaning Up," 27–42. **22.** Barnaby J. Feder, "In the Clutches of the Superfund Mess," *The New York Times,* 16 June 1991, sec. 3, 1, 6; Steven Brostoff, "Superfund Program Ripe for Overhaul, AIA Says," *National Underwriter,* 16 March 1992, 3, 28. **23.** Feder, "In the Clutches of the Superfund Mess," sec. 3, 6; Atwood, "Superfund," 9E; "Throwing Good Money After Bad Water Yields Scant Improvement," *The Wall Street Journal,* 15 May 1991, A1, A6. **24.** Bobbi Igneizi, "The Enforcer," *San Diego Union,* 9 May 1989, C-1, C-2. **25.** James R. Healey, "Audi Drives to Polish Its Image,"

USA Today, 23 March 1988, 1B, 2B. **26.** Steven Waldman, "Kids in Harm's Way," *Newsweek,* 18 April 1988, 48. **27.** John Carey and Zachary Schiller, "The FDA Is Swinging 'A Sufficiently Large Two-by-Four,'" *Business Week,* 27 May 1991, 44; Barbara Presley Noble, "After Years of Deregulation, a New Push to Inform the Public," *The New York Times,* 27 October 1991, sec. f, 5; Marian Burros, "F.D.A. Plans to Take the Fantasy Out of Labels," *The New York Times,* 18 September 1991, sec. b, 1, 6; James G. Dickinson, "FDA Draft Rules Go Back to the Drawing Board," *Medical Marketing & Media,* March 1992, 48–52; Maggie Mahar, "Under a Microscope but FDA Chief David Kessler Keeps His Cool," *Barron's,* 2 March 1992, 12–15. **28.** Patricia Sellers, "How to Handle Customers' Gripes," *Fortune,* 24 October 1988, 88–100. **29.** Joel Russel, "Mentor-Protégé: A Difficult Birth," *Hispanic Business,* September 1991, 26, 28, 30. **30.** Alan Farnham, "Holding Firm on Affirmative Action," *Fortune,* 13 March 1989, 87, 88. **31.** Sylvia Nasar, "Women's Gains Will Keep Coming," *U.S. News & World Report,* 2 April 1990, 45; Charlene Marmer Solomon, "Careers Under Glass," *Personnel Journal,* April 1990, 97–105. **32.** Diane Crispell, "Women's Earnings Gap Is Closing—Slowly," *American Demographics,* February 1991, 14. **33.** Amy Saltzman, "Trouble at the Top," *U.S. News & World Report,* 17 June 1991, 40–48. **34.** Saltzman, "Trouble at the Top," 40–48. **35.** Elizabeth Kolbert, "Sexual Harassment at Work is Pervasive, Survey Suggests," *The New York Times,* 11 October 1991, sec. a, 1, 11; Chris Lee, "Sexual Harassment: After the Headlines," *Training,* March 1992, 23–31; Jeffrey P. Englander, "Handling Sexual Harassment in the Workplace," *CPA Journal,* February 1992, 14–22; Ellen Gragg, "Sexual Harassment: Confronting the Issue of the '90s," *Office Systems,* February 1992, 33–36; Susan L. Webb, "Dealing with Sexual Harassment," *Small Business Reports,* January 1992, 11–14. **36.** Joann S. Lublin, "Companies Try a Variety of Approaches to Halt Sexual Harassment on the Job," *The Wall Street Journal,* October 11, 1991, B1, B10; Stephanie Strom, "Many Companies Assailed on Sex Harassment Rates," *The New York Times,* 20 October 1991, 1, 15. **37.** Robert Pear, "U.S. Proposes Rules to Bar Obstacles for the Disabled," *The New York Times,* 22 January 1991, A1, A12. **38.** Otto Johnson, ed., *The 1991 Information Please Almanac* (Boston: Houghton Mifflin, 1990), 818; Ron Winslow, "Safety Group Cites Fatalities Linked to Work," *The Wall Street Journal,* 31 August 1990, B8. **39.** Milo Geyelin, "Study Faults Federal Effort to Enforce Worker Safety," *The Wall Street Journal,* 28 April 1989, B1; Robert D. Hershey, Jr., "Budget Office Blocks Job Health Rules," *The New York Times,* 16 March 1992, C10+; "California Ranks No. 1 in Worker-Safety List," *The Asian Wall Street Journal,* 2 January 1992, 2; "Group Ranks California First on Worker Safety," *The Wall Street Journal,* 3 January 1992, A3+; Marc Kauffmann, "Services: Your Competitives Edge," *Telemarketing Magazine,* January 1992, 32–34. **40.** Dana Milbank, "Companies Turn to Peer Pressure to Cut Injuries as Psychologists Join the Battle," *The Wall Street Journal,* 29 March 1991, B3, B3. **41.** Jane Bryant Quinn, "Why Tele-Crooks Are Still on the Line," *Washington Post,* 25 March 1990, H11; Jerry Gray, "'900' Phone Operation Draws a Lawsuit; New Jersey Wants to Shut Down Infotrax Communications," *The New York Times,* 28 February 1992, B5+; Ray Py, Candace D.

Sams, and Susan J. Aluise, "History of Federal Policy in 900 Industry," *Long-Distance Letter,* 24 February 1992, 4; Richard Devine, "900 Numbers: The Checkered Image Gradually Fades," *Puget Sound Business Journal,* 28 February 1992, 19. **42.** Earl C. Gottschalk, Jr., "'Con Artists' Charged in California Sting," *The Wall Street Journal,* 26 April 1991, C1, C16. **43.** Kevin Kelly and Joseph Weber, "When a Rival's Trade Secret Crosses Your Desk . . . ," *Business Week,* 20 May 1991, 48; Jerry W. Mills, "Copyright Won't Work? Call It a Trade Secret," *Computerworld,* 24 February 1992, 104; Mary Kathleen Flynn, "Keeping Secrets," *PC Magazine,* 28 April 1992, 32; M. Margaret McKeown and Gregory J. Wrenn, "The Stakes Are Rising," *The National Law Journal,* 24 February 1992, 27+; James Lyons, "Ask Before You Pack," *Forbes,* 16 March 1992, 106. **44.** Milo Geyelin and Beatrice E. Garcia, "GE Is Fined $10 Million in Criminal Case," *The Wall Street Journal,* 27 July 1990, B5. **45.** Neal Templin, "Chrysler Faces $7.6 Million Fine for Mail Fraud," *The Wall Street Journal,* 13 August 1990, A2. **46.** Stanley J. Modic, "Corporate Ethics: From Commandments to Commitment," *Industry Week,* 14 December 1987, 34. **47.** "Written Honesty Tests," *Small Business Report,* June 1987, 15. **48.** Frank Edward Allen, "McDonald's to Reduce Waste in Plan Developed with Environmental Group," *The Wall Street Journal,* 17 April 1991, B1, B2; Joan S. Lublin, "'Green' Executives Find Their Mission Isn't a Natural Part of Corporate Culture," *The Wall Street Journal,* 5 March 1991, B1, B8. **49.** William H. Miller, "Those Stingy American Companies," *Industry Week,* 21 January 1991, 48–53. **50.** "U.S. Spends Big to Clean Up Pollution," *San Diego Union,* 23 December 1990, A-1, A-18; "$40 Billion Reported Spent on Illegal Drugs," *San Diego Union,* 20 June 1991, A-2. **51.** See note 1. **52.** Adapted from Robert Johnson, "With Its Spirit Shaken But Unbent, Cummins Shows Decade's Scars," *The Wall Street Journal,* 13 December 1989, A1.

CHAPTER 5

1. Adapted from Allen R. Myerson, "Setting Up an Island in the Soviet Storm," *The New York Times,* 30 December 1990, sec. 3, 1, 6; Anthony Ramirez, "Soviet Pizza Huts Have Local Flavor," *The New York Times,* 11 September 1990, C18; Mark Berniker, "Pizza Hut Succeeds in Soviet Challenge," *Journal of Commerce,* 10 September 1990, 1A, 5A; Stuart Elliot, "Pizza Hut Managers Drill Soviets in Art of Service," *USA Today,* 2 October 1990, 2B; "Red Tape Greets Moscow Pizza Hut," *USA Today,* 2 October 1990, 2B; Interview with Donald Kendall, "Go There and Get the Business," *Directors-Boards,* Winter 1991, 15–19; Rajan Chaudhry and Brian Quinton, "Operators Team Up to Stand Out," *Restaurants & Institutions,* 8 January 1992, 94–102; Joel Ostrow, "Fast-Food Prices Jump in Russia," *Advertising Age,* 6 January 1992, 1, 22. **2.** Adapted from Barry Schiller, *The Economy Today,* Fifth Edition (New York: McGraw-Hill, 1991) 856–857. **3.** Alex Groner, *The American Heritage History of American Business and Industry* (New York: American Heritage, 1972), 321; U.S. Department of Commerce, *Statistical Abstract of the United States, 1985* (Washington, D.C.: Government Printing Office, 1984), 810. **4.** Peter Passell, "America's Position in the Economic Race: What the Numbers Show and Conceal," *The New York Times,* 4 March 1990, sec. 4, 4, 5; Leonard Silk, "Triple Play: The Rich Nations Get Richer. And Then?" *The New York Times,* 1 July 1990, sec. 4, 1, 5; Thomas A. Stewart, "The New American Century," *Fortune,* Spring–Summer 1991 (Special Issue), 12–23. **5.** Louis Uchitelle, "Dollar's Decline as Export Engine," *The New York Times,* 26 February 1991, D2. **6.** Robert B. Reich, "Who Is Us?" *Harvard Business Review,* January–February 1990, 53–64. **7.** Jim Powell, "Who Owns the U.S. and Does It Matter?" *World Monitor,* June 1990, 58–64; Richard D. Besser, "Change Needed to Improve US Outlook," *Assembly,* January 1992, 48. **8.** Sylvia Nasar, "A Gain in Trade from Gulf War," *The New York Times,* 13 March 1991, C1, C2; "U.S. Posts a Surplus in Trade," *The New York Times,* 12 June 1991, C1; Michael Sesit, "U.S. Investment by Foreigners Plunged in 1990," *The Wall Street Journal,* 4 April 1991, C1, C21; "Revival of EC/Gulf Trade Talks?" *Europe 2000,* March 1992, R65+; Max Gates, "Progress Reported in Trade Talks," *Automotive News,* 2 March 1992, 37; "Chinese Trade Talks," *Israel Business Today,* 21 February 1992, 12; John Maggs, "Lawmaker Calls for Openness on North American Trade Talks," *Journal of Commerce and Commercial,* 26 February 1992, 3A; "How to Grow Poorer," *The Washington Post,* 21 March 1992, A22+; "U.S. Assailed over Trade," *The New York Times,* 22 February 1992, 41+. **9.** Powell, "Who Owns the U.S.?" 58–64. **10.** Robert H. Bork, Jr., "'New Protectionism' to Fit the Times," *U.S. News & World Report,* 6 April 1987, 44. **11.** Robert J. Shapiro, "A Battle Royal over Food," *U.S. News & World Report,* 23 May 1988, 56; Benjamin Fulford, "Rice Maneuvers," *Business Tokyo,* 1 September 1991, 28; Howard La Franchi, "Officials Hope to Resolve GATT," *The Christian Science Monitor,* 26 August 1991, 4; Robert J. Samuelson, "The Absurd Farm Bill," 6 August 1990, 51. **12.** Bork, "'New Protectionism' to Fit the Times," 45. **13.** "The Unique Japanese," *Fortune,* 28 November 1986, 8; Fulford, "Rice Maneuvers," 28. **14.** Work and Black, "Uncle Sam as Unfair Trader," 42–44; Jacob, "Export Barriers the U.S. Hates Most," 88–89. **15.** Work and Black, "Uncle Sam as Unfair Trader," 42–44. **16.** Peter Passell, "Adding Up the Trade Talks: Fail Now, Pay Later," *The New York Times,* 16 December 1990, sec. 4, 3. **17.** Robert J. Shapiro, "A Hidden Tax on All Our Houses," *U.S. News & World Report,* 21 March 1988, 52. **18.** Edwin A. Finn, Jr., and Kathleen Healy, "We've Met the Enemy and They Are Us?" *Forbes,* 9 February 1987, 83. **19.** Work and Black, "Uncle Sam as Unfair Trader," 42–44. **20.** R. C. Longworth, "World Trade System Won't Be the Same After Failure of GATT Talks," *San Diego Union,* 9 December 1990, A-2, A-19. **21.** Clyde H. Farnsworth, "Trade Focus Has Changed," *The New York Times,* 28 May 1991, C1, C9. **22.** "Ambition Giving Way to Reality," *San Diego Union,* 23 June 1991, I-1, I-8; Mark M. Nelson and Martin Du Bois, "Pact Extends Europe's Common Market, *The Wall Street Journal,* 23 October 1991, A12. **23.** Peter Truell, "Free Trade May Suffer from Regional Blocs," *The Wall Street Journal,* 1 July 1991, A1. **24.** John W. Wright, ed., *The Universal Almanac, 1991* (Kansas City, Mo.: Andrews and McMeel, 1990), 322. **25.** "To Him That Hath Not," *The Economist,* 27 April 1991, 82; "Poor Countries Victim of U.S. Budget Deals,"*Forbes,* 2 September 1991, 37. **26.** Francis X. Clines, "Kremlin to Look for Investments at London

Summit," *The New York Times,* 10 July 1991, A1, A4; Steven Prokesch, "Caution on Helping Soviet Economy Is Emphasized by Industrial Nations," *The New York Times,* 10 July 1991, A4. **27.** Mark Robichaux, "Federal Export Programs Overlap Despite Changes," *The Wall Street Journal,* 26 June 1991, B1. **28.** Susan Dentzer, "The Coming Global Boom," *U.S. News & World Report,* 16 July 1990, 22–28. **29.** Press release, Export Now, 1988. **30.** John O'Dell, "Franchising America," *Los Angeles Times,* 25 June 1989, sec. IV, 1, 5. **31.** Steven Greenhouse, "Chip Deal Ties IBM to Siemens," *The New York Times,* 5 July 1991, C1, C4. **32.** Maria Shao, Robert Neff, and Jeffrey Ryser, "For Levi's, a Flattering Fit Overseas," *Business Week,* 5 November 1990, 76–77. **33.** John Hoerr, Leah Nathans Spiro, Larry Armstrong, and James B. Treece, "Culture Shock at Home: Working for a Foreign Boss," *Business Week,* 17 December 1990, 80–84; Joann S. Lublin, "The American Advantage," *The Wall Street Journal Special Report on Executive Pay,* 17 April 1991, R4. **34.** Hoerr, Spiro, Armstrong, and Treece, "Culture Shock at Home," 80–84. **35.** See note 1. **36.** Adapted from Fred Martin, "Heard the One About the Copy Shop in Budapest?" *The New York Times Magazine,* 16 December 1990, 42–48; Ralph S. Blackman, "A Hungary Market for U.S. Goods," *Small Business Reports,* July 1990, 20–24; Steven Weiner, "On the Road to Eastern Europe," *Forbes,* 10 December 1990, 193–200; Ray Converse and Shelley Galbraith, "New Frontier for Business: Eastern Europe," *Business America,* 18 June 1990, 2–7; Kate Bertrand, "Marketers Rush to Be First on the Bloc," *Business Marketing,* October 1990, 20–23; John Templeman, Ken Olsen, David Greising, Jonathan Kapstein, and William Glasgall, "Eastward Ho! The Pioneers Plunge In," *Business Week,* 15 April 1991, 51–53.

CHAPTER 6

1. Adapted from Brenton R. Schlender, "Bill Gates Sets a New Target," *Fortune,* 25 February 1991, 12–13; *Microsoft Corporation 1990 Annual Report,* 1990, 1–18; Evelyn Richards, "A Hard-Nosed Businessman with a Certain Boyish Charm," *Washington Post,* 30 December 1990, H3; Carrie Tuhy and Greg Couch, "Software's Old Man Is 30," *Money,* July 1986, 54–55; Brenton R. Schlender, "How Bill Gates Keeps the Magic Going," *Fortune,* 18 June 1990, 82–86, 88–89; G. Pascal Zachary, "Operating System: Opening of 'Windows' Shows How Bill Gates Succeeds in Software," *The Wall Street Journal,* 21 May 1990, A1, A4; Mary Jo Foley, "Boy Wonder: Microsoft's Bill Gates," *Electronic Business,* 15 August 1988, 54–56; D. Ruby, S. Kanzler, R. Glitman, and T. Pompili, "Can Microsoft Blend Blue Jeans and Gray Flannel?" *PC Week,* 21 October 1986, 57, 59, 72–74; Daniel Ruby and Stephen Kanzler, "Is IBM–Microsoft Relationship Near Its End?" *PC Week,* 21 October 1986, 57, 74; "Microsoft's Network Is a Model for Corporate Communications Systems," *PC Week,* 21 October 1986, 73; Richard A. Chafer, "The Growth of Microsoft," *Personal Computing,* June 1986, 29; Jonathan B. Eleven, "Microsoft: Recovering from Its Stumble over 'Windows,'" *Business Week,* July 22, 1985, 107–108; James Daly, "Suit May Hurt Microsoft Users," *Computerworld,* 24 February 1992, 37, 44; Kathy Rebello, "Microsoft: Bill Gates's Baby Is on Top

of the World. Can It Stay There?" *Business Week,* 24 February 1992, 60–64; "Top of the World: Microsoft," *The Economist,* 4 April 1992, 88+; Lawrence Minard, "A $7 Billion Boo-Boo," *Forbes,* 13 April 1992, 14. **2.** David H. Holt, *Management: Principles and Practices,* 2nd ed. (Englewood Cliffs, N.J.: Prentice Hall, 1990), 10–12; James A. F. Stoner, *Management,* 4th ed. (Englewood Cliffs, N.J.: Prentice Hall, 1989), 15–18. **3.** Brian S. Moskal and Thomas M. Rohan, "A Much Tougher Line Faces Line Managers," *Industry Week,* 18 April 1988, 29–30; Richard M. Davis, Jeffrey M. Corbin, Joycelyn D. Stabler, and Charles G. Weller, "The Planned Evolution of a Team Culture," *Journal for Quality and Participation,* January/February 1992, 24–31; Sheila Rothwell, "The Development of the International Manager," *Personnel Management,* January 1992, 33–35. **4.** Robert L. Katz, "Skills of an Effective Administrator," *Harvard Business Review,* September–October 1974. Reprinted in *Paths Toward Personal Progress: Leaders Are Made, Not Born* (Boston: Harvard Business Review, 1983), 23–35. **5.** Robert H. Lengel and Richard L. Daft, "The Selection of Communication Media as an Executive Skill," *Academy of Management Executive,* 11, no. 3 (1988): 225–232. **6.** Lengel and Daft, "The Selection of Communication Media," 225–232. **7.** Kathryn M. Bartol and David C. Martin, *Management* (New York: McGraw-Hill, 1991), 268–272; Richard L. Daft, *Management,* 2nd ed. (Chicago: Dryden, 1991), 188–195; Ricky W. Griffin, *Management,* 3rd ed. (Boston: Houghton Mifflin, 1990), 131–137. **8.** Bill Saporito, "How Quaker Oats Got Rolled," *Fortune,* 8 October 1990, 131–138. **9.** Daft, *Management,* 180–184. **10.** Mark B. Roman, "The Mission," *Success,* June 1987, 54–57. **11.** Fred R. David, "How Companies Define Their Mission," *Long Range Planning,* 22, no. 1 (February 1989): 90–97. **12.** Daft, *Management,* 128; Bartol and Martin, *Management,* 157–159. **13.** Daft, *Management,* 132–136; Bartol and Martin, *Management,* 172–173. **14.** Daft, *Management,* 130. **15.** Daft, *Management,* 460. **16.** Alan M. Weber, "Corporate Egotists Gone with the Wind," *The Wall Street Journal,* 15 April 1991, A14. **17.** Walter Kiechel III, "Wanted: Corporate Leaders," *Fortune,* 30 May 1983, 135ff. **18.** Bartol and Martin, *Management,* 506–508. **19.** Bartol and Martin, *Management,* 506–508. **20.** Harry Bacas, "Who's in Charge Here?" *Nation's Business,* May 1985, 57. **21.** Mark Frohman, "Participative Management," *Industry Week,* 2 May 1988, 37–42; Paul A. Whiting, "Should Agency Owners Choose Their Successors?" *Insurance Review,* March 1992, 43–46; Matthew P. Gonring, "The Communicator's Role in Leading Corporate Cultural Change," *Communication World,* February 1992, 25–28; Edward A. Kazemek and Daniel M. Grauman, "Teamwork Approach to Strategy Keeps CEOs in Tune with Players," *Health Care Strategic Management,* February 1992, 16–17; A. C. Hyde, "Feedback from Customers, Clients, and Captives," *Bureaucrat,* Winter 1991–1992, 49–53; George Milite, "Participative Management: Pros and Cons," *Supervisory Management,* January 1992, 10. **22.** Joani Nelson-Horchler, "The Magic of Herman Miller," *Industry Week,* 18 February 1991, 11–17. **23.** Peter Nulty, "The National Business Hall of Fame," *Fortune,* 11 March 1991, 98–102. **24.** William C. Symonds, "How Companies Are Learning to Prepare for the Worst," *Business Week,* 23 December 1985, 74–76; "StarKist Opens Doors Nearly 3 Years

After Tainted Tuna Scandal," *Montreal Gazette,* 11 September 1988, A8; Eileen Murray and Saundra Shohen, "Lessons from the Tylenol Tragedy on Surviving a Corporate Crisis," *Medical Marketing & Media,* February 1992, 14–19. **25.** Sharon Y. Lopez, "Managing Through Tough Times," *Black Enterprise,* January 1986, 57ff; Symonds, "How Companies Are Learning to Prepare for the Worst"; Carla Lazzareschi, "How 2 Firms Coped With Riots," *The Los Angeles Times,* 11 May 1992, D1, D6. **26.** See note 1.

CHAPTER 7

1. Larry Carpenter, "How to Market to Regions," *American Demographics,* November 1987, 44–45; Barbara Hetzer, "Pushing Decisions Down the Line at Campbell Soup," *Business Month,* July 1989, 62–63; David Wellman, "Campbell: The Next Generation," *Food & Beverage Marketing,* August 1990, 16–19; Tom Peters, "There Are No Excellent Companies," *Fortune,* 27 April 1987, 341–344, 352; Kevin T. Higgins, "Firms Tune Up Their Management," *Marketing News,* 25 September 1989, 2, 26; "Campbell Soup," *The Wall Street Transcript,* 16 March 1992, 104646; Ronald Fink, "Campbell Soup: Can the Stockpot Keep Bubbling?" *FW,* 31 March 1992, 16; "Campbell Creates 2 New Divisions," *Supermarket News,* 3 February 1992, 14; Stuart Elliott, "Campbell Shapes Up All Around," *The New York Times,* 29 January 1992, C5+; "Campbell Soup Co.," *The Wall Street Journal,* 29 January 1992, B12+. **2.** James E. Grunig, "Communication Is Not Enough," *Communications Briefings,* July 1987, 4; John H. Sheridan, "Aligning Structure with Strategy," *Industry Week,* 15 May 1989, 15–23; Richard L. Daft, *Management,* 2nd ed. (Chicago: Dryden, 1991), 246. **3.** Jim Brokaw, "Dr. Pepper, Sealtest and the Wood Brothers," *Motor Trend,* March 1974, 102. **4.** Kathryn M. Bartol and David C. Martin, *Management* (New York: McGraw-Hill, 1991), 336. **5.** Bartol and Martin, *Management,* 345. **6.** Daft, *Management,* 249. **7.** John S. McClenahen, "Flexible Structures to Absorb the Shocks," *Industry Week,* 18 April 1988, 41, 44. **8.** Bartol and Martin, *Management,* 349. **9.** John S. McClenahen, "Managing More People in the '90s," *Industry Week,* 20 March 1989, 30–38. **10.** Bartol and Martin, *Management,* 352. **11.** Richard T. Pascale, "Fit or Split?" *Across the Board,* June 1990, 48–52. **12.** Bartol and Martin, *Management,* 345. **13.** Bartol and Martin, *Management,* 370–371. **14.** Daft, *Management,* 256–259. **15.** Daft, *Management,* 259–262; Bartol and Martin, *Management,* 373–377. **16.** Daft, *Management,* 260. **17.** Daft, *Management,* 261; Bartol and Martin, *Management,* 376. **18.** Daft, *Management,* 262; Bartol and Martin, *Management,* 376. **19.** John Hoerr, "Work Teams Can Rev Up Paper-Pushers, Too," *Business Week,* 28 November 1988, 64–68, 72; Paul E. Brauchle and David W. Wright, "Fourteen Team Building Tips," *Training & Development,* January 1992, 32+; Dan Margolies, "Hi Ho, Hi Ho, It's Off to Manage Ourselves We Go!" *Kansas City Business Journal,* 21 February 1992, 1+; Tom Brown, "Why Teams Go 'Bust'," *Industry Week,* 2 March 1992, 20. **20.** Daft, *Management,* 266. **21.** Daft, *Management,* 264; David Pinto, "Wal-Mart, P&G Alter Retail Trade," *Chain Drug Review,* 9 March 1992, 1+; "The Big Gamble," *Adweek,* 9 March 1992, 9. **22.** Jolie B. Solomon

and John Bussey, "Pressed by Its Rivals, Procter & Gamble Co. Is Altering Its Ways," *The Wall Street Journal,* 20 May 1985, 1, 16. **23.** Joseph Weber, "A Culture That Just Keeps Dishing Up Success," *Business Week Innovation,* 1989, 120–123. **24.** Neal Boudette, "Networks to Dismantle Old Structures," *Industry Week,* 16 January 1989, 27–31. **25.** Daft, *Management,* 272–273. **26.** Christopher A. Bartlett and Sumantra Ghosal, "Matrix Management: Not a Structure, a Frame of Mind," *Harvard Business Review,* July–August 1990, 138–145. **27.** Daft, *Management,* 280–281; Bartol and Martin, *Management,* 357–358. **28.** Daft, *Management,* 282. **29.** Boudette, "Networks to Dismantle Old Structures," 27–31. **30.** Thomas M. Rohan, "Whitecollar Wisdom," *Industry Week,* 3 September 1990, 32–34. **31.** Daft, *Management,* 282; Bartol and Martin, *Management,* 360–361. **32.** Daft, *Management,* 283; Bartol and Martin, *Management,* 361. **33.** Daft, *Management,* 284. **34.** Charles Hall, "The Informal Organization Chart," *Supervisory Management,* January 1986, 41. **35.** Fred Luthans, "Successful vs. Effective Real Managers," *Academy of Management Executive,* 2, no. 2 (1988): 130. **36.** Princess Jackson Smith, "Networking: What It Is, What It Can Do for You, How You Do It," *Vital Speeches of the Day,* 15 September 1983, 712–713; John P. McDermott, "Professional Networking Can Heighten Perspective," *Pacific Business News,* 27 January 1992, 28. **37.** F. J. Lunding, G. L. Clements, and D. S. Perkins, "Everyone Who Makes It Has a Mentor," *Harvard Business Review,* July–August 1978. Reprinted in *Paths Toward Personal Progress: Leaders Are Made, Not Born* (Boston: Harvard Business Review, 1983), 135–147. **38.** Terence E. Deal and Allan A. Kennedy, *Corporate Cultures: The Rites and Rituals of Corporate Life* (Reading, Mass.: Addison-Wesley, 1982). **39.** Lawrence A. Bossidy, "Why Do We Waste Time Doing This?" *Across the Board,* May 1991, 17, 20–21. **40.** "What's Your Corporate Culture?" *Effective Manager,* December 1982, 4–5. Based on Deal and Kennedy, *Corporate Cultures.* **41.** See note 1. **42.** Adapted from "Lessons from a Successful Intrapreneur," *The Journal of Business Strategy,* March–April 1988, 20–24; Charles J. Murray, "Why 3M Values 'Intrapreneurship'," *Design News,* 4 April 1988, 111–118; Art Fry, "The Post-it Note: An Intrapreneurial Success," *Advanced Management Journal,* Summer 1987, 4–9.

CHAPTER 8

1. Adapted from Vaughn Beals, "Harley-Davidson: An American Success Story," *Journal for Quality and Participation,* June 1988, A19–A23; "Quality and Productivity: The Harley-Davidson Experience," *Survey of Business,* Spring 1986, 9–11; Sharon Brady, "School of Hard Knocks," *Software Magazine,* April 1988, 37–44; Shirley Cayer, "Harley's New Manager-Owners Put Purchasing Out Front," *Purchasing,* 13 October 1988, 50–54; Claudia H. Deutsch, "Now Harley-Davidson Is All Over the Road," *The New York Times,* 17 April 1988, sec. f, 12; Holt Hackney, "Easy Rider," *Financial World,* 4 September 1990, 48–49; Roy L. Harmon and Leroy D. Peterson, "Reinventing the Factory," *Across the Board,* March 1990, 30–38; John Holusha, "How Harley Outfoxed Japan with Exports," *The New York Times,* 12 August 1990,

sec. f, 5; Peter C. Reid, *Well Made in America* (New York: McGraw-Hill, 1990); "How Harley Beat Back the Japanese," *Fortune,* 25 September 1989, 155–164; Kevin Kelly and Otis Port, "Learning from Japan," *Business Week,* 27 January 1992, 52–60; James Sterngold, "American Business Starts a Counterattack in Japan; Long-Term Commitment Is Needed for Success," *The New York Times,* 24 February 1992, A1+; "Harley: Serious about Success," *Production,* February 1992, 10. **2.** Gene Bylinsky, "The Race to the Automatic Factory," *Fortune,* 21 February 1983, 51+. **3.** Wickham Skinner, *Manufacturing: The Formidable Competitive Weapon* (New York: Wiley, 1985), 216. **4.** George Stalk, Jr., and Thomas M. Hout, *Competing Against Time* (New York: Free Press, 1990), 2, 52, 58. **5.** Dwight B. Davis, "Apple: Harvesting the Macintosh," *High Technology,* May 1985, 39–40. **6.** "Could a Robot Do That Job?" *Industry Week,* 10 June 1985, 5; "Brother Robot," *The Economist,* 14 March 1992, S23+; Colleen Moynahan, "Robot Enables Safer, Faster Finishing Operation," *Apparel Industry Magazine,* January 1992, 36. **7.** Kathryn M. Bartol and David C. Martin, *Management* (New York: McGraw-Hill, 1991), 688. **8.** Doris Jones Yang, "Boeing Knocks Down the Wall Between the Dreamers and the Doers," *Business Week,* 28 October 1991, 120–121. **9.** Bob Davis, "Computers Speed the Design of More Workaday Products," *The Wall Street Journal,* 18 January 1985, 19. **10.** Bartol and Martin, *Management,* 687. **11.** Stephen Kreider Yoder, "Putting It All Together," *The Wall Street Journal,* 4 June 1990, R24. **12.** Bylinsky, "The Race to the Automatic Factory." **13.** Bylinsky, "The Race to the Automatic Factory." **14.** James O'Toole, "Eli Whitney, You've Met Your Waterloo," *Across the Board,* November 1985. **15.** Gary S. Vasilash, "A Working FMS!" *Production,* December 1990, 50–52. **16.** James B. Dilworth, *Production and Operations Management: Manufacturing and Nonmanufacturing,* 3rd ed. (New York: Random House, 1986), 566. **17.** Wickham Skinner, "The Focused Factory," *Harvard Business Review,* May–June 1974, 115. **18.** Roger W. Schmenner, *Production/Operations Management: Concepts and Situations,* 2nd ed. (Chicago: Science Research Associates, 1981), 281. **19.** Dilworth, *Production and Operations Management,* 356. **20.** Milt Freudenheim, "Removing the Warehouse from Cost-Conscious Hospitals," *The New York Times,* 3 March 1991, sec. c, 5. **21.** "Production Problems Become More Manageable," *Business Week,* 25 April 1983, 70+. **22.** Schmenner, *Production/Operations Management,* 618. **23.** "Quality: The U.S. Drives to Catch Up," *Business Week,* 1 November 1982, 66+; Rick Van Sant, "The Quest for Quality," *Cincinnati Business Courier,* 24 February 1992, 13; Peter Adrian, "Cost-Cutting, Quality Improvement Insufficient to Ensure Manufacturing Success," *Manufacturing Automation,* November 1991, 2; Candice Goodwin, "The Stamp of Quality Approval," *Accountancy,* December 1991, 114+; John Butman, "Quality Comes Full Circle," *Management Review,* February 1992, 49+. **24.** David A. Garvin, "Product Quality: Profitable at Any Cost," *The New York Times,* 3 March 1985, sec. 3, 3; Maurice Jeffrey, "Quality in Product Development," *Candy Industry,* November 1991, 49. **25.** Richard T. Schonberger and E. M. Knod, *Operations Management,* 4th ed. (Homewood, Ill.: Irwin, 1991), 872. **26.** Schmenner, *Production/Operations Management,* 209. **27.** Garvin, "Product Quality: Profitable at Any Cost." **28.** Jeremy Main, "Ford's Drive for Quality," *Fortune,* 18 April 1983, 62+. **29.** Courtland L. Bovée and John V. Thill, *Marketing* (New York: McGraw-Hill, 1992), 729. **30.** Schmenner, *Production/Operations Management,* 209. **31.** Dilworth, *Production and Operations Management,* 618. **32.** Marilyn Joyce, "An Ergonomics Primer Part 1: Office Considerations," *Management Solutions,* April 1988, 38–45. **33.** Dilworth, *Production and Operations Management,* 608–609. **34.** Main, "Ford's Drive for Quality"; "Ford Uses Employee-Involvement Groups to Improve Quality," *Automotive News,* 28 February 1983, 4. **35.** Peter F. Drucker, "The Emerging Theory of Manufacturing," *Harvard Business Review,* May–June 1990, 94–102. **36.** Gilbert Fuchsbert, "Gurus of Quality Are Gaining Clout," *The Wall Street Journal,* 27 November 1990, B1. **37.** John H. Sheridan, "World-Class Manufacturing," *Industry Week,* 2 July 1990, 36, 38, 40–46; Obie O. Mason, "Toward a World Class Manufacturing," *America's Textiles International,* February 1992, 54+; Thomas Schuler, "World Class Manufacturing on Your Doorstep: What to Do about It. . . ," *Nonwovens Industry,* January 1992, 22+. **38.** Jonathan P. Hicks, "Making Steel Cheaper and Faster," *The New York Times,* 27 February 1991, sec. d, 7. **39.** Amil Kumar Naj, "Industrial Switch: Some Companies Cut Pollution by Altering Production Methods," *The Wall Street Journal,* 24 December 1990, 1, 21; Juanita Darling, "Mexico's Anti-Smog Plan Meets Industry Resistance," *The Los Angeles Times,* 25 March 1992, A4+; Sarah Lubman, "Rockwell Settles Pollution Charge; Criticizes Agency," *The Wall Street Journal,* 27 March 1992, A16+. **40.** Keith H. Hammonds and Monica Roman, "Itching to Get onto the Factory Floor," *Business Week,* 14 October 1991, 62, 64. **41.** Dilworth, *Production and Operations Management,* 551–556. **42.** Bartol and Martin, *Management,* 307–308. **43.** See note 1. **44.** John Teresko, "Making CIM Work with People," *Industry Week,* 2 November 1987, 50–65; Thomas M. Rohan, "Whipping Resistance," *Industry Week,* 2 November 1987, 68–84; Therese R. Welter, "Getting Set for Implementation," *Industry Week,* 2 November 1987, 86–92; Kenneth R. Sheets with Robert F. Black, "America's Blue Collars Get Down to Business," *U.S. News & World Report,* 29 February 1988, 52–53; Alan Halcrow, "Employee Participation Is a Sign of the Times in LA," *Personnel Journal,* January 1988, 10–11.

CHAPTER 9

1. Adapted from Thomas M. Rohan, "Maverick Remakes Old-Line Steel," *Industry Week,* 21 January 1991, 26–30; "Nucor's Ken Iverson on Productivity and Pay," *Personnel Administrator,* October 1986, 46–52, 106–108; John Merwin, "People, Attitudes and Equipment," *Forbes,* 8 February 1988, 68–72; "Empowering Employees," *Chief Executive,* March–April 1989, 44–49; Michael A. D'Amato and Jeremy H. Silverman, "How to Make Money in a Dull Business," *Across the Board,* December 1990, 54–59; Richard Preston, "Annals of Enterprise; Hot Metal-I," *The New Yorker,* 25 February 1991, 43–71; Frank Haflich, "Nucor Looks Westward but Scrap Holds Keys," *American Metal Market,* 27 March 1992, 1+; Erle Norton, "Nucor to Spend $170 Million on Plant Expansion," *Business*

Journal Serving Charlotte and the Metropolitan Area, 27 January 1992, 1+. **2.** Bernard M. Bass, *Leadership and Performance Beyond Expectations—Executive Book Summaries,* 8, no. 6 (June 1986): 6. **3.** "New Findings About What Makes Workers Happy," *Working Woman,* February 1985, 22. **4.** Dennis C. Kinlaw, "What Employees 'See' Is What Organizations 'Get,'" *Management Solutions,* March 1988, 38–41. **5.** Elton Mayo, "Hawthorne and the Western Electric Company," in *Classics in Management,* edited by Harwood F. Merrill (New York: American Management Association, 1960). **6.** Abraham H. Maslow, "A Theory of Human Motivations," *Psychological Review,* July 1943, 370; *Motivation and Personality,* 2nd ed. (New York: Harper & Row, 1970). **7.** Frederick Herzberg, *Work and the Nature of Man* (New York: World, 1971). **8.** David A. Nadler and Edward E. Lawler III, "Motivation—A Diagnostic Approach," in *Perspectives on Behavior in Organizations,* edited by Richard Hackman, Edward E. Lawler III, and Lyman W. Porter (New York: McGraw-Hill, 1977). **9.** Walter B. Newsome, "Motivate, Now!" *Personnel Journal,* February 1990, 51–54; Marjorie Wold, "Making Workers Happy: It Takes More Than a Paycheck to Motivate Your Employees. Here Are Some Owners Who Take a Personal Interest in Their Workers, with Impressive Results," *Progressive Grocer,* March 1992, 44+; "Educate, Motivate to Compete in the 90s," *Modern Materials Handling,* January 1992, 62+. **10.** Douglas McGregor, *The Human Side of Enterprise* (New York: McGraw-Hill, 1970). **11.** Christopher Byron, "An Attractive Japanese Export: The XYZs of Management Theory Challenge American Bosses," *Time,* 2 March 1983, 74; William G. Ouchi, *Theory Z: How American Business Can Meet the Japanese Challenge* (Reading, Mass.: Addison-Wesley, 1981). **12.** U.S. Department of Labor Statistics. **13.** Anne B. Fisher, "The Downside of Downsizing," *Fortune,* 23 May 1988, 42. **14.** John Case, "The Real Age Wave," *Inc.,* July 1989, 23. **15.** Kathleen McKay-Rispoli, "Small Children: No Small Problem," *Management World,* March–April 1988, 15. **16.** "Workforce 2000 Is Welcome Today at Digital," *Business Ethics,* July–August 1990, 15–16. **17.** "12 Companies That Do the Right Thing," *Working Woman,* January 1991, 57–59. **18.** Fisher, "The Downside of Downsizing," 42; Daniel Goleman, "When the Boss Is Unbearable," *The New York Times,* 28 December 1986, sec. 3, 29. **19.** Janice Castro, "Where Did the Gung Ho Go?" *Time,* 11 September 1989, 53. **20.** Joani Nelson-Horchler, "When the Escalator Stops . . . ," *Industry Week,* 8 December 1986, 62. **21.** Alan Deutschman, "What 25-Year-Olds Want," *Fortune,* 27 August 1990, 43. **22.** Edwin A. Locke and Gary P. Latham, *Goal Setting: A Motivational Technique That Works!* (Englewood Cliffs, N.J.: Prentice-Hall, 1984). **23.** Robert W. Goddard, "Well Done!" *Management World,* November–December 1987, 14–15. **24.** Michael LeBoeuf, "The Greatest Management Principle in the World," *Working Woman,* January 1988, 70–72+. **25.** Ronald Whipple, "Rewards Have Value," *Personnel Journal,* September 1990, 92–93. **26.** John Holusha, "Detroit's New Labor Strategy," *The New York Times,* 13 May 1983. **27.** Terrence Roth, "Employee Involvement Gains Support," *The Wall Street Journal,* 12 December 1984, 35; Jonathan Lee, "Sonoco Stresses Employee Involvement to Alter Company's Safety Performance," *Pulp & Paper,* March 1992, 198+; Robert L. Masternak and Timothy

L. Ross, "Gainsharing: A Bonus Plan or Employee Involvement?" *Compensation and Benefits Review,* January/February 1992, 46+. **28.** "A Work Revolution in U.S. Industry," *Business Week,* 16 May 1983, 100+. **29.** "A Work Revolution in U.S. Industry." **30.** "USA Snapshots," *USA Today,* 20 November 1990, 1D. **31.** Hewitt Associates, reported in Cathy Trost and Carol Hymowitz, "Careers Start Giving In to Family Needs," *The Wall Street Journal,* 18 June 1990, 9E. **32.** Dennis J. Kravitz, *The Human Resource Revolution—Executive Book Summaries,* 11, no. 7 (July 1989): 4. **33.** Deirdre Fanning, "Fleeing the Office, and Its Distractions," *The New York Times,* 12 August 1990, sec. 3, 25. **34.** Julie A. Cohen, "Managing Tomorrow's Workforce Today," *Management Review,* January 1991, 19; Bob Cohn, "A Glimpse of the 'Flex' Future," *Newsweek,* 1 August 1988, 39. **35.** Carey W. English, "Job Sharing Gains Ground Across U.S.," *U.S. News & World Report,* 14 October 1985, 76. **36.** Tracy E. Benson, "Empowered Employees Sharpen the Edge," *Industry Week,* 19 February 1990, 18. **37.** Michael A. Verespej, "When You Put the Team in Charge," *Industry Week,* 3 December 1990, 30–32. **38.** Kevin M. Paulsen, "Gain Sharing: A Group Motivator," *MW,* May–June 1989, 24–25. **39.** "Where Ducks and Fun Mean Success," *Industry Week,* 18 March 1991, 29. **40.** See note 1. **41.** Adapted from Alan Halcrow, "A Gold Medal Boost to Morale at Domino's Pizza," *Personnel Journal,* August 1987, 23, 25.

CHAPTER 10

1. Adapted from "Changing a Corporate Culture," *Business Week,* 14 May 1984, 130–138; *The Johnson & Johnson 1990 Annual Report*; "Shrinking, Changing Labor Force Prompts Johnson & Johnson Family Issues Policies," *Employee Benefit Plan Review,* September 1989, 57–60; "What Makes Sales Forces Run?" *Sales & Marketing Management,* 3 December 1984, 24–26; Susan Dentzer, "Excessive Claims," *Business Month,* July 1990, 52–63; Evelyn Gilbert, "Benefits No 'Soft' Issue: J&J Official," *National Underwriter,* 10 December 1990, 15, 21; Christopher Power, "At Johnson & Johnson, a Mistake Can Be a Badge of Honor," *Business Week,* 26 September 1988, 126–128; Lee Smith, "J&J Comes a Long Way from Baby," *Fortune,* 1 June 1981, 58–66; Neal Templin, "Johnson & Johnson 'Wellness' Program for Workers Shows Healthy Bottom Line," *The Wall Street Journal,* 21 May 1990, B1, B6; Barbara Scherr Trenk, "Corporate Fitness Programs Become Hearty Investments," *Management Review,* August 1989, 33–37; Michael A. Verespej, "A Ticket to Better Health," *Industry Week,* 4 February 1991, 24–25; Joseph Weber, "No Band-Aids for Ralph Larsen," *Business Week,* 28 May 1990, 86–87. **2.** Ellen Brandt, "Global HR," *Personnel Journal,* March 1991, 40. **3.** James W. Walker, *Human Resource Planning* (New York: McGraw-Hill, 1980), 4. **4.** Joel Dreyfuss, "Get Ready for the New Work Force," *Fortune,* 23 April 1990, 172. **5.** "Job Puzzle: Skilled Workers Scarce Even as Layoffs Mount," *San Diego Tribune,* 1 October 1991, A-1. **6.** Peter T. Kilborn, "Part-Time Hirings Bring Deep Changes in U.S. Workplaces," *The New York Times,* 17 June 1991, A1. **7.** Max Messmer, "Strategic Staffing for the '90s," *Personnel Journal,* October 1990, 94. **8.** David Kirkpatrick, "Smart New Ways to Use

Temps," *Fortune,* 15 February 1988, 110–116; "Part-Time, Work-At-Home Add Flexibility," *Employee Benefit Plan Review,* March 1992, 26–28; Debra Tomchek, "Part-Time Professional: Making it Work," *Bureaucrat,* Winter 1991–1992, 54–56. **9.** "The Interviewing Process," *Small Business Report,* December 1987, 61–66. **10.** "Drug Testing," *The Wall Street Journal,* 19 March 1991, A1. **11.** Carl Camden and Bill Wallace, "Job Application Forms: A Hazardous Employment Practice," *Personnel Administrator,* March 1983, 31+. **12.** Jean Sensel and Dianne MacDonald, "Dragging Employers into Child Support," *Nation's Business,* October 1991, 34–35. **13.** Marj Charlier and Wade Lambert, "McDonald's Told to Pay $210,000 Damages in Negligent-Hiring Case," *The Wall Street Journal,* 15 March 1991, B4. **14.** "New-Employee Orientation," *Small Business Report,* April 1984, 37–40. **15.** Robin Bergstrom, "Hard Times," *Production,* July 1990, 50. **16.** "The Three R's on the Shop Floor," *Fortune,* Education 1990, 87. **17.** Susan E. Kuhn, "How Business Helps Schools," *Fortune,* Education 1990, 91. **18.** "The Three R's," 88. **19.** Brian S. Moskal, "Just a Degree of Confidence," *Industry Week,* 19 February 1990, 65–66. **20.** *World Almanac and Book of Facts: 1992* (New York: Pharos Books, 1991), 177. **21.** Joani Nelson-Horchler, "CEO Pay," *Industry Week,* 15 April 1991, 13. **22.** Janice Castro, "How's Your Pay?" *Time,* 15 April 1991, 40; John A. Byrne, "The Flap over Executive Pay," *Business Week,* 6 May 1991, 90. **23.** Edward C. Baig, "The Great Earnings Gamble," *U.S. News & World Report,* 17 September 1990, 65, 68. **24.** John Greenwald, "Workers: Risks and Rewards," *Time,* 15 April 1991, 42–43. **25.** Greenwald, "Workers: Risks and Rewards." **26.** Earl Ingram, "Compensation: The Advantages of Knowledge-Based Pay," *Personnel Journal,* April 1990, 138–140. **27.** U.S. Chamber of Commerce, *Employee Benefits* (Washington, D.C.: GPO, 1991), 34–36. **28.** *Statistical Abstract of the United States: 1991* (Washington, D.C.: GPO, 1991), 430. **29.** Roger Thompson, "The Threat to Pension Plans," *Nation's Business,* March 1991, 18–24; "How Safe Are Pension Plans?" *Journal of Accountancy,* February 1992, 16; Linda Thornburg, "The Pension Headache," *HRMagazine* January 1992, 38+. **30.** Christopher Power, "Pension Raiding, 1983 Style," *Forbes,* 20 June 1983, 130. **31.** John Hoerr, "ESOPs: Revolution or Ripoff?" *Business Week,* 15 April 1985, 94–108; William Smith, Harold Lazarus, and Harold Murray Kalkstein, "Employee Stock Ownership Plans: Motivation and Morale Issues," *Compensation and Benefits Review,* 1 September 1990, 37; Margaret Lund, "ESOPs Gaining Popularity as Business Tool," *National Underwriter Property & Casualty-Risk & Benefits Management,* 23 March 1992, 20+; "ESOP Seen as 'Win-Win' for Company, Employees," *Milling & Baking News,* 11 February 1992, 18. **32.** "Taking Baby Steps Toward a Daddy Track," *Business Week,* 15 April 1991, 90. **33.** Carol A. Perkin, "Help for Workers Who Care for Their Parents," *The New York Times,* 4 June 1989, sec. 3, 19. **34.** Julie A. Cohen, "Keeping Kids at Work," *Management Review,* January 1991, 27–28. **35.** Donald L. Parks, "Time Off in the Future," *Pension World,* March 1991, 42–43. **36.** "Flexible Benefit Plans Popular with Small Companies," *Small Business Report,* November 1985, 34. **37.** "Why We Should Invest in Human Capital," *Business Week,* 17 December 1990, 89. **38.** Templin, "Johnson & Johnson's 'Wellness' Program," B1. **39.** Julie A.

Cohen, "Managing Tomorrow's Workforce Today," *Management Review,* January 1991, 21. **40.** Michael J. Major, "Employee Assistance Programs: An Ideal Whose Time Has Come," *Modern Office Technology,* March 1990, 76. **41.** Maria Helene Sekas, "Dual-Career Couples—A Corporate Challenge," *Personnel Administrator,* April 1984, 37–45. **42.** William McWhirter, "Major Overhaul," *Time,* 30 December 1991, 56–58. **43.** "Farewell Fast Track," *Business Week,* 10 December 1990, 193. **44.** Survey Research Center, Economic Policy Division, Chamber of Commerce of the United States, *Employee Benefits 1981* (Washington, D.C.: Chamber of Commerce of the United States, 1981). **45.** "Helping Squeezed Executives When the Belt Gets Tighter," *Insight,* 26 November 1990, 39. **46.** Kirkland Ropp, "Downsizing Strategies," *Personnel Administrator,* February 1987, 61–64; Paul M. Forbes, "Winning in the New Neighborhood," *National Petroleum News,* March 1992, 65. **47.** Daniel Forbes, "The No-Layoff Payoff," *Dun's Business Month,* July 1985, 64–66. **48.** Bill Saporito, "Cutting Costs Without Cutting People," *Fortune,* 25 May 1987, 27–32. **49.** Donald C. Bacon, "See You in Court," *Nation's Business,* July 1989, 17. **50.** Joann S. Lublin, "Firing Line: Legal Challenges Force Firms to Revamp Ways They Dismiss Workers," *The Wall Street Journal,* 13 September 1983. **51.** Robert A. Snyder and Billie Brandon, "Riding the Third Wave: Staying on Top of ADEA Complaints," *Personnel Administrator,* February 1983, 41–47; Arnold H. Lubasch, "U.S. Court Decides Cases on Age Bias," *The New York Times,* 16 December 1982; Aaron Bernstein, "Putting Mandatory Retirement Out to Pasture," *Business Week,* 10 June 1985, 104–105. **52.** Irene Pave, "They Won't Take It Anymore," *Across the Board,* November 1990, 20. **53.** Sandra Evans, "Today's Elderly: Healthier, Happier," *Washington Post,* 9 March 1986, A1. **54.** See note 1. **55.** Adapted from Seth H. Lubove, "Pivotal People," *The Wall Street Journal,* 3 August 1987, 1. Reprinted by permission of *The Wall Street Journal,* © Dow Jones & Company, Inc., 1987. All Rights Reserved Worldwide.

CHAPTER 11

1. Adapted from Morgan O. Reynolds, "Unions and Jobs: The U.S. Auto Industry," *Journal of Labor Research,* Spring 1986, 103–126; William A. Nowlin, "Restructuring in Manufacturing: Management, Work, and Labor Relations," *Industrial Management,* November–December 1990, 5–9, 30; Anne B. Fisher, "Behind the Hype at GM's Saturn," *Fortune,* 11 November 1985, 34–49; Donald Ephlin, "Saturn's Strategic Role in Industrial Relations," *Survey of Business,* Summer 1986, 23–25; Alex Taylor III, "Back to the Future at Saturn," *Fortune,* 1 August 1988, 63–72; "GM–Auto Workers Saturn Contract," *Monthly Labor Review,* October 1985, 48–50; Bryan H. Berry, "It's Now or Never for World-Class Automaking at GM," *Iron Age,* 7 November 1986, 34A1–35; James B. Treece, "Here Comes GM's Saturn," *Business Week,* 9 April 1990, 56–62; Maralyn Edid, "How Power Will Be Balanced on Saturn's Shop Floor," *Business Week,* 5 August 1985, 65–66; Ben Fischer, "Finishing Out the Century," *Journal for Quality and Participation,* March 1991, 48–52; Doron P. Levin, "Reality Comes to G.M.'s Saturn Plant," *New

York Times,* 14 November 1991, sec. c, 1, 5; "Saturn Unit's Workers Pass Labor Pact by 72% to 28%," *The Wall Street Journal,* 15 November 1991, A2; Kathleen Morris, "Sales: Saturn-GM," *FW,* 14 April 1992, 48; Terrence O'Hara, "At Long Last, Saturn Cars Go into Orbit," *The Washington Business Journal,* 17 February 1992, 1+; Jim Henry, "Saturn Has Made Business Fun Again," *Automotive News,* 10 February 1992, 88+; Bob English, "Saturn Has the Ring of Success; GM Subsidiary Taking Customers Away from the Imports," *The Financial Post,* 15 February 1992, A2+; "Saturn Will Make Money within Five Years," *Ward's Auto World,* March 1992, 30. **2.** Clemens P. Work, "Making It Clear Who's Boss," *U.S. News & World Report,* 8 September 1986, 43. **3.** Peter F. Drucker, "Peter Drucker Asks: Will Unions Ever Again Be Useful Organs of Society?" *Industry Week,* 20 March 1989, 18–19. **4.** James Cook, "Collision Course," *Forbes,* 13 May 1991, 81. **5.** "The Good Guy Finally Won," *Time,* 23 December 1991, 56. **6.** Ephraim Lewis, "BW/Harris Poll: Confidence in Unions Is Crumbling," *Business Week,* 8 July 1985, 76. Reprinted by special permission, copyright © 1985 by McGraw-Hill, Inc. **7.** Thomas A. Kochan and Harry C. Katz, *Collective Bargaining and Industrial Relations* (Homewood, Ill.: Irwin, 1988), 165. **8.** Kochan and Katz, *Collective Bargaining and Industrial Relations,* 166. **9.** Barry Schiffman, "Tougher Tactics to Keep Out Unions," *The New York Times,* 3 March 1991, sec. 3, 8. **10.** Kochan and Katz, *Collective Bargaining and Industrial Relations,* 173. **11.** Terry Schraeder, "Decertification Elections: An Opportunity for Employers," *PIMA Magazine,* October 1990, 10. **12.** Kochan and Katz, *Collective Bargaining and Industrial Relations,* 176, 238. **13.** *World Almanac and Book of Facts* (New York: Scripps Howard, 1989), 161. **14.** Aaron Bernstein, "The Secondary Boycott Gets a Second Wind," *Business Week,* 27 June 1988, 82. **15.** David Benjamin/Jay, "Labor's Boardroom Guerrilla," *Time,* 20 June 1988, 50. **16.** Facts on File, 15 July 1988, 514; Personal communication, Ben Albert of COPE. **17.** "Next!" *Forbes,* 18 July 1983, 149; "Paper Avoids a Replay of J. P. Stevens," *Business Week,* 27 June 1983, 33+. **18.** Bob Baker, "Riding Out the Strike," *Los Angeles Times,* 26 August 1990, D1–D3; Peter T. Kilborn, "Ban on Replacing Strikers Faces Veto Threat," *The New York Times,* 7 March 1991, A10. **19.** "'Telescabbing': The New Union Buster," *Newsweek,* 29 August 1983, 53–54. **20.** "NLRB Permits Replacements During Legal Lockout," *Personnel Journal,* January 1987, 14–15. **21.** Daniel D. Luria, "New Labor–Management Models for Detroit?" *Harvard Business Review,* September–October 1986, 27. **22.** "Strikes and Lockouts in U.S. Now on Rise," *The New York Times,* 12 March 1987, A28. **23.** U.S. Department of Labor, Bureau of Labor Statistics, *Current Wage Developments* (Washington, D.C.: GPO, February 1991), 4. **24.** Clarence R. Deitsch and David A. Dilts, "The COLA Clause: An Employer Bargaining Weapon?" *Personnel Journal,* March 1982, 220–223; Kenneth B. Noble, "Workers Aren't Betting on Inflation," *The New York Times,* 27 April 1986, E4. **25.** John J. Lacombe II and Fehmida R. Sleemi, "Wage Adjustments in Contracts Negotiated in Private Industry in 1987," *Monthly Labor Review,* May 1988, 23; U.S. Department of Labor, Bureau of Labor Statistics, *Compensation and Working Conditions* (Washington, D.C.: GPO, August 1991), 49. **26.** Edward M. Coates III, "Profit Sharing

Today: Plans and Provisions," *Monthly Labor Review,* April 1991, 19. **27.** Gary W. Florkowski, "Profit Sharing and Public Policy: Insights for the United States," *Industrial Relations,* Winter 1991, 98; Henry L. Turner, III, "Qualified Plans Fail the 'True Economics' Test," *National Underwriter Life & Health–Financial Services Edition,* 2 March 1992, 20+. **28.** Florkowski, "Profit Sharing and Public Policy," 98. **29.** "Bell System's Breakup Is Jarring the Unions," *Business Week,* 30 May 1983, 76+; "The Sudden Uncertainties of Working for Bell," *Business Week,* 20 June 1983, 26. **30.** Gregory A. Patterson, "Blue Collar Boon: Hourly Auto Workers Now on Layoff Have a Sturdy Safety Net," *The Wall Street Journal,* 29 January 1991, A1; Gregory A. Patterson and Joseph B. White, "GM–UAW Pact Allows Company to Cut Payroll in Return for Worker Buy-Outs," *The Wall Street Journal,* 19 September 1990, A3. **31.** Jeremy Main, "Anatomy of an Auto-Plant Rescue," *Fortune,* 4 April 1983, 108+. **32.** Daniel Seligman, "Who Needs Unions?" *Fortune,* 12 July 1982, 54+.; *Fortune* Panel, "Are the Unions Dead?" **33.** Donald Thompson, "New Role for Labor Unions," *Industry Week,* 9 February 1987, 35. **34.** Richard Leonard, "ESOPs Bring Participation Home," *Management Review,* November 1990, 45–49; Howard Banks, "Who Guards the Public Interest?" *Forbes,* 11 April 1983, 39+; Kenneth Labich, "A Steel Town's Bid to Save Itself," *Fortune,* 18 April 1983, 103+; "The Next Step for Weirton's Workers," *Business Week,* 28 March 1983, 39; William Serrin, "Employees to Buy Huge Steel Works in $66 Million Pact," *The New York Times,* 14 March 1983, 1; "The Fortune 500 Special Report," *Fortune,* 28 April 1986, 174. **35.** Aaron Bernstein, "Move Over Boone, Carl, and Irv—Here Comes Labor," *Business Week,* 14 December 1987, 125. **36.** Michael A. Verespej, "Unions Seize Opportunity," *Industry Week,* 2 May 1988, 22. **37.** David Pauly, "2001: A Union Odyssey," *Newsweek,* 5 August 1985, 40. **38.** Seligman, "Who Needs Unions"; *Fortune* Panel, "Are the Unions Dead?" **39.** "Next a Valet with Each Job?" *Time,* 2 March 1987, 55. **40.** See note 1. **41.** Francine Schwadel, "Nordstrom Workers Reject Their Union in Voting at Five Seattle-Area Stores," *The Wall Street Journal,* 22 July 1991, B4; "Briefly: Employees Want Nordstrom Union Booted," *Los Angeles Times,* 4 May 1991, D2; "NLRB Clears Nordstrom of Unfair Labor Practices," *Women's Wear Daily,* 10 April 1991, 22; Charlene Marmer Solomon, "Nightmare at Nordstrom," *Personnel Journal,* September 1990, 76–83; Linda Darnell Williams, "Nordstrom Pact Aims to Resolve Labor Dispute," *Los Angeles Times,* 18 August 1990, D1, D2; Francine Schwadel, "Irate Nordstrom Straining in Labor Fight," *The Wall Street Journal,* 5 April 1990, B1, B6; Stuart Silverstein, "Taking On Nordstrom," *Los Angeles Times,* 12 March 1990, D1, D4.

CHAPTER 12

1. Dori Jones Yang and Robert Buderi, "Step by Step with Nike," *Business Week,* 13 August 1990, 116–117; "The '80s: What a Decade!" *Advertising Age,* 1 January 1990, 25; Kate Fitzgerald, "Nike Flexes Muscle for Kids," *Advertising Age,* 10 July 1989, 51; "The Billboard Is Back! Nike Captures Award as Decade's Best," *PR Newswire,* 5 December 1989; Sheryl Franklin, "The Other Side," *Bank Marketing,* August 1987, 62; "Nike Outdoes Competition in Delivery to Customers," *Global Trade,* March 1988, 8; Ellen Benoit, "Lost Youth," *Financial World,* 20 September 1988, 28–31; Robert F. Hartley, *Marketing Successes, Historical to Present Day: What We Can Learn* (New York: Wiley, 1985), 214–224; Marcy Magiera, "Nike Edges Reebok; L.A. Gear Sprinting," *Advertising Age,* 25 September 1989, 93; Douglas C. McGill, "Nike Is Bounding Past Reebok," *The New York Times,* 11 July 1989, sec. d, 1–4; Barbara Buell, "Nike Catches Up with the Trendy Frontrunner," *Business Week,* 24 October 1988, 88; Pat Sloan, "Reebok Runs Harder to Keep Lead," *Advertising Age,* 24 July 1989, 6; G. Christian Hill, "Nike Posts Big Gains in Sales and Profit; Reebok Hopes Pump Will Help It Keep Up," *The Wall Street Journal,* 19 December 1989, B10; Pat Sloan, "Reebok Gets Pumped for 1990," *Advertising Age,* 20 November 1989, 35; Bruce Horovitz, "Athletes Team Up for New Nike Campaign," *Los Angeles Times,* 27 June 1989, sec. IV, 6; Dori Jones Yang, "Swoosh: The Unauthorized Story of Nike and the Men Who Played There," *Business Week,* 6 April 1992, 10. **2.** "AMA Board Approves New Marketing Definition," *Marketing News,* 1 March 1985, 1. **3.** Franklin S. Houston, "The Marketing Concept: What It Is and What It Is Not," *Journal of Marketing,* April 1986, 81–87. **4.** George S. Day and Robin Wensley, "Assessing Advantage: A Framework for Diagnosing Competitive Superiority," *Journal of Marketing,* April 1988, 1–20. **5.** Janice Castro, "Mr. Sam Stuns Goliath," *Time,* 25 February 1991, 62–63. **6.** Michael E. Porter, *Competitive Advantage* (New York: Free Press, 1985), 14. **7.** Courtland L. Bovée and John V. Thill, *Marketing* (New York: McGraw-Hill, 1992), 188. **8.** John F. Cady and Robert D. Buzzell, *Strategic Marketing* (Boston: Little, Brown, 1986), 13. **9.** Roy Furchgott, "Skinny Beef Joins the Light Lineup," *Adweek,* 3 November 1986, 26. **10.** Kathleen M. Berry, "Diversifying to Counter a Slump on the Slopes," *The New York Times,* 6 January 1991, sec. 3, 4. **11.** Ronald Alsop and Michael Waldholz, "Aspirin Makers Gear Up to Profit from New Study on Heart Attacks," *The Wall Street Journal,* 28 January 1988, A27. **12.** Al Ries and Jack Trout, "Marketing Warfare," *Journal of Consumer Marketing,* Fall 1986, 78. **13.** Charles D. Schewe, *Marketing Principles and Strategies* (New York: Random House, 1987), 50. **14.** Schewe, *Marketing Principles and Strategies,* 52–55. **15.** Geoffrey Colvin, "The Wee Outfit That Decked IBM," *Fortune,* 19 November 1990, 165, 168. **16.** Annetta Miller and Dody Tsiantar, "A Test for Market Research," *Newsweek,* 28 December 1987, 32. **17.** Jack J. Honomichl, *Honomichl on Marketing Research* (Lincolnwood, Ill.: NTC Business Books, 1986), 74–84. **18.** Claudia H. Deutsch, "What Do People Want, Anyway," *The New York Times,* 8 November 1987, sec. 3, 4. **19.** Robert Johnson, "General Mills Risks Millions Starting Chain of Italian Restaurants," *The Wall Street Journal,* 21 September 1987, A1; Gail Bellamy, "Menus That Sell," *Restaurant Business,* March 1992, 72–80; Nancy Brumback, "Crashing Down," *Restaurant Business,* 1 March 1992, 58–62; Rajan Chaudhry, "R & I Presents America's Choice in Chains," *Restaurants & Institutions,* 12 February 1992, 76–96; Carol Casper, "Market Segment Report: Italian," *Restaurant Business,* 20 January 1992, 127–136. **20.** "Top 50 Growth Chains," *Restaurant Business,* 20 July 1991, 117–130. **21.** Stephen Rosen, "Cost-Conscious Market Research," *The Wall Street Journal,* 25 April 1988, B24. **22.** Letter to owners, from Infiniti Division of Nissan Motor Corporation, 23 July 1991. **23.** Robert B. Settle and Pamela Alreck, "How to Be Class Conscious," *Success,* June 1987, 8, 10. **24.** "Roper's America: A Small, Outspoken Group Forms Majority of Opinions," *Adweek,* 25 April 1988, 16. **25.** "The Customer Isn't Always Rational," *Adweek,* 7 December 1987, 36. **26.** "The Customer Isn't Always Rational," 37. **27.** Francine Schwadel, "Shoppers' Blues: The Thrill Is Gone," *The Wall Street Journal,* 13 October 1989, B1–B2; Betsy Morris, "As a Favored Pastime, Shopping Ranks High with Most Americans," *The Wall Street Journal,* 30 July 1987, 1, 16. **28.** Robert Kearns, "Is Everybody Happy?" *Business Marketing,* December 1989, 30–32, 34, 36. **29.** Michael H. Morris and Jeanne L. Holman, "Source Loyalty in Organizational Markets: A Dyadic Perspective," *Journal of Business Research,* 16, no. 2 (1988): 117–131. **30.** Ernest F. Cooke, "What Is Business and Industrial Marketing?" *Journal of Business and Industrial Marketing,* Fall 1986, 9–17. **31.** Morris and Holman, "Source Loyalty in Organizational Markets," 118; Cooke, "What Is Business and Industrial Marketing?" 11. **32.** Haken Hakansson, ed., *International Marketing and Purchasing of Industrial Goods* (New York: Wiley, 1984). **33.** Ronald Alsop, "Firms Send Brands to College to Cultivate New Consumers," *The Wall Street Journal,* 31 July 1986, B25; Joanne Lipman, "Spring Break Sponsors in Florida Find Too Much of a Good Thing," *The Wall Street Journal,* 21 March 1989, B1, B7. **34.** Fabian Linden, "New Money and the Old," *Across the Board,* July–August 1985, 43–49. **35.** Faye Rice, "Making Millions on Women over Thirty," *Fortune,* 25 May 1987, 75. **36.** Maria Shau, Christopher Power, and Laura Zinn, "Suddenly, Asian-Americans Are a Marketer's Dream," *Business Week,* 17 June 1991, 54–55. **37.** Larry Carpenter, "How to Market to Regions," *American Demographics,* November 1987, 45. **38.** Martha Farnsworth Riche, "Psychographics for the 1990s," *American Demographics,* July 1989, 53–54. **39.** Leslie Wayne, "Carnival Cruise's Spending Spree," *The New York Times,* 28 August 1988, sec. 3, 1; Ernest Blum, "Carnival Marks 20th Year with Bright Outlook for Its Future," *Travel Weekly,* 19 March 1992, 1+. **40.** Wayne, "Carnival Cruise's Spending Spree," sec. 3, 1. **41.** Stan Rapp and Thomas L. Collins, "The Great Turnaround: Selling to the Individual," *Adweek's Marketing Week,* 27 August 1990, 20–26. **42.** See note 1. **43.** John Koten, "Giving Buyers Wide Choices May Be Hurting Auto Makers," *The Wall Street Journal,* 15 December 1983. Reprinted by permission of *The Wall Street Journal,* © Dow Jones & Company, Inc., 1983. All Rights Reserved Worldwide.

CHAPTER 13

1. Brian K. Burton, "Tops in Popcorn: Indiana Is the World's Largest Producer," *Indiana Business,* October 1987, 18–24; Robert Runde, "Fortunes from Scratch: A Popcorn King Who's in the Chips," *Money,* November 1979, 106, 108, 110, 112, 114; Orville Redenbacher, "The Funny-Looking Farmer with the Funny-Sounding Name," *Guideposts,* January 1990, 2–5; Frazier Moore, "A Corn for Connoisseurs," *Madison Avenue,* May 1985, 14, 16–18; Bernice Kanner, "Kernel Knowledge," *New York,* 11 January

1988, 14–15; Lori Kesler, "Personalities Pitching Products," *Advertising Age,* 3 May 1984, M30, M34, M38; Laura Klepacki, "Popping Up; Light Microwave Popcorn May Be Low in Fat and Low in Salt, but Sales Are Airborne," *Supermarket News,* 9 March 1992, 13+. **2.** Advertisement for the French Redevelopment Agency, *Electronic Business,* 17 September 1990, 1. **3.** Walter J. Salmon and Karen A. Cmar, "Private Labels Are Back in Fashion," *Harvard Business Review,* May–June 1987, 99. **4.** Ronald Alsop, "What's in a Name? Ask Supermarket Shoppers," *The Wall Street Journal,* 9 May 1988, 21. **5.** "How to Break Loyalty to the Competition" (interview with Andrew Parsons and James Schroer), *Boardroom Reports,* 1 April 1987, 3. **6.** Bill Saporito, "Has-Been Brands Go Back to Work," *Fortune,* 28 April 1986, 124; Christine Donahue, "Marketers Restore Old Masters," *Adweek,* 14 September 1987, 4. **7.** Ronald Alsop, "To Know a Brand Is Not to Love It," *The Wall Street Journal,* 15 June 1988, 25. **8.** Anne B. Fisher, "Coke's Brand-Loyalty Lesson," *Fortune,* 5 August 1985, 46. **9.** Fisher, "Coke's Brand-Loyalty Lesson," 44, 45. **10.** Howard Schlossberg, "Brand Value Can Be Worth More Than Physical Assets," *Marketing News,* 5 March 1990, 6. **11.** Courtland L. Bovée and John V. Thill, *Marketing* (New York: McGraw-Hill, 1992), 260. **12.** Donahue, "Marketers Restore Old Masters," 14. **13.** Steven Flax, "The Big Brand Stretch," *The Marketer,* September 1990, 32–35; Michael McDermott, "Too Much of a Good Thing?" *Adweek's Marketing Week,* 4 December 1989, 20–25; Tom Bunday, "Capitalizing on Brand Extensions," *Journal of Consumer Marketing,* Fall 1989, 27–30; Joshua Levine, "But in the Office, No," *Forbes,* 16 October 1989, 272–273. **14.** Warren Berger, "What's New in Corporate Trademarks: Licensing for Fun and Profit—and Free Exposure," *The New York Times,* 24 April 1988, sec. 3, 13. **15.** "The Packaging Investment," *In Business,* March–April 1988, 40. **16.** Jack G. Vogler and Steven Lawrence, "Packaging Better," *Boardroom Reports,* 1 June 1987, 10. **17.** "Budget Gourmet's Downscale Look (and Its Upscale Taste) Whetted Consumers' Appetites," *Adweek,* 3 August 1987, 30; Rebecca Fannin, "The Right Stuff: The Budget Gourmet," *Marketing & Media Decisions,* Winter 1986, 14+; "Good and Cheap," *Packaging Digest,* November 1984, 62+. **18.** Pamela G. Hollie, "Importance of Color Packaging," *The New York Times,* 20 August 1985, 55, 19. **19.** Jacob M. Schlesinger, "Firms Strive to Improve Basic Products," *The Wall Street Journal,* 8 October 1985, B1. **20.** James Cox, "Boom Year for New Products," *USA Today,* 12 January 1988, 1B. **21.** "New Product Winners—And Losers," *In Business,* April 1985, 64. **22.** Anna Sobczynski, "New Product Success Can Be All in the Timing," *Advertising Age,* 3 May 1984, M15. **23.** *Tools of the Trade* catalog from Smith & Hawken, 1990, 17. **24.** Kenneth Labich, "The Innovators," *Fortune,* 6 June 1988, 56. **25.** Toni Mack, "Let the Computer Do It," *Forbes,* 10 August 1987, 94. **26.** Nancy Madlin, "Streamlining the Test-Marketing Process," *Adweek,* 11 November 1985, 10. **27.** Donahue, "Marketers Restore Old Masters," 4. **28.** Clare Ansberry, "Kodak Suspends Its Production of Disk Camera," *The Wall Street Journal,* 2 February 1988, A4; Clare Ansberry, "Battery Makers See Surge in Competition," *The Wall Street Journal,* 30 November 1987, A8. **29.** Jack Willoughby, "Endgame Strategy," *Forbes,* 13 July 1987, 181. **30.** "The Pricing Decision: Part I—The Corner-

stone of the Marketing Plan," *Small Business Report,* May 1985, 73. **31.** Christine Ammer and Dean S. Ammer, *Dictionary of Business and Economics* (New York: Free Press, 1977), 327. **32.** Norton E. Marks and Neely S. Inlow, "Price Discrimination and Its Impact on Small Business," *Journal of Consumer Marketing,* Winter 1988, 31–38. **33.** Thomas T. Nagle, *The Strategy and Tactics of Pricing* (Englewood Cliffs, N.J.: Prentice-Hall, 1987), 335–336. **34.** Kent B. Monroe, *Pricing: Making Profitable Decisions* (New York: McGraw-Hill, 1990), 406. **35.** Charles D. Schewe, *Marketing Principles and Strategies* (New York: Random House, 1987), 336. **36.** See note 1. **37.** Marlys Harris, "The Success of Sweet Smells," *Money,* October 1985, 78–86.

CHAPTER 14

1. Joseph Weber, "Black & Decker Cuts a Neat Dovetail Joint," *Business Week,* 31 July 1989, 52–53; Janet Meyers, "Black & Decker Ups Share in Hardware," *Advertising Age,* 24 July 1989, 28; Rebecca Fannin and Laura Konrad Jereski, "Black & Decker Powers into Housewares," *Marketing & Media Decisions,* August 1985, 34–40, 109; Bill Kelley, "Black & Decker Rebuilds," *Sales & Marketing Management,* June 1987, 49; Christopher S. Eklund, "How Black & Decker Got Back in the Black," *Business Week,* 13 July 1987, 86, 90; James A. Constantin and Robert F. Lusch, "Discover the Resources in Your Marketing Channel," *Business,* July–September 1986, 19–26; Paula Schnorbus, "B&D Turns On the Power," *Marketing & Media Decisions,* May 1988, 57–58, 62, 64; John Huey, "The New Power in Black & Decker," *Fortune,* 2 January 1989, 89–91, 94; "Winning Turnaround Strategies at Black & Decker," *Journal of Business Strategy,* March–April 1988, 30–33; "Black & Decker to Send Sales Specialists into Industrial and Construction Markets," *Industrial Distribution,* April 1987, 4; Deborah Schondorf, "Home Appliance Industry," *Value Line Investment Survey,* 20 March 1992, 128+; Kurt Kleiner, "Black & Decker Takes Aim at Japanese with New Tool Line," *Baltimore Business Journal,* 7 February 1992, 3. **2.** Rom Markin, *Marketing Strategy and Management,* 2nd ed. (New York: Wiley, 1982), 297. **3.** Alix M. Freedman and Thomas R. King, "Perrier's Strategy in the Wake of Recall: Will It Leave Brand in Rough Waters?" *The Wall Street Journal,* 12 February 1990, B1, B3. **4.** Milind Lele, "Matching Your Channels to Your Product's Life Cycle," *Business Marketing,* December 1986, 64. **5.** Cynthia Crossen, "B. Dalton Plans to Shut Out Small Publishers," *The Wall Street Journal,* 2 February 1988, 25. **6.** Bill Saporito, "Discounters in the Dumps," *Fortune,* 3 August 1987, 109. **7.** Lisa Gubernick, "Movie Madness," *Forbes,* 8 February 1988, 37. **8.** Joseph Pereira, "Toys 'R' Us: Big Kid on the Block, Won't Stop Growing," *The Wall Street Journal,* 11 August 1988, 6. **9.** Raymond Roel, "Doubleday Redux," *Direct Marketing,* October 1987, 34–36, 40–42, 44, 46. **10.** Bert Rosenbloom, *Marketing Channels* (Chicago: Dryden, 1987), 431. **11.** Louis Rukeyser, ed., *Louis Rukeyser's Business Almanac* (New York: Simon & Schuster, 1988), 649. **12.** Steven P. Galante, "Distributors Switch Strategies to Survive Coming Shakeout," *The Wall Street Journal,* 20 July 1987, B21. **13.** Janice Castro, "No Holds Barred," *Time,* 11 April

1988, 46. **14.** Susan Caminiti, "The New Champs of Retailing," *Fortune,* 24 September 1990, 85–86, 90, 94, 98, 100. **15.** Rukeyser, *Louis Rukeyser's Business Almanac,* 595. **16.** Jo Ellen Daily, "One-Stop Shopping for the Woman on the Go," *Business Week,* 18 March 1985, 116. **17.** Jack G. Kaikati, "Don't Discount Off-Price Retailers," *Harvard Business Review,* May–June 1985, 86. **18.** Kaikati, "Don't Discount Off-Price Retailers," 91. **19.** Gary Strauss, "Warehouse Clubs Heat Up Retail Climate," *USA Today,* 7 December 1990, 1A–2A; Ann Hagedorn, "Warehouse Clubs, Plentiful but Profit-Poor, Face a Shakeout," *The Wall Street Journal,* 7 May 1987, A1; "Clubs Deliver 26 Percent Price Advantage: Study," *U.S. Distribution Journal,* 15 March 1992, 9+; "Warehouse Clubs Becoming More Established," *Food Institute Report,* 7 March 1992, 3+; Ronald A. Margulis, "Competing with the Clubs," *The U.S. Distribution Journal,* 15 February 1992, 29+; "Who Buys from Clubs?" *Supermarket Business Magazine,* January 1992, 28+. **20.** Deirdre Fanning, "Only the Best for the Bergdorf Man?" *The New York Times,* 16 September 1990, sec. 3, 23. **21.** "Supermarkets' Lean Margins," *USA Today,* 18 December 1990, 1B. **22.** N. R. Kleinfield, "Even for J. Crew, the Mail-Order Boom Days Are Over," *The New York Times,* 2 September 1990, sec. 3, 5. **23.** David Wessel, "Computer Finds a Role in Buying and Selling, Reshaping Businesses," *The Wall Street Journal,* 18 March 1987, A1, A25. **24.** Howard Rudnitsky, "Play It Again, Sam," *Forbes,* 10 August 1987, 48. **25.** John Yoo, "Bad Trip: As Highways Decay, Their State Becomes Drag on the Economy," *The Wall Street Journal,* 30 August 1989, A1, A8; Daniel Machalaba, "Push for Long Trucks Hits Bumpy Road," *The Wall Street Journal,* 9 May 1990, B1–B2; Debra Lynn Dadd and Andre Carothers, "A Bill of Goods? Green Consuming in Perspective," *Greenpeace,* May–June 1990, 8–12. **26.** See note 1. **27.** Adapted from Dougald MacDonald, "Overnight Success (Or Failure)," *New England Business,* 21 April 1986, 57–64; Dean Foust, "Mr. Smith Goes Global," *Business Week,* 13 February 1989, 66–72; "Federal Express Spreads Its Wings," *Journal of Business Strategy,* July–August 1988, 15–19; Carl Williams, "A Company Study: The Challenge of Retail Marketing at Federal Express," *Journal of Services Marketing,* Summer 1987, 25–38; Dean Foust, "Why Federal Express Has Overnight Anxiety," *Business Week,* 9 November 1987, 66; Peter Bradley, "Good Things Come in Small Packages," *Purchasing,* 9 November 1989, 61, 64.

CHAPTER 15

1. Michael Murphy, "Apple Abides," *Computing Decisions,* 26 February 1985, 62, 66; Katherine M. Hafner, "Apple's Comeback," *Business Week,* 19 January 1987, 84–89; Katherine M. Hafner, "Apple Goes for a Bigger Bite of Corporate America," *Business Week,* 24 August 1987, 74–75; Brian O'Reilly, "Growing Apple Anew for the Business Market," *Fortune,* 4 January 1988, 36–37; Felix Kessler, "Apple's Pitch to the Fortune 500," *Business Week,* 15 April 1985, 53–56; William Pat Patterson, "Polishing the Corporate Apple," *Industry Week,* 7 January 1985, 61–62; Thane Peterson, "Apple Takes a Bigger Bite Out of the Continent," *Business Week,* 19 December 1988, 104; Len Strazewski, "Apple Uses New

Marketing Strategy to Take a Slice of Competition's Pie," *Marketing News,* 12 September 1988, 7, 12; Jonathan Joseph, "Apple Tries Again to Blast Off in Japan," *Electronics Week,* 10 June 1985, 34–35; "Apple-IBM Alliance Is Cleared by Regulator," *The Asian Wall Street Journal,* 6 January 1992, 5. **2.** Nanci Hellmich, "Big Changes Proposed for Food Labels," *USA Today,* 6 November 1991, 1D. **3.** George P. Dovel, "Stake It Out: Positioning Success, Step by Step," *Business Marketing,* July 1990, 43–44, 46, 48–51. **4.** Louis Rukeyser, ed., *Louis Rukeyser's Business Almanac* (New York: Simon & Schuster, 1988), 35. **5.** "Sales Costs Higher for Small Firms," *Small Business Report,* November 1990, 18. **6.** Lynn Asinof, "Telemarketing Makes Rapid Strides at U.S. Corporations," *The Wall Street Journal,* 21 July 1988, A1. **7.** Laurie Peterson, "900 Numbers: A Mixed Blessing for Marketers," *Adweek's Marketing Week,* 7 October 1991, 9; Leonard Wiener, "Dollars for Dialing," *U.S. News & World Report,* 17 June 1991, 60–61. **8.** Courtland L. Bovée and John V. Thill, *Marketing* (New York: McGraw-Hill, 1992), 602. **9.** George R. Walther, "Reach Out to Accounts," *Success,* May 1990, 24. **10.** Eugene Johnson, David Kurtz, and Eberhard Scheuing, *Sales Management Concepts, Practices, and Cases* (New York: McGraw-Hill, 1986), 81–82. **11.** Kenneth R. Sheets, "3-D or Not 3-D? That's the Question for Advertisers," *U.S. News & World Report,* 25 January 1988, 59; Authors' estimates. **12.** Rukeyser, *Louis Rukeyser's Business Almanac,* 356, 361. **13.** "Down to Business, Chapter VII: Everything You Always Wanted to Know About Advertising—Cheap!" *Entrepreneur,* May 1985, 84. **14.** Janet Neiman, "The Trouble with Comparative Ads," *Adweek's Marketing Week,* 12 January 1987, 4–5. **15.** Neiman, "The Trouble with Comparative Ads," 4–5; Joseph B. White, "Ford Decides to Fight Back in Truck Ads," *The Wall Street Journal,* 28 February 1989, B1, B6. **16.** Bruce Buchanan and Doron Goldman, "Us vs. Them: The Minefield of Comparative Ads," *Harvard Business Review,* May–June 1989, 38–40, 42, 44, 48, 50; William T. Neese, "Comparative Ads Work Well Even for 'Help Wanted': Strategy Is Best for Mature Markets," *Marketing News,* 20 January 1992, 13. **17.** Jeffrey A. Trachtenberg, "New Law Adds Risk to Comparative Ads," *The Wall Street Journal,* 1 June 1989, B6. **18.** Paul Duke, Jr., and Ronald Alsop, "Advertisers Beginning to Play Off Worker Concern Over Job Security," *The Wall Street Journal,* 1 April 1988, A11; Ronald Alsop, "More Food Advertising Plays On Cancer and Cardiac Fears," *The Wall Street Journal,* 8 October 1987, 33; George E. Belch and Michael A. Belch, *Introduction to Advertising and Promotion Management* (Homewood, Ill.: Irwin, 1990), 186. **19.** "Emotions Important for Successful Advertising," *Marketing News,* 12 April 1985, 18. **20.** Jeffrey A. Trachtenberg, "Marketing Against the Mainstream," *Forbes,* 25 July 1988, 184, 186. **21.** Joanne Lipman, "Ads of the '80s: The Loved and the Losers," *The Wall Street Journal,* 28 December 1989, B1, B4; Cyndee Miller, "Hey Dudes: Fox TV May Have a Cash Cow in Its Licensing Deals," *Marketing News,* 11 June 1990, 1; Joanne Lipman, "Name Two U.S. Stars Reluctant to Appear in TV Ads in Japan," *The Wall Street Journal,* 4 November 1987, A1, A19. **22.** "American Voice," *American Demographics,* December 1990, 14; "USA Snapshots: Ads We Find Least Convincing," *USA Today,* 9 March 1988, 1D; Alix Freedman, "Mar-

riages Between Celebrity Spokesmen and Their Firms Can Be Risky Ventures," *The Wall Street Journal,* 22 January 1988, A23; Christian Ryssel and Erich Stamminger, "Sponsoring World-Class Tennis Players," *European Research,* May 1988, 110–116. **23.** Joshua Levine, "Fantasy, Not Flesh," *Forbes,* 22 January 1990, 118–120. **24.** Ronald Alsop, "Can Honda Scooter Ads Get Any More Offbeat Than This?" *The Wall Street Journal,* 4 June 1987, B25. **25.** James Cox, "Infiniti's Epiphany," *USA Today,* 15 January 1990, 6B; Lipman, "Ads of the '80s"; Ronald Alsop, "Surreal Ads Startle—But Do They Sell?" *The Wall Street Journal,* 20 October 1988, B1; Stuart Elliott, "Eternal Wait for Infiniti," *USA Today,* 29 August 1989, 2B. **26.** Courtland L. Bovée and William F. Arens, *Contemporary Advertising* (Homewood, Ill.: Irwin, 1989), 259–261. **27.** Joanne Lipman, "Ad Industry's Health Draws Mixed Prognoses," *The Wall Street Journal,* 23 September 1987, B7. **28.** Warren Berger, "We're So Sorry," *Inside Print,* January 1988, 34–36, 38, 40, 44. **29.** David Ogilvy, *Ogilvy on Advertising* (New York: Vintage Books, 1983), 112. **30.** Dennis Kneale, "'Zapping' of TV Ads Appears Pervasive," *The Wall Street Journal,* 25 April 1988, 21. **31.** Stuart Elliott, "'Chameleon' Ads Mimic TV," *USA Today,* 12 June 1989, 5B. **32.** Larry Armstrong, "'Honey, Let's Tape Some Commercials for the Weekend,'" *Business Week,* 9 December 1991, 42. **33.** William R. Morrissey, "Gain Competitive Edge with Data-Based Direct Marketing," *Marketing News,* 15 March 1985, 22–23. **34.** Richard P. Kern, "1984 Survey of Selling Costs: Something Old, Something New," *Sales & Marketing,* 20 February 1984, 12+. **35.** Rukeyser, *Louis Rukeyser's Business Almanac,* 580. **36.** Paragraphs on media adapted from Belch and Belch, *Introduction to Advertising and Promotion Management,* 311; Tom Eisenhart and Sue Kapp, "Orchestrating Your Media Options," *Business Marketing,* April 1990, 38–41, 44–47. **37.** Kristine Stiven, "Leading Media Companies 1988 Edition," *Advertising Age,* 27 June 1988, S4. **38.** Hanna Rubin, "Home Video," *Adweek's Marketing Week,* 11 September 1989, 166, 168; Amy Zipken, "Direct Marketing," *Adweek's Marketing Week,* 11 September 1989, 228, 230; "Calculators on Shopping Carts Can Add Up to Good Business," *The San Diego Union,* 23 December 1991, A-22. **39.** Paul Holmes, "Public Relations," *Adweek's Marketing Week,* 11 September 1989, 234–235. **40.** "To the Winners Belong the Spoils," *Marketing News,* 10 October 1986, 1, 13. **41.** Cyndee Miller, "VNRs Are Still Hot, But They're Drawing Fire," *Marketing News,* 12 November 1990, 6. **42.** John Philip Jones, "The Double Jeopardy of Sales Promotions," *Harvard Business Review,* September–October 1990, 145–152; Laurie Petersen, "The Pavlovian Syndrome," *Adweek's Marketing Week,* 9 April 1990, P6–P7; Belch and Belch, *Introduction to Advertising and Promotion Management,* 524–526. **43.** Jeffrey A. Trachtenberg, "Does Sports Marketing Make Sense?" *The Wall Street Journal,* 19 April 1989, B1; Dan Cook, "Nothing Sells Like Sports," *Business Week,* 31 August 1987, 48–53; William George Shuster, "How Sports Marketing Helps Watches Score Big," *Jewelers Circular Keystone,* February 1992, 206+. **44.** Richard Gibson, "Latest in Corporate Freebies Try to Be Classy Instead of Trashy," *The Wall Street Journal,* 7 August 1989, B4. **45.** Monci Jo Williams, "Trade Promotion Junkies," *The Marketer,* October 1990, 30–33; Margaret Littman, "The Death of Advertising?" *Pre-

pared Foods,* February 1992, 25; Anil Jagtiani, "How to Make Money on Trade Promotions," *Foods & Beverage Marketing,* February 1992, 21+; Michael McCarthy, "The Empire Strikes Back," *Adweek,* 24 February 1992, 1+; Al Urbanski, "Blame It on the Trade," *Food & Beverage Marketing,* January 1992, 28+. **46.** "Trade Shows: An Alternative Method of Selling," *Small Business Report,* January 1985, 67. **47.** See note 1. **48.** Ronnie Gunnerson, "Spanish Gold," *Target Marketing,* February 1987, 14, 17, 21; Laurence Jolidon, "Advertisers Make Pitch for Hispanics," *USA Today,* 7 October 1987, 1B, 2B.

CHAPTER 16

1. Adapted from Dennis Livingston, "American Express Reins in the Paper," *Systems Integration,* May 1990, 52–58; James A. Rothi and David C. Yen, "Why American Express Gambled on an Expert Data Base," *Information Strategy,* Spring 1990, 16–22; Patrick Lyons and Anthony Fabiano, "Using Expert System Technology to Foster Innovation," *Review of Business,* Fall 1990, 33–38; John Paul Newport, Jr., "American Express: Service That Sells," *Fortune,* 20 November 1989, 80–94; Steve Fluty, "American Express Goes the Distance," *Inform,* January 1987, 34–36; Eva Kiess-Moser, "Customer Satisfaction," *Canadian Business Review,* Summer 1989, 43–45; "American Express: Focus on Management," *Incentive Marketing,* January 1989, 32–33; Jill Andresky Fraser, "James D. Robinson III: Member Since 1969," *Inc.,* September 1990, 159; Robert Teitelman, "Image vs. Reality at American Express," *Institutional Investor,* February 1992, 36+; Bruce Caldwell, "Amex's Data Center Shuffle: Unloading an Overbuilt Facility Has Proven Daunting," *Information Week,* 10 February 1992, 30+. **2.** Paul Kondstadt, "Ship 54—Where Are You?" *CIO,* May 1990, 80–81, 84, 86. **3.** Kathryn M. Bartol and David C. Martin, *Management* (New York: McGraw-Hill, 1991), 703–705. **4.** Bartol and Martin, *Management,* 707. **5.** Bartol and Martin, *Management,* 709–710. **6.** Meghan O'Leary, "Putting Hertz Executives in the Driver's Seat," *CIO,* February 1990, 62, 66, 68–69. **7.** William F. Allman, "A Sense of Where You Are," *U.S. News & World Report,* 15 April 1991, 58–60. **8.** Donald H. Sanders, *Computers Today* (New York: McGraw-Hill, 1988), 118. **9.** Sanders, *Computers Today,* 122. **10.** Jan Larson, "Expert Systems Save Time," *American Demographics,* July 1990, 23. **11.** Sanders, *Computers Today,* 121–122. **12.** Sanders, *Computers Today,* 27. **13.** Adapted in part from Sanders, *Computers Today,* 27; Timothy Trainor and Diane Krasnewich, *Computers!* (New York: McGraw-Hill, 1989), 32. **14.** This section generally adapted from Trainor and Krasnewich, *Computers!,* 24–48. **15.** Trainor and Krasnewich, *Computers!,* 24. **16.** Charles S. Parker, *Management Information Systems, Strategy and Action* (New York: McGraw-Hill, 1989), 54. **17.** Gary Hoover, Alta Campbell, and Patrick J. Spain, *Hoover's Handbook* (Austin, Tex.: The Reference Press, 1990), 67. **18.** Hoover et al., *Hoover's Handbook,* 193. **19.** Hoover et al., *Hoover's Handbook,* 193. **20.** Trainor and Krasnewich, *Computers!,* 90. **21.** Trainor and Krasnewich, *Computers!,* 90–91. **22.** Sally Cusack, "Reading with Electronic Eyes," *Computerworld,* 1 October 1990, 41. **23.** Stephen G. Kochan and Patrick H. Wood, *Exploring the UNIX System* (Indianapolis: Hayden, 1989), 1. **24.** Paul B. Carroll, "IBM to Unveil Plan to Build Clone of Apple's Macintosh," *The Wall Street Journal,* 2 October 1991, A3, A4. **25.** *Database Catalog* (Palo Alto, Calif.: Dialog Information Services, 1991). **26.** Sanders, *Computers Today,* 406. **27.** Information on Associate obtained from *Business Software Database,* Ruth Koolish Information Sources. **28.** *Knowledge Index User's Workbook* (Palo Alto, Calif.: Dialog Information Services, 19 September 1988). **29.** The section on languages is generally adapted from Sanders, *Computers Today,* 501–517. **30.** Adapted from an example in Trainor and Krasnewich, *Computers!,* 41. **31.** Trainor and Krasnewich, *Computers!,* 161–163. **32.** Richard Brandt, Deidre A. Depke, Geoff Lewis, Keith H. Hammonds, and Chuck Hawkins, "The Personal Computer Finds Its Missing Link," *Business Week,* 5 June 1989, 120–128. **33.** Gary Forger, "Slashing Lead Times with Quick Response," *Modern Materials Handling,* July 1989, 77–78; James A. Senn, *Information Systems in Management* (Belmont, Calif.: Wadsworth, 1990), 611–615. **34.** Forger, "Slashing Lead Times," 77–78. **35.** See note 1. **36.** Eliot Marshall, "The Scourge of Computer Viruses," *Science,* 8 April 1988, 133–134; Philip Elmer-DeWitt, "Invasion of the Data Snatchers!" *Time,* 26 September 1988, 62–67; Asra Q. Nomani, "Byteing Back: Bug Busters Devise Electronic Vaccines for Computer Viruses," *The Wall Street Journal,* 17 June 1988, 1; William E. Halal, "Computer Viruses: The 'AIDS' of the Information Age?" *The Futurist,* September–October 1988, 60.

CHAPTER 17

1. Adapted from Debbie Berlant, Reese Browning, and George Foster, "How Hewlett-Packard Gets Numbers It Can Trust," *Harvard Business Review,* January–February 1990, 178–183; Ed Sperling, "HP Riding High on Downsizing," *Systems & Network Integration,* 16 March 1992, 12+; Robert D. Hof, "Suddenly, Hewlett-Packard Is Doing Everything Right," *Business Week,* 23 March 1992, 88+; John A. Young, "Quality Lessons from Hewlett-Packard," *Manufacturing Engineering,* January 1992, 14, 16. **2.** Personal communication, American Institute of Certified Public Accountants, New York, 1992. **3.** Personal communication, American Institute of Certified Public Accountants, New York, 1992; Spencer Phelps Harris, ed., *Who Audits America* (Menlo Park, Calif.: Data Financial Press, 1990), 283. **4.** Paul Schneider, "'Til Retirement Do Them Part," *Business Month,* July 1990, 14–15; "Less Is More Among the Bean Counters," *U.S. News & World Report,* 17 July 1989, 11; David Greising, Leah J. Nathans, and Laura Jereski, "The New Numbers Game in Accounting," *Business Week,* 24 July 1989, 20–21; "The Big Eight, Seven, Six . . . ," *Time,* 17 July 1989, 77. **5.** Ellen Benoit, "The Bean-Counter Blues," *Financial World,* 22 January 1991, 38–39. **6.** Lee Berton, "Accountants Issue Guidelines to Prevent Manager Fraud; Legislator Assails Them," *The Wall Street Journal,* 13 March 1991, A2; Lee Berton, "Guides to Prevent Fraud in Business Are Slated Today," *The Wall Street Journal,* 12 March 1991, C21; Alison Leigh Cowan, "Accountants Fear S. & L. Backlash," *The New York Times,* 31 July 1990, sec. c, 1. **7.** Susan Goodwin and Edward W. Younkins, "How the Expanding Scope of CPA Services Threatens Accountants' Claim to Independence," *Practical Accountant,* September 1990, 92–99; March Leepson, "Taking Off by the Numbers," *Nation's Business,* August 1987, 49. **8.** Lee Berton, "FASB Rule Requires Public Companies to Issue Annual Cash-Flow Statements," *The Wall Street Journal,* 23 November 1987, 10. **9.** Steven Waldman and Rich Thomas, "How Did It Happen?" *Newsweek,* 21 May 1990, 27–28, 32; Jonathan Beaty, "Running with a Bad Crowd," *Time,* 1 October 1990, 36–40; Howard Rudnitsky, "Good Timing, Charlie," *Forbes,* 27 November 1989, 140–144. **10.** Dana Wechsler Linden, "Lies of the Bottom Line," *Fortune,* 12 November 1990, 106, 108, 112; Terence P. Paré, "Cute Tricks on the Bottom Line," *Fortune,* 24 April 1989, 193, 196. **11.** Robert Mulligan, "Ice Cream," *Starting Out Series,* No. 142, U.S. Small Business Administration, September 1980 (republished 1983). **12.** See note 1. **13.** Jack E. Kiger, Stephen E. Loeb, and Gordon S. May, *Accounting Principles,* 2nd ed. (New York: Random House, 1987), 148.

CHAPTER 18

1. Adapted from Peter Nulty, "America's Toughest Bosses," *Fortune,* 27 February 1989, 40–46, 50, 54; Robert Bruce Slater, "The Architect of NCNB's First Republic Buyout," *Bankers Monthly,* May 1989, 26–27; Richard I. Stillinger, "NCNB Strikes Gold in Texas," *Bankers Monthly,* August 1989, 73; James Srodes, "A Tale of Two Banks: East Coast Wisdom . . . ," *Financial World,* 6 February 1990, 26–30; Gary Hector, "The Brash Banker Who Bought Texas," *Fortune,* 27 August 1990, 54–62; Mary Colby, "Southeast Superregionals Go to the Mat," *Bank Marketing,* November 1990, 40–45; Jerry Barry, "Staking New Claims," *World,* 1990, 16–27; Betsy Morris, Fred Bleakley, and Martha Brannigan, "Power Shift: In New Merger Wave, Superregional Banks Are Grabbing the Lead," *The Wall Street Journal,* 28 June 1991, A1–A6; Kenneth Cline and James R. Kraus, "C&S–Sovran Forced to Play a Weak Hand," *American Banker,* 9 July 1991, 1, 7; Martha Brannigan, "NCNB C&S–Sovran Agree to a $4.26 Billion Merger," *The Wall Street Journal,* 22 July 1991, A3; Martha Brannigan, "NCNB—C&S Merger Will Stir Up South," *The Wall Street Journal,* 23 July 1991, A2; David Mildenberg, "NCNB Faces the Nation," *Business North Carolina,* January 1992, 20+; Rudolph A. Pyatt, Jr., "Missing the Boat on Interstate Banking," *The Washington Post,* 6 January 1992, WB3+. **2.** "88% of U.S. Currency Unaccounted For, Study Says," *San Diego Union,* 11 February 1986, A-2. **3.** Carol Boyd Leon, "Why Americans Are Writing More Checks," *American Demographics,* February 1987, 35. **4.** Patricia M. Scherschel, "Why There's Such a Rush to Deal Out Credit Cards," *U.S. News & World Report,* 11 November 1985, 84. **5.** Jeff Bailey, "Major Credit-Card Issuers Tighten Grip on Market Despite High Interest Charges," *The Wall Street Journal,* 29 July 1988, A15. **6.** Bailey, "Major Credit-Card Issuers Tighten Grip on Market," 15; Howard Rudnitsky, "An Excess of Plastic," *Forbes,* 4 February 1991, 52, 56. **7.** Terence P. Pare, "Tough Birds That Quack Like Banks," *Fortune,* 11 March 1991, 79–84. **8.** Nyra Krstovich, Reference Librarian at Federal Reserve Bank of San Francisco, Personal communication, 28 September 1991. **9.** Nathanial Nash, "Death Rattle for a Dated Industry," *The New York Times,* 19 February 1989, sec. 3, 1, 26; Larry Martz, Rich Thomas, Carolyn Friday, John McCormick, Ginny Carroll, Andrew Murr, and Peter Katel, "Bonfire of the S&Ls," *Newsweek,* 21 May 1990, 20–25; John Meehan, Mike McNamee, Gail DeGeorge, and Joan O'C. Hamilton, "Is There Any Bottom to the Thrift Quagmire?" *Business Week,* 4 March 1991, 62–63; Krstovich, Personal communication; John Pickering, "RTC Set to Unlock Legal Floodgates," *Accounting Today,* 6 April 1992, 1; Resolved: Resolution Trust Corp. Is Doing a Credible Job," *Business Week,* 20 April 1992, 100+; "Don't Derail the S&L Bailout," *Business Week,* 20 April 1992, 126. **10.** Frank McCoy, "Toward a More Perfect Union," *Black Enterprise,* October 1989, 87–90. **11.** Pare, "Tough Birds That Quack Like Banks," 79–84; Catherine Yang, Howard Gleckman, Mike McNamee, Chuck Hawkins, and Peter Coy, "The Future of Banking: Banks Must Be Free—and Willing—to Change, or They May Die," *Business Week,* 22 April 1991, 72–76. **12.** Michael Quint, "Balances Without Any Checks," *New York Times,* 11 September 1991, sec. c, 1, 5. **13.** Vicky Cahan, "Banks Are on the Brink of Breaking Loose," *Business Week,* 7 March 1988, 99. **14.** "Spreading Financial Networks," *Nation's Business,* June 1985, 42. **15.** Julie Stacey, "USA Snapshots: Bank Failures," *USA Today,* 23 May 1991, 1B; Fred R. Bleakley, "Bank Industry Had Dismal '90, Survey Shows," *The Wall Street Journal,* 11 February 1991, A3, A6; Kenneth H. Bacon, "Big Banks Would Gain Vastly Broader Powers Under Treasury's Plan," *The Wall Street Journal,* 6 February, 1991, A1–A4; Stephen Labaton, "Top U.S. Auditor Predicts Banks May Be Headed for Large Bailout," *The New York Times,* 12 June 1991, sec. a, 1, sec. c, 3; Leonard Silk, "The Argument over Banks," *The New York Times,* 8 February 1991, sec. d, 2. **16.** Steve Lohr, "Banking's Real Estate Miseries," *The New York Times,* 13 January 1991, sec. 3, 1–6; Lowell Bryan, "Two Enemies of Sound Banking," *The Wall Street Journal,* 29 April 1991, A14; Jerd Smith, "Big Banks Cut Commercial Loans, Real Estate Returned," 28 February 1992, 1; "Adriane B. Miller, "Kinder, Gentler Lenders Keep Home Foreclosure Rates Down," *The Baltimore Business Journal,* 21 February 1992, 13; T. L. Gage, "Regulatory Thaw Could Revive Bank Real Estate Lending," *Corporate Cash Flow Magazine,* February 1992, 19–20. **17.** Jonathan Fuerbringer, "Commercial Paper Has Troubles, Too," *The New York Times,* 10 February 1991, sec. f, 4; John Meehan, Catherine Yang, Geoffrey Smith, Joan O'C. Hamilton, and Walecia Konrad, "Banks: Is Big Trouble Brewing?" *Business Week,* 16 July 1990, 146–152. **18.** Robert Guenther, "Business Bulletin: Foreign Banks Take a Greater Share of U.S. Corporate Business," *The Wall Street Journal,* 16 March 1989, A1. **19.** Steve Lohr, "For Lagging American Banks, Survival Means Consolidation," *The New York Times,* 21 July 1991, sec. 4, 5; Liz Mullen, "California Thrift Agencies Face Consolidation as Number of Governed Institutions Dwindles," *The Los Angeles Business Journal,* 3 February 1992, 8A; "Bank Reform: Is Bigger Necessarily Better," *Bankers Magazine,* January–February 1992, 22+; Norman Katz, "The Unfolding Trends in Bank Consolidation," *Bankers Magazine,* January–February 1992, 12; Catherine Reagor, "Bankers See More Consolidation in '92," *The Business Journal,* 6 January 1992, 1+. **20.** Kenneth H. Bacon, Ron Suskind, and Paulette Thomas, "U.S. Recession Claims Bank of New England as First Big Victim," *The Wall Street Journal,* 7 January 1991, A1, A6; Steve Lohr, "One Bank's Experience of Failure: U.S. Presence Soothes the Fearful," *The New York Times,* 18 February 1991, sec. 1, 33; Mindy Fetterman, "BNE Bailout Spells Trouble for Northeast," *USA Today,* 7 January 1991, 1B–2B. **21.** Stephen Labaton, "Administration Presents Its Plan For Broad Overhaul of Banking," *The New York Times,* 6 February 1991, sec. a, 1, sec. d, 6; Kenneth H. Bacon and Paulette Thomas, "Big Banks Would Get Vastly Broader Powers Under Treasury's Plan," *The Wall Street Journal,* 6 February 1991, A1, A4; Stephen Labaton, "House Panel Backs Broad Changes in Bank Rules," *The New York Times,* 29 June 1991, 17–18. **22.** Fred R. Bleakley and Martha Brannigan, "In New Merger Wave, Superregional Banks Are Grabbing the Lead," *The Wall Street Journal,* 28 June 1991, A1, A6; Leslie Wayne, "Fleet's Big Bet on New England," *The New York Times,* 24 April 1991, sec. c, 1, 6; Joshua Hammer and Bruce Shenitz, "The New Giant on the Block," *Newsweek,* 29 July 1991, 36–37; Steve Lohr, "The Best Little Bank in America," *The New York Times,* 7 July 1991, sec. 3, 1, 4; Charles McCoy and Ralph T. King, Jr., "Add Security Pacific to BankAmerica: The Result Is Clout," *The Wall Street Journal,* 13 August 1991, A1, A10. **23.** Steve Lohr, "Recasting the Big Banks: Weakened Giants, in Humbling Mergers, Are Fighting to Regain Their Dominance," *The New York Times,* 17 July 1991, sec. a, 1, sec. c, 6; Michael Quint, "Bigger Banks, But Better Banking?" *The New York Times,* 23 August 1991, sec. c, 1, 4. **24.** Pamela J. Podger, "Bank Start-Ups Draw Interest of Small Firms," *The Wall Street Journal,* 28 December 1990, B1–B2. **25.** Steven V. Roberts and Gary Cohen, "Villains of the S&L Crisis," *U.S. News & World Report,* 1 October 1990, 53–59; G. Christian Hill and Paulette Thomas, "Big Thrift-Rescue Bill Is Likely to Realign the Financial System," *The Wall Street Journal,* 7 August 1989, A1, A6; Monroe W. Karmin, "Oh, That Costly S&L Mess!" *U.S. News & World Report,* 9 April 1990, 37–38; "Bailout Agency for S&L's Plans to Begin Dismantling," *The New York Times,* 24 March 1992, D2; William P. Barrett, "Stooling Wanted," *Forbes,* 13 April 1992, 21; S&L's Assets Down, but Stable," *The Denver Business Journal,"* 14 February 1992, 10; High Rollers: Inside the Savings and Loan Debacle," *Business Credit,* March 1992, 31. **26.** Lohr, "One Bank's Experience of Failure," sec. 1, 33. **27.** Associated Press, "47% of Bankers Have Doubts About FDIC," *Arizona Republic,* 8 October 1991, C14. **28.** William M. Isaac, "Wrong Time to Soak the Banks," *The Wall Street Journal,* 29 January 1991, A16. **29.** Associated Press, "47% of Bankers Have Doubts About FDIC," C14; Stephen Labaton, "Bank Deposit Fund Nearly Insolvent, U.S. Auditor Says," *The New York Times,* 27 April 1991, sec. 1, 31; Stephen Labaton, "Bank Fund Outlook Is Bleaker," *The New York Times,* 28 June 1991, sec. c, 1, 9. **30.** Paul Duke, Jr., "S&L Mess May Spark a Thorough Overhaul of Deposit Insurance," *The Wall Street Journal,* 3 July 1990, A1, A10. **31.** Labaton, "Administration Presents Its Plan for Broad Overhaul of Banking," sec. a, 1, sec. d, 6; Louis Uchitelle, "Reforms in Banking Call For a Shrinking U.S. Role," *The New York Times,* 21 February 1991, sec. a, 1, sec. d, 6. **32.** "A Guide Through the Banking Maze," *USA Today,* 25 February 1985, 3B. **33.** See note 1. **34.** Ronald Grzywinski, "The New Old-Fash-

ioned Banking," *Harvard Business Review,* May–June 1991, 87–98; Amy Bodwin, "Banking on the Future: Chicago Idea Could Aid City," *Crain's Detroit Business,* 30 September 1991, 13–14; Robert Reed, "Thinking Small," *Crain's Chicago Business,* 16 July 1990, 17–19; David Osborne, "Bootstrap Banking," *Inc.,* August 1987, 69; Steve Mills, South Shore Turns Itself Around While Showing How a Bank Can Help," *The American Banker,* 16 April 1986, 24.

CHAPTER 19

1. Adapted from Lewis J. Wright, president and CEO of Emerald Homes, Phoenix, Arizona, personal communication, November 1991; Emerald Homes L.P., 1990 annual report. **2.** John J. Curran, "Hard Lessons from the Debt Decade," *Fortune,* 18 June 1990, 76–81; Robert F. Black, Don L. Boroughs, Sara Collins, and Kenneth Sheets, "Heavy Lifting," *U.S. News & World Report,* 6 May 1991, 52–61. **3.** Kate Ballen, "The New Look of Capital Spending," *Fortune,* 13 March 1989, 115–120; Michael F. Smith, "Capital Investment Budgeting," *Small Business Reports,* December 1988, 80–88. **4.** "Assets and Liabilities of Commercial Banking Institutions," Table 1.25, *Federal Reserve Bulletin,* October 1991, A18. **5.** Ellyn E. Spragins, "Low-Brow Finance," *Inc.,* May 1990, 109–110. **6.** Vivian Brownstein, "Who's Afraid of Inventories?" *Fortune,* 29 February 1988, 61, 64; Thomas C. Hayes, "Behind Wal-Mart's Surge, A Web of Suppliers," *The New York Times,* 1 July 1991, sec. d, 1–2. **7.** See note 1. **8.** Richard W. Stevenson, "Carolco Flexes Its Muscle Overseas," *The New York Times,* 26 June 1991, sec. c, 1, 17; Roger Smith, Carolco, personal communication, 21 October 1991; Adam Bryant, "Carolco in Agreement for Financing Package," *The New York Times,* 25 March 1992, C4; John Lippman, "Carolco Pictures Sells Some Film Rights to Raise Cash," *The Los Angeles Times,"* 13 February 1992, D2; "Downsizing," *Broadcasting,* 17 February 1992, 8; Jim McCullaugh, *Billboard Magazine,* 1 February 1992, 85.

CHAPTER 20

1. Adapted from William A. Francis, vice president, Landes Associates, Inc., Wilmington, Delaware, personal communication, 7 October 1991; Charles R. Day, "Kingdom's Magic Really Isn't," *Industry Week,* 6 April 1992, 6; Glenn Withiam, "The Mouse Stays Home," *The Cornell Hotel & Restaurant Administration Quarterly,* February 1992, 12; "Disney Outlines the Keys to Successful Customer Contacts," *Pets-Supplies-Marketing,* March 1992, 90+. **2.** William Power, "Small Investors Are Punier Than Many Think," *The Wall Street Journal,* 28 March 1989, C1, C10; Jordan E. Goodman, "Small Investors Favor Funds 7 to 1 to Stocks," *Money,* April 1992, 70; William Power, "Small Investors Trade Heatedly in U.S. Market," *The Asian Wall Street Journal,* 24 January 1992, 9; William Power, "Small Investors Are Trading with Vigor, but Brokers Still See Caution, Not Frenzy," *The Wall Street Journal,* 23 January 1992, C1. **3.** Anise C. Wallace, "How the Little Guy Is Playing the Market," *The New York Times,* 3 September 1989, sec. 3, 1, 10. **4.** Martin L. Leibowitz and Stanley Kogelman, "Asset Allocation Under Shortfall Con-

straints," *Journal of Portfolio Management,* Winter 1991, 18–23. **5.** Burton G. Malkiel, "Is the Stock Market Efficient?" *Science,* 10 March 1989, 1313–1318; Simon M. Keane, "Paradox in the Current Crisis in Efficient Market Theory," *Journal of Portfolio Management,* Winter 1991, 30–34; William E. Sheeline, "Who Needs the Stock Exchange?" *Fortune,* 19 November 1990, 119–124; David Zigas, Gary Weiss, Ted Holden, and Richard A. Melcher, "A Trading Screen on Every Floor," *Business Week,* 5 November 1990, 128–130. **6.** Jeffrey B. Little and Lucien Rhodes, *Understanding Wall Street,* 2nd ed. (Blue Ridge Summit, Pa.: Liberty House, 1987), 128. **7.** Gary Weiss, "The Long and Short of Short-Selling," *Business Week,* 10 June 1991, 106–108; Derek T. Dingle, "How to Keep Making Money When Stock Funds Decline," *Money,* April 1992, 51+; Kathy M. Kristof, "Short Sellers Have Hard Year as Market Booms," *The Los Angeles Times,* 22 March 1992, D4+; "A Correction: Short Sales," *The New York Times,* 2 April 1992, C12+; Eric Reguly, "Short-Sellers Hanging In: Despite Market Surge, Some See Good Risk Rewards," *The Financial Post,* 18 January 1992, 17; Alison Leigh Cowan, "No Guts, No Glory: Short-Selling in a Bull Market," *The New York Times,* 12 January 1992, sec. 3, F5+. **8.** Sumner N. Levine, ed., *The Dow Jones–Irwin Business and Investment Almanac* (Homewood, Ill.: Dow Jones–Irwin, 1988), 453. **9.** Sheeline, "Who Needs the Stock Exchange?" 119–124. **10.** Sheeline, "Who Needs the Stock Exchange?" 119–124. **11.** Craig Torres and William Power, "Big Board Is Losing Some of Its Influence over Stock Trading," *The Wall Street Journal,* 17 April 1990, A1, A6; Floyd Norris, "A Look Ahead for the Big Board," *The New York Times,* 7 January 1992, C8+. **12.** Robert Ferri, National Association of Securities Dealers, New York, personal communication, December 1991; "NASDAQ International to Start Up in January," press release, National Association of Securities Dealers Automated Quotation System, 10 October 1991. **13.** Sheeline, "Who Needs the Stock Exchange?" 119–124; Richard L. Stern, "A Dwindling Monopoly," *Forbes,* 13 May 1991, 64–66; Torres and Power, "Big Board Is Losing Some of Its Influence over Stock Trading," A1, A6. **14.** Diana B. Henriques, "Ignore Foreign Stocks at Your Peril," *The New York Times,* 7 July 1991, sec. 3, 13; Rudiger von Rosen, "What Europe Can Teach the S.E.C.," *The New York Times,* 29 March 1992, sec. 3, F13+; Jonathan Clements, "'Buy Foreign,' Strategists Urge U.S. Investors," *The Wall Street Journal,* 3 March 1992, C1+; Tom Petruno, "Why Foreign Stocks Are Slipping; Other Economies Are Down; A U.S. Recovery May Not Help Them," *The Los Angeles Times,* 13 March 1992, D1+; Tom Petruno, "Good Year for Foreign Stocks?" *The Los Angeles Times,* 3 January 1992, D1; William Power, "Big Board Chief Renews His Pitch on Foreign Stocks," *The Wall Street Journal,* 7 January 1992, C14+. **15.** John Collins, director of news media services, Investment Company Institute, Washington, D.C., personal communication, December 1991. **16.** Diana B. Henriques, "In World Markets, Loose Regulation," *The New York Times,* 23 July 1991, sec. c, 1, 6–7. **17.** John J. Curran, "Finding a Path Between Greed and Fear," *Fortune 1986 Investor's Guide,* Fall 1985, 9. **18.** Louis Rukeyser, ed., *Louis Rukeyser's Business Almanac* (New York: Simon & Schuster, 1988), 305. **19.** John Heine, deputy director of the office of public affairs, Securities and Exchange Commission, Washington, D.C., personal communication, December 1991. **20.** Theodore Focht, president and general counsel at the Securities Investors Protection Corporation, Washington, D.C., personal communication, December 1991. **21.** See note 1. **22.** Adapted from Floyd Norris, "Forcing Salomon into Buffett's Conservative Mold," *The New York Times,* 29 September 1991, sec. 3, 8; Linda Sandler, "For Buffett, Salomon Isn't Sole Worry," *The Wall Street Journal,* 22 August 1991, C1–C2; Tatiana Pouschine and Carolyn Torcellini, "Will the Real Warren Buffett Please Stand Up?" *Forbes,* 19 March 1990, 92–98; Joshua Hammer, Joanna Stone, and Marc Levinson, "'I Will Be Ruthless,'" *Newsweek,* 9 September 1991, 62; Thomas McCarroll, "Salvaging Salomon Brothers," *Time,* 2 September 1991, 59; John Train, *The Money Masters* (New York: Harper & Row, 1980), 1–41; Paul Sweeting, "Carolco Stock Drops After Rumors of Partner Pullouts," *Billboard Magazine,* 18 January 1992, 78; Richard W. Stevenson, Carolco Stock Reaches an Accord on Its Plan for Revamping," *The New York Times,* 17 January 1992, 15; David J. Jefferson, Carolco Says Foreign Partners to Invest $45 Million, Allow Payment Deferral, *The Wall Street Journal,* 17 January 1992, B3; Michael Lewis, "The Temptation of St. Warren: Buffett's Principles—and Wall Street's," *New Republic,* 17 February 1992, D5; Allan Sloan, "Warren Buffett Looks Like a Winner in a White Hat," *The Los Angeles Times,* 6 January 1992, D5; Allan Sloan, "Beauty and the Beasts," *The Washington Post,* 7 January 1992, C3.

CHAPTER 21

1. Adapted from Matthew Cooper, Dorian Friedman, and John Koenig, "Empire of the Sun," *U.S. News & World Report,* 28 May 1990, 44–51; Gail DeGeorge, "A Sweet Deal for Disney Is Souring Its Neighbors," *Business Week,* 8 August 1988, 48–49; Kevin Johnson, "Plan Unveiled for Huge Disneyland Expansion," *Los Angeles Times,* 9 May 1991, A1, A30–A31; Chris Woodyard and Kevin Johnson, "How Disney Park Would Benefit 2 Sites," *Los Angeles Times,* 5 June 1991, D3; Jeffrey A. Perlman, "Disney's 21st Century Transit Plan Rides on Old Standby—the Car," *Los Angeles Times,* 9 May 1991, A3, A26; Mark Gladstone, "Disney Seeks a Special Law for Long Beach Park," *Los Angeles Times,* 9 April 1991, B1, B4; Mark Gladstone and Ralph Frammolino, "Disney Becoming Mouse That Roared in the State Capitol," *Los Angeles Times,* 22 April 1991, A3, A21–A22; Mark Gladstone, "Coastal Panel Vote Aids Disney Plan for Park," *Los Angeles Times,* 12 June 1991, A3, A18; Mike Davis, "Will Cities Enter Mickey Mouse Deals to Survive?" *Los Angeles Times,* 11 August 1991, M1, M6; Faye Fiore, "Disney's Florida Critics Warn of a Greedy Monster," *Los Angeles Times,* 20 February 1991, A1, A22–A23; Kevin Johnson, "Disney's Expansion Plans Are Not a Free Ride," *Los Angeles Times,* 12 May 1991, A3, A19; Kevin Johnson, "Disney Deal Is a Tall Order for Cash-Strapped Anaheim," *Los Angeles Times,* 10 May 1991, A3, A41; Dave McNary, "Disney," *UPI News,* 12 December 1991. **2.** *Survey of Current Business* (Washington, D.C.: GPD, September 1991), 3, 8. **3.** Bartley A. Brennan and Nancy Kubasek, *The Legal Environment of Business* (New York: Macmillan, 1988), 317. **4.** Douglas Whitman and John William Gergacz, *The Legal Environment of* Business, 2nd ed. (New York: Random House, 1988), 353. **5.** Brennan and Kubasek, *The Legal Environment of Business,* 361. **6.** George A. Steiner and John F. Steiner, *Business, Government, and Society* (New York: McGraw-Hill, 1991), 345. **7.** Clemens P. Work, "Return of the Big Stick," *U.S. News & World Report,* 4 June 1990, 54. **8.** Andy Pasztor and Timothy K. Smith, "FTC Opposes Purchase Plans by Coke, Pepsi," *The Wall Street Journal,* 23 June 1986, A2. **9.** Tim Smart, Michele Galen, Gail DeGeorge, and Paul Angiolillo, "The Crackdown on Crime in the Suites," *Business Week,* 22 April 1991, 102. **10.** Work, "Return of the Big Stick," 54; U.S. Antitrust Action Against Keirtsu Unlikely," *Comline News Service,* 12 November 1991. **11.** Jacqueline Mitchell and Neal Templin, "Nissan Will Buy More Auto Parts Made in the U.S.," *The Wall Street Journal,* 8 November 1991, A2. **12.** Susan B. Garland, "What a Way to Watch Out for Workers," *Business Week,* 23 September 1991, 42; Tim Smart and Dean Foust, "The Supreme Court: Leave it to the States," *Business Week,* 8 July 1991, 32; Michael Galen, "The Crackdown on Crime in the Suites," *Business Week,* 22 April 1991, 102–104. **13.** "Don't Mess with Us," *Adweek's Marketing Week,* 1 July 1991, 22; Steve Lohr, "The Nation: War and Recession Speed Up the Airlines' Flights to Oblivion," *The New York Times,* 17 February 1991, sec. e, 5. **14.** Steiner and Steiner, *Business, Government, and Society,* 302. **15.** Brennan and Kubasek, *The Legal Environment of Business,* 111. **16.** Michael Kranish, "Bush Relies on Quayle; Critics Say He's Lap Dog for Business," *San Diego Union,* 16 November 1991, A–1. **17.** Donald L. Barlett and James B. Steele, "'NOL' Is the Magic That Makes Your Money Theirs," *San Diego Union,* 17 November 1991, A–15. **18.** Warren T. Brookes, "Higher State Taxes Are Hurting the National Economy," *The San Diego Union,* 22 December 1991, C-4. **19.** *Survey of Current Business* (Washington, D.C.: GPO, 1991), 7. **20.** Anna Cifelli Isgro, "The Tax Upheaval: What It Means for Business," *Fortune,* 9 June 1986, 21. **21.** Richard L. Berke, "Donors to Parties Sidestepped Rules," *The New York Times,* 18 May 1991, sec. b, 7. **22.** "Growth in PAC Donations Stalls," *Facts on File,* 2 May 1991, 317. **23.** Berke, "Donors to Parties Sidestepped Rules," sec. b, 7. **24.** Brennan and Kubasek, *The Legal Environment of Business,* 32. **25.** Steiner and Steiner, *Business, Government, and Society,* 149. **26.** Brennan and Kubasek, *The Legal Environment of Business,* 17. **27.** Thomas W. Dunfee, Frank F. Gibson, John D. Blackburn, Douglas Whitman, F. William McCarty, and Bartley A. Brennan, *Modern Business Law* (New York: Random House, 1989), 164. **28.** "Justices Uphold Punitive Damages in Awards by Jury, *The New York Times,* 5 March 1991, sec. a, 1; L. Gordon Crovitz, "With Punitive Damages, Let the Foreigner Beware," *The Wall Street Journal,* 18 March 1992, A15; Milo Geyelin, "Product Suits Yield Few Punitive Awards," *The Wall Street Journal,* 6 January 1992, B1. **29.** Brennan and Kubasek, *The Legal Environment of Business,* 183. **30.** Brennan and Kubasek, *The Legal Environment of Business,* 184. **31.** Dunfee et al., *Modern Business Law,* 200. **32.** "Clorox Faces Negligence Suit," *San Diego Union,* 13 April 1990, A–12. **33.** Dunfee et al., *Modern Business Law,* 211–212. **34.** Dunfee et al., *Modern Business Law,* 558. **35.** Alex Finkelstein, "Mississippi Man's Estate Sues Disney," *The Orlando Business Journal,* 3 June 1990, 1. **36.** Brennan and Kubasek, *The Legal Environment of Business,* 187–189; Whitman and Gergacz, *The Legal Environment of Business,* 482–483. **37.** Brennan and Kubasek, *The Legal Environment of Business,* 192–195; Whitman and Gergacz, *The Legal Environment of Business,* 486. **38.** Dunfee et al., *Modern Business Law,* 569. **39.** Ronald A. Anderson, Ivan Fox, and David P. Twomey, *Business Law* (Cincinnati: South-Western Publishing, 1987), 497. **40.** Robert J. Posch, Jr., "Contractual Protection of a Firm's Confidential Data," *Direct Marketing,* 6 January 1984, 114–117. **41.** Dunfee et al., *Modern Business Law,* 576. **42.** Brennan and Kubasek, *The Legal Environment of Business,* 198–199. **43.** Dunfee et al., *Modern Business Law,* 236. **44.** Brennan and Kubasek, *The Legal Environment of Business,* 124. **45.** Dunfee et al., *Modern Business Law,* 284–297; Brennan and Kubasek, *The Legal Environment of Business,* 125–127; Whitman and Gergacz, *The Legal Environment of Business,* 196–197; *The Lawyer's Almanac* (Englewood Cliffs, N.J.: Prentice Hall Law & Business, 1991), 888. **46.** Brennan and Kubasek, *The Legal Environment of Business,* 128. **47.** Brennan and Kubasek, *The Legal Environment of Business,* 144. **48.** Milo Geyelin, "Feuding Firms Cram Courts, Study Says," *The Wall Street Journal,* 31 December 1990, A9. **49.** Dunfee et al., *Modern Business Law,* 745, 749. **50.** Anderson, Fox, and Twomey, *Business Law,* 684. **51.** Brennan and Kubasek, *The Legal Environment of Business,* 152–153; Whitman and Gergacz, *The Legal Environment of Business,* 252. **52.** Madeline Argher, "You Can't Take It with You," *Savvy,* March 1983, 25, 29; Clemens Work, "When a Key Worker Leaves with Secrets," *U.S. News & World Report,* 7 October 1985, 67. **53.** Brennan and Kubasek, *The Legal Environment of Business,* 160; Whitman and Gergacz, *The Legal Environment of Business,* 260. **54.** Anderson, Fox, and Twomey, *Business Law,* 635. **55.** Brennan and Kubasek, *The Legal Environment of Business,* 516–517. **56.** Don L. Boroughs, "It Pays to Go Broke," *U.S. News & World Report,* 8 April 1991, 49. **57.** Wallecia Konrad, "Battered but Not Broke," *Working Woman,* October 1985, 66–68. **58.** See note 1. **59.** Adapted from Johnnie L. Roberts, "Pitney Bowes Thrives from Close Relations with Postal Service," *The Wall Street Journal,* 4 April 1991, A1, A6; Niels Erich, "The Mail Must Go Through," *D&B Reports,* March/April 1989, 56–57; Alan Farnham, "What Goes On in Your Mailroom?," *Fortune,* 27 February 1989, 105–108; Gary Slutsker, "Mail Smart," *Forbes,* 12 December 1988, 246, 248.

CHAPTER 22

1. Adapted from Kathryn J. McIntyre, "1991 Risk Manager of the Year: Growing with Marriott," *Business Insurance,* 29 April 1991, 142–156; Pamela Taulbee, "Corralling Runaway Workers' Comp Costs," *Business & Health,* April 1991, 46–55; Carol Cain, "No Kidding About Safety: Great American Keeps Comp Losses Down, Despite Very Young, Seasonal Workforce," *Business Insurance,* 8 August 1983, 3, 37; Mary Jane Fisher, "Informed Workers Make Wise Health Care Users," *National Underwriter,* 2 May 1988, 10–11; Kathy Seal, "Marriott Hotels Get Green Light from EPA," *Hotel & Motel Management,* 24 February 1992, 26. **2.** George J. Church, "Sorry, Your Policy Is Canceled," *Time,*

24 March 1986, 20. **3.** Harrison L. Moore, "Can Your Product Stand the Test of Time?" *Inc.,* April 1980, 60–64. **4.** George L. Head, "The Steps in Risk Management," in *The Risk Management Process* (New York: Risk and Insurance Management Society, 1978), 12. **5.** "Ashland Oil's Cleanup Bills for Oil Spill Pass $4 Million," *Business Insurance,* 18 January 1988, 1. **6.** Much of the material related to the three steps of the risk-management process is adapted from Head, "The Steps in Risk Management," 12–15. **7.** Eileen Z. Joseph, "Getting Past the Liability Crisis," *Nation's Business,* August 1986, 69–70; Christopher Farrell and Kimberly Carpenter, "Business Gets the Hang of Do-It-Yourself Coverage," *Business Week,* 21 July 1986, 112–114; "Self-Insurance Booms," *Nation's Business,* June 1988, 24; Christopher Farrell, Resa King, and Joan O'C. Hamilton, "The Crisis Is Over—But Insurance Will Never Be the Same," *Business Week,* 25 May 1987, 122–123; Stephen Waldman, Daniel Shapiro, and Tom Schmitz, "The Surge in Self-Insurance," *Newsweek,* 7 March 1988, 74–75; Karen Munson and David Israel, "Self-Insurance Check-Up," *HRMagazine,* February 1992, 83+; Brigitte Maxey, "Surge in Self-Insurance Erodes Underwriters' Role," *The Journal of Commerce and Commercial,"* 12 February 1992, 1A; Gwen Moritz, "Risk, Advantages Debated with Self-Insurance Policies," *The Memphis Business Journal,* 27 January 1992, 14. **8.** "The Budget Dollar," *The San Diego Union,* 30 January 1992, A–7. Mark R. Greene and James S. Trieschmann, *Risk and Insurance* (Cincinnati: South-Western Publishing, 1988), 81. **9.** Mark Hoffman, ed., *The World Book Almanac and Book of Facts, 1992* (New York: Pharos Books, 1991), 690. **10.** Greene and Trieschmann, *Risk and Insurance,* 81 **11.** "America's Insurers: No Thrift Crisis, This," *The Economist,* 20 April 1991, 78, 80, 82. **12.** Kerry Pechter, "Preparing for Perils Abroad," *North American International Business,* August 1990, 26. **13.** "Insurers to Get Bill in Toxic Waste Cleanups," *San Diego Union,* 16 November 1990, A-14. **14.** Beatrice E. Garcia, "Insurers Slip into Cyclical Downturn," *The Wall Street Journal,* 14 February 1989, A1. **15.** Susan Pulliam, "Nowhere to File: Blue Cross Collapse in West Virginia Puts Many in Dire Straits," *The Wall Street Journal,* 8 March 1991, A1. **16.** Richard W. Stevensen, "Worry for an Industry Selling Peace of Mind," *The New York Times,* 12 May 1991, sec. 4, 5; Frederick Rose and David B. Hilder, "Brought to Earth: Junk-Bond Deals Trip Insurer as State Seizes Unit of First Executive," *The Wall Street Journal,* 12 April 1991, A1. **17.** Eric N. Bert, "Insurance Giants No Longer Ask to Be All Things to All People," *The New York Times,* 7 February 1991, sec. a, 1. **18.** John D. Long and Davis W. Gregg, eds., *Property and Liability Insurance Handbook* (Homewood, Ill.: Richard D. Irwin, 1965), 829ff. **19.** Jane Easter Bahls, "The Rewards of Risk Management," *Nation's Business,* September 1990, 58. **20.** Greene and Trieschmann, *Risk and Insurance,* 530. **21.** C. Arthur Williams, Jr., and Richard M. Heins, *Risk Management and Insurance,* 6th ed. (New York: McGraw-Hill, 1989). **22.** David Warner, "Benefits Update," *Nation's Business,* April 1991, 33. **23.** Leonard Sloane, "Worker Insurance Evolution," *The New York Times,* 6 December 1983. **24.** "Controlling Insurance Costs," *Inc.,* April 1988, 128. **25.** American Institute of Certified Public Accountants; Church, "Sorry, Your Policy Is Canceled," 20; Lee Berton, "The CPA Jungle: Accounting Profession, Once a Staid Field, Is Torn by Incivility," *The Wall Street Journal,* 24 July 1991, A1. **26.** Stephen H. Collins, ed., "Practitioner's Update: Liability Crisis Ahead?" *The Practical Accountant,* November 1990, 19. **27.** Martha Glaser, "Managed Care Bites Benefit!" *Business and Health,* May 1991, 71–72, 74, 76, 78. **28.** Personal communication, Jennell Patterson, Public Relations Office, Health Insurance Association of America, 1989. **29.** Greene and Trieschmann, *Risk and Insurance,* 298. **30.** Personal communication, Patterson, Health Insurance Association of America, 1989. **31.** Health Insurance Association of America. **32.** Ellen Paris, "Sigmund Freud, Meet Jean-Baptiste Say," *Forbes,* 19 February 1990, 148. **33.** Maureen Weiss, "The High Cost of Klutzmanship," *Across the Board,* May 1991, 59. **34.** Milt Freudenheim, "Health Care a Growing Burden," *The New York Times,* 29 January 1991, sec. c, 1. **35.** Ron Winslow, "Medical Costs Soar, Defying Firms' Cures," *The Wall Street Journal,* 29 January 1991, A1. **36.** Philip J. Hilts, "Say Ouch: Demands to Fix U.S. Health Care Reach a Crescendo," *The New York Times,* 19 May 1991, sec. 4, 1; Paul Dwyer and Susan B. Garland, "A Roar of Discontent," *Business Week,* 25 November 1991, 28–30. **37.** "U.S. to Meet with Major Health Insurers," *The New York Times,* 24 September 1991, sec. a, 19; "Medical Rationing," *U.S. News & World Reports,* 7 January 1991, 85. **38.** Sidney Marchasin, "Cost Shifting: How One Hospital Does It," *The Wall Street Journal,* 9 December 1991, A10. **39.** Ron Winslow, "Medical Experiment: Some Companies Try 'Managed Care' in Bid to Curb Health Costs," *The Wall Street Journal,* 1 February 1991, A1; Sally Berger and John Abendshien, "Questions to Mull on Managed-Care Pacts," *Modern Healthcare,* 16 March 1992, 54; Christine Woolsey, "Risks of Managed Care," *Business Insurance,* 23 March 1992, 2; Lauren Haworth, "Traditional Health Plans Give Way to Managed Care," *The Business Journal—Portland,* 24 February 1992, 9. **40.** Joyce E. Santora, "Allied-Signal's Network Cuts Health Care Costs," *Personnel Journal,* May 1991, 41. **41.** Edmund Faltermayer, "Strong Medicine for Health Costs," *Fortune,* 23 April 1990, 221, 226. **42.** Faltermayer, "Strong Medicine," 224, 226. **43.** *Employee Benefits* (Washington, D.C.: U.S. Chamber of Commerce, 1991), 28. **44.** *1991 Life Insurance Fact Book, Update* (Washington, D.C.: American Council of Life Insurance, 1991), 4. **45.** See note 1. **46.** Adapted from Jill Andresky Fraser, "A Fresh Look at Insurance," *Inc.,* December 1990, 153–154; Henry A. Revzan, "Controlling Insurance Costs," *Small Business Reports,* April 1991, 62–67; Greene and Trieschmann, *Risk and Insurance,* 44.

PHOTO CREDITS

2 Hiroyuki Matsumoto/Black Star 4 The Photo Works 10 Shones/Gamma-Liaison 12 Courtesy Taco Bell Corporation 18 Paul Conklin/Monkmeyer 21 FPG 26 Spencer Grant/Photo Researchers 27 Courtesy Johnson Publishing Co., Inc. 32 Visual Images West/The Image Works 39 Courtesy Moneysworth & Best Shoe Repair, Inc. 40 Kevin Horan/Stock, Boston 43 Steve Payne 44 Courtesy T-Bones Steakhouses 53 Ty Greenlees, Dayton, Ohio 56 Montes de Oca 60 Arnold John Kaplan/The Picture Cube 64 Frank Siteman/Monkmeyer 67 Steve Woit 68 Rob Crandall/Stock, Boston 74 Bill Ray 77 Courtesy Nevica Skiwear 81 Mark Zemnick 85 Richard Howard 88 Simon Fraser/Science Source/Photo Researchers 91 J.D. Sloan/The Picture Cube 99 Mark Zemnick 101 Tom McCarthy/The Picture Cube 112 Robert Rathe/Stock, Boston 116 Montes De Oca 118 Lee Holden/Courtesy Ben & Jerry's Ice Cream 122 Michal Heron/Woodfin Camp & Associates 125 P. Vauthey/Sygma 127 Fujifotos/The Image Works 134 Rameshwar Das/Monkmeyer 142 Courtesy Avon Cosmetics Inc. 147 Courtesy Pizza Hut 152 Tom Carroll/International Stock Photography 154 Courtesy McDonnell Douglas Corporation 157 Greg Pease 160 Greg Pease 167 Greg Pease 169 Michael Baytoff/Black Star 171 Lisa Quinones/Black Star 176 Wayne Eastep/The Stock Market 178 Tim Carlson/Stock, Boston 181 Ken Kerbs 183 Greg Pease 184 Michael L. Abramson/Woodfin Camp & Associates 198 Courtesy Texaco, Inc. 200 Courtesy Campbell Soup Company 204 Brownie Harris/The Stock Market 208 Courtesy Ford Motor Company 209 Matthew Borkoski/Stock, Boston 215 Dick Luria/Science Source/Photo Researchers 216 Andrew Sacks/Black Star 217 Steven Kahn 227 Courtesy Harley-Davidson, Inc. 232 Tom Sobolik/Black Star 234 David Perry/Rockwell International Corporation 244 John A. Gallagher 250 Top, Dean Abramson; bottom, Michael Hart/Borden 253 Rothstein/Redstone Stock Agency 254 Courtesy Westinghouse Electric Corporation 256 Courtesy Nucor Corporation 260 Telegraph Colour Library/International Stock Photo 263 Shelly Katz/Black Star 265 Michael Newman/PhotoEdit 267 Courtesy Whirlpool Corporation 274 Courtesy Motorola, Inc. 282 Rick Friedman/Black Star 283 Jim Wilson/Woodfin Camp & Associates 289 Pete Byron/Black Star 294 Spencer Grant/Photo Researchers 297 Courtesy Steelabor 303 Courtesy Steelabor 308 Okoniewski/The Image Works 313 Courtesy General Motors 315 Alan Tannenbaum/Sygma 319 Top, Ken Kerbs/DOT; bottom, courtesy United Auto Workers 326 Gabe Palmer/The Stock Market 329 Courtesy Domino's Pizza 335 Doug Mazzapica/Black Star 336 Mark Perlstein/Black Star 337 Courtesy 3M 340 Courtesy Perez Hernandez Promotions 351 Courtesy NIKE, Inc. 356 William Waterfall/The Stock Market 358 Ken Kerbs/DOT 363 Courtesy Philips Medical Systems 366 Courtesy of Collgate-Palmol-

ive Company 371 Brownie Harris 374 Jim Pozarik/Gamma-Liaison 378 L. Fleming/The Image Works 381 Courtesy Hunt-Wesson, Inc. 386 Calvin Larsen/Photo Researchers 390 Courtesy Emerson Electric 392 Seth Resnick/Stock, Boston 397 Courtesy Mail Boxes Etc. 404 Mark Antman/The Image Works 406 David Yang-Wolff/PhotoEdit 407 Mark Perlstein/Black Star 410 Courtesy The Black & Decker Corporation 416 Jon Burbank/The Image Works 419 Rich Iwasaki/Allstock 423 Peter Menzel/Stock, Boston 424 Frank Siteman/The Picture Cube 431 Top, courtesy North Beach Leather Stores; bottom, courtesy of Amoco Chemical Company 439 Courtesy of the Institute of Outdoor Advertising 443 Michael Grecco/Picture Group 450 John Michael/International Stock Photo 459 Top, courtesy Unisys; bottom, courtesy of Honeywell 460 Ron Watts/Black Star 462 Paul Shambrrom 470 Courtesy Unisys 476 John S. Abbott 480 Ed Wheeler/The Stock Market 486 David Bentley 502 Blair Seitz 507 Courtesy Debra Berlant, Hewlett-Packard Company 512 Al Clayton/International Stock Photo 516 Jim Amos/Photo Researchers 522 Mark Zemnick 523 Gregory Heisler/The Image Bank 524 Mark Antman/The Image Works 528 George Goodwin/The Picture Cube 535 Rob Kinmonth 540 Frank Siteman/The Picture Cube 542 Mark Zemnick 549 Peter Kane/Courtesy Mead Corporation 552 Julius Blumberg 559 Julius Blumberg 561 Julius Blumberg 565 Courtesy Lewis J. Wright 570 Johnny Stockshooter/International Stock Photo 572 Seth Resnick/Stock, Boston 575 Courtesy Fidelity Investments 576 Courtesy Department of the Treasury 577 Luc Novovitch/Gamma-Liaison 582 Larry Kolvoord/The Image Works 584 Michael Melford/The Image Bank 586 Catherine Ursillo/Photo Researchers 587 Left, Wesley Boxco/Photo Researchers; right, Lisa Quinones/Black Star 596 Courtesy Bill Francis, photo by Bill Lindsey 602 Chad Ehlers/International Stock Photo 605 David J. Sama/Texas Reprint 611 Dennis Brack/Black Star 613 Courtesy Ralston Purina Company 621 Allen Tannenbaum/Sygma 623 Courtesy William Morris Agency 624 Diana Walker/Time Magazine 627 Art Seitz/Sipa 632 Ron Frehm/International Stock Photo 635 Top, courtesy Sure-Grip International; bottom, Bryce Flynn/Stock, Boston 638 Mathew Naytho/Stock, Boston 645 John Ficara/Woodfin Camp & Associates 646 Geoffrey Clifford/Wheeler Pictures 648 Ken Kerbs/DOT 652 Seth Resnick

ILLUSTRATION AND TEXT CREDITS

CHAPTER 1

6 **Exhibit 1.1,** adapted from *World Tables 1991* (Baltimore, MD.: Johns Hopkins University, 1991), 85, 185, 241, 617; *Information Almanac* (Boston: Houghton-Mifflin, 1990), 259.

7 **Exhibit 1.2,** adapted from Samuel C. Certo, Max E. Douglas, and Stewart W. Husted, *Business,* Second Edition. Copyright 1984 by Allyn and Bacon, Inc. Reprinted with permission; and William F. Schoell and Joseph P. Guiltinan, *Marketing: Contemporary Concepts and Practices,* 5th Edition, Copyright © 1992 by Allyn & Bacon. Reprinted by permission, 215.

8–9 Adapted from World Resources Institute, "Managing Earth's Resources," Special Advertising Supplement, *Business Week,* 18 June 1990, 5, 6, 56, 57; Emily T. Smith, Vicki Cahan, Naomi Freundlich, James E. Ellis, and Joseph Weber, "The Greening of Corporate America," *Business Week,* 23 April 1990, 96–103; Thomas DiLorenzo, "Does Free Enterprise Cause Pollution?" *Across the Board,* January–February 1991, 35–41; Gretchen Morgenson and Gale Eisenstodt, "Profits Are for Rape and Pillage," *Forbes,* 5 March 1990, 94–100.

23 Adapted from John W. Wright, ed., *The Universal Almanac 1991* (Kansas City, Mo.: Andrews and McMeel, 1990), 215; Eva Pomice, Robert Black, and Dana Hawkins, "When Will the Recession End?" *U.S. News & World Report,* 18 March 1991, 62–64; Paul Duke, Jr., "Economic Signals Suggest Worst Is Over," *The Wall Street Journal,* 3 June 1991, A2.

25 **Exhibit 1.6,** adapted from John W. Wright, ed., *The Universal Almanac 1991* (Kansas City, Mo.: Reprinted by permission of Andrews and McMeel, all rights reserved, 1990), 223.

CHAPTER 2

35 **Exhibit 2.1,** adapted from *The World Almanac and Book of Facts, 1992* edition, (copyright Pharos Books 1991, New York, NY 10166), 142.

36 Adapted from John W. Wright, ed., *The Universal Almanac, 1991* (Kansas City, Mo.: Andrews and McMeel, 1990), 106–108; Otto Johnson, *The 1991 Information Please Almanac* (Boston: Houghton Mifflin, 1991), 61–63; Jon Cooney, ed., *Louis Rukeyser's Business Almanac* (New York: Simon & Schuster, 1988), 133–143; Eugene Carlson, "Privatization Lets Small Firms Manage Everything from Libraries to Golf Courses," *The Wall Street Journal,* 2 April 1991, B1; Barnaby Feder, "Cutting Big Government, Round 2," *The New York Times,* 12 February 1989, sec. 3, 4.

37 **Exhibit 2.2,** adapted from *Survey of Current Business* (Washington, D.C.: GPO, September 1991), S-10.

41 Exhibit 2.3, adapted from the *Statistical Abstract of the United States: 1990* (Washington, D.C.: GPO, 1990), 522, 523.
42 Exhibit 2.4, adapted from Bartley A. Brennan and Nancy Kubasek, *Legal Environment of Business.* Reprinted with the permission of Macmillan Publishing Company. Copyright © 1988 Macmillan Publishing Company, Inc., 216.
50 Adapted from Jaclyn Fierman, "Deals of the Year," *Fortune,* 28 January 1991, 90–92.
50–51 Adapted from Sharon G. Hadary, "Think Big," *National Business Employment Weekly, Managing Your Career,* Spring 1990, 11–12; Kevin Gudgridge and John A. Byrne, "A Kinder, Gentler Generation of Executives," *Business Week,* 23 April 1990, 86–87; Jerry Buckley, "The New Organization Man," *U.S. News & World Report,* 16 January 1989, 41–43.
54 Exhibit 2.7, adapted from Judith H. Dobrzynski, "The Top One Hundred Deals," *Business Week,* April 5, 1991, 26–28; Susan Antilla and Gary Strauss, "Takeovers Revert to Cash, Stock," *USA Today,* December 4, 1990, 1B; and *Statistical Abstract of the United States: 1990,* Washington, D.C.: Government Printing Office, 1990), 518.

CHAPTER 3

63 Adapted from "Checklist for Going into Business," Management Aid No. 2016 (Washington, D.C.: U.S. Small Business Administration, 1977).
65 Exhibit 3.1, adapted from Dun & Bradstreet, Economic Analysis Department, "New Incorporations Decrease 6.8 Percent in Decamber *Current Economic Indicators,* 32, no. 12 (December 1990): 4–5; Dun & Bradstreet, *Business Failure Record,* (New York: The Economic Analysis Department, The Dun & Bradstreet Corporation, 1991), 4. (From the Economic Analysis Department, The Dun & Bradstreet Corporation, 1992.)
66 Exhibit 3.2, adapted from Ellen Graham, "The Truth About Start Ups." Reprinted with permission, *Inc.* Magazine, January 1988. Copyright 1988 by *Inc.* Publishing Company, 38 Commercial Wharf, Boston, MA 02110, adapted from Ellen Graham, "The Entrepreneurial Mystique," in *The Wall Street Journal Special Report on Small Business,* May 20, 1985. Reprinted by permission of *The Wall Street Journal Special Report on Small Business,* © 1985 Dow Jones & Company, Inc. All Rights Reserved Worldwide. sec. 3, p. 4C.
67 Exhibit 3.3, adapted from John Case, "Disciples of David Birch," *Inc.,* January 1989. 41, Reprinted with permission, *Inc.,* magazine, January 1989. Copyright © 1989 by Goldhirsch Group, Inc., 38 Commercial Wharf, Boston, MA 02110. 60.
70 Exhibit 3.4, adapted from Geoffrey N. Smith and Paul B. Brown, "Sweat Equity." Excerpted in *Macmillan Executive Summary Program,* December 1986, 3, 4.
73 Exhibit 3.6, adapted from "The 1990 Guide to Small Business," *U.S. News & World Report,* November 23, 1989, 78, [copyright, 1989, U.S. News & World Report.] And from "How to Bankroll Your Venture," Reprinted by permission from the September, 1985 issue of *Changing Times Magazine,* copyright © 1985 The Kiplinger Washington Editors, Inc., 41.
76 Exhibit 3.7, adapted from Carrie Dolan, "Entrepreneurs Often Fail as Managers," *The*

Wall Street Journal, May 15, 1989, (Reprinted by permission of *The Wall Street Journal,* © 1989 Dow Jones & Company, Inc. All Rights Reserved Worldwide.) B1.
78 Adapted from Mark Stevens, "Seven Common Mistakes Small Businesses Make—And How to Avoid Them," *Working Woman,* January 1986, 44–48. Reprinted with permission from *Working Woman* Magazine. Copyright 1986 by W.W.T. Partnership.
80 Exhibit 3.8, adapted from *Statistical Abstract of the United States: 1991* (Washington, D.C.: GPO, 1991), 778.
83 Exhibit 3.9, adapted from Alfred Edmond, Jr., "The B. E. Franchise Start-Up Guide," *Black Enterprise,* September 1990, (Reprinted by permission of Earl G. Graves Publishing Co.) 75.

CHAPTER 4

93 Adapted from Lowell G. Rein, "Is Your (Ethical) Slippage Showing?" *Personnel Journal,* September 1980, 740–743.
95 Adapted from Shawki Barghouti and Guy Le Moigne, "Irrigation and the Environmental Challenge," *Finance & Development,* June 1991, 32–33.
105 Exhibit 4.4, adapted from "Outlook: 1990–2005: Labor Force Projections," *Monthly Labor Review,* November 1991, and "Employed Civilians by Detailed Occupation, Sex, Race, and Hispanic Origin," *Employment and Earnings,* January 1991, pp. 185–190; U.S. Bureau of Labor Statistics, Washington, D.C., 33.
107 Exhibit 4.5, adapted from Stephen Wermeil, "Supreme Court, in 6–3 Vote, Backs Hiring Goals to Correct Sex Bias," *The Wall Street Journal,* 26 March 1987, 3; Adam Clymer, "Rights Bill Passes in House but Vote Is Not Veto-Proof," *The New York Times,* 6 June 1991, A1, A12; adapted from Albert B. Crenshaw, "Appeals Court Upholds Order to Make Woman a Partner," *Washington Post,* December 5, 1990, G3; William L. Kendel, "Antonio and Betts: Burden of Proof and Other Barriers to Plaintiffs in Wholesale Litigation under ADEA and Title VII," *Employee Relations Law Journal,* Autumn 1989, 267–280; Kenneth L. Karst, "Private Discrimination and Public Responsibility: Patterson in Context," *Supreme Court Review,* Annual 1989, 1–51; and Michael S. Vogel, "The Remains of Title VII after Lorance v. AT&T Technologies," *Columbia Human Rights Law Review,* Fall 1990, 73–95.
109 Exhibit 4.6, adapted from Amy Saltzman, "Trouble at the Top," *U.S. News & World Report,* June 17, 1991. Copyright, 1991, U.S. News & World Report, 40–48.
111 Exhibit 4.7, adapted from National Safety Council, "Accident Facts, 1991 Edition" (Chicago: National Safety Council, 1991), 43, 47–49; Dana Milbank, "Companies Turn to Peer Pressure to Cut Injuries as Psychologists Join the Battle," *The Wall Street Journal,* March 29, 1991, B1. [Reprinted by permission of *The Wall Street Journal,* © 1991 Dow Jones & Company, Inc. All Rights Reserved Worldwide.] And from "Accident Facts, 1991 Edition," National Safety Council, 1991 43, 47–49.
114–115 Adapted from Jeffrey A. Fadiman, "A Traveler's Guide to Gifts and Bribes," *Harvard Business Review,* July–August 1986, 122–136. Reprinted by permission of *Harvard Business Review.* An excerpt from "A Traveler's Guide to Gifts and Bribes," by Jeffrey A Fadiman, July/

August 1986. Copyright © 1986 by the President and Fellows of Harvard College; all rights reserved.

CHAPTER 5

128 Exhibit 5.1, adapted from Peter Passell, "America's Position in the Economic Race: What the Numbers Show and Conceal," *The New York Times,* 4 March 1990, sec. 3, 4, 5; Leonard Silk, "Triple Play," *The New York Times,* 4 March 1990, sec. 4, 1, 5; Carole Gould, "A Steady March into Funds,"; Ed Rubenstein, "Still Number One," *The National Review,* 23 July 1990, 15.
129 Exhibit 5.2, adapted from Christopher Farrell, Michael J. Mandel, Keith Hammonds, Dori Jones Yang, and Paul Magnusson, "At Last, Good News," reprinted from June 3, 1991 issue of *Business Week,* by special permission copyright © 1991 by McGraw-Hill, Inc.
130–131 Adapted from Ann Reilly Dowd, "Viva Free Trade with Mexico!" *Fortune,* 17 June 1991, 97–100; Blayne Cutler, "Welcome to the Borderlands," *American Demographics,* February 1991, 44–57; Roberto Sero, "Border Boom's Dirty Residue Imperils U.S.–Mexico Trade," *The New York Times,* 31 March 1991, sec. 1, 1, 15; John Hilkirk, "Foreigners Flood Mexico with Plants," *USA Today,* 11 March 1988, 111B–112B; Brian O'Reilly, "Business Makes a Run for the Border," *Fortune,* 18 August 1986, 70–76; Mariah E. deForest, "Offshore Across the Border," *Manufacturing Systems,* February 1987, 37–40; Janice Castro, "Yankee! Welcome to Mexico!" *Time,* 1 June 1987, 51; Stephen Baker with Adrienne G. Bard and Elizabeth Weiner, "The Magnet of Growth in Mexico's North," *Business Week,* 6 June 1988, 48–50; Brian O'Reilly, "No Picnic in Mexico," *Fortune,* 15 August 1988, 8–9.
131 Exhibit 5.3, adapted from Sylvia Nasar, "A Gain in Trade from Gulf War," *The New York Times,* 13 March 1991, C1.
138 Adapted from Ford S. Worthy, "Making It in China," *Fortune,* 17 June 1991, 103–104; Keith Bradsher, "U.S. Weighing Concessions to Keep China Trade Status," *The New York Times,* 10 July 1991, A4.
139 Exhibit 5.4, adapted from John Labate, "The World Economy in Charts: Special Report—Gearing Up for Steady Growth," *Fortune,* 29 July 1991, 99 © 1991 The Time Inc. Magazine Company. All rights reseved.
141 Exhibit 5.5, based on information from U.S. Department of Commerce, *Survey of Current Business* (Washington, D.C.: GPO, 1991), 88; Texaco 1990 Annual Report; Johnson & Johnson 1989 Annual Report; Pan Am 1989 Annual Report; Gillette 1990 Annual Report; Merck 1990 Annual Report; Bankers Trust 1990 Annual Report; Abbott Laboratories 1989 Annual Report; Eastman Kodak 1989 Annual Report; Deere & Company 1989 Annual Report; Texas Instruments 1989 Annual Report; Apple Computers 1990 Annual Report; Annabella Gabb, "Heinz Meanz Brandz," *Management Today,* 1 July 1989, 64.
143 Exhibit 5.6, adapted from Jim Powell, "Who Owns America and Does It Matter?" *World Monitor,* June 1990, 58–64; and from John Hoerr, Leah Nathans Spiro, Larry Armstrong, and James B. Treece, "Culture Shock at Home: Working for a Foreign Boss," reprinted from December 17, 1990 issue of *Busi-*

ness Week by special permission, copyright © 1990 by McGraw-Hill, Inc.
144–145 Adapted from David Ricks, "How to Avoid Business Blunders Abroad," *Business,* April–June 1984, 3–11.

CHAPTER 6

158–159 Adapted from Lyn Taetzsch and Eileen Benson, "Taking Charge of Yourself and Your Job." Reprinted by permission of the publishers, from *Supervisory Management,* October 1978, 6–9. Copyright © 1978. American Management Association, New York. All rights reserved.
161 Adapted from Kenneth R. Andrews, "Ethics in Practice," *Harvard Business Review,* September–October 1989, 99–104; Andrew S. Grove, "What's the Right Thing? Everyday Ethical Dilemmas," *Working Woman,* June 1990, 16–18; John Case, "Honest Business," *Inc.,* January 1990, 65–59.
163 Exhibit 6.2, adapted from Management, Second Edition, by Richard L. Daft, copyright © 1991 by The Dryden Press, reprinted by permission of the publisher. Based on information in the Christie Brown, "Sweat Chic," *Forbes,* September 5, 1988, p. 130.
166 Adapted from Ricardo Semler, "Managing Without Managers," *Harvard Business Review,* September–October 1989, 76–84.
167 Exhibit 6.3, reprinted by permission of *Harvard Business Review,* an excerpt from "How to Choose a Leadership Pattern" by Robert Tannenbaum and Warren H. Schmidt, May/June 1973. Copyright © 1973 by the President and Fellows of Harvard College; all rights reserved.
173–174 Adapted from Alan M. Webber, "Consensus, Continuity, and Common Sense: An Interview with Compaq's Rod Canion," *Harvard Business Review,* July–August 1990, 115–123; "Compaq in Shift as Exec Exits?" *Electronic News,* 28 January 1991, 6; Laura Brennan, "Once-Invincible Compaq Beset by Midlife Crisis," *PC Week,* 6 May 1991, 1; Mark Ivey, "How Compaq Gets There Firstest with the Mostest," *Business Week,* 26 June 1989, 146–150; Mark Land, "Big Loss Forces Compaq Layoffs," *USA Today,* 24 October 1991, B-1; John Schneidawind, "Compaq at Crossroads," *USA Today,* 28 October 1991, B-1, B-3.

CHAPTER 7

180 Adapted from Steven Prokesch, "Edges Fray on Volvo's Brave New Humanistic World," *The New York Times,* 7 July 1991, sec. 3, 5.
182 Adapted from Paul Klebnikov, "The Powerhouse," *Forbes,* 2 September 1991, 46–52; Jules Arbose, "ABB the New Energy Powerhouse," *International Management,* June 1988, 24–30.
186–187 Ronald Henkoff, "Cost Cutting: How to Do It Right," *Fortune,* 9 April 1990, 40–53; Andrall E. Pearson, "Tough-Minded Ways to Get Innovative," *Harvard Business Review,* May–June 1988, 99–106; David Woodruff, "Carving a Niche in Surgical Tools," *Business Week Innovation,* 1989, 126–129; John H. Sheridan, "Aligning Structure with Strategy," *Industry Week,* 15 May 1989, 15–23; Michael Beer, Russell A. Eisenstat, and Bert Spector, "Why Change Programs Don't Produce Change," *Harvard Busi-*

ness Review, November–December 1990, 158–166; Patricia Sellers, "Pepsi Keeps on Going After No. 1," *Fortune,* 11 March 1991, 62–70; James A. Belasco, "Teaching the Elephant to Dance," *Executive Book Summaries,* 12, no. 11, part 3 (November 1990): 1–8; John Markoff, "The Smart Alecks at Sun Are Regrouping," *The New York Times,* 28 April 1991, sec. F, 4; "Bubble Chart Sends Message," *Pryor Report,* July 1990, 4; Amanda Bennett, "Downsizing Doesn't Necessarily Bring an Upswing in Corporate Profitability," *The Wall Street Journal,* 6 June 1991, B1; Richard W. Stevenson, "Battling the Lethargy at Douglas," *The New York Times,* 22 July 1990, sec. 3, 1; Pascal Zachary, "Bruised Apple: Computer Firm's Chief Faces Slowing Growth, Discord in the Ranks," *The Wall Street Journal,* 15 February 1990, A1; Tom Peters, "Creating the Fleet-Footed Organization," *Industry Week,* 18 April 1988, 35–39.
188 Exhibit 7.5, Copyright 1984 Time Warner Inc. Reprinted by permission.
189 Exhibit 7.6, adapted from Steven Burke, "Shake-Up at IBM Is Seen as Blow to Aker's Authority." Reprinted from *PC Week,* 2 February 1988, 121. Copyright © 1988 Ziff Communications Company.
190 Exhibit 7.7, Copyright 1984 Time Warner Inc. Reprinted by permission. Copyright © Harald Sund/Courtesy *Life* Magazine. Richard Mackson/*Sports Illustrated.* Reprinted from the April, 1984 issue of *Money* Magazine by special permission. *Fortune* is a registered trademark of Time Warner Inc. *People* Weekly is a registered trademark of Time Warner Inc.
191 Exhibit 7.9, Copyright 1984 Time Warner Inc. Reprinted by permission.

CHAPTER 8

213 Adapted from E. J. Muller, "Harley's Got the Handle on Inbound," *Distribution,* March 1989, 70, 74; Arjan T. Sadhwani, M. H. Sarhan, and Dayal Kiringoda, "Just-in-Time: An Inventory System Whose Time Has Come," *Management Accounting,* December 1985, 36–39, 42–44; E. J. Muller, "Airfreight Makes Service Levels Soar," *Distribution,* January 1989, 58–63; Steven P. Galante, "Distributors Bow to Demands of Just-in-Time Delivery," *The Wall Street Journal,* 30 June 1986, 25.
214 Exhibit 8.3, adapted from Sylvia Nasar, "A Grain in Trade from Gulf War," *The New York Times,* March 13, 1991. Copyright © 1991 by The New York Times Company. Reprinted with permission, C1.
217, Adapted from Janet Endrijonas, "Acer Pres Says Taiwan-Bashing Ended," *Newsbytes* (press-release database), 27 March 1990; Fred Langa, "Taiwan, the Soviet Union, and You, Part 2," *Byte,* October 1990, 10; "Altos Computer System to Join the Acer Group," *Business Wire* (press-release database), 5 July 1990.
218 Adapted from "Next Touts 86% Increase in Sales of Its Computers," *San Jose Mercury News,* 1 August 1991, C3; Mark Alpert, "The Ultimate Computer Factory," *Fortune,* 26 February 1990, 75–79; Neal E. Boudette, "Creating the Computer-Integrated Enterprise," *Industry Week,* 18 June 1990, 62, 65–66.
220 Exhibit 8.4, adapted from "Choosing the Right Site," Mark L. Goldstein, *Industry Week,* 15 April 1985, 58. Reprinted with permission from *Industry Week,* 15 April 1985. Copyright, Penton Publishing, Inc., Cleveland, Ohio.

225 Exhibit 8.7, adapted from Gerald H. Graham, *The World of Business* (Reading, Mass.: Addison-Wesley, 1985), 199.

CHAPTER 9

239 Exhibit 9.3, adapted from Richard L. Daft, *Management,* Second Edition (Ft. Worth: Dryden Press, 1991), 406.
240 Exhibit 9.4, adapted from Walter B. Newsome, "Motivate, Now!" *Personnel Journal,* February 1990, reprinted by permission of A. C. Croft, Inc., 53.
243 Exhibit 9.5, adapted from "Ages of the Work Force," *Workforce 2000.* Copyright © 1987, Hudson Institute. Reprinted with permission; Department of Labor, Bureau of Labor Statistics, *Outlook 2000* (Washington, D.C.: GPO, April 1990), 105.
244 Adapted from William B. Johnson, "Global Work Force 2000: The New World Labor Market," *Harvard Business Review,* March–April 1991, 118–119.
245 Exhibit 9.6, adapted from Bureau of Labor Statistics, *Outlook 2000,* (Washington, D.C.: GPO, April 1990), 105–106; *Statistical Abstract of the United States: 1991* (Washington, D.C.: GPO, 1991), 391.
246 Exhibit 9.7, Marcy E. Mullins, "USA's Changing Demographics," *USA Today,* 26 August 1991, 9A.
246–247 Adapted from Joseph D'Obrian, "Only English Speakers Need Apply," *Management Review,* January 1991, 41–45; Seth Mydans, "Pressure for English-Only Job Rules Stirring a Sharp Debate Across U.S.," *The New York Times,* 8 August 1990, A12; L. Erik Bratt and Fred Alvarez, "English-Only Memo Outrages Employees," *San Diego Union,* 15 September 1990, C-1.
248 Exhibit 9.8, adapted from Suzy Parker, "A Look at Statistics That Shape Your Finances," *USA Today,* 24 January 1990, copyright 1990, *USA Today,* reprinted with permission, 1B.

CHAPTER 10

264 Exhibit 10.2, adapted from John C. Szabo, "Finding the Right Workers," *Nation's Business,* February 1991, copyright 1991, U.S. Chamber of Commerce, copyright 1990 Towers Perrin, from Workforce 2000, Competing in a Sellers Market: Is Corporate America Prepared? A survey report on Corporate Responses to Demographic and Labor Force Trends. 16–22.
266 Exhibit 10.3, adapted from *37th Annual Salary Survey Report,* The Port Authority of NY and NJ, June 1984.
268 Exhibit 10.4, adapted from "The Interview Process," *Small Business Report,* December 1987, 64.
270–271 Adapted from John S. McClenahen, "The Privacy Invasion: In a Job Setting, How Personal Is Too Personal?" *Industry Week,* 11 November 1985, 50–53; John Corbett O'Meara, "The Emerging Law of Employees' Right to Privacy," *Personnel Administrator,* June 1985, 159–165; Patricia Amend, "High-Tech Surveillance: The Boss May Be Watching," *USA Today,* 14 March 1990, 11B; Tony Mauro and Julia Lawlor, "More Bosses Set Rules for After Hours," *USA Today,* 13 May 1991, 1A; Jane Easter Bahls, "Checking Up on Workers," *Nation's Business,* December 1990, 29–31.

272 Tom Peters, "The German Economic Miracle Nobody Knows," *Across the Board,* May 1991, 47–48.

273 Adapted from Shirley Sloan Fader, "What Your Boss Wants You to Know," *Business Week's Guide to Careers,* October 1985, 43–44; "How to Climb up the Job Ladder," *Glamour,* December 1982, 170–171; Gloria Norris and Jo Ann Miller, "Pacing Your Career: Long-Term Strategies for Success on the Job," *Vogue,* September 1979, 338+.

278 Exhibit 10.6, adapted from National Institute of Business Management; "Compensation and Benefits," *Small Business Reports,* October 1990, 49.

278 Exhibit 10.7, adapted from *Statistical Abstracts of the United States: 1991* (Washington, D.C.: GPO, 1991), 419.

279 Exhibit 10.8, adapted from *Statistical Abstracts of the United States: 1991* (Washington, D.C.: GPO, 1991), 420.

284 Exhibit 10.9, adapted from Katherine C. Naff and Paul van Rijn, "The Next Generation: Why Are They Leaving?" *The Bureaucrat,* Summer 1990, reprinted by permission of the Bureaucrat, Inc., 39–43.

CHAPTER 11

299 Exhibit 11.2, adapted from Bureau of Labor Statistics, Bureau of National Affairs, reported in *Business Week,* 8 July 1985, 72; Peter Fullam, "Organized Labor at Crossroads," *Indianapolis Star,* 2 September 1991, CO4.

302 Adapted from John Hoerr, "What Should Unions Do?" *Harvard Business Review,* May–June 1991, 44–45; "Labor Letter," *The Wall Street Journal,* 26 February 1991, A1; Dana Milbank, "Far from the Mill," *The Wall Street Journal,* 23 May 1991, A1.

306 Adapted from Frank Swoboda, "Greyhound Declares Strike Over," *Washington Post,* 8 May 1990, A8; Peter T. Kilborn, "Small Towns Grow Lonelier as Bus Stops Stopping," *New York Times National,* 11 July 1991, A8; Albert R. Karr, "Rail Unions, Carriers Fail to Reach Pact," *The Wall Street Journal,* 17 April 1991, A3; James R. Healey and Mark Memmott, "Businesses Felt Rail Strike Most," *USA Today,* 18 April 1991, 1A; "Casey Jones Walks Out," *Time,* 29 April 1991, 65; "High Court Ruling to Help Hospital Unions Organize," *San Diego Union,* 24 April 1991, A-2; Linda Greenhouse, "High Court Eases Rule on Unionizing Hospital Workers," *The New York Times,* 24 April 1991, sec. A, 1.

307 Adapted from Rose Tamburri, "Canadian Government Workers Launch National Strike to Protest Wage Controls," *The Wall Street Journal,* 10 September 1991, A16; Jeffrey Ulbrich, "Canadian Strike Is 'Massive,'" *San Diego Union,* 10 September 1991, A-1, A-10.

311 Exhibit 11.6, adapted from *Statistical Abstract of the United States: 1988* (Washington, D.C.: GPO, 1988); Bureau of Labor Statistics, *Current Wage Developments,* (Washington, D.C.: GPO, March 1991), 67; *Statistical Abstracts of the United States: 1991,* (Washington, D.C.: GPO, 1991), 474.

316 Exhibit 11.7, adapted from John Hoerr, "Beyond Unions: A Revolution in Employee Rights Is in the Making," *Business Week,* 8 July 1985, 73. Reprinted by special permission. Copyright © 1985 by McGraw-Hill, Inc.; Joan Biskopic, "Bush Signs Anti-Job Bias Bill Amid Furor over Preferences," *The Congressional Quarterly Weekly Report,* 23 November 1991, 3463.

CHAPTER 12

330 Exhibit 12.2, adapted from Charles D. Schewe, Marketing Principles and Strategies. Copyright © 1987, reprinted by permission of McGraw-Hill, Inc., 35.

331 Exhibit 12.3, adapted from Courtland L. Bovée and John V. Thill, *Marketing* (New York: McGraw-Hill, 1992), 14.

334 Exhibit 12.4, adapted from Charles D. Schewe, *Marketing Principles and Strategies* (New York: Random House, 1987), 35.

338–339 Adapted from R. C. Baker, Roger Dickinson, and Stanley Hollander, "Big Brother 1994: Marketing Data and the IRS," *Journal of Public Policy & Marketing,* 5 (1986): 231; "Is Nothing Private?" *Business Week,* 4 September 1989, 74–82; "Privacy vs. Free Speech," *Direct Marketing,* May 1989, 42; Robert J. Posch, Jr., "Can We Have à la Carte Constitutional Rights?" *Direct Marketing,* July 1989, 76.

345 Exhibit 12.6, adapted from William F. Schoell and Joseph P. Guiltinan, *Marketing: Contemporary Concepts and Practices,* 3rd ed. (Boston: Allyn & Bacon, 1988), 215. Copyright © 1988 by Allyn & Bacon. Reprinted with permission; adapted from Samuel C. Certo, Max E. Douglas, and Stewart W. Husted, *Business,* 2nd ed., Allyn & Bacon, 1988.

346 Exhibit 12.7, adapted from "More Bang for the Ad Dollar," Niles Howard, *Dun's Review,* November 1978. Reprinted with the permission of *Dun's Business Month,* November 1978. Copyright 1978, The Goldhirsch Group, Inc.

347 Adapted from "Dutch Women: The Individualization Trend," *Market: Europe,* December 1990, 3–4.

348 Exhibit 12.8, adapted from William Zikmund and Michael D'Amico, *Marketing,* 2nd ed. (New York: Wiley, 1986), 99. Reprinted by permission of John Wiley & Sons, Inc.

349 Adapted from John Thackray, "Much Ado About Global Marketing," *Across the Board,* April 1985, 38–46; Perry Pascarella, "In Search of Universal Designs," *Industry Week,* 22 July 1985, 47–52; William W. Locke, "The Fatal Flaw: Hidden Cultural Differences," *Business Marketing,* April 1986, 65, 72–76; Alice Rudolph, "Standardization Not Standard for Global Marketers," *Advertising Age,* 27 September 1985, 3–4.

CHAPTER 13

359 Exhibit 13.1, adapted from Courtland L. Bovée and John V. Thill, *Marketing* (New York: McGraw-Hill, 1992), 253; and reprinted with permission of Macmillan Publishing Company from *Marketing,* Third Edition by Joel R. Evans and Barry Berman. Copyright © 1987 by Macmillan Publishing Company, 615.

360 Adapted from Tracy E. Benson, "Product Liability: Deep Waters to Debate," *Industry Week,* 6 August 1990, 46–63; Marisa Manley, "Product Liability: You're More Exposed Than You Think," *Harvard Business Review,* September–October 1987, 28–40; "Limits to Liability," *San Diego Union,* 1 October 1990, B-6; Marisa L. Manley, "Controlling Product Liability," *Inc.,* February 1987, 103–107; Gail Greco, "Product Liability Bill On Its Way," *Entrepreneur,* October 1990, 192–193.

364 Exhibit 13.2, adapted from Anne B. Fisher, "Coke's Brand-Loyalty Lesson," *Fortune,* 5 August 1985, 46; John Koten, "Why Do Hot Dogs Come in Packs of 10 and Buns in 8s and 12s?" *The Wall Street Journal,* September 21, 1984. Reprinted by permission of *The Wall Street Journal,* © 1984 Dow Jones & Company, Inc. All Rights Reserved Worldwide. A1, 15.

366 Exhibit 13.3, adapted from Ronald Alsop and Bill Abrams, eds., "Getting an Edge with Better Packages," in *The Wall Street Journal on Marketing* (New York: New American Library, 1986), 140–141. Dow Jones Irwin, Inc.

367 Adapted from John Koten, "Why Do Hot Dogs Come in Packs of 10 and Buns in 8s and 12s?" *The Wall Street Journal,* 21 September 1984, A1, A15.

371 Exhibit 13.5, adapted from Charles D. Schewe, *Marketing: Principles and Strategies* (New York: McGraw-Hill, 1987), 294.

373 Exhibit 13.6, adapted from Courtland L. Bovée and John V. Thill, *Marketing* (New York: McGraw-Hill, 1992), 290.

376 Adapted from Kent B. Monroe, *Pricing: Making Profitable Decisions* (New York: McGraw-Hill, 1990), 406.

377 Exhibit 13.7, adapted from Thomas C. Kinnear and Kenneth L. Bernhardt, *Principles of Marketing,* 3rd ed. (Glenview, Ill.: Scott, Foresman/Little, Brown, 1990), 610; *Principles of Marketing,* Third Edition, by Thomas C. Kinnear and Kenneth L. Bernhardt, p. 610. Copyright © 1990, 1986, 1983 Scott, Foresman and Company. Reprinted by permission of Harper-Collins Publishers.

CHAPTER 14

389 Exhibit 14.1, adapted from Theodore Beckman, William Davidson, and W. Wayne Talarzyk, *Marketing,* 9th ed. (New York: Ronald Press, 1973), 307.

391 Adapted from Philip R. Cateora, *International Marketing* (Homewood, Ill.: Irwin, 1990), 582.

394 Exhibit 14.3, adapted from Charles D. Schewe, *Marketing Principles and Strategies* (New York: Random House, 1987), 399.

395 Gregory Stricharchuk, "Card Makers' Tough Tactics Belie Sweet Verse as Competition Rises," *The Wall Street Journal,* 24 December 1987, A11; Denise M. Topolnicki, "Greetings from the Rack Race," *Venture,* February 1988, 44–48; Hallmark Cards press release, 24 October 1988; Michael Booth, "Sweet Talk, Tough Tactics," *The New York Times,* sec. f, 6+.

399 Exhibit 14.4, adapted from Charles D. Schewe, *Marketing Principles and Strategies* (New York: Random House, 1987), reprinted with permission of McGraw-Hill, Inc., 435–436.

401 Exhibit 14.5, adapted from Courtland L. Bovée and John V. Thill, *Marketing* (New York: McGraw-Hill, 1992), 455; and Exhibit from *Retail Management* by Avigit Ghosh, copyright © 1990 by the Dryden Press, reprinted by permission of the publishers.

402–403 Adapted from Kathryn Graven, "For Toys 'R' Us, Japan Isn't Child's Play," *The Wall*

Street Journal, 7 February 1990, B1; "Toys 'R' Us Goes Overseas—And Finds That Toys 'R' Them, Too," *Business Week,* 26 January 1987, 71–72; Michael Salter, "Big Stores, Bigger Sales: Canada," *McLean's,* 15 December 1986, 42–43; Joseph Pereira, "Toys 'R' Us, Big Kid on the Block, Won't Stop Growing," *The Wall Street Journal,* 11 August 1988, B6.
408 Exhibit 14.7, adapted from Thomas A. Foster, "Logistics: Our Economy's Engine," *Chilton's Distribution,* July 1991, 6–14.

CHAPTER 15

419 Adapted from Courtland L. Bovée and William F. Arens, *Contemporary Advertising* (Homewood, Ill.: Irwin, 1989), 638–639.
420 Exhibit 15.1, adapted from William Zikmund and Michael D'Amico, *Marketing,* 2nd ed. (New York: Wiley, 1986), 479.
425 Exhibit 15.2, adapted from Courtland L. Bovée and John V. Thill, *Marketing* (New York: McGraw-Hill, 1992), 590.
430 Exhibit 15.3, adapted from Bureau of Labor Statistics (Employment); *Advertising Age,* 27 March 1986; John P. Cortez, "Coen Expects '92 Recovery, 9% Ad $ Hike," *Advertising Age,* 28 October 1991, 1, 53; Martin Fleming, "Media Spending in the 1990s," *American Demographics,* September 1991, 48–50, 52–53.
436 Exhibit 15.4, adapted from "U.S. Advertising Volume," *Advertising Age,* 6 May 1991, 16.
437 Exhibit 15.5, adapted from Christopher Gilson and Harold W. Berkman, "Advantages and Disadvantages of Major Advertising Media," in *Advertising: Concepts and Strategies* (New York: McGraw-Hill, 1980), 274–275.

CHAPTER 16

453 Exhibit 16.1, reprinted with permission of Macmillan Publishing Company from *Systems and Design: A Case Study Approach* by Robert J. Thierauf and George W. Reynolds. Copyright © 1980 by Merrill Publishing Company an imprint of Macmillan Publishing Company, Inc., 69.
455 Exhibit 16.2, adapted from Kathryn M. Bartol and David C. Martin, *Management* (New York: McGraw-Hill, 1991), 708.
463 Adapted from Erin Kelly, "First Steps: Questions to Ask Yourself Before You Start Shopping," *USA Today,* 23 September 1985, 4E; John Hillkirk, "Let Your Needs Guide Computer Choice," *USA Today,* 10 June 1985, 3E.
471 Exhibit 16.6, adapted from Timothy Trainor and Diane Krasnewich, *Computers!* (New York: McGraw-Hill, 1989), 41.
472–473 Adapted from Fidelity Investments, *Fidelity Focus,* Summer 1991, 20–25; PR Newswire, "Fidelity Announces FOX and TouchTone Trader," 20 February 1992; PR Newswire, "Fidelity Reports Surge in IRA Accounts," 10 February 1992; Julie Rohrer, "Money Management's Brave New World," *Institutional Investor,* March 1991, 39–44; Jaclyn Fierman, "Fidelity's Secret: Faithful Service," *Fortune,* 7 May 1990, 86–92; David Churbuck, "Watch Out, Citicorp," *Forbes,* 16 September 1991, 38–39; Hank Gilman, "Fidelity's 2d Round of Layoffs Removes 500 Jobs in City Office," *Boston Globe,* 1 March 1988, C 1.

CHAPTER 17

484 Exhibit 17.2, adapted from "As Many of the Big Eight Centralized, Price Waterhouse Bucked the Trend," reprinted from October 24, 1983 issue of *Business Week* by special permission, copyright © 1983 by McGraw-Hill, Inc.
487 Adapted from Peter Fuhrman, "Doing Business in the Dark," *Forbes,* 19 February 1990, 50, 54.
495 Adapted from Elizabeth S. Lewin, "How Much Are You Really Worth?" *Sylvia Porter's Personal Finance Magazine,* February 1986, 66, 68; *Sylvia Porter's Money Book* (New York: Avon, 1976), 36–37; M. Herbert Freeman and David K. Graf, *Money Management* (Indianapolis: Bobbs-Merrill, 1980), 10–11; Desmond A. Jolly, *Personal Financial Statement,* University of California, Division of Agricultural Sciences, February 1979, 2–3.
498–499 Adapted from Manual Schiffres, "All the Good News That Fits," *U.S. News & World Report,* 14 April 1986, 50–51.

CHAPTER 18

515 Exhibit 18.1, adapted from *Survey of Current Business* (Washington, D.C.: GPO, September 1991), S-15.
518–519 Exhibit 18.2, adapted from "Banks by Other Names: Who Offers What Services," *Money,* September 1985, 80–81; Personal communication, Federal Reserve Bank, 1988; Personal communication, National Credit Union Administration, 1988.
521 Exhibit 18.3, adapted from "The State of American Banking," *The New York Times,* 20 February 1991, sec. d, 6; "Top Banks in Acquired Deposits," *American Banker,* March 26, 1992, 31A; and "Top Commercial Banks in Deposits and Assets," *American Banker,* March 26, 1992, 28A.
525 Adapted from "Poland to Take Bank Private," *The Wall Street Journal,* 16 September 1991, A12.
526–527 Adapted from Steven R. Weisman, "Two Japanese Banks Merging in Preparation for New Era," *The New York Times,* 30 August 1989, sec. d, 1, 4; Brian Robins, "Meanwhile, Back at the Ranch . . . ," *The Banker,* January 1991, 44–46; Brian Robins, "Shotgun Marriages," *The Banker,* January 1991, 47–49; James Alexander, "Gung Ho, Go Slow," *The Banker,* January 1991, 50; Jim Impoco, "Japan's Banking Blues," *U.S. News & World Report,* 25 February 1991, 50, 51; Gale Eisenstodt, "Good News for U.S. Banks," *Forbes,* 10 December 1990, 38, 40; "Are All Banks Equal?" *The Economist,* 23 March 1991, 84, 86; "The Japanese Way," *The Banker,* January 1991, 12.
528–529 Adapted from Jonathan Beaty and S. C. Gwynne, "The Dirtiest Bank of All," *Time,* 29 July 1991, 42–47; John Greenwald, "Feeling the Heat," *Time,* 5 August 1991, 44–46; Michael Quint, "The Luster Fades at First American," *The New York Times,* 22 July 1991, sec. d, 1, 3; Neil A. Lewis, "Clark Clifford, Symbol of the Permanent Capital, Is Faced with a Dilemma," *The New York Times,* 5 April 1991, sec. a, 14; Jim McGee, "Document Challenges Clifford, Altman on Stock Deal, Policies," *Washington Post,* 5 August 1991, A4; Marjorie Williams, "Clark Clifford: The Rise of a Reputation," *Washington Post,* 8 May 1991, D1, D8; Jonathan Beaty and

S. C. Gwynne, "Is That All There Is?" *Time,* 30 December 1991, 59.

CHAPTER 19

546 Adapted from John Evans, "Citicorp Said to Be Mulling Sale of Consumer Unit in Italy," *American Banker,* 9 September 1991, 8.
546 Exhibit 19.4, adapted from "Prime Rate Charged by Banks," Table 1.33, *Federal Reserve Bulletin,* October 1991, A22.
547 Exhibit 19.5, adapted from Louis E. Boone and David L. Kurtz, *Contemporary Business,* 5th ed. (Chicago: Dryden, 1987), 562.
548 Exhibit 19.6, adapted from "Interest Costs Exceed Profits," *The San Diego Union,* 8 September 1989, E-1; Vivian Brownstein, "Profits: Wait Till Next Year," *Fortune,* 12 August 1991, 21–22; Gene Koretz, "Now, Business Is Borrowing Just to Cut Back," *Business Week,* 17 December 1990, 20.
548 Exhibit 19.7, adapted from "Percentage Long-Term Letter®-Rating Upgrades & Downgrades, by Year, 1970–1990," Figure 2, *Moody's Special Report: Changes in Corporate Credit Quality, 1970–1990,* February 1991, 5; "Number of Defaulting Issuers," Figure 6, *Moody's Special Report: Corporate Bond Defaults and Default Rates, 1970–1990,* January 1991, 9.
554–555 Adapted from Kenneth W. Sparks, "Successful Business Borrowing: How to Plan and Negotiate a Loan," *Macmillan Executive Summary Program,* December 1986, 2–8.
556 Exhibit 19.9, adapted from "Commercial Paper and Bankers Dollar Acceptances Outstanding," Table 1.32, *Federal Reserve Bulletin,* October 1991, A22.
563 Adapted from "Companies Gain Funds by Speeding Intakes and Slowing Outgoes," *The Wall Street Journal,* 31 July 1974, 1; "Top U.S. Title Insurer, TI Corp., Indicted for Fraud in Huge Check-Kiting Scheme," *The Wall Street Journal,* 15 January 1976, 6; Irwin Ross, "The Race Is to the Slow Payer," *Fortune,* 18 April 1983, 75–80.

CHAPTER 20

577 Exhibit 20.1, based on information from Kate Ennis, communications coordinator, Standard & Poor's Corporation, New York, personal communication, December 1991; David M. Blitzer, "GNP Benchmark Revisions," *Standard & Poor's Industry Surveys: Trends and Projections,* 14 November 1992, 5; Marc Levinson, "Living on the Edge," *Newsweek,* 4 November 1991, 22–25.
583 Exhibit 20.2, adapted from William Power, "Regional Exchanges Consider a New Option: Merging," *The Wall Street Journal,* 8 February 1991, C1, C15; and reprinted by permission of *The Wall Street Journal,* © 1991 Dow Jones & Company, Inc. All Rights Reserved Worldwide.
589 Exhibit 20.3, adapted from "A Centennial View: Dow Jones Industrial Average," *The Wall Street Journal,* centennial edition, B15; and reprinted by permission of *The Wall Street Journal,* © 1991 Dow Jones & Company, Inc. All Rights Reserved Worldwide.
590–591 Adapted from Jordan E. Goodman, "Stock Analysis Checklist," *Money,* September 1983, 69. Excerpted from the September 1983

issue of *Money* magazine by special permission. © 1983, Time, Inc.

592 Adapted from Peter C. Du Bois, "How to Buy Foreign Stocks . . . Hong Kong Marches On," *Barron's*, 29 July 1991, 56.

592 Exhibit 20.4, reprinted by permission of *The Wall Street Journal.* © Dow Jones & Company, Inc., 1989. All rights reserved.

593 Exhibit 20.5, reprinted by permission of *The Wall Street Journal.* © Dow Jones & Company, Inc., 1989. All rights reserved.

593 Exhibit 20.6, reprinted by permission of *The Wall Street Journal.* © Dow Jones & Company, Inc., 1989. All rights reserved.

594 Exhibit 20.7, reprinted by permission of *The Wall Street Journal.* © Dow Jones & Company, Inc., 1989. All rights reserved.

CHAPTER 21

608 Exhibit 21.1, based on information from the *Code of Federal Regulations,* Titles 9, 21, Pts. 100–169, 200–N, Superintendent of Documents, GPO, Washington, D.C.

610 Exhibit 21.2, adapted from "Deregulating America," *Business Week,* 28 November 1983, 80–81; Donald L. Barlett and James B. Steele, "Deregulation Decimated Airlines, Truck Industry—Are the Banks Next?" *San Diego Union,* 19 November 1991, A-1, A-4; George A. Steiner and John F. Steiner, *Business, Government, and Society* (New York: McGraw-Hill, 1991), 307–309.

612 Exhibit 21.3, adapted from *Facts and Figures on Government Finance,* 23rd ed. (Washington, D.C.: Tax Foundation, Inc., 1986); "How to find Your Market," *Changing Times,* September 1985, 36 and 67; David A Westenberg, "What's in a Name? Establishing and Maintaining Trademark and Service," *Business Lawyer,* November 1986, 65–89; and Ernest E. Helms, "Protecting Your Ideas—and Your Money," *Black Enterprise,* September 1986, 65–69.

617 Exhibit 21.4, adapted from Bartley A. Brennan and Nancy Kubasek, *The Legal Environment of Business* (New York: Macmillan, 1988), 24; Douglas Whitman and John Gergacz, *The Legal Environment of Business,* 2nd ed. (New York: Random House, 1988), 22, 25.

618 Adapted from Daniel C. Carson, "'Hired Guns' Aim to Keep Veil of Secrecy on Product Dangers," *San Diego Union,* 4 May 1991, A-3; "U.S. Orders Recall of Heart Valves," *San Diego Union,* 24 April 1991, A-3; Jeff Bailey, "Fears over Pfizer Heart-Valve Fractures Lead to Patients' Suffering and Lawsuits," *The Wall Street Journal,* 21 June 1990, B1; "Ford to Pay Couple $6M in Fatal Crash," *USA Today,* 5 April 1990, 1A; Jonathan Weber, "Heart Valve Case Leaves Pfizer Under a Cloud," *Los Angeles Times,* 1 April 1990, D1.

625 Adapted from Robert Sam Anson, "In Thailand, Don't Even Ask If It's Real," *Business Month,* October 1989, 23–25.

626 Adapted from "How to Find Your Market," *Changing Times,* September 1985, 36, 37. Adapted with permission from *Changing Times* Magazine. © Kiplinger Washington Editors, Inc.,

1985; David A. Westenberg, "What's in a Name? Establishing and Maintaining Trademark and Service," *Business Lawyer,* November 1986, 65–89; Ernest E. Helms, "Protecting Your Ideas—And Your Money," *Black Enterprise,* September 1986, 65–69.

CHAPTER 22

638 Exhibit 22.1, adapted from Mark R. Greene and James S. Trieschmann, *Risk and Insurance* (Cincinnati: South-Western Publishing, 1984), 25.

641 Adapted from "Setting Limits at Lloyd's," *Business Week,* 27 January 1992, 41.

646–647 Adapted from Beatrice E. Garcia, "Who Ya Gonna Call If a Ghostbuster's Proton Pack Breaks?" *The Wall Street Journal,* 24 August 1989, A1, A4; Deanna Hodgin, "Insurers Play Backup for the Band," *Insight,* 23 July 1990, 38–39.

648 Adapted from "'Wellness' Plans: An Ounce of Prevention," *Newsweek,* 30 January 1989.

649 Exhibit 22.4, adapted from "Pinned Down by Medical Bills," *Time,* 30 June 1986, 64; Joseph Carey, "Health Benefits for Employees Enter New Era," *U.S. News & World Report,* 22 July 1985, 73; Personal communication, Employee Benefit Research Institute, Washington, D.C., 1989.

GLOSSARY

A

absolute advantage Nation's ability to produce a particular product with fewer resources (per unit of output) than any other nation (125)

accountability The necessity to report results to supervisors and justify outcomes that fall below expectations (181)

accounting Process of recording, classifying, and summarizing the financial activities of an organization (482)

accounting equation Assets equal liabilities plus owners' equity (487)

accrual basis Accounting method in which revenue is recorded when a sale is made and expense is recorded when incurred (493)

acquisition Combination of two companies in which one company purchases the other and remains the dominant corporation (51)

activity ratios Financial ratios that indicate the amount of business a company is doing (505)

actuaries Persons employed by an insurance company to compute expected losses and to calculate the cost of premiums (639)

administrative law Rules, regulations, and interpretations of statutory law set forth by administrative agencies and commissions (616)

administrative skills Technical skills in information gathering, data analysis, planning, organizing, and other aspects of managerial work (156)

advertising Paid, nonpersonal communication to a target market from an identified sponsor utilizing mass communications channels (420)

advocacy advertising Ads that present a company's opinions on public issues such as education and health (430)

affirmative action Activities undertaken by businesses to recruit and promote minorities, based on an analysis of the work force and the available labor pool (106)

agency Business relationship that exists when one party (the principal) authorizes another party (the agent) to act on her or his behalf, while controlling the agent's conduct (622)

agency shop Workplace requiring nonunion workers who are covered by agreements negotiated by the union to pay service fees to that union (310)

amortization Accounting procedure for systematically spreading the cost of an intangible asset over its estimated useful life (491)

analytic system A production process that breaks incoming materials into various component products (207)

application software Programs that perform specific functions for users, such as word processing or spreadsheet analysis (466)

Pages on which the glossary terms appear are indicated by the numbers within parentheses.

G-0

arbitrage Simultaneous purchase in one market and sale in a different market with a profitable price or yield differential (583)

arbitration Process for resolving a labor-contract dispute in which an impartial third party studies the issues and makes a binding decision (304)

artificial intelligence Use of computers to mimic human thought processes (457)

artwork The visual, graphic part of the ad (435)

assembly language One level above machine language; it consists of fairly cryptic low-level commands that initiate CPU commands (470)

assembly line Series of work stations at which each worker performs a specific task in the production process (207)

assembly-line layout Method of arranging equipment in which production is a flow of work proceeding along a line of work stations (222)

asset allocation Method of shifting investments within a portfolio to adapt them to the current investment environment (574)

assets Physical objects and intangible rights that have economic value to the owner (487)

auction exchanges Centralized marketplaces where securities are traded by specialists on behalf of investors in auctions (582)

audit Accountant's evaluation of the fairness and reliability of a client's financial statements (484)

authority Power granted by the organization and acknowledged by the employees (181)

authorization cards Sign-up cards designating a union as the signer's preferred bargaining agent (302)

authorized stock Shares that a corporation's board of directors has decided to sell eventually (560)

autocratic leaders Managers who centralize authority and do not involve others in decision making (165)

automated teller machines Electronic terminals that permit people to perform simple banking transactions without the aid of a human teller (523)

automation Process of performing a mechanical operation with the absolute minimum of human intervention (207)

average Number typical of a group of numbers or quantities (675)

average markup Constant markup percentage used in setting prices for all products in a product line (378)

B

balance of payments Sum of all payments one nation has made to other nations minus the payments it has received from other nations during a specific period of time (129)

balance of trade Relationship between the value of the products a nation exports and those it imports (127)

balance sheet Financial statement that shows assets, liabilities, and owners' equity on a given date (489)

bankruptcy Legal procedure by which a person or a business that is unable to meet financial obligations is relieved of debt (625)

barriers to entry Factors that make it difficult to launch a business in a particular industry (38)

bartering Trading by exchanging goods or services directly rather than through a medium like money (5)

batch processing A computing method in which "jobs" are submitted to the computer in "batches" at regular intervals, so users must wait for their results (460)

bear market Falling stock market (588)

behavior modification Application of punishments and rewards, with the aim of improving human behavior (249)

behavioral segmentation Categorization of customers according to their relationship with products or response to product characteristics (346)

beneficiaries People named in a life-insurance policy who are paid by the insurer when the insured dies (651)

bill of materials Listing of all parts and materials in a product that are to be made or purchased (221)

bit A single unit of information; can consist of either a 1 or a 0 (464)

blacklist Secret list circulated among employers to keep union organizers from getting jobs (305)

blue-chip stocks Equities issued by large, well-established companies with consistent records of price increases and dividend payments (578)

board of directors Group of people, elected by the shareholders, who have the ultimate authority in guiding the affairs of a corporation (48)

bond Certificate of indebtedness that is sold to raise funds (557)

bonus Cash payment in addition to the regular wage or salary, which serves as a reward for achievement (277)

bookkeeping Recordkeeping, clerical phase of accounting (486)

boycott Union activity in which members and sympathizers refuse to buy or handle the product of a target company (305)

branch office Producer-owned operation that carries stock and sells it (398)

brand Any name, term, sign, symbol, design, or combination used to identify the products of a firm and to differentiate them from competing products (363)

brand equity The overall strength of a brand in the marketplace and its value to the company that owns it; increasingly, companies are trying to assign financial value to brand equity (365)

breach of contract Failure to live up to the terms of a contract, with no legal excuse (622)

break-even analysis Method of calculating the minimum volume of sales needed at a given price to cover all costs (379)

break-even point Sales volume at a given price that will cover all of a company's costs (379)

broker Individual registered to sell securities (585)

brokers Agents that specialize in a particular commodity (398)

budget Financial plan for company's future activities that estimates revenues and proposed expenditures and that forecasts how expenditures will be financed (483)

bull market Rising stock market (588)

bulletin board systems The electronic equivalents of traditional bulletin boards; users can "post" messages, data, and programs for other people to access (468)

business agent Full-time union staffer who negotiates with management and attempts to resolve grievances brought up by union members (300)

business cycle Fluctuations in the rate of growth that an economy experiences over a period of several years (19)

business-interruption insurance Insurance that covers losses resulting from temporary business closings (644)

byte A collection of eight data bits (464)

C

calendar year Twelve-month accounting period that begins on January 1 and ends on December 31 (489)

call option The right to buy shares at a specified price and sell at a market price (580)

callable bonds Bonds that a company can redeem before the stated maturity date (558)

canned approach A selling method based on a fixed, memorized presentation (428)

capital Funds that support a business and its tools (machines, vehicles, and buildings) to produce goods and services (4)

capital budgeting Process for evaluating proposed investments in select projects that provide the best long-term financial return (549)

capital gains Difference between the price at which a financial asset is sold and its original cost (assuming the price has gone up) (573)

capital-intensive businesses Businesses that require large investments in capital assets (38)

capital investments Money paid to acquire something of permanent value in a business (549)

capital items Relatively expensive organizational products that have a long life and are used in the operations of a business (362)

capital structure Financing mix of a firm (546)

cartel Association of producers that attempts to control a market and keep prices high by limiting output and dividing market shares among the members (21)

cash basis Accounting method in which revenue is recorded when payment is received and expense is recorded when cash is paid (493)

cash discount Discount offered to buyers who use cash instead of credit (380)

central processing unit The core of the computer, performing the three basic functions of arithmetic (addition, etc.), logic (comparing numbers), and control/communication (managing the computer) (463)

centralization Concentration of authority and responsibility at the top (185)

certificate of deposit Note issued by a bank that guarantees to pay the depositor a relatively high interest rate for a fixed period of time (521)

certification Process by which a union is officially recognized by the National Labor Relations Board as the bargaining agent for a group of workers (302)

certified management accountants Accountants who have fulfilled the requirements for certification as specialists in management accounting (486)

certified public accountants Professionally licensed accountants who meet certain requirements for education and experience, and who pass an examination (485)

chain of command Pathway for the flow of authority from one level of an organization's employees to the next (183)

channel captain Channel member that is able to influence the activities of the other members of the distribution channel (396)

chattel mortgage Agreement that the movable property purchased through a loan belongs to the borrower, although the lender has a legal right to the property if payments are not made as specified in the loan agreement (553)

chief executive officer Person appointed by a corporation's board of directors to carry out the board's policies and supervise the activities of the corporation (48)

chief information officer A top corporate executive with responsibility for information and information systems (453)

circular flow Continuous exchange of goods and services for money among the participants in an economic system (15)

claims Demands for payment by an insurance company due to some loss by the insured (639)

classical theory of motivation The view that money is the sole motivator in the workplace (236)

closed shop Workplace in which union membership is a condition of employment (310)

closing The point at which a sale is completed (429)

code of ethics Written statement setting forth the principles that should guide an organization's decisions (114)

cognitive dissonance Anxiety following a purchase that prompts buyers to seek reassurance about the purchase (341)

coinsurance The share of medical costs the patient picks up to supplement the remaining costs paid by the insurer (648)

collateral Tangible asset a lender can claim if a borrower defaults on a loan (552)

collective bargaining Process used by unions and management to negotiate work contracts (303)

commercial banks Traditional banks offering savings, checking, and loan services (517)

commercial paper An IOU issued by corporations to raise short-term capital (525), (554)

commercialization Large-scale production and distribution of a product (370)

commissions Payments to workers who achieve a certain level of sales (277)

commodities Raw materials used in producing other goods (581)

commodities futures Contracts for commodities that will be delivered at a future date (582)

commodity business Business in which products are undifferentiated, so that price becomes the chief competitive weapon (40)

commodity exchanges Marketplaces where contracts for raw materials are bought and sold (584)

common law Law based on the precedents established by judges' decisions (616)

common stock Shares whose owners have the last claim on distributed profits and assets (560), (578)

communication Transmitting information from one person to another (157), (235)

communication media Channels of communication (157)

communism Economic system in which all productive resources are owned and operated by the government so that there is no private property (8)

comparative advantage Nation's ability to produce a given product at a lower opportunity cost than its trading partners (125)

comparative advertising An advertising technique in which two or more products are explicitly compared (431)

compensating balance Portion of an unsecured loan that is kept on deposit at the lending institution to protect the lender and increase the lender's return (554)

compensation Payment to employees for their work (275)

competitive advantage Quality that makes a product more desirable than similar products offered by the competition (332)

competitive advertising Ads that specifically highlight how a product is better than its competitors (430)

comprehensive general liability insurance Liability insurance that covers a wide variety of losses, except certain losses specifically mentioned in the policy (645)

computer languages Sets of programmable rules and conventions for communicating with computers (469)

computer-aided design Use of computer graphics in the development of products or processes (208)

computer-aided engineering Use of computers for engineering (209)

computer-aided manufacturing Use of computers to control production machines (209)

computer-integrated manufacturing Computer-based systems that coordinate and control all the elements of design and production, including CAD and CAM (209)

concentrated marketing Marketing program aimed at a single market segment (348)

concept testing Process of getting reactions about a proposed product from potential customers (369)

conceptual skills Ability to understand the relationship of parts to the whole (159)

conglomerate mergers Combinations of companies that are in unrelated businesses, designed to augment a company's growth and diversify risk (53)

consent order Settlement in which an individual or organization promises to discontinue some illegal activity without admitting guilt (616)

consideration Bargained-for exchange necessary to make a contract legally binding (621)

consortium Group of companies working jointly to promote a common objective or engage in a project of benefit to all members (52)

consumer market Individuals who buy goods or services for personal use (333)

consumer promotions Sales promotions aimed at final consumers (440)

contingency leadership Leadership style promoting flexibility and adoption of the style most appropriate to current conditions (166)

contingent business-interruption insurance Insurance that protects a business from losses due to an interruption in the delivery of supplies (644)

continuity The pattern according to which an ad appears in the media; it can be spread evenly over time or concentrated during selected periods (436)

contract Exchange of promises enforceable by law (621)

controller Highest-ranking accountant in a firm, responsible for overseeing all accounting functions (486)

controlling Process of ensuring that organizational objectives are being attained and of correcting deviations if those objectives are not being reached (167)

convenience products Products that are readily available, low priced, and heavily advertised and that consumers buy quickly and often (361)

convenience stores Food stores that offer convenient locations and hours but stock a limited selection of goods (404)

conversion process Sequence of events (input → transformation → output) for transforming materials into goods and services (206)

convertible bonds Bonds that offer the buyer the option of converting them into a stated number of shares of common stock (559), (577)

cooperative advertising Joint efforts between local and national advertisers, in which producers of nationally sold products share the costs of local advertising with local merchants and wholesalers (432)

cooperatives Associations of people or small companies with similar interests, formed to obtain greater bargaining power and other economies of scale (52)

copy The verbal (spoken or written) part of an ad (435)

corporate culture Organizational climate or set of values that guides and colors the atmosphere within a company (198)

corporation Legally chartered enterprise with most of the legal rights of a person, including the right to conduct a business, to own and sell property, to borrow money, and to sue or be sued (44)

correlation Statistical relationship between two or more variables (678)

cost-benefit analysis Comparison of the costs and benefits of a particular action for the purpose of assessing its desirability (609)

cost of capital The average rate of interest a firm pays on its combination of debt and equity (544)

cost of goods sold Cost of producing or acquiring a company's products for sale during a given period (494)

cost-of-living adjustment Clause in a union contract ensuring that wages will rise in proportion to inflation (311)

cost per thousand The cost of reaching 1,000 people with an ad (436)

cost shifting Hospitals and doctors boosting their charges to private paying patients to make up for the shortfall in government reimbursements for their Medicare and Medicaid patients (649)

couponing Distribution of certificates that offer discounts on particular items (440)

craft unions Unions made up of skilled artisans belonging to a single profession or practicing a single craft (297)

creative selling The selling process used by order getters, which involves determining customer needs, devising strategies to explain product benefits, and persuading customers to buy (423)

credit life insurance Coverage that guarantees repayment of a loan or an installment contract if the borrower dies (644)

credit unions Cooperative financial institutions that provide loan and savings services to their members (518)

crime insurance Insurance against loss from theft (644)

crisis management System for minimizing the harm that might result from some unusually threatening situations (169)

critical path method Scheduling method that estimates the smallest amount of time in which a whole project can be completed by projecting the time needed for completion of the longest sequence of tasks (the critical path) (225)

currency Bills and coins that make up the cash money of a society (516)

current assets Cash and other items that can be turned back into cash within one year (489)

current liabilities Obligations that must be met within a year (491)

current ratio Measure of a company's short-term liquidity, calculated by dividing current assets by current liabilities (504)

customer divisions A divisional structure that focuses on customers or clients (191)

customized marketing A marketing program in which each individual customer is treated as a separate segment (350)

customs duties Fees imposed on goods brought into the country (614)

cyclical variation Change that occurs in a regularly repeating pattern (677)

D

damages Amount a court awards a plaintiff in a successful lawsuit (634)

data Recorded statistics, facts, predictions, and opinions; data need to be converted to information before they can help people solve business problems (452)

data communications The process of connecting computers and allowing them to send data back and forth (472)

database A collection of related computer files that can be cross-referenced in order to extract information (452)

database management software Programs designed to create, store, maintain, rearrange, and retrieve the contents of databases (469)

database marketing Direct marketing in which advertisers take advantage of comprehensive information on customers, including purchase behavior, demographics, and lifestyle (438)

dealer exchanges Decentralized marketplaces where securities are bought and sold by dealers out of their own inventories (582)

debentures Bonds not backed by specific assets (558), (577)

debit card Form of plastic money that automatically decreases a person's bank account when used (523)

debt Funds obtained by borrowing (72)

debt ratios Financial ratios (sometimes called coverage

ratios) that indicate the extent of a company's burden of long-term debt (505)

debt-to-equity ratio Measure of the extent to which a business is financed by debt as opposed to invested capital, calculated by dividing the company's total liabilities by owners' equity (505)

debt-to-total-assets ratio Measure of a company's ability to carry long-term debt, calculated by dividing total liabilities by total assets (505)

decentralization Delegation of authority and responsibility to employees in lower positions (185)

deceptive pricing A range of pricing and promotion practices that are considered misleading by government regulators (376)

decertification Process workers use to take away a union's right to represent them (302)

decision support systems Extensions of management information systems that provide managers with the tools and data they need for decision making (456)

deductible Amount of loss that must be paid by the insured before the insurer will pay for the rest (639)

deed Legal document by which an owner transfers the title to real property to a new owner (624)

default Failure of issuers to meet their contractual principal and interest obligations (577)

delegation Assignment of authority, responsibility, and accountability to lower-level employees (181)

demand Specific quantity of a product that consumers are willing and able to buy at various prices at a given time (13)

demand curve Series of points on a graph showing the relationship between price and quantity demanded (13)

demand deposit Money in a checking account that can be used by the owner at any time (516)

democratic leaders Managers who delegate authority and involve employees in decision making (166)

demographics Study of the statistical characteristics of a population (345)

denomination Face value of a single bond (557)

dental and vision insurance Insurance that covers a portion of the costs of dental and eye care (648)

department stores Large retail stores that carry a wide variety of merchandise (399)

departmentalization Grouping people within an organization according to function, division, teams, matrix, or network (187)

departmentalization by division Grouping departments according to similarities in product, process, customer, or geography (189)

departmentalization by function Grouping workers according to their similar skills, resource use, and expertise (188)

departmentalization by matrix Permanently assigning employees to both a functional group and a project team (thus using functional and divisional patterns simultaneously) (193)

departmentalization by network Breaking major functions into separate companies that are electronically connected to a small headquarters organization (194)

departmentalization by teams Assigning employees to functional departments but also assigning them to teams either permanently or temporarily (192)

dependent variables Events that change as the independent variables change (674)

depreciated value Value of something after it has been in use for a time, which is less than its value when new (643)

depreciation Accounting procedure for systematically spreading the cost of a tangible asset over its estimated useful life (491)

deregulation Removal or relaxation of rules and restrictions affecting business (609)

desktop publishing The ability to prepare documents using computerized typesetting and graphics processing capabilities (468)

differentiated marketing Marketing program aimed at several market segments, each of which receives a unique marketing mix (350)

direct mail Advertising sent directly to potential customers, usually through the U.S. Postal Service (438)

directing Process of getting people to work effectively and willingly (164)

disability income insurance Insurance that protects an individual against loss of income while that individual is disabled as the result of an illness or accident (650)

discount brokerages Financial-services companies that sell securities but give no advice (588)

discount pricing Offering a reduction in price (380)

discount rate Interest rate charged by the Federal Reserve on loans to member banks (532)

discount stores Retailers that sell a variety of goods below the market price by keeping their overhead low (400)

discretionary order Market order that allows the broker to decide when to trade a security (586)

discrimination In a social and economic sense, denial of opportunities to individuals on the basis of some characteristic that has no bearing on the ability of these persons to perform (104)

disinflation Economic condition in which the rate of inflation moderates (21)

disk drive The most common mechanism for secondary storage; includes both hard disk drives and floppy disk drives (465)

disk operating system The most common operating system for microcomputers (466)

dispatching Issuing work orders and routing papers to department heads and supervisors (226)

distributed processing An approach to computer network design in which processing power is spread out among the various computers attached to the network (473)

distribution centers Warehouse facilities that specialize in collecting and shipping merchandise (407)

distribution channels Systems for moving goods and services from producers to customers (388)

distribution mix Combination of intermediaries and channels that a producer uses to get a product to end users (388)

diversification Assembling investment portfolios in such a way that a sudden loss in one investment won't affect the value of the entire portfolio (574)

divestiture Sale of part of a company (51)

dividends Payments to shareholders from a company's earnings (560), (578)

division of labor Specialization in or responsibility for some portion of an organization's overall task (180)

double-entry bookkeeping Way of recording financial transactions that requires two entries for every transaction so that the accounting equation is always kept in balance (488)

downsizing Laying off employees in an effort to become more profitable (185)

due process System of procedures and mechanisms for ensuring equity and justice on the job (314)

dumping Charging less for certain goods abroad than at home (133)

E

earnings per share Measure of a firm's profitability for each share of outstanding stock, calculated by dividing net income by shares of stock outstanding (503)

ecology Relationship among living things in the water, air, and soil, as well as the nutrients that support them (95)

economic order quantity The optimal, or least-cost, quantity of inventory that should be ordered (564)

economic system Means by which a society distributes its resources to satisfy its people's needs (4)

economies of scale Savings from manufacturing, marketing, or buying large quantities (64)

effectiveness Increasing competitiveness through efficiency, quality, and improved human relations (207)

efficiency Minimizing cost by maximizing the level of output from each resource (207)

efficient market hypothesis Theory that the market finds its true value quickly and efficiently (574)

elastic demand Situation in which a percentage change in price produces a greater percentage change in the quantity sold (377)

electronic funds transfer systems Computerized systems for performing financial transactions (523)

electronic mail The transmission of written messages in electronic format between computers (468)

embargo Total ban on trade with a particular nation or in a particular product (133)

employee assistance programs Company-sponsored counseling or referrals for employees with personal problems (283)

employee stock-ownership plan Program enabling employees to become owners or part owners of a company (281)

empowerment Giving employees greater involvement in the day-to-day workings of a company (254)

endowment insurance Life insurance that guarantees death benefits for a specified period, after which the face value of the policy is paid to the policyholder (651)

entrepreneurs People who accept the risk of failure to organize the other three factors of production in order to produce goods and services more efficiently (4)

equilibrium price Point at which quantity supplied and quantity demanded are in balance (14)

equity Funds obtained by selling shares of ownership in the company (72)

ergonomics Study of human performance in relation to the tasks performed, the equipment used, and the environment (216)

exchange process Act of obtaining a desired object from another party by offering something in return (329)

exchange rate Rate at which the money of one country is traded for the money of another (139)

excise taxes Taxes intended to help control potentially harmful practices or to help pay for government services used only by certain people or businesses (613)

exclusive distribution Approach to distribution in which intermediaries are given the exclusive right to sell a product within a given market (393)

executive information systems Similar to decision support systems, but customized to the strategic needs of executives (456)

expectancy theory The idea that the amount of effort a worker expends will depend on the expected outcome (239)

expense items Relatively inexpensive organizational products that are generally consumed within a year of their purchase (362)

expenses Costs created in the process of generating revenues (492)

experience curve Predictable decline of all costs associated with a product as the total number of units produced increases (375)

experiment Data-collection method in which the investigator tries to find out how one set of conditions will affect another set of conditions by setting up a situation in which all factors and events involved may be carefully measured (674)

expert system A computer system that mimics the thought processes of a human expert who is adept at solving particular problems (457)

exporting Selling and shipping goods or services to another country (127)

express contract Contract derived from words, either oral or written (621)

external data Facts obtained from sources outside the records of the business itself (671)

extra-expense insurance Insurance that covers the added expense of operating the business in temporary facilities after an event such as a fire (644)

F

factoring Sale of a firm's accounts receivable to a finance company, known as a factor (553)

factors of production Resources that a society uses to produce goods and services, including natural resources, labor, capital, and entrepreneurship (4)

family branding Using a brand name on a variety of related products (365)

Fed funds rate Interest rate charged for overnight loans between banks (532)

fidelity bond Coverage that protects employers from dishonesty on the part of employees (643)

FIFO First in, first out: method of pricing inventory under which the costs of the first goods acquired are the first ones charged to the cost of goods sold (498)

finance companies Unregulated companies that specialize in making loans (518)

financial accounting Area of accounting concerned with preparing financial information for users outside the organization (482)

financial futures Legally binding agreements to buy or sell financial instruments at a future date (581)

financial management Effective acquisition and use of money (542)

first-line managers Those at the bottom of the management hierarchy whose power and responsibility are limited to a narrow segment of the organization's activities; also called *supervisory managers* (155)

fiscal policy Use of government revenue collection and spending to influence the business cycle (20)

fiscal year Any 12 consecutive months used as an accounting period (489)

fixed assets Assets retained for long-term use, such as land, buildings, machinery, and equipment (491)

fixed costs Business costs that must be covered no matter how many units of a product a company sells (375)

fixed-position layout Method of arranging equipment in which the product is stationary and equipment and personnel come to it (223)

flat structure Structure having a wider span of management and fewer hierarchical levels (185)

flexible manufacturing Production use of computer-controlled machines that can adapt to various versions of the same operation; also called *soft manufacturing* (210)

flextime A scheduling system in which workers are given certain options regarding time of arrival and departure (252)

floating exchange rate system World economic system in which the values of all currencies are determined by supply and demand (139)

focused factory Manufacturing facility that deals with only one narrow set of products (210)

foreign exchange Foreign currency that is traded for domestic currency of equal value (139)

foreign sales corporations Tax-sheltered subsidiaries of U.S. corporations that engage in exporting (138)

form utility Consumer value created when a product's characteristics are made more satisfying (329)

for-profit corporations Companies formed to earn money for their owners (45)

forward buying Retailers' taking advantage of trade allowances by buying more products at discounted prices than they hope to sell (441)

four Ps Marketing elements—product, price, place, and promotion (333)

fourth-generation languages A collective name applied to a variety of software tools that ease the task of interacting with computers; some let users give instructions in natural languages such as English (471)

franchise Business arrangement in which an individual obtains rights from a larger company to sell a well-known product or service (80)

franchisee Person or group to whom a corporation grants an exclusive right to the use of its name in a certain territory, usually in exchange for an initial fee plus monthly royalty payments (80)

franchiser Corporation that grants a franchise to an individual or group (80)

free-market system Economic system in which the way people spend their money determines which products will be produced and what those products will cost (7)

free trade International trade unencumbered by any restrictive measures (135)

frequency The average number of times that each audience member is exposed to the message (equal to the total number of exposures divided by the total audience population) (436)

fringe benefits Compensation other than wages, salaries, and incentive programs (278)

full-service brokerages Financial services companies with a full range of services, including investment advice, securities research, and investment products (588)

G

gain sharing Earning short-term monetary rewards based on team performance (254)

Gantt chart Bar chart used to control schedules by showing how long each part of a production process should take and when it should take place (224)

general expenses Operating expenses such as office and administrative expenses not directly associated with creating or marketing a good or service (494)

general obligation bonds Municipal bonds backed by the issuing agency's general taxing authority (576)

general partnership Partnership in which all partners have the right to participate as co-owners and are individually liable for the business's debts (43)

generally accepted accounting principles Professionally approved standards used by the accounting profession in preparing financial statements (483)

generic products Products in plain packaging that bears only the name of the item, not of its producer (363)

geographic divisions A divisional structure based on location (191)

geographic segmentation Categorization of customers according to their geographic location (345)

glass ceiling The invisible barrier that keeps women out of the top positions in business (107)

goal Broad, long-term target or aim (162)

goal sharing Plan for rewarding employees not on the basis of overall profits but in relation to cost savings resulting from increased output (277)

going public Act of raising capital by selling company shares to the public for the first time (75)

goods-producing businesses Businesses that produce tangible products (34)

goodwill Value assigned to a business's reputation, calculated as the difference between the price paid for the business and the underlying value of its assets (491)

grapevine The communication network of the informal organization (197)

grievances Employee complaints about management violating some aspect of a labor contract (314)

gross domestic product Dollar value of all the final goods and services produced by an economy during a specified period (usually a year); includes profits from foreign-owned businesses within a nation's borders, and excludes receipts from overseas operations of U.S.-based companies (5)

gross national product Total value of all the final goods and services produced by an economy over a given period of time; includes receipts from overseas operations of U.S.-based companies, and excludes profits from foreign-owned businesses within a nation's borders (5)

gross profit Amount remaining when the cost of goods sold is deducted from net sales (496)

gross sales All revenues received from the sale of goods or services (494)

group norms Standards of behavior that all members of a given group accept (237)

growth stocks Equities issued by small companies with unproven products or services (578)

H

hard manufacturing Use of specialized production equipment that cannot readily be moved (209)

hardware The physical components of a computer system, including integrated circuits, keyboards, and disk drives (462)

Hawthorne effect Improvement in performance as a by-product of attention, revealed in the Hawthorne studies of worker productivity (237)

health maintenance organizations Prepaid medical plans in which consumers pay a set fee in order to receive a full range of medical care from a group of medical practitioners (650)

hedge An investment that protects the investor from suffering loss on another investment (581)

hierarchy Pyramidlike organizational structure comprising top, middle, and lower management (155)

high-growth ventures Small businesses intended to achieve rapid growth and high profits on investment (62)

high-level languages The computer languages most people are familiar with, such as BASIC, Logo, and C; single commands accomplish the equivalent of several assembly-language commands, and the language is easier for humans to read and write (470)

holding company Company that owns most, if not all, of another company's stock but that does not actively participate in the management of that other company (46)

horizontal conflict Conflict between channel members at the same level in the distribution chain (396)

horizontal mergers Combinations of companies that are direct competitors in the same industry (52)

horizontal organization Structure to coordinate activity by facilitating communication and information exchange across departments (194)

hospitalization insurance Health insurance that pays for most of the costs of a hospital stay (648)

hostile takeovers Situations in which an outside party buys enough stock in a corporation to take control against the wishes of the board of directors and corporate officers (52)

human relations The way two or more people interact with one another (234)

human relations skills Skills required to understand other people and to interact effectively with them (157)

human resource management The specialized function of planning how to obtain employees, oversee their training, evaluate them, and compensate them (262)

hygiene factors Aspects of the work environment that are demotivating only if deficient (238)

I

implied contract Contract derived from actions or conduct (621)

importing Purchasing goods or services from another country and bringing them into one's own country (127)

incentives Cash payments to workers who produce at a desired level or whose unit (often the company as a whole) produces at a desired level (276)

income statement Financial statement showing how a business's revenues compare with expenses for a given period of time (492)

independent variables Events that are controlled by outside factors (674)

index number Percentage used to compare such figures as prices or costs in one period with those in a base or standard period (676)

indexing Assembling investment portfolios by selecting securities that together reflect the profile of the market as a whole (575)

individual retirement account Type of savings account that provides tax and interest-rate advantages to depositors who are building a fund for retirement (521)

individual rights Philosophy used in making ethical decisions that aims to protect human dignity (92)

industrial unions Unions representing both skilled and unskilled workers from all phases of a particular industry (297)

inelastic demand Situation in which a percentage change in price produces a smaller percentage change in the quantity sold (377)

inflation Economic condition in which prices rise steadily throughout the economy (20)

informal organization Organizational characteristics and relationships that are not part of the formal structure but that influence how the organization accomplishes its goals (196)

information A specific collection of data that pertain to a particular decision or problem (452)

information systems All written and electronic forms of sharing information, processing data, and communicating ideas (195)

injunction Court order directing someone to do something or to refrain from doing it (309)

insider trading Employee's or manager's use of information gained in the course of his or her job and not generally available to the public in order to benefit from fluctuations in the stock market (113)

institutional advertising Advertising that seeks to create goodwill and to build a desired image for a company rather than to sell specific products (430)

institutional investors Companies that invest money entrusted to them by others (47), (572)

insurable risk Risk for which an acceptable probability of loss may be calculated and that an insurance company might therefore be willing to cover (638)

insurance Written contract that transfers to an insurer the financial responsibility for any losses (637)

intangible assets Assets having no physical existence but having value because of the rights they confer on the owner (491)

integrated circuits Electronic components that contain thousands of transistors and can therefore perform complicated tasks, such as arithmetic and data storage (459)

intellectual property Intangible personal property such as ideas, songs, or any mental creativity (624)

intensive distribution Approach to distribution that involves placing the product in as many outlets as possible (392)

intentional tort Willful act that results in injury (618)

interlocking directorates Situation in which members of the board of one firm sit on the board of a competing firm (606)

internal data Facts available in a company's own records (671)

inventory Goods held on hand for the production process or for sales to final customers (211)

inventory control Method of determining the right quantity of various items to have on hand and of keeping track of their location, use, and condition (211), (407)

inventory turnover ratio Measure of the time a company takes to turn its inventory into sales, calculated by dividing cost of goods sold by the average value of inventory for a period (505)

investment banks Financial institutions that specialize in helping companies or government agencies raise funds (520)

investment portfolios Assortment of investment instruments (574)

involuntary bankruptcy Bankruptcy proceedings initiated by a firm's creditors (625)

issued stock Authorized shares that have been released to the market (560)

J

job analysis Process by which jobs are studied to determine the tasks and dynamics involved in performing them (265)

job description Statement of the tasks involved in a given job and the conditions under which the holder of the job will work (266)

job enrichment Dividing work in an organization so that workers have more responsibility for the total process (251)

job sharing Splitting a single full-time job between two workers for their convenience (253)

job shop Firm that produces dissimilar items or that produces its goods or services at intervals (210)

job specification Statement describing the kind of person who would be best for a given job—including the skills, education, and previous experience that the job requires (266)

joint venture Enterprise supported by the investment of two or more parties for mutual benefit (52)

junk bonds Bonds that pay high interest because they are below investment grade (558)

justice Philosophy used in making ethical decisions that aims to ensure the equal distribution of burdens and benefits (94)

just-in-time inventory control A computerized system of managing inventory (564)

just-in-time system A continuous process of inventory control that, through teamwork, seeks to deliver a small quantity of materials to where they are needed precisely when they are needed (212)

K

Keogh account Type of retirement savings account for the self-employed that provides tax and interest-rate advantages (521)

key-person insurance Insurance that provides a business with funds in compensation for loss of a key employee (647)

knowledge-based pay Pay keyed to an employee's acquisition of skills (277)

L

labor federations Umbrella organizations of national unions and unaffiliated local unions that undertake large-scale activities on behalf of their members and that resolve conflicts between unions (300)

labor-intensive businesses Businesses in which labor costs are more important than capital costs (38)

labor unions Organizations of workers formed to protect and advance their members' interests (296)

laissez-faire leaders Managers who lead by taking the role of consultant, leaving the actual decision making up to employees (166)

law of large numbers Principle that the larger the group on which probabilities are calculated, the more accurate the predictive value (639)

lead times Periods that elapse between placement of a purchase order and receipt of materials from the supplier (212)

leadership The ability to motivate someone to do something (234)

leading Aspect of directing that involves guiding employees in a job (165)

lease Legal agreement that obligates the user of an asset to make payments to the owner of the asset in exchange for using it (557), (624)

legal detriment The assumption of a duty or the forfeit of a right, which is necessary to make a contract legally binding (621)

leverage Use of borrowed funds to finance a portion of an investment (542)

leveraged buyout Situation in which an individual or a group of investors purchases a company with the debt secured by the company's assets (51)

liabilities Debts or obligations a company or government owes to other individuals or organizations (487)

liability insurance Insurance that covers losses arising either from injury to an individual or from damage to other people's property (644)

licensing Agreement to produce and market another company's product in exchange for a royalty or fee; or giving rights to a company to use a well-known name or symbol in marketing its products (141), (365)

lifestyle businesses Small businesses intended to provide the owner with a comfortable livelihood (62)

lifetime security Arrangement that gives workers some protection against temporary layoffs during an economic slowdown and against job loss during a downsizing or plant closing (312)

LIFO Last in, first out: method of pricing inventory under which the costs of the last goods acquired are the first ones charged to the cost of goods sold (499)

limit order Market order that stipulates the highest or lowest price at which the customer is willing to trade securities (586)

limited liability companies Organizations that combine the benefits of S corporations and limited partnerships without the drawbacks of either (46)

limited partnership Partnership composed of one or more general partners and one or more partners whose liability is usually limited to the amount of their capital investment (43)

line-and-staff organization Organization system that has a clear chain of command from the top down but that also includes functional groups of people who come under the heading of staff (183)

line of credit Agreement stating the amount of unsecured short-term loans that the lender will make available to the borrower, provided the lender has the funds (554)

line organization Chain-of-command system that establishes a clear line of authority flowing from the top down to subordinates (183)

liquidity An asset's ease of conversion to cash (49)

liquidity ratios Financial ratios that indicate how quickly a company can repay obligations (504)

lobbies Groups who try to persuade legislators to vote according to the groups' interests (614)

local advertising Advertising sponsored by a local merchant (432)

local area network A computer network that encompasses a small area, such as an office or a university campus (472)

locals Relatively small union groups, usually part of a national union or a labor federation, composed of those who work in a single facility or in a certain geographic area (300)

lockout Management activity in which union members are prevented from entering a business during a strike, to force union acceptance of management's last contract proposal (308)

long-term liabilities Obligations that fall due more than a year from the date of the balance sheet (492)

long-term loans Debt that must be repaid over a period of more than a year (557)

loss exposures Areas of risk in which a potential for loss exists (635)

M

M1 That portion of the money supply consisting of currency and demand deposits (515)

M2 That portion of the money supply consisting of currency, demand deposits, and time deposits (515)

machine language The "lowest" level of computer language, consisting entirely of 1's and 0's; the only level of computer language that hardware understands (470)

mail-order firms Companies that sell products through catalogs and ship them directly to customers (404)

mainframe computers With the exception of supercomputers, the largest and most powerful computers (461)

major-medical insurance Insurance that covers many medical expenses not covered by other health-insurance plans (648)

malpractice insurance Insurance that covers losses arising from damages or injuries caused by the insured in the course of performing professional services for clients (647)

managed care Health care set up by employers (usually through an insurance carrier) who provide networks of doctors and hospitals that agree to discount the fees they charge in return for the flow of patients (650)

management Process of coordinating resources to meet an objective (154)

management accounting Area of accounting concerned with preparing data for use by managers within the organization (482)

management by objectives Control tool in which managers are given the opportunity to structure their personal objectives and work procedures to mesh with the organization's goals (168)

management by walking around A communication technique used by managers to talk directly to employees and learn what's going on (157)

management information systems Systems that supply periodic, predefined reports to assist in managerial decision making (456)

managerial integrator Manager who coordinates activities of several functional departments but belongs to none (195)

mandatory retirement Required dismissal of an employee who reaches a certain age (288)

mandatory subject Topic that must be discussed in collective bargaining (304)

manufacturer's agents Wholesalers that do not take title to products but that receive a commission for selling products (398)

manufacturing resource planning Companywide computer system that coordinates data from all departments in order to maintain minimum but sufficient inventories and a smooth production process (213)

margin requirements Limits set by the Federal Reserve on the amount of money that stockbrokers and banks may lend customers for the purpose of buying stocks (533)

margin trading Borrowing money from brokers to buy stock, paying interest on the borrowed money, and leaving the stock with the broker as collateral (587)

market People who need or want a product and who have the money to buy it (333)

market economies Economic systems in which goals are achieved by the action of the free market, with a minimum of government intervention (7)

market indexes Measures of security markets calculated from the prices of a selection of securities (575)

market makers Dealers in dealer exchanges who sell securities out of their own inventories so that a market is always available for buyers and sellers (583)

market order Authorization for a broker to buy or sell securities at the best price that can be negotiated at the moment (586)

market segmentation Division of a market into subgroups (344)

market segments Groups of individuals or organizations within a market that share certain common characteristics (333)

market share Percentage of total industry sales that are made by a particular company (336)

market-share liability Concept that extends strict product liability by dividing responsibility for injuries among all manufacturers in an industry according to their market share at the time of the injury (620)

marketable securities Stocks, bonds, and other investments that can be turned into cash quickly (562), (572)

marketing Process of planning and executing the conception, pricing, promotion, and distribution of ideas, goods, and services to create exchanges that satisfy individual and organizational objectives (328)

marketing concept Belief that a business must determine and satisfy customer needs in order to make a profit (331)

marketing intermediaries Businesspeople and organizations who channel goods and services from producers to consumers (388)

marketing mix Blend of elements satisfying a chosen market (333)

marketing research Process of gathering information about marketing problems and opportunities (338)

marketing strategy Overall plan for marketing a product (332)

markup Amount added to the cost of an item to create a selling price that produces a profit (378)

markup percentage Difference in percentage between the cost of an item and its selling price (378)

mass production Manufacture of uniform products in great quantities (207)

master limited partnership A business partnership that acts like a corporation, trading partnership units on listed stock exchanges; if 90 percent of income is passive, MLPs are taxed at individual rates (43)

matching principle Concept that long-term projects should be funded with long-term sources of capital, whereas short-term expenditures should be funded from current income (546)

material requirements planning Method of getting the correct materials where they are needed for production and doing it on time and without unnecessary stockpiling (212)

materials handling Activities involved in moving, packing, storing, and inventorying goods (407)

mean Sum of all the items in a group, divided by the number of items in the group (675)

mechanization Use of machines to do work previously done by people (207)

media Communications channels, such as newspaper, radio, and television (435)

media mix The combination of various media options that a company uses in an advertising campaign (435)

media plan A written plan that outlines how a company will spend its media budget, including how the money will be divided among the various media and when the advertisements will appear (435)

median Midpoint, or the point in a group of numbers at which half are higher and half are lower (675)

mediation Process for resolving a labor-contract dispute in which a neutral third party meets with both sides and attempts to steer them toward a solution (304)

mental-health insurance Insurance that covers the costs of psychiatric care, psychological counseling, and substance abuse treatment programs (649)

mentor Experienced member of an organization who serves as a guide and protector to a lower-level employee (198)

merchant wholesalers Independent wholesalers that take legal title to products (398)

merger Combination of two or more companies in which the old companies cease to exist and a new enterprise is created (51)

methods improvement Examining all aspects of a job or task in order to improve efficiency levels (216)

microcomputer The smallest and least-expensive class of computers, such as the Apple Macintosh and the IBM PS/2 (460)

microprocessors Advanced integrated circuits that combine most of the basic functions of a computer onto a single chip; sometimes called "computers on a chip" (459)

middle managers Those in the middle of the management hierarchy who serve as a conduit between top and first-line management, implementing the goals of top managers and coordinating the work of first-line managers (155)

minicomputers Computers that fall between workstations and mainframes in terms of cost, size, and performance (461)

minorities In a social and economic sense, categories of people that society at large singles out for discriminatory, selective, or unfavorable treatment (104)

mission Overall purpose of an organization (161)

mission statement Putting the organization's mission into words (161)

missionary salespeople Salespeople who support existing customers, usually wholesalers and retailers (424)

mixed capitalism Economic system in which operation of the free market is influenced to some degree by government involvement (7)

mode Number that occurs most often in any series of data or observations (676)

modem A hardware device that allows a computer to communicate over a regular telephone line (472)

monetary policy Tactics for expanding or contracting the money supply as a means of influencing the economy (20), (531)

money Anything used by a society as a token of value in buying and selling goods and services (514)

money-market accounts Bank accounts that pay money-market interest rates and permit the depositor to write a limited number of checks (521)

money-market funds Mutual funds that invest in short-term securities (580)

monopoly Market in which there are no direct competitors so that one company dominates (19)

morale General outlook in regard to a job or an organization (235)

mortgage bonds Corporate bonds backed by real property, not by mortgages (577)

motivating Aspect of directing that involves giving employees a reason to do the job and to put forth their best performance (165)

motivation Giving employees a reason to do their jobs and to perform at their best (235)

motivators Factors of human relations in business that may increase motivation (239)

MRO items A common term for supply products purchased by organizational customers; it stands for maintenance, repair, and operating items (362)

multinational corporations Firms with operations in more than one country (127)

multiplier effect Chain reaction whereby a change in one economic variable affects other variables, resulting in a ripple of changes throughout an economic system (17)

municipal bonds Debt issued by a state or a local agency; interest earned on municipal bonds is exempt from federal income tax and from taxes in the issuing jurisdiction (576)

mutual company Nonprofit insurance company owned by the policyholders (641)

mutual funds Pools of money raised by investment companies and invested in stocks, bonds, or other marketable securities (580)

N

national advertising Advertising sponsored by companies that sell products on a nationwide basis; refers to the geographic reach of the advertiser, not the geographic coverage of the ad (432)

national banks Banks chartered by the federal government (517)

national brands Brands owned by a manufacturer and distributed nationally (363)

national union Nationwide organization representing workers in a particular craft or industry (300)

natural-language processor A system or software program that converts a natural language to a computer language; natural-language processing is the primary feature of fourth-generation languages (457)

need-satisfaction approach A selling method that starts with identifying the customer's needs and then creating a presentation that addresses those needs; this is the approach used by most professional salespeople (428)

needs Things that are necessary for a person's physical, psychological, and social well-being (329)

negative correlation Statistical relationship in which a change in one variable is associated with the other variable's change in the opposite direction (678)

negligence Failure to observe a reasonable standard of care in order to protect others from unreasonable risk of injury (619)

net income Profit or loss of a company, determined by subtracting expenses from revenues (492)

net sales Amount remaining after cash discounts, refunds, and other allowances are deducted from gross sales (494)

network A collection of computer, communications software, and transmission media line (such as a telephone) that allows computers to communicate (472)

networking Seeking to broaden one's effectiveness in an organization or industry by forming relationships with others in the same and related fields (197)

no-fault insurance laws Laws limiting lawsuits connected with auto accidents (645)

not-for-profit corporations Incorporated institutions whose owners have limited liability and that exist to provide a social service rather than to make a profit (45)

not publicly traded corporations Corporations that withhold their stock from public sale (closed corporations) (45)

NOW account Interest-bearing checking account with a minimum-balance requirement (521)

O

objective Specific, short-range target or aim (162)

observation Technique of watching or otherwise monitoring all incidents of the particular sort that the investigator wants to study (673)

odd-even pricing Setting a price at an odd amount slightly below the next highest dollar figure (380)

off-price stores Retailers that offer bargain prices by maintaining low overhead and acquiring merchandise at below-wholesale costs (401)

office automation systems Computer systems that assist with the tasks that people in a typical business office face regularly, such as drawing graphs or processing documents (455)

oligopoly Market dominated by a few producers (19)

open-book credit Payment terms that allow the purchaser to take possession of goods and pay for them later (550)

open-market operations Activity of the Federal Reserve in buying and selling government bonds on the open market (533)

open order Limit order that does not expire at the end of a trading day (586)

open shop Workplace in which nonunion workers pay no dues (310)

open systems Operating systems (such as UNIX) that run on a wide variety of computers and don't restrict users to a single company's hardware (466)

operating expenses All costs of operation that are not included under cost of goods sold (494)

operating income Amount remaining when operating expenses are deducted from gross profit (496)

operating systems The class of software that controls the computer's hardware components (466)

operational objectives Objectives that focus on short-term issues, are set by first-line managers, and describe the outcomes necessary to achieve tactical objectives and strategic goals (162)

operational plans The actions designed to achieve operational objectives and to support tactical plans, usually defined for less than one year and developed by first-line managers (162)

opportunity cost Value of using a resource; measured in terms of the value of the best alternative for using that resource (11), (125)

order getters Salespeople who are responsible for generating new sales and for increasing sales to existing customers (423)

order processing Functions involved in receiving and handling an order (406)

order takers Salespeople who generally process incoming orders without engaging in creative selling (423)

organization Group of people whose interactions are structured into goal-directed activities (178)

organization structure Formal patterns designed by managers to divide labor and assign formal tasks, to define the span of management and the lines of authority, and to coordinate all organizational tasks (178)

organizational market Customers who buy goods or services for resale or for use in conducting their own operations (333)

organizing Process of arranging resources to carry out the organization's plans (164)

orientation Session or procedure for acclimating a new employee to the organization (272)

outplacement Job-hunting and other assistance that a company provides to laid-off workers (286)

over-the-counter market Network of dealers who trade securities that are not listed on an exchange (584)

owners' equity Portion of a company's assets that belongs to the owners after obligations to all creditors have been met (487)

P

par value Arbitrary value assigned to a stock (559)

parallel processing The use of multiple processors in a single computer unit, with the intention of increasing the speed at which complex calculations can be completed (460)

parent company Company that owns most, if not all, of another company's stock and that takes an active part in managing that other company (46)

participative management System for involving employees in a company's decision making (166)

partnership Unincorporated business owned and operated by two or more persons under a voluntary legal association (43)

pattern bargaining Negotiating similar wages and benefits for all companies within a particular industry (311)

pay for performance Accepting a lower base pay in exchange for bonuses based on meeting production or other goals (277)

payee Person or business a check is made out to (516)

penetration pricing Introducing a new product at a low price in hopes of building sales volume quickly (375)

pension plans Company-sponsored programs for providing retirees with income (280)

performance appraisal Evaluation of an employee's work according to specific criteria (274)

perks Special class of fringe benefits made available to a company's most valuable employees (278)

permissive subject Topic that may be omitted from collective bargaining (304)

personal property All property that is not real property (624)

personal selling In-person communication between a seller and one or more potential buyers (420)

physical distribution All the activities required to move finished products from the producer to the consumer (405)

picketing Strike activity in which union members march before company entrances to persuade nonstriking workers to walk off the job and to persuade customers and others to cease doing business with the company (305)

piecework system The practice of paying workers a certain amount for each unit produced and paying those who surpass a stated quota at a higher rate for *all* units produced (236)

place utility Consumer value added by making a product available in a convenient location (329)

plan The system designed to achieve goals and objectives (162)

planned economies Economic systems in which resource-allocation decisions are made by the central government (8)

planning Establishing objectives for an organization and determining the best ways to accomplish them (161)

point-of-purchase display Advertising or other display materials set up at retail locations to promote products to potential customers as they are making their purchase decisions (441)

political action committees Groups formed under federal election laws to raise money for candidates (614)

pollution Threats to the physical environment caused by human activities in an industrial society (94)

Ponzi scheme Form of fraud in which money received from later investors is used to pay off the earlier investors (112)

positioning The process of achieving a desired position in the minds of potential customers (422)

positive correlation Statistical relationship in which an increase or decrease in one variable is associated with another variable's change in the same direction (678)

possession utility Consumer value created when someone takes ownership of a product (329)

power of attorney Written authorization for one party to legally act for another (622)

preferred-provider organizations Health-care providers offering reduced-rate contracts to groups that agree to obtain medical care through the providers' organization (650)

preferred stocks Shares that give their owners first claim on a company's dividends and assets (579)

premium Fee that the insured pays the insurer for coverage against losses (637)

premiums Free or bargain-priced items offered to encourage consumers to buy a product (441)

press conference Gathering of media representatives at which companies announce new information; also called a press briefing (440)

press relations The process of communicating with reporters and editors from newspapers, magazines, and radio and television networks and stations (439)

press release A brief statement or video program released to the press announcing new products, management changes, sales performance, and other potential news items; also called a news release (440)

price discrimination Offering a discount to one customer but not to another, with the intention of restraining competition (376)

price-earnings ratio Comparison of a stock's market price with its earnings per share (589)

price fixing The illegal cooperation between two or more companies that agree on prices in order to reduce competition (376)

price leader Major producer in an industry that tends to set the pace in establishing prices (377)

price lining Offering merchandise at a limited number of set prices (380)

primary data Facts gathered for the study of a specific problem (671)

primary storage devices Storage for data and programs while they are being processed by the computer; also called RAM (465)

prime interest rate Lowest rate of interest charged by banks for loans to their most credit-worthy customers (532)

principal Amount of a debt, excluding any interest (557)

private accountants In-house accountants employed by organizations and businesses (486)

private brands Brands that carry the label of a retailer or wholesaler rather than a manufacturer (363)

private corporations Companies owned by private individuals or companies (45)

private law Law that concerns itself with relationships between individuals, between an individual and a business, or between two businesses (617)

probability Likelihood, over the long run, that a certain event will occur in one way rather than in another way (672)

process divisions A divisional structure based on the major steps of a production process (190)

process layout Method of arranging equipment so that production tasks are carried out in discrete locations containing specialized equipment and personnel (221)

product Good or service used as the basis of commerce (358)

product advertising Advertising that tries to sell specific goods or services, generally by describing features, benefits, and occasionally price (430)

product-development process Stages through which a product idea passes—from initial conceptualization to actual appearance in the marketplace (368)

product differentiation Features that distinguish one company's product from another company's similar product (332)

product divisions A divisional structure based on products (190)

product liability Company's responsibility for injuries or damages that result from use of a product the company manufactures or distributes (645)

product-liability law Law that holds a manufacturer liable for injuries caused by a defective product (619)

product life cycle Stages of growth and decline in sales and earnings (370)

product lines Groups of products that are physically similar or that are intended for similar markets (372)

product mix Complete list of all products that a company offers for sale (372)

production Transformation of resources into forms that people need or want (206)

production and operations management Coordination of an organization's resources in order to manufacture its goods or produce its services (218)

production control Production planning, routing, scheduling, dispatching, and follow-up and control in an effort to achieve efficiency and high quality (219)

production forecasting Estimating how much of a company's goods and services must be produced in order to meet future demand (219)

productivity The measured relationship of the quantity and quality of units produced and the labor per unit of time; indicates the efficiency of production (38)

professional corporations Companies whose shareholders offer professional services (medical, legal, engineering) and set up beneficial pension and insurance plans (46)

profit Money left over after expenses and taxes have been deducted from revenue generated by selling goods or services (11)

profit sharing System for distributing a portion of the company's profits to employees (277)

profitability ratios Financial ratios that indicate to what extent a company is making a profit (503)

program evaluation and review technique Scheduling method similar to the critical path method but relying on statistical estimates of how long each task should take (225)

program trading Investment strategy using computer programs to buy or sell large numbers of securities, thereby taking advantage of price discrepancies between stock index futures or options and the actual stocks represented in those indexes (583)

programming Process of creating the sets of instructions that direct computers to perform desired tasks (458)

programs Organized sets of instructions, written in a computer language, that perform designated tasks such as word processing (462)

project management Assigning employees to a functional group but also temporarily assigning them to a specific project (194)

promissory note Unconditional written promise to repay a certain sum of money on a specified date (551)

promotion A wide variety of persuasive techniques used by companies to communicate with their target markets and the general public (418)

promotional mix The particular blend of personal selling, advertising, public relations, and sales promotion that a company uses to reach potential customers (420)

property Rights held regarding any tangible or intangible object (624)

property insurance Insurance that provides coverage for physical damage to, or destruction of, property (643)

proprietary operating systems Operating systems that run on only one brand of computer; they offer users a limited selection of hardware and software choices (466)

protectionism Government policies aimed at shielding a country's industries from foreign competition (132)

prototypes Working samples of a proposed product (369)

proxy Document authorizing another person to vote on behalf of a shareholder in a corporation (48)

proxy fight Attempt to gain control of a takeover target by urging shareholders to vote for directors favored by the acquiring party (52)

psychographics Classification of customers on the basis of their psychological makeup (347)

public accountants Independent outsiders who provide accounting services for businesses and other organizations (484)

public corporations Government-owned corporations formed for a specific public purpose (45)

public goods Goods or services that can be supplied more efficiently by government than by individuals or businesses (18)

public law Law that concerns itself with relationships between the government and individual citizens (617)

public relations Nonsales communication that businesses have with their various audiences (includes both communication with the general public and press relations) (421)

publicly traded corporations Corporations that actively sell stock on the open market (open corporations) (45)

pull strategy Promotional strategy that stimulates consumer demand, which then exerts pressure on wholesalers and retailers to carry a product (422)

pure capitalism Capitalism in its ideal state, in which all resource allocations are controlled by the unfettered operation of the free market (7)

pure competition Situation in which so many buyers and sellers exist that no single buyer or seller can control the price of a product or the number of units sold (19)

pure risk Risk that involves the chance of loss only (634)

push strategy Promotional approach designed to motivate wholesalers and retailers to push a producer's products to end users (422)

put option The right to buy shares at market price and sell at a specified price (581)

Q

qualified prospects A potential buyer who has both the money needed to make the purchase and the authority to make the purchase decision (425)

quality assurance A companywide system of practices and procedures to assure that company products satisfy customers (215)

quality circles Regularly scheduled meetings of about five to fifteen workers to identify and suggest solutions to quality, safety, and production problems (216)

quality control Routine checking and testing of a product or process for quality against some standard (214)

quantity discount Discount offered to buyers of large quantities (380)

quasi-public corporations Public utilities having a monopoly to provide basic services (45)

quick ratio Measure of a company's short-term liquidity, calculated by adding cash, marketable securities, and receivables, then dividing that sum by current liabilities (504)

quotas Fixed numbers of minority-group members to be hired, or fixed limits on the quantity of imports a nation will allow for a specific product (108), (132)

R

rack jobbers Merchant wholesalers that are responsible for setting up and maintaining displays in a particular store area (398)

random access memory (RAM) Primary storage devices in a computer (465)

random sampling Selecting a sample in a way that gives all items or persons in the larger group an equal chance of being selected (673)

rate of return Percentage increase in the value of an investment (574)

ratification Process by which union members accept or reject a contract negotiated by union leaders (304)

ratio analysis Comparison of two elements from the same year's financial results, stated as a percentage or a ratio (502)

reach The total number of audience members who will be exposed to a message at least once in a given period (436)

read only memory (ROM) Special circuits that store data and programs permanently but don't allow users to record their own data or programs; a common use of ROM is for the programs that activate start-up routines when the computer is turned on (465)

real property Land and everything permanently attached to it (624)

real-time processing A method of information processing in which the computer's files are updated as soon as new information arrives (460)

recession Period during which national income, employment, and production all fall (19)

recruiters Members of the human resource staff who are responsible for obtaining new job candidates (266)

repetitive manufacturing Repeated, steady production of identical goods or services (210)

replacement cost Cost of replacing a lost or damaged item with a new one (643)

reserve requirement Percentage of a bank's deposits that must be kept on hand (531)

reserves Funds a financial institution keeps on tap to meet projected withdrawals (531)

responsibility The obligation to perform the duties and to achieve the goals and objectives associated with a position in the organization (181)

restructuring Process of changing the nature of a company by reordering its ownership, composition, operation, or work force (285)

résumé Summary of education, experience, and personal data compiled by the applicant for a job (267)

retailers Firms that sell directly to the public (397)

retained earnings Net increase in assets (cash and outstanding receivables) for an accounting period; part of owners' equity (488)

return on investment Ratio between the income earned by a firm and total owners' equity (374), (503)

return on sales Ratio between income before taxes and net sales (503)

revenue bonds Municipal bonds backed by revenue generated from the projects financed with the bonds (577)

revenues Amount of sales of goods or services and inflow from miscellaneous sources such as interest, rent, and royalties (492)

reverse channels Distribution channels designed to move products from the customer back to the producer (391)

revolving line of credit Guaranteed line of credit (554)

right-to-work laws Laws giving employees the explicit right to keep a job without joining a union (311)

risk The threat of loss (634)

risk-control techniques Methods of minimizing losses (636)

risk-financing techniques Paying to restore losses (636)

risk management Process of evaluating and minimizing the risks faced by a company (635)

roles Behavior patterns (154)

routing Specifying the sequence of operations and the path the work will take through the production facility (221)

S

S corporations Corporations with no more than 35 shareholders that may be taxed as partnerships (46)

salaries Weekly, monthly, or yearly cash compensation for work (276)

sales office Producer-owned operation that markets products but doesn't carry any stock (398)

sales promotion A wide range of events and activities (including coupons, rebates, contests, in-store demonstrations, free samples, trade shows, and point-of-purchase) designed to stimulate interest in a product (421)

sales support personnel Salespeople who facilitate the selling effort by providing such services as prospecting, customer education, and customer service (423)

sample Small part of a large group (672)

savings and loan associations Banks offering savings, interest-bearing checking, and mortgages (517)

savings banks Mostly in New England, banks offering interest-bearing checking, savings, and mortgages (517)

scrambled merchandising Policy of carrying merchandise that is ordinarily sold in a different type of outlet (400)

seasonal variation Regular, predictable change over a year's time (677)

secondary data Facts previously produced or collected for a purpose other than that of the moment (671)

secondary storage Computer storage for data and programs that aren't needed at the moment (465)

secular trend Pattern of growth or decline in a particular business, industry, or economy that occurs over a long period of time—say, 20 or 30 years (678)

secured bonds Bonds backed by specific assets (558)

secured loans Loans backed up with something of value that the lender can claim in case of default, such as a piece of property (552)

selective credit controls Federal Reserve's power to set credit terms on various types of loans (533)

selective distribution Approach to distribution that relies on a limited number of outlets (392)

self-insurance Arrangement whereby a company insures itself by accumulating funds to pay for any losses, rather than buying insurance from another company (636)

selling expenses All the operating expenses associated with marketing goods or services (494)

seniority Longevity in a position or company, frequently used as a basis for making human resource decisions (compensation, termination, and so on) (286)

serial bonds Bonds from a single issue that must be repaid at intervals (558)

service businesses Businesses that provide intangible products or perform useful labor on behalf of another (34)

setup costs Expenses incurred each time a producer organizes resources to begin producing goods or services (210)

sexual harassment Unwelcome sexual advance, request for sexual favors, or other verbal or physical conduct of a sexual nature within the workplace that affects a person's job prospects or job performance (110)

shareholders Owners of a corporation (45)

shop steward Union member and worker who is elected to represent other union members and who attempts to resolve employee grievances with management (300)

shopping products Products for which a consumer spends a lot of time shopping in order to compare prices, quality, and style (361)

short selling Selling stock borrowed from a broker with the intention of buying it back later at a lower price, repaying the broker, and pocketing the profit (579)

short-term debt Borrowed funds used to cover current expenses (generally repaid within a year) (550)

sinking fund Account into which a company makes annual

payments for use in redeeming its bonds in the future (558)

situational management Management style that emphasizes adapting general principles to the specific objectives of one's own business (166)

skimming Charging a high price for a new product during the introductory stage and lowering the price later (375)

slowdown Decreasing worker productivity to pressure management (305)

small businesses Companies that are independently owned and operated, that are not dominant in their field, and that meet certain criteria for number of employees or annual sales revenue (62)

socialism Economic system characterized by public ownership and operation of key industries combined with private ownership and operation of less vital industries (10)

software The instructions that drive computers (462)

sole proprietorship Business owned by a single individual (41)

span of management Breadth of a manager's authority; also known as *span of control* (184)

specialty advertising Advertising that appears on various items such as coffee mugs, pens, and calendars, designed to help keep a company's name in front of customers (441)

specialty products Products that a consumer will make a special effort to locate (361)

specialty shops Stores that carry only particular types of goods (402)

speculative risk Risk that involves the chance of both loss and profit (634)

speculators Investors who seek large capital gains through relatively risky investments (573)

spot trading Trading in commodities that will be delivered immediately (582)

spreadsheet A program that organizes and manipulates data in a row–column matrix (467)

staff Those who supplement the line organization by providing advice and specialized services (183)

staffing Process of matching the right people with the right jobs (164)

stakeholders Individuals or groups to whom business has a responsibility (90)

standardization Uniformity in goods or parts, making them interchangeable (207)

standards Criteria against which performance may be measured (168)

stare decisis Concept of using previous judicial decisions as the basis for deciding similar court cases (616)

start-up company New venture (66)

state banks Banks chartered by a state government (517)

statement of cash flows Financial statement that summarizes receipts and disbursals of cash in three areas: operations, investments, and financing (496)

statistical process control Monitoring the production process using control charts (215)

statistical quality control Use of random sampling to test the quality of production output (215)

statistics Factual data that can be presented in numerical form (674)

statutory law Statute, or law, created by a legislature (615)

stock Shares of ownership in a corporation (45)

stock certificate Document that proves stock ownership (559)

stock company Profit-making insurance company owned by shareholders (641)

stock exchanges Facilities where shares of stock are bought and sold (562)

stock option Contract allowing the holder to buy or sell a given number of shares of a particular stock at a given price by a certain date (580)

stock specialists Intermediaries who trade in particular securities on the floors of auction exchanges; "buyers of last resort" (582)

stock split Increase in the number of shares of ownership that each stock certificate represents (561)

strategic goals Goals focusing on broad issues (162)

strategic plans The actions designed to accomplish strategic goals, usually defined for periods of two to five years and developed by top managers (162)

strict liability Concept of liability even in cases where the defendant has used reasonable care (619)

strict product liability Concept that assigns product liability even if the company used all reasonable care in the manufacture, distribution, or sale of its product (620)

strike Temporary work stoppage aimed at forcing management to accept union demands (305)

strikebreakers People who cross a picket line to work (307)

subsidiary corporations Corporations whose stock is owned entirely or almost entirely by another corporation (46)

super NOW account Interest-bearing checking account with a relatively high minimum-balance requirement (521)

supercomputers Computers with the highest level of performance, often boasting speeds greater than a billion calculations per second (462)

supermarkets Large departmentalized food stores (403)

supply Specific quantity of a product that the seller is able and willing to provide at various prices at a given time (13)

supply curve Series of points on a graph showing the relationship between price and quantity supplied (14)

surety bond Coverage that protects companies against losses incurred through nonperformance of a contract (643)

surgical and medical insurance Insurance that pays for the costs of surgery and physicians' fees while a person is hospitalized or recovering from hospitalization (648)

survey Data-collection method in which the subjects are asked questions to determine their attitudes and opinions (674)

synthetic system A production process that combines two or more materials or components to create finished products; the reverse of an analytic system (207)

T

table Grid for displaying relationships among words and numbers, particularly many precise numbers (680)

tactical objectives Objectives focusing on departmental issues, set by middle managers, and describing the outcomes necessary to achieve the results required by the organization's strategic goals (162)

tactical plans The actions designed to achieve tactical objectives and to support strategic plans, usually defined for a period of one to three years and developed by middle managers (162)

tall structure Structure having a narrower span of management and more hierarchical levels (185)

target markets Specific groups of customers to whom a company wants to sell a particular product (333)

tariffs Taxes levied on imports (132)

task force Group of people from several departments who are temporarily brought together to address a specific issue (195)

tax credit Amount deducted from the income on which a person or business is taxed (611)

team Two or more people working together to achieve a specific objective (164)

technical salespeople Specialists who contribute technical expertise and other sales assistance (424)

technical skills Ability to perform the mechanics of a particular job (156)

telecommuting Working from a home office, commuting via telephone, computer modem, and fax (252)

telemarketing Sale of goods and services by telephone (404), (424)

tender offer Invitation made directly to shareholders by an outside party who wishes to buy a company's stock at a price above the current market price (52)

term bonds Bonds from a single issue that must be repaid simultaneously (558)

term insurance Life insurance that provides death benefits for a specified period (651)

termination Act of getting rid of a worker (285)

test marketing Product-development stage in which a product is sold on a limited basis (369)

Theory X Set of managerial assumptions about workers' motivations that coincide with an authoritarian management style (241)

Theory Y Set of managerial assumptions about workers' motivations that coincide with a participative management style (241)

Theory Z Human relations approach that seeks to encourage worker involvement by satisfying a wide range of needs (242)

time deposits Bank accounts that pay interest and restrict withdrawals to a specified time (516)

time-sharing system An approach to computer design in which the computer's time is divided among a number of independent terminals, each of which perceives that it has the computer's undivided attention (460)

time utility Consumer value added by making a product available at a convenient time (329)

title Legal ownership of property (624)

top managers Those at the top of an organization's management hierarchy, having the most power and responsibility in the organization (155)

tort Noncriminal act (other than breach of contract) that results in injury to a person or to property (617)

total quality management An all-encompassing philosophy of management based on a vision of quality and customer satisfaction (215)

trade allowance A discount offered by producers to wholesalers and retailers (441)

trade credit Credit obtained by the purchaser directly from the supplier (550)

trade deficit Negative trade balance (127)

trade discount Discount offered to a wholesaler or retailer (380)

trade promotions Sales promotion efforts aimed at inducing distributors or retailers to push a producer's products (441)

trade salespeople Salespeople who sell to and support marketing intermediaries by giving in-store demonstrations, offering samples, and so on (424)

trade show A gathering where producers display their wares to potential buyers; nearly every industry has one or more trade shows focused on particular types of products (441)

trademark Brand that has been given legal protection so that its owner has exclusive rights to its use (363)

trading blocs Organizations of nations that remove barriers to trade among their members and that establish uniform barriers to trade with nonmember nations (136)

transaction Exchange between parties (329)

transaction costs Costs of trading securities, including broker's commission and taxes (588)

transaction processing system A computerized information system that processes the daily flow of customer, supplier, and employee transactions, including inventory, sales, and payroll records (455)

transactional leadership Traditional function of management involving motivating employees to perform at expected levels, structuring employee roles and tasks, and linking rewards with goal achievement (165)

transfer payments Payments by government to individuals that are not made in return for goods and services (18)

transformational leadership Beyond the scope of the traditional management function, involving motivating performance above expected levels, inspiring employee concern for broader issues, and instilling in employees confidence in their ability to achieve the leader's lofty visions of the future (165)

Treasury bills Short-term debt issued by the federal government (576)

Treasury bonds Debt securities issued by the federal government that mature in 10 to 30 years (576)

Treasury notes Debt securities issued by the federal government that mature within 1 to 10 years (576)

trend analysis Comparison of a company's financial data from year to year to see how they have changed (501), (677)

trust Arrangement in which people owning stock in several companies give control of their securities to trustees who then gain control of and manage the companies; sometimes used to buy up or drive out smaller companies, thus giving monopolistic powers to the trusts (606)

trusts Monopolistic arrangements established when one company buys a controlling share of the stock of competing companies in the same industry (52)

turnover Number of times that average inventory is sold during a given period (378)

two-tier wage plans Compensation agreements in which new employees are put on a wage scale lower than that of veteran employees (311)

tying contracts Contracts forcing buyers to purchase unwanted goods along with goods actually desired (606)

U

umbrella policies Insurance that provides businesses with coverage beyond what is provided by a basic liability policy (646)

underground economy Economic activity that is not reported (5)

underwriters Insurance company employees who decide which risks to insure, for how much, and for what premiums (639)

undifferentiated marketing Marketing program that offers a single standard product to all consumers (347)

unemployment insurance Government-sponsored program for assisting workers who are laid off or, to a lesser extent, who quit their jobs (279)

unfunded pension liabilities Amount by which a company's estimated future pension obligations exceed the funds set aside to cover those obligations (501)

Uniform Commercial Code Set of standardized laws that govern business transactions and that have been adopted by most states (615)

uninsurable risk Risk that few, if any, insurance companies will assume because of the difficulty of calculating the probability of loss (637)

union shop Workplace in which the employer may hire new people at will but only for a probationary period, after which they must join the union (310)

unissued stock Authorized shares that are to be released in the future (560)

universal life insurance Combination of a term life insurance policy and a savings plan with flexible interest rates and flexible premiums (651)

UNIX The most prominent open operating system; it can run on a wide variety of machines from microcomputers to supercomputers (466)

unlimited liability Legal condition under which any damages or debts attributable to the business can also be attached to the owner, because the two have no separate legal existence (43)

unsecured bonds Bonds backed only by the reputation of the issuer (558)

unsecured loan Loan requiring no collateral but a good credit rating (553)

U.S. savings bonds Debt instruments in small denominations sold by the federal government (576)

utilitarianism Philosophy used in making ethical decisions that aims to achieve the greatest good for the greatest number (92)

utility Power of a good or service to satisfy a human need (329)

V

value-added taxes Taxes paid at each step in the distribution chain on the difference between the cost of inputs and the price obtained for outputs at that step (613)

variable costs Business costs that increase with the number of units produced (375)

variable life insurance Whole life insurance policy that allows the policyholder to decide how to invest the cash value (651)

variables Changeable factors in an experiment (674)

venture capitalists Investment specialists who provide money to finance new businesses or turn-arounds in exchange for a portion of the ownership, with the objective of making a considerable profit on the investment (74)

vertical conflict Conflict between channel members at different levels in the distribution chain (396)

vertical marketing systems Planned distribution channels in which members coordinate their efforts to optimize distribution activities (396)

vertical mergers Combinations of companies that participate in different phases of the same industry (53)

vertical organization Structure linking activities at the top of the organization with those at the middle and lower levels (180)

voluntary bankruptcy Bankruptcy proceedings initiated by the debtor (625)

W

wages Cash payment based on a calculation of the number of hours the employee has worked or the number of units the employee has produced (276)

wants Things that are desirable in light of a person's experiences, culture, and personality (329)

warehouse Facility for storing backup stocks of supplies or finished products (407)

warehouse clubs Low-priced stores that sell memberships to small retailers and consumer members (401)

warranty Guarantee or promise (620)

wheel of retailing Evolutionary process by which stores that feature low prices are gradually upgraded until they forfeit their appeal to price-sensitive shoppers and are replaced by new competitors (400)

whole life insurance Insurance that provides both death benefits and savings for the insured's lifetime, provided that premiums are paid (651)

wholesalers Firms that sell products to other firms for resale or for organizational use (397)

work rules Policies set during collective bargaining that govern what type of work union members will do and the conditions under which they will work (313)

work sharing Slicing a few hours off everybody's workweek and pay in order to minimize layoffs (253)

worker buyout Distribution of financial incentives to

workers who voluntarily depart, usually undertaken in order to shrink the payroll (288)

workers' compensation insurance Insurance that partially replaces lost income, medical costs, and rehabilitation expenses for employees who are injured on the job (645)

workgroup computing A computing arrangement in which teams can easily work together on projects (472)

working capital Current assets minus current liabilities (504)

workstation A recently developed class of computers with the basic size and shape of microcomputers but with the speed of traditional minicomputers (traditionally, the term was applied to any terminal at which computer users work) (461)

wrongful discharge Firing an employee with inadequate advance notice or explanation (287)

yellow-dog contract Agreement forcing workers to promise, as a condition of employment, not to join or remain in a union (305)

NAME AND COMPANY INDEX

SUBJECT INDEX

How far can you get in the stock market on just $12?

Details on the other side of this page.